ISRAFEL

The Life and Times of Edgar Allan Poe

If *I could dwell*
W*here Israfel*
  H*ath dwelt, and he where I,*
He *might not sing so wildly well*
  A *mortal melody,*
W*hile a bolder note than this might swell*
  F*rom my lyre within the sky.*

BOOKS BY HERVEY ALLEN

PROSE

TOWARD THE FLAME: A War Diary
Illustrated by Lyle Justis

ISRAFEL: The Life and Times of Edgar Allan Poe
Two volume edition 1926
One volume edition 1934
Both Illustrated   •

POE'S BROTHER: The Life and Poetry of William Henry Leonard Poe
(With Thomas Ollive Mabbott)
Illustrated

ANTHONY ADVERSE:
One volume edition—standard—1933
Three volume edition—de luxe limited—1933
Two volume edition—1933
Two volume edition—illustrated by N. C. Wyeth—1934

POETRY

WAMPUM AND OLD GOLD

CAROLINA CHANSONS
(With DuBose Heyward)

THE BRIDE OF HUITZIL: An Aztec Legend
Designed by Bruce Rogers

THE BLINDMAN

EARTH MOODS AND OTHER POEMS

SONGS FOR ANNETTE

SARAH SIMON

NEW LEGENDS
Large de luxe limited edition
Standard edition

Edgar Allan Poe as a Young Man

From a daguerreotype, probably taken in Baltimore in the early 1840's
Courtesy of the Maryland Historical Society

ISRAFEL

The Life and Times of

EDGAR ALLAN POE

BY

HERVEY ALLEN

FARRAR & RINEHART, INC.

ON MURRAY HILL · NEW YORK

1934

For
Mary Lucy Allen

PREFACE TO THIS EDITION

ISRAFEL was originally issued in a two-volume edition. In that form it went through a number of printings here and abroad and a certain amount of emendation. During the process a considerable demand for a less expensive and more convenient format developed to which this one-volume edition is the publisher's answer.

The book has not been reprinted from the old plates but completely reset, and I have taken advantage of the opportunity thus provided to make a number of minor corrections not only as to the publishing details of some of Poe's writings but in regard to the spelling of certain names of those associated with the poet. In a few cases these spellings are still doubtful, due to the lapse of years or the difficulty of making out old handwriting. As far as possible I have agreed with Professor Woodberry in the use of proper names, for the sake of standard practice, although in one or two cases I depart from his usage where an error seems obvious. The references in the footnotes have also been brought more up to date and in a large number of notes references have been changed in order to provide the casual reader with a more available text or to direct the more scholarly to the prime source rather than to a commentator.

Since the publication of this biography not a great deal of important new material about Poe, from a biographical standpoint, has come to light. What of interest has been recently turned-up by scholars I have sometimes availed myself of, now and then, incorporating a few minor new facts into the text with necessary acknowledgment and reference. In that connection it is proper to say that I have not felt it incumbent upon me to mention in the body of the text the so-called "letter" from Dumas the elder to an Italian officer of police, which purports to tell of Dumas's meeting with Poe and Fenimore Cooper in the year 1832 in Paris, although through the courtesy of the present owner I was permitted to examine that "letter" and the material connected with it.

In one or two cases illustrations have been changed or shifted and I have also here and there taken the opportunity of correcting and, I hope, of improving, the diction and the style of the book in general.

I have been urged by some authorities, whose opinions properly convey great weight in all matters concerning Poe, to "tone down" my assertion in the text that a secret marriage took place between Poe and Virginia Clemm in Baltimore previous to their marriage in Richmond. After careful and long considered reweighing of all the evidence I am still of the opinion that the secret marriage did take place as I state in the text. My reasons for not altering my opinion are, in brief : The marriage license was issued and is on record; Mrs. Clemm made a statement in a conversation that was taken down in shorthand that the marriage took place; curious circumstances strongly point to the expediency of the secret marriage. In this case, as in general throughout the book, I have taken contemporary authentic documents and the statements that eyewitnesses made about Poe as being more valid in evidence toward establishing a biographical fact than any post-mortem speculations or doubts possibly can be, no matter by whom advanced. The careful reader, however, is urged to examine the evidence for himself in this particular.

Israfel is not "fictionized biography." Even very small circumstances and particulars about Poe, the people he knew, and his surroundings as described in the text, are for the most part literal. Where I have been forced to reconstruct from scattered evidence I have been painstaking and conservative. The reader is asked out of fairness to bear in mind that this biography does not contain *all* the facts about Poe, nor does any other; also that *Israfel* is a biography and not a textual critique or bibliography of Poe's writings. Those who wish minute and detailed facts about Poe's publications should consult Professor Killis Campbell's "Poe Canon" (in his book *The Mind of Poe*), and other textual comments and commentators.

I should also state that the purpose of this biography precluded the possibility of any extensive asides in literary criticism. The attempt here has been to tell the story of Poe's life in more than usual detail; to get the essential narrative of time, place, events and personalities that constitute Poe's life-story in proper sequence and truthful relationship. I am conscious of the fact that in some places I have laid an emphasis on details which appear trivial in themselves and which even seem to put me in the position of overemphasizing the importance of Poe himself. That is not so. Nearly everything about Poe has either been a matter of bitter dispute or has become needlessly legendary. To offset that I have been under the necessity of presenting evidence even in minute detail in order to make the record clear.

In preparing this text I have frequently availed myself of the corrections and right criticisms of former editions, which the comments of many Poe specialists provided me. In particular, I wish to thank Professors Killis Campbell, Thomas Ollive Mabbott, and S. Foster Damon for their emendations, and Miss Julie Eidesheim for her invaluable assistance in reading the proof.

HERVEY ALLEN

October, 1934

PREFACE

IT IS not the intention in this preface to attempt to present, in condensed form, a critical estimate of the great figure whose semblance, at least, walks through the pages of this biography. A long, laborious, and conscientious consideration of the immense amount of material concerning Poe has convinced the author that any brief, comfortably-clever, and convenient presentation of his character, from either a literary, a psychological, or a romantic standpoint is bound to be misleading. So diverse, so conflicting, and so astoundingly confusing were the life experiences of Edgar Allan Poe that, in comparison, the lives of most other men of letters are a simple tale.

The method followed here has been to disregard, for the most part, the findings of all other biographers who have worked in the field and to depend largely upon source material drawn from contemporary documents, letters, and the evidence given by those who saw, talked with, and, to some extent, knew the man. No matter how great the authority or scholarship of those who lived after Poe died, it is felt that the evidence of those who affirm, "I saw him, talked with him, on such and such an occasion he did, or said, or appeared thus and thus," is of more value than theories, be they ever so erudite and clever.

This biography, then, is the *story* of Edgar Allan Poe, and the strange formative America in which he lived, and perished, reconstructed from the direct evidence latent in the documents, letters, books, and illustrations of the period from about 1800 to 1850. Neither expense, effort, nor meticulous care was spared in assembling this data, in which process the courtesy, advice, and enthusiasm of those who were drawn upon for aid, or for source material in their right or custody, were truly encouraging and, indeed, made this work possible.

There are a great many Lives of Poe. This differs from all others in that, for the first time, it tells the complete story of the man, from birth to death, and makes reasonably clear the mystery which hitherto surrounded the first half of his life and the formative processes of youth. Former biographers, because of the inaccessibility of material, withheld for curious personal reasons, had been largely compelled to project Poe as a somewhat enigmatical torso, with the base draped in convenient and impressive folds.

It was purely an accidental circumstance, but nevertheless, an important one, that the passing of time had brought about the release of sources, hitherto inaccessible, which also make it possible to tell amply the strange and startling story of Poe's youth. There is no longer any necessity for talking about "the Poe mystery," indeed, it is no exaggeration to say that there are few other literary figures whose personal life is so fully documented. There exists in the files of the firm of *Ellis & Allan,* the business house in which Poe's guardian was a partner, a surprisingly complete record of the daily life of the family and community in which Poe lived during his youth. These papers were purchased some years ago by the Economic Section of the Library of Congress, presumably as source material for the study of an early nineteenth century Virginia mercantile firm. There are thousands of papers comprising the business and personal correspondence of Poe's guardian, John Allan, and his partner, Charles Ellis, covering a quarter of a century contemporaneous with Poe's youth. During this time, Poe was in John Allan's house, or in correspondence with him. There is, in this store of material, a constant running reference to "Edgar" from childhood to manhood, some items in his own hand, and many letters concerning him and his guardian. The author and other researchers have sifted this mass of documents, and from it drawn the material for the story of Poe's childhood and youth. The story which emerged is startling, strange, and contradictory of many assertions and legends hitherto accepted about Poe and his early environment.

For the most part, the statements made in this text are heavily documented by footnotes, but the reader is asked to remember that many assertions made in the body of the work, about the character of those who had the molding of the young Poe in their keeping, are made from a knowledge of the complete material as a whole. To quote sources in every case would require an annex volume of references alone.

In addition to the *Ellis & Allan Papers,* the publication of the correspondence between Poe and John Allan by the Valentine Museum in 1925, amply covered the period between 1826 and 1832. By good fortune, the author was able to locate the wills of William Galt and John Allan, which are here published in full, in the appendix, and from a synthesis of all three sources: *Ellis & Allan,* the *Valentine Museum Poe Letters,* and the wills mentioned, to present his conclusions. It is proper to state here that the construction put upon the relations between Poe and his guardian is not an effort to exonerate Poe. The domestic affairs of John Allan have, as a matter of fact, been treated *with considerable reserve.* There is no desire to make "startling revelations" in this biography. Collateral material, bearing upon events and persons not concerned with Poe, has been carefully excluded. It is also pertinent to state that, in the author's opinion, the attempt by John Allan to throw a shadow on the name of the poet's mother was without foundation, and a doubtful gesture of desperate self-defense.

A much closer and more affectionate relation between Edgar Poe and his elder brother, William Henry Leonard Poe, than had hitherto been suspected, was brought to light by the discovery by Thomas Ollive Mabbott of Henry Poe's poems and prose bearing upon Edgar. The above-mentioned material was generously supplemented, and made more or less complete, by the letters and data supplied to the author by the late Edward V. Valentine, Esq., of Richmond, related to Poe's foster-mother, and one of the few persons recently still living, known to have seen Poe, and to have had immediate knowledge of his character, his family, and personal friends. In this matter, and in others, the author remains in great debt to Mr. Valentine.

Although Poe was an extraordinary, and unique character, in attempting to reconstruct his life it soon became apparent that, without a recall of the lost but swiftly changing world through which he moved amid the kaleidoscopic incidents of his environment, it would be hopeless even to approach an understanding of the man. Yet if Poe's reactions to his environment were peculiar to himself, it is in those very peculiarities that his essential literary character is to be glimpsed, and that his triumphs and failures are to be found. Because, for many intricate historical reasons, the America from 1800 to the Civil War and, particularly, the America of the 1830's and 1840's was long allowed to lapse into oblivion, only the lyrical and romantically-imaginative work of Poe is generally known to the present generation.

The peculiar and intense difficulties with which the writers of the "Middle American" period struggled, and to which most of them capitulated, are now much less evident, even to Americans, than those of the environment of Restoration London,—or almost any other era. In this study, the intellectual and physical background of the central figure has therefore been reproduced with considerable care.

America has been gradually becoming aware of its past. Suddenly realizing that, for some reason, the balance of influence in the planet may have been conferred upon her, she is now looking about, and behind, and wondering why. It is ludicrous to suppose that the three generations, from the founding of the Federal Union to the Civil War, were merely so many old-fashioned nobodies. We have already begun to be intrigued by their furniture and costumes, and more recently to commence to look beneath the surface. Whether we admire or not is inconsequential. The type of culture which has now acquired a fearsome momentum was then getting under way among Americans, its future direction was being settled—so that, it is now little short of a necessity to become familiar with some of its background. It seems startling, at first thought, to insist that in the Baltimore, or Philadelphia, or Boston of the 1830's and 1840's or even earlier, there were tides of thought, intellectual movements, and political theories that congealed in literature. But is was so, and, without understanding them, and resurrecting them, we cannot understand ourselves.

It is, therefore, earnestly hoped that, in this biography, the attempt to suggest some of the social values of the "Middle American scene" will become evident. Poe's own comment was couched in a style and with an irony that made it distasteful, and even madly iconoclastic, to his contemporaries. Yet right now a great deal of his criticism of social, political, and literary life in America rings with a strangely modern sound. It is significant that, while conservative academic circles still continue to yawn through Mr. Emerson's doubtful *Compensations,* there is little knowledge of, or comment upon, what Mr. Poe had to say of democracy, science, and unimaginative literature about the same time. The croak of the raven is conveniently supposed to be purely lyric. In that direction, the discussion of Poe's contribution to American letters may be said to be presented here in a modern aspect.

The contribution to imaginative literature is, always, the main and most pertinent claim for attention that an author can have upon posterity. Whatever may be the eventual niche accorded to Edgar Allan Poe in the literature of English, and estimates vary, the great importance of his place in the field of American letters cannot be successfully denied.

The legend of the man is enormous. One of the few American literary names that cannot be mentioned without awakening interest, anywhere in the United States, is that of Edgar Allan Poe. He is one of the few of our poets who enjoy the perquisites of completely general fame. This is, in itself, for whatever reason, a giant achievement, and deserves the attention of careful and complete biography, free from sectional propaganda, the pet theories of specialists, and sentimental or moralistic twaddle. But there is something more than that; for those who care nothing, even for those who deprecate his contributions to literature, the story of the man, as a mere human adventure, must, by force of its inherent, dramatic, genuinely romantic, and strange psychological values, be found intriguing to the last degree. Though we may find it impossible to love, and even difficult to admire, we cannot help being intensely interested. The bare material of the man's biography is fascinating. Its events constitute a series of human accidents out of which the *timbre* of personality, and the notes on the staff of incident, have produced the harmony and dissonance of an orchestrated tragedy. With so great a theme, the present biographer can only hope that his audience will not be repulsed by the many difficulties which, he is the first to acknowledge, he has frequently been unable to surmount.

References in the text to authorities, sources, and the author's comments, are made in a series of running footnotes numbered consecutively. Cumbersome Latin abbreviations have been left out, *and the numbers may refer to footnotes either backward or forward.* In using those references, the reader is asked to bear in mind that the footnotes run from 1 to 938, and that a reference to a note *may* also imply and include a reference to the discussion in the text upon the same page where the footnote occurs. Duplication of footnotes and cumbersome requoting of authorities have thus been avoided.

The illustrations are all from contemporary sources, and have been chosen and arranged, not only to illustrate a particular place in the text, but also to make clear the background of the period in which Poe moved, and the panorama of the changes which occurred. For the convenience of Poe scholars and collectors, the title pages of Poe's *bound works,* issued during his lifetime, are here reproduced, together with the photographs of rare newspapers, and a periodical to which he contributed. In each case, these accompany a discussion and description of the publication in the text.

No reference in the biography is made to the "Quarles" pamphlet supposed, by some, to have been issued by Poe as a reply to Dickens' *American Notes.* In the opinion of the author, based on a thorough investigation, this is not an item that can be assigned to the pen of Poe. The discussion of Poe's "war" with Longfellow and of his association with Dr. Thomas Holley Chivers has, for reasons of space, been only indicated. There is now available an able biography of Chivers by S. Foster Damon. The relations between Edgar Allan Poe and his older brother, Henry, have only been touched on in the text. A full discussion of the two brothers will be found in *Poe's Brother, The Poetry of William Henry Leonard Poe,* by Hervey Allen and Thomas Ollive Mabbott, Doran, 1926, an excerpt from which is here printed in Appendix IV. It should also be noted that this biography ends with the death of Poe, and does not purport to detail the aftermath of the Griswold controversy, and other posthumous matters.

In conclusion, the author desires to make evident his profound sense of gratitude and indebtedness to the following persons, publishers, and institutions, for their invaluable aid, and generous contributions of advice and data:

To the Edgar Allan Poe Shrine of Richmond, Virginia, and to Mr. and Mrs. Archer Jones, personally, for their invaluable assistance, access to important stores of Poe material, and for illustrations; to Granville S. Valentine, Esq., and to Miss Julia Sully, both of Richmond, Va., to W. G. Stanard, Esq., President of the Virginia Historical Association, and to Mrs. Mary Newton Stanard for several valuable facts, reminiscences, illustrations, and helpful observations; to Edward V. Valentine, Esq., for excerpts from his diary, and permission to reprint letters from the Allan-Galt correspondence; to James Southall Wilson, Edgar Allan Poe Professor of Literature at the University of Virginia—in particular for his generous attitude about the title "Israfel"—and for access to the Ingram collection, diaries, and Whitman correspondence at the University of Virginia, as well as permission to quote sundry items, and for his helpful advice; to William Van R. Whitall, Esq., of Pelham, New York, for the loan of essential texts from his library and collection, and for his advice and comment; to John T. Snyder, Esq., of Pelham, New York, for the use of rare Poe items, and first editions in his collection; to S. Foster Damon, Esq., of Brown University, for advice and information; to a New York "Poe Collector," who desires to remain anonymous, for the loan of texts; to James F. Drake, Esq., for the loan of three letters, and permission to reprint; to Miss Laura M. Bragg, Director of the Charleston Museum, and to John Bennett, Esq., for information dealing with Poe in Charleston, and *The Gold-Bug;* to Theodore Spicer-Simson, Esq.,—and to Miss Elena von Feld, of the American Museum of Natural History, for the illustrations of Poe's Gold Bug Synthesis; to Edwin M. Anderson, Esq., Librarian of the New York Public Library; to Francis Rawle, Esq., President of the Pennsylvania Historical Society; to the Librarian of the Century Association; to the Maryland Historical Society, in particular for rare files of newspapers and illustrations; to the Librarian of the Virginia State Library; and to the Custodian of the *Ellis & Allan Papers* at the Library of Congress.

The author also desires to express his appreciation for the release of copyrights on various and sundry items and illustrations to Houghton Mifflin Company, Thomas Y. Crowell and Company, Harper & Brothers, the Century Company, the University of Virginia, the Columbia University Press, the Lewiston Journal Company, Charles Scribner's Sons, The Valentine Museum, of Richmond, Va., and J. B. Lippincott Company—Also to Professor George E. Woodberry, Professor James A. Harrison, Professor Killis Campbell, and Dr. Thomas Ollive Mabbott particularly, for the benefit of their labors in the Poe field, without which no competent comment on Poe would now be possible.

HERVEY ALLEN

CONTENTS

ILLUSTRATIONS

ISRAFEL

ISRAFEL

CHAPTER ONE

A DRAMATIC PROLOGUE

MRS. PHILLIPS was a milliner who lived on Main Street in Richmond, Virginia, near that part of the town known as the "Bird in Hand." In the year 1811, in addition to her usual summer creations of silk, lavender-ribbon and lace,—which were said to have occasionally attained the distinction of good taste,—she was also doing a more than usually thriving trade in perfumes and cosmetics, owing to the gathering next door at the *Indian Queen Tavern*[1] of Mr. Placide's Company of *Richmond Players* about to open the local theatrical season.

Sometime in August the personnel of Mr. Placide's troupe was further augmented by the arrival from Norfolk, where she had lately been playing, of a young actress then twenty-six years of age, Mrs. Elizabeth Arnold Poe, whose beauty, voice and terpsichorean accomplishments had made it worth while for Mr. Placide to pay her way from Norfolk to Richmond, since her failing health, the presence of two young children, and the death or absence of her husband seem to have left her stranded in the former place, despite the fact of a performance having been lately advertised there for her benefit.[2]

Mrs. David Poe, for Poe had been her second husband's name, was accompanied by her two children, Edgar and Rosalie, and was then, or later, given rooms in Mrs. Phillips' establishment, probably owing to the fact that the inn next door was already crowded, and that the nature of the entertainment provided there was at times too Bohemian and convivial to suit the needs of a young actress in delicate health, the mother of a family.

---

[1] Mrs. Phillips' shop, which is still standing in an altered shape, was next door to a hostelry famous as the haunt of actors in a part of town where there were a number of inns. Among those nearby, and one of the oldest, was the *Bird in Hand*, from which that portion of town took its name. Mrs. Phillips has been called "Mrs. Fipps" heretofore, but in the Richmond directories of the time she appears as "Mrs. Phillips." Fipps was evidently the Scotch equivalent adopted by tradition.

[2] Norfolk, Virginia, *Herald* for July 26, 1811.—"Misfortunes have pressed heavily upon Mrs. Poe, who has been left alone, the support of herself and several young children."

Of the two children, Edgar was the older, then going on to three years of age. He had been born in Boston on January 19, 1809,[3] while his mother and father were playing in that city at the old Federal Street Theater. At the time of his arrival in Richmond, Edgar was a handsome, sturdy little boy with large, dark gray eyes, long, dark brown hair, and an engaging countenance. His sister Rosalie was then a child in arms, having been born most probably in December, 1810, in Norfolk, Virginia.[4] A third and eldest child, William Henry Leonard Poe, had been left shortly after his birth, in the Summer of 1807, in the care of his paternal grandfather, "General" David Poe, at 19 Camden Street, Baltimore.

Edgar Allan Poe, for that was the full name which the son of the young actress was later to receive, was the child of strolling actors, if so leisurely a word as "strolling" can be applied to the painful and varied peregrinations of his parents, David and Elizabeth.

Elizabeth Arnold (Poe), the poet's mother, was the daughter of an actor, Henry Arnold, and an actress, Elizabeth Smith, both of the Covent Garden Theater, London. The marriage bans of the couple were published at St. George's Church in London in 1784, and the couple were married in June of that year. Elizabeth, their daughter, was born in the Spring of 1787. Henry Arnold, Poe's maternal grandfather, appears to have died in the early Winter of 1790, as his name disappears from the play bills about then. His widow continued to play at Covent Garden for the next six years, but left London at the beginning of November, 1795, for the United States, taking her daughter Elizabeth along with her. They landed in Boston from the ship "Outram" on January 3, 1796, as a shipping notice two days later in the *Massachusetts Mercury* shows. Miss Arnold was then nine years old. The passenger list of the "Outram" included a number of emigrating English actors among whom was one Charley Tubbs.

In February, 1796, Mrs. Arnold made her American début at Boston with considerable success.[5] A little later she and her daughter, accompanied by Mr. Tubbs, after a brief tour through part of New England, arrived at Portland, Maine; where the young Miss Arnold made her

---

[3] This date has been agreed upon after the careful investigations of Prof. Woodberry. All other dates, whether given by Poe himself, or the members of the Poe family, can be confidently disregarded. Poe's autobiographical notes given to Griswold on the back of an old envelope are particularly misleading. See note on Poe's parentage and heredity in Appendix I.

[4] Accounts of Rosalie Poe upon her adoption by the Mackenzies a few months later speak of her as much older and as "running about" even at the time of Mrs. Poe's arrival in Richmond.

[5] *Massachusetts Mercury* for February 16, 1796: "We have had the pleasure of a complete fruition in the anticipation of the satisfaction a Boston audience would receive from the dramatic abilities of Mrs. Arnold. The theater never shook with such bursts of applause, as on her first appearance, on Friday last," etc.

first appearance (*sic*) at a vocal concert on June 1, 1796, singing some songs, suited to her childish age and part. It was about this time, if not earlier, that the attractive widow Mrs. Arnold became the spouse of the genial but superficial Mr. Tubbs.[6] He accompanied her upon the pianoforte and supported her in minor parts. During the Summer and Fall of 1796 they attemped to organize at Portland, Maine, what may be quaintly regarded as the first "little theater" in America.

Mr. and Mrs. Tubbs and the young Elizabeth Arnold were the stars of the company, the other members appear to have been recruited mainly from the local amateur talent. One winter's experience of the coldness of the climate and the frigid dramatic enthusiasm of the Puritans appears, however, to have been blighting, and in January, 1797, Mr. and Mrs. Tubbs, together with the ten-year-old girl, "the beautiful Miss Arnold whose powers as an actress command attention,"[7] attached themselves to Mr. Solee's Company of *Boston and Charleston Comedians* and started for South Carolina. On the way down the coast, they stopped in New York to give two performances at the John Street Theater, when an epidemic of yellow fever intervened and the company was scattered to reunite again in Charleston, S. C. The Tubbses arrived on the sloop "Maria" and went to board with Colonel Maybery on Bay Street.

In Charleston, performances were given all Winter. The season opened November 9, 1797, and Mr. Solee engaged both Mr. and Mrs. Tubbs for light comedy parts and songs, and the young Miss Arnold in childish rôles such as "Cupid," and "a nymph."[8]

In the Spring of 1798, just before the season was over, Mr. Tubbs, together with two other actors of the company, Edgar and Whitelock, caused such disaffection in the troupe as to result in a dissension in its ranks. Some of the actors, among whom were Mr. and Mrs. Tubbs and the young Miss Arnold, were forced to leave the city temporarily. Mr. Tubbs was described by the manager, Mr. Solee, as the "least member of the company and a vermin." These disgruntled players were later gathered together again in Charleston by Mr. Edgar, and for a month after the close of the season by the Charleston Company, continued to give performances under the name of the *Charleston Comedians*.

---

[6] Mr. Tubbs may have married Mrs. Arnold before they left England. The actress naturally retained her old name on theater bills and the matter is therefore difficult to trace. Woodberry is followed here. The story that Poe's mother was born at sea is a legend with no basis of fact, it may be noted.

[7] The *Eastern Herald and Gazette of Maine,* December 12, 1796.

[8] Elizabeth Arnold made her début on the Charleston boards November 18, singing *The Market Lass,* and her first "important" theatrical appearance December 26, as the "Duke of York" in *Richard III.* The family continued playing in Charleston through the Spring of 1798.

It was in this troupe that Poe's mother, Elizabeth Arnold, ceased to take only juvenile parts and found herself described as an actress.[9] Mr. Edgar, the pseudo-manager of the new troupe, appears to have been a drunkard with a disputatious disposition. Owing to this, and the fact that the secession of his cast from the ranks of the *Charleston Players* had been viewed unfavorably by the public and press, the notices which he and his people received were by no means favorable. To this, however, both Mrs. Tubbs and Miss Arnold were notable exceptions.

It is about this time that all references to Mr. and Mrs. Tubbs cease. They disappear from the scene; and it is quite possible that the grandmother of Edgar Allan Poe rests in some unmarked grave in Charleston, S. C., the victim of "Yellow Jack," the terrible fever, which for years haunted the old port epidemically and perennially, claiming even a half century later, the brother of the English poet, Hugh Clough, and many another.[10] There is some tradition of Poe's grandmother having appeared later in Baltimore but it rests on a shadowy foundation. That she accompanied Mrs. Poe and the children to Richmond in 1811 has no basis of fact.

In the late Spring or early Summer of 1798, apparently without her mother or stepfather, Elizabeth Arnold in the care of a Mr. Usher,[11] and a Mrs. Snowden came North to Philadelphia where they joined the dramatic company then playing in that city, and acted for the next four seasons, until 1802, with occasional appearances in Washington, Southwark, and other places.

In March, 1800, the company with which the future Mrs. Poe was then playing was joined by a Mr. C. D. Hopkins, comedian. On July 4, 1802, Miss Arnold was given a benefit performance in Baltimore, and it *may* have been at that time that she was first seen by young David Poe, then about twenty-five years old and engaged in studying law [12]

---

[9] *South Carolina State Gazette* for April and May, 1798: Miss Arnold's new parts at this time were: "Anna" in the *Death of Major André;* "Miss Biddy Bellair" in *Miss in Her Teens;* "Nancy" in *Three Weeks after Marriage;* "Pink" in *The Young Quaker;* "Sophia" in *The Road to Ruin;* and "Phoebe" in *The Reapers.*

[10] Epitaph in St. Michael's Churchyard, Charleston, S. C.

GEORGE AUGUSTUS CLOUGH

A NATIVE OF LIVERPOOL,

DIED SUDDENLY OF "STRANGERS FEVER"

NOV'R 5TH 1843

AGED 22

A careful search of available records in Charleston, S. C., made by the author in 1923-4, failed, however, to reveal any trace of either Mr. or Mrs. Tubbs' being interred there.

[11] The name "Usher" thus appears early in the history of Poe.

[12] He was born "certainly not later than 1780." John Poe, Esq., to Prof. Woodberry, June 19, 1883. The statement that David Poe eloped with Miss Arnold about this time as related by Ingram is not true. He was misinformed.

with Henry Didier and others. This meeting, however, is only a possibility. David Poe went South to an uncle in Augusta, Ga., and in July, 1802, Elizabeth Arnold was married to Mr. Hopkins whose principal comic rôle was that of "Tony Lumpkin." The couple continued to play in Alexandria, Norfolk, Petersburg, and Richmond [13] as members of the *Virginia Players*. Of this union there were no children.

In the meantime, young David Poe, who seems to have had more interest in amateur theatricals—where his appearance had met some encouragement—than in "Blackstone," left his uncle's house in Augusta and went to Charleston, S. C., where he made his "second appearance on any stage" December 5, 1803.[14] Despite his desire for theatrical fame, David Poe seems to have been of a retiring and even bashful disposition. In addition, he was delicate and tubercularly inclined, which probably partly accounts for the fact of an awkwardness and self-consciousness that precluded him from success in any but the most minor rôles.[15] His amateur manner remained, and whatever his talents, it may be definitely stated that they were always far below those of the young actress whom he afterward married.[14] Nevertheless, the young actor's first press notices [16] were not unfavorable, and he seems to have met with considerable encouragement in Charleston, then one of the principal theatrical centers, where he appeared during the entire Winter of 1803 [17] under the management of Mr. Placide of the *Charleston Players,* who had succeeded Mr. Solee.

[13] The plays and the rôles in which Mr. and Mrs. Hopkins appeared can be found in the contemporary newspaper files of the towns mentioned.

[14] The *Charleston City Gazette* for December 1, 1803, advertises David Poe's first appearance in a pantomime, *La Pérouse*—as "An Officer." For a full discussion of the relative dramatic abilities of both of Poe's parents, see Woodberry's *Life*, 1909, vol. I, chap. I. I have somewhat curtailed it here as being of minor importance in connection with Poe himself and have contented myself by introducing some new material not given by or accessible to former biographers.

[15] *George Barnwell*—"Young Poe begins to emerge from the abyss of embarrassment in which natural diffidence, from his first appearance until two or three of his last performances had plunged him so deep as to deprive him of all power of exertion. But he must have not only courage but patience: 'slow rises the Actor.' " Information from a contemporary dramatic criticism in a Charleston newspaper supplied by Eola Willis of Charleston, S. C.

[16] "The *Charleston Courier* at this time had an official critic, 'Thespis'—(Mr. C. C. Carpenter), a cultivated Englishman, who not only wrote dramatic criticisms of a peculiarly honest and helpful nature, but took a keen fatherly interest in the advancing careers of the young members of the company. His sympathy and understanding must have been very comforting to the tyros who were trying to prove their worth to the Manager's satisfaction."—Eola Willis in the *Bookman.*

[17] The characters acted by David Poe at the Charleston Theater in 1803 were: "Belmore" in *Jane Shore;* "Laertes" in *Gustavus Vasa;* "Harry Thunder" in *Wild Oates;* "Donalbain" in *Macbeth;* "Grimm" in *The Robbers;* "Falliero" in *Abaellinor or the Great Bandit;* "Stepheno" in *The Tale of Mystery;* "Young Woodland" in *Cheap Living;* "Williams" in *John Bull;* "Don Pedro" in *Much Ado About Nothing;* "An Officer" in *La Pérouse;* "Tressel" in *Richard III;* "Pedro" in *The Voice of Nature;* "Allan-a-Dale" in *Robin Hood;* "Thomas" in *The Marriage Promise;*

The best portrait of Edgar Allan Poe's father that remains is to be found in the dramatic criticism of a contemporary Charleston newspaper describing his first speaking appearance:[16]

Of the Young Gentleman who made his first appearance on any stage, it would be hazardous to take an opinion from his performance this evening. For some time he was overwhelmed with the fears incident on such occasions to an excess that almost deprived him of speech. A first appearance is a circumstance of novelty, and the audience therefore did not, as the European audiences do, on such occasions, greet the newcomer with encouraging plaudits; nor did the young gentleman receive one token of welcome or approbation till it was earned by him. Though he could not, even to the last, divest himself of his fears, we thought he disclosed powers well fitted for the stage. His voice seems to be clear, melodious and variable; what its compass may be can only be shown when he acts unrestrained by timidity. His enunciation seemed to be very distinct and articulate; and his face and person are much in his favor. His size is of that pitch well fitted for general action if his talents should be suited to, sock and buskin. On the whole, we think that if the young gentleman has a passion for histrionic fame he may promise himself much gratification. What he did disclose was greatly in his favor; and extreme modesty, though it may operate as a temporary impediment, will be considered by every judicious person, as a strong prognostic of merit, and earnest of future excellence!

That neither the professional performance nor the type of plays in which David Poe acted entitled him to any claim upon "histrionic fame," both the criticism of the time and the play bills with the small parts in which he appeared confirm.[17]

In the Fall of 1804 David Poe had evidently come North, for we find him joining the *Virginia Players* in company with his future wife, and playing in Petersburg and throughout the entire circuit of that company. The season of 1805 was opened in Washington under the management of Mr. Green. It was unfortunate in several ways; financially, and from the loss of the company's star comedian, Mr. Hopkins, who died after a very brief period of illness on October the 26th. His widow, the former Miss Arnold, did not remain long unconsoled, for in a surprisingly short time afterward she was married to young David Poe, who borrowed money from a friend for the expenses of the occasion. Whether the young widow's haste was due to the natural ardor of her temperament or the failure of the deceased to engage her affections, must remain in those realms of speculation sacred to theologians.

The Poes remained with the *Virginia Players* until May, 1806, when

---

"Trueman" in *George Barnwell;* "Carmillo" in *Julia or the Italian Lover;* "Trifle" in *The East Indian;* "Dennis Crackskull" in *The Scheming Lieutenant;* "Don Garcia" in *A Bold Stroke for a Husband;* "Mezetin" (Pantomime) in *The Touchstone of Truth;* "Don Antonio Gaspard" in *Liberty in Louisiana;* "Hunter" in *The Fatherless Children;* "Hortensio" in *Catherine and Petruchio;* "Sebastian" in *Charlotte and Werter;* and "Lover" in *The Old Soldier.*—Eola Willis in the *Bookman,* from files of contemporary Charleston newspapers.

they went North to Boston, stopping on the way for summer engagements at Philadelphia and New York. By October they had rejoined their old friends the Ushers of the *Boston and Charleston Players,* whose influence may have been responsible, together with the Poes' former appearance with the company, for their engagement at the Federal Theater in Boston.

The Poes remained in Boston for three years. Mrs. Poe played several major Shakespearean rôles from time to time, "Blanche," "Ophelia," "Cordelia," "Juliet," and occasionally "Ariel." She appeared frequently as a dancing partner with her husband, dancing the Polish Minuet or singing between his clogs, reels, hornpipes, and Scotch flings.

A digest of the criticisms which Mrs. Poe received shows her to have been more gifted with diligence in her art than by native talent, and deserving of praise rather than of admiration. David Poe found his natural level in minor parts, or in appearing as an entertainer and dancer, supported by the acceptable voice of his wife. Together they managed to make a bare living.

It was during this Boston sojourn that the two boys were born: William Henry Leonard probably sometime during the early months or in the Summer of 1807,[18] as the records of Mrs. Poe's unbroken appearances preclude any other time; and Edgar in January, 1809, when Mrs. Poe was again absent from the theater from January 13th to February 8th.[19] At this time the family was living at 33 Hollis Street.

As a great deal has been made in some quarters of the fact that Poe was born in Boston and of his later brief association with the place, it must always be kept in mind that he was *born* there and nothing more. Even a genius can scarcely be expected to have memories of the first six months of his life, even though they be passed in New England. "Because kittens may be born in an oven, that does not make them loaves of bread." Edgar Allan Poe was not a Bostonian, despite the claim, largely one of sentiment and convenience, on the title page of his first book. By education, association, preference, and prejudice, Poe was a Virginian,[20] and throughout all of his wanderings Richmond was his home.

David and Elizabeth Poe continued to play in Boston after the birth of Edgar until the end of the theatrical season. How poor these actors

---

[18] Almost certainly during the early months of 1807 as this child, William Henry Leonard Poe, was left with his grandparents in Baltimore during the Summer of 1807, the theatrical vacation. If he had been born there, this might account for the story in the Poe family that Edgar had been born in Baltimore.

[19] Mrs. Poe is advertised to appear in January, 1809, on the 6th, 9th, 13th, 20th as the "Peasant" in *The Brazen Mask,* a pantomime. Her next appearance was on February 8th. Her confinement probably took place between January 13th and February 8th, the notice for the 20th having probably been inserted some days before the event.

[20] By "Virginian" I do not mean an "American"; the distinction, which was once a real one, has since become blurred.

were, is shown by the fact that three weeks after Edgar's birth his little sylph-like mother was back on the boards dancing and singing, her first appearance after the arrival of her son having taken place on February 8, 1809, and not two days later as the newspaper notices indicate.[21] The sudden popularity of the boy actor, John Howard Payne, who made his first appearance in Boston in 1809, seems for a time to have threatened the Poes' livelihood. "Master Payne," however, evidently had his heart in the right place, for on April 19th the following notice appeared in a Boston newspaper:

BOSTON THEATRE

For the Benefit of Mrs. Poe

MRS. POE RESPECTFULLY INFORMS THE PUBLIC, THAT IN CONSEQUENCE OF REPEATED DISAPPOINTMENTS IN OBTAINING PLACES DURING,

Master Payne's

ENGAGEMENT, HE HAS CONSENTED TO PLAY ONE NIGHT LONGER—AT HER *Benefit*
THIS EVENING, APRIL 19TH (1809) WILL BE PRESENTED, FOR THIS NIGHT ONLY, THE CELEBRATED PLAY CALLED *Pizzaro*:
ROLLO (*First Time*) . . . *Master* PAYNE

Two nights before, Mrs. Poe had played "Ophelia" to Payne's "Hamlet." Such a concession as the benefit must have been necessary to keep the wolf away from "Ophelia's" door.

Mrs. Poe's last appearance in Boston took place at the *Exchange Coffee House* where she sang on May 16, 1809. September found the family in New York at the Park Theater, where both she and her husband played, mostly in light comedy, until July 4, 1810. Her husband's press notices were now often unfavorable, and it is about this time that David Poe apparently disappears. He deserted his wife or he died, and there is no further authentic mention of him. The tradition is that he died of consumption. If so, the sound of the small applause which had occasionally been his must have been effectually muffled by the clods of the potter's field.

The "disappearance" of David Poe in July, 1810, dates the beginning of a Poe family mystery about which there has been a good deal of futile speculation. It gave rise to suspicions that later on played an

---

[21] Original play bill of the Boston Theater. *False Alarms, Brazen Mask,* Mr. and Mrs. Poe in the cast of the latter, February 8, 1809. This bill is of peculiar interest because it shows that Mrs. Poe appeared two days earlier, after Edgar's birth, than the date which Prof. Woodberry records. A pathetic sidelight is that the rôle chosen for Mrs. Poe was "little more than a walking part." See note in the Catalogue of the American Art Association Inc., for Poe items in sale of April 28, 29, 1924, No. 932.

important part in the life of the poor actor's famous son. According to one legend, with little basis of fact, David Poe deserted his wife for a Scotch woman and went to live with her abroad. By her he is reputed to have had a son with whom Poe is supposed to have gone to school at Irvine, Scotland, a circumstance that laid the basis for the plot of *William Wilson*. This can all be safely dismissed as imagination not to be described as pure. A more credible Richmond tradition supposes that David Poe died in Norfolk, Virginia, which one detached and untraced newspaper clipping tends to confirm, giving the date as October 19, 1810. This tradition is all very nebulous, however, and the historical record of the poet's father ends with July, 1810, in New York.

Whatever may have been the cause of David Poe's final disappearance, there was something about it that afterward caused great uneasiness to the son of the little actress. She treasured some unfortunate correspondence, almost her sole legacy to her son, Edgar, which he too cherished while he lived, but left directions that at his death it should be burned. The request was carried out by his mother-in-law and aunt, Maria Clemm. What part David Poe, the poet's father, played in this, if any, it is therefore impossible to say and useless to guess. The position of Mrs. Poe, however, is considerably clearer.

Deprived of her husband either by death or conjugal misfortune, probably the former, she left New York in the Summer of 1810 and went South to Richmond. There she was once more engaged to play on the Southern circuit, where she was already well and favorably known. She was accompanied from place to place by the child Edgar, now only two years old, but even then involved in the maze of tragedy. Edgar was already separated from his older brother by the poverty of his parents, who had been forced to leave Henry in Baltimore. Mrs. Poe had now lost her husband and was striving to support herself and her child. She must already have been far gone in tuberculosis, of which she died only a year later, yet she was forced to appear by the dire necessity of her poverty, dancing and singing in motley, night after night. To cap the climax she was pregnant with a posthumous child. For an actress ill and without resources, a helpless woman without a husband, engaged in a profession at which the age was only too prone to point the finger of scorn, it was a dreadful and precarious plight. There can be no doubt, that even while he was learning to talk, the little Edgar was clasped, with many a dark foreboding of natural terror, to his mother's heart.

Keeping Edgar with her, Mrs. Poe continued to play in Richmond and Norfolk, although her time was approaching. While in Norfolk (at the *Forrest House* on December 20, 1810) according to the Mackenzie family Bible, Mrs. Poe gave birth to a daughter, Rosalie.

That David Poe was not with Mrs. Poe in Norfolk at this time, is shown by the fact that Rosalie's birth took place so long after the death or disappearance of her husband that doubt was afterwards thrown on the paternity of the child.[22] It is an ungrateful task thus even to touch upon the reputation of this unfortunate young actress who gave to the world what art she had, and bequeathed to her adopted country one of its greatest geniuses in the person of her son. But the facts of the situation should no longer be suppressed as they undoubtedly affected the relations of Edgar Poe with his guardian, and his own family later on. It was this story, or the echoes of it, which long afterwards caused Poe to put the deaths of his father and mother "within a few weeks" of each other.[23]

All the authentic dates and the known facts show that the suspicion which was thus afterward thrown upon the memory of Mrs. Poe was not only cruel but untrue. That it was thrown upon her, however, there is no doubt. With the use that was made of it, and its effect upon the character of her son Edgar, it will be necessary to deal.

Soon after the birth of Rosalie, Mrs. Poe was again appearing in various parts, continuing a now hopeless struggle to support herself and her two "infants" despite her fast-failing health. The earnings of a minor actress on the early American stage were at best pitiable, and all the incidents of the life were ignoble, squalid, and precarious. The hardships of travel were great, and the places of entertainment rarely comfortable and not always respectable. For a sensitive woman with two babies to care for, it was a difficult and exhausting mode of life. Mrs. Poe's misfortunes and condition were evidently the cause of solicitude to her fellow actors, as frequent appeals for herself and her fatherless children in the columns of old newspapers still meet the curious eye. In Charleston, Norfolk, and Richmond, she was accorded frequent benefits at which the charitable public was urged to assist.

From Norfolk Mrs. Poe went to Charleston, S. C., where she played in the Winter and Spring of 1810 and 1811. In April of the latter year her health was evidently failing, for she was given a special benefit performance. In the notice of this, which appeared in the Charleston papers, her ill health was specifically mentioned. From Charleston the

---

[22] See the letter from John Allan to William Henry Leonard Poe in Baltimore, dated Richmond, November 1, 1824, in which among other things he says: . . . "At least she is half your sister and God forbid, my dear Henry, that we should visit upon the living the errors and frailties of the dead." This letter is to be found in the *Ellis & Allan Papers* in the Library of Congress, photostat in the possession of the author. For a full discussion of this see page 103.

[23] Poe's own statement (Poe to William Poe, Richmond, August 20, 1835) that "my father David died when I was in the second year of my age . . . my mother died a few weeks before him," is of a piece with the rest of his muddled autobiographical data and shows that he was either ignorant of the facts (*sic*), or rightly anxious to shield the reputation of his mother and sister.

Mrs. David Poe

née Arnold

who died in Richmond, Va., December the eighth
1811, leaving her son EDGAR POE an infant orphan

From a miniature long cherished by Poe

The House in which *Mrs.* David Poe died in Richmond, Virginia

Views from left to right show: 1. Rear Court, 2. Mrs. Phillips' House,
3. Bricked-up arch to old "Indian Queen Tavern"

Courtesy of the Edgar Allan Poe Shrine, Richmond, Virginia

young actress and her family returned to Norfolk, where she was obviously in failing health and destitute.[24]   The article about her there is lengthy and appealing, and stresses the point that she "has been left alone, the support of herself and several children."   Evidently the response was not great, and in August we find her again returning to Richmond, where she was always most popular, in time for the opening of the season.

It was to be the last of her many weary journeys with her young and doubtless often fretful family.   Her little space of comedy was about to end in a tragedy, one of many which pursued her son Edgar through the remainder of his astonishing life.   As she drove through the brick arch [25] into the wagon yard of the old *Indian Queen Tavern* and ensconced herself in the rooms behind and over the milliner shop of the good Mrs. Phillips, she entered upon the last scene of the last act. Perhaps in her heart she knew it, for she had already been very ill and must have been, from the nature of the events which were soon to follow, in a consumptive condition and a low state of health.

For an account of Mrs. Poe in the heyday of her fame, we have the description of one who had seen her as a care-free girl.[26]   Although the description is evidently taken from the miniature of Mrs. Poe which Edgar long cherished, a copy of which was sent to Ingram, Poe's first competent biographer after Poe's death,[27] it, and the miniature itself, are the best memorials of the poet's mother which exist.   This description shows Mrs. Poe to have had

the childish figure, the great, wide open, mysterious eyes, the abundant curling hair confined in the quaint bonnet of a hundred years ago and shadowing the brow in raven masses, the high waist and attenuated arms clasped in an Empire robe of faint, flowered design, the tiny but rounded neck and shoulders, the head proudly erect.   It is the face of an elf, a sprite, an Undine who was to be the mother of the most elfish, the most unearthly of poets, whose luminous dark gray eyes had a glint of the supernatural in them and reflected as he says in one of his earlier poems, "the wilder'd" nature of the man.

Such was the charming young actress who, with her attractive little boy Edgar, and her baby daughter Rosalie, took up her abode with Mrs. Phillips, the milliner at Richmond, sometime in August, 1811, "above that part of the town known as the 'Bird in Hand.'"   For the mother of Israfel it was the next to the last remove.

---

[24] Norfolk, Virginia, *Herald* for July 26, 1811.
[25] Since bricked up but still visible.
[26] Beverley Tucker, a contributor to the *Southern Literary Messenger*, and the author of *The Partizan Leader*.   The description was written in 1835.
[27] The *Ingram Papers* and Manuscript in possession of the University of Virginia Library.

CHAPTER TWO

THE TWO ORPHANS

THE arrival of Mrs. Poe at the *Indian Queen Tavern,* as the star of the little troupe of actors then gathered there, was no doubt the signal for a good deal of comment in local dramatic circles. Rehearsals and performances soon began.

Mrs. Phillips' small shop at that time stood some little distance back from Main Street, abutting the purlieus of the Tavern on the corner of Main and Twenty-third. There was a neat walk up through the dooryard, then lined with shade trees under which the young child Edgar immediately after his arrival in Richmond must first have played.[28]

According to the testimony of a lady from Norfolk [29] who, as a little girl, remembered seeing Mrs. Poe play there in 1811, and made friends with her children who lodged nearby on Bermuda Street (at Norfolk), —the family was then accompanied by a Welsh nurse who looked after the children and nursed Mrs. Poe. This evidence is extremely legendary, however, and there is no authentic mention whatever of the nurse's presence in Richmond.[30]

Mrs. Poe's bright little lad would no doubt have been a favorite with the members of the *Virginia Players* and the hangers-on about the *Indian Queen* next door, and he must often have sat on the knees of his father's and mother's friends before the great open chimney of the inn. The hostelry was the center of the professional dramatic life of old "Richmond City" and was also frequented by the hangers-on and stage-door Lotharios of the theater, together with a few teamsters and travelers. But its principal business was that of a theatrical lodging house and its coterie.

---

[28] For the description of the house in which Mrs. Poe died and its environs, I am indebted to information supplied me by the present owner of the property in whose family it has been for many years, and under whose hands it has passed through successive building changes greatly altering it and the old inn next door, both belonging to the same owner. A personal visit was made to the spot, and photographs of the premises made and compared with old ones, in July, 1925. The former house of Mrs. Phillips is now inhabited by negroes and surrounded by a tenement, all in a shocking state of neglect and disrepair. The former front yard of her shop is occupied by a building erected some time since. The inn archway is bricked up.

[29] Afterwards a Mrs. Archer of Richmond, mother of Mrs. S. A. Weiss.

[30] Although there is some doubt about this "nurse" having been with Mrs. Poe, the evidence from this account and several others is too precise to be *ignored.* I am inclined to accept it as accounting for the persistent rumors that Mrs. Tubbs, for whom the nurse was mistaken, accompanied Mrs. Poe to Richmond.

Mrs. Poe, who was in increasing ill health, as the frequent interruptions of her appearances at the theater showed, must have been glad to have had the children taken care of by anyone who would do so. Often enough, perhaps, there was no one at all. Mrs. Phillips, who appears to have been a kind woman, had probably taken the burden of the two little ones and the partial care of their sick mother upon herself—as any good woman might—between the intervals of waiting upon her customers in the little front room with a low fireplace and small square window panes, where her scanty stock of ribbons, poke bonnets, lace caps, cosmetics and perfumes was on display.

Mrs. Phillips' clientele was of two strata: that of the fashionable ladies of Richmond who looked to her for the latest creations, and the dramatically inclined persons from the theatrical hotel next door, who, no doubt, found upon her counters the faultlessly blooming roses which have always enhanced the cheeks of "the profession" both on and off the stage.

Thus there was ample opportunity for the ladies of the better families of Richmond, who would not otherwise in those days have been introduced to members of the theatrical profession off-stage, to become acquainted with the fact that a young actress, the mother of the handsome little fellow playing about the dooryard, was ill in the rooms immediately behind the shop of Mrs. Phillips. There can be no doubt either, that Mrs. Poe, as the star of Mr. Placide's company, the mother of a family, and an actress who, by repute and appearance, was well known to all of fashionable Richmond, was held in a different estimate than some of her more humble sisters in the theatrical boarding house next door. These, too, however, were occasionally honored by fashionable visitors who desired to testify to their admiration in a more ardent manner than a discreet applause from a seat in the theater might express. And among the most gay and ardent, if contemporary accounts are to be credited, none were more so than the members of a numerous circle of prosperous and pious Scotch merchants.

The theater in which Mrs. Poe and Mr. Placide's Company of *Virginia Players* acted stood on the present site of the Monumental Episcopal Church, on the block between Twelfth and Fourteenth Streets on Broad, known at the time as Theater Square.[31] In order to reach this

---

[31] The Richmond Theater was on the site of a frame building which had been built by a remarkable Frenchman in 1786 as an Academy in which he attempted to introduce many new ideas in education and the fine arts into America; among other things, theatricals, painting, and sculpture. The first classic plaster casts for models ever seen in America were shown here. M. Quesnay's scheme failed. The Academy was afterwards used for the Virginia Convention which ratified the Federal Constitution, and in 1802, the building having been destroyed by fire, its site was occupied by the new Richmond Theater, a brick and frame structure also destroyed by fire in 1811. As many of Poe's earliest and most intimate associations are connected with this spot it has been thought worth while to give the above facts.

from the lower part of Main Street where Mrs. Poe lived, it would have been most convenient to pass along Fourteenth Street to Broad.

At the corner of Fourteenth Street and Tobacco Alley was the residence of Mr. John Allan, the junior partner of *Ellis & Allan,* Scotch merchants doing a general merchandising business in the city and the region about, and trading by chartered ships and by cargo at home and abroad. The store was not under the residence, as has heretofore always been asserted, but was around the corner on Thirteenth Street about a block away on premises which were leased by the firm and purchased later on,[32] in April, 1812.

During the late Summer and the Fall of 1811, Mrs. Poe must have often passed the house of John Allan, probably occasionally taking little Edgar with her to performances or rehearsals at the theater. It is quite possible that Edgar may have sometimes appeared on the stage in an infantile rôle; [33] his juvenile repertoire of poems and recitations was known to have caused comment upon private occasions a little later. That he must have gone to and fro with his mother, past the door of John Allan, there can be little doubt.

Mrs. Frances Keeling Allan, the first wife of the merchant, had at this time been married to him for eight years, but was without children and undoubtedly longed for them with all the yearning of her sex and the tenderest desires of a noble but lonely and disappointed heart. The household consisted of John Allan himself, his wife Frances, her sister Anne Moore Valentine, and the negro servants or slaves. It is probable that either or both the ladies may have made the acquaintance of Mrs. Poe and her handsome boy, by whom Mrs. Allan was greatly attracted, as they passed the door from time to time; a speaking acquaintance may have been struck up with the popular young actress and Edgar offered apples,[34] a fruit as much prized in Southern towns as oranges were in the North, and one with which the Allan house was always well supplied.[35] Whether it was in this way, or at the shop of the milliner, Mrs. Phillips, certain it is that Frances, wife of John Allan,

---

[32] *Ellis & Allan Papers,* Library of Congress, Washington, D. C. — Articles of agreement made and entered into the 22nd day of April in the year of our Lord 1812, between Anthony R. Thornton of the Town of Fredericksburg and State of Virginia, of the first part and Charles Ellis and John Allan, Merchants and partners trading under the name of *Ellis & Allan.* (Consideration one thousand pounds of current money on or before the 22nd day of April, 1817, with interest.) To sell and convey to the said *Ellis & Allan* a house on Thirteenth Street, etc.

[33] Edward V. Valentine to the author at Richmond, Virginia, July, 1925.

[34] Frances Allan seems to have been the *active* factor in Edgar's "adoption" from the first.

[35] John Allan to Charles Ellis in New London, Connecticut, from Richmond, Virginia, October 26, 1812.

"P. S. I wish you would procure for me a barrel of nice green pippins on your return to New York." For this and similar items see the *Ellis & Allan Correspondence,* Library of Congress, Washington, D. C.

merchant, became acquainted with and more than casually interested in the fate and fortunes of Elizabeth Poe and her fatherless children. Through Mrs. Allan, too, doubtless came the interest and help of Mrs. William Mackenzie, a charitable and motherly woman, the wife of one of Mr. Allan's closest friends, already provided with two children of her own, John and Mary. It was, indeed, for both Mrs. Poe and her children, a benign combination of circumstances, whatever they may have been, which brought these two good women to her bedside in the house of the little Scotch milliner.

The Scotch circle in "Richmond City" was at that time a peculiarly close one. One of the Mackenzies afterwards remarked that "Mrs. Phillips came of a good family," [36] and doubtless both the kind ladies who had taken an interest in the young actress were provided with news as to Mrs. Poe's condition, and in return provided for her the necessities of life in the form of occasional gifts of food and clothing.

During the late Fall of 1811 Mrs. Poe's condition grew rapidly worse. The burden of supporting her two infant children must have fallen with crushing weight upon her narrow and consumptive shoulders. Her appearances at the theater grew fewer and farther apart; they finally ceased. Mr. Placide, the manager, doubtless did what he could for so important a member of his company, because all of these actors lived from hand to mouth. Mrs. Phillips must soon have been contributing the room rent free, as Mrs. Poe's stipend ceased with her appearances; and doubtless Edgar was very much about the shop, much to the good woman's terror for her poke bonnets and falderals, whose rigid repose upon uprights would have been grievously disturbed by the play of a vigorous three-year-old lad.

The rooms behind Mrs. Phillips' shop were not the best place in the world for an invalid. There was one fireplace downstairs, but whether there was any fuel to burn there, is another question. The lower part of Main Street, a few blocks away, was subject to periodical invasions of the River James which took every occasion to overflow its banks. The season had been an exceptionally rainy and unhealthful one throughout tide-water Virginia, as the letters of that date show; mosquitoes must have been rife,[37] and this had added constantly recurring attacks of malaria to her poverty and deprivations, to deplete further the ebbing strength of the consumptive young actress.

The little upstairs room in which she lay dying had the scantiest of furnishings: a miserable bed for herself on a straw mattress,[38] with

---

[36] Meaning a good "Scotch" family.
[37] Letter from Pedlar Mills, Virginia, from Joshua L. Ellis to Mr. Charles Ellis at Richmond, August 13, 1811, and others of like import at later dates. "The rains have been greater here than I have ever seen them." *Ellis & Allan Papers,* Library of Congress, Washington, D. C.
[38] This is specifically mentioned in some accounts.

perhaps a woven coverlet and a blanket contributed by Mrs. Phillips; one or two old chairs; probably a trundle bed for the children, a cot upon which a nurse, if present, slept; and some bottles with candle ends in them. Mrs. Poe's effects would have been of the most meager description. A few soiled odds and ends of dramatic costumes, tawdry splendors of her past triumphs; a small trunk or chest in which some relics and letters of the vanished Harlequin were cherished by his widowed Columbine; the scanty remnants of even scantier meals; and the children's tattered clothes. In such a room lay dying the mother of Edgar Allan Poe.

In her poverty-stricken condition medical attendance must have been nil, probably luckily for her, as the science had not yet passed beyond regarding the lancet and the barber's bowl as the panacea for all ills. She must have lain through the shortening days, as November waned into December, striving to read the darkness of the future, which for her was dark enough, trying to still the noisy and peevish crying of little Rosalie, listening to the voices of Mrs. Phillips' customers in the room below or to the feet of her little son as they stumbled up the narrow stairs.

Her hopeless darkness, however, was lightened from time to time by visits to the squalid, but interesting garret of the dying actress and her charming children, by the *grandes dames* and lesser ladies of Richmond, who sought the latest mode in bonnets at the hands of Mrs. Phillips. She, indeed, poor woman, we may be sure, had done her full part to interest her customers in the misery of her guests, and had received perhaps an unexpected reward at finding her little shop the center of considerable interest, not all of which could have been in vain.

Those who care to search the Richmond papers of that time will find in the *Enquirer* of November 25, 1811, an appeal for Mrs. Poe "to the kind hearted of the city," inserted no doubt by the thoughtful hands of Manager Placide, for four days later one comes across the advertisement of a benefit to be repeated for the *second* time, "in consequence of the serious and long continued indisposition of Mrs. Poe, and in compliance with the advice and solicitation of many of the most respectable families."

Among the "ladies of the most respectable families" who visited Mrs. Poe and her children, as her tragedy neared the end of its last act, none were more welcome and efficacious to the little family in the dingy upstairs room than Mrs. Frances Allan and Mrs. William Mackenzie.

It is not hard to imagine what must have been the thoughts and emotions of Mrs. Allan, the tenderly inclined, childless woman, as she sat in that bare garret with the handsome, curly-headed young Edgar Poe in her yearning arms, talking to him; and with the girlish mother on the bed, against whose soiled pillows the black hair of the invalid lay tangled in dark disarray. Nor could she have been oblivious to the silent appeal of the haunted, "wildered" eyes of the young actress which shifted tragically from the baby face of young Rosalie, resting trustfully against the bosom of Mrs. Mackenzie, to that of her little son smiling sadly back at her from the chair of Mrs. Allan. There was a silent appeal here which even a rough man might understand. To these good women, as the future proved, it was not made in vain. A few days later there was an appeal of a more obvious kind—

☛ TO THE HUMANE HEART

> On this night *Mrs. Poe,* lingering
> on the bed of disease and surrounded
> by her children, asks your assistance:
> and *asks it perhaps for the last time.*
> For particulars, see the Bills of the day.

It was indeed, "for the last time!" [39] Death had finally appeared in one of his favorite guises, pneumonia: and the tragedies of the little doll actress were over. "Ariel" had received release; the tinsel stars of the wand were laid away with the paper flowers of "Ophelia"; "Juliet" was tricked out in her best paste jewels, and, for a few hours, lay in squalid state in the milliner's attic, where all those who had made her small world, and who had cared a little, might come to see. Among these, we may be sure, were the members of Mr. Placide's company from the tavern next door, Mrs. Phillips, Mrs. Allan and Mrs. Mackenzie and their husbands, who by this time had been interested in the startling little tragedy on lower Main Street to the extent of taking the arrangements for the funeral into their own hands.

It would be easy enough to pull out the *vox humana* for the final scene when Edgar and Rosalie Poe were at last parted from that which had been their mother. For the not unimaginative the facts will suffice: Mrs. Allan and Mrs. Mackenzie came for the children the morning after their mother's death. One can imagine the sudden hush about the old inn and the milliner's shop. The broad Scotch lamentations of Mrs. Phillips, the moment when the two children were held up to look for the last time upon their little doll-like mother, now waxen, indeed, and lying upon the bed, dressed in some high-waisted Empire slip of the period. Certainly, as the custom then was, some toll was taken of her long, dark locks, and before the children left the room little Rosalie was

---

[39] Mrs. Elizabeth Arnold (David) Poe died December 8, 1811. On December 9th Mrs. Mackenzie took Rosalie home, and Mrs. Allan carried Edgar to her house. (Statement by Mary Mackenzie, Rosalie's foster-sister.)

In the newspaper notice quoted on this page there was an error in spelling which has not been reproduced.

given an empty jewel case, the modest contents of which had long ago vanished to put food in her mouth. For Edgar there was a miniature of his mother, and a painting by her of Boston Harbor, upon the back of which in her own pitiful cipher she had charged her little son to "love Boston, the place of his birth, and where his mother found her best and most sympathetic friends." [40] Like many another death-bed admonition it was to be in vain, for her son always found there the reverse of his mother's experience. This, together with a certain weakness of constitution, was the entire inheritance of the orphans of David and Elizabeth Poe.[41]

Outside the little shop some of the members of Mr. Placide's company doubtless gathered to say, on the part of the women at least, a tearful farewell to the little gray-eyed boy who had been their pet. Some of them may have accompanied Mrs. Poe to her last resting place in St. John's Churchyard where Mr. Allan and Mr. Mackenzie, who were members of the congregation, had arranged for her burial, not without protest from certain members of the vestry who shared the prejudices of their time and were reluctant to see even the mortal remains of an actress sheltered by consecrated ground. Fittingly enough she was buried "close to the wall." There is an entry for the burial, but it is without name, and the grave was for over a century left unmarked.[42]

Young as he was, Edgar Poe could scarcely have remembered the actual scenes surrounding the final tragedy of his young mother, but even a child of three may be conscious at the time that its own familiar little world has suddenly gone to pieces about it. When Edgar got to the street in front of Mrs. Phillips' shop he was parted from his baby sister, Rosalie, and suddenly found himself alone with an affectionate but nevertheless strange woman. The soft and always comforting presence known to all children as "mama" had disappeared. The doubtless protesting sister Rosalie had mysteriously vanished in the arms of another unknown person. As the boy rattled over the old, cobbled streets of "Richmond City" in Mrs. Allan's hired hack [43] he must dimly have experienced for the first time, in an emotion without words, the extreme sense of fear and utter loneliness which was to follow him to the grave. The tenderness of the strange woman who sat beside him could never supply the intimate sense of well-being and

---

[40] Woodberry, 1909, vol. I, page 14, and other authorities. Ingram I, 6, etc.
[41] There was also a bundle of letters, and as it now appears from a poem by Henry Poe recently discovered, a pocket book with locks of hair of both parents. See *Poe's Brother*, Doran, 1926.
[42] A fitting monument has recently been provided.
[43] John Allan did not at this time own a horse and carriage, but he was at considerable expense for hack hire. For the frequent bills from Richard E. Wortham & Co., for hack hire through 1811 and 1812, see the *Ellis & Allan Papers*, Library of Congress, Washington, D. C. Receipt for 12th of November, 1812, etc.

spiritual safety which a real mother confers naturally upon her child. Ishmael was gone forth to dwell in other tents, and the hand of the stranger was henceforth mysteriously against him.

Looking back after more than a hundred years, to us the bitter end of the little tragi-comedy of Mrs. Poe seems to be one of those petty victories of which even Death might be ashamed. To young Israfel, whose trembling little mouth was for the time being stopped by the bread and kisses of charity, it was the first and perhaps the most decisive of the many tragedies which the Dark Angel was bidden to confer upon him.

CHAPTER THREE

LADY BOUNTIFUL CLAIMS ISRAFEL

THE household in which the orphan child Edgar found himself ensconced, if not entirely welcome, was, as we have seen, that of John Allan, the merchant, and Frances Keeling [44] his wife, a charming young woman then twenty-seven years old. With them at this time and for many years thereafter lived Mrs. Allan's elder sister Anne Moore Valentine, soon to become known to Edgar as "Aunt Nancy," a lady whose affection, like that of her married sister, never failed to follow Edgar Poe till death stilled her loyal heart.

The house at the corner of Fourteenth Street and Tobacco Alley was neither "one of a row of dingy three story dwellings" nor a "princely Southern Mansion," as it has been variously described, but a well-built, rather spacious brick structure of the Georgian type with three floors containing three or four rooms each, and a garret which at that time had a small hall and two rooms. In the rear there was probably provision for the housing of the servants, of which at this time Mr. Allan is known to have kept three and possibly more,[45] not at all unusual in slave times, nor indicative of wealth. Either upon the first or second floor, there was a large dining room with folding doors that opened into a drawing room or library, which in all probability did not contain many books, as the owner was of a practical cast of mind. Most of the rooms contained open fireplaces which at one time must have possessed handsome Georgian mantelpieces to match the style of the finely turned mahogany banisters with delicate uprights that still remain.[46] It was

---

[44] Frances Keeling (Valentine) Allan born 1784, her sister Anne Moore Valentine was born the previous year.

[45] I find record of this transaction in the *Ellis & Allan Papers:* "Jan. 1st, 1811, a negro woman named Judith hired from Master Cheatham for the sum of £25 to be retained clothed as usual under a bond of £50." Judith was retained for some years. See also J. H. Whitty *Memoir—The Complete Poems of Edgar Allan Poe,* large edition, note page xxii for the names of the servants some years later. Also will of William Galt, Appendix III.

[46] The author visited this house in July, 1925, and found the lower story still occupied as an office. The house has passed through many vicissitudes, having at one time been the most notorious in Richmond. The partitions have been torn out to make storage space, but their location can still be seen as well as one old mantelpiece, the rest of which have been replaced by Victorian marble insults. Viewed from the front, a very deceptive idea of the size of the place is given, as it is in reality quite large. A great many of the absurdities in some of Poe's biographies could have been avoided by a visit to the houses where he and his friends lived, many of which are still standing in Richmond and elsewhere.

in short an excellently comfortable though not pretentious or impressive dwelling. The house was then owned by William Galt.

As the long residence, cherishing, breeding, and education received in the home of John Allan is perhaps the central fact in Poe's story,—since the vital formative years of his life were largely spent there, and since the relations between Poe and his foster-father were in a sense decisive as to the poet's future,—it is the purpose here to discuss the character and affairs of John Allan and his family relations at some length and with a considerable degree of candor.[47]

Much more than a century has elapsed since the events and the persons involved in them troubled the world of men, and it is now high time to set forth the facts. That the reputations of those involved have all been carefully shielded, except that of the name which has caused their several obscurities to be remembered, is already a smoking sacrifice to family pride.

John Allan was a native of Irvine, Scotland, where he had been born in 1780 and received at least an ordinary but sufficient education, of which he states, that at the age of fifteen his foster-son Edgar had already received a better one.[48] Whatever formal education he had was considerably augmented by a gift of keen natural parts and a mercantile familiarity with the forms of business correspondence, legal papers and accounts. His letters are couched in a style which stamps their writer as a man of decided and astute personality, not without a pleasant and softer gleam here and there, but only too often with the glitter of steel and an affected piety. In early youth he had been left an orphan[49] and emigrated from Scotland to settle in Richmond, having been brought up in the store, counting house, and ships of his uncle, William Galt, a rich Scotchman doing a prosperous mercantile and tobacco trade at home and overseas,—said to have accumulated before

---

[47] The relative importance of the time spent in Mr. Allan's house by Poe can probably be brought home most vividly in a graphic form. Representing the whole of Poe's life by a straight line, the time spent with Mr. Allan and his family is shown by the heavier portion. The influences, of course, extended much further. The scale is one inch to each decade of Poe's life.

1809 1811 1827 1849

[48] Letter to William Henry Leonard Poe from John Allan, dated Richmond, November 1, 1824.

[49] The Allans and Galts were petty traders and smugglers about the ports of Greenock and Irvine toward the end of the 18th century. John Allan's mother, whom one of the Galt cousins once hoped to marry, kept a tea shop in Greenock. For the life of the place and time, including characters from the Allan and Galt families, see the works of the Scotch novelist, John Galt, the friend of Byron, also see Chapter V, note 126.

his death one of the largest fortunes in Virginia. Mr. Galt's generosity and native clannishness were the mainstay, the hope, and the means of final gratification of a host of squabbling, poor Scotch relatives.[50]

On a stool in the same counting house, where he had been brought up with John Allan, was another young Scotchman, Mr. Charles Ellis, also provided with previously settled relatives who were already trading to some advantage. After having served for some time about Mr. Galt's establishment, the two young clerks set up for themselves as partners in a general mercantile and trading business by sea and land, in which tobacco buying and selling was the most profitable transaction. They were in all probability backed by William Galt and Josiah Ellis, their two uncles respectively, either by a capital stock or an advance of credit sufficient to set up the new firm which traded under the name of *Ellis & Allan*. In the meantime both the young partners had married.

The nature of the trade carried on by the firm of *Ellis & Allan,* the aroma and atmosphere of it, which literally and figuratively permeated and dominated the household and the environment in which Poe spent his boyhood, is not well described by the term "Tobacco Merchants." The firm dealt in everything under the sun, and would do or perform anything which was probably profitable and ostensibly lawful. Peace could not satiate nor did war abate the infinite variety of their correspondence and their ways of gathering pence.[51]

Shortly before the outbreak of hostilities between Great Britain and the United States we find Mr. Charles Ellis dashing off in great trepidation to New London, Connecticut, and later on beseeching Mr. James Pleasants [52] in the Halls of Congress to aid in liberating the good ship "Georgiana," which had sailed a little too close-hauled into the weather eye of the embargo law. Nor did the commencement and duration of hostilities apparently cause any cessation in the correspondence with the British and foreign merchants, or with Mr. Allan's family in Scot-

---

[50] For the statements made in this and the next paragraphs I am indebted to the correspondence between John Allan, and his sisters and brother-in-law in Scotland anent family affairs in general, Mr. William Galt of Richmond, and the troubles arising about his will. All in the *Ellis & Allan Files* at the Library of Congress.

[51] One of the ten thousand various items in the *Ellis & Allan Papers:*

Messrs. ELLIS AND ALLAN   *Powhattan,* Jan. 6th, 1811

This will be handed you by my son John E. Meade who wants a few articles of clothing. Will you be so good as to furnish him on my acct, and oblige yours respectfully,

D. MEADE

[52] Afterwards governor of Virginia.

John Allan, Merchant

The foster-father of Edgar Allan Poe

Born at Irvine, Ayrshire, Scotland, in 1780, died at Richmond, Virginia,
March 27, 1834

From a silhouette

*Signatures
of the partners*

land. Some means were found, by cartel or privateer, and the letters slipped through.[53]

In addition to the great item of tobacco (in which most of the imported merchandise purchased from the firm by Virginians was paid for in kind) the partners dealt in wheat, hay, maize, corn meal, grains, fine teas and coffees, cloth, clothing of all kinds, flowered vest stuffs, seeds, wines and liquors (especially Philadelphia claret); outfitted slaves; supplied plantations with agricultural implements, nails and hardware; chartered ships and coastwise schooners; imported tombstones,[54]—and, as a side issue, were not above trading in horses, Kentucky swine from the settlements, and old slaves whom they hired out at the coal pits till they died.[55] The concern also advanced money; dabbled occasionally in city real estate; and both of the partners or their families had plantations in the country, John Allan's at "Lower Byrd's" and the Ellises' at "Red Hill" and "Pedlar's Mills." These also were expected to pay. It was on the whole a thrifty, a Scotch, and sometimes a sordid atmosphere in which Charles Ellis and his partner moved.[56] But for all that it was not a narrow, and never a stingy one, until years later when it might have been more generous still.

For over it all was the variety and the romance of the sea that floated up the James to the thriving port at the Falls, the long splendor of Virginia sunshine, the syrupy perfume of tobacco, and the almost magic life of old Richmond. About the warehouse and docks of Poe's foster-father crowded the foreign and coastwise shipping of square-rigged days.[57] Martingales sprang away from the proud double curve of mirrored bows, brass glittered, sails flapped, and the bo'suns' whistles sang like frantic canaries. Drays laden with great tuns of fragrant Virginia leaf rattled over the cobbles. Dark stevedores answered the hails and songs of passing barges and canal boats; and the yellow river

---

[53] The correspondence of the firm is interesting from the standpoint of showing that the merchants on both sides of the water regarded the War of 1812 purely as a quarrel between two governments and as an unmitigated nuisance. In particular the Regent (George IV) comes off rather roughly in the candid opinions exchanged.

[54] These for Charlottesville seemed to have always had the names and dates wrong, doubtless to the present confusion of antiquaries. The New England stonecutters evidently had little reverence for Virginia families.

[55] Memorandum marked "Old Papers 1811-1812." "In re. McCaul-Stevens and Eudocia. Stephens hired to McGrouder at the Coal Pits, Eudocia hired to Dan'l Woode's son not far from Col. Saunders." (This girl was bought from John McCaul January 2, 1811.) Also "tell Mrs. F. McCaul at Hennrico her old man died last night."

[56] Letter from R. S. Ellis to Mr. Charles Ellis, his brother, from Red Hill, Virginia, December 11, 1811. *Ellis & Allan Papers*. "Mr. Were has returned the horse we sold him saying he was lame and too small, Brother Joshua was married on 3rd instant., all your hogs are disposed of except 3," etc.

[57] This warehouse was rented from Joseph Gallego for $137.50 a quarter. *Ellis & Allan Papers*.

stuttered and clucked, as the siphon of the tides rolled it backward and forward under the piles and slivered planks.

At the store, planters rode up and tethered their horses; wagons loaded for the Western settlements with blankets, ginghams, and the little puncheons of rum and powder, while the clerks weighed out the rolls of ponderous lead. Students on their way to William and Mary presented letters of credit from their up-country sires. Ladies came to make choice of taffetas and brocade stuffs, young gentlemen pursers, in semi-nautical garb, strolled in and out with accounts and moneys, while Ellises, Allans, Mackenzies, McMurdocks and MacDougals punctuated the snuff-dusty air with the *burr* of broadest Scotch, and John Allan strolled off down Tobacco Alley with some British or Yankee captains to dinner at the cozily furnished house around the corner. Here their weathered seamen's countenances looked masterfully across the table at the engaging Miss Valentine and the wide-eyed young Edgar Poe, as Frances Allan brewed a strong dish of the best of Imperial Gunpowder Tea, and her husband spoke feelingly of the fine nappy ale of Kilmarnock.[58]

The conversation was of the decline in the flax prices at Lisbon, of the latest alarms and excursions of Bonaparte, the Orders in Council, and the prices last fetched at Liverpool for the best Virginia leaf. To this board and household the young housewife of twenty-seven summers and her sister Miss Valentine brought a fresh blond beauty and the traditions of grace and ease of Virginia planters, together with an unfailing feminine tenderness in which a sensitive little orphan boy basked. It was the atmosphere of the old, vanished Eastern Seaboard, the South of slavery and the days of sailing ships, something to be recalled over a glass of old port and a churchwarden's clay pipe. Out of this, it had pleased the wayward ways of fate to conjure a master of dreams.

Despite the considerable volume of business carried on by the partners, the condition of John Allan's affairs in December, 1811, were not such as to permit the addition of another soul to his permanent household without his pausing to take thought.[59] When Frances Allan brought young Edgar Poe home the day after the death of his mother, her husband no doubt regarded it as the kindly and impulsive act of a woman, but as the days and weeks passed and the problem of what to do with the two orphans grew pressing with both the Allans and Mackenzies, it became evident that the hands of the pretty young boy

---

[58] Letter from Allan Fowlds, Kilmarnock, Scotland, 4th of January, 1812. "Mrs. F. is keeping for you some fine nappy ale," etc. *Ellis & Allan Papers.*

[59] The somewhat detailed account of the firm's affairs given above should not lead the reader to suppose that at this time, 1812, Mr. Allan was a wealthy man. The business was as yet a young one, the firm was new and struggling, and entering upon a period of general commercial stagnation.

An Off-Hour at *Ellis & Allan*

From an old print of a contemporary establishment

had twined very deeply in the heartstrings of the childless merchant's wife—that she could not bear to part with him. Doubtless he clung to her; his beauty and already romantic story were appealing—to the child-hungry woman it was enough.

With her husband, however, it was different.[60] He was willing and kindly enough to indulge his lovely wife in a temporary charitable impulse, against which no one but a boor would protest, but to make the object of it his legal son and heir, with all that would be involved, was a horse of a different color. That he was altogether justified in this hesitancy, few, who can imagine themselves confronted by a like problem, will deny. Left an orphan himself, he could not but have been moved by the fate of the child who rode cock-horse so engagingly, or sat upon his knee. But it was by no means sure that he and his wife might not yet have children themselves—she was twenty-seven and he was thirty-one—and the prospects of his own issue sharing alike with strangers, even in future time, might well daunt him. Besides, to put it coldly, and he was capable of doing that, the brat of strolling play actors, as his Scottish tongue would frame it, was perhaps not the best of blood to claim as his own. That he had his doubts about Mrs. Poe, we have already seen. David Poe he must have seen upon the stage, and he was capable of drawing his own conclusions. Besides John Allan had social ambitions as the future showed. What of the whispers about his "son"? In addition there were other more practical, and at that time secret, but cogent reasons, which might well make him pause.

In the first place, the condition of his affairs was not at that time such as to warrant the additional burden of the keep and education of a child. In March, 1811, he had sailed to Portugal[61] with a considerable cargo on the ship "Sylph" in company with one or two other vessels employed by the Ellises, himself, and Mr. Galt, in expectation of selling provisions to the British Army under Lord Wellesley, just then about to open the Peninsular Campaign. Prices were high and some profit resulted, but owing to the precarious situation of affairs in America just prior to the then imminent war, the gain had been

---

[60] As a great deal of criticism has been leveled against John Allan for not legally adopting Poe and making him his heir, the question will be presented here with the facts which have not heretofore been aired.

[61] Letter from John Allan to Charles Ellis in the *Ellis & Allan Papers,* postmarked New York, June 16, 1811, and dated—Lisbon, April 28, 1811, Ship "Sylph" off Bellumcastle—"Dear Charles: I am happy to inform you that we arrived in safety here on the 26th about 12 A.M. after a most boisterous passage of 23 days from the roads."

Also John Allan from Lisbon, May 31, 1811—

"McLurin Scott has taken passage on board of the Ship 'Telegra' for New York to sail the 2nd or 3rd of June. I shall not be long after him." Josiah Ellis accompanied Mr. Allan on the voyage. It was the intention of both of them to visit Scotland on their way back, but this had to be deferred.

swallowed up, and he had returned to Richmond in the Summer to meet a decidedly serious and widespread financial situation owing to the Embargo and Non-Intercourse Acts.

In addition, his whole family relationship was liberally provided with orphans. He, and four partially dependent sisters at Irvine and Kilmarnock, Scotland, were orphans. The children of at least one of his married sisters were the object of the bounty of himself and his wife, a niece being Mrs. Allan's namesake. There was an old Aunt Jane, "the only surviving member of our father's family," and four young orphan boys, cousins, by the name of Galt. These boys had to be, and were, well taken care of by remittances from Mr. William Galt, the wealthy Richmond uncle. That orphans and their doings were much in Mr. Allan's mind about this time, and that he might well shrink from adding another and gratuitous one to the family roll of charity, a few extracts from the family correspondence will make startlingly clear.[62]

Kilmarnock, 4th Jan. 1812.

My Dear Brother: [read brother-in-law]

I wrote you some time back with the Melancholy News of the Death of my Little Boy William which I hope you have received. I had your favor of the 6th of August . . . which gave us all great pleasure to hear that you and Mrs. A was in good health, and received from Mr. Kerr the coral Necklace and Braceletts as a present from Mrs. Allan to her Little Namesake. I am glad to inform you she is getting quite about and is I trust beginning to walk, the rest of the children is all at school. . . . I had another from your uncle Mr. Galt, and I cannot help thinking he is one of the best-hearted Men, his great anxiety for the Education and support of those Little Orphan Boys the Galts show it in a clear point of view he has appointed me to look after them and see everything done for their interest . . . they seem smart fine children. . . . Your Uncle was so very kind as to send Mrs. Fowlds a present for the education of my children one hundred pounds sterling. . . . Dear Brother we are fully expecting to see you and Mrs. Allan this summer. . . . Your sisters Mary, Jean, and Elizabeth are well. . . . Elizabeth is at Mrs. Galts at Flowerbanks. Mrs. Fowlds desires me to say to you that she received the five guineas for which please accept her warmest thanks . . . etc.

I am My Dear Brother
Yours sincerely,
Allan Fowlds

Some time later we get further news of the orphans from Mrs. Fowlds, John Allan's sister:

My Dear Brother:

Your Letters of Feby. 3rd and July 6th I duly record. . . . I was extremely sorry to observe by it the account my Aunt has given of poor Thomas Galt. I

---

[62] From the *Ellis & Allan Papers,* Library of Congress, Washington, D. C.

William Mayo

The Master of "Powhatan Seat"

A plantation on the site of an old Indian settlement in the suburbs of
Richmond, Va.

A gentleman of the Old Virginia school, a type familiar to POE during the days of his
childhood. *Mr.* MAYO was a member of POE's church, a customer of *Ellis & Allan,*
and a friend of POE's foster-father

By permission of Mrs. Mary Mayo Ingle, a great-granddaughter

flatter myself he is not so bad as has been represented he is an Orphan, John, and I am convinced, none of his faults will be hid; my Aunt and him had not sorted well some how or other; but sister Jane blamed the Maid for it: however, she was so displeased she would not allow him to sleep in the House last time he was at home and Robt. Gemmel took him and I heard the vessel was to be laid up for the Winter and I wished him to stay with me as . . . was informed the Owners were going to put him on board another vessel so his education will be kept back this Winter he is a clever Boy I am told and an excellent scholar and I have no doubt not withstanding all his boyish faults he will be a clever Man he is the best Looking of the whole. *I myself know what it is to be an Orphan they require to walk very circumspectly indeed to escape the censours of a criticising World.* . . .

But the tale of family troubles is not quite complete, John Allan's sister it appears may have had her own reasons for suspecting the frailty of womankind,—the same letter continues—

. . . I was extremely happy to observe that Jane and you were come to an understanding, nothing gives me greater uneasiness than friends quarrelling. Were you not extremely sorry when you heard Cousin William had acted so very foolishly, she was young and thoughtless no doubt but no such apology can be offered for a Man at least 28 or 30 years older than her the betraying the trust Mrs. Galt [63] had reposed in him was not honorable and is what aggravated the trial to think she had encouraged a man to go about her house who was doing everything in his power to destroy the peace of it. However, Mrs. G. is reconciled. . . . I hope Uncle William will forgive her and not let her impropriety have any influence on him as she was a good hearted Girl and had an innocent gaiety about her. I would have not have thought her capable of so imprudent a step. . . . Jean Guthrie calls often and asks for her Johnny she was here yesterday inquiring for you . . . etc.

As Mr. John Allan, merchant, then in some financial perplexity, turned these and other family matters over in his mind, he cannot be entirely blamed for a certain lack of enthusiasm and pessimism about orphans. But there were several other reasons why he could not acquiesce in the immediate adoption of the boy Edgar Poe, reasons of which there is every right to suppose he did not and could not present to his wife. He was already a father, by two other women in Richmond, of two children, a daughter by one and a son by the second.[64] One of these, a son, by a Mrs. Collier, he was then, or a few months later, educating if not supporting, as is shown by the following receipt from William Richardson, a Richmond schoolmaster.[65]

---

[63] This is a Mrs. Galt at "Flowerbanks" on Cree Water. See Chapter V, page 58.
[64] John Allan's illegitimate children at the time that Poe was taken into his household were certainly two, *i.e.,* a daughter by a "Mrs. Wills" and a son by a "Mrs. Collier." There are traces of still others a little later not mentioned here or in the will. Young Poe was sent to school with Edwin Collier. For further complications as late as 1834, see John Allan's will, Appendix III.
[65] *Ellis & Allan Papers,* Library of Congress, Washington, D. C. The evidence does not rest on this one item by any means.

1812   *Mr.* John Allan, *Dr.*
                     To William Richardson
    Oct.
    5th   To three Months Tuition of Edwin Collier — $5—
                                       Received payment
                                   William Richardson

That the good Scotch merchant was not cast down entirely by these
responsibilities, that he had the solace which is said to soothe the breast,
and was willing to pay for it, as for his other pleasures, is brought out
nicely by another item of about the same date—[65]

Mr. J. Allan   14 *Oct.* 1812 [66]
                         Bought @ Auction
    I Flute .... $21—
                 Received payt. for Foster and Satchell
                                              Th. Foster

It is, in all probability, the same flute upon which Edgar Allan Poe
afterwards learned to play in those early, easy days in Richmond which
were to permeate his dreams, for circumstances and Frances Allan
prevailed, and Edgar Poe became the foster-child of John Allan.

The circumstances which added the force of public opinion to the
already patent desire of his wife to retain Edgar, and which was the
immediate decisive factor in persuading John Allan to acquiesce in her
desire, was one of those fearful tragedies whose only mitigation lies
in the fact that they arouse universal charity. On December 26, 1811,
only about two weeks after Mrs. Poe had been buried at St. John's,
the Richmond Theater, where she had so often played, took fire from
the stage chandelier during a presentation of *The Bleeding Nun* by
Mr. Placide and his Company to a packed house. It was the night
after Christmas. The results were for a generation memory-searing.
Among the seventy-three persons who are known to have perished was
the Governor of Virginia.

On that night an Herculean negro blacksmith strode through the
flames along with other persons engaged in the work of rescue: heroism,
pathetic sacrifice, and children in the fire moved to one outcry the then
not too United States. The Federal Senate purchased crape sleeve

---

[66] *Ellis & Allan Papers,* Library of Congress, Washington, D. C.

bands, and even the Legislature of Massachusetts was melted to official tears. This letter will give some idea of how John Allan felt about it at the time, and why he and all his family escaped. It is from a friendly commercial correspondent.

New York, Jany. 8th, 1812

JOHN ALLAN, *Esq.,*

    DEAR SIR:

    I received your favor of the 3rd inst. . . . Of the Horrible Catastrophe which befel your city I have indeed had too correct information—, it was first announced here by a gentleman from Washington who reported, that as he was leaving, the mail arrived from Richmond announcing it. My Fears were it would prove too true and knowing the confined manner in which the Stairs were built I felt confident [I] would hear of the loss of some Friends, which the next day's mail brought, and with it, a detail of all the Horror of that Fatal night—*How fortunate, that yourself and Family went out of Town* and what a consolation that Mr. Richard and family escaped as they did with the exception of poor little George Dixon whose fate I must lament with you. . . . My God what must be the feelings of Mr. Gallego and Mayor Gibson and Family, but I must stop I am going too far. . . . .

W. WHITLOK, *Jun.*[67]

    Miss Valentine escaped too, having been on a holiday visit with the Ellises in the country to see "Uncle Joshua" married.[68] John Allan had good reason to congratulate himself, doubtless he felt grateful that so far he had escaped the flames, and reflected that a little insurance with Providence as to the future might pay. All of Richmond was at that time busy in works of charity. Orphans were being cared for by wholesale, and the upshot of the matter was that the Poe children remained where they had been taken; Edgar in John Allan's house, and little Rosalie at Mr. William Mackenzie's.

    In Edgar's case, that his fostering in the house where he had been sheltered was mainly due to the intercession and insistence of Frances Allan there can no longer be any doubt. There is the direct statement of one of the family servants to that effect and even *the possibility* that Frances Allan was so anxious to keep the beautiful young boy in lieu of the child which nature denied her, that she failed to answer the inquiries of his anxious grandparents in Baltimore, "General" David

---

[67] *Ellis & Allan Papers,* Library of Congress, Washington, D. C.
[68] From Eliza M. Hunter, niece of Charles Ellis, at Red Hill, Virginia, January, 1812, to Charles Ellis of *Ellis & Allan* at Richmond. "Nancy went home about four weeks ago with Cousin Betsy to Cynthia Hunter. They came up to the wedding and spent a few weeks with us."

Poe and his wife,[69] and Edgar's Aunt, Eliza Poe. Even after more than a hundred years there is something touching in the beseeching tone of this long dead voice speaking out of the dry mold of government archives with the deep anxiety of tears.

Baltimore, Feb. 8th, 1813

'Tis the Aunt of Edgar that addresses Mrs. Allen for the second time, impressed with the idea that a letter if received could not remain unacknowledged so long as from the months of July, she is induced to write again in order to inquire in her family's as well as in her own name after the health of the child of her Brother, as well as that of his adopted Parents. I cannot suppose my dear Mrs. Allen that a heart possessed of such original humanity as yours must without doubt be, could so long keep in suspense, the anxious inquiries made through the medium of my letter by the Grand Parents of the Orphan of an unfortunate son, surely ere this allowing that you did not wish to commence a correspondence with one who is utterly unknown to you had you received it Mr. Allen would have written to my Father or Brother if it had been only to let them know how he was, but I am confident that you never received it, for two reasons, the first is that not having the pleasure of knowing your christian name I merely addressed it to Mrs. Allen of Richmond, the second is as near as I can recollect you were about the time I wrote to you at the springs where Mr. Douglas saw you, permit me my dear madam to thank you for your kindness to the little Edgar— he is truly the child of fortune to be placed under the fostering care of the amiable Mr. and Mrs. Allen, Oh how few meet with such a lot—the Almighty Father of the Universe grant that he may never abuse the kindness he has received and that from those who were not bound by any ties except those the feeling and humane heart dictates—I fear that I have too long intruded on your patience, will you if so have the goodness to forgive me—and dare I venture to flatter myself with the hope that this will be received with any degree of pleasure or that you will gratify me so much as to answer it—give my love to the dear little Edgar and tell him tis his Aunt Eliza who writes this to you, my Mother and family desire to be affectionately remembered to Mr. Allen and yourself—Henry frequently speaks of his little brother and expresses a great desire to see him, tell him he sends his very best love to him and is greatly pleased to hear that he is so good as also so pretty a Boy as Mr. Douglass represented him to be—I feel as if I were writing to a sister and can scarcely even at the risk of your displeasure prevail on myself to lay aside my pen — With the hope of your indulgence in pardoning my temerity I remain my Dear Mrs. Allen yours

with the greatest respect

ELIZA POE

Mrs. Allen the kind Benefactress of the infant Orphan Edgar, Allen, Poe.[70]

Now there are some remarkable things about this letter. In the first place Rosalie is not mentioned at all for which there are several possible

---

[69] The reader will doubtless recall the fact that Edgar's elder brother, William Henry Poe, was already residing with this couple, having been left with them by his parents in 1807. See page 4 for this. For a further account of "General" David Poe see Chapter VII, note 172.

[70] The letter is printed, of course, with the original spelling and punctuation carefully reproduced from a photostat of the original in the *Ellis & Allan Papers.* "Allen" is spelt "Allen" by Eliza Poe.

explanations that suggest themselves,[71] secondly this letter definitely disposes of the story repeated by so many Poe biographers that either the Allans or the Mackenzies entered into correspondence with the Poes in Baltimore who refused *on account of poverty* to take in the two orphans. Evidently nothing of the kind had occurred, and as a matter of fact the shoe was on the other foot. In a letter which Poe wrote to his guardian from West Point in 1830, he specifically mentions the fact that John Allan had followed his own desire, or the desire of his wife to adopt Edgar Poe, despite the express wishes of the grandfather, "General" David Poe, to have the care of his favorite grandchild. Poe represents that his grandfather was *in good circumstances at the time,* and that in order to induce the Poes to allow Edgar to remain with the Allans, John Allan had held out strong inducements for them to do so by promises of adoption and liberal education. This letter Poe says was at that time (January 3, 1830) in possession of the members of the Poe family in Baltimore.[72] The implication is clear, once having determined to gratify the fond wishes of his wife for the "adoption" of Edgar, John Allan carried the matter off with his usual vigor and determination.

Hence Eliza Poe seems more than doubtful as to whether her letter to Lady Bountiful is going to be answered. It is also interesting to observe that two commas in the last line quite subtly, and thus early assert the boy's right to his own name. There is a tradition but no record to show that both Edgar and Rosalie were baptized respectively as Edgar Allan [73] and Rosalie Mackenzie, but as neither was ever *legally* adopted they remained "Poe," as they had been born.[74] Thus the boy came by the name of Edgar Allan Poe, which he has successfully projected into time. Aside from this, the baptismal water left very little trace.

Like other mortals the young Poe was subject to those internal frailties and afflictions which cause parents endless anxiety, and Mrs. Allan must often have found herself, with this rather delicate and pretty

---

71 There are several explanations of this possible:
   1. Eliza Poe simply failed to mention Rosalie or chose not to.
   2. She did not care to confuse issues with Mr. Allan by mentioning Rosalie.
   3. The Poes did not know there was such a child.
   4. The Poes were already in communication with the Mackenzies.
72 Poe to John Allan from West Point, New York, January 3, 1831. See the *Valentine Museum Poe Letters,* letter No. 24, page 253.
73 J. H. Whitty says, probably as early as December 11, 1811, in the case of Edgar. See his *Memoir* to *The Complete Poems,* page xxii, large edition. There is also a tradition that both the children were baptized by the Reverend Mr. Richardson of St. John's.
74 Legal adoption outside of the ties of blood was almost unknown in the South at this time. Prof. James Southall Wilson to the author, July, 1925.

little boy, filling the rôle of mother in grim earnest. Let it be solemnly recorded then for the first time, that in May, 1812, Edgar Poe was afflicted with the croup for which his foster-father paid the bill. As the earliest documentary evidence of Poe's being in John Allan's household it is not without a genuine element of interest:

Mr. JOHN ALLAN

To P. THORNTON

1812

May 21st	To Visit and medicine to child.............	$1.50
22nd.	To Visit	1.00
23rd.	To Visit and Vial Pectoral Mint...........	1.50

$4.00

Rect. payment

PHILIP THORNTON [75]

In July, as we have seen, the family visited the Springs where Edgar was evidently noticed by a Mr. Douglas of Baltimore who remarked upon his great beauty to his aunt Eliza Poe. That the young boy was a really lovely child, whose winsome appearance and romantic story appealed to all tender hearts, there is a mass of testimony and tradition to attest. Frances Allan was evidently in love with her little pet, now nearly three years old, an affection which he is known to have passionately returned. Sometime in the Fall the family returned to Richmond, probably after having visited Mrs. Allan's relatives, the Valentines, near Staunton, as it was their custom to do. During the Winter of 1812 we find them in Richmond as usual living at the corner of Fourteenth Street and Tobacco Alley. "Uncle" William Galt seems to have been living with them then. Edgar was by this time for better or for worse a fixture in the household, where he was often seen by an Abner Lincoln of Boston who was at this time a frequent guest together with Dr. Thornton and the Ellises at John Allan's table.

Mr. Allan was in considerable difficulties, one of his ships having been seized by the customs authorities at Norfolk, and as he sat in front of the coal fire, pondering the style of his "prayer for release" to the Federal Court, his thoughts must have wandered over the water to the orphans at Kilmarnock or have paused between the wailing notes of his new flute to consider the future of the little orphan whose bare feet could be heard padding about upstairs while he was being put to bed by "Ma" or "Aunt Nancy." John Allan, too, had his softer moods, and in the years ahead, he conceived a pride and a tenderness for the

---

[75] Philip Thornton was a doctor, the personal friend of John Allan. He is frequently mentioned in correspondence. The receipt is from the *Ellis & Allan Papers.*

little lad whom he came to regard as his son. It was this which his proud heart never forgave; that the youth to whom he had once unbent and unbosomed would not obey his behest was unpardonable. For as with everything else that the merchant dealt in, there was a price to be paid for his affections, a price which the poet in Poe found too great to pay. It was the control of his heart and soul. But now, for a while at least, Lady Bountiful and her husband were in control of the clay, if not the spirit of the boy, and that momentous modeling had begun which was to make and mar the man.

CHAPTER FOUR

"THE LITTLE ANGEL" TRIES HIS WINGS

FRANCES ALLAN would undoubtedly have liked to adopt the young Edgar Allan Poe formally and legally but her husband continued to demur. It was only after considerable persuasion and the unexpected force of circumstances that he had at length consented to receive the boy permanently into his household. At first blush his refusal to adopt the child legally, after consenting to his becoming a fixture in the family circle and lending him his name, may seem a captious distinction, but from his point of view many poignant reasons continued to operate for refusing or at least deferring indefinitely such an irrevocable act. In addition to those which have already been rehearsed, there must have been a deep-seated feeling that in a certain way he would be over-riding Providence by adopting a child that it had not pleased God to send him in the ordinary course of nature. The Scotch sense of literal reality is almost morbidly honest, and John Allan could not allow even his sympathy and affection to deceive him into believing by legal fiction what was in reality not true. He was willing to indulge his wife, with and for whom he doubtless felt a great sympathy in their mutual child-lessness, but he was not willing to commit himself, without further demonstration as to the character of his ward, into declaring him to be the inheritor of his property. All this, and a certain instinctive sense of the vast gulf which separated the temperaments of himself and his ward, something which both of them must have instinctively felt almost from the first—all this must have decided him that delay was the best policy, and as the good old Scotch adage has it, he had best "bide a wee."

In this decision he differed profoundly from the feminine impulsive-ness of his wife, but the overwhelming desire of a childless woman for an object upon which to lavish the pent up tenderness of thwarted maternity, and the unemotional foresight of a clear-headed man of affairs are two different things. It is impossible to say, even now, which was right,—the blind love of the foster-mother, or the oblique though logical view of the man; possibly the former.

Had Edgar been legally adopted, it is possible that the feeling of eating the bread of strangers of in the final analysis being an object of charity, of which fact he was often reminded,—it is quite probable that this feeling of inferiority against which he built up an almost morbid pride, destined to be one of the controlling factors in his character, would never have been present at all or would have vanished as time went on.

As it was, Poe was compelled to move in a world of uncertainties, one where the deepest and most intimate ties of life were, as he increasingly realized with the years, dependent upon the impulses of charity. The illusion of the permanence of home and the immutability of the paternal and maternal relations are the twin rocks upon which a well-integrated personality is built and stands. Shatter these, or give them the quality of uncertainty, and the spirit becomes one with the quicksand upon which it feels that life rests.

Even in the endearments of his foster-mother, Poe must have come to realize that he was a substitute for her own child. Her affections were great, but the fact remains that she was not his own mother. If he did not sense it, Mr. Allan on several well-authenticated occasions took care to make it painfully clear. As a very young child, Edgar would have actually missed the physical presence of his own mother; as he grew older and her memory dimmed, he must have sought for compensation elsewhere. There seems every reason to feel that Frances Allan met this situation with a plenitude of endearments that undoubtedly had an effect upon Poe's character. Mrs. Allan's unusual fondness for children and for her foster-son in particular was the cause of remark at the time and later.[76] That her affection for the little boy was one of the holiest and finest of his many feminine contacts does not lessen the probabilities of its far-reaching effects. In the same house was also his "Aunt" Nancy Valentine who seems to have been only a little less fond. In the light of modern psychology, it may well seem to many that this is alone sufficient to account for many of the apparent motions of his later life. It may be that from the first Edgar Allan Poe was embarked upon one of those hopeless quests of the soul that drive many artists to the greatest heights of creation and the lowest depths of despair.

As a little boy it seems that he cared more for the company of little girls than of boys of his own age, and that his schooldays were lonely and unhappy.[77] Though not unhealthy he was delicate, a condition in which his foster-mother indulged him, for he was brilliant and beautiful, and soon became the pet of the household and its friends. At a very early date he is said to have shown an innocent but passionate attachment for Catherine Elizabeth Poitiaux, a pretty little girl, who

---

[76] See Mrs. Galt's letter to Frances Allan about the Galt children from Irvine, Scotland, in 1818, Chapter V, page 61.

[77] Poe in *Burton's Gentleman's Magazine* for April, 1840. "Since the sad experience of my schoolboy days to this present writing, I have seen little to sustain the notion held by some folks, that schoolboys are the happiest of all mortals."

as Mrs. Allan's godchild was one of his first playmates.[78]   It was also
Mrs. Allan's particular delight to take him upon calls to her various
friends and relations, upon which occasions she is said to have dressed
him in a charming costume of a peaked, purple velvet cap with a gold
tassel from which his dark curls flowed down, like those of a Restoration periwig, over an ample tucker that disappeared into small baggy
trousers of yellow Nankeen or silk pongee.   Seated upon a davenport,
swinging his little buckled shoes in the air, he would gravely look on,
while the assembled ladies dressed in the semi-classic Empire costumes
of the day, with fillets in their hair, chattered about the latest war news
and sipped tea.

Sometimes he would be called upon to amuse the company by standing upon a high-backed chair to recite jingles.   Tradition has it that
the company was both delighted and amused.   Even John Allan was
not insensible to his juvenile talents, and we have a picture of the young
Poe, mounted shoeless upon the long, shining dining room table, after
the dessert and cloth had been cleared away, to dance; or standing
between the doors of the drawing room at the Fourteenth Street house
reciting to a large company, and with a boyish fervor, *The Lay of the
Last Minstrel*.   "He wore dark curls and had brilliant eyes, and those
who remembered him spoke of the pretty figure he made, with his
vivacious ways." [79]   The reward for such occasions was to pledge the
healths of the company in sweetened wine and water.   Much has been
made of this fact, which in all conscience seems harmless and trivial
enough.[80]

Of the early life in Richmond of this delightful little boy, who later
on felt competent to exchange places with the Archangel Israfel, there
remain a mass of legend and some few authentic facts.   Perhaps it will
not be entirely without some contribution as to the nature of the man
as a human being to get a few glimpses of him trying out his young
wings even before he aspired to leave the nest.

Some of the earliest and dearest associations of Poe's life clustered
about the old Memorial Church on Broad Street which had been erected
on the site of the Richmond Theater as a memorial to those who had perished in the fire.[81]   John Allan and Charles Ellis had both subscribed to
the fund for its erection, the latter twice as much as his partner,[82] and
both had taken out their membership there after leaving St. John's.

---

[78] J. H. Whitty, *Memoir,* large edition, page xxiv.
[79] Woodberry.
[80] See the discussion of Poe's early drinking in Chapter IX, page 137.
[81] The history of this church is in itself very interesting and closely connected with
the successful reëstablishment of the Protestant Episcopal Church in Virginia which
had suffered a serious eclipse during the Revolution.   Among those prominently concerned with it were Bushrod Washington and Chief Justice Marshall.
[82] The bills and receipts for this are in the *Ellis & Allan Papers* at Washington.

Frances Keeling Allan

née Valentine

First Wife of JOHN ALLAN, merchant, of Richmond, Virginia, Beloved
foster-mother of EDGAR ALLAN POE

Born February 14, 1784; adopted by JOHN Dixon, printer, January 12, 1795;
married JOHN ALLAN 1803; died February 28, 1829

[Data courtesy of Edward F. Valentine]

From a portrait by Thomas Sully, owned by Edward V. Valentine
Courtesy of the Valentine Museum, Richmond, Virginia

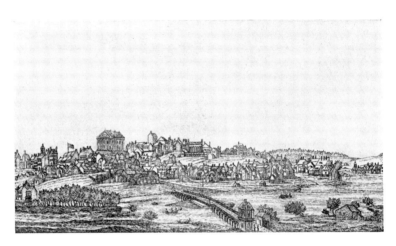

The Richmond of Poe's Early Childhood

From a rare old print
Courtesy of the Edgar Allan Poe Shrine, Richmond, Virginia

The Burning of the Theater in Richmond, Virginia
on the Night of December 26, 1811

This was the theater in which ELIZABETH ARNOLD POE, mother of EDGAR
ALLAN POE, was acting shortly before her death on December 8, 1811

The Monumental Church, Richmond, Virginia

Mr. ALLAN and his partner held pew 80, where the young POE sat with his foster-parents

From a very rare old print

Courtesy of the Edgar Allan Poe Shrine, Richmond, Virginia

Rt. Rev. Richard Channing Moore

Protestant Episcopal Bishop of Virginia and
First Rector of the Monumental Church, Richmond, Virginia

Where EDGAR POE attended with his foster-parents

The Monumental Church was completed in 1814 on the site of the burned "Richmond Theater," in which POE's mother had often played, and where she received two benefits while on her death-bed. JOHN ALLAN's pew was No. 80, directly in front of the pulpit; there POE sat and looked up into *Bishop* MOORE's face

By permission of Mrs. Mary Mayo Ingle

This was consonant with a well-marked determination to better the social status of the "firm."

The building was an impressive one with a monument to the sufferers of the fire at the entrance, a rather naïve fresco of the heavenly regions on the ceiling, tablets with the Ten Commandments, and a great gold lettered text, "Give Ear O Lord," just over the chancel. It was the custom of all the children to try out their spelling on this, and Mary Brockenbrough, a little girl one year younger than Poe, remembered looking back and seeing Poe, "a pretty little boy with big eyes and curly hair" hypnotized by the text.

The Allans had pew 80 and, from the end where he usually sat, Poe could see the back of little Mary's head obliquely in front. Just across the nave was the front pew of Chief Justice Marshall and his long-legged son who sat with the gate open and his feet in the aisle. The Allan pew was directly before the pulpit in which the stout Bishop Moore, rector of the church at that time, held forth, to what effect upon young Poe we can only surmise, probably the usual one.

It was here that Poe first met his youthful companion Ebenezer Burling, of whom more hereafter, and laid that foundation of familiarity with the Bible and the church services and singing which he never lost.[83] One biographer has averred "that phrenologically considered," the bump of reverence was entirely lacking in both Poe and Rosalie and that they never evinced any interest in the saving works of religion.[84] However that may be, to church he went regularly in the company of Mrs. Allan who was extremely pious. From his foster-father who had a more eighteenth century and encyclopedic attitude and philosophy, Edgar undoubtedly received or overheard opinions which made him one of the first poets in America to view the world minus the explanation of a miracle working deity, and to take a metaphysical interest in the growing data of science.

Among the many visitors to the house then and later, was Mr. Edward Valentine, a cousin of Mrs. Allan, who was very fond of the boy. He was a great practical joker and by way of being somewhat of a merry rogue himself.[85] This young gentleman taught young Edgar several amusing tricks. One of these was the ancient amusement of snatching a chair away from someone about to sit down. Unfortunately the newly acquired talent was tried upon the person of a portly

[83] I am indebted to the kindness of Mrs. Mary Newton Stanard for the reminiscences of her grandmother, Mary Brockenbrough, here included. See also J. H. Whitty's *Memoir*, large edition, page xxv. Also Mrs. Shew's account of Poe in church, taken from the *Ingram Papers*.

[84] Mrs. Susan Archer Weiss in *The Home Life of Poe*.

[85] For several amusing facts about this gentleman I am indebted to Mr. Edward V. Valentine, the well-known sculptor, of Richmond, Virginia, which he related to me in July, 1925.

and extremely dignified lady caller, and tradition has preserved for us the picture of John Allan leading his too pert young charge away for chastisement after the old-fashioned manner, and of Mrs. Allan with tears in her eyes hurrying upstairs shortly after to quiet the lamentations of her pet.

As a counterbalance to his wife's indulgence, Mr. Allan conscientiously set about to train up the boy according to his more severe ideas of the proper way in which the twig should be bent. Consequently, when the child was "good," he was indulged, but any exhibition of waywardness or disobedience brought down on him the usual punishment of the time which, it was said, was administered to him upon divers occasions with undue severity. To save him from this was the constant aim of the ladies, and even the servants of the household. With their connivance the boy soon learned to shield himself by means of petty subterfuges upon his own part which were doubtless more clever than manly.

The child's education was early well looked after. As a very little boy, there is a trustworthy legend that he was sent to a "dame school," which would correspond most nearly to the modern kindergarten, minus much of the element of organized play. This was said to have been kept by an old Scotch lady with a broad Lowland accent, doubtless in itself a recommendation to the parents of many of her charges. Of her, very little is remembered except a rumor that she called Edgar "her ain wee laddie," and in after years was said to have brought him presents of the best smoking tobacco she could obtain (sic).[86] Poe also indicates in a seemingly autobiographical passage in *The Narrative of Arthur Gordon Pym*, "He [Mr. Allan] sent me at six years of age to the school of old Mr. Ricketts, a gentleman with only one arm, and of eccentric manner." It has since been found that there was in Richmond about that time a one-armed schoolmaster by the name of "Ricketts."[87] One William Richardson also kept a boys' school where John Allan sent some of the other children in whom he was interested in 1813-14. The truth is, it is not definitely known exactly where and to whom Poe first went to school.

It is fairly certain, however, that shortly before the departure of the Allans for England in 1815, Poe was a student with a Mr. William Ewing who kept a boys' school in Richmond at that time.[88] Ewing from his letters seems to have had a dry sense of humor, and in addition to have taken a real interest in his young charge, remarking in a letter

[86] This story rests upon evidence that can be questioned.
[87] I am indebted for the sources of this information to Mr. J. H. Whitty's *Memoir* to *The Complete Poems*.
[88] Letter from William Ewing dated Richmond, November 27, 1817, to John Allan in London.

some two years after the lad had left him that "He is a charming boy," and inquiring what he was reading. Evidently, even by 1814 or 1815, Poe was one of those strange freaks of nature in a school, a boy who took a lively interest in his books. Mr. Ewing also received payments from John Allan for Edwin Collier, the natural son, from March 15, 1815, to March 15, 1818. In all probability young Collier attended the school in 1815 at the same time as Edgar Poe.[89] There are also indications that Mr. Allan was educating others of his progeny about this time elsewhere, as the firm of *Ellis & Allan* was called upon by other teachers for their tuition.[90]

There is another side to Edgar Poe's childhood for which, by the nature of things, there can be very little documentary evidence, yet one that careful inference has every right to draw. It is that of his intimate association with negroes as a Southern boy brought up in Richmond during the days of slavery, and of the profound effect which their rhythms, melodies, and folk-tales must have had upon his imagination.

From earliest childhood Poe must also have listened to a continuous stream of oral narratives and exploits related by the sea captains, merchants and adventurers who sat at his foster-father's table and later on unburdened themselves before the fire. It seems a warrantable inference that much of his flair for sea narrative was the result of this.

That the boy often found himself seated by the glowing hearth of many a negro cabin, or in the slave quarters, listening to the weird tales of the dark tenants and swaying to the syncopations of their songs is inevitable. Northern critics and biographers seem, largely, to have forgotten that Edgar Allan Poe was a Southerner raised in the South. To them, the importance of his early environment, and the romantic and grotesque incidents of the life about him in his early but impressionable boyhood, must for the most part, on account of their lack of sympathy with something which they have never experienced or suspected, be forever a closed book.

For if there is one thing more than any other which sets off that portion of the Union where Poe was raised, the Old South, "Uncle Sam's Other Country," from all other sections, it is the exotic and withal grotesque presence and influence of the negro. He, more than

---

[89] Letter from William Ewing to John Allan from Richmond, Virginia, November 29, 1815.
Letter from John Allan to William Ewing from London, England, March 21, 1818.
[90] Young Collier seems to have been withdrawn from his former schoolmaster, William Richardson, sometime in 1814 and to have been entered with William Ewing, March, 1815. Whether Poe went to school also under William Richardson, or whether Ewing succeeded Richardson in the business is not clear. The whereabouts and names of the other children have only a remote connection with Poe at this time, and, for obvious reasons, they are not elaborated upon in the text.

any other factor, he and the soft languor of its subtropical springs and summers are responsible for the combined squalor and glamour of its ancient villages and towns. Here, transplanted to a new environment in a more boreal continent, the negro has created for himself another native habitat, and no one who lives there can fail to come under the peculiar and ofttimes fatal influence of his methodical-chaos of life. To this influence the receptive and imaginative mind of young Poe was constantly subjected during the most impressionable years of his childhood.[91]

Like all well-bred Virginia boys, he had his own negro "mammy" up to the time when the family left for England in 1815.[92] The life of the white man overshadows and often checks the exuberance and strangeness of the *modus vivendi* of the darkey; the "black secrets" and the magic of his real existence are seldom penetrated by the adult members of the dominant race. Children, however, are always privileged characters, and young Edgar, as a prime favorite and pet of the family, must often have sat by their firesides in the rooms of his foster-father's house-servants in Richmond, or in the slave quarters and cabins upon the plantations at which he was a frequent visitor.

There he must have feasted upon corn-pone and listened, while many a tale of Brer Rabbit and his ilk went round, while the ghosts, and "hants" and spooks of an ignorant but imaginative and superstitious people walked with hair-raising effect, and songs with melancholy harmonies and strange rhythms beat themselves into his consciousness with that peculiar ecstasy and abandon which only children and the still half-savage individuals of a childish race can experience. Here it was then, rather than upon some mythical journey to France or Russia, that he first laid the foundation for his weird imaginings and the strange "new" cadences which he was to succeed later on in grafting upon the main tree of English poetry. Here, too, may have arisen his flair for the bizarre, and the concept that birds and animals were speaking characters, and that fear of graves and corpses and the paraphernalia of the charnel, so peculiarly a characteristic of the negro, which haunted him through the rest of his life. Reliable tradition, indeed, has preserved some incidents which confirm the probability.

One Summer, when Edgar was about six years old, the Allans paid a visit to one of the smaller Virginia Springs, and on their way back to Richmond stopped to visit Mrs. Allan's relatives, the Valentines, at Staunton. Edward Valentine, whose interest in Edgar has already

---

[91] One biographer avoids much of this by saying, "The psychology of a poet's boyhood is obscure."

[92] Possibly the "Judith" or the "Eudocia" mentioned by receipts and the bills of sale as being in John Allan's household. See note 45.

been remarked, was fond of organizing wrestling matches for small
money prizes between Edgar and the little pickaninnies with whom he
played. He would also take young Poe about the country driving, or
seated behind him on horseback. Valentine is responsible for the story
that once as they were returning from the country post office, where
Edgar had astonished the rustics with his infant learning by reading a
newspaper aloud to them,[93] on the way home, they passed a log cabin
near which were several graves. The boy betrayed such nervous terror that Mr. Valentine was forced to take Edgar from his seat behind,
and hold him before him on the horse, while the boy kept crying out,
"They will run after us and drag me down." Upon being questioned
later, he admitted that it had been the custom of his "mammy" to take
him at night to the servants' quarters—"where many a tale of graveyard ghost went round"—and he had been regaled with gruesome
stories of cemeteries and horrible apparitions. To such incidents as
these there can be little doubt that American Literature owes a considerable debt. The time had come, however, when Edgar Poe was
to be removed temporarily from such plantation influences and plunged
into the midst of an older, and perhaps more civilized and complicated
world. With the cessation of hostilities after the Treaty of Ghent in
1815, John Allan had decided to pay a long deferred visit to England
and Scotland, and the family went abroad.

The early Spring and Summer of 1815 must have been largely occupied by the family preparations for the voyage in which Edgar would
naturally have taken a lively interest. Frances Allan had been hurt in
an accident and the departure was delayed. We catch a final authentic
but fleeting glimpse of the boy at this time, when the easy flow of his
happy childhood in Richmond was about to be interrupted by an important remove. From the reminiscences of one Dr. C. A. Ambler,[94]
afterwards a well-known physician, we learn that about this time he
used to swim with Edgar Poe at a pool in Shockoe Creek, then situated
where the shops of the C. & O. Railroad now stand. Dr. Ambler says
that he stripped with Edgar day after day, and that the boy was of a
delicate physique and rather timid disposition, taking to the water a

---

[93] There is an interesting letter in the *Ellis & Allan Papers* which throws considerable light on the state of culture among the poorer up-country whites at this time, in
which one of the Ellises depicts their incredulity over his prediction of an eclipse of the
sun, and their superstitious astonishment at its fulfillment. The mental condition of
these "poor whites" seems to have approached that of the medieval peasant during the
early Renaissance.

[94] This information is given in a letter from Dr. Ambler to Edward V. Valentine of
Richmond, which the latter read to the author in July, 1925. The story of Shockoe
Creek and its peregrinations and floods is closely interwoven with the history and fate
of Richmond. In the early Nineteenth Century, a sudden flood in this stream prevented
the perpetration of a massacre by an uprising of the slaves.

bit reluctantly.[95]   The testimony as to Poe's physical development in childhood is not without value, and in many particulars confirms the evidence as to his early appearance.   That he was about to be removed to a more bracing climate and exposed to the vigorous and sometimes brutal influences of the playgrounds of English schools for the next five years marks the beginning of a new and powerful influence upon his mental and physical equipment.   The sunlight of Virginia and the mists and snows of Scotland and Stoke Newington are two different things.

---

[95] Dr. Ambler states Poe was about "nine years old at this time." As Poe was in England during his ninth year, the doctor is mistaken on this point. Poe's later prowess as a swimmer is in contrast with this early timidity.

CHAPTER FIVE

THE correspondence of Poe's guardian John Allan with his relatives in Scotland during the years 1811 and 1812, and from then on to the end of the war, the letters from his sisters and brother-in-law at Irvine and Kilmarnock [96] fairly teem with references and invitations to him and his wife to revisit the haunts of his youth. In 1811 he had intended to return from Lisbon by way of Great Britain, when the imminence of hostilities intervened. The war, of course, had enforced the postponement of the family wishes, and his own, for some years. Now, at last, he was about to see them realized.

There were, in addition, business reasons the most urgent. The cessation of trade between England and America had borne peculiarly heavily upon the Virginia tobacco merchants. Accounts for cargoes shipped just before the war were still unsettled, and it was necessary to close these and to reëstablish personal relations with English houses in a market where tobacco prices were extraordinarily high, due to the cessation of supply, but which might be expected to be glutted as soon as intercourse was resumed, from the immense reserve stocks on hand. All of this required the personal presence of at least one member of the firm, and it was the junior partner who, combining his personal desires and business advantage, undertook the mission to establish a foreign branch.[97]

Personally it must have been with a good deal of pleasure that John Allan looked forward to a reunion with his family upon his native heath. It had now been many years since he had left Scotland a penniless youth to make his fortunes in the land where fortunes were then to be made. The pot at the end of the rainbow had not proved a mere legend. The orphan was returning to Scotland in comfortable circumstances. He had before him, the prospect of his uncle's ample fortune, and he brought with him a beautiful young wife and sister-in-law, for Miss Valentine accompanied him. Perhaps not the least factor in his natural pride of accomplishment was the presence of his handsome, brilliant, and lovable little foster-son, Edgar, a living testimony to the charitable inclinations and capacity of his purse. Some stress has already been

---

[96] See the letters in the *Ellis & Allan Papers,* Library of Congress, Washington, D. C., from John Allan's sisters, Mary, Elizabeth, Jane, and his brother-in-law, Allan Fowlds, from 1811 to 1814.

[97] Woodberry, 1909, vol. I, page 20.

laid on the less appealing aspects of John Allan's character. It is only just to make the point, at this juncture, that there was also in the man a deep and abiding generosity and capability for the finer manifestations of human affection. Like most of us, this wily Scot had contradictions in his nature. He was capable, at once, of a generous bounty and a mean parsimony, a large tolerance and a bigoted determination to dominate. During his association with him, Edgar Poe experienced the entire gamut of the capabilities of a nature, the vigor of which can only be described by the adjective "tremendous." It was no dovecot into which the lost fledging had fallen, but the nest of a hawk, whose wings were strong to protect, but with talons that clutched, and a beak that might pierce to the heart.

At the time when John Allan and his family sailed for England, the child Edgar had been taken not only into the house, but into the arms and heart of his foster-father. The merchant's correspondence at this date and afterwards bears unmistakable evidence of the pride, the affection and the hopes which he cherished for the boy, and it is safe to say that from 1815 to 1820, and for a year or two after, John Allan looked upon little "Edgar Allan" as he would have regarded the child of his loins. As for his wife, Frances, and her sister,—they were completely under the boy's spell. Only the cloud of his schooldays cast a shadow on an otherwise sunny landscape.

Before leaving Richmond, Mr. Allan auctioned his household furniture and some personal effects through the commission house of Moncure, Robinson & Pleasants, drew £335.10.6 from his own firm, had his goods conveyed by dray and boat to the ship "Lothair" anchored in the James, and, on June 17, 1815, set sail for England with his wife, Miss Valentine, and Edgar. From these facts it can be seen that he contemplated a stay of some duration.[98] Edgar left behind him his little sweetheart Catherine Poitiaux of whom, even at this early age, he was very fond.

As the custom then was, Mr. Allan provided his own stores for the voyage. These he purchased partly in Richmond, while the rest came on board at Hampton Roads, sent over from Norfolk by the firm of Moses Myers & Sons. A few brief glimpses can be caught of the family during their voyage of thirty-six days. The "Lothair" sailed from the "Roads" on June 22, 1815, and a letter brought back by the pilot boat tells us that, "Ned [Edgar] cares but little about it, poor fellow." From later letters, from the other side, we learn that Edgar soon re-

---

[98] Letters in the *Ellis & Allan Papers,* also see letter from Col. Thomas Ellis to Prof. Woodberry, from Baltimore, May 28, 1884. The author of the school texts was Lindley Murray, and the *Reader* was / "The eleventh Philadelphia edition, / published by Johnson & Warner, / at their Stores in Philadelphia, and Richmond (Vir). / John Bouvier, Printer, / 1814. /

covered, however, and inferences show us John Allan, or his pretty wife with the child on her lap in the cabin, instructing him out of *Murray's Reader, The Olive Branch,* or *Murray's Speller* which had been provided for the purpose at a cost of 16s. 6d.

They arrived at Liverpool July 28, 1815, and next day Mr. Allan writes his partner Charles Ellis that, "The ladies were *verry* sick. . . . Edgar was a little sick but had recovered." In Liverpool John Allan had business to transact with Ewart Myers & Company.

Apparently family ties in Scotland were powerful, for business detained them only a short while, and a few weeks later we find them at Greenock in Scotland, where they had probably just arrived, or had come over from Irvine only a few miles away in order to catch an outbound American mail. Evidently they succeeded, for we have this hurried letter from John Allan to Charles Ellis, his partner, written with the family hanging over him with messages for home, and little Edgar pleading, "Pa, say something for me."

D. CHARLES, *Greenock,*[99] Sept. 21, 1815

I arrived here about a half an hour ago . . . finding some American vessels on the eve of sailing I avail myself of the chance to write a few lines, though I cannot say much about our business . . . [evidently the time was too short. Here follow some price quotations of tobacco, of which he continues.] I flatter myself from the small quantity in London & the Postieur of affairs on the Continent that our sales will be profitable.

It would appear that France and the Allies have concluded a Treaty but it has not been promulgated—the Allies will hold the strong posts for a while until the refractory spirit of some of the old adherents of Bonaparte has subsided. France is far from being settled. Louis is too lenient & too peaceable the French delight in War I believe they care but little who rules them provided that ruler indulges them in their Habit which 25 years of war has so strongly fixed upon them.

Provisions of every description are extremely low here and in this quarter they are in the midst of Harvest, the crops are abundant and I think will be got in well. . . .

Frances says she would like the Land and lakes better if it was warmer and less rain, she bids me say she will write Margaret [Mrs. Ellis] as soon as she is settled but at present she is so bewildered with wonders that she *canna* write. Her best Love to Margaret & a thousand kisses to Thos. [Thos. Ellis a playmate of Poe] Nancy [Miss Valentine] says give my love to them all—Edgar says Pa say something for me, say I was not afraid coming across the Sea. Kiss Theo, [?] for him. We all write our best Love to my Uncle Galt and old Friends.

I am—etc. JOHN ALLAN [100]

(Postscript) Edgars Love to Rosa & Mrs. Mackenzie.

[99] A seaport of Renfrewshire about twenty-three miles from Glasgow on the Firth of Clyde. At this time it was one of the chief ports for American trade.

[100] The letter is evidently very hurriedly written, a little difficult to read in some places, which is unusual with John Allan, whose handwriting is large, round, and clear. The lapse into Scotch is unusual and testifies to his agitation, or the effect of a return to early associations.

Frances Allan's remarks about the weather in that part of Scotland where the Allans had gone to visit were by no means purely conversational. Greenock is officially the town with the heaviest rainfall in Scotland,[101] and that is saying a good deal for the rain. It may have been that some early memories of this "dewey, misty" climate and

> . . . the chill seas
> Around the misty Hebrides !

were so thoroughly soaked into Edgar Poe that he long remembered the plashy fields about Irvine and Kilmarnock.

Another great poet tramping through Kilmarnock only three years later was overtaken by a rain in the very town, from whereabouts John Keats writes to Reynolds on July 13, 1818, that the rain had stopped him on the way to Glasgow. Mrs. Allan's meteorological observations are therefore confirmed by great authority, in which His Majesty's Weather Reports concur, so we may be *definitely* sure that rain it did.

For *a' that,* however, Irvine in Ayrshire, where the Allans "settled down," is in the heart of the Burns country, and was at that time a lovely little seaport on the north bank of the river of the same name crossed by a picturesque old stone bridge. Here Poe must often have stood to watch the ships, or have crossed on excursions with his father's young cousins and nephews, the Galt or Fowlds boys, over the river to Seagate or Stonecastle nearby, both picturesque ruins. An academy had been founded at Irvine centuries before the Allans arrived, and there during the Summer of 1815 he was sent to school, doubtless in company with several of his "cousins."[102]

The country about fairly swarmed with John Allan's relatives and friends, all anxious to welcome him, to see his beautiful wife and the "little boy," and to hear about the health of their rich uncle in Richmond, a theme of considerable family interest. A married sister and her husband, Allan Fowlds, lived at Kilmarnock with several children, among them Frances, the namesake to whom Mrs. Allan had sent the coral bracelet some years before. One cannot help wondering if Mrs. Fowlds had really saved some of her "nice nappy ale" for her brother, and if Jean Guthrie *did* come asking for "her Johnny," how Mrs. Allan took it.[103]

At Irvine itself, where the Allans seem to have set up some sort of

---

[101] "64 inches."

[102] J. H. Whitty *Memoir*. The rest of the information is gathered from a mass of family correspondence in the *Ellis & Allan Papers* and from competent descriptions of the places themselves.

[103] Extracts from a letter to John Allan from his sister, Jane, at Irvine :

housekeeping while Edgar went to the Academy, lived three other sisters, Eliza, Mary, and Jane, together with other relatives, the Walshes [104] and some friends, a Capt. James Solomon, whom Mr. Allan had befriended while a prisoner of war in America,[104] and Mr. Ferguson "who kept a fine gig and dashed about at a great rate.[105] There is also some reference to "little brothers,"[106] perhaps a term of affection for the Galt children, the orphans.

At any rate, despite the rain and the Scotch mist, we may be sure it was a merry little society and a pleasant home-coming, and that young Edgar Poe and Nancy Valentine shared in the welcome. The bonds of family in Scotland are close, and these two fell within the magic circle. The country about is beautiful, and aroused Keats' admiration three years later, on his walking trip with Charles Armitage Brown.[107]   At Kilmarnock, Poe could not escape hearing about Bobby Burns; "Highland Mary" is buried at Greenock; and the poet's lines and songs were at that time and for a generation to come on everyone's lips. Here they saw the strange effect of the long northern twilight and the eery red shadows of the sunsets long after the hour of a Virginia night-fall. Even in England in July the twilight does not end until about 10 P.M., and Poe reveled in just such light effects afterward, and strange valleys—

> In the midst of which all day
> The red sunlight lazily lay.

Here, too, he was moving in the very scenes which Scott describes.   If these things did not leave a direct mark upon his style, his foreign experiences must at least have enhanced and made vivid his future delving into the literature of Britain, amid scenes of which he had personal knowledge.

About thirty miles south of Irvine and Kilmarnock on the Cree Water,[108] in a country of beautiful private parks and small lochs, lived the Galts at a handsome estate called "Flowerbanks" that overlooked

---

[104] "Mr. Walsh has purchased the great part of a galeaat and sails out of Irvine." There were Mr. and Mrs., and Jane Walsh in this family.
[105] "A very agreeable young man; I had the pleasure of being his bridesmaid."
[106] "All our little brothers are well and are making fine scholars."
[107] Extract from Keats' letter upon entering Ayrshire: "We · came down upon everything suddenly—there were on our way the "bonny Doon," with the Brig that Tam o'Shanter crossed, Kirk Alloway, Burn's Cottage, across the Doon; surrounded by every Phantasy of green in Tree, Meadow, and hill.—The stream of the Doon, as a Farmer told us, is covered with trees 'from head to foot'—you know these beautiful heaths so fresh against the weather of a summer's evening. . . ."—*John Keats, Amy Lowell,* vol. II, page 46.
[108] A river between Wigton and Kirkudbrightshire in Scotland. The description of "Flowerbanks" is from a letter of Mary Allan, who says, "I could be happy to live here forever."

a charming prospect in the Cree Valley where the fishers could be seen drawing their nets. This is close to the "Bride of Lammermoor" country, and is one of the most charming sections of Scotland. The Allans visited their relatives here and evidently stayed for some little time with the family, which seems to have consisted of an aunt, Mrs. Elizabeth Galt; William Galt and his wife, "Cousin Jane"; and the orphans, four or possibly three Galt boys,—for Thomas seems to have gone to sea. Here doubtless Poe played about the country with these children, with whom he had ample time to become intimate then and later on, amid scenes the charm of which could not have been wasted, even upon his extreme youth. This was probably in the late Summer of 1815.[109]

"Flowerbanks," however, was not the only place visited by the Allans. From Kilmarnock the family went to visit in Greenock, and from thence to Glasgow and Edinburgh. Mr. Allan doubtless combined his business and pleasure at these places,[110] but he was accompanied by his family and little Edgar Poe, who certainly could not have been oblivious to the attraction of strange sights for young eyes. Whether all of the Galt orphans went along is uncertain, but it is known that one of them, James Galt, then about fifteen years old, was of the company, and to his later reminiscences we are indebted for the facts. This nephew, it seems, was a favorite of old William Galt in Richmond who to some extent kept a tab on John Allan through the boy's letters.[111]

It had been John Allan's intent to leave Edgar at School at Irvine during this pleasure trip, and upon his return to England, but both Mrs. Allan and Miss Valentine objected, an attitude ably seconded by young Poe himself, so that it was agreed to allow Edgar to make the Scotch "grand tour" and return to London with the ladies, provided he would go back to Scotland later to attend school at Irvine with young James Galt. This early rift in the family over Edgar's care and whereabouts is not without significance as it shows plainly that Mrs. Allan was still the main protagonist for the boy, while her husband was anxious to settle matters, even then, by packing him off to school, a device to which he was to resort later on when the household became divided over more important matters in Richmond.

In the Fall, the family returned to England, stopping at Newcastle and Sheffield on the way, and landing in London on October 7, 1815. Here was another sea voyage, part of the way, amid notable scenery, at a time when Poe was beginning to awaken to himself and the world

---

[109] As late as December 30, 1846, Poe wrote one A. Ramsay of Stonehaven, Scotland, inquiring after *his* (Poe's) Allan and Galt relatives.

[110] Charles Denny was the Glasgow merchant with whom Mr. Allan transacted much of his business.

[111] J. H. Whitty, *Complete Poems,* large edition, Appendix, page 202.

about him.   It may have been that he saw Ailsa Rock glimmering far out at sea of which Keats wrote about the same time:

> . . . thou art dead asleep;
> Thy life is but two dead eternities—
> The last in air, the former in the deep;
> First with the whales, last with eagle skies—

These coasts seem to have affected the sea poetry of Keats, and it is certain that much of the poetry of Poe deals with a craggy and mist-veiled region.

The Allans did not immediately find lodgings, but, upon their arrival at London, stopped at *Blake's Hotel,* where on October 10, 1815, John Allan wrote Charles Ellis that they had arrived three days before from Glasgow, and that their satisfaction with the Scottish sights was "high in all respects."   A few days later they found a satisfactory residence in Russell Square, on the present site of the *Bedford* and *West Central* hotels.   From here on October 15, 1815, John Allan writes that he is sitting before "a snug fire in a nice little sitting parlor in No. 47, Southampton Row, while Frances and Nancy are sewing and Edgar is reading a little story book."   How we should like to know what it was!   Evidently Edgar read a good deal even at seven years of age.

Sometime later, probably about the end of 1815, Poe returned with James Galt to Scotland to attend once more the grammar school at Irvine.[112]   Edgar, it seems, was very unwilling to part with the family and the womenfolks pleaded to keep him in London, but in vain.   Poe's character even at this time began to manifest its willful characteristics. James Galt says that on the voyage back from London to Irvine, Edgar was very querulous all the way.   Young Poe had started for Scotland very unwillingly, and he evidently intended to let the world know the state of his feelings.

At Irvine, Edgar Poe and James Galt lived with Mary Allan, John Allan's sister, while the two boys went to school.   The house where they stayed, called the Bridgegate House, was till lately still standing. There, James Galt and the young Edgar Poe occupied the same room, and from the lips of the older boy we begin to get a definite impression of Poe's character.   He was, it seems, very mature for his age, full of old-fashioned talk, filled with a great self-reliance and absolutely devoid of fear.   Life with "Aunt Mary" and at the Academy did not suit him, and he made "plans" to go back to America, perhaps with Catherine in mind, or to run away to London, probably back to his dear "Ma," and "Aunt Nancy," but certainly not back to his dear "Pa," who had so nonchalantly packed him off from all those he loved.   This is the first of Edgar's many plans to run away, and in a little lad of seven or eight years at most, it shows a spirit of adventure, self-confidence, and obstinacy that is to be remarked. Evidently "Aunt Mary Allan," who, from her letters, seems to have been a kindly and knowing person, had a rapid time of it with the fiery little boy storming about her quiet old house.

In the canny and dour atmosphere of the Scotch village, Poe undoubtedly missed the note of gaiety and the warm, generous influences of his Richmond home. Frequent services at the Irvine and Kilmarnock kirks were long and lugubrious; the discipline at the Academy, a school with medieval traditions, was strict and probably corporeal; one of the exercises in writing was the copying of epitaphs from the old graves in the kirkyard close by, and there was doubtless no lack of *"auld licht"* sermons by Dr. Robertson, to the accompaniment of frequent reversals of the hour glass,—all the atmosphere of Protestant piety which had so outraged Burns a few years earlier. Indeed, in the very square with the Allan house at Irvine was Templeton's bookshop where Burns had gone to turn over many a sheet of old songs.[112]

There were mitigating circumstances, however; visits to Allan Fowlds, the merry nurseryman, and his family at Kilmarnock a few miles away; games in Nelson Street with Jock Gregory and Willie Anderson, who, as an old man in 1887, recalled Edgar Poe as much fussed over by the Allans, and a lively apt youngster with a will of his own;—and there was a ghost-walk just opposite in the garden of Lord Kilmarnock's mansion which the lord's lady was said to haunt.

Certainly Edgar was restless, and much affected the old, red, creaking-wheeled riding carts of the country upon which he rode gaily beside the driver; a little gray-eyed, dark, curly-headed boy dressed in a green duffle apron and thick-napped, red Kilmarnock tam o' shanter,—drinking in the strange sights of the old Scotch villages all about—but still making trouble for "Aunty Mary." She, at last, poor soul, could stand it no longer, and in a burst of exasperation packed up his clothes and shipped him back to London,[112] doubtless to the annoyance of John Allan, and the rapturous kisses of "Ma" and "Aunt Nancy." James Galt seems to have gone with him, for, not long after, there are letters to Richmond from the former. Mrs. Allan was very fond of these Galt children, too, and in October, 1818, the curtain lifts on the little family for a brief glimpse, when Mrs. Galt of "Flowerbanks" writes to John Allan in London, and encloses a message to his good wife.

---

[112] For the facts detailed here I am indebted to extracts from the *Ellis & Allan Papers;* Prof. Killis Campbell's *Unpublished Documents Relating to Poe's Early Years, The Sewanee Review;* XXI, 212-221, April, 1912, and his article in the *Dial* for February, 1916; and J. H. Whitty, *Memoir,* large edition, section VI, Appendix, pages 201-209.

Oct. 24, 1818

. . . Tell Mrs. Allan that her attention and great kindness to my children can never be forgotten as in every letter they are extolling her goodness. . . . My kind love to Miss Valentine and if she is half as good as she is represented to me she must be everything that anyone would wish. Compliments to Mrs. A., Miss V., little Edgar and Jane. . . .

Your affectionate Aunt
ELIZABETH GALT [113]

This letter is interesting as supplying the names of the persons in John Allan's household in London, and is one of the many proofs of the love for children shown by Frances Allan. "Jane" is John Allan's own sister.

There is an earlier glimpse than this, though, some two years before. Edgar could not have remained very long at Irvine, for he seems to have returned early in 1816 to London where a letter reached him written from Richmond in the Spring. It was from his little sweetheart Catherine Poitiaux, Mrs. Allan's godchild. As the first of the many love letters that Poe received, and from a little girl seven or eight years old, now dead for nearly a century, it is not without a quaint interest of its own.

Richmond, 18, 1816

. . . Give my love to Edgar and tell him I want to see him very much. . . . I expect Edgar does not know what to make of such a large City as London, tell him Josephine and all the children want to see him. . . . [114]

Evidently Edgar *was* missed and remembered!

Upon his return to London in 1816, Poe was sent to the Misses Dubourg's[115] boarding school at 146 Sloane Street, Chelsea, not far from the South Kensington Museum, where he continued to live, making short visits to the family, probably until the end of the Spring of 1817 or later. The Misses Dubourg were the sisters of a clerk in the employ of *Ellis & Allan* during 1816 and 1817, but of them little is known. The record of Poe's life at this school is now confined to the following bill for tuition, which tells a rather complete story for such a document. Among other things we learn that Edgar was known as "Master Allan."

---

[113] The extracts from this letter of Mrs. Galt to John Allan have been supplied the author by the kindness of Mr. Edward V. Valentine of Richmond, who has the correspondence in his possession.
[114] *Ellis & Allan Papers,* Library of Congress, Washington, D. C.
[115] "Pauline Dubourg" is the laundress in the *Murders in the Rue Morgue.*

Masr. Allan's School Acct. to Midsummer 1816

Board & Tuition ¼ year	7	17	6
Separate Bed	1	1	0
Washing	0	10	6
Seat in Church	0	3	0
Teachers and Servants	0	5	0
Writing	0	15	0
Do. Entrance	0	10	0
Copy Books, Pens, etc., etc..	0	3	0
Medicine, School Expenses	0	5	0
Repairing Linen, shoe strings etc. . .	0	3	0
Mavor's Spelling	0	2	0
Fresnoy's Geography	0	2	0
Prayer Book	0	3	0
Church Catechism Explained	0	0	9
Catechism of Hist. of England . . .	0	0	9
	12	2	0

Receipted, July 6, 1816
sgd. GEORGE DUBOURG

On the back we find that, "School recommences Monday the 22nd of July."[116]

During the stay of the family in England there are several mentions of Mrs. Allan's being in ill health, a more or less chronic condition, judging by other frequent references in family correspondence of later date, that was to play a considerable part in the relations later between Edgar Poe and John Allan. In a letter written to his uncle in Richmond as early as 1816, John Allan specifically states that his wife is in poor health. The earliest mention of any letters of Poe occurs in connection with his foster-mother's illness. In August, 1817, John Allan took his wife Frances to Cheltenham where she seems to have improved, and on August 14th of that year he writes his bookkeeper George Dubourg in London, enclosing a letter from the boy, and saying that if Edgar, who was evidently left behind at school, wishes to write at all he must send his letters to his mama, "as I do not think she will return with me." Mrs. Allan, finding the waters of benefit, wished to give them a longer trial. Why John Allan should have returned the letter is not clear unless it was to place it in the office files (*sic*). In any event it appears he did not wish to receive the boy's communications. Such incidents as these would be trivial did they not show definitely from which direction the warm and cold winds blew, even as early as this.[117]

---

[116] This receipt has been published in the *Dial* for February, 1916, and is to be found in the *Ellis & Allan Papers,* Washington, D. C. Courtesy of Prof. Killis Campbell.

[117] The full text of Allan's letter is in the Valentine Museum, Richmond, Virginia, and a quotation from it is given in the *Valentine Museum Poe Letters* (published in 1925), on page 17, introduction.

In the Summer of 1817 about the time that Edgar left the Misses Dubourg's school, John Allan moved from 47, Southampton Row to what is now number 83. This house was still standing in 1915, and is the same one that Poe mentions in *Why the Little Frenchman Wears his Hand in a Sling,* as "39, Southampton Row, Russell Square, Parish o' Bloomsbury."[557] Here they remained till shortly before they left London.

While in that city, John Allan had his place of business at 18 Basing Hall,[118] under the name of *Allan & Ellis,* a reversal of style that is said not to have pleased his partner at home. Most of his business was with Thomas S. Coles and A. Saltmarsh, his "inspectors," and with the firm of John Gilliat & Co. His affairs did not prosper, and that certain other worries followed him overseas, this rather snappy glimpse of home correspondence not without direct interest in itself, and bearing directly upon Poe, will testify. The letter is from William Ewing, Edgar's former schoolmaster in Richmond, which reached Mr. Allan in London March 7, 1818.

Richmond, Novr. 27th, 1817

Dr. Sir

I take upon myself the liberty of writing to you this note, relative to Master Edwin Collier, whom you placed under my tuition in the spring of the year 1815 and who has regularly attended my school since that period. His mother informs me that she has frequently reminded your partner Mr. Ellis to mention Edwin's situation to you, but thinks that amid the hurry of important communications he had omitted the subject altogether. She has accordingly solicited me to write to you, and to present a statement of Edwin's account from his first entrance to the end of the year. It is as follows;

Mr. Allan	To Wm Ewing, Dr.		
For Master Edwin Collier's tuition from March 15th			
1815 to March 14 1818 at $42 per annum			$126.00
Cr. June 1815 by cash from Mr. Allan	$12.25		
Oct. 1816 by cash from Mr. Ellis	$29.75		42.00
	To Balance		84.00

Thus there will be a balance due me of $84 on the 14th of March next—You will confer a favor on me, and equally so on Mrs. Collier, by dropping a few lines to me through the medium of your firm, first opportunity, expressive of your concern for the tuition and education of the above child, as far as you may deem proper in regard to the future. It is proper here also to add, that no improper step was taken by me, or any call made on any of your friends here for the payment of my bill, but on Mr. Ellis, who informed me, that some teacher had warranted the firm of *Ellis and Allan,* which induced him to refer any claims of this sort to your own inspection—I mention this, lest you might have imagined it to have been done by me.

---

[118] From addresses in letters to John Allan at that date. Also Mary Newton Stanard to the author on August 21, 1925.

I trust Edgar continues to be well and to like his school as much as he used to when he was in Richmond. He is a charming boy and it will give me great pleasure to hear how he is, and where you have sent him to school, and also what he is reading. There is no news here at present. . . . Poor Potter ended his earthly joy and miseries last week, so also died L. Joseph and Miles L., the latter was found dead by his own door supposed to have fallen in drink and to have expired under the consequences. . . . Let me only beg of you to remember me respectfully to your Lady Mrs. Allan and her Sister who I hope are well and do not forget to mention me to their august attendant, Edgar.

I am, etc.,

WILLIAM EWING

To this, in a somewhat less merry mood, John Allan replies,

London March 21, 1818

Mr. WILLIAM EWING

SIR —

I received your favor of the 27th Nov. last post the "Albert" that arrived here on the 7th inst having your account for the education of Edwin Collier . . . which sum Mr. Ellis will pay you; but I cannot pay any more expense on account of Edwin, you will therefore not consider me responsible for any expenses after the 15th of the month.

I cannot conceive who had a right to warrant *Ellis and Allan* on my account.

Accept my thanks for the solicitude you have so kindly expressed about Edgar & the family, Edgar is a fine Boy and I have no reason to complain of his progress.

I am etc.

JOHN ALLAN [119]

Mr. Allan's solicitude for his progeny was evidently in inverse ratio to their distance. But we do not hear what Edgar is reading which would, indeed, have been an interesting thing to know.

Probably in the Fall of 1817,[120] Poe was entered at the Manor House School of the Reverend "Dr." Bransby at Stoke Newington, then a suburb of London, which still retained the separate identity and the antique atmosphere of an old English village. The Academy was exclusively for young gentlemen, of the fairly well-to-do, and it was here that the young poet laid the first firm basis for an education.[121] He was

---

[119] Both of these letters are from the *Ellis & Allan Correspondence,* Library of Congress, Washington, D. C.

[120] The reasons for supposing this date are arrived at by the dates of correspondence and the fact that young Poe was in Scotland during part of 1815. In 1816, when he is known to have been living in London, Poe first attended the Misses Dubourg's school and would probably remain for the full term. This would bring his entry at the Stoke Newington Academy to some time in 1817. Poe afterward spoke of a "five years' schooling in England." The "year" at Irvine, a year with the Misses Dubourg, and three years with "Dr." Bransby cover this satisfactorily as to the time elapsed. The Allans sailed for home in the early Summer of 1820.

[121] The Academy stood on the northeast corner of Church Street and what is now Edwards Lane. Prof. Lewis Chase in the *London Athenaeum* for May, 1916, pages 221-222.

The Grammar School at Irvine, Scotland
Which Poe attended for several months in 1815
From a pen and ink sketch. Courtesy of R. L. McTavish

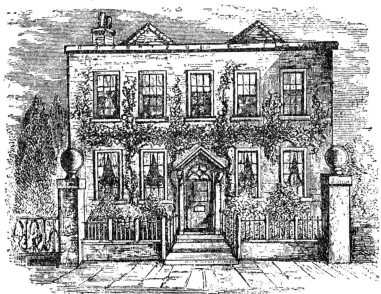

The Manor House School at Stoke Newington
London, England
Which Poe attended from 1817 to 1820. *From an old print*

now nearly ten years of age and entering upon that period of life when the lineaments of character begin to make themselves visible and reflect most forcibly the modeling of environment.

From Poe's own lips in the strange autobiographical and tragic story of *William Wilson* we have the poet's confession that in the old school at Stoke Newington began one of those spiritual struggles in the personality of a genius, the results of which have become significant to literature. Both the school itself and its haunted surroundings were well calculated to stir his imaginings, and despite his extreme youth, the capacity of the boy to be moved by it cannot be doubted. "In childhood I must have felt with the energy of a man what now I find stamped upon my memory as the *exergues* of the Carthaginian medals"—this was written years later about his schooldays at Stoke Newington—, and *"Oh, le bon temps que ce siècle de fer,"* says Poe, sighing in nostalgic retrospect in spite of the shadow of loneliness which he claimed had been cast upon him!

In 1818 the ancient village of Stoke Newington, which has since been absorbed by the growth of London, was a dream-like and spirit-soothing place, "a misty village of Old England," as Poe recalled it, rambling along an old Roman road bordered with a vast number of gnarled elm trees and ancient houses dating from the days of the Tudors. "At this moment," he says, writing many years later, "I feel the refreshing chilliness of its deeply-shadowed avenues, inhale the fragrance of its thousand shrubberies, and thrill anew with indefinable delight, at the deep, hollow note of the churchbell, breaking, each hour, with sudden and sullen roar, upon the stillness of the dusky atmosphere in which the fretted Gothic steeple lay imbedded and asleep." It does not, therefore, seem to be straining things too far to say that from this ancient place steeped in the memories of a millennium, where objective reminders of the past still lingered so romantically, some of the foreign coloring, the minute descriptions of ancient buildings, and the love for the "Gothic" and medieval atmosphere, in which he so often reveled later, may have originated.

For just off the village green among deeply shaded walls stood the ancient house of that Earl Percy who was the unfortunate lover of Anne Boleyn, and the mansion of Queen Elizabeth's noble favorite, the great Earl of Leicester. To the west of the little open square, green, shady lanes melted into the cool and misty meadows, while the school itself was situated on the east of the town on a quaint street of Queen Anne and Georgian houses, "haunts of ancient peace," carpeted about with darkly-shaded English lawns and bordered by hedges. Behind its own box bordered parterre, on this very street, stood the Manor House Academy, a large, white, rambling mansion of various architectures, with a roof that sloped away in the rear to a massive brick wall pierced by ponderous, iron-studded gates.   One cannot do better than to let Edgar Poe himself describe it and the life he led there:

The house I have said was old and irregular. The grounds were extensive, and a high and solid brick wall, topped with a bed of mortar and broken glass, encompassed the whole. This prison-like rampart formed the limit of our domain; beyond it we saw but thrice a week—once every Saturday afternoon, when, attended by two ushers, we were permitted to take brief walks in a body through some of the neighboring fields—and twice during Sunday, when we were paraded in the same formal manner to the morning and evening service in the one church of the village. Of this church the principal of our school was pastor. With how deep a spirit of wonder and perplexity was I wont to regard him from our remote pew in the gallery, as, with step solemn and slow, he ascended the pulpit! This reverend man, with countenance so demurely benign, with robes so glossy and so clerically flowing, with wig so minutely powdered, so rigid and so vast,—could this be he who, of late with sour visage, and in snuffy habiliments, administered, ferule in hand, the Draconian Laws of the academy? Oh, gigantic paradox, too utterly monstrous for solution! At an angle of the ponderous wall frowned a more ponderous gate. It was riveted and studded with iron bolts, and surmounted with jagged iron spikes. What impressions of deep awe did it inspire! It was never opened save for the three periodical egressions and ingressions already mentioned; then, in every creak of its mighty hinges, we found a plentitude of mystery—a world of matter for solemn remark, or for more solemn meditation. The extensive enclosure was irregular in form, having many capacious recesses. Of these, three or four of the largest constituted the playground. It was level, and covered with fine hard gravel. I well remember it had no trees, nor benches, nor anything similar within it. Of course it was in the rear of the house. In front lay a small parterre, planted with box and other shrubs; but through this sacred division we passed only upon rare occasions indeed—such as a first advent to school or final departure thence, or perhaps, when a parent or friend having called for us, we joyfully took our way home for the Christmas or Midsummer holidays. But the house!—how quaint an old building was this!—to me how veritably a palace of enchantment! There was really no end to its windings—to its incomprehensible subdivisions. It was difficult at any given time, to say with certainty upon which of its two stories one happened to be. From each room to every other there were sure to be found three or four steps either in ascent or descent. Then the lateral branches were innumerable—inconceivable—and so returning in upon themselves, that our most exact ideas in regard to the whole mansion were not very far different from those with which we pondered upon infinity. During the five years of my residence here, I was never able to ascertain with precision, in what remote locality lay the little sleeping apartment assigned to myself and some eighteen or twenty other scholars. The school room was the largest in the house—I could not help thinking, in the world. It was very long, narrow, and dismally low, with pointed Gothic windows and a ceiling of oak. In a remote and terror-inspiring angle was a square enclosure of eight or ten feet, comprising the *sanctum,* 'during hours,' of our principal, the Reverend Dr. Bransby. It was a solid structure, with massy door, sooner than open which in the absence of the 'Dominie,' we would all have willingly perished by the *peine forte et dure.* In other angles were two other similar boxes far less reverenced, indeed, but still greatly matters of awe. One of these was the pulpit of the 'classical' usher, one of the 'English and mathematical.' Interspersed about the room, crossing and recrossing in endless irregularity, were innumerable benches and desks, black, ancient, and time-worn, piled desperately with much-bethumbed books, and so beseamed with initial letters, names at full length, grotesque figures, and other multiplied efforts of the knife, as to have entirely lost what little of original form might have been their portion in days long departed. A huge bucket with water stood at one extremity of the room, and a clock of stupendous dimensions at the other.[122]

This description, however, is not to be taken too literally. It is quite possibly a synthesis of both Irvine and Stoke Newington, and in one particular quite misleading,—the description of the headmaster, Dr. Bransby.[123]

In the first place the good man was not a "Doctor" at all, or so only by courtesy. He appears on his bills as the "Rev^d. John Bransby." Nor was he "old" when Poe was at his school, being at that time, 1817, only 33 years of age. The Reverend John Bransby was an M. A. of St. John's College, Cambridge. He seems to have been a merry, Tory clergyman with a large family and convivial habits, very fond of field sports; the cleaning of his gun was a signal to the boys that he was off for the day. "He was a classical scholar of no mean stamp possessing a large fund of miscellaneous information, both literary and scientific . . . and combined an enthusiastic love of nature with an extensive knowledge of Botany," and gardening. "Dr." Bransby wrote political pamphlets and looked upon the days at Stoke Newington as "a bright spot in his life." He was much beloved by his scholars.

These facts give us quite a different picture, indeed, from that drawn by Poe in *William Wilson*. John Bransby in after years was said to have been considerably nettled by the use of his name in the story, and to have been quite reticent about Poe, remarking, only, that he had liked the boy, who went under the name of "Allan," but that his parents spoilt him by allowing him too much pocket money. "Allan," he said, "was intelligent, wayward, and wilful," which testimony agrees with James Galt's.

Of Poe's associations with his schoolmates nothing definite is known. We have his own statement, however, to the effect that, even thus early, his dominant characteristic of pride began to make itself felt. "The ardor, the enthusiasm, and the imperiousness of my disposition, soon rendered me a marked character among my schoolmates,—gave me an ascendency over all not greatly older than myself." Master Ewing, his former Richmond schoolmaster, had desired himself to be remembered

[122] The quotations descriptive of Poe's schooldays are from his story *William Wilson*.
[123] The description of Poe's schoolmaster, the Reverend John Bransby is taken from the *London Athenaeum* No. 4605 for May, 1916, pages 221-222, an article by Prof. Lewis Chase, part of which is quoted. In this connection note that the pictures in several biographies of Poe purporting to be those of "Dr." Bransby are in reality a likeness of Dr. William Cooke, a rector of Stoke Newington who died when Bransby was thirteen years old. John Bransby was born in 1784 and died March 5, 1857.

to the "august" Edgar, so that there is some confirmation of the statement. Pride is not a trait that would have tended to make him companionable, and it is probable that much of the complained-of loneliness sprang from this. There is also some indication that the boys revenged themselves upon him for his over-bearing attitude by an annoying repetition of his name which probably, from the Southern twist of his Virginia accent, gave them ample opportunity for a rather obvious and humble pun upon his patronymic.[124] The results upon his diction of a long residence in England and Scotland and of the Scotch dialect so frequently heard in his foster-father's house are not to be overlooked.

Bills from the Manor House School rendered for "Master Allan," which have recently come to light,[125] give us the only direct insight to the life of the schoolboy, Edgar Poe, at Stoke Newington that we possess. From these it appears that like other lads he played hard, and was ruthless on shoe leather. A pair of shoes evidently lasted him a month, by which time they went on the docks for repairs. The total bill for the summer term of 1818, it appears, was £1. 15s. 6d. which includes two new pairs, three mendings, and no less than six shillings' worth of laces consumed in that period! For the rest, Poe's memoirs of the Reverend John Bransby's sermons in *William Wilson* are confirmed, and we learn in addition that the boys were charged extra for listening to them, as John Allan is billed 3s. 6d. for pew-rent, and a charity sermon for Edgar's share. Poe had a single bed at this school, as he had at the Misses Dubourg's, and for "board and education" was charged £23. 12s. 6d. a term. He took dancing as an extra at £2. 2s., and had the services of a "hairdresser" or barber for 2s. a term. The school allowance of pocket money it seems was 5s. the term, which, as it is certainly not the "extravagant amount" that "Dr." Bransby mentions, must have been supplemented by "dear Ma," and "Aunt Nancy." On August 31, 1818, he seems to have hurt his hand somewhat badly, for his foster-father is charged with an item 10s. 6d. for having it dressed, and 2s. 6d. for ointment and lint a month later. The boy is charged with two large slates, but there is no mention of school texts by title. The whole cost for the term at this excellent English school came to £23. 2s. 11d. By January 25, 1819, Poe was back at school from the Christmas holidays which he must have spent with the Allans in London, for at that date the vacation came to an end.

Unfortunately, then, we do not know what, if any, were the books that Edgar may have read at Stoke Newington. Master Ewing's inquiry shows that he was reading. There must have been something

---

[124] David Poe was listed on the tax returns in Boston for 1809 as "David Poo," with taxables of $300 in personable property.

[125] *Valentine Museum Poe Letters,* Bills from Reverend John Bransby to John Allan for "Master Allan," see pages 319-327.

more than mere textbooks about the school somewhere, although English grammar schools of the period were amazingly innocent of anything but the dog-eared Latin grammars, spellers, cheap editions of Homer, Virgil, and Cæsar, and the ponderous arithmetics of the period. Whether the boys ever went to the theater is doubtful, although Edgar probably saw the sights of London with his "mother" during the holidays,—the Tower and Westminster, at least, and perhaps the Elgin Marbles, then newly arrived.

Let the searchers for the literary inspirations of Poe's boyhood make the most of the fact that he was in London at school when the first edition of *Christabel* and *Kubla Khan* appeared from John Murray's; but it is not likely that any of this magic fell upon his ears until years later. That was "modern poetry" then, and so we may be sure taboo in the schools where Pope still reigned. "Byron" was a thing for young gentlemen ushers to chuckle over in a knowing way, and conceal from the innocent eyes of their charges. As for Shelley, if he were known at all to any of the faculty at Stoke Newington, what chance would the works of an avowed atheist have under the watchful, churchly eye of the Reverend and forceful "Dr." Bransby? That Poe was in the same city at the time when Coleridge, Wordsworth, and Keats were meeting about the same fire with Haydon is a temporal and geographic fact without literary significance, despite the attempt to make it so from some quarters.[126]

On Christmas, mid-term holidays, and week-ends Edgar must have visited the Allans at their London lodgings. One thing is certain, John Allan is not likely to have become acquainted with any of the literary figures of the day. The Virginia tobacco trade, and the social circle which it implies, cannot by the wildest stretch of imagination be advanced as a source for even juvenile literary inspirations or associations. If Edgar saw anyone at his guardian's house while in London, besides the immediate members of his family, they were probably merchants who had business with the firm and discussed, in a broad lowland accent, the prices current of Virginia leaf, or the vicissitudes of American ships. Mrs. Allan, however, seems to have gathered about her a more congenial and interesting group, for, while Edgar was at school, Mrs. Allan, whose health continued to be precarious, traveled about from place to

---

[126] Owing to the fact that John Galt, the Scotch novelist, and a friend of Byron, hailed from Irvine and Kilmarnock and was a connection of the Galt family, cousins to the Allans, some attempt has been made to connect Poe's foster-parents with the literary life of the London of the time. There is not a shadow of proof, however, on which to rest the assumption. John Galt *was*, however, in London at the same time as the Allans. The following *occurs* in a letter from Byron to John Murray dated Bologna, September 17, 1819.

"Dear Sir:—I have received a small box consigned by you to a Mr. Allan with three portraits in it."—etc. *The Works of Lord Byron,* edited by Rowland E. Prothero, M. A., John Murray, London, 1900, vol. IV, page 353.

place, in company with Jane Galt and others, as a letter from Damlish written by Miss Galt to "Miss [Mary] Allan" at 38, Southampton Row, Russell Square, London, on October 24, 1818, shows. At that time Mrs. Allan did not intend to return to London till November.

. . . I think she regrets leaving this part of the country. Mr. Dunlop has been persuading her to remain for some time—he will leave her in charge of the beaus (army officers) who winter here, Major Court and Captain Donnal who she is sure will take good care of her and he would take a nice little cottage for her. What do you think of that arrangement? Don't you think we plan very well. Mrs. Allan drank tea last evening at Mr. Dunlops. They leave this Monday. Mr. Leslie who has been with them for some time is quite delighted with the country. He has been very busy taking views of the different places around. Mrs. Allan is much about the same as when I wrote, I regret often that we have not you all here to enjoy the beauties of Devonshire. . . . There is one view here which reminds me very much of the first look you get at Ayrshire from—— . . . accepts our best regards to Miss Valentine and Mr. Allan. . . .

By which it would seem that Edgar's "Aunt Nancy" kept house in London, while his invalid foster-mother was in Devonshire, assisted by one of John Allan's sisters. A little glimpse into the family circle of over a century ago in England is thus afforded. Evidently Edgar was then well tucked away at "Dr." Bransby's.

Leslie, the artist referred to, was E. C. R. Leslie, R. A., who was born in London of American parents in 1784. His parents returned to America and he was later a student at the Royal Academy, exhibiting there the year this letter was written. He later returned to America and became professor of drawing at West Point. It is just possible that Leslie who was in close touch with the Allans painted a portrait of "Master Allan" in England.[127]

The references to Mrs. Allan's constant ill health continue steadily in nearly all the correspondence from now on until she died over a decade later in Richmond.

Before leaving England, John Allan's affairs were in bad shape and generally complicated. The tobacco market was poor, and he had adventured considerably with a merchant by the name of William Holder who writes in January, 1820:

I cannot express my dear Sir what I feel at this moment for your *kind, humane* & feeling conduct toward me & my two unprovided daughters at present I can only offer you my sincere *thanks*. . . . It would be the proudest hour of my life to make you ample restitution . . . etc.

In March, Mr. Allan was attacked by a dropsy, of which he nearly died, and he was not able to get to the counting house until April 3rd to

[127] The letter from Jane Galt and the reference to Leslie came from Edward V. Valentine, Esq., of Richmond, Virginia, from his diary, and from letters given him to copy by Miss Sallie Galt on July 12, 1915, from the Galt-Allan correspondence.

wind up his affairs. He found that in the meantime he had been robbed by a clerk by the name of Tayle, and gives the details in a letter to Charles Ellis marked "private," in which he adds, London, April 18, 1820:

Would say we are all tolerably well, I certainly am much better, Frances complaining a good deal & Ann & Edgar are quite well. . . .

The final crash financially came over the confusion between *Ellis & Allan* in Richmond and *Allan & Ellis* in London, both of which firms tried to collect a sum of £2700 due from the estate of a Mr. Guilles of Glasgow, debtor to William Galt. Gravely in debt and cast down by his failure, Mr. Allan rented his household effects and house (for he hoped to return), took Edgar out of school, and prepared to depart for America. Had he been successful, Edgar Poe would have been raised in England. On May 20th, Mr. Allan writes home from London:

. . . I trust to be off by the June Packet & when I arrive I shall use every exertion of which I am capable to complete our engagements to our creditors. . . . Mrs. Allan is in better health than usual, Ann quite well & so is Edgar, as for myself I was never better. . . . The arrival of the Queen produced an immense sensation. Few thought she would return, but the bold & courageous manner by which she appeared . . . has induced a vast number to think her not guilty. She was received with immense acclamation & the populace displaced her horses, drew her past Carlton House and thence to Alderman Wood's House South Audley St. The same day the King made a communication to the House of Lords charging her with High Treason. . . .

From which it is quite plain that Edgar Poe, just before he left England, probably saw the unfortunate Queen Caroline drawn through the London streets. It was probably his first and last glimpse of royalty, and his last of London.

On June 9th we find the family at Liverpool where they arrived the day before, waiting for the Packet.

[Mrs. Allan] . . . felt much indisposed. I hope the trip to Virginia [?] will be of service to her, she has yet to learn what a pleasing sensation is experienced on returning Home—Even in verry Hot weather. We will trust to God that our congratulations on the Birth of another Daughter to your family will be . . . finally realized . . . make my best respects to our dear Margaret [Mrs. Ellis] & all the children. Mrs. A. & Ann desire their love to you, Margaret & the young ones. Remember us all to Mr. and Mrs. Richard, Doct. and Mrs. Thornton, the children, Rose [Poe], Mr. and Mrs. Mackenzie. . . . Mrs. Mackenzie of Forest Hill called and addressed her love to Mrs. Mackenzie, they are all well.

In a few days, apparently about the end of June, 1820, Mr. Allan and the family with young Edgar set sail for New York.

The net result of Poe's boyhood experience in England and Scotland seems to have been a precious store of rather distinct and romantic memories, a lively young body hardened by the sturdy games of the

English school ground and climate, a little Latin, some mispronounced French, and an ability to work problems in simple arithmetic. Perhaps also, a too well developed self-confidence and boyish pride. In addition, young Poe had seen, long before most American youths, the beginnings of the age of industrialism, in England and Scotland, factories operated by steam, and the beginnings of railways.[128] His horizons had been widened, the provincialism of a Virginia-bred youth inoculated with a valuable antidote, and he had heard and been instructed in English spoken at the source.

In June, 1820, however, he left behind him forever the quaint English town, and the rambling mysterious corridors and alcoved dormitories of the old school where he had spent a considerable portion of his boyhood, to return with Mr. Allan and his family to the United States.

---

[128] "Railways"—see a letter from Allan Fowlds written from Kilmarnock, Scotland, as early as January 4, 1812, to John Allan at Richmond, Virginia, in which Fowlds says, . . . "we are getting a fine new Harbor at the Troon with 3 or 4 fine dry docks, the railway from the Troon to Kilmarnock is almost completed, they are shipping great Quantity of Coals for Ireland"—etc. Steam engines were not used *there* at that time.

CHAPTER SIX

ISRAFEL MEETS HELEN

THE voyage from England to America was made in thirty-six days, a fairly average passage for the time. Mr. Allan and his family arrived in New York on July 21, 1820, accompanied by young James Galt, then about twenty years old, who came to Richmond apparently at the behest of his wealthy uncle there.[129]

Ships and the sea, which always have a fascination for boys of an adventurous turn,—and by this time Edgar was certainly that,—exercised a peculiar charm for young Poe if one can judge anything from his later stories, so many of which have their scenes laid in a maritime setting. Along with young Galt he would not have failed to take delight in the always-to-a-landsman novel incidents of a transatlantic voyage, and to have become somewhat familiar with the picturesque setting and life of the jack-tar on the sailing ships of the age. Nor could the busy life of the London and New York docks and waterfronts have been lacking in an appeal to his imagination.

A port of the early twenties of the nineteenth century, filled with the square-riggers, barks, Indiamen, Blackwall frigates, and men-of-war of the time, presented a romantic aspect even to contemporary eyes. Gleaming sails, black and yellow hulls careening to the wind, and painted with white stripes along the rows of square grinning port-holes, flashing brasses, bells and cannon, and the chanteys of sailors as the capstan clanked and the anchors walked home to the catheads,—would not have been waste material upon the retina of Edgar Poe even when only twelve years of age. A great full-rigged ship under all sail, with a "bone-in-her-teeth," graceful gilded figurehead and fluted stern galleries, home from the Indies with all her national bunting and house-flags flying, was a good thing for a young poet to see, something which has unfortunately perished from the earth.

Poe's sea stories, even the most fanciful, such as *The Narrative of Arthur Gordon Pym,* exhibit a familiarity with nautical ways and terms which much actual experience at sea was the cause of supplying. Two transatlantic voyages before the age of manhood, and a life spent about the docks, and in seaports, was an unusual and valuable experience for one of the coming figures in American literature. In his voyages upon army transports from Boston to Charleston, and upon his return thence

---

[129] Woodberry, 1909, vol. I, page 24.
"Galt"—J. H. Whitty, *Memoir,* large edition, Appendix, page 206.

to Hampton Roads, Poe was at a later time to renew his direct acquaintance with the ocean for a brief time at least.[130]   The magic sights and
sounds of the sea have been caught up into lines of his prose and
poetry, notably in *Annabel Lee* and *The City in the Sea*.   One can hardly
quote even the titles without making the fact self-evident.   In this, Poe
has carried on one of the great traditions of English verse, the sea
influence, and that he was able to do so is partly the happy result of
experience rather than a literary *tour de force*.

The letters of Mr. Allan's partner, Charles Ellis, written from the
new offices of the firm on Fifteenth Street opposite the *Bell Tavern*
(whither they had moved in September, 1817) to his wife, then in the
mountains, afford an unusually intimate glimpse into the events upon the
return of the Allans and young Poe to Richmond, and of the kind of
world with which the youth was about to renew a long broken tie.

It was a hot, fever-ridden community to which they were returning,
with customs quite different from those current at Russell Square or
Stoke Newington.

Mr. Hughes of the house of Hughes & Armistead stabbed a Mr. Randolph son
of Wm. Randolph of Cumberland the other night, at the time it was thought to
be mortal, as the dirk punctured the left side just above the hip to a considerable
depth, but Dr. Nelson who attended him, tells me no unfavorable symptoms exist
now.   Mr. H. is out of town & perhaps will not return. . . .

Of the slaves working about the docks and ships in the sweltering
summer weather, Mr. Ellis remarks June 27, 1820, shortly before the
Allans returned:

. . . The Richmond gang look as if they would rather be at home, but all goes
on very well except the elopement of that troublesome fellow Nelson who went
off last Wednesday and has not been heard of since.   He is one of the best hands
for work I ever saw, but he vexes me exceedingly when he goes off, especially in
busy times, little Bill goes about and does some light work, but still complains a
good deal, Africas feet is nearly well and indeed I hear no complaining among
any of the People except Caty's child, it is very poor.   She says it is very sick.   It
has no fever nor complaint of the bowels.   I hear it is neglected, I have sent it
some chicken every day sence I have been up. . . .

So the days had been going on in the little town along the James to
which the young Poe was returning to spend the rest of his boyhood and
to become familiar with the life of a plantation founded community.
On July 3rd, Mr. Ellis writes his wife:

. . . Mr. and Mrs. Allan are at last arrived in New York, and as soon as they get
on, and settle down a little I shall leave them the bag to hold, and flee to the mountains. . . .   Mr. Allan would set out from New York last Friday via Norfolk
and I suppose will be here on Friday or Saturday.   Mrs. Allan was rather unwell

---

[130] See Chapter XI.

The Home of Charles Ellis, partner of John Allan

Franklin and Second Streets, Richmond, Virginia

Here Poe lived with his foster-parents a short while after returning from England in August, 1820. "The Enchanted Garden" was directly across the street from this house. This was one of Poe's boyhood haunts

Courtesy of the Edgar Allan Poe Shrine, Richmond, Virginia

"The Mother's Chamber" in the Ellis House

Occupied by Frances Allan in 1820

Photograph 1877

Courtesy of the Edgar Allan Poe Shrine, Richmond, Virginia

A Poem by Edgar Poe

Found in the 1822 files of *Ellis & Allan*

This poem, obviously in a childish hand, was found by Prof. Killis Campbell. The lines are not signed but are almost certainly Poe's. The treatment of the theme is characteristic. The poem may belong to the early "lost volume" mentioned by Poe's schoolmaster, J. W. CLARKE

Photostat supplied to the Library of Congress by Prof. Killis Campbell after original manuscript was lost

The House of Poe's "Helen," Jane Stith Stanard

Capitol Square, Richmond

(The house behind the statue of Henry Clay)

The chimney to the right was on BUSHROD WASHINGTON's office. It was in this house that POE met the mother of his schoolmate, ROBERT STANARD. This lady influenced his whole life, and has been immortalized in one of POE's greatest poems, *To Helen*

Probably the only extant photograph

Courtesy of the Edgar Allan Poe Shrine, Richmond, Virginia

The Earliest Known Lines of Poetry
with Signature of Edgar A. Poe

" Last night with many cares and toils oppress'd
Weary . . I laid me on a couch to rest —"

These lines, found by the author in the *Ellis & Allan* files for November, 1824, are written on a sheet of paper covered by JOHN ALLAN's figures dealing with his precarious financial situation at the time. They show POE in a typical melancholy mood alluded to in JOHN ALLAN's letter to HENRY POE. This couplet, which antedates *Tamerlane* by three years, is here first published. It confirms POE's statements that he wrote poetry as a young boy

& was resting. The rest was hearty, don't give yourself any uneasiness about my health. . . . The inhalation of the exhilirating nitric acid gas in this place has gained some amusement among the curious and idle, I have not seen or felt the effects.

The city is healthy, except for children teething, and many of them suffer greatly. . . .

CHARLES

The Allans with Miss Valentine and Edgar arrived at Richmond, after a voyage down the coast to Norfolk, on August 2nd, and went to stay at the house of Mr. Ellis as this letter shows.[131]

Richmond, August 7th, 1820.

Your letter of the 4th inst. by last nights mail affords me great pleasure, and that of Mr. and Mrs. Allan who are at our home receiving the congratulations of their friends. Mrs. Allan could she be as even tempered and as accommodating as she has been sence her return, she would make the path through life much more even to herself. . . . I find Mr. Allan can't do much yet, it will take some time to obtain a knowledge of our affairs & he is engaged in seeing his old friends. Mr. and Mrs. Allan will continue at our home, they are all well but complain of the warm weather. . . .

On August 8th, Robert S. Ellis writes to congratulate Mr. and Mrs. Allan upon their safe return, and on August 14th from Charles Ellis, in another letter to his wife, we learn that:

Our friends Mr. and Mrs. Allan, Nancy, and Edgar are very well & you would be surprised to see what health and color Mrs. A. has. They are quite well and satisfied at our house & make out pretty well altho not as well as you would do. They are a little Englishised but it will soon wear off. They talk of going to Stanton. . . .

Edgar Poe remained for the entire Summer at the Ellis house. "Nancy and Edgar stay well," says John Allan in September. He was now "holding the bag" in good earnest, and not very much in it—and goes on to gossip about cleaning up the old garden across the street, about an old slave who could work no more as her hip "seemed to be dislocated" . . . and prices current on tobacco. The old house on Tobacco Alley and Fourteenth Street was still rented. Mr. Allan set about looking up a new house and secured one fronting west on Clay Street beyond old St. James Church. Nearby lived Dr. Ambler and Bishop Moore "right across on the corner from Clay Street." It was probably now that Edgar first took to swimming in Shockoe Creek with young Ambler, and to wandering about again with Ebenezer Burling, whose father Thomas printed the *Journal* of the State Senate. "Aunt" Nancy Valentine was a pleasant companion with a broad humorous face, good for a ramble with the boy out to the Hermitage, or for a game of

---

[131] Also Woodberry, Weiss, etc.

chess with him when "Ma" was ill, or on rainy days sat sewing by her mahogany work stand. "Pa" was no longer so pleasant as in times past, even more stern than before. A great many things financial and domestic preyed upon his mind. Edgar began more and more to step over to the Mackenzies to see "Rose" and to play with Jack, to stay at Burling's over night or with the Ellises. England seemed a dream, a new life had begun. Somehow he was already quite lonely and beginning to wonder about it all. Not long afterward he began to write poetry.

Richmond in the 1820's was a good place for a boy to live in. The meadows, streams, swamps, and forests around about were beautiful, and the valley of the James from Church Hill and the Bluffs, with the yellow river winding away into the distance, or dashing among the wooded islands at the Falls, would present to European eyes, perhaps, a magnificent spectacle, for it is at least five times as large as the Marne and several times greater than the Thames,—like the rest of America upon a continental scale.

The little capital of Virginia had, at that time, a population of about twelve thousand souls. The porches of its pillared churches and political buildings looked down, with a semi-classic stare from its hills, over Georgian houses set amid spacious gardens and green lawns. At its foot ran the key-like flanges of docks, and the black warehouses edged with a tangled fringe of masts, sails, and flags; while around the curve of Penitentiary Hill came gliding the canal boats drawn by tinkling bell-hung mules. Boys swam in the river and creeks; over the fields sounded the plantation bells, or the sonorous roar of the conch-bugle calling the slaves from the fields; the tobacco waved,—and the fortunes of the planters grew.

No community in America had retained more of its pre-revolutionary traditions than tide-water Virginia. It was the home of an aristocracy born in the great houses of gentlemen, surrounded by servants and family portraits, the life of a flourishing colony projected forward into another time.

Upon Poe's return to Richmond in 1820, save for the domestic chimneys, there could scarcely have been a smoke-stack in the place.[132] Planters rode about the streets on blooded horses; the carriages of the local gentry whirled by with black coachman and footman; the governor, if he was so minded, and he often was, kept at least a provincial court; the legislature met, and great lawyers argued at the bar. There was a brilliant round of social activities in which the Allans were soon to take their part, an intense local pride, a taste for the arts, and a respect for tradition and inherited rank. In all this, the young Edgar Poe moved and breathed, and had the roots of his being.

------

[132] Many old prints of Richmond show this delightful condition.

Immediately across from Mr. Ellis' house at Second and Franklin Streets there was then, and for many years later, a beautiful landscaped garden filled with lindens and the scent of winter-blooming roses. Amid its walls and nooks took place many of the incidents of one of the great romances of the poet's life, and it still flourishes in the lines which have fixed some of its scenes permanently upon the memories of men. But of that hereafter.[133]

The family did not remain very long with Mr. Ellis, but moved in the Autumn of 1820 into their new home,[134] where Edgar must have renewed with peculiar intensity many of the scenes of his earliest recollections, and greeted with mutual curiosity the now budding young ladies and gentlemen with whom he had played as a child.

One of these was Ebenezer Burling whom Poe had met at the Memorial Church. He resided with his widowed mother at a house in Bank Street, and seems to have played a not unimportant rôle in some of the major incidents of the poet's youth.[135] With Burling, Poe read *Robinson Crusoe* and the boys then had a boat on the James which seems to have been the genesis of the little pleasure yacht mentioned at the beginning of *Arthur Gordon Pym.* Burling, it is said, had previously taught Poe to swim.[136] In 1836 Poe wrote the *Southern Literary Messenger,* harking back to old "Robinson Crusoe days":

How fondly do we recur in memory to those enchanted days of our boyhood when we first learned to grow serious over Robinson Crusoe!—when we first found the spirit of wild adventure enkindling within us, as by the dim firelight we labored out, line by line, the marvelous import of those pages, and hung breathless and trembling with eagerness over their absorbing—over their enchanting interest. Alas! the days of desolate islands are no more.

At any rate, the boys had many a lark together in "Richmond City" and the country about. A Mrs. C. E. Richardson afterward kept a tavern in Richmond which at one time sheltered Poe in a day of adversity, and Ebenezer, it is said, developed the drink habit early, which may have had some influence upon Poe in company with him there, but that was later on.[137] This Ebenezer Burling, or *Berling,* as it is sometimes spelled, was not a schoolmate of Poe but attended the school of one William Burns, a Scotch gentleman, who boarded at Parson Blair's house.[138]

If by some magic we could return to Richmond, Virginia, in the late Autumn of the early twenties after the harvest had been gathered, we

---

[133] See Chapter VIII.
[134] E. V. Valentine to the author, Richmond, July, 1925.
[135] J. H. Whitty *Memoir,* large edition, page xxiv.
[136] J. H. Whitty *Memoir,* large edition, page xxv.
[137] J. H. Whitty *Memoir,* large edition, page xxix.
[138] Information gathered from the *Ingram Papers.*

might come across Edgar Allan Poe, a well-knit, broad-browed, curly-headed lad with astonishing long-lashed, deep gray eyes, seated with his best chums Jack Mackenzie, Rob Sully, little Bobby Stanard, and Robert Cabell upon a rail fence like so many crows, each munching a tender juicy turnip, or a raw sweet potato with a little salt on it, which, as many a Southern boy knows, is not half bad. On Saturdays there were fish-fries by the river and tramps through the luxuriant Virginia woods above the James after wild grapes and chinquapins.

Edgar was well to the forefront in all of this. Much of the delicate timidity of his baby days had been, superficially at least, cast off. The playgrounds of the schools at Irvine and Stoke Newington had made him an able runner and jumper,[139] and had given him the English schoolboy's technique and readiness in fisticuffs which must have compelled the respect of his companions and have enabled him to indulge to the full a merry propensity for practical jokes. At one time he appeared as a ghost in the middle of a late card party in Richmond at which General Winfield Scott was present. It is worthy of note that Jack Mackenzie, the foster-brother of Rosalie, who knew him extremely well, and saw him often in his own house where Rosalie Poe had been given refuge and tender care, remarked of him, "I never saw in him as boy or man a sign of morbidness or melancholy, unless it was when Mrs. Stanard ('Helen') died, when he appeared for some time grieving and oppressed. Aside from this, cards, raids on orchards and turnip patches, swimming in Shockoe Creek, and juvenile masquerades seem to have been the normal order of life."[140]

That there was another side, though, is abundantly evident from other accounts. The truth is, that even at this early date, Edgar Allan Poe began to develop that strange diversity, and the contradictory sides to his personality that have so puzzled and will long continue to intrigue the world. That he was a merry companion in minor ways, many of his little friends have left their testimony. But that he was also a lonely and sometimes a morbid little boy, already torn and troubled by the riddles of existence, the demands of an esthetic nature for the unattainable, and satisfactions not to be found in the objective life of his companions, is equally certain. We hear of long lonesome tramps, of attempts at juvenile self-expression with both the pen and brush, which only secrecy could save from the inevitable ridicule of boyhood and the ponderous misunderstanding of adults. He was much given to daydreams and reveries, and to the plucking of flowers and the reading of books. Where the University of Richmond now stands was once a

---

[139] There are several stories and authentic ones of Poe's powers as a runner and jumper.

[140] Mrs. Susan Archer Weiss in her *Home Life of Poe,* not always reliable, gives John Mackenzie's *own* account of the intimacy between Poe and himself.

meadow where the young Israfel culled violets. These, with other "feminine" characteristics, must inevitably have relegated him to a world apart from men and little boys. It was the world of vision and of dear-bought dreams.

Considerable mention is made of Poe's enthusiasm for drawing, and there remains at least one drawing of his own hand, around which cluster the tenderest and saddest of memories. Poe seems always to have visualized with a keen eye for shadow and color, and with sufficient vividness to make him desire to reproduce his impressions. In this propensity he doubtless met some sympathy at the hands of young Robert Sully[141] who came of a family of artists, and became a creditable one himself in after life. From Sully one gets a softer and more endearing picture. Young Sully was somewhat delicate, and so sensitive and irritable that few of his companions could remain on good terms with him for long periods. In view of this, the little glimpse he gives us of Poe is doubly interesting. "I was a dull boy at school," Sully says, "and Edgar when he knew that I had an unusually hard lesson would help me with it. He would never allow the big boys to tease me, and was kind to me in every way. I used to admire and envy him, he was so bright, clever and handsome. He lived not far from me, just around the corner, and one Saturday he came running up to our house, calling out, 'Come along, Rob! We are going to the 'Hermitage Woods' for chinquapins, and you must come, too. Uncle Billy is going for a load of pine-needles, and we can ride in his wagon.'" In the shadow that soon falls over the life of this child of misfortune, the picture of the "bright" young Edgar and his little friend Rob rattling off with their childish arms around each other in Uncle Billy's old wagon, is like a gleam of sunlight across a somber landscape. In the future it was not often the clouds parted, even for so brief a glimpse as this. No wonder that later he was to look back upon these halcyon days in Richmond as a Utopia of memory in which to take refuge from a cruel world.

That the friendship with the Sullys was a close one is shown by the fact that Robert's uncle, Thomas Sully, the well-known American artist, some time later made a miniature portrait of the young Poe, then at the beginning of his fame, in the attitude of one of the portraits of Byron.[142]

Immediately upon his returning to Richmond John Allan placed his foster-son in the English and Classical School of one Joseph W. Clarke, of Trinity College, Dublin, who has been described as a fiery, pompous, and pedantic Irishman, making his living by assuming the rôle of pre-

---

[141] Nephew of the American artist, Thomas Sully.
[142] The author has certain intelligence of the existence of this portrait but is not at liberty to divulge full information owing to the restrictions of the owner.

ceptor to the sons of the more fashionable families of Richmond.[143] Like most Irishmen, however, indications are not lacking that he possessed a softer and more genial side.

The curriculum was that of the old-fashioned preparatory school of the day, a continuation of the Latin, French, and primary mathematics of the English Schools which Poe had already attended. In America, perhaps, there was even then some attempt at actually teaching the spoken language, and of reading some of its more classic literature, Johnson, Addison, Goldsmith or Pope. That Edgar was well advanced in Latin for a boy of his years, and that the cost of his education was not unduly heavy, this interesting receipt found among his foster-father's papers will testify:

Mr. JOHN ALLAN, *Dr.*
    To present quarters tuition of
Master Poe from June 11th to Sept 11—1822 . . . . $12.50
   1. Horace 3.50, Cicero de Off. 62½ 4.12½
   1. Copy book, paper Pen & Ink 87½

                                               $17.50
                            Rec'd pay.
                                Jos. W. CLARKE[143]

On another bill dated March 11, 1822, there is a charge of $1 for a "Portion of Fuel."[143] No further textbooks are mentioned.

At this rate young Edgar's schooling could not have cost much over $60.00 a year. Even this, however, is paid in installments during 1822, which jibes with the accounts of Mr. Allan's financial embarrassment at the time.[143]

Mr. Allan's English ventures had not been successful, and had displeased both his partner, Charles Ellis, and his uncle, William Galt, upon the backing of whose fortune, in the final analysis, rested the credit of the firm. Mr. Allan was at one time forced to a personal assignment to his creditors, but, by a special arrangement, was left in actual possession of his various properties.[144] The record of mortgages upon the family real estate immediately prior to the year 1823 show that, to say the least, Edgar's guardian must have been forced to live with considerable prudence and an eye to the pennies.[144] This in conjunction with the legends as to the early pampering of Edgar by "a

---

[143] Receipts for Poe's tuition under Master Clarke in the *Ellis & Allan Papers.* Photostats in possession of the author. Also see Woodberry, 1909, vol. I, page 24.

[144] Woodberry, 1909, page 27, etc., the assets of *Ellis & Allan* were bought in at public auction by John Allan's uncle William Galt who in 1825 returned them by bequest. See Appendix III.

princely merchant," and the possible result of the effect of business worries upon John Allan's none too affable temper, may have a direct bearing upon the early life of Poe. There must have been times when the atmosphere of the family circle, despite the gentle presence of Frances Allan and the gaiety of Anne Valentine, reeked with Scotch gloom.

During these periods of gloom and family friction, Edgar would spend the night at Burling's house which met with strong disapproval from Mr. Allan.

As to what went on in the garret of the house on the corner of Clay and Fifth Streets, it is not hard to hazard a fairly accurate guess. There can be no doubt that it was very early Edgar Allan Poe's ambition to be a poet.[145] Some of his schoolmates in Richmond early noted in him a certain aloofness, and a tendency to withdraw to his room and shut himself up to scribble verses. That the desire for creative writing was so strong upon a lad of fourteen or fifteen that he would leave the games and pastimes of his schoolfellows to go alone to his room and write verses is something of major importance in the story of his life.

Poetry, in the frankly objective civilization of the United States, which has largely given itself over to the conquest of a continent and a preoccupation with things for their own sake, is a lonely, and in all save its last honorable stages, a discounted art. The physical form in which it congeals is expensive to produce, requires the coöperation of others, is silent in itself, and has almost no marketable value. Hence, the young person who chooses the art of poetry in which to embody the forms and imagery of his imagination, is suspected to be doing nothing at all, or to be a little mad. In any case, his interruption upon the slightest pretext is thought of as being of no importance whatever. The inevitable and unhealthy conclusion is therefore forced upon such a one by the entire world that he is a being set apart. That his art may be part and parcel of his surroundings and of vital importance to his neighbors is usually a posthumous discovery. To write poetry he must dream with an intensity that transcends reality; to focus his dreams he requires uninterrupted leisure; and to find this he must hide himself. The result is only too often the feeling of a hunted thing, a sense of remoteness from the life about, and a nervous system jangled by the million interruptions of family and economic life. Above all there is no one to whom he may go to learn his art; or if there is, the result is usually fatal. It is essential, then, that any great poet should begin young, or by the time he has mastered his tools he may be too old to produce. That all of this, including the nervous stress of contempt and inter-

---

[145] For the statements here, I am relying on statements in the preface to Poe's first book in 1827, and many other indications gleaned from various sources too numerous to list.

ruptions, played its part in the experience of Poe is an almost inevitable conclusion.

It is pertinent to note, therefore, that like Keats and Shelley, Poe began to write very early. Some of the contents of his first book, he claims to have composed at the age of fourteen; nor is this at variance with what we know of his rather precocious development which James Galt noticed even in the conversation of the little boy at Irvine. That he was encouraged at home by Frances Allan, both tradition and the knowledge of his foster-mother's character seem definitely to indicate. Even John Allan is said to have taken a secret pride in the boy's effusions and to have read them upon occasions to the amusement of his friends, who pronounced them "trash."[146] At any rate, sometime toward the end of Edgar's attendance upon Master Clarke, John Allan is known to have shown the Irish schoolmaster a whole manuscript of collected verses by his youthful ward.[147]

These do not seem to have been simply the occasional doggerel which all sentimental young fellows at some time during their life write to the eyebrows of their calf-loves, but a whole "volume" of verses to an entire townful of young ladies. The object cannot have been to make *all* the girls love him at once, such Mormon propensities in an adolescent boy would, indeed, have been alarming. Even at the risk of rating the attraction of the ladies to be secondary, it looks very much as if the primary interest of the young poet must have been in the poems themselves. These must have been completed before Edgar was fifteen, as old Master Clarke, the schoolmaster, said that Mr. Allan showed them to him with a view of getting his judgment upon the wisdom of their publication, before the Fall of 1823 when that worthy Irishman retired from the headship of the Academy, vice Master Burke. As to what his comments were, we can guess. It has often been claimed that some of these early verses were those printed in Baltimore in 1823, signed "Edgar," but since there is neither direct nor literary evidence to warrant the assumption, the "fact" can be dismissed.

More amorous verses, however, continued to drip from the enamored pen of the young author, if the statements of several Richmond ladies are to be relied on. These particular ones about 1823 or 1824 seem to have been addressed largely to the belles of a fashionable boarding school kept by Miss Jane Mackenzie, the sister of the Mrs. William Mackenzie who had taken Rosalie into her home. "She was," says a lady biographer,[148] "tall and stately, prim and precise, and was attired generally in black silk and elaborate cap and frizette, a very lady-

---

[146] R. H. Stoddard *Memoir,* page 27. Stoddard is to be taken with a grain of salt.
[147] Statement by Master Clarke.
[148] Mrs. Susan Archer Weiss.

prioress sort of person. . . . When Edgar was about fifteen or sixteen he began to make trouble for Miss Jane."

This "trouble" took the form of clandestine correspondence with the fair virgins immured behind the walls of Miss Jane. The missives were, it appears, supplemented by candy and offerings of "original poetry." It was Edgar's habit to make pencil sketches of the girls who had most smitten his fancy, and to request these favored maidens to attach locks of their hair to the cards. Little sister, Rosalie, who is described at this time as a "pretty child with blue eyes, rosy cheeks, and of a sweet disposition," was the postman for Eros until the indignation of Miss Jane and the slipper of Mrs. Mackenzie rudely discouraged the messenger of romance.

Rosalie appears to have been very fond of her brother, whom she saw frequently at church and as a constant visitor at the Mackenzies', the home of one of Edgar's closest chums, young Jack. She followed the two boys about after school, and romped with them whenever she could. Later on this propensity to follow Edgar was to become embarrassing, due largely to an unfortunate development, or rather lack of development, which came over the girl when she was about twelve years old. Up to that age she seems to have developed in a healthy and usual way, but from then on she ceased to function as a normal human being. Probably due to a defective heredity, the sister of Edgar Allan Poe, while apparently healthy physically, retained the mentality of an adolescent. To the extent that Edgar was plus, Rosalie was minus. Viewed in the cold light of modern psychology, there can be little doubt that they were both abnormal types. Poe was a genius; Rosalie was a high grade moron.

The recollections of this period of Poe's youth, both apocryphal and genuine, are many and various. Even some of those which are well authenticated, however, are not at all pertinent to his development, and for the most part assume the nature of irrelevant small-talk and gossip. But a few of the memories of Col. Thomas H. Ellis, the son of Charles Ellis, who was on peculiar terms of intimacy with both Poe and the Allans are worth recording.[149]

Among other things about Poe, he says that "He was very beautiful, yet brave and manly for one so young. No boy ever had a greater influence over me than he had. He was indeed a leader among his playmates." Tom Ellis remembered that one day Edgar Poe took him off into the fields and woods near Belvedere, an estate that then belonged to Judge Bushrod Washington, and kept the little fellow there all day, while he shot a lot of the good judge's domestic fowls. For this Mr. Allan gave his "son" a good whipping when he returned late

[149] Harrison's *Life of Poe,* pages 23, 24, 25.

that evening. Poe also taught Tom how to shoot, swim, and play bandy, and once "rescued" the little chap from drowning after throwing him into the river at the Falls in order to teach him to swim. Edgar also chased Tom's little sister Jane into hysterics with a toy snake which caused considerable family difficulties. The Allans it seems, significantly enough, would have liked to adopt this little girl as their daughter, and showered the family of the "senior partner" with the "largest Christmas and birthday gifts which they received." Colonel Ellis recalled Poe's having taken first prize in elocution when he competed with Channing Moore, Cary Wickham, Andrew Johnston, Nat Howard and others. "He was trained in all the habits of the most polished society. There was not a brighter, more graceful, or more attractive boy in the city than Edgar Allan Poe." Of the social affairs in the Allan household about this time, however, we get a somewhat different picture from young Jack Mackenzie.

That young gentleman, it appears, could not abide the ordeal of a meal at the Allans'. "Mr. Allan was a good man in his way," he said, "but Edgar was not fond of him. He was sharp and exacting, and with his long, hooked nose, and small keen eyes looking from under his shaggy eyebrows, he always reminded me of a hawk. I know that often when angry with Edgar he would threaten to turn him adrift, and that he never allowed him to lose sight of his dependence on his charity." The Allans, who were fond of giving teas and "sociables," required Edgar to be present, usually with one or two boy friends, and occasionally he was given a party of his own when both boys and girls were invited. On such occasions, despite the charm of Mrs. Allan and the good fun of "Aunt Nancy" Valentine, a rigid etiquette reigned, and Mr. Allan used these occasions quite obviously to cultivate in Edgar the stilted manners which the code of the time prescribed, a type of social behavior more consonant with the inclinations and training of Mr. Allan, than that of higher Virginia society.

Formalities, important as Mr. Allan may have thought them to be, could not have troubled Edgar very much at this time. He seems to have led a double life of dreaming and verse making on the one hand, and a thoroughly harum-scarum existence on the other. He was fond of stealing off with three or four cronies to swim in the James near *Rocketts* or the pool below the Falls, where he met, and apparently enjoyed, the society of the young toughs of that neighborhood known to all boys of Richmond as "Butcher Cats." When the water was low, they would wade over the rocky bed of the James to the far bank and set fish-traps along the shores of its willow-islands. Here Edgar with Burling and others led a more or less "Huck Finn"–"Tom Sawyer" kind of existence during the Summers, and developed a wholesome, and, for a boy of his years, an unusual physique—in muscle at least.

On the James, indeed, occurred the "great" feat of his boyhood, when he more than satisfied the Byronic tradition. Poe himself was proud of his athletic accomplishment, and as late as May, 1835, wrote to Mr. White the editor of the *Southern Literary Messenger* about some mention of the incident which was remembered for years in Richmond:

> The writer seems to compare my swim with that of Lord Byron, whereas there can be no comparison between them. Any swimmer 'in the falls' in my days, would have swum the Hellespont, and thought nothing of the matter. I swam from Ludlow's wharf to Warwick (six miles), in a hot June sun, against one of the strongest tides ever known in the river. It would have been a feat comparatively easy to swim twenty miles in still water. I would not think much of attempting to swim the British channel from Dover to Calais.[150]

Edgar was evidently considerable of a hero. Quite a little crowd gathered to see him start. Master Burke, the schoolmaster, followed in a boat; with Robert Cabell, little Robert Stanard, and some others trying to keep abreast of them along the banks. Poe succeeded in reaching his goal and walked home afterwards apparently none the worse for wear, and in triumph. Such, however, was not the experience of little Rob Stanard who returned home very late, covered with mud and soaked. His excuse to his father, Judge Robert Stanard, was that "he had been walking down the river bank watching Edgar Poe swim to Warwick."[151] As to what followed immediately history is silent. Yet the acquaintance of these two lads was important. Out of it sprang the first great emotional experience of Edgar Poe's life, and one of the supreme lyrical utterances of romantic poetry.

The tie which often exists thus between an older and a younger playmate is one of the dearest and most serene of human associations. It is not a complicated one, and there are no mean motives in it. The recognition and protection of the older boy, whose superior mental and physical development give him an almost magic superiority, the recognition of which is delightful, is returned whole-heartedly by the younger partner in the form of undisguised admiration, trust, and affection, to which only the term, "hero worship," can apply. Between Edgar Poe and Rob Stanard such a friendship seems to have existed. It is probable that Poe found in the high bred delicacy and sensitive nature of the younger boy, for such from many accounts he appears to have been, a refuge from the more boisterous and insensate natures about him. What more natural, then, than that little Rob should take his hero Edgar home and exhibit him proudly to the family, who had doubtless

---

[150] Published in the *Southern Literary Messenger* and also quoted by Ingram. For the incident see also Harrison, Woodberry, etc.

[151] Reminiscences of John C. Stanard furnished to the author by W. G. Stanard, President of the Virginia Historical Association, August, 1925. The latter, in several conversations with the author during the preparation of this biography, also discussed the character of Jane Stith Stanard and the family traditions about her.

been regaled with accounts of his charm, prowess, and virtues. It is the essence of a hero that he has no faults.

So it came about, one important day for poetry, that Rob Stanard took Eddie Poe home to show him his pet rabbits and pigeons. After these were duly, and no doubt satisfactorily admired, for Edgar was always very fond of pets, as he thought that animals are in many respects superior to men, young Bob probably invited him into the house to meet his mother, Mrs. Jane Stith Stanard. One can imagine the two quaintly dressed boys entering the old house together to meet "mother." That meeting was to be the awakening encounter and emotional inspiration of his manhood.

Both from the accounts of those who knew her and from her portrait, it is quite evident that Mrs. Stanard was a woman of great beauty and of a somewhat classic countenance. The style of dress of the period, with its decidedly statuesque outlines, lines that had about them at least the suggestion of something out of antique times, something of grandeur and nobility, must have suited her type of beauty to perfection. Her family and relatives have preserved into modern times the memory of one unusual for her warmth of heart and graciousness in an age of gracious manners.[152]   In short, Mrs. Stanard is known to have been a beautiful woman, a splendid hostess, and possessed of a peculiarly radiant and extraordinary and memorable personality. Her house was an exceedingly delightful one, bathed in sunshine from the great garden beyond. By the young poet, "Helen" seems always to have been remembered as a person who radiated light.

Poe went home in a dream from which he never fully aroused himself.[153]   In Mrs. Stanard he had found the chivalrous ideal of a young boy's first idolatry and the material comfort of sympathy and appreciation, for it is tradition that to Mrs. Stanard he read his verses, and received from her both helpful criticism and wise encouragement. What she meant to him only an aspiring young poet, left an orphan, and a worshiper of beauty could know. That there were many visits to her house during the course of several years, and not one only, as has been so often stated, is certain.

Judge Robert Stanard's house, where Poe's "Helen" and his little friend Robert lived, is still standing. It is on Ninth Street facing Capitol

---

[152] There is, of course, no precise contemporary account of the actual scene of this meeting. I am giving the descriptions from a knowledge of the house and descriptions of a portrait of Jane Stith Stanard. The poem *To Helen* seems to be the first hand impression of a beloved person bathed in and radiating light.

[153] Poe's own statement to Mrs. Helen Whitman that Jane Stith Stanard was his "Helen" is attested beyond all dispute by the knowledge of the Stanard family, and a copy of the 1845 edition of Poe's poems given to Mrs. Whitman by him. On page 91 of the first volume, the poem *To Helen* appears, beside the title of which is the word "Stanard" written in Poe's own hand in pencil. Catalogue of American Artists' Association, April 28, 1924.

Square in Richmond, and in the days of Poe's boyhood had a portico and marble stoop with brass rails in front. Its garden, which was a beautiful one, occupied almost the entire square. Here in the midst of fragrant Southern bloom and the sudden wings of little Rob's pigeons, Edgar must often have sat in some quiet nook with Rob and his mother, read his poems, and listened to the words of encouragement which fell with a double value from such beautiful lips. There are many recollections in the Stanard family of young Poe's intimacy with all the inmates of the house, and the sweet tie of sympathy existing between Mrs. Stanard and the handsome young lad was remarked by all. John C. Stanard, a nephew of Robert's father, remembers coming to the house one day and knocking for some time without any response. He finally heard steps as if someone inside were trying to make as little noise as possible. Then the door was opened by little Robert Stanard and Edgar Poe, both of whom looked embarrassed. He found that the family was out, and that the servants had taken advantage of their absence to go out, too. The two boys had been playing a forbidden game of cards, and after his knock were hiding the pack before they let him in. In the face of such testimony it is idle to say that Poe met "Helen" only once.[151]

Both Mrs. Stanard and Edgar Poe were types of those super-sensitive natures whose higher inner processes take place in that holy land of sensibility, the western border of which so often marches with the kingdom of insanity. Both of them were to trespass over this boundary in the dark caravan of melancholy, Edgar for occasional sojourns, but "Helen" to be lost permanently amid the strange gleams and shadows of that realm only a few years later. Between these kindred there had arisen an instinctive and instant bond of sympathy. For an instant before they passed into the night, their fingers touched, and Edgar for once was completely happy in another's presence.

> I *have been* happy, tho' but in a dream.
> I have been happy—and I love the theme,

wrote Poe three or four years later in his first book.

Thus to have found this first real love and the maternal tenderness, which filled the greatest need in his life, combined in a single person was a piece of psychic good fortune of momentous import to Poe. What was said in their conversations is too long in the past to know, probably nothing of great verbal import. These talks, however, seem to have marked those periods, when for a few instants there were memorable interludes when Edgar Allan Poe found himself completely at home in this world.

They were interrupted by the advance across the dial of the shadow which was completely to envelop "Helen" and to wrap her from the sight of Edgar. Mrs. Stanard was going insane. In April, 1824, she died at the age of thirty-one. Death had scored *two* in what was to be an increasingly intimate association with Poe. Jane Stith Stanard was buried in Shockoe Cemetery where she now lies with the other members of her family, among them "little Bob." A pall of violets, those "myriad types of the human eye," has filled the little inclosure with eternal spring.[154]

There is an immortal story that Poe haunted the spot. He said that he did, in a confession to another Helen years later, and tradition seems to confirm the tale. That his great grief was noted even by his companions is a matter of record. Undoubtedly behind the little gate rests the most ideal love of the man's soul. There is another inscription upon the stone, but for posterity there is only one epitaph—

TO HELEN

Helen, thy beauty is to me
  Like those Nicean barks of yore,
That gently, o'er a perfumed sea,
  The weary, wayworn wanderer bore
To his own native shore.

On desperate seas long wont to roam,
  Thy hyacinth hair, thy classic face,
Thy Naiad airs have brought me home
  To the glory that was Greece
And the grandeur that was Rome.

Lo! in yon brilliant window-niche,
  How statue-like I see thee stand,
  The agate lamp within thy hand!
Ah, Psyche, from the regions which
  Are Holy Land!

[154] The epitaphs of the Stanard family read: "Jane Stith Stanard . . . departed this life on the 28th of April, in the year 1824, in the 31st year of her age." "Robert Stanard (*husband*) born 17th Aug. 1781, died 14th May, 1846."
"Robert Craig Stanard [Poe's playmate] born on the 7th of May, 1814, and died in Richmond on the 2nd of June, 1857." Hence Poe was about fifteen when he first saw "Helen," and little Rob, ten.

CHAPTER SEVEN

ISRAFEL SALUTES THE MARQUIS

OVER a third of the span of the days allotted to Poe had already flashed their way through the kaleidoscope of their seasons, before "Helen" was borne to her final refuge. The fiery, sensitive young boy was fast budding into the even more sensitive man, a process which seems to have taken place rather precociously in Poe, for all accounts agree that, both mentally and physically, the young poet developed "beyond his years." That his nature and temperament discovered themselves in an accelerated, but accentuated, and rather brief period, the history of his parents and the evidence about him seems to indicate. He was a lamp which burned intensely in response to the current of a life which was so strong, and which alternated so violently between hope and despair, that the filament was soon burnt out. In the course of the next few years, from 1823 on, he was to experience a nervous tension and undergo trials, the nerve-racking effect of which undoubtedly left him unstrung, and followed him through the remaining lustra of his life. To a finely organized body and intellect, the trials of adolescence are often sufficient in themselves to dictate the future motions of the man; add to this the body-blows of death, an unhappy and harassed love affair, a complete change in the methods of living of one's family, with all the adjustments of environment involved, accompanied by an agony of domestic dissensions, and it does not require the prophetic offices of a psychologist to predict the result.[155] Through such an experience the young Poe was about to pass. For several reasons, then, the year 1823 may be said to mark definitely the end of his childhood.

One of the minor changes, but nevertheless, to a youth, an important one, was the resignation of Master Joseph Clarke as the headmaster of the school which Poe attended, the somewhat flamboyant régime of the Irishman giving way to that of the new incumbent, Master William Burke, a man of sounder learning and more rigid discipline, the rod being by no means a stranger to his strong right hand. In the Fall of 1823, Edgar Allan Poe was the star pupil in the ceremony attendant

---

[155] The evidence of the growing tension from this time on in the Allan household rests upon such a variety of indications that, to present all the proof, would turn this chapter into an exhibition of stray phrases and hints from documents. A few of the more important will be presented.

upon the change of school administrations, and addressed his retiring master in an English ode, written by himself for the occasion.[156] The delighted old Irishman never forgot this, and, years later in Baltimore, recalled of his famous pupil that "Edgar had a very sweet disposition, he was always cheerful, brimful of mirth and a very great favorite with his schoolmates. I never had occasion to speak a harsh word to him, much less to make him do penance. He had a great ambition to excell." Master Clarke also remembered that during the vacation of 1822 two of his pupils, Edgar Poe and Nat Howard, had each written him a complimentary letter in Latin and that Edgar's had been in verse. That before he was sixteen, Poe could manage Latin verses, and compose and deliver in English a school ode for an audience of his schoolmates and parents, may be minor exhibits, but they are at least tell-tale straws on the current of his literary progress.[157]

With the advent of Master Burke, a less happy period of every-day and school life seems to have fallen upon Poe. Not that the new schoolmaster was responsible, indeed, it was noted by Edgar's schoolmates that Poe was almost alone among them in escaping condign attentions, but the young scholar seems to have developed an aloofness and moodiness, a tendency to withdraw himself more than ever from the generally all-absorbing activities of school life, so engrossing to the average boy, which was the cause of remark and distinctly remembered by his fellows.[158] Looking backward, it is not hard to understand what must have been a mystery to his schoolmates.

Mrs. Stanard was going insane and dying. About this time the visits to her house must have had to cease, and we can imagine Edgar's anxious inquiries morning after morning of little Robert before school, the mournful replies of his little friend, and the vision of a loved face, seen through a haze of secret tears, glimmering vaguely upon the pages of Latin texts. Decidedly, this would not be understood by the boys on the benches about him, nor was it a subject which he desired to have discussed. The repression and depression of secret sorrow had already begun to erect its barrier between him and the bright juvenile world about. There were also, in all probability, other reasons for sullen irritation and disquiet, reasons the most profound.

About this time the health of Poe's foster-mother again becomes the subject of anxious remarks in the annals of the family correspondence,[159] and it seems probable that Frances Allan began about now to pass into

---

[156] Woodberry, 1909, vol. I, page 25, and others.
[157] Recollections of Joseph Clarke, Poe's schoolmaster, when interviewed by a Baltimore reporter.
[158] Recollections of John Mackenzie and Dr. Creed Thomas of Richmond, Poe's schoolmates.
[159] See *Ellis & Allan Papers,* Washington, D. C., in the letters between John Allan and his sisters about the Galt will this subject is incidentally mentioned.

John Allan Esq To *J. W. Clarke Dr.*

To tuition of son Edgar Poe from June 11th
to Sept. 11th — — — — — — — $12⁵⁰

Rec'd payt. in advance

J. W. Clarke

Bill of J. W. Clarke

Richmond schoolmaster, to John Allan for tuition
of "son," Edgar Poe

From the Ellis & Allan Papers

the state of ill health and decline which in the space of three or four years was to stretch her not far from Mrs. Stanard in Shockoe Cemetery.

Poe loved Frances Allan with one of the greatest loves of his life,[160] the ties of gratitude and natural affection which bound him to her were as great as can exist. In addition, she possessed that quality of physical beauty which he worshiped, and by this time he must have long known that it was to her and her sister, to his "dear Ma, and Aunt Nancy" that he owed his preservation and his continued cherishing in the house of John Allan. What were the physical causes of Mrs. Allan's continued illness, and whether they were connected with her childlessness, is a question which by its inevitable and proper privacy precludes both the material and the desire to discuss it. That Poe pondered it, however, in his heart seems hardly problematical. He was now a man, possessed of the mature knowledge and feelings which often come early to Southern youths, and he lived in an age and place where the frankness and outspoken habits of the late Eighteenth Century still lingered strongly. What he knew, or thought, about this problem which affected him and his family circle so vitally, we can never know, but it is probable that results of his speculations may have strongly affected him in his attitude towards his foster-father. They were facing each other now in the same house as man to man. It was no longer, as in England, "little Edgar" and "Pa," but Edgar Allan Poe, poet, looking searchingly into the eyes of John Allan, merchant. Upon occasions it must have been a type of scrutiny which even John Allan found somewhat disconcerting.

In 1823-24 Richmond, Virginia, was a small town according to modern standards, of whose inhabitants a large proportion were slaves. The conventions of society were strict, and the confines of the white community in the city were numerically narrow. The wireless was yet to be invented, but news of a certain character undoubtedly radiated rapidly, and, from the nature of the conditions existing in the Allan household from about this time until the death and the filing of the will of John Allan, which confirmed certain rumors, it seems warrantable to infer that Frances Allan was by now aware of the fact that she had not been the sole object of her husband's affections.[161]

That the intelligence would be disturbing to her, and to the little circle over whose destinies she had watched with tender love and solicitude,

---

[160] The letters of Poe to his foster-mother a few years later were said to have been couched in terms of passionate endearment.

[161] Just when, or how, Frances Allan came to suspect this cannot, of course, be shown. From all indications, the life of the family while in England had been very happy. Between 1820 and 1824 *something* occurred to change this. Mrs. Allan's health began seriously to fail, we find John Allan and Poe at serious odds, and Edgar very gloomy. From later correspondence it is known that Poe took his foster-mother's part in the family dissensions. Miss Valentine's sympathy was naturally with her sister. It appears that about this time Edwin Collier or one of the other illegitimate sons of Allan was taken from Richmond and sent to school in Washington, D. C.

it seems fatuous to remark. Whether she confided immediately in Edgar no one can know. It seems unlikely. Her loyalty to her husband, and her regard for the tender feelings of the sensitive schoolboy would probably forbid, but Poe would be quick to sense the electricity in the atmosphere of trouble, and in the inevitable family alignment which was to follow, he could not have helped taking the side to which sympathy, and, a little later, full knowledge of the facts impelled him. It was, of course, that of his "mother."

During the period of financial embarrassment leading up to the mortgaging and assignment of his property [162] after the return from England, John Allan's temper could not have been of the best, and this too would have added to the stresses in the household. Two years later, on March 26, 1825, however, Mr. Allan was relieved of the shadow on this side of his affairs by the death of his uncle, William Galt, who left him the bulk of a great fortune, the Allans, Galts, and other relatives in both America and Scotland coming in for minor shares. It was an event which had been anticipated with various feelings by a large number of those who expected to benefit. Poe afterwards stated that the fortune amounted in all to $750,000. Whether that is substantially correct or not, it is difficult at this date to ascertain.[163] Suffice it to say, that John Allan found himself the recipient of a fortune in cash, merchandise, slaves, securities and real estate, which would in modern times entitle him to be described as a millionaire. The readjustments involved in his life, status, and social ambitions, and the effect of these upon his immediate family were various and not altogether restful, nor entirely happy.

As one of the richest men in Virginia, he would inevitably become the object of considerable attention and remark, a condition which, owing to certain aspects of his private affairs, was not altogether to be relished. Envy was, as always, present to drop a little vitriol into the Falernian. John Allan was troubled with a lame foot and raised his cane high when he walked—"So Galt has left all his money to old swell-foot Allan" was the remark made by a Richmond acquaintance in a letter to a friend when he heard the news.[164] Perhaps the feeling of such an attitude in the background brought the cane down a little more firmly, and gave a firmness and breadth to certain plans for the future in which a grand family mansion played a part; plans that might otherwise have been

---

[162] The year 1823 had been one of extreme financial depression amounting to panic. William Galt's death, later, came in the nick of time to save John Allan.

[163] Letter from Poe to William Poe dated, Richmond, August 20, 1835, "Brought up to no profession, and educated in the expectation of an immense fortune [Mr. A. having been worth $750,000] the blow has been a heavy one. . . ." etc. See Harrison, vol. II, page 15. See also the will of William Galt, Appendix III.

[164] The author does not feel at liberty to quote the source. See also a letter concerning William Galt printed in Appendix III.

conceived upon a somewhat less impressive scale. There was trouble in Scotland over the administration of the will, too, and threats to appeal to the law. In the eyes of certain relatives the shares which they received appeared attenuated,[165] and the brisk correspondence which ensued reeked with Caledonian frankness, to which the replies were carefully pondered.

All this was not conducive to the peace of mind of John Allan or Edgar Allan Poe. The world about was troubled by many things, its vistas were suddenly strangely widened, the prime affections upon which it hung were becoming frayed, and in the meanwhile Mrs. Stanard was slowly and awfully dying. Of these days, Creed Thomas, Poe's schoolmate, says [166]—"It was a noticeable fact that he never asked any of his schoolmates to go home with him after school. The boys would frequently on Fridays take dinner or spend the night with each other at their homes, but Poe was never known to enter into this social intercourse. After he left the school ground we saw no more of him until next day." Where was the merry and popular Edgar Poe of other days? The shadows, it would seem, had already begun to fall.

In April, 1824, occurred the death of Mrs. Stanard. It is not known definitely whether her unhappy young admirer was present at her burial or not. He was a close friend of little Rob, and well liked by the family, but the chances are against it, as the nature of "Helen's" taking off had been so peculiarly tragic that even the presence of dear "strangers" would have been painful to the family. If Poe haunted her grave at night as tradition asserts, the nature of his experiences in a dark cemetery with the sound of the night wind through the funereal gratings and tall grave grasses must have been searing to the soul of one who was scarcely more than a boy. Nor could a reckless abandonment to even so extreme and natural a grief have failed to give a morbid cast to his thoughts, and have tried his already taut nervous system. The truth is that Poe's weeping by night at the grave of "Helen" is one of the episodes in his life which probably can never be reduced to a certainty. The main evidence for it rests upon his own account given years later to Mrs. Helen Whitman, when he was under every inducement to render as romantic as possible every association which hung about the name of "Helen," past and present. The story is almost too dramatically pat, and episodically fortunate, to be taken as wholly true. It agrees

---

[165] Letter from John Allan to one of his sisters, even some years later, from Richmond, March 27, 1827. ". . . Perhaps the four first Legatees named in my Uncle's Will do not attach sufficient importance to Capt. and Jane Walsh's lawyer's letter, you are out of the scrape, unless indeed Capt. Walsh can prove as he has written that there can be no doubt but Jane is entitled to the whole residue. I think this rather too absurd, but will scuffle for her third in place of a Seventh. . . ." etc., for three long pages. *Ellis & Allan Papers*, Washington, D. C.

[166] Dr. Creed Thomas, afterward a well-known Richmond physician.

too well with the legend which he built up about himself later, and with
the lugubrious sentimentality of the time.   It is what he would like to
have had happen, and that, only too often, was sufficient for Poe to
"make it so."   That he was afraid of the dark and a prey to terrifying
visions is against the probability of his watching by a new made grave
at night, nor was the cemetery in those days of medical license without
proper caretakers.   It is also true that other sad associations of the
place were later added to burden his memory.[167]   A visit to the spot with
the facts in mind will best enable one to decide.   That his grief was a
great one, and lasting, no one can ever doubt.

About this time Poe seems to have first been haunted by nightmares,
of which John Mackenzie heard him say afterward, "that the most horrible thing he [Poe] could imagine as a boy was to feel an ice-cold hand
laid upon his face in a pitch dark room when alone at night; or to
awaken in semi-darkness and see an evil face gazing close into his own;
and that these fancies had so haunted him that he would often keep his
head under the bed-covering until nearly suffocated."   Here at least
is something to make the psychologist ponder and the philosopher start.
What may be the significance of cold, dead hands laid at midnight upon
the brow of a shuddering boy must be left to them.   The dead, however,
at this time were by no means the entire preoccupation of young Poe.

In the Autumn of 1824 not only the City of Richmond but the entire
State of Virginia was looking forward feverishly and preparing dramatically for the approaching visit of the Marquis de La Fayette.[168]
It was the greatest national event of a personal nature since the death
of Washington, and it occurred at a period when there was nothing of
much importance to occupy the mind of the public politically or inter-
nationally.   By the end of the first quarter of the Nineteenth Century,
La Fayette had outlived nearly all of his great revolutionary contemporaries, and he personified to the new generations, and to the already
awakening giant of the young Western Republic, the ideals which in
theory at least were held most dear.   No doubt had as yet been entertained as to their efficacy to bring about the millennium, and in the romantic, affable, and intriguingly hawk-like little Frenchman, the sons
and daughters of the generation of the Revolution beheld the foe of
tyrants, the friend of Washington, a great soldier, and the symbol of
the triumph of the doctrines of Jefferson, and the philosophy of Rous-

---

[167] The author ventures it as his *opinion* here that Poe's terrible grief upon returning
from the army in 1829 and finding Frances Allan dead, and his well-authenticated
despair at her grave after the funeral, was later on confused in his own mind, and in the
recollections of others, with a more romantic legend about Mrs. Stanard.   The reader
is left to his own inferences.

[168] If the reader should think that the incident is given undue prominence here, let
him turn to the newspapers and letters of the time.   The importance of La Fayette's
visit as a turning point in Poe's experience has never been made clear.

seau.   Here was a perfect hero in fact and body, and the reception tendered him throughout the Union took on all the guise of a patriotic
triumph.   Nor was it without justification.   It was received on the part
of the honor guest with a tact and grace, the memory of which played
its part in one of the side shows of the World War a century later.   In
the life of Poe, it provided the first opportunity for the young poet to
participate in the affairs of this world in the rôle of a man.   What he
learned while La Fayette was in Richmond, and the effect of his active
part in the military pomp and ceremonial display of the occasion, bore
fruit in the future actions and movements of the man.   It was his confirmation into the affairs of adult life.

Virginia was under peculiar debt to La Fayette, his campaign against
Arnold and his gallantry at Yorktown were remembered as a part of
her history, and the Old Dominion determined to surpass herself in the
tradition of open-handed hospitality.   Letters began to pour in to Governor Pleasants from all over the state.

Fredericksburg, Oct. 6th, 1824

JAMES PLEASANTS, *Esqr.*

DEAR SIR:
Under the impression that Genl La Fayette on his route to York will pass
through this town the citizens are making preparations to receive him.

Connected with these arrangements, it is wished to know the views of the
Executive of the State on this subject after the example of other States, is it
intended that you meet him at the State line in person or by deputation, and what
mode of conveyance is intended for him?   I am requested by our Committee of
arrangements here to ask your reply to the above.

Should you pass through this town to meet him on the Potomac, our citizens
will be pleased of the opportunity of testifying the respect which they entertain
towards you.

Respectfully,
GARRETT MINER [169]

To a great soldier the chief honors were, of course, to be military,
and in addition to the letters from patriotic citizens, there were many
from the commanding officers of the State Militia asking to be provided with arms for the occasion from the State Arsenals.   The helpless
state of the militia, indeed, is not without its alarming and amusing
sides. [170]

In Richmond the excitement and anticipation were intense, and in no
circles more so than among the young gentlemen of Burke's Academy
and other well-born youths of the town.   A military company, called the
"Richmond Junior Volunteers" or "Morgan Legion," was organized

---

[169] This and the letters immediately following are from the archives of the Virginia
State Library.

[170] See a characteristic letter from Yorktown, Virginia, dated 25 September, 1824, to
George Pleasants requesting arms for the local militia unit, signed John B. Christian,
Capt.,—Virginia State Library *Archives.*

and provided with a uniform of the fringed hunting shirts of the frontier. Of this proud little company John Lyle was elected Captain, and Edgar Allan Poe Lieutenant, a distinct tribute to Poe, for the offices were doubtless much coveted. The next thing on the *tapis* was to provide the organization with arms, the details of which transaction seem to have been managed by the two young officers.

In the carefully fostered legend of the faithfulness and contentment of the slaves under the ancient régime in the old South, it has been conveniently forgotten that one of the ever present fears under which a slave-holding community lived was the nightmare of a rebellion of the blacks. Nor was it an idle dream. There had been in Virginia already several alarming, though abortive, attempts on the part of the negroes which, however futile, had sufficed to raise the "goose flesh" of the planters and the inhabitants of towns. In Richmond a regiment of the State Guards was kept ready for emergencies at all times, and a portion known as *"the* guard," was always under arms at the penitentiary where the barracks were. The officers were required to appear upon all occasions in uniform. In order to welcome La Fayette it was proposed to march the 19th, Richmond, Regiment out of the city. As it would never do to leave the town entirely unguarded, an arrangement was made to distribute arms to volunteer militia which this letter records.

Sir
    Dr. Adams the Mayor of the City of Richmond has suggested the propriety on my part as the Col. of the 19th Regiment of applying to the Executive for a number of arms to be used by the militia during the absence of the many persons who are about to leave the City for York, which can be returned after the particular necessity for them ceases. In furtherance of his views I have thought it proper to make the application and would be pleased if the Executive would communicate their determination to the Mayor.

I am Sir, etc.
L. B. Darvie [169]
Col. 19th Regt., Va. Inf.

The permission was granted and among those applying for arms was the Company of Junior Morgan Riflemen, the application being signed by John Lyle, Captain, and Edgar A. Poe, Lieutenant. The matter-of-fact endorsement on the outside

Richmond Oct. 13, 1824

To the Governor and Council
    Gentlemen :
    The subscribers to the inclosed list having associated for the purpose of forming a patrol, for the protection of the City during the absence of the Volunteer Companies, respectfully ask through me that they may be furnished with the necessary Arms and Acoutrements.

Respectfully
Inman Baker, Jr. [169]

can scarcely convey the pride and sense of rapture which must have filled the hearts of the Richmond Junior Volunteers, who were included in the list, as they put real guns over their shoulders, or of Lieutenant Edgar Poe as he girt a sword on his thigh and sallied forth to meet La Fayette.

La Fayette,[171] clad in a cocked hat and short trousers, a style then almost extinct, arrived on a steamer from Norfolk. "Along with John C. Calhoun and two members of the visiting committee, he was drawn in a carriage by four horses while the Fayette Guard marched in front, and young George Washington La Fayette followed in similar state behind. This procession of carriages, filled with officers and worthies of the Revolution, passed to a double arch of evergreens, in front of the *Union Hotel,* at the corners of which were four beautiful young ladies posed as living statues." Here the Marquis was greeted by forty officers of the Revolution, his comrades in arms of as many years before. Not the least moving sight of the procession which followed, and certainly the proudest of all, was the company of "pretty boys" called the "Richmond Junior Volunteers," which headed by Captain John Lyle and Lieutenant Edgar Poe, with their swords at salute, now passed in review.

The boys of this company, as representing some of the best families of Richmond, seem to have acted as a bodyguard for the old patriot, and there is a well-founded tradition of their escorting him to the Memorial Church with Chief Justice Marshall, where Captain Lyle and Lieutenant Poe accompanied him up the aisle to the Marshall pew.

Poe would have been doubly proud, for he must have been noticed and have become personally known to La Fayette as the grandson of "General" David Poe of Baltimore. On his visit there La Fayette is said to have gone especially to the grave of the old Revolutionary hero and exclaimed, *"Ici repose un cœur noble."* [172] The knowledge of this fact, which could scarcely have been unknown to Poe who was in correspondence with his brother William Henry,[173] and other relatives in

---

[171] For a complete and excellent description of La Fayette's visit to Richmond see *Richmond, Its People and Its Story,* by Mary Newton Stanard, chapter XVI.

[172] Here, indeed, rested a noble heart—David Poe, Assistant Deputy Quartermaster for Baltimore during the Revolutionary War, had been one of the foremost of the young patriots who had cleared the British out of Maryland. Notable among his deeds was the leading of a mob that drove out the Royal Sheriff and made one William Goddard, editor of a Tory sheet which had attacked Washington, feel the weight of patriotic wrath. "General" Poe, as he was called, not only fought for his country but, out of his own scant savings, advanced certain sums to the cause which were never repaid. In 1814, at the age of seventy-one, he again volunteered and saw active fighting against the British in the Battle of North Point. Many years after his death in Baltimore, his widow, then in greatly reduced circumstances, received a pittance from the Republic.

[173] Edgar had received a letter from Henry Poe in Baltimore while La Fayette was in Richmond—See John Allan's letter to Henry Poe, page 103.

Baltimore, must have quickened his sense of family pride on his paternal side, and have drawn his attention to a military career. At any rate, less than three years later we find him joining the army.

The effect of a boys' cadet company upon the psychology of its members is more lasting and goes deeper than most casually minded parents realize. The pride of gold lace and brass buttons, the fine feathers of the young warrior, their effect upon the young ladies of his acquaintance, and the gang spirit engendered by the organization which develops the chief virtue of youth, loyalty, is often character-fixing in its effect. Poe, as an officer, had exercised authority, its taste was sweet, beyond doubt, and his pride and self-reliance had been aroused. That the "Richmond Junior Volunteers" were a great success is evident from the fact that they did not disband, and, a month after La Fayette's visit, they are to be found still drilling and petitioning for the permanent possession of their arms.

Richmond, Nov. **17,** 1824

To the Governor:

At the request of the members of the Richmond Junior Volunteers, we beg leave to solicit your permission for them to retain the arms which they lately were permitted to draw from the Armorey. We are authorized to say that each individual will not only pledge himself to take proper care of them, but we ourselves will promise to attend strictly to the order in which they are kept by the company.

We are, etc.
JOHN LYLE
EDGAR A. POE [174]

As to Governor Pleasants' reply, the records are silent, but for Poe the end of his military juvenilia was not yet.

During his association with the members of other military organizations and various persons with whom this new freedom of experience brought him in contact, young Poe seems for the first time to have ranged the city rather freely, and to have been treated as a man. It cannot be positively stated, but it seems highly probable, that the effect of this experience at a time of open house and *mardi gras* while La Fayette was being fêted, was to bring him in contact with new acquaintances of a type who regaled his ears in no uncertain terms with the details and circumstances of his foster-father's indiscretions; so that he gathered from a portion of the community, with which he had not heretofore been familiar, a more precise idea of the estimation in which, in some quarters, his guardian was held.

---

[174] *Calendar of Virginia State Papers,* X, 518 (1892). The original letter has been lost.

Be this as it may, at any rate there is direct evidence of the fact that about this time his moodiness and general attitude began to give his guardian considerable alarm. Inference seems to warrant the assumption that the severe visitations of John Allan's discipline could not have been received at this time by Edgar with the purely regretful protests of childhood. As the rod fell on shoulders which had just worn epaulets, or upon that humbler locality where the rods of parents are wont to descend, it is highly probable that the hurt pride of "Lieutenant Poe," lately attached to the Marquis de La Fayette, replied to the reproaches of his guardian in a truthful but disrespectful manner; or that he sulked like a young bear and indicated that there were good reasons why. John Allan was not only displeased, he was alarmed; and shortly after the departure of the Marquis we find him justifying himself to the Almighty and fortifying himself in the regard of Edgar's brother in Baltimore in a rather interesting style. The letter is to William Henry Leonard Poe then seventeen years old.

Richmond Nov. 1824

DEAR HENRY:

I have just seen your letter of the 25th ult. to Edgar and am much afflicted he has not written you. He has had little else to do, for me he does nothing and seems quite miserable and sulky and ill tempered to all the Family. How we have acted to produce this is beyond my conception, why I have put up so long with his conduct is little less wonderful. The boy professes not a spark of affection for us, not a particle of affection for all my care and kindness towards him. I have given [him] a much superior Education than ever I received myself. If Rosalie has to relie on any affection from him God in his mercy perserve her—I fear his associates have led him to adopt a course [?] of thinking and acting very contrary to what he professed when in England. I feel proudly the difference between your principles and his and hence my desire to stand as I ought to do in your Estimation. Had I done my duty as faithfully to my God as I ought to Edgar, then had Death, come when he will have no terrors for me, but I must end this with a devout wish that God may yet bless him and you and that success may crown all your endeavors and between you, your poor Sister Rosalie [175] may not suffer. At least she is half your sister and God forbid my dear Henry that we should visit upon the living the errors of the dead. Believe me Dear Henry we take an affectionate interest in your destinies and our United Prayers will be that the God of Heaven will bless and protect you. Rely on him my Brave and excellent Boy who is ready to save to the uttermost. May he keep you in Danger, preserve you always is the prayer of your

Friend & Servant

[JOHN ALLAN]

---

[175] In the *Ellis & Allan Papers,* from which this letter is taken, are found about this time nine charges by John Allan against both Edgar and Rosalie for small amounts of postage.

On the back of the copy of this note, there is, characteristically enough, a calculation for compound interest of a certain sum at six per cent in the same pious hand.[176]

Perhaps the cold palm which Edgar had felt upon his brow was not altogether a dream. To be able in the same breath to defend oneself, by endeavoring to cause dissension between brothers, while casting a slur on the mother of the same youth on whose head the divine blessing is invoked—and calmly to turn over the same sheet of paper and calculate the amount of compound interest due, is to proclaim oneself in the possession of qualities which, if not human, are certainly not divine. Such was evidently the spirit of the man who devoutly consigned the future of the Poe orphans to the mercy of God.

Keeping in mind the spiritual vista thus opened to us by John Allan's own pen, his more mundane proceedings can now be chronicled. The old house at the corner of Fourteenth Street and Tobacco Alley once more comes into view. It had been left John Allan as part of the Galt estate, and to it the family now moved once again for a while, but not for long. It is this house, still standing, with which the most intimate and earliest memories of Poe must be associated when thinking of his boyhood in Richmond. Strangely enough it has been almost overlooked, doubtless eclipsed by the traditions of Edgar Poe which gathered about a grander and more impressive mansion to which the family next removed.

Naturally enough the inheritance received from William Galt in 1825 changed the social outlook and the mode of life of John Allan and his family. Coincident with the turn for the better in their circumstances there had been, despite Mrs. Allan's precarious health, an increase in the round of social gaieties, and the old house at Fourteenth Street, so convenient from a business standpoint, was found inadequate for their different needs.[177]

On June 28, 1825, only three months after the probating of his uncle's will, Mr. Allan bought at auction a large house on the southeast corner of Main and Fifth Streets for the sum of $14,950.[178] It was a good bargain as the former owner had paid $19,100 for it, but died before he completed payments. The house had been built by David Meade Randolph, but was afterward purchased and much im-

---

[176] Photostat of this letter in the possession of the author. The letter was a copy kept in the *Ellis & Allan Files,* the original, of course, having gone to Henry Poe. No doubt the copy was retained to show to Edgar. The copy is unsigned, but is in John Allan's own hand.

[177] William Galt's will was signed March 25, 1825, and probated March 29, 1825. The house at Tobacco Alley and Fourteenth Street was a bequest to John Allan. See Appendix III.

[178] Letter of Col. Thomas Ellis to George E. Woodberry dated Baltimore, May 28, 1884.

proved by Señor Joseph Gallego, a rich Andalusian merchant of Richmond, who had indulged his Spanish fancy for landscaping by planting a double garden below the house; that on the east being for vegetables, while the slope of the hill on the south, which the house overlooked, was green with abundantly bearing grape-vines, fig trees, and raspberry bushes; nor were flowers, vines, and shrubs lacking with bloom and sweet scent. Here was a garden, indeed, for a certain young poet who loved flowers, and was doubtless not averse to figs.

In this house, since torn down, occurred the most momentous passages of Poe's early life; it is forever connected with his name and that of John Allan in Richmond; some of its furnishings have achieved a permanent place in our literature, and to it, in his thoughts, Edgar Poe forever returned "home." In view of this, a description of it, as a background for the life he led there, will assume more than an antiquarian interest.

From its windows there was a magnificent sweep of scenery to be seen, a view of the valley of the James stretching away into Henrico and Chesterfield Counties, and of Manchester, on the south bank, then a delightful little village. This with its bridges, its islands, its river, falls, meadows, woods and hamlets was the country of Poe's boyhood. The generous doorway of the mansion opened into a spacious hall, on the right of which was the morning reception and tea room. Just across the hall from the front room was the dining room, octagon in shape, and beautifully lighted. On the second floor was the large octagon parlor or ball room, famous for many a brilliant affair, while John Allan's own chamber was immediately over the front door, with windows that overlooked the drive and front yard. On the same floor were three other bedrooms, one occupied by Miss Valentine, another spare room for guests, and a third which was Edgar's.

Poe's room was at the end of a hall that ended in a wedge-shaped alcove just beyond a rather dark twist in the stairs.[179] In this recess, so that it protruded somewhat beyond the door, was a table upon which stood an *agate lamp,* always kept burning at night, because of the dark stairs and hall. On this table it was Poe's habit to throw his coat as he entered the room. The chamber had two windows, one fronting north, and one east with an extensive view, for at that time there were no other buildings upon Mr. Allan's square. There was in addition to the usual bedroom furniture, a comfortable lounge where Poe loved to lie and read; a table for his books; and a wardrobe well furnished—we hear of occasions upon which young visitors to the house were sup-

---

[179] For some of the details as to Poe's room in the Allan house I am indebted to a Richmond antiquary, to the recollection of Thomas Bolling, a visitor to Poe's room, and to articles still preserved at the Poe Shrine in Richmond and elsewhere, and to the letter of Col. Thomas Ellis to Prof. Woodberry—see note 178.

plied with extra clothing from Edgar's store. This, especially, must have been grateful to Poe, who was at this time by way of being a bit of a dandy,—neat and careful of his rather distinguished person at all times, except when in the clutches of poverty later on, or during one of his sprees. In short, his appearance was always a barometer of his mental and financial condition. By inclination and training he was orderly in his living and punctilious about his dress.

We are told by one who had often been there, that against the walls of Poe's bedroom in the Allan house was a modest shelf of books, and at this time there would certainly have been more in his "father's" library. In view of the fact that many of these books must have been instrumental in shaping the man's imagination, it is interesting to speculate what volumes may have been there. Nor is this a mere guess; books were infinitely less numerous then than they are now, literary taste was more fixed, and the sources of the boy's lines in his first volume of poetry, most of which goes back to Richmond or University days, are often quite obvious.

On the shelves and table of his room where he studied there were, of course, his textbooks, among them some of the classics, Homer, Virgil, Cæsar, Cicero, and Horace. There would have been old grammars, dog-eared spellers, readers, and French readers,—some of them perhaps brought back from England,—English and American histories, some of the Gothic romances, and probably a manual or two on military tactics. Byron, Moore and Wordsworth we may be sure were present, with Coleridge and Keats, and more doubtfully Shelley, certainly some of the old eighteenth century poets with which the libraries of Southern gentlemen were so liberally stocked. *Don Quixote, Gil Blas* and *Joe Miller* we hear of later in a letter. Milton was there, the boy knew him, Burns, of course—Mr. Allan was a Scotchman. Campbell and Kirke White can be added to the list and perhaps E. C. Pinkney.[180]

Of novelists, Poe would by this time have come across Scott, Cooper, Charles Brockden Brown, and some of the earlier things of Irving, and he would have made the acquaintance of Macaulay and other English essayists and reviewers in the pages of the *Edinburgh Review* and *Blackwood's* which were largely subscribed to in Richmond. Certainly he must have read the poetical effusions of local and contemporary, but now long forgotten, "bards" and "bardesses" in both the American and British periodicals and newspapers of the day.

There is direct evidence of an abundance of these. Richmond and his "father" were in close touch with England through foreign trade and family relations, and one of the obliging side issues of the firm of *Ellis & Allan* was to act as agents for subscriptions to newspapers and

---

[180] For the last three names I am indebted to Dr. Thomas Ollive Mabbott.

other publications. During part of the firm's history it handled popular London periodicals and even sheet music. These were kept upon the second floor of the *Ellis & Allan* establishment, and Poe's fondness for the spot was a matter of note. Although the boy was rather shy, it was remembered that upon occasions he would recite some favorite poem to those about the place. Among the periodicals which Poe is known to have seen there beyond all peradventure, were the London *Critical Review of Annals of Literature* from 1791 to 1803 in thirty-nine bound volumes, and the *London Ladies' Magazine* for the same period bound in thirty volumes. Moore, Byron, and Goldsmith seem to have greatly interested him.[181] Along with the rest of the world he must have been familiar with Scott. This together with the books in the libraries and upon the tables of his friends, his formal instruction at school, but, above all, the stock of volumes and periodicals over the offices of his "father's" firm, seems to have constituted for the most part the literary background of Edgar Allan Poe. For that time, at least, it was by no means a scant one. He was an accurate and omnivorous reader.

Frances Allan furnished the new house lavishly but in good taste. There were many rich hangings and some busts by Canova of Dante and Mary Magdalene, both of which seemed to have remained in Poe's mind. The furniture was in a graceful late Empire style with gilt brass inlay. Poe seems to have had a desk in his room, or at least a table, upon which was a handsome brass inkstand and sand-caster, purchased by his foster-father and marked "John Allan '13." [182] These Poe afterward took with him among the few things which he carried from John Allan's home, and kept them by him for a long time.

The most delightful feature of the new dwelling, however, was the long portico extending the full depth of the house. The reception and dining room opened out upon it on the first floor, and Mr. Allan's room and the parlor upstairs. Here through the long Virginia Spring, Summer, and Fall the family spent most of their time together with their constant guests. There was "a splendid swing" on the upstairs porch, and a telescope through which the young folks, particularly, loved to peep at the stars and the country across the James. Through its lenses the eyes of young Poe first became familiar with those stars and constellations, the lovely names of which are strewn through his poetry, and, while his passion for astronomical and cosmic speculations

---

[181] Prof. Killis Campbell is to be credited with first extracting many of these facts from the *Ellis & Allan Papers*. I am also in possession of book and newspaper lists ordered by the firm. Also see Killis Campbell, *Poe's Reading,* The University of Texas *Studies in English*, No. 5.

[182] Now in possession of the Bucks County Historical Society at Doylestown, Pennsylvania, with an interesting record of their history. The style of the furniture shows that the house was furnished by Frances Allan about 1825.

was being aroused, through the same glass he became familiar with the quaint face and the dead mystery of the moon.[183, 761]

But not all of Poe's time during the Spring and Summer of 1825 was spent reading in his room or at *Ellis & Allan,* swinging on the porch, or peering through telescopes. There was other and more serious game afoot.

---

[183] See *The Adventure of Hans Pfaall, The Balloon Hoax.* In the latter story Poe's knowledge of much astronomical lore is mathematically correct. The mathematics of the stars interested him as well as their poetical names. Poe certainly knew sufficient mathematics to navigate.

The Allan House, "Moldavia"

At the corner of Fifth and Main Streets, Richmond, Virginia

The home of JOHN ALLAN's better fortunes, connected with some of the most
intimate and important events in the life of EDGAR ALLAN POE

From a photograph originally in the possession of Ingram, Poe's English biographer

John Allan

The foster-father or guardian of Edgar Allan Poe

From a portrait by an unknown artist, probably painted after *Mr.* ALLAN
inherited his uncle's fortune

Photograph of the picture
Courtesy of the Edgar Allan Poe Shrine, Richmond, Virginia

Sarah Elmira Royster
Portrait drawn by Edgar Allan Poe

The little girl who was engaged to POE just before he left for the University in 1826. In 1849 *Miss* ROYSTER, then *Mrs.* SHELTON and a widow, again promised to marry POE. His death in Baltimore in 1849 prevented the consummation of the early romance of his youth

Courtesy of J. K. Lilly, Jr., Indianapolis, Indiana

"A Fountain and a Shrine"

Garden and Fountain of the Edgar Allan Poe Shrine
Richmond, Virginia

Showing the rear of the "Old Stone House" fronting on Main Street not
far from where *Mrs.* POE died

The Poe Shrine at Richmond is the legitimate center of interest and activity in
preserving material and relics connected with EDGAR ALLAN POE, and in
perpetuating his memory

CHAPTER EIGHT

ELMIRA AND THE ENCHANTED GARDEN

WHERE "Linden Row" now stands in Richmond, Virginia, at the corner of Franklin and Second Streets, there was once a beautiful garden that Edgar Poe loved more than well.[184] Even its story was romantic. Thomas Jefferson had once sought to use the space of ground that it occupied in order to erect a prison in which to carry out one of his favorite theories in regard to the reform of prisoners, but one Colonel Thomas Rutherford arranged to exchange the property, and under the care of well-trained gardeners the spot became one of the most beautiful on a once lovely old street. The prisoners which dwelt behind its high brick wall were roses, honeysuckle, jasmine, and the flowering myrtle.

From childhood it had been familiar to Israfel, who on his way to and from school, or on play-larks with little Tom Ellis, caught the scent of Southern Spring as it drifted over the old walls, arresting passers-by with its perfumed invitation from many flowers, and inviting them to leave the white sunshine in the quiet, warm streets, and tarry for a while amid its green coolness.

Charles Ellis, of *Ellis & Allan,* lived just across the street on the opposite corner, in the long frame house with five dormer-windows and double chimneys where the Allans had visited after their return from England.[184] From the front windows, the whole of the block across the street stretched away in a green and flowered vista, musical with birds, a labyrinth of mystery for childhood, and a seat of shade for old age. The place was tended by Mr. Ellis' gardener [185] and must have been a favorite haunt for the solitary hours beloved by Poe.

In his story, *The Landscape Garden,* he has left us the unperishable memory of its delights in the form of a fantasy upon the art of land-

---

[184] See Chapter VI, page 79.
[185] In Poe's story, *The Landscape Garden,* the hero is "Ellison, my young friend." It now appears that the land upon which this garden was situated actually belonged to Poe's guardian, for in William Galt's will among other bequests to John Allan is, "my vacant lot corner of F and 2nd Streets, opposite the residence of Charles Ellis." See Appendix III.

scape gardening, and in a half-homesick mood afterward recalls it by
a quotation from Giles Fletcher:

> The garden like a lady fair was cut,
> That lay as if she slumbered in delight,
> And to the open skies her eyes did shut;
> The azure fields of heaven were 'sembled right
> In a large round, set with flowers of light:
>> The flowers-de-luce, and the round sparks of dew
>> That hung upon the azure leaves, did show
> Like twinkling stars, that sparkle in the evening blue.

Here was a retreat, indeed, where he could forget the world of docks
and ships along the river banks below, and the interminable babble of
prices and merchandising at his foster-father's counter and table. For
Edgar Poe, it was the setting and the background of a world of dreams.

"Helen" was dead, but Israfel was still moving in the world of men;
he looked about him and saw that their daughters were fair, and he
walked with them in the enchanted garden. It was there that he brought
Sarah Elmira Royster and whispered to her through her tangle of
unforgettable curls. She was one of the first, and was destined to be
the last, love of a life star-crossed by many women.

Elmira, for by that name the young lady was known, was the daughter of one of the neighbors.[186] She at one time lived just across the
street from Edgar's school.[187] Propinquity at any rate was present.
Young Poe was not one to overlook the charming because they were
near, and at the time she "swims into our ken" she was about fifteen
and dowered with a trim little figure, an appealing mouth, large black
eyes, and long, dark chestnut hair. The combination was irresistible
to Poe.

He had probably known her since 1823, certainly during 1824, and
after the gloom of "Helen's" passing and during the days of change
and trouble in the Allan household, the walks with Elmira, or "Myra,"
as he called her, along the quiet streets of old Richmond, or in the
woods and fields about, must have been a balm, and have brought a
glow of strange unwonted happiness to his lonely heart.

But it was to the enchanted garden above all that he brought her,
to sit there in the myrtle shades, and talk to her about his love and
dreams. Here it was that he recalled her, in the troubled days of after-
times. Looking back, the dream seemed idyllic, and the light that lay

---

[186] The Roysters were well known to both John Allan and Charles Ellis. This
connection afterward was probably fatal to Poe's hopes. Miss Royster became Mrs.
Shelton. In 1810 I find that the Roysters loaned money to John Allan, charged to
his personal account, *Ellis & Allan Papers*—a receipt dated Richmond, December
22, 1810.
[187] Old Richmond directory.

upon it with such peculiar glory he has caught up and left for us in some of his finest lines:

> Thou wast that all to me, love,
>   For which my soul did pine—
> A green isle in the sea, love,
>   A fountain and a shrine,
> All wreathed with fairy fruits and flowers,
>   And all the flowers were mine. . . .
>
> And all my days are trances,
>   And all my nightly dreams
> Are where thy grey eye glances,
>   And where thy footstep gleams—
> In what ethereal dances,
>   By what eternal streams.

The stuff that dreams are made of, in the case of Poe, has had a strange power of congealing. The garden, its brick walls, its roses and Elmira, have long vanished into the gulf that waits for all things, but as a memorial to the poet's dream, and to the fresh young beauty of the little girl who would have been Poe's wife if Fate had not intervened, there has arisen a memorial [188] nearby, which like its original, the enchanted garden, is also

A Fountain and a Shrine.

Before John Allan moved to the mansion of his better circumstances on Main and Fifth Streets, the Roysters lived in a frame house still standing across lots, or as it was then, across gardens, on Second Street. From Edgar's window where he was then living to the back of Elmira's house there was at that time an unbroken view, and it was the custom of the two young lovers to conduct a handkerchief flirtation, Edgar from his window, and Elmira from the casement at the head of the landing on the stairs. One can imagine their hearts fluttering with every wave of the white signals, and Elmira must have looked up many a night and seen the lamp glowing in the room of the young boy she loved. Nor were these signals purely sentimental. From after events it is known that Mr. Royster did not look too favorably upon the obvious attentions of young Poe, and certainly John Allan's sympathy must at this time have been, to say the least, attenuated.

But the canny Scot along with the other increased ambitions and more impressive mode of life which his uncle's fortune brought into prospect, seems to have changed somewhat his plans for the education of Edgar. Up until the receipt of the Galt estate in 1825, it is prob-

---

[188] The Edgar Allan Poe Shrine in the Old Stone House, Main Street, Richmond, Virginia, is one of the most beautiful memorials to literary genius in the United States. See the illustration at page 109.

able that if John Allan had any plans at all for the future of his brilliant young foster-child, they centered about the store and warehouse
of *Ellis & Allan,* where the practical-minded merchant probably visualized Edgar Poe as occupying a stool and working his way up to
a possible share in the business, or to the point where he could start
out on a mercantile career of his own, as he and Charles Ellis had done
years before. Nor was it by any means an unkindly vista. That Edgar
was much employed about the store, we know, and that he occasionally
served behind the counter as a dry-goods clerk, or as a messenger
carrying papers and valuables to and fro, was afterward recalled by
many who saw him there. Of the use to which he put the book and
periodical department we have already seen. Here he also met the
book lovers, journalists, and *literati* of the town, and occasionally favored the clerks and customers about the place with the recitation of
some favorite poem, a song—for he sang well—or a conversation upon
literature, the world of which had become known to him in the articles
and reviews between the covers of the magazine counter stock of *Ellis
& Allan.* There is no record of his being carried upon the firm's pay-
rolls, though. Quite reasonably enough, his guardian seems to have
charged up his small services against his board and keep. Whatever
pocket money he had came from his "Ma" and "Aunt Nancy." Their
generosity, as his companions and schoolmates testify, supplied him
with a more than usual amount which seems to have been as easily and
generously spent as it was given.

So far, Poe had received as good an education as any boy in Richmond. With the new house, and the higher social status to which his
"father" aspired, seems to have come a different idea as to the possible future and training of the foster-son. Edgar's abilities at decla-
mation, and his leaning toward literature and the world of the intellect,
may have caused John Allan to ponder the manifest advantages of a
professional career, the law,[189] with perhaps the Halls of Congress in
view; nor was he, it is only right to say, oblivious to the remarkable
qualities of Edgar's mind. There was another factor, too. A course
at the University would take him out of the house, and out of the house
for reasons that we have seen, Mr. Allan was very anxious at this time
that the foster-son should go. At any rate, the University began to
be talked of, and in March, 1825, Edgar Poe was removed from Master Burke's school.[190] He was put under the care of private tutors with
an early entrance at the University of Virginia directly in view.

Of the interviews with John Allan and of his life about the warehouse of *Ellis & Allan* together with the provincial and mercantile

---

[189] Both Poe and Mr. Allan specifically mention "law" in later correspondence.
[190] Woodberry, 1909, vol. I, page 29.

clap-trap of the conversation enjoyed there, Poe has left us a neat but sardonic picture in the thinly disguised autobiographical satire of *The Literary Life of Thingum Bob, Esq.*—nor does he forget in an amused way to hint at his own naïve literary aspirations. With even a small knowledge of his life in Richmond about this time, the whole thing is reasonably clear. Even his middle name with the ironical thoughts it afterwards occasioned, creeps into the satire.

Of one's *very* remote ancestors it is superfluous to say much.[191] My father, Thomas Bob, Esq., stood for many years at the summit of his profession, which was that of a merchant-barber,[192] in the city of Smug. His warehouse was the resort of all the principal people of the place, and especially the editorial corps— a body [193] which inspires all about it with profound veneration and awe. For my own part, I regarded them as gods, and drank in with avidity the rich wit and wisdom which continuously flowed from their august mouths during the process of what is called "lather." My first moment of positive inspiration must be dated from that ever-memorable epoch, when the brilliant conductor of the 'Gad-Fly,'[194] in the intervals of the important process just mentioned, recited aloud, before a conclave of our apprentices, an inimitable poem in honor of the "Only Genuine Oil-of-Bob" (so called from its talented inventor, my father), and for which occasion the editor of the 'Fly' was remunerated with a regal liberality, by the firm of Thomas Bob and Company, merchant-barbers.[195]
The genius of the stanzas to the "Oil-of-Bob" first breathed into me, I say, the divine *afflatus*. I resolved at once to become a great man and to commence by becoming a great poet. That very evening I fell upon my knees at the feet of my father.
"Father," I said, "pardon me!—but I have a soul above lather. It is my firm intention to cut the shop. I would be an editor—I would be a poet—I would pen stanzas to the 'Oil-of-Bob.' Pardon me and aid me to be great!"
"My dear Thingum," replied my father (I had been christened Thingum after a wealthy relative so surnamed), "My dear Thingum," he said, raising me from my knees by the ears—"Thingum, my boy, you're a trump, and take after your father in having a soul. You have an immense head, too, and it must hold a great many brains.[196] This I have long seen, and therefore had thoughts of making you a lawyer. The business, however, has grown ungenteel, and that of politician don't pay. Upon the whole you judge wisely;—the trade of editor is best:—and if you can be a poet at the same time—as most of the editors are, by-the-by,—why you will kill two birds with one stone. To encourage you in the beginning of things, I will allow you a garret; pen, ink, and paper; a rhyming dictionary; and a copy of the 'Gad-Fly.' I suppose you would scarcely demand any more."
"I would be an ungrateful villain if I did," [197] I replied with enthusiasm. "Your generosity is boundless. I will repay it by making you the father of a genius."

---

[191] A covert reference to his real parents seems quite evident.
[192] *I.e.,* a merchant who gave his customers a close shave.
[193] Poe had all the delight of the day in puns. Like Keats he reveled in them.
[194] A reference to Poe himself and his editorial criticisms that stung deeply, and his recitations of poetry about the office.
[195] No salary was given him by the "close shaving" firm, hence the irony.
[196] A study of Poe's portraits will make this literal description of himself plain.
[197] "Ungrateful" was John Allan's favorite reproach of Poe.

And he did!

Here we have the whole bucketful in a thimble, the cursory allusion to his real parents, "the remote ancestors of whom it is superfluous to say much," "my father, the close-shaving merchant," the cheap lather of conversation about the warehouse, the Genuine Oil-of-Bob of family pride, and the applause of the clerks which aroused Poe's ambition—and John Allan—"raising me from my knees by the ears." It is all quite palpable, and very, very tragic. How could he demand more than a garret, pen and paper; would he not be an "ungrateful villain" if he did?

John Allan had provided the garret, the pen and paper, the clothes, and the food. That as he grew older he was incapable of providing more for "the immense head that must hold a great many brains," and for the heart that was beating so highly and proudly, was the beginning of a tragedy that has had no end.[198] The duel between these two giants, for they were both that, and duel it was, echoes even now in a subtle way in the melancholy and morbid cast of much of Poe's work. Without a thorough understanding of the relations of these two extraordinary men there can be no comprehension whatever of the motions of Poe. For almost a full half of its life one of the most delicately adjusted and sensitively organized nervous systems that the world has ever seen was subject to the ceaseless and exacting dominance of a potent, a massive and a gigantically virile will. It was not *Ariel* at the beck of *Caliban,* the colors will not stand that, but it was *Hamlet* fostered by a Northern *Shylock,* a central fact in Poe's life that the world, which is seldom subtle, will probably not take the trouble to understand.

The relation of father and son is one that has been left strangely undissected in our literature, while its feminine counterpart has been unduly exploited. In John Allan *vs.* Edgar Poe the perturbations of father and son were raised by circumstances to the *n*th degree of possibilities—and the result was in proportion to the cause. The relation between them was one of the most perplexed, complicated, and subtle in the whole range of life or literature, and therefore doubly hard to understand. But it is also one of the most interesting, for as always in the case of Poe, it was cast dramatically and carried in its involved ramifications, domestic secrets, hidden and damaging letters, unforgiving pride, and the sorrow and death of a beautiful woman beloved by both of them. As we have already taken some pains to look at the physical furnishings in the Allan house, let us for a few moments retire behind the arras.

When John Allan permitted his wife to take the infant Edgar Poe into her house and arms, it was, as we have seen, a little reluctantly.

---

[198] From his influence upon Poe's life, John Allan becomes automatically one of the great secondary characters of literary annals.

Once the fact was accomplished, however, it must also be said that his acceptance of it was more than generous. The child, and John Allan was fond of children, seems to have undoubtedly crept very deeply into his affections, to such an extent that there can be little doubt that for many years he accepted him as his son. In England he went by his foster-father's name, and John Allan made statements to his Scotch relatives that can only indicate that he regarded him then as his heir. Tradition as to Mrs. Allan's coddling and Mr. Allan's undue severity with frequent corporal punishments, in reality means little. Frances Allan was a childless woman whose indulgence her husband corrected in the universal manner of mankind. In plain English, Edgar was probably a naughty and willful little boy who took no harm from being spanked. The situation thus created, however, grew more serious later as a basis for a dangerous family alignment, one which John Allan could not help but resent more than if the boy had been his own. The charges that the older man wounded the pride of the boy by constantly reminding him of his dependence upon charity are more serious, and from much direct testimony appear to be true.

As they grew older, the gulf between their temperaments began to widen. Most men, even of a thick fiber, have a tenderness and fondness, though a hidden one, for little children. Edgar's beauty and "his vivacious ways" no doubt appealed for a while to John Allan. As the boy became more the man, the natural indifference and antagonism of male for male began to play their part in his foster-father's attitude. There was, too, probably unknown to them both, a jealousy for the affection of Frances Allan so strongly concentrated on Edgar, one which even a real father sometimes experiences, as his part in the life of the woman is replaced by the advent of children; and in John Allan's case this was accentuated by the actual fact of the extra-parentage of the child.

As he increased in years, the older man seems to have lost, as often happens, some of the more endearing and easy youthful sides of his nature which he undoubtedly, at one time, possessed; and he became harder-grained, closer, short-tempered, and obstinate. Quite incapable, in short, of appreciating the possibilities in the more delicate aspects of Edgar, and perhaps dissatisfied in a certain way with his wife. He had wronged her, but by that very fact he knew the reason why he had no legitimate children; as he became less attached to Edgar and the possessor of a great estate, he was more than ever desirous of a natural heir. In the meantime, while his wife's affections for young Poe increased with the fine promise of Edgar's young manhood, his own had waned. This seems to have been about the situation when he fell heir to the Galt fortune, and to have warranted Poe later in his statement that "He treated me as kindly as his gross nature would permit." Edgar had been provided with a home and education—the garret and the pens and ink—but he missed in his foster-father what was of much more importance to a boy of genius, the sympathy and understanding of a generously responding temperament.

The situation was tragic and, as is nearly always the case, an ironical one. Into the house of a hard-headed, literal, and commercially-minded Scotch merchant, the eccentricities of Fate had introduced one of the most cunningly and highly strung instruments that has ever trembled to the delicate breath of song, combined with an esthetic ego that later could hardly bear to contemplate the idea that even God was its superior. Add to this, the ugly noise of domestic dissension under the stress of secret sorrow, and the curious stage is set for an inevitable tragedy, a favorite one of the Infernal Mimes, known as the "Breaking Heart of Youth."

For it was not mere incompatibility of natures that brought about the inevitable; *that,* perhaps, as in many another family, might have spent itself in minor ways, but sometime between the return of the family from England and La Fayette's visit to Richmond, Frances Allan seems to have become aware of her husband's unfaithfulness, and the knowledge which was then or afterward shared by Edgar brought the two together in an aggrieved compact that was inevitably against, and probably supremely exasperating to, John Allan. Miss Valentine's position as a dependent upon her brother-in-law's bounty was anomalous, but it is not hard to guess where her sympathies lay, and upon occasions they must have shown. But this was by no means all.

When Mrs. Poe, Edgar's mother, died, John Allan had come into the possession of her letters, and, among these, there was some family secret that was extremely damaging to the Poes. Mrs. Clemm, Poe's mother-in-law, said that years later she destroyed the correspondence after her "Eddie" died, in order to keep the fact from ever becoming known to the world.[199] Just what it was can therefore never be proven, but there is a strong suspicion that it in some way compromised David or Elizabeth Poe and dealt with the paternity of Rosalie. In the family scenes which occurred, for under the conditions they were bound to, it was this secret which John Allan reserved to add the last sting to the reproaches of ingratitude, which he heaped on the foster-son who now dared to sympathize with her whom he had come to regard as his mother. No scribe was present to record this as a fact for posterity, but what John Allan had written albeit shamefacedly, in a letter to Henry Poe,[200] he would scarcely in his rage withhold from Edgar. To

---

[199] See the mention of these letters Chapter II, page 20, note 41.
[200] Letter of John Allan to William Henry Leonard Poe, quoted page 103, *ante,* "God forbid, my dear Henry," etc.

have stones cast at his dead mother and his little sister, from the hands of one who should have been the last to throw them, was something which no lad of spirit could stand. That Edgar replied ably, and perhaps out of all bounds, is a warrantable guess.

In the Spring of 1824, Mrs. Stanard had died; Mrs. Allan's health was failing through sorrow or some other cause; and the gloom in the privacy of John Allan's house must have been quiet and deep, when it was not stormy. A few months later, we find John Allan writing Henry Poe that Edgar is moody and adding, hypocritically enough, "I cannot imagine what *we* have done to deserve this." [200] There is not a word of pride over Edgar's escorting La Fayette, or of his excellent record at school. Only a vague and irritated reproach. In the light of all the facts, it can now only seem that the letter to Baltimore was a gesture of precaution, on the part of John Allan, and a deliberate attempt to malign Edgar Poe.

Sometime in the Summer of 1825, however, Henry paid a visit to his brother Edgar in the new house on Main Street. Doubtless the brothers had much to talk about. They had seen each other, at most, upon only two or three occasions before. Some of the contents of John Allan's letter may well have been on their minds. Henry, it seems, was considerably upset and impressed by the innuendoes, and as late as 1827 published in the *North American* in Baltimore a poem entitled *Lines on a Pocket Book* in which "Rosalie" is addressed as being of doubtful paternity. This poem constitutes the closest approach to an explanation of the Poe family mystery that exists.[201]

William Henry Leonard Poe was a rather delicate and tubercularly inclined boy of some literary promise, as his few published poems show. He and Edgar may have had a good deal in common and enjoyed each other's society. It was only upon rare occasions that Poe could "open up" with the freedom and confidence that a blood relative of sympathetic temperament inspires. At this time Henry Poe seems to have been in the navy or the merchant marine. On this visit to Richmond he wore a nautical uniform and, upon one occasion at least, in company with Ebenezer Burling, the boys called upon Elmira Royster. If Rosalie came over from the Mackenzies' to visit her two big brothers, it was one of the few occasions when all of the children of Elizabeth Poe sat together in the same room.

Rosalie was at this time a dull and undeveloped little girl of about fourteen or fifteen. She could have been in her condition only an annoyance and a sorrow to Edgar Poe. He was on close terms of friendship with the Mackenzies, whose kindness and care of Rosalie had continued, and was a frequent visitor in their house. Mrs. Mackenzie

---

[201] See *Poe's Brother,* by Hervey Allen and Thomas Ollive Mabbott, Doran, 1926.

he often called "Ma," and upon several occasions was heard to remark that he wished he had been adopted by them instead of the Allans, words which could not have failed to reach his guardian's, by this time, burning ears. About this time, too, it is said he began to talk to the Mackenzies about running away to sea, and to complain frequently of Mr. Allan.[202] To the Mackenzies, Mr. Allan replied that Edgar did not know what gratitude was. Nevertheless, Mrs. Allan and Mrs. Mackenzie were still fast friends and continued so till the end.

Through the Summer and Autumn of 1825 Edgar Poe continued his work with tutors, looking forward to his entrance at the University of Virginia. Despite the trouble in the background, he could not have eluded a certain joy in the new variety of contacts in the life which surrounded him now in the new house. The Allans, as part of the social campaign for the position to which their wealth now entitled them, gave many entertainments and the house was noted for its hospitality. John Allan's generosity in the manner of his way of life is not to be impugned. Thomas Ellis speaks of the many young folks and children who ran in and out, to peep through the telescope, or to see Edgar. Doubtless Elmira's curls were no strange sight in the garden on the slope of the hill when the grapes were ripe. An arbor is an excellent place to exchange kisses. Poe seems to have idolized her, and a study of the changes in the text of *Tamerlane* will result in some interesting speculations about this little girl.[203]

Poe's family moved in the best of Richmond society. Some of John Allan's neighbors were Thomas Taylor, whose daughter William Galt married; Mr. Joseph Tate, Major James Gibbon, Mr. Joseph Marx and Thomas Gilliat. "These gentlemen were of the highest social position in Richmond" and were associates of Chief Justice Marshall, Colonel Ambler, Dr. Brockenbrough, Judge Cabell, Judge Stanard and others famous for good dinners and whist parties. In such houses young Poe was welcome, and the associations of such an environment stamped upon him the attitude and the mode of conversation of a gentleman. It was the Virginia of the Old School, a school for manners.

Doubtless the possibility of Edgar's being Mr. Allan's heir did not escape the speculation of certain mamas with eligible daughters, young people married early then, but young Poe was becoming more and more

---

[202] New light is thrown on Edgar's desire to go to sea by the fact that, shortly after the visit to Richmond noted above, Henry sailed as a midshipman (*sic*) on the U.S.S. "Macedonian" for South America. See note 201.

[203] In the accounts of Elmira (Mrs. Shelton) and her accounts of Poe, I have followed carefully the letters from her to Ingram, published in his biography of Poe, and other letters of interviews with Mrs. Shelton by Edward V. Valentine of Richmond, later sent to Ingram and now at the University of Virginia. Some of these latter have never been published.

interested in Elmira and the visits to her house were frequent. From her lips we get a fresh and vivid account of the young Poe.[203]

It was Edgar's habit, during the Summer and Fall of 1825, to slip over to the Royster House nearby and to spend long hours in the parlor with Elmira. She played the piano and they would sing together, Edgar in a fresh young tenor voice, or he would accompany her upon the flute which he played quite well. Sometimes, but not often, Ebenezer Burling would go along. But Elmira does not seem to have cared much for him. The conversation was of the news of the younger set of the day. Once, upon her repeating a brisk remark of a young lady acquaintance, Poe replied that he was surprised that Elmira would associate with anyone so unladylike. Years later she remembered this. There must also have been certain moments upon the sofa, or upon the window seat on the landing upstairs, when the conversation was of a decidedly endearing nature and more than mere words were exchanged, for before Poe left for the University, Elmira had promised to be his wife, a promise which was kept a secret, probably on account of the parental attitude toward the match.

Elmira said that Poe was shy but very handsome, with large dark gray eyes and rather august manners. In short, we get the feeling that little Elmira was carried off her feet by quite an impressive and princely young man. There was talk of books and poetry, and perhaps some verses in Elmira's album,[204] the custom of the day, and when other amusements failed, Edgar drew pictures and sketches for his sweetheart. One of these, a portrait of Elmira herself by Poe's own hand, has come down to us as a record of some of the happiest hours of his life. One can imagine the little girl sitting on the sofa in the Royster parlor, the sheets of music and the flute lying upon the open pianoforte, while Edgar Poe, pencil in hand, sketched the wistful little face that still looks out at us from the yellow paper, after more than a hundred years. There is certainly a very fetching flaunt to the tangle of pretty curls. One can almost hear their fresh voices blending in *The Last Rose of Summer,* through the half-open window; or the tinkle of the piano and the low bubbling notes of the flute.

Mrs. Allan does not seem to have looked upon Edgar's approaching departure with anything but sorrow. Doubtless, her husband's anxiety to have Edgar out of the house could not be concealed, and she may have had a feminine foreboding that it was the beginning of the end. Her health was rapidly failing, and the thought of being left alone in the house, to confront the Scotch harshness of her masterful husband, was probably more than she could bear. Perhaps she had some inkling of his future intentions as to Edgar, and knew that although his means

---

[204] This is inference. Mrs. Shelton does not say so.

for charity were now ample, the will for bounty had run out. That it was a gloomy time, the servants have testified. The antagonism between John Allan and his ward was extreme. On this account, and because of her great love for Edgar, Frances Allan seems to have deferred her parting with him to the uttermost. She resolved to accompany her son to Charlottesville, and to see him settled at the University. Christmas that year, despite the ample setting at the Allan house, must have been, at best, a gloomy affair.

Of Poe's parting with John Allan there is no record. Let us hope there was a gleam of the old affection. Of admonitions and promises we can be certain. Perhaps Elmira's kisses and avowals served somewhat to soften the admonitory thumping of the lame man's cane; there was at least a fond farewell from "Aunt Nancy" Valentine. One of the new Allan carriages was ordered out, Edgar's small baggage lashed at the back, and with old Jim on the box,[205] Frances Allan and Edgar Allan Poe drove away from the great house down Main Street. The black coachman remembered that they were both very sad. It was just about Valentine's Day in February, 1826.

While they trotted along in the new family carriage, perhaps Mrs. Allan remembered another ride down Main Street, in a hired hack, some fifteen years before, and once again clasped warmly the hand of the same orphan who still sat by her side. She at least had given him all that any mother could. It was the end of the first momentous act. As Jim cracked his whip over the straining horses along the road to Charlottesville, and the spires and pillared porches of Richmond disappeared behind the snowy hills, Edgar's boyhood with its homes, and warehouses, ships, "Helen," Elmira and the Enchanted Garden, disappeared into the irrevocable past. As if in final farewell Poe entrusted a love letter for Elmira to be delivered to her by the hands of James Hill, the coachman. It was the last message which she was destined to receive from him for a long time.[206] In addition to the letter Poe left with Elmira a mother-of-pearl purse marked with her initials in which the engraver had made an error. On February the fourteenth, 1826, Poe matriculated at the University of Virginia.[207]

---

[205] James Hill was the name of Mr. Allan's coachman. Edward V. Valentine to the author at Richmond, July 16, 1925. The carriage belonged to Mrs. Allan, having been left to her by William Galt. See his will, Appendix III.

[206] J. H. Whitty *Memoir,* large edition, page xxvii.

[207] Entry in the University of Virginia *Records.*

CHAPTER NINE

ISRAFEL IN CAP AND GOWN

THOMAS JEFFERSON, that dreamer of dreams and political-romanticist, had a great vision. From his high place of Monticello in Albemarle County, Virginia, he looked down across the green slopes of the South-West Mountains and beheld

> In the greenest of our valleys
> By good angels tenanted,
> Once a fair and stately palace—
> Radiant palace—reared its head.
> In the monarch Thought's dominion.—[208]

The valley was the little vale where the hamlet of Charlottesville nestled, and the palace was his vision of the classic courts and cloisters of the University of Virginia.

During his gigantically active intellectual life, Jefferson wrote some thirty thousand letters, and among these, not a small proportion was devoted to the bringing about of what has in the end proved to be, perhaps, his most solid and far-reaching achievement—"The Oxford of the New World." Through the barriers of the ignorant indifference of legislatures and the parsimony of selfish individuals, the mercurial eloquence of his restless pen penetrated with a Midas touch; public and private purse strings were loosened for his "Educational Fund," and in the wild heart of the Alleghanies the domes and colonnades, the serpentine walls, and the five-fold terraced campus of the new University arose as if by magic.

In October, 1823, near the close of his long career, we find Jefferson writing to his friend John Adams—"Against . . . *tedium vitae,* however, my dear friend, I am now fortunately mounted on a hobby, which, indeed, I mounted some thirty or forty years ago, but whose amble is still sufficient to give exercise and amusement to an octogenarian writer. This is the establishment of a University for the education of all succeeding generations of youth in this Republic." [209] On Monday, March 7, 1825, this vision and hobby became a fact, when without ceremony or ostentation, the University of Virginia opened its doors and fifty

---

[208] There is no attempt here, of course, to imply that *Poe* meant these lines to apply to the University.

[209] The letter is given here as it was partly quoted by Edwin A. Alderman, President of the University of Virginia, in the *Virginia Quarterly Review* for April, 1925, pages 78-84. To Dr. Alderman I am also indebted for other facts.

youths matriculated, followed by sixty-six more during the first session.

The second session began February 1, 1826, when thirty-four students entered, who by the middle of the month had increased to one hundred and thirty-one. On St. Valentine's Day the University records show that five students matriculated, and among them is the illustrious name of Poe. The exact entry, spelling and all, is as follows:

Edgar A. Poe: / 19 January, 1809 / John Allen Richmond, Va. / and the Schools of Ancient and Modern Languages.[210]

Poe's entry is number one hundred thirty-six in a total enrolment of one hundred and seventy-seven for the entire session, which ended at Christmas, 1826.[210]

Of the parting with Frances Allan nothing is known. No mother leaves her boy at a University without realizing that she has resigned her complete control, and has committed her son to the doubtful currents of adult life. The peculiar tenderness of the tie which bound her to Edgar must have wrung both their hearts, for the future was troubled. Doubtless she saw him "settled," and drove back over the cold February hills with a troubled heart to the disturbing situation in her own house at Richmond, which she must now face alone; nor could her knowledge of her foster-son's impulsive and passionate temperament have left her without forebodings about the months to follow. For the first time in his life, Poe was left completely alone. He was about to be subjected to the difficult test of freedom, and the environment into which he had been thrown was not without decided temptations.

Jefferson's ideas about the University were peculiar; in some respects they were the most advanced of their age, and in others they partook of that idealistic and unpractical turn of mind, which, arising from a too fond estimate of human nature, has in some of its major aspects proved almost fatal to the Republic over which the soul of the philosopher yearned. It was only by the early modification of some of his pet theories that the University was saved from anarchy.

From an educational standpoint, the organization of the new school was forward-looking, a radical departure from established methods, but on the whole excellent. A highly competent and learned faculty had been cajoled by the glowing letters of the "Old Man Eloquent" into lending the luster of their foreign degrees and exotic reputations to the traditionless school which needed them. In 1826 six out of the eight professors were foreign born, and were irreverently referred to by the students as "those damned foreign professors." The faculty in Poe's day consisted of Professors Blaettermann, Bonnycastle, Dunglison, Em-

---

[210] Harrison, *Life and Letters of Edgar Allan Poe*, vol. I, page 38. Note that Poe did *not* give the place of his birth as Woodberry states vol. I, 1909, page 32. "Allen" is a misspelling, of course.

met, Key, Lomax, Long, and Tucker. Seven of these men bore the best of scholastic reputations, being for the most part Englishmen from Cambridge and Oxford, with the exception of Professor Blaettermann, who was a German of profound and pedantic classical learning. George Tucker had been persuaded to leave a career in the Halls of Congress to undertake the Chair of Moral Philosophy. He was the Chairman of the Faculty, which frequently met for disciplinary sessions, and afterward distinguished himself as an economist, essayist, historian, and biographer of Jefferson.[211]

The courses were of a continental character that was probably too advanced to suit the preparatory and secondary education of the American youths who were then subjected to them, but to Poe, who had received a more ample and thorough grounding in English schools, they offered an opportunity of which he took advantage. A field in which, as the records prove, he distinguished himself. This field, as might be supposed, for a young poet in love with words, was that of language.

Jefferson himself, while Governor of Virginia at an earlier date, had first introduced the formal study of modern languages into America. The organization of "his" new University offered him the opportunity for further educational innovations. Among the most notable of these was the abolition of the class system in favor of a modified form of the elective system of German Universities, the introduction of an optional period of training in military drill, the establishment of workshops for practical education, somewhat along the lines of modern industrial training, the encouragement of vaccination by gratis treatment, and the permission of optional attendance at chapel. Over all of these, the reactionary pedagogues shook their doubtful heads, and none more doubtfully than George Ticknor at Harvard. Some of these departures, though philosophically sound, were too far ahead of their time and went down to defeat.[212]

Above all, of course, or it would not have been Jeffersonian, the University of Virginia was to be democratic; the students were to govern themselves as individuals, and when discipline became necessary, it was to be by the intervention of the local arm of the civil law. This item in particular, naturally enough broke down completely. Scholastic anarchy and student escapades disturbed the peace of the College, Charlottesville, and the plantations about, until the faculty threatened

---

[211] *Life and Letters of Edgar Allan Poe,* J. A. Harrison, Chapter II. Also various brief articles and pamphlets dealing with the establishment of the University of Virginia.

[212] Reminiscences of William M. Burwell from the *New Orleans Times-Democrat* for May 18, 1884. Burwell's facts about Poe are not always to be taken without reservations, but his descriptions of contemporary life with Poe, when at the University, there is no reason to doubt as they are in many other ways confirmed. The text here is an excerpt from the *Alumni Bulletin,* University of Virginia, for April, 1923.

to resign in a body and obtained the authority to exert a sufficient internal control from above, and the establishment of a more efficient method of police. In the midst of this era of airy confusion and adolescent nonsense, young Poe arrived. That, in some sense, he was its victim there can be little doubt. One of his college-mates has left us an excellent picture of the times.[212]

To the first sessions of this admirable school poured in the Southern youth, most of them intent upon availing themselves of the advantages afforded. Among them, however, were many who had little other object than to combine enjoyment with the preparatory routine of a liberal education. Some of this class arrived with unlimited means, others with elegant equipages. One came from the Eastern Shore with a tandem of blooded horses, a servant, a fowling-piece, and a pointer or two. Some were afflicted with habits of extravagance and contempt for the toilsome acquisition of knowledge. These not only indulged in unseemly fun in the college, but invaded the little courthouse town of Charlottesville, where they were objects of admiration, with those at least who had goods to sell or horses to hire. Mr. Jefferson having assumed that these high-spirited coadjutors in the defense of our constitutional ramparts comprehended his patriotic motives, had provided no discipline for their scholastic deportment. He confided that the restraints of propriety would be sufficient to make them behave themselves as gentlemen. They certainly did behave themselves as gentlemen of the highest style. They gamed, fought duels, attended weddings for thirty miles around, and went in debt in the most liberal manner. Mr. Jefferson often invited some of the students to dine at Monticello, where they were entertained with that urbane hospitality for which he was so remarkable. The repasts inclined no doubt to the French style of cookery, which had led Patrick Henry to close a diatribe against his doctrines with the crowning charge, "He hath abjured his native victuals!" Little is remembered of these honored entertainments except that the great statesman commended a Swiss wine of the most acid and astringent character, then regarded as a sorry substitute for the "peach and honey" of the period. . . .

The buildings first completed stood in the midst of uncultivated fields and other unattractive scenery. The county of Albemarle contained many families of the highest worth. Indeed, it had furnished many of the most eminent men in the State's history. Mr. Jefferson, Lewis, the explorer of the Missouri, and perhaps Clark, who captured Kaskaskia from the British; the Minors, Gilmers, Carters, Carrs and others were all natives of Albemarle, but these families were scattered over a large country. The courthouse town of Charlottesville had been the place near which the prisoners captured at Saratoga had been confined. It had been the temporary seat of the Legislature during the invasion or raid by Tarleton. It had a population of several hundred, but at the period now spoken of Mr. Jefferson has recorded, as one of the religious tolerations, that there being no church in the village, each of the principal church persuasions held its services in the courthouse under a rotation agreed on among themselves. The families of the professors were too limited to furnish social facilities to the students. So far, then, from there being at or around the University a social intercourse of sufficient extent to have provided even reasonable recreation for so many young men, there was not even a public opinion strong enough to rebuke their excesses.

In this there was nothing strange. Station an army or a belligerent body in a small village, and a large element in that body will be demoralized by the ennui of idleness. The same body would find social and public enjoyment in a large city. Systematic drunkenness or persistent gaming are restrained, if not prevented entirely, by the variety of attractions and by the positive enforcement of law in every great metropolis.

The public opinion and corporate ordinances of the village were alike disregarded. The disorder and dissipation of the students were subjects of indignant censure. The few merchants and hotels found their account in this extravagance, though the reckless creation of debt led to the enactment of a statute subsequently by which such debts, when beyond the reasonable wants of a student were declared void. A party of students on a frolic were coming along the road between the village and the University when they suddenly encountered the professor of moral philosophy and political economy. Most of the party escaped; but one, afterward a distinguished advocate, disdained concealment. "I am," said he, "K.M.M., of Tuskaloosa, Alabama—too firm to fly and far too proud to yield." "And," said the professor, "Mr. M. might have added, almost too drunk to stand." . . .

The habits of this *jeunesse dorée* had attracted the reprobation of the municipal authorities, and it was decided to extend the jurisdiction of the commonwealth over these elegant young outlaws. At a session of the grand jury, impaneled for the county of Albemarle, process was issued summoning some of the students to testify as to any violations of the gaming act known to them. No sooner was this summons known than every one who could have criminated his associates left the University and took refuge in a little wooded knoll a mile or so west, determined to remain until the great inquest of the county should have adjourned. The rendezvous then assumed the aspect of a gypsy camp. There was a clear running stream, huge rocks and a surrounding forest. The darkies, delighted with the excitement, ran between the camp and the village bringing supplies of food and drink and intelligence of the hostile movements. With a glass, indeed, the high road and buildings were distinctly visible. Of course, the laws which they had violated received additional infractions, as there was reckless pleasure in playing cards on a table of gneiss or granite and in employing pebbles for counting.

The conjoint effect of legal penalties, scholastic discipline and parental authority, however, terminated these excesses. A few of the richer and more reckless went away, the rest settled down to their legitimate duties, and in two years the excellent faculty of the University had inaugurated the system and standard of study which gradually ripened into its present reputation for solid and universal learning.

Such, in some of its more objective lineaments, was the scholastic community in which Poe found himself. Like a great many other American Universities, then and now, the learning seems to have been available and the organization of social life nil.

Upon his first matriculating, Edgar Poe was assigned a room on the "West side of the Lawn" from which he soon afterwards removed, for what cause is not known, to room number 13 West Range, the chamber which is now known at the University of Virginia as "Poe's Room," being kept vacant and sacred to his memory. The story that Poe first roomed with one Miles George and soon afterwards fought with him, the quarrel being the occasion of Poe's move, is now known to be untrue.[213] He did, it seems, have a fist fight with young George, with the usual result of a closer friendship between them, but there are no records of his ever having a roommate, and at number 13 West Range he certainly roomed alone.

Poe's room was pleasantly situated under the second arch to the left, from the walk that divides the west dormitory arcades. It was a combined study and sleeping apartment, about fifteen by twenty feet, with a latticed and a solid door opening out upon the arcade, from which there was then a distant view of the Ragged Mountains. One window looked to the rear over a lawn, then, it seems, used as a wood yard. There was a mantelpiece and a small open fireplace.[214]

Here the young poet undoubtedly passed most of his time while at the University, held his long remembered readings and parties, and wrote home the pathetic letters to his family, and those beseeching lover's complaints and declarations which little Elmira never saw,—or saw too late.[215] The room is dark; it is on a level with the ground, and has in common with other dormitories at the University of Virginia, a quaint, but rather cell-like and faintly melancholy air. In the winter it could not have been anything but cold. The heating arrangements of the time, and of many Southern homes and institutions even to-day, are constructed with an eye to the long Summer, and seem to ignore the Winter and late Fall. Of other facilities there were none. The architects of the period were engrossed with the façades of the ancients, but the *baths* of Caracalla remained, as in the Middle Ages, unstudied and unknown.[216]

From the mass of records and reminiscences now available it is possible to reconstruct, with some degree of accuracy, the character of the life and even the daily routine of the students while Edgar Allan Poe was in "cap and gown," a medieval idea which, by the way, America had not then adopted.

Poe was awakened every morning, probably about half-past five, by

---

[213] Letter of Dr. Miles George to Mr. Edward V. Valentine of Richmond, later sent to J. B. Ingram and now in the Ingram collection of Poe Papers at the University of Virginia, printed in the *Alumni Bulletin,* University of Virginia, for April, 1923. This letter contradicts flatly and ultimately many of Thomas Goode Tucker's "too complete memories" which have been so often followed by Poe biographers.

[214] From data gathered on a visit to the University of Virginia in July, 1925.

[215] Few of Poe's biographers seem to have realized that the young student who inhabited No. 13 West Range in 1826 was under stress of great anxiety about home matters. An unhappy love affair, plus home dissensions and great financial embarrassment, all of which Poe experienced here, is enough to unsettle any college freshman. Henry Poe was away on a cruise.

[216] Even the means of obtaining fire was still in the flint and tinder age. Pocket matches, at a considerable cost, were introduced from England about a year later.

William Wertenbaker, secretary to the faculty, librarian and general *factotum,* whose duty it was to see that the students were up, dressed, and ready for work. There was probably some sort of hurried ablutions, and then a rush for breakfast to some boarding house nearby, followed, in Poe's case, by early morning recitations. His schedule shows that these fell between the hours of seven and nine A.M., and that his course consisted of lectures in Latin, Greek, French, Spanish and Italian.[211] One of his classmates, remembering these occasions, afterward described Poe, "as having been an excellent French and Latin scholar; he could read and speak both languages with great ease, although he could hardly be said to have known either language thoroughly. Greek he read indifferently. Time and again he would enter into the lecture room [Pavilion V, or Pavilion VI where Professors Long and Blaettermann lived] utterly unprepared to recite if called upon. But his brain was so active and his memory so excellent, that only a few moments' study was necessary, and then he was ready to make the best recitation in the class. To have an opportunity of 'reading ahead' . . . was all that Poe desired when unprepared. As a consequence of this wonderful faculty he was able to maintain a very high position in his classes, and win for himself the admiration, but more often the envy of his fellow students." [217] In this account there is an indication of a certain superficial cast to Poe's learning which agrees well with his immense affectation of it in later times. Tradition has it that the classes of young Dr. Blaettermann, who had come to the University via London, with a pleasant English bride, were particularly lively. The doctor's strong German accent, penchant for puns, and inability to keep order brought about, it seems, some memorable and amusing scenes which Poe must have witnessed but does not seem to have taken an active part in. Indeed, both his scholastic and disciplinary records were officially excellent. The University minute books yield these items:

At a meeting of the Faculty, December 15th, 1826,—

Mr. Long made a report of the examination of the classes belonging to the School of Ancient Languages, and the names of the students who excelled at the examination of these classes:

Senior Latin Class:

GESSNER HARRISON of Rockingham.
ALBERT L. HOLLADAY of Spottsylvania.
BERTHIER JONES of Amelia.
EDGAR A. POE of Richmond City., etc.

---

[217] Reminiscences of Thomas G. Tucker, confirmed by similar memories of other classmates of Poe, and by the University records. Tucker wrote an article called *Edgar Allan Poe while a Student at the University of Virginia,* much quoted from.

II

The names of the students who excelled in the Senior French Class as reported by the Professor of Modern Languages were as follows:

PHILIP ST. GEORGE AMBLER of Richmond City.
JOHN CARY of Campbell.
GESSNER HARRISON of Rockingham.
WM. MICHIE of Hanover.
CONWAY NUTT of Culpepper.
EDGAR A. POE of Richmond City.
WM. SELDEN of Norfolk.
HENRY TUTWILER of Rockingham.

Poe also did excellent work in Italian, and was at one time complimented by Professor Blaettermann for a translation from Tasso. Evidently one poet moved another.

The names on the class lists of these long dead lads bring back vividly the air of the vanished classroom with all the pathos that an old teacher feels as he turns over the faded leaves of some dusty roll book of years before, while the names and images of those long lost to conscious memory leap out at him with the recollection of half-forgotten incidents, recalling the ghosts of happy and laughing faces turned to dust, or long hardened into caricatures of their youthful beauty by the grim mold of manly metal. Wiping such secret, but withal not unkindly mistiness from a pair of pedagogical spectacles, the years of a century roll back before us, and we stand in Professor Blaettermann's classroom in Pavilion VI at the University of Virginia in the Spring of 1826.

The tousled heads of ten or twelve boys in their late teens, at their early morning recitation, are dotted lackadaisically about the whittled benches, trying to imbibe by inspiration from the puzzling text, what they should have learned by candle-light the night before. A mumbled conversation, despite the glare of Professor Blaettermann, is going on in one corner of the room; and on a bench near the front, seated with his cronies Tom Golson, Upton Beale or Philip Slaughter, their faces shining from the early morning pump and the run to the classroom, sits Edgar Allan Poe. "Mishter Chorge," says the young German at the desk, "are you prepart?"—silence—"Vel den, Mishter Long! Haf you prepart your Tasso? *Cherusalem Delifered,* virst stanssa, pegin'"— George Long, a mild youth of some eighteen summers, given to dining with visiting ex-presidents rather than to the midnight oil, arises and fumbles out some lines. "Ach Gott! dot vill do, Mishter Long, I see you are not *Long* for dis blace" (laughter and stamping of feet). "Mishter Poe. . . ."

Edgar gets up. He is a little flushed, his large eyes shining with eagerness; a rather slender and delicate boy of seventeen, with a mass

of dark hair and an easy carriage.   On the little room falls the spell of
his low but arresting and unforgettable voice.[218]

The lines roll on with something in them of the sonorous Italian.
The surprised class grows hushed; Professor Blaettermann beats time
ecstatically with a muttered, *"Das is gud, gud!"* then—the bell—and
the whole class laughing and slapping Poe on the back for having actually
wrung an encomium from *one of those damned foreign professors,* pours
out under the peristyle and rushes shouting, boy-like, into the bright
spring sunshine of one hundred years ago.

Classes over, the day was Poe's, and the night too.   There were certain periods of military drill taught at that time at the University of
Virginia by Mr. Mathews, a West Point graduate.[219]   This was one of
Jefferson's hobbies, who felt that the future leaders in the Republic
should be trained to arms, and Poe seems to have elected to take the drill
probably from the flair given to his military ambition aroused as an
officer in the Richmond Junior Volunteers.   La Fayette's praise was
evidently not forgotten, nor the exploits of Grandfather David Poe.
Edgar seems to have nourished the military tradition considerably, and
in a few months it was to bear bitter fruit.   The military instructor
afterwards recalled Poe, as, "thick-set with a jerky gait and bandy legs,"
but as this jars with nearly all other descriptions of the young poet at
this time, we may feel certain that the instructor's recollection was at
fault, or that he confused someone else with Poe.[220]

Monday mornings the colored washerwomen made their rounds, of
whom no less than seven afterwards asserted that they had all washed
for "Marse Eddie Poe," and quarreled over the honor much as the Greek
Cities over Homer's birth.   The afternoons were spent at the library,
at the stores, or about "hotels" in Charlottesville, a mile or so away, and
there was swimming in the yellow Rivanna, and rambles amid the
Ragged Mountains nearby.   Lessons, however, were not neglected, and
the Reading Room of the Library, then located in Pavilion VI, saw Poe
often and deeply immersed in his books.

William Wertenbaker, the librarian, recollected Poe as, "then little
more than a boy . . . about five feet two or three inches in height, somewhat bandy legged, but in no sense muscular or given to physical exercises.   His face was feminine, with finely marked features, and eyes
dark, liquid and expressive.   He dressed well and neatly.   He was a
very attractive companion, genial in his nature, and familiar by the

---

[218] The scene is reproduced here from contemporary accounts of such recitations and
the peculiarities of Professor Blaettermann.   Poe's translation of *Tasso* is specifically
mentioned.

[219] J. H. Harrison, *Life and Letters of Edgar Allan Poe,* chapter II, page 39.

[220] Mr. Mathews, the drill master, seems to have followed Thomas Tucker's description which is at fault.

varied life that he had already led, with persons and scenes new to the unsophisticated provincials among whom he was thrown. . . . What, however, impressed his associates most were his remarkable attainments as a classical scholar. . . ." Poe was often found in the Library which was then open from three-thirty to five o'clock where he seems to have reveled in the rare and fine collection of standard authors assembled by Jefferson himself. The records show that Edgar A. Poe borrowed these books from the Library, a list which gives us some inkling of his interests outside of class work.

Histoire Ancienne	— Rollin
Histoire Romaine	— Rollin
America	— Robertson
Washington	— Marshall
Histoire Particulière	— Voltaire
Nature Displayed	— Dufief [221]

The mixture of romantic history and natural science is characteristic. To the same reading room came Jefferson himself; his well-known figure about the University must have been familiar to Poe. They must have been together frequently in the Library, and it is scarcely possible that at some time some conversation was not exchanged. For all that, Jefferson left no mark on the imagination of Poe. Their worlds of thought, indeed, were universes apart.

Poe's life at the University of Virginia has hitherto had to be constructed solely from the testimony and reminiscences of his classmates; it is now possible, however, for the first time to add to it the facts given in his own letters to John Allan.[222] Only two of these written from the University remain. It is probable that he wrote several others to his foster-mother but these, if they exist, and they probably do not, have not come to light. In May, 1826, Poe writes to John Allan that he has received from home a uniform coat together with six yards of striped cloth for pantaloons, and four pair of socks. He says that the coat, which is a beautiful one, fits him exactly. It seems that at this period some of the students, those at least who took military drill, wore a sort of cadet uniform which accounts for the word "uniform." The disturbances caused among the student body by the meeting of the local grand jury also comes in for brief mention. Poe says his guardian will no doubt have heard about them by that time and tells us that those

---

[221] Recollections of William Wertenbaker, Librarian of the University of Virginia, in *The Independent* for September, 1900.

[222] The facts narrated in this and the ensuing paragraph are taken from two of Poe's own letters to John Allan while at the University, first published in the *Valentine Museum Poe Letters*, pages 37-44, "letters Nos. 1 and 2." now available for the first time.

whose names had been put upon the sheriffs' lists had gone on their travels into the woods and mountains taking their bedding and provisions along with them.   Poe himself is evidently not among them. The *Hegira,* it seems, took place the first day of the fright.   Finding that those who were "wanted" were thus disappearing into remote places, the faculty now took a hand in the affair and issued a sort of proclamation confining the student body to the dormitories between the hours of eight and ten A.M. during which time the visitation and inquisition of the sheriffs was to take place.   Little attention was paid to this, however, and those with troubled consciences took to the woods freely a second time.   In consequence of this the faculty the next morning reprimanded several, suspended for two months James Abbot Clarke of Manchester, one of Poe's old schoolmates at Burke's Academy, and Armstead Carter from near Charlottesville for the rest of the session. Thomas Barclay was dismissed.

The constant fighting, dueling and bickering of the student body also comes in for mention.   It was a rude age in some respects and among the students lingered many of the barbarous customs of the American frontier.   Poe tells us that a common fight was such an ordinary occurrence that no notice was taken of it.   A more savage and feudistic affair between Turner Dixon and one Blow from Norfolk attracted more lasting notice.   In the preliminary scuffle Blow, it seems, had the advantage, but Dixon took revenge by posting him in most indecent terms. This, and Blow's reply, was for a week the main topic of conversation. All the pillars in the University were turned white with scribbled reminders and counter replies, until finally Dixon was provoked into making another assault on Arthur Smith, one of Blow's Norfolk friends, by striking him on the head with a stone.   At this Smith pulled out a pistol and would have ended the controversy then and there if the weapon had not missed fire.   Finally the Proctor of the University took a hand, summoned all the aggrieved parties before a magistrate, and bound them over to keep the peace.   The picture given of the lax discipline of the student body at this period, and the hot-headed bickering of young Southern gentlemen brought up in the traditions of the dueling code is illuminating.   Poe closes the letter with affectionate messages home to the ladies of the household and a request for a copy of Tacitus' *Historiæ* and a further supply of soap! [364]

In a second letter from the University, written to John Allan on September 21, 1826, Poe tells us of the consternation among the student body at the announcement of the examinations to be given in the following December.   As the University had been under way for only two years, he thinks it doubtful whether any diplomas or degrees will be conferred.   Other institutions require three or four years before a degree is conferred, he tells us, and there was evidently some feeling that it would be unfair to examine those who had been there only one session, in the same requirements, along with those who had been attending lectures for two. This, of course, covers his own case. Nevertheless, he seems fairly confident. He has been studying hard, he says, in order to prepare, and expects to come off as well as the rest, provided he is not too nervous.

Among other things, we also learn that the Rotunda was at that time nearly finished and the pillars of the Portico completed, to the great improvement of the appearance of the campus. The books, of which he says there was a fine collection, had recently been moved into the new Library. Another, and peculiarly brutal fight to the finish is also described. Poe saw the entire affair which came off just in front of his door.

One Wickliffe, who, it will appear from the sequel, must have been well versed in the tactics of gouging and biting, then prevalent in the Western settlements, retired behind West Range to settle his differences with another student, and being the stronger, soon had the latter down and completely at his mercy. Not content with that, he then proceeded to bite his antagonist from the shoulder to the elbow. Poe says that he saw the arm afterwards and that the flesh was so seriously torn as probably to necessitate the cutting out of pieces as big as his hand. Poe adds without further explanation, that Wickliffe was from Kentucky. Scarcely a generation before, the same customs had disturbed the constitutional convention when it met at Richmond, Virginia. With such wolfish tactics still lingering about, the situation of Poe when he enraged the young bloods among the gamblers of the place by failing to meet his card debts may be imagined. Poe's September letter from the University also informs us that John Allan had already paid him a visit sometime before, and suggests that business may require his presence in Charlottesville about examination time in December. What that business eventually turned out to be, and how momentous the visit was to Poe, must be related shortly.

Of the life about the little hamlet of Charlottesville, then confined to the valley below the college, there remain many authentic traditions. With the opening of the University and the consequent influx of gilded youth, there sprang up a parasitical commercial group which lived upon and exploited the students.[223] Chief among these were the hotel and boarding-house keepers who supplied the young gentlemen scholars with apple-toddy, egg-nog, mint slings, and the famous "peach and honey" of the neighborhood, or who kept dogs for the students, and connived at their clandestine affairs and gambling parties. There is some mention

---

[223] In a letter from West Point to John Allan, dated January 3, 1830, Poe specifically states that he was compelled to borrow money from "Jews" in Charlottesville at exorbitant rates of interest.

of Poe's paying some attention to a daughter of one of the boarding-house keepers and taking her to dances, but he does not appear to have taken any unusual part in the bucolic revels of the place, nor to have fallen at any time under the formal censure of the University authorities. The legend that he was expelled has, of course, long ago been exploded.[224] The University records, however yield us this:

The Faculty met December 20th, 1826

Present: JOHN T. SOMES, *Chairman*
DR. DUNGLISON
DR. BLAETTERMANN
MR. BONNYCASTLE
MR. TUCKER
MR. KEY

The Chairman presented to the faculty a letter from the Proctor giving information that certain Hotel Keepers during the last session had been in the habit of playing at games of chance with the students in their Dormitories—he also gave the names of the following persons who he had been informed had some knowledge of the facts, Edgar Mason, Turner Dixon, William Seawell, E. Le Branche, Edgar Poe, Drummond Emmanuel Miller, Hugh Pleasants and E. G. Crump who having been summoned to appear . . . etc.

Poe with some others said he knew nothing about it and the matter was dismissed. Evidently, in common with the other schoolboys, Edgar Poe did not make a very good witness. That he was a devotee of, if not an adept at, gaming, however, the amount of his losses later bears a better witness than he himself did.

The merchants of the town evidently did a thriving trade, mostly, of course, on credit. The parents of the students were required to give surety that their bills would be settled, although there was also an act of the legislature that absolved a student from debts which were found to be "unjust." [225] The relation existing between careless and spendthrift youths, whose expenses were guaranteed, and irresponsible and avaricious shopkeepers was one which lent itself to exploitation. In Poe's case, the situation was undoubtedly aggravated by conditions which have only lately come to light.

Young Poe was known to be the ward, and was said to be the heir of

---

[224] William Wertenbaker's recollections made in 1869—"I was myself a member of the last three [Poe's] classes, and can testify that he was tolerably regular in his attendance, and a successful student, having attained distinction at the Final Examination in Latin and French; and this was at that time the highest honor a student could obtain. The present regulations in regard to degrees had not been adopted. Under the existing regulations he would have graduated in the two languages above named, and have been entitled to diplomas."—*The Independent* for September, 1900.

[225] It was probably this statute that John Allan afterward took as a legal ground for refusal to pay Poe's debts. Bills of merchandise purchased by Poe from Charlottesville merchants were rendered to the firm of *Ellis & Allan* as late as 1835. These items are to be found in the *Ellis & Allan Papers,* Library of Congress, Washington, D. C. See page 150 this volume.

one of the richest men in Virginia.[226]   It was probably not only easy
and possible for him to exploit his credit to an unusual degree, but he
was almost certainly pressed to do so by the shopkeepers who were
familiar with his "father's" circumstances.   It would seem that in the
matter of clothes particularly, Poe soon ran into considerable debt.
This, in itself, would have been a minor extravagance—all the clothes
that even a young man of dandiacal inclinations could wear in one session would not have been a serious matter to a father in John Allan's
circumstances—but Poe, it seems, used his clothes and orders upon his
tailors to pay his gambling debts.   He developed a great leaning for
cards and no less than seventeen broadcloth coats [227] are *said* to have
failed amply to satisfy his ill luck at Loo and Seven-up.   This, on the
surface, has an ill look for Poe, and that he was culpable to some degree
cannot be denied.   The real reason for Poe's "passion for gaming"
which his classmates soon noticed has, however, never been told.   Family
letters which have recently come to light put a new face upon the matter,
a face with a strange and serious expression.

John Allan, it seems, retained such a lively memory of the household
controversies prior to Poe's departure for the University, that, either
through previous deliberate intention, or an after-developed unwilling-
ness to give where it hurt—probably the latter—his remittances to his
foster-son were not only inadequate but almost nil.   In the light of later
events, it is scarcely too much to say that the firm Scotch merchant and
"millionaire" had embarked upon a policy of embarrassing his foster-son.

Without the revelations contained in some of Poe's letters which have
recently been published (September, 1925), his embarrassed and
harassed condition while at the University would never have been
suspected.[228]   Upon leaving for Charlottesville, John Allan provided
him with $110.   The expenses of attendance were, Poe assures his
foster-father, at the lowest possible estimate, $350 a year, and he item-
izes his immediate outlay *in advance* as follows:

For Board	$ 50.00
For lectures under 2 professors	60.00
Room rent in the University	15.00
For bed	12.00
For room furniture	12.00
Total	$149.00

[226] Poe seems to have made considerable capital of this on various occasions.
[227] R. H. Stoddard *Memoir,* page 34, W. J. Widdleton, publisher, 1875.
[228] The facts in the discussion which follows are taken from the *Valentine Museum
Poe Letters* published by Lippincott of Philadelphia, in 1925, and hitherto inaccessible
to former biographers.   See particularly letter "No. 24" dated at West Point, January
3, 1830, pages 253-258.

Thus Poe was already $39.00 in debt immediately upon arrival at the University, and, as he says, he had the mortification of being regarded as a beggar because he owed for public property.

In reply to Poe's expostulations, John Allan did not neglect the opportunity of reproaching his foster-son for not attending *three* lectures and subjected him to the utmost abuse as if the boy were "the vilest wretch on earth" for running in debt.   In compliance with the suspicious Scotchman's "command," Poe wrote him a letter giving an itemized account of his expenditures.   To cover the debt of $39 the merchant sent Poe a check for $40 leaving $1 for "spending money."   Textbooks at that time were furnished from home.   Of these John Allan sent him those which were evidently in stock at *Ellis &Allan,* among them a *Cambridge Mathematics* in two volumes, and a set of *Gil Blas* which had no connection with the courses which Poe was taking.

Poe was obliged to hire a servant and pay for fuel, laundry, and all other expenses and as a consequence again "ran into debt."   It was then, he says, he became "dissolute," meaning probably that he played cards for money, and adds touchingly that he calls God to witness that he never loved dissipation, but that even the hollow profession of friendship of his companions was a comfort to one whose only crime was that he had never had anyone on Earth who cared for him.   His letter is, indeed, a cry of pathetic despair, and the indubitable proof of a parsimony, on the part of his guardian, which, if it was not premeditated, brands him as one of the meanest of mankind.   In any event it is beneath contempt.

Poe wrote a letter to James Galt asking for relief which Galt was unable at the time to afford him.   Knowing that John Allan was one of the richest men in Virginia, the other Scotchman may well have hesitated.   After this he became desperate, Poe says, and involved himself irretrievably in gambling.   Towards the end of the term John Allan sent him $100, but it came too late to afford him relief, and he seems to have been literally hounded from the University.   Thus, in all, during the entire year at Charlottesville, Poe's guardian sent him $250, a sum which, *in toto,* was $100 less than the expenses required.   The inference is plain.   The result was, that Poe returned to Richmond followed by warrants and under the stigma of "extravagance."   Mr. Allan's position is clear, for he not only refused to meet the debts of honor but even the bills for sweeping out his "son's" room and making his bed.[229]

Had John Allan been in straitened circumstances, there might have been some excuse for this strange parsimony, but he was now in the full enjoyment of his uncle's ample fortune and, at that time, planning expenditures which make Edgar's expenses, debts and all, seem a baga-

---

[229] See the letter from Geo. W. Spotswood, Chapter X, page 154, also note 263.

telle in comparison. The plain ugly fact seems to be that he disliked the boy because of what he knew, and that Edgar Allan Poe was already cut off with a shilling, and a Scotch shilling at that. Between the two men and an open rupture was only the fast-wasting form of Frances Allan. To prevent it, even at the last, was the prayer literally on her dying lips as her breath failed.[230]

To pay his way, and even at various times to obtain food and fuel, Poe was thus reduced to the necessity of exploiting his credit in Charlottesville, and to playing cards for what he could make out of them. As always happens in such cases, he was unlucky; the debts remained unpaid, and as a consequence he began to lose caste. Even a gentleman gambler is supposed to play for the excitement and amusement; once his necessities become apparent, he enters a professional but unhonored class. Among the Virginia planters' sons and Southern youths with whom Poe played, this was particularly true. Even the labor of hands for gain was despised as being performed by slaves; to play for it was beyond the pale.

But there was cause of more heart-torturing worry than unpaid debts or the unflattering opinions of his classmates; no word had come from Elmira. All his ardent, beseeching, and heart-broken letters remained unanswered at a time when, to a young lover, silence is despair. Mr. Royster had intercepted the lovers' correspondence, and both her parents were pressing upon Elmira the suit of an older, and, in their eyes, a more acceptable man, one Mr. A. Barrett Shelton, a persistent young bachelor, and a man of means and some social distinction. Thinking that Edgar had forgotten her, the little girl reconsidered her promise to Poe and unwillingly acquiesced. That there must have been some collusion between Mr. Royster and John Allan seems an unavoidable conclusion. The two men were friends, and if Mr. Royster had thought that Poe was even to share in John Allan's estate there can be little doubt that he would have regarded him with more complacence as a son-in-law. From whom he learned that this was not to be the case is not certain, but it is not hard to guess.[231]

Poe's condition at the University of Virginia was therefore a peculiarly trying one to a sensitive young lad of seventeen "with a feminine face." Outwardly he was the spoiled and petted heir of a wealthy man with a dangerous but enviable credit among the shopkeepers, a well-dressed, handsome, and brilliant young scholar who played too much Loo; inwardly he was the prey to exasperating and debilitating anxieties, worried at the unexpected, unjust, and embarrassing withholding of funds, tortured by the inexplicable silence of the girl whose

[230] See Chapter XII, page 187, also James Galt's testimony given by J. H. Whitty *Complete Poems of Edgar Allan Poe,* large edition, appendix page 195.
[231] See Chapter VIII note 186, page 110.

promise and kiss had gone with him when he left Richmond, and torn between his fear of, and duty towards his guardian, and his sympathy for his foster-mother. What he knew, he durst not tell, and it would have done him no good if he had. The letters from John Allan were wormwood and gall, and there was no one to whom in this dilemma he could turn for advice. Then too, what of the future? This also was to be considered. It is not stepping out of the surrounding frame of facts to say that it was a situation so exquisitely perplexing, that at times it was more than he could bear. In an evil hour he resorted to the temporary oblivion and releasing excitement of the bottle.

The motives which first led, and later compelled Poe to resort from time to time to drink are not mysterious, and are certainly not inexplicable, but they are difficult to discuss and to place in their true light especially in the United States. In a country and age where the mere transportation of alcohol once became a crime and its interdicted consumption an event of cheap bravado, the visualization of an era when a glass of wine or beer was regarded in the same light, and as inevitable, as turkey soup after Thanksgiving still requires an effort of the imagination which the average person can scarcely be expected to exert. Drinking has become romantic; in Poe's day the spigot was associated with, and for gustatory reasons preferred to, the pump. The gentleman of taste saw to it that his wines were old and properly served, just as the good housewife now exerts herself to have the fish reasonably fresh and not too thoroughly fried. It is true that there were even then total abstainers, but there were also then, as there are now, vegetarians. Tipsiness, especially after dinner, was regarded as enviable; drunkenness was unfortunate,—only when the habit became inveterate and disgusting did it really enter the realm of morals. To understand the cause and nature of Poe's drinking is essential to the understanding of his character; to misunderstand it is ignorantly to malign the man. Just as De Quincey is forever associated with opium in the minds of his readers, Poe has been credited with the bottle as the source of his inspiration. Mention him in any company, and like a reflex action comes the inevitable question, "Did he drink?" The answer is, "He did"; but to the moral indictment implied, it is no answer at all.

The first mention of Poe's drinking crops up while he was at the University of Virginia. To be sure, some capital has been made of the fact that on various occasions Poe is known to have tasted wine before. To anyone who is not hopelessly bigoted about the matter, however, these stories can be dismissed as futile attempts by special pleading to lay emphasis on facts which, by their nature, can have no significance. To say that Poe on this or that occasion in his childhood tasted wine, a beverage which in the age of its universal use *must* have been in the houses of his foster-father and his friends, is of no more significance than to say that he drank coffee. Had Poe not over-indulged upon occasions some years later, such tittle-tattle would now no more be mentioned than the news that he ate several meals every day. Up until the time of his arrival at the University of Virginia, there is, meticulously speaking, not the slightest trace or indication, nor any evidence upon which to base even a supposition, that he had ever been intoxicated, or that he cared particularly for liquor.

That alcohol played a large and important part in determining the events of his career cannot be denied, but that it was *the* determining and most important factor is a false conclusion.[232] The proof of these statements will be found in the facts of the poet's life already related, and those to be set forth in the narrative which is yet to follow.

At the University, Poe for the first time began to drink. The motives which led to this seem to have been somewhat involved and various. In the first place, from his method of imbibing, Poe does not seem to have liked the taste. Your drinkers may be grouped into four several kinds: sippers, tipplers, gulpers, and guzzlers. The Sipper is your exquisite gentleman who inhales the bouquet, is particular as to the temperature, and tastes drop by drop, to the last in his delicate glass, the rare aroma of an old vintage whose date he judges not by figures but by flavor. Tipplers are those who drain the glass in private, slowly but often, judging the brew by the quality and duration of the dreamful aftermath. Gulpers are those who care nothing for the taste, but with a single direct motion send the drink home for the result. Your Guzzler is he who drinks all, as rapidly, as frequently, and as persistently as he can. In this convivial category our hero was of the third degree, a Gulper. "He would always seize the tempting glass, generally unmixed with sugar or water, —in fact perfectly straight and without the least apparent pleasure, swallow the contents, never pausing until the last drop had passed his lips. One glass at a time was all that he could take; but this was sufficient to rouse his whole nervous nature into a state of strongest excitement which found vent in a continuous flow of wild, fascinating talk that enchanted every listener with siren-like power."[233]

---

[232] Many of the "Medical," "Psychological," and "Psychoanalytical," etc., etc., lives of Poe are vitiated by the fact that the premise of biographical facts from which their conclusions are drawn is at fault, due to the statements of old biographies that rest on legendary sources. To put the case mildly, for instance, very little is really known of Poe's heredity. The real character of his parents and immediate grandparents cannot be ascertained with sufficient clearness to warrant any *scientific* conclusions. See Appendix I for a discussion of Poe's ancestry.

[233] Reminiscences of Thomas G. Tucker, Poe's classmate. Peter the Great of Russia had caused a great furor in England in the Seventeenth Century by a similar method of drinking. Bishop Burnett says it was Peter's custom to drink large bumpers of brandy, raw, before breakfast, and to gulp them down. The Muscovite seems to have derived much pleasure from the performance, and in contradistinction to Poe, "liked the taste."

Edgar's revels were held in his own room.   A good fire would be lit, the furniture or other odds and ends sometimes serving for fuel (if the wood yard outside the window was not privateered upon), the table was drawn out and the game begun.   Several of those who were present at such times have testified to the fact that Poe seemed under great nervous strain and excitement.   When the means for his daily needs depended upon the run of cards, we can understand this.   Ill luck would make it worse.   Of the strain he was under from other causes, his class-mates could, of course, have known nothing.   Poe's drinking, which at worst seems to have been very occasional at the University, probably took place for a variety of reasons.

In the first place as we have seen, it was the custom of the time and the fashion at the University.   There must also have been a certain amount of bravado in the young student, in common with many others at a similar stage of development, who want to "play the man" and impress the world with their manly sophistication.   Poe seems rather to have affected the rôle of the finished youth.   His experience abroad, his com-ing from Richmond, the "big town" of his group, and the reputed wealth of his "father," all led him to live up to the jejune ideal which he as-sumed the others to demand of him.   It was the boy's aim to impress and to be remarkable.   There was also another motive, perhaps not a con-scious one, but a powerful one.   Poe was not to the manner born.   In the group of "F.F.V.'s" in which he found himself, he desired to be accepted without question, and the social doubt that his birth implied drove him not only to equal, but to try to exceed his companions in their own modes; to be a remarkable, a strange, and a good fellow.   As always the thing was overdone.   Those who are sure of themselves never need to impress.   So the fire burned more brightly, the stakes were perhaps a little higher, and the drinking a little deeper than was necessary.   Lastly, but most important of all, in the temporary excitement of wine came self-confidence and oblivion.   It made him confident, and it made him forget.   This, at all times, then and in the future, was the main reason for his drinking.

The effect upon Poe of even a small quantity was out of all usual proportion.   He seems to have been so sensitively organized, that a dram, which to the average man caused only a faint glow, was sufficient to make his actions and conversation unusual.   One glass was literally too much; two or three were disastrous; and a continued round of pota-tions reduced him to a quivering caricature of himself, a libel on genius, and a portent of fallen humanity.   The aftermath was physical torture, spiritual despair, and the remorse of a "lost" but abnormally sensitive soul.   These manifestations are discussed here in the light of what was to follow rather than in connection with Poe's imbibing at the University, which is important as a beginning and a tendency rather than for its immediate importance.

While at Charlottesville, Poe's drinking seems to have been noted for its unusual effects upon an already remarkable personality rather than for its frequency. It was not habitual but rare. A visit to his room while one of his parties is under way, in the company of one of his classmates, will perhaps serve to make this clear. A classmate says: [234]

> Poe roomed on the West side of the Lawn, I on the East, he afterwards moved to the Western Range [Number 13]—I was often in both rooms and recall the many hours spent therein. . . . He was very excitable and restless, at times wayward, melancholic and morose, but again in his better moods frolicsome, full of fun and a most attractive and agreeable companion. *To calm and quiet the excessive nervous excitability under which he labored,* he would too often put himself under the influence of the "Invisible Spirit of Wine."

Another companion remarks: [235]

> The particular dissipation of the University at this period was gaming with cards, and into this Poe plunged with a recklessness of nature which acknowledged no restraint. . . . It led to a loss of caste among his high spirited and exclusive associates.

Tom Tucker also tells us: [236]

> Poe's passion for strong drink was as marked and as peculiar as that for cards. It was not the taste of the beverage that influenced him; without a sip or smack of the mouth he would seize a full glass, without water or sugar, and send it home at a single gulp. This frequently used him up; but if not, he rarely returned to the charge.

Such drinking bears all the marks of being a very juvenile performance, indeed, Baudelaire has called it potations *en barbare,* but it has about it, laying aside the pitiably boyish bravado, a certain gesture of childlike despair that is significant. No letter from Elmira and several from John Allan—down goes a nasty dram which "frequently used him up"—and no wonder, the "peach-honey" of the University was a man's drink.

West Range was known in Poe's day as "Rowdy Row" and there were strict rules that the students' doors must be unbarred when a professor tapped on them, a rule hard to enforce. But not all of the parties in Number 13 were given over to cards and convivialities; these, it seems, in the light of after events have been overstressed. The real boy who dwelt there was of another stamp, or there would not now be over the door of Number 13 "Rowdy Row" a bronze tablet with—

---

[234] Dr. Miles George in a letter to Edward V. Valentine of Richmond, May 18, 1880. This letter is now in the Ingram collection at the University of Virginia.

[235] William M. Burwell, May 18, 1884, in the *New Orleans Times-Democrat.*

[236] Thomas Goode Tucker to Douglas Sherley—letter—April 5, 1880. Also quoted by Prof. Woodberry, 1909, vol. I, page 33.

The University of Virginia about Poe's Time
West Front
From an old print

Professor George Tucker

One of the Faculty at the University of Virginia at the
time Poe attended in 1826

Courtesy of the University of Virginia Alumni Association

No. 13 West Range

Poe's room at the University of Virginia. Now used as a
memorial to the poet

From a photograph taken in 1926

Bill for a Suit of Clothes

Made for Poe to wear home for the Christmas Holidays from the University of Virginia in December, 1826, rendered to John Allan by Samuel Leitch, Jr., apparently a Charlottesville tailor. Poe was anxious to make a good appearance in the eyes of Miss Royster, who, although he did not know it, was already engaged to another man through parental persuasion

From the Ellis & Allan files

Edgar Allan Poe
MDCCCXXVI
Domus parva magni poetæ [237]

Many a long hour in the little dormitory was spent poring over favorite poets, Shelley, Keats, Coleridge, and Wordsworth, present now beyond all doubt, and the old favorites Byron and Moore. Here, too, first began to take shape *Tamerlane,* through which moved the ghost of Elmira as he imagined her, and longed for her walking with him through the wild glens of the Ragged Mountains, that, with *Kubla Khan's* magic on his lip, he called the "Mountains of Belur Taglay." Why were his letters never answered? Did he suspect the truth before the term was over—

> I pictured to my fancy's eye
> Her silent, deep astonishment,
> When, a few fleeting years gone by
> (For short the time my high hope lent
> To its most desperate intent,)
> She might recall in him, whom Fame
> Had gilded with a conqueror's name
> (With glory—such as might inspire
> Perforce, a passing thought of one,
> Whom she had deem'd in his own fire
> Wither'd and blasted; who had gone
> A traitor, violate of the truth
> So plighted in his early youth,)
> Her own Alexis, who should plight
> The love he plighted *then*—again,
> And raise his infancy's delight,
> The bride and queen of Tamerlane.—[238]

Ah, yes! He would show her that he was faithful, he, whom she had thought forgetful. To her he would return and make her his bride and queen when fame was his! How delightful, how youthful, and how pathetic! In the meanwhile he crammed his mind from "many an ancient volume of forgotten lore," and treasured all those honeyed fancies that cloy the too sweet lines of *Al Aaraaf.*

> The Sephalica, budding with young bees,
> Upreared its purple stem around her knees :—

he writes, culling the rich vowels of the flower's name from the pages of *Nature Displayed* flung at random on the table—"bees—bees"—there occurs the ready rhyme of "knees" and the vision of a certain intriguing petticoat flaunted from a sofa in a parlor on Second Street in

---

[237] The inscription seems to be after that on the house of Erasmus in the Hoogestraate, Rotterdam.
[238] From the 1827 version of *Tamerlane,* stanza XII.

Richmond, then Elmira standing up to her knees among flowers in the Enchanted Garden just as they were said to have sprung about the feet of Sappho, and the lines say themselves. But that will never do. No, he is the scholar now, too, and the young poet solemnly notes of the *sephalica,* "This flower is much noticed by Lewenhoeck and Tournefort. The bee, feeding upon its blossom, becomes intoxicated." [239] One wonders how anybody with a name like *Leeuwenhoek* could have noticed anything so charming. Nor did he keep these fancies entirely to himself. "Poe was fond of quoting poetic authors and reading poetic productions of his own, with which his friends were delighted and entertained; suddenly a change would come over him; then he would with a piece of charcoal evince his versatile genius by sketching upon the walls of his dormitory, whimsical, fanciful and grotesque figures, with so much artistic skill, as to leave us in doubt whether Poe in future life would be a painter or a poet." [240] Among these sketches were grotesques of the plates of an edition of Byron. What an enthusiasm and a necessity for self-expression were pent up in these close walls!

The company that gathered about the fire in Number 13 to listen to some of the early American Short Stories and the impassioned voice of Poe reciting his own poetry was a brilliant one and comprised some of the future leaders of the time.[241] Those who listened to Poe then never forgot him. Between the glasses of hot apple-toddy, the bursts of laughter and the green oaths of youth, the anecdotes about the campus queans, the idiosyncrasies of the faculty, and the latest student duel, Poe would read something he had just written, putting his whole soul into his gestures and the low melodious modulations of his voice, while the fire flickered and the long candle shadows waved to and fro. Then followed an open expression of opinions. [242] "On one occasion Poe read a story of great length to some of his friends who, in a spirit of jest, spoke lightly of its merits, and jokingly told him that his hero's name 'Gaffy' occurred too often. His proud spirit would not stand such open rebuke, so in a fit of anger, before his friends could prevent him, he had flung every sheet into a blazing fire, and thus was lost a story of more than ordinary parts which, unlike most of his stories, was intensely amusing, entirely free from his usual somber coloring and sad conclusions merged in a mist of impenetrable gloom. He was for a long time afterwards called by those in his particular circle 'Gaffy' Poe, a name that he never altogether relished." And so, as might have been expected,

---

[239] See Poe's own notes to *Al Aaraaf.*

[240] Dr. Miles George to Edward V. Valentine, letter, May 5, 1880, now in the Ingram collection, University of Virginia.

[241] For a long list of the distinguished men who were at the University of Virginia with Poe, see Harrison, *Life and Letters of Edgar Allan Poe,* vol. I.

[242] Thomas Goode Tucker is quoted here.

the proud "Alexis" who was to come back as the conquering hero, "gilded by fame," to make Elmira his queen and his bride, had become "Gaffy"! The name followed him to West Point. But there is nearly always affection in a nickname, even ridicule is familiar, and Poe was evidently liked. "Whatever Poe may have been in after years," says a classmate and intimate friend, "he was at the University as true and perfect a friend as the waywardness of his nature would allow. There was never then the least trace of insincerity."

With all of its distractions, this was seed-time for a great harvest. Under Professor Long, who had a passion for geography in its relation to history, may have first arisen Poe's minute knowledge of the bizarre facts in the customs and landscapes of "far countrees," and the curiosity to continue the research out of which tales could be fabricated with that "imaginative-realism" in which he delighted. Professor George Tucker, who touched even the dry data of statistics and treatises on population with the virile wand of interest, could scarcely have failed to attract Poe, for while Poe was at the University, Tucker was writing a story called *A Voyage to the Moon*,[243] in somewhat the manner followed later by his pupil in his *Balloon Hoax, Hans Pfaall,* and the like. Poe not infrequently visited the faculty at home and such things as lunar voyages may have been discussed. It was a topic upon which Edgar would love to enlarge. Keats longed for the moon like a child; Poe with his combined mathematics and poetry imagined that he reached it.

And there were the Ragged Mountains!—Poe knew a private and little-trod path that led there, to glens glistering in the Spring with the bleached flame of the dogwood blossoms, or brilliant beyond European imagination after the first frosts with the pied motley of the scarlet and golden Virginia Fall. Here he could find solitude and dream of Elmira, and make poems "upon a dim, warm, misty day, toward the close of November, and during the strange *interregnum,* of the seasons which in America is termed the Indian summer." [244] Of what he saw and thought there, let him speak for himself when ". . . attended only by a dog upon a long ramble among the chain of wild and dreary hills that lie westward and southward of Charlottesville."

The thick and peculiar mist, or smoke, which distinguishes the Indian summer, and which hung heavily over all objects, served no doubt, to deepen the vague impressions which these objects created. So dense was this pleasant fog that I could at no time see more than a dozen yards of the path before me. This path was excessively sinuous, and as the sun could not be seen, I soon lost all idea of the direction in which I journeyed. . . . In the quivering of a leaf—in the line of a blade of grass—in the shape of a trefoil—in the humming of a bee—

---

[243] Published in the *American Quarterly Review* in 1827. A comparison of Tucker's work with Poe's shows, however, no traceable connection.

[244] The quotations here are from Poe's *Tale of the Ragged Mountains,* published in *Godey's Lady's Book* for 1844.

in the gleaming of a dew drop—in the breathing of wind—in the faint odors that came from the forest there came a whole universe of suggestion—a gay and motley train of rhapsodical and immethodical thought.

This was a very excellent classroom, indeed, for a poet, and there is no better incubator in the world for dreams than the sun diffused in warm mist.

Thus slipped the months away. On July 4th Jefferson had died and Poe heard the old University bell tolled for the first time to mark his passing. Edgar was himself secretary of the "Jefferson Literary Society," [245] a type of organization that in the college life of the time provided not only literary and oratorical occasions, but became a convenient means for the formal recognition of cliques; it filled very largely the place of the modern fraternity. In a Southern college, the death of its great founder would not fail to be marked by the student orators of the time. It was still the age of the spoken word.[246] But the Fall of 1826 was marked for Edgar Poe by an event which must have caused him more immediate and genuine sorrow than the death of Jefferson. Some time in the late Autumn of the year John Allan seems to have visited Charlottesville. It was no mere matter of academic interest that drew his reluctant feet to the University; certain manuscripts bearing his foster-son's signature had come to light, not poems, but bills payable.

As the term drew to its close near the Christmas holidays, the merchants of Charlottesville who supplied the University students, doubtless began to want to see the color of money before their gay young customers departed from the neighborhood. Bills were sent home and the usual difficulties began. Owing to his guardian's untimely parsimony in sending Edgar almost no cash allowance at all, the boy had no doubt had to use his credit to an unusual extent to begin with.

One can imagine the almost apoplectic effect of the cold record of his ward's progress along the primrose path, when presented in dollars and cents to the purse-careful Scotchman. John Allan seems to have called James Hill, ordered out the carriage, and driven post-haste over to Charlottesville. Nor would two days' journey over the mountain roads of Virginia, in the McAdamless year of grace 1826, have served to smooth

---

[245] Some doubt has been thrown on the authenticity of Poe's signature as the secretary of this society.

[246] When the *History of Oratory in the United States* is written, as it ought to be, the large part played in national political movements by the literary societies in American schools and colleges will become apparent. Starting as genuine debating groups, in which argumentation was actually studied and practiced, these forensic-social groups gradually deteriorated; parliamentary procedure devolved into a patter and ritual; the laws of evidence were disregarded, and the palm awarded to the loquaciously-eloquent, whose flights were unhindered by the weight of logic. One of these "orators" from Buncombe County, North Carolina, who was elected to the United States Congress, has added a new word to the language, *buncombe,* later shortened to *bunk*. The necessity for the word is by no means sectional.

his wrath. He had plenty of time to think over what he would do and say, and as usual his action was vigorous and his remarks characteristic.

The interview between Edgar and his guardian at Number 13 must have been a fiery one. Poe's proceedings had been, indeed, most unfortunate. The result was fraught with tremendous consequences to his future. Mr. Allan no doubt found a rather recalcitrant and exasperated youth to deal with; the whole story came out inevitably, as the bills were there to expose it; and Poe was curtly informed that his University career was over.

Whatever drinking there had been, must have been made the most of, and the gambling debts were, of course, inexcusable in the eyes of the older man. These, Mr. Allan refused to pay. He may have settled some of those for which he was legally responsible and afterward have driven away in high dudgeon, nor would it be any balm to his feelings, under the circumstances, that to a certain extent his attempt to put his ward on short commons had resulted in his having to pay more in the end. Edgar's brilliant scholastic record gave him nothing to complain of, so the affair was entirely financial. When all is said and done, a few appletoddies could not have weighed very heavily in the scale except to lend extra force to the older man's invective. Poe's predicament will scarcely be evident to modern eyes. In his day, imprisonment for debt was still in full force; the laws of Virginia were stringent, and the boy, as soon as the news of his guardian's attitude got about, which must have been instanter, *would find himself pursued by warrants.* [247] Until the debts were satisfied, he could not return to the county where they had been contracted, and in a short while processes were issued which drove him from the state. By simply withholding his aid, John Allan automatically made Poe's return impossible. Whatever indiscretions Poe may have committed, there is no evidence that he deserved a punishment which involved the whole of his future. Mr. Allan was not legally responsible for the gambling debts, but a few hundred dollars would have staved off the merchants at Charlottesville. The cold fact remains that the good merchant did not think that his foster-son was worth this. The threat to his Scotch purse was unforgivable. A few years later he made ample provision for his natural children in his will, legacies which, although a long and scandalous litigation was involved, his second wife undertook to set aside. In possession of a great fortune, $250 was the extreme limit of his effort to carry out his promise to give Poe a liberal education. In short the "jig was up." Poe had lost his opportunity of a University education, and had to face alone the demands for the payment of his debts of honor, doubtless to him the most unpleasant aspect

---

[247] In Poe's last letter to John Allan from West Point he specifically states that he was hounded out of Richmond by warrants. See *Valentine Museum Poe Letters,* letter No. 24, page 256.

of the affair. As a result of the situation he seems, as one of his class-mates says, "to have lost caste." The last of the Charlottesville episode closed in gloom. From William Wertenbaker, who was a close friend of Edgar, we have a vivid description of the final hours at the University.

On the night of December 20, 1826, or thereabouts, the two young men spent the early hours of the evening at the house of one of the fac-ulty, probably Professor Tucker, or Professor Blaettermann, whose conversation and young English wife must have attracted the boys to the fireside. After the visit, Wertenbaker and Poe walked over to "the small dwelling of a great poet" in West Range, where Poe began to smash up the furniture. This he burned with sundry papers and the accumulated rubbish of the term in the little fireplace, meanwhile telling his troubles, in a gloomy and foreboding vein, to William Wertenbaker, a sympathetic listener.

It was a cold night in December, and his fire having gone pretty nearly out, by the aid of some tallow candles, and the fragments of a small table which he broke up for the purpose, he soon rekindled it, and by its comfortable blaze I spent a very pleasant hour with him. On this occasion he spoke with regret of the large amount of money he had wasted and of the debts he had contracted during the session. If my memory is not at fault he estimated his indebtedness at $2000, and, though they were gaming debts, he was earnest, and emphatic in the declaration that he was bound by honor to pay, at the earliest opportunity, every cent of them.[248]

William Wertenbaker probably went home about midnight, leaving Edgar to fall asleep by the flickering shadows of the dying fire as the last sticks of his little table, upon which *Tamerlane and Other Poems* had come into being, slowly turned into ashes, the ashes of lost opportunity.

The next day be climbed on the Charlottesville coach in company with Philip St. George Ambler, Robert Hunter, Zaccheus Lee, Creed Thomas, and other youths of Richmond, Washington, and the vicinity, and started for home. They must have stopped overnight on the way, and arrived in Richmond the day before Christmas, 1826. Poe brought with him a small trunk, in which were the remnants of a considerable wardrobe, the spoil of the Charlottesville merchants, a few cherished books, and the manuscripts of some of the poems which appeared in Boston about six months later.[249] The prodigal had returned. As he ran up the steps of the big house on Main Street, dressed in a "London hat, a super-blue broadcloth suit with gilt buttons, a velvet vest and

---

[248] This is one of the most authentic glimpses of Poe at the University that we have. William Wertenbaker afterward became Librarian of the University of Virginia. It was his "profession" to cherish the literary memories of the place.

[249] *Tamerlane and Other Poems.* It is also even possible that the notes and many of the lines of *Al Aaraaf* were in existence at this date as it bears the stamp of having been conceived where a library was available and leisure to use it. *Al Aaraaf* was published in 1829. Poe afterward used it as a mine for later poems, *Zante*, etc.

drab pantaloons," [250] he probably had no hallucinations as to the fatted calf, or that John Allan, under the circumstances, would rehearse the paternal rôle in the parable.   But he seems to have been met with fondly welcoming arms by Frances Allan and his dear "Aunt Nancy."   Holly was in all the windows, and mistletoe festooned the chandeliers, but where was Elmira?

---

[250] Poe purchased these articles on December 4, 1826, from Samuel Leitch, Jr., a Charlottesville merchant.   Mr. Allan refused to pay the bill, now in the *Ellis & Allan Papers,* Library of Congress, Washington, D. C., Poe's name on the bill is misspelled *Powe.*

CHAPTER TEN

ALIAS HENRI LE RENNÉT

SO the prodigal found himself, suddenly, in Richmond again. Ill at ease, too, for he had now given John Allan real cause for complaint, and his position in the household was essentially uncomfortable; lawyers were trying to force Mr. Allan to recognize his foster-son's gambling debts which, it appears, in all totaled about $2500,[251] when the final sums came in. These John Allan resolutely refused to recognize, and his exasperation seems to have been so extreme then, or later, that he would not even settle for accounts that were legitimately contracted.[252] The greeting between the two could only have been curt.

Poe must have felt his position keenly. The other boys, to some of whom he doubtless owed money, were also home for the holidays. For them it was Christmas and a merry time. Poe, in his chagrin, would scarcely care to see them. There would be no happy return on a noisy coach to Charlottesville after New Year's. He was no longer the brilliant young student and sport of his set, with a literary career ahead, but the prodigal whose brief career of glory was over, whose social position with his own friends was compromised by unpaid debts of honor, with the dubious prospects of *perhaps* a place on a stool in the counting house of *Ellis & Allan*. The pill was a bitter one, and it was made no easier by his discovery of the truth about Elmira. Luckily, it is not hard to piece out the events of the first day at home, the day before Christmas.

Edgar must have had a long talk with his "mother" and "Aunt Nancy"; that at least we can be sure was comforting. On his drive to the University, the February before, it seems that he had even then broached the subject to Frances Allan of leaving John Allan's house, and making his own way in the world. She, however, had persuaded him to go on to Charlottesville.[253] The return of Poe in "disgrace" must have again aroused apprehensions that he would leave her, and she was anxious to soften the hard places of his fall, and make him welcome again by the fireside which she had done so much to make happy.

---

[251] Statement made by Col. Thomas H. Ellis in a letter to the editor of the *Richmond Standard,* April 22, 1881. Lawyers' letters relating to collection of these debts are still extant in Richmond, Virginia.
[252] See specifically the letter of Edward G. Crump to Poe, March 25, 1827, on page 163.
[253] Statement made by James Hill, the Allans' coachman, who drove Mrs. Allan and Poe to Charlottesville in 1826. See Whitty *Memoir,* large edition, page xxvii. Also close of Chapter IX, this volume.

Nothing is more indicative of her affection than the fact that she had arranged for him, that very night, a Christmas Eve party to which his friends were to be invited, as a formal advertisement of the fact that he was still at home as the beloved foster-son of a hospitable house. Nor was this in reality putting much of a strain on the circumstances surrounding Poe's withdrawal. That John Allan permitted it shows that even he acquiesced.[254]

It must be remembered that Edgar had not in any official way disgraced himself.[255] That he had gambled, and upon occasions overstepped the mark in the drinking bouts, was true, but it was also true of nearly all the other students. He had not incurred the displeasure of the authorities, and been dismissed; his guardian had withdrawn him, not so much because of the "immorality" of his conduct, as on account of his debts.[256] In the final analysis this was what worried Mr. Allan most, as it would worry any Scotchman or commercial-minded man. Had Edgar's waywardness been of an inexpensive type it might have been censured, but no very drastic action would have followed. The tune of $2500 for one term was a melody which did not appeal to a Scotch ear, however, and as Mr. Allan had to pay the piper, he had decided to put a period to the dance. It was, in the opinion of him who had to bear the expense, not worth the cost. At best, Mr. Allan's enthusiasm over a liberal education for the foster-child must have been limited. That limit had already been exceeded during the first year of the cultural interlude, and, as a consequence, Master Edgar found himself suddenly very much at home. It was this financial aspect, too, in a more personal and proud way, rather than the pricking of bad conscience, which appears to have worried young Poe the most. The drinking escapades, on which so much emphasis has been laid, could not have caused him much self-reproach at the time. He could not see them as the evil portents of the future. He must have been a little ashamed of the fact that his head was not as hard as the heads of his mates who could carry their liquor better than he, but, that he had taken a not unusual part in what was then expected and practiced by every live young gentleman at college, did not cause him much spiritual dismay we may be sure. Drinking in all its aspects stood on a different moral plane in 1826 than it does now. What did worry and cause him

---

[254] Thomas Bolling, a young friend of the Allan family and an acquaintance of Poe, visited the Allan house in Richmond the day before Christmas and was invited to this party. The Bolling family was settled in Goochland County at "Bolling Hall" and "Bolling Island" Plantations. John Allan's plantation was in the same neighborhood. See page 687.

[255] See John Allan's letter to the Secretary of War from Richmond, May 6, 1829. "I have much pleasure in asserting that he [Poe] stood his examination at the close of the year with great credit to himself."

[256] John Allan says in the same letter referred to in note 255, "He left me in consequence of some gambling at the University at Charlottesville," etc.

chagrin, perhaps even a feeling of disgrace, was the remembrance that a goodly number of ex-college mates possessed certain I. O. U.'s for not inconsiderable amounts, notes which his foster-father had refused to honor. These in the boy's eyes were debts of honor; in Mr. Allan's they were debts of dishonor, and in legal fact to him did not exist. The fact that his disappointing and troublesome foster-son might lose prestige among the members of a fast young set, whose good opinion Mr. Allan did not think worth having, especially at a great price, left him unmoved.

Edgar, on the other hand, like most boys of his age, probably felt, and valued more keenly, the attitude of his fellows than the opinions of his parents.[257] This, coupled with an inability to appreciate the nature and difficulty of acquiring what was so easy to spend, undoubtedly contributed the main stress in an already strained condition of affairs.

With the women of the household this monetary consideration could not have been the most important one. Like most women, they regarded the situation in its purely human and personal aspect as a conflict of personalities. They were more apt to condone what in their eyes was, at worst, the result of the natural exuberance and inexperience of a handsome boy under whose more manly clothes beat the romantic heart and pulsed the warm body which they had loved and cherished since childhood. It is scarcely possible that Mrs. Allan ever forgot the purple cap with the gold tassel, the Nankeen trousers and the buckled shoes. No good woman ever would.

So there was to be a party! We can imagine Edgar's reception of the news, his appreciation of all that it meant, and his passionate gratitude to his "mother." What would he do without her? She who was frail and ill, his "dear, dear Ma!"—Now he would run over and see Elmira. . . .

The blow was a staggering one. "No, she is not at home. Miss Royster has left Richmond." The door closed, shutting out the little parlor where the flute had once warbled and the piano tinkled, leaving him, can we doubt it, in tears. Someone must have told him, and some-one must have left him in despair.[258]

It was all plain now. He could hear John Allan and Mr. Royster

---

[257] One of the main motives for Poe's leaving Richmond and assuming an alias was undoubtedly his desire to avoid the unbearable contacts with those to whom he owed debts of honor.

[258] There is, of course, no "document" describing this visit to the Roysters'. Poe may have learned of Elmira's plight even before he left the University, or from the servants or his foster-mother. In any event, the result of the news would have been the same. In *The Pirate,* a story published in the *Baltimore North American* for 1827, there is, however, a melodramatic description of what is probably Edgar Poe's version of his last scene with Elmira. See Appendix IV.

talking it over, see all of his pathetic letters opened by an unfeeling hand, the amused grins over the ardent lines, and a little girl in tears. Then the advent of the unwelcome Mr. Shelton, his plausible talk, and Elmira at last sent away where her lover could not find her to tell her he still loved her, that it was all a cruel lie, and that her Prince Charming had come back to claim his princess after all. How dreary the Enchanted Garden now, and how cold the snow looked on the roofs as he stared across to the Roysters' and saw the empty window where a handkerchief had once waved! It was all like a bad dream. As he unpacked the mementoes of his lost room at the University, who can doubt that the lines of certain manuscripts indited to a lost little lady swam dizzily before him through the mist of his despair. Could she, had she actually forgotten him? Most of Poe's historians have dismissed the "Elmira incident" as an amusing story of puppy-love. They forget that in 1826-27, especially in the South, marriage took place *commonly* in the teens. Poe had not simply lost a nice little sweetheart but his promised *wife*. Elmira *married* Mr. Shelton the next year. She had two children by him, both named Sarah Elmira, who died in infancy, and a son. This "affair" was in reality a great emotional crisis, and a frustration in the life of Edgar Allan Poe. The home-making instinct here received its deathblow, with a consequent tendency towards *wanderlust*. It was one of the deepest sources of Poe's melancholy.

In considering Poe's parting and break with his guardian, during the months of December, 1826, and January, 1827, the fact of his broken engagement and the resulting irritation and wound to his pride and hopes must be included. The spectacle of a pretty young girl, from whose lips both the promises and pledges of affection have been freely received but a few months before, in the arms of an ardent young rival is not one well calculated to soothe the smart of misfortune. For with even the affectation of Byronic pride and passion, and Poe had more than that, it was a choking piece of humble pie. Hence the little *Song* from poems written in youth and dated by its allusion.

I saw thee on thy bridal day—[259]
When a burning blush came o'er thee,
Though happiness around thee lay,
And the world all love before thee:

And in thine eye a kindling light
(Whatever it might be)
Was all on Earth my aching sight
Of Loveliness could see.

[259] Written after the marriage of Elmira to Mr. Shelton and undoubtedly addressed to her.

Nor were a few rather poor lines the end of Elmira. After the exit of Mr. Shelton she was to come on the stage again with Israfel to take part in the last brief, hopeful, sunset glow of his final act. But in December, 1826, the end seemed inevitable—a merry Christmas, indeed! The scene now shifts to a little later on in the afternoon.

We are indebted to the testimony of Thomas Bolling,[254] a former schoolmate of Edgar's, to whom Mr. Allan had extended a cordial invitation to call, sometime before when he was on a visit to the country, for a description of the events at the Allan house on Christmas Eve, 1826. The young man, who was about Edgar's age, had taken the opportunity of paying his respects to Mr. and Mrs. Allan during the afternoon of the 24th, and was somewhat embarrassed to see that preparations for an entertainment were under way. He at once rose to leave, but was stopped by Mr. Allan, who cordially insisted upon his staying, explaining that Edgar had just returned from the University, and that some of his young friends and acquaintances had been asked in to meet him. Young Bolling replied that he was not suitably dressed, whereupon Mr. Allan bade him, "Go up to Edgar's room. He will supply you with one of his own suits." The remarkable extent of Poe's wardrobe was now probably thoroughly impressed on Mr. Allan's mind.

Upon going upstairs, Tom Bolling found Edgar lying on a lounge in his own room reading. "A handsomely furnished room, with books and pictures arranged in bookcases around the wall." One cannot help wondering if the little picture of Boston with the pathetic lines on the back was among the rest. Edgar welcomed his friend cordially, and threw open the doors of his well-stocked wardrobe, giving Tom his choice. Both of them then went downstairs to the drawing room where Edgar did his part in welcoming his guests. As the evening wore on, Poe seems to have become as impatient as usual with the formal social scene, and pulling young Bolling aside, he quietly proposed that they slip off down street and have a private spree of their own. Bolling replied at first "That it would never do," but his friend was so urgent that he finally yielded, and the company was left to enjoy themselves as well as they could without the presence of the "honor guest."

Just what led Poe to do this, it is not hard to guess. The reception of friends who knew the story of his fiasco at the University was probably no easy matter, Elmira must have been keenly on his mind, and the festivities of a Southern Christmas Eve thoroughly out of keeping with his mood. In company with Bolling, we can imagine him retiring to Mrs. E. C. Richardson's tavern, a favorite haunt, where he may have found Ebenezer Burling, and over a few comforting cups confided the perplexities of his situation, while the festivities went on at home minus the presence of the young host.

Poe's accounts to his friends of his University career were, as might have been expected, not the whole truth. In self-defense he seems to have assumed a rather lofty indifference, and to have tried with a college boy's braggadocio to impress his acquaintances with the "sporty" side of his life. His debts he explained by saying that he wanted to see how much of the old man's money he could spend,[260] and the seventeen broadcloth coats were an item in his remarks. This, if it came to Mr. Allan's ears, could not have helped to heal matters. Of the real reasons, neither he nor Poe would have been anxious to talk. The deserted party must also have been oil on the flames rather than a domestic lubricant. One is warranted in picturing Mr. Allan as very angry, and "Ma" perhaps in tears, when the boys returned that night, if either of the couple was inclined to sit up that long. The holly at the Christmas breakfast table could scarcely have expressed the spirit of the occasion for Frances Allan any more than the mistletoe did for Edgar.[261] It was all very tragic, and it was all very human. There was right and wrong on both sides, a determined, exasperated, and incensed older man, and a despairing, sensitive, and love-sick boy. Out of such stuff the world's tragedies are conveniently made.

The Christmas Holidays of 1826 marked the last passing phase of Poe's boyhood. New Year's, 1827, dawned and Poe was in reality, if not wholly in years, a man. Like everyone who is not born with at least a plated spoon in his mouth, he was now confronted with the prime question of every man's life—"Wherewith should he eat and where-withal should he be clothed?" The store of *Ellis & Allan* seems to have been the most obvious answer, but this distasteful solution was not offered him. Conditions at home must have been unusually uncom-fortable and, for a time, probably during the last of the holidays, Poe went down to his "father's" plantation, "The Lower Byrd" in Gooch-land County, to avoid the painful scenes in the big city house, and the trials of seeing his friends depart for the University leaving him be-hind. In the country, too, he could escape those who were hounding him for his debts, for he was now pursued by warrants.

He seems to have returned to Richmond sometime in January and to have talked about, and even begun the reading of law.[262] But this was not definite enough for Mr. Allan who seems to have considered that young Poe had forfeited his chance to become a professional man

[260] R. H. Stoddard *Memoir*. See note 146.

[261] Christmas breakfast in the South often assumes the importance of the Christmas dinner in the North.

[262] Poe's visit to the country and his attempt to read law are given on the double evidence of James Galt, and Poe himself in one autobiographical story published in Richmond, 1835, see note 150.

by his conduct. The older man on his part, however, offered no help in Poe's attempts to obtain employment, although he reproached the boy for "eating the bread of idleness." The stories, related by former biographers, that he was given work in the store of *Ellis & Allan* are now shown by the dates of letters which have come to light, and the nature of their contents, not to be true. Poe's situation was, indeed, desperate. John Allan would not pay off his debts, or make any compromise which would allow him to return to the University. Neither would he aid him in getting employment, while at the same time he excoriated him for being idle. In the household, Edgar's position had become anomalous; he was, it appears, subject even to the whims, not only of the whites, but of the slaves, too. Indeed, he specifically complains of this. For a young Virginian this was the lowest rung of domestic tyranny. He was in fact trapped, and there is every indication that his foster-father took the occasion to rub it in. Probably he deliberately improved the opportunity to make clear to Poe the lesson that the way of the evil doer is hard, and to impress upon him the value of money by allowing him to remain without any at all, and no means of making any. Fiery interviews must have occurred upon the receipt of such letters as this from Charlottesville:

JOHN ALLAN, *Esq., Richmond*

DEAR SIR,

I presume when *you sent* Mr. Poe to the University of Virginia you felt yourself bound to pay all his necessary expenses—one is that each young man is expected to have a servant to attend his room. Mr. Poe did not board with me, but as I had hired a first rate servant who cost me a high price, I consider him under greater obligations to pay me for the price of my servant. I have written you two letters and have never received an answer to either. I beg again, sir, that you will send me the small amount due ($6.25). I am distressed for money and I am informed that you are Rich both in purse and Honor.

Very respectfully,
GEO. W. SPOTSWOOD [229, 263]

From later indications it appears that this bill, along with the others, was never paid. John Allan at one time seems to have planned a public career for Poe, but in his indignation he allowed his foster-son to hang about the house, subject to the petty tyranny of his servants and his own reproaches, and pursued by warrants, which, about the middle of January, it appears began to make Poe's future residence in Richmond, without the aid of his guardian, an impossibility.

Poe was not merely passive under this. He is known to have written a letter to the *Mills Nursery Company* of Philadelphia, a firm with

[263] The date of this letter is 1st of May, 1827. The other letters, before, were written a month apart. The photostat of one written April 2, 1827, is also in the possession of the author. Poe may have received the first himself. It has not been found.

which *Ellis & Allan* had dealings, asking them for employment in that city.[264] His letter was, it appears, referred back to his guardian, who with the written evidence in his hands of Poe's intentions to leave the house, seems to have precipitated a scene more violent than any which had preceded it. Even with a full knowledge of John Allan's character, it would seem impossible that he should be keeping Poe at home merely to make him suffer. He may have had some plan in mind for the boy later, and have simply used the opportunity to impress Poe with the results of extravagance. A little pursuit by bailiffs might perhaps, he may have thought, be a salutary lesson to be more careful in the future, but the evidence all points to the fact that this was not the case. He must have known that his own parsimony was, in the final analysis, the cause of Poe's having run into debt, and, as he made no move to secure his "son" any employment, nor to save him from impending imprisonment, while he continued to reproach him for not paying for his keep, the inference is forced upon us that he desired to have him out of the house; to have done with his interference in the discords of the family; and be rid of the young upstart, "the black-heart," as he called him later, who could if he desired make the family skeletons dance. The scene now shifts again to the library of the Allan house sometime after supper in the evening of March 18, 1827.

The great quarrel, resulting in his leaving the house of John Allan, was the crisis of Poe's life. In point of time it falls about midway in his span of days. In a certain sense, all the events of his youth led up to it, and its results never ceased to affect his manhood. Things were said by both men, which could never be forgiven; it was the decisive turning point in Poe's career. From the mass of evidence now at hand, and the knowledge of the personality and character of those involved, it is amply possible to reproduce what took place.[265]

John Allan must have confronted Poe with the Mills Nursery letter, and have demanded of him whether it was his intention to leave Richmond as he indicated, or stay and work off his debts. Stared in the face by his own handwriting, Poe took the bit in his teeth and spoke his mind, reproaching his guardian for his parsimony to him in the University. John Allan could counter this by denouncing Edgar's ex-

---

[264] J. H. Whitty *Memoir,* large edition, page xxix.

[265] The publication of the *Valentine Museum Poe Letters* in September, 1925, including correspondence between Poe and John Allan the two days immediately after the quarrel show exactly what took place. The story of this momentous event in Poe's life has hitherto, of necessity, rested on guesswork. The exact date of the quarrel is arrived at by a series of deductions from the dates of correspondence during this period of the end of March, 1827, *viz:* a letter written by John Allan to a sister in Scotland, March 27, 1827. A letter from Poe's creditor Crump, dated March 25, 1827. Poe's two letters to John Allan after the quarrel, and the latter's reply. For the deductions from these I am frankly indebted to Prof. Killis Campbell, and Mrs. Mary Newton Stanard's excellent comments in the *Valentine Museum Poe Letters.*

travagance and dissipation there, which must have brought up the subject of the gambling debts, a sore point with them both.   This seems
to have been the main bone of controversy.   Poe urged that he be
allowed to continue his course at the University by having his just debts
paid there; the rest he felt he could shoulder later himself.   His conduct during the last three months at the University, probably since John
Allan's visit, had, he represented, been exemplary, and he had stood
high in his classes.   John Allan absolutely refused to send him back
to Charlottesville.   He seems to have had an idea that Poe should have
continued at home to complete his studies.   "French, mathematics, and
the classics," he afterward specifically mentions.   Evidently he had
some vague idea of a professional career for Poe still in mind.   It was
this rock upon which their further possibility of voyaging together
split.   From Poe's and John Allan's letters of the two days immediately
following the quarrel it is quite evident that Poe desired to continue his
course at the University with the idea of a literary future in mind.
Even while so harassed in Richmond between January and March,
1827, it is probable that he continued to work upon his poems.   John
Allan regarded his time spent on these as idling, and he seems to have
made it a condition that if Poe remained in the house it must be on his
guardian's terms.   Poe could either remain and pursue the studies which
would "promote the end,"—the "eminence" in public life to which John
Allan says he had taught him to aspire,—or he could get out!   For a
literary career the older man had no sympathy and he would not permit
his "son" to idle around the house while engaged in any scribbling, nor
would he make it possible for him to return to the University with such
an end in view, indeed, he would not permit that at all.   The reading
of law is rather clearly implied, and Poe, it seems, was given the night
to think it over.   He was left for a few hours definitely at the parting
of the ways.

During the night of March 18, 1827, Edgar Allan Poe, lying in his
bed in his room in the Allan house after the momentous interview with
his guardian, made the great decision of his life.   He decided not to
submit to John Allan's dictation of his future, nor to accept the conditions laid down, even if forced out upon the world.   Let us be fair,
there were some ugly connotations to this determination; it was "ungrateful," and it would bring pain to several yearning hearts, among
them Poe's, but it was nevertheless a great decision and a brave one.
Comfort had been weighed in the balance with pride and the potentialities of genius, and comfort had been found wanting.   The possibility of fame and honor had deliberately been preferred to wealth.
More, although perhaps he could not know it, starvation and poverty
had been chosen.   That they were risked, Poe must have known.

From his letter to John Allan later, on the afternoon of the same day, it is plain that the final break occurred on the morning of the nineteenth of March. The discussion was probably resumed at the breakfast table. No doubt John Allan asked for Poe's decision and Poe told him what it was. In addition he said that it was his opinion that John Allan's real reason for not sending him back to the University was that he was too parsimonious to do so. This declaration seems to have been followed by an outburst of extreme anger on the part of the older man, who had a violent temper and a sharp tongue. By this time the whole house must have been in an uproar, the harsh voice of the furious Scotchman and the pounding of his cane on the floor advertised to the household the extremity of his anger, nor could the shrill strained tones of Edgar's replies have reassured the frightened ladies and scared servants. That the young upstart whom he regarded as the object of his charity was about to shake off his dominance must have come as a terrible shock to the older man. The scene seems to have ended in a furious round of mutual insults; both had a gift of irony and were in possession of facts that hurt. Poe's self-confidence in his future seemed insufferable—"let him find out what it means to starve," thought John Allan—predicted that Poe would soon be starving in the streets—and ordered him to quit the house. His command was carried out immediately and literally, for Poe dashed out the door with nothing but what he had on.

From the letters between the two which immediately followed, it is now possible for the first time to follow Poe's movements accurately.[265] Poe left John Allan's house on the morning of Monday, March 19, 1827. Having no place to go, characteristically enough, his first place of refuge was a tavern. On the afternoon of the same day he writes John Allan from the *Court House Tavern,* Richmond, a three page letter. The letter is headed "Richmond, Monday," and is undated.[265] He addresses his "father" as "Sir."

Poe says that after his treatment of the day before and the quarrel which had taken place that morning, he hardly expects John Allan to be surprised at the contents of the letter. His determination is at last taken unalterably, however, to find some place in the wide world where he will not be treated as his guardian has treated him, and that, as he has been long considering such a move, Mr. Allan need not think that his departure is the result of passion, and that he is already hoping to return. Poe then proceeds to rehearse his reasons for his decision.

From the time he has been able to think on any subject, he says, he had been ambitious, and had been taught by John Allan himself to hope for a high position in public life. Therefore, a college education was what he most ardently desired. He continues by asserting that this had been denied him in a moment of caprice because he disagreed with his guardian in an opinion. This meant that he told John Allan the real reason for his keeping him from college was that he was too parsimonious to send him there. Naturally enough the older man would not have agreed to that, in spite of the fact. Poe also tells his "father" that he has overheard him telling others that he had no affection for his ward, and as John Allan could not have known that Poe was listening, his assertion could only be taken to be true. Furthermore, John Allan had ordered him to quit the house ("often" seems to be understood here) and had continually upbraided him for eating the bread of charity while at the same time refusing to remedy the conditions by obtaining work for him. Lastly,—and the charge is significant from so proud a spirit as Poe's,—his guardian had taken a cruel delight in exposing the boy before those from whom he hoped to obtain advancement, and had subjected him, he says, completely, not only to the members of the white family, but to the slaves. The slaves were very fond of him.

He ends by entreating his "father" at least to send him his trunk containing his clothes and books, and a sum of money sufficient to pay his way to some Northern city and support him there for a month until he can obtain a position and earn enough to keep himself at the University. He asks that his trunk and effects be sent to him at the *Court House Tavern* with some money, as he is in dire need, and he adds, that if the request is not complied with, he trembles at the consequences. A postscript informs his guardian that it depends upon him whether he sees or hears from the writer again.

The letter bears every impress of being written by one who found himself insulted and wronged beyond all bearing. The hint of suicide is significant; evidently Poe would rather kill himself than return. He was already undergoing the pains of hunger.

Having received no answer to this, the next day, Tuesday, Poe writes John Allan again. He begs him to send him his trunk and his clothes, doing his guardian the grace to say that, as he had not received his clothes, he must suppose John Allan had not got his first letter. His necessity, he says, is extreme. He has not tasted any food since the morning before, has no place to sleep, and is roaming about the streets almost exhausted. His guardian's prediction will be fulfilled unless he obtains his trunk and clothes and enough money to go to Boston, $12.00. If John Allan will not give the money to him, Poe asks him to lend it till he can obtain a position. He says he sails Saturday,—the day he refers to in 1827 fell on March 24th,—and he closes by a pathetic message of affection and love to all at home, and a postscript saying he has not a cent in the world with which to buy food.

John Allan sent neither the trunk nor the money. Before receiving the second of Poe's letters, he had replied to the first. In justice to the older man it must be said that his letter shows no trace of passion, it is, indeed, so calm and judicial as to be utterly cold. Its studied periods, to one who had been without food for a day when he received it, must have been far from satisfying.

Mr. Allan says that he is not surprised at anything that Poe may do or say, he reminds him of his debt for his rearing and education already received and admits that he had taught him to be ambitious for a high place in public life, but he adds, *Don Quixote, Gil Blas, Joe Miller* and such books could not be expected to promote such a career. Evidently these had been a bone of contention, and John Allan did not approve of reading "novels." We also learn elsewhere that he abhorred Byron. He defends himself from Poe's charges (and he is distinctly on the defensive in this letter) by saying that his reproaches for Poe's idleness were only made to urge him to perfect himself in the mathematics and the languages. *That Poe has not shown any intention to comply with his wishes* (evidently in the matter of the direction which his studies were to take) *is the only subject upon which he says he cares to be understood.* He also adds, and we are bound to credit him in this with being sincere, that unless Poe's heart is made of marble, he can judge for himself whether he has not given his foster-father good reason to fear for him in more ways than one. He insists that his only reason for reprimanding his "son" was to correct his faults, and that for the rest of the charges he has no answer, as the world will reply to them. But he ends with a taunt. Now, he says— since Poe has declared his independence—the first result is that he must tremble for the consequences unless the man, whose support he has just shaken off, will send him some *money*. With that word his correspondence with his foster-son ceased for two years.

If any doubt remains, this letter makes ultimately clear that the cause of Poe's final break with John Allan was the latter's determination to force Poe into a career he did not care to follow. As one reads the confident and admonitory periods of this self-contained letter, addressed by the man in the comfortable house in Richmond to the youth who was hungry on the city streets, it is only natural to recall the remark of Cromwell made upon another pregnant occasion to some self-righteous gentlemen, "Bethink you, bethink you, in the Bowels of Christ, ye may be wrong!" Such a possibility seems never to have troubled John Allan. Strangely enough, in the matter of his choice as to the future career and the treatment of his foster-son, he appeals in the same letter to the judgment of the world. All the world now knows the answer. But, perhaps, this is unfair,—what could one expect of a youth who deliberately preferred *Don Quixote* to insults and mathematics?

Poe says that he is sailing for Boston on the next Saturday, March 24th, after the writing of the letter, but he also says he is penniless. It would seem as if his sailing were largely contingent upon the receipt of the $12 which he says the passage will cost. From the copy of John Allan's letter, originally in the *Ellis & Allan Files,* it is evident he sent Poe no money. The immediate sailing for Boston must, therefore, have been deferred. Tradition, circumstantial evidence, and direct testimony all point to the fact that it was.[266]

Poe tells his "father" that he will receive letters at the *Court House Tavern;* evidently this was a temporary arrangement, as he had no money, he could not have stayed there. He seems to have gone to stay at Mrs. Richardson's tavern where he was known, and where his friend Ebenezer Burling was an habitué about the bar. That *Richardson's Tavern* was Poe's hiding place during the few days that he remained in Richmond after the quarrel with John Allan, rests on direct testimony, for Dabney Dandridge, one of the slaves of the Allan household, told persons still living in Richmond that he carried packages from the Allan household to Poe while he was there, but "Dab" did not dare to reveal the fact to the members of the family. "Mars Eddie" was a favorite with the servants, and it is probable, that finding John Allan would not send him his clothes, he prevailed on the house servants to bring them to him. In this way, too, he must have got the manuscripts of his poems published a month or so later. *These he would hardly have had in his hand when he ran out of the house.* Dabney Dandridge also said that during this time he carried notes for Poe to a young lady of the neighborhood whom his young master admired. She was at that time boarding with a Mrs. Juliet J. Drew nearby.

It is very likely that Frances Allan saw Poe's letters to her husband. At any rate she seems to have become aware of Poe's intentions to leave Richmond, and must have created a scene, for she prevailed on Mr. Allan to stop Poe's departure and the captains of the ships about the port were warned not to take him. Not caring to offend the head of a great firm with whom many of them traded, the avenue of departure was closed to Poe by the ship captains. Frances Allan must have been hoping for a reconciliation, and her husband doubtless thought that his recalcitrant ward would soon be starved into submission. Both

---

[266] The editor of the *Valentine Museum Poe Letters,* Mrs. Mary Newton Stanard, has very cleverly, and in a scholarly way, suggested that Poe sailed from Richmond on the ship "Carrier," Captain Gill. The deduction is made from the dates of letters and the files of the *Boston Commercial Gazette* between March 26 and April 7, 1827. If so, Poe arrived in Boston on April 7, 1827. The author, here, is inclined to think that, for the reasons given in the text, the weight of evidence is against Poe's having sailed on the "Carrier" as early as March 24th.

Mrs. Allan and Miss Valentine appear to have supplied Poe with some small sums of money, as he must have had some upon which to live during the interim.[267] John Allan did not send it, and in Poe's condition of debt he could scarcely have borrowed any. The amount at best was small, and only sufficed to last him for a few weeks, until May twenty-sixth to be exact.

In order to save himself from being arrested on a debtor's warrant, and to conceal his departure, Poe now assumed the name of Henri Le Rennét, and having persuaded Burling to join him, left Richmond, probably on some coastwise vessel for Norfolk. Burling had a small boat on the James in which the two boys had formerly made many a "voyage," and they seem now to have joined company for a real adventure.

Exactly what took place in Norfolk will probably never be known. Burling was drunk when he left Richmond, and he began to take a melancholy view of the future as he sobered up. Probably there was some difficulty in obtaining a berth aboard a ship. Burling returned to Richmond, evidently before Poe sailed, saying he had gone abroad. Either there had really been some talk of this, or the tale had been agreed upon to throw the family off the scent, and to put a quietus on the warrants. The latter was probably the main factor in Poe's *incognito,* then and for sometime afterward. That Frances Allan thought Poe had gone abroad is shown by the fact that four or five persons afterward saw two letters which she wrote to him with a foreign address. Burling simply got "cold feet" and dropped out. He was a weak and dissipated youth who died some few years later of cholera, and disappears from the record. Poe, however, did not go abroad, but persisted in his decision to get to Boston, probably because of its being a literary center, where, if his contemplated book of poems was published, it would receive a better chance of being noticed than if it emanated from Richmond. He may also have been influenced in his decision by his mother's injunction "to cherish the city of his birth," and have intended to look up the old friends of his parents. At any rate he arrived in Boston certainly by the middle of April, 1827. There is some evidence that he worked his way north on a coal-ship.[268]

Frances Allan is said to have been heart-broken; to one in her condition, the bitter quarrel between the two men of her household, followed by the loss of her "dear boy," must have been crushing. Poe

---

[267] The traditions to this effect seem to have come later from Miss Valentine herself.
[268] In many of the stories which Poe afterward told of these adventures, a "coal-ship" remains a constant factor among much romance. See specifically Woodberry, 1909, vol. I, page 67—Poe's story in Baltimore to Nathan C. Brooks. Not much stress can be laid on this evidence, however.

never saw her again.[269] Her affection attempted to follow him across the sea where she and John Allan thought he had gone,[270] for Poe received from her, sometime during 1827, two letters which are said by those who saw them to have exonerated him from all blame in the dissensions of the Allan household. These may have reached him at Boston or Fort Moultrie, or he may have received them after their return to the writer when he came back home. At any rate their existence is too well established to doubt.[271] Poe's arrival in Boston sometime in the first half of April of 1827 is now no longer a matter of conjecture and all stories about his going to Greece, getting in trouble over passports at St. Petersburg, Russia, and being rescued by the intervention of the American Consul, Henry Middleton, the visit to France, and having his portrait painted by Inman while in London, are at once and forever dismissed as legends. Poe's movements from January, 1827, to February, 1829, are no longer "mysterious" but a matter of record.

In the meantime things at the Allan house in Richmond seem to have taken their usual way—that of John Allan. Mrs. Allan grew feebler, and the master of the establishment went grimly about his affairs, except for the anxiety of his wife, taking matters very coolly. In a letter written from Richmond, March 27, 1827, to one of his sisters in Scotland, he covers three pages defending his administration of his uncle's will and ends with a few significant sentences about domestic affairs:

. . . though Mrs. Allan (is) occupying one of the airiest and pretty places about Richmond, it seems to make no improvement in her—it is indeed a lovely spot. . . . Miss Valentine is as fat and hearty as ever, I'm thinking Edgar has gone to Sea to seek his own fortunes. . . .[272]

How obstinate of Mrs. Allan not to improve in so "airy" a mansion when her sister was heartier than ever! What could be the reason? Perhaps the air was not so salubrious after all; even Edgar seems to have sought a different atmosphere. "I'm thinking," says John Allan

---

[269] Poe returned just too late to attend her funeral. See Chapter XII, page 188.

[270] In his letter to his sister in Scotland, dated March 27, 1827, John Allan specifically says, "I'm thinking Edgar has gone to Sea . . . etc." This looks as if at that date Mr. Allan was *not at all sure where* Poe had gone, despite Poe's earlier statement. John Allan never trusted Poe's statements then or later, especially in letters.

[271] These letters were long cherished by Poe. His wife, Virginia, is known to have had them about the time of her death, when she read them to Mrs. Shew. See the letter from Mrs. Shew to Ingram, Poe's biographer, now in the Ingram collection, University of Virginia. In this, Mrs. Shew (then married a second time) says these letters were the *second* Mrs. Allan's. This is an obvious error, although she is quoting from her diary (*sic*). It can positively be stated that the second Mrs. Allan never wrote any letters to Poe.

[272] From the *Ellis & Allan Papers,* Library of Congress, Washington, D. C., photostat in possession of the author. Also referred to in connection with the William Galt will, Chapter VII, page 97, this volume. Also for further quotation, see note 165.

—one wonders. By this time he knew most of the story of the runaway, even to the name which Poe assumed, for on the very desk upon which he wrote the "airy" letter to Scotland, was some mail which the fortune-hunting Edgar never received. Among it was this letter:[273]

Dinwiddie County, March 25, 1827

(*Mr.* EDGAR A. POE)

DEAR SIR:

When I saw you in Richmond a few days ago I should have mentioned the difference between us if there had not been so many persons present. I must of course, as you did not mention it to me, enquire if you ever intend to pay it. If you have not the money, write me word that you have not, but do not be perfectly silent. I should be glad if you would write to me as a friend. There can certainly be no harm in your avowing candidly that you have no money, if you have none, but you can say when you can pay me if you cannot now. I heard when I was in Richmond that Mr. Allan would probably discharge all your debts. If mine was a gambling debt I should not think much of it. But under the present circumstances I think very strongly of it. Write to me upon the receipt of this letter and tell me candidly what is the matter.

Your friend EDWARD G. CRUMP

Under the endorsement "to E. A. Poe" John Allan has added in his own hand "alias—Henri Le Rennét." Poe never got the letter, and it remains to this day in the file where his guardian quietly placed it. Meanwhile, what of Henri Le Rennét?

Upon his arrival in Boston, Poe probably tried to look up some of the old friends of his mother and father. His knowledge of such, at best, must have been slight; his parents had been obscure, and they had been forgotten in Boston for sixteen years.

In some way or other he became acquainted with a youth of about his own age of the name of Calvin Thomas. There was *said* to have been some connection between the families of the two boys which was not a pleasant one. A Miss Thomas had at one time been in the same theatrical company with the Poes.[274] Young Thomas and his people

[273] Crump's letter was written in Dinwiddie County on March 25th and must have taken a day or so for transmittal and delivery at Richmond. John Allan writes his sister from Richmond on March 27th. Both letters therefore must have been in his hands about the same day.

[274] The *Norfolk Herald,* July 6, 1811—From this probable accidental resemblance of names there has been an attempt in some quarters to connect the name of David Poe and the actress, Miss Thomas. There is no evidence that this Miss Thomas was a relation of Calvin Thomas, the printer. Poe may never, as Prof. Woodberry thinks (*Atlantic Monthly,* December, 1884), have told his real name to Thomas. The printer never seems to have known that he *had* known Poe despite the latter's great fame afterward. Thomas was a very obscure person. He later moved to New York, Buffalo, and Springfield, Missouri, where he died in 1876. Communications from a Miss Martha Thomas, daughter of Calvin, elicited the information that the Thomases knew nothing about Poe and had no records of the Boston print shop nor any copies of *Tamerlane and Other Poems.* See letter of Miss Martha Thomas to Prof. Wood-

had at one time lived in Norfolk and came later to Boston, with their grandmother, who wished to educate them there. They were originally New Yorkers. Whether there had really been any family intimacy between the Poes and Thomases seems very doubtful. One thing is certain, however, the two youths became friends, the result of which was the publication of Poe's first volume.[275]

Calvin F. S. Thomas was the proprietor of a little job printing shop at "No. 70, Washington Street, Boston, Corner of State Street." The style of type fonts and printer's ornaments which he used show that he had *newly* set up in a small business, which he had probably recently bought from someone else. He was about nineteen years old and could have had little more than an apprentice's brief experience at his trade. To the hands of this tyro Poe confided the printing of a book which is now one of the most sought-after and most costly in the English language. It was *Tamerlane and Other Poems*. This was probably sometime about the beginning of May, 1827. The time of Poe's arrival in Boston precludes its being much earlier, and the date of his ensuing enlistment in the army fixes it as being sometime within the month of May.

Where and how Poe was living at this time is unknown. Probably on the remnants of his Richmond money. There is a story of his having obtained work on a Boston newspaper. The preparation of even this little volume for the press, together with the inevitable revision of the text, must have consumed considerable time and have precluded other work. By the time the book was printed he must have been penniless. Thomas, of course, was only a printer and had no means of publishing, so that the bulk of the edition,—said to have been forty or fifty copies at most,—remained on his hands. Poe probably bought a few copies himself with the last of his dwindling stock of coins; two books are known to have been sent out to reviewers.[276] Poe afterward said that the edition "was suppressed for private reasons." The "private reasons" are not hard to guess! There was no way to distribute the book when it was printed; no one who would buy it, if it had been put on sale; and the author was out of funds. *Tamerlane and Other*

berry—Woodberry, 1909, vol. I, Notes, page 360. Also *Atlantic Monthly,* December, 1884. The matter is very obscure and equally unimportant. The fact that both Poe and Thomas had lived in Virginia may have brought them together. The real point is that Calvin Thomas was a printer who printed Poe's first book.

[275] Poe's idea of earning money to go back to the University seems to have quickly disappeared at this time under the stress of poverty and no work. That he persevered in publishing his poetry shows how vital a place his desire for literary recognition held in his mind. The pitiable result of this sacrifice was the practical suppression of the volume.

[276] The *United States Review and Literary Gazette,* August, 1827. *The North American Review* for October, 1827. For a full description of *Tamerlane* see Killis Campbell, *Poems of Poe,* New York, 1917.

Poems was a pamphlet of about forty pages, 6⅜ by 4⅛ inches, bound in yellow, tea-colored covers. There have been at least three reprints but only four genuine copies of the first edition are known to exist. The author's name is not printed, the title page giving only "By a Bostonian," and a motto which happens to be the same as that chosen for Tennyson's first book, *Poems by Two Brothers.*

Just why Poe published the book anonymously is an interesting speculation. Evidently from this, and the fact that he later enlisted under an assumed name, he was very anxious not to have his whereabouts known, probably mainly to prevent his being followed by duns and warrants. "By a Bostonian" certainly looks as if he did not desire to hail from Richmond. Poe knew that the book would have a better chance of being reviewed in the Northern magazines if it came from Boston, or it may have been merely a sentimental compliment to his mother and the lines she had written on the back of her picture of that city. It was, of course, the city of his birth, but the place where he was starving could have been little more.

We should like very much to know just what Edgar Poe carried with him from the house of John Allan in Richmond. He must have rescued from his room the manuscripts of the poems which appeared in Boston a few months later. Among them were probably some of those which Mr. Allan had shown a few years before to the schoolmaster, Mr. Clarke. There were enough of them, and some of them were of such length, as to show conclusively that their composition must have covered a period of several years prior to their printing. They prove Poe to have been hard at work at his craft, consciously and determinedly a poet. In his preface he says in part:

The greater part of the poems which compose this little volume were written in the year 1821-2, when the author had not completed his fourteenth year. They were of course not intended for publication; why they are now published concerns no one but himself. Of the smaller pieces very little need be said, they perhaps savour too much of egotism; but they were written by one too young to have any knowledge of the world but from his own breast. . . .

It is chiefly for the knowledge of that young breast, which they reveal, that the poems are of value now. *Tamerlane* is an ambitious piece, which seems to have been written later than the others, at the University,[277] as it bears the ear-marks of the type of verse and the kind of semi-classical theme which the influences of the formal education of the day would supply to scribbling youth. It is chiefly of interest, though, in the light of what followed later, and as an indication of the kind of material which attracted Poe. For the rest, they show us a sensitive boy with an innate sense of melody, a surprising order of

---

[277] Its connection with Elmira has already been noted. This also helps to place it as later work.

technique for one so young, and a spirit, which, while it found great charm in nature and the people with whom it came in contact, valued landscapes and persons less for themselves than for the dreams and moods which they invoked. Thus Poe already possessed the two main artistic factors that make a poet. He had moods which were of enough value to be worthy of being recorded; and he had the artistry to record them successfully. In *Tamerlane and Other Poems* these qualities are best exhibited in *Dreams* and *The Lake*—

> In youth's spring, it was my lot
> To haunt of the wide earth a spot
> The which I could not love the less;
> So lovely was the loneliness
> Of a wild lake, with black rock bound,
> And the tall pines that tower'd around.
> But when the night had thrown her pall
> Upon that spot—as upon all,
> And the wind would pass me by
> In its stilly melody,
> My infant spirit would awake
> To the terror of the lone lake.
> Yet that terror was not fright—
> But a tremulous delight,
> And a feeling undefin'd,
> Springing from a darken'd mind.
> Death was in that poison'd wave
> And in its gulf a fitting grave
> For him who thence could solace bring
> To his dark imagining;
> Whose wild'ring thought could even make
> An Eden of that dim lake.

This poem is doubly interesting because it is the first which shows definitely how early the strange spell of melancholy and the preoccupation with death entered into his work. The young boy who wrote it must clearly have had periods of extreme sensitivity when physical existence became actually painful, together with a weird sense of the mystery of inanimate things that was to haunt him through life. So far as we know, his real mother and Mrs. Stanard were the only two instances in which he had actually, thus far, experienced the trial of death. That a sense of grief and a feeling of brooding sorrow were thus early engraved on him, the lines bear witness. It is true that early youth is more often preoccupied by the themes of death and mutability than middle age, but there seems to be an unusual sense of them expressed here.

The realization that his poems were to become irrevocable in print would spur Poe to further revisions, so that while he tells us that, "the greater part of the poems which compose this little volume were written . . . when the author had not completed his fourteenth year," we can take this with a grain of salt, as they undoubtedly had been much revised at home, at the University, and in Boston where they went to the press. The format, printing, and punctuation [278] of the book show that Poe appreciated the importance of the mechanical side of his art, and possessed both the education and the inclination to turn out a literate, although a typographically bungled piece of work. Thomas, the printer, who was only a year older than Poe, could not have been a past master in his art [279] and the passable result, despite some mistakes, must largely be attributed to the active collaboration and supervision of Poe himself.

With the publication of *Tamerlane and Other Poems,* Poe's funds (or the patience of his landlady) seem to have been completely exhausted. His situation was desperate; he was not capable of sustained physical labor, even if he could have secured employment, and an appeal to Richmond was unthinkable. In this extremity of pride and hunger he remembered his former military episodes in the "Junior Richmond Volunteers," or on the drill ground at the University, and joined the army.

The War Department records show that Poe enlisted in the United States Army on May 26, 1827, under the assumed name of Edgar A. Perry.[280] He gave his age as twenty-two years, although he was only eighteen, and stated that he was born in Boston and was by occupation a clerk. The enlistment records describe him as having gray eyes, brown hair, a fair complexion, and a height of five feet, eight inches. Without further delay the new recruit was assigned to Battery "H," of the First Artillery then stationed in Boston Harbor at Fort Independence.[281] In the barracks there, Poe spent the time from the end of May to the end of October, 1827. During this period he must have undergone his training as a recruit, but he seems early to have gravitated into the quartermaster's department where his clerical training and mercantile experience with *Ellis & Allan* would recommend him. The assertion that Poe enlisted in the army as a result of a spree had no foundation in fact and little probability behind it. From the time of his enlistment to his discharge we know that his conduct was so exemplary as to lead to his rapid promotion, and he was officially recommended upon discharge as being "sober," an unusual military virtue at that time.

Nevertheless, Poe's enlistment is significant of the fact that he already found himself unable to cope with the world in civilian life.

---

[278] The punctuation already shows many of Poe's peculiarly individual ideas about this "art," later developed to a "science" after his connection with the *Southern Literary Messenger.*

[279] Thomas was not even a member of the local printers' union.

[280] All of the War Department records relative to Poe's connection with the United States Army are taken from the text of the documents as given by Prof. Woodberry in his article in the *Atlantic Monthly* for December, 1884. The search for this material was made by direction of the President of the United States.

[281] Poe seems to have joined his command about June 1, 1827.

His tender rearing, his education, his desire for leisure and solitude and, above all, his nervous, impulsive, and erratic characteristics, which the events of the last few years had tended to accentuate, now undoubtedly began to be tremendous handicaps in a world which despises a dreamer, and puts a premium on physical endurance and insensibility. Poe was stretched from now on between two drums of a rack that kept turning slowly, torturing him until they pulled him apart. Every turn of the screw of the one to which his feet were bound, was bent on dragging him down to the callous level of the mediocrity about him, while the cords about his head dragged him ever upward, insisting that to be a poet and a dreamer, he must become hyper-sensitive, see colors beyond the visible spectrum, and hear whispers of voices inaudible to the average ear. It was to the latter world that he belonged. Stretched between the two he was torn apart; he occasionally relieved the tension of the unremitted torture by the anesthetics of feminine sympathy, alcohol and, towards the last,—opium, the result of each attempt at relief being, of course, a lowering of his power to withstand. Combined with this was, perhaps, an unfortunate heredity.

Of the life of the young artilleryman at Fort Independence, Boston Harbor, in the Summer of 1827, there is very little trace. It was afterward said that at some time during the army episode he wrote letters to his foster-mother dated from St. Petersburg, Russia (*sic*). Some record of his doings at this time has recently come to light through the discovery of an old Baltimore publication of 1827 called *The North American*.

To this obscure periodical the elder Poe brother, William Henry Poe, contributed steadily from the Summer of 1827 to the end of the year and the demise of the magazine. His contributions were in both prose and poetry, usually signed "W. H. P." From the nature of these it now seems certain that he was in touch with his brother Edgar in Boston and, perhaps, later from Charleston, for more particularly in a story called *The Pirate,* W. H. Poe treats romantically the episode of the love affair of Edgar with Elmira Royster, and republishes in two instances poems from *Tamerlane* over his own initials and as extracts. *Dreams* in a new version appears signed "W. H. P."

From this evidence, it seems undeniable that Edgar, while in the army, corresponded with Henry and sent him a copy of *Tamerlane* from Boston.[282]

It is possible that if, at this period of his life, Poe could have found

---

[282] *The Happiest Day, the Happiest Hour,* from *Tamerlane and Other Poems,* 1827. Republished by Henry Poe, 1827. The credit for the discovery of *The North American* containing the work of Henry Poe belongs to Dr. Thomas Ollive Mabbott and Captain F. L. Pleadwell. It is possible that portions of *The Pirate* are Edgar Poe's. Dr. Thomas Ollive Mabbott and I have collected all this material in *Poe's Brother,* Doran, 1926, a book to which the reader is referred.

the shelter of some sympathetic and understanding influence capable of imparting a feeling of calm and security to his intellect, and physical comfort conducive to the free working and growth of his mind, this continent might have seen the flowering of a genius which would have demanded a respectful and unqualified admiration for its unblighted blossoming, rather than a belated recognition in which scorn and pity have slowly given way to acceptance. Instead of that, the most sensitive nervous system, and one of the keenest intellects then extant in North America, was treated to a round of spiritual and mental outrage inherent for any higher nature in the ranks of a regular artillery regiment lying idle in barracks during a time of profound peace. The army of one of the most warlike republics which has ever troubled the world is not to be blamed if it is not so organized as to provide an ideal home for neurasthenic young poets; its domestic economy is bound to be of a different order. That Poe did not die at about the same age, and of similar complaint to Chatterton's, in a garret in Boston, Massachusetts, is due to the food, clothes, shelter, and refuge from the civil society of the time provided by Battery "H" of the First Regiment of United States Artillery. Of his not unimportant adventures under the eagle, under various circumstances and upon distant shores, we shall shortly learn. In the meantime his physical continuity was assured, but—

> The happiest day—the happiest hour
>   My sear'd and blighted heart hath known,
> The highest hope of pride and power,
>   I feel hath flown.
>
> Of power! said I? yes! such I ween;
>   But they have vanish'd long, alas!
> The visions of my youth have been—
>   But let them pass.
>
> And, pride, what have I now with thee?
>   Another brow may even inherit [283]
> The venom thou hast pour'd on me—
>   Be still, my spirit!

It is a pitiful farewell to youth, an acknowledgment of the futility of the Byronic formula, and a foreboding of the future. The shades of the prison house had begun to descend upon Poe, but in them his spirit was never to be "still."

On October the 31st, 1827, his Battery was ordered to Fort Moultrie on Sullivan's Island at the mouth of Charleston Harbor, in South Carolina.

---

[283] This line and the one following can refer only to the fact that Poe felt that a possible heir of his guardian might "inherit" the "venom" which had been heaped on him. It seems to be a patent reference to conditions "at home."

CHAPTER ELEVEN

ISRAFEL IN CAROLINA

TROOP movements, in the leisurely days before the coming of railroads, were by water. Outward bound from Fort Independence, Boston Harbor, the army transports moved through the flashing November weather of 1827, sinking the sand dunes of Cape Cod and the blue haze of Nantucket behind them, as they stood far out into the Atlantic to be rid of the perils of the coast. There was, at least for Poe, the pageantry of adventure about it; the sparkle of brass buttons and uniforms; the call of bugles from ship to ship; the bright sails and the banners.[284]

Poe's company embarked on the brig "Waltham," Captain Webb, and sailed from Boston, Thursday, November 8, 1827. From the ship notices of the time it is even possible to ascertain that among her "passengers," Lieut. H. W. Griswold, U.S.A., Lady and child, Lieut. J. Howard, U.S.A., Lady and three children, and Dr. J. Dodd, U.S.A.," were those officers of his own company who afterwards, in April, 1829, provided him with testimonials as to his meritorious service in the army.[287] The voyage down the coast took eleven days, the "Waltham" arriving at Charleston, Sunday, November 18, 1827.[285]

The whole interlude of Poe's life in the army, taken in connection with the places he visited, affords a remarkable example of the method the man sometimes followed in working directly from his environment. The story of it might almost be called *How Poe Gathered His Material for a Short Story*. Contrary to the fond and oft repeated opinion of many critics, Poe often found his material in the life and the place about him, and then worked only in a secondary and indirect way from literary sources. He visualized even imaginary localities strongly, and his scenery, although often a synthesis of the hills of one place and the lowlands of another, nevertheless, sprang directly from the vistas which he had seen. Out of the strange and impressive environ-

---

[284] It may be suggested that Henry Poe's having joined the *navy* may have influenced Edgar's joining the *army* in hopes of adventure. Edgar, we now know, became the Byronic hero of Henry's group in Baltimore and the subject of their poetic effusions in *The North American*. See L. A. Wilmer's *Merlin* afterward referred to by Edgar Poe in a complimentary manner.

[285] "Ship News" from *The Charleston Courier* and *The City Gazette and Commercial Daily Advertiser*, Charleston, S. C., for November 19, 1827. See *Poe in Charleston, S. C.*, by William Stanley Hoole, Duke University, *American Literature*, March, 1934, pages 78-80.

ment into which he was about to be plunged for a year, free from the problems of sustenance and with the opportunity for considerable leisure, came directly much of his material for *The Gold-Bug, The Oblong Box, The Man that was Used Up, The Balloon Hoax,* and bits of the melancholy scenery, and sea and light effects which, from the time of his sojourn in Carolina, haunt so much of his poetry. A comparison of his 1827 and 1829-31 volumes will at once make this apparent. A familiarity with the peculiar nature of the landscape and the section where Poe was about to tarry during 1827-28 will explain the "exotic" sources from which many of his descriptions in prose and poetry are derived.

From November 19, 1827, to December 11, 1828, he did garrison duty at Fort Moultrie on Sullivan's Island. One Sunday, early in November, 1827, the army transports from Boston found themselves ". . . in full view of the low coasts of South Carolina," [286] and anchored just under the lee of the walls of the old fortress, near the back channel, where they discharged Battery "H" of the First United States Artillery, bag and baggage, officers and men, among whom was Private Edgar A. Perry, *alias* Henri Le Rennét, *alias* Edgar Allan Poe, doing duty even then as a company clerk. [287] He must have been given quarters somewhere within the bastions of the old fort.

Style is very often the result of the impact of a new environment upon the unsuspected potentialities of artistic personality. "For the first and only time in his life, Poe now found himself in a sub-tropical environment," a district with a highly differentiated fauna and flora, utterly different from anything he had seen so far, either in Virginia or abroad. [288] In addition to this, the place was full of piratical and Revolutionary lore, the very island and the bay upon which he looked had been famous as the haunt of pirates. To the south and west, Fort Sumter, only then beginning to assume the formidable shape of brick and stone so familiar to the reading public of the '60's, looked across a narrow channel at its sister, Fort Moultrie, while a few miles up the harbor could be seen the pillared porches and spires of Charleston, a port which was alive then with ships from all over the world. [289]

Northward and eastward stretched away from the barracks windows the long, low beaches of Sullivan's Island some miles away to an inlet which separated it from the Isle of Palms where the prospect was re-

---

[286] From *The Balloon Hoax.*
[287] See the letter of Lieut. J. Howard given to Poe on his discharge, page 194.
[288] Prof. C. Alphonso Smith to the author, July 23, 1921, "The point you make seems to me a good one and so far as I know the matter has never been presented as you propose. So far as I know, this was the only really 'tropical' background that Poe had ever seen."
[289] At the time of Poe's service at Fort Moultrie, Charleston, South Carolina, was one of the great American ports, hundreds of ships clearing weekly.

peated.   The inlet could be breasted by a powerful swimmer like Poe
with a few vigorous strokes.   The young soldier had only to pass
through the portcullis to find himself upon a magnificent beach washed
by a summer sea, a firm strand that stretched for miles, with the Gulf
Stream on one side, and a low range of sand hills inland, covered with
scrub palmetto and myrtles, the home of strange birds, sand butter-
flies, amusing beetles, and the haunt of great sea-turtles that crawled
out by moonlight to lay their eggs.   Here and there, at long intervals,
was the hut of a lonely hunter or fisherman, far from the little summer
settlement then confined to the immediate vicinity of the fort.   The
one overpowering impression of the place is the continual bell-like breaking of the "sounding sea," the eye-puckering glare of the lime-white
sun, and the dirge of the wind through the myrtles, accompanied by a
faint, clacking sound like an overtone of eery applause caused by the
clapping together of the palms of the palmettos.

This island of sea-weathered monotonies, driven into Poe's consciousness by the long hours of an idle year, is the home of the Gold-
Bug.   At the beginning of the story he has described it himself.[290]

This island is a very singular one.   It consists of little else than the sea-sand,
and is about three miles long.   Its breadth at no point exceeds a quarter of a
mile.   It is separated from the mainland by a scarcely perceptible creek, oozing
its way through a wilderness of reeds and slime, a favorite resort of the marsh-
hen.   The vegetation, as might be supposed, is scant, or at least dwarfish.   No
trees of any magnitude are to be seen.   Near the western extremity, where Fort
Moultrie stands, and where are some miserable frame buildings, tenanted, during
summer, by the fugitives from Charleston dust and fever, may be found, indeed,
the bristly palmetto; but the whole island with the exception of this western
point, and a line of hard beach on the sea-coast, is covered with a dense under-
growth of the sweet myrtle so much prized by the horticulturists of England.[291]
The shrub here often attains the height of fifteen or twenty feet, and forms an
almost impenetrable coppice, burdening with its fragrance.

Such remote places, haunted by blue herons and other rare and shy
bird-life, are, even to-day, the retreats of eccentric characters who find
their compensation for loss of contact with their fellows in the observation of nature.   Amid the lonely scrub forests of Sullivan's Island
during the long hours of his rambles about the place, Poe seems to
have encountered such a person, for he says, "In the inmost recesses of
this coppice, not far from the eastern or more remote end of the island,
Legrand had built himself a small hut which he occupied when I first,
by mere accident, made his acquaintance."

---

[290] It must be borne in mind that Poe did not write *The Gold-Bug* until many years
later, 1842.   The beach at Sullivan's Island seems to have been "photographed" on
his retina.
[291] Poe is probably thinking of the Rev. "Dr." Bransby's garden at Stoke Newington, where he cherished exotic shrubs.   See Chapter V, page 69.

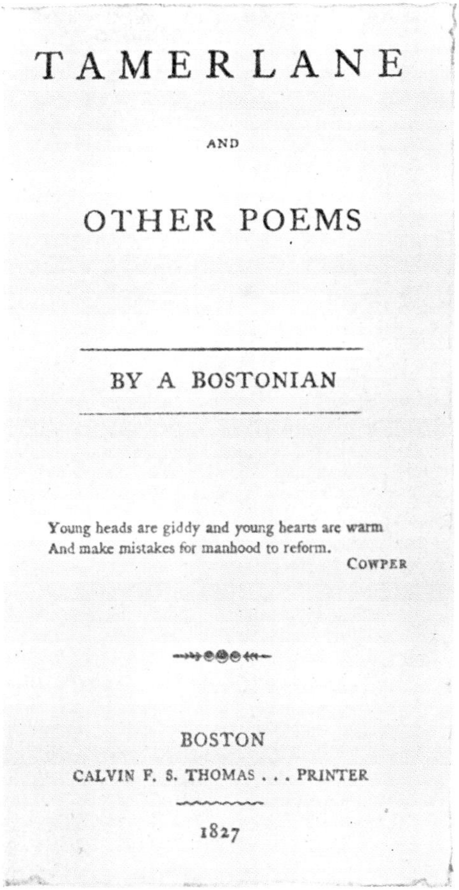

TAMERLANE

AND

OTHER POEMS

BY A BOSTONIAN

Young heads are giddy and young hearts are warm
And make mistakes for manhood to reform.

COWPER

BOSTON

CALVIN F. S. THOMAS . . . PRINTER

1827

Title Page of *Tamerlane and Other Poems*
Boston 1827
Edgar Allan Poe's first published volume

The Front and Back Wrappers of *Tamerlane and Other Poems*

Containing the advertisement by the printer of his trade and place of business. *Grace Poe Items*

Reproduction from photographs. Courtesy of John J. Snyder, Esq., of Pelham, N. Y.

TAMERLANE

AND

OTHER POEMS.

BY A BOSTONIAN.

Young heads are giddy, and young hearts are warm,
And make mistakes for manhood to reform.—COWPER.

BOSTON:
CALVIN F. S. THOMAS....PRINTER.

1827.

Printing.

CALVIN F. S. THOMAS

CONTINUES TO EXECUTE

BOOK & JOB PRINTING

IN ALL ITS BRANCHES.

INCLUDING

Books, Pamphlets, Catalogues, Cards,
Show Bills, &c. &c.

ON THE MOST REASONABLE TERMS

NO. 70,

WASHINGTON-STREET, BOSTON,

CORNER OF STATE STREET.

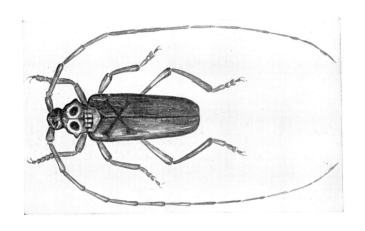

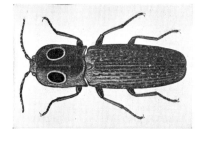

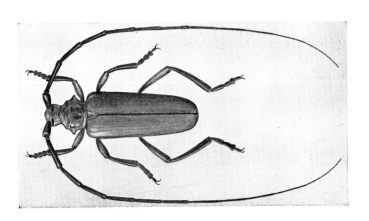

Poe's Gold Bug Synthesis

Suggested by Prof. Ellison Smyth, Jr.

what | scribed, and we again set to work with the | the nature of things, for any negro's visage to
is the | spades. I was dreadfully weary, but, scarcely | assume. He seemed stupified—thunderstricken.
let go | understanding what had occasioned the change | Presently he fell upon his knees in the pit, and,
| | burying his naked arms up to the elbows in gold

easy
it for

e for

iter's
h he
it the
be of
tting
l the
theus
owed
grand
with
ame-
com-
tring

o the
e lay,
t tape
point
st the
, and
alrea-
e and
upiter
ythe-
; was
circle,
aking
upiter
about
k the
muse-

F.O.C. DARLEY DEL.   GILBERT SC.

mo- | let them there remain, as if enjoying the luxury | gold of antique date and of great variety—
ed it; | of a bath. At length, with a deep sigh, he ex- | French, Spanish, and German money, with a
much | claimed, as if in a soliloquy, | few English guineas, and some counters of
| "And dis all cum ob de goole bug' de putty | which we had never seen specimens before.

at imme- | refer only to the position of the skull upon the | remove all participants in his secret. Perhaps
arrange- | tree, while 'shoot from the left eye of the | a couple of blows with a mattock were suffi-
| death's-head' admitted, also, of but one inter- | cient, while his coadjutors were busy in the pit;
e known, | pretation, in regard to a search for buried trea- | perhaps it required a dozen—who shall tell?"

n charac-
tute dots,

f evident
hree new
and 3.
he cipher
we find,
arrange-

the word
d, repre-
tree,' we

, and re-
fore, we

e of the
us with
ted by 6

; of the

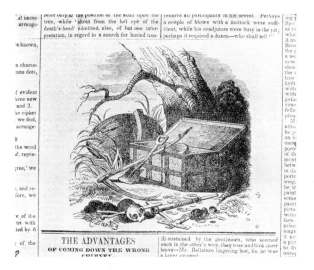

THE ADVANTAGES
OF COMING DOWN THE WRONG
CHIMNEY.

ill-sustained by the gentlemen, who seemed
each in the other's way, they rose and took their
leave—Mr. Bellaire lingering last, for he was
a lover avowed

Original illustrations for *The Gold Bug*

Published with the text for Poe's $100 prize story in The Philadelphia *Dollar
Newspaper* for Wednesday, June 28, 1843. The illustrations were by F. O. C.
DARLEY, the Philadelphia artist retained by POE to illustrate *The Stylus*,
which never appeared. Discovered by Prof. Killis Campbell.

From a file of the Dollar Newspaper
Courtesy of the Maryland Historical Society

That Poe had a generous amount of idle time on his hands while at Fort Moultrie there can be no doubt. He was a member of a coast-guard regiment at a remote and little inspected post during a long era of profound peace. There were not even any lawns to be cut, and the situation of the fort, cut off from the world by what was then a row or sail of several miles from Charleston, curtailed even the social ambitions of the officers, and prevented the garrison from being kept busy about the multifarious trivialities necessarily required of the soldier at a "smart post." The nearest hamlet was Mt. Pleasant, a community whose amusements were strictly confined to the raising of children and the delirious concerts of an orchestra of frogs. Leave in Charleston was the only relaxation of the garrison ("the facilities of passage and repassage," says Poe, "were far behind those of the present day!") To these pastimes, Poe seems to have added some conversation with the more cultivated of the officers, swimming, the study of the strange shapes of nature about him, the polishing of verses, excursions into the pages of Moore and Byron, and long hours of wandering along the sounding beaches and the "coppice" of Sullivan's Island.

The orders of the day governing the routine and discipline of the force at Fort Moultrie show that the garrison rose about five-thirty A. M., policed, breakfasted, and engaged in a short morning's infantry drill, varied from time to time by exercises at the great guns. The passage of time was punctuated by the sharp reports of the sunrise and sunset gun, the strains of the bugles at meal times and retreat, and by nothing more. Beyond this, there was little to do except to play Seven-up on a blanket, or roll dice. Even from these strenuous duties Poe seems to have absolved himself by assuming clerical work with the consequent familiarity and favor of his officers which it entailed. After a few hours of "paper work," we can imagine him "calling it a day," and going outdoors to roam the beaches. To this mode of life, the climate was conducive, and he says:

The winters in the latitude of Sullivan's Island are seldom very severe, and in the fall of the year it is a rare event indeed when a fire is considered necessary. About the middle of October 18—, there occurred, however, a day of remarkable chilliness. Just before sunset I scrambled my way through the evergreens to the hut of my friend, whom I had not visited for several weeks. . . . A fine fire was blazing upon the hearth. It was a novelty, and by no means an ungrateful one. I threw off an overcoat, took an armchair by the crackling logs, and awaited patiently the arrival of my host.

In such a scene as this *The Gold-Bug* begins.

There are several prime factors to the story: The first is the eccentric character of "Mr. William Legrand"; he was of an ancient Huguenot family. The next is "Jupiter," the negro servant, and the others are Poe himself, slightly disguised by the first person pronoun, a wonderful, golden, skull-marked beetle, the solution of a mysterious mathematical cipher, a buried pirate treasure, and the meticulous description of the locality. As an example of Poe's method of assembling material for his *more objective kind* of short story, it is the purpose here to suggest briefly the probable sources of *The Gold-Bug*.

The idea of buried treasure is one which would inevitably associate itself in Poe's mind with Sullivan's Island, which was from early colonial times the haunt of pirates. Stede Bonnet himself was captured by a Colonel Rhett of Charleston only a few miles north of Fort Moultrie, and the port itself was early blockaded and its citizens held for ransom by Black Beard. Poe gives his pirate the generic name of "Captain Kidd," who is supposed to have buried his fabled treasure on Long Island, New York. In Poe's day the Isle of Palms immediately north of Sullivan's Island was known as Long Island, and so appears on all old maps. That the suggestion of buried treasure was present, seems fairly clear. "Legrand," the principal figure in the story, although Poe himself is the real hero who *so* cleverly solves the cryptogram,[292] was probably suggested by the very prevalent Huguenot name of Legaré (pronounced Le Gree) among the many descendants of French settlers upon the Carolina "sea-islands." There was a minor poet of this name, which is also common in Louisiana. According to the story, "Legrand" hailed from New Orleans. Into the mouth of "Jupiter," the slave or valet, Poe puts the negro dialect of Virginia with which he was familiar, rather than the flat, quacking Gullah *patois* of the Carolina Low Country. "Jupiter" talks like a Richmond darkey. So much for the human elements. When we come to the gold-bug itself, "the queerest scarabæus in the world," there is a synthesis of material which is perhaps even more interesting and original.

POE'S GOLD-BUG SYNTHESIS

The genesis of Poe's "gold-bug" seems to have been beyond peradventure some of the beetles which he noticed on his rambles among the sand dunes of Sullivan's Island. A clever synthesis of several of these, together with the legends of pirates, the strange aspects of the lonely landscape, and his well-known flair for the solution of ciphers, give all the necessary factors for the plot. Our immediate concern is with the beetles. In the story, the descriptions are scattered; brought close together in connection with one another, their origin becomes startlingly plain.

To make his "gold-bug," Poe evidently superimposed one upon another several of the beetles common to the Island, taking the long

---

[292] Poe prided himself upon his ability to solve cryptograms—see Woodberry, 1909, vol. I, pages 303-304, and his own articles on the subject in *Alexander's Messenger*, Dec. 18, 1839, *Graham's*, July, 1841, etc. This was a later development and the cryptogram in the story belongs to the Philadelphia period of about 1842.

antennæ and the golden tint from one, and the skull markings and shape from another. These when assembled became the *Scarabœus Caput Hominis,* a bug never seen before or since upon sea or land. We can imagine him, upon some idle sunny day, the young soldier in the scarlet and blue uniform of the artillery, lying upon his stomach amid the sand dunes amusing himself with a piece of manuscript and the gyrations of some unfortunate beetle. The one of which "Jupiter" says, "I nebber did see sich a *deuced* bug—he kick and he bite eberyting what cum near him.[293] . . . I didn't like de look ob de bug mouff, myself, no how, so I wouldn't take hold ob him wid my finger, but I cotch him wid a piece ob paper . . . and stuff a piece of it in his mouff—dat was de way" [294]—and that is the way we can easily see several beetles going home to Fort Moultrie in the pockets of one Edgar Allan Poe, *alias* Perry, to be duly drawn upon paper that evening under the light of the glimmering barracks lantern by a semi-scientific young poet who combined imagination with observation and the use of the artistic pencil. Indeed, it is this very operation of drawing beetles in which we surprise "Legrand" at the opening of the story.

. . . he seated himself at a small table on which were a pen and ink, but no paper. He looked for some in a drawer, but found none. 'Never mind,' said he at length, 'this will answer'; and he drew from his waistcoat pocket a scrap of what I took to be very dirty foolscap, and made upon it a rough drawing with the pen. . . . When the design was complete, he handed it to me without rising. . . . 'Well!' I said, after contemplating it for some minutes, 'this *is* a strange *scarabœus,* I must confess; new to me: never saw anything like it before—unless it was a skull, or a death's-head, which it more nearly resembles than anything else that has come under my observation.' 'A death's-head!' echoed Legrand. 'Oh—yes—well, it has something of that appearance upon paper, no doubt. The two upper black spots look like eyes, eh? and the longer one at the bottom like a mouth—and then the shape of the whole is oval.' . . .

Elsewhere "Legrand" says of the bug, "It is a brilliant gold color— about the size of a large hickory nut, with two jet black spots near one extremity of the back, and another somewhat larger, at the other. . . ." The antennæ, we also learn, are long and accentuated, and the beetle had powerful jaws. With these descriptions in mind we can now proceed to see how Poe played with his beetles to the tune of a charming medley in fact and fancy, the theme of which was the gold-bug.

The reader is now asked to accompany an enthusiastic "bug-hunter" upon Sullivan's and Long Island, South Carolina, about one hundred years after Poe's historic visit, and to partake vicariously of the excitements of the chase. Some years ago, it appears, a noted entomol-

[293] In corrections in his own hand in the Century Association copy of *The Collected Works* once owned by Poe and Griswold, Poe has changed *deuced* to "d——d." See note 299.

[294] The quotations are, of course, from *The Gold-Bug.*

ogist,[295] armed with the classic butterfly net of science, crossed over from Sullivan's Island to Long Island to collect insects. While he was forcing his way through a dense thicket, a large beetle lit on the end of the dagger leaf of a bristling Spanish bayonet. The insect was new to him and most beautiful,—nothing like it, he thought, was to be found out of the tropics. It was gleaming with fiery gold, soft satiny green, and dull old-gold—the antennæ nearly three inches long extended in front of the insect as it stood *at attention*.[296]

In his excitement, the scientific gentleman missed it with his net, but some years later when visiting the same locality he managed to snare several by the pleasant and magic formula of anointing tree trunks in daytime with an alluring mixture of stale beer, rum, and brown sugar. Their fondness for sap, it seems, suggested his "sugaring for them" as moth collectors do. A specimen of the beetle itself, it appears, must be closely examined if its beauty is to be fully appreciated. A large specimen is about an inch and a half long and about half an inch wide; they have black antennæ that sometimes measure over two inches in length, while the head and prominent prothorax are glittering with fiery gold sometimes shot with iridescent green. The fore-wings are satiny green and, when opened, discover the full-gold of the abdomen beneath, so that old "Jupiter's" description of, "Solid goole inside and all sep hum wing," fixes it as Poe's very "gold-bug," indeed.

But how about the skull markings? These, it appears, we do not have to go far to seek, as they are also forthcoming from a beetle very common to the locality of Fort Moultrie. Mr. Smyth, for such was the scientific gentleman's name, upon this same "sugaring expedition" was so fortunate as to capture upon the same tree, side by side with the golden *Callichroma,* one of the common big "Click Beetles" of the vicinity, which is known to bug men as *Alaus Oculatus* and to small boys as "The Jumping Jack." It is about the same size as the gold-beetle (*Callichroma*), but flatter and more oval. It has a background of black, thickly spotted with white, and its very large prothorax is provided with two oval, eye-like black spots edged with white that give it a decidedly piratical and skull-like appearance.[297]

---

[295] Ellison A. Smyth, Jr.—the author is frankly indebted to Prof. Smyth of the Virginia Polytechnic Institute for the description of the capture of the beetles, and for the idea which they suggested to him which are taken from his article in the *Sewanee Review.* for January 1, 1910, *Poe's Gold-Bug from the Standpoint of an Entomologist.* The text of the article was supplied the author by the Charleston Museum, Charleston, South Carolina, together with specimens of the beetles described, captured on Sullivan's Island.

[296] "At attention"—with antennæ pointing. This is the position which suggested to Poe his idea for using the beetle as a "treasure pointer."

[297] The drawings of these insects have been made for the author (from specimens captured on Sullivan's Island within a few miles of Fort Moultrie) by Miss Elena von Feld of the American Museum of Natural History, New York City; specimens furnished by Miss Laura M. Bragg, Director of the Charleston Museum.

Mr. Smyth was then visited, he said, by a "scientific revelation," and a moment of literary insight, in which he saw that Poe's gold-bug was a composite, and that by placing *Alaus Oculatus, I,* the "skull-bug," on *Callichroma, II,* the gold-bug, he had what the printer has so obligingly done for us here, Edgar Allan Poe's clever little synthesis, or "*Scarabœus Caput Hominis,*" Poe's gold-bug.[298]

The description of the beetle which "Legrand" finally places in the hand of Poe is now complete:

It was a beautiful *scarabœus,* and, at that time, . . . unknown to naturalists—of course a great prize in a scientific point of view. There were two round black spots near one extremity of the back and a long one near the other. The scales were exceedingly hard and glossy, with all the appearance of burnished gold. The weight of the insect was very remarkable. . . .

The weight was necessary if the insect was to be used as a plummet and a divining rod, as it was used in the story. The black marks at the rear making cross-bones can, of course, be left to Poe's imagination, but it is all very typical of the young Poe, of his imaginative fancy, his preoccupation with semi-scientific observation, and his love of a good hoax.

There are many elements in *The Gold-Bug,* indeed, which indicate Poe's insatiable curiosity, his live interest in many things. The long antennæ of the beetle, which when lowered through the eye of the skull, point to the treasure, imply a knowledge of the old legends of the divining rod. There is also an understood element of sympathetic magic, for the golden bug is attracted by the golden treasure,—like attracts like—and there is, last of all, the delightful poetic fancy that the very soil of the island, where pirates have buried their doubloons and jewels, bred an insect that partakes of the nature of the golden treasure and the fearsome markings of the "Jolly-Roger" itself.

Indeed, confirmation of this association of the ideas in the story with the pirate flag is unexpectedly forthcoming from the pen of Poe himself. In an 1845 edition of *The Raven and Tales* which he corrected for himself, Poe has inserted these paragraphs in his own hand with the evident intention of including them in a reprint of the text. These changes appear to have been overlooked or disregarded by Griswold, Poe's editor, and they should now be added to all texts of *The Gold-Bug* which is otherwise incomplete. The paragraphs show the hero of the story and "Legrand" talking—[299]

---

[298] Arrangement for the synthesis of *Callichroma* and *Alaus Oculatus* designed by Theodore Spicer-Simson, Esq. to conform with Poe's own description in *The Gold-Bug.*

[299] These paragraphs added by Poe himself, are inserted in the present text of *The Gold-Bug* immediately *before* the paragraph beginning, "but your grand eloquence . . ." etc., and are taken from Poe's own copy of *The Raven and Other Poems* by Edgar A. Poe, New York, Wiley and Putnam, 161 Broadway, 1845. 12 mo.

(*Hero*) I presume the fancy of the skull—and of letting fall a beetle through the skull's eye—was suggested to Kidd by the piratical flag. No doubt he felt a kind of poetical consistency in recovering his money through his *ominus insignium.*

(*Legrand*) Perhaps, still I cannot help thinking that common-sense had quite as much to do with the matter as poetical consistency. To be visible from the Devil's seat, it was necessary that the object, if small, should be *white;* and there is nothing like your human skull for retaining and even increasing its whiteness under exposure to all vicissitudes of weather.

In this bit of dialogue, the double attitude of "poetical consistency" and "common-sense," which Poe constantly employed in his stories, is nicely stressed and the effect of pirate legends upon the plot definitely confirmed.

For the rest, the remaining elements of the story are part and parcel of romance. In the "high rugged country behind Sullivan's Island," Poe introduces some of the scenery of the Ragged Mountains into South Carolina, for the country back of the sea-islands is in reality excessively low and flat.[300] The tree, however, is true to life. In the huge tulip trees and live oaks of the district,[301] covered with the funereal plumes of Spanish moss waving eerily like the canopy of a catafalque, who better than the young Poe could see something charnel-like, or provide a grinning skull among the gloomy labyrinth of branches? Nor is the size of the tree exaggerated. There are many near Fort Moultrie, a little way inland, even more gigantic and incredible than the one introduced in the story itself. The two guardian skeletons buried with the treasure are part of pirate lore. Stevenson uses the same device in *Treasure Island,* and such, in reality, seems to have been the gruesome custom of the buccaneers. But nothing can exceed the skill with which every item of fact and fancy is combined in the story to lead the reader on and up to the climax of the finding of the treasure when "Jupiter" is digging under the great tree by the glimmer of a lantern, and the dog—

---

and *Tales,* by Edgar A. Poe, New York, Wiley and Putnam, 1845. 12 mo. "The above two works are bound together, the first precedes." This was Poe's own copy, with many manuscripts, marginal corrections and additions, evidently intended as the basis for a new edition, afterward the property of R. W. Griswold, Poe's editor, with his autograph on a fly leaf. It was bequeathed by J. L. Graham to the Century Association of New York. Quotations here by the courtesy of the Librarian of the Century Association.

[300] Prof. Basil L. Gildersleeve in writing Prof. Harrison says . . . "I am old enough to remember what an excitement his *Gold-Bug* created in Charleston when it first appeared, and how severely we boys criticised the inaccuracies in the description of Sullivan's Island." Harrison's *Life and Letters of E. A. Poe,* vol. I, page 315. Prof. Gildersleeve knew the failings of his home town. Even Poe could not improve on scenery that was "already perfect."

[301] On Fairfield Plantation on the Santee, some miles from Sullivan's Island, there is a live oak which requires thirteen persons to span it. Many other large trees abound.

leaping into the hole, tore up the mould frantically with his claws. In a few seconds he had uncovered a mass of human bones, forming two complete skeletons, intermingled with several buttons of metal, and what appeared to be the dust of decayed woolen. One or two strokes of a spade upturned the blade of a large Spanish knife, and, as we dug further, three or four pieces of gold and silver coins came to light . . . , (then the iron bound box, with its heavy lid and two sliding bolts!) These we drew back trembling and panting with anxiety. In an instant a treasure of incalculable value lay gleaming before us. As the rays of the lanterns fell flashing within the pit, there flashed upward a glow and a glare, from a confused heap of gold and of jewels, that absolutely dazzled one's eyes.

In other stories and poems there are to be found distinct traces of his visits to Charleston and the hinterland. The house of Usher, itself, may well be some old, crumbling, and cracked-walled colonial mansion found moldering in the Carolina woods, as it was left desolate by the hands of the marauding British, surrounded by its swamps and gloomy woods, its cypress-stained tarns, and its snake-haunted Indian moats. To see these, is instantly to be reminded of descriptions by Poe. The whole country about, in fact, was one peculiarly in sympathy with his more lonely and melancholy moods. The vault described at the end of *The Sleeper,* a poem written in its first form about 1831, recalls almost literally some of the great family tombs on the plantations about Charleston, with the semi-feudal pomp that surrounds them.[302] And Poe saw this country, it must be remembered, before the devastations of war had laid low the glories of its old royal grants and baronies. As a disinherited son he must have envied, and as a Virginian sympathized with, its prodigally-generous plantation life.

The young soldier seems to have risen rapidly in the estimate of his officers. Doubtless his gentlemanly manners and appearance soon recommended him. With this and his education, he would, indeed, have stood out in sharp contrast to the average regular army recruit of the period. His attention to duty was strict and evidently satisfactory, for on May 1, 1828, we find him being appointed "artificer," [303] a title which does not necessarily carry any mechanical duties with it, but is merely the first rung in promotions carrying higher pay and leading to the higher non-commissioned grades. He had already served as company clerk and assistant in the commissariat department, and was evidently about headquarters where he attracted attention and gave satisfaction. The Colonel himself must have had his eye on him, for his rise through all the non-commissioned grades seems to have taken place between May and December, 1828, and on January 1, 1829, he was appointed regimental sergeant major at Fortress Monroe, Virginia. Naturally enough, with added responsibility went the compensation

---

[302] Typical of these is the family tomb at Middleton Gardens near Charleston.
[303] One biographer is somewhat confused by Poe's being appointed an "artificer."

of greater personal freedom. Poe would have had little difficulty in obtaining considerable leave, and there is evidence that he spent part of it in visits to the nearby city of Charleston. Here was a city with whose quaint streets and high-walled gardens he must have had considerable contact. The wanderings of a young soldier upon leave are not always without romance, and the unique and foreign aspect of the place could not have been lost upon him. Perhaps he knew that he had been there before, as a child in arms, with his even-then dying mother, in 1811, [304] and so sat through some play given upon the stage of the theater where she had trod the boards in *The Wonder* seventeen years before. Mr. Placide, the manager of Mrs. Poe's company, had been succeeded in Charleston by his son, and it is by no means impossible that Poe, who was on the hunt for information about his parents, may have looked him up.

At any rate, certain passages in *The Oblong Box* show that he was familiar with the departure of the Charleston sailing packets and the life along the docks, and he may have visited the "Old State House" (the rooms of the Charleston Library Society were located in the same building) and turned over some of the colonial records in the Probate Court relating to pirates and shipwreck, material which seems to have affected *The Gold-Bug*. [305]

For the rest, oblivion has it in its quiet keeping. The officers of Poe's regiment died before they could be questioned as to the details of his life at Charleston, and almost nothing but the official records are left. Here is a whole year whose social and whose human contacts are nearly blank. Of its dreams we know more, for *Al Aaraaf* is the monument.

This is the longest poem that Poe wrote. Its story-plot and general architecture are negligible, although the conception is poetic. Into it the young poet poured, during the lonely hours at Fort Moultrie, a wealth of imagination, lovely sound, and airy fancy that entitle the work, for such it is, to a higher consideration than it has ever received. It has inspired other young poets to first take flight, and it remained for years a poetical bank upon which he continued to draw. Despite its frequent echoes, no one in America up to that time had ever written so many magic lines. Poe's dreams of the region between earth and paradise, however, were rudely interrupted by the place from which interruptions so often come—home.[306]

---

[304] This is doubtful, however, as Poe knew almost nothing about his family until he lived among his relatives in Baltimore in 1829. See his mistake in regard to being Benedict Arnold's grandson, Chapter XII, page 201.

[305] In 1745, the ship "Cid Campeador," commanded by one Julian de Vega, was wrecked off the coast of South Carolina. Some of the affidavits preserved in the *Probate Court Records* at Charleston when compared with *The Gold-Bug* suggest that Poe may have seen them (*sic*).

[306] See note 350, Chapter XII, referring to *Al Aaraaf*.

His hardship after leaving the house of John Allan, and the opportunity for considerable contemplation which the stay at Fort Moultrie afforded, seems to have confirmed Poe in his ambitions for a literary career.   He felt, he says, that the prime of his life was passing, yet three years of his five year term of enlistment remained to be served, with no prospects but barracks life beyond that. Sometime during the close of the year 1828 [307] he seems to have got into communication with his foster-father, either by letter or through the good offices of friends, and expressed a desire to obtain his guardian's help in leaving the army.   Mr. Allan's permission, it seems, was required, for Poe's company commander, Lieutenant J. Howard, had become much interested in the brilliant young soldier and had promised to discharge him, if a reconciliation between John Allan and Poe could be confirmed. The communications between Richmond and Fort Moultrie were made through the medium of a Mr. John O. Lay who seems to have been a friend of the Allan family.[308]

Although aware now of the whereabouts of his foster-son, John Allan did not write him directly, but wrote Mr. Lay that he thought a military life was a good one for Poe, and evidently indicated that he was quite content to allow him to remain where he was.   Nothing is more indicative of John Allan's utter coldness of heart than this.   The letter was inclosed by Mr. Lay to Lieutenant Howard, and must have brought a sinking sense of disappointment to the homesick and ambitious young soldier.   For the time being, his hopes were dashed to the ground and doubt cast upon all his statements to Lieutenant Howard.

With resumption of intercourse between "father" and "son," a new factor begins to creep into John Allan's attitude to "the son of actors" —snobbishness.   After inheriting his uncle's ample fortune, the older man developed social aspirations in conformity with the large mansion in Richmond, and these, it would appear, he felt were somewhat threatened by the fact that his "son" had enlisted as a private soldier. The descendant of Scotch smugglers, to judge from expressions in the correspondence which took place, felt that to have Poe return in the uniform of anything less than an officer would be to have entailed upon him a portion of Poe's "infamy"; nevertheless, he feels a military career is the thing for Poe.   "He had better remain where he is until the end of his enlistment."

In a letter written by Poe to John Allan from Fort Moultrie on December 1, 1828, Poe protests against this, tells of his concern at learning that John Allan had been ill, and speaks with pardonable pride of

---

[307] The facts related here which conflict with certain "standard" biographies come from the new published letters of the Valentine Museum, Richmond. See particularly letter 6, page 75.

[308] Some authorities say, "a relative of Mrs. Allan."

his own satisfaction at his rapid promotion. He stresses his determination to leave the army unless absolutely forbidden to do so by his "father," and states that army regulations do not permit of promotion from the ranks, and that his age precludes West Point. It is now that the first mention of West Point occurs.

This letter shows Poe's character to have considerably hardened during his army career. His promotions seem to have given him self-confidence and poise, and he says that he is no longer a wayward boy but a man with a work to do in the world. His future greatness he successfully predicts, for "he feels that within him" which will make him fulfill John Allan's wishes, and he excuses his self-confidence by saying that conviction of success is the only thing that can make ambitions and talent prosper. "I have thrown myself on the world like the Norman conqueror on the shores of Britain and, by my avowed assurance of victory, have destroyed the fleet which could alone cover my retreat—I must either conquer or die—succeed or be disgraced." Poe makes plain that he is not asking for money—a letter to Lieutenant Howard assuring that officer of the reconciliation that would procure his release is all he asks—and—"my dearest love to Ma—it is only when absent that we can tell the value of such a friend"—yours respectfully and affectionately.

This cry from the high heart of ambitious and fiery youth in the agony of frustration and the prison-house of military barracks received as a reply a complete silence. In the arctic labyrinth of John Allan's brain it was locked away as utterly and securely as some pathetic secret in a vault of cold marble.

One ponders wearily such facts, startled by the amazing possibilities of human nature, wondering a little about the wet eyes of the fragile, failing wife in the great house at Richmond, of what her husband thought when he found his prediction about the boy's starving in the streets had not been fulfilled—not completely, that is—whether he was glad or sorry, annoyed or simply surprised. Was there not some sorrow and yearning left in the man—or was he, after all, this strong prophet of lean years, who saw to it that his predictions were fulfilled—disappointed? Who knows—even Fate must have been astonished—John Allan had raised a poet!

In the meantime, Edgar Poe had sailed northward.[309] On December the first, he writes that his regiment was under orders to sail for Old Point Comfort. The low coasts of Carolina faded away forever under

[309] *Charleston Courier* and *Charleston Gazette* for December 3, 1828: "*In the offing:* The ship *Harriet,* (of Bath) Johnson from Baltimore, *via* Norfolk, with two companies of U. S. Troops for [relief of] the Garrison in the Harbor, anchored below yesterday." Notices from the same papers for December 5 and 12, 1828, show that the "Harriet" remained in harbor a week and on December 11, 1828, left for Norfolk. *Charleston Gazette* for December 22, 1828, notes from a

the eyes of "Edgar A. Perry," First United States Artillery; the ship "Harriet" sailed up the coast with the warm current of the Gulf Stream; the hours passed calmly while the men played cards in their bunks under the light of whale-oil lanterns. Fortress Monroe drew swiftly nearer. Certainly a letter would be there to release him from all this! Only a few lines would do the trick—would save three years of youth from being wasted. Even "Pa" would not fail him there. What had he done anyway to be thought so "degraded"? Played cards for money and read novels, drunk a little heady peach-and-honey, insisted upon being a poet. For that he had done penance in uniform and barracks for two long, lost years. Surely that was enough! It was getting near Christmas time. Perhaps, they would let him come home? *Home!* —he could anticipate old black "Dab" crying out over him as he opened the big door; "Ma" coming weakly down the steps half blind with joy, "Aunt Nancy's" hearty rapture, even John Allan's amused ironical smile and, "Weel, weel, my ain proud cockerel, fluttered back, eh!" Then the glow of the agate lamp in his own quiet room and the books. . . . The ship, with its burden of artillery, lurched another wave-length northward. To Israfel it seemed to be making no perceptible progress. He was already a little, just a little weary of another voyage which was now half over. Within a few weeks of reaching Fortress Monroe he was twenty years old. *Tamerlane* had probably been destroyed in Boston, almost the whole edition. There had not been even a flash in the pan.

"correspondent": "Norfolk, December 15: The ship *Harriet,* Johnson, fm [*sic*] *Charleston,* with two companies U. S. Artillery, anchored off Old Point this afternoon." See *Poe in Charleston, S. C.,* by William Stanley Hoole, Duke University, *American Literature,* March, 1934, pages 78-80.

CHAPTER TWELVE

COLD MARBLE

POE'S regiment would have been completely disembarked and in quarters at Fortress Monroe, Virginia, about the middle of December, 1828.[309] By the transfer from Fort Moultrie, only the scene of his monotony had been shifted. Old Point Comfort at that time was scarcely a village. What little gaiety it offered centered largely about a hotel where the officers occasionally held dances, sometimes attended by ladies from Washington, Baltimore, or Richmond. For the enlisted men, the fort, cut off by water as it was, could have offered almost nothing, beyond the squabbles of the married quarters, to relieve the tedium of artillery practice and guard duty. Poe seems to have made friends with the non-commissioned officers of his old company; he specifically mentions Sergeants Benton, Griffith, and Hooper in a letter written later to Sergeant Graves, more familiarly known as "Bully," whose wife, and one "Duke" are also included in his salutations.[310] Occasional leave to Norfolk, nearby, was probably the most abandoned form of entertainment known to the post.

It is no wonder, then, that the young soldier with *Al Aaraaf* in his pocket, and *Tamerlane* completely revised and ready for print, under the urge of literary ambition, became impatient and felt that the prime of his life was being wasted. Three more years of military office routine would be fatal. He had already written Mr. Allan from Fort Moultrie that it was now high time that he should leave the army. To find no letter awaiting him at Fortress Monroe filled him with a growing despair as day after day slipped by and the silence in Richmond continued. A week or so after arriving at Fortress Monroe, Poe again wrote his guardian expressing his sorrow at not hearing from him, and his fixed determination to leave the service.[311]

This letter is remarkable. It shows how thoroughly Poe's personality had become integrated by his army experience, and throws a vivid emphasis upon his literary aspirations. Despite the fact, says Poe, that his ambition has not taken the direction which his guardian desired, he is determined to follow his own bent. Richmond and the United

---

[310] Poe to Sergeant Samuel Graves from Richmond, May 3, 1830, *Valentine Museum Poe Letters,* No. 21.

[311] Poe to John Allan from Fortress Monroe, December 22, 1828, *Valentine Museum Poe Letters,* No. 27. Poe indicates in this letter that unless he receives help, he contemplates going abroad, probably to London (*sic*).

States are all too narrow a sphere for him, and the world will be his theater. As for the army, he wishes to be gone. The undoubted conviction of genius rests heavily upon him. The letter is one of the most prophetic. In it he emphatically, but with great dignity, denies the imputation that he is degraded. *I have in my heart what has no connection with degradation and can walk amidst infection and be uncontaminated,* is a close paraphase of his words. How heavily the sights and sounds of barracks life, the crassness, the coarseness, the association with those who were personally repulsive, together with the utter lack of all touch with the subleties of another world in which he lived—how heavily these weighed upon him, leaps forth at us from the fevered writing on the yellowed page. If John Allan is determined to abandon him, Poe warns him, although neglected, he will be doubly ambitious, and the world will undoubtedly hear of the son whom the older man thought beneath his notice. With this letter the relations of "father" and "son" begin to enter upon their final phase.

Lieutenant Howard, Poe tells us, had already introduced him to Colonel James House who had known "General" David Poe, the poet's grandfather. The Colonel and the other officers all feel that Poe might be got into West Point, despite his age, if John Allan will only aid him . . . etc., etc., but to this there was no reply. John Allan was probably too much absorbed in the important affairs of the world of reality to be moved by the prayers of a "son" whose avowed ambition was to be a poet. Whether he conveyed Poe's oft-repeated messages of affection to his "dear Ma" is not known. At least he paid no attention to her constant appeals to be allowed to see her "dear boy," now only a few miles away from Richmond. And this plea was refused with a more than Spartan fortitude on the part of her husband, for Frances Allan was dying. In the big house at Richmond, the long physical and spiritual agony of the childless woman was about to receive its final anodyne. Worry over her mortal illness might be accepted as a sufficient reason for John Allan's disregard of his troublesome "son," if it was not definitely known that it was the constant prayer of his fast sinking wife that she might be allowed to see "Eddie" [312] before she died.

Shortly after Poe's arrival at Fortress Monroe, his own assertions as to the good opinion in which he was held by his officers were confirmed by his promotion to the highest rank which an enlisted man can attain, short of a commission. We have already seen that Lieutenant

[312] Testimony of James Galt which Mr. J. H. Whitty prints in his *Memoir:* This is to the effect that Mrs. Allan's dying desire was to hold Poe in her arms before she died. In case she passed away before Edgar arrived home, she asked not to be buried until her foster-son should see her. The Galts, it will be remembered, were cousins of John Allan.

Howard had introduced the young soldier to the Colonel of the Regiment. This, and the fact that he had long been employed upon military clerical work by his other officers, apparently to their complete satisfaction, probably procured his final promotion. A few days after disembarking at Old Point Comfort, probably about December 20, 1828, Poe was detailed to Regimental Headquarters.

"Private Perry's" performance of duty at regimental headquarters was evidently eminently satisfactory, for ten days later, on January 1, 1829, he was appointed regimental sergeant major and is so carried on the morning report of the day following.

Poe's appointment to be regimental sergeant major is undoubtedly a compliment to his trustworthiness and executive ability. The entire correspondence of a command passes through the hands of that noncommissioned officer. He is often in a position to cause serious trouble even for commissioned officers, and must perforce possess the confidence and trust of the regimental staff. The regiment, of which Poe was the senior enlisted member at Fortress Monroe in January, 1829, was a composite one, being composed of companies detailed from various commands to make up an "artillery practice school," a use to which the old fort has frequently been put. Among the officers present at that time was one Lieutenant Joseph Locke with whom Poe came in touch, not altogether affably, later on at West Point. The fact that he had reached the top of the ladder as a private soldier, with peculiar opportunities to learn the mystery of artillery, undoubtedly helped him greatly in obtaining letters to the War Department.

Sometime during January, 1829, Poe was ill in the military hospital at Fortress Monroe where he was attended by the Post Surgeon, a Dr. Robert Archer, with close relatives in Richmond.[313] The young soldier seems to have been prostrated by some sort of fever. No doubt his uneasiness and anxiety were a contributing cause. Dr. Archer was greatly attracted by the brilliant young soldier whose manners were so evidently those of a gentleman. After some little time, Poe confessed to the surgeon, who seemed to be his friend, that he was the "son" of John Allan of Richmond and serving in the army under an *alias*. Dr. Archer, who must have known Poe's story through his Richmond connections, interested himself in the young man's behalf. It may have

---

[313] Dr. Archer was an uncle of Mrs. Susan Archer Weiss, one of Poe's minor biographers. Under the circumstances of this close relationship I have followed *her* account of Poe's contact with this army surgeon which is somewhat more complete and convincing, in this particular, than Prof. Woodberry's. It is now certain, from letters unknown to either Prof. Woodberry or Mrs. Weiss, that Dr. Archer did *not* suggest to Poe the West Point scheme which he (Poe) had already conceived at Fort Moultrie some months before. Dr. Archer was appointed to the United States Medical Corps, August 5, 1826, and stationed at Fortress Monroe. *National Calendar,* vol. IV, page 158.

been in this way that Frances Allan first heard that her foster-son was at Fortress Monroe.

By this time Poe was thoroughly aware of the fact that his guardian would not help him to a discharge, with a literary career in view. The West Point idea seems to have been the only form of compromise, so letters were again written to John Allan suggesting aid in procuring a substitute, and his influence for a cadet's appointment. Dr. Archer enlisted the aid and aroused the interest of the officers. What, if anything, was Mr. Allan's reply is not known. The first direct message from Richmond which Poe received from his guardian was a summons to the death-bed of "mother."

Frances Allan's frantic requests had at last prevailed. Realizing that she was indeed in her last agony, even the cold marble seems to have been touched, but it was too late. On Saturday, February 28, 1829, Sergeant Major "Edgar A. Perry" is carried as present on the muster roll of his regiment, and on the same day, a few miles away in Richmond, Mrs. Allan died.[314] Knowing full well the mettle of the man with whom she was having her last dealings, with her dying breath she extorted from him a solemn promise that he would not abandon Poe.[315] It was her last wish that she might not be buried until he saw her. It is impossible to contemplate this gentle woman, waiting in vain for the beloved and eagerly expected footstep of her "dear boy," while the darkness closed in upon her; or the stern heart that sat beside her, only melting at the last, without a solemn wonder at the different capabilities of human nature. With her had departed the sweetest and truest friend that a certain poet ever knew. "If only *she* hadn't died," said Poe afterward.

On the afternoon of Sunday, March 1, 1829, by far the most conspicuous passenger on the Norfolk stage bound for Richmond must have been a young sergeant major in the uniform of the First Artillery, with a hospital pallor under his sunburn, and obviously nervous and excited by every delay. Frances Allan had died on the morning of the twenty-eighth of February, she must have been sinking for two days before, yet it was only at the last that she had prevailed on her husband to send for Poe. Some hours would have been consumed in getting a leave granted, if the message was received the next day, and Poe could

---

[314] *Richmond Whig*, Monday, March 2, 1829. "Died on Saturday morning last, after a lingering and painful illness, Mrs. Frances K. Allan, consort of Mr. John Allan, aged 47 [*sic*] years. The friends and acquaintances of the family are respectfully invited to attend the funeral from the late residence on this day at 12 o'clock." Clipping by courtesy of Edward V. Valentine, Esq.

[315] Mrs. Allan had a small income of her own from certain parcels of real estate which, it appears from transactions of assignment in 1822, were held in her name. It may be that she suggested to her husband that some of the proceeds from this property might be devoted to Poe. There is no direct evidence that she did so, however.

hardly have started till the afternoon of March 1st.[316]   While he was engaged in making the journey between Fortress Monroe and Richmond, Mrs. Allan was being buried.   Perhaps there were good reasons for this; in any event, her last request was not carried out.

The return of a young soldier to his home town after an absence of two years cannot fail to awaken in him a flood of memories.   One can imagine Poe's impatience at the stages where the negro horse boys slowly unhitched and hitched the relays of horses, and the thousand recollections that thronged upon him as, towards the close of a gloomy March evening,[317] the conveyance rattled, all too slowly, into the dimly lit streets of Richmond.   Once arrived, he must have dashed up Main Street to the corner of Fifth, through the gate leading into the circular drive before the familiar house, and run with all his might up the steps.   The crape was not there, perhaps he was not too late after all?   A hundred things that he had been saving up to say to his "mother" for the past two years crowded to his lips.   The door swung open, and in a few instants he knew that it was all over.

The scene of Poe's tragic home-coming was said to have been so harrowing as to be unbearable to those who witnessed it.   Frances Allan had been greatly loved by her whole household, the demonstrative negro servants were in tears.   Miss Valentine, inconsolable and worn out by her long vigil by the bedside, could not have met Poe with much fortitude.   Even John Allan was profoundly moved; he stayed away from the office next day, and he was so agitated as to misdate a document.   Be it set down to his credit that it was an order for some mourning clothes for Poe.[318]   The dying whispers of his wife not to forget "her dear boy Edgar" were too near a thing for him to disregard utterly, and a flood of old tender memories of the dead woman in front of the fire, with the boy upon her knee, many and many an evening, must have revived in him some of the old affection.

Soon after his return, probably the next day, Poe visited Shockoe

---

[316] In his letter to John Allan from Fortress Monroe of March 10, 1829, Poe showed that the journey from Richmond to Norfolk took a day and a night.   As he arrived home "the evening after the funeral," March 2nd, he must have left Old Point Comfort sometime the day before, probably on the afternoon stage unless he went by water.   The latter method was slower, and therefore probably not employed in this race with death.

[317] It must be remembered that in Poe's day the term "evening" meant any time after three o'clock P. M. until darkness.   In some parts of the South the word is still used that way by the older generation.

[318] *Ellis & Allan Papers*—"Mr. Ellis, please to furnish Edgar A. Poe with a suit of clothes, 3 pairs of socks or thread hose.   McCrery will make them.   Also a pair of suspenders, and hat and knife, pair of gloves."   This is in the handwriting of John Allan, but dated March 3, *1828*, probably due to Mr. Allan's troubled state of mind at his wife's death, as the slip belongs in the records of 1829.   Poe was not in Richmond in 1828.

Cemetery where Mrs. Allan had been buried. The empty room had been bad enough; close to the actual presence of death in the graveyard, now for the second time, Poe must have sounded the last fathom of despair. The future author of *The Conqueror Worm* and the philosophy of *Eureka* could not have been, even at that time, under any comforting illusions about the hereafter of death. On the way to the new grave they passed the tomb of Mrs. Stanard, just to the left of the road, a combination of sorrow that in Poe's state must have been well-nigh unbearable. It seems to have been so, for he is said to have cast himself down exhausted by the last resting place of Frances Allan. The servants remembered helping him into the carriage which bore him away.

Perhaps it may have occurred to his "strong-minded guardian," while his wife was being buried and his "son's" heart had almost stopped beating at her grave, that there were a good many things in heaven and *earth* that had hitherto not been thought of in his philosophy. The wife, who had, at least, been allowed to share his bosom, later received a "fitting marble monument." Even in that, however, she was not alone. For the time being, though, John Allan was shaken. It was some weeks before another piece of marble that had originally been quarried in Scotland resumed its normal mean temperature.

Of the details of this Richmond visit in the Winter of 1829 not very much is known. Poe probably saw most of his old friends who were not away at the University. The Galts seem also to have been most kind, and the young sergeant major undoubtedly visited his sister Rosalie at the Mackenzies'. Probably the most important of his visits was at the Roysters'. Poe is said to have called upon the parents of his sweetheart and to have created a scene when he learned that during his absence Elmira had been married to Mr. Shelton. This was contrary to the assurances he had received from them upon his return from the University in 1827.[319] The young poet undoubtedly felt that both he and Elmira had been tricked, and every advantage taken of his absence to influence her. He is said to have reproached Mr. and Mrs. Royster bitterly, and to have demanded an interview with Elmira. This, of course, was refused, and Mr. Shelton was warned. It appears that one of Poe's letters to Elmira from the University had fallen into her hands after her marriage, and that as a consequence she had made things unpleasant for her husband and parents. The marriage was a fact, however; Poe had lost his "Lenore," and this grief was added to his already overwhelming sorrow over the death of Mrs. Allan. From later devel-

[319] The Roysters had talked to Poe after his return from the University and it had been agreed to defer the marriage for a year. At any rate, Elmira then married Mr. Shelton while Poe was away and *not* just before his return from the University, as several biographers aver.

opments, it is known that he was by no means satisfied as to the state of Elmira's feelings, and there can be no doubt that he cherished her memory, was haunted by dreams of her as long as he lived, and felt determined to have an interview at the first opportunity. This, however, did not occur while he was in Richmond in 1829. No doubt there were precautions taken to prevent it.

Poe's leave of absence was the usual ten-day furlough granted for such emergencies in the army. During the few days that he was in Richmond, the West Point scheme was talked over with John Allan, who was probably willing to listen to it because it seemed to offer a final solution as to his ward's future and definitely removed him from the household.[320] A complete reconciliation was impossible under the circumstances, but a more amicable feeling undoubtedly existed between them when Poe left for Fortress Monroe, than had been the case for a long time.

The young soldier left Richmond early on the morning of the ninth of March, 1829. He went to his "father's" room to bid him good-bye, but finding him asleep, he did not awaken him to the consciousness of grief. Immediately on arriving at Old Point Comfort, on the morning of the tenth, he wrote back home.[321] He says he is well, and there is a note of joy in the letter at the reconciliation with his guardian, for he tells us, that if it were not for Mrs. Allan's death, he would now be happier than he has been for a long time. The rest of the letter is given up to saying how anxious he is to retrieve his good name and reëstablish himself in the good opinion of his guardian, and to suggestions as to those who might aid in obtaining an appointment to West Point, now taken for granted. Evidently, during the visit home, the matter had been talked over, and John Allan's consent obtained.

From many indications, it is certain that, from the first, the whole West Point plan was on Poe's part merely a concession to his guardian's idea of what his future career should be. The young soldier would have liked to free himself entirely from the army to give himself up to writing. On this point, however, as upon his "son's" returning to Charlottesville, John Allan was adamant. Poe was himself a little wiser now. He had learned how futile it was to woo the muse with no bread in his stomach, and no oil in the lamp; and he was prepared to compromise, rather than to walk out of the house again to starve. Frances Allan's promise, that she had extorted from her husband, had

---

[320] Definite moves to obtain letters of influence to the War Department for a cadet's appointment all follow this time, and Poe's proceedings to get clear of the army from the time of this visit show that the understanding with his guardian was reached at this time, and not before by previous correspondence.

[321] Poe to John Allan, March 10, 1829. Letter No. 9, *Valentine Museum Collection.*

paved the way for a reconciliation. With temporary acquiescence to his guardian's wishes, and a repetition at West Point of his success in the ranks, Poe felt that there was a real hope of being reinstated in Mr. Allan's good opinion if not in his affection. In the meantime, the Military Academy offered board, bed and education; a specious combination that has appealed to a great many poor but ambitious youths. To share, even partially, in John Allan's large fortune was also highly desirable. Even a modest legacy would bring Poe the possibility of the leisure for his writing which he so much desired—desired, indeed, above all things—and relief from the haunting fear of poverty. This choice, therefore, which circumstances had so largely thrust upon him, was the lesser horn of a dilemma rather than a thirst for the glory of arms. The result of it was to be the almost utter waste of two years out of a short life.

From the standpoint of literature, it is unfortunate that John Allan could not change his mind. A little concession, on his part, to the darling wish of his "son's" heart would have allowed the world to have heard from Poe oftener and sooner. It might have saved him, even then, from the nerve-shattering effects of the poverty and deprivations to follow. But to the potentialities of his ward, John Allan was blind. West Point, to the good merchant, seemed an ideal solution. Edgar would there be under that discipline of which the Scotchman felt he was in such need; it relieved Mr. Allan of personal expense by casting him on the public charge; and it removed Poe from the household and assured him a future. By such an arrangement the older man could at once assoil himself of his promise to his dead wife, and be honorably rid of the young genius who had become a spiritual, an intellectual, and a physical nuisance. There comes a time in every man's life when he feels that he is entitled to what he calls "peace." Death had removed John Allan's wife. He was now looking forward to a new era of existence, and in the scheme of that life there was no place for a reminder, a painful reminder, of the old order of things.

No one can blame Mr. Allan for this. A lack of psychic insight and artistic prevision, however desirable, must be forgiven—a man cannot be reproached for the lack of qualities with which he has not been endowed—but there was something more than this. When John Allan "adopted" the helpless child whom he took into his house, whether willingly or not, he assumed certain responsibilities. It is the ruthlessness of his shaking these off, from the time of Poe's sojourn at Charlottesville until after the West Point interlude, of which posterity has a right to complain. The dying prayers of his wife seemed temporarily to arouse in him a sense of the fact that fatherhood does not consist simply in cramming a child's stomach, and then throwing it out of the nest.

As the days slipped by, however, the repugnance to having Poe in the house returned, and the memory of the promise waned. It is this process that the correspondence between the years 1829 and 1833 shadows forth. The beginning, as might be expected, was more favorable than the end.

Most of Poe's time when he got back to the Fort was taken up in making arrangements for his discharge, getting letters from his officers to the War Department, and finding a substitute willing to serve out the remainder of his enlistment, about three years. A few weeks after his arrival, arrangements were complete, and the Colonel of the Regiment wrote the following letter to the General commanding the Department of the East. As usual in Poe's case, most of the biographical data is inexact. The story which Poe told his commanding officer can be read between the lines.

> *Fortress Monroe,*
> March 30, '29

GENERAL,—I request your permission to discharge from the service Edgar A. Perry,[322] at present the Sergeant-Major of the 1st Reg't of Artillery, on his procuring a substitute.

The said Perry is one of a family of orphans whose unfortunate parents were the victims of the conflagration of the Richmond Theatre in 1809.[323] The subject of this letter was taken under the protection of a Mr. Allan, a gentleman of wealth and respectability, of that city, who, as I understand, adopted his protegé as his son and heir; with the intention of giving him a liberal education, he had placed him at the University of Virginia from which, after considerable progress in his studies, in a moment of youthful indiscretion he absconded,[324] and was not heard from by his Patron for several years; in the meantime he became reduced to the necessity of enlisting into the service,[325] and accordingly entered as a soldier in my Regiment, at Fort Independence, in 1827. Since the arrival of his company at this place he has made his situation known to his Patron, at whose request the young man has been permitted to visit him; the result, is an entire reconciliation on the part of Mr. Allan, who reinstates him into his family and favor, and who in a letter I have received from him requests that his son may be discharged on procuring a substitute, an experienced soldier and approved sergeant is ready to take the place of Perry as soon as his discharge

---

[322] The request for discharge of course had to be in the same name as that under which the soldier was enlisted.

[323] The Colonel evidently had the story from Poe and from John Allan's letter to him, but he is somewhat mixed as to dates and precise facts. The theater burned in 1811. That Poe used it as a convenient method of explaining his adoption seems likely. It is also a more romantic reason, the kind that Poe liked to fill into his "autobiography."

[324] The use of the word "absconded," carrying with it the idea of financial defaulting, may indicate that, in his letter to the Colonel, John Allan made mention of Poe's running away on account of debts.

[325] "Reduced to the necessity," etc.—this is an interesting comment on the Colonel's own opinion of the enlisted personnel of that day, and Poe's desperate straits in Boston in 1827. Evidently "enlisting" was one step short of suicide.

can be obtained.[326] The good of the service, therefore, cannot be materially injured by the discharge.

I have the honor to be,

With great respect, your obedient servant,

JAS. HOUSE,
Col. 1st Art'y.

To the General Commanding the
E. Dept. U. S. A., New York.

Permission was granted by General E. P. Gaines commanding the Eastern Department, from New York headquarters in an order dated April 4th, and in compliance with this, "Edgar A. Perry" was discharged from the service of the United States on April 15, 1829, a sergeant—as the Colonel notes—then being ready to take his place as substitute. As this transaction was later used as the basis of a serious charge against Poe by the second Mrs. Allan, it is important to note that Poe was discharged from the army in a little over a month from the time that he returned from furlough to Richmond. Apparently, the whole matter was easily arranged. Allowing for the time which the mail then required between New York and Fortress Monroe,[327] and for the usual delays of official correspondence, it is hard to see how it could have been done more speedily.

Poe's own description of the transactions involved in his discharge is now available.[328] On the date of his discharge it appears that both Colonel House and Lieutenant Howard, his regimental and company commanders, were absent. Had they been present, either one, it would have been possible to have mustered in the first recruit who offered as a substitute, which would have cost Poe only the usual bounty of $12. Poe had told John Allan that it would only cost that much, when he was in Richmond, it appears. With the officers absent who were competent to enlist a *new* recruit in his place, Poe was forced to pay $75 to the sergeant who took his place. This he did by giving the substitute $25 cash and a note for $50, which he afterwards took up out of $100 sent him from home. As Poe's explanation agrees with the army regulations in force at the time, both John Allan's suspicions, and the charge of embezzlement made against Poe by the second Mrs. Allan in her only

[326] The wording here strongly suggests that the approved sergeant was ready to fill the post of sergeant major to which he would at the same time have to be promoted by regimental order. The point should be noted.

[327] Then at least three or four days each way. The orders would also be a day or so in being approved, written, and transmitted. It evidently took the Colonel's letter three days to get to New York and the confirming order at headquarters was issued on the fourth. The order for discharge is dated ahead to the fifteenth of April because it allows a month's half pay and is convenient to compute. This completely does away with the second Mrs. Allan's story of delay during which the aggrieved substitute "grew tired waiting and wrote to Mr. Allan."

[328] From various letters from Poe in the *Valentine Museum Collection* dated from Baltimore in the Summer of 1829, written to John Allan in Richmond.

known printed statement about him, published long after his death, are both shown to be wrong.

Years after the events just described, when every move of Poe had become a matter of public interest, the second Mrs. Allan, then a widow, wrote to Colonel Thomas H. Ellis at that time living in Baltimore, an "explanation" of the estrangement between Edgar Poe and John Allan. The letter is quoted in part:

> Mr. Poe had not lived under Mr. Allan's roof for two years before my marriage, and no one knew his whereabouts; his letters were very scarce and were dated from St. Petersburg, Russia, although he had enlisted in the army at Boston. After he became tired of army life, he wrote to his benefactor, expressing a desire to have a substitute if the money could be sent to him. Mr. Allan sent it, Poe spent it; and after the substitute was tired out, waiting and getting letters and excuses, he [the substitute] enclosed one of Poe's letters to Mr. Allan, which was too black to be credited if it had not contained the author's signature. Mr. Allan sent the money to the man, and banished Poe from his affections; and he never lived here again.[329]

An examination of the statements in this letter, together with the known facts and movements of Poe and John Allan, and other letters dealing with the young poet's period of army service and discharge, prove that Mrs. Allan's letter is incorrect, not only in its charge of the misuse of funds, but in nearly every other item. Poe did, it is now known, still owe money to some of the non-commissioned officers in his regiment when he left Fortress Monroe. A letter of Poe's written to one of these men later on fell into the second Mrs. Allan's hands. This, together with her husband's suspicions, and the nature of Poe's statements about his guardian in the epistle itself, perhaps led Mrs. Allan to make the statement that she did make.

The absence of Lieutenant Howard, on the date of Poe's discharge, April 15th, probably accounts for the fact that Poe did not, although anxious to secure his cadet appointment, leave Fortress Monroe until almost a week after his release. He was waiting to obtain letters from Lieutenant Howard and the other officers to aid him in his application. These letters were given gladly, and show clearly the high estimation in which Poe was held by his superiors. The blamelessness of his conduct during his two years in the army is clear. His company and battalion commanders write:

> *Fortress Monroe, Va.* 20th April, 1829.
> Edgar Poe, late Sergt-Major in the 1st Arty, served under my command in "H," company 1st Reg't of Artillery, from June 1827, to January 1829, during which time his conduct was unexceptionable. He at once performed the duties

---

[329] This letter was afterward published by Colonel Thomas H. Ellis, the son of Charles Ellis, in the *Richmond Standard* for April 22, 1880. Louise Allan Mayo also gave further publicity to this unfortunate epistle in *Historic Homes of Richmond*. The *Richmond News, Illustrated Saturday Magazine*, July 28, 1900.

of clerk and assistant in the Subsistent Department, both of which duties were promptly and faithfully done. His habits are good and entirely free from drinking.

J. Howard,
Lieut. 1st Artillery

In addition to the above, I have to say that Edgar Poe [erased Perry] was appointed Sergeant-Major of the 1st art'y; on the 1st of January, 1829, and up to this date, has been exemplary in his deportment, prompt and faithful in the discharge of his duties—and is highly worthy of confidence.

H. W. Griswold,

Bt. Capt. and Adjut. 1st Art'y

To this is a third endorsement by the Lieutenant Colonel of the regiment, W. J. Worth,[330] who joins most heartily adding some further praise of his own. The letter, in short, covers the entire period of Poe's service in the army under all three officers.

With these letters in his pocket, young Poe left Old Point Comfort and set out for Richmond where he seems to have been occupied during the latter part of April, 1829, and the first week of May in obtaining political influence for his appointment. John Allan bestirred himself in the matter and obtained a letter from Andrew Stevenson, the Speaker of the House, and a Major John Campbell, who remembered having seen Edgar Poe as a boy at "The Springs" in 1812.[331] While Poe was still in Richmond, Colonel Worth, the Representative in Congress from the district, was also prevailed upon to write the Secretary of War in the young man's behalf, and to these letters and the eulogies of Poe's former officers, John Allan added his own. Pen in hand, the nature of the older man's feelings toward his ward could not be forced beyond the following arctic "recommendation":

Richmond, May 6, 1829.

Dr. Sir,—The youth who presents this, is the same alluded to by Lt. Howard, Capt. Griswold, Colo. Worth, our representative, and the speaker, Hon'ble Andrew Stevenson, and my friend Major Jno. Campbell.

He left me in consequence of some gambling at the University at Charlottesville, because (I presume) I refused to sanction a rule that the shop-keepers and others had adopted there, making Debts of Honour of all indiscretions. I have much pleasure in asserting that he stood his examination at the close of the year with great credit to himself. His history is short. He is the grandson of Quartermaster-General Poe, of Maryland, whose widow as I understand still receives a pension for the services or disabilities of her husband. Frankly, sir, do I declare that he is no relation to me whatever; that I have many whom I have taken an active interest to promote theirs,[332] with no other feeling than that,

---

[330] The endorsement of this letter by the Lieutenant Colonel of the Regiment shows that the Colonel *was* absent as Poe states.

[331] See Chapter III, page 38.

[332] This may refer to the "children," probably not to anyone in Scotland as William Galt had cared for them in his will.

every man is my care, if he be in distress. For myself I ask nothing, but I do request your kindness to aid this youth in the promotion of his future prospects. And it will afford me great pleasure to reciprocate any kindness you can show him. Pardon my frankness; but I address a soldier.[333]

Your Ob'd't se'v't,
JOHN ALLAN

The Hon'ble John H. Eaton, Sec'y of War, Washington City.

With this gloomy document from the frank altruist who felt that "every man is my care, if he be in distress—" to fire the enthusiasm of the Secretary of War in his behalf, Poe left Richmond on or about May 7, 1829, and went to Washington to present the letters to the Secretary of War in person.

John Allan's letter must have been meant for the eyes of Poe himself as much as for the Secretary of War.[334] It was plain notice to the young poet that his guardian considered him as merely an object of charity, and that beyond his efforts to get him off his hands and into West Point, he had no further interest. "Frankly, sir, do I declare that he is no relation to me whatever," did not mean that he was about to make Poe his heir, or at home any more in his house. In formally carrying out his promise to his dead wife, only John Allan's honor, and not his affection, was involved. The result of Poe's application was the usual one. The letters were put on file in the War Department and nothing happened for months.

Mr. Allan had given Poe $50 when he left Richmond. Poe apparently merely stopped off in Washington to present his letters at the War Department and then went on to Baltimore, where we find him before the middle of May, 1829. Poe immediately proceeded to look up his own relatives, and, on May 20th, he writes John Allan that he has succeeded in finding his aged grandmother, Mrs. (General) David Poe and his other relations. In the meantime he had drawn on Richmond for an additional $50, a draft which his guardian honored. On May 18th, John Allan writes from Richmond telling Poe that Colonel Preston had written a warm letter of recommendation in his behalf, and at the same time enclosing a check for $100 with the admonition to *be prudent and be careful*. Colonel Preston's letter which John Allan is evidently somewhat astonished to find so "warm," was as follows:

Richmond, Va., May 13, 1829.

SIR,—Some of the friends of young Mr. Edgar Poe have solicited me to address a letter to you in his favor, believing that it may be useful to him in his applica-

---

[333] Hon. John H. Eaton, then Secretary of War, also bore the title of "Major." In the South this would not be forgotten. See also James Preston's letter.

[334] Hon. John H. Eaton of Tennessee, was Secretary of War in Jackson's cabinet 1829-1937. He was a politician of great influence in the Jackson "democracy" and did not escape without grave scandals being connected with his name. John Allan was evidently not anxious to be beholden to him—"For myself I ask nothing."

tion to the Government for military service. I know Mr. Poe and am acquainted with the fact of his having been born under circumstances of great adversity. I also know from his own productions and other undoubted proofs that he is a young gentleman of genius and taleants. I believe he is destined to be distinguished, since he has already gained reputation for taleants and attainements at the University of Virginia. I think him possessed of feeling and character peculiarly intitling him to public patronage.

Very respectfully your obt. serv't,
JAMES P. PRESTON

Major John Eaton, *Sec'y of War,* Washington.

This letter is more than a formal recommendation obtained by political influence; it is the warm recognition of Poe's "taleants" by a friend and neighbor who had known him from childhood.[335] Despite his unusual spelling, James Preston had sufficient literary foresight to be distinguished as the first person who linked the word *genius* with the name of Poe.

Poe had several good reasons for going to Baltimore from Washington. In the first place, he must have been thoroughly advertised of the fact that by this time he was no longer welcome "at home." With the waning of John Allan's "affection," he also felt the desirability of establishing more firmly the family ties with his blood relations in Baltimore, and the importance of obtaining from them whatever influence the name of his grandfather, who had been Quartermaster in the Revolutionary War, might have with the War Department.[336] Poe's ignorance about his own family up until this time seems to have been almost complete. Grandfather Poe's exploits in the Revolution had taken on an importance by family recital and the lapse of time which had already breveted him "General." Edgar was delighted. He was, in short, only now beginning to find out who he really was. "Edgar Allan" was about to become completely metamorphosed into "Edgar Poe." There was also another reason why Poe desired to be in Baltimore, one which he had not so far dared to reveal to his guardian. His real interest in life was now centered upon getting out another volume of poems. With May, 1829, the long and indomitable struggle for literary recognition really begins.

Once in Baltimore, Poe lost no time in pushing the publication of *Al Aaraaf* and the new and revised poems which he now had on hand. His experience with *Tamerlane and Other Poems* had taught him the

---

[335] The Hon. James P. Preston—"Mr. Preston," was the father of young Preston who had been one of Poe's rather intimate playmates at Mr. Clarke's school; they sat on the same bench together there, and young Preston had at one time been in the habit of taking home some of Poe's schoolboy verses for his mother's criticism. In the letter which Mr. Preston gave Poe to the Secretary of War there is a patent reference to this.

[336] Preference of appointment was given to the descendants of Revolutionary officers.

futility of merely printing his own work with no means of publication or public notice, and he now set about preparing the way for his next book in the manner which he followed for the rest of his life. · This was to send his work to some well-known writer or influential person, and, under the guise of soliciting their criticism, to obtain a hold on their interest and influence.

A day or so after his arrival in Baltimore, May 11, 1829, he called upon William Wirt,[337] the author of the then well-known *Letters of a British Spy.* Poe had met Mr. Wirt previously in Richmond, and he now left with him the manuscripts of *Al Aaraaf,* telling him that he was submitting it immediately to a Philadelphia publisher. He also asked for Mr. Wirt's comment, doubtless hoping for a letter that would have influence with publishers. Wirt, who was a semi-literary person, was completely mystified by the imagery of *Al Aaraaf,* a poem that still continues to trouble the "well ordered" and academic mind. He, however, replied the same evening—having evidently put in the day somewhat badly with "Nesace" in the limbo of *Al Aaraaf*—yet with kindly feelings withal for the young author to whom he writes:

Baltimore, May 11, 1829.

. . . I am sensible of the compliment you pay me in submitting it to my judgment and only regret that you have not a better counsellor. But the truth is that having never written poetry myself, nor read much poetry for many years, I consider myself as by no means a competent judge. . . . This is no doubt an old-fashioned idea resulting from the causes I have mentioned, my ignorance of modern poetry and modern taste. You perceive therefore that I am not qualified to judge of the merits of your poem. It will, I know, please modern readers—the notes contain a good deal of curious and useful information, but to deal candidly with you (as I am bound to do) I should doubt whether the poem will take with old-fashioned readers like myself. . . . I would advise you, therefore, as a friend to get an introduction to Mr. Walsh or Mr. Hopkinson or some other critic in Philadelphia, versed in modern . . .[338]

Armed or disarmed with this letter from a legal critic who thought that, "the notes contain a good deal of curious and *useful* information," Poe set out at six o'clock the next morning on the steamboat for Philadelphia with his manuscript in his pocket.

In Philadelphia, Poe submitted his poems to Messrs. Carey, Lea &

---

[337] William Wirt had just retired to Baltimore as ex-U. S. Attorney General. In 1831 he represented the Cherokee Indians in their famous suit before the Supreme Court of the United States, to retain their lands (the Cherokee Nation *vs.* the State of Georgia). The court held that it had no jurisdiction in the case. An important constitutional principle was involved, and Wirt's arguments were most able (Niles XXXVI. 231, 258.9; Stat. Man., II, 709). See also (Wooster *vs.* the State of Georgia), 1832, for an interesting sidelight on this case.

[338] From the mutilated manuscript in William Wirt's handwriting, with the conclusion of the letter and the signature missing, now in the Boston Public Library. Dr. Thomas Ollive Mabbott is to be credited for making public this letter.

Carey, and had a short interview with Mr. Lea at the firm's office on Chestnut Street, in which Mr. Lea suggested that the "author" might contribute some poems to the *Atlantic Souvenir*. Meanwhile, he took the manuscript of *Al Aaraaf* under advisement while Poe returned to Baltimore.

Before the end of the month, Poe probably received from the Philadelphia firm the usual reply of publishers to a young poet, saying that if they could be guaranteed from all loss, they would undertake publication. Hence on May 29, 1829, we find Poe writing to John Allan inclosing him William Wirt's letter, enlarging on the importance of a young poet's being *brought before the eye of the world* early, and asking his guardian to write the publishers, guaranteeing the book to the extent of $100. In making this request, Poe assures Mr. Allan that he has long ago given up Byron as a model.[339] The merchant's reply, which was unusually prompt, was to refuse sternly all aid, and "strongly censure" Poe for his "conduct."

More correspondence about *Al Aaraaf* followed between "father and son," [340] but although Poe grew humbler, Mr. Allan remained as always—firm. The incident seems to have affected their relations seriously. John Allan was both disgusted and alarmed at this token that Poe's literary ambitions were unchanged, and he seems to have felt that his ward was not very much in earnest about West Point. Although it was obviously not Poe's fault that the appointment was not forthcoming, and equally patent that he would have to exist in the meantime, John Allan, while he retired to his plantation during the summer days, seems to have left his "son" to shift largely for himself. Poe would have liked to come home he tells his guardian, but the latter replied that he was not especially anxious to see him, and let it go at that. By the end of July, 1829, the young poet was in precarious circumstances. Finally, on July 26th, John Allan sent him a little money with the suggestion that a man of genius ought not to have to apply for aid; to which taunt Poe replied, that a little more timely assistance would prevent the application.

As John Allan's suspicions of Poe's honesty and ability in money matters have to a certain extent been handed down as part of the Poe

---

[339] This remark arouses interesting speculations. Byron, and the influence of the Byron cult on young Poe was doubtless something which John Allan abhorred and had held responsible for many of his ward's "immoral" flirtings with literature. The reader will remember that *Don Quixote* and *Gil Blas* were also on the Scotchman's *index expurgatorius,* although he had sent Poe a copy of the latter himself—see page 135.

[340] Poe seems to have replied at the same time to Carey, Lea & Carey asking them to hold his poems until they heard further. The manuscript of *Al Aaraaf* remained with them up until the end of July, 1829, by which time all hope of Mr. Allan's help was at an end and Poe wrote them withdrawing it.

tradition, a brief examination of Poe's financial transactions at this time may be of value in making plain his typical difficulties.

By John Allan's own accounting on the back of one of Poe's letters, it appears that from about the middle of May to the nineteenth of July, 1829, the merchant provided Poe in all with $200. On this amount the youth was expected to board and clothe himself for a period of ten weeks, pay his traveling expenses from Richmond to Washington, and from Washington to Baltimore—then a matter of about a day each way—and take care of all contingent expenses, in short, as John Allan recommended, "be prudent and be careful." The young man was just out of the army, and except for the suit of mourning which was given to him in Richmond, he was without civilian clothes. Allowing for the value of money at that time, $200 might have covered this, had there been no extra expenses. But Poe tells his guardian that he had to take up the note of $50 which he had given to his substitute, and we know also that he had gone to Philadelphia and returned to Baltimore in May. Allowing for the money he sent the substitute, we now learn that Poe had spent $104 between early May and June 22, 1829, when he tells his guardian that he was robbed of $46, "all I had," while sharing a room with Mosher Poe in the *Beltzhoover Hotel* in Baltimore. By searching the pockets of his cousin, who thus immortalized himself, Poe was able the next night to recover $10. The man begged not to be exposed on account of his wife, although Poe gives his name in the letter to John Allan.[341] The next remittance which Poe received from Mr. Allan was on July 26th.

It would therefore appear that during the Summer of 1829, for a period of one month at least, Edgar Allan Poe managed to exist on $10, probably with the connivance of his landlady and his relations. The exact form of dissipation in which the young poet indulged at 33 cents a day does not appear at this writing to be clear. Nor was this all, John Allan's censure of his extravagance was bitter and his expression of his suspicions extreme. For even suggesting the publication of the poems, Poe is now full of apologies. Nevertheless the manuscript was still left with Carey, Lea & Carey, and Poe, meanwhile, had succeeded in getting an introduction to Mr. Walsh, the editor of the *American Quarterly Review,* and obtained the promise of his help. In the interim there was no word from the War Department about the appointment.

During the entire period of young Poe's stay in Baltimore from May, 1829, until the end of that year, the letters he received from John

---

[341] This name has been deleted from the *Valentine Museum Poe Letters,* letter No. 13. Mosher Poe was a second cousin of Edgar's. There is no doubt the story is true or Poe would not have dared to give his cousin's name to John Allan. In one facsimile reproduced in the *Valentine Letters* the name "Mosher" occurs.

Allan were filled with sarcasms, suspicions, and reproaches. An occasional remittance generally came in time to save him from being thrown into the street, but the anxiety with which he accounts to his guardian for every penny gives indubitable evidence of the spirit in which the help was conferred. Aside from "blowing the boy up" for thinking of wasting money on poems, the chief bones of contention were the older man's suspicion about the amount of money given to the substitute—which no end of obvious facts and explanation served to allay—and the constant doubts expressed to Poe about his zeal in the matter of obtaining the appointment. A letter from Poe in which he told his guardian that he had just found out that he was a grandson of General Benedict Arnold [342] must have caused Mr. Allan to exclaim "I might have known it," for such were his sentiments. It seems probable that at the time Poe himself may have thought this to be true. The story, of course, came from the fact that his maternal grandmother's name *had* been Arnold. Aside from this, there was nothing in it. Perhaps, after all, it was only a sly little hoax on the part of Poe who enjoyed a well-fabricated fib, and knew the exact expression that it would summon upon John Allan's countenance—the grim mouth relaxing for a moment into a sardonic but withal annoyed smile. Whatever may have been his motive, however, in conveying to Richmond this devastating piece of information, which certainly would not have aided him with the War Department,[343] he lost no opportunity of proving to his guardian his earnestness about West Point. Poverty spurred him to it, an effect that may have been calculated by his guardian, and on July 23rd he set out on foot for Washington, the payment of a board bill of $40 having exhausted the larger part of a long expected remittance from Richmond received the day before.

After walking to Washington, Poe had a personal interview with the Secretary of War who told him there was a surplus of ten cadets then on the roll at West Point. But he advised him not to withdraw his letters of recommendation "for use elsewhere," as Poe says, because of the numerous resignations at West Point which usually took place during the summer encampment. If these resignations should exceed ten, Poe would be sure of his appointment in September; if not, Mr. Eaton assured him he would be among the first appointed for the following year. Poe was afraid that his age might interfere, but he was assured by the Secretary of War that he might call himself twenty-one until he was twenty-two. The interview ended with a remark from Mr. Eaton that the trip to Washington had been unnecessary. After which the young man had the pleasure of walking back to Baltimore.

[342] Poe to John Allan, June 25, 1829, Letter No. 13, *Valentine Museum Collection.*
[343] Had Poe not succeeded in getting the appointment, this story would have been an excellent excuse. See note 304.

From Baltimore he writes John Allan on July 26th, that he has explained
everything to him that needed explanation and left no stone unturned
in the pursuit of his object.   In great perplexity he adds that he wishes
Mr. Allan would give him directions as to what course he is to pursue.
He says that he would have returned home to Richmond but for the
fact that his guardian had said he was not especially anxious to see him.

Poe's position was in fact at this time most trying.   His guardian had
told him that he was "forgiven," yet the tone of his letters, and his continuing to keep him at arms' length, and on starvation allowance, were
proofs of how he really felt.   If this were not enough, there was the
letter to the Secretary of War which Poe must have seen, as it was given
to him as a personal introduction to Major Eaton.   All this was puzzling and painful to the young man; again and again he begs his "father"
to come out in the open, assuring him pathetically that since Charlottesville he has done nothing to offend him.

> . . . I thought *that had been forgiven,* at least you told me so—I know that I
> have done nothing since to deserve your displeasure—.   As regards the poem,
> I have offended only in asking your approbation—I can publish it upon the terms
> you mentioned—but will have no more to do with it without your entire appro-
> bation—I will wait with great anxiety for your answer.   You must be aware
> how important it is that I should hear from you soon—as I do not know how
> to act.

But his anxiety was not relieved for a fortnight.   In the meantime
under date of August 4th, Poe writes again saying how anxious he
is to return home.   With almost nothing to live on in Baltimore, and
no assurance of more, the "anxiety" is not hard to understand.   No
reply having come from Richmond, on July 28th, Poe had written
Carey, Lea & Carey, asking for the return of his manuscript, for which
he bravely says he has made a better disposition than he could have
hoped for.   Whether he had really done so is doubtful.   The expression
was probably meant to cover his own disappointment while leaving the
best of impressions upon the Philadelphia publishers.

Baltimore
July 28th 1829
Rec'd *July* 30"
Ans"*Aug.* 3"

Messrs. Carey, Lea & Carey

Gentlemen—
Having made a better disposition of my poems than I had any right to expect,
(inducing me to decline publication on my own account) I would thank you to
return me the MSS: by the gentleman who hands you this—mail.

I should have been proud of having your firm for my publishers & would have
preferred publishing, with your name, even at a disadvantage had my circumstances admitted of so doing.

Perhaps, at some future day, I may have the honor of your press, which I
most sincerely desire—

Mr. Lea, during our short interview, at your store, mentioned *The Atlantic Souvenir* and spoke of my attempting something for that work. I know nothing which could give me greater pleasure than to see any of my productions, in so becoming a dress & in such good society as "The Souvenir" would ensure them— notwithstanding the assertions of M^r. J^n Neal to the contrary, who now & then hitting, thro' sheer impudence, upon a correct judgment in matters of authorship, is most unenviably rediculous whenever he touches the fine arts—

As I am unacquainted with the method of proceeding in offering any piece for acceptance (having been sometime absent from this country)[344] would you, Gentlemen, have the kindness to set me in the right way—

Nothing could give me greater pleasure than any communication from Messrs Carey Lea & Carey—

With the greatest respect
& best wishes
I am Gentlemen
Your most ob^d Servt.
EDGAR A. POE

On August 10th, Mr. Allan again sent his ward a remittance, apparently accompanied by bitter complaints about the money spent on the substitute, despite the fact that the necessity for the expenditure had been amply explained several times before. Poe says that he can live on $8 or $10 a month, "anything with which you think it is possible to exist," and ends with a request to have his trunk sent to Baltimore in care of H. W. Boal, Jr. This trunk contained some books and papers. On August 19th, Mr. Allan sent Poe $50 on which he existed for three months. During that time Mr. Allan went to the Hot Springs, a visit that marks the second attack of a complaint that finally proved fatal some five years later. In the meantime Carey, Lea & Carey had returned *Al Aaraaf* and Poe was trying to place it in Baltimore.

August, 1829, marks the beginning of an association that was a vital one in Poe's life. He had gone to live with the Clemms. At that time Mrs. Maria Clemm, Poe's aunt, was living in a two-story house with an attic in Mechanics Row, Milk Street. She seems to have occupied the upper part of the house together with her little daughter Virginia, her son Henry, old Mrs. David Poe (the poet's grandmother), and William Henry Leonard Poe. The addition of Edgar was undoubtedly a heavy burden on her already overcrowded household. Poe tells his guardian that old Mrs. Poe was a paralytic, that Mrs. Clemm was, if possible, in a still worse case, and that his brother Henry was so far gone in drink as to be unable to help himself.

The poverty-stricken Clemm-Poe household seems to have existed, and they could have done little more than that, on a small pension received by Mrs. "General" Poe, the pittance of Henry Clemm, a mason's

---

[344] Poe's *seeming* allusion here to a trip abroad is the first evidence of his intentions to cover up the period of his army service by claiming for himself the prestige of foreign travel: John Allan had impressed upon him the social disgrace of enlistment.

apprentice, the driblets of money received by Edgar from Richmond, and the sewing which Mrs. Clemm worked on, when she was able. Henry Poe was for a time after his return from sea employed as a clerk in the law offices of one Mr. Henry Didier, but he was dying of tuberculosis and given up, as Poe says, to drink.

Edgar apparently shared a back attic room with his elder brother, and probably helped to nurse him even at this time. In this house the poet first met his cousin, Virginia Maria Clemm, then a little girl seven years old who later became his wife.

Virginia seems at that time to have been a merry little schoolgirl, rather plump, with brown hair, violet eyes, and a disposition that was her chief charm. Doubtless she romped about the house with big Cousin Eddie, who called her "Sis" or "Sissie," and the childlike and helpless affection, one of complete trust on her part, and of protection and solicitude on Poe's, now began. Despite the fond assertions of innumerable romantic biographers, it is extremely unlikely that it ever amounted to much more. Mrs. Clemm was a woman whose maternal instinct was tremendously accentuated. She appears to have taken her young nephew to her heart from the first. A paralytic mother, a troublesome son, a dying nephew, and an utterly dependent daughter were not sufficient to satisfy her all-inclusive motherliness. To these she now added the sore pressed Edgar Allan Poe. For him it was the beginning of one of the most benign and, at the same time, devastating influences of his career.

Warned by the complete demise of his first book—owing to the lack of any adequate public notice, from the rear garret of Mrs. Clemm's house in Baltimore, Poe now began to send out through the Autumn and early Winter of 1829 letters and poems to editors and critics in order to prepare the way for the volume containing *Al Aaraaf,* which he was determined to publish in spite of John Allan, West Point, poverty, and the interruptions of a closely-packed household.

To this career of literary ambition he was driven by the double necessity of expressing the intense desires of his nature, even by this time thwarted in many ways, and that vivid sense of the reality and all-importance of the ego known as pride, a pride that Poe identified with the archangel Israfel, but which, in some of its aspects, belonged equally to Lucifer. It was no accident that the young poet had already years before taken Byron for his master, not only in attitude and verse, but in spirit. From Baltimore, Poe, as we have seen, had written Mr. Allan that he had given up Byron as a model, and in a certain sense he had, for he was now mature enough to realize that no mere follower can ever achieve. The necessity for originality, even in adaptation from others, was firmly fixed in his mind. But the pride was not gone. Above all obstacles it rose supreme, the inward sense of power, the

Baltimore, about the time of Poe's first stay there in 1829 and 1830

Showing the effect of BYRON's and MOORE's "Oriental Poems," and such works as IRVING's *Alhambra*, on the American landscape. The artist here makes Baltimore look like Bagdad. The dome of the Roman Catholic Cathedral and the shaft of the Washington Monument become the domes and minarets of mosques. Note the Arab steeds in the foreground. Compare this picture with the picture of Baltimore facing, page 237

From an old print.   Courtesy of the Maryland Historical Society, Baltimore, Maryland

Baltimore Assembly Room

Baltimore City Fountain

Scenes in Early Baltimore familiar to Poe

From two old illustrations
Courtesy of the Maryland Historical Society

AL AARAAF,

TAMERLANE,

AND

MINOR POEMS.

BY EDGAR A. POE.

BALTIMORE:
HATCH & DUNNING.

1829.

Title Page of *Al Aaraaf, Tamerlane, and Minor Poems, Baltimore, 1829*

Edgar Allan Poe's second published volume

NOTE: A title page with the imprint "1820" is known to exist. This was a printer's error

Courtesy of John T. Snyder, Esq., of Pelham, New York

The United States Military Academy

West Point on the Hudson, about 1830

From an old print

Courtesy of the New York Public Library

necessity for justification, the sense of the importance of his utterance, was now more than ever fixed upon him.   Hence his unequivocal prophecies of ensuing greatness which so disgusted John Allan, the force which insulated him to a great extent from all outward circumstances—always in the end unimportant to those who live within themselves—and such lines as these in *Tamerlane:*

> . . . There *is* a power in the high spirit
> To *know* the fate it will inherit)
> The soul, which knows such power, will still
> Find *Pride* the ruler of its will.[345]

Thus, despite all untoward and often degrading circumstances, the great work went on in the back garret of Mrs. Clemm where Henry lay coughing himself to death, in the same room with Edgar, or stumbled in late at night in his cups to boast drunkenly of his exploits in South America and other romantic lands beyond the seas he had traversed some years before, exploits to which Edgar listened eagerly, and made his own.

In the room downstairs Mrs. Clemm sewed while Virginia ran back and forth carrying things to the helpless grandmother.   She, poor lady, doubtless reminisced, as old people will, of the time when in her youth, as the wife of a Quartermaster of the Continental Armies, her husband had provided money and forage for La Fayette and his soldiers, while she and the girls of Baltimore with their own hands cut out five hundred pairs of trousers for the breechless troops of Washington—"and now, how small her pension was!"   Towards evening, young Clemm would come home covered with stone dust; Edgar from wandering about the docks or haunting the office of the *Federal Gazette and Baltimore Daily Advertiser* on the corner of St. Paul and Bank Streets, perhaps with the manuscript of *Al Aaraaf* in his pocket which he had shown to William Gwynn, the editor, and got small encouragement. David Poe had once worked for Gwynn when he kept a law office, and knowing the family traits, Mr. Gwynn had remarked, when he saw the poetry of the runaway actor's son, that it "was indicative of a tendency to anything but the business of matter-of-fact life."   A remark which time has shown to be true, but, as so often happens, irrelevant.

After nightfall, with the sewing laid aside, the family would gather about the table by the feeble light of a few tallow dips to sup on the single dish which Mrs. Clemm had cooked, and sometimes, by her importunity with friends or relatives, provided.   Grandma Poe would be drawn up close to the small coal fire, and they would discuss the last depressing letter from "Pa" in Richmond, while Virginia chattered, or did her sums with "Cousin Eddie" to help.   Then bed-time, for bed-

---

[345] The italics are Poe's.

time came early in those days to folk with a scant stock of candles, only
one for Henry and Edgar as they climbed to their attic, Henry complaining, and coughing himself into a restless slumber, while Edgar,
as long as the candle lasted, bent over his papers, driving the pen on
and on toward that far-off shining goal. He was arrested at last by
the midnight ghosts of "Helen" and Elmira, or his dear "Ma" with
the agate lamp in her hand in the old house on Tobacco Alley. There
the air from the docks used to blow in, waving the curtain fitfully—
as it did here—reminding him exquisitely, but exquisitely painfully, of
the vanished home in Richmond. The clothes that he took off were
a little more ragged every night, despite the obstinate needle of Mrs.
Clemm. Undressing under the eaves of the low-ceilinged room, Poe
brushed them and folded them carefully, before he lay down by the side
of the brother whose face was flushed, but whose hands and feet had
already begun to take on an eternal cold.

September, 1829, passed and there was no cadet's appointment from
the War Department. The few letters from Richmond became more
urgent and severe. Mr. Allan was greatly alarmed. Suppose, after all,
that his convenient plan for providing for Edgar at the public cost had
failed! He accused Poe of having deceived him in regard to Mr.
Eaton's promise for September appointments. In reply Poe refers him
to his former letters giving the Secretary of War's exact words, pointing out that his guardian is "mistaken." He will, he says, go to Washington, however, and get the Secretary to give him his appointment in
advance together with an order to repair to West Point for examination
the following June. These letters he will ask the Secretary of War
to forward to Mr. Allan "so that all doubts will be removed"—and
he adds with a touch of irony, "I will tell him (the Secretary of War)
why I want it at present and I think he will give it."

But Poe did not do this. He was without sufficient funds when
he wrote this letter (October 30th) even to walk to Washington again.
The offer, however, seems to have quieted John Allan, who probably
did not care to be put into the position of doubting the good faith of
the Secretary of War. Nevertheless, he did not reply, and two weeks
later Poe is forced to write him again telling his guardian that (November 12th) he is almost without clothes and about to be ejected by his landlady,[346] as he has received nothing from home since the middle of
August. John Allan at last replied and sent him $80. Nearly all of

---

[346] This would seem to indicate that Poe did not live continuously with the Clemms.
His places of abode were no doubt largely contingent upon the state of the supplies
from Richmond, and both the Herring and Poe cousins doubtless gave him shelter
from time to time. Mrs. Clemm, however, says that Poe lived with her while in
Baltimore in 1829. The statement does not necessarily mean "all the time." Prof.
Woodberry doubted Mrs. Clemm's statement, but the *Valentine Museum Poe Letters*
now confirm it.

this was already due for board and in the next letter Poe was forced to beg his "father" to get half a strip of linen from Mr. Galt, which Aunt Maria Clemm would make up into sheets "without charge."

It must be remembered that in making these appeals, Poe was carrying out Mr. Allan's own desire of waiting for the cadet's appointment, and that while so waiting he could not obtain employment when it was known that, at any moment, he might have to leave his job and be ordered off to West Point. Furthermore, the youth who was without clothes in Baltimore in November, 1829, was the ward of a rich man whose prosperous warehouse was piled high with goods. Yet, says Poe, "if you could send me a piece of linen, or a half piece at *Mr. Galt's* . . . I could get it made up *gratis* by Aunt Maria." . . . One wonders if "dear Pa" actually loosened up and did send the linen on by the boat, or whether Aunt Maria provided that *gratis,* too. The letter containing this modest request is the last on record that Poe wrote to his "father" from Baltimore in 1829. Something had happened which mollified even John Allan, and the world now first began to take a faint notice of Edgar Allan Poe.

Not very far from Mrs. Clemm, on Exeter near State Street, lived Mr. Henry Herring who had married Poe's Aunt Eliza, the same who had written the touching letter to Frances Allan many years before.[347] There were five children in the Herring House, cousins with whom young Poe was soon on intimate terms, writing poetry in his Cousin Mary's album, and being much about the place. Aunt Eliza had died some years before, but Mr. Herring, who seems to have been acquainted with a number of literary men and editors about Baltimore, succeeded in interesting them and some other of the Poe cousins in Edgar's work. Both Mr. Herring and George Poe had known a Mr. John Neal when he had been in Baltimore as an editor a short while before. They had all belonged to the Delphian Club on Bank Lane, better known as "The Tusculum." Mr. Gwynn, to whom Poe had lately shown *Al Aaraaf,* was also a member.

John Neal, who wrote under the pen name of "Jehu O'Cataract," had gone North to start a paper in Portland, Maine. This, he afterwards continued as the *Yankee and Boston Literary Gazette,* in whose columns his literary criticisms were received as oracles. George Poe, the father of Neilson Poe, seems to have used his influence with his old friend John Neal, and to have suggested to his literary cousin Edgar that he send Neal some poetry for editorial comment. This Poe did and was rewarded soon after by the following notice in the columns of the *Yankee* for September, 1829:

If E. A. P. of Baltimore—whose lines about "Heaven" though he professes to regard them as altogether superior to anything in the whole range of American

---

[347] See Chapter III, page 38.

poetry, save two or three trifles referred to, are, though nonsense, rather exquisite nonsense—would but do himself justice might [*sic*] make a beautiful and
perhaps a magnificent poem.　There is a good deal here to justify such a hope.

These words, said Poe, were, *"The very first words of Encouragement
I ever remember to have heard."* [348]　But Neal ends the little critique
with, "He should have signed it Bah!　We have no room for others."
　　Nevertheless, Poe took the criticism in good part and in the December
issue of the *Yankee* he was allowed to print a letter covering four pages
containing copious selections from the forthcoming volume.　Among
other things Poe says of himself:

> I would give the world to embody one half the ideas afloat in my imagination.
> . . .　I appeal to you as a man who loves the same beauty which I adore—the
> beauty of the natural blue sky and the sunshiny earth. . . .　I am and have been
> from childhood, an idler.　It cannot therefore be said that
>> 'I left a calling for this idle trade,
>> A duty broke—a father disobeyed.'
> for I have no father—nor mother.

John Allan's reproaches were evidently in his mind, and as he was often
without resources in Baltimore, the censure of his relatives for writing
poetry instead of "going to work" may possibly be reflected here.
　　The whole letter is typical of Poe's method of puffing his own work.
It amounted, in short, to a long announcement of his forthcoming
volume.　John Neal prefaced it with these editorial remarks:

> The following passages are from the manuscript works of a young author,
> about to be published in Baltimore.　He is entirely a stranger to us, but with
> all their faults, if the remainder of *Al Aaraaf* and *Tamerlane* are as good as
> the body of the extracts here given, to say nothing of the more extraordinary
> parts, he will deserve to stand high—very high, in the estimation of the shining
> brotherhood, etc.

This editorial prelude concludes with some highly moral and patronizing advice to the poet's extreme youth, quite typical of the time.
　　The notice in the September *Yankee* by the famous John Neal was
probably of direct service to Poe in two ways.　It must have been drawn
to John Allan's attention by the admiring Nancy Valentine, or Poe's
good friends the Galts, and caused Mr. Allan to reflect a little.　At any
rate, about the middle of December, Poe received $80 from his guar-
dian, and then or later, permission to return home.　With Neal's puff
in hand Poe was also enabled to approach the publishers in Baltimore,
the favorable notice of a Northern critic of note being then, as now,
impressive in the South, which pays no serious attention to its own
writers until they are praised elsewhere.　The result, in Poe's case, seems

---

[348] Poe means by an editor in the public prints.　It must be remembered that Poe's
"attack" on Neal in the letter to Carey, Lea & Carey was made two months *before*
Neal's remarks in the *Yankee*.　See "Poe and John Neal" in Appendix IX.

to have been that his book was accepted. On November 18th, in the "linen" letter, he writes John Allan that his poems have been accepted upon advantageous terms by Hatch & Dunning of Baltimore, "they to print, and give the author 250 copies of the book." Mr. Dunning, Poe adds, well knowing that his guardian might suspect that some expense was involved, would confirm the terms himself upon an immediate visit to Richmond.

Heralded thus somewhat dubiously, but on the whole in a not unkindly way, Poe's second volume, *Al Aaraaf, Tamerlane, and Minor Poems,* appeared in Baltimore in December, 1829, published by Hatch & Dunning, and printed by Matchett & Woods, the same firm which then printed the *Baltimore Directory*. It was a thin octavo volume bound in blue boards, containing seventy-one pages padded out with a considerable number of extra fly-leaves upon which appeared mottoes quoted from English and Spanish poets. The margins were more than ample. The dedication, a line from Cleveland, reads:

Who drinks the deepest?—here's to him.

In this book, *Al Aaraaf* and *Tamerlane* were the principal offerings. The latter was dedicated to John Neal, "respectfully," with the advertisement,

This poem was printed for publication in Boston, in the year 1827, but suppressed through circumstances of a private nature.[349]

As a matter of fact, it was completely rewritten in conformity with the outcome of the adventure with Elmira, and, from a literary standpoint, greatly improved. The two main long poems were followed by a brief preface, and nine miscellaneous short poems of which three are revised reprints from the Boston volume. The second of the nine, beginning "I saw thee on thy bridal day," obviously refers to Elmira Royster, by this time Mrs. Shelton. *Al Aaraaf* is an attempt on the part of the youthful poet to put in the form of an allegory his philosophy of beauty.[350] The allegory is obscure, but the poem contains many exquisite lines.

---

[349] See Chapter X, page 164.

[350] *Al Aaraaf* is the region placed by the Arabian poets between the upper and nether regions, neither hell nor heaven, where those spirits who deserve to enter neither, dwell. Poe has personified his ideal of beauty in a beautiful maiden by the name of "Nesace" who dwells in a distant star—

"—for there
Her world lay lolling on the golden air,
Near four bright suns—"

Poe has caught some of the tremendous sweep of space from Milton, and there are reminiscences of *Queen Mab,* with a strange admixture of Moore and Byron and perhaps a trace of Pinkney. Despite this, the fault of a young poet, it is peculiarly his own. The universe is ransacked for beautiful things to make up its lines, with notes, in which the young poet takes a pardonable pride.

In general it may be said that Poe's second book with all of its juvenile faults was his first real approach to a contribution to American poetry. It marked a distinct advance over his first volume of two years before, and embodied in its lines some of his characteristic landscapes tinged with his mystical melancholy and the autobiographical records of his love affairs. The gain in his handling of rhythms is marked. Certainly the landscapes bear indubitable marks of his South Carolina sojourn.[351]

Poe remained in Baltimore until the end of 1829 seeing his book off the press and dispatching copies to editors for review and notice. On December 29, 1829, he sent a copy to his friend John Neal, the editor of the *Yankee* in Boston, with this characteristic letter:

> I thank you, sir, for the kind interest you express for my worldly as well as poetical welfare—a sermon of prosing would have met with much less attention.
>
> You will see that I have made the alterations you suggest . . . and some other corrections of the same kind—there is much, however, (in metre) to be corrected—for I did not observe it till too late.
>
> I wait consciously for your notice of the book—I think the best lines for *sound* are those in *Al Aaraaf*—
>
> > *All Nature speaks and ev'n ideal things,*
> > *Flap shadowy sounds from visionary wings.*
>
> I am certain that these lines have never been surpassed.—
>
> > *Of late, eternal Condor years*
> > *So shake the very Heaven on high,*
> > *With tumult as they thunder by,*
> > *I have no time for idle cares*
> > *Through gazing on the unquiet sky.*
>
> 'It is well to think well of one's self'—so says somebody. You will do me justice, however.
>
> > Most truly yours,
> > EDGAR A. POE

After which Poe said good-bye to the Clemms, and the Herring and Poe cousins, packed up what little belongings he had, and taking advantage of John Allan's permission to return home in the luster of his new laurels, went to Richmond before the holidays were over, taking along a generous supply of the copies of the new book for distribution among his friends.

Upon his return to Richmond, Poe found his old room ready for him at the Allan house. It was then and long afterwards known as "Edgar's Room" to all the servants and the friends of the family. Dur-

---

[351] This is the "foreign influence" pointed out by numerous critics in Poe's second volume, due to his trip abroad in 1827, now known to be a pure myth.

ing the second Mrs. Allan's régime the name was probably suppressed. After Mrs. Clemm's crowded and humble quarters, the spaciousness, the luxury, and the gardens of the big house must have been delightful. The kindly black faces of Jim and Dabney were there to welcome him, and their hands to serve him, while "Aunt Nancy's" affection was as loyal as ever. But with what memories must he have wandered about the house! Frances Allan was gone, her room was empty, and there was no Elmira to come and sit in the swing or look through the telescope. That Poe was in Richmond by the first week in January, 1830, is certain, as he was supplied with clothes at that time by orders upon *Ellis & Allan,* among other things, a fine "London hat." Probably, despite the darning needle of Mrs. Clemm, his wardrobe was in a sad condition after the period of poverty in Baltimore.

The second night after his return, Poe met Thomas Bolling, his old University of Virginia acquaintance (altogether, as his letters show, a charming fellow), at Sanxey's Book Store then at 120 Main Street, Richmond. Tom Bolling was home for the holidays from Charlottesville, and the two boys had many reminiscences to exchange, not having seen each other for two years. Poe gave Bolling a copy of *Al Aaraaf* and regaled him with an apocryphal account of his "trip abroad," since the real facts of his rather uneventful life in the army as an enlisted man did not supply the adventurous background which the author of two volumes of poetry required. Bolling was much impressed, and we may be sure carried back to the University the news of the brilliant and interesting career of "Gaffy," news which no doubt helped to clear the atmosphere there of the cloud which rested upon the erstwhile young gambler on account of unpaid debts.

Thus the "Poe legend" was already beginning to take shape with Poe himself as the prime source.[344] All of this was at that time due to his desire to appear a man set apart, an adventurous fellow, who had left the University to see the world, and had succeeded.[352] In these stories he seems always to have embodied some of the actual experiences of his brother Henry.[353]

For the rest, Poe was much about town, seeing his old friends and distributing to them in person, or by orders on the Richmond bookstore, copies of *Al Aaraaf.* As few were capable of understanding the poems,

[352] A Richmond newspaper for January 19, 1830, Poe's twenty-first birthday, prints the acknowledgment of the receipt of *Al Aaraaf,* etc.

[353] The persistence of the story about Poe's "trip abroad" is incredible. Russian encyclopedias give detailed accounts of his "arrest in St. Petersburg," and confusing the title of Henry Middleton, the American Consul with that of "minister," have translated the word "priest." So we have Poe, drunken, of course, being rescued from prison and Siberia by the "Rev. Middleton," Bible in hand. Absurdity can go no further! Henry Poe, Edgar's brother, *may* have been to St. Petersburg while in the navy or merchant marine. There is no proof. Poe probably "annexed" some of his brother's adventures. Henry died soon after, so that the rest is silence.

an attitude of amusement, always a convenient mask for ignorance, was the general result.   In this the wiseacres of the town were confirmed by a review J. H. Hewitt is supposed to have written for the Baltimore *Minerva and Emerald,* poking fun unmercifully at the new poet.   The paper's editor was Rufus Dawes, and Poe may have been mindful of this when he skinned the man alive in *Graham's Magazine.*[354]

Not a great deal is known of this, Poe's last, sojourn in the Allan house at Richmond, in the Spring of 1830.   He was still waiting for his appointment to West Point and for that reason was tolerated as a temporary inmate of the establishment, rather than the "son" of the house.   John Allan had not long before returned from "The Springs." He was not in very good health, was still troubled over his wife's death and revolving in his mind the fact that he had no heir nor wife to pre-side over his household, although Miss Valentine remained and took her sister's place most acceptably as later events show.   Poe probably came and went as he pleased, being left to his own desires and his room with the beloved books, where the further revision of his poems with new ones was already under way.   He probably saw a good deal of the Mackenzies at Duncan Lodge where Rosalie still lived in the atmosphere of affection which her brother so lacked.   Mr. Allan may have tried at times to drown his memories after a not unusual method, although he was by no means given to drink.   There is a good reason to believe, however, that with the first signs of advancing age and ill health and the loss of his life partner of many years' standing, at this particular time he sometimes indulged too freely.   If so the results were not such as to make things happier for the members of his household.   Shortly after the beginning of the year he began to find solace for his sorrows in the companionship of one who had already borne him a daughter. The natural result proved doubly disturbing to his peace of mind.

On May 3, 1830, he had a violent quarrel with Poe.[355]   Probably a recurrence of the old charges of idleness and living upon his bounty, in which he heaped reproaches upon his ward, and ended by roundly insulting the young poet about his family, at a time, says Poe, "When you knew my heart was almost breaking."   The uncertainty of living in Richmond waiting for the appointment, while the carping and fault-finding tongue of his guardian let no old fault rest, when, too, Frances Allan and Elmira were haunting him like ghosts—all this made such

---

[354] "We now hesitate not to say, that no man in America has been more shamefully over-estimated," etc. Poe's article on Rufus Dawes. See Chapter XXI, page 439. The real author of the review of *Al Aaraaf* is doubtful.
[355] *Valentine Museum Poe Letters,* letter No. 24, page 257. If the young Poe had any knowledge of his guardian's mode of life at this time, and it is quite probable that he had, in view of his great reverence for the memory of his foster-mother, his indignation over his guardian's actions becomes only too clear. The situation does not need to be elaborated

scenes doubly hard to bear, sometimes almost insufferable. The alternative was starving, nakedness, and the loss of opportunity.

A few minutes after this scene Poe wrote to an old army acquaintance at Fortress Monroe, apparently a sergeant in his old company to whom he owed money. Poe addressed him as "Bully," and says that the reason he had not paid the debt was because he could not get the money out of his guardian, although he had tried dozens of times. Poe, it seems, owed sums to several other non-commissioned officers in the old regiment, amounts which he had probably borrowed in the Spring of 1829 on the prospects of the "reconciliation" with Mr. Allan after Frances Allan's death. The small sums he had received from home had not permitted a settlement. From other statements in this letter, it appears that he could not be frank with his guardian about the matter. The trouble John Allan had raised over the extra amount necessary to procure a substitute was probably a sufficient warning that any further revelations about expenditures would be met with a burst of wrath. One Downey from Fortress Monroe had already called upon John Allan and received an answer not satisfactory to Poe's "creditors," and this reply Poe is at haste to explain away by saying that *Mr. Allan was not very often sober* and his words could be discounted.

This statement about John Allan is one of the most discreditable and unfortunate that Poe ever made. Whatever the provocation, it was unwise, defamatory to his "father," and eventually the final cause and plausible excuse for his being "disinherited." On this letter the second Mrs. Allan also based her charge that Poe had spent the money provided for the substitute. Sergeant Graves, or "Bully," to whom Poe wrote was not the substitute, however, but simply one of several soldiers about Fort Moultrie to whom the ex-sergeant major owed various small sums. Poe promises payment, and in a most familiar tone, ends by informing "Bully" that the writer is now a cadet. This looks very much as if the Secretary of War had already given Poe the letters to report at West Point for examination, as the latter had suggested that he would in an earlier letter to Mr. Allan while in Baltimore. Only the official confirming letters were now needed; perhaps the exact weight of political influence was still lacking, and events now shaped themselves in such a way as to cause Mr. Allan to secure this and get Poe finally off his hands.

John Allan was now a widower, and a very eligible one in point of fortune, at least. His former wife's sister, Miss Valentine, was running his establishment, and it seems to have occurred to the thrifty merchant that the arrangement already in force might as well be made permanent. About a year before Frances Allan's death he remarked in a letter that Miss Valentine was "as fat and hearty as ever." Doubtless her figure had lost nothing in attractiveness during the interim;

she was acquainted with how much sugar he liked in his coffee, she was near at hand, and they were intimately "at home." The result was that he began to pay her marked attentions. What the lady's sentiments were, we do not know. To remain in the same household where she had already lived for twenty-five years, and to become the presiding mistress of one of the finest establishments in Richmond, may not have been without its attractions. Poe, however, seems to have been outraged. Frances Allan was dead scarcely a year, and he was under no hallucinations as to the delicacy of his guardian's tender emotions. He seems to have protested and to have reminded his "Aunt Nancy" of her dead sister's wrongs. Perhaps he even intruded upon some sentimental scenes. At any rate Miss Valentine refused John Allan's offer, probably influenced by Poe's advice, and the effect was devastating upon what remained of Frances Allan's household. John Allan's indignation must have been implacable. Was he never to be quit of this young upstart, or the household rid of his interference in his perfectly logical and natural plans? He seems to have forthwith determined to put an end to it once and for all. Poe has been accused of trying to prevent his foster-father from having a legitimate heir, but the "other reasons" seem to be sufficient and much more probable. Whatever the *reasons* may have been, the *results* are not in doubt. Poe was packed off forthwith to West Point. General Scott's influence seems to have been obtained, [356] and through John Allan's partner, Mr. Charles Ellis, a letter was secured from the latter's younger brother, Powhatan Ellis, then United States Senator from Mississippi, recommending Poe to the Secretary of War. As usual, a senator's letter turned the trick with the War Department, and on March 31, 1830, we find Poe's guardian signing this document at Richmond, probably not without extreme satisfaction:

SIR—as the guardian of Edgar Allan Poe I hereby signify my assent to his signing articles by which he shall bind himself to serve the United States for Five years, unless sooner discharged, as stipulated in your official letter appointing him cadet.

Respectfully,
Your obt.—servant.
JOHN ALLAN

The Hon. Sec'y of War
Washington

---

[356] This is not certain but probable. General Scott had known Poe as a boy; John Allan knew him; a volume of Poe's early poems was afterward found in the General's library; several of Poe's West Point classmates assert that General Scott helped Poe. At a much later date General Scott gave money to a collection taken up to help Poe, etc., etc. Also see letter No. 23, *Valentine Museum Poe Letters* (November 6, 1830).

The state of affairs at home may be inferred from the fact, that once in the possession of his appointment the new cadet did not linger any longer than he had to. From Mr. Allan's letter it seems clear that Poe received his cadet's warrant at the end of March, 1830. Examinations at West Point were in June, yet by May 12th, he was preparing to depart, for on that date John Allan is charged on the books of his firm with a pair of blankets for Poe's outfit, and it seems likely that, about the same time, the young man left Richmond for the United States Military Academy. Mr. Allan accompanied him to the steamboat leaving for Baltimore, and shook hands with him. Poe says that he knew it was meant for a final farewell.[357]

Poe must have arrived in Baltimore about the middle of May, 1830, where he seems to have gone to live temporarily with his Aunt Maria Clemm, as letters from Richmond were afterward addressed to him in care of his brother Henry, who also resided with her. The affection of Mrs. Clemm, and the doubtless spontaneous welcome of little Virginia, no doubt formed a warm contrast to the atmosphere he had just left. The fact that he was about to enter the military profession, presumably for life, did not interfere with his literary aspirations. Poe doubtless had his reservations about the permanence of his career in the army, even then. He must already have been at work on some of the poems which appeared the year following, and he doubtless hoped that by pleasing his guardian and becoming an officer he would solve the problem of existing, and later on be in a position to rely on Mr. Allan's patronage in the work which lay nearest to his heart.

Indeed it is safe to say that from the first, "Cadet Poe" had no enthusiasm for West Point. His two years of army service could leave him no illusions as to what was to come afterward. And the outward glitter—the uniforms, and the parades—did not have the attraction for him by this time that they have for the average youngster who first encounters them. A long experience on the inside of a military tunic had already proved to him how tight and narrow was the fit. He was now twenty-one years old and capable of estimating his chances for the future.[358] With his temperament, his literary propensities, and the circumstances under which he entered the Military Acad-

---

[357] *Valentine Museum Poe Letters*, letter No. 24, page 257.

[358] Some of Poe's biographers make capital of Poe's being over twenty-one at the time of his entrance at West Point, and to accuse him of "duplicity." As a matter of fact to this day both at Annapolis and West Point various "dodges are worked" by candidates to circumvent the letter of the law about appointments: mail is sent to establish "legal residence" in other districts than that from where the candidate hails, etc. Poe's age was afterward a joke at West Point. See Chapter XIII, page 222. It is now known that the Secretary of War himself gave Poe assurance that he could call himself twenty-one until his twenty-second birthday. See this chapter, page 201, also *Valentine Museum Poe Letters*, letter No. 15, page 159.

emy, it was almost a foregone conclusion that he would not stay long in a place where even determination and military ambition are often not sufficient to produce a diploma. Two years in barracks had already informed him as to the amount of freedom that he could expect, and the discipline at West Point was even stricter. Nevertheless, there was no alternative. John Allan's help was contingent upon his making the most of the opportunity, and there was nothing else to do but to starve. Up until the last, however, Poe continued to further his literary plans, for while in Baltimore on his way to West Point he took the occasion to call on Mr. Nathan C. Brooks of semi-literary character to whom he read some of his manuscripts and promised to send a poem for an annual that Brooks then had under way. This Poe never did. It seems also that he borrowed some money from a former schoolmate to whom he imparted another version of his legendary adventures abroad.[359]

Poe probably went by way of Philadelphia to New York, and thence to West Point,[360] where he arrived in time to take the examinations for admission during the last week of June, 1830. On June 28th, he writes John Allan that the examinations for admission are just over, and adds with a true Virginian naïveté that a great many cadets of "good family" have been rejected. Even the son of a governor was found deficient! Mr. Allan's remarks upon the Poe family were probably remembered. Doubtless, to the aspirant for social honors in Richmond, the shot went home. Evidently young Poe was somewhat taken aback by the businesslike air of the Military Academy for he is careful to impress his guardian, as if in preparation for possible snags ahead, that less than a quarter of those who enter ever graduate. "I will be much pleased," he adds, "if you will answer this letter." He was not quite sure how the wind blew in Richmond,—then, too, during the first few days in uniform, it is strangely comforting to hear from home. On July 1, 1830, Poe took the oath at West Point "to preserve the Constitution of the United States and serve them against all their enemies whomsoever." The next morning, with a veteran's disgust, he found himself being awakened in a tent by the familiar sound of reveille, and donning a cadet's uniform.

About the same time that Cadet Edgar Allan Poe was going through the manual of arms, with astonishing facility for a *plebe,* on the summer parade ground at the United States Military Academy, Mr. Allan

---

[359] Woodberry, 1909, vol. I, page 67.

[360] This is not certain. It is thought that Poe took the opportunity to call on some literary friends in Philadelphia, as well as upon Carey, Lea & Carey. It may be that he arranged to publish the sonnet *To Science* in the *Casket* while in Philadelphia at this time. The poem appeared a few months later, October, 1830, and L. A. Wilmer is thought to have been connected with the *Casket* and the *Saturday Evening Post* about this time.

was enjoying the hospitality of his friend John Mayo at Belleville Plantation near Richmond, despite a very annoying complication in his private affairs at home. Among the house guests was Miss Louisa Gabriella Patterson (the niece of Mrs. Mayo), a strong-minded lady from New York, about thirty years of age. Mr. Allan was attracted by her; the attentions of the rich widower were well received, and they shortly afterwards became engaged. It was the stroke which severed Poe forever from the home of his youth. He was now finally and irretrievably an exile in a world hostile to dreamers. For a while he tarried as a stranger in the tents of the Military.

CHAPTER THIRTEEN

THE WEST POINT INTERLUDE

THE not inconsiderable period of his short life which Poe spent at West Point, trying to carry out John Allan's idea of what his career should be, may be considered, for the most part, as a spiritual and mental interlude. It lasted from June 25, 1830, to February 19, 1831,[361] and marked the passing of the days when he made his final decision to cast off all outside dictation and to follow, without further delay or indirection, a literary career. During the periods of drill and recitation his body and the secondary part of his mind were marched back and forth on the parade ground or to the classroom, but his spirit and desire were elsewhere.

Upon arrival, in the last week of June, 1830, he seems to have passed the entrance examinations without difficulty, and to have been received by a Captain Hitchcock and a Mr. Ross, to whom he was previously known or bore letters of introduction. On July 1st, as we have already seen, he took the oath, and as the custom then was and still is, he immediately went to live under canvas in the annual summer encampment of the cadets. His tent mates were Cadets Read, Stockton from Philadelphia, and Henderson, the last a nephew of the Secretary of War.[362]

Upon arrival at "The Point," Poe had found waiting for him a letter from his guardian which had been forwarded by his brother Henry from Baltimore, containing a $20 bill, and a complaint that he had taken some articles from home which did not belong to him. These, it appears from his reply, were some books from his own room and probably a brass inkstand, sand caster, and pen holder marked with John Allan's name and the year '13.[363] These articles must have been

---

[361] These dates are deduced from the *Valentine Museum Poe Letters*. Poe arrived at West Point in time to take the entrance examinations, which lasted two days. He probably arrived the day or the afternoon before. On June 28, 1830, he writes John Allan saying the examinations are over. The date of his leaving is from the letter written to John Allan from New York, February 21, 1831, in which he says he left West Point two days before. This for the first time gives Poe's stay at West Point its proper duration.

[362] This, and some of the other material not hitherto included in Poe's biographies, has been taken from the *Valentine Museum Poe Letters*, Nos. 22, 23, 24, and 25, all but the last written by Poe from West Point, and all covering the period with interesting new data.

[363] As Poe had these with him for years, and at no time *after* the Spring of 1830 had an opportunity of taking any "souvenirs" from the Allan house, it is reasonably certain he brought them from Richmond when he left for West Point. See also Chapter VII, page 107, note 182.

in Poe's possession for years in his own room, some of the books were doubtless the gift of Frances Allan, or his own scant little library. Nothing shows the strength of Mr. Allan's overpowering sense of property, and his petty parsimony more than this incident.

Financially Poe's experience at West Point was largely that of the fiasco at Charlottesville. The $20 was evidently to see him through the Military Academy. It, and the pair of blankets which he drew from *Ellis & Allan* in May, were the last evidences of any warmth which he received from his guardian, who now felt that on the generous cadet's salary of $28 a month, and rations, Poe was amply upon his own. It was customary for the parents of cadets to make a deposit for the boys to draw upon, for their instruments, books, clothes, and other incidentals. But this was not done for Poe, although he writes later asking for "instruments and a *Cambridge Mathematics,*" but the letter received no reply. Indeed, his guardian did not communicate with him at all between June, 1830, and January, 1831. From the day Poe took the oath, it is quite obvious that John Allan considered and hoped that their intimate association was at an end.

About the year 1830, the Military Academy at West Point consisted of five fairly large stone buildings for administrative purposes, classrooms, and dormitories scattered about the "parade," the heights above the Hudson. There were, in addition, six brick buildings for the officers and professors near the river, and some old military store houses of Revolutionary date for arms and equipment. The original barracks had been burnt some years before Poe's arrival.

In 1830, the Academy was twenty-eight years old and there were some thirty-odd professors, instructors, and assistants for a corps of about 250 cadets. First preference in appointment was given by law to the descendants of Revolutionary officers, which accounts for Poe's anxiety in looking up his grandfather's record in Baltimore,—the sons of the officers of 1812 coming next. The legal age for appointees was between fourteen and twenty-one, most of the boys being admitted in the early teens, so that Poe was far more mature than the average cadet of his time, in both years and experience.

The course lasted four years, but was by no means so rigidly organized as at present. Under the conditions, Poe's hope of receiving advanced standing owing to his previous military experience and attendance at the University of Virginia, might possibly have been accorded him had he consistently distinguished himself. Some of the more advanced cadets were allowed to take part as instructors, for which they received additional pay. A cadet's salary was fixed by law at $330, with certain allowances for rations and permission to purchase

equipment at army rates.   Textbooks, and articles of personal use were
not provided, however, and Poe soon found himself in debt for necessaries which the parents of the other students either furnished or provided by deposit.   In his final letter from West Point, he complains
bitterly of this and of the similar lack of the small necessities of life
which John Allan's parsimony had also inflicted upon him at the University of Virginia.   To be without soap, candles, writing materials,
room furniture, fuel, and clothing; to be forced to borrow even the
minor articles for personal cleanliness and comfort is a situation which
is essentially exasperating and degrading.   Poe took a peculiar pride
in the neatness and care of his person and complains justly of the
unnecessary "fatigues and degradations" which he was forced to undergo.   The household economy of the time, particularly the Virginia
plantation, supplied many of the articles, which are now purchased as a
matter of course.   In Poe's day it was difficult, sometimes even impossible to buy them at all. [364]   Such a situation does not need to be
enlarged upon.

At Charlottesville the story of his birth had undoubtedly somewhat
compromised his social position with the sons of Virginia aristocrats.
At West Point this condition did not exist; Poe, indeed, seems to have
definitely allied himself there with Virginians, who, up until the Civil
War, constituted themselves a group apart,—yet the Military Academy
was by no means democratic.   It had its own peculiar snobbery.   This
consisted in affecting to look down on one who had served in the ranks.
Future officers, and the sons of officers had their own opinion about
one who had so far erred as to have been a common soldier.   He did
not "belong," and his mannerisms, especially since they were marked,
were doubly open to suspicion.   In Poe's history at West Point this
played its part, and helped to make the already bitter, a little salt.   To
offset this, Poe gave himself out as a young man of many adventures,
one who could tell much of strange places if he cared to.   Thus the
"mystery" was continued.

As for the rest, there was certainly something to be gained:

The Course of Study is completed in four years, each being devoted to a
class; and includes the French language, drawing, natural and experimental

---

[364] Soap, candles, toilet preparations, minor articles of clothing, mattresses, towels,
linen of all kinds, and articles of knit and woven wear were made at home for the
most part.   Not to have these, argued oneself homeless, and a nobody.   With no
cash to buy these, Poe's condition at Charlottesville and West Point can be imagined.
It was one of the things that not only made life unbearable but compromised his
social position.   A borrower is always a nuisance.   Poe had been sent to West Point
with a handshake and $20, the rest was silence.   He was right in resenting this
bitterly.

philosophy, chemistry, and mineralogy, geography, history, ethics, and national law, mathematics in the highest branches, and lastly artillery and engineering.[365]

The country about the Academy was not without its attractions, had there been any time to enjoy them. The view from West Point down the gorge of the Hudson as far as Horse Race and Anthony's Nose is peculiarly beautiful and was impressed firmly on the young poet's memory. Old Fort Putnam on the hill behind the barracks had at that time the remains of various subterranean chambers, the Catskills, which had already been celebrated by Irving, were nearby, and in the neighborhood of the post was Stony Point, the scene of Major André's sad adventure and the treason of General Arnold, in which, as we have seen, Poe might feel himself entitled to take a peculiar interest. But there was no time to wander among the hills as there had been at Charlottesville. A paternal government claimed his time and the intervals of leisure were few. Nevertheless, West Point left its mark, and later appears vaguely in some of Poe's descriptions of New York scenery.

The cadets rose early; breakfasted, we may be sure, frugally; attended lectures; dined; and about four P.M. returned to the barracks to get into uniform for the "parade" or drills which occupied the bulk of the remaining hours of daylight. After supper there was a study period, with call to quarters about nine o'clock and early taps. Leaves were few and far between, with holidays even rarer. Here was scant time for dreaming.

From the West Point period, the beginning of Poe's physical troubles definitely dates.[366] It is reasonably certain that he was of a type which matured early; he probably reached the prime of life before the full strength of manhood in many others began. Despite his early prowess as a swimmer, it is known that he was generally averse to physical exercise and easily fatigued.[367] He had a weak heart and little energy. Any long continued regimen of drill and exercise must have left him morose and unstrung. The conditions at West Point were precisely the worst that he could be called upon to undergo, because the most vigorous, and there was no time at all for escape and solitude. Every incident of his daily routine, and the forced intimacy of tent and barracks life, was an interruption to that stream of consciousness which, to a man of Poe's type, was all in all—the reverie from which he hoped from time to time to snatch something worth preserving.

The ordinarily constituted man, certainly the cadets who surrounded

[365] *The Northern Traveller,* third edition, revised and extended, published by G. & C. Carvill, New York, 1828 (and after). "A reliable guide book and compilation of information for travelers from official sources."
[366] See Poe's own statement, *Valentine Museum Poe Letters,* letter No. 24.
[367] Testimony of classmates at the University of Virginia.

Poe, could never have an inkling of the sense of hopelessness, nervous irritability, and spiritual frustration which comes to the artist as he feels those rare periods when consciousness becomes creative being interrupted by the trivialities of petty conversation, the necessity to appear polite, or the call of duty to some ultimately useless task. The result is like losing something out of the mouth while dining. No matter how much is eaten afterward the sense of loss is still there. Six months of this seems to have been sufficient to prostrate Poe and send him into a nervous collapse.[368] A boyhood in the same house with John Allan, followed by a period of wild anxiety, starvation, the loss of his sweetheart, and the death of his "mother," was an excellent preparation. Whether this entitled Poe to sympathy is not the question to be raised; the facts, and their result on the man who was subjected to them, are, however, pertinent matter of inquiry.

The drills, during the summer encampment at West Point, are notoriously severe. It is then that the raw *plebes* are knocked into some kind of form for the coming academic year by the combined efforts of the military instructors, and the officious attentions of the upper classmen known as "hazing," which is as much, and as important a part of the character and life-forming aim of the Military Academy as the textbooks or the sermons in Chapel.

Poe seems to have escaped some of the attention of the upper classmen by the fact that he had already passed two years in the army, and bore somewhat the character of a veteran. His age, which was several years greater than most of the others, and his evident maturity seem also to have distinguished him from the rest and to have aided in building up a certain glamour and curiosity about his name and antecedents. He became known for his aloofness and pride, and the joke was circulated that having obtained an appointment for his son who had died, Poe had himself taken the boy's place and entered West Point. It was the dignified "father" whom they now beheld. All this the ex-sergeant major seems to have taken not too good-naturedly while he added to his prestige by indicating that he was a youth with a romantic and thrilling past. Brother Henry's adventures were now liberally drawn upon again for his own account, and to them Poe added certain other items about voyages to the Mediterranean, and experiences while penetrating the mysterious interior of Arabia that probably reflect the sources of his reading for *Israfel,* and the secondary Oriental literature which engaged his attention about this time. That anyone could imagine such vivid experiences was probably beyond the literal horizon of his fellow cadets. The aura of the legend which Poe undoubtedly

---

[368] *Valentine Museum Poe Letters,* letter No. 25. Poe from New York to John Allan just after leaving West Point.

began to build up about himself, even at the University of Virginia, now took on a more definite form, and the stories of his "foreign voyages" were long remembered by his West Point classmates, stories that come to life years later in their reminiscences to confirm the myth for biographers.[369] Even the cold records of the War Department have scarcely been able to destroy their effect. Someone at West Point also heard the story (which Poe had a year before written to John Allan) that the romantic looking cadet was a grandson of Benedict Arnold, and this tale began to be whispered about the corridors of South Barracks. A friend at last made bold to ask Poe himself, and there is good authority for the statement that he would neither deny nor affirm it. The truth seems to be that Poe really knew so little about his mother and her antecedents that he was not sure himself. Her maiden name, he knew, had been Arnold, and he knew little more; in addition the tale undoubtedly added a strange, and to him a delightfully diabolic color to his reputation.

Part of this desire for a mysterious notoriety was undoubtedly due to Poe's own feeling of the necessity for padding out his personality in certain directions in which it lacked or had been frustrated, and for making a frame for the strange face in the portrait of himself, that he early set about painting. Both the frame and the countenance that looked out from it were largely artificial, but they were nevertheless works of art. A delight in gulling the simplicity of those about him, a belief in their simplicity which begot in him a dangerous sense of superiority and contempt, was also present. As he grew older this sense of superiority became more and more necessary to his own thought to offset the sense of weakness that came to afflict him, as he began to disintegrate physically and psychically. The romantic hero was the first to appear, only to be replaced later by the perfect logician.

It would have been an excellent thing for the young gentleman adventurer known as Cadet Edgar Allan Poe, whose critical intellect had already freed him from the narrow enthusiasm of patriotism, and unmasked for him the empty banality behind the brassy glitter of military life, if, at this period of his existence, he could have been removed by some miracle to an environment where he might have listened to and taken part in the debates and conversation of his superiors and equals. As it was, there was no one about him with whom he could talk. The personnel at the Academy, while he was there, seems to have been without exception of the completely usual stamp. No one of his classmates had any mental ambitions, and none of them ever achieved any distinc-

---

[369] Allan B. Magruder, a classmate of Poe, to Prof. George E. Woodberry, April 23, 1884. See Woodberry, 1909, vol. I, page 70.

tion beyond that of brevet-general or pastor *emeritus* of an evangelical church. To them, Poe's babel of critical remarks about poets and philosophers of whom they had never heard before, and seldom heard mentioned again in the warlike or peaceful events of their hide-bound lives, must have been incomprehensible and suspect.

The truth is that, even at the age of twenty-two, Poe had few contemporaries in the United States.[370] There were a few circles in Boston, New York and Philadelphia where his remarks might have found an audience. Baltimore was later on to provide another. For the rest, the old tradition of classical culture was fast disappearing along with the old generation which had founded the "Republic." The new Jacksonian "Democracy" was already climbing into the saddle, the frontier democracy, which the followers of Jefferson mistakenly took for their own. It was no longer fashionable to be a "gentleman," or to know anything. The tide of romanticism and secondary German philosophy, which Longfellow and Emerson were later on to introduce in America, had not yet begun to be mentioned. So far Poe had spoken in an atmosphere so rarefied that it could not produce even an echo. At West Point the vacuum was complete.

American history has produced no more ludicrous paradox than this young literary genius shut up in an institution which was then, and for some years later, partly given up to educating and providing the military technique for many of those who were later on to use the knowledge they had so gained in trying to destroy the nation which provided the means for so doing. The world in which Poe moved had nothing to do with all this. The sectionalism which was even then beginning to divide the nation, the controversy over slavery, the awakening of industrialism, and the mewling and puking of the young democracy, even then beginning to strike out against all those who raised their heads above its level of thought or morals, did not exist for him. His world lay in the realms of thought, criticism, and the philosophy of European molding which he had first found in the pages of the English reviews upon the counters in the book loft at *Ellis & Allan*. Here he had met the young Macaulay, and "Christopher North," had become interested in Shelley, Keats, and Byron, Wordsworth, and the giant Coleridge, and it was with them that he thought, and out of them that he moved forth armed with a genuine comment on the philosophy of the time and the only lasting creative urge in romantic poetry that the United States produced. Longfellow and Emerson translated, re-

---

[370] It must be remembered that Poe's environment, even in Richmond, was largely Scotch; his primary education was founded in English schools, and his reading had been largely in the English periodicals found at *Ellis & Allan*. At the University of Virginia he had come across the rare Germanic influence then scarcely known in this country. Poe read French, Italian, and Latin.

molded, and explained, but Poe took the data of romanticism and out of it created something new, a unique utterance in poetry, and a critical comment and application of philosophy to his time and environment that is only now beginning to become appreciated.[371] His art in prose and verse has already won its cloud-streaked place in the sun. In the scattered leaves of his critical and philosophical comments lie some of the earliest suggestions of the possible results of science upon the world and the spirit of man, doubts as to the ultimate self-sufficiency of democracy, queries as to the human value of a society which made physical comfort its goal, strange philanderings in psychology, and in the mathematics of astronomy.

As yet it was all very vague and youthfully crude, yet it was there, in embryo, in the young man in a swallow-tail coat and bowler shako, who was being marched back and forth on the hot August parade ground at West Point, learning the precise angle at which the rifle must be held at "port arms," and how to salute the flag which did not represent anything that he really cared very much about, and a great deal that was positively distasteful to him. For this performance he received three meals and about ninety cents a day. The strange result was that, in spite of it, he evolved from Coleridge and others his own critical theory of poetry and somehow, somewhere, continued to write poetry, poetry which did not view the change which even then he saw creeping across the machineless world into which he had been born with the undivided enthusiasm of most of his contemporaries.[372] In the *Philadelphia Casket* for October, 1830, appeared reprinted from the 1829 volume the young West Point cadet's

SONNET—TO SCIENCE

Science! true daughter of Old Time thou art!
  Who alterest all things with thy peering eyes.
Why preyest thou thus upon the poet's heart,
  Vulture, whose wings are dull realities?
How should he love thee? or how deem thee wise,
  Who wouldst not leave him in his wandering
To seek for treasure in the jewelled skies,
  Albeit he soared with an undaunted wing?

[371] This "comment" is scattered and sometimes dulled by Poe's aping of greater knowledge than he possessed, and carelessness about facts, but it is there, nevertheless, in his criticism, his stories, and in *Eureka*. Lowell said, "As it is, he has squared out blocks enough to build an enduring pyramid, but left them lying careless and unclaimed in many different quarries." J. R. Lowell in *Graham's Magazine*, 1845, vol. XXVII, no. 2, page 50.

[372] The cocksure optimism of Victorianism is utterly lacking in Poe. He was one of the few to see the implications of harm in the age of machinery just coming into its own. His chief quarrel with it was that it destroyed beauty and leisure. As a Virginian and an egoist Poe despised mobocracy and a Santa Claus view of science; as an artist he depicted the ugliness of industrialism.

Hast thou not dragged Diana from her car?
  And driven the Hamadryad from the wood
To seek a shelter in some happier star?
    Hast thou not torn the Naiad from her flood,
The Elfin from the green grass, and from me
The summer dream beneath the tamarind tree?

In the meantime, General Scott had visited West Point on a tour of inspection, probably, about the end of the summer encampment, and was, so Poe tells his guardian in a letter written home that Fall, most cordial in his attentions to the young Virginian.[373]   General Scott was probably more than casually interested, for John Allan was by that time engaged to a lady who was one of his relations.

The Summer of 1830, indeed, had been a crucial one in the changes which it brought about in Poe's relations with John Allan, and any projects which he may have had for the future favors of his guardian. None of Poe's letters home had been answered.   Mr. Allan was summering on his Lower Byrd Plantation in Goochland, and passing the time most pleasantly in courting the lady of his choice at Mr. Mayo's on Belvedere.   Poe no doubt heard of the turn which affairs had taken through the visit of some Virginia friends to West Point, Mr. Chevallee and Mr. Cunningham.[373]   He could not help being much interested for he must have realized that in a very real sense he had interests at stake.   The possibility of a legitimate heir would undoubtedly greatly weaken the already slender claim which he might still feel he had upon the favor and affection of John Allan.   On October 5, 1830, Mr. Allan was married in the Patterson house in New York to his second wife, the wedding being attended by the Galts and other Richmond friends and relatives.   The happy pair returned to live in Richmond.   Poe tells his "father" that he had hoped to have a visit from him at "The Point," as the other boys were visited by their relatives, but such an event was probably the last idea in John Allan's mind.[373]   With the new wife, both the dark and the bright memories of the first were swept away.   John Allan had confessed the faults and the results of former indiscretions to his new partner before his marriage,[374] he had been accepted in spite of them, and naturally enough he did not care to renew the past, or the possibility of future complications by even a mention of Poe.   He belonged to the realm of Frances Allan, and that world, for the good merchant, now enjoying an Indian Summer of youth, had completely passed away.   To the new wife, Edgar Allan Poe was a name, the son of actors and a scribbler; to her husband, a troublesome memory.   It was hard,

---

[373] *Valentine Museum Poe Letters,* letter No. 23.
[374] John Allan in his will made at Richmond, Virginia, April 17, 1832.   See the copy of John Allan's will, Appendix III.

almost impossible for Poe to believe this. He still continued to write "affectionately" to "Dear Pa." But there was no answer.

At the end of the Summer the battalion of cadets moved into their winter quarters. Poe's room, which he shared with two others, was Number 28 of the old South Barracks, and here the final phase of Israfel in brass buttons dragged its way to an abrupt end through the Fall and Winter of 1830-31.

Number 28 was furnished, as were all the rooms in the barracks, with a more than Spartan simplicity. There were three beds, perhaps as many chairs, and a table shared in common by the inmates. A wardrobe for each contained their equipment and clothes, for which a precise position was indicated by the regulations. No ornaments or pictures were tolerated, but as a special concession, certain *lares* might be "displayed," upon the upper shelf of the cupboard. A broom, a few basins, slop tubs, and pitchers completed the domestic scene of a cadet's background, to which an open fire, if the room was fortunate enough to abut on a chimney flue, and a few candlesticks contributed the sole touches of warmth and light. Compared with this, Number 13 "Rowdy Row" at the University of Virginia had been a luxurious apartment and a haven of private refuge. To the usual assortment of textbooks, Poe somehow or other had contrived to add some genuine literature. These works of imagination consumed by far the larger portion of his study hours as well as his spare time. Even a drill or formation was insufficient at times to interrupt a favorite passage, yet, despite this, until he deliberately set out to neglect his studies, he stood high in his classes at the end of the semi-annual examination: third in French, and seventeenth in mathematics, in a class of eighty-seven.

There is a studied confusion about the incessant routine of a military academy that no haphazard method of existence can hope to equal. The method itself is beyond approach for producing a continuous series of events that perpetually threaten to make everyone late to something. As a consequence, the unfortunate young gentlemen subjected to the process are forever rushing about changing clothes or books, dashing up and down stairs, arising, going to bed, winding themselves in long sashes, buckling on swords, answering oral orders bawled through the long corridors, or stampeding off to formations and yelping "here" to their names at roll call thousands of times. The method of existence is so complicated that living is impossible.

The life of the inmates of Number 28 was further made more interesting, if less tolerable, by the visits at both stated and unexpected hours of the various officers of military and academic discipline who were charged with enforcing the list of thirty-three disciplinary "don'ts," each with its ingenious penalty; or by the intrusions of upper classmen who were tacitly licensed by the traditions of the place to inflict the peculiarly exasperating personal annoyances of the code of hazing at any hour of the day or night. The blare of bugles and the crash of drums announced the beginning and close of the various and numerous periods into which the day was divided, a schedule which took no account of the value of leisure. There was literally no provision at all for privacy in barracks, and the cadets ate together in a large mess hall under the eyes of the officers. The hours of leave were so short as to preclude any trips into the country about, and if they had not been, there would have been no place to go. The observances of the ritual of rank and military restrictions made visits to the married quarters of the officers uncomfortable when they were possible.

West Point was, at that time, remote from all places of any size and the visits of relatives and parents were perforce laborious, brief, and far between. In short, there was no social life at all. The only relief to the bareness and monotony of the place seems to have been a combination store and illicit groggery run by "Old Benny Haven," who exchanged various petty, luxurious tidbits, and bottles of brandy for the small change of the cadets, when they had any, and lacking that, conducted a usurious form of barter in the clothes, blankets, equipment, and even the soap and candles of the young gentlemen. His place just off the post was, of course, out of bounds, and, although frequently visited by the officers for convivial refreshment, was at once the only solace and the main cause of trouble for the cadets. In addition to Old Benny's place, as often happens about military posts, the Commissary seems to have provided a loafing place at odd times. Here Poe became acquainted with the Commissary Clerk, at that time one J. Augustus Shea, who it seems had some literary propensities as he afterward published poems. Little George Shea, the clerk's son, then a small child running about the grounds, was afterward recalled by Poe. Both father and son heard the poet deliver *The Raven* in New York fifteen years later when he was at the crest of his fame, and had renewed the old West Point intimacy.[669] In such surroundings the young Poe, who loved to imagine himself in luxurious and semi-Oriental apartments, surrounded by sweeping draperies, a gloomy, religious light, and tripods of incense, found himself "at home."

Number 28 South Barracks early attained the reputation of being a "hard" room. Those who aspired to a minimum of appearances on the rolls of discipline soon learned to avoid its precincts. From it, from time to time, issued pasquinades and diatribes in rhyme upon the officers and faculty which were clever enough both to amuse and to annoy. Lieutenant Joseph Locke of Savannah appears to have distinguished himself as a merciless enforcer of discipline, and his doubtless too frequent visits to Number 28 were soon celebrated by the pen which has alone preserved him to fame:

As for Locke, he is all in my eye;
  May the d——l right soon for his soul call.
He never was known to lie—
  In bed at a reveille 'roll-call.'

John Locke was a notable name;
  Joe Locke is a greater: in short,
The former was well known to fame,
  But the latter's well known "to report."

Even Colonel Thayer, the Superintendent, did not escape, although Poe seems to have found in him one of the few men he could admire while at the Military Academy.

Cadet T. H. Gibson was Poe's roommate, and from him, although he set down his memories many years later, we are indebted for what is probably the most authentic picture of "Cadet Poe": [375]

. . . The first conversation I had with Poe after we became installed as room-mates was characteristic of the man. A volume of Campbell's *Poems* was lying upon our table, and he tossed it contemptuously aside with the curt remark: 'Campbell is a plagiarist'; then without waiting for a reply he picked up the book, and turned the leaves over rapidly until he found the passage he was looking for.

'There,' he said, 'is a line more often quoted than any other passage of his: "Like angel visits few and far between," and he stole it bodily from Blair's *Grave*. Not satisfied with the theft he has spoiled it in the effort to disguise it. Blair wrote: "Like angel visits *short* and far between," Campbell's "Few and far between" is mere tautology.'

Poe at that time, though only twenty years of age,[376] had the appearance of being much older. He had a worn, weary discontented look, not easily forgotten by those who were intimate with him. Poe was easily fretted by any jest at his expense. . . . Very early in his brief career at the Point he established a high reputation for genius, and poems and squibs of local interest were daily issued from Number 28 and went the round of the classes. . . .

The studies of the Academy, Poe utterly ignored. I doubt if he ever studied a page of Lacroix, unless it was to glance hastily over it in the lecture room, while others of his section were reciting. It was evident from the first that he had no intention of going through with the course, and both Professors and Cadets of the older classes had him set down for a *January Colt* before the corps had been in barracks a week.

From a letter written to John Allan before he entered the Military Academy, it is evident that Poe counted confidently upon his former army experience and his preparation at the University of Virginia to get him through the course at West Point in short order. He tells his guardian that he hoped to complete it in six months. It is probable

---

[375] *Harper's New Monthly Magazine,* November, 1867.
[376] He was actually twenty-two, but had given his age in the records at West Point as nineteen years and some months.

that he found it, from the nature of the arrangement of the curriculum, rather than from the difficulty of the subjects themselves, impossible to carry out the prediction. This miscalculation of the results of his abilities, combined with the prospect of the increased length of stay at West Point which it involved, and the growing distaste for the bare existence he found there, probably accounts for the discontented and haggard look which his roommate recalled over thirty years later. In the army itself Poe had found means to escape much of the physical drudgery of drills, and the way to considerable leisure for his dreams and composition by engaging in the clerical work which conferred such privileges. At West Point there was no way of avoiding the ironclad routine, and the young poet found himself bound, and turning ceaselessly upon a wheel where the torture became more irksome with each revolution. To look forward to an endless life of that kind of thing was not to be contemplated without despair. Indeed, it is probable that even the unexpected lengthening of its temporary continuance was more than he cared to face, and that he had, as his roommate seems to think, made up his mind to shake the dust of the place from his feet as early as the Fall of 1830. In addition there was the change in the affairs of John Allan which probably removed from Poe the last incentive to continue the situation.

Mr. Allan's marriage had interfered sadly with these hopes. That it made Poe uneasy there can be no doubt. It was for that reason that he wrote John Allan in November that he regretted that his guardian had not felt it worth while to come up from New York to pay him a visit, although a sight of the man who had so often reviled and reproached him could have brought little satisfaction. Doubtless there was some element of affection due to memories of old and happier times, but these were now remote. Nevertheless, Mr. Allan's indifference, and the fact that he had ignored Poe, was alarming, so the November letter to Richmond may be regarded as a "feeler-out." Poe tells his guardian that he has found West Point not unpleasant and that he is at that time (November 6, 1830) standing first in all his sections.

The roommate's inference and recollection that Poe neglected his classes probably arises from composite memories set down years later. That Poe was on the whole discontented and nervous there is every reason to believe to be correct.

Poe's standing academically, however, was not much affected. He probably did not have to study much; he was brilliant; had an excellent preparation, and seems to have found no difficulty in distinguishing himself in languages and mathematics. When he did decide to go, as he did, it was not by the route of failure in the classroom, but by disregarding the rules of discipline. For a little while he was not sure enough of the actual state of affairs in Richmond to cut the last tie which bound him to his past without some further thought.

This was probably the condition of his affairs, an uneasy condition, through the Fall and early Winter of 1830. It was a state of spiritual limbo that must have been particularly trying. Nevertheless, he was not quite ready to take so irrevocable a step on his own initiative. Nor can we blame him, for by this time he knew full well what it meant to starve. Even *he* could not afford to be independent on nothing at all. Byron, and not Chatterton was his model.

During this interlude he again began to drink. As nearly always just a little; but that little for him was a great deal too much. It probably helped to deplete his nerves already badly strained. Having experienced the effects of gulping, he now took to sipping. The stories as to his being raving drunk in the guard house are not true. Had they been so, he would not have been under the necessity of deliberately neglecting his duty to procure his release. There was, however, it seems, often enough a bottle of brandy present in Number 28, occasionally resorted to in company with such friends as its contents and the inspired conversation of the owner might attract. About the time of the letter home, Poe's roommate again pulls aside the curtain for a brief glimpse at Number 28:

It was a dark, cold, drizzling night, in the last days of November, when this event came off. The brandy bottle had been empty for two days, and just at dusk Poe proposed that we should draw straws—the one who drew the shortest to go down to Old Benny's and replenish our stock. The straws were drawn, and the lot fell on me.

Provided with four pounds of candles, and Poe's last blanket, for traffic (silver and gold had we none, but such as we had we gave unto Benny), I started just as the bugle sounded 'to quarters.' It was a rough road to travel, but I knew every foot of it by night or day, and reached my place of destination in safety, but drenched to the skin. Old Benny was not in the best of humors that evening. Candles and blankets and regulation shoes, and similar articles of traffic, had accumulated largely on his hands, and the market for them was dull in that neighborhood. His chicken suppers and bottles of brandy had disappeared very rapidly of late, and he had received little, or no money in return.

At last, however, I succeeded in exchanging the candles and blankets for a bottle of brandy, and the hardest-featured, loudest-voiced old gander that it has been my lot to encounter. To chop the bird's head off before venturing into barracks with him was a matter of pure necessity; and thus, in fact, Old Benny rendered him before delivery. I reached the suburbs of the barracks about nine o'clock. The bottle had not as much brandy in it as when I left Old Benny's, but I was very confident I had not spilled any. I had carried the gander first over one shoulder and then over the other, and the consequence was that not only my shirt front, but my face and hands were as bloody as the entire contents of the old gander's veins and arteries could make them.

Poe was on the lookout and met me some distance from the barracks, and my appearance at once inspired him with the idea of a grand hoax.[377] Our plans were perfected in an instant. The gander was tied, neck and feet and wings together, and the bloody feathers bristling in every direction gave it a nondescript appearance that would have defied recognition as a gander by the most astute naturalist on the continent. Poe took charge of the bottle, and preceded me to the room. 'Old P.' was puzzling his brains over the binomial theorem and a visitor from the North Barracks was in the room awaiting the result of my expedition.

Poe had taken his seat, and pretended to be absorbed in the mysteries of *Leçons Françaises*. Laying the gander down outside the door, I walked or rather staggered into the room, pretending to be very drunk, and exhibiting in clothes and face a spectacle not often seen off the stage. 'My God! what has happened?' exclaimed Poe, with well-acted horror.

'Old K—old K—!' I repeated several times, and with gestures intended to be frantically savage.

'Well, what of him?' asked Poe.

'He won't stop me on the road any more'—and I produced a large knife that we had stained with the few drops of blood, that remained in the old gander. 'I have killed him!'

'Nonsense!' said Poe, 'you are only trying one of your tricks on us.'

'I didn't suppose you would believe me,' I replied, 'so I cut off his head and brought it into barracks. Here it is!' and walking out of the door I caught the gander by the legs, and giving it one fearful swing around my head dashed it at the only candle in the room, and left them all in darkness with what two of them believed to be the head of one of the professors. The visitor leaped through the window and alighted in the slop tub, and make fast time for his own room in the North Barracks, spreading, as he went, the report that I had killed old K—, and that his head was there in number 28. The story gained credence, and for a time the excitement in barracks ran high. When we lit the candle again, "Old P." was sitting in one corner, a blank picture[378] of horror, and it was some time before we could restore him to reason.

So the barracks were able to credit even murder to the discontented occupant of Number 28. A strange fellow after all! There was something about him one could not understand. Almost anything might be suspected of one who actually dared to be different—and was proud of it. "Benedict Arnold's grandson!" Interesting no doubt, but dangerous. And so he continued here, as elsewhere, lonely; sad that he was set apart, and yet proud of it. It was this combination of pride, loneliness, and homesickness—the necessity of expressing his sense of malaise, and the desire for the comfort that nothing but dreams could bring him,

---

[377] Poe's ceaseless desire to perpetrate hoaxes was not due solely to a sense of humor. The feeling of superiority which it conferred on him as the person who stood behind the curtain was the main motive. This is frequently one of the minor manifestations of an exaggerated ego.

[378] "Old P." was the other roommate, it appears. See the apocryphal, for the most part, reminiscences of Timothy Pickering Jones, "Poe and I were classmates, roommates, and tent mates." *New York Sun,* May 10, 1903.

which seems to have memorably combined at West Point and to have projected itself for the first time into great poems.

One can imagine him, after taps, waiting for the roommates to drift off into the dreamless sleep which was so often denied him by their mutterings, and by the beating at the bars of the restless wings of his own spirit,—one can imagine him getting up in the bare, cold room, and by the light of a carefully shaded candle, setting down the proud words of *Israfel*. How could they know, these heavy sleepers, these solemn memorizers of the banalities of textbooks—that in their midst, brooding over them in the long hours of the night, sat a spirit whose song was sweeter and clearer than that of the archangels of God! How human and earthy, and how comforting to his own feelings it was, to imagine that even in heaven his voice would be heard above all others, and be found more acceptable. Out of this gigantic and almost insane pride of heart welled up the lines of the poem ending at last in the majestic pæan:

> If I could dwell
> Where Israfel
>   Hath dwelt, and he where I,
> He might not sing so wildly well
>   A mortal melody,
> While a bolder note than this might swell
>   From my lyre within the sky.[379]

It was to Richmond, and the happier early days with Frances Allan and the friends of childhood, that he returned in homesick reveries, for homesick he was. Poe was one of those sensitive natures to which the incidents of existence were often painful. Ensconced in the old and familiar, this feeling was lulled; bleak and new surroundings became, by contrast, unbearable and served to make the past a heaven by contrast. Besides, his own intense consciousness of self, a consciousness so supreme as to render the outside world pale and remote, was of the type which tends to extend much of its self-love to the places where it has dwelt, so that a town, a room, or even a tree that has been a refuge becomes romantic and important, as do all things that have been pleasantly familiar in the past.

All this seemed true now of Richmond; the houses, the fields, the river, the ghostly figures that walked in the past of his boyhood, moved in a golden and vernal landscape, with something sacred about it,—a shrine, a green isle in the sea. Oh, the lost loved faces! the silent tones of voices! the dear, dear past forever wild with all regret! It was the only time when he had been happy, at one with himself, and beloved. This is the grand nostalgia, the immortal regret, the famished yearning

---

[379] The last verse of *Israfel* is quoted here as given in the 1845 version. The 1831 text shows numerous variations.

out of which so often springs great poetry. It was the only thing that comforted him, the idealized images of the past, witness:

> Helen, thy beauty is to me
> Like those Nicean barks of yore,
> That gently, o'er a perfumed sea,
> The weary, wayworn wanderer bore
> *To his own native shore* . . .

and the lines written some years later to Sarah

> When melancholy and alone,
> I sit on some moss-covered stone
> Beside a murm'ring stream;
> I think I hear thy voice's sound
> In every tuneful thing around,
> Oh! what a pleasant dream—

and Poe's dreams of the past were so vivid that he heard voices of the dead and lost speaking; not only the eye but the ear also had its memories:

> The bowers whereat, in dreams, I see
> The wantonest singing birds,
> Are lips—and all thy melody
> Of lip-begotten words–

Amid this longing for the past, in the presence of an always unbearable present, his spirit constantly stood—

> A voice from out the Future cries,
> "On! on!"—but o'er the Past
> (Dim gulf!) my spirit lies
> Mute, motionless, aghast!

And it was into this gulf, which he so brooded upon during the long hours of the night, while the rest of the inmates of the barracks slumbered around him, that Poe let down the leaky bucket of inspiration and drew forth *To Helen, The Sleeper, The Pæan, Fairy-land,* and *The Valley of Unrest,* that most beautiful of all his reveries. These poems are rich with the dark jewels of sorrow, the dim Northern twilight of Scotland and the Celtic folk tales he heard from the old people at Irvine, the mystic landscapes of Carolina, and the exotic compound of his "Oriental" readings best exemplified, perhaps, by *The City in the Sea.* These he felt were worth preserving and adding to his already published verses. Before he left West Point he had made arrangements to do so.

The new manuscript collection, which included the poems published in Baltimore, and the new ones written at Mrs. Clemm's, in Richmond, or at the Military Academy, he seems to have submitted to Colonel Thayer, who approved of them, and granted permission to allow the members of the cadet corps to subscribe towards their publication at seventy-five cents a copy (*sic*), the amount to be deducted from their pay. This permission and Colonel Thayer's probable appreciation of Poe's work, expressed perhaps in some personal interview, seem to account for the young man's admiration of that officer, the only personal enthusiasm of which we have any mention during the West Point interlude. Possessed of a guaranteed sale in advance of several hundred copies—nearly everyone seems to have subscribed—Poe wrote to Elam Bliss, a New York publisher, who, it seems, came personally to West Point, sometime about the end of 1830, and made arrangements with the young author to bring out the volume.

The enthusiasm for it among the cadets was by no means literary. They had no idea of the real nature of the book to which they subscribed, but undoubtedly thought it would contain a collection of the humorous verse satirizing the officers and the faculty, which had from time to time proceeded from the strange but clever fellow who inhabited Number 28. Poe on his part undoubtedly knew this, but he used the opportunity to get out his book, probably knowing full well that he would not be present to receive the personal expressions of disgust and disappointment, when its real nature became known. Some of the pearls, as the preface to the book shows, were intended to be cast where they might be audibly appreciated,—as for the grunts of disapproval from the ostensible audience, Poe would neither hear nor care. The important thing was, that a new book was under way. Mr. Bliss, or his agent, returned to New York with the manuscript ready for the printer, and with little or no effort the cost of the forthcoming volume was guaranteed.

How long Poe would have lingered at West Point doing "fours right" and "shoulder arms," it is hard to tell. His decision to depart was undoubtedly hastened by an event in Richmond that, as the future proved, removed him from all prospects of any immediate or death-bed generosity which John Allan might fondly be hoped to display. The event was unexpected and uncomfortably disconcerting.

Sergeant Graves, "Bully," had evidently waited up until about the end of the year (1830) in hopes that the money owed him, about which Poe had written so reassuringly the previous May, might be forthcoming. By that time, the patience of the soldier, who was still at Fortress Monroe, was exhausted, and he wrote to John Allan himself in no uncertain terms, demanding that the matter should be settled at once. As Poe had informed this soldier that Mr. Allan was seldom sober, the nature of the information which he possessed must have insured the prompt payment of his demand. It would never do, for a newly married man in Mr. Allan's situation, to have allowed a common soldier to go about with a letter from his adopted "son" which plainly made such damaging assertions. In the concise words of the second wife "Mr. Allan sent him the money . . . and banished Poe from his affections." That much, at least, of the good lady's explanation seems to be literally true. The rest of her statements may well have been the convenient interpretation which, out of self-defense, her husband was forced to put upon it. No one can blame John Allan, in this instance, at least, for being outraged. The fact that Poe had never meant the letter to come home to roost does not excuse his lack of loyalty in writing it. It is impossible at once to claim the benefits of intimate association and to violate its confidences. Sergeant "Bully" Graves of the First United States Artillery had, by reason of the writings which he possessed, fallen heir to the only financial "legacy" that the Galt-Allan fortune was to contribute to the name of Edgar Allan Poe! An unfortunately flourishing signature of that young gentleman adorned the bottom of the fatal letter. Not only the cat, but all expectation of kittens, was now let out of the well-known bag.

Mr. Allan wrote Poe a furious letter, which must have been a masterpiece of invective. It reached Poe just in time to wish him a happy New Year for 1831. He was informed that he was disowned and that no further communications from him were desired. On January 3, 1831, Poe replied in what is probably the most literally autobiographical letter that he ever wrote.[380]

The mask, that the sense of favors to come, or the lingering traces of real affection which Poe may have still retained—the necessity for patience and dissimulation that these had enforced in previous letters to his guardian, was now removed. With nothing to be lost by open defiance, he spits back the bitter truth.

The letter to "Bully" is acknowledged and the charge of Mr. Allan's drinking reaffirmed. The truth, he says, he leaves to God, and John Allan's conscience. The rest of the letter is given up to a multitude of reproaches, which, even when every allowance is made, still remain as a tremendous indictment of the character of John Allan. The parsimony so fatal at Charlottesville had also done its sharp work at West Point, but, above all, Poe in effect reproaches his guardian for his lack of affection and tells him that it was only Frances Allan who cared for him as for her own child. "If she had not died while I was away, there would have been nothing to regret."

Perhaps, the most significant sentences of all, in this burning letter, are those in which Poe speaks of his own health. Despite the undoubted presence of some self-pity, there is a hopeless truth in his statements that he knows he will not live long—"Thank God!"—and that his future will be one of indigence and sickness. He says, and this statement seems to be especially significant, that he has no energy nor health left, and he complains of the fatigues of "this place"—fatigues which his absolute

---

[380] *Valentine Museum Poe Letters,* letter No. 24. The Allan-Poe controversy cannot be understood thoroughly without a knowledge of this letter.

POEMS

BY

EDGAR A. POE.

TOUT LE MONDE A RAISON.—ROCHEFOUCAULT.

SECOND EDITION.

New York:
PUBLISHED BY ELAM BLISS.

1831.

Title Page of *Poems*—Second Edition

Published in New York by Elam Bliss in 1831

EDGAR ALLAN POE's third published Volume usually known as the "West Point Book"

Courtesy of a New York Collector

On the Philadelphia-Trenton Line

From an old print
Courtesy of the Pennsylvania Historical Society

Philadelphia from the Navy Yard

From an old print
Courtesy of the Pennsylvania Historical Society

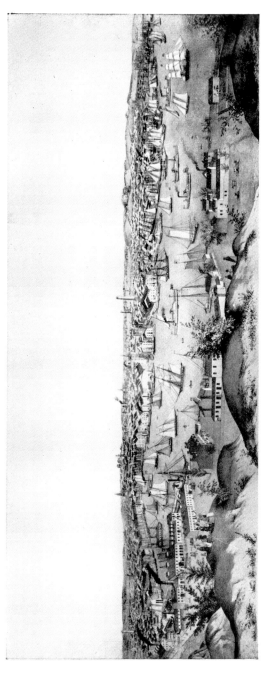

Baltimore in the Early 1830's

During the time of Poe's residence there with his
Aunt Maria Clemm

From an old print

Courtesy of the Maryland Historical Society

Part of a Page on which Poe's prize story of "The MS. Found in a Bottle" first appeared

This was his first decided success

From a very rare file of the Saturday Visiter. Courtesy of the Baltimore Historical Society

BY CLOUD & POUDER.

SOUTH GAY-ST., ONE DOOR FROM THE CORNER OF MARKET-ST.

SATURDAY, OCTOBER 19, 1833.

VOLUME 3—NUMBER 38.

TWO DOLLARS PER ANNUM. IF PAID IN ADVANCE.

LITERARY.

PRIZE POEM.

SONG OF THE WIND.

PRIZE TALE.

MS. FOUND IN A BOTTLE.

want of necessities had subjected him to.   The letter concludes with the
announcement that he intends to resign.   If the permission is not granted
from home, he curtly informs John Allan that from the date of the letter
he will neglect his studies and duties.   Should the permission not be
forthcoming he will leave West Point in ten days.   Otherwise, says he,
"I should subject myself to being dismissed."   Poe's resolution was
evidently made while he was reading John Allan's letter.   The careful
phrasing of the indignant reply evidently occupied a day or so in which
the exact course to be pursued was turned over in Poe's mind most carefully.   This letter to John Allan, begun on the third of January, 1831,
was not mailed till the fifth.   A few days later in Richmond John Allan
himself endorsed upon it:

> I rec'd this on the 10th and did not from its conclusion deem it necessary to
> reply. I made this note on the 13th and can see no good Reason to alter my
> opinion. I do not think the boy has one good quality. He may do or act as he
> pleases tho' I would have saved him but on his own terms and conditions since
> I cannot believe a word he writes. His letter is the most bare-faced one-sided
> statement.

A careful comparison of dates in the case of this letter may serve to make
clear exactly what happened.   Poe's last letter from West Point was
begun on the third, mailed on the fifth (postmark), and received by Mr.
Allan on the tenth of January.   John Allan then considered his decision
about it for three days before making his endorsement on the thirteenth.
*But the court-martial records show that after January seventh Edgar
Allan Poe ceased to function as a cadet at West Point.*   In other words,
he did not *wait* to hear from Mr. Allan, for, before the letter got to
Richmond, Poe was already "on strike."

There were, in reality, only two parties in this passage at arms.   Between the granite-like obstinacy of John Allan and the final, nervous
explosion of Poe's indignation, West Point was a mere incident.   If Mr.
Allan's consent to a resignation had been obtained, Poe would have
profited to the extent of the traveling expenses which he needed—and
that would have been all.   Mr. Allan's guardianship was at an end.   The
letter of January 3, 1831, to Richmond was the young poet's moral
Declaration of Independence.

There was, indeed, a much deeper cause for the declaration than has
heretofore been suspected.   A comparison of certain passages in John
Allan's will with the date of Poe's letter to Sergeant Graves ("Bully"),
and the mention of the quarrel between "father" and "son" on the same
date (" . . . The time was within half an hour after you had embittered
every feeling of my heart against you by your abuse of my *family,* and
myself, under your own roof—and at a time when you knew that
my heart was almost breaking . . .") gives rise to some pertinent
speculations.

Why had Mr. Allan been drinking about this time; why did he quarrel with Poe; and above all, why did he abuse Edgar's *family?* Poe underscores the word *family,* and it can scarcely refer to anything else but the sore point about Mrs. Poe and Rosalie.[381] Nothing would be more likely to drive the foster-son out of the house immediately. But why drive him out, why! What *was* the motive? One sentence from John Allan's will illuminates all these old letters, like switching on a light in a dark room full of musty documents:

> The twins were born some time about the first of July 1830.

They were illegitimate. No wonder Mr. Allan was then "seldom sober." That was why he was frantic with anxiety to get Edgar out of the house when he did return to Richmond in 1830, and why he kept urging and urging Poe to get his appointment and even tried to hurry the War Department. The appointment came in March; but Poe did not leave. On May 6th Mr. Allan picked a violent quarrel with his ward, the old calumny against Edgar's mother was revived as a desperate but sure expedient to get rid of him—"under your own roof—at a time when you knew my heart was almost breaking."[355] A few days later Poe drew the blankets from *Ellis & Allan,* and left via Baltimore. "When I parted from you at the steamboat, I knew that I should never see you again." The same day that Poe took the oath at West Point, the twins were born in Richmond.

So it was not so very simple after all! Like all important and long enduring human relationships it was very, very complex. John Allan and Edgar Poe loved each other. In the inmost realm of the spirit they were father and son. Time and fate had made them so. That is the only satisfactory explanation of the enormous agitation behind their correspondence; the reason, why, in spite of all, they could never quite break it off. Even on the last West Point letter, the older man endorses: "He may do or act as he pleases tho' I would have saved him *but on his own terms. . . ."* In the last analysis it was John Allan's sensuousness and obstinacy that ruined the two finest associations of his remarkable life. They killed Frances Allan, and they blasted Poe. The strange, Scotch parsimony was only a concomitant. Even after his second marriage the revelation of "Bully's" letter was a sore blow. The raveled thread was snapped; Poe left West Point, and went into a nervous collapse. If this was not tragedy, the word to describe it has not been coined.

The process of cutting the bonds of military discipline was more protracted than Poe surmised. Mr. Allan's consent was not forthcoming,

---

[381] Mr. Allan would scarcely "abuse" Mrs. Clemm or Edgar's paralyzed grandmother. The Poe cousins were not known to him personally. Henry *might* have come in for a tongue-lashing, but all the probability here points to Edgar's parents, "my family, and myself." He may have included Mosher Poe in his remarks.

so the young man had to set about it the next way. The manner was simple enough; it consisted in taking the path of least resistance. After the receipt of the letter from Richmond, Poe simply gave up. Although the plan was deliberate, it also bears out his own testimony that he was too physically ill to go on. From January 7, 1831, he absented himself from all military formations, recitations, and from church,—and he disobeyed the orders of his superiors when he was directed to take part. The prime military virtue of obedience was thus hopelessly insulted, beyond that there was no "moral offense" involved. The story that he deserted either from the army proper or from the Military Academy is a legend which it is scarcely necessary to deny.

On January 5, 1831, it appears that a court-martial under the presidency of Lieutenant Leslie of the Engineers was convened at West Point to try several cadets for offenses against discipline. For some reason the sittings of the court were postponed until January 28th. During the two weeks prior to that event there were scarcely any duties which Cadet Poe did not ingeniously manage to neglect. As a consequence after disposing of some other cases—[382]

The Court next proceeded to the trial of Cadet E. A. Poe of the U. S. Military Academy on the following charges and specifications:—

CHARGE 1st—GROSS NEGLECT OF DUTY

Specification 1st—In this, that he, the said Cadet Poe, did absent himself from the following parades and roll calls between the 7th January and 27th January 1831. . . .

Specification 2nd—In this, that he, the said Cadet E. A. Poe, did absent himself from all Academical duties between the 15th and 27th January 1831. . . .

CHARGE 2nd—DISOBEDIENCE OF ORDERS

Specification 1st—In this, that he, the said Cadet Poe, after having been directed by the officer of the day to attend church on the 23rd of January 1831, did fail to obey such order. . . .

Specification 2nd—In this, that he, the said Cadet Poe, did fail to attend the Academy on the 25th January 1831, after having been directed to do so by the officer of the day.

Poe pleaded *guilty* to all but the first specification of the first charge, to which he pleaded *not guilty*. As that charge was automatically proven by the rollbooks for formations, he thus put himself beyond all recommendations for mercy. "After mature deliberation on the testimony deduced," the "prisoner" was found "Guilty on all the charges and specifications," and it was adjudged "that he, Cadet E. A. Poe, be *dismissed* the service of the United States." [382] The sentence was made

---

[382] An abbreviated transcript of *Military Academy Order No. 7*, Engineer Department, Washington, February 8, 1831. Prof. James H. Harrison prints this, vol. II, pages 374-376, from Ingram.

effective as of March 6, 1831, in order to provide sufficient sums out of his pay to satisfy his indebtedness to the Academy. On that date Poe was officially discharged with a balance to his credit of twenty-four cents. Long before that, however, he was on his way to New York City.

The findings of the court-martial were approved by the Secretary of War on February 8, 1831, and seem to have taken a week or so before they were returned to West Point. Poe must have had some qualms imagining the face of Major Eaton as he read the record of the trial and called to mind the enthusiastic promises of a certain Richmond youth a little over a year before, one who had walked from Baltimore to plead his case personally. That, however, deterred neither Mr. Secretary nor Cadet Poe, and on February 17th or 18th he was given his release.

One can imagine him upon the evening of that eventful day packing up his books, John Allan's inkstand, a few uniforms which he kept to remind him of past glories, and the *lares* and *penates* which accompanied even the poorest of waif poets in the iron-bound trunk that John Allan had sent him by steamboat to Baltimore. Then he made the rounds, saying good-bye, not without a certain relish for the brief glamour that surrounds a departing spirit at the Military Academy, who has dared to defy the delegated authority of the United States—and survived. And we can imagine him, too, selling off for what he could get, a few *picayunes* and *fipenny bits* at most, the scanty remains of his outfit. Perhaps there was a shako, or a slim sword exchanged next morning at Old Benny's for a thin second-hand suit of citizen's clothes, a parting nip with the old rascal "on the house," with "here's luck." It was, we know, a cold, a very cold day.

On February 19, 1831, the steamboat from Albany stopped at the desolate West Point wharf to take on board a lonely figure dressed in a nondescript costume consisting of a thin and badly worn suit of second-hand clothes rendered somewhat grotesque by a cadet's overcoat and a battered hat. A small iron-bound trunk was trundled on board, and the old side-wheeler "Henry Eckford" thrashed her way down stream toward New York.[383] The young man on the deck shivered and fingered the lonely coins in his pocket somewhat apprehensively. No one, who saw the nervous trembling of the bird-like fingers, would have suspected that they had just relinquished the sword and were already reaching ambitiously for a mightier weapon. The fare was at least seventy-five cents, and that was about all he had. The two freight barges

---

[383] From *The Northern Traveller,* a guidebook of the time, and a contemporary steamboat schedule, it appears that the steamer "Henry Eckford," with two freight barges in tow, plied between New York and Albany and made local stops. The fare from New York to Albany was $1.00. The "Henry" called at West Point Dock, February 19, 1831, on the down trip.

An Early Steamboat on the New York to Albany
Route in the days of Poe

From an old print
Courtesy of the Pennsylvania Historical Society

behind the "Henry" took up the slack of the tow line with a swish and trailed on behind; the departing wail of the steamer's whistle echoed up the gorge of the Hudson, to be answered by the notes of a bugle from the heights above. Future generals of the United States and the Confederacy were on their way to recitation and the several stars that afterwards adorned their shoulders or collars. Edgar Poe was following his own.

CHAPTER FOURTEEN

THE WEARY, WAYWORN WANDERER

POE arrived in New York about February 20, 1831, and seems to have remained there until the end of March of that year. During this sojourn, his movements and doings are exceedingly obscure. The young man who took up lodgings somewhere close to Madison Square can best be described in his own words as "a weary, wayworn wanderer." He was literally penniless, and thinly clad. There was no *Ellis & Allan* to draw upon for even a mourning suit now; he was just out of West Point and without sufficient civilian clothes. His scheme seems to have been to obtain literary work of some sort, probably with the newspapers, while the forthcoming volume held out some hopes of a small return. But in the meantime he must eat, and he was also very ill.

In the last letter from West Point, Poe had assured John Allan that he would never trouble him again. Faced by starvation and the prospect of a serious illness, however, he was once more forced to eat humble pie, lacking anything more substantial. Two days after leaving the Military Academy he writes in his New York lodging from what he feels is probably his death-bed, asking his "father" to send him enough to keep from starving.

The break at West Point and the severance of all home ties, with the consequent necessity of making an immediate *about face* in his plans and order of life, had undoubtedly entailed a fierce mental and spiritual struggle. He was, in fact, in one of those nervous emotional crises which make or mar a career.[384] This was reflected in his physical condition. He left West Point in a depleted and fatigued state. The trip down, we are told, was bitterly cold, and he had no adequate clothing,— "no cloak"—he says, although it is known that he brought with him from the Military Academy his cadet's overcoat and wore it years later even at Fordham.[385] However that may be, he contracted an almost fatal "cold," complicated by ear trouble. The result seems to have been one of those periods of complete nervous and psychic exhaustion that occasionally overtook him from now on, in which a weak heart played

---

[384] New light upon Poe's condition, and the date of his arrival in New York, has been thrown on this period by the *Valentine Museum Poe Letters,* letter No. 25, New York, February 21, 1831.

[385] This coat, and various other items of military attire, evidently relics of West Point days, are mentioned by several persons who knew Poe from this time on.

an important part.[384] In the midst of this he wrote the despairing letter to Richmond.[384]

In this letter, in addition to his desperate appeals for help, which even the disordered and blotted writing stamps as genuine, Poe attempts to defend himself for his course of procedure; lays the blame for being "dismissed" on his guardian's refusal to give him permission to resign; and expatiates on his excellent standing in class, and the sympathy of his superiors and classmates. This sympathy, he says, he possessed; adding that sickness was the real cause of his dropping out,—and everybody at "The Point" knew it. In the meantime he is writing from his "death-bed," and a little help during his last hours would be grateful.

The letter is undoubtedly exaggerated in its self-pity, but it was written during a time of great pain from a discharging ear, with the horror of starvation near, alone in a strange city, and by a terrified and delicately sensitive young man. Where else could he appeal but to "Dear Pa" and "home"? "Do not tell my sister," he pleads—"I shall send to the post office every day." But he sent in vain. That home which he addressed was his no longer. The letter was smugly filed away to receive over two years later a coldly furious endorsement from a stern hand.

Somehow, doubtless to his own surprise, Poe recovered in a week or so and found himself able to read proofs at the office of Elam Bliss at 111 Broadway, where "the second edition" of *Poems* was under way. Mr. Bliss, who was a kindly man, may also have taken pity on the young poet and have invited him to dine with him at his home at 28 Dey Street, where we may be sure the hospitality was, to the guest at least, no empty formality.

One of the few reminiscences of Poe at this time comes from Peter Pindar Pease, an erstwhile clerk at a Charlottesville store, who says he had met Poe in Boston when in similar desperate circumstances and who now ran across him again in New York.[386] From him it seems that it was Poe's custom to walk under the elm trees in Madison Square, and that, upon one occasion, Poe dined with Peter Pindar Pease and informed him that he had at last "struck it hard"; meaning that he was in good luck, and probably referring to the new book. The statement is characteristic. Nothing could tame the young poet's pride; the possibility of fame from the book must have filled his mind. Despite the indications of poverty which Pease noted, he found Poe in a confident and boastful mood. Who paid for the dinner, we do not learn.

At this period Inman, the artist, had his studio at 48 Vesey Street, and it was now, *if at any time*, that he painted the portrait of Poe with

---

[386] From an untraced clipping from an article. "P. P. Pease" is alluded to elsewhere as an early prohibitionist and anti-saloon man. Dr. Mabbott suggests *The Outlook*. I have been unable to verify this as the source.

which he has been credited. It is doubtful if he really did so, however, as the picture does not resemble the other known authentic likenesses of Poe in later life. All that can be said is that it shows a well-dressed, rather slight, sensitive featured, and delicately bred young man in his early twenties, and that it *might* be Poe. If so, it is the earliest picture of the poet known. Mr. Bliss may have arranged for it on the strength of the forthcoming book, but it is *extremely unlikely*. Poe was penniless and unknown, and there is no indication that Inman was his close friend. The picture may be any young dandy in the costume of the time.

It was a hard time financially, too. Jackson's fast and loose fiscal policy was already beginning to make money tight, and the times were distinctly close ones for the inhabitants of the avenues as well as Grub Street.[387] Evidently the bulk of the money for the new book was not forthcoming until it was delivered at West Point. Perhaps a few advances saved the day. So it was hard sledding at best. Poe wrote to his brother Henry, for whom he had already gone into debt, but his brother was now dying in Baltimore and could not aid him. By the beginning of March it was evident that New York would not afford a living to an unknown pen, and we find the young poet writing to Colonel Thayer, the Superintendent at West Point, whose favor he seems to have overestimated. Colonel Thayer had probably been "kind," but he doubtless, for all that, had his reservations about young gentlemen who were dismissed for not attending church, even when directed to do so by the officer of the day! Temporarily, Poe seems to have considered becoming a soldier of fortune.

The letter read:

New York, *March* 10, 1831.

Sir;—Having no longer any ties which can bind me to my native country—no projects—nor any friends—I intend by the first opportunity to proceed to Paris with the view of obtaining through the interest of the Marquis de La Fayette an appointment (if possible) in the Polish Army.

In the event of the interference of France in behalf of Poland this may easily be effected— [388] at all events it will be my only feasible plan of procedure.

The object of this letter is respectfully to request that you will give me such assistance as may be in your power in furtherance of my views.

A certificate of 'standing' in my class is all that I have any right to expect.

---

[387] Andrew Jackson was attacking the charter of the Bank of the United States, and the period of financial chaos, state banks, and "wild cat" money was being ushered in. While Poe was in New York in February, 1831, the attack was going on in Congress. (Benton, *View,* I. 187-325; Deb., XI. 143-61.) The effect was alarming.

[388] In 1830-31 the Poles rebelled against the tyranny of Tsar Nicholas I. Patriotic secret societies drove the Russians out of Warsaw, November 29, 1830. On January 25, 1831, the independence of Poland was proclaimed; the help of France was hoped for. A few months later the rebellion was suppressed with frightful cruelty on both sides. Poe evidently watched these events carefully.

Anything further—a letter to a friend in Paris—or to the Marquis—would be a kindness which I should never forget. Most respectfully,

Yr. obt. s't.,

EDGAR A. POE

Col. S. Thayer, Supt. U. S. M. A. [389]

What an impression La Fayette had made on Poe, and how much he counted on the influence of his grandfather's friend, is plainly shadowed forth in this letter. Colonel Thayer did not reply, it seems, and the young writer evidently soon gave up all thought of following a military career any longer. It was the last gesture in that direction, and a desperate one at that, but it is interesting to note that, even at this date, Poe felt it might be well for him to go abroad. Perhaps he felt instinctively that his talents might be appreciated where he, indeed, first received the greatest recognition. There was evidently no place for him in New York. Assured of this, he began once more to turn his thoughts toward Baltimore. Richmond offered nothing. In Baltimore, at least there were family relations, and, through them, he might hope to gain friends. If nothing else, Mrs. Clemm's house offered maternal affection and a roof. In the meantime the poems had appeared, and Poland was collapsing. In that, the letter to Colonel Thayer had received a conclusive answer.

Sometime about the end of March, 1831, Elam Bliss seems to have completed *Poems* by Edgar A. Poe, "second edition," and the cadets at West Point were pondering and grumbling over the incomprehensible lines of *Israfel, To Helen, Lenore, The Sleeper,* and *The Valley of Unrest.* Nor did the inscription

TO THE U. S. CORPS OF CADETS

THIS VOLUME

IS

RESPECTFULLY DEDICATED

tend to ease the sting of having been gulled. No one, of course, suspected that it was the most enduring compliment that a certain "corps" could receive. For a few minutes, the dark figure that had been a stranger among them was recalled. Then the busy bugles blew again drowning out the disgruntled laughter. It seemed as if for a third time the young poet's assault upon oblivion had called forth nothing but derision, and a few, a very few coins. On these he remained some days longer in New York, and on the remainder, a very scant remainder, set out wayworn and weary shortly afterward for Baltimore. It was at least a move towards his own native shore. The loadstone of "home,"

---

[389] Printed in the *New York Sun* for October 30, 1902, from manuscripts left to the Association of West Point Graduates by General Cullum.

however, still fluttered the directing needle because, for Poe, Richmond never lost the peculiar quality of a magnet. Elmira was still there, and all the other invisible lines of magnetism were set strong.

Poe's third book, *Poems* (second edition), New York, published by Elam Bliss, 1831, was a duodecimo volume of 124 pages bound in pale green boards, and rather poorly printed on ordinary rag paper. The exact number of the edition is not known, but it certainly did not exceed five hundred.[390] The title page bore the line from La Chaussée,[391] *"Tout le monde a Raison,"* this sentiment being a sort of plea for a liberal attitude toward the contents of the book and for the critical theories which it advocated in the preface entitled, "Letter to Mr. —— ——." This anonymous person is addressed as "Dear B," and may have been Elam Bliss himself. The poems were here reprinted in revised form from the earlier Baltimore edition of 1829. In that sense only the 1831 *Poems* was a second edition.

The "Letter to Mr. B" is somewhat rambling, and was evidently written in off-hours at West Point, whence it is dated. In this preface, Poe informs us, amid a rather youthful parade of erudition resounding with the names of Shakespeare and Milton, that in his revisions of earlier work he has learned the lesson of the shears, and that these poems now appear with "the trash taken away from them in which they were embedded." The most interesting thing in the epistle to "Mr. B," however, is the appearance here for the first time of Poe's theory of poetic criticism. Literary reputation, he says, percolates the social pyramid from "a few gifted individuals who kneel around the summit, beholding, face to face, the master spirit who stands upon the pinnacle." After a brief comment on the difficulty of an American author being taken seriously he contines:

You are aware of the great barrier in the path of an American writer. He is read, if at all, in preference to the combined and established wit of the world. . . . Our antiquaries abandon time for distance: our very fops glance from the binding to the bottom of the title-page, where the mystic characters which spell London, Paris, or Geneva, are precisely so many letters of recommendation. . . .

After this brief beginning of what was later to develop into one of the favorite themes of his acrid criticism, Poe leaps rapidly past Aristotle, taking the opportunity to shy a brick at didactic poetry, which leads him to Wordsworth whom he handles roughly. Coleridge he mentions next with reverence. To him indeed, he owed most of his theory

---

[390] This is a liberal estimate and allows for the number distributed at West Point, and about two hundred fifty for general distribution—half and half—a not improbable arrangement.

[391] Dr. Thomas Ollive Mabbott finds that this line, heretofore attributed to Rochefoucauld, is from La Chaussée, the whole quotation meaning, "When all the world is wrong, all the world is right."

of poetry with which he ends this rather remarkable but nevertheless
jejune preface:

A poem, in my opinion,[392] is opposed to a work of science by having, for its *imme-diate* object, pleasure, not truth: to romance, by having for its object an *in-definite* instead of a *definite* pleasure, being a poem only so far as this object is
attained: romance presenting perceptible images with definite, poetry with
*in*definite sensations, to which end music is an essential, since the comprehension
of sweet sound is our most indefinite conception. Music, when combined with
a pleasurable idea, is poetry: music, without the idea, is simply music: the idea,
without the music, is prose from its very definiteness.

This was the germ of the famous lecture of years later on *The Poetic
Principle,* and the source, having its roots, in the discussions of Coleridge, from which he developed and elaborated his own canons for both
writing and criticizing verse. Like nearly all poetic criticism by poets,
it was, in its final analysis, a special and ingenious plea for the kind of
poetry he himself wrote. Despite the leaven of considerable truth, it
remains as an interesting example of "rationalization."

The body of the book contained eleven poems, notably: *To Helen,
Israfel,* and *The Doomed City,* the first version of the latter a much improved *City in the Sea. To Helen* has, in its revised form, taken its
place as one of the great lyrics of the language, while *Israfel* is undoubtedly the first, wildly clear burst of song of the "bitter, bright, cold morning" of a winter day that was to end, like all winter days, in early night.
No more golden notes of prideful promise have ever been uttered as a
prelude. As usual the sources of the poems betray a strange mixture of
autobiography, with real and imaginary landscapes.

> I could not love have except where Death
> Was mingling his with Beauty's breath—
> Or Hymen, Time, and Destiny
> Were stalking between her and me.

strongly recalls the experiences of the past decade with the tragic death
of Mrs. Stanard and Frances Allan, the unfortunate outcome of the
affair with Elmira Royster, and the troubles at home. The figure of the
"Lost Beloved" now first comes strongly into its own. "Helen" is probably a combination and imaginative synthesis of Jane Stith Stanard and
Frances Allan with the abstract longing for the perfect Belovéd common
to all young men. *Lenore* seems to be more definitely applicable to
Elmira. As for *Israfel,* it is undoubtedly about Poe himself. *The City
in the Sea* and *The Valley of Unrest* combine the peculiar effects of
browsings in Oriental literature, and the memories of Scotland and the
Carolina Low Country fused with a mystical magic. Some of the lines,

---

[392] With the exception of the words "in my opinion," this theory is lifted verbatim
from Coleridge's *Biographia Literaria,* chapter XIV. I am indebted to Mr. Joseph
Wood Krutch for this reference showing the early effect of Coleridge on Poe.

and even whole poems, approach perilously near the banal, but they are nearly always saved by a certain distinction.   Many of the selections, notably *Irene,* later called *The Sleeper,* owed their fame to the revisions of later years.   But despite all this, there are many great lines in the book, and it can safely be said that it constitutes an important addition to American poetry.   *Al Aaraaf* again appeared together with *Tamerlane,* now, for the second time, considerably revised.   *Israfel* itself still waited the sure and final touches of the now rapidly maturing hand.   For the first time Poe had written poems which in conception, music, and content were wholly and peculiarly his own.

For the time being, however, the inward knowledge of this accomplishment had to be its own reward.   The only concrete evidence of public approbation was a few dollars left over from the subscription which Mr. Bliss paid to the poet, several author's copies, and the following obscure notice whose very source has been forgotten.

The poetry of this little volume has a plausible air of imagination, inconsistent with the general indefiniteness of the ideas.   Everything in the language betokens poetic inspiration, but it rather resembles the leaves of the sybil when scattered by the winds. . . .[393]

Packing a few copies of his poems and his pitiably scant "wardrobe" in what must have been a very cheap or second-hand carpetbag, Poe took the few dollars that remained to him, after Mr. Elam Bliss and the printers were satisfied, and made his way to Baltimore, probably immediately after his writing the letter to Colonel Thayer.   That seems to have been a final gesture of sheer desperation.[394]

A guidebook of the time,[365] evidently written for prudent and conservative travelers, informs the wary voyager that in New York "it is best to go to the steamboat ten or fifteen minutes before the time of departure to avoid the crowd which always collects at the dock.   *Caution,* if luggage is sent by a porter, ask him for his number, so that if he is negligent or dishonest, he may be reported at the police office."   This caution we may be sure Poe did not have to observe upon the blustering March day in 1831, when he set out for Baltimore via Philadelphia.   If the iron-bound trunk largely filled with *Poems,* second edition, accompanied him, it must have done so upon a wheelbarrow, side by side with the faded flowers upon a carpetbag, and the "crowd" at the docks just above the Battery doubtless looked somewhat askance at the starved and Spanish-looking young gentleman attired in a cadet's overcoat and a beaver hat.   A pair of clumsy army boots disguised what would otherwise have been a rather neat and delicate foot.

---

[393] From a review in the *New York Mirror* of May 7, 1831.
[394] The letter to Colonel Thayer was written from New York on March 10, 1831; on May 6, 1831, he wrote in Baltimore to William Gwynn.

There were at that time four steamboat lines connecting with Philadelphia, the first stage of the journey taking the traveler as far as Perth
Amboy or New Brunswick.   The boats left from "downtown" docks,
and, as they pulled out for the Jersey side of the Hudson, the little city
of New York lay spread before one.   It was a delightful old town.   A
dash of green along the Battery—"on summer evenings the place is supplied with music, and often fireworks . . . and Castle Garden has a fine
promenade. . . . Broadway, the most fashionable promenade in the
city, is most crowded with passengers between one and three o'clock, or
in hot weather, after dinner."   There were forty-two fire engines, besides *two hook and ladder companies!*—Eight (8) large brick school-
houses, "averaging nearly forty-two by eighty-five feet in size," where
no less than five thousand children enjoyed the maps, globes, and
libraries, and the uniform system of the Lancastrian Plan at $1.25 a
quarter, although two of them were "given over" to Africans.[365]   The
mass of low-roofed, white frame and brick houses topped by a few flat
steeples, extended in a solid mass as far north as Washington Street.
"The village of Hoboken is seen a mile or more up the river and the
hills of Weehauken, but on the eastern shore of the river opposite the
Palisades . . . the soil is inferior; and the woodland encroaches too
much upon the fields and orchards."   Here, in the middle distance,
glimmered the spire and the farmhouses of Greenwich Village.   "The
Lunatic Asylum, about seven miles from the city, is a large building of
hewn stone, occupying a commanding position."

The world across which the young Poe moved from New York to
Baltimore wore, as yet, an ancient face.   It was the world which had remained largely stationary from Julius Cæsar to Napoleon.   Its rhythms
were those of the coach horse and the water mill, and its thoughts were
secondary reflections on the sages and poets of Palestine, Greece, and
Rome.   Only here and there a subtle change was beginning to come
across it.   Now and then white sails were prophetically veiled by steamer
smoke, here and there a factory chimney disputed the eminence of the
church steeple; the prisms of canals cut across the landscape, or groups
of surveyors began to whisper through the yet colonial countryside the
strange syllables of "railroad."   Groups of farmers would shortly be
gathering to toss up their hats as their first *iron-horse* roared by.   The
quiet of the landscape was, however, deceptive, for, in the towns, the
giant of an industrial democracy had already begun to stretch himself.
The unexpected surplus in the Federal Treasury was being divided
among the states for "national improvements."   Under the eager demands of the Western voters who had left the stains of their muddy
boots on John Quincy Adams' aristocratic furniture, as Andrew Jackson entered the White House with a whoop,—canals were already
stretching their arms across the mountains, and railway routes were

following fast.   The making, the carrying, and the marketing of things as an end in itself, was about to become the be-all and the end-all here. It was the last comprehensive glimpse at the undisturbed world into which he had been born that Poe was to have.   In a few years a gigantic change was to sweep across the landscape, altering the very aspect of things, disturbing that subtle balance and blend of objects, the eternal fitness of one thing with another, which only nature can produce on a grand scale, and which men have called "beauty."   Nor was this process, which went on so rapidly and, in its first crude essays, under the eyes of Poe, unseen by him or uncommented upon.   The young poet who had already written

> Science! true daughter of Old Time thou art!
> Who alterest all things with thy peering eyes.
> Why preyest thou thus upon the poet's heart,
> Vulture, whose wings are dull realities?

was thoroughly aware of the secrets which the "peering eyes" had found, secrets that were being applied to "dull realities" to "alter all things, to drive

> . . . the Hamadryad from the wood
> To seek a shelter in some happier star . . ."

He too sought a shelter in a happier star.   It was the sphere of his dreams, made up largely of the visions of the early more integrated world of his childhood and the reveries extracted from the literature of other epochs.   This was the world for which he longed, and looked back upon with a heart-uneasy homesickness, that strange longing which lends a romantic retrospect, and a mystic delight, to the many hermitages he evoked with words: *The Valley of the Many-Colored Grass, The Landscape Garden, The Domain of Arnheim.*   Along with this desire "to return," so impossible of fulfillment, as he grew older, was the ever-widening angle between himself and the world of reality around him, a progressive and cumulative advance of nervous and psychic incompatibility that made him less and less capable of coping with an environment which grew more and more out of harmony with his desires. From now on, this divergence must be reckoned with as we watch Poe tossed from horn to horn of an impossible dilemma; that of a personality without a neighborhood.   The refuges, and anodynes, the seductive subterfuges to which he resorted were often more fatal than the trouble itself.   Indeed, the very medicines which their victim prescribed, were, in a large sense, the symptoms of the progressive disease which he sought to allay.   It was a strange acceleration of blended cause and effect that fused into one tremendous cause, destined finally to hurl him out of a world which he found intolerable, a cumulative tragedy, that ended in a smash resounding through time. Fortunately, for us, the spectators, both the victim and the rapidly shifting world across which he moved were strangely, almost grotesquely, interesting.

Poe had been born into the easy-going, sedate, and in many ways self-sufficient world of the early Republic, its conventions were those of a primarily agricultural society. Its methods and means of life had culminated in attitudes which were the result of generations of experience, and its taste was reflected in the semi-classical costume, architecture, and furniture of the day. That, in short, was its objective comment upon life. It was a world of gentlemen and ladies, who regarded themselves in the half-English, half-Roman Republic that they founded, as the natural directors and patrons of the society which they were born to administer. Across this quiet picture the hand of "progress" suddenly moved an erasive sponge dipped in a solvent of the new ideas and forces released by mechanical science, and the drab wash of a frontier democracy without tradition. For a few decades all the colors in the social picture ran and blended; outlines and perspective were lost in the total effect of a crude smear. It was through these decades that Poe lived; at the end of the incredible forties, when he died. He disliked the strong solution on the sponge, and he doubted the direction of the hand which employed it. From this disturbed picture of running colors in the stage of solution, the domains which he perfected in literature were his escape. Like other men he could not climb completely out of his own time, but the physical means which he employed to escape out of its rococo frame constitute the story of his own undoing.

In 1831, the first daubs of the sponge were just beginning to be apparent. The Republic was ended and the Democracy had begun. Andrew Jackson had introduced the spoils system.[395] It was a political idea that had many social ramifications.

Poe had seen the port of New York in 1820, upon his return from England. It was then scarcely more than an enlarged and hustling colonial town enmeshed in a mass of yards and rigging of the sail-borne argosies of the world. In 1831, a new note was upon the water and the landscape. Here and there a factory chimney raised its dark plumed head amid the steeples, and against the snowbanks of sails crossed the nervous spider web of walking-beams driving over half a hundred side-wheel steamers that, even at that date, threaded the harbor and rivers of Manhattan. Their paddles ate steadily into the problem of distance with an astonishing and prophetic speed. Characteristically enough, the passengers did not care very much where they were going; all that they knew was that they were going faster. For them, and for

---

[395] During the first year of Jackson's presidency about 690 officers were removed. The subordinates removed by these swelled the number of those who lost their positions to about 2000. The total number of removals by all former Presidents was 74.

their descendants, it has been enough.   The age of marvels had begun.

The "Philadelphia Steam Boat Line" at that time ended at New Brunswick in New Jersey where travelers took up the second lap of the journey on the "Forenoon Line" of stages, after staying at the hotel all night.   We are assured by good contemporary authority [365] that "the view is pretty from the hill . . . whence public buildings appear to good advantage, particularly the Theological Seminary, which is under the synod of the Dutch Reformed Church"—thence the route led to Princeton, covered behind laboring post horses, with dinner at the stage-house just opposite *Nassau Hall* in the center of the town. Just across the street was the large college yard, the heavy shade trees, and the "fashionable burying ground," where "sober" travelers could walk off the fumes of poker-heated toddy by perusing the edifying epitaphs of Aaron Burr, Jonathan Edwards, Samuel Davis, Samuel Finley, John Witherspoon, and even Samuel S. Smith.   Then it was only ten miles by way of Lamberton and the State Prison to Trenton, over a bridge on the Delaware, "a handsome structure with five arches" that gave approach to "a town of considerable size, with a great number of stores and the aspect of business."   Doubtless Poe took it all in from the less comfortable but cheaper and more "aspect-informing" top of the "Forenoon Line."

At Trenton, the Union Line Steamers left for Philadelphia, "except when the water is low," paddling by Coal Haven—a little cove on the west side of the river where "arks" laden with coal from the Lehigh mines waited to be towed to Philadelphia [396]—and thence past Bordentown on a steep sandbank through which a road cut down to the dock. Just north of the village stood the long white house of Joseph Bonaparte, the Count de Survilliers—and one time King of Spain—with the two low square towers at the end, and a great shot tower near it on the river.   Bristol was passed next, "where a number of gentlemen's seats adorned the river banks with much admired flower gardens along the verge ornamented with fine weeping willows."   A little beyond, lay Burlington with a row of fine residences facing the river.   Before it ran a wide, grassy street with a beautiful sloping embankment.   Below Burlington, the banks of the Delaware widen and flatten out into a low and marshy country on the eighteen mile run to Philadelphia.   It is, says the *Northern Traveller,* "quite unfriendly to the picturesque"—but it was then the haunt of reed birds, and wild, crimson-breasted ducks who fed sedately upon the edible cresses of the salt marsh, riding the

---

[396] "At Philadelphia is located the Bank of the United States, an institution, which, while it has signally failed in its prime object of producing a stable national currency, is heated by a furnace centrally located and fructified twice daily by Lehigh coals." Extract from a notice evidently written by a Jackson man, in a contemporary (1831) guidebook.   This sentence is peculiarly explanatory of the times.

waves of the passing steamers so confidently that they became the
temptation of traveling sportsmen, who shot at them from the decks
of steamboats, tilting their beaver hats back and discommoding their
stocks to draw a bead along the elegantly chased barrels of English
fowling pieces belching forth a deal of white smoke and a loud
"bang." [397]

About here supper was ready.   The captain sat at the head of the
long, white table set with a profusion of side dishes and thick, ruddy
glasses, while overhead the chain chandeliers jangled musically at every
down stroke of the simple engine; the whistle wailed away over the
marshes; the alternate jets of steam darted upward, now to port, and
now to starboard from the stand-pipes, and the smoke rolled backward
from the trim smoke-stacks topped with the prim lace of pointed
iron-cuffs.

Over this placid fertile Delaware valley, which had been the home of
Mark Woolston, Cooper's hero of the *Rancocus* and *The Peak*—stories
that were familiar to Poe—young Poe gazed from the hurricane deck
of the Union Line Steamer on a March day in the early thirties, when
around a great bend in the river a distant steeple and a high shot tower
overtopping the low roofs of the Quaker City came into sight.

Three glass-houses near the water, with white walls and black roofs,
next engaged the attention of the curious traveler, with the shipyards
behind; then the boat-house in the Navy Yard rising over a little island
in the river loomed up, and the steamer swung into the Market and
Arch Street wharves.   There was a tangle of the spars of square-
riggers along the waterfront, gilded figure-heads leaping out from the
arch bows of fast clippers loading for London, China, and the wide
world; a rumble of drays along the cobbled quays—and the crowd of
gentlemen with high hats and gold-knobbed canes, ladies in rustling
silk skirts with bustles, poke bonnets, absurd little cloth slippers peeping
in and out under their dresses, and little girls with lace frilled pantalettes
rushed out of the dock-houses to climb high busses with eagles and landscapes painted on their sides, or to be bustled, valises, leather trunks
and all, into high-backed carriages that rumbled and swayed homeward
over the joggling flagstones of the narrow streets, lit dimly here and
there by a chained whale-oil lamp.

The sanded floor of some waterfront tavern where candles burned
dimly in the small square-paned windows probably extended its humble
hospitality to Poe.   Like Franklin, a century before, he had arrived in
Philadelphia with only a few pennies in his pockets.   There was, of
course, the *United States Hotel* on Chestnut Street opposite the Great
Bank, or the *Mansion House* on South Third, or, for the more do-

---

[397] The habit of shooting at game from public conveyances was an American custom
upon which foreign travelers of the time comment with disgust.

mestically inclined, Mrs. Sword's on Walnut Street, whose scrapple and sausage breakfasts were famous, or Mrs. Allen's on Sixth Street near the State House, who went in for "sparrow-grass" and reed birds smothered in butter—but all of these implied the possession of bank notes. Besides, New York money was at a discount in Pennsylvania. We may be sure that a certain young man, the author of three books of poems, lately dismissed from West Point, dried his army overcoat before a far less pretentious fire somewhere near the Market.

About the same time a poor youth by the name of Horace Greeley arrived in New York with all his worldly goods bundled in a handkerchief.

Whether Poe called on his friend, Mr. Lea, at Carey & Lea, the publishers, or on the editor of the *Philadelphia Casket* during this sojourn of a few hours in the Quaker City is not known. He seldom missed an opportunity to cultivate an editor, but this time he was provided with neither the clothes nor the mood to make an impression, and it is not probable that he was advertising the fact in influential quarters that he had been dismissed from West Point. The state of his purse also admitted of no delay, and the day after his arrival probably saw him on the way to Baltimore on the steamboat line by which he had made the trip two years before.

Baltimore was then the third city in the United States. Owing to the development of ship canals between it and Philadelphia, and the building of the Baltimore and Ohio Railroad, it was like many other American towns of the time, just entering upon a period of surprising enterprise. Along with this, there was a considerable publishing business of newspapers and more or less intermittent periodicals sponsored by various literary groups. "The harbor in the Patapsco River has a narrow entrance and is well protected by high ground. On the side opposite the city is an abrupt elevation of considerable size, where is a fort, and whence a commanding view is enjoyed." The city itself consisted of broad streets with a number of public monuments and imposing public buildings whose architecture was largely confined to their façades. Above the low, black roofs projected the dome of the cathedral, the turreted Washington Monument, the steeple of St. Paul's Church, and the strange round cylinder of a high shot tower. The river front itself was a mass of red brick warehouses bordering long slips which gave the harbor somewhat the appearance of the keys of a piano. Along these lay steamers with the rakish lines of Aladdin's slippers, and crescent paddle boxes blazoned with their names; also schooners, lumber and produce rafts, and the rake-masted Baltimore clippers.[398]

---

[398] The description of Baltimore, which provided the scene in which Poe was to move for the next few years, has been taken from old prints and letters of the day.

Fells Point, about a mile below the more fashionable higher levels, was the business section where most of the stores and shipping interests were situated. It was in this district, in Mechanics Row on Milk Street (now Eastern Avenue), where Poe's aunt, Maria Clemm, still resided.

Here it was that sometime about the end of March, 1831, Poe came home. One can imagine the ecstatic welcome of Virginia ("Sis" was now grown to be quite a fair-sized girl) as Cousin Eddie came into the upstairs room with his wonderful soldier coat on, and Mrs. Clemm dropping her sewing to welcome home the wanderer with a somewhat perplexed but nevertheless hearty hug from her strong motherly arms. There was also a feeble but well-meant handshake from the pale and hollow-cheeked Henry, and a wan smile from paralytic Grandmother Poe, now completely bedridden. That night "Muddie" set another place at the table, and put another cup of water in the soup, while Eddie unpacked his few clothes and disposed his books and papers on the third floor. He was back in the attic room with Henry again. Thanks to Mrs. Clemm, there was a roof over them both, and something to eat. For Edgar it was a permanent arrangement. Henry was dying.

CHAPTER FIFTEEN

"THE MYSTERIOUS YEARS"

SPEAKING of Poe many years later, in New York, Elizabeth Oakes Smith, one of the *literati*, remarked, "men, such as Edgar Poe, will always have an ideal of themselves by which they represent the chivalry of a Bayard and the heroism of a Viking, when, in fact they are utterly dependent and tormented with womanish sensibilities." [399] There can be little doubt that, in this estimate, Mrs. Smith was essentially correct. Baltimore, 1831, marks the beginning of the period, which extended through all the rest of his life, when Poe gave himself up, in his domestic life, to a complete dependence for sympathy and physical comfort upon his aunt, Mrs. Clemm. As time went on, his cousin Virginia gradually took her own peculiar place in the circle of domestic pillars upon which he leaned. All attempt to realize objectively the Viking-military ideal had passed with West Point—the letter to Colonel Thayer, with the contemplated trip abroad to enter the Polish Army, was the last move in that direction. But the romantic, Bayard-chivalric idea still lingered, and was evident to the end in the various episodes with women, more especially in the juvenile affairs of the years in Baltimore and Richmond.

Hence, one of the first glimpses we have of the young poet after his arrival in Baltimore,[400] is his calling in full cadet regalia, and in company with Brother Henry, upon a young lady by the name of Kate Bleakely who lived nearby. Miss Bleakely was the daughter of Matthew Bleakely, the proprietor of the *Armistead Hotel* on Short Swan Street between Jones Fields and the Market Space. She was probably one of the elder brother's flames. They sat together in the hotel parlor. Kate seems to have been considerably impressed, and not a little flattered, by the attentions of "Mr. Allan Poe," as he called himself, and by the pale, rather willowy elder brother. Edgar enlarged upon his prospects in Richmond, and later on addressed verses to the young woman, who was, of course, flattered. The combination of brass buttons and poetry is a solvent one upon the young female heart, and perhaps Poe played the part well even in a hotel parlor. Kate's heart was fluttered, while Edgar had merely provided for himself a little stage upon which he

---

[399] Selections from the *Autobiography of Elizabeth Oakes Smith,* edited by Mary Alice Wyman, Lewiston Journal Company, Lewiston, Maine, page 119.
[400] Information supplied from letters by a member of the Poe family in Maryland.

might strut in costume, with a mild glow about the heart. The incident ended there. What Henry thought we do not know.

Edgar was tolerantly fond of his older brother who also wrote heart-smitten lyrics, and supplied an audience for the new book. Whether Henry was still attempting work in Mr. Didier's office is doubtful. He was far gone in consumption and lapsed frequently into drink. The two young men probably still shared Mrs. Clemm's attic room together. A good deal of the time of the younger brother must have been taken up nursing Henry, as the periods of his prostration became longer and more frequent. The nature of tuberculosis was still a mystery. It was then a "poetic," and a "genteel" disease.[401]

As early as May, Poe was casting about for steady literary work. On May 6, 1831, he wrote to William Gwynn of Baltimore, editor and owner of the *Federal Gazette,* asking him for work on a salary basis.[402] Mr. Allan's marriage, Poe said, had completely changed his prospects, and his guardian was anxious that he should remain in Baltimore.[403] Poe, it seems, had already quarreled with Gwynn, probably over the latter's treatment of *Al Aaraaf.*[404] For this he now apologized and asked the editor's indulgence. Neilson Poe had only recently left Mr. Gwynn's employ, and Edgar may have had some hopes of supplying his place in some humbler manner. But Mr. Gwynn did not see fit to reply. Poe was unable to see him personally as he (Poe) was confined to his room by "a severe sprain to his knee." The next move was to write his friend Dr. Nathan C. Brooks, upon whom he had called on his way to West Point,[405] asking him for a position as an usher (assistant-teacher) in a boys' school which Dr. Brooks had lately opened, at Reisterstown, Maryland. The position was already filled. The possibility of teaching, Poe seems to have kept in mind during most of the Baltimore sojourn.[406] It implied, at least, the possibility of salary and some leisure for the never-forgotten writing.

---

[401] The statement is nowhere directly made in any correspondence that Henry Poe died of tuberculosis. From various indications and references to his ill health, his early death, the long period of his illness, and the fact that no specific name is given to his complaint, it is morally certain that consumption complicated by alcoholic excess was the cause.

[402] A Baltimore correspondent sends information of a Balloon-hoax story contributed by Poe to a Baltimore newspaper about April 1, 1831. It has not been possible to verify this. Dr. Mabbott informs me he "doubts it."

[403] This was pure fiction on Poe's part as there had been no communication between him and John Allan since the letter of February 21, 1831, in New York. The only basis for the statement is that Mr. Allan was certainly desirous of Poe's staying away from Richmond. Poe evidently still counted on his guardian's help, and therefore hoped to seem to act according to his desires. It will be remembered that Mr. Gwynn had been a law student with David Poe, the poet's father.

[404] See Chapter XII, page 211. Also Poe to Gwynn, Baltimore, May 6, 1831.

[405] See Chapter XII, page 216. Brooks continued Poe's friend for years; also Chapter XIX, page 354.

[406] See Poe to Kennedy, Baltimore, March 15 (1835).

A little later Mrs. Clemm's sore pressed household was relieved of one of its helpless burdens by the prime remover of all difficulties. The *Baltimore American* for Tuesday, August 2, 1831, contained this notice :

Died last evening, W. H. Hope aged 24 years. His friends and acquaintances are invited to attend his funeral this morning at 9 from the dwelling of Mrs. Clemm in Milk Street.—

Henry was buried in the graveyard of the old First Presbyterian Church.

So June and July of 1831 must have been pretty well taken up with nursing the dying brother. As John Keats sat beside the bedside of his dying brother Tom, so Edgar Poe watched the passing of Henry under the spell of the same dread disease. There could have been time for very little work, and the whole process was enormously depressing, complicated as it was by a terrible poverty.

One can recall a little group of friends and relatives gathered upstairs at Mrs. Clemm's on a hot August morning in Baltimore. The depressing old hymns, little Virginia's terror, and the faint bird-like calls of the paralyzed grandmother as the shuffling feet carried the long burden downstairs, Mrs. Clemm in her widow's weeds, weeping. After the short journey to the churchyard, Edgar returned to find himself the sole occupant of the attic room. Perhaps a physical relief, but there was no one there now to whom to read *The Valley of Unrest* or to help cap rhymes. Henry's only legacy to his brother was the memory of his adventures and a debt, both of which Edgar claimed.[407] Only a dim memorial of Henry exists in a few obscure amorous verses published in the columns of the extinct Baltimore *North American* in 1827. Save for the curiosity of antiquaries and the reflected glory of Edgar, whose talents and vices Henry seems to have shared, William Henry Leonard Poe is a wasted and youthful shadow. The Poe and Herring cousins may have helped, probably with food. Edgar is known to have contracted a debt of $80 during his stay in Baltimore in 1829, part of which, he says, was for Henry.[407] The difficulties resulting from this debt occupy the chief place in the story of the remainder of the year. John Allan again figures in it largely.

For the time being, Poe evidently did not consider Henry's debt as his own, for on October 16, 1831, he wrote John Allan an affectionate and homesick letter in which he tells him that he is clear of the difficulty that he spoke of in his last letter (Poe may have been writing to Richmond after settling in Baltimore, but these letters have been lost). This letter,[408] however, completely does away with the story that at this

---

[407] The debt was *probably* a note, endorsed for Henry in 1829 to help pay for doctors and medicines.
[408] *Valentine Museum Collection,* letter No. 26.

time the young poet was receiving an allowance from John Allan; evidently nothing of the kind occurred, for Poe distinctly says that he grieves that it is so seldom he hears from John Allan or even of him. He is now writing, he says, because he has nothing to ask; but being by himself, and thinking over old times and "my only friends," his heart is full. The letter contains a note of self-reproach, and, despite the possibility of mercenary interest—a possibility which Poe carefully counters—the letter can only be taken for a genuine expression of regret and affection. He ends with a postscript asking if his "father" will not write one word to him. The letter is addressed in care of William Galt.[409] Poe hoped that this good friend would learn of its contents when he put it in John Allan's hands. It would thus be delivered by a messenger in favor. The epistle is, when all is said and considered, nothing short of the cry of an exiled soul for news from home.

Poe had now had ample opportunity to reflect and feel the effects of his own total neglect of John Allan's advice. Despite the enormously complicated and aggravated circumstances of their long association, there was still an element of affection between them which cannot be denied. The very fact, that each could forever hurt the other, shows that a tie still existed, despite the written denials of both. Underneath the events of both their lives, the unshed tears of a father and son lost to each other murmured dismally in the deepest caverns of being. John Allan could not understand how he could ever lose anything that he had once possessed; Edgar Poe could not conceive how anyone could be finally angry with him. Call it sentimental or what not, but "Dear Pa," says Edgar, "God bless you." In Richmond, John Allan kept turning over the old letters from Poe, endorsing them from time to time with evident emotion.

Yet all the ramifications of their long and bitter quarrel were at work in the inevitable chain of cause and effect. The letter which John Allan had written to Henry Poe in 1824 [410] complaining of Edgar, must inevitably have had its effect upon the Baltimore relatives. Henry would almost surely show it to his cousins. Its vague attack on Edgar, and the dark insinuations which it contained against Mrs. Poe and Rosalie, made Mrs. Clemm forever uneasy. From time to time she hinted that there was "a great mystery." [411] From Mrs. Poe's letters, that Edgar

---

[409] Mr. Galt was looking after the business at *Ellis & Allan* for Mr. Allan who was now often absent. The address to William Galt thus insured its not being read by the clerks, and its getting into the correct hands. Poe was evidently anxious to reopen communication with Richmond; the long silence had greatly alarmed him.

[410] See Chapter VII, page 103.

[411] Mary Devereaux spoke of this remark by Mrs. Clemm, see this chapter, page 269. Mrs. Clemm was not referring to conditions in Richmond, but to a Poe family mystery as she continued to hint of it years later after the Allan affairs were aired in court.

so carefully guarded, she knew the truth, whatever it was, and this evidently was troubling enough. The Poes and Herrings, on their part, must have viewed the situation somewhat practically. Edgar, so far as they knew, seemed to have lost a literally golden opportunity. He had cast off the care of a rich guardian, and somehow or other managed to get disowned. The reasons for it could not be plain. It must have been, and as a matter of fact it was, partly his own fault, so what he said was discounted. In the meanwhile, here was an unknown scribbler apparently content to live on Mrs. Clemm. One might help her, but, as for Edgar, it was well to be a little wary, especially as he fascinated one's daughters. All this affected Poe's attitude towards his cousins, particularly the Neilson Poes, and played its part shortly in his approaching clandestine marriage with Virginia.

Mrs. Clemm, on the other hand, took a more "motherly" view. With Henry dead and her own son "of not much account" (it is said he later ran away to sea), she felt strongly the necessity of a man in her household who was at least a protection and a putative bread-winner. Anyone who could get money for stringing words, she thought, must be a genius, and, above all this, she loved Edgar Poe. His personality, appearance, and blood-relationship were enough. To a woman of her nature, the fact that he needed help was an irresistible appeal. From the day that he entered her door in 1831, he was at once sheltered and bound in the strong arms of a powerful and masterful, yet completely feminine woman, who only surrendered him at last, and then with a supreme and touching reluctance, to death. The marriage with Virginia was the cementing bond of the most overpowering relationship of the latter half of his life. For in the last twenty years of Poe's existence Maria Clemm assumed the major rôle in his affairs that John Allan had occupied during the first. Otherwise there was no comparison. A just and clear understanding of Mrs. Clemm's vital influence upon Edgar Allan Poe is one with the comprehension of the man himself.

Maria Poe Clemm was born March 17, 1790, the younger sister by some five or six years of the poet's father, David. Her parents, "General" David, and Elizabeth Cairnes Poe were then living in Baltimore. On July 13, 1817, at the age of twenty-seven, she married William Clemm, Jr., a widower with five children, a little property, and some prospects, the ceremony taking place at St. Paul's Church, Baltimore. Mr. Clemm died February 8, 1826, leaving Mrs. Clemm penniless with two living children of her own: Henry, born September 10, 1818, and Virginia Maria, born August 15, 1822.[412] A third child, Virginia Eliza

---

[412] There is some conflict about dates here, August 12, and August 22, 1822, are also given by family tradition. The church record is followed, and from St. Paul's Parish, Baltimore, see Woodberry, 1909, vol. I, page 137, note 1. The thanks of the author are also due to Mrs. Sally Bruce Kinsolving for making a search of the St. Paul's *Parish Records*.

(named for Mrs. Herring, Poe's aunt), died in infancy. What little property Mr. Clemm had left, had gone to the children by the first wife or was in litigation. Henry, the son, was, as we have seen, a stone-cutter. But he was of little real help, being an intermittent drinker. His movements and whereabouts are as obscure and uncertain as his character. Thus, in a double sense, Edgar Poe came into the life of Mrs. Clemm to take the place of a son. The tragic picture of the household was complete with Mrs. Elizabeth Poe, Virginia's and Edgar's grandmother, who had become bedridden in 1827 from paralysis, and, except for an insignificant pension, was totally dependent upon Mrs. Clemm. Edgar was thus living with the closest relations he had left, his aunt, and his full cousin Virginia. In 1831, Virginia was only nine years old, yet it was only four years later that she became Poe's wife. How important or significant either her inclination or judgments were in the marriage, can best be arrived at by a comparison of date. A full discussion of this must be deferred to its proper place in the calendar while, in the meantime, the little girl goes to school.

During the Summer of 1831 Poe tried to alleviate the distressing conditions at the house in Milk Street, while he was still helping to nurse Henry, by competing for a $100 prize offered by the *Philadelphia Saturday Courier,* a paper like the old *Saturday Evening Post.* The prize was for a short story. Poe submitted a number of tales but the award went to a Mrs. Delia S. Bacon for a story called *Love's Martyr.* Poe's effort was not entirely unsuccessful, however, for the editor accepted his *Metzengerstein* which appeared in the *Philadelphia Saturday Courier,* January 14, 1832. It was his first short story to be published (*sic*), and shows that he was turning his attention from poetry to the more lucrative field of prose. It is possible that without the merciless spur of poverty he might never have done so. In verse, the dreamer found his true dream within a dream—and received only a dreamful compensation.

The sale of a story in January, 1832, nevertheless, did not serve to put anything on the table through the Summer of 1831. Mrs. Clemm was probably under the necessity of going elsewhere than to the market with her market basket, a large wicker affair, vividly recollected by many who were repeatedly called upon to contribute to its contents, notably the Neilson Poes and the Herrings. Mrs. Clemm in her widow's cap and large motherly person, her broad benign face troubled with an eleemosynary woe, was wont to appear at irregular but disconcerting intervals, the basket upon her arm, her fine gray eyes yearning with stark anxiety, and a tale of dole upon her lips that would have drawn tears from the mask of Comedy. No one was proof against her; for what she had to say was always painfully true: Virginia was naked; "dear Eddie" was *so* ill; or old Mrs. Poe was about to die (had been about to die indeed for five years); she herself was a poor widow; Henry was unsteady again;

the fire had gone out—and there was nothing to eat! What could one do in her large, neat, appealing, and irrefutable presence? The only reply was a contribution to the basket. Its wide and insatiable mouth gaped darkly, engulfing a child's garment, a chicken, half a peck of potatoes, turnips, or loaves of bread—shut to the tune of her departing blessing, and it and the incident were both temporarily closed. But never completely so. It was impossible that the conjunction of all the ill luck which was so generously hers could ever end. Fortunately for a great poet, Mrs. Clemm had a knack, a technique, indeed, which she soon acquired, of cutting under all intelligence and stabbing straight for the heart. She belonged in one part of her nature to that great, dark-garmented sisterhood that her own black widow's weeds recalled, those who are forever flitting from door to door reminding the conventionally prosperous that poverty, bastardy, and suffering are mysteriously present facts and that alms are in order. Much as, from innate respectability, she hated her rôle, Mrs. Clemm played it surpassingly well. She was in this respect a little half-sister of St. Francis. Her lips, her gestures, and her own sacrifices pleaded for starving old age, childhood, and irresponsible genius. Only editors could resist, and even they did so with tears. On several occasions Mrs. Clemm actually borrowed money from an anthologist. Charity records no more signal triumph.

Yet sometimes her greatest skill was in vain. On November 7, 1831, Edgar Allan Poe was arrested in Baltimore for a debt—"which I never expected to have to pay." [413] It was the $80, *probably* the note which he had endorsed for Henry, who was now free from all but celestial duns.[407] Edgar immediately wrote to John Allan. Prison was staring the young poet directly in the face. He was in bad health and he says he cannot undergo as much hardship as formerly. The debt laws in Baltimore were strict. One could then be confined for a debt of $5, and citizens of another town were not allowed the relief of bankruptcy. Besides, the debt was already two years old and it was Winter. "P. S.," he adds, "I have made every exertion but in vain." The letter was written on the eighteenth but it received no reply. Over two weeks later, on December 5th, Mrs. Clemm seconded the appeal to Richmond in a heart-rending letter to John Allan [414] that in both style and content does her credit. She had herself by some miracle raised $20, but that was not sufficient. She reminds Mr. Allan that Poe has no other place to which to appeal; says that besides this $80 he is not in debt; and closes by stating that the young man had been extremely kind to her so far as his opportunities would permit. There is some indication

---

[413] *Valentine Museum Poe Letters,* letter No. 27, Baltimore, Maryland, November 18, 1831 (Friday). See also note 407.
[414] *Valentine Museum Poe Letters,* letter No. 28.

in this letter that Mr. Allan had "refused" to help Edgar, but it probably refers only to his long silence.

Ten days later Poe again writes to John Allan in sheer desperation. The prison door is evidently yawning. The letter is one of the most pitiable that a poet was ever forced to write to a patron.

Balt. *Dec.* 15th, 1831 [415]

DEAR PA,
I am sure you could not refuse to assist me if you were well aware of the distress I am in. How often have you relieved the distress of a perfect stranger in circumstances less urgent than mine, and yet when I beg and entreat you in the name of God to send me succour you will still refuse to aid me. I know that I have no longer any hopes of being again received into your favour, but for the sake of Christ, do not let me perish for a sum of money which you would never miss, and which would relieve me from the greatest earthly misery. . . .

Poe then contrasts the blessings of wealth and happiness which his guardian was then enjoying with his own terrible misery, and adds:

If you wish me to humble myself before you I am humble—Sickness and misfortune have left me not a shadow of pride. . . .

How differently he would act, were their situations reversed, is the burden of the letter's close. It reminds one of the last stanza of *Israfel*. Alas, for a poet in a world of sweets and sours so strangely portioned!

John Allan was not really so emotionally unassailable as this letter would indicate, although the accidental cause of events warranted Poe in thinking so. Mrs. Clemm, as we have seen, had written Mr. Allan on December 5th; on the seventh, Mr. Allan had warranted John Walsh, a Baltimore correspondent of *Ellis & Allan* to "procure Poe's liberation and give him $20 besides to keep him out of further difficulties," but for some reason unknown, the merchant neglected to mail the letter until January 12, 1832. Mr. Allan was considerably troubled by this, an unusual oversight on his part in a financial transaction, for he endorses on the back of Poe's letter of December 15th. "Then put it in the [post] office myself." This letter, *written* two days later, was evidently intended to answer Mrs. Clemm's letter of the fifth.

In the meantime, of course, Poe knew nothing of all this. Christmas Day, 1831, must have passed in an agony of suspense, and, on December 29th, he again wrote to Richmond making a final curt appeal. [416] The letter begins "Dear Sir," and contains a reminder that it is from one who in old times once sat upon the knees which the writer is now forced to embrace. Some two weeks later Poe was probably startled by the unexpected intervention of Mr. Walsh. It was after the crisis was over.

---

[415] *Valentine Museum Poe Letters,* letter No. 29.
[416] *Valentine Museum Poe Letters,* letter No. 30.

What had happened is not exactly clear. Poe does not seem to have been actually imprisoned. Probably some one of the cousins intervened to save the family name from disgrace; the importunate creditors were prevented; and Edgar Poe was absolved from the misery of hearing the New Year's bells of 1832 ring through prison walls. For an under-fed young man with a weak heart and a tendency toward melancholy, it was more than a fortunate escape—it was an extension of his lease on existence. The nadir had been reached.

The year 1832 still remains the most mysterious in the annals of Edgar Allan Poe. In many respects it is a blank, there is no corre-spondence covering the period, and his exact whereabouts during part of the time is open to reasonable doubt. The preponderance of evi-dence, however, points to the fact that he was in the garret of Mrs. Clemm's Milk Street house, and that the stories which began to appear in 1833 in the *Baltimore Saturday Visiter, The Tales of the Folio Club,* and *The Coliseum* were under way there.[417] The short stories which appeared in the *Philadelphia Saturday Courier* during 1832, of which there were five, probably represent the work of 1831.

Although it is impossible to present the events covering this "mysteri-ous year" with any assurance as to the precise order of time in which they occurred, there is a considerable mass of evidence relating to the stay of Poe in Baltimore, some of which undoubtedly tends to fill in what has long remained more or less a blank. Before touching on this, it should be stated that none of the traditions of this time indicate that the young poet was dissipated. The reliable facts, indeed, prove the reverse. He was, it seems, in ill health part of the time, probably caused by the weak heart that threatened to cease to beat altogether two years later, after the extreme poverty and deprivations that he was forced to undergo. It is now definitely known that absolutely no help was received from Richmond. The aid received from John Allan in January, 1832,

---

[417] Several legends about Poe's going abroad in 1832, and of his being in Baltimore unknown to the Clemms, exist. I have assembled the bulk of the material dealing with this year and considered all the correspondence before and after it, and all the circum-stances implied. There is no genuine *evidence* to imply that Poe was not in Baltimore in 1832, and all the implications are that he was. The *Valentine Museum Poe Letters* are silent but indicate, at the last, that Poe had remained in poverty in Baltimore. Mary Devereaux's story shows Poe very palpably *a year or two before* John Allan's death in 1834, and must necessarily cover part of the "mysterious" period. The amount of manuscript material which Poe had on hand a year or so later, taken together with the work that he is known to have done in 1831, shows that he must have been writing through 1832. Had he made all of the "voyages" and trips, been dying of fever, in jail, etc., etc., during this time, we would have some authentic record, or some real evidence about it. The blank simply means an unknown author hard at work on his manuscripts. The account given here has been put together with painstaking analysis; where surmise has been resorted to it is the result of the elimination of the impossible.

was the last help he was ever to experience from that quarter.[418] Writing was Poe's sole resource.

Among other places where Poe is known to have been seen about this time was E. J. Coale's bookstore on Calvert Street, which he is said to have haunted, and Widow Meagle's Oyster Parlor on Pratt Street near Hollysworth. Here he met a sailor by the name of Tuhey who played the flute. The proprietress was a good-natured Irish woman who made much of the "Bard," as he was called. Persons who went there, afterward remembered hearing Poe recite his own poetry, and the flute playing of Tuhey beside the inn fire.[419] The Tavern was a resort of sea-faring men, and those who gathered there were wont to exchange stories. Poe was still forced, it appears, to wear various articles of his West Point uniform, partly from necessity, probably, and partly from desire. There is some tradition of his drilling the street gamins about the neighborhood of Fells Point, and the young lads of the vicinage were said to have been fond of him, and to have followed him whenever he went through the streets. The Baltimore Library, then at the corner of Holliday and Fayette Streets, seems also to have been a refuge, and to have provided the source for the many literary and historical gleanings that appeared a few years later in the *Southern Literary Messenger* as *Tid-bits*. There may have been some "flying visits" to Philadelphia when the purse permitted, probably to see the editors of the *Courier*.[420]

The chief event of this period, however, was a romantic affair with a Miss Mary Devereaux, a neighbor of the Clemms. The recollections of that young lady were not contributed until about forty years afterward, so that the exact time which they covered cannot be definitely ascertained, but, from numerous indications, it appears that part of the events which she described took place during the year 1832.[417]

Mrs. Clemm's attic room looked out upon the rear of the houses upon Essex Street, in "Old Town." Poe was much in this attic, writing, and, as he looked out of the third story window one day, across the fluttering

---

[418] As this statement contradicts that of all other biographers and Poe himself to John P. Kennedy, the reader is referred to the *Valentine Museum Poe Letters* covering the second Baltimore period, 1831-1833, which show beyond peradventure that John Allan did *not* give Poe an "annuity." During the period, John Allan probably (*sic*) sent Poe a small gift in November, 1831, the $80 to save him from prison, too late, "and $20 besides." In his last letter to John Allan (Poe from Baltimore, April 12, 1833,) the latter says, "It is now more than two years since you have assisted me . . . three since you have spoken [written] to me." Poe would scarcely lie to John Allan about what Mr. Allan had done himself. Prof. Woodberry's contrary statements were made before the complete evidence was available.

[419] See J. H. Whitty's *Memoir,* large edition, page xxxv. There are also other accounts confirming this.

[420] This is conjectural, although there are some doubtful references to it by Mary Devereaux.

clothes in the backyards between Milk and Essex Streets, he noticed a pretty girl who wore her auburn hair in "frizzed puffs," as the style then was. She was sitting in the rear window of a house opposite. A handkerchief flirtation began in which another girl, Mary Newman, who lived next door to Mary Devereaux on Essex Street, soon joined.[421] The white signals were alluring, and soon led to a closer acquaintance. Both the girls knew that Poe was a young soldier and a poet, and their hearts as well as the handkerchiefs seem to have been agitated. A battle-dore and shuttlecock game of kisses was soon being played with hands for rackets, until Mrs. Devereaux once inquired, "What takes you upstairs so much, Mary?"

One summer afternoon when Mary Devereaux and Mary Newman were seated talking together on their adjoining front stoops on Essex Street, with only a balustrade between them,[422] Edgar Poe passed "as usual" on his way home to Mrs. Clemm's.[421] The impressive Edgar stopped and bowed. Virginia, it seems, had already been sent to Mary Devereaux for a lock of the bright hair which had first attracted his attention. The favor had been granted. One can therefore imagine the excitement of the two Marys as the romantic figure of the Milk Street window actually seemed about to speak. "Do you know him?" whispered Mary Newman to Mary Devereaux. "No," replied Miss Devereaux, lying valiantly despite the burning lock of hair. "Why, that's Edgar Poe who has recently come from West Point. He writes poetry, too. Why, I declare! There he comes across the street. Oh! Isn't he handsome!" With a few omissions, perhaps, "Poe's Mary" can best tell the rest of the story for herself.[422]

Mr. Poe, having crossed the street, came up the Newman's stoop. As he did so, I turned my back, as I was then young and bashful. He said 'How do you do, Miss Newman?' She then turned and introduced him to me, and then happened to be called into the house. Mr. Poe immediately jumped across the balustrades separating the stoops, and sat down by me. He told me I had the most beautiful head of hair he ever saw, the hair that poets always raved about. . . . From that time on, he visited me every evening for a year, and during that time, until the night of our final lover's quarrel, he never drank a drop, as far as I know . . . Affectionate! . . . he was passionate in his love. . . . My intimacy with Mr. Poe isolated me a good deal. In fact my girl friends were many of them afraid of him and forsook me on his account. I knew more of his male friends. He despised ignorant people, and didn't like trifling and small talk. He didn't like dark-skinned people. When he loved, he loved desperately. Though tender and very affectionate, he had a quick, passionate temper, and was very jealous. His feelings were intense and he had but little control of them. He was not well

[421] It is said that Poe for awhile boarded at the Newmans', but Mary Devereaux's story indicates that he knew Miss Newman as a neighbor and lived at the Clemms' whence Virginia carried notes.

[422] The account here given and the conversations are taken from *Poe's Mary* by Augustus Van Cleef, *Harper's New Monthly Magazine,* March, 1889, pages 634-640. Also see note 745.

Street Scene in Baltimore of the 1830's

Showing a street scene of about a century ago in Poe's day

From an old print

Courtesy of the Maryland Historical Society

John P. Kennedy

Poe's Baltimore Patron, author of *Horseshoe Robinson*, *Swallow Barn*, etc. Member of Congress, attorney, and famous host

After a painting by Wilson

Courtesy of the English Bookman

Yours &c
T. S. Arthur

Author of "Ten Nights in a Barroom"

A friend of Poe in Baltimore

From an etching in Godey's Lady's Book *for 1844*

The *Southern Literary Messenger* Building
and the offices of *Ellis & Allan* to the right

Two buildings in Richmond, Virginia, intimately connected with Poe. Many
months were passed under both roofs as a clerk in his foster-father's warehouse
and as an editor on the *Messenger*

balanced; he had too much brain. He scoffed at everything sacred and never went to church.[423] If he had had religion to guide him he would have been a better man. He said often that there was a mystery hanging over him he never could fathom. He believed he was born to suffer, and this embittered his whole life. *Mrs. Clemm also spoke vaguely of some family mystery, of some disgrace.* . . .[411] Mr. Poe once gave me a letter to read from Mr. Allan, in which the latter said, referring to me, that if he married any such person he would cut him off without a shilling.

Eddie and I never talked of his poetry then or in later years. He would not have done that; he would have considered it conceited. We were young, and only thought of our love. Virginia always carried his notes to me. . . . Eddie's favorite name was 'Mary,' he said. He used often to quote Burns, for whom he had a great admiration. We used to go out walking together in the evenings. We often walked out of the city and sat down on the hills.

One moonlight summer night we were walking across the bridge, which was not far from our house. At the other end of the bridge was a minister's house. Eddie took my arm and pulled me, saying, 'Come, Mary, let us go and get married; we might as well get married now as any other time.' We were then but two blocks from home. He followed, and came in after me. We had no definite engagement, but we understood each other. He was then not in circumstances to marry. When my brother found that Mr. Poe was coming so often he said to me: 'You are not going to marry that man, Mary?—I would rather see you in your grave than that man's wife. He can't support himself, let alone you.' I replied, being as romantic as Eddie was, that I would sooner live on a crust of bread with him than in a palace with any other man. . . . The only thing that I had against him was that he held his head so high. He was proud and looked down on my uncle whose business did not suit him. He always liked my father, and talked with him a good deal. . . .

One evening a friend of my brother's, a Mr. Morris, was visiting us. He knew that Mr. Poe's favorite song, which I often sang him, was *Come Rest in This Bosom.* He asked me to sing it in order to tease Mr. Poe. I went to the piano to sing. Mr. Morris stood by me and turned the leaves. Mr. Poe walked with one hand behind his back, up and down the room, biting the nails of the other hand to the quick, as he always did when excited. He then walked over to the piano, and snatched the music and threw it on the floor. I said that it made no matter, and that I could sing the song without music, and did so. Mr. Morris, knowing me well, called me 'Mary.' That also made Eddie jealous. He stayed after Mr. Morris left, and we had a little quarrel.

Our final lovers' quarrel came about in this way: One night I was waiting in the parlor for Eddie, and he didn't come. My mother came into the room about ten o'clock and said, 'Come Mary, it's bed-time.' The parlor windows were open, and I lay with my head on my arms on one of the window sills. I had been crying. Eddie arrived shortly after my mother spoke to me, and he had been drinking. It was the only time during that year that I ever knew him to take anything. He found the front door locked. He then came to the window where

---

[423] This implied a much more definite philosophy at that time than now. To be "a free thinker" was a serious charge in 1832. The author has contemporary letters showing that young men who took Sunday walks had to hide the wild flowers they picked on such sinful rambles under their beaver hats on returning to town *or they would lose their jobs.* See *The Young Man's Sunday Book*, Philadelphia, Desilver, Thomas and Co., 1836, for some startling remarks on young men who do *not* go to church.

I was, and opened the shutters, which were nearly closed. He raised my head, and told me where he had been. He said he had met some cadets from West Point when on his way across the bridge. They were old friends, and took him to *Barnum's Hotel*,[424] where they had a supper and champagne. He had gotten away as quickly as possible, to come and explain matters to me. A glass made him tipsy. He had more than a glass that night. As to his being an habitual drunkard, he never was as long as I knew him.

I went and opened the door and sat on the stoop with him in the moonlight. We then had a quarrel, about whose cause I do not care to speak.[425] The result was that I jumped past him off the stoop, ran around through an alleyway to the back of the house, and into the room where my mother was.

She said, 'Mary! Mary! what's the matter?'

Mr. Poe had followed me, and came into the room. I was much frightened,[425] and my mother told me to go upstairs. I did so.

Mr. Poe said, 'I want to talk to your daughter. If you don't tell her to come down stairs, I will go after her. I have a right to!'

My mother was a tall woman, and she placed her back against the door of the stairs, and said, 'You have no right to; you cannot go upstairs.'

Mr. Poe answered, 'I have a right. She is my wife now in the sight of Heaven!'

My mother then told him he had better go home and to bed, and he went away.

He didn't value the laws of God or man. He was an atheist. He would just as lief have lived with a woman without being married to her as not. . . . I made a narrow escape in not marrying him. I don't think he was a man of much principle.

After the quarrel . . . I broke off all communication with Mr. Poe, and returned his letters unopened. My mother also forbade him the house. He sent me a letter by Virginia. I sent it back unopened. He wrote again, and I opened the letter. He addressed me formally as 'Miss Devereaux,' and upbraided me in satiric terms for my heartless, unforgiving disposition. I showed the letter to my mother, and she in turn showed it to my grandmother, who was then visiting us. My grandmother read it, and took it to my uncle James. My uncle was very indignant, and resented Mr. Poe's letter so much that he wrote him a very severe, cutting letter, without my knowledge. Mr. Poe also published at the same time in a Baltimore paper a poem of six or eight verses, addressed *To Mary*. The poem was very severe, and spoke of fickleness and inconstancy. All my friends and his knew whom he meant. This also added to my uncle's indignation.

Mr. Poe was so incensed at the letter he received that he bought a cowhide, and went to my uncle's store one afternoon and cowhided him. My uncle was a man of over fifty at the time. My aunt and her two sons rushed into the store, and in the struggle to defend my uncle tore his assailant's black frockcoat at the back from the skirts to the collar. Mr. Poe then put the cowhide up his sleeve and went up the streets to our house as he was, with his torn coat, followed by a crowd of boys. When he arrived at our house he asked to see my father. He told him he had been up to see his brother, pulled out my uncle's letter, said he

---

[424] This hotel, *Barnum's,* was a famous Baltimore hostelry noted for its diamond-back terrapins, and canvas-back ducks "done rare." The place was built in 1827. The Post Office was on the ground floor. This was the end of the Philadelphia stage line, just then (1832) about to go out of business.

[425] "Mr. Poe" had evidently carried matters to extremes. The reader is asked to note this passage for future reference.

resented the insult, and had cowhided him. I had been called down-stairs, and when Mr. Poe saw me, he pulled the cowhide out of his sleeve and threw it down at my feet, saying, 'There, I make you a present of that !'

Shortly after this exciting and melodramatic scene, the Devereaux' moved away from Baltimore [426] and did not come across Poe until many years later. There are one or two very significant things about Mary Devereaux's account, evidently by an uneducated but intelligent girl, it bears considerable weight as the direct evidence of one who knew him exceedingly intimately. The extreme difficulty of living with a man of Poe's nervous and excitable temperament needs little comment. It is a further testimony to Mrs. Clemm's everlasting affection and patience, while the picture of Virginia as a mere child and the bearer of love notes sets aside completely the absurd romantic rubbish that has been built up about this little maiden at that time.

Evidently she was a nice little schoolgirl in gingham and pigtails, who carried and fetched for big Cousin Eddie, probably with a mischievous thrill in the case of Mary Devereaux. This can scarcely mean that, "from the first Edgar Poe recognized in her the one over-powering affection of his heart." If he did so, asking her to trot around the block to fetch him a lock of red hair from Mary's was a passing strange way of manifesting his "soul's worship" for Virginia. It is quite obvious to all but the sentimentally purblind that the only "throne in the house of the great poet" occupied by his *spiritu-el* cousin" was a chair at the table three times a day, when the state of Mrs. Clemm's larder permitted it. Mary says that Virginia was plump and hearty and a nice little schoolgirl with a pleasing disposition, "her chief charm." Perhaps, Mrs. Clemm had her plans, but of these, like a wise mother, she said nothing then, we may be sure.

The end of the affair with Mary was to be typical of several to follow later. She bears testimony that Poe was passionate. Evidently he meant to have what all men desire—"He didn't value the laws of God or man"—and the cause of the quarrel on the stoop Mary didn't care to talk about,[425] but it is also evident that the great excitement of sex, like all other "stimulants," completely unnerved Poe. He was never capable of remaining calm and collected, even rational enough, to overcome the normal and proper difficulties that stood between love and the prize. Before marriage was possible, the emotional pressure became so great that it exploded along some other paths, anger, jealousy,— exasperation of some kind, ending in sheer exhaustion and in later years followed by collapse. Uncle So-and-so was cowhided, the husband, or prospective mother-in-law fearful for the family real estate, with other relatives, became alarmed, and the world always heard about

---

[426] To Philadelphia ——, and afterward to Jersey City.

it later through the secondary literary manifestations of poems or tales of woe. Of course, the neighbors talked, and in Poe's case the gossip has become immortal.[427]

About the same time, when, according to Mary, John Allan was threatening to cut Poe off "without a shilling," in case he married her, that gentleman in Richmond was making his will. This ode on the intimations of mortality was drawn April 17, 1832, due to the fact that, since his visit to the Hot Springs in 1829, Mr. Allan's health had been steadily failing, and the "intimations" were now again assuming a dropsical turn.[428] Poe seems to have got wind of this. A printer by the name of Askew is known to have carried letters back and forth for Poe from Richmond.[429] The old servants in the house, who had not forgotten either the old days or "Marse Eddie," occasionally sent him news, or he may have heard through the Mackenzies, who were still intimate with Miss Valentine, of the doings at the big mansion. Rosalie Poe was still living with the Mackenzies.

There were a hundred motives to take Poe to Richmond. Aside from going "home," and that was much, the chance of a favorable reception by his "father" might mean the immediate relief of his desperate circumstances and a change in his entire future. Undoubtedly, too, there were other than mercenary motives. Perhaps they would let him rest in his old room. "Aunt Nancy" would still be there, and after all "Pa" *had* saved him from prison. He must care a little. A rumor of the making of the will,[430] of Mr. Allan's ill health, or some chance kindly expression from John Allan may have been the deciding factor. We can be sure his heart was beating fast as he packed his bag and said good-bye to Mrs. Clemm. The steamboat left early.

It was sometime in June, 1832, when Poe arrived in Richmond after an absence of over two years.[431] The return to an old scene revives all the familiar attitudes and emotions that go with it. The little Virginia capital could scarcely have changed at all since he had left it, the very patterns of the vines on the walls of houses were old friends. It must have seemed impossible as he opened the gate of the well-known

---

[427] In Richmond, Baltimore, and Charlottesville, Poe is still gossiped about as though he were alive. Some of the legends are ingenious.

[428] John Allan had nearly died of dropsy in March, 1820. John Allan to Charles Ellis, London, March, 1820. *Ellis & Allan Papers.*

[429] Information given to the author in Richmond, July, 1925.

[430] Robert Cabell was one of the witnesses of the will. Young Robert Cabell was a close friend of Poe and may have been in touch with him.

[431] This date has been placed a year earlier and a year later by various biographers. The making of the will, and the known movements of Poe in 1831 and 1833, place it in 1832 by elimination. The birth of young William Galt Allan, after which, according to the Allan tradition, Poe appeared, seems to fix it about June. Poe could not have appeared "after the birth of the first child" as he is said to have done, as that was at a time when he is known to have been elsewhere.

walk that he was not really "going home." All that lay about him was at the core of his dreams. Old "Dab," the butler, opened the door, and Poe told him to take the bag to "his room." It was not the gesture of presumption but the motion of old habit. At the same time he asked for Miss Valentine. She, it appears, must have been out, and the old butler informed him that "Marse Eddie's room" was now a guest chamber! There appears to have been some argument with old Dandridge about this. Poe regarded the room as his peculiar domain. His things, he thought, were still there.[432] The old darkey must have been in a quandary. Poe then asked for Mrs. Allan who came down to the parlor.

Here she found a young man, a stranger, acting like a member of the family. To her amazement, she found herself being reproached for having ordered her own house to suit herself. Poe on his part, as usual under the stress of great excitement, could not control his feelings and found himself reproaching "the strange woman" who seemed to have usurped Frances Allan's place. The voice of an "heir" upstairs did not tend to soothe him. It is said that even the child came in for some acrid remarks on Poe's part, and that in his excitement he went so far as to hint that Mrs. Allan had not been without mercenary motives in marrying. The lady is said to have replied that, far from considering Poe a member of the family whose wishes were to be consulted in the plans of the household, she knew him to be nothing more than a mere pensioner on her husband's bounty. The interview was undoubtedly acrimonious and, no doubt, enormously exasperating to them both. To Mrs. Allan, Poe's presence must have been an insufferable reminder, and an assertion of the rights of the beloved foster-son of the first wife, that struck at the very basis upon which her own existence and her children's lives, for there were now two of them, must rest. She sent for Mr. Allan, who was at the office, and is said to have coupled her message with the assertion that "Edgar Poe and herself could not remain a day under the same roof." Poe was inclined for a moment to stand upon "his rights," and seems to have remained seated in the parlor, but the emphatic sound of the lame man's cane clicking up the walk, and the clump of a well-known foot was sufficient to change his mind if not his feelings. He

---

[432] These, it appears, had been "moved out," a fact that enraged Poe. The story of this visit comes from two distinct angles: the legends according to the Allan tradition, and the version derived from the Mackenzies to whom Poe went immediately after the event. I have tried to reconstruct the incident taking into consideration the personalities involved and the standpoints from which the stories were afterwards told. Mrs. Susan Archer Weiss and others, afterwards presented the Mackenzie-Poe version. For the Allan version see the letters of Miss Mayo and Colonel Ellis—also see Woodberry, 1909, vol. I, pages 95-96. The *Valentine Letters* show *no* indication of a visit in 1831. The only possible time was the early Summer of 1832. The second visit to the Allans took place shortly before Mr. Allan's death in 1834. Poe's memorandum to Griswold we now know refers to letters written and received at West Point. *Valentine Museum Poe Letters,* Nos. 22-24.

crossed the hall to the front door about the same instant that John Allan let himself in by the side entrance.

Poe went to the Mackenzies', where he told his story. They were simple and kindly folk who understood. Rosalie was still there, and Jack Mackenzie his staunch boyhood friend. Rosalie had grown up, but she was still a little girl. Miss Valentine, who must have been out when Poe "called" at the big mansion, sent him money. The Mackenzies also probably contributed. After a short time Poe returned to Baltimore.

Then the Richmond gossip began. It was rumored that Poe had thrust himself past the butler and gone to Mrs. Allan's room where she lay in bed with a new-born infant in her arms. There he had "reviled her and the child" and had been thrown out by the servants after which he threw stones at the house. Only the arrival of Mr. Allan had prevented goodness knows what! Poe must, of course, have been drunk. What could one expect of the son of actors, a mad poet,—after all Mr. Allan's kindness, too! A hundred eager Penelopes now took up the shuttle of rumor, platting and unraveling the endless web of petty scandal, as the domestic knitting needles were laid aside, in order to weave the most delightful incident that had been suggested to designers along the James for years.

Before the shuttles were discarded, a whole grotesque panel in the tapestry of the adventures of Israfel was completed for the corridors of legend. It was such an intriguing work of art that it appeared later as a lunette in one of the side halls of history.

In the meantime, Mr. Allan's generosity had crystallized in his will in the form of certain codicils regarding the education of twin boys, on a side street in Richmond, who were now just two years old. Perhaps, the once beloved foster-son's indignation and the nervousness of the second Mrs. Allan had roots which even the longest knitting needle could not probe. Whatever may have been said between them that morning in the big octagon parlor, on Poe's part, the world was never the wiser. Others were not so reticent about him.[433]

---

[433] The second Mrs. Allan and her family, together with Colonel Thomas Ellis and a certain social group in Richmond, later on became the source of much invidious anti-Poe propaganda. They had had the advantage of living after Poe died, when all fear of the devastating reply that he might have made was removed. Then the world was informed of Poe's ingratitude to his "generous benefactor," forgery, and the embezzlement of the substitute's money. At the time that these assertions were allowed to "emanate," the documents which disproved them were in the hands of those who originated the stories. Only two conclusions are possible: either these people fabricated the legends, or they were too purblind to understand the letters which they themselves possessed. Considerable authority was attached to their assertions as coming from persons who had personal knowledge of the facts, as well as documents to which biographers were denied all access. The impression grew that the real facts were scandalous—they were—but not about Poe. The story of Poe's visits to Richmond was the beginning of this kind of thing. It is now high time, a century later, to lift "the mysterious veil."

The news of the outcome of the visit to Richmond could have brought very little cheer to the poverty-stricken hearth of Mrs. Clemm in Baltimore. If anything, Poe had only "succeeded" in making his alienation the more complete. John Allan never communicated with him (Poe) again, and Poe attempted to do so only once with him. There was nothing left but for the pen in the garret to scratch on and on, with only the most glimmering prospects that the fine chirography of its industrious characters would ever be translated into print. There was a whole volume of stories at hand, the famous *Tales of the Folio Club.*

Meanwhile, at the Baltimore Library, the same pair of eyes were eagerly scanning *The Tales of Hoffmann,* German Philosophy, largely in a denatured and secondary English form, foreign and American newspapers and magazines.

In the Autumn of 1832, there is a legend and some evidence that Poe made an ocean voyage as a sailor before the mast to the coast of Wexford in Ireland.[434] But both the legend and the evidence are uncertain. The incident remains to be proved, and the probabilities are that Poe remained in Baltimore. Henry Clemm may have accompanied Poe to Ireland, but Mary Devereaux says he went West, about this time. An old acquaintance and boyhood chum also removed from Virginia into an even vaguer beyond. In the Fall of 1832, Ebenezer Burling died of cholera in Richmond. Whether Poe heard about it then we do not know.

Edgar was much at his cousins' house as well as at the Clemms'. At the corner of Bounty Lane and Caroline Street lived a cousin, Mrs. Beacham, with several in her family. Here Poe was a frequent visitor, as well as at Mr. George Poe's house. A good deal of his time was spent at Mr. Henry Herring's on Asquith Street near Pitt. Mr. Herring was a prosperous lumber dealer and was able to afford a pleasant social background for his daughter. A circle of young girls met frequently at her house, and Poe seems to have been much in demand, reciting poetry, and writing in his cousin's album, a custom of the time which was so universal as to develop a distinct type of parlor literature. Poe seems to have been extremely fond of this Miss Herring, if not in love. She married a year or two later and left Baltimore to live in Virginia. The Cairnes, family relatives of old Mrs. David Poe, were also kindly and hospitable,[435] and there was a neighbor, a Mrs. Samuel F.

---

[434] J. H. Whitty mentions this in his biographical sketch to the *Complete Poems,* Houghton Mifflin. The story comes from the memories of Poe's friend, F. W. Thomas, who said that he knew a sailor by the name of Tuhey, who played the flute, and that the sailor told him that Poe had gone with the said Tuhey to Ireland and back. The story is at best extremely doubtful.

[435] According to F. W. Thomas, Tuhey, the sailor, was also a guest at this house and Poe was so much in love with one of the Cairnes girls that, when she refused him, he went to Ireland in despair. See note 419 for the source of this.

Simmons, who was extremely kind. In recognition of this, she received sometime later the manuscript of *Morella* in the neat scribal characters that mark it as part of *The Tales of the Folio Club*. About the same time, Poe was engaged in writing his only attempt at drama, *Politian*.

It is noticeable that most of the houses which Poe frequented were the homes and rendezvous of pretty young girls. In their company, rather than in the companionship of youths of his own age, he seems to have been most at home. With them he doubtless found himself the object of interest and considerable admiration, an atmosphere in which he expanded. Seated on the Empire sofas, just then beginning to go out of fashion, in a parlor adorned with *genre* pictures of the day, each conveying an obvious but edifying moral, he wrote sentimental poems in the red morocco, brass-bound and betasseled albums, or looked at the incredible flounced nymphs simpering from the pages of a genteel magazine, with the head of a living replica tantalizingly near. Then, with a faint rustle of ruffles and the twinkle of low-heeled, beaded cloth slippers, they would all gather about the piano where the candles would be lit in the little brass side-sconces, brightening white lace-covered hands that leapt along the keys. A certain young gentleman with soulful gray eyes turned the music, whose quaint notes as large as tadpoles wriggled their way through the faint-ruled lines of an old song. Outside the passer-by paused to be quaveringly informed that a young lady within was extending a contralto invitation to *Come Rest in This Bosom*. Then there was currant cake and a little sweet elderberry wine. The conversation was in strict keeping with the refreshments. In winter-time the black lumps of cannel coal melted slowly in the arabesqued cast-iron paunch of an urn-topped stove; *parchesi* draughts advanced or returned on candle-lit squares; the strange designs of dominoes grew and dissolved on deal tables, amid breathless giggles; and there was an ancient game, never old, played with a handkerchief or a pillow. Baltimore, after all, had its relaxations. Above the monotone of poverty, if one listens carefully, can be heard the quaint grace notes of a thin piano and the whisper of skirts over carpets where the flowers of Victoria had not yet bloomed. Half a century later an old lady remembered a young man: [436]

Mr. Poe was about five feet eight inches tall, and had dark, almost black hair, which he wore long and brushed back in student style over his ears. It was as fine as silk. His eyes were large and full, gray and piercing. He was entirely clean shaven. His nose was long and straight, and his features finely cut. The expression about his mouth was beautiful. He was pale, and had no color. His skin was of a clear, beautiful olive. He had a sad, melancholy look. He was very slender . . . but had a fine figure, an erect military carriage, and a quick

---

[436] Mary Devereaux in 1888-9. *Harper's New Monthly Magazine,* December, 1889. See note 422, page 268.

step. But it was his manner that most charmed. It was *elegant*.[437] When he looked at you it seemed as if he could read your thoughts. His voice was pleasant and musical but not deep. He always wore a black frock-coat buttoned up, with a cadet or military collar, a low turned-over shirt collar, and a black cravat tied in a loose knot. He did not follow the fashions, but had a style of his own. His was a loose way of dressing as if he didn't care. You would know that he was very different from the ordinary run of young men.

Thus, we get a fairly complete picture of Poe in the early 1830's. In the Fall of 1832, Mrs. Clemm moved from Milk Street to Number 3 Amity Street where she resided until the entire family left for Richmond in 1835. She was accompanied to the new dwelling by Virginia, "a handful of furniture," and her nephew Edgar, who, although nobody knew it but himself, was just on the threshold of fame.

---

[437] For a person born in the 1820's and reared in the decades that followed, "elegant" was the last word of praise. The word has lost its glory. "Elegance" was interred at Frogmore.

CHAPTER SIXTEEN

BOTTLED FAME

VERY scanty was the success that had met any of Poe's efforts, thus far, to obtain either sale or fame for the work of his pen. Here and there, one of his poems warmed someone capable of feeling the divine fire, and his immediate acquaintances spoke and thought of him as a poet. Beyond that, the three little books seemed to have dropped into a void. *Belles-lettres,* it was only too painfully evident, would have led to the garret of Chatterton if it had not been for the garret of Mrs. Clemm. Poe, as we have seen, had therefore turned his efforts in a more marketable direction. The journalism of his time now commenced to claim his attention seriously, and he began to study the contemporary prints, both newspapers and magazines, especially the latter. The result was two-fold: he now earnestly began to write prose—during 1832, five of his tales, the first of his published short stories, were published in the *Philadelphia Saturday Courier,* where he had competed unsuccessfully for a prize,—the other facet of his immediate interest was the beginning of his theories about American magazines and literary criticism. In the meanwhile, the muse did not entirely languish, *The Coliseum,* at least, was under way and even an attempt at drama, *Politian.* What he lacked was some point of publishing contact. So far, he had not been able to accomplish that in Baltimore.[438] The stories, and the first three books of poems, together with the cruder attempts at short stories which Poe is said to have written at the University of Virginia and to have destroyed there, represented the results of the longings of his youth, and the later and riper harvest of his first creative urge. But for awhile, especially in the Winter of 1833, it looked as if the stories were to die as unnoted and as unlamented as the poems.

It was remarkable that Poe had been able to complete this considerable volume of literary output during the harassed years between 1827 and 1833. It was more than remarkable, and speaks plainly for his overmastering desire to create, that he had been able to do anything at all. The Winter of 1833, in particular, must have been a starving time. There are many indications that the period of collapse and illness in New York was indicative of the too heavy drafts upon his physical

---

[438] It is said that he had published verses in Baltimore newspapers, but the evidence is doubtful.

capital. A disintegration seems to have followed, partly perhaps upon the lines which heredity dictated. A weak heart, which sometimes completely prostrated him, shattered nerves, and the beginnings of the conditions which afterward led to disturbed mental states, all played their several parts from now on. For, from the time of his escape from West Point, it is safe to say that he was never a completely well man.[439] There were, from now on, periods of vigor and creation; but there were also recurring and accentuated periods of collapse. Starvation, anxiety, disappointment, and dissipation all contributed to the final tragic result, only sixteen years later, in the same city where he had first found shelter with Mrs. Clemm.

During the Winter of 1833, Poe must have been much about the streets of Baltimore trying to pick up odd jobs. The newspapers, despite the efforts of Neilson Poe, had failed to take him on.

In all this year, there is only one letter to break the silence, and it speaks in the tones of despair. On April 12, 1833, Poe wrote his last letter to John Allan.[440] He says in it that Mr. Allan has not assisted him for over two years, nor "spoken" (written) to him for three, and that, although he has little hope of any answer, he cannot refrain from attempting to make one more attempt to interest his guardian. Poe says that he is utterly without friends and therefore without the means of obtaining employment, and that he is perishing, literally perishing for want of help. Yet, he adds pathetically, he is not idle, nor addicted to any vice, nor has he offended society in any way which should bring the fate of starvation upon him. "For God's sake pity me, and save me from destruction," was the last line that he ever wrote to his guardian. It reveals a soul in a waking nightmare and it received no reply.

John Allan, indeed, was on the verge of a country where no postman could follow him. His dropsy was fast gaining upon him. During the Winter and Spring of 1833, he was, from time to time, engaged in writing various codicils in his will, the nature of which were so intimate that he employed his own handwriting in order to avoid the necessity of witnesses. In March, one of the illegitimate twins had died [441] which

---

[439] Prof. George E. Woodberry also dates the failure of Poe's health from about this time. See his *Life of Edgar Allan Poe,* 1909, vol. I, pages 122-123: "He had begun normal, healthy and well; at twenty-five he was no longer so, nor was he ever to regain sound health," etc.

[440] One of the most remarkable coincidences in the annals of literary correspondence is connected with this letter. On the very same day that Poe wrote this letter in Baltimore, April 12, 1833, perhaps at the same hour, John Allan in Richmond was endorsing on the back of another letter of Poe's, written from New York, February 21, 1831, the following: "April 12, 1833, it is now upwards of two years since I received the above precious relict of the Blackest Heart and deepest ingratitude, alike destitute of honor and principle every day" . . . etc., etc. The reader should compare letter No. 25 with letter No. 31 of the *Valentine Museum Poe Letters,* a comparison that provides a strangely intimate glimpse into the past.

[441] See the statements in the will of John Allan, Appendix, or page 289 this chapter.

required further alteration in his will, but the removal of this claim on "charity" did not induce him to extend it to another claimant in Baltimore who had at least a moral hold on his interest.

Towards the end of July, Mr. and Mrs. Allan, Miss Valentine, two baby boys, two nurses, two drivers, five horses, and two carriages, all set out for Virginia Hot Springs in considerable style. One of the babies, Willie Galt, was teething; and Mr. Allan himself was almost helpless from dropsy, yet not too weak to take a considerable pleasure in the important figure which he cut. "In fact," said he, "we made quite a little cavalcade." [442] He had attained all that the world could give him, wives, concubines, children, slaves, horses and the envy of his neighbors.[443] The note of satisfaction is strong, but the cavalcade was nearing the end of the journey. In the meantime, a young man in Baltimore, who had refused at a great price to become an appendage of the caravan, had definitely started on the career which has caused the little domestic procession over the Virginia hills to be remembered.

In July, 1833, the *Baltimore Saturday Visiter,* an ephemeral weekly newspaper then edited by a Mr. L. A. Wilmer with considerable local success, offered a prize of $50 for the best short story and $25 for the best poem to be submitted within a given time.[444] The judges appointed by the editor were John P. Kennedy, Dr. James H. Miller, and J. H. B. Latrobe, who has left us the story of what happened:

> We met one pleasant afternoon in the back porch of my house on Mulberry Street, and seated round a table garnished with some old wine and good cigars, commenced our critical labors. As I happened to be the youngest of the three, I was required to open the packages of prose and poetry, respectively, and read the contents. Alongside of me was a basket to hold what we might reject.
>
> I remember well that the first production taken from the top of the prose pile was in a woman's hand, written very distinctly, as indeed, were all the articles submitted, and so neatly that it seemed a pity not to award it a prize.[445]

---

[442] Information gleaned from various items and letters in the *Ellis & Allan Papers.*

[443] Despite the "swank" attached to "The Springs," an English traveler a year later, 1834, informs us that "The Springs" were incredibly crude and uncomfortable. A Mr. Fry and his son, both great dancers, kept the place. The food was disgusting, the meat was carved by Mr. Fry himself, dressed in a dirty blue smock, who made a point of dropping the knife to escort ladies to their seats with gallantry. There were not enough "servants," *i.e.,* slaves and guests were awakened early in the morning by throat-clearing, shouts for hot water, and the sound of slops being poured from the windows. The beds did not permit a night's undisturbed rest. Sanitary conditions were those of the frontier. Only Virginia chivalry could survive the roads. A plague of flies added the last delightful touch.

[444] The statement of the amount of the prize has often been wrongly given heretofore as $100. It was, as a matter of fact, $50 for a story, and half that for a poem; Mr. Latrobe himself, one of the judges, afterwards misstated the amount which biographers have followed.

[445] In his egregious sketch of Poe, Dr. Rufus W. Griswold afterward tried to rob Poe of all credit in this matter by stating that the prize was awarded to the best written manuscript in point of penmanship. This was a sneer at Poe's beautiful Roman holograph of the *Folio Club Tales.*

It was ruthlessly criticized, however, for it was ridiculously bad—namby-pamby in the extreme and of the school known as the *Laura Matilda* school. . . . Of the remaining productions I have no recollection. Some were condemned after a few sentences had been read. Some were laid aside for consideration—not many. These last failed to pass consideration afterwards, and the committee had about made up their minds that there was nothing before them to which they would award a prize, when I noticed a small quarto-bound book that had until then accidentally escaped attention, possibly because so unlike, externally, the bundles of manuscript that it had to compete with. Opening it, an envelope with a motto corresponding with one in the book appeared, and we found that our prose examination was still incomplete. Instead of the common cursive manuscript, the writing was in Roman characters—an imitation of printing.

I remember that while reading the first page to myself, Mr. Kennedy and the Doctor had filled their glasses and lit their cigars, and when I said that we seemed at last to have a prospect of awarding the prize, they laughed as though they doubted it, and settled themselves in their comfortable chairs as I began to read. I had not proceeded far before my colleagues became as much interested as myself. The first tale finished I went to the second, then to the next and did not stop till I had gone through the volume, interrupted only by such exclamations as 'Capital!' 'Excellent!' and the like from my companions. There was genius in everything they listened to; there was no uncertain grammar, no feeble phraseology, no ill-placed punctuation, no worn truisms, no strong thought elaborated into weakness. Logic and imagination were combined in rare consistency. . . . There was an analysis of complicated facts—an unravelling of circumstantial evidence that won the lawyer judges—an amount of accurate scientific knowledge that charmed . . . a pure classic diction that delighted all three.

When the reading was completed there was a difficulty of choice. Portions of the tales were read again, and finally the committee selected *A Ms. Found in a Bottle.* One of the series was called *A Descent into the Maelström,* and this was at one time preferred . . . all the circumstances of the selection ultimately made have been so often since referred to in conversation that my memory has been kept fresh, and I see my fellow judges over their wine and cigars, in their easy chairs—both genial, hearty men, in pleasant mood, as distinctly now as though I were describing an event of yesterday. . . .

Refreshed by this most unexpected change in the character of the contributions, the committee refilled their glasses and relit their cigars, and the reader began upon the poetry. This, although better in the main than the prose, was bad enough, and, when we had gone more or less thoroughly over the pile of manuscript, two pieces only were deemed worthy of consideration. The title of one was *The Coliseum,* the written printing of which told that it was Poe's. The title of the other I have forgotten, but upon opening the accompanying envelope, we found that the author was Mr. John H. Hewitt.[446] I am not prepared to say that the committee may not have been biased in awarding the [poetry] prize to Mr. Hewitt by the fact that they had already given the [prose] . . . prize to Mr. Poe. I recollect, however, that we agreed that, under the circumstances, the excellence of Mr. Hewitt's poem deserved a reward, and we gave the smaller prize to him with clear consciences. I believe that up to this time not one of the committee had ever seen Mr. Poe. . . .

---

[446] Mr. Hewitt's poem was entitled *The Song of the Winds* under a pen-name —"Henry Wilton."

Not long afterward the *Saturday Visiter* for October 19, 1833, appeared with the following notice that must have come to Poe's eye with almost the relief of a reprieve.

. . . Amongst the prose articles were many of various and distinguished merit, but the singular force and beauty of those sent by the author of *The Tales of the Folio Club* leave us no room for hesitation in that department. We have accordingly awarded the premium to a tale entitled *The Ms. Found in a Bottle.* We cannot refrain from saying that the author owes it to his reputation, as well as to the gratification of the community, to publish the entire volume. These tales are eminently distinguished by a wild, vigorous, and poetical imagination, a rich style, a fertile invention, and varied and curious learning.

Signed   JOHN P. KENNEDY
J. H. B. LATROBE
JAMES H. MILLER

In the same number in which this notice appeared, the prize story was published.

At a time when prizes for literary effort are so many and various as to have almost ceased to attract attention, the significance of this award can scarcely be appreciated. Not only was the cash itself supremely grateful, but, for the first time, the attention of a fairly large public was now focused upon Poe, for the news of the award was not confined to the pages of *The Visiter.* Poe had at last emerged from the shadow of the wings. The limelight had been definitely focused upon him, and, from this time on, his various entrances and exits on the literary stage, although they were not always accompanied by applause, were nevertheless followed by the magic glare. Perhaps of more immediate importance was the fact that he had gained some influential friends. Among the most important and constant of these was a benevolent and wise gentleman, then a well-known Baltimore author, John P. Kennedy, Esquire.[447]

The Monday after the announcement of the award in the *Saturday Visiter* was used by Poe to call upon all the members of the committee in order to thank them. Mr. C. F. Cloud,[448] the owner and publisher of the paper, had, it seems, already called on Mr. Kennedy on Sunday morning and given him such an account of the young author that the good gentleman's curiosity and sympathy were both thoroughly awakened. When Poe was introduced next day, he was cordially received, and the interesting reports about him fully confirmed by his conversation and appearance. He was invited to return to the house, then

---

[447] *Swallow Barn* was Mr. Kennedy's *magnum opus.* His kindness to Poe is his only genuine claim to literary remembrance. His work was like its author, urbane and impeccable. He commanded at one time a considerable and highly respectable public, especially in Baltimore. He is also "remembered" for *Horseshoe Robinson.*
[448] Descendants of Mr. Cloud in Catonsville, Maryland, have the only complete file of the *Baltimore Saturday Visiter* extant, I am informed by a Baltimore collector.

one of the most important from a literary as well as a social point of view in Baltimore—in short, in a limited but very definite and helpful way, Mr. Kennedy became Poe's patron. Never was a young poet more in need of one.

An hour or so after the call upon Mr. Kennedy, Poe introduced himself to Mr. Latrobe, another one of the judges, in his office.[449] From him comes a full and interesting account of the interview:

I was seated at my desk on the Monday following the publication of the tale, when a gentleman entered and introduced himself as the writer, saying that he came to thank me as one of the committee, for the award in his favor. Of this interview, the only one I ever had with Mr. Poe, my recollection is very distinct, indeed,—He was if anything, below the middle size, and yet could not be described as a small man. His figure was remarkably good, and he carried himself erect and well, as one who had been trained to it. He was dressed in black, and his frock coat was buttoned to the throat, where it met the black stock, then almost universally worn. Not a particle of white was visible. Coat, hat, boots, and gloves had evidently seen their best days, but so far as mending and brushing go, everything had been done apparently, to make them presentable.[450] On most men his clothes would have looked shabby and seedy, but there was something about this man that prevented one from criticizing his garments, and the details I have mentioned were only recalled afterwards. The impression made, however, was that the award in Mr. Poe's favor was not inopportune. Gentleman was written all over him. His manner was easy and quiet, and although he came to return thanks for what he regarded as deserving them, there was nothing obsequious in what he said or did. His features I am unable to describe in detail. His forehead was high, and remarkable for the great development at the temple. This was the characteristic of his head, which you noticed at once, and which I have never forgotten.[451] The expression of his face was grave, almost sad, except when he became engaged in conversation, when it became animated and changeable. His voice I remember was very pleasing in its tone and well modulated, almost rhythmical, and his words were well chosen and unhesitating. . . . I asked him whether he was then occupied with any literary labor. He replied that he was then engaged on *A Voyage to the Moon,* and at once went into a somewhat learned disquisition upon the laws of gravity, the height of the earth's atmosphere, and capacities of balloons, warming in his speech as he proceeded.[452] Presently speaking in the first person, he began the voyage . . . leaving the earth, and becoming more and more animated, he described his sensation as he ascended higher and higher . . . where the moon's attraction overcame that of the earth, there was a sudden *bouleversement* of the car and great confusion among its tenants. By this time the speaker had become so excited, spoke so rapidly, gesticulating much, that when the turn upside-down took place, and he clapped his hands and stamped with his foot by way of emphasis, I was carried along with him. . . . When he had finished his description he apologized for his excitability, which he laughed at himself. The conversation then turned upon other subjects, and soon afterward he took his leave. . . .

---

[449] The Mechanics Bank Building—later.
[450] So much for Mrs. Clemm!
[451] Phrenology was then taken in all seriousness.
[452] See Chapter VII, page 108.

In his calls on the judges, Poe did not forget Dr. James Miller with whom he also struck up an acquaintance that later led to some letters between them. The friendship with Lambert Wilmer, the editor of *The Visiter,* was kept up for some time. He and Poe discussed together the founding of a magazine in Baltimore and were evidently fairly intimate. It was the first of the many magazine projects which from this time on became a preoccupation with Poe and absorbed much of his thought and energy. Two items were always lacking in these schemes to found the great American periodical; *i.e.,* capital, and sta‚ bility in the character of the proposed managing editor.

Wilmer describes Poe as the "most passionless" of men that he ever knew. His opinion seems to have been based for the most part on Poe's writing and an innate delicacy in his friend which he mistook for lack of vigor. As he must have known of the horsewhipping incident, which raised not a little dust in the neighborhood, his statement cannot have the force which the words alone would imply. Wilmer was doubtless soon sorry enough that the poetry prize had been given to Hewitt, for that young gentleman soon worked himself into the good graces of the owner of the paper, Mr. C. F. Cloud, and usurped the editor's chair. Wilmer was forced to leave Baltimore in 1834, penniless and on foot. The prospectus with which Poe provided him, outlining the plan for a magazine to be published in Baltimore, fell by the wayside.[453] The *"bouleversements"* of the fly-by-night journalism of the time were generally sudden and often merciless and tragic, as Poe himself was to find out later. Even the modicum of humanity usually embodied in the ethics of an organized profession was still lacking.

Hewitt's complication with Wilmer did not, however, prevent Poe from becoming close friends with the former. The two poets were in a sense rivals, Hewitt had once been on the staff of the *Minerva and Emerald* which had handled *Al Aaraaf* so nonchalantly, but their mutual interest in poetry seems to have brought them together frequently. There were long rambles in the country about Baltimore during which literature was the topic of conversation, and Hewitt has left us a picture of Poe in Byron collars and a black stock, one who "looked the poet all over." Yet all this did not prevent Poe, when the occasion offered, from explaining just how it was that Hewitt had received the prize. After Wilmer left, the columns of *The Visiter* do not seem to have been so hospitable to Poe. That paper fell later into the hands of T. S. Arthur,[454] who in turn yielded to Dr. J. E. Snodgrass, the physician who was Poe's friend to the last. It was thus peculiarly linked with Poe's name, and with all of those connected with it he was for

---

[453] When Wilmer left Baltimore, Poe sent him a prospectus for a Baltimore magazine. It was the first of many similar schemes.
[454] See the portrait included in this volume.

long, then and afterward, more or less associated. Lambert Wilmer remembered Poe particularly well:

. . . His time appeared to be constantly occupied by literary labors; . . . he lived in a very retired way with his aunt Mrs. Clemm, and his moral deportment as far as my observations extended was altogether correct. . . . In his youthful days Poe's personal appearance was delicate and effeminate, but never sickly or ghastly, and I never saw him in any dress which was not fashionably neat with some approximation to elegance. Indeed, I often wondered how he could continue to equip himself so handsomely, considering his pecuniary resources were generally scanty and precarious enough. My intercourse with Poe was almost continuous for weeks together. . . . His general habits at that time were strictly temperate, and but for one or two incidents I might have supposed him to be a member of the cold-water army. . . .

"The one or two incidents" were the occasion of the cadets' supper at the *Barnum Hotel* and a single instance when Poe took Wilmer home and offered him some Jamaica rum after the universal custom of the time. Aside from these, there is no authentic, indeed not any attempt to indicate drinking episodes during the entire period of the poet's residence in Baltimore. He was, as a matter of fact, unusually abstemious for a young man of the time much about a convivial Southern town.

During the time of Poe's stay in Baltimore, from 1831 to 1835, there were two distinct literary groups in the city. The first of these gathered about John P. Kennedy, William Gwynn, and others of the old "Tusculum" Club. These were more literary than journalistic. The second group consisted of men, then only beginning to be known as writers, such as Arthur, Brooks, Dawes, Carpenter, Hewitt, and MacJilton. These represented rather ably the various tendencies in cheap verse, magazine stories, and the more "popular" writing of the time. Their names are to be found frequently associated with that of Poe in the newspapers and magazines of the period, and the decades to follow, and they were, at least during his lifetime, in some sense his rivals. It was from the first group that Poe, for the most part, received his inspiration and his aid, principally from John P. Kennedy. The inference cannot reasonably be avoided that it was Mr. Kennedy who really smoothed the path, not only by advice and influence, but by actual physical help. He was one of the few friends that Poe kept to the very end, one to whom he was permanently grateful.

The suggestion that the remaining *Tales of the Folio Club* should be published, was not lost upon Poe, and towards the end of 1833 he seems to have gone personally to Philadelphia, to try to prevail on his old acquaintance, Carey & Lea, to bring out the collection of tales to which others, it appears, were later added. Mr. Kennedy's help was probably largely instrumental. In addition to this, *Godey's Lady's Book* was induced to accept one of the series, *The Visionary*, which appeared in the issue of that magazine for January, 1834.

Nevertheless, the last months of 1833 and the greater part of 1834 were a starving time for Poe in the little two-story brick house with a dormer window and double chimneys on Amity Street. Mrs. Clemm's basket must have frequently made the rounds for requisitions, her needle could not be busy enough. At one time she is said to have tried to eke things out by teaching school. With nothing but prospects in view, the Winter of 1833 came to an end for the Poe-Clemm household in Baltimore. It had been a memorable year, the path ahead was smoother and brighter. It was the question of continuing to exist, until the editorial barriers were passed, that was now most perplexing. In the meanwhile, Virginia was entering upon womanhood, propinquity was at work, and a cousinly affection was ripening into something more definite. With the opening of the new year the rumor of an approaching event, in which Poe could not help being vitally interested, claimed his presence at Richmond. John Allan was dying.

Sometime during the latter part of the Winter of 1833-34, probably in February, Poe, therefore, again found himself before the familiar mansion in Richmond with the firm intention of having an interview with "Pa." His object must have been to plead his "rights," and to make plain his necessities; perhaps, once and for all to explain away all differences and, in the forgiving mood which he might expect to find at a death-bed, to be received again as a son who could hope to share in the benefits of affection. Evidently he had been reliably warned that the end was near, and there was a chance, even in the remote possibility of a reconciliation, which he could not afford to neglect. All the memories of a lifetime and the vital element of self-interest combined to make a motive powerful enough to cause him to try to force his way into the house where his last reception could leave no doubt as to the nature of his welcome as a member of the family.

After the visit of the Spring before, the servants had doubtless been instructed by both their master and their mistress how to receive "Marse Eddie." But prophetic foresight here seems to have been of little avail. Poe arrived, is said to have thrust himself past the butler, and to have run upstairs to the big front room overlooking the lawn. Mr. Allan was seated, with his cane beside him, propped up with pillows, and reading a newspaper. He was helpless from dropsy. The lines of youthful and amused irony that had once given him an almost sweet expression about the mouth had long ago faded, and the hawk face and black eyebrows lowered menacingly at the lines of the daily news. Suddenly the small piercing eyes looked over the edge of the *Richmond Whig,* and beheld in the doorway an apparition from the past. The young foster-son was standing there as if the years had rolled back, gazing appealingly at his "father," and, as always in that presence, looking ill at ease. For a moment they must have stared thus at each other, these two strongly opposed spirits, for the last time. Then Poe tried to make some advances to the older man, probably pitiful enough,—he tried to come into the room. As if he were being attacked, John Allan seized the cane by his armchair and flourished it in the air. A torrent of imprecations and reproaches rolled from his lips. He threatened to beat Poe if he approached him, rising up in his invalid's chair like a dying eagle, dangerous, implacable, and able to strike till the last. His cries brought his startled wife and the servants to the room, and Poe was ignominiously thrust by the slaves from the door. One can imagine the invalid trembling and exclaiming, and the young poet returning to Baltimore, sorrowful and shaken, even to the roots of his ego, by the spectacle and the strange fact of someone who hated him to the last. Had either of them cared less, the last infernal scene would have been impossible. Devastating demonstrations are not manifested by indifference.

It is now time to relate the passing of the man whose shadow of influence lies across the life of Poe from first to last. Edgar's visit to Richmond may well have hastened the end. That the intimations of his departure had lain heavily upon John Allan for almost two years, the dates, and the nature of his will, show clearly. In December, 1833, he was busy winding up the affairs of *Ellis & Allan* with his old partner, Charles Ellis. Poe's visit to Richmond followed a few weeks later, after which time Mr. Allan failed rapidly. On March 19th, Miss Valentine stopped in at *Ellis & Allan* to tell the clerks that Mr. Allan "was a very sick man." About a week later the end came. At eleven o'clock on the morning of March 27, 1834, Mrs. Allan was in her husband's chamber attending to some of the duties of the sickroom, when a terrified scream from her brought the family and the servants hurrying in. John Allan had died suddenly in his easy-chair. The jaw had dropped. Up until the very last instant of life it had remained absolutely firm. There was only one thing that he could not overcome.

Even about the semblance of the man who sat there propped up amid the pillows, there must have been something tremendous. The hands which had, at last, relaxed had never relented, and even after death they reached out strongly into time. By every worldly standard John Allan was a success. He had begun with nothing, but he died in full possession of ample moneys, a handsome mansion, broad fertile acres,—the arbiter and absolute master of over half a hundred human souls.[455] Two ladies of considerable force, beauty, and attainments had been his wives; at least two other women had shared his favors; he was the father of seven children [456] for his second wife had presented him with three.

---

[455] Slaves, immediate family, and a host of relatives in Scotland. See his own, and the will of William Galt, Appendix III.

[456] Edwin Collier, twin sons and a daughter by Mrs. W., two sons by his second wife, and an infant daughter. Mr. Allan never "acknowledged" the daughter by Mrs. W., but left her and her mother jointly $3000. See the will.

Of all those upon whom the dominant shadow of his personality had so heavily fallen, Edgar Allan Poe was the only one that had completely eluded him. That John Allan is remembered by the one and only item that he failed to possess completely is a comment which a generation that ignored irony failed to understand. The influence which finally relaxed the grasp of the Scotch merchant on the twenty-seventh of March, 1834, was a powerful one. It is no wonder that Mrs. Allan screamed.

The will, in which there was not even an allusion to Poe, was a curious human and quasi-legal document containing clauses which throw a new light on the troubles that had long disturbed the Allan household, troubles in which the foster-son had played such an important part. There were, it now appears, a disconcerting number of children to provide for, and a domestic situation already so perplexing that the testator might well overlook a mere foster-child (who had merely been raised as the son of his bosom) in favor of those who were of his own blood. But, even of that motive, no one can be certain. If the intentions of the testator were benign, they were also unfortunately obscure, for both the grammatical and the legal phraseology of the will was so faulty [457] as to arouse the justifiable suspicion that it was meant to protect the posthumous reputation of the testator rather than to confer benefits upon the legatees. Whatever the motives or the intentions, they were not carried out. The widow refused to abide by the will itself, and, in a long and scandalous litigation, carried her case to the State Supreme Court, where she successfully established her intestate rights. To the proud and firm-minded relict, who buried her husband in Shockoe Cemetery at noon, sharp, on Saturday the twenty-ninth of March, 1834, the sorrow of his taking off was somewhat mitigated by certain considerations to which the world at large was not then privy. The nature of these was revealed in his will: [458]

In the name of God, Amen: I John Allan, of the City of Richmond, being of sound mind and disposing memory, do make and ordain this my last will and testament, revoking all other wills by me heretofore made. [*Then follow items, and a provision constituting his beloved wife, Louisa Gabriella Allan, James Galt, and Corbin Warwick, executrix and executors. This part of the will is dated April 17, 1832, and is witnessed by Th. Nelson, M. Clark, and Robert L. Cabell. On December 31, 1832, in a second section of the will without witnesses, the intent of the first part of it was reiterated with some curious additions:*]

Mrs. Louisa Gabriella Allan, wife of John Allan
John Allan, child and 1 *enseignt*
(. . . . .)
1st pay all my debts.
2nd. My whole estate to be kept under the management of my exors, hereinaftei

---

[457] For a legal analysis of the will, see Appendix III.

[458] The part of John Allan's will given here and the complete text given in the appendix are from a certified copy supplied the author by Mr. Charles O. Saville, Clerk of the Chancery Court of the City of Richmond, Virginia.

mentioned until my eldest child becomes of age, the house and all the ground contiguous and attached to the same, I hereby authorize and empower my executors, or such of them as may act, to sell if they shall think it advisable after the expiration of 5 years from this date, also lot at intersection of F and 2nd Street, opposite Mr. Ellis's . . . ⅓ of the net annual income of my whole estate to be paid to my beloved L. G. A. during her natural life or until my eldest child becomes of age. At the division of my estate I desire that my wife shall have one-third of my estate for life. . . .

To Miss Ann Moore Valentine $300 per annum and her board lodging and washing to be paid and found her out of my estate during her natural life, and this provision is to be in lieu of $2000 which I hold of her money, and of which my estate is to be discharged if she accepts this bequest.[459] To each of my sisters Nancy Fowlds, Jane Johnston, Elizabeth Miller £300 Sterling, and to my sister Mary Allan £100 Sterling, all residing in Scotland.[460] I devise the whole of my estate among my children which may be alive at the time of my death and of such as my wife may at that time prove to *ensignt,* in case they should be all boys I then desire that the estate may be equally divided among them in case of the birth of a daughter or daughters then I desire that my son or sons as the case may be shall be entitled to double what my daughters may have, my children to take the part of such of them as may die under age. In case of the death of all my children without being married or arriving at the age of 21 years I then give and devise to my relations Wm. Galt & Jas. Galt and to Corbin Warwick and to their heirs, exors, and administrators all the estate given to my children . . . the remaining ⅕ part I wish disposed of in such manner as I may hereafter appoint by codicil. I desire that my executors shall out of my estate provided give to ——————— a good english education for two boys sons of Mrs. Elizabeth Wills, which she says are mine, I do not know their names, but the remaining fifth, four parts of which I have disposed of must go in equal shares to them of [or] the survivor of them but should they be dead before they attain the age of 21 years their share to go to my sister's Fowlds children in equal proportions with the exception of three thousand dollars, which must go to Mrs. Wills and her daughter in perpetuity.

JOHN ALLAN, Dec. 31st, 1832

This memo. in my handwriting is to be taken as a codicil and can easily be proven by any of my friends.

The notes preceding are in the handwriting of my friend, Jno. G. Williams.

The twins were born sometime about the 1st of July 1830. I was married the 3rd October 1830 in New York, my fault therefore happened before I ever saw my present wife and I did not hide it from her. In case therefore these twins should reach the age of twenty-one years and from reasons they cannot get their share of the fifth reserved for them, they are to have $4000 each out of my whole estate to enable them to prosecute some honest pursuit, profession or calling.

March 15th, 1833, I understand one of Mrs. Wills' twin sons died some weeks ago, there is therefore one only to provide for. [*With this happy natural simplification of so plural a difficulty, the testator then delicately adds*]: My wife is to have all my furniture, books, bedding, linen, plate, wines, spirits, etc., etc., Glass and China ware.

JOHN ALLAN

---

[459] This money had been left to Miss Valentine by William Galt in 1825. See his will, Appendix III.

[460] See Chapter III and Chapter V for other mention of these relatives.

Even the "wines, spirits, etc., etc.," however, do not seem to have had the desired cordial effect.

At a Circuit Superior Court of Law and Chancery held for Henrico County at the Capital in the City of Richmond, the 8th day of May 1834. . . . Louisa G. Allan, widow and relict of the said John Allan, deceased . . . appeared in Court and renounced the Executorship, and also declared that she will not take or accept the provision of any part thereof. . . .

The second Mrs. Allan survived her husband by almost half a century, during a considerable portion of that time, several gentlemen practicing before the Richmond bar were able to join in the refrain of an old English song:

God bless the testator who draws his own will

discreetly, but with substantial reasons for appreciation of the professional sentiment.

There can be little doubt that even the hope of a legacy in Richmond had kept the young poet in Baltimore restless. John Allan *could* be, and we know often was, prevailed upon to help from time to time, so that the feeling of there being a final refuge, someone to depend upon in time of desperate need, had never been entirely absent in his former ward. The rôle of the cast-off rich man's son, even of the prodigal who might be forgiven at the last, was also a pleasant and interesting background which Poe never entirely abandoned. He was delighted to refer to it from time to time in letters, and we have already seen how frequently it cropped up in his conversation. Mr. Allan's death had now put an end to this so far as the reality went. The last ties of self-interest and lingering sentiment with the past were now demonstrably dissolved. "Dear Pa" was now beyond the appeal of even the most needy "man of genius"; and the will, silent about Poe, had been probated. The doubtless disappointed young man in Baltimore could no longer deceive even himself about the past. In grim earnest he must now look to the future for the tying of any ties that might bind. Those of his youth were now only the figments of memory.

There was a certain side of Poe's nature which made him admire and lean upon those who were capable of overcoming the difficulties of a physical world. He was, in a large sense, incapable of doing so himself, like so many other artists who find the ultimate reality in dreams, yet he instinctively felt the need and the worth of practical capacity. It was for that reason that he had never been entirely able to shake himself clear of John Allan, even in his own mind. He was not entirely selfish in this, it was merely the necessity of self-protection, a means by which he tried vicariously to complement an accidental lack in his own character. Yet strangely enough he was never willing to admit that dependence implied possession. It was always at that point that the break inevitably came, and a new pillar was sought to lean upon, or another breast upon which to rest "a proud but weary head." The situation, in various disguises, occurred again and again in the future, as it had in the past, for instance:

Once having freed himself from John Allan, starvation forced Poe to depend upon another guardian, the army; finding that intolerable, he went through exactly the same motions with precisely the same persons at West Point; free of that, with John Allan beyond recall, he sheltered himself upon the wide and willing breast of his Aunt Maria Clemm. It seemed providential to both of them, and psychologically it was so. On the return from the visit to Richmond in the early months of 1834, Poe must have realized in his inmost being that the little house on Amity Street, and not the great mansion in Richmond, was "home."

Consequently, it was natural enough that it should occur to both Poe and Mrs. Clemm, if it had not been in their thoughts even earlier, that the arrangement, already in force at Amity Street, might be made permanent by a marriage with Virginia. She was still young, very young, only in her twelfth year in fact, but she was budding into womanhood, and marriage at that time, especially in the South, often took place very early. Many a girl was the mother of a family at sixteen. Edgar's affairs with other girls must have alarmed Mrs. Clemm. She could see herself left alone if Poe married, or making room for a young bride in her household, to the numbers of which, death only had brought relief. In addition she loved Poe, there can be no doubt of that. He was of her own blood, and she regarded herself now as his mother. It would be an excellent family arrangement, and some sort of an understanding was certainly arrived at by the young people. Henry Clemm had gone away, and his mother was anxious to have the protection and the support which Edgar's presence promised. Much has been made of this "romance." In sober reality it can scarcely be regarded as more than an acknowledgement of general convenience. Virginia was still too young for an immediate ceremony and there was grave objection to an immediate marriage on the part of the Neilson Poes.

Poe, on his part, was troubled in his heart by the fact that Virginia was his full cousin, and by her extreme youth. He was troubled and yet attracted. The truth seems to be that he was a type which is so hypersensitive as to be somewhat revolted by the fully developed womanly form, and some of its more hearty implications. The infantile, and very youthful, bore a strange attraction for him that satisfied a craving for the abnormal manifest in other directions. Baudelaire describes it well. Poe was at once excited and repulsed. The relations with Virginia lie very close to the core of his inner mystery; they explain many of his heroines. It was not the charming and simple affair

that those in love with convention would have us believe. About it
was the haunted gray twilight of near incest that troubled his deepest
dreams. He was twenty-five and she was about thirteen. The neurolo-
gist's eye is needed to probe deeper. One feels very near here to the
secret of a strange soul. What were the real incidents of the wooing,
no one will know. The kind Poe cousins were evidently alarmed, and
are known to have remonstrated with Mrs. Clemm.[461] Thus matters
remained for about a year.

During the latter part of 1834 despite the brighter prospects opened
up by the *Saturday Visiter* prize and a certain amount of "fame" which
went with it, Poe's condition was more than usually desperate. No
word had come from Carey & Lea, in Philadelphia, about the volume
of short stories, and there seems to have been no remunerative work
of any kind. Mrs. Clemm's entire attention must have been taken up
by ministering to the old grandmother who was fast approaching her
end. Edgar himself was in ill health, approaching one of those periods
of utter depression, due to nerve strain and a weak heart. The neurasthenic hero of the stories written during the Baltimore period
shadows forth his own condition. *The Visiter* had published his poem,
The Coliseum, earlier in the year. But even its columns were now less
hospitable, as his friend Wilmer had been forced out of the editorship
into circumstances of great poverty and his place taken by Hewitt, who
was a competitor of Poe and probably could not forget that Poe had
approached him once asking him to allow the facts of the poetry award
to become known. Finances for the little family on Amity Street were
now at their lowest ebb, and in November, 1834, alarmed and dismayed
by hearing no word from Philadelphia, Poe wrote the following letter
to his friend Mr. Kennedy:

Baltimore *Nov.* 1834 [462]

DR. SIR,—I have a favor to beg of you which I thought it better to ask in
writing, because, sincerely, I had not the courage to ask it in person. I am indeed well aware that I have no claim whatever to your attention, and that even
the manner of my introduction to your notice was, at best equivocal. Since the
day you first saw me my situation in life has altered materially. At that time
I looked forward to the inheritance of a large fortune, and in the meantime was
in receipt of an annuity sufficient for my support. This was allowed to me by a
gentleman of Virginia (Mr. Jno. Allan) who adopted me at the age of two years
(both my parents being dead) and who, until lately always treated me with the
affection of a father.[463] But a second marriage on his part, and I dare say many
follies on my own at length ended in a quarrel between us. He is now dead and

---

[461] Neilson Poe, who had a large place just outside of Baltimore, a little later offered
to take Virginia and keep her as one of his family until she was eighteen. The objection was not to Virginia's marrying Poe, but on account of her extreme youth. The
fact is significant. See Woodberry, 1909, vol. I, pages 137 and 144.
[462] A letter in the *Kennedy Manuscripts.*
[463] This is all "poetic license" on Poe's part, of course.

has left me nothing. I am thrown entirely upon my own resources with no profession, and very few friends. Worse than all this, I am at length penniless. Indeed no circumstances less urgent would have induced me to risk your friendship by troubling you with my distresses. But I could not help thinking that if my situation was stated—as you could state it—to Carey and Lea, they might be led to aid me with a small sum in consideration of my Ms. now in their hands. This would relieve my immediate wants, and I could then look forward more confidently to better days. At all events receive the assurance of my gratitude for what you have already done.

Most respy, yr, obt. st.,

EDGAR ALLAN POE

Mr. Kennedy was just stepping into a carriage to go to Annapolis when he received Poe's note. He remained there for some time and did not reply to Poe until December 22, 1834, in part as follows:

. . . I requested Carey immediately upon the receipt of your first letter to do something for you as speedily as he might find an opportunity, and to make some advance on your book. His answer let me know that he would go on to publish, but the expectation of any profit from the undertaking he considered doubtful— not from want of merit in the production, but because small books of detached tales, however well written, seldom yield a sum sufficient to enable the bookseller to purchase a copyright. He recommends, however, that I should allow him to sell some of the tales to the publishers of the annuals. My reply was that I thought you would not object to this if the right to publish the same tale was reserved for the volume. He has accordingly sold one of the tales to Miss Leslie for the *Souvenir,* at a dollar a page, I think with the reservation above mentioned—and has remitted me a draft of fifteen dollars which I will hand over to you as soon as you call upon me, which I hope you will do as soon as you can make it convenient. If the other tales can be sold in the same way, you will get more for the work than by an exclusive publication.

Yours truly,   JOHN P. KENNEDY

This little snatch of correspondence lowers us like a diving bell into the depths, where for a little space we can look around us in the darkness of a young poet's despair. Both letters are characteristic of their writers. Poe's one of restrained desperation, with the characteristically garbled autobiographical statements, altered to suit the occasion; Mr. Kennedy's kindly, wise, and supremely tactful—"My reply was I thought you would not object to this"—and the "draft of fifteen dollars which I will hand over to you as soon as you call upon me which I hope you will do as soon as you can make it convenient"—how *soon,* and how *convenient* it was, we may be sure that Mr. Kennedy knew only too well.

Nor did the kind offices of the older man end here. The $15 must have been eked out to the last penny, but in the middle of March, 1835, Poe again wrote Mr. Kennedy asking his influence with the Public School Commissioners to enable him to obtain a position as a school teacher, ". . . Have I any hope? . . . the 18th is fixed for the de-

cision of the commissioners, and the advertisement has only this moment caught my eye." Mr. Kennedy's reply written the same day,
Sunday, March 15, 1835,[464] was the famous invitation to dinner. In
reply to this Poe dispatched the following pathetic note, perhaps the
wide-eyed little Virginia carried it, as she had carried notes of a different kind before:

DR. SIR,—Your kind invitation to dinner today has wounded me to the quick.
I cannot come—and for reasons of the most humiliating nature in my personal
appearance. You may conceive my deep mortification in making this disclosure
to you—but it was necessary. If you will be my friend so far as to loan me $20,
I will call on you tomorrow—otherwise it will be impossible, and I must submit
to my fate.

Sincerely yours,
E. A. POE

Sunday 15th.

The little note was the turning point in Poe's literary career. Poe must,
indeed, have been desperate before his pride, his governing motive, could
have surrendered so far. Mr. Kennedy was touched to the quick. He
now fully realized the situation that the letter revealed. The curtains
in the windows of a proud little home had been drawn back for an instant and revealed the ill-clad family who dwelt there sitting about an
empty table. The good man bestirred himself, as he would doubtless
have done before had he known. Poe was provided with clothes, invited to the Kennedy house, made much of at the generous board,—
doubtless Mrs. Clemm's basket profited, too—and Edgar was even
loaned Mr. Kennedy's horse "for exercise." The last was indeed the refinement of courtesy to a Virginian. Once on horseback, Edgar Poe
felt himself to be a gentleman again. Nor will the sneers of Griswold
a quarter of a century later, at all these items, suffice to convince the
world that it was merely a beggar who went riding.

But the greatest service of all was Mr. Kennedy's introduction of the
young author to the editor of the *Southern Literary Messenger* in Richmond, to whom, upon the advice and recommendation of his patron,
Poe submitted some of his tales. *Berenice* was accepted, and appeared
in the March, 1835, number of the *Messenger* with a highly laudatory
editorial notice. The editor was much impressed and followed up Poe's
reference to Mr. Kennedy with a letter of inquiry. Mr. Kennedy replied to Mr. White:

Baltimore, *Apr.* 13, 1835

DEAR SIR,—Poe did right in referring to me. He is very clever with his pen
—classical and scholar-like. He wants experience and direction, but I have no
doubt he can be made very useful to you. And, poor fellow, he is *very* poor. I

---

[464] This note has been correctly dated as of 1835 by Prof. Woodberry, and not 1833
as given by Prof. Harrison.

told him to write something for every number of your magazine, and that you might find it to your advantage to give him some permanent employ. . . . The young fellow is highly imaginative and a little *terrific*. He is at work upon a tragedy, but I have turned him to drudging upon whatever may make money. . . .

The hint from Mr. Kennedy went home. *Berenice* was the entering wedge, and every number of the *Messenger* for sometime afterward contained a story and some criticism or reviews by Poe. John P. Kennedy had not only saved him; he had "made" him. Poe never forgot this as long as he lived and, many years later, remarked to Thomas Stoddard with an undimmed sense of gratitude, "Mr. Kennedy has been, at all times, a true friend to me—he was the first true friend I ever had—I am indebted to him for *life itself.*"

Thomas Wylkes White, editor of the *Southern Literary Messenger,* was a native of Virginia,[465] and a member of the numerous tribe of itinerant printer-publishers who, in the 1830's, were filling the ephemeral editorial chairs of various will-o'-the-wisp magazines that glowed faintly here and there all over the United States, and for the most part died away painlessly, after giving off a faint gaseous light. Mr. White was more able than most, however, and a happy combination of circumstances and personalities permitted him to continue the *Southern Literary Messenger* with unusual success. In 1834, he went to Richmond—where nine numbers of the *Messenger* had already appeared under the editorship of Mr. James Heath, author of *Edge Hill.*[466] There White became a sort of combined printer-business-manager-and-editor of the sheet, Mr. Heath continuing for some time to act in an unpaid advisory capacity. White was a good business man, with a pleasant personality, although shrewd, but he lacked the background, the literary qualities, and the editorial vision to make the magazine a complete success. In 1834, there were only a few hundred subscribers. In Poe, Mr. White soon recognized the very type of man which his paper most needed, and the correspondence, stories, reviews, and articles which Poe contributed through the Spring of 1835 led up to a suggestion of permanent employment on the staff. On June 2, 1835, Poe wrote White a long letter on various topics concerning the magazine, in which he says:

. . . You ask me if I would be willing to come to Richmond if you should have occasion for my services during the coming winter. I reply that nothing would give me greater pleasure. I have been desirous for some time past of paying a visit to Richmond, and would be glad of any reasonable excuse of so doing. . . .

Aside from the fact that Richmond was always home to Poe, there was a particular, and peculiar personal reason, over and above the op-

---

[465] The statement that Mr. White was a Northerner, born in Yorktown, Pennsylvania, etc., etc., is incorrect.

[466] *Edge Hill,* a novel then rather widely read, by James Heath.

portunity offered by White, why he "would be glad of any reasonable excuse of paying a visit to Richmond." The reason belonged to the realm of the romantic.[467]

Miss Mary Winfree of Chesterfield, Virginia, a young lady who had formerly enjoyed Poe's passing attentions, and who had never forgotten him, had come to visit in Baltimore sometime before Poe's marriage with Virginia. She was, perhaps, the first of the several Marys to whom Poe had confided the touching fact that she bore his favorite name. At any rate, her interest was sufficient to cause her to seek him out. She did not, of course, know that Poe was thinking of marrying Virginia, and it is not likely that he enlightened her. Miss Winfree was a close friend of Elmira Royster (Mrs. Shelton), and, in discussing the past with Poe, the interesting and disturbing information came to light that Elmira was not altogether happy with her husband, and that she had never ceased to love Poe. The deception which her parents had practiced upon her had, as we have seen, come to light through the finding of one of Poe's letters to her from the University, and her first romantic attachment flamed up anew. Miss Winfree brought with her a little book called the *Bijou,* one of the ubiquitous parlor annuals of the time, to whose pages Mrs. Shelton had contributed a story signed with her initials, in which, to those who knew her past, the meaning was clear. She was, it appears, languishing for a glimpse of her true love, and the pain could not be assuaged. Despite the fact that "Hymen [in a double sense] and Time and Destiny were now stalking between" him and her—Poe seems to have determined to see her at least once again, to let her know that he still loved her, and to justify the past. How far he intended to go it is impossible to say. Circumstances would doubtless dictate that, as they did. It was a sentimental and dangerous situation that appealed to his romantic heart. Once in Richmond, time would provide the opportunity. What was Virginia's status in the triangle it is hard to say.

For a time, however, the move to Richmond had to be deferred. Mr. White was not yet ready, and old Mrs. Poe was dying. A few checks now and then for $5 and $10 amounts from the *Messenger* served to back the wolf off the front stoop, at least, while the pen in the little room on Amity Street went forward. . . . The mail was robbed by one William Jones and Poe found himself the loser "to a small amount." Poe purchased some especially fine printer's ink for Mr. White and took it to the steamboat himself. John Marshall, the great Chief Justice, died. Poe remembered him well from the old family pew in the Monumental Church. He, too, was now added to the names of the past recorded in

___

[467] I am indebted to a Richmond acquaintance who desires to remain anonymous for part of the information dealing with this little known episode. This acquaintance has the copy of the *Bijou.*

Shockoe Cemetery, and a little paragraph from the hand of the boy who had known him appeared in the *Messenger* soon after:

> . . . Our great and lamented countryman, fellow-townsman, neighbor and friend —for by all these names did a fortuitous conjunction of circumstances, including his own kind and prideless heart, entitle us to call him. . . .[468]

On May 30, 1835, Poe wrote to Mr. White in Richmond alluding to a serious breakdown about that time:

> I have not seen Mr. Kennedy for some days, having been too unwell to go abroad . . . at the time I wrote the hasty sketch I sent you I was so ill as to be hardly able to see the paper on which I wrote, and finished in a state of complete exhaustion. . . .

On June 12th, he again writes White:

> I am glad to say that I have entirely recovered—although Dr. Buckler, no longer than three weeks ago, assured me that nothing but a sea-voyage would save me. . . .

Evidently this was no ordinary indisposition. Dr. Buckler would not have ordered a sea-voyage to a poverty-stricken young poet unless he had good cause for alarm. He thought it was the only thing that would *save* his patient. And this illness was only a repetition of several that had preceded it in the previous four years. Poe had specifically mentioned his ill health in letters to John Allan, as we have seen.

An understanding and some explanation of Poe's physical and mental condition is, from now on, fundamental even to a partial understanding of his character. A completely satisfactory understanding of a matter necessarily nebulous and of a character so strangely contradictory and complex must perhaps forever elude our grasp. There are, however, certain indications inherent in the symptoms of his condition, and the work which he produced, that tend to throw a light upon some of the darker phases of his nature. Any study of the man, which obstinately refuses to recognize the unpleasant and unfortunate aspects of his nature, or to explain his tragedy by assuming and asserting that his misfortunes were due merely to persecution, an unappreciative world, and a perverse fate, must disregard, ignorantly or deliberately, some of the outstanding and most incontestable facts of his career. Poe's human misfortunes cannot be laid in the main upon the shoulders of the epoch and the world in which he moved; they were, for the most part, caused by the early break-up of his physical health, due to his unhappy youth and heredity and the stimulants which he used to counteract their effects.

---

[468] Chief Justice Marshall had been injured in a stagecoach accident in the Spring of 1835. He went to Philadelphia for medical treatment where he died on July 6th. Poe was at work on a review of the second edition of Marshall's *Life of Washington,* in two volumes, 1832. Marshall's death had an important bearing on the trend of national events, see note 500, Chapter XVIII, page 331.

Paradoxically enough, out of the mental state evolved from ill health and one of the stimulants he resorted to, flowed much of the creative work of the artist which insured his literary success. That there was, in addition to this, a third factor, the unique humanity of the man himself, goes without saying. Every human being is different from all others. The exact and unique flavor of a personality can never be completely caught in any literary reconstruction. The hint of the peculiar genius of a man can only be partly reflected in the glass of his actions. These are being detailed here, and, from them, the reader must largely be left to make his own reconstruction. The more physical aspects, however, bear analysis, and it is necessary now to attempt some evaluation of them in the interplay of ill health and the effects of nostrums. Combining the last two with the reflection of the man's self in his actions, at least, a credible ghost may be invoked.

Poe was afflicted with a weak heart. There is, later on, direct medical evidence of a doctor and a professional nurse of long experience to that effect. In addition to this, the long tragedy of his youth had, as we have seen, exhausted him nervously. The effect of these two conditions was to subject him to a general feeling of depression due to subnormal vitality, culminating frequently in periods of more or less complete prostration or threatened collapse. A specious, and apparently easy "remedy" for this feeling of debility, induced by a weak heart and exhausted nerves, was the use of stimulants or sedatives. It seems transparently evident that, when a period of collapse overtook him, Poe resorted to one of two drugs, either alcohol or opium. There is direct evidence, as we have seen, of his use of alcohol in 1826 at Charlottesville and in 1830 at West Point. Even a very little was, to him, peculiarly disastrous. With the advent of the Baltimore period, there are powerful reasons to lead one to believe that, from that date on, Poe now resorted, *from time to time,* to the use of opiates.

In the first place, it must be remembered that in his condition, if he was to continue to work, perhaps at times even to survive, drugs were in order. He had tried alcohol and found it more or less disastrous. Opium, for Poe, involved a peculiarly seductive temptation. It removed him completely from the world of reality which he largely disliked; it enormously increased the bounds of his imagination; and it coincidentally vastly stimulated his creative faculty while soothing his nerves. At the same time its effects were so subtle as to escape immediate observation and comment, while, at least at first, it did not produce the violent reactions and periods of mania which followed his resort to drink. For the time being, it seemed to solve all difficulties and to provide a sovereign panacea.

During the stay in Baltimore from 1831 to 1835, there can be no moral doubt that Poe was using opium, at least from time to time. The indubitable evidence of the fact lies in the work which he produced. *The Tales of the Folio Club* are replete with opiate dreams, and when they fell into the hands of Baudelaire, some years later, caused him to shed tears of joy as he recognized the very features of his own reveries as it were endowed with life. Such stories as *Ligeia* and *Berenice* illustrate this directly, especially the latter. They provide not only direct references to the drug, but the imagery, the irrational associations, and the very use of words are characteristic. To those who have no knowledge or familiarity with the effects of opium, and they are, of course, the majority, the evidence may seem insufficient; to those who have, the turning of these pages tells an irrefutable tale. There is evidence by witnesses that Poe took opium in Philadelphia. In 1847, he tried to commit suicide with laudanum. The inference is that he had tried the use of opiates before. Rosalie Poe, his sister, says that in 1848, at Fordham, he "begged for morphine." In June, 1884, Dr. John Carter of Baltimore who had considerable knowledge of Poe from his brother, another physician who had treated the poet in Richmond in 1849, wrote to Professor Woodberry that, while he had no direct personal evidence, "I may state, in a matter of so leading importance, that I incline to the view that Poe began the use of drugs in Baltimore, that his periods of abstinence from liquor were periods of at least moderate indulgence in opium, . . ." etc.

During the Baltimore period, Poe is known to have abstained almost totally from liquor. Although he was ill and in the greatest poverty, as his own letters at that time abundantly attest, he nevertheless contrived to produce a large mass of creative work. That when so ill, and under such difficult living conditions, he could produce at an hitherto unexampled rate, indicates an unusual cause. But when the work itself produced under such conditions is examined and found to contain, not only direct references to the use of opium, but to be of a type produced by a consciousness laboring under the effects of the drug, the chain seems complete. Besides this, there were also secondary manifestations of a decided change in his character through the Baltimore years which tend to confirm the suspicion.

In the first place, from 1831 to 1834, Poe remained almost unknown. The records of his existence for part of that time are amazingly obscure, and for a considerable portion of the period absolutely lapse. This means, if anything, that he was largely confined to the garret of Mrs. Clemm. Ill health, poverty, and pen-driving will not entirely explain the fact that a young soldier and a fairly athletic young man of a few years before had suddenly become a complete recluse. He was not ill all the time, but at periods, yet he obtained no steady employment for a period of almost five years in the prime of youth. Thousands of the young men in Baltimore at the same time, despite the severe financial stricture, were successfully employed. What was Poe doing? Dreaming in Mrs. Clemm's attic, and the records of those dreams are strongly tinged with opium. Alcohol he did not take because he did not need it. Mrs. Clemm's influence is of course to be reckoned with here.

Another startling change also overtook him now. From 1832 to 1847, Mary Devereaux is the only record of a really normally passionate love affair that Poe was engaged in. Up until that time, all through his youth, his interest in girls and women had been varied and constant. These now suddenly cease. Now, one of the notorious effects of opium is the eventual weakening of sexual desire. This condition now suddenly seems to present itself. At the end of the period in 1835, he had deviated so far from the normal as to be able to marry, apparently both willingly and apathetically, a thirteen-year-old child. That there were other and more profound sexual disturbances in Poe's nature, the sadistic trend of a considerable body of his work indicates. The lessening of desire, and the strange conditions of his marriage are the principal matters, however, to be reckoned with. During the latter half of his life, his trend from the normal was marked. What had produced such an effect upon one who, in boyhood, appears to have been somewhat precocious may well cause one to ponder. In the understanding of Poe's character during the latter half of his life, the problem is a central one. He was now entering upon a new phase.

For the Baltimore period and the home on Amity Street were about to close. One cannot help wondering about the life that went on in the little house with the single dormer window and the end chimney. Mrs. Clemm was preoccupied night and day with the duties of the household and the dying grandmother, she and Edgar gathered about the little dining-room table with the always snowy cloth and the spotless china, listening to the childish talk of the childish cousin, whose great eyes looked at Edgar only half comprehendingly.—What did Poe think of it all?—the ambitious young man with the soaring mind. And what of the more intimate and tender episodes? There was something strange about that, something infantile with the quality of a day-dream come true. Strange and yet alluring. An inscrutable experience was having its subtle way. "Ligeia" had become a reality. She was beginning to dominate his dreams, and yet was she? There was still Elmira.

On July 7, 1835, Mrs. David Poe died at Amity Street. She was seventy-eight years old. Her death could, in the nature of things, have been nothing but a relief. Mrs. Clemm could now turn all her attention to Edgar and Virginia. The household was reduced to the final number to which there was never any natural addition—and Poe was free to follow his star.

Under the beat of the steamer's paddles, Baltimore faded for the time being into a dream. Richmond was calling with all the force of

"Sunday Evening at the Yarrington's"

From an old illustration

The Poet of the Latter Years
Edgar Allan Poe about the Autumn of 1848
From a photograph of the "Whitman" daguerreotype

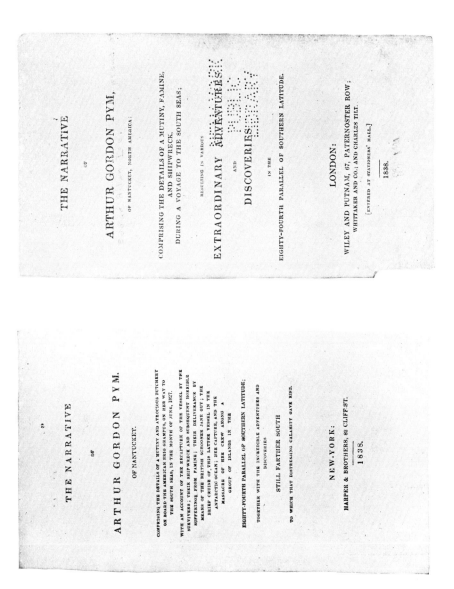

Title Pages to the English and the American Editions of *The Narrative of Arthur Gordon Pym*, Edgar Allan Poe's fourth published volume

THE GREAT FIRE.

We present to our readers, in our extra, issued this day, at 1 o'clock, not only a description, but a GRAPHIC SKETCH of the dreadful fire which last night created so much devastation. We reached the scene about 9 o'clock, this morning—drew a hasty picture of it, and, by 12 o'clock, Johnson, the artist, had the above representation ready for the press. So much for enterprize!

A Characteristic Incident in
Philadelphia of the 1840's

And a bit of the enterprising journalism of the
day concerned with firemen and engravers

the past and a brighter future.   The dream of Poe's life was coming true—he was going "home" with foreign laurels.   They were not bright yet, but they were visible, and they became him well.   Mrs. Clemm remained behind in the house on Amity Street, awaiting the outcome of a long litigation over her husband's will,[469] and to watch over Virginia. It was about midsummer of the year 1835.   Only fourteen years later the curtain fell.

---

[469] This "litigation" if it can be termed that, had to do with Mrs. Clemm's and her children's share in the property of Mrs. Catherine Clemm of Mount Prospect, Maryland.   She was, it seems, entitled to one-third—the children of the first wife of William Clemm made trouble.   Poe was exceedingly anxious to obtain this legacy, a small amount, to help set up his own house with Mrs. Clemm.   See Poe to Kennedy, Richmond, January 22, 1836, etc.   The matter later called Poe to Baltimore from Philadelphia.

CHAPTER SEVENTEEN

THE VALLEY OF THE MANY-COLORED GRASS

ABOUT the person of the young man, who reappeared in Richmond in the early August days of 1835, there was, beyond peradventure, something distinguished: a certain knack of tying the black stock; a precise and studied nonchalance about the buttoning of the tight, double-breasted waistcoat over the impeccable linen—carefully mended by "Muddie"—that was somehow arresting. The large beaver hat, then universally worn by all who pretended to the name of gentleman, sat a little to the side, tilted a bit backward, accentuating an already prominent brow, and curling in an arch way over a delicate ear. Under the flare of its small brim drooped a tangle of black-brown hair blanching an olive, oval face from which looked, unforgettably, two large and haunted gray-blue eyes. The mouth was small, a little weak, and slightly twisted by pain. The lips and chin were clean shaven, and there was the faintest suggestion about them of a whimsical and ironical smile out of a wisp of side-burns. It was the countenance of one who regarded his world as a dream within a dream.

The erect figure of the man dressed in a raven-black and meticulously brushed flare-tail coat, with the roll collar left open, contrived to be impressive by just avoiding being dapper. The shoulders were thrown back, showing too narrow a chest, and vest buttons that gleamed like medals over the stomach. The metal tassel of a long, knit, ring-fastened purse dangled from the slant vest pocket, anchored there by nothing more than a Mexican half-dollar of a few "levies," and a nervous brisk gait was accentuated by the ripple in an ample pair of Nankeen, diapered pantaloons, strapped under the boots. Such was Mr. White's brilliant young editor, going calling in Richmond some weeks after the last purple blooms had disappeared from the paulownia trees. Those who passed him in the street felt they had encountered a presence, and both men and women remarked and remembered, "There goes Edgar Poe."

For the first few days he probably stopped at Duncan Lodge with the Mackenzies. Rosalie was there, happy, unshadowed by any future, a fully grown child. Mr. and Mrs. Mackenzie never failed to make him welcome, and there was always Jack—bluff and hearty. Perhaps "Aunt Nancy" dropped over quietly from the Allan house to tell him about Pa's last hours, and whisper about the will. She, at least, was secure in $300 a year and her board and washing. Her revelations could not have been much of a surprise to Poe, who would certainly ascertain for himself the exact provisions of a certain document.[470]   But it must have been strange to pass the big house with its drawn curtains; to hear the shouts of John Allan's eldest boy in the old garden; to be stopped in the streets by the affectionate greeting of the old house-servants, and yet to know, beyond doubt, that in all that he was never, nevermore, to have any part.   How curious, too, when passing the store of *Ellis & Allan* to look in at the door!   The very shadows and odors were familiar [471]— John Allan's desk was there in the office, and a trunk with letters—but "Pa" was inevitably gone.

The past was not forgotten, however.   The strange record of it lay there in the old trunk, and in the hearts of those who now occupied the big house.   Poe's arrival, although she took no notice of it, was undoubtedly a source of anxiety to Mrs. Allan.   Already she was in trouble about the will.   Poe knew too much, if he had cared to say anything. It would pay to be careful, above all to avoid any more scenes.   So the big door never swung open to him again, and other doors in certain other places were quietly and mysteriously closed.   *Sub rosa,* in certain circles the word went around.   In the end it made a difference, especially when the Allan children grew up.   At that time they were only cutting their teeth.[472]

For the most part, though, the old friends remained true, Jack Mackenzie, of course, and Bob Cabell, Rob Stanard especially, and the Galts. Poe was welcome at many homes, for himself alone.   Many knew enough to take the talk of ingratitude to John Allan with the proper grain of salt; card playing at the University had been heard of before. It was not a sin which debarred one from dances.   Even old I. O. U.'s could be overlooked when a charming young man in the way of fame was to be forgiven, and invited in to add to the conversation.   On the whole it was at first rather a triumphant return.   There were a few discreet smiles, no doubt, at the expense of a certain proud lady, *not* a Virginian, who kept a large house.   But Frances Valentine's foster-son was not overlooked.   After Baltimore and poverty it seemed brilliant. There was wine at every table, music, pretty girls, and a certain defer-

---

[470] Poe would almost certainly acquaint himself with the nature of John Allan's will probated in public court.   He would take no chances.

[471] After the death of the first Mrs. Allan, John Allan removed a trunk containing his first wife's correspondence and probably other data to *Ellis & Allan*.   In this he put Poe's letters from 1824 on.   The trunk fell into the hands of James Galt as John Allan's executor and was by him removed to Fluvanna Plantation.   There the second Mrs. Allan had access to it and removed from it some of Poe's letters now in the *Valentine Museum Collection.*   She appears to have destroyed others.   Only one letter in Frances Allan's handwriting is known to exist.   James Galt said there were "other letters" that remained in the trunk.   Whose, it is not known.

[472] John Allan's last child, referred to in his will, survived her two brothers, who died young.

ence to "literature." On some occasions all this seems to have gone
to the head.

After a short stay at the Mackenzies', Poe took up lodgings with Mrs.
Poore, who kept one of those peculiarly genteel Southern boarding
houses on Bank Street, Capitol Square. The weather was fine, Mr.
White was more than cordial, and Eliza, his daughter, could recite
Shakespeare "elegantly." She had "remarkable eyes." Elmira was
near and not forgotten. A little after the arrival of the young poet in
Richmond, the *Southern Literary Messenger* found its columns em-
bellished with the following lines contributed by "Sylvio."

TO SARAH

. . . The silvery streamlet gurgling on,
The mock-bird chirping on the thorn,
Remind me, love, of thee.
They seem to whisper thoughts of love,
As thou didst when the stars above
Witnessed thy vows to me;—

The gentle zephyr floating by,
In chorus to my pensive sigh,
Recalls the hour of bliss,
When from thy balmy lips I drew
Fragrance as sweet as Hermia's dew,
And left the first fond kiss. . . .

As Mrs. A. Barrett Shelton suddenly ran across these yearning
rhymes in the *Messenger,* her eyes may possibly have become too
dimmed to note the exact expression on the face of her husband comfortably seated at his breakfast coffee. Many must have known who the poet
on the *Messenger* was, "Sylvio" could not have been an impenetrable
disguise. If so, the enlightening Miss Winfree was Elmira's bosom
friend. In the meantime Edgar went every morning to his desk at the
Messenger office, sometimes, too often perhaps, taking a bracer from
the decanter on Mrs. Poore's sideboard, which made him superbly confident—a superbness that did not altogether recommend itself to Mr.
White.[473] Otherwise they got along famously.

The offices of the *Southern Literary Messenger* were situated at the
corner of Main and Fifteenth Streets, in a substantial three-story brick
building with a steeply-pitched slate roof topped by a squat brick chimney. Underneath was Archer's shoe shop, the *Messenger* being on the
second floor. Poe reached his sanctum by an outside stairway from
Fifteenth Street and held forth in the rear room. It was a neighborhood with which he was uncannily familiar, for right next door (one
could hear the clerks shouting through the walls) were the store and

---

[473] Mr. White, it will be remembered, specifically warned Poe against morning drinking. See White to Poe, Richmond, September 29, 1835, printed on page 310.

lofts of *Ellis & Allan*. Poe had gone to work that way before! The very slight rise in the brick pavement starting up Fifteenth from Main was familiar. Even now the click of a cane upon it, and the ring of a boot must have made him start.

In the same office with Poe sat Mr. White,[474] a stocky, good-natured man with a florid face. Visitors, local literary lights and authors, dropped in frequently for a chat or to solicit a favor. In front could be heard the Scotch-tinged conversation of the foreman, William McFarland, and John Fergusson as they clapped the frames on the round, black-faced presses or fluttered their hands magically over the square cases of type. Proofs hung upon rusty hooks; the mail was heavy, and piled up mainly upon Poe's desk. Copies of books for review kept coming in, so the young editor was very busy.

The office was left very much alone to Poe, as Mr. White, once the literary capacity of his assistant became apparent, went about the state and the neighboring towns soliciting subscriptions. There were only 700 subscribers when Poe came. With the combined efforts of the young man's brilliant pen and Mr. White's junketings, they now mounted with a bound. So there was no time left to dream. In the little office, where the light filtered blankly through the square, dusty panes, someone was always holding forth and squirting tobacco juice about. There were volumes to review; McFarland was howling for copy; or the latest edition was to be bundled up, addressed by hand, and sent out. Whale-oil lamps and printer's ink scented the air. Only on the way home in the evening, as the strong sugary smell of Virginia tobacco surged out at him from the door of *Ellis & Allan,* the past, all the lost past, rolled down upon Poe overpoweringly, in a cloud of sweet odor, for he was peculiarly sensitive to perfume. To his dying day the scent of orris root made Frances Allan live again, standing as she used to in her bedroom, looking into her glass before an open bureau drawer.[475] Then he went "home" to dine at Mrs. Poore's in Capitol Square.

Behind it all there was, already, a vast melancholy. If "Muddie" and "Sis" could only come to Richmond! Perhaps a little later? Just now his "salary" was only $10 a week.

One day Poe received an invitation to attend a party at a big house "across the river." He went early.[476] Elmira, he heard, was going to be there. The stairs, in this mansion of a memorable meeting, curved in a double arc to a landing with a bay window from which opened a

---

[474] The author is in possession of abundant material for a literal description of the *Southern Literary Messenger* offices, the vicinity, and the personnel. The building was removed in 1908, much of the material in it being taken over for the Poe Shrine. The description of T. W. White is from a portrait.

[475] Poe spoke of this memory-odor as late as 1849.

[476] Mrs. Shelton herself authenticated this incident.

spacious drawing room. At the end of this, in a window niche, Poe took his stand and waited. The gentlemen left their hats in the hall; the ladies left their wraps in an anteroom off the stairs. Presently Elmira appeared. She was coming up the stairway alone and still beautiful. The September sunshine caught, with a well-known glint, in her auburn hair. Poe watched it while she took off her hat. Then she turned to enter the room, but she did not do so. Something stopped her at the threshold more powerful than a restraining hand. It was an unforgettable and devouring pair of eyes.

Mrs. Shelton said, years later, that it seemed to her as if there were nothing else in the room.[476] It seemed as if they shed darkness in the place, the shadows of longing and reproach. For a moment they stood and exchanged glances, then her husband came. He took in the situation at a glance; almost carried his wife away; put on her cloak himself as he led her to the door, and drove off furiously down the road.

Poe had, indeed, lost his "Lenore." He did not see her again for more than ten years. Both the Sheltons and Roysters were much alarmed. Elmira was, after this, both recalcitrant and ill, and her husband intimated that if Poe tried to meet her again, there would be a violent reckoning. Nor was this an idle threat, for, along the James and farther South,[477] the *code duello* was at that date, and for years to come, by no means a dead letter, as many another editor had good cause to know.

Poe was greatly depressed and, about that time, news came from Baltimore that threw him into despair. The Neilson Poes, it appears, had taken advantage of his absence to break off the affair with Virginia and were bringing pressure upon Mrs. Clemm to let the young girl come and live with them. It seemed as if once more his hopes of a home were to be dashed to the ground—or at least intolerably deferred. There was something peculiarly repulsive to Poe about a boarding-house table. The purely accidental association of insufferable personalities who sought to gorge their appetites and curiosity about the same board, the landlady introducing "our poet," the suspicion which followed one who desired privacy, the five-year-old conversation, and the ignorant gossip, were enough to drive him mad. How could the gods afflict him with great dreams and the love of "all the beauty that we worship in a star," while seating him at a board where any remark above an inanity made all the heavy feasters choke or stare? It was a divine jest! Worse than the army mess, for there was no escape whatever. So Poe kept longing for the refuge of a home. As early as August 20th he remembered that he had well-to-do cousins in Georgia, and wrote to William

---

[477] Dueling lingered in Virginia and the Carolinas long after it went out of fashion in the North. A notorious case occurred in Charleston, South Carolina, just before the Civil War, in which an editor was killed.

Poe of Augusta giving a detailed account of the family and his life history, and soliciting aid for Mrs. Clemm:

. . . In conclusion I beg leave to assure you that whatever aid you may have it in your power to bestow upon Mrs. Clemm will be given to one who well deserves every kindness and attention. Would to God that I could at this moment aid her. She is now, while I write, struggling without friends, without money, and without health to support herself and two children. I sincerely pray God that the words which I am writing may be the means of inducing you to unite with your brothers and friends, and send her that *immediate* relief which it is *utterly* out of my power to give her just now, and which, unless it reach her soon will, I am afraid, reach her too late. Entreating your attention to this subject, I remain

Yours very truly & affectionately
EDGAR A. POE

The taking over of a new position or a decided change in one's mode of life and residence is, like New Year's, very often the occasion for trying to put good resolutions into effect. Upon assuming the new position in Richmond, Poe evidently undertook to shake off his dependence on stimulants of any kind, while, at the same time, he forced himself at the new work. The combined effort was more than he could support; he had evidently tried to bolster himself up by drinking, and the result was a collapse. The letter which he now wrote to Mr. Kennedy is the expression of one who finds the terrible drabness of the real world intolerable as he struggles to abandon a habit. What the real reason is, Poe carefully conceals:

Richmond, *Sept.* 11, 1835

DR. SIR,—I received a letter yesterday from Dr. Miller [478] in which he tells me you are in town [Baltimore]. I hasten therefore, to write you,—and express by letter what I have always found impossible to express orally—my deep sense of gratitude for your frequent and effectual assistance and kindness. Through your influence Mr. White has been induced to employ me in assisting him with the Editorial duties of his Magazine—at a salary of $520 per annum. The situation is agreeable to me for many reasons—but alas! it appears to me that nothing can now give me pleasure—or the slightest gratification. Excuse me, my Dear Sir, if in this letter you find much incoherency. My feelings at this moment are pitiable indeed. I am suffering under a depression of spirits such as I have never felt before. I have struggled in vain against the influence of this melancholy—*you will believe me* when I say that I am still miserable in spite of the great improvement in my circumstances. I say you will believe me, and for this simple reason, that a man who is writing for effect does not write thus. My heart is open before you—if it be worth reading, read it. I am wretched, and know not why. Console me—for you can. But let it be quickly—or it will be too late. Write me immediately. Convince me that it is worth one's while, that it is necesasry to live, and you will prove yourself my friend. Persuade me to do what is right. I do not mean this—I do not mean that you should consider what I now write you a jest—oh pity me! for I feel that my words are inco-

---

[478] *Kennedy Manuscripts.*

herent—but I will recover myself. You will not fail to see that I am suffering under a depression of spirits which will ruin me should it be long continued. Write me then, and quickly. Urge me to do what is right. Your words will have more weight with me than the words of others—for you were my friend when no one else was. Fail not—as you value your peace of mind hereafter.

E. A. Poe

This terrible letter was evidently written in the access of remorse which followed an application to the bottle, and in a state of physical and mental collapse. Poe was, for the first time, completely in a vicious circle. Trying to escape from his troubles he had delivered himself to another torment. The angel of oblivion, which he sought to invoke, now first revealed itself as a demon from which he could not escape. The thought was maddening. Had all the slavery in time of starvation, the escape from John Allan, the dreams of ambition been in vain? Elmira was gone. Virginia, it appeared, and with her the strength of Mrs. Clemm upon which he leaned, was about to be snatched from him, too. At Mrs. Poore's for the first time, Poe heard unmistakably the faint tapping at the window pane of the inexorable beak of the bird of despair that later invaded his chamber to perch triumphant over the personification of knowledge and art. It was the hand of a drowning man who had gone down for the first time, and felt the water close over him, that Mr. Kennedy was asked to take. There was a postscript almost as long as the letter in which Poe discusses the fate of his tales with Carey & Lea and rails against a fellow author for stealing (*sic*) some of his ideas from *Hans Pfaall*. It seems almost as if the man had developed two minds, a personal and an editorial self. The manifestations of the dual nature and the occasional visits of the demon were to continue. A few days later Mr. Kennedy replied:

Baltimore, *Sept.* 19, 1835

My Dear Poe,—I am sorry to see you in such a plight as your letter shows you in.—It is strange that just at the time when everybody is praising you and when Fortune has begun to smile upon your hitherto wretched circumstances you should be invaded by these villainous blue devils.—It belongs, however, to your age and temper to be thus buffeted,—but be assured it only wants a little resolution to master the adversary forever,—Rise early, live generously, and make cheerful acquaintances and I have no doubt you will send these misgivings to the Devil.—You will doubtless do well henceforth in literature and add to your *comforts* as well as to your reputation which, it gives me great pleasure to tell you, is everywhere rising in popular esteem. Can't you write some farces after the manner of the French Vaudevilles? If you can—(and I think you can—) you may turn them to excellent account by selling them to the managers in New York. I wish you would give your thoughts to this suggestion. . . .

An excellent suggestion, too—a few light farces to take his mind out of the strange ghoul-haunted hinterland where it too often wandered, and the first hint of New York. Mr. Kennedy understood suggestion better than he knew. But the "adversary" was not such a simple one as he imagined. It was much "stranger" than he knew and had delivered a knockout in the first round. It is doubtful if Poe received Mr. Kennedy's letter in Richmond. He had parted with Mr. White and had gone back to Baltimore. Matters there had evidently come to a crisis with the Poes, Mrs. Clemm and Virginia, and on September 22, 1835,[479] he was secretly married in St. Paul's Episcopal Church to his little cousin. Mrs. Clemm was the only witness present and the minister, possibly at the solicitation of Poe himself, who was anxious to keep the matter from coming to the ears of his cousin Neilson, did not even make an entry in the parish register. Only the record of the city license and Mrs. Clemm's word remain. There can be little doubt, however, that the clandestine marriage took place.

Poe arrived in Baltimore somewhere about the twentieth in a highly agitated state. He had been dismissed by Mr. White and he thought he was going to lose Virginia. The house at Amity Street no doubt echoed with his pleadings and explanations. Once the clandestine marriage was suggested, Mrs. Clemm saw the way out of an immediate imbroglio with her relatives, and doubtless acquiesced willingly in an arrangement which she undoubtedly had much at heart. Virginia must have been at once terrified by the state that Edgar was in, and excited by the thought of being married, a step to adult dignity and an event in which, for the first time, she found herself indispensable and of genuine importance. But her disappointment at having no one but her mother present must have been extreme. The entire setting of a ceremony so dear to the feminine heart was entirely lacking. Not even a veil! One can imagine "some natural tears were shed." Yet worst of all, no one was to know afterward. It was a matter that later on had to be remedied by an ingenious device. In the meantime Edgar was calmed. His hints of suicide made in Mr. Kennedy's letter were probably renewed before Virginia and Mrs. Clemm.[480] What could they do? The women would be terrified. So it happened that the momentous step was taken. Edgar Allan Poe was provided with a home; whether he had also gotten a wife in the full sense of the word has been doubted. No one will ever surely know. In striving to understand the man, however, the speculation is not entirely idle.

A few days after the very quiet and more than obscure ceremony, Poe must have written to Mr. White asking him to take him back on

---

[479] Prof. J. A. Harrison gives the date as September 22, 1834, but Prof. Woodberry, 1835. The latter is correct as I have been at some pains to ascertain. The correspondence in the appendix from St. Paul's Parish shows no records of the marriage. Mrs. Clemm was afterward much "upset" when she was questioned about it.

[480] The reader will recall that Poe frequently threatened suicide in letters to John Allan, indirectly at least.

the *Messenger* and promising to behave, for Mr. White replied in a letter which reveals him as a kindly and wise friend whose patience had evidently been tried. A full understanding of the situation can best be arrived at by allowing White to speak for himself:

Richmond *Sept. 29,* 1835

DEAR EDGAR,—Would that it were in my power to unbosom myself to you in language such as I could on the present occasion, wish myself master of. I cannot do it—and therefore must be content to speak to you in my plain way.

That you are sincere in all your promises, I firmly believe. But Edgar, when you once again tread these streets, I have my fears that your resolves would fall through,—and that you would sip the juice, even till it stole away your senses. Rely on your own strength and you are gone! Look to your Maker for help, and you are safe.

How much I regretted parting with you, is unknown to anyone on this earth, except myself. I was attached to you—and am still, and willingly would I say return, if I did not dread the hour of separation very shortly again.

If you could make yourself contented to take up your quarters in my family, or any other private family, where liquor is not used, I should think there were hopes of you.—But, if you go to a tavern, or to any other place where it is used at table, you are not safe. I speak from experience.

You have fine talents, Edgar,—and you ought to have them respected as well as yourself. Learn to respect yourself, and you will very soon find that you are respected. Separate yourself from the bottle, and bottle companions, forever! Tell me if you can and will do so—and let me hear that it is your fixed purpose never to yield to temptation.

If you should come to Richmond again, and again be an assistant in my office, it must be expressly understood by us that all engagements on my part would be dissolved, the moment you get drunk.

No man is safe who drinks before breakfast! No man can do so, and attend to business properly. . . .

I am your true Friend
T. W. WHITE

E. A. POE, *Esq.*

In the face of this letter, attempts to sweeten the reason for the first parting between Poe and White can scarcely be regarded as a contribution to biography, however kindly in motive. Mr. White addresses Poe almost in the tone of a father. Evidently the sight of the vacant chair in the office in Richmond caused the good man to yearn over the brilliant and wild young figure that had lately occupied it. What the real cause for Poe's "sipping" was, Mr. White could have had no idea. That his loss by Poe's absence was financial as well as personal is not sufficient to account for a ring in the lines that is not metallic. Poe must have made the promise, for in a few days he returned to Richmond. Mrs. Clemm made arrangements to follow speedily. Her protection, as she knew, was urgently needed. The house in Amity Street was broken up in October, 1835, and the ghosts of poor Henry and Grandmother Poe left to twitter there alone.

Upon his return to Richmond, Poe was welcomed back by Mr. White, who was doubtless reassured by hearing that his aunt and cousin were about to come from Baltimore to provide the domestic influence which the good man had so strongly advised. Mrs. Clemm and Virginia followed a short time afterward, and the newly married couple and mother-in-law took up their abode at a Mrs. Yarrington's boarding house, also overlooking Capitol Square, in the same neighborhood as Mrs. Poore's.

Mrs. Yarrington's was on the southeast corner of Bank and Eleventh Streets, a two-story brick house with large green shutters of a type then common in Richmond. The Poes occupied a front room above the parlor, the windows of which gave a pleasant view of the garden-like Capitol Grounds. The exact nature of the domestic arrangements is not known. Nothing was said about the marriage at all. Poe's friends were simply informed that his aunt and little cousin, who were dependent upon him, had come to live with him. Virginia did not impress those who saw her as being a woman. Her actions were rather those of a merry schoolgirl, which, after all, was no more than could be expected of a child of thirteen. She was rather small for her age, "plump, pretty, but not especially so, with sweet and gentle manners and the simplicity of a child."

Rosalie, or "Rose Poe," as she was more generally known, was now twenty-five years old, but only about Virginia's age mentally. She was, it appears, somewhat of an annoyance to Edgar, who was then called "Buddie" by his family circle. Rose would follow him about with a patient, lamb-like admiration that was, at times, embarrassing. The games of childhood still occupied her attention, and she and Virginia played like two little girls together at the Mackenzies', screaming in a swing under the trees at Duncan Lodge or skipping rope together in the yard. A brief glimpse at this kindergarten eclogue of Poe's early married life has been preserved by Mrs. William Mackenzie, who remembered that one afternoon "Buddie" came up to the Lodge to fetch home Virginia who met him with such "abandon" that Mrs. Mackenzie's Victorian sensibilities were shocked.

The sad truth seems to be that Virginia very closely resembled Rosalie. She, too, never fully developed. When she was twenty-odd it was noticed by competent persons [481] that she did not appear to be over fifteen. Her mind developed more normally than her cousin's, but her body was never wholly mature. It was the reverse in the case of Rose.

In Richmond, even in 1835, it was remarked that the otherwise childish prettiness of Virginia was marred by a chalky-white com-

---

[481] Elizabeth Oakes Smith and others of the *literati* in New York in the late '40's. When in Philadelphia, in 1842, a friend took her to be only fourteen.

plexion, a pastiness that later became waxen. Such a detail would be unimportant if it were not for the fact that she developed tuberculosis a few years later, and finally died of it. Virginia had been raised in the same house where Henry Poe died of the disease; a certain strain in the Poe family seems to have been predisposed to it, and the frequent short commons at Mrs. Clemm's was certainly a contributing factor. The affliction, the appearance, and some of the more ethereal and abnormal characteristics of the little child-wife have been transferred into literature.

For Poe the "delicacy" which the advancing stages of the dread, but then fashionable and romantic, disease, conferred on his wife—the strange, chalky pallor tinged with a faint febrile rouge, the large, haunted liquid eyes—gradually acquired a peculiar fascination. From the wide and later on terror-stricken depths of those eyes looked forth the spirit of one who had been robbed of life, a mind which had outgrown its body, simple, and yet wise enough to sense its own tragedy. Her whole being slowly became morbidly ethereal. The plumpness remained to the last,[482] yet somehow it suffered a subtle earth-change as if Death himself were amorous. To the man who was irretrievably linked to her, she became part and parcel of his own tragedy. His capacity for love, perhaps even his potentiality for sensuousness, was metamorphosed into a patient and tragic sympathy—the truly magnificent and loyal sorrow of one who beheld in his bed, in his garden, and at his table a constant and pathetic reminder of the omnipotence of the conqueror worm. On the whole, aside from his great art, his abiding tenderness for Virginia must remain as his greatest claim for a hold on the average human heart. She was the key that completely unlocked for him the house of shadows. She is the prototype of his heroines.

Virginia became his "Ligeia," his "Eulalie," "Eleonora," the sister in the *House of Usher,* perhaps even his "Annabel Lee," "Berenice," for instance.

Berenice and I were cousins, and we grew up together in my paternal halls. Yet differently we grew—I, ill of health, and buried in gloom—she, agile, graceful, and overflowing with energy. . . . O gorgeous yet fantastic beauty! O sylph amid the shrubberies of Arnheim. . . . And then—then all is mystery and terror, and a tale which should not be told. Disease, a fatal disease, fell like the simoon upon her frame; and, even while I gazed upon her, the spirit of change swept over her, pervading her mind, her habits, and her character, and, in a manner the most subtle and terrible, disturbing even the identity of her person. . . .

So they all were, always subtly different from Virginia, and yet always the same; dying, corpse-like ladies usually related to their lovers,

---

[482] See the picture of Virginia made *after* her death at Fordham in 1847, page 581.

with the pale suggestion of incest just around the corner of the family tomb. It was a page, many pages, from his own experience.

It seems strange that this should have been so, but it must be remembered that Virginia Clemm in her actual appearance and life history approached the ideal of the desired feminine type of the time. Delicate, consumptive, given to fainting, and languidly lying upon invalid couches; saying incredibly refined and sentimental things, and listening to denatured artificial rhapsodies,—they wasted away in their wailing lovers' arms, leaving them stricken with sorrow or touched by madness to haunt the lonely grave, forever inconsolable.

Poe, as it happened, had married a little girl who, as time passed, approximated the fashionable ideal of the romantic Victorian heroine more nearly than any other whom he might have chosen. The real story of her tragedy is like an excerpt from a novel of the day. That Poe etherealized and enormously improved it, there can be no doubt. His particular etherealizations were not sentimental mockeries, because behind them lay the grim spiritual reality of a human tragedy that was horribly, pitiably true. That he sometimes sought to escape from it into the more robust world of reality, only proves that he was human after all.

In Richmond, Poe began in leisure hours to teach Virginia to chatter a little French and to play the harp. She sang in a sweet, high, girlish voice, trilling, as the fashion then was, like a bird. Mrs. Clemm did the work. But with the unwonted plenty and comparative peace at Mrs. Yarrington's she began to recover her health. The basket for a few months was temporarily forgotten, nor was she by any means oblivious, then or later, to the necessity of providing a background of respectability for Edgar. Now for a little time, however, she was able to sit in the parlor with the stuffed birds, rocking, in her white cap, her white starched cuffs, and her widow's weeds, while she sewed for the two over whom her grandly simple heart yearned maternally— chatting with the other boarders, or Mrs. Mackenzie—supported like a real lady by a professional man, and entirely, impeccably genteel. On Sundays, Poe read by the parlor lamp while she sat opposite him, her hands unwontedly idle.

Through the week, Poe on his part was busy—for the time being completely absorbed by his work at his desk in the office of the *Southern Literary Messenger*. The young man was actually becoming a force, if not a figure, in contemporary national journalism and literature. During the year 1835 he published in the *Southern Literary Messenger* thirty-seven reviews of American and foreign books and periodicals, nine tales, four poems, and excerpts from his drama *Politian*.[483] In

---

[483] The bibliography is taken from Harrison, and is probably incomplete.

addition to this there were critical notes and notices, a general editorial supervision of the contents of the magazine, and an active correspondence.

His work had already fallen inevitably into the two main categories in which it continued, from then on, to manifest itself; *i.e.,* the critical, and the creative. For the time being, due to the fact that his editorial duties gave him no leisure time, the creative faculty slumbered. Most of the tales and several of the poems were drawn from the reservoir of manuscript which Baltimore and the past had provided. The poems were minor affairs such as *To Sarah, To Mary, The Hymn* (from *Morella*) or excerpts for *Politian.* One or two new stories of minor importance were produced, but, for the most part, they were drawn from the already prepared *Tales of the Folio Club.* The bulk of the work, however, was critical. It was in the pages of the *Messenger* that Poe first appeared in the American arena as the greatest literary gladiator of his time. American critics up until that era had generally conducted their mock combats with blunt or, at best, lead weapons. Poe now appeared in their midst with a bright sword that bit deep and drew blood. He began to be feared, hated, and admired. He was, despite peculiar personal reservations, a *Humanist.*

The texts which the young man in Richmond reviewed in 1835-36 the world has for the most part comfortably contrived to forget, a fact which has pulled the same damp blanket of oblivion over the work of their only able critic. Yet this fact, naturally enough, did not then detract from its contemporary importance. The books, periodicals, speeches, and poems which Poe passed upon in the 1830's, constituted his education in the current literature of the day and a soft bone on which to cut his eye-teeth. For the most part, with the single exception of Carlyle, time has confirmed his judgments.

His aptitude for the work was deeply rooted in the intricate folds of his nature. In the first place, he had a genuine respect for real literature that endowed him at times with a sixth sense as to the acid effect of time. His background, from a constant and early reading of foreign periodicals,[484] was genuinely cosmopolitan instead of local. Great critics of the English reviews, particularly Macaulay, were his models. His artistic idealism and his materialistic philosophy gave him a hatred of cant; and his youthful experience with a provincial aristocracy in a small Southern town made him dislike snobs—even from New England. Poe had a genuine love for literature; it was his great passion; he was in earnest about it. He could not therefore abide dilettantes, and it was insufferable to him that the prize for which he had starved and worked should be dropped even ephemerally into the hands

---

[484] This familiarity extended back at least as far as 1824.

of those whose sole art consisted in the clever manipulation of little feeble "puffing." The sappy sentimentalism of the time, although it did not fail to leave its mark on him, was nevertheless the great god Sham against which he mainly tilted. As a great lyricist in prose and poetry he could not abide a mock emotion, and he was unerring in smelling it out. Mixed with all this was a tendency to the pedantic that became more marked, as the necessity for confirming the belief in his own logical mental processes began to require a secret assurance, and above, and finally dominating all, was an ego that felt itself exalted because it was able to abase. It was an almost insane desire for fame, the last infirmity of noble minds.

Out of such an exalted head the critic on the *Messenger* was suddenly born. Mr. White received protests. From time to time he and others remonstrated. Libel suits might follow—enemies would be, in fact, were made—even New York began to take notice. But the subscription list bounded from three, well up into four figures; esteemed contemporaries watched and reprinted. The audience became large, very large. The salary if it did not leap, at least wriggled to $15 a week and a few extras. While Virginia and Rose skipped rope at the Lodge, the pen at the *Messenger* went back again and again into the ink and the acid. At last, it was making an immediate and an effective noise.

For some time after his return from Baltimore, Poe must have kept his promise to Mr. White. Years later, J. W. Fergusson, one of the printers, remarked, "There never was a more perfect gentleman than Mr. Poe when he was sober," (but at other times,) "he would just as soon lie down in the gutter as anywhere else." The "other times" must have come later, and perhaps cast some light on the reasons for Poe's finally parting with Mr. White. Through the Winter of 1835-36, indeed till sometime late in 1836, there could not have been many lapses, if any at all. The proof lies in the crowded columns of the *Messenger*.

Poe found most of his social relaxation with the Mackenzies at Duncan Lodge, at the Sullys', and with Dr. Robert G. Cabell. His boyhood friend, Bob Stanard, "Helen's" son, he regarded with a peculiar affection which was heartily returned. But there were some rents in the social pavilion which let in a stinging rain. Two of his old schoolmates refused to attend with him a party given by the mother-in-law of General Scott,[485] and some of the old hostility from the University and from friends of the Allans troubled him. Troubled him more, perhaps, than will ever be known. Part of his spare time was spent at Sanxey's bookstore or with Eliza White, who was rather a beauty and bookishly inclined. She was the daughter of his employer, so both inclination and interest dictated that he should be attentive. A great deal of nonsense

---

[485] A Mrs. Mayo with some pretense to "literary" fame.

was afterward talked about this, based largely on the fact that the lady never married. Poe was undoubtedly intimate with her, and she was present, years later, as an old friend, at the death-bed of Virginia at Fordham. The effort to throw a romantic atmosphere about every woman with whom the poet came in contact on an intimate basis is, of course, nonsense.

Of the house and the domestic circle at Mrs. Yarrington's, we know very little. Certain it is, though, that both Poe and Mrs. Clemm longed for their own home and continued to work for it. One of the cousins, George Poe, of Mobile, Alabama, was now in turn appealed to about the beginning of the new year. The glimpse is rather intimate:

DEAR SIR,—I take the liberty of addressing you in behalf of a mutual relative, Mrs. William Clemm, late of Baltimore—and at her earnest solicitation. . . .

Having lately established myself in Richmond, and undertaken the Editorship of the *Southern Literary Messenger,* and my circumstances having thus become better than formerly, I have ventured to offer my Aunt a home. She is now therefore in Richmond, with her daughter Virginia, and is, for the present boarding at the house of a Mrs. Yarrington. My salary is only, at present, about $800 per ann: and the charge per week for our board (Mrs. Clemm's, her daughter's and my own), is $9. I am thus particular in stating my precise situation that you may be the better enabled to judge in regard to the propriety of granting the request I am now about to make for Mrs. Clemm.

It is now ascertained that if Mrs. Clemm could obtain the means of opening, herself, a boarding-house in this city, she could support herself and daughter comfortably with something to spare. But a small capital would be necessary for an undertaking of this nature, and many of the widows of our first people are engaged in it and find it profitable. I am willing to advance, for my own part, $100, and I believe that William and R. Poe will advance $100. If then you would so far aid her in her design as to loan her, yourself, $100, she will have sufficient to commence with. I will be responsible for the repayment of the sum, in a year from this date, if you can make it convenient to comply with her request. . . . I feel deeply for the distresses of Mrs. Clemm, and I am sure *you* will feel interested in relieving them.

[*Signature cut off*]

P. S.—I am the son of David Poe, Jr., Mrs. Clemm's brother.

On the receipt of such letters as these—several of the relatives did respond—the reason for keeping the first marriage secret now becomes clear. Once married, Poe would be appealing on behalf of himself. With the marriage a secret he could, with good grace, as a relative supporting his aunt and cousin out of the kindness of his heart, ask the rest of the family to chip in. It was, perhaps, a justifiable subterfuge. Mrs. Clemm certainly needed help. That she and Poe connived, there can be no doubt. Things on the whole were looking up for Edgar. A few days after the letter to George Poe he wrote to Kennedy:

Richmond, *Jan.* 22, 1836

DEAR SIR,—Although I have never yet acknowledged the receipt of your letter of advice some months ago, it was not without great influence on me. I have since then, fought the enemy manfully, and am now, in every respect, comfortable and happy. I know you will be pleased to hear this. My health is better than for years past, my mind is fully occupied, my pecuniary difficulties have vanished. I have a fair prospect of success—in a word all is right. I shall never forget to whom all this happiness is in a great degree to be attributed. I know that without your timely aid I should have sunk under my trials. Mr. White is very liberal and beside my salary of $520, pays me liberally for extra work, so that I have nearly $800. Next year that is at the commencement of the second volume, I am to get $1000. Besides this, I receive from publishers, nearly all new publications. My friends in Richmond have received me with open arms, and my reputation is extending—especially in the South. Contrast all this with those circumstances of absolute despair in which you found me, and you will see how great reason I have to be grateful to God and to yourself. . . .

Yours very truly

EDGAR A. POE

J. P. Kennedy

During the Spring of 1836 Poe conducted, among others, a heavy correspondence with Beverley Tucker of Williamsburg, Virginia, a critic who admired his work but was careful in his praise. Some comments which Tucker made to White in a letter about Poe caused the young author some uneasiness as to the effect they might have on his employer. Poe consequently wrote explaining the situation to Tucker who immediately responded by writing White a reassuring letter containing some additional good advice meant for Poe. The manuscript of the *Tales of the Folio Club* which still remained with Carey & Lea in Philadelphia had not been published by them. In February, 1836, the manuscript was returned by them to Poe with one story missing. Most of those stories had appeared in the *Messenger*.

Poe now wrote to J. K. Paulding in New York City, asking him to submit the volume to Harpers, which he did. The book was refused, and on March 3, 1836, Mr. Paulding wrote to White:

. . . I regret this decision of the Harpers, though I have not opposed it, because I do not wish to lead them into any measure that might be accompanied by a loss, and felt as I would feel for myself in a similar case. . . .

Exactly two weeks later Paulding wrote to Poe saying he was returning the manuscript in a box of books that Haynes was sending for review. Poe, it appears, had requested Paulding to submit it to another publisher but he was unable to do so. In this letter, he suggests to Poe, "I think it would be worth your while, if other engagements permit, to undertake a Tale in a couple of volumes, for that is the magical number." Out of this suggestion grew *Arthur Gordon Pym*, which shortly afterward began to appear serially in the *Messenger*. It was the only notable piece of creative writing which occupied Poe in Richmond. An effort was now made to get the *Tales* published in England through Sanders & Ortley of New York. Poe's friend, Edward W. Johnson of the College of South Carolina, performed the good offices of a go-between, and the New York publishers were ready to send the book to England in the Fall of 1836, when Poe asked to have it returned for further revision. He was not satisfied to let it go to England as it stood. Nothing further came of the matter. In the meanwhile, Poe was married a second time to Virginia. This time the ceremony was public. It took place at Mrs. Yarrington's house, in Richmond, on May 16, 1836.

The reasons for a second ceremony, although complex, are not at all mysterious. As we have seen, the chief reason for the clandestine marriage in September, 1835, had been the opposition to it on the part of the Poe connection. Since then Poe and Mrs. Clemm had been receiving contributions "to help Mrs. Clemm," Edgar acting as the nephew who had charitably assumed the chief responsibility of maintaining his Aunt Maria and *Cousin* Virginia. No mention was made of her being his wife. The cousin Poes would by no means have contributed toward setting up a house for a young man already on his own salary so that he could live with a full cousin who was in their judgment too young to marry. It would never do now suddenly to throw off the mask and reveal the fact that the relatives had simply been fooled. Family complications would follow, when it was important to keep on good terms. The easiest solution, therefore, was simply to have a new ceremony. By the removal from Baltimore the influence of Neilson Poe had been dodged, and Poe now had the argument that he was already supporting his aunt and cousin. In addition to this, the revelation in Richmond that he was already married to a little girl when she was only thirteen would have been extremely uncomfortable, and the statement might have been met with doubt. There is also the very likely possibility that Poe and Virginia had not been living together as man and wife, but that there had been an understanding at the time of the first marriage that he was to wait till Virginia was mature. Both Virginia and Mrs. Clemm undoubtedly desired the social distinction of even a simple public ceremony. The other affair without ring, cake, or guests could scarcely have seemed a marriage to them at all. Now, with Edgar's unexpected "affluence," a regular marriage was possible. By a second marriage all of these difficulties were solved and an endless round of explanations avoided. But the extreme youth of the bride was still a source of embarrassment and was carefully concealed.

The marriage bond, which was signed in the Hustings Court of the City of Richmond on May 16, 1836, shows that oath was made before Charles Howard, the Clerk of Court, by Thomas W. Cleland as witness that "Virginia E. Clemm is of the full age of twenty-one years." She was, as a matter of fact, thirteen years, nine months and one day old.[486] The discrepancy is glaring. Cleland, who was a friend and fellow boarder of Poe, is known to have been a pious Presbyterian and he would scarcely have taken oath to what he did not believe to be true. Despite the extremely youthful appearance of the bride, he must have been assured of her age by Poe, Mrs. Clemm, and, of course, Virginia. She, poor child, was probably eager enough for a "real wedding" to say anything "Muddie" and "Buddie" suggested.

On the day of the marriage, Jane Foster,[487] a friend of Mrs. Yarrington, who lived outside of Richmond, came to visit her friends in town. She found Mrs. Yarrington and Mrs. Clemm busy baking a wedding cake and was informed that a marriage was to be performed at the house that day. Jane watched the cake while the two older women concerned themselves about the other simple preparations. Late in the afternoon, the Virginia "evening," the guests began to arrive. Mr. White and his daughter Eliza, Mr. and Mrs. Cleland, William McFarland and John Fergusson, the printers on the *Messenger,* Mrs. Yarrington, Mrs. Clemm, and Jane Foster constituted the little party. The marriage was performed in the boarding-house parlor by the Reverend Amasa Converse, a Presbyterian divine, at that time the editor of the *Southern Religious Telegraph.* Virginia was dressed in a traveling dress and a white hat with a veil; Poe was, as usual, in a black suit and the omnipresent black stock. Jane Foster, who was herself scarcely more than a child, remembered the very youthful appearance of Virginia. The nuptial scene was reflected in a looking glass on the parlor wall, and little Miss Foster was surprised to note that the mirror did not show Virginia to be any older when she passed out than when she walked in. Marriage, she was sure in her naïve way, would magically remedy the contrast between the little bride and the mature bridegroom, for Poe was twenty-seven. The Reverend Amasa Converse remarked that the bride had a pleasing air, but *did* seem young. Mrs. Clemm he noted as "being polished, dignified, and agreeable in her bearing" and that she gave Virginia away "freely." In the parlor after the ceremony Mrs. Clemm was in her element when her fellow boarders were called in while the happy event was announced, and wine and cake were served. It

---

[486] For a discussion of Virginia's date of birth see Woodberry, 1909, vol. I, page 137.
[487] Afterward Mrs. Stocking. The account of the wedding given here is taken from various documentary sources and from an account given personally to the author in Richmond in July, 1925, by a niece of Mrs. Jane Stocking (Miss Foster) who was fond of relating the details of the occasion to members of her family. Mrs. Stocking was a close friend of Mrs. Yarrington, who was a planter's daughter and risked the anger of her family by "marrying beneath her." In order to help her husand "to get along faster" she had started a boarding house.

was doubtless then that the Reverend Amasa noted that the widow was "agreeable in her bearing."

After the humble felicitations, a hack was called to the door, and Virginia and Edgar drove off together on their honeymoon. One catches a glimpse of the waving hands of the boarders, the fat stack of the little, wood-burning locomotive throwing sparks on Virginia's traveling dress on the short journey to Petersburg, and a round of entertainments at various friends' houses in the quiet little town basking in the sunlight and perfume of a Virginia May. The paulownia trees were in bloom.

The Poes spent their honeymoon at the house of Mr. Hiram H. Haines of the Petersburg, Virginia, *Constellation,* Democratic in its journalistic policy, we solemnly learn. There were also visits to the house of Edwin V. Sparhawk, another journalistic friend, and Dr. William M. Robinson entertained them at a party and noted that Poe's conversation was brilliant. Poe no doubt noticed, although he enjoyed it, that the conversation of the others was somewhat bucolic. He was already longing for more cultivated fields in which to converse largely.

Before the end of May, the young editor and his child-wife returned to Richmond. The Stanards, the Sullys, and young Dr. Ambler called, the latter doubtless recalling two little boys who once swam together in Shockoe Creek twenty years before. Mr. White promised the young husband a raise in salary. He was to receive "$20 after November."

It was now Summer, and the hot valley of the James took on the glittering green of June woodlands and the pied hues of many-colored grass. The calmest hours that Poe was ever to know in manhood were swiftly passing, a brief respite between poverties and tragedies, the memory of this time he has preserved in the tropical idyl of *Eleonora:*

> She whom I loved in youth, and of whom I now pen calmly and distinctly these remembrances, was the sole daughter of the only sister of my mother long departed. Eleonora was the name of my cousin. We had always dwelled together, beneath a tropical sun, in the Valley of the Many-Colored Grass. No unguided footstep ever came upon that vale; for it lay far away among a range of giant hills. . . . Thus it was that we lived all alone, knowing nothing of the world without the valley,—I, and my cousin, and her mother.

"Knowing nothing of the world . . ." unfortunately it was true. Now they were married, Poe was making every effort to have his own home where the illusion of the secluded valley might be continued. Only a few weeks after the return from the honeymoon he wrote Kennedy, again unfolding his domestic and financial circumstances to the faithful friend in Baltimore.

Richmond, *Va.,* July 7, 1836

DEAR SIR,—Having got into a little temporary difficulty I venture to ask you, once more, for aid, rather than apply to any of my new friends in Richmond.

Mr. White, having purchased a new house at $10,000, made propositions to my aunt to rent it to her [*sic*], and to board himself and family with her. This plan was highly advantageous to us, and, having accepted it, all arrangements were made and I obtained credit for some furniture, etc., to the amount of $200, above what little money I had. But upon examination of the premises purchased, it appears that the house will barely be large enough for one family, and the scheme is laid aside, leaving me now in debt, (to a small amount), without those means of discharging it upon which I had depended.

In this dilemma I would be greatly indebted to you for the loan of $100 for six months. . . .

"But upon examination of the premises purchased"—one cannot help but smile a little, and yet want to cry too with Mrs. Clemm and Virginia over the disappointment about the "premises" so carefully examined *after* the purchase had been made! One wonders—Mr. White would scarcely buy a house before he had looked at it. "This plan," says Poe, "was highly advantageous *to us.*" Then he continues to Kennedy:

. . . Have you heard anything farther in relation to Mrs. Clemm's estate?

Our *Messenger* is thriving beyond all expectations, and I myself have every prospect of success. It is our design to issue, as soon as possible, a number of the Magazine consisting entirely of articles from our most distinguished *literati.* . . . Could you not do me so great a favor as to send me a scrap, however small, from your portfolio? Your name is of the greatest influence in that region where we direct our greatest efforts—in the South.

Any little reminiscence, tale, *jeu d'esprit,* historical anecdote,—anything, in short, *with your name,* will answer all our purposes. I presume you have heard of my marriage.

With sincere respect & esteem
Yours truly,
EDGAR A. POE

"Our *Messenger*" may have been thriving, but Mrs. Clemm and Virginia shared only in the glory. The grand scheme of the $10,000 boarding house having been abandoned, perforce, the little family moved from Mrs. Yarrington's on Capitol Square to "a cheap tenement on Seventh Street," [488] where they sublet rooms. Mrs. Clemm went back to her dressmaking; there were generally a few boarders at the table. Virginia was a little more silent now, the honeymoon was over, some of the patches of many-colored grass were probably becoming a little parched, even for her, life had a few surprises. She was trying as hard as she could to grow up—

Nearly twenty years after this time there were persons living on Main Street who remembered almost daily to have seen about the Old Market, in business hours, a tall, dignified looking woman, with a market basket on one arm, while on the other hung a little girl with a round ever-smiling face, who was addressed as "Mrs. Poe !" She, too, carried a basket.[488]

---

[488] Mrs. Susan Archer Weiss, *Home Life of Poe.* A few facts regarding Richmond occurrences of which Mrs. Weiss was reliably informed are culled here from an otherwise inaccurate biography.

Mrs. Yarrington's parlor mirror had been right after all. The marriage had worked no magic for Virginia.

Poe was now seldom to be found at home. "Graceful, and with dark, curling hair and magnificent eyes, wearing a Byron collar and looking every inch a 'poet,' " he preferred the recitations of Eliza White doing "Lady Macbeth" in the house that was too small for two families, the lurid remarks of journalistic brethren at the office, the excitement of a correspondence with J. Q. Adams or Mrs. Sigourney, supper at the Sullys', or an evening at the *Court House Tavern*. There were many places he could go, and every place he went he was offered wine. Sometimes he took it. Then he was very ill and went home, to spend several days in bed. "Dear Eddie's health was so bad, no, he could not get down to the office to-day," was Mrs. Clemm's version. And she loved him so much that at last she came to believe it, although she knew it was not true.

Towards the end of 1836 the days in bed became more frequent. Mr. White, it appears, became annoyed and then alarmed. Yet he was loath to force a parting. His young editor had become invaluable. There was a good deal of idle gossip about it all,—about Poe, the Allans, Elmira, Eliza White, Virginia, and Mrs. Clemm. "There was a general prejudice against her on account of her having made or consented to the match between her little daughter and a man of Poe's age and dissipated habits."[488]

As usual, the gossips, with the unerring instinct of their race, had aimed the barb for the heart. For back of it all, then and forever afterward, remaining even after Poe was removed from the scene, was the grand simple heart, the strong arms, and the maternal bosom of Maria Clemm. If there be anything at all in the tradition of the test of sacrifice and abnegation, she loved him better than all the other women who crossed his path. She it was who never doubted or faltered in her belief in the immortal part of the man; who, after the mortal had been removed, continued nobly to cherish the memory of his genius. She washed for him, worked for him, begged for him, nursed him and comforted him. Before her simple "Eddie, Oh God, my dear Eddie!"— all the mud of Mrs. Ellet, the vitriol of Griswold, and the sugar of Helen Whitman is dried up and blown away while Mrs. Clemm's cry remains to *keen* in our ears. Small persons, who called upon her later when smug society and the legacy of fame had driven her half crazy, saw nothing in her but an old bereaved woman with a broad face, roughened hands, and an ignorant manner of speech.[489] Pharisees like

---

[489] See R. H. Stoddard's account of Mrs. Clemm, after Poe's death. *Lippincott's Magazine,* January, 1889, page 112. One of the most self-complacent articles ever written.

Stoddard departed making long the fringes of their phylacteries—laughing, and thanking God they were not like that. Thackeray, who knew nothing at all of one Virginian, drew large genteel audiences in Richmond, and exchanged aristocratic repartee with ladies in Charleston—and departed. Charles Dickens returned to the States on his second tour. In a certain obscure Episcopal Church Home in Baltimore, erected on the same spot where a great poet had died only a few years before, the author of *Bleak House* called on a tearful old woman whose last days were being prolonged by Christian charity. It was "Muddie," whose reward for exorcising the demons down under the sea was the contempt of mankind and a saintlike face. Mr. Dickens left behind a present of money pressed into a rheumatic old hand. Only he and Lowell were fully aware who it was that had made the croaks of the raven in *Barnaby Rudge* audible to the entire world.

By December, 1836, Richmond and the South no longer offered a broad enough field for a rising young author and editor who desired to try sinking his plowshare into more fertile literary soil. During the year, Poe's tremendous critical fertility had continued.

No less than eighty-three reviews, six poems, four essays, and three stories had appeared in the *Messenger*,[483] besides, there was correspondence which its editorial duties necessitated and the writing of the narrative of *Arthur Gordon Pym* that Poe hoped to sell to Harpers after publishing it in the *Messenger* in serial form. The reviews ranged through almost the entire gamut of contemporary literature from *Recollections of S. T. Coleridge*[490] to Mrs. Sigourney's *Letters to Young Ladies*. The poems were mostly old ones revived, some of them changed into masterpieces. *To Helen* had appeared in March, *Irene, or The Sleeper,* in May, and *Israfel* now wonderfully perfected in August. Besides this, there had been the lovely sonnet, *Zante,* and some additional scenes from *Politian*. Poe's study of poetical criticism was having a memorable effect upon his own early work. His poems were now pruned and grafted to last through the winter of time. The stories, *Metzengerstein, The Homo-Camelopard* and the like, were still drawn from the old reserve supply, but the essays were new. Chief of these was *Maelzel's Chess-Player* in which he exposed the method by which a dummy chessman, that had gone the rounds of American cities winning games with living opponents, was operated. It is possible that Poe's interest in this automaton was early aroused by an article in the Baltimore *North American* to which Henry Poe had contributed in

---

[490] *Letters, Conversations, and Recollections of S. T. Coleridge,* New York, published by Harper & Brothers, No. 28 Cliff Street, 1836. Another Harper book reviewed by Poe who was anxious to publish *Arthur Gordon Pym* through Harpers. Poe was much in debt to this book for many ideas he later developed. Poe's critical debt to Coleridge cannot be too strongly stressed.

1827. Many persons had been more mystified than amused by the maneuvers of the automatic man, and the *exposé,* although only partly correct, created quite a little furor. It was the first of Poe's work in which he emerged as the unerring, abstract reasoner, and foreshadowed the method he followed later in his detective stories such as the *Murders in the Rue Morgue,* a method which has been embalmed in the triumphs of "Sherlock Holmes."

Pinakidia, another type of contribution, were selections from the author's notebook, selections which throw an interesting sidelight on his literary and journalistic pilferings, nearly always from secondary sources. By a mistake, obviously made in the composing room, they were printed in the *Messenger* as "original" instead of the opposite.

Like so many other literary and curious persons of his epoch, Poe kept a commonplace book. Into it went from time to time cullings from a thousand books, magazines and newspapers, copies of which came under his editorial eye. Nor was he by any means blind to the dusty shelves and remote alcoves of libraries public and private. He made the most of, and he improved such opportunities for browsing as *Pinakidia* and the later *Marginalia* show. These grains of gold sifted out of dust and refuse were not so valuable in themselves, but they provided an inexhaustible source upon which he drew for items of curious knowledge, for a parade of learning, and for quotations that temporarily lulled or alarmed even the learned. Above all, here was the store of ammunition for charges of plagiarism which he loved to ram home. From his careful gleaning over wide fields, there was scarcely any figure in poetry, or any idea, which Poe could not show had been used before. Often the charge was true; always it was plausible. In the great shallow lakes of American crudity, the well of erudition of the young Richmond critic seemed deep—even profound.

But there was something more to it than that. This habit of clipping and noting exercised a valuable curiosity. Out of a dead book or a banal news-sheet, Poe developed the habit of culling the one living incident, the pertinent fact, or the picturesque scene. He remembered it, and when the time came the shot was there, carefully greased and labeled, in the right locker. It was later always delivered with telling effect, and in a direction that associated it with the living thought of his time. That the French of obscure titles, the original sources, and the precise wording of quotations were sometimes garbled, is of importance only in the cemetery of the scholastic mind, for, by the living use of such matter, Poe frequently conferred upon it the only gleam of vitality which it ever possessed. Even in 1836, he stood out boldly and alone as the only arresting critic of contemporary literature in the United States.

His rise to that position had been meteoric. It was the *Southern Literary Messenger* which had conferred upon him the opportunity to claim the title. In less than two years that obscure magazine claimed the attention of the nation on an equal footing with *The New Englander* and the *Knickerbocker,* and was even beginning to disturb the complacent local religion of the *North American Review,* to which, heretofore, nothing south of the Delaware had been audible.

In the late Fall of the previous year (1835), Theodore S. Fay, a young author who had many friends in the literary circles of New York and among the editors of the Knickerbocker journals, published a novel called *Norman Leslie.* It was greeted by a howl of metropolitan acclaim that found the usual servile echo in the provinces. The book was unusually poor, and the reverberations in the canyon of criticism were more than usually grand. In December, 1835, Poe reviewed *Norman Leslie* in the columns of the *Messenger.* Both the book and, by implication, the author were reduced to the light powder of which they were actually composed, but in a manner so trenchant, so vividly interesting and unanswerable, that the public in general became interested, subscribed in numbers, and eagerly hoped for more.

The New York papers, at first, maintained a discreet and dignified silence, but the cat was out of the bag and scratching so hard that the pose of dignified silence became too painful to maintain. On April 9, 1836, the *New York Mirror* with a display of no less than four scornfully pointing, printed hands drew attention to a column on another page in which Poe was satirized in his own style for his methods of criticisms, his minute analyses, and his accusations of plagiarism. The notice itself accused him of striving for notoriety "by the loudness of abuse," hinting that he was actuated by jealousy because he "knows by experience what it is to write a successless novel." This doubtless referred to some rumor of the collected tales which Harpers had refused.

In the April number of the *Messenger* Poe replied. The statement about "a successless novel," not being true, was easily refuted, and the young editor took the occasion to make his views on the necessity for a broad attitude in criticism clear:

. . . We are becoming boisterous and arrogant in the pride of a too speedily assumed literary freedom. We throw off with the most presumptuous and unmeaning hauteur *all* deference whatever to foreign opinion—we forget, in the puerile inflation of vanity, that *the world* is the true theatre of the biblical histrio—we get up a hue and cry about the necessity of encouraging native writers of merit—we blindly fancy that we can accomplish this by indiscriminate puffing of good, bad, and indifferent, without taking the trouble to consider that what we choose to denominate encouragement is thus, by its general application, precisely the reverse. In a word, so far from being ashamed of the many disgraceful literary failures to which our own inordinate vanities and misapplied patriotism have lately given birth, and so far from deeply lamenting that these daily puerilities are of home manufacture, we adhere pertinaciously to our original blindly conceived idea, and thus often find ourselves in the gross paradox of liking a stupid book the better because sure enough, its stupidity is American.

Poe's view that the world, by which he unconsciously meant the world of European culture, was the only background which provided the correct perspective in which to judge one's own work or that of others, was, of course, by no means new. It has been consciously or unconsciously adopted by many of the greatest writers of other periods, and it jibed with the private opinions of many readers at the time. But in some quarters it was essentially uncomfortable. In such a "world vista" as Poe proposed, what would become of America's literary Holy Land, New England? Besides this, the new prophet had arisen on the wrong side of Jordan. In certain quarters the stone heaps were prepared. The *New York Commercial Advertiser* pronounced him anathema. W. G. Clark of the *Philadelphia Gazette* pounced on him and the war was even carried south of the James. For the most part, though, the South rallied around him. For it, the position of the Jordan was reversed. But Poe understood that, and how little it meant. He had raised the *view halloo* under the palace windows and he longed to follow the quarry whither it fled—northward.

Once dip your pen in acid and it becomes difficult to convince even a friend that a compliment is not meant for an innuendo. Poe's reputation for critical savageness has been over-strained. A letter by Poe to a complaining contemporary in September, 1836,[491] provides an answer to those who complain of his severity which an examination of the columns of the *Messenger* also refutes. For the most part, indeed almost without exception, time has confirmed the justness of his criticism. *Sartor Resartus* alone survives. Nor would it be reasonable to expect Edgar Allan Poe to be in sympathy with the style of Thomas Carlyle. It is doubtful if Poe ever descended into those turgid and strangely agitated depths. Yet here was the only "world book" that met his view.

It was the "world view," however, that moved Poe northward in 1837. Ten years before, he had written from Fortress Monroe to John Allan, "Richmond and the United States were too narrow a sphere and the world shall be my theater."[492] This fine ambition had never died. Poe knew the South too well to put any value on its acclaim. He was not deceived because three, or even five thousand persons [493] there had

---

[491] Poe to the *Richmond Courier* and *Daily Compiler,* Richmond, September 2, 1836, . . . "But this charge of indiscriminate 'cutting and slashing' *has never been adduced* —except in four instances, while the rigid justice and impartiality of our Journal had been lauded even *ad nauseam* . . ." etc. The letter is detailed and convincing.

[492] *Valentine Museum Collection,* letter No. 7, Poe to John Allan, December 22, 1828.

[493] Prof. J. A. Harrison, *Life and Letters,* vol. I, p. 125, gives the increase of subscribers on the *Messenger* as from seven hundred to five thousand. Prof. Woodberry is more conservative and puts the last figure at thirty-five hundred. The last is correct. Poe gave the larger.

subscribed to the *Messenger*. That was mainly because out of an honest literary opinion he had happened to criticize the North. There were probably not five hundred souls all told, anywhere, who knew what he was really talking about. South of the Potomac, literature was "cherished" as the decent avocation of a gentleman who might otherwise have to work with his hands. Hayne and Simms met the same situation in South Carolina a little later—and lost. What could one do in a section which gave its praise easily and so took it with a private grain of salt,—where every crowing plantation Chanticleer or twittering Jenny Wren was acclaimed as a poet; a *province* that talked of "Southern Literature" and preferred foreign books, a locality whose estimate of style was theatrically forensic?[246] One could live there comfortably and become, possibly, an obscurely honored local bard, the schoolboy's aversion and the old maid's pride. Horrible thought! Every day that he had spent in England, every page of the foreign reviews in the loft of *Ellis & Allan*, every contact with the great, wide, oblivious world cried out against it. "The world shall be my theater!" and the world won. In January, 1837, the following notice appeared in the *Southern Literary Messenger:*

Mr. Poe's attention being called in another direction, he will decline, with the present number, the Editorial duties on the *Messenger*. His Editorial Notices for this month end with Professor Anthon's *Cicero*—[404] what follows is from another hand. With the best wishes to the Magazine, and to its few foes as well as many friends, he is now desirous of bidding all parties a peaceable farewell.

Mr. Poe's urge for exit, however, was not purely literary. Encounters with the glass toward the end of 1836 had evidently been at least occasional, consequently his health was again "bad." Despite his increased salary, now over $1000 a year, he had, it seems, involved himself in debt. Mrs. Clemm's boarding-house venture was evidently not a paying one. Increasing fame had also added a certain arrogance that even his friends deprecated. Mr. White had been patient, but probably annoyed by irregularities; and no one enjoys being patronized. They parted friends, however. The young editor's copy on hand was to be exhausted rapidly, as the pages of the *Messenger* show, but Poe was to continue some contributions. He was particularly anxious to finish the serials of *Arthur Gordon Pym*.

About the middle of January, 1837, we find Poe in bed winding up his correspondence and making his last acceptances for the *Messenger*, articles which did not please Mr. White.[495] There is a tradition that Poe asked to be reinstated but it is a doubtful one that would naturally

---

[404] Poe was expecting to go to New York, where Prof. Anthon lived, and had therefore probably picked his book for favorable notice.

[495] See the correspondence between White and Poe in January, 1837.

be cherished by a magazine. During his régime it had increased its circulation from 500 to 3500 copies; [493] Poe had developed, by valuable experience, some well-defined ideas about the possibilities of a truly national publication. He was the first journalist to conceive of a magazine on a huge modern scale. That was the great idea he hoped to put into operation. He saw clearly, even then, that it would have to be done from Philadelphia or New York.

What little furniture they had was probably sold. "Muddie" and Virginia accompanied him. The little wife had matured considerably. There is a brief silence, and then we find them in New York. In Richmond he left behind him a few virulent enemies and a large number of friends. The great experiment had begun.

CHAPTER EIGHTEEN

THE journey from Richmond to New York occupied several weeks. Poe was accompanied by his little family through Baltimore and Philadelphia, where, in both cities, various relatives, friends, and literary acquaintances were called upon. In Baltimore there can be little doubt that Poe conferred with Kennedy, who was thoroughly acquainted with the reasons for the move. The severance of the connection with Mr. White of the *Messenger* was a serious matter, in point of salary and influence. There must have been personal complications between the older man and his brilliant young assistant which induced Mr. White to part with Poe more readily than might otherwise have been the case. From a purely business standpoint, there was every reason why Mr. White should desire him to remain. The "other reasons" were afterward referred to vaguely by both Mr. Kennedy and Poe himself. Kennedy says that "He [Poe] was irregular, eccentric, and querulous, and soon gave up his place," and this statement is largely borne out by Poe himself some years later:

For a brief period while I resided in Richmond and edited the *Messenger*, I certainly did give way, at long intervals, to the temptation held out on all sides by the spirit of Southern conviviality. My sensitive temperament could not stand an excitement which was an everyday matter to my companions. In short, it sometimes happened that I was completely intoxicated. For some days after each excess I was invariably confined to bed.[496]

The last glimpse that we have of Poe in Richmond shows him thus "confined to bed." Kennedy undoubtedly heard about such occasions from White later on. We can be sure that Poe himself, in talking the move over with Kennedy and others, would enlarge on the prospects of the wider field offered in the North, and on the pet project of the great national magazine. Mrs. Clemm and Virginia must have seen the Baltimore relatives, with whom, since Virginia's marriage with the rising young editor, they would now be on a more satisfactory basis. From Baltimore, the journey was continued to Philadelphia after a brief sojourn.

There were considerable inducements for Poe to remain in the Quaker City, where, indeed, we find him two years later. He already had acquaintances among publishers and editors there, and Philadelphia was

---

[496] See the *Baltimore American* for 1881—Poe to Dr. Snodgrass, April 1, 1841.

at that time the great publishing center. These, however, were not sufficient to detain him. He was then, through correspondence from Richmond, in touch with Dr. Francis Lister Hawks, a North Carolinian, at that time rector of St. Stephen's Episcopal Church and editor of the *New York Review,* to which he had already asked Poe to contribute. It is quite possible that Poe hoped to be able to occupy on that magazine much the same position he had held with Mr. White on the *Messenger,* and, with the aid of his friends, Professor Charles Anthon, and James K. Paulding,[497] and others to build up for himself rapidly a national reputation in the field of literature and journalism. In this hope, he was soon to be disappointed.

Poe, Mrs. Clemm, and Virginia arrived in New York about the end of February, 1837. Passers-by in the street must have turned to notice the three, evidently Southerners by their clothes. The distinguished air of the Byronic-looking man, the modest but appealing beauty of the young girl, and Mrs. Clemm's matronly expansiveness, as they went about looking for lodgings, would have attracted attention.

To Poe· and his family, New York was an utterly new experience. There were·no old acquaintances to stop them in the streets for a village chat, no friends or kin, as in Richmond and Baltimore. They were uncannily alone with no one to whom to turn. What little money they had saved for the move must have been nearly exhausted. Poe had resigned from the *Messenger* on January 3, 1837, and it was now more than six weeks since the last payment by Mr. White.[498] In the meantime installments of *Arthur Gordon Pym* had been appearing in the *Messenger,* and there may have been some return due from that and other items Poe was to send to Richmond. The connection there was by no means severed and relatives were still friendly. But, at best, the resources of the three were small., What goods, if any, Mrs. Clemm brought to New York must remain unknown.

The Poes first took up residence in Manhattan in a rather dilapidated old brick building at the corner of Sixth Avenue and Waverley Place where they shared a floor with a Scotchman by the name of William Gowans, who was then, and for many years after, a well-known bookseller about New York.[499] At that time he conducted business at 169

---

[497] Considerable correspondence with Hawks, Anthon, Paulding, and others, had been carried on by Poe from Richmond in 1836.

[498] Thos. W. White to Poe in Richmond, January 17, 1837. " . . . You are certainly as well aware as I am, that the last $20 I advanced to you was in consideration of what you were to write for me by the piece. I also made you a promise on Saturday that I would do something for you today . . . and though it is entirely out of my power to send you up anything this morning, yet I will do something more sure, before night or early tomorrow if I have to borrow it from my friends. T. W. W."—Poe was evidently gathering funds for the move at that time.

[499] William Gowans (1803-1870). In 1842, Mr. Gowans removed his business to 204 Broadway, and later, in 1846, to 63 Liberty Street. At both of these places Poe was a visitor to the Scotch bookseller who remained his friend to the last.

Broadway in quarters that were known as the "Long Room." Mr. Gowans soon became a firm friend of Poe and his family, and later on followed Mrs. Clemm as one of her boarders when she moved elsewhere. He, more than anyone else, seems to have afforded Poe an important point of literary contact. Poe was much in his bookstore browsing among the volumes, and the early experiences of the young poet in Scotland, plus a knowledge of the Scotch temperament which he possessed from the long association with the clans in Richmond, now stood him in good stead. A warm bookstore and the personalities it attracted were not to be despised.

Literary progress, however, was unexpectedly difficult and disappointingly slow. There were several contributory causes. Poe had arrived in New York during the height of the financial panic of 1837. Since the latter part of 1835, the country had been experiencing the painful results of Jackson's fast and loose fiscal policy, and the mercurial phenomena of the tariff under the alternate heat and cold of sectional attacks. The dying convulsions of the Bank of the United States left the nation at the mercy of petty financiers and the mad fluctuations of credit expansion due to Western land speculation made possible by the "wild cat" paper issues of state banks. An added impetus was given to the Western boom by the distribution of funds from the federal treasury to the several states, and from them to local banks.[500] Consequent easy credit permitted immense sums to be borrowed and invested in worthless public lands purchased with equally worthless "wild cat" money. The federal treasury then suddenly required that payments be made in specie, and the bubble burst. Thousands of people were ruined and the failure of long-established firms became the chief item of news. April 6, 1837, was long remembered in New York as the day of terror and gloom. Flour and other necessities rose to preposterous heights. The rich trembled and the poor starved.

A natural repercussion of this state of affairs was the suspension of numerous magazines and newspapers, and the reluctance of publishers to take risks on any but the best known English authors. The *New York*

---

[500] Under the Act of Congress of June 23, 1836, relating to the distribution of the surplus federal revenue, the money in the federal treasury on January 1, 1837, with the exception of $5,000,000, was to be deposited with the several states in proportion to their representation in Congress. The Western land boom was thus accelerated by three successive installments of $28,000,000 in all, paid to the states and never returned. Most of this was wastefully squandered. A fourth installment on account of the crisis of 1837 was postponed and never paid. It is safe to say that, had John Marshall lived, this policy could not have been carried out. His death had permitted Jackson to appoint Roger B. Taney as Chief Justice, and four other Supreme Court judges were also appointed by Jackson. The policy of the Court now changed towards upholding states rights and state banking laws. See Brisco *vs.* the Bank of Kentucky on the question of the issue of bills on state credit conflicting with Craig *vs.* the State of Missouri, an earlier decision.

Review, which Poe had so much counted on, suspended until October, 1837. It was all but impossible to get cash for articles or stories of any kind. Poe haunted the sanctums of various editors. His work on the *Messenger* was so well known as to get him a courteous reception, but the interviews all ended in an exchange of amenities and no promise of work. Poe's attacks on various contemporaries, especially Fay, were now quietly remembered against him; Paulding was preparing to leave New York for Washington; and Anthon, although he remained cordial, was, at best, only a minor prop. The sledding was undoubtedly hard and might have ended in a smash had it not been for the maintaining strength of Mrs. Clemm, who, despite the high cost of living, now once more undertook to provide food and shelter by the expedient of taking in boarders. Sometime during the Spring of 1837 [501] the family moved to an old frame house at 113½ Carmine Street, situated near St. John's Church on the west side of the street above Varick. The house was a dingy structure with a high-pitched roof topped by a single brick chimney. There were seven shuttered windows that stared uncompromisingly at the front, and a flat Georgian doorway at one end, approached by a front stoop with wrought-iron railings. The rooms were more than ample for the little family circle to which Mrs. Clemm perforce added two or three boarders. William Gowans now accompanied the Poes from Sixth Avenue to the new residence. He boarded with them for a long time and has left us an intimate picture of his friends at this period:

> For eight months or more one house contained us, as one table fed! During that time I saw much of him [Poe], and had an opportunity of conversing with him often, and I must say, that I never saw him the least affected by liquor, nor ever descend to any known vice, while he was one of the most courteous, gentlemanly, and intelligent companions I have met with during my journeyings and haltings through divers divisions of the globe; besides, he had an extra inducement to be a good man as well as a good husband, for he had a wife of matchless beauty and loveliness; her eye could match that of any *houri,* and her face defy the genius of a Canova to imitate; a temper and disposition of surpassing sweetness; besides, she seemed as much devoted to him as a young mother is to her first-born. . . . Poe had a remarkably pleasing and prepossessing countenance, which the ladies would call decidedly handsome.

Mr. Gowans has been called "the wealthy and eccentric bibliopolist" who lived with the Poes, so some allowance must be made for the contemporary exuberance of his style. Undoubtedly, though, the family circle was pleasing and Virginia unusual. The description of her "houri eyes" brings up the liquid and glittering glances of one already afflicted with tuberculosis. Evidently she was more womanly and mature by now, and very fond of Poe. There still remains the tradition of the

---

[501] Poe wrote to Anthon from Carmine Street on May 27, 1837.

The Philadelphia Markets and the Horns of Plenty

THE

CONCHOLOGIST'S FIRST BOOK:

OR,

A SYSTEM

OF

TESTACEOUS MALACOLOGY,

Arranged expressly for the use of Schools,

IN WHICH

THE ANIMALS, ACCORDING TO CUVIER, ARE GIVEN WITH THE SHELLS,

A GREAT NUMBER OF NEW SPECIES ADDED,

AND THE WHOLE BROUGHT UP, AS ACCURATELY AS POSSIBLE, TO THE PRESENT CONDITION OF THE SCIENCE.

BY EDGAR A. POE.

WITH ILLUSTRATIONS OF TWO HUNDRED AND FIFTEEN SHELLS, PRESENTING A CORRECT TYPE OF EACH GENUS.

PHILADELPHIA :

PUBLISHED FOR THE AUTHOR, BY

HASWELL, BARRINGTON, AND HASWELL,

AND FOR SALE BY THE PRINCIPAL BOOKSELLERS IN THE UNITED STATES.

1839.

The Conchologist's First Book: or, A System of Testaceous Malacology

Philadelphia, 1839

EDGAR ALLAN POE's fifth published volume

A piece of hack work characteristic of American publishing of the era to which Poe lent his name as editor

Courtesy of a New York Collector

Philadelphia in the 1840's

From an old print
Courtesy of the Pennsylvania Historical Society

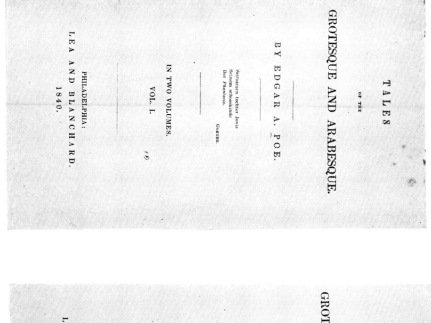

Title Pages of *Tales of the Grotesque and Arabesque*
Philadelphia, December, 1839
Edgar Allan Poe's sixth published book (2 *volumes*)

Poe's Residence at 113½ Carmine Street,
New York City, in 1837

From a sketch

girl calling to her husband from the upstairs windows of the Carmine Street house, and of their walks together at twilight among the tombs in St. John's graveyard nearby.

Certainly, Mr. Gowans was a good friend. On March 30, 1837, the booksellers of New York gave a dinner at the *City Hotel* to which various literary figures and some well-known artists were invited. Among them were Washington Irving, William Cullen Bryant, James K. Paulding, Fitz-Greene Halleck, and Chancellor Kent; the artists were Henry Inman and Trumbull. Gowans invited Poe. The affair was rather a brilliant one and marked the first appearance of the young Southern critic and poet among the Knickerbockers. No doubt he took care to improve the opportunities of the occasion.[502]

The only other record of Poe about this time, aside from his personal correspondence with Professor Anthon and others, shows that during the Winter of 1837, which was a peculiarly severe one, Poe called at the Northern Dispensary, still located at Waverley Place and Christopher Street, to obtain medicine for a severe cold. This was probably when on his way home to lodgings at Sixth Avenue and Waverley Place. An interesting fact about this isolated record is that Dr. Valentine Mott and Mrs. Shew were both on duty at the Northern Dispensary in 1837, and that Poe may then have met, for the first time, the two persons with whom he was to be closely associated some years later.

From an artistic standpoint, the young critic's release from the *Southern Literary Messenger* was fortunate. As usual, when all his time and energy was not consumed by journalism and correspondence, his creative capacity came to the fore. Poe found almost no work in New York and so turned his attention again to his stories.

The year 1837-38 marks the beginning of a second creative period; the first having come to an end two years before in Baltimore. At Carmine Street he finished *Arthur Gordon Pym* and saw the first printing of *Siope*, or *Silence—A Fable*, taken all in all, as a pure work of art, his most majestic contribution to prose. Here, more than ever, he now began to realize the truth of the lines he had written seven years before in *Al Aaraaf*:

> Ours is a world of words: Quiet we call
> 'Silence'—which is the merest word of all.

Siope was first published in the Fall in the *Baltimore Book,* edited by W. H. Carpenter and T. S. Arthur, Poe's old friend of the *Baltimore Saturday Visiter,* but it bears the marks of having been under way for

---

[502] This dinner, in a certain way, marked the end of the ascendancy of the "Knickerbocker Writers." The newer *literati* and the stars of the new journalism were about to appear. Lowell, Longfellow and others were just on the horizon. The men at the dinner were members of a literary generation that preceded Poe in reputation.

some time before the move to New York. In June, 1837, the *American Monthly Magazine* published a tale by Poe called *Von Jung, the Mystific,* that belongs to his stories of the grotesque. It and *Siope* mark the continuation of his interest in the psychological and the morbidly mystical. *Siope* was presented, "in the manner of the psychological autobiographists." There is a trace of Coleridgian and German metaphysics in its manner, and a morbid "spiritualism" in both the new stories which suited the trend of the times. Transcendentalism and spiritualism were already in the air. To these Poe added his own gruesome touch.

About the young dreamer who, perforce, whiled away most of his idle time on his manuscripts at 113½ Carmine Street in the Summer of 1837, there was certainly something morbid. It was true that ever since the furor for Gothic romances the public's thirst for horror had always been acute. Such tales as *Frankenstein* and the like, and some of the German offerings, although they contained spinal thrills, were, when all is considered, at best simply shivers *à la mode,* and at worst purely literary. Their wax-work characters never came to life, and their corpses were only conveniently dead. But in the stories which Poe had now begun to write, the atmosphere was, in reality, charged. Both his physical and psychic horrors seemed to be the transcripts of actual suffering, terror and torment. The breeze which blew through his pages carried the awful reek of charnels. His murders were grisly, and his corpses seethed. It was a new and a genuine note. No one, not even Coleridge, had so successfully exploited the psychology of fear. Coleridge always left off where beauty refused to follow; with Poe in the realm of prose, there were no confines to horror whatsoever, and he was artistically successful in overstepping the former frontiers. Only some of the drawings of Leonardo da Vinci approached the delineation of the emotions and the details which he describes. With Leonardo the sketches were records made with an almost divine curiosity; they were to him simply part of the data of life, which had a horrible side. With Poe it was different. He seemed at times to be almost in love with the fearsome, and to have taken a strange pleasure in its delineation. The very fact that he was so successful in portraying it implies a satisfaction in imagining the causes of the emotion of fear, which only a morbid cast in his character could account for. Poe was not generally sadistic, but he was at times curiously close to the edge of the gulf into which the genial Marquis so notably plunged. After a day spent in piling up horrors and cannibal feastings in the chapters of *A. Gordon Pym,* one can easily imagine him going for a walk with the pallid Virginia amid the graves of old St. John's. There was, to him, an inevitable attraction in such places. His mind must have traveled back frequently to Shockoe Cemetery, or to the ancient epitaphs copied over and over upon the slates of the schoolboy at Irvine. There, on the graves of the Allan relatives, a carven ship bellied its stone sails to an eternal breeze from the realms of nowhere. In such spiritual monsoons, while he sensed the odor of corpses and asphodels, he widened his sensitive nostrils. The emblem of his time, whose sentiments were lugubrious, was a weeping willow tree. To his own and other generations it was left to him to whisper the hair-lifting secrets *underneath* the roots. Here he was dealing, as most great artists do, with an eternal theme.

Amid Poe's various orchestral fugues and lyric songs composed upon the theme of fear, *The Narrative of Arthur Gordon Pym* may be regarded as a somewhat fumbling prelude to the masterpieces which were to follow. Both Captain Marryat and Cooper had set the pace for sea stories. The public at that time was greatly interested in an expedition, under government auspices, that was then fitting out for the Antarctic, chiefly fathered by one J. N. Reynolds, with whom Poe was probably personally acquainted.[503] This was the sea of mystery of the *Ancient Mariner,* and Poe was strangely fascinated by what might lie beyond its wall of ice. He was also well acquainted with Morrell's *Narrative of Four Voyages to the South Sea and the Pacific,* and with *The Mutiny of the Bounty,* lately issued by Harpers, which may have raised his hopes of being able to sell to them his own story along somewhat the same lines. Irving's *Astoria* was also familiar to Poe, and he was reviewing Stephens' *Travels in Arabia Petræa.* These, together with his own avidity for horrors, amply satisfied by reading which reeked with blood-curdling murders, mutiny, and shipwreck, constituted his sources for his fourth book and first volume of prose that was announced in May and issued by Harper and Brothers in July, 1838. It was described by the publisher as follows:

The Narrative of Arthur Gordon Pym, of Nantucket; comprising the Details of a Mutiny and Atrocious Butchery on board the American Brig Grampus, on her Way to the South Seas—with an Account of the Recapture of the Vessel by the Survivors; their Shipwreck, and subsequent Horrible Sufferings from Famine; their Deliverance by means of the British Schooner Jane Gray; the brief Cruise of this latter Vessel in the Antarctic Ocean, her Capture, and the Massacre of her Crew among a Group of Islands in the 84th Parallel of Southern Latitude; together with the incredible Adventures and Discoveries still further South, to which that distressing Calamity gave rise. 12 mo., pp. 198. New York: Harper and Brothers, 1838.

In this story, the author is at his best at the first and last of the narrative. The scene is supposed to open in Nantucket, but, as in reality

[503] Although Poe's association with J. N. Reynolds is obscure, the personality of the man and the episodes which he related to Poe must have made an undying impression, for, sixteen years later, Poe cried out to him continually during the night he was dying. This tends to strengthen the idea that the material and associations of *A. Gordon Pym* go much deeper in Poe's nature than has hitherto been suggested. See the latter part of Chapter XXVII.

Poe knew little about the locality which Melville so vividly presents in *Moby Dick,* he gives us some autobiographical details from his early life in Richmond.[504]   The yacht which the two friends own, at the commencement of the story, goes back to the boat in which Poe and Ebenezer Burling early adventured together upon the James.   Even the name of an early Richmond schoolmaster, Ricketts, is recalled, together with some reference to schooldays "on the hill" as part of Richmond was called in Poe's day.   The final escape of the two friends on shipboard is an imaginative rendering of Poe's flight with Burling from Richmond in March, 1827.   "Pym's" testy old grandfather with the umbrella is too close a portrait of John Allan to be mistaken.   The main and central part of the story is largely a compilation of the mutinies, murders, and the sufferings of shipwrecked mariners taken sometimes almost *verbatim* from the literary sources mentioned.   The curious emphasis upon cannibalism is perhaps psychic.   Towards the last of the story, as the hero moves into the Antarctic realms of mystery, the author's better imagination again takes full sway, and the effects are at times sublime, recalling some of the descriptions in *The Ancient Mariner.*   The Island of Tsalal is especially well imagined.   Poe took the strange characters, which he describes upon the walls of the caves, from the descriptions of the hieroglyphs in the caverns of Mt. Sinai found in Stephens' *Arabia Petræa.*   The note on the hieroglyphs, at the end of the story, is the first instance of Poe's interest in cipher, and the device of the brief preface, which purports to be written by "Pym"—who, however, mentions Poe—has about it all the machinery of the hoax in which the real author so delighted.   J. K. Paulding was instrumental in getting Harpers to accept the story, which had a very small success.   It was reviewed rather extensively in the United States and was republished by Wiley & Putnam in England,[505] in which country the rural readers are said to have been taken in.   From Harpers, Poe received very little, and from the English publishers, as the custom then was, nothing at all.

One of the few pieces of work which have definitely been traced as Poe's, during this first New York sojourn, is a review of Stephens' *Arabia Petræa* which appeared in Dr. Hawks' *New York Review* for October, 1837.   As Poe's procedure in this review was peculiarly characteristic, it is worth while to consider it here as a type of his method

---

[504] Poe's description, however, was not superficial as this letter shows: Carter to Poe, Cambridge, Massachusetts, June 19, 1843. " . . . Within a week I have read for the first time, *Pym's Narrative.* I lent it to a friend, . . . a brother of Dr. O. W. Holmes, yet he is so completely deceived by the minute accuracy of some of the details, the remarks about the statements of the press, the names of people at New Bedford, etc., that though an intelligent and shrewd man he will not be persuaded that it is a fictitious work," etc.

[505] Wiley & Putnam, London, two printings, 1838, 1841.   These editions were presumably authorized. A pirated edition appeared, London, 1844.

in such work. Poe has been accused of making a parade of classical and scientific learning which he did not possess. In certain respects the accusation is true; on the other hand, it should be said that he was unusually conscientious about his reviews and went to no little trouble to look up authorities and to correspond with living scholars who might aid him in throwing light on the matter in hand. *Arabia Petræa* was a peculiarly erudite work, a record of travels in a land upon which, even now, modern archeology is only beginning to lift a doubtful curtain. It took the reader into the waste and desert places of a vanished civilization amid the doubtful shadows of pedantic classical, and Biblical learning. Poe's own argument from a religious standpoint was orthodox enough to satisfy the clergyman in whose magazine the review appeared. The rest of his material was made up by extract and paraphrase from the book itself, aided by some comments culled from a work on prophecy then recently published by a Dr. Keith. The main attempt at criticism turned on the exact meaning of two verses from the Bible, *Isaiah* 34.10, and *Ezekiel* 35.7, for an interpretation of which Poe wrote to his friend Professor Anthon, who replied [506] giving a careful rendering from the original Hebrew that Poe printed *verbatim*. No credit was given to Anthon, and Poe used the material as his own on several subsequent occasions. The impression given was that Poe knew Hebrew; the result was a rather erudite review. As it was *unsigned,* and was later attributed to Secretary Case, much of the criticism leveled against Poe in this instance is without force. His re-use of Anthon's material was, however, typical.

Of the intimacies of the inhabitants of 113½ Carmine Street between the Spring of 1837 and Midsummer, 1838, less is known than of almost any other epoch in their careers. For Poe, owing to the financial stress of the day, it was largely an era of marking time. The grand magazine scheme had to be postponed, but it was still carefully cherished. Gowans had introduced the Poes to James Pedder and his family. Pedder was an Englishman, a writer of juvenile stories, and a man of some charm. In 1838, he went to Philadelphia to edit the *Farmer's Cabinet* which he continued successfully until 1850. Pedder's removal to Philadelphia undoubtedly influenced Poe to turn his eyes in that direction. New York seemed to offer nothing. The Winter of 1838 was a bitter and terrible one. Combined with the money stringency, the suffering had been intense. Despite the efforts of Mrs. Clemm, the young author once more found himself in debt. He appears to have written to his friend Kennedy to obtain help in his always "temporary difficulties," but Mr. Kennedy was in straits himself and this time could do

---

[506] Anthon to Poe, New York, June 1, 1837.

nothing.[507] It is probable that, by the Summer of 1838, Poe and Mrs. Clemm were no longer able to meet the rent. A move was imperative.

During the eighteen months or so which the family had passed in New York in 1837-38, it is likely that Poe and Virginia, with Mrs. Clemm, were sometimes seen at old St. Stephen's where the Reverend Dr. Hawks of North Carolina held forth, or perhaps St. John's, near the Carmine Street house, occasionally received more than graveyard visits. There must also have been Sunday walks on the Battery and the promenade of old Castle Garden where the band played. Bowling Green, past the genteel boarding houses opposite the *Adelphi House,* then in all its regal splendor, was a favorite place for a stroll. On the roof of the New York Exchange fronting Wall Street—"built of white Westchester marble with four classic columns on the front"—one could watch the semaphore telegraph signaling to the vessels at Sandy Hook. For one shilling, the round trip on the Jersey City Ferry could be made on summer evenings from the foot of Cedar and Cortlandt Streets, and, from the Fulton Street slip, one could take the boat up the East River past Hell Gate to Prince's Linnæan Garden at Flushing—

> The proprietor exerts himself to obtain all native productions as well as interesting exotics. The village is small but pleasant. The garden of Mr. Prince will supply strangers of taste and science with rare seeds, flowers and trees, and has done much to introduce beautiful varieties into this country . . . the 4 hothouses contain about 20,000 plants in pots; and the garden covers at [*least*] 30 acres.

From passages in *The Landscape Garden* it seems highly probable that a certain traveler of decided taste, and a considerable pretension to science, visited Mr. Prince's Linnæan Gardens with a pale little girl on his arm.

Perhaps the good Mr. Gowans or other friends sometimes supplied theater tickets. These were the days when Edwin Forrest had just returned from his first English tour, and was going about playing Bulwer-Lytton's *Lady of Lyons* to ecstatic audiences. He was later on to supply America with its first great divorce trial. Joseph Burke, a young Irish lad of twelve years, was appearing in *Norval,* a Scottish pastoral drama, in which for a reason impenetrable to this generation, the appearance of an adolescent Highland shepherd in kilts, strutting and mouthing the lines:

> My name is Norval: on the Grampian hills
> My father feeds his flocks; a frugal swain . . .

caused old gentlemen in black stocks to clear their throats and delicate young ladies to weep. Maria Tree was singing *Home, Sweet Home!*

---

[507] See Poe to Brooks, Philadelphia, September 4, 1838. The name of the "friend" is left blank but understood between them.

from John Howard Payne's opera of *Clari,* and making the song immortal. *The Old Oaken Bucket* was roared stridently by all the good
fellows in beaver hats who could crowd themselves into the bar of the
old *Broadway National House.* G. P. Morris had just written *Woodman, Spare that Tree,* and *Zophiel, or The Bride of Seven* was being
memorized in the schools. Progress was just getting under way; the
godless, scandalous, candle-lit Eighteenth Century was patronizingly referred to as "the former age"; while the new gas footlights were soon
to be turned up for Thackeray, Longfellow, "purety," gentility—and
the ruthless assault upon Mexico. Tables and telegraph instruments
were both about to rap messages.

In the Summer of 1838, when hoopskirts were beginning to drive out
flounced petticoats, and some gentlemen were commencing to be cir-
cumspect about after-dinner drinking, Poe somehow or other borrowed
enough money to join his friend Pedder in the Quaker City. Mrs.
Clemm closed the house on Carmine Street and followed with Virginia.
Before the end of August, the whole family were boarding in Philadelphia. Prospects were again beginning to brighten. It even looked for
a time as if the great national magazine might soon be got under way.
The field was ripe, and a prospectus of it was forever running in the
head of its "editor."

CHAPTER NINETEEN

IN the Summer of 1838, probably toward the end of August, Poe and his little family journeyed to Philadelphia and took up their residence with James Pedder in a boarding house that was kept by the Pedder sisters on Twelfth Street, a little above Mulberry (Arch).[508]

Pedder, the Englishman previously mentioned, had already established for himself magazine connections in Philadelphia, and it may have been through his advice and probably his assistance that Poe had been induced to change his residence. The boarding house was evidently a temporary arrangement until Poe could obtain employment and settle himself some place else. Long unsuccess in New York had left him poor again. The money for the move had been borrowed, and there is some evidence that, before leaving New York, Mrs. Clemm had again been forced to beg and find loans where she could. A gentleman by the name of Bayard had been the victim this time, apparently unknown to Poe. The move was by no means ill-advised as the town chosen for the new home was the center of journalistic activity in the United States. Poe was simply taking his wares to the most promising market.

A few weeks after his arrival in the city that was to be his home for the next six years, Poe and his family moved from the Twelfth Street boarding house to another boarding establishment at Fourth and Arch (then Mulberry).[509] The move "down town," nearer to the district where the publishers' offices and printers' shops were then located, would seem to indicate that, at an early date after his arrival in Philadelphia, Poe had already found literary employment. *Tales of the Grotesque and Arabesque* were partly prepared at this Arch Street boarding house, to which Lowell came later, in 1845, bringing his bride. Mrs. Lowell wrote a letter from there during her honeymoon days and described the

---

[508] The locations of Poe's places of abode, offices of magazines, and the addresses of persons with whom he was intimately acquainted in Philadelphia have been arrived at by a careful comparison of his own correspondence and letters about him, consultation of contemporary city directories, magazine and newspaper headings, and the city records dealing with the transfer of real estate and street and lot numbers. Wherever possible both the old and new street numerals are given. It has thus been possible to reconstruct Poe's Philadelphia haunts fairly accurately. The sojourn of Poe with the Pedders rests on the recollections of the Pedder sisters to whom Poe afterward presented some of his manuscripts.

[509] Poe was known to have been at this house till the beginning of September, 1838. See Poe to N. C. Brooks, Philadelphia, September 4, 1838. "I am just leaving Arch Street for a small house," etc.

house as being then 127 Arch Street, at the northeast corner of Fourth
and Arch, kept by Mrs. Parker, a Quakeress. It was clean and neat
with a genteel reputation, the upper rooms in the rear being light and
airy with white curtains and green trimmings. The Poes remained there
until the beginning of September, 1838.[510]

At the end of the 1830's, Philadelphia was the second city of the
Union, surpassed in population by New York City alone. The building
of the Erie Canal, the access of population due to the first strong inset
of the tide of immigration, and the trade of the then flourishing American merchant marine had given New York the lead some decades before; but it was by no means an overwhelming one, and, as Philadelphia
was also a great seaport and was developing its hinterland by both railways and canals, there was then no certainty that the lead of Manhattan was to be permanent.[511]

It was just about the turn of the tide in the race between those communities that depended upon their natural native increase for growth
and those which were to grow by foreign accretion. Philadelphia belonged predominantly to the former class. It was, and it continued to
be for many years, a peculiarly American city, with a culture surpassed
by no other town on the continent. Its rapid commercial development
and the vast changes wrought by industrialism in Pennsylvania have
tended to obscure the city's intellectual and political importance in the
past. Nevertheless, for those who desire to study a flowering of intellectual and literary activity, peculiarly American in its nature, it is to
Philadelphia as well as to Boston that one must turn.

Indeed, it was the peculiarly native fervor of the Philadelphia intel-
lectuals, the too often provincial nature of their development, which
has caused them to be forgotten; while the New Englanders, who concerned themselves with the movements of world literature and continued in control of a national press, have continued to be more notably

---

[510] From a letter of the first Mrs. James Russell Lowell, written during her honeymoon about the end of May, 1845. The character of Poe's residences is given carefully
here as it indicates his mode of life, financial and social conditions.

[511] The author is greatly in the debt of Francis Rawle, Esq., President of the Pennsylvania Historical Association, for free access to the library, catalogues, collections of
prints, paintings, and the invaluable original manuscripts and literary correspondence
in its possession. The preparation of Poe's contemporary Philadelphia background
ranged over a wide field of material. Some of the more accessible references are:
Oberholtzer, E. P., *The Literary History of Philadelphia,* Geo. W. Jacobs & Co.,
Publishers; the same, *Poe's Philadelphia Homes;* Smyth, A. H., *The Philadelphia
Magazines and their Contributors,* Philadelphia, Robert M. Lindsey, 1892; files of
Burton's, Graham's, Godey's, and other magazines to which Poe contributed; files of
contemporary newspapers. Descriptions of persons and places are taken from contemporary engravings, paintings, and other illustrations. Maps, almanacs, book catalogues, time tables, directories, first editions of Poe and other authors, and files of
correspondence of literary and other persons connected with Poe directly, or with his
environment, have been consulted.

remembered. To those who are interested, however, in the literary, periodical, and journalistic output which most generally affected the contemporary American scene from the latter part of the Eighteenth Century well up until the middle of the Nineteenth, Philadelphia is all-important.

It was no mere boyish adventure which drew Benjamin Franklin from his brother's printing establishment in Boston to the Quaker City, even as early as 1723. It was merely an early exercise of his preëminent sagaciousness, for even at that time Philadelphia was the great publishing center of the Colonies.[512] From its presses issued a flood of religious and political tracts, important newspapers, and the immortal sayings of "Poor Richard" himself. In Philadelphia appeared the first American editions of Shakespeare and Milton, *Pamela,* and *The Vicar of Wakefield,* and, in 1782, the first English Bible printed in the United States. In 1764 the first American religious journal had appeared in that city, and the record was continued well into the next century which saw the founding there, in 1802, of the *Juvenile Magazine;* the first native daily newspaper, the *American Daily Advertiser;* the first penny paper, the *Cent,* in 1830; the first monthly magazine in the country, and a mathematical journal. It was in Philadelphia, too, that there first appeared that outstanding feature of modern American journalism, the illustrated comic. The importance of the place as a center for political publication during and after the Revolution needs no comment. It was there that the Continental Congress sat and the Constitutional Convention convened. The ensuing ten years as the national capital continued to lend it a peculiar importance with a marked effect upon the circulation of its schoolbooks and newspapers.[513] All of this publishing activity, naturally enough, did not go on without a cultural and literary background.

Some of the early efforts of the local literary lights are to be found embalmed in the pages of the *Columbian Magazine,* which issued during the last two decades of the Eighteenth Century. These for the most part partook of the classical inanities of the period. Various gentlemen contributed translations, in couplets, from the Latin poets, or contented themselves with putting nursery jingles into Latin that attempted to

---

[512] The important rôle which mechanical advances in printing have played in the spread of intellectual enlightenment has seldom been fully stressed. The mission of Franklin to England, at the behest of Governor Keith of Pennsylvania, to provide the best of type and presses then obtainable, immediately placed Philadelphia a century ahead of the other colonies in publishing. Seventeenth century presses continued to be used elsewhere in America well up into Revolutionary times. The lead was long maintained in Philadelphia, where, in 1819, the art of lithography was introduced into the United States in the pages of the *Analectic Magazine.* Revolution in illustration followed.

[513] Poe's own early schoolbooks had been printed there. See note 98, page 54.

render the exact tang of "hot butter blue beans" into the idiom of Cicero, with consequent learned controversies. The only excursions into the realms of light were confined to some local descriptions and political articles not without merit but of a secondary order. The *Columbian* upon its demise was succeeded by the *Analectic* which condescended, though in a restrained manner, to deal with the existing world. There was also later the *North American Quarterly* which attempted, not without some success, to fulfill the function on this side of the water of the English reviews of the early Nineteenth Century. It dragged on a meritorious but somewhat dull life for some time.[514]

The comparative failure of the more pretentious literary efforts of Philadelphians, to gain and maintain a national or international reputation, may largely be set down to the nature of the social matrix in which they were fixed.[515] This did not apply so strongly to the journalistic and publishing groups that escaped the inherently warping effects of those who wrote from the background of Philadelphia bluestocking society, priding itself on exclusiveness, an exclusiveness which forgot that sequestration worked both ways.

The social group of *littérateurs* gathered most notably about Dr. Wistar who resided in a house at the southwest corner of Fourth and Locust Streets, long famous for its hospitality and the notables who gathered there. These gatherings indeed became traditional, and even after the death of the good doctor were carried on formally as "Wistar Parties." A picture of their founder appeared on the card of invitation, and was referred to as late as 1855 by Thackeray, as the "hospitable pig-tailed shade." Washington Irving, who occasionally visited his Quaker neighbors, complained of suffering, at Philadelphia literary gatherings and tea parties, "from an artillery of glances from long rows of young ladies."

There were, however, several groups where real discussion went on, and a world of ideas was developed and proposed which never wholly succeeded in getting born. It was an interesting world for all that, and at the time a real one; one which later surprised and delighted Thackeray who wrote home to his wife, "Do you know there are 500,000 people in

---

[514] Poe had undoubtedly pored over the pages of these and similar publications in Richmond at *Ellis & Allan,* who took subscriptions for such periodicals. His curious tendency to the semi-classical and the pedantic is largely to be explained by a reference to the magazine literature of his boyhood. The background of American writers of the '40's to the '60's cannot be understood without a familiarity with the early nineteenth century magazines and newspapers upon which they were raised. Illustrations are often the primary source of literary inspirations. Philadelphia provided the best of these—see note 512.

[515] This does not apply to the political pamphlets and tracts. It must be remembered that the bulk of the Revolutionary doctrines, the only part of American literature that gained the ear of the world in the Eighteenth Century, was *printed* in Philadelphia where the best brains of the Colonies gathered.

Philadelphia? I dare say you had no idea thereof, and smile at the thought of there being a *monde* here and at Boston and New York." Mr. Thackeray was then being received with enthusiastic and substantial appreciation, so his wife might well smile. Yet there was a *monde* sure enough. The "Carey Vespers" succeeded the "Wistar Parties" but sounded a knell, the echoes of which can be heard even to-day by those who live South of Market.

Yet it was Philadelphia that produced the first genuine American literary figure, the curious novelist Charles Brockden Brown, whose triple name has set the style for so many thrice-named and third-rate American authors. About Brown there is an undoubted air of minor genius. It was his novels which in reality reproduced the American scene rather than the later, romantic and naïve frontier stories of Cooper, whose realities are confined largely to the sea. The neglected story of Charles Brockden Brown is one of the most interesting in American literature. Both his life story and his work had engaged the attention of Poe as early as Richmond boyhood days.[516]

By 1830, the first efflorescence of early nineteenth century magazine activity had pretty well worked itself out in Philadelphia and a new generation of editors, writers, and publishers had lately appeared on the scene. Graham, Burton, Godey, the Petersons, and many others were already active in the magazine world. The *Saturday Evening Post* had been begun in Franklin's old print shop, and, since March, 1833, John Greenleaf Whittier had been editing the *Pennsylvania Freeman* at 31 North Fifth Street.

The chief idea of the new journalism was the exploitation on a larger scale than ever before of the now literate middle classes and a deliberate appeal to the feminine reader, with all the moralistic, democratic, and namby-pamby tendencies which the attempt and the age implied.[517]

The first transition from the more robust, though stuffier, classically-minded literature of the old school was noticeable in the sudden popularity of the Parlor Annuals and Ladies' Gift Books which, from about 1825 on, began to roll off the press in Philadelphia. The first of these had been imported from England, but the large success of the *Atlantic Souvenir,* the *Bijou,* and later comers attracted a host of others to the field. Tennyson had found them in England a fertile field in which to sow lyrics, and Poe, as we have seen, had already "appeared." The realm of the "Parlor" was soon invaded more energetically by a host of ladies' and gentlemen's magazines.

---

[516] Poe's early fascination for Brown may perhaps be explained by a remark which Brown made about his own work: His books he said had, "great efficacy in beguiling his body of its pains and thoughts of their melancholy; in relieving the head and heart of their aches."

[517] The announcements and editorials of the magazines of the era make their publishing philosophy sufficiently clear.

By the time of Poe's arrival in Philadelphia in 1838, *Godey's* Magazine or *Lady's Book, Graham's Casket, Burton's Gentleman's Magazine,* the *United States Military Gazette, Alexander's Weekly Messenger,* and a small host of others, all issued from the Quaker City, together with a crop of annuals and several flourishing newspapers. The town had attracted to it many editors of great ability from other places, chief among whom was Louis A. Godey, the editor of the *Book* which bore his name, the *Ladies' Home Journal* of its time. He had associated with him Mrs. Sarah J. Hale—author of *Mary Had a Little Lamb*— and formerly editress of a Boston journal,[518] and Louis M'Michael. It was Mr. Godey who first successfully reached the audience of American womanhood. To this audience, he and his staff catered most deliberately with the peculiarly pure and pretty sentimentality of the early American-Victorian scene.

The democratic theory of universal literacy was already beginning to provide an audience on a scale hitherto undreamed of. It was an audience of which Poe was one of the first to become aware, and it was composed of both men and women of all classes. But in Poe's case, there was a peculiar situation. Writers had hitherto, for the most part, addressed themselves perforce to those who could read. But those who could read had constituted an exclusive intellectual minority necessarily tinged with classic ideals and aristocratic convictions. The generation at the end of the '30's in the United States was the first to come to maturity under the public school system. The situation was now changed and Poe was aware of it. He desired to become generally known to this uneducated but reading generation, yet he continued to address them as if they were all capable of desiring serious literature, universally thoughtful, hopeful of being cleverly amused, and interested in genuine criticism. In this he was mistaken. Poe's commercial hypotheses for a great magazine were well laid, but his own unadulterated message was

---

[518] Mrs. Sarah J. Hale published a pamphlet of child's verses, Dr. Lowell Nason of Boston, publisher, 1830. It is now exceedingly rare and contains some of the best known children's lyrics in the language.

> "Mary had a little lamb,
> Its fleece was white as snow,"

and—

> "If ever I see on bush or tree
> Young birds in a pretty nest,
> I must not in my play
> Steal the young birds away
> To grieve their mother's breast."

Mrs. Hale had known of Poe since 1827, and had written a letter to her son, at West Point in 1830, inquiring about him. This partly explains Poe's frequent appearance in *Godey's* where Mrs. Hale held sway for years with telling effect on the American feminine world.

far over the heads of his audience. It was only when it was controlled
and altered by the influence of his proprietors and boss editors that it
found a large contemporary reception. Yet it was this very process of
adulteration and artistic cheapening that his literary ideals and self-
confident ego could never stomach.

For such reasons, and the philosophy that lay behind them, Poe was
successful in increasing the circulation of the *Messenger, Burton's,* and
Graham's, and for the same reasons, coupled with his own infirmities,
he forever failed in launching any successful magazine of his own. For
literature and posterity the outcome has been fortunate. Neither Poe
nor his successive employers fully realized the anomaly inherent in the
facts, and Israfel continued, inadvertently, to address himself to an
audience élite enough to be capable of remembering and cherishing what
was valuable.[519]

All else in his work, all that was purely contemporary, has suffered
the inevitable canker of ruthless time. It is a strange paradox, for the
very quality which has preserved him to fame was fatal to the financial and physical prospects of the man. He was doomed forever to
struggle with a hopeless and degrading poverty.

Other writers of the age avoided poverty by various expedients:
Longfellow was a professor, Emerson was a minister, Holmes was a
doctor, Hawthorne found refuge in a minor government employ that
Poe tried to obtain in vain; Lowell escaped by several routes. Poe
alone of his generation, unable to long cope with the world in any
practical way, remained the poet, the dreamer, and the artist, dependent
solely upon the motion of his pen from left to right for a precarious
living. He was the prime example in his generation in America of the
detached literary type, the traditional starving poet.[520] There was no
system of patronage, no benevolent government, no aristocracy; and
he starved. For this, his practical countrymen have from time to time
pointed the finger of scorn. There are even now many school texts
which hold Poe up as a genius but a horrible moral example. Thus
mediocrity is confirmed in its mistrust of the unusual, and dullness comforted by respectability.

The galaxy of publications already noticed as appearing in Philadelphia in 1838-39 were not without the ample aid of the crafts which pro-

---

[519] George R. Graham, however, afterwards commented on this in his defense of Poe.
Graham's Magazine, 1850:
"The character of Poe's mind was of such an order as not to be very widely in demand. The class of educated mind which he could readily and profitably reach was
small—the channels through which he could do so at all were few . . ." etc. Mr.
Graham was the most successful magazine editor of his era and deserves respectful
attention in his estimate of Poe.
[520] It is characteristic of the age that the poet Longfellow, who embodied the genius
of mediocrity, received a bust in Westminster Abbey while Poe's obscure grave in
Baltimore was sown with thistles.

duced them. Thither had flocked artists, able and humdrum illustrators, printers, engravers, lithographers, designers, and binders. The town was full of their shops and haunts; and in these places and among their coteries Poe spent much of his time.

Printing and publishing was thus taking on many of its modern aspects. The printing was largely bad or mediocre, but in the field of illustrations, despite much execrable taste, there was considerable mechanical advance. Steel engraving, lithographing, and woodcuts were much in vogue. There was even an adventuring on the part of publishers into the domain of stenciled and lace perforated offerings of valentine-like aspect, tinsel trimmings, and ornamented hand stamps and decalcomanias.[521] An examination of *Godey's Lady's Book,* say for the year 1844, will not be without profit for those interested. The partly hand-colored fashion plates have a value of their own.[522]

Against the tawdry, the cheap, the pretty and the sentimentally moral illustrators, Poe struggled and resolutely set his face. It was one of the chief items of complaint against the periodicals of the day which he constantly reiterates. His own ideal was to employ only woodcuts, comparatively simple, and executed by competent artists. In his correspondence with Lowell the point is frequently stressed.[523] Such an item, although comparatively unimportant, yet gives an insight into the well-rounded artistic probity of the man. His own juvenile predilection for the pencil was not without result.[524] In this connection one more point must be noticed.

Stereotyping had now been in successful use in the United States for about ten years. The first largely successful application of the principle had been in *Harper's Family Library,* which dated from the early '30's.[525] Books could now be printed rapidly from plates; the chances of reduplication were enormously enhanced; and the output, in an age when all type was hand-set, was vastly increased and made cheaper.[512] It was a mechanical advance which directly affected the type of works in which Poe found himself engaged; *i.e.,* textbooks, the publication of collected works, and the printing of periodicals.

The old publishing firm of Carey, Lea & Carey, to whom Poe was

---

[521] Louis A. Godey was once described as a "decalcomaniac."

[522] It is not to be supposed that people actually appeared as the fashion plates of any period show them. The point is that the spirit of the times can be glimpsed in fashion plates, because that is the way people *desired* to appear.

[523] See also Poe's prospectus for the *Penn* and the *Stylus* and his contract with the artist, F. O. C. Darley.

[524] One of these portraits of Elmira was lately in the collection of C. H. Barney of Richmond, Va., direct from Mrs. S. E. Shelton. See page 119.

[525] A good example of this *Family Library* is *A description of Pitcairn's Island and its Inhabitants with an Authentic account of the Mutiny of the Ship Bounty,* J. Harper, New York, 82 Cliff St., 1832. Harper's stereotype edition. Poe's *Arthur Gordon Pym* had been made possible by cheap printing processes used by the Harpers.

known since Baltimore days, after undergoing the change of Lea & Carey, had an off-shoot in Lea & Blanchard.[526] Both firms were now briskly engaged in flooding the American market with reprints of Byron, Scott, and later of Dickens, upon which, under existing copyright laws, the matter of authors' royalties was a mere courtesy. With these firms and with the copyright situation, Poe was soon greatly interested.

For the rest, Philadelphia was a pleasant place to be. Living was cheap. The markets were not second even to those of Baltimore. Rents in town were reasonable, while the country about was verdantly fertile and contained some of the most satisfactory landscape in the eastern United States. The pastoral and romantic aspects of the Delaware, the Schuylkill and the Wissahickon valleys had already attracted the brush and pencil of various foreign artists as early as the Eighteenth Century. Over it all was the peculiarly tranquil and yet alluring legend of the peaceful experiments of William Penn.

The city itself was at that time (1838) composed almost exclusively of red brick dwellings with white stone trimmings and smooth marble stoops. The streets were paved with round cobbles, broken by flagstones at the crossings, and stone gutters down the center, but provided with broad brick pavements well shaded in all the residential and even the business districts. There were many walled gardens, churchyards, and open spaces, particularly Franklin Square with a then famous fountain, for the town prided itself on its water-supply, one of the finest in the world.

One of the peculiarities of Philadelphia was the faucet which had replaced the earlier pump before every house. From these every morning a gushing stream was turned over the sidewalks and streets. Housemaids flourished brooms, and even scrubbed the brick pavements with flat stones and sand, while the gleaming brass rails, door knockers and knobs were the remarked objects of their peculiar and inveterate attention. Water was dashed about freely. In the early mornings it ran down the central gutter in a veritable river, imparting a spotless air to the town, but endangering the apparel of Captain Marryat and other British travelers who insisted upon their customary morning constitutionals.

The plan of the town was then unusual, consisting, for the most part, of regularly numbered streets crossing each other at right angles, a

---

[526] Mathew Carey, an economist of considerable influence, was the "ancestor" of various Philadelphia publishing houses, in which the name "Carey" appears even now. He was a great high tariff man, also famous for his "standing Bible type" from which over two hundred thousand impressions were struck between 1804 and 1825. The forms stood till 1844. Carey was also influential in introducing Didot's stereotyping process into the United States. Carey, of Carey & Lea, was his son. Poe was much about the plant and dealt with the junior partner, Mr. Lea, in 1829 and the '30's, and corresponded with the firm. See Chapter XII, page 202.

scheme whose literal convenience has unfortunately spread over the rest of the country. The houses with their singularly regular and precise system of numbering bespoke the somewhat prim and staid nature of their owners by displaying their large unmistakable brass numerals with glittering pride. The whole impression of the place was one of comfortable and prosperous order. There was not wanting, however, a decided and peculiar charm to the scene.

The architecture still bore, predominantly, the cast of the Eighteenth Century and the Colonial, but it was, by now, largely and not inharmoniously mixed with the columns, façades, and the straight, brick fronts of the early Republic. The roofs, and the quaint angles of the forest of domestic chimneys lent a picturesque guise. There were many notable public buildings: the Mint, and the Pennsylvania Hospital, the simple but impressive Quaker Meeting House, and Christ Church in the manner of Sir Christopher Wren. With the aspect of all of these, Poe was to become particularly familiar; and with the shops, the old *United States Hotel,* and the Exchange.

The Post Office, a place of frequent resort for the whole town, was at Independence, then known as Congress, Hall. Here Poe called often for his own mail and that of the magazines with which he was connected. In 1838 there were two ordinary mails to New York and "down east" that closed at five A.M. and five P.M., and there was a daily mail south and west. The Post Office kept open from sunrise until eight P.M. but for only one hour on Sunday. Stamps were not used until about ten years later, nor envelopes,[527] and "gentlemen of reputation" could establish credit at the Post Office and settle their bills monthly.

One of the sights of Philadelphia was the office of the principal mail contractor, a little two-story building on the west side of Third Street, where the stages and expresses departed for all directions. The contractor was a well-known local character, one Jim Reeside, nicknamed "The Admiral," a tremendous man, with whose wife it was well for the editors of magazines to be friends. Mr. Reeside kept famous gray horses, and a huge dog which slept in front of the office on the brick pavement while the patrons of the United States mail awaited the end

---

[527] Poe's correspondence with Dr. Snodgrass and others in the latter '30's and early '40's is still carried on with folded foolscap paper and wafer seals, the postage being prepaid. Postage was often a serious item with Poe. The rates were high, averaging ɔ cents for a prospectus of the *Penn* or *Stylus,* for instance. Private "letter mail" companies attempted to compete with the government but were closed up by federal action. The American Letter Mail Co. of Philadelphia early used stamps. Poe once cautions a correspondent to use Harnden's Express instead of the Post Office on account of cheaper rates. See Poe to Lowell, February 4, 1843.

of his nap.   His repose was dangerous to disturb, and the world, for the most part, possessed itself in patience or went around.[528]

Poe's business in Philadelphia for the most part took him into the lower part of town, down the broad "S"-shaped sweep of the wide Dock Street, past the white pillared Merchants Exchange.   Here the newspaper, magazine, printers', and engravers' offices were located, about whose haunts on Front and Dock Streets he was frequently seen.   The river front was a mass of shipping whose masts and sails topped the flat roofs of blank-faced brick warehouses separated by narrow, stone-paved alleys.   Drays, Dearborn wagons, York carryalls, coaches, and trotting wagons rumbled past over the cobbles, laden with heavy bales of merchandise or sedate passengers, making a frightful din punctuated by the oaths of the drivers and the incessant cracking of long whips.

Ladies from the fashionable districts came shopping in coaches, and little one-horse hacks.   At five o'clock the merchants' sulkies and the bankers' carriages gathered in front of the money-changers' offices where messengers and merchants' clerks rushed in and out, exchanging at the latest quotations their wild-cat money and state banknotes.   Jay Cook and other rising young financiers stood on tables, quoting from memory the latest price on Louisiana or Arkansas money, picking out with unerring eye the lamentably frequent counterfeit bills.   At closing time apprentices put up the wooden shutters across the square-framed shop windows; hatters took in their hooked poles upon which were hung rows of high beaver hats; the white canvas awnings in front of general stores, which gave the street in daytime the aspect of an arcade, were rolled up, and the world, that could afford it, crowded on to the Chestnut Street accommodation stages and rode off home.

For the most part, however, it was a world that walked, nor was it much of an effort.   A stroll of twenty or thirty "blocks" in almost any direction took one into the country.   The night watchmen then began to make their rounds, stopping at the little sentry-box stations at the corners to light the whale-oil lights, to rattle their sticks, and to proclaim the time of the night with an "all's well."

But the nights were, by no means, all peaceful.   If any city in the Union could have inspired a poet to write *The Bells,* it was Philadelphia!   One of the outstanding features of life in that place was the frequent fire alarms, real and imaginary.   Scarcely a night passed without a rushing to and fro of the volunteer fire companies to a great clanking of gongs, blowing of bugles and ringing of bells.   The great bell at

---

[528] The apparently disconnected anecdote is introduced here to show the vast change that has taken place since Poe's day.   A visit to the present Philadelphia Post Office with this little incident in mind will serve to bring home the enormous gulf between the world of Poe's day and our own.   Tons of mail now leave the Philadelphia Post Office daily.   The entire United States in Poe's era did not furnish this quantity.

Congress Hall tapped the signal of the quarter in which the fire lay. Thither the volunteer firemen rushed, clad in all the splendors of leather helmet, varnished hip boots, and oil-cloth cloaks,—only to find the alarm a false one, or to stage a disgraceful riot caused by professional jealousies while some unfortunate's house went up in flames. These fire companies provided, for many, the only social and political organization that they knew, and were at once the despair and the pride of the municipality which they kept in perpetual turmoil.

In the early morning, the town awoke to the rumble of market carts and farmers' wagons and the clatter of the shaggy hoofs of rural nags ridden by buxom, red-cheeked German girls clutching brown crocks of butter, and panniers swollen with loaves of rye bread, *pumpernickel,* and cheese. Such made their way to the long, low market buildings that stretched for squares along lower High (Market) Street, high-roofed sheds set upon pillars, with walled stalls, where the generous products of one of the most fertile farm regions in the United States astonished the foreign traveler.

Sixteen pound turkeys could be bought for $2. Wild game, rabbits, partridges, pheasants, quail, and venison were exposed in abundance. The butchers slaughtered frequently and made the occasion a fête day, parading through the town in white smocks to the noise of trumpet and drum, with skinned calves, the carcasses of pink scrubbed pigs with carrots in their mouths, or even an occasional bear, displayed in their carts. Such occasions were advertised widely, when the weather was hot, and the meat was bought up quickly.

Ducks, shad, and reed birds; great crocks of eggs, and strings of fowl decorated the market arcade for blocks. Here, amid piles of apples, heaps of red carrots, the long, green ears of maize, and bushels of glistering pea pods, the ladies of Philadelphia, despised by their Boston sisters for their early marketing habits, moved amid a crowd of prim-bonneted Quaker maidens and their broad-brimmed papas. Buttonless Dunkards, yellow-turbaned negresses purchasing sturgeon meat at one cent the pound were to be seen, and shovel-bearded Moravians in from Bethlehem in covered wagons rubbing shoulders with the eagerly buying pursers of departing ships in smart shore togs and varnished hats. Here, Mrs. Clemm and Virginia were glad to come with a market basket to be cheaply filled, and through these arcades Poe passed many a morning on his way to work at *Graham's* near the old Exchange.

It was a prosperous and hearty world, one in strange contrast to the grotesque dreams of the Dreamer who had come to live there. It was the upper strata of its population, which marketed with such gusto and fed upon scrapple and blood sausages for breakfast, that now composed a large part of his audience, and there were only a few of them to whom he could really speak.

> They, content with the glow of carefully tempered twilight,
> Measured pulses of joy, and colorless growth of the senses,
> Stand aghast at my dream of the sun, and the sound, and the splendor.[529]

To the inner circle of the Wistar Parties, Poe never penetrated. His outer semblance was for a brief time known to the proprietors of magazines and the editors of newspapers. Among them he moved, a strange, marked figure, clad nearly always in shabby black, his eyes forever turned inward, beholding little but his dream. Even this, as he said, was a dream within another dream—the outside world which he so little marked and with whose various embodied shapes he conversed, as with ghosts.

Yet in Philadelphia, for a short time, he was to know the most prosperous if not the happiest days of his manhood. The shadow, which lay somberly over its clean-swept streets and spotless houses, was the steadily failing health of his girl-wife. For the next decade Virginia was slowly dying. As it was, for her, and for her debt-burdened husband, the brief stay in the respectable, if not fashionable, boarding house on Arch Street with the Pedders had drawn to a close.

About September 5, 1838, Poe removed from the house at Fourth and Arch Streets to a new dwelling located at Sixteenth near Locust. He describes it as a "small house."[530] Less is known about this residence than of any other which the family occupied while in Philadelphia. The building has long since been torn down, and even the exact extent of the stay there is not known. This seems to be the house which Captain Mayne Reid, who about that time became acquainted with the Poes, describes as "a lean-to of three rooms (there may have been a garret with a closet) of painted plank construction, supported against the gable of a four-story brick house." Reid's description could apply to no other dwelling occupied by the Poes while in Philadelphia.[531] Most of the fresh material which was written for Burton must have been prepared at the Sixteenth Street residence during the Fall and early Winter of 1839.

The day before moving from Arch Street, Poe wrote to his old Baltimore friend, Nathan C. Brooks, telling him that on account of

---

[529] Writing from Kennett Square near Philadelphia some years later, Bayard Taylor bursts into an ecstasy of indignation against the Philadelphia environment and its smugness. He knew it only too well.

[530] Poe to N. C. Brooks, September 4, 1838. Also reminiscences of John Sartain, Mayne Reid, etc.

[531] Reid's description may apply to the Spring Garden Street house occupied by the Poes three years later. That was a three-story brick house, however, and the descriptions cannot be reconciled. Reid's recollections may confuse both places *(sic)*.

two important affairs then under way he could not undertake to write a critical article on Washington Irving which Brooks had previously requested.[530]   At that time Brooks had just bought out the *North American Quarterly Magazine of Baltimore* and changed it to a monthly under the name of the *American Museum of Literature and the Arts*.   Poe's remarks about Irving and his own methods of criticism are not without interest:

My main reason for declining is . . . I could not do the review well at short notice. The truth is, I can scarcely say I am conversant with Irving's writings, having read nothing of his since I was a boy, save his *Granada*. It would be necessary to give his entire works a perusal. . . . Irving is much overrated, and a nice distinction might be drawn between . . . what is due to the pioneer solely, and what to the writer.

The merit, too, of his tame propriety and faultlessness of style should be candidly weighed. He should be compared with Addison, something being hinted about imitation. . . . A bold and a prior investigation of Irving's claims would strike home, take my word for it. The American literary world never saw anything of the kind yet. . . .[530]

Brooks was at this time printing a good deal of the work which Poe must have done in New York.   What the two important matters were, which Poe had on hand at that time and alleges as the reason for refusing an Irving article to Brooks, cannot be definitely stated.   One of them, however, was the preparation of material for a textbook on conchology.

The Conchologist's First Book: or, A System of Testaceous Malacology, arranged expressly for the use of schools, etc., was the fifth volume to which Poe lent the force of his name.   It was published in April, 1839, in Philadelphia by Haswell, Barrington & Haswell.   The number of the first edition is not known.   The book is bound in brown paper boards with an outside cover with stamped illustrations of shells, weeds, and grasses, and although for the most part simply a rearrangement of the work of others, it is copyrighted in Poe's name ("Edgar A. Poe").

The volume was purely a piece of hack work upon which Poe hoped to realize enough from its sale as a textbook to support him till he could find literary connections in Philadelphia.   Pedder acted as the go-between with Haswell, Barrington & Haswell and Professor Wyatt probably furnished Poe with the English text from which, for the most part, the work was taken.   It was probably the definite engagement upon this book, arranged by Pedder with the publishers, which had finally induced Poe to leave New York.   Philadelphia, on account of the many engravers then engaged there, was a peculiarly good place to issue a volume which demanded extensive technical illustration.

The publisher's office was located at 293 Market Street, and there, during the Autumn of 1838 and the early months of 1839, Poe spent much of his time working on the volume on shells. He was assisted in his labors by a Mr. Isaac Lee, and Professor Thomas Wyatt, a neighbor, who was really responsible for the volume, and supplied most of the necessary scientific information. Wyatt had previously issued through Harpers "his late excellent *Manual of Conchology,*" a book which had proved so expensive to publish that Harpers could not afford to reprint it. Wyatt went about lecturing and selling his books, and, it is said, paid Poe $50 for the use of his name on the title page, as being one which would be likely to further sales. The whole scheme was obviously carefully arranged to avoid trouble over copyright with Harpers, the effect of which was to alienate the "affections" of that firm from Poe and to stand in his way six years later when he wished them, through Professor Anthon, to issue his collected works. To avoid any other legal troubles the work was deliberately based on an English text.

The Conchologist's First Book, 1839, 12 mo. pp. 156, had a preface and introduction written by Poe and signed "E.A.P." which contained an explanation of the terms together with acknowledgments to Lee and Wyatt. This was followed by three pages of an introduction in which Bergman, De Blainville, and Parkinson are quoted, followed by twelve pages of engraved and beautifully colored plates of shells and their parts, boldly lifted *in toto* from an English book, *The Conchologist's Text Book,* by Captain Thomas Brown, to whom no credit is given. Poe simply paraphrased in the body of the book from Wyatt for his nomenclature and descriptions of shells. This, of course, was by arrangement. For the description of the animals, Poe, who had now become deft, translated from Cuvier, giving that author credit. The unfortunate Brown, however, was completely left out.[532] Professor Wyatt concluded the volume with a glossary and an index written by himself. There was a second edition with ten added pages in 1840, under Poe's name, a third anonymous one in 1845 by the same Philadelphia publisher. The book was reprinted in England, and in all no less than nine editions have been traced.

It was not long before Poe was accused of stealing the work entirely from Brown. Poe replied indignantly, "I wrote the Preface and Introduction, and translated from Cuvier the accounts of the animals, etc. *All* school-books are necessarily made in a similar way." He then goes on to describe the usual procedure of "quacks" and claims that

---

[532] "Poe added such important integral portions to *his* book . . . that the name of 'Brown' was later dropped from the title page by the publishers, and Poe's ideas worked into the new edition. This is the first time that this fact has ever been stated. . . ." A Richmond correspondent to the author, March 10, 1926.

he did not intend to give the impression that the work was original with him. His defense is only partly sustained by the facts, and at best the book remains an unfortunate literary transaction. It later brought him more obloquy than money, but undoubtedly served to turn his attention to the outrageous condition of international copyright, a subject which he afterward discussed with Dickens and which led subsequently to Poe's taking up the study of law and registering as a law student.

Poe has also been credited with a translation and digest of Lemonnier's *Natural History,* that was published in the Spring of 1839 under Wyatt's name. In a review of the book in *Burton's Gentleman's Magazine* for July, 1839, Poe said that he wrote "from personal knowledge, and the closest inspection and criticism." This simply means that, at the time, he and Wyatt were working on the *Conchology,* the latter was also translating Lemonnier, and Poe perhaps occasionally helped. His review is an obvious puff for a friend's book and not one of his own. From this work, however, the poet acquired not a little definite technical knowledge. Even the printing of textbooks was grist to his mill.

The rest of Poe's time, in the Spring of 1839, was taken up with the free-lance publishing of articles in various magazines to which he was already known, and with the making of contacts in Philadelphia with the local press, where his old friend L. A. Wilmer, who had left Baltimore on foot when ousted from the editor's chair of the *Visiter,* was now in one of his frequently shifted saddles. Consequently, in May, the *Saturday Evening Chronicle* published Poe's grotesque story of *The Devil in the Belfry,* a satire on the credulity and conventionality of the mob. About a month before, his poem, *The Haunted Palace,* which was introduced into *The House of Usher,* appeared in the *Baltimore Museum.* This poem is an allegory depicting the progress of madness, and is the first thoroughgoing intimation from Poe that he could detect, in himself at least, the possibility of the final *dénouement* of the hero of the poem and of *The House of Usher.* That he, himself, and the strange conditions of his marriage are in part the subjects of the story and the poem, there can remain no doubt. The description of Roderick Usher is the most perfect pen-portrait of Poe himself which is known. It might be labeled "Self-Portrait of the Artist at the Age of Thirty."

The character of his face had been at all times remarkable. A cadaverousness of complexion, an eye large, liquid, and luminous beyond comparison; lips somewhat thin and very pallid, but of a surpassingly beautiful curve, a nose of a delicate Hebrew model, but with a breadth of nostril unusual in similar formations; a finely moulded chin, speaking, in its want of prominence, of a want of moral energy; hair of a more than web-like softness and tenuity;—these features, with an inordinate expansion above the regions of the temple, made up altogether a countenance not easily to be forgotten.

Certain passages in *The House of Usher,* chiefly those dealing with "a small picture . . . of an immensely long and rectangular vault and tunnel . . . a flood of intense rays rolled throughout and bathed the whole in a ghostly and inappropriate splendour," and "the morbid condition of the auditory nerve," suggest unmistakably that previous to this time Poe was at least familiar with the effects of opium as, indeed, *Ligeia* also strongly implies.[533] And it is Virginia, too, who is embodied in the wasting frame of the Lady Madeline. "The disease of the Lady Madeline had long baffled the skill of the physicians. A settled apathy, a gradual wasting away of the person," her strange relations with her brother in the story, and his unmentionable reason for wishing to entomb her alive, all recall the long tortures that Poe underwent by the bedside of his slowly fading *wife* and *cousin.*

It is, indeed, in the order of the event of his heroes and heroines that the progress of the phases of Poe's inner life, its integration and disintegration, are to be read. He had, by now, well developed all of his ideal types except one. The Byronic hero of the prideful youth had gone with little Elmira Royster, the princess of *Tamerlane.* "Helen," the yearning and mourned for heroine, a compound of Mrs. Stanard and Frances Allan, had been duly celebrated in pæans and lyrics; "Ligeia," the strange mental opposite of Virginia and her prototypes had arisen to give him ghostly comfort in the barren cave of his marriage. Illness and early death overtook them all in the pages upon which they strangely moved. In Baltimore and New York, Poe's hero had become neurasthenic and hypochondriac, haunted by incest and mystery, the drug addict and the victim of supernatural fears. All of these were Poe himself and the women he loved, simulacra or defense mechanisms to compensate him in the realm of dreams for the sorrows and disappointments of his own life. All the apartments, the houses, the very gardens in which these dream-phantoms moved, were furnished with a magnificence which arabesquely caricatured the grotesque bareness of his real dwellings and the sordid places in which fate compelled him to dwell.

Let us look for a moment at an ideal chamber in which Poe sees the happy owner peacefully asleep. Who that sleeper was, can be safely left to the reader: "The Proprietor lies asleep on a sofa—the weather is cool—the time is near midnight: we will make a sketch of the room during his slumber": [534]

---

[533] See Chapter XVI, page 299, for a full discussion of this. It is not the intention here to show that Poe was an habitual user of opium. That he resorted to it from time to time is plainly indicated. Also see Chapter XXIII and Chapter XXVI, pages 559 and 650.

[534] From Poe's *Philosophy of Furniture, Burton's Magazine,* May, 1840.

Poe's Ideal Room

. . . It is oblong—some thirty feet in length and twenty-five in breadth—a shape affording the best (ordinary) opportunities for the adjustment of furniture. It has but one door—by no means a wide one—which is at one end of the parallelogram, and but two windows, which are at the other. These latter are large, reaching down to the floor; have deep recesses, and open on an Italian veranda. Their panes are of a crimson-tinted glass, set in rosewood framings, more massive than usual. They are curtained within the recess by a thick silver tissue adapted to the shape of the window, and hanging loosely in small volumes. Without the recess are curtains of an exceedingly rich crimson silk, fringed with a deep network of gold, and lined with the silver tissue, which is the material of the exterior blind. There are no cornices; but the folds of the whole fabric (which are sharp rather than massive, and have an airy appearance) issue from beneath a broad entablature of rich giltwork, which encircles the room at the junction of the ceiling and walls. The drapery is thrown open also, or closed, by means of a thick rope of gold loosely enveloping it, and resolving itself easily into a knot; no pins or other such devices are apparent. The colors of the curtains and their fringe—the tints of crimson and gold—appear everywhere in profusion, and determine the *character* of the room. The carpet—of Saxony material—is quite half an inch thick, and is of the same crimson ground, relieved simply by the appearance of a gold cord (like that festooning the curtains) slightly relieved above the surface of the ground, and thrown upon it in such a manner as to form a succession of short irregular curves, one occasionally over-laying the other. The walls are prepared with a glossy paper of a silver-gray tint, spotted with small arabesque devices of a fainter hue of the prevalent crimson. Many paintings relieve the expanse of the paper. These are chiefly land-scapes of an imaginative cast; such as the fairy grottos of Stanfield, or the lake of the Dismal Swamp of Chapman. There are, nevertheless, three or four female heads, of an ethereal beauty—portraits in the manner of Sully. The tone of each picture is warm, but dark. There are no 'brilliant effects.' Repose speaks in all. Not one is of small size. Diminutive paintings give that *spotty* look to a room, which is the blemish of so many a fine work of Art over-touched. The frames are broad but not deep, and richly carved, without being *dulled* or filagreed. They have the whole lustre of burnished gold. They lie flat on the walls, and do not hang off with cords. The designs themselves are often seen to better advan-tage in this latter position, but the general appearance of the chamber is injured. But one mirror, and this not a very large one is visible. In shape it is nearly circular, and it is hung so that a reflection of the person can be obtained from it in none of the ordinary sitting-places of the room. Two large low sofas of rosewood and crimson silk, gold-flowered, form the only seats, with the excep-tion of two light conversation chairs, also of rosewood. There is a pianoforte (rosewood, also), without cover, and thrown open. An octagonal table, formed altogether of the richest, gold-threaded marble, is placed near one of the sofas. This is also without cover; the drapery of the curtains has been thought sufficient. Four large and gorgeous Sèvres vases, in which bloom a profusion of sweet and vivid flowers, occupy the slightly rounded angles of the room. A tall cande-labrum, bearing a small antique lamp with highly perfumed oil, is standing near the head of my sleeping friend. Some light and graceful hanging shelves, with golden edges and crimson silk cords with golden tassels, sustain two or three hundred magnificently bound books. Beyond these things, there is no furniture, if we except an Argand lamp, with a plain crimson-tinted ground-glass shade, which depends from the lofty vaulted ceiling by a single slender gold chain, and throws a tranquil but magical radiance over all.

Now this is something more than a room to be used as a standard for better home furnishings by the readers of the *"Gent's Mag."* It is in reality the secret inner chamber of the poet's dreams, and as such it is worthy of considerable attention from a psychological point of view. It is the same room, slightly altered, in which "Ligeia" strove to enter the corpse of "Rowena," the apartment of "Roderick Usher," and the room where the "Raven" appeared. It is the scarlet and gold apartment where "Prince Ego" lies asleep in the soporific fumes of a perfumed lamp, carefully curtained from the world, suffused by a bloody-scarlet glow of magic and mystery, where the feminine faces that look from the wall are not those of real women but of the beloved "ethereal" dream faces. The landscapes are gloomy—of the dismal swamp—and no one, no one ever comes there—"The door is by no means wide." There "my sleeping friend," Poe's own half-drugged, perfumed soul, lies forever dreaming, undisturbed by reality. The curtain cords "knot easily," and even the mirror is carefully placed so that from no ordinary position in the room can the inhabitant thereof catch a glimpse of his real physical self. Only the red rays of the lamp depending from the lofty ceiling on the golden chain save it from the gloom of the sepulcher.

One can scarcely refrain now from smiling at all this (the rococo taste, and the insane coloring), but the actual picture of the real room in which "our sleeping friend" lay *awake,* and the real trouble in the wide, sleepless eyes wipes the superior curl from our lips. And there is something more than this, too. Every time has its ideal abodes and favorite characters. These are perfectly, and always impossibly expressed for it by its artists, none of whom can completely escape the ideal longings of the world in which they move. Somehow or other, by the magic of personality and the accidents of circumstance, Edgar Allan Poe was able to embody for his contemporaries not only the fragile, spiritual beings which they hoped and played that they were, but also the very houses and rooms in which they longed to move.[535] The taste of the time was bad; its human ideals were exaggerated and impossible, but in Poe, through the magic of art, they were removed into the world of ideality and became the shadowy prototypes of his era. There, like all imponderable things, they remain, made permanent in time.

---

[535] The ideal of the Victorian heroes and heroines seems to have been the creation of a completely masculine and feminine type. Much of the fiction of the Twentieth Century stresses the strange results of a mixture of the two types in one person, and the neurasthenic results. The effect upon the costume of the two sexes, by these various ideals, at different epochs provides a field for an interesting study.

It was in Philadelphia, too, that Poe fully developed the last of his heroes to appear in prose. With the first intimations of a disintegrating mind, he began to console himself by imagining in himself the opposite.[536] Consequently the next dream-self which developed was the hero whom he projected as the inhuman reasoner of the tales of ratiocination, the solver of puzzles, the unerring reader of cryptograms, the successful finder of treasure, and the detector of mysterious crimes. This hero was a new contribution to literature, and is, taken all in all, the most popularly successful of those which Poe created. There had been only a few hints of him before in Poe's writing, but in the Spring of 1839, if not earlier, Poe became definitely interested in the solutions of cryptograms, of which the mysterious hieroglyphs in *Arthur Gordon Pym* are perhaps an earlier symptom. In January (*sic*), 1840, he published in *Alexander's Weekly,* an obscure Philadelphia magazine, "a challenge to the world," in which he offered to solve any and all cryptograms submitted. As "the world" reached by Mr. Alexander consisted of a few hundred readers at most, Poe was successful in solving the few specimens sent in. As we shall see, the scheme was later repeated on a larger scale in *Graham's,* where Poe proved himself to be rather adept with ciphers.

Another obscure contribution of Poe, about this time, was the review of N. P. Willis' *Tortesa,* which appeared in the *Literary Examiner and Western Monthly Review* for July, 1839. This was a Pittsburgh publication, fathered by one E. Burke Fisher, a former contributor to the *Messenger* while Poe was editor, and a Mr. Whitney. Pittsburgh was largely devoid of any literary interest. Several local magazines had already been laid to rest in that locality, and the *Western Monthly Review* expired painlessly in August, 1839, without paying Poe, who has caused its editor to be faintly remembered by remarking, "No greater scamp ever walked."[537]

The personal doings of Poe and his family during the first six months of their stay in Philadelphia are mostly unrecorded. For his various contributions here and there in newspapers and magazines he received almost nothing. The financial panic was still on, and the wolf must have been seated before the door at Sixteenth near Locust Street, where the family seems to have remained until about the Fall of 1839.[538] Mrs. Clemm and Virginia are said to have resorted again to taking in sewing. Of boarders we hear nothing. There was probably little enough to divide

---

[536] For a detailed account of this disintegrating process the reader must turn to the evidence in Chapter XXII and chapters following.

[537] Poe to Dr. Snodgrass, Philadelphia, July 12, 1841. Dr. Thomas Ollive Mabbott says that there were probably two items that appeared in the *Western Monthly Review* about this time.

[538] Woodberry, 1909, vol. II, note 3, pages 34 and 35, notes the removal about this time, but ignores the Sixteenth Street residence.

among three.   This now habitual stringency was relieved by the engagement of Poe for the part-time editing and contributing to *Burton's Gentleman's Magazine and American Monthly Review.*   Just how Poe
met Burton is not certain, possibly through Brooks or Wilmer, who
were early contributors to *Burton's.*   In April Burton had reviewed
Arthur Gordon Pym and handled it rather sarcastically.   Despite that,
the author soon after applied to the editor for employment and received
this answer:

Philadelphia, May 10, 1839

Edgar A. Poe, *Esq.:*

My dear Sir,—I have given your proposal a fair consideration.   I wish to
form some such engagement as that which you have proposed, and know of no
one more likely to suit my views than yourself.   The expenses of the Magazine
are already awfully heavy; more so than my circulation warrants.   I am certain
that my expenditure exceeds that of any publications now extant, including the
monthlies which are double in price.   Competition is high—new claimants are
daily arising.

Shall we say ten dollars per week for the remaining portion of the year.   Should
we remain together, which I see no reason to negative, your proposition shall be
in force for 1840.   A month's notice to be given on either side previous to a
separation.

Two hours a day except occasionally, will, I believe, be sufficient for all required except in the production of any article of your own.   At all events you
could easily find time for any other light avocation—supposing that you did not
exercise your talents in behalf of any publications interfering with the prospect
of the G.M.

I shall dine at home today at 3.   If you will cut your mutton with me, good.   If
not, write or see me at your leisure.

I am, my dear Sir, your obedt. Servt.
W. E. Burton

Mr. Burton was an Englishman.   There is something Pepysian in
his invitation "to cut mutton," a phrase that at that time could scarcely
have been lost on Poe.   He, indeed, must often have thought with a
sigh of the generous Virginia board set by Frances Allan, with all the
foreign comestibles of John Allan's warehouse at her command.   Doubtless at three o'clock on the Saturday afternoon of May 10, 1839, he sat
across the table from burly Billy Burton, who looked like an apotheosis
of John Bull himself, and doubtless discussed the future of the *Gentleman's Magazine* and the mutton, both at considerable length.

No one could talk more divinely than Poe, when the occasion was
auspicious.   In certain aspects, his conversation at times resembled that
of Coleridge.   But it was not often that he talked so, and when he did,
alas, in America there was no Charles Lamb, no Keats, and no Haydon
or Wordsworth before whom to pour forth the ambrosia from the
arabesqued golden bowl of his dreams.   Lowell could have been such
a friend, but he was far away.   What was said intimately between

them was committed to paper and therefore dulled For the most part this ethereal talk wasted itself upon the dull ears of a White, a Griswold, a Burton, or a Graham. Even they, however, remembered it, although it left them amazed. Ethereal conversation is the greatest gift of the gods. The gods of Ireland had bestowed it magnificently upon Poe—but there is always a fairy curse that goes with this gift; it vanishes instantly into thin air. Only Johnson possessed a Boswell. It would have been fortunate, amusing, exasperating, and mystifying had someone so dogged Poe, for there were also occasions when he opened his lips with the same effect that at a more remote epoch was produced by opening the lid of Pandora's box.

Mr. Poe's arrangement with Mr. Burton was not unlike the contract which he had formerly made with Mr. White, and it commenced with the same salary—but there was one important reservation, at least on Poe's part. Mr. Poe was even then engaged in a scheme to start a magazine of his own, and he did not intend to sell himself so fully to his editor as upon a former occasion. He was simply to write *for* Mr. Burton, and when that gentleman soon afterward printed his name on the July number, the first to which Poe contributed, it is said to have led to their first misunderstanding. At any rate, Poe did not identify himself with *Burton's* to anything like the degree or in the same manner that he had with the *Messenger.*

The *Gentleman's Magazine,* to which Poe now found himself a contributor and, willy-nilly, an editor, had been founded in 1837 by William Evans Burton, an English comedian. Mr. Burton was a man of great practical ability and a deal of pretension. He claimed to be a graduate of St. John's College, Cambridge (*sic*), and was not only desirous of being known as a comic actor and a manager, a career in which he had achieved some success, but was also covetous of literary fame in his adopted country. In his own words, *Burton's Magazine* was to be worthy of a place "upon the parlour table of every gentleman in the United States." To that end he had seen fit to try a cast of the dice in the magazine field in the very midst of the financial panic, and it is no small compliment to his practical ability to chronicle the fact that he abundantly succeeded where others longer established in the same domain had failed. Joseph Jefferson has left us an excellent picture of the man.[539]

Burton was thoughtful and saturnine . . . one of the funniest creatures that ever lived. . . . As an actor of the old broad farce comedy Mr. Burton had no equal in his day . . . 'Captain Cuttle,' and 'Micawber' were his great achievements; his face was a huge map on which was written every emotion that he felt. . . .

[539] *Autobiography of Joseph Jefferson,* the American actor, page 100.

Some of these ill-concealed emotions Edgar Poe did not like. He could not, from the first, help despising that part of Burton's nature which he later described not inaccurately as the "buffoon." [540]

Mr. Burton was at first both owner and editor, and the magazine consequently partook somewhat of the rather stodgy nature of its father. The poems resembled heavy crusts of half-baked pies, while the stories were the lightest pastries imaginable. These, however, seem to have been relished by several thousand subscribers, mostly in Philadelphia, where the padding out of frills of translations and book reviews, obtained by a brutal use of the tailor's shears, was mistaken for the latest cut of literary fashion. Much of the "Quaker" following was due to the fact that Burton opened his pages generously to local poets and poetesses, novelists, and journalists. These in turn provided an enthusiastic *claque*. Neither the noise of their grateful applause nor the fervency of their contemporary din now annoys the ears of posterity. In addition to this, Mr. Burton also committed the then customary international burglary upon the literary effects of various British authors, among whom Leigh Hunt was the most famous. Such was the state of affairs when Mr. Poe appeared rather unwillingly upon the scene.

To come across Poe's work suddenly in *Burton's* is like finding a sonnet by Michelangelo in a bizarre scrapbook. To the August number, Poe contributed *The Man that was Used Up;* in September, *The Fall of the House of Usher;* October and November saw *William Wilson* and *Morella* respectively; and the end of the year *The Conversation of Eiros and Charmion.* Besides this, there were several rather perfunctory book notices and some reprinted, but, as always, improved versions of formerly printed poems. *To Ianthe in Heaven* and *Spirits of the Dead* were an addition to his verse, the former of considerable merit. [541]

The office of *Burton's Gentleman's Magazine,* irreverently referred to by Poe as the *Gent's Mag.,* was at Bank Alley and Dock Street, now Lodge and Dock. Just at this point Dock Street makes one of its wide, sweeping curves, and where Lodge Street joins it there is a little rounded corner, in Poe's day covered by a canvas awning from the shop then located there. Under this he was occasionally to be seen loitering and

---

[540] Poe to Snodgrass, April 1, 1841. See also Poe to Thomas, November 23, 1840, and Poe to Snodgrass, January 17, 1841, for further jibes at Burton's expense.

[541] A typical Poe legend is connected with the lines *To Ianthe.* In the Summer of 1838, Poe is said to have made a trip to Po Valley, Center County, Pennsylvania, where he engaged the affections of no less than two maidens, visited a cave, carved his initials, and gave the original manuscript of *To Ianthe* to a young woman who was conveniently buried with the poem—and the proof. The hope of a legacy from some collateral relatives settled in Pennsylvania is said to have caused the trip. This is, of course, pure fiction. See *A Modern Petrarch (A Story of Alexander's Stream)* in *The Seven Mountains,* H. W. Shoemaker, Bright Printing Co., Reading, Pennsylvania, 1913.

BURTON'S

GENTLEMAN'S MAGAZINE.

EDITED BY

WILLIAM E. BURTON AND EDGAR A. POE.

VOLUME V.

FROM JULY TO DECEMBER.

By a gentleman, we mean not to draw a line that would be invidious between high and low, rank and subordination, riches and poverty. No, *The distinction is in the mind.* Whoever is open, just, and true; whoever is of a humane and affable demeanor; whoever is honourable in himself, and in his judgment of others, and requires no law but his word to make him fulfil an engagement;—such a man is *a gentleman;*—and such a man may be found among the tillers of the earth as well as in the drawing rooms of the high born and the rich.

DE VERE.

PHILADELPHIA.
PUBLISHED BY WILLIAM E. BURTON,
DOCK STREET, OPPOSITE THE EXCHANGE.

1839.

Title Page of *Burton's Gentleman's Magazine*
Showing Poe's name carried as Editor in July, 1839
Courtesy of Maryland Historical Society

The Pagoda

A pavilion and race track near POE's Coates Street residence in Philadelphia,
built by "PAGODA-ARCADE" BROWN, and a familiar sight to POE and his family.
POE later on comments caustically on the "pagodas "of American architecture

From a contemporary drawing
Courtesy of the Pennsylvania Historical Society

George Rex Graham

Founder and owner of *Graham's Magazine*

An able and kindly man, a pioneer in the American magazine field. Under Poe's editorship *Graham's Magazine* was one of the first to attain a circulation on a modern scale

Courtesy of the Pennsylvania Historical Society

William Burton

An English comedian known as "Bully Burton," and one of the many Philadelphia magazine owners of the early 1840's. Editor-publisher of the *Gentleman's Magazine*. Mr. Burton was one of the minor interesting figures of the day who came in contact with Poe

Courtesy of the Pennsylvania Historical Society

Yours very sincerely,

Rufus W. Griswold.

The Rev. Rufus W. Griswold
"Ludwig"

Author of the most popular anthologies of the era, and the editor of Poe's Works
after his death, which Griswold prefaced with a virulent biography of the poet

*From a portrait by J. B. Read, about the time Poe first met Griswold in
Philadelphia*

From "Our Contributors" in Graham's

Courtesy of the Edgar Allan Poe Shrine, Richmond, Virginia

talking. The classic front of the Exchange was just across the curve of Dock Street, then full of drays passing to and from the waterfront just below, and in the same vicinity along Front Street and the neighboring alleys, were located the printers', engravers', and binders' offices. Here Poe strolled about on various errands and was frequently seen in company with one Alexander, Mr. Burton's printer, English, and others. There were several newspapers published nearby.

There were also frequent visits to Congress Hall for the mail of the magazine, and it was Poe's custom, on warm days, to sit dreaming or reading his letters on the benches under the shade trees in Independence Square, staring at the dark, stone walls of the great prison along Walnut Street. Then, too, one could always while away an afternoon at Mr. Sully's exhibitions of "ethereal paintings" just opposite the State House, perhaps remembering schooldays in Richmond with Robert Sully, the nephew of the painter, or talking to the artist himself, to whom Poe was known.[542]

By strolling through the arcade from Chestnut Street to La Fayette, with a few idle moments to spare, one could see the curiosities in Mr. Peal's collection in the long upper room where dances were frequently held, or examine the lines of stuffed birds in glass cases under the rows of paintings hung above them. Most intriguing of all was the skeleton of a mammoth partly restored in plaster. It may possibly have been those very bones that inspired Hirst's remarkable poem on *The Coming of the Mammoth,* which Poe afterward reviewed, remarking, "Eight miles!" against the stanza in which Mr. Hirst, in the careless fervor of poetic license, makes the Mammoth jump across the Mississippi River.[543]

In addition to the Arcade, a curious structure with restaurants and shops downstairs, conceived by an eccentric architectural genius known as "Pagoda-Arcade Browne," there was also the Museum at Ninth and George Streets, with Nathan Dunn's Chinese collection upstairs. Here there was always something going on. In 1839, George Combe, "the eminent lecturer on the science of Phrenology," a science in which Mr. Poe was a dabbler, lectured to a small group of five hundred, while upstairs over two thousand people listened to the strains of Frank Johnston's famous negro brass band. It was the beginning of the age of

---

[542] Thomas Sully painted a portrait of Poe in Philadelphia.

[543] Stan V. Henkels & Son, Philadelphia, Catalogue No. 1388, March 19, 1926. *The Coming of the Mammoth, The Funeral of Time, and Other Poems,* by Henry B. Hirst, Boston. Published by Phillips & Sampson, 1845. 12mo, original boards; printed label partly missing.

An autograph presentation copy: "To Edgar A. Poe, Esq., with the regards of his friend Hirst, June, 1845." Dr. Thomas Ollive Mabbott, in a letter dated New York, September 29, 1924, says this book has quite a number of annotations throughout in Poe's hand.

pseudo-science and savage music. Both the pseudo-science and the strange rhythms intrigued Mr. Poe. He was also quite proud of the great "bump of ideality" that bulged upon his brow.

The theater was on Chestnut Street between Sixth and Seventh. The theatrical Mr. Burton no doubt occasionally arranged to take his young editor there, to see Edwin Forrest rant and tear, or home evenings to his own hospitable house at 158 North Ninth Street, where the dinners and suppers were ample; the guests, literary, dramatic, and convivial.

Poe, on his part, was at this time not imbibing. For several years past nothing more than water had passed his lips.[544] His virtue in one case was probably offset and made possible by the use of a more subtle and even more fatal stimulant.[533]

The days with Burton, however, laid the basis for many lasting and important associations. One day in 1839, at the magazine office, he met a rather quizzical gentleman by the name of Thomas Dunn English, who describes Poe as being dressed in a black suit, well brushed, with very clean linen, rather an unusual thing then, apparently, for an editor. They walked down Chestnut Street together as far as Third, where English later on had his offices, writing drivel for a juvenile magazine called the *John Donkey.* They parted at that time both well pleased. The intimacy grew and finally led to an association in New York and a famous libel suit later on. In Philadelphia, English visited the Poes at home, where he described Mrs. Poe as a delicate gentlewoman and noticed that Mrs. Clemm was more of a mother than mother-in-law. Mr. English was by way of being a poet himself. He wrote a once famous old song called *Ben Bolt,* of lachrymose tendencies, and later introduced Poe to another young poet about town who was studying law. This was Henry Beck Hirst of *Mammoth* fame, of whom more hereafter.

All this time, nevertheless, Poe had not forgotten his scheme to launch a magazine of his own, the plans for which were rapidly maturing in his own head. Mr. Burton, on his part, was revolving further ventures into the dramatic field as a theater owner. His plan of a business activity took him frequently to New York. More and more of the routine work was thrust upon Poe, who was perhaps justified in feeling that the terms of agreement were being imposed upon. He was at

---

[544] Poe to Dr. Snodgrass, Philadelphia, April 1, 1841. Speaking of his experience with Burton, Poe says . . . "From the hour on which I first saw this basest of calumniators to the time in which I retired from his office . . . I pledge you, before God, the solemn word of a gentleman . . . *nothing stronger than water ever passed my lips* . . . *after* leaving Burton . . . I was induced to resort to the occasional use of *cider,* with the hope of relieving a nervous attack. . . ." See Thomas' remark about Poe's use of cider, Chapter XXI, page 447. Mrs. Clemm also bore testimony as to Poe's sobriety in the early Philadelphia days.

times irregular, which exasperated Burton, and the first warmth of their mutual cordiality began to wane rapidly. By the end of the year they were both quite cool.

September, 1839, marked the beginning of a busy time for Poe after a less than usually productive period. He was now preparing for the appearance of his collected tales in two volumes, final arrangement for the publication of which had been made about the end of the month, September 28, 1839, with Lea & Blanchard. The edition was to be at the risk of the publishers, and the author waived any claim for royalties unless the venture was successful.

Poe was very desirous of obtaining quotable criticisms for his work, to be used in inspired notices, and it was now that he began a rather extensive correspondence with literary friends and editorial acquaintances with that object in view. Such men as Washington Irving, James E. Heath, then editor of the *Southern Literary Messenger,* Philip Pendleton Cooke of Charles Town, Virginia, an author of some note, and a Dr. J. Evans Snodgrass of Baltimore, associated for some time with Brooks on the *Museum,* an abolitionist, and a man of some local fame, were among those appealed to. The mass of these letters gives a rather intimate record of Poe's activities about this time, and shows him in touch with a wide range of literary personalities. In addition to this, they are an excellent example of how he smoothed the path for his own work by "soliciting criticisms," and spread the news of his publications by calling the attention of his various correspondents to favorable notices in current periodicals, quoting the encomiums of one man to another. The whole provides a rather interesting glimpse into the contemporary literary frog pond.

To Irving, Poe sent copies of *Burton's* containing *The House of Usher* and *William Wilson,* as they appeared. Irving replied to both, and upon receipt of the latter tale wrote Poe: [545]

I repeat what I have said in regard to a previous production, [*The House of Usher*], which you did me the favor to send me, that I cannot but think a series of articles of like style and merit would be extremely well received by the public.

I could add for your private ear, that I think the last tale [*William Wilson*] much the best, in regard to style. It is simpler. In your first you have been too anxious to present your picture vividly to the eye, or too distrustful to your effect, and have laid on too much coloring. It is erring on the best side—the side of luxuriance. There is no danger of destroying its graphic effect which is powerful. . . .

Time has not confirmed Irving in his judgment. It has been the very graphic effect in *The House of Usher* which has caused it to be remembered where *William Wilson* is often forgotten.

---

[545] Washington Irving to Poe, Newburgh, November 6, 1839.

The correspondence with P. P. Cooke largely concerned *Ligeia*. Cooke's letter is most charming and exhibits a Virginia gentleman enjoying to the full the life of his time.

. . . My wife enticed me off to visit her kins-people in the country, and I saw more of guns and horses and dogs than of pens and paper. Amongst dinners, barbecues, snipe-shooting, riding parties, etc., I could not get my brains into humor for writing to you or to anybody else.[546]

He then follows with a long discussion of *Ligeia*. The letters between Poe and Cooke plainly develop the fact that in his prose tales Poe followed much the same method of reconstruction as in his poems, *i.e.,* the theme in one story was further developed and perfected in another of later date. In this case the fact is plainly brought out that *Morella* and its theme found its perfect and final expression in *Ligeia,* which Poe considered his best story.

The most intimate, indeed almost affectionate, correspondent at this time was Dr. J. E. Snodgrass.[547] The poet asks him many small favors, and confides in him to the extent of much pertinent small talk. In one letter in a postscript Poe says:

P. S. I have made a profitable engagement with 'Blackwood's Mag': and my forthcoming *Tales* are promised a very commendatory review in that journal from the pen of Prof. Wilson. Keep this a secret, if you please, for the present.

At a later date Poe told Griswold that he had contributed to two foreign (English) magazines. These contributions have never been definitely traced, but it seems possible that certain articles bearing upon the question of international copyright, which afterward appeared in *Blackwood's* and the *Edinburgh Review,* may be by Poe, who was constantly fishing for English connections in several directions, then and later. To the correspondence with Heath of the *Messenger,* there will be occasion to refer later. In a letter to Snodgrass, at the end of October, Poe asks the doctor to forward him, if possible, some back files of the *Messenger,* evidently with the idea of reprinting from them some of his redacted poetry which appeared later in *Burton's.*[548] He had neg-

---

[546] P. P. Cooke to Poe September 16, 1839. Cooke writes from Charles Town, Va. (now W. Va.), at that time one of the strongholds of Virginia plantation life at its best.

[547] Dr. James Evans Snodgrass of Baltimore had been one of the associates and contributors with Brooks on the *Museum.* These letters were in part published in the *New York Herald* for March 27, 1881. The more exact text appears in Woodberry. Harrison also includes them with a running comment.

[548] Poe requests from Snodgrass especially No. 7, vol. I, to No. 6, vol. II, of the *Southern Literary Messenger.* He undoubtedly desired these to republish and revamp his old work in Richmond for Philadelphia publications. Snodgrass does not seem to have been able to supply these as Poe later, through Henry B. Hirst, borrowed several copies of the *S.L.M.* from William Duane, Secretary of the Treasury. These borrowed volumes gave rise to an unfortunate and mistaken charge against Poe by Duane. See Chapter XXII, page 468. Also Woodberry, 1909, vol. II, appendix II.

lected to keep by him, he soon afterward told Lowell, any volumes of any of his own poems.

Sometime towards the end of 1839 or the beginning of the new year, the time cannot be fixed exactly, Poe and his family moved from Sixteenth near Locust Street to a new dwelling on Coates Street just overlooking the banks of the Schuylkill River.[525] This was at the opposite end of town from the offices of *Burton's Magazine,* and entailed a walk of between two and three miles, unless the Chestnut Street stages were used, which, since 1829, had been running from the Coffee Houses on Front Street to the Schuylkill. If Poe walked, his route lay by the long gloomy walls of the Eastern Pennsylvania State Penitentiary, "large and imposing like the sight of a fortress." Past this reminder of misery—"the prisoners are all to be kept in solitary confinement . . . and the arched roofs reverberate every sound"—[365] the poet went back and forth between the town and his little house.

The dwelling stood until the late 1920's, a three-story brick house with a white marble doorstep, situated on a little triangle of ground made by the junction of Coates Street, Fairmount Drive, and an alley. This was by far the most comfortable house in which Poe had lived for any length of time since the Richmond days. The country all about, at that period, was open, with only a few buildings scattered here and there, and, although the railroad yards were near, where cars were then shifted by horses, there was a beautiful view up the river and across to the opposite bank.

Just below the house, on the river flat, was a curious structure known as the Pagoda which had been erected by Browne, the eccentric designer of the Arcade. Its Chinese proportions overlooked an abandoned race track, which had been part of Browne's scheme. Here some of the sporting gentlemen of Philadelphia could still be found, in high-wheeled racing carts, exercising their blooded nags and smart tandems. Just above the house was a high shot tower, for long a feature of the Philadelphia landscape. The house itself had two good rooms on the ground floor and several ample bedrooms above. Poe used the front parlor with a black slate mantel for his study, while the rear chamber appears to have been the dining-room; there being a cellar kitchen below, at that time. It was in the front room at Coates Street that most of the articles and stories which appeared in *Graham's* must have been written, and it is highly probable that it was here, too, that the first faint taps of the *Raven* began to be heard, and to be put down upon paper. In the bedroom upstairs, Poe lay ill for weeks at a time.[549]

The proximity to the river allowed Poe to indulge in the only form of

---

[549] Description from a visit made by the author to the Coates Street house in March, 1926.

physical exercise for which he cared, and it was from the time of moving into the Coates Street house that his interest in the landscape and the country about Philadelphia may be dated. There were, it appears, picnics and boating excursions up the Schuylkill and Wissahickon with occasional hunting trips. Some neighbors of the Poes, who lived in the Lemon Hill district, remembered a shooting expedition to Gray's Ferry in a rowboat after reed birds. Characteristically enough the Virginian did the shooting while one of the Detwiler lads plied the oars. It was remembered that the mysterious looking gentleman made good use of his fowling-piece, and secured a good bag.[550]

Although the new "mansion" was to see Poe in the most prosperous days that he ever knew—those of his period as editor of *Graham's Magazine,* when, for a while, the howls of the wolf were succeeded by the notes of Virginia's little piano—the first few months in the residence at Coates Street were sad ones. The connection with *Burton's* was severed, and Mr. Graham had not yet employed Poe. It was a time of scarcity and living on hopes of prospects for the *Penn.* Even the three-cent postage for the circulars must have been hard to find, and they were often mailed in bundles to his friends for distribution. Nothing, however, ever kept the home from having about it a spotless, a neat, and an attractive air of comfort imparted by the incessant and loving labor of the mother-in-law, who was the mother of both her "children." If the walls were not hung in scarlet and gold, they were at least a complete refuge from the world. It was remarked that Mrs. Clemm kept no servant, but that Virginia was often seen working about the garden in front, where she raised fruit and flowers, while her widowed mother did the housework. The slightest patch of ground was always sufficient excuse for Virginia to provide her Eddie with a nosegay and a pot in the window. Poe had, by this time, become more than ever attached to her whose frail childlike person he had come to idolize and to confuse with the "Ligeia" of his dreams. It was not the full, hearty love of manhood for a healthy, competent woman, but a tenderness made poignant by a constantly increasing dread, a pity that longed to wrap her from sorrow and every care. Such a tenderness is often more enduring than passion. In the evenings she sang to him by the fire while Mrs. Clemm sewed; or he read to them, from his long rolls of perfectly written manuscript, some poem or weird tale in a voice that seemed to summon presences from the shadows,[551] while Catarina, the cat, then in

---

[550] From an anonymous clipping. Contemporary records show the Detwilers to have been neighbors of the Poes in the "Lemon Hill" district.

[551] F. O. C. Darley, the artist, tells of Poe's reading the manuscripts of *The Gold-Bug* and *The Black Cat* to him later. "The form of Poe's manuscripts was peculiar. He wrote on half sheets of note paper, which he pasted together at the ends, making one continuous piece, which he rolled up tightly. As he read he dropped it upon the floor. It was very neatly written and without corrections apparently." Darley to Woodberry, February, 1884.

her burgeoning kittenhood, purred on the ample plateau of Mrs. Clemm's lap.[552]   But there were gloomy days, too, when Virginia was faint and ill, when Eddie was in the depths of melancholia, or in one of those fits of abstraction, utter lassitude, or even semi-madness induced by a drug. Then he would get up and wander off, God knows where, to be brought back raving by staring neighbors or cajoled by "Muddie."   He would then collapse and lie for days helpless and despondent, half mad with remorse and exhaustion, upon the upstairs bed.   Towards the end of 1839 those fits began to gain upon him.   Finally he went into a nervous collapse.   He was fighting off an old demon and, as a compromise, began to drink hard cider.[544]   These periods of absence from the magazine and the severity of some of Poe's criticism had evidently gone far towards complicating matters with Mr. Burton, for it was about this time that Poe seems to have attempted to sever connection with the *Gentleman's,* to have repented, and to have written the editor a despairing and supplicating letter.   Mr. Burton replied.   His letter is undated:

I am sorry you have thought it necessary to send me such a letter. Your troubles have given a morbid tone to your feelings which it is your duty to discourage. I myself have been as severely handled by the world as you can possibly have been, but my sufferings have not tinged my mind with melancholy, nor jaundiced my views of society. You must rouse your energies, and if care assail you, conquer it. I will gladly overlook the past. I hope you will as easily fulfill your pledges for the future. We shall agree very well, although I cannot permit the magazine to be made a vehicle for that sort of severity which you think 'so successful with the mob!' . . . I accept your proposition to recommence your interrupted avocations with the *Maga*. Let us meet as if we had not exchanged letters. Use more exercise, write when feelings prompt, and be assured of my friendship. You will soon regain a healty activity of mind and laugh at your past vagaries.[553]

This is certainly charitable, thoughtful, and the advice is good, yet a glance at Mr. Burton's jolly comedian's countenance will at once explain his faith in the power of simple remedies to bring health and peace to a face that wore far different lineaments from his own.   The truce, however, was arranged and Poe's contributions continued.   He was now at work upon a serial story called *The Journal of Julius Rodman,* being an account of the "First Passage across the Rocky Mountains of North America ever achieved by Civilized Man." [554]   The story appeared

---

[552] This cat is mentioned by name in Poe's own letters to Mrs. Clemm, and afterward accompanied the family to New York where she was seen by visitors to the Fordham cottage, and specifically mentioned. See Poe to Mrs. Clemm, New York, April 7, 1844, page 466, and Chapter XXIV, page 598.

[553] It will be remembered that both Mr. White of the *Messenger* and Mr. Kennedy also advised exercise for Poe. This is a confirmation of Poe's sedentary and unhealthy mode of life, probably due to his lack of energy, a bad heart and poverty. He seems at times to have attempted to follow out the advice.

[554] First traced by Ingram, Poe's English biographer.

anonymously in *Burton's* from January to June of the following year (1840). This tale is perhaps the least worth while of any of Poe's longer works and resembles *Arthur Gordon Pym* in its method and style. The story professes to describe the adventures of a young Kentucky traveler on a trapping expedition up the Missouri in the last decade of the eighteenth century. The Rocky Mountains are crossed in 1792, and the hero returns to Virginia, where, for insufficient motives, he carefully secretes his diary. The interest in the West was then strong, and Poe was simply writing for an audience. The narratives of Lewis and Clark, Sir A. Mackenzie, and Washington Irving's *Astoria* were the sources drawn upon.[555] It is only occasionally, in this tale, that Poe attains to a faint glow of his better self. In the meantime, the last month of the year finally saw the publication of the collected tales an accomplished fact at last.

Tales of the Grotesque and Arabesque, the sixth work appearing under Poe's name, was published in December, 1839, at Philadelphia by Lea & Blanchard, the title page bearing the date 1840. The edition consisted of 750 sets of two volumes each, and was dedicated to Colonel William Drayton. The first volume of 243 pages contained a preface in which Poe strove to counter the charge of German influence, and to lay stress on the fact that the collection possessed a spiritual coherence, having been written with a view to publication in collected form "to preserve, as far as a certain point, a certain unity of design." This was followed by fourteen tales. The second volume contained ten stories and an appendix. In the *Foreign Quarterly Review* for July, 1827, appeared an article by Sir Walter Scott which suggested the title.[556] This comprised a collection of all the tales published up until that time with the addition of *Why the Little Frenchman Wears his Hand in a Sling.*[557] In them, all the types of the heroes and heroines which Poe was to create, appeared fully developed except that of the "Unerring Reasoner." That was to await the tales of ratiocination soon to follow.

Poe had now been for a year and a half in Philadelphia. He had made many valuable acquaintances and increased his fame. . . . The year 1839 closed having seen two works issued under his name, and the publication of some of the greatest of his tales. The financial return had been almost nothing, and he was now once more despondent.

---

[555] *Astoria,* Washington Irving, Philadelphia, two volumes, 1836. A narrative deduced from the fur trading records of the Northwest and John Jacob Astor's ventures and adventures. An important piece of Americana. Poe's use of sources, contrasted with Irving's method, is apparent here.

[556] Woodberry, 1909, vol. I, page 223, note 1.

[557] Republished in the *Broadway Journal,* November 9, 1845. See also Chapter V, page 63, for the source of this story.

In addition to this, the troubles with Burton were rapidly drifting to a close.

The opening of the year 1840 found Poe with several irons very much in the fire. He was still contributing perfunctorily to *Burton's,* but his main interest was now engrossed in the grand scheme to launch a magazine of his own, of which he was to be sole editor and proprietor. As he had no capital, his campaign for starting the journal, to be called the *Penn Magazine,* was pressed along three separate lines, *i.e.,* the favorable announcement of its approaching advent by other publications, the securing of distinguished contributors, each with his own following, and the assurance of sufficient subscribers, in advance, to provide the initial financial backing.

For the securing of all three essentials, Poe relied perforce upon the coöperation and confidence of his personal and literary friends. His correspondence at this time is almost entirely given over to matters concerning the *Penn,* and for the most part embraced the members of his own family in Baltimore, old friends in Richmond, correspondents in the West, particularly St. Louis, and various magazine editors upon whose fear or favor he might safely rely. John Tomlin of Tennessee, Dr. Thomas Holley Chivers of Georgia, both poets, and Frederick William Thomas were now added to the list.

Poe had met Tomlin through magazine correspondence at an earlier date. Chivers had already published poems which had attracted Poe's notice, and the correspondence which now sprang up between them was the beginning of an association which later had curious ramifications in their mutual effect upon each other's poetry. Thomas was a poet and novelist, the author of *Clinton Bradshaw, Howard Pinckney, East and West,* and other forgotten works. He was also a minor journalist and dabbled not unsuccessfully in politics. At the time their correspondence began, Thomas was living in St. Louis. Through Baltimore connections, he already knew of Poe and was prepared to admire him. It was the beginning of the closest friendship which Poe contracted during his manhood.[558]

Poe's theory of issuing a magazine of his own was, that once rid of the thwarting influence of an editor such as Mr. White or Mr. Burton, and with the policies of the magazine entirely in his own hands, he would be able to appeal to a larger and, at the same time, more select audience by the fearlessness of the criticism and the quality of the contributions offered. In this connection, Lowell's description of the literary conditions in the United States a few years later was equally applicable to 1840.

---

[558] For a full history of Thomas see Appendix VI.

The situation of American literature is anomalous. It has no center, or, if it have, it is like that of the sphere of Hermes. It is divided into many systems, each revolving round its several suns, and often presenting to the rest only the faint glimmer of a milk-and-water way.[559]

In 1840, and for some years later, these several centers may be said to have been located at Boston, New York, Philadelphia, and Baltimore. The West was nebulous and the faint glow at Charleston, which became visible just before the Civil War with the issue of *Russell's Magazine* there, had not yet troubled the horizon.

It was Poe's plan to disregard all of these local groups with their mutual and petty internal jealousies, and to found a periodical which would not only be national, but even international in its scope.

Unlike nearly all the other editors and critics of his time, Poe was aware of the movements and the orbits of stars in both English and German literature. There were only two magazines in the country that would have been rivals—the *North American Review* and the *Knickerbocker*, which represented the New England and Manhattan groups respectively. Towards the former, with the exception of James Russell Lowell, Poe was peculiarly hostile. Part of this hostility to New England was due to personal jealousy and Southern traditions, but the major part of it can now candidly be acknowledged to have had its source in a just anger at the preposterous assumptions of the New England group and their clannish log rolling. To a man of Poe's critical acumen and artistic instinct, this was like a red rag to a bull. The assumption of the superiority of the New England brand of culture and virtue has been swallowed by the American people with an ease that is only to be explained by their almost complete indifference to the facts of their own history, and an admiration for persistent propaganda. To Poe, raised in Virginia, and a member of Thomas Jefferson's own university, the assumption was intolerable. Nor is the fact unimportant in Poe's history. Through its curious ramifications, his reputation has suffered. The Puritan has withdrawn the fringes of his robes lest they take stain from the contact; Emerson called him the "jingle man," and went on cogitating "Compensations"; and Longfellow, the carefully bibulous and benign, assumed the throne in solitary state, where he has reigned for two generations as the greatest American poet. In the meantime, every schoolboy learned that Edgar Poe was a drunkard, and the faintly heard echoes of Baudelaire's twisted horn confirmed from France the certainty that he was "immoral." In the United States he became the *enfant terrible* of American literature, and abroad one of the two "world artists" we have produced.

---

[559] Lowell's sketch of Poe, *Graham's Magazine,* February, 1845.

In 1840, Poe was hoping to give a center and an intellectual direction to the current in the muddy swimming hole of American literature. It is a great pity that he failed. Artistically he was the foremost creative mind of his literary generation in America; in the final analysis it was his physical infirmities which doomed him to fail. Poe's own prospectus for the *Penn,* which was circulated about a year later (he probably delighted in the pun on the name), gives most satisfactorily the basis upon which he built his hopes. Naturally enough, the complete philosophy behind it is not fully developed in a document whose aim was so practical as the

Prospectus

of

THE PENN MAGAZINE

A Monthly Literary Journal

To be edited and published in the city of Philadelphia
By EDGAR A. POE

To The Public:—Since resigning the conduct of the *Southern Literary Messenger,* at the commencement of its third year, I have always had in view the establishment of a Magazine which should retain some of the chief features of that journal, abandoning or greatly modifying the rest. Delay, however, has been occasioned by a variety of causes, and not until now have I found myself at liberty to attempt the execution of the design.

I will be pardoned for speaking more directly of the *Messenger.* Having in it no proprietary right, my objects too being at variance in many respects with those of its very worthy owner, I found difficulty in stamping upon its pages that *individuality* which I believe essential to the full success of all similar publications. In regard to their permanent influence, it appears to me that a continuous definite character, and a marked certainty of purpose, are requisites of vital importance; and I cannot help believing that these requisites are only attainable when one mind alone has the general direction of the undertaking. Experience has rendered obvious—what might indeed have been demonstrated *a priori*—that in founding a Magazine of my own lies my sole chance of carrying out to completion whatever peculiar intentions I may have entertained.

To those who remember the early days of the Southern periodical in question, it will be scarcely necessary to say that its main feature was a somewhat overdone causticity in its department of Critical Notices of new books. The *Penn Magazine* will retain this trait of severity insomuch only as the calmest yet sternest sense of justice will permit. Some years since elapsed may have mellowed down the petulance without interfering with the vigor of the critic. Most surely they have not yet taught him to read through the medium of a publisher's will, nor convinced him that the interests of letters are unallied with the interests of truth. It shall be the first and the chief purpose of the Magazine now proposed to become known as one where may be found at all times, and upon all subjects, an honest and a fearless opinion. It shall be a leading object to assert in precept, and to maintain in practice, the rights, while in effect it demonstrates the advantages, of an absolutely independent criticism; a criticism self-sustained; guiding itself only by the purest rules of Art; analyzing and urging these rules as it applies therein; holding itself aloof from all personal bias; acknowledging no fear save that of outraging the right; yielding no point either to the vanity of the author, or to the assumptions of critical prejudice, or to the involute and anonymous cant of the Quarterlies, or to the arrogance of those organized *cliques* which, hanging like nightmares upon American literature, manufacture, at the nod of our principal booksellers, a pseudo-public opinion by wholesale. These are objects of which no man need be ashamed. They are purposes, moreover, whose novelty at least will give them interest. For assurance that I will fulfill them in the best spirit and to the very letter, I appeal with confidence to those friends, and especially to those Southern friends, who sustained me in the *Messenger,* where I had but a very partial opportunity of completing my own plans.

In respect to the other characteristics of the *Penn Magazine* a few words here will suffice.

It will endeavor to support the general interests of the republic of letters, without reference to particular regions—regarding the world at large as the true audience of the author. Beyond the precincts of literature, properly so called, it will leave in better hands the task of instruction upon all matters of *very* grave moment. Its aim chiefly shall be *to please*—and this through means of versatility, originality, and pungency. It may be as well here to observe that nothing said in this Prospectus should be construed into a design of sullying the Magazine with any tincture of the buffoonery, scurrility, or profanity, which are the blemish of some of the most vigorous of the European prints. In all branches of the literary department, the best aid, from the highest and purest sources, is secured.

To the mechanical execution of the work the greatest attention will be given which such a matter can require. In this respect it is proposed to surpass, by very much, the ordinary Magazine style. The form will somewhat resemble that of the *Knickerbocker;* the paper will be equal to that of the *North American Review;* pictorial embellishments are promised only in the necessary illustration of the text.

The *Penn Magazine* will be published in Philadelphia, on the first of each month; and will form, half-yearly, a volume of about 500 pages. The price will be $5 per annum, payable in advance, or upon receipt of the first number, which will be issued on the first of March, 1841. Letters addressed to the Editor and Proprietor,

Edgar A. Poe

Philadelphia, *January* 1, 1841

In this prospectus for the *Penn,* somewhat toned down for popular consumption, we have, in a thimble, the outstanding critical and publishing theories of Poe, *i.e.,* his insistence that the unity of a vivid personality would impel success, his purpose to criticize without fear or favor, a refusal to pander to local prejudices or sectional cliques, the theory of the world as an audience, a freedom from didactic tendencies and ephemeral propaganda, pleasure as the aim of literature, the avoidance of the profane or the erotic, and a format which relied on good printing and legitimate illustration of the text rather than upon sentimental embellishment. The theory was fairly sound, but it is an open question whether, if financial circumstances had permitted it, the personality of the "Editor and Proprietor" would have allowed him, particularly in the realm of criticism, to have carried it wholly into effect. He, too, had peculiar prejudices and particular friends.

The responses to Poe's appeals by correspondence were on the whole rather reassuring. Promises of support by subscribers, and of articles from various literary friends accumulated encouragingly, and it seemed for a while as if the *Penn* might actually appear in January, 1841, as an announcement in the *Philadelphia Saturday Chronicle* for June 13, 1840, indicated. A series of unforeseen events, and an unlooked-for change in Poe's prospects, now, however, suddenly intervened, and the date of the first appearance of the magazine was deferred. These events were a nervous crisis, a final quarrel with Burton, and the absorption of Poe in his work as the editor of another important periodical.

Through the latter part of the Winter and the early Spring of 1840, Poe had continued his work with Mr. Burton, although unwillingly. Their growing tension was now made even more tense by a scheme of prizes which Burton began to offer under the guise of "premiums," sums which Poe said Burton never intended to pay. It was a method of obtaining authors' manuscripts, by dangling a precarious bait before their eyes, which disgusted Poe. He is said to have protested to Burton, but in vain.

Also about this time, the proprietor of the *Gentleman's* began to become more interested in his theatrical than in his journalistic ventures, and quietly commenced to negotiate for the sale of the magazine without saying anything to Poe. Poe on his part was conducting his negotiations for the *Penn* without saying anything to Burton, when about the same time, apparently, the news of the several private activities of each came to both their ears. Poe is said to have availed himself of Burton's lists for the *Penn,* but as many of the subscribers and contributors had been obtained by his own efforts, the charge against him is not clear. Poe's irregularities and fitfulness were doubtless irritating; on the other hand, he had been ill. As usual there was much to be said, on all sides, when the final break came. Burton's quarrels with various theatrical managers had determined him to buy a theater of his own, and he now, without saying anything to Poe, advertised the magazine for sale. It was then, perhaps, when he attempted to remonstrate with his editor about the lists, that Poe told him that he "looked upon him as a blackguard and a villain." In addition to all this, Burton had been absent from the magazine offices on theatrical business quite frequently. In February, he is known to have been in New York. This threw a double burden upon Poe, who became tired of the whole thing, and upon one of these occasions made his attitude in the matter clear by staying away himself. The final *dénouement* is graphically given by one of Poe's friends, a Mr. Rosenbach, whose father was interested in the magazine. On returning, Mr. Burton opened the office door to find the desk piled high with manuscripts and letters, Poe absent, and the layout for the next number unprepared:

> Burton immediately sought my father at his house, and it was about midnight when he found him. He came in a carriage with a large bundle of manuscripts, from which they made selection. They worked until morning when they sent me with copy to the printer, Charles Alexander, in Franklin Place, Chestnut Street. Alexander hunted up some extra compositors, and by dint of hard work and hurried proofreading, the *Gentleman's Magazine* appeared as usual. Poe was discharged for his negligence. . . .[560]

One can imagine the roast-beef tinge of the comedian-editor's countenance as he arrived at Mr. Rosenbach's about midnight, "in a carriage piled high with manuscripts." And of the remarks anent Mr. Poe as "some selection was made"—frantically—under the rays of the astral lamp while dawn slowly paled into morning. For some time afterward, both Mr. Burton and Mr. Poe were heard by mutual acquaintances to be indulging themselves in libelous asides at each other's expense. After this affair, which occurred sometime in the Spring of 1840, Poe did not again appear at the office of the *Gent's Mag.* There were, however, a number of personal matters left in the air by his withdrawal, about which Burton addressed a letter to Poe at the end of May. The nature of these, and the state of the controversy can best be understood by giving Poe's carefully pondered reply:

> SIR,—I find myself at leisure this Monday morning, June 1, to notice your very singular letter of Saturday. . . . I have followed the example of Victorine and slept upon the matter and you shall now hear what I have to say. In the first place, your attempts to bully me excite in my mind scarcely any other sentiment than mirth. When you address me again, preserve if you can, the dignity of a gentleman. . . . As for the rest you do me great injustice and you know it. As usual, you have wrought yourself into a passion with me on account of some imaginary wrong; for no real injury, or attempt at injury, have you ever received at my hands. As I live, I am utterly unable to say why you are angry, or what true grounds of complaint you have against me. You are a man of impulses; have made yourself, in consequence, some enemies; have been in many respects ill-treated by those whom you looked upon as friends—and these things have rendered you suspicious. You once wrote in your magazine a sharp critique

---

[560] See also Alexander to Clarke, October 20, 1850, *Gill*, page 97. "The absence of the editor on professional duties left the matter frequently in the hands of Mr. Poe, whose unfortunate failing may have occasioned some disappointment in the preparation of a particular article expected from *him*, but never interfering with the regular publication of the *Gentleman's Magazine*, as its monthly issue was never interrupted upon any occasion, either from Mr. Poe's deficiency, or from any other cause, during my publication of it, embracing the whole of Mr. Poe's connection with it. . . ." This somewhat conflicting testimony is given here as a matter of justice.

upon a book of mine—a very silly book—*Pym*. Had I written a similar criticism upon a book of yours, you feel that you would have been my enemy for life, and you therefore imagine in my bosom a latent hostility towards yourself. This has been a mainspring in your whole conduct towards me since our first acquaintance. It has acted to prevent all cordiality. In a general view of human nature your idea is just—but you will find yourself puzzled in judging me by ordinary motives. Your criticism was essentially correct, and therefore, although severe, it did not occasion in me one solitary emotion either of anger or dislike. But even while I write these words, I am sure you will not believe them. Did I not still think you, in spite of the exceeding littleness of some of your hurried actions. a man of many honorable impulses, I should not now take the trouble to send you this letter. I cannot permit myself to suppose that you would say to me in cold blood what you said in your letter of yesterday. You are, of course, only mistaken in asserting that I owe you a hundred dollars, and you will rectify the mistake at once when you come to look at your accounts. . . . Your error can be shown by reference to the Magazine. During my year with you I have written:

In July	5 pp.	
" August	9 pp.	
" September	16 pp.	
" Oct.	4 pp.	
" Nov.	5 pp.	
" Dec.	12 pp.	
" Jan.	9 pp.	
" Feb.	12 pp.	
" March	11 pp.	
" April	17 pp.	
" May	14 pp.+5 copied	—Miss McMichael's Ms.
" June	9 pp.+3 "	—Chandlers

132   (*An error in addition*)

Dividing this sum by 12, we have an average of 11 pp. per month—not 2 or 3. And this estimate leaves out of question everything in the way of extract or compilation. Nothing is counted but *bona fide* composition. 11 pp. at $3 per p. would be $33, at the usual Magazine prices. Deduct this from $50, my monthly salary, and we have left $17 per month, or $4.25 per week, for the services of proof reading; general superintendence at the printing office; reading, alteration, and preparation of Mss., with compilation of various articles, such as Plate articles, Field sports, etc. Neither has anything been said of my name upon your title page, a small item—you will say—but still something, as you know. Snowden pays his editresses $2 per week each for their names solely. Upon the whole I am not willing to admit that you have greatly overpaid me. That I did not do four times as much as I did for the Magazine was your own fault. At first I wrote long articles, which you deemed unadmissable, and never did I suggest any to which you had not some immediate and decided objection. Of course, I grew discouraged, and could feel no interest in the journal.

I am at a loss to know why you call me selfish. If you mean that I borrowed money of you—you know that you offered it, and you know that I am poor. . . . Place yourself in my situation and see whether you would not have acted as I have done. You first 'enforced,' as you say, a deduction of salary; giving me to understand thereby that you thought of parting company. You next spoke disrespectfully of me behind my back—this as an habitual thing;—to those whom you supposed your friends, and who punctually reported to me, as a matter of course, every ill-natured word which you uttered. Lastly, you advertised your magazine for sale without saying a word to me about it. I felt no anger at what you did—none in the world. Had I not firmly believed in your design to give up your journal, with a view of attending to the Theatre, I should never have dreamed of attempting one of my own. The opportunity of doing something for myself seemed a good one—(and I was about to be thrown out of business)— and I embraced it. Now I ask you, as a man of honor and as a man of sense,— what is there wrong in all this? What have I done at which you have any right to take offence? I can give you no definite answer (respecting the continuance of *Rodman's Journal*) until I hear from you again. The charge of $100 I shall not admit for an instant. If you persist in it our intercourse is at an end, and we can each adopt our own measures. In the meantime, I am,

Yr. Obt. St.,
Edgar A. Poe

To have admitted the charge of $100, which was more than he actually did owe Burton, would have necessitated the continuance of the *Rodman Journal* for nothing at all. Mr. Burton, who had several manuscripts of Poe's on hand, refused to publish them, and also annoyed Poe by pretending not to be able to find the manuscripts sent in to the magazine by several of his former contributors. About the middle of June, Poe wrote to Snodgrass saying:

I would go down to the office, open the drawer in his presence, and take the MS. from beneath his nose. I think this would be a good deed done, and would act as a caution to such literary swindlers in the future. . . . [561]

Even as late as April, 1841, Poe again writes:

In regard to Burton I feel indebted to you for the kind interest you express; but scarcely know how to reply. My situation is embarrassing. It is impossible, as you say, to notice a buffoon and a felon, as one gentleman would notice another. The law, then is my only recourse. . . . [540]

Poe felt that he was being libeled. But nothing came of his talk of the law, and both he and Burton gradually cooled off. Burton's "libels" had to do with assertions on his part that Poe's irregularities and idiosyncrasies, while employed on the *Gentleman's Magazine,* were due to drinking. Mr. Burton was mistaken, but honestly so. Poe had, indeed, been wayward and fitful, but as will be shown shortly, he was not drinking at this time.[544] His eccentricities arose from another source. The *Penn Magazine* project may be regarded as having caused the main trouble with Burton, as it did later on with Graham.

---

[561] Poe to Snodgrass, Philadelphia, June 17 (1840). This is a characteristic Poe letter full of bluster. After calling Burton many hard names he became friends with him a year or so later.

In the meantime, in May, 1840, Poe had met personally, and became in a few days intimately acquainted with, his lifelong friend, F. W. Thomas, who had stopped off at Philadelphia on his way home to St. Louis from the Whig presidential convention held in Baltimore the same month.[558]   Thomas visited the Poes at Coates Street where the family was still living.   They were all much taken with one another. Thomas was especially delighted with Virginia and Mrs. Clemm, and evidently won his way to the heart of Poe, who afterward mentions his conversation turning frequently "upon the one loved name."   It was Frances, the name of Poe's beloved foster-mother.[562]

There were many associations which drew these two young men together.   In the first place, both were writers, poets, and editors; both had been raised in the South and had known of each other through mutual friends for a long time.   Thomas, like Poe, suffered from ill health.   He was a cripple, probably due to tuberculosis of the bones, and his struggles for recognition had been long and hard.   In Baltimore, while Poe was in the army, Thomas had known Poe's brother Henry well, and they had been rivals in a love affair.[563]   It was then that he had first learned of Poe and his work.   Poe had been especially interested in Thomas' novel, *Clinton Bradshaw,* because it depicted persons then living in Baltimore, whom he knew.   In Philadelphia, both of them became intensely interested in each other.   There were long conversations upon poetry and other literary topics.   Poe gave Thomas much good advice about style and method in novel writing, and the evenings at Coates Street were enlivened by Virginia's singing in her sweet, high voice one of Thomas' songs, *It is said that "Absence Conquers Love."*   Thomas loved this composition and once, when in Philadelphia, ill and in hard luck, he had stopped in front of a house on Chestnut Street to listen to a lady's voice singing a familiar tune— it was his own song.

While in Philadelphia in May, 1840, Thomas made a speech for "Tippecanoe and Tyler too"—and was pelted by a mob of the Locofocos. The young politician was a lawyer and a personal admirer of the Whig candidate—

One of the first persons who noticed me in the West was General Harrison, who shortly after my arrival in Cincinnati invited me to the 'Bend,' where I went and was his guest for some weeks,—I was engaged there in one of my first law cases against his eldest son (now dead), William Harrison.[563]

---

[562] Thomas was referring to his sister Frances.   This remark of Poe's is peculiarly significant as showing how strongly he cherished the memory of his foster-mother. Thomas to Poe August 3, 1841, "I remarked one day to my sister *Frances* . . ." etc.
[563] Thomas to Poe, Washington, August 3, 1841.   An autobiographical letter evidently sent by Thomas to his friend for purposes of reviewing.   Full text in Griswold collection.   See "Poe and Thomas," Appendix VI.

It is impossible now, almost a century later, to recall to the present generation the fervency of the presidential campaign of 1840. It marked the beginnings of the insurgence of the idealism and the hopes which two decades later placed Abraham Lincoln in the White House. It was a progressive movement that centered itself about Harrison, a rather futile old military hero, but it was pregnant with the energy and lyric enthusiasm of youth. The Whigs were a young man's party and the campaign marked a departure from old-time methods. There were torchlight processions, speeches by young madcaps in oil-cloth cloaks, glistening with the reflections of rockets and red fire, and, above all, the sound of young, manly voices raised in a national enthusiasm of song while the barbecued ox sizzled before some great bonfire in the prim public squares. Both Poe and Thomas felt the breeze raised by the passing wings of the angel of youth and both wrote political songs. "I battled with right good will for Harrison," says Poe.[564] Thomas was later rewarded with a public office, the benefits of which he tried hard to obtain for Poe. They both met at a time of considerable spiritual enthusiasm, and forever remained firm friends. Most of the biographies of Poe have overlooked the great friendship of Poe's later years. It was a fine one. Their conversation and correspondence were affectionate, and their rare times together fondly cherished. Those who assert that Poe was incapable of true friendship must explain away the contrary evidence of these sometimes touching letters. "You have shown yourself, from the first hour of our acquaintance, that *rara avis in terris*—a true friend. Nor am I the man to be unmindful of your kindness." [565] Poe on his part did many literary favors for Thomas.

Poe's resources, already of the scantiest, were reduced to nil after his parting with Burton. The last of his contributions to the *Gentleman's* ceased in June, 1840. During the past six months his most important critical contributions had been a highly appreciative critique of De la Motte Fouqué's *Undine,* the effect of which is largely overcome by finding the same critic praising, *ad nauseam,* Moore's *Alciphron.* From old association Poe was more than partial to Moore, who had a contemporary reputation now difficult to understand. Poe had also found opportunity to take Longfellow to task for bungling in *Hyperion,* when the stuff of his prose gave him, Longfellow, a great artistic opportunity. Longfellow's treatment of *Hyperion* was more personal and autobiographical than Poe knew, and dealt with the events of the death of his first wife and his second marriage.

---

[564] Poe to Thomas, August 26, 1841. Undated by Stoddard. The date comes from Thomas' reply of July 1, 1841. Thomas' father was also an active Whig, see Appendix VI.

[565] Poe to Thomas, May 25, 1842.

With the advent of Summer, however, Poe's opportunities for publishing were, as we have seen, withdrawn. His contributions from June, 1840, to January, 1841, when he began to write for *Graham's,* were mostly fugitive and certainly obscure. Some went to the Philadelphia newspapers, *Alexander's Weekly Messenger,* to the editor of which he was already known since the cryptogram articles, and a few paragraphs to the *United States Military Magazine.* This comprehended the extent of his publishing until December, 1840.

The rest of the time was taken up by his correspondence concerning the *Penn,* his supervision of the printing and mailing out of the prospectus already noticed, dated January 1, 1841. It was during this interlude that he approached his cousin, William Poe of Baltimore, with an appeal for aid in his venture. The paucity of his work at this time may also be attributed to the approach, through the Fall of 1840, of the sickness which confined him to bed in the December and January following. After the flare-up with Burton there had been a well-authenticated nervous collapse. Which was the cause, and which the effect, it is impossible to ascertain. The ramifications and implications are various.

Suffice it to say, that Poe was far from a well man in heart, brain, or nerves. To this condition was now added the additional strain of no occupation with a consequent return of dire poverty. Once more, for a brief period, his entire support was Mrs. Clemm. In addition to supplying the larder by some beggar's magic, she also nursed both Poe and Virginia. In the Summer, she had received a temporary respite by an absence from Philadelphia "on a six weeks' visit to New Jersey," perhaps to Mary Devereaux, who was then married and living in Jersey City.

In October, 1840, Burton succeeded in selling the *Gentleman's Magazine* outright for $3500 to George R. Graham, the owner of *Atkinson's Casket,* an anemic monthly that had then fluttered harmlessly through ten puerile volumes. Mr. Burton sold out his literary aspirations and used the cash to purchase Cook's Olympic Circus, between Eighth and Ninth Streets in Philadelphia, where he now once more appeared in his true character as manager and chief clown. Graham was thus left in sole charge of both magazines which he continued separately, up until the new year, when their destinies and identities were merged in a new publication called *Graham's Magazine.* Mr. Burton, at the time of the merger, a process lamentably familiar to the readers of modern American periodicals, boasted 3500 subscribers, and Mr. Graham, 1500. The new magazine therefore started with about 5000 for its audience. In a few months it had increased under Poe's editing to over 37,000. It was the largest monthly in the world, the first of the huge modern

American magazines. The inference from these figures speaks loudly for Poe. It was then an unprecedented triumph in the field of journalism.

Graham's Monthly, in some of its respects, may be compared with the present *Saturday Evening Post,* or the *Ladies' Home Journal.* It aimed to appeal to a large audience of both sexes of the middle classes, and it succeeded. Strangely enough, Mr. Graham was at that time a part owner in the contemporary *Saturday Evening Post.* In some respects, except for the fact that he was extravagant and died in poverty, George R. Graham was the Curtis or the Munsey of his time. Behind his first success was the able editor Edgar Allan Poe, for whom, after all, Burton, it appeared, had deep in his heart a real liking. When the negotiations for the sale of the *Gentleman's* were completed, Burton turned to Graham and remarked, "There is one thing more, I want you to take care of my young editor." It was one of the most telling and kindly lines that actor ever spoke. Sometime between October and December, 1840, Mr. Graham came into contact with Poe, for in the last number of the *Gentleman's* under Graham's management, appeared Poe's remarkable tale of conscience, *The Man of the Crowd.* It is a curious combination of a "hero" under the effect of remorse for crime, and the scenes of London which Poe recollected from his sojourn there with the Allans, now grotesquely recalled through the cloud and pall of a dream.

From the blank of the remaining months of the year, only a few glimpses can be snatched. The hunt for a legacy was still on: the old one of William Clemm, Sr., Virginia's grandfather, of Mount Prospect, Maryland. Legal business in connection with this matter seems to have taken Poe to Baltimore in the Summer and Fall of 1840.[469] Mrs. Clemm's lawyer had his offices in the basement of *Barnum's Hotel,* at the intersection of Fayette and Calvert Streets, where Poe was occasionally found. Poe seems to have stayed with the family of Mr. William J. High, an artist, and at that time had a daguerreotype taken by Stanton & Butler at 79 Fayette Street.[566]

This picture he gave to the Highs for their kindness. It afterward seems to have fallen into the hands of some of the Baltimore Poes.

On November 23, 1840, Poe was at home in Philadelphia answering a letter from F. W. Thomas, which—"I only received . . . about an hour ago, having been out of town for the last ten days. . . ." This, and a similar reference to an absence from town in August of the same year, possibly refers to the occasional trips to Baltimore. The rest of Poe's activities at this time related, for the most part, to his efforts to launch the *Penn Magazine.* In his letter to Thomas, Poe continues—

[566] From the history of this daguerreotype, furnished by a Baltimore friend, it has been possible to reconstruct the story of these obscure trips.

Thank you a thousand times for your good wishes and kind offers. I shall wait anxiously for the promised article. I should like to have it, if possible, in the first sheet, which goes to press early in December. But I know that I may depend upon you, and therefore say no more upon this head. For the rest, your own experience and friendship will suggest the modes by which you may serve me in St. Louis. Perhaps, you may be able to have the accompanying 'Prospectus' (of the *Penn*) (which you will see differs from the first) inserted once or twice in some of the city papers—if you can accomplish this without trouble I shall be greatly obliged to you. Have you heard that illustrious graduate of St. John's College, Cambridge (Billy Barlow) [a reference to Burton] has sold his magazine to Graham, of the *Casket?*

Mrs. Clemm and Virginia unite with me in the kindest remembrance to yourself and sister—with whom your conversation (always turning upon the 'one loved name') has already made us so well acquainted. How long will it be before I see you again? Write immediately.

It was probably in November, 1840, that Poe and Mr. Graham first met and talked over the proposition of Poe's assuming charge of the new magazine that was to appear the first month of the new year. The definite engagement did not take place till later, but, as has been noticed, Poe contributed a story to the last number of the *Gentleman's* and his hand is found in the columns of the new monthly as early as February, 1841. That he did not contribute more, or appear largely in the first number, was due to the fact that he was now overtaken by one of those periods of illness, nervous collapse, and prostration which were so significant in his career. It was this, and the expectations of an arrangement with Graham which now perforce deferred the appearance of the *Penn,* and brought him to the verge of a physical and mental crisis.

CHAPTER TWENTY

H I G H   T I D E

MR. GRAHAM had not overlooked Burton's final admonition not to forget his young editor, and, by the middle of January, 1841, Mr. Poe was up and about again, for on the eighteenth of that month he had an interview with the proprietor of the two newly-merged magazines, at which a satisfactory arrangement was made. The agreement with Mr. Graham promised to be the most liberal engagement with any magazine owner, which Poe had so far contracted. He had evidently learned something from his twin experiences with both Mr. White and Burton, and was now, from the first, frank about his desire to start a magazine of his own and to have a large part in shaping the policies of *Graham's,* should he undertake its editorial chair. An arrangement that bore some of the features of a compromise was therefore put in force.

The idea of the *Penn* was not to be abandoned, but was to be held in abeyance. If Poe proved himself capable, Mr. Graham, it appears, would either back him in the new venture or give him an interest in the magazine, as circumstances might dictate. In the meantime Poe was to have a large, if not a directing share in the policies of *Graham's;* to supply stories, articles, poetry, and criticism; and above all, to induce the best known literary characters of the time to lend the luster of their names and the drawing power of their contributions to its pages.[567]

It is certain that this arrangement had been thoroughly discussed between them prior to January, 1841, for, to the last number of *Burton's,* in December, 1840, Poe, as we have seen, had contributed the story of *The Man of the Crowd,* when the expiring *Gentleman's* had been under the management of its new editor. Poe's illness had delayed his assuming complete charge of the first number of *Graham's* which appeared in January, 1841, in all the triumph of fresh format and lavish illustration.

Soon after, the jocular Mr. Burton, who had completely withdrawn from the magazine field, having bought out a bankrupt theatrical manager in Baltimore, opened up in Philadelphia with a blaze of glory in

---

[567] The nature of Poe's "interest" with Mr. Graham is plainly to be pieced together from Graham's statement in his own magazine in 1850 in reply to Griswold's Poe obituary article. More specifically, the terms are plain in Poe's own correspondence after his withdrawal from *Graham's.* See Poe to Daniel Bryan, July 6, 1842, etc.

the New National Theater with *The Rivals* and *A Roland for an Oliver,* as the first bill on August 31, 1840. Mr. Burton's new theater was the finest in America; its scenery, its curtain, and its chandelier were "the marvels of the age." All of this, however, did not prevent its failure. The desire of the Englishman was to repopularize the stock company method which had undergone a serious decline in America, due to the then new "star system," and the exploitation of a new style of hectic publicity. After long vicissitudes, he finally succeeded in New York. With the beginning of 1841, except for a few acid references in his former editor's correspondence, he passes out of the life of Poe.

George Rex Graham (1813-1894), who now became a new and important factor in Poe's career, was a remarkable and, on the whole, an able man. He was the son of a Philadelphia merchant who had lost his fortune in one of the then frequent panics. At an early age he had learned the trade of cabinet-maker. Later on, he studied law and was admitted to the bar in 1839. About that time, he became one of the editors of the *Saturday Evening Post,* and the owner of the *Casket.* He also dabbled a good deal in the purchase of shares and merging of magazines, his final merger of the *Casket* and *Burton's* having involved Poe. With the launching of *Graham's* in 1841, he entered upon the most prosperous and important period of his career. He was the first to undertake successfully a great national magazine in the United States with an audience which numbered many thousands. In short, *Graham's* may be regarded as the forerunner of the large, modern American magazines. In this venture, the experience, the theories, and the abilities of Mr. Poe were attractive to Mr. Graham, who was skilled in his choice of subordinates. These abilities, we may be sure, and not Mr. Burton's advice, were the deciding factors in the choice of an editor.

Mr. Graham announced that "he sought to find a mean between the uninteresting and severe literature that only Tories read and the namby-pambyism which was the ruling note of the age." In addition to this, he inaugurated the policy of paying his authors liberally. Mr. Longfellow received $50, and often more, for a poem. The song writer, George P. Morris, received that much in advance for any song he chose to write, no matter how bad it might be. Fenimore Cooper was paid $1800 for *The Islets of the Gulf (Jack Tier),* which Graham himself admitted did not bring him a single new subscriber, and others were well paid in proportion. Engravings sometimes cost from $100 to $200 a plate, and with printing and fancy paper ran well up to $500. In short, Mr. Graham was lavish in his outlay, and it paid. Unfortunately there was one exception to this policy of generosity. The young editor of *Graham's Lady's and Gentleman's Magazine*—"embracing every department of literature, embellished with engravings, fashions, and music arranged for a piano-forte, harp and guitar"— received a salary which can be described only as meager. It was $800 a year.

For the articles and poems, that he contributed in addition to his regular work, Poe was doled a small rate per page that made the remuneration of Longfellow, and others, look princely. Perhaps this private fact was not without its bearing upon Poe's attitude towards some of the more fortunate New Englanders, the luster of whose names was, at least in this respect, more golden. There can be no doubt that he had been prevailed upon to suspend the *Penn* only by the promise from Mr. Graham of a substantial increase of salary at the end of six months, and the prospect of a partial ownership in his magazine at the end of a year. Mr. Graham began with 5000 subscribers; in about a year and a half he had nearly 40,000. Whatever part the proprietor's business judgment may have played in this then phenomenal success, it must be admitted that most of it was due to Poe, who, from February, 1841, to April, 1842, practically reigned supreme.

Yet, tragically enough, it was this very success that made Mr. Graham reluctant to share it with his editor, or to take part with him in his darling free-lance venture. Poe, however, continued to cling to the idea of his own magazine to the last. His experience with George Rex Graham was only a repetition, on a larger and more affable scale, of his associations with White and Burton. Again the fatal "irregularities" played their part, this time more seriously, and again the ghost of being his own manager haunted the scene and kept him from giving himself wholly to his position.

Small as was the remuneration which Poe received from Mr. Graham in comparison with that of other contributors,[568] it constituted the best offer which he had ever received, one which, in his desperate circumstances, he could not think of disregarding. The *Penn* project was therefore temporarily allowed to lapse, and on February 20, 1841, the *Saturday Evening Post* announced that the *Penn* was "suspended," because of the extreme financial stringency of the times, from which magazines were the first to suffer. Nor was this an unlikely excuse. The Bank of the United States had closed its doors after borrowing some $13,000,000 from other Philadelphia banks, many of which immediately succumbed. Poe was paid a considerable compliment in the notice, and it was announced that this "stern, just, and competent critic would now assume the editorial chair at *Graham's.*" Many of Poe's

---

[568] The salary agreed upon is said to have been $1500 a year with promise of increase. There is considerable conflict about this item which ranges from $1400 to $2000 in various accounts. Poe received a salary of $800!

friends, especially at the South, were greatly disappointed by the announcement. John Tomlin wrote him from Jackson, Tennessee, "Have you indefinitely postponed the publication of the *Penn Magazine?* If so, your friends here are grievously disappointed . . . ," and F. W. Thomas, from Washington where he had lately gone to obtain a government position:

Washington City, *March 7*, 1841

My DEAR POE,—Your humble servant hails for the present from this land of excitement and rascality. I am here scribbling about matters and things. I have been in Washington this week past. Dow, whom I see frequently, told me that you had given up the idea of the *Penn* and was engaged with Graham. I regret that you have been prevented from carrying out that glorious enterprise at present, but you'll do it yet. . . .

I hope, my dear Poe, that you are well and doing well; before long, that is, in a month or so, I hope to take you by the hand. My respects to your mother and lady. Dow is well—and I hope in spite of his Locofocoism will retain his office. Write me if you please, as soon as convenient, as I must answer the proposition I have spoken of above.

P. S. Please direct to me to *Washington* and not St. Louis.

"The proposition" was a proposal by Thomas to write a serial novel for *Graham's Magazine,* to which end the good offices of Poe might be expected. Nor was Thomas' removal from St. Louis to the capital, and his reference to politics, without a particular bearing upon Poe. Thomas, as we have seen, had been a hearty supporter of Harrison, who had been inaugurated only nine days before this letter was written. Harrison had known Thomas' father very well, and soon found a government position for the son. It was the purpose of Thomas to obtain a government clerkship for Poe, which he would very likely have done, had not the death of the old Whig hero on May 4, 1841, upset not only the plans of his friends, but the entire policy of his party. Tyler succeeded, to whom Thomas was less well known, and the effect was adverse to Poe as we shall see.

The offices of *Graham's Magazine* were located at Third and Chestnut Streets, on the top floor of the old *Philadelphia Ledger* Building, and the *Dollar Newspaper,* in which Poe afterward published *The Gold-Bug,* was on the floor immediately underneath. Here Poe came regularly almost every day, from the house on Coates Street, clear on the other side of town. It was from this chair in Graham's office that he now began to turn off the reviews and the stories which, for the next year and a half, continued to thrill the readers of the magazine and to add so much to his own reputation. Some of his best work was done here between periods of opening the mail, sorting the manuscripts, and preparing the copy for new issues—an editorial function, which, with his knowledge and interest in printing, and the methods of illustration then in vogue, he was able to perform peculiarly well.

In the mornings, it was the custom of Mr. Graham and his wife, who now lived in considerable style, to drive up in their carriage; climb up the three flights to the office; and scissor the piles of morning mail, taking out the bank notes and bills that now rolled in with increasing regularity, but leaving the answering of the correspondence to Mr. Poe and his assistants. Graham and his spouse then departed with the roll of money to change it as rapidly as possible, and to the greatest advantage, at the shops of the money-changers along the street just below. This regular matutinal pilfering undoubtedly disgusted the young editor upon whose shoulders most of the burden fell, and played its part in his leaving the paper soon after. The morning harvest for the next two years was always large, but in it he had little share. By July, 1841, the subscription list had risen to 20,000, which promised a gross harvest of about $60,000 to Mr. Graham for the first six months of his venture, and brought a profit to him of about $15,000 at the end of a year.

Graham's, indeed, rapidly came to be the most important and busiest magazine office in the United States. Situated in the great publishing center of the country, about it gathered a bevy of interesting personalities—writers, artists, printers, and engravers—and if nothing else, the worldly importance which the chair at its editorial desk temporarily conferred upon Poe was grateful to a soul which hungered and thirsted for admiration and recognition.

In the same room with Poe, but at another desk, sat Charles J. Peterson, an able assistant editor. He was of Swedish descent, and one of a family of Philadelphia magazine dabblers and printers. His brothers, Theophilus Beasely, George W., and Thomas Peterson, were much in and out, being minor editors and publishers themselves. A little later they set up shop at 306 Chestnut Street, and began to issue cheap stereotyped books of popular authors at twenty-five cents a copy and less, an unheard-of feat at that time. All the latest publishing and printing ideas were in the air, and were discussed diligently by the black-stocked and flare-tailed gentlemen who dropped in to listen to George Graham's sprightly and pleasant conversation, in hopes, perhaps, of an invitation to his famous dinner table.

There were also artists: Thomas Sully, occasionally, who did much work for Graham; a host of minor but clever illustrators; Darley, and the Englishman John Sartain, one of the foremost engravers of the time, whom Sully had prevailed upon to come to America, where he throve at his art and made enough money to enter the magazine field later on, to his own undoing, with *Sartain's Union Magazine*. It was Sartain to whom Poe afterward offered the final manuscript of *The Raven,* and it was he who published posthumously the last draft of

The Bells. Thomas Dunn English was much about the place, as was Captain Mayne Reid, a rather charming novelist who looked like Napoleon III, and was the author of a novel called *Afloat in the Forest,* a tale of a white family adrift on a huge log down the Amazon, that appeared serially in *Our Young Folks,* and intrigued a generation of breathless little boys. He and English frequently walked home with Poe to Coates Street, and later on to the Spring Garden house. Charles Alexander, Burton's printer, had been retained. He was a good friend of Poe. Nor was there any lack of more distinguished visitors.

These made it a point when in the "Quaker City" to call upon Mr. Graham and the much feared Mr. Poe to peddle their wares to the highest bidder then in the field; and always to take dinner with Mr. and Mrs. Graham, who spent much of their new wealth on a lavish table and house, bidding all the live spirits of their world in to dine on the best the land afforded. These parties were brilliant, and were long remembered.

Mr. and Mrs. George Rex Graham had provided themselves with a rather handsome house on Arch Street, whence Mrs. Graham drove out daily behind a fine team of grays that attracted attention even in Philadelphia, a city that went in for smart turnouts. It was her custom at times to call for Virginia, when the pair would drive back down Chestnut Street shopping at the smart Philadelphia stores, after the manner of womankind. To be sure, Mrs. Graham did all of the shopping, although this was the most prosperous time that Virginia and Mrs. Clemm were ever to know. Poe had provided Virginia with a harp, a little pianoforte, and a few luxuries of prettiness in dress in which she and her mother reveled.[569] Sometimes the trip may have ended, as many such a trip did terminate, at Eugene Roussel's store at 114 Chestnut Street, with the black bear in the window, where one of the earliest soda-water fountains in the country was installed. Such trips would be rare, however, and long remembered. The year 1841 was the last in which Virginia was really able to go about much. Speaking of Poe's manner of life at this time, Graham afterward remarked:

I shall never forget how solicitous of the happiness of his wife and mother-in-law he was, whilst one of the editors of *Graham's Magazine,* his whole efforts seemed to be to procure the comfort and welfare of his home. Except for their happiness and the natural ambition of having a magazine of his own, I never heard him deplore the want of wealth. The truth is he cared little for money, and knew less of its value, for he seemed to have no personal expenses! What

---

[569] Mr. Graham himself tells of Poe's buying some luxuries, and his uneasiness until they were paid for. Both Graham and his wife were much at the Poes' house, and he specifically mentions taking Poe and Virginia out to drive. This was certainly not a solitary instance. Roussel's was a well-known rendezvous in the '40's.

he received from me in regular monthly installments went directly into the hands of his mother-in-law for family comforts; and *twice* only I remember his purchasing some rather expensive luxuries for his house, and then he was nervous to the degree of misery until he had, by extra articles, covered what he considered an imprudent indebtedness. His love for his wife was a sort of rapturous worship of the spirit of beauty which he felt was fading before his eyes. I have seen him hovering around her when she was ill, with all the fond fear and tender anxiety of a mother for her first born—her slightest cough causing in him a shudder, a breast chill that was visible. . . .[570]

It seems certain that the year 1841 was one of the times when Poe was most free from his besetting troubles, poverty, and the depressed physical state which led to the use of stimulants. It was probably at this time that Mrs. Clemm began to gather about her a few household articles, the straight-backed flower painted chairs, the brown china with the Chinese river scenes on it,[571] the four-poster beds, curtains, a tea set, and deep-grained, red carpets in which Poe so delighted. All of these were lost a few years later in the desperate poverty that overtook her before the move to New York.

The warning of the breakdown at the end of 1840 had not been without its lesson, and for the next nine months or so, during the first part of his reign at *Graham's,* Poe braced up, as the importance of his new position demanded. Then the old troubles returned and he began to be "irregular." This period marks a peak, perhaps the crest, of his creative faculties.[572] As it was, even then life was not without its temptations. There were those suppers and dinners at Mr. Graham's on Arch Street.

To facilitate hospitality, Mr. Graham had a door broken through the party wall between his own house and that of Elijah Van Sychel, a wine merchant on Second Street, and the best of vintages flowed, from an inexhaustible supply, through this private way onto the great oval table in Graham's dining room beneath a chandelier of bubble crystals purchased from a defunct theater. Here, about a table set under the crystal-twinkling candles, in a room full of mirrors, Poe's especial abomination, Mr. Graham gathered about him the writing and artistic fraternity of the city: the artists Thomas

---

[570] G. R. Graham's *Defense of Poe, Graham's,* 1850.

[571] The description of these articles is literal. Some of the chairs are still in Philadelphia. The second landlord of the Spring Garden house also remembered articles left behind in 1844, in lieu of rent. Mr. William Owens, the late tenant (1926) at 530 North Seventh Street, had a unique relic of the Poe china. Also see reminiscences of T. C. Clarke, Sartain, Graham, and *Poe in Philadelphia* by Alexander Harvey, the *Press,* Philadelphia, June 19, 1892.

[572] The "peak" does not imply that the best or most perfect items of his creative faculty were turned off while Poe was editor of *Graham's,* but that during that period as both a critic and an artist he functioned importantly, consistently, and for a considerable time during which his contact with various important personalities was especially significant.

Sully, Darley, Robert Bud, and Sartain; N. P. Willis, when he was in Philadelphia; Judge Conrad, Thomas Dunn English, Louis A. Godey, Mrs. Hale, the Petersons, T. C. Clarke, Rufus Griswold, and the "sweet lady writer," Grace Greenwood. Even Henry Clay came there once to dine, and to toast the delightful Mrs. Graham, who presided over the Philadelphia prodigality of her table with a happy and memorable charm.[573] Poe was often seen at the board, coming with a sleeveless mantle thrown over one shoulder; in the inevitable suit of raven black, hoping to be seated next to Thomas Sully, to whom he could talk of Robert and of old Richmond days, and hear of his friends. Here it was, too, that he often, and for a while pleasantly, found himself face to face with his future biographer, Griswold, while story and anecdote followed the bowl, and the bottles appeared mysteriously through the so-convenient private door. The candles frequently burned low before they rose. It was delightful, and it was hard to withstand.

But there was a reverse to this convivial and social medal which was not so bright. Mrs. Clemm, it appears, was much worried by these dinners at Graham's and would wait late in the kitchen to take Poe home. Characteristically enough, she also brought a basket, and fragments of the feast accompanied her home with Eddie, who otherwise was given to dropping in for a few brandies with Henry B. Hirst, or absinthe with Sartain—then almost anything might happen. It might be Front Street or Lower Dock, and another spell in bed. For a while, though, all went well—Mr. Poe was regularly and hard at work.

Besides the usual routine involved in the editing and make-up of a large magazine, Poe proved himself of great value to his proprietor by his ability to secure for the columns of his periodical the magnet of well-known names. A considerable portion of his time through the Spring of 1841 was taken up in writing to various American authors asking them to contribute. This correspondence frequently took the form of circular letters, only slightly altered to suit the individual case. He was quite skillful in drafting these, and the response was often cordial. Poe had followed the same scheme successfully with both White and Burton, but in Graham's case he had the added bait of high pay to sweeten the lure, and the pages of a really important publication to open to his correspondents.

In the Spring and Summer of 1841, he wrote to Washington

---

[573] When Mr. Graham was ending his days poor and infirm at Orange, New Jersey, in the early 1890's, the lavish dinners of his prosperous days were recalled by the few who remembered a discarded but once important figure in American journalism. John Sartain, T. C. Clarke, N. P. Willis, and others have left accounts of Graham in his heyday.

Irving, Fenimore Cooper, Fitz-Greene Halleck, N. P. Willis, and several others, asking their coöperation. These letters were peculiar, however, in that they were not only a plea in disguised form for *Graham's,* but also show that Poe had taken seriously Mr. Graham's promise to aid in the establishing of the new magazine in which Poe was to have a proprietary interest. In short, Poe could not drop the darling idea of the *Penn* or a similar periodical, as this letter to Longfellow, typical of many others, plainly shows:

Philadelphia, *June* 22, 1841

DEAR SIR,—Your letter of the 19th May was received. I regret to find my anticipations confirmed, and that you cannot make it convenient to accept Mr. Graham's proposition. Will you now pardon me for making another?

I need not call your attention to the signs of the times in respect to magazine literature. You will admit the tendency of the age lies in this way—so far at least as regards the lighter letters. The brief, the terse, the condensed, and the easily circulated, will take the place of the diffuse, the ponderous, and the inaccessible. Even our reviews, (lucus a non lucendo) are found too massive for the taste of the day. I do not mean for the taste of the tasteless, but for that of the few. In the meantime the finest minds of Europe are beginning to lend their spirit to magazines. In this country, unhappily, we have not any journal of the class which either can afford to offer pecuniary inducement to the highest talent, or which would be, in all respects, a fitting vehicle for its thoughts. In the supply of this deficiency there would be a point gained; and in the hope of at least partially supplying it, Mr. Graham and myself propose to establish a Magazine. . .

Poe then continues with a description of the format which he regards ideal, the hope of gaining noted contributors, and a request to Longfellow to furnish one paper each month—"prose or poetry, absolute, or serial."

This letter, and its several copies dispatched to others, is remarkable for bringing out the strong and weak points of Poe's judgment. His literary analysis of the time is excellent. Indeed, many of his remarks about the reviews and the reviewing fraternity apply today, but his lack of foresight and a knowledge of human nature in supposing that Mr. Graham would give up the then so profitable magazine he already owned, to embark on a totally new venture, merely to carry out the pet literary theories of his assistant editor, is almost childish. Nor is it likely that Graham relished the implied criticism of the magazine which Poe was then editing for him in such letters as these. News of such correspondence as this must inevitably have come to his ears, as it had come to Burton's and have made the ensuing parting with Poe less hard to bear. Poe had also written John P. Kennedy a somewhat similar note in June, in which he also asked for a novel. Mr. Kennedy had been elected to Congress, however, and did not comply.[574]

Through the Summer and Fall of 1841, Poe also continued his quite intimate correspondence with Dr. Snodgrass of Baltimore, who contributed several items to *Graham's,* one of which Poe says the "proof reader" spoiled. At the same time, its author was appearing in *Godey's.* A contract to write exclusively for *Godey's* prevented N. P. Willis from contributing to *Graham's.*[575] The first correspondence between him and Poe bears the date of November 30, 1841, but there had evidently been considerable previous intercourse. Mr. Willis was later on to play an important rôle in the affairs of Poe. Poe had evidently been using a little "diplomacy" to get around the contract difficulty with Godey, and Mr. Willis' letter appears to be a little surprised in tone.

That Poe regarded even the important post on *Graham's* as only a temporary makeshift, and that he chafed under his poverty, is plainly brought out as early as May 20, 1841, when the first definite suggestion of a federal office, which for the next two years continued to agitate them both, was made by his friend, F. W. Thomas, himself on the national payroll at Washington. Mr. Thomas' account of the duties implied, and the leisure left over for literary-minded gentlemen, is alluring:

MY DEAR POE:

. . . How would you like to be an office holder here at $1500 per year payable monthly by Uncle Sam, who, however slack he may be to his general creditors, pays his officials with due punctuality. How would you like it? You stroll to your office a little after nine in the morning leisurely, and you stroll from it a little after two in the afternoon homeward to dinner and return no more that day. If, during office hours, you have anything to do, it is an agreeable relaxation from the monotonous laziness of the day. You have on your desk everything in the writing line in apple-pie order, and if you choose to lucubrate in a literary way, why you can lucubrate. . . .

We can be sure that Mr. Poe would have liked this very well indeed. The young man who had found time to compose poems on the counter at *Ellis & Allan,* some years before, would have known well how to take advantage of the strolling leisure and the writing materials in "apple-pie order." Mr. Thomas was already "lucubrating" considerably himself while drawing down $1000 a year. Poe

---

[574] Poe's faith in Mr. Kennedy's kindness must have been at times a little onerous to his early patron. A little later he appeals to him again for political influence; another appeal, still later, is made for money. Cash loans Mr. Kennedy refused, perhaps with good reason. In all else he helped when he could. See also Chapter XVIII, note 507.

[575] The items mentioned here are to be found in the correspondence with the persons mentioned about this date, September and November, 1841.

replied on June 26, 1841, congratulating Thomas, and suddenly discovering that he himself was an ardent Whig,—one who had "battled with right good will for Harrison, when opportunity offered." Alas! that good man was dead! "With Mr. Tyler I have some slight personal influence, although it is a matter which he has possibly forgotten," Poe adds—but, "I am a Virginian—at least I call myself one"—and it is not to be forgotten that President Tyler had been born in old Charles City County, the oldest part of the Old Dominion.

A few days later Thomas writes again, urging Poe to come to Washington, and suggesting that his old friend John P. Kennedy might be induced to help with his newly-acquired Congressional influence.[574] Poe would like to have gone and replied:

> I wish to God I could visit Washington, but—the old story you know—I have no money; not enough to take me there, to say nothing of getting back. It is hard to be poor, but as I am kept so by an honest motive I dare not complain. . . . I would be glad to get almost any appointment, even a $500.00 one, so that I have something independent of letters for a subsistence. To coin one's brain into silver, at the nod of a master, is, to my thinking, the hardest task in the world. . . .

Here in a nutshell we have Poe's own objection to magazine work, and here the matter rested for some time. Thomas saw Kennedy, who promised to help, and drew the attention of the President's sons to Poe's articles. Poe on his part began to find great merits in Robert Tyler's poetry—the matter dragged on.[576]

The Spring of 1842 had been productive of many interviews and meetings which initiated some of the most important friendships and acquaintances of Poe's life. Perhaps the most far-reaching of these was his encounter with Rufus Wilmot Griswold.

The Reverend Mr. Griswold, for such was the gentleman's rightful title, had been born at Benson, Vermont, in 1815, and in his early days had traveled both abroad and in the United States. He had been a kind of printer-publisher's apprentice for some time, but had later on taken up the study of theology and become a Baptist clergyman. He left that, even then, unlucrative profession, to become an editor, a compiler, and perhaps, on the whole, the most competent hack writer about personalities in the United States. There were no authors, then of any note or even glimmering obscurity in the United States, whom Mr. Griswold did not in a sketchy way know all about. His editing of various works of sundry kinds and his connections with various periodicals had given him a cannily clever

---

[576] Robert Tyler, the President's older son, was a frequent contributor to magazines and newspapers in both prose and verse. He had married Priscilla Cooper, a daughter of Thomas Cooper. She was then mistress of the White House, the President being a widower.

Laurel Hill Cemetery

A favorite Sunday Afternoon Saunter in the 1840's in Philadelphia

From an engraving in Godey's Lady's Book *for 1844*

A Pic-nic on the Wissahickon

Showing the effect of romantic literature on the landscape and flora
about Philadelphia in the 1840's

From Graham's Magazine *edited by Poe*
Courtesy of John T. Snyder, Esq., of Pelham, New York

A Philadelphia Shop of the Early 1840's

A typical engraved card of the era
Courtesy of the Pennsylvania Historical Society

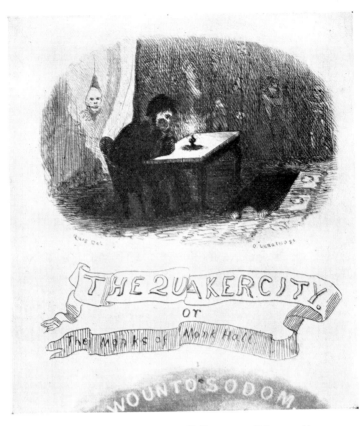

Title Page to one of George Lippard's
Philadelphia Novels

LIPPARD was a friend of POE in Philadelphia, and later on, in 1849, helped to save his life. Such books as LIPPARD's uncover a forgotten vein in American romantic-Gothic novels and stories that help to explain the contemporary literary atmosphere in which POE lived

Faithfully yours
Charles Dickens

The famous English novelist about the time of his interviews with Poe in
Philadelphia at the United States Hotel

*From an engraving of a portrait D. Maclise, A. R. A., issued by Lea and
Blanchard in 1840*

Courtesy of the Edgar Allan Poe Shrine, Richmond, Virginia

insight into the lives, tendencies, and ambitions of his contemporaries. In addition to this he possessed a too shrewd natural insight. Had he not been so shrewd about personalities he might have been more literary. The Reverend Doctor's attack on Poe after the latter's death, and a certain flair of petty treachery, combined with his subtle methods of invigorating truth with a specious dose of probable lies, has induced a large number of his commentators, and especially the protagonists of Poe, to surmise that Rufus Griswold was provided with a dash of canine blood on his mother's side. Lowell, who was not given to invective, once remarked that "the Reverend Mr. Griswold is an ass, and, what's more, a knave." This was going it a bit too far, however. The truth seems to be that his knavery was very careful and his asininity somewhat encyclopedic. Perhaps the most serious charge against him is that he was the first "great" American anthologist.

Poe met Griswold in Philadelphia sometime in the early Spring of 1841, when the Doctor was engaged in preparing for publication his *Poets and Poetry of America,* a book that appeared in April, 1842, and subsequently went through some twenty-nine editions. Poe had not been writing poetry for some time. Prose, and the press of much journalistic business had forbidden. He had not forgotten, however, his first literary love. The three early volumes had been constantly called upon for revised republication here and there, and Griswold's anthology was an opportunity not to be missed. Griswold, on his part, was anxious to do a favor for the rising young editor of *Graham's;* and in March, 1841, some correspondence and talk evidently passed between them, with the result that several of Poe's poems and a sketch of his life—very sketchy and misleading, indeed—were included in the new anthology with a modest meed of praise by Griswold.[577] The most memorable poem of Poe's which was accepted was *The Haunted Palace,* which Poe claimed, but mistakenly, that Longfellow had plagiarized in his *Beleaguered City.* Significantly enough, Poe remarks to Griswold that, "by the 'Haunted

---

[577] These autobiographical sketches, the data for which were furnished by Poe to Griswold, Hirst, Thomas, Lowell, etc., etc., from time to time are not to be taken seriously as evidence against Poe's veracity. Almost any author of any note can recall furnishing *A Sketch of My Life,* on the sudden demand of a publisher or correspondent, that was sufficient unto the hour and was never expected to stand up under careful scrutiny. There is no intent to deceive in this type of "biography," but simply a desire to please. Poe substituted an interesting trip abroad, which he meant to take, for a boresome year in the army, and moved up his birthday a precocious notch or two. Such fibs were the common stock in trade of innumerable writers. The President of the United States must be born in a log cabin, and every American poet must live, at least for a while, in London or Paris. This is simply the orange juice that enables the public to swallow the man. The creation of a personal legend is the necessity of genius. The gods live by myths.

Palace' I meant to imply a mind haunted by phantoms—a disordered brain." For the time being, all was pleasant between these two young men, whose association was so mutually disastrous.

The first feeling of jealousy arose between them because Griswold, above all things, hoped to be a poet himself, but his performance in the creative field was lamentable, and Poe took no care to disguise his contempt. On the other hand, no praise which Griswold could have bestowed on Poe would have been sufficient to the poet's praise-hungry ears. The modest draught which he did receive, he felt to be an insult. In short, he was classed as an equal of many and the inferior of a few. It was a critical estimate which he never forgave. Shortly afterward, Griswold appeared as an editorial rival for Poe's own chair; Poe made fun of the anthology in a public lecture; and the foundations for a hatred that has followed both beyond the grave were thus satisfactorily laid. These petty causes seem out of all proportion to the dire results. Yet no one could be more biting than Poe when he chose to be. Speaking of the *North American Review* and its coterie, which he especially loathed, he once closed an acid paragraph with an extract from Sterne's *Letter from France:* "As we rode along the valley we saw a herd of asses on the top of one of the mountains—how they viewed and reviewed us!"

About midsummer Poe again addressed Lea & Blanchard on the subject of getting out another edition of *Tales of the Grotesque and Arabesque,* in which were to be included his new stories of *The Murders in the Rue Morgue* and *The Descent into the Maelström,* lately brought out in *Graham's.* "The new pieces will be eight in number, making the entire collection thirty-three, which will occupy two thick novel volumes." Once again, he was forced to propose that all the profits should go to the publishers, his only reward to be twenty copies for himself. Even this, however, was not attractive to Lea & Blanchard, who replied immediately:

August 16, 1841

EDGAR A. POE

. . . In answer we very much regret to say that the state of affairs is such as to give little encouragement to undertakings. As yet we have not got through the edition of the other work, and up to this time it has not returned us the expense of the publication . . . etc.

"The state of affairs" obviously refers to the chronic condition of financial panic and publishing difficulties at the time, from which Poe suffered in several ways. It is safe to say that the same tales have, in various editions and publications, been reprinted thousands of times in many languages. To their author they brought nothing but a few complimentary copies, and the small price paid for them by magazines. Fame has been his only reward.

Poe, like all the other American authors of his time, suffered from a publishing and printing situation in the United States, purely legal and economic in its nature, which for many decades, from 1815 to the early '90's of the last century, exercised a controlling influence on American literature. The erudite and abstract minds which, for the most part, in critical and academic circles manufacture the literary comment and authoritative judgments upon the literature of the past, seem wholly ignorant of or oblivious to the fact that, in order to have any voice in the choir of his era, an author must first get himself printed and then widely published, *i.e.,* distributed. In this mechanical and economic process, his artistic or purely literary merit is, during his lifetime, only too often a negligible factor. No matter what the literary merit of a work may be, unless it be embodied in a book it can never be known. This patent and obvious fact, and the purely practical factors which govern it, are scarcely even commented upon by those who deal, afterward, with the content of literature from a detached and artistic standpoint.

That the clauses of a nation's copyright laws may very largely determine the forms of its literature and dictate inevitably the whole trend of a literary epoch is too obvious a consideration to intrigue the minds of critics intent upon nice abstractions. A study of the correspondence of American publishing houses during the last century largely explains, upon this practical basis, the whole trend and condition of American literature. As one turns the faded leaves of the copy books of, say, Harpers, Carey & Lea, Longman & Company, etc., it soon becomes patent that the popularity of foreign authors in the United States and the permanence of their reputations were more the result of the conditions of copyright law, than of their own inherent merit. In all this, the advance in the art of printing, the skill and the wages of the printer and binder, and the ethics of the book trade played an inevitable part.

The result of the law of copyright in the United States during the Nineteenth Century, and the publishing conditions it evoked, was to create for all American novelists, poets, and authors of any books whatsoever a tremendous handicap in the race for fame in America, particularly with English writers. In the final analysis it was a wall *which no single American author of the early Nineteenth Century* was ever *fully* able to surmount during his lifetime.[578]

---

[578] An excellent, and one of the few available texts on this important aspect of American letters is *Mathew Carey, A Study in American Literature,* Earl L. Bradsher, the Columbia University Press, 1912, to which the following brief discussion is frankly in great debt. Thanks are due to Dr. Bradsher for permission to quote from the correspondence of Carey & Lea embodied in his text, and from his own text.

Stated briefly and baldly, the situation of American publishing, and therefore of American letters, from the close of the War of 1812, and for many decades thereafter, was conditioned by the fact that the financial survival of American printers and publishers was wholly dependent upon the number and the rapidity with which they could pirate the editions of English and other current foreign books. Up until 1812 the processes of printing and the means of transportation were so slow and precarious that, although there was a considerable reprinting and importation of English classics through ordinary channels, there was no thought or opportunity of exploiting such a trade, any more than a publisher might now be said to be "exploiting" Byron by offering a new edition of his works. With the new generation after the War of 1812, however, both the taste for reading and the facilities for printing and importation had entirely altered. Letters from even such then remote places as Pittsburgh, Pennsylvania, and Augusta, Georgia, show that cheap English novels were all the rage. To publish an American novel or any native book implied the purchase of copyright from the author, or at least a royalty, followed by the laborious printing of it from handwritten manuscript. On the other hand, to bring out an English novel, or an English translation of a French or German book, required no payments to the author whatever. All that was necessary was a single copy of the book. The main point of success was to be first in the field. Thus the publishing house that *first* obtained a copy of a new foreign book skimmed the cream off the sales. To obtain such copies even a few hours in advance, there were no lengths to which publishers were not prepared to go.

Large publishing houses had their English scouts, sometimes an employee of an English firm, or the firm itself. These agents forwarded the proof or the advance copies of a first edition by "the first and swiftest sailing vessel." Swift schooners and sloops were employed to meet these vessels at sea, or at the outer anchorage, where the books were transferred and brought in a few hours or a day in advance, thus insuring a gain in time, which was the deciding factor. Travelers were importuned, and their books bought at preposterous prices. Many an English gentleman found that the novels he had laid in, to while away the tedious hours of a voyage, constituted an unexpected and handsome investment. The volume having once been obtained, its binding was torn off; the leaves distributed among a gang of swift compositors, and, without even the trouble of calculating the page make-up, by evening the work was in frames; the presses went all night, and by evening of the next day, a new American edition of Scott, Byron, Miss Porter, Miss Edgeworth,

Moore, Burney, Lady Morgan, Leigh Hunt, or someone else was on its way to booksellers all over the country. If necessary, all the seats in the outgoing stages would be hired to carry the books. For instance, one publisher writes:

MR. JOHN MILLER, *June* 17, 1823,

We have rec'd *Quentin Durward* most handsomely and have the Game completely in our own hands this time. In 28 hours after receiving it, we had 1500 copies sent off or ready to go, and the whole Edition is now nearly distributed. In two days we shall publish it here and in New York and the Pirates may print it as soon as they please. The opposition Edition will be out in 48 hours after they have one of our copies but we shall have complete and entire possession of every market in the Country for a short time. Independently of profit, it is in the highest degree gratifying to be able to manage the matter in our own way without fear of interference . . . etc.[578]

This was publishing with a vengeance! A whole volume might be devoted to the elaboration and proof of the strange conditions of bookselling and publishing in early nineteenth century America. Even a glimpse is illuminating. The opinion, so generally held, that the intellectual and social background of America was incapable, for a long period, of producing any considerable number of able writers, rests on a conclusion which has been arrived at for the most part without a knowledge of the controlling facts. Under the existing copyright laws, the only salvation for American authors lay in the limited output of English books. Unfortunately for Americans, the English were prolific.

When Scott appeared, one immensely popular novel followed another in quick succession. The American public after devouring the latest, looked for the next. Hardly had Scott ceased to produce when Dickens, ably seconded by Marryat, began a series equally popular; and, when Marryat fell out, Benjamin Disraeli was ready to fill the gap. From *Waverley* in 1814, to *The Mystery of Edwin Drood,* 1870, the year that did not produce at least one highly popular British novel was a barren one. Against this continuous stream the American novelist was compelled to wage a bitter struggle.[578]

The struggle, from the standpoint of the creation of a native literature in the United States, was largely in vain. America was annually flooded with English books; the prestige of wide and international fame went to foreigners; and the native writer had to combat, not only the vast difficulty of getting published at all, but along with it, the suspicion that he was a provincial tyro. "Who reads an American book?" asked a famous English critic. Who, indeed! When six books out of ten that got printed even in the United States were English.

Against this condition and the reading prejudices which it evoked, Poe with others wages a ceaseless and a futile battle. That his collected tales did not sell even 750 copies in a single year was no comment on their literary quality; the miracle was that they had been published at all. "The state of affairs is *such*," say Lea & Blanchard—and it certainly was. Only by waiving his royalty could Poe appear at all. The price of American books was always higher than that of English, as the royalty was necessarily included in a native production. Cooper went through a series of failures. Carey & Lea lost $2600 on one of Cooper's novels alone. Washington Irving, by the 1840's, found difficulty in getting his work published with even a decent royalty, and was thwarted in obtaining an edition of over 2500. His hopes for fine editions and an adequate format were regarded as the dreams of eccentric luxury. In March, 1842, he is offered "the . . . present arrangement for two years at one thousand dollars per annum and *include* the right to publish *Astoria, Miscellany,* etc., in it. Or if you wish to publish *Mahomet* this spring and the two volumes of tales mentioned in your letter . . ." and this represented the *ne plus ultra* to the "prince of American authors." Dorr's Rebellion in Rhode Island, the failure of the United States Bank, the suspension of interest, even on state deposits, by banks in Maryland and Pennsylvania, and the disastrous disorganization of the currency, completed the scene of gloom in which Poe had appeared with his *Grotesques and Arabesques.* Poe was only one of many. He was in fact typical of all:

J. Fenimore Cooper *Esq.,* Nov. 13, 1834

We wish to remark that we have been *compelled* to sell Books cheaper than we did formerly. When your early works were published English novels retailed for $1.50 and American could be sold at $2. Now the other retails at $1, and the other at about $1.50 less. . . .[578]

William Gilmore Simms labored under similar difficulties and could get his books set up only slowly, chapter by chapter in small editions, while his publishers were using as many as ten or twelve printing firms at a time to rush through an English novel. This discouraging process is shown in the following letter to Robert Carey, the publisher in Philadelphia:

Woodland, 5th *May*

Dear Sir:

I sent you some time since seven Chapters of B. B.—To Mr. Beite. I have just transmitted the conclusion of Vol. 1 together with a portion 64 pages—of Vol. 2 inc. I trust you receive [them] safely . . .etc.[579]

The result of all these exasperating delays, small royalties and failures, lack of prestige, and ceaseless competition was to discourage any but the most determined American writers from writing

[579] From a letter of William Gilmore Simms belonging to the author.

novels or works that required the dignity of book form. Hence innumerable magazines flourished, and the short story became the favored medium and fast developed form. Poe wrote short stories, not because he regarded them as a great art form, but because no other form would pay. American novels were almost driven out of existence, verse was confined to magazines, and the cheap pamphleted English plays flooded the market. The only recourse for an American writer was to write for the magazine, or even newspaper field; or to become one of a group such as the transcendentalists, who manufactured their own audience. In the sparsely settled South, plantation distances made such groups impossible. Coteries were therefore confined to New England, or to one or two cities where a few American authors asserted themselves like Kennedy, Bayard Taylor, or the Knickerbockers. New England was the most self-conscious and best organized native audience, and there a few American books actually sold. Elsewhere the foreign flood washed clear over literary heads. Philadelphia was the great American publishing center, but it published English books. The cause had been enacted by the Congress into a federal statute for the encouragement and protection of authors.

In considering the desperate and sometimes ignoble and petty lengths to which Poe, Longfellow, Lowell, and others went to obtain publication and an adequate hearing, the conditions of the time must be borne in mind. Had even the best of authors not done so, the ranks of the mute and inglorious Miltons would have been augmented, and posterity have been none the wiser. The end, in this case, justified the means. It was a case of survival and existence; right and meet so to do. The protests of two generations of thwarted and impoverished American authors were inaudible at Washington. At last, the publishers, and the printers' union took a hand in the matter, the copyright law was changed, and the professors and critics began to proclaim a new era in American literature. The cause was so close under their noses that they had overlooked it entirely. Only the publishers knew, and with them it was a trade secret.

Despite the failure of Poe's friends to obtain a government sinecure for him by political influence, and the refusal of his publishers to bring out a new edition of his tales, there was never a time in his life when there were so few clouds visible on the horizon; when his prospects appeared so bright as in the Summer and Autumn of 1841. He was, apparently for him, fairly well; and, for the time being, he braced himself to meet the responsibilities of a new position by letting stimulants alone. He was the respected and feared editor and critic of an important, if not the most important, magazine in

the country. Although comparatively poor, his home was comfortable and even pretty. Virginia's health had not yet broken fatally,
and she was still able to accompany him on Sunday rambles or picnics up the Wissahickon. Above all he was growing in fame, and,
for the time being, seemed surrounded by friends old and new. These
delighted to gather at the Coates Street house, kept spotless by Mrs.
Clemm, who managed Poe's bank account carefully.[570] She and
Virginia added all they could by taking in sewing. Virginia was now
eighteen, but a friend who knew her then says, ("She hardly looked
more than fourteen." One can see her in a poke bonnet with "her
round full face and figure, pouting lips, a forehead too high and
broad for beauty, and big, dark eyes and ravenblack hair, contrasting
almost startlingly with a white colorless complexion," [580] dressed in
some simple white dress, and leaning upon Edgar's arm as he wandered
with her on Sunday afternoons through the fashionable shades of
Laurel Hill Cemetery, among the cypress and weeping willow trees.
Other gentlemen with tall beaver hats, with other drooping ladies,
also leaning upon black broadclothed arms, passed them solemnly.
The birds sang and flashed from tomb to tomb. "It is a theme,"
says the editress of *Godey's Lady's Book,* "upon the beauties of which
we could expatiate for hours"—and she did.[581]

Summer afternoons, the gentlemen exercised their tandems about
Browne's Chinese Pagoda, or there were walks to be taken over the
old, arched, covered bridge (which looked like a long, badly bent
canal boat with Grecian ambitions) to the Fairmount Water Works,
where the white Ionic pillars were mirrored in the river and the reservoirs. Poe must have gone swimming in the river when it was hot.
Virginia loved to watch him, as she did later on in New York. And
there were boat trips, perhaps with the Detwilers. The family appears never to have gone to church. On "First Day" mornings (for
Philadelphia kept Quaker Sabbath rather than Sunday) Poe would
sometimes rise early and scull up to the then remote and rural valley
of the Wissahickon to dream beside some quiet meadow bank. Of
one such adventure, perhaps of many, he has left a delightful record—

MORNING ON THE WISSAHICCON [582]

by *Edgar A. Poe*

It was not until Fanny Kemble, in her droll book about the United States,
pointed out to the Philadelphians the rare loveliness of a stream which lay at

---

[580] For this, and several other remarks upon Poe's marriage and Virginia's appearance, see Mrs. Susan Archer Weiss' *Home Life of Poe.*
[581] *Godey's Lady's Book,* March, 1844, page 107.
[582] From the *Opal* for 1844, an annual published by N. P. Willis. This little pseudo-
pastoral of Poe's is little known in comparison with many of his popular stories.

their own doors, that this loveliness was more than suspected by a few adventurous pedestrians of the vicinity. But, the *Journal* having opened all eyes, the Wissahiccon, to a certain extent, rolled at once into notoriety. I say 'to a certain extent,' for, in fact, the true beauty of the stream lies far above the *route* of the Philadelphian picturesque-hunters, who rarely proceed farther than a mile or two above the mouth of the rivulet—for the very excellent reason that here the carriage-road stops. I would advise the adventurer who would behold its finest points to take the Ridge Road, running westwardly from the city, and, having reached the second lane beyond the sixth mile-stone, to follow this lane to its termination. He will thus strike the Wissahiccon, at one of its best reaches, and, in a skiff, or by clambering along its banks, he can go up or down the stream, as best suits his fancy, and in either direction will meet his reward.

I have already said, or should have said, that the brook is narrow. Its banks are generally, indeed, almost universally, precipitous, and consist of high hills, clothed with noble shrubbery near the water, and crowned at a greater elevation with some of the most magnificent forest trees of America . . . that define the moss covered bank, against which the pellucid water lolls its gentle flow, as the blue waves of the Mediterranean upon the steps of her palaces of marble. Occasionally in front of the cliffs, extends a small definite *plateau* of richly herbaged land, affording the most picturesque position for a cottage and garden which the richest imagination could conceive. The windings of the stream are many and abrupt, as is usually the case where banks are precipitous, and thus the impression conveyed to the voyager's eye, as he proceeds, is that of an endless succession of infinitely varied small lakes, or more properly speaking tarns. . . .

Not long ago I visited the stream by the route described, and spent the better part of a sultry day in floating in a skiff upon its bosom. The heat gradually overcame me, and resigning myself to the influence of the scenes and of the weather, and of the gently moving current, I sank into a half slumber, during which my imagination revelled in visions of the Wissachiccon of ancient days— of the 'good old days' when the Demon of the Engine was not, when picnics were undreamed of, when 'water privileges' were neither bought nor sold, and when the red man trod alone, with the elk, upon the ridges that now towered above. And, while gradually these conceits took possession of my mind, the lazy brook had borne me, inch by inch, around one promontory and within full view of another that bounded the prospect at the distance of fifty yards. It was a steep rocky cliff, abutting far into the stream, and presenting much more of the Salvator character than any portion of the shore hitherto passed. What I saw upon this cliff, although surely an object of very extraordinary nature, the place and season considered, at first neither startled nor amazed me—so thoroughly and appropriately did it chime in with the half-slumberous fancies that enwrapped me. I saw, or dreamed that I saw, standing upon the extreme verge of the precipice, with neck outstretched, with ears erect, and the whole attitude indicative of profound and melancholy inquisitiveness, one of the oldest and boldest of those identical elk which had been coupled with the red men of my vision.

I say that, for a few moments, this apparition neither startled nor amazed me. During this interval my whole soul was bound up in intense sympathy alone. I fancied the elk repining, not less than wondering, at the manifest alterations for the worse, wrought upon the brook and its vicinage, even within the last few years, by the stern hand of the utilitarian. But a slight movement of the animal's head at once dispelled the dreaminess which wrested me, and aroused me to a full sense of the novelty of the adventure. I arose upon one knee within the skiff, and while I hesitated whether to stop my career, or let myself float nearer to the object of my wonder, I heard the words 'hist! hist!' ejaculated quickly but cautiously, from the shrubbery overhead. In an instant afterward a negro emerged from the thicket, putting aside the bushes with care, and treading stealthily. He bore in one hand a quantity of salt, and, holding it towards the elk, gently yet steadily approached. The noble animal, although a little fluttered, made no attempt to escape. The negro advanced; offered the salt; and spoke a few words of encouragement or conciliation. Presently, the elk bowed and stamped, and then lay quietly down and was secured with a halter.

Thus ended my romance of the elk. It was a *pet* of great age and very domestic habits, and belonged to an English family occupying a villa in the vicinity.

This charming but now little read sketch of Poe's shows him in the midst of his dreams in the kind of landscape that evoked them. How great was the influence of the artists and engravers of the time upon their own generation, and more particularly upon the landscapes, descriptions of which reappear in Poe's stories, can only be understood by becoming familiar with the publications of the day. It is not an exaggeration to affirm that, through the medium of romantic art, they beheld a different world from ours; that their eyes were altered. It was the evoking of the dreams of his time in their *perfect melancholy types,* in both prose and poetry, which partly explains Poe's place in literature. The perfection of the dreams of any age is always interesting. But there is another element that enters here. The complaint about the devastating hand of the utilitarian is typical. In the march of industrialism, Poe beheld the hand that was ruining the pastoral world into which he had been born, and still loved. Chimneys were already blowing their black clouds across his valley of the many-colored grass. He was one of the first to understand their implication and to complain. Where the elk stood, is to-day a landscape that is humanly intolerable, and "progress" is still at work.

"Never sing the Three so well as when penniless," remarked Poe in a review, but his whole life was a refutation of the theory that the poet is nourished by starved muses. Comfort and prosperity mark on the whole the most active creative period of his life.[572] Poe contributed largely to every number of *Graham's Magazine* during that time, conducted an active correspondence, and overflowed into other public prints. In the two years mentioned he turned off no less than fifty-one reviews, nine new stories, and fifteen essays; reprinted two revised poems, and published two new ones. Besides all this, there may be some still untraced items, and there are definite indications that he was at work at home on some material which followed later.

The temper of Poe's criticism in *Graham's* had not changed essentially from that contributed to the *Southern Literary Messenger* some years before. It was, to be sure, a little more urbane and a little more worldly wise—and in this more kindly attitude he was warranted—for the books which now came to his hand for review happened to be on the whole rather better than those of the previous decade. The poetry was not *quite* so saccharine, and the prose at least pretended, at times, to deal with the actual world. A review of Moore's *Alciphron* in January, 1840, showed that Poe was under the spell of the age himself and still admired one of his first masters in poetry, for he hailed it as a masterpiece.[583] Longfellow came in for praise, and condemnation as a mere copyist, while Tennyson drew forth Poe's whole admiration as the "greatest" of all English poets. It was probably more Tennyson's skill in language than his philosophy which brought forth the praise. The prose reviews ranged from Seba Smith's *Powhatan* to Macaulay's *Critical and Miscellaneous Essays*. The total impression after turning over these now faded reviewer's columns, dealing with for the most part forgotten books, is that a brilliant critical mind, steeped in the maxims of Coleridge, and provided with curious insight and a clever dialectic, has been compelled to waste itself upon small fry.

When the occasion offered, there was never lacking something succinct and glittering to say. Unfortunately the occasional blast of a cannon meant for battle is lost amid the sometimes petty, and often pedantic, crackle of firecrackers in which a Seba Smith goes down to a cricket's Waterloo. Poe has been blamed for descending to correct the grammar or criticize the rhetoric of those he reviewed. At the time, this was one of the most valuable and practical services which an American critic could perform for his minor contemporaries. Macaulay used it in his reviews when necessary (that of the Reverend Robert Montgomery's poems, for instance), and evinced the same anger at the vicious puffing which could project illiterate balderdash onto the library shelves of gentlemen. It was no small gain at the time to have it noised abroad that there was a critic on *Graham's* whose sense of humor and sound technique delighted in exposing the ridiculous in grammar, logic, and imagery. A study of these, and the rest of Poe's reviews, shows that from them may be culled expressions and dicta which shadow forth a critical philosophy, one of the most far-ranging of its time and place. Above all they escaped the taint of being provincial, and were a genuine contribution to the body of American critical letters.

It was at this time, too, that Poe developed fully the tale of ratiocination and wrote *The Murders in the Rue Morgue, The Mystery of Marie Rogêt,* and *A Descent into the Maelström.* These stories pre-

---

[583] In this review Poe admired Moore's skill and "ingenuity" in the construction of a long narrative poem.

sent us with the last and most original prose hero he was to perfect, that of the Perfect Logician. In them the logical processes are stressed to the last degree.

Poe must have been considerably disturbed mentally by the kind of imagery and incident which he had found forced upon himself, by the dictates of his own nature, in the *Tales of the Grotesque and Arabesque*. He could not fail to recognize that many of the implications of these stories were distinctly abnormal, particularly those which reveled in the horrible rendings of human flesh, blood, and the strange sex or sexless relations of the heroes and heroines. He now began to struggle against this—in 1841—when for a while the stimulants seemed temporarily to have been let alone. Most alarming of all, perhaps, had been the fact that what he had so far written seemed inevitably to be thrust upon him. Now he determined to construct logically, to pick, and to choose deliberately.

Hence, the next dream-self or literary hero, who appears, is supposedly endowed with almost superhuman reason. He is the detective by logical method, the enemy of crime. The heroes of the stories no longer indulge in cannibal feasts themselves, or the rendings of bodies, but are the hunters down and the putative preventers of such things. Indeed, says Poe to himself, in effect, such things are not done by men—and he introduces a horrible ape to perform the abominations which his consciousness still insisted upon presenting.

The body was quite warm. Upon examining [584] it, many excoriations were perceived, no doubt occasioned by the violence with which it had been thrust up [the chimney]. Upon the face were many severe scratches, and, upon the throat dark bruises, and deep indentations, of finger nails as if the deceased had been throttled to death. . . . The party made its way into a small paved yard in the rear of the building, where lay the corpse of the old lady, with her throat so entirely cut that, upon an attempt to raise her, the head fell off. The body as well as the head, was fearfully *mutilated*—the former so much so as scarcely to retain any semblance of humanity. . . .

So in a vicious circle the "expert reasoner" came around again in spite of himself to the very thing he was trying to escape—dead women, their bodies horribly mutilated. There was no way out. Yet how desperately he tried. In the quiet Coates Street house, with Virginia or Mrs. Clemm sewing before the fire, visions of scenes so terrible as to sear the minds of generations thronged through the bulging head of the young man, who inscribed them carefully, in wonderful, sonorous English on rolls of blue paper meticulously pasted together.

The bedraggled corpse of Marie Rogêt lay before him on the banks of the Seine; or an enormous ape stuffed the naked body of a young

---

[584] From *The Murders in the Rue Morgue*.

girl, bitten and excoriated, up a lethal chimney. The tell-tale heart, his own diseased and palpitating organ, beat till it almost set its unhappy owner crazy; and he could feel it in imagination, throbbing there, a complete and horrible entity below the floor. Of all these things "Muddie," poor simple "Muddie," never complained. Her needle went on, and little Sis went upstairs coughing, to go to bed with Catarina the cat.

It was certainly one of the strangest households in the world. While Mrs. Clemm peeled potatoes, an ape plucked the hair off its victims. There is no use in detailing the fact that years before Poe may have read of an escaped orang-outang in the files of an obscure Pennsylvania newspaper; or that a contemporary murder in New York filled the papers with the usual sickening details.[585] These may have pulled the trigger inside the head with the strange brain, but they do not account for the tremendous explosion which followed.

But, for the time being, the young editor at *Graham's* continued to insist that he was the *most* reasonable of men. There was no cryptogram so subtle but that he could solve it. The magnificent (though imaginary) triumph of Poe in the "challenge to the world" issued some time before in *Alexander's Weekly* was now recalled, to a larger "world." In August, 1841, Poe solved in *Graham's* a cryptogram sent him by Thomas from Washington, who replied that Poe's articles on cryptography had there attracted much attention and had even been brought to the notice of the President's sons. This, of course, with the federal job in view. (A system for the solution of puzzles might well interest the politicians!)

As a matter of fact, Poe did solve a number of cryptograms rather cleverly, and was forced to enter into an extensive correspondence with a number of people on the subject. By a wrong guess as to the author, he returned one to his friend Tomlin in Tennessee about this time and complains of the work involved. All of this was the same kind of thing that soon after entered into the exhibition of cipher solving in *The Gold-Bug*. It was a mysterious realm in which he

---

[585] In August, 1841, an unfortunate woman named Mary Cecilia Rogers, who lived at 114 Liberty Street, New York, was murdered under atrocious circumstances by her lover, who then committed suicide. The newspapers of the day made it their usual game. Poe's *Mystery of Marie Rogêt* was based on this crime. See Poe to Roberts, Philadelphia, June 4, 1842:

". . . I, in reality enter into a very long and rigorous analysis of the New York tragedy. No point is omitted. I examine, each by each, the opinions and arguments of the press upon the subject, and show that this subject has been, hitherto, unapproached. In fact I believe not only that I have demonstrated the fallacy of the general idea—that the girl was the victim of a gang of ruffians—but have *indicated the assassin* in a manner which will give renewed impetus to investigation. . . . It has occurred to me that you would be willing to purchase it for the forthcoming *Mammoth Notion.* . . ."! This is *all* enormously characteristic of the time and the man.

could seem to reign triumphant and alone, and so comparatively easily convince himself, and the world (for that was necessary before he could have faith in his own powers), that here was a very great reasoner indeed. There is some legend of his visiting the Harvard Library about this time to obtain texts on cryptography, but although the sources from which he drew his information are apparent, no such trip can be accounted for by time and his known whereabouts.[586]

The Perfect Reasoner began very early to manifest himself on the critical side also. In February, 1841, Poe wrote a review of *Barnaby Rudge* for *Graham's* in which he undertook to predict the plot of the story which was appearing serially. In this he was successful and, it is said, caused Dickens to explain that "the man must be the devil" (*sic*). At any rate it was in *Barnaby Rudge* that Poe first met the raven which he soon afterward made his own—of the bird in *Barnaby Rudge* he says:

> The raven, too, intensely amusing as it is, might have been made, more than we now see it, a portion of the conception of the fantastic Barnaby. Its croakings might have been *prophetically* heard in the course of the drama. Its character might have performed in regard to that of the idiot, much the same part as does, in music, the accompaniment in respect to the air. Each might have been distinct. Each might have differed remarkably from the other. Yet between them there might have been wrought an analogical resemblance, and although each might have existed apart they might have formed together a whole which would have been imperfect in the absence of either.[587]

This is undoubtedly the germ of thought and the artistic philosophy out of which fluttered Poe's own "raven." Lowell noticed it in his *Fable for Critics*.[588] *The Raven*, indeed, is more logically constructed and approaches nearer to Poe's ideal of the artistic faculty in control of the logical than many of his critics are prepared to admit. Its genesis, at least, lay in an able criticism of a great book.

There is another type of writing embodied in some of the essays and colloquies that Poe produced during the Philadelphia period, which at that time was almost peculiar to him. It is so customary to regard him as a romanticist and a lyric poet that, for the most part, his interesting speculations upon, and projections of the future; his awareness of the changes being wrought in society by medical and mechanical advance; and his dissent from the prevailing political and economic philosophy of his era, have been overlooked or forgotten. It is true that the liter-

---

[586] Howard Paul in *Munsey's Magazine*, September, 1892. Paul tells of a visit of Poe to the Harvard Library to read "Trithemius, Vignere, and Niceron" on cipher writing and says Poe had only *one* response sent in to his challenge to solve cryptograms. The first statement is unsupported, and the last demonstrably fails to convince, because of contradictory letters in Poe's correspondence: Thomas, Tomlin, Snodgrass, etc.

[587] Poe's review of *Barnaby Rudge*, one of the most able of his criticisms.

[588] See Chapter XVII, page 323, and Chapter XXII, page 487.

ary form in which he chose to embody these is much less memorable than his other work, but in the study of the man they cannot be overlooked. Here, for instance, is a comment on the architecture of American cities that goes home even to-day. It is from an article entitled *The Business Man.*

> . . . Whenever a rich old hunks or prodigal heir or bankrupt corporation gets into the notion of putting up a palace, there is no such thing in the world as stopping either of them, and this every intelligent person knows. The fact in question is indeed the basis of the Eye Sore trade. As soon therefore, as a building project is fairly afoot by one of these parties, we merchants secure a nice corner of the lot in contemplation, or a prime little situation just adjoining, or right in front. This done we wait until the palace is half-way up, and then we pay some tasty architect to run us up an ornamental mud hovel, right against it; or a Down-East or Dutch pagoda, or a pig sty, or an ingenious little bit of fancy work, either Esquimeau, Kickapoo, or Hottentot.

"I am a business man. I am a methodical man. Method is *the* thing, after all"—begins this article.

As we have seen, Poe was peculiarly obsessed with, and convinced of, the possibility of human flight. The dirigible balloon was much on his mind. He even foresaw the skyscraper and speaks of the "twenty story" buildings in Manhattan. In predicting many changes in the physical aspect of civilization he was often most happy in his guesses, sometimes coming startlingly close to present facts, but unlike nearly everyone else at that time he did not believe in the inevitable benefits of "progress," and saw the opening and raw seams in a society which was built purely upon material welfare. "Comfort" he did not regard as the final ideal. The absence of an aristocracy as a guide to taste he lamented—in *The Philosophy of Furniture* he says:

> We have no aristocracy of blood, and having therefore as a natural, and indeed as an inevitable thing, fashioned for ourselves an aristocracy of dollars, the *display of wealth* has here to take the place and perform the office of the heraldic display in monarchial countries. By a transition readily understood, and which might have been as readily foreseen, we have been brought to merge in simple *show* our notions of taste itself.

More remarkable still is the fact that Poe was practically the only American writer of his age who foresaw some of the inevitable weaknesses inherent in the democratic theory and boldly commented upon them. Up until the Civil War, the doctrines of the Revolution were practically unquestioned. In *Mellonta Tauta,* a conversation supposed to take place in A.D. 2848, Poe makes the following observations on democracy in the United States:

. . . They started with the queerest idea conceivable, viz: that all men are born free and equal—this in the very teeth of the laws of *gradation* so visibly impressed upon all things both in the moral and physical universe. Every man 'voted,' as they called it—that is to say meddled with public affairs—until, at length, it was discovered that what is everybody's business is nobody's, and that the 'Republic' (so the absurd thing was called) was without a government at all. It is related, however, that the first circumstance which disturbed, the self-complacency of the philosophers who constructed this 'Republic,' was the startling discovery that universal suffrage gave opportunity for fraudulent schemes, by means of which any desired number of votes might at any time be polled, without the possibility of prevention or even detection, by any party which should be merely villainous enough not to be afraid of the fraud. A little reflection upon this discovery suffered to render evident the consequences, which were that rascality *must* predominate—in a word, that republican government *could* never be anything but a rascally one. While the philosophers, however, were busied in blushing at their stupidity in not having foreseen these inevitable evils, and intent upon the invention of new theories, the matter was put to an abrupt issue by a fellow of the name of *Mob,* who took everything into his own hands and set up a despotism, in comparison with which those of the fabulous Zeros and Hellofaga-baluses were respectable and delectable. This Mob (a foreigner, by-the-by) is said to have been the most odious of all men that ever encumbered the earth. He was a giant in stature—insolent, rapacious, filthy; had the gall of a bullock with the heart of an hyena and the brains of a peacock. He died, at length, by dint of his own energies, which exhausted him . . .

by which it is plain to be seen that the magic of the ballot box had little attraction for Poe.

Although Poe has been accused of "dabbling in science," his interest and speculations about it were at least a half century in advance of his time:

Last night had a fine view of Alpha Lyrae, whose disk, through our captain's spy glass, subtends an angle of half a degree [*Poe supposes the drift of the solar system toward this star produced this result*] looking very much as our sun does to the naked eye on a misty day. Alpha Lyrae although so *very* much larger than our sun, by-the-by, resembles him closely as regards its spots, its atmosphere, and in many other particulars. It is only within the last century, Pundit tells me, that the binary relation existing between these two orbs began to be suspect. . . .[589]

That in the 1840's Poe should suggest in a popular magazine that the sun-spot periods and atmosphere of the stars might serve to relate them to our own sun, is little short of startling. It was a theory which

---

[589] During the year 1840-41 occurred the longest sun spot in the annals of astronomy. This lasted eighteen months. About the same time Schwabe was conducting his inquiry into the periodicity of sun spots. In 1843 he announced his discovery of the average period of 11.13 years. Discussion was therefore going on in scientific publications about sun spots in the early '40's.

even astronomers had only begun to discuss.[590] Although not original with him, he was quick to grasp its immense significance, when few, very few indeed, knew what he was talking about. In other words, Poe was one of the first of our literary men really to have his imagination stirred by science. He predicted the trans-oceanic telegraph and wandered strangely in the realms of galvanic resuscitation. For him, almost alone as a writer, electricity *was* in the air.

Of the poetry of the Philadelphia period, there is not much to say. *To Helen* and *Israfel,* the latter again improved, were both again republished. *The Island of the Fay* is obviously a study for *The Landscape Garden. The Raven,* either in mind or on paper, was already under way. It probably first began to take on a vague form at the Coates Street house. Otherwise there was small time to dabble in verse, his most loved form of expression.

One of the peculiar features of this period was Poe's return to his youth for source material. Pauline Dubourg, the washerwoman in *The Murders in the Rue Morgue,* was the name of a former schoolteacher in London.[115] *The Man of the Crowd* reveals impressions of the visit to London with the Allans, as does *Why the Little Frenchman Wears his Hand in a Sling.*[557] *The Gold-Bug* was soon to revive with startling detail the army experience on Sullivan's Island in 1827-28, and *The Literary Life of Thingum Bob, Esq.,* is in part Richmond and *Ellis & Allan* brought to life. *William Wilson* was, of course, an "allegory" of English schooldays and the self-conflict in Poe's dual nature, in some places literally delineated.[122] Besides this, there were numerous other lapses of the pen into the man's past. The distinct trace of opium in the confusion of the senses (taste and smell) meets us startlingly in *Monos and Una.*[591] There is direct evidence by Poe's cousin, Miss Herring, that, soon after he wrote this, August, 1841, he was using opium to excess.

But there was still another important characteristic present in his writings, which provides a convenient loophole to the man's soul—it is what made him laugh. Edgar Allan Poe, like most essentially egotistic people, had a private sense of humor. He seemed to regard the world from an

---

[590] "The sun-spot curve (period) . . . resembles the light curve of the average variable star of long period . . . from the researches of Abbot . . . the total radiation of the sun varies, in amount, and as a consequence *the sun must be regarded as a variable star of long period." Eclipses of the Sun,* S. A. Mitchell, pages 119-120.

[591] From the *Colloquy of Monos and Una:*

". . . Volition had not departed but was powerless. The senses were unusually active, although eccentrically so, assuming often each other's functions at random. The taste and smell were inextricably confounded, and became one sentiment, abnormal and intense. . . ." The rest of the description amounts to a delineation of the symptoms of a drug addict. Compare this description of Poe's with Baudelaire's descriptions of opium dreams. See especially *Charles Baudelaire, A Study,* Arthur Symons; also *Les Paradis artificiels opium et hashchisch* by Charles Baudelaire, Paris, 1864.

immense pinnacle, on an assumed basis of superiority necessary to his own comfort, from which the race of men resembled some grotesque inhabitants of a planet about which he was curious, but not sympathetic. From time to time he descended amongst this race of flies, who had stung him, and broke their bones, or otherwise hurt them. This was partly abnormal, and partly in revenge for his own troubles.[592]

There are, also, those stories in which Poe takes a delight in mystifying and cheating his fellow men. *Diddling Considered as one of the Exact Sciences* is a case in point. Such imaginings helped his sense of inferiority and allowed him a laugh all by himself. In perusing those pages, others find it hard to join in the mirth because the writer seems to take an unholy joy in the weakness and the ignorance of his fellow men. There is too sardonic a gusto about it all. A large part of Poe's satire is directed against the literary and journalistic sentimentality of his time. This would be well enough, but there is no esthetic moral involved in his viewpoint. "Look at these poor fools," says Poe in effect—"and despise them." The tongue in the cheek forever precludes a smile, and we are simply wearied.

Poe's humor generally falls flat and constitutes one of his great failures. Part of this failure, at the present time, is due to the fact that the conventions of wit have largely changed since his day. Wit, like other things, goes in fashion, and the wit of Poe's day is not that of ours. He laughed in the convention of *Southern* wit, which in a *literary* form has nearly always congealed in the bandyings of "jokes" that rest upon puerile pedantries in which only the classically learned are supposed to be initiates. Often it was based upon a comedy of manners that no longer exists. The semi-classical names, strangely compounded, assumed by *literati,* and an enormous delight in the absurdities of bombastic verbosity were its distinguishing marks. There are, about the mossy cloisters of some Southern universities, a few professors who still indulge in this convention in their communications and mimic battles with the great unknown wits of their section. To modern ears the jargon is unintelligible. It is the thin snickering of ghosts.

Yet Poe himself satirized this type of humor in the opening of *The Tales of the Folio Club,* which cleverly enough took off the proceedings of certain gentlemen in Baltimore who met at the "Tusculum" and invited Lord Byron to become an honorary member of their pompous

---

[592] "And he [Poe] remains still a kind of enigma. . . . Yes, enigmatical in various points : as to his not giving even the breath of life to the few ghosts of women who cross his pages; of never diving very deeply into any heart but his own. Are not most of his men malign, perverse, atrocious, abnormal, never quite normal, evocations of himself? From Dupin to Fortunato, from the Man in the Crowd to the Man in the Pit, from Prince Prospero to Usher, are not these *revenants,* in the French sense?" Arthur Symons, *Charles Baudelaire, A Study,* pages 42-43.

circle, without receiving a reply. The gentlemen were too steeped in their own gravy to detect its musty aroma.

But there was something more than this. To Poe, all the world was grotesque. He viewed it from an immense distance and all the actions of all its funny little ephemera were alike mechanical to him. To the normal man, such a view is horrible, and there laughter ends. But to Poe it was funny. It fed his sense of importance. Everything grinned at him and gesticulated in a distorted glass at the end of the enormous perspective of a telescope reversed—and *he* laughed. His sorrow and pity were peculiarly private, as well as his humor. In short, he could be sorry only for himself. In the fate of humanity he saw his own predicament, but it was over his own, and not theirs that he lyrically mourned. In Philadelphia this culminated in *The Masque of the Red Death,* and later on, in the vision of the world as a cemetery where the corpses writhed in their tombs (*Premature Burial*). Yet about it all there was an ecstasy, a satisfaction in the triumph of death and the feast which follows, that has lent these compositions the reality of the horrors they depict. The ruthlessness of nature has been dramatically and successfully evoked. The curious thing is, that Poe could be ecstatic about it, and so endow it with poetic life. That he both entices and repulses is the peculiar quality of his own horror, humor, pity—and genius.

There has seldom, if ever, been in the annals of English literature so contradictory a nature as Poe's. If he dreamed terrible things, he also dreamed surpassingly beautiful ones; and he blent both horror and beauty so that, by the strange chemistry of his nature, they became one. This is his great triumph, the strange aspect of beauty that he constantly insists upon. There are few, however, who can successfully appropriate this Baconian formula. It is only similar natures that can mix them with like result.

By the end of 1841, it had become amply evident to Poe that Mr. Graham was not going to support him in starting a new magazine, and abandon an already successful enterprise. Nor would he allow Poe a proprietary share in a harvest which had proved so unexpectedly rich. Mr. Graham was of a nature so easy and affable that there was no excuse for even Poe to quarrel with him, and Graham was above many of the petty devices for annoyance by which Mr. Burton had moved his former assistant's contempt. Nevertheless, the refusal to back Poe in a new venture, or to give him a share in the magazine which he had so largely built up, constituted, at least in the mind of the young editor, a violation of the fundamental part of their agreement.

It is altogether likely that Graham was loath to part with a man who was able to increase his subscription list at the rate of several thousands a month, yet Poe on his part was dissatisfied, and was, no doubt, at times his usual overbearing self. The acid in his criticism always worried those *for* whom he wrote as well as those *at* whom he wrote.

Then, during the early months of the new year, an event transpired in the bosom of Poe's home circle which once again induced him to relapse into those irregularities the causes of which were so complex. The comparative good health and abstinence of a year were now about to end, and the beginning of the final descent into the maelstrom was soon under way. The immediate and tragic cause of the disasters which followed must now be related.

CHAPTER TWENTY-ONE

ONE evening towards the end of January, 1842, the twentieth, there was a small party gathered for the evening at Poe's Coates Street house. There was a coal fire, and Mrs. Clemm, with the cat following her about, was preparing to preside at the coffee urn in which she delighted, and to dispense some simple evening hospitality while Eddie read or talked. The birds were asleep, with a cloth drawn over their cage. Virginia, as she often did, was to provide the music for the occasion. Poe took a special pride in this, as he had taught her nearly all the simple accomplishments that she knew—a little French and some songs. The harp was brought out, and the girl-wife with the large bright eyes and the waxen face ran her childish hands over the wires and began to sing. There was something peculiarly angelic and ethereal about this sight of Virginia playing the harp in the parlor by her own fireside, that almost transported Poe. She was delicately, morbidly angelic. Everybody noticed that, and upon such occasions her voice came to him like that of "Ligeia" or "Eleonora" speaking to him in his most paradisiacal dreams. It was indeed her voice that gave a color to them all. Dressed in white, singing in the glow of the lamplight, she became the personification of the Victorian heroine.

The notes mounted higher, very true and clear—suddenly she stopped, clutched her throat, and a wave of crimson rushed down over her breast. Poe—all of them sprang to her.[593] For a while it seemed certain that she must die. Stained with her life blood, he carried her upstairs and laid her on her bed. While Mrs. Clemm wrung out cold cloths, and used her simple housewife skill, Eddie went for the doctor.

It was a trip clear across town. Dr. John Kearsley Mitchell lived at 228 Chestnut Street. He must have found a frantic young man pulling at his brass bell-knob that January night, and have driven back

---

[593] Poe's cousins, the Herrings, formerly of Baltimore, had come to live in Philadelphia sometime in 1840 or 1841. See Woodberry, 1909, vol. II, appendix, page 429. She, Mrs. Warden, formerly Miss Herring, then a widow, had gone to live with her father in Philadelphia and met Virginia and Mrs. Clemm unexpectedly one day on Chestnut Street. The Herrings were present on the evening when the misfortune overtook Virginia. The account comes from them, and from Poe to G. W. Eveleth, New York, January 4, 1848, *The Letters of Edgar A. Poe to George W. Eveleth*, edited by Prof. James Southall Wilson, *Alumni Bulletin*, University of Virginia, January, 1924, pages 18-19. Ingram, I, page 215. There are also accounts by a neighbor of the Poes at Fordham, of a similar attack of Virginia's in 1847, see page 572, Chapter XXIII.

to Coates Street madly. No doubt before the lights on the river came into view again, and they drew up at the white doorstep of the little house, an eternity had passed for Poe. His sanity was, in a peculiar way, bound up with the life of Virginia. She embodied, for him, the only possible physical compromise with reality, in a sexual predicament so complex and subtle that it can scarcely be understood in all its vital ramifications. The very thought of losing her was a species of madness. He had always feared it and trembled. Now that the first unmistakable scarlet flag of danger had been displayed, the world seemed to reel and the sky to totter.

This fatal warning at the evening party in January, 1842, marked not only the beginning of the end for Virginia, but nervous disorganization for Poe. Dr. Mitchell in reality had two patients on his hands, and, as a matter of fact, found Poe's condition more perplexing than his wife's, whose complaint, if then incurable, was at least not a puzzle to diagnose.[594] There are indications that, from this time on, things began to go awry at the office. Mr. Poe was often "irregular" and now again began to drink. Virginia continued to have relapses, each one of which drove her husband to despair. He would go out, take a drink, and sometimes be absent for days. Towards the end of the Winter these periods were evidently frequent. There was an attack of his old heart trouble in the Spring. Mr. Graham was forced to call in outside editorial help. It was Griswold.

Of the cause of the resort to stimulants which, from now on, more or less beset him, Poe wrote in 1848 in answer to a friend who had questioned him about the "irregularities":

You say, "Can you *hint* to me what was the 'terrible evil' which caused the 'irregularities' so profoundly lamented?" Yes, I can do more than hint. This 'evil' was the greatest which can befall a man. Six years ago [*1842*], a wife, whom I loved as no man ever loved before, ruptured a blood-vessel in singing. Her life was despaired of. I took leave of her forever and underwent all of the agonies of her death. She recovered partially, and I again hoped. At the end of a year, the vessel broke again. I went through precisely the same scene. . . . Then again—again—again—and even once again, at varying intervals. Each time I felt all the agonies of her death—and at each accession of the disorder I loved her more dearly and clung to her life with more desperate pertinacity. But I am constitutionally sensitive—nervous in a very unusual degree, I became insane, with long intervals of horrible sanity. During these fits of absolute unconsciousness, I drank—God only knows how often or how much. As a matter

---

[594] The attitude of the age toward tuberculosis is now almost impossible to understand. All its *symptoms* were delicate, poetic, and fashionable. The disease itself was, like cancer, then considered shameful and mentioned only by a pretty name. One went into a fashionable "decline," which was later whispered to be "consumption." Paradoxically, it was something to be proud and ashamed of at the same time. It is forgotten attitudes like this that explain and govern the lives of humanity, and remain enigmas to other epochs.

of course, my enemies referred the insanity to the drink, rather than the drink to the insanity. I had, indeed, nearly abandoned all hope of a permanent cure, when I found one in the *death* of my wife. This I can endure as becomes a man. It was the horrible never-ending oscillation between hope and despair which I could *not* longer have endured, without total loss of reason. In the death of what was my life, then, I receive a new but—Oh, God!—how melancholy an existence.[595]

As a matter of fact he never did attain a "permanent cure"; the descent, from 1842 on, was at a constantly accelerated rate.

Poe had become acquainted with a young lawyer of a pleasing and endearing personality, but with rather eccentric habits. This friend was Henry Beck Hirst, whose law office was on Prince Street. Poe was much interested in copyright law at that time, a subject which he and Thomas mention occasionally in their correspondence, so Poe spent a great deal of time at Hirst's office. His interest in copyright arose from the international situation, then as now far from satisfactory, but infinitely worse then, as the rights of both English and American authors in the "other man's country" were mutually and inevitably disregarded by the publishers.[596] Poe was always anxious to publish in England. His experience with the English edition of *Arthur Gordon Pym* had been a case in point, and he may have had some sort of a clandestine arrangement for articles with the *Edinburgh Review* or *Blackwood's*.[597] Besides all this, it was noised about that Charles Dickens was coming to Philadelphia in March, 1842. Poe intended to see Dickens, hoping to gain his help in placing a book of collected stories in London, while at the same time he thought to secure his aid in agitating for better international copyright conditions.

There must have been much more behind all this than the mere references in correspondence indicate. Poe undoubtedly devoted much time to informing himself about the legal status of copyright. The pub-

---

[595] Poe to G. W. Eveleth, New York, January 4, 1848, see note 593.
[596] Over 15,000 copies of Macaulay's *History of England* had been sold in the United States without any return to the author. Macaulay made a famous speech in Parliament which secured the English Copyright Act of 1842. In the same year an attempt was made to get Congress to change the American copyright law, but in vain. The matter was much in the air. Such men as Poe and Charles Dickens, who understood the importance of the measure, were vitally interested in having adequate laws and international agreement. See the account of Poe's interview with Dickens on page 424. Dickens' letters to Lea & Blanchard in *Mathew Carey*, Bradsher, Columbia University Press, appendix IX.
[597] The evidence for this rests upon Poe's own statements in his correspondence, and upon certain articles on internatioal copyright in English magazines, anonymous but apparently from his pen. See Poe to Snodgrass, September 11, 1839, and June 7, 1841. Mention of being in touch with Disraeli—Poe to Cooke, September 21, 1839. In notes furnished to Griswold, March 29, 1841, Poe says "[I] lately have written articles continuously for two British journals whose names I am not permitted to mention." Prof. Wilson *may have* brought some of these out in *Blackwood's Magazine* as anonymous pseudo-editorial matter on copyright (*sic*).

lishing aspects were only too well known to him already. He seems
to have had some idea of persuading Thomas and others to use their
influence in getting a new copyright bill through Congress. Mr. Kennedy, of course, would be asked to help. Nor was this entirely visionary. With the editorial influence Poe had, and his knowledge of newspaper manipulating for his own ends, something might really have
been done. The upshot of all this sudden interest in law was that
Poe found himself thrown quite frequently with the decidedly interesting young law student. For such Hirst was when the two first met
in November, 1841.

Henry B. Hirst was by no means absorbed by the law. His family—
whom he afterwards alienated by an unwelcome marriage—seems to
have been moderately well off, and Henry found himself more interested
in studying birds, collecting their nests and eggs, and writing poetry,
than in memorizing what Mr. Blackstone has to say about torts. He
was much given to rambling about the country.

Hirst was a friend of George Lippard, a young Philadelphia eccentric of the day, who wore his hair in long shaggy locks. He dressed in
a blue coat buttoned tight at the waist, and flourished a scalloped velvet
collar in total disregard of prevailing fashions.

It was Lippard's custom, by night, to shelter in a large abandoned
building near Franklin Square, whose one hundred vacant rooms were
open to various types of tenants by squatters' right. Lippard used to sleep
there with his head on a carpetbag and imagine terrible things. He
called the place "Monk Hall" and wrote a mad "Gothic" romance about
it in which skulls grinned, hooded figures vanished up halls, and strange,
coffin-like shadows lay upon the moonlit floor.[598]

Conditions under the blind and stolid respectability of Philadelphia
were then, as now, surprising to the respectable. From his house at
Apple Street, near Jefferson, Lippard poured forth novels and plays
characterizing the city with "Wo Unto Sodom"—books which aroused
howls of protest, and a mob headed by the mayor to stop a play. This
"young petrel who swooped, gyrated and cut his circles over the roofs
and chimney tops of Philadelphia, sailing up the Wissahickon and down
the Brandywine, now scouting its romantic history and now its foolish-
ness and vice, was as odd a creature as is known to the literary annals
of the neighborhood." [599] We must leave him being married in Indian
costume by moonlight on the Wissahickon. Through Hirst, it is likely
that Lippard first met Poe. In a way they were three of a kind.

It was Hirst's custom to visit Joseph Bonaparte, the ex-King of
Spain, at his home in exile near Trenton, where, for a time, the young

[598] See illustration of title page, page 397. These stories of Lippard's represented a
tendency in the literature of the time which left its trace on Poe in a vague way.
[599] The description is taken from E. P. Oberholtzer's *Literary History of Philadelphia*.

lawyer was welcome. Hirst mixed drinks excellently well and knew good wine, which seems to have been the ostensible cause of both his friendship and sudden parting with Napoleon's brother, and others. He and Poe used to drop in frequently at John Sartain's printing office. Sartain drank absinthe, Hirst loved brandy, so these late parties of the artist-engraver, the mad young bird-nesting law student, and the author of *The Raven* undoubtedly caused "Muddie" considerable alarm.[600]

Next to F. W. Thomas, Hirst was the closest friend that Poe had in the Philadelphia days. Thomas lived in Washington, and the touch with him was mainly by letters, or much enjoyed but rare visits. Just as Poe had rambled about Baltimore with Wilmer, he now did the same with Hirst around Philadelphia, walking out towards Doylestown, where solemn Dunkards and bearded Moravians passed along the pike in long, canvas-covered wagons, the buckets slung beneath, while the two young men talked poetry and literature, and rambled.

The Raven, it seems, which was now under way, was much discussed. Some of its ideas and figures must have been thrashed out between them. Hirst, whose mind gradually became befuddled by drink, recalling those excursions afterward, "remembered" that it was he who had "written" it. This he stubbornly maintained in after years, and since his close association with Poe was well known to many persons in Philadelphia, there were, as usual, a few to be found who pitied him and believed. John Sartain, who also saw Poe in a period of madness, had a somber last recollection of Hirst, poor, and wrecked mentally and physically, trying to write a line of poetry in a half-witted and muttering way.

The only certain recollection of the conversation that took place upon these excursions and rambles, comes from the pen of Poe himself in his sketch of Henry B. Hirst.[601] Finding some secluded nook, the two young poets would read their poetry to each other. Poe was especially fond of Hirst's little poem about *The Owl:*

> When twilight fades, and evening falls
>   Alike o'er tree and tower,
> And Silence, like a pensive maid,
>   Walks round each slumbering bower,—
> When fragrant flowrets fold their leaves,
>   And all is still in sleep,
> The hornéd owl on moon-lit wing
>   Flies from the donjon keep.

---

[600] *Poe in Philadelphia,* by Alexander Harvey, the *Press* (Philadelphia), Sunday, June 19, 1892. Sartain contributed reminiscences to the author of this article, who also had considerable local knowledge about Hirst.

[601] *Henry B. Hirst,* by E. A. Poe. See *Poe's Collected Works* in four volumes, vol. III, pages 209-12, W. J. Widdleton, New York, 1868. Much is to be gathered from this sketch, especially between the lines.

And he calls aloud—'tu-whit! tu-whoo!'
 And the nightingale is still,
And the pattering step of the hurrying hare
 Is hushed upon the hill;
And he crouches low in the dewy grass,
 As the lord of the night goes by,
Not with a lordly whirring wing,
 But like a lady's sigh.

Hares, donjon keeps, and nightingales are rarely met with about Philadelphia—yet there is a "pensive charm" about these lines that gives one a glimpse of a wistful, weak young law student reciting them hopefully to his critical friend as they sauntered in chestnut shade down some lane out Westchester way. "No one," says Poe, moved by the memories of those times—even after a quarrel with his friend—"No one, but a poet at heart could have conceived these images, and they are embodied with much skill."

It was in all probability on these rambles with Hirst that the "Raven" first began to croak his "Nevermore," for Poe had then lately discovered him in *Barnaby Rudge*. Hirst on his part read his own poetry to Poe. Some of the poems of both young men, when they were published a few years later, bore indubitable evidence of their authors' close association. Hirst closed the last stanza of his long poem of *Endymion*, which he published complete in *Graham's* for January, 1844, with the following lines:

Both hands upon his brow—terror, and sadness
 And horror in his eyes, with speechless face,
 He pierced the depths of space,
Glaring, like one struck dumb with sudden madness,
 While in the distance died that sad "For ever!
 For ever and for ever!"

In the *Southern Literary Messenger* for July, 1844, Hirst published the first canto of *Endymion*, which shows that the poem was already under way some time before, during his association with Poe.

The admirably contrasted figures of "Astarte" and "Dian," which Poe afterwards used in *Ulalume*, seem also in a general way to be traceable to Hirst. In Hirst's *Endymion* "Dian" shines approvingly on the hero of the poem. "Venus" and "Dian" are, however, identified in canto I, stanza 20 of *Endymion*, quoted by Poe. The idea of contrasting the two ideas, and using "Astarte" as a personification of lust, while "Dian" represents a noble and chaste love, the central theme in *Ulalume*, may have been suggested to Poe by Thomas Holley Chivers' poem of *Nacoochie*, where such a contrast of the two actually occurs. Hirst, however, closes his *Coming of the Mammoth* volume with a sonnet called *Astarte* that contains both "Astarte" and "Dian," and Poe noticed this sonnet particularly, toward the close of his review of the *Mammoth* in 1845, shortly before *Ulalume* appears to have been written.

In 1849 Hirst published a volume of poems called *The Penance of Roland*. In this book, in a poem called *Berenice* (on page 99), a poet lies at his lady's feet and gazes at

> The radiant glory of a face
> Which even in dreams adorns the Italian skies
> Of passionate love,—the Astarte of their space!

On the very next page—

> We'd pause, entranced by Dian's amber light.

It is very difficult to tell in this case whether Poe was borrowing from Hirst, or Hirst from Poe. *Ulalume* had been published by 1849. On the other hand, *The Penance of Roland* is full of Poeisms, and in the poem of that name published in *Graham's,* January, 1848, Hirst actually "lifted" phrases from *Lenore,* and embodied the demon eye of the "Raven," and the apostrophe to the bird. Hirst had already complained in an anonymous article in the *Philadelphia Saturday Courier* of Poe's borrowing from his *Endymion.* Poe, in 1845, has made a similar complaint of Hirst in the *Broadway Journal.* Thus the unfortunate controversy continued. Poe made the nature of his borrowing sufficiently clear in the sketch he did of Hirst. It was the old story, genius had appropriated from mediocrity and created something immortal; mediocrity went muttering to its grave, forgotten except for the vital contact. "To be a good imitator of Henry B. Hirst," said Poe with his tongue in his cheek, "is quite honor enough for *me.*" [601]

But in Philadelphia their rambles went on for two or three years. They continued firm friends; sipped absinthe with John Sartain; forgathered at Hirst's little law office on Prince Street; drank brandy; read copyright law or poetry—and talked. On Sunday mornings, Hirst repaired to Poe's little house near Spring Garden Street for breakfast. There is one record of an especially sumptuous repast of potted Delaware shad and baked potatoes, while "Muddie" supplied the plates of smoking Maryland waffles.

Early in March, 1842, when Poe's relations with Mr. Graham were beginning to get involved, Charles Dickens came to Philadelphia to lecture and stopped at a then famous hostelry which displayed the screaming eagle, he so much detested, as its sign. It was the old *United States Hotel* on Chestnut Street. Dickens' immense popularity in America can scarcely be understood now, by a generation which reads him little except at school. Reading aloud after supper was then, with family prayers, the regular routine of hundreds of thousands of firesides where the grown-ups gathered about the hearth eagerly, and the children laughed and sobbed over "Little Dorrit," "Tiny Tim," and "Oliver Twist." There were literally thousands of persons who had pages of Dickens by heart. His advent on the western side of the Atlantic was more of a triumph than a tour. Men, women, and children loved the man who had conjured for them, as no one else has ever done in English prose.

Poe could not have been so ardent an admirer of someone else's work, but he did not neglect the opportunity of making himself known. He wrote to Dickens at the *United States Hotel,* enclosing his forecast of the plot in the review of *Barnaby Rudge,* together with the two volumes of his published *Tales of the Grotesque and Arabesque.* Mr. Dickens was interested and immediately replied:

United States Hotel, March 6, 1842

MY DEAR SIR,—I shall be very glad to see you whenever you will do me the favor to call. I think I am more likely to be in the way between half past eleven and twelve than at any other time. I have glanced over the books you have been so kind as to send me, and more particularly at the papers to which you called my attention. I have the greater pleasure in expressing my desire to see you on this account. Apropos of the 'construction' of *Caleb Williams,* do you know that Godwin wrote it *backwards,* the last volume first,—and that when he had produced the hunting dream of Caleb and the catastrophe, he waited for months, casting about for a means of accounting for what he had done?

Faithfully yours always,
CHARLES DICKENS

It is probable that, in his letter to Dickens asking for the interview, Poe alluded to a similarity between the man hunt in the Gordon Riots at the end of *Barnaby Rudge* and a scene in Godwin's novel. Dickens says *"apropos"* of *Caleb Williams.* It was characteristic of Poe that he could always find "the similarity"—that was annoying—but it always secured attention. Even Charles Dickens seated before his coal fire at the *United States Hotel,* eating Philadelphia scrapple, which he called, "a kind of black pudding," blinked at the "similarity" as he opened his morning mail and read the beautiful, clear handwriting of "your obedient servant, Edgar Allan Poe." Here was a young Yankee it might be well to meet. Poe had two long interviews.

Dickens had suffered greatly from having his work pirated in America. Philadelphia, with its many publishers, was one of the most offending of localities, so the malodorous condition of international copyright was much on his mind. The conversation between him and Poe turned on that matter and Poe's hope of obtaining recognition in England. He asked Dickens' aid in placing a volume in London which the latter promised willingly.[602] Evidently the big-bearded man with the deep

---

[602] Later on in the Summer of 1842 Poe became impatient at not hearing from Dickens on the subject, and appears to have written him again in care of Putnam's, just before Dickens left New York. Dickens did not receive the letter until sometime later in

eyes, bright green necktie slipped through a diamond ring under the then unusual stiff linen collar, and a velvet vest with a gold chain and cameo charm dangling across it,[603] found the young man with the olive complexion, the raven black hair, scrupulously brushed and oiled beaver hat, and mended gloves, an interesting person. Poe came back again to talk with his friend in the dressing-gown with quilted violet facings, probably to impress further the importance of his work on the Englishman. There was also some talk of Tennyson, and Poe read a poem by Emerson. Dickens was impressed, he never forgot Poe, and on his second visit looked up Mrs. Clemm in Baltimore after Poe had died.[604]

Since their realms of imagination and interest were worlds apart, it seems a strange quirk of fate that Charles Dickens should have suggested *The Raven* to Edgar Allan Poe.

Dickens' own visit was only an interlude, however important, in a time of general disintegration for Poe. Through the entire Spring of 1842, Virginia's condition was most precarious, and this was reflected in Poe's conduct. By April, matters had almost come to an impasse with Graham. There is no doubt that Poe was exceptionally hard to get along with at this time. Charles Peterson, who was a man of considerable vigor, and felt his subordinate position in the office at times keenly, became engaged in an argument with Poe one day while Mr. Graham was present.[605] This brought matters to a climax. Although Mr. Graham, in later defending Poe from Griswold's ruthless attacks, softened the story down, he is known to have told a friend, Professor A. H. Smyth of Philadelphia, that he discharged Poe, and he confirmed the statement later to Mr. Sartain saying, "Either Peterson or Poe would have to go—the two could not get along together." [600]

The truth is Mr. Graham was most loath to part with Poe. He understood the cause of his editor's troubles, and was in all ways most sympathetic. Although there was certainly a great disappointment on Poe's part, and dissatisfaction with Mr. Graham for not carrying out his promise to help found the new magazine, yet there was never any per-

---

England, when he replied, November 27, 1842, saying he had never forgotten his promise. He tried in vain, with Moxon, to place some work of Poe's, probably the *Tales*— "I have mentioned it to publishers with whom I have influence, but they have, one and all, declined the venture. . . . Do not for a moment suppose that I have ever thought of you but with a pleasant recollection; and that I am not at all times prepared to forward your views in this country . . ." etc. See Woodberry, 1909, vol. I, pages 328-29.

[603] Description of Dickens taken from a portrait of him painted in Philadelphia.

[604] See Chapter XVII, page 323.

[605] Some doubt has been cast on this, as on May 31, 1842, Peterson wrote to Lowell: "Poe is a splendid fellow, but as unstable as water." Something had evidently occurred to call for faint praise. Both Peterson and Graham probably understood the cause of Poe's moods. Graham's own statements to Sartain tend to confirm the fact that the office was at times pretty lively—for the source see note 600. Also see Woodberry, 1909, vol. I, page 330.

sonal quarrel between them as there had been with Burton. The parting resembled more the parting with Mr. White of the *Messenger* some years before. Throughout Virginia's illness, the Grahams remained solicitous, calling with the carriage and the grays to take her out riding. This reminiscence of Mr. Graham's probably belongs to 1842.

> I rode out one summer evening with them, and the remembrance of his watchful eyes, eagerly bent upon the slightest change of line in that loved face, haunts me yet as the memory of a sad strain. It was this hourly anticipation of her loss that made him a sad and thoughtful man, and lent a mournful melody to his undying song. [*i.e.,* the theme of the "Lost Beloved."]

One day in April, when Poe came to the office after an absence, he found the Reverend Rufus Griswold occupying the editorial chair. Poe took the situation in at a glance, turned on his heel and never entered the place again.

Force of circumstances and his own failings had produced the result, rather than any direct action on the part of Graham. Nevertheless, it was an accomplished fact. Griswold's assertion that Poe never contributed again to *Graham's* was untrue; Griswold himself must have seen the manuscripts from Poe's pen that continued to come to the office even while the latter was editor. From time to time after leaving, Poe contributed altogether fifty items to *Graham's*. April, 1842, indeed, saw the important review of Longfellow's *Ballads and Other Poems*, and in May *The Masque of the Red Death*. A review of Hawthorne's *Twice-Told Tales* was continued in May from the April number, which was the last that Poe edited. In June, there was a review in *Graham's* from Poe's hand of Griswold's anthology, after which there was a hiatus through the Summer, while he was away and ill, until September. Poe's own account of the parting with Graham is contained in a letter he wrote a few months later.[606]

> . . . My connection with *Graham's Magazine* ceased with the May number, which was completed by the first of April—since which period the conduct of the journal has rested with Mr. Griswold. . . . I have no quarrel with either Mr. Graham or Mr. Griswold—although I hold neither in especial respect. I have much aversion to communicate with them in any way, and perhaps it would be best that you should address them yourself. . . . I am making earnest although secret exertions to resume my project of the *Penn Magazine,* and I have every confidence that I shall succeed in issuing the first number on the first of January [1843]. You may remember that it was my original design to issue it on the first of January 1842. I was induced to abandon the project at that period by the representations of Mr. Graham. He said that if I would join him as a salaried editor, giving up for the time my own scheme, he himself would unite with me at the expiration of six months, or certainly at the end of a year. As Mr. Graham was a man of capital and I had no money, I thought it most prudent to fall in with his views. The result has proved his want of faith and

---

[606] Poe to Daniel Bryan, Esq., of Alexandria (then D. C.), July 6, 1842.

my own folly. In fact I was continually laboring against myself. Every overture made by myself for the benefit of *Graham,* by rendering that Magazine a greater source of profit, rendered its owner at the same time less willing to keep his word with me. At the time of our bargain (a verbal one), he had 6,000 subscribers—when I left him he had 40,000. It is no wonder that he has been tempted to leave me in the lurch. . . .

As usual, most of the resentment was on the part of Poe. Neither Graham nor Griswold was even cool, and both continued to be most friendly, the latter at least in appearance, when occasion served. Even Peterson wrote to Lowell trying to reassure him in a vague way about Poe.[605] Peterson and Griswold did not get along, and Mr. Graham said he afterward discharged Griswold for writing a treacherous and secret attack on Peterson while they were both on *Graham's*.

The loss of the important position on the magazine he had done so much to build up was not taken so coolly by Poe as his letters seem to indicate. In the first place, he was plunged into immediate poverty by the situation. There is some doubt as to just where he was living in Philadelphia at this time, as the Coates Street house seems to have been abandoned in the Spring of 1842. This is doubtful, though. There is, however, no doubt whatever about his physical condition. Desperate over the loss of his position and Virginia's health, he was now for the first time drinking heavily. The curtain, at this time, must again be raised for us by Mary Devereaux, Poe's former Baltimore sweetheart, who had married and was living in Jersey City.[422]

While Virginia was lying on what seemed her death-bed, probably at Coates Street in Philadelphia, Poe went on a spree and finally arrived in New York, where he looked up Mary's husband and obtained her address.[607] On the way over to Jersey City on the ferry boat he forgot it, and attracted much attention by wandering up and down, asking everybody whom he met for Mary's address. The ferry boat arrived in Jersey City and returned with Mr. Poe still aboard. Another trip was made, and the boat returned with Mr. Poe still aboard. Still another trip was made, and yet another, with what the passengers took to be a lunatic questioning them. Finally Poe found a deck hand who knew where the former Miss Devereaux resided. As the hatless man in the very black stock fixed him with eyes that did not focus, and insisted with mouth awry, that the address he would get if he "had to go to hell for it," the navvy, faced by the imperious Virginian, hastily complied. When Mary's husband later returned from work on the

---

[607] On July 6, 1842, see note 606, Poe writes Daniel Bryan, "Upon my return from a brief visit to New York a day or two since . . ." etc. This may date the visit to Mary (*sic*). Or it may have been earlier just after losing his position at *Graham's*. The author of *Poe's Mary*, see note 422, dates the occurrence at that time, and says Poe found Griswold in charge when he returned. The exact date is doubtful but "Mary" says, "in the Spring of 1842."

same boat, he was informed that a "crazy man had been looking for his wife." In the meantime Poe had found Mary.

When Mr. Poe reached our house I was out with my sister, and he opened the door for us when we got back. We saw he was on one of his sprees, and he had been away from home for several days. He said to me: 'So you have married that cursed ——— ! Do you love him truly? Did you marry him for love?' I answered, 'That's nobody's business; that is between my husband and myself.' He then said, 'You don't love him. You do love me. You know you do.'

As to whose business this was, we do not learn. Mr. Poe, we are informed, stayed to tea, of which he drank only one cup. Even this, however, had an astonishing effect, for during the conversation at the table he became very much excited, and seizing a dish of radishes before him, took up a table knife and proceeded to reduce them to mincemeat with such enthusiasm that "the pieces flew over the table, to everybody's amusement." After "tea," Mr. Poe insisted upon music, and that Mary should sing him the old Baltimore song, his favorite, *Come Rest in This Bosom.* He then departed for parts unknown.

A few days later Mrs. Clemm, half frantic, having left Virginia in the care of the neighbors, appeared looking for "Eddie dear," whom she had evidently tracked from Philadelphia to Jersey City and Mary's house. Virginia, she said, was crazy with anxiety.

By this time, perhaps, no one was very much amused. A kindly posse of obliging citizens from Hoboken and its vicinity, together with "Muddie" and Mary, then set out in search, and the author of *The Imp of the Perverse* was finally found in the woods on the outskirts of Jersey City. Mosquitoes were then not unknown, even in that neighborhood, and the single cup of tea at Mary's is the last record of "food" some days before. "He was," she says, "wandering about like a crazy man. Mrs. Clemm took him back with her to Philadelphia." There would be an agony of penitence and several days in bed. Virginia would be coughing in one room and Eddie delirious in another—and there was no money. Only Mrs. Clemm knew how to weather this. It must often have been the basket again; there was no other way. But it was always mercifully and carefully hidden from the callers. Only those awful home-comings! The neighbors could not fail to see them.

Not long after severing connection with *Graham's,* Poe and the family moved from Coates Street to a house much nearer the then publishing district of Philadelphia.[608] The new abode was a three-story,

---

[608] This house, which is still standing on the present Brandywine Alley, in the rear of 530 North Seventh Street, Philadelphia, was visited by the author in April, 1926. The then tenant of the Poe quarters was a Mr. William Owens and his family. The place was little altered, but in poor repair. The pear tree was blown down in a storm some years before. Contemporary descriptions are taken from T. C. Clarke, Sartain,

In 1842; about the time of his correspondence with POE about contributing
to *Graham's Magazine*

From "Our Contributors" in Graham's
Plate supplied by the Edgar Allan Poe Shrine, Richmond, Virginia

Poe's "Spring Garden Street House"

The rear of 530 N. Seventh Street, corner of Brandywine Alley
Philadelphia

Now maintained as a memorial by the generosity of
Richard Gimbel, Esq., of Philadelphia

From a photograph taken for the author in 1926

Captain Mayne Reid
Author of *Afloat in the Forest, The Desert Home*, etc.

A friend of Poe in Philadelphia who has left a description of domestic scenes in the Poe house

From a steel engraving

Courtesy of John T. Snyder, Esq., of Pelham, New York

(Almost forgotten in the United States, Mayne Reid's delightful adventure stories are still remembered and read in England, where his fame continues.)

THE DOLLAR NEWSPAPER.

A FAMILY PERIODICAL—Devoted to Literature, Domestic and Foreign News, Agriculture, Education, Finance, Amusements, &c.—INDEPENDENT ON ALL SUBJECTS.

PUBLISHED BY A. H. SIMMONS & CO., S. W. CORNER THIRD AND CHESNUT STREETS—$1 PER YEAR, IN ADVANCE.

PHILADELPHIA, WEDNESDAY MORNING, JUNE 28, 1843.

NO. 23.

VOL. I.

STANZAS FOR MUSIC.

THE OLD NIGHT OWL.

BY JAMES REES.

ORIGINAL STORIES.

THE GOLD-BUG.

BY EDGAR A. POE.

Reproduction of a Page of the Philadelphia *Dollar Newspaper*

In which Poe's $100 prize story of *The Gold Bug* appeared in 1843

Also showing one of Darley's illustrations

From a rare file of the Dollar Newspaper.   *Courtesy of the Maryland Historical Society*

(*The discovery of Prof. Killis Campbell*)

brick building in the rear of a typical Philadelphia residence, situated
at 234 (now 530) North Seventh Street.[609] The house appears to have
been built originally for servants' quarters, and stands in a rear lot, a
short block from Spring Garden Street. The door opened on Brandywine Alley, then Wistar Lane, there being a private school between Poe's
house and Spring Garden Street from 1842 to 1844.

No other house occupied by the poet during his manhood, with the
possible exception of the Fordham Cottage in New York City, is so
closely related with the intimate joys and tragedies of Poe's life as this
brick cottage. It was under its roof that the last vestiges of his brief
prosperity disappeared, and that the swift descent into the whirlpool of
despair took on an accelerated motion.

This house, which is now maintained as a memorial in much the same
condition in which Poe left it, connected with the front quarters of the
landlord, who was, in 1842, a Mr. Alburger. It is of solid brick construction with a basement that, in Poe's day, contained a cistern. There
were large paneled doors with wrought-iron locks, and three rows of
square-paned windows, those on the third floor being casements. It
contained a living room on the first floor with an open fireplace and
a rather handsome mantel. There was a small hall with narrow stairs,
across which lay the kitchen, where "Muddie" spent most of her time,
and two rooms on the second floor.

The front room, with a black slate mantel, was Poe's, the other being
the guest chamber. Mrs. Clemm's and Virginia's apartments on the
third floor were reached by narrow stairs. Mrs. Clemm had the rear
room just across the hall from Virginia. "Sis," for the most part, lay
ill in a small low-ceilinged bedroom containing three little casement windows almost like ships' ports, an open fireplace, and two large cupboards,
more than ample for her scant wardrobe.

The house was, at first, fairly well furnished with items which gradually disappeared as Mrs. Clemm, during the next two years, was forced
to pawn them piece by piece. Virginia's piano, now silent, was in the
little downstairs living room, with "a large hair-lined mahogany sofa."
The white curtains, flowers, painted chairs, potted plants, framed engravings and woodcuts from magazines, and the caged birds, served to
give the house an air of homelike comfort and charm which all who
came there noticed. Poe's scant library, and a profusion of flowering

---

Griswold, Graham, Thomas, Mayne Reid, and others. By the generosity of Richard
Gimbel, Esq., of Philadelphia, the house has since been purchased, repaired, and is
now open to the public as a Poe memorial.

[609] Poe to Thomas, May 25, 1842: "I have moved from the old place, [*Coates Street*]—
but should you pay an unexpected visit to Philadelphia, you will find my address at
Graham's." This looks as if Poe were not yet certain of his new residence and was
boarding for a while.

plants blooming even in the wintertime, helped to complete a background for the poet which none who partook of Mrs. Clemm's excellent repasts—served on snowy cloths in the sitting room with a bright fire glinting on the simple china—failed to remark. No matter how extreme the poverty, "the small dwelling of a great poet" was always spotless. By the grace of "Muddie" and Virginia, it cast a charm.

Poe, too, contributed and helped. To him the place was his only refuge from a hostile universe, his dwelling in Arnheim, the land of dreams. Some years later he wrote a letter defending himself against accusations made by a small magazine called the *Weekly Universe*. Since it details his mode of private life, it is entitled to be constantly kept in mind: [610]

The fact is thus:—My *habits* *a*re vigorously abstemious, and I omit nothing of the natural regimen requisite for health—*i. e.,* I rise early, eat moderately, drink nothing but water, and take abundant and regular exercise in the open air. *But this is my private life—my studious and literary life—and of course escapes the eye of the world.* The desire for society comes upon me only when I have become excited by drink. Then *only* I go—that is, at these times only I *have been* in the practice of going among my friends; who seldom, or in fact never, having seen me unless excited, take it for granted that I am always so. Those who *really* know me, know better. . . .

Poe, of course, like everyone else suffered from the fact that one's frailties and idiosyncrasies attract public attention and become the stuff of remark, gossip, and anecdote, while the long blameless hours of domestic innocence are too trite to stain any page, even a white one. And there is something pathetic and plaintive about this short paragraph of defense against a chorus of abuse, which, whatever its cause, was afterward coarse and unwarrantably profuse. It is the confession of a sensitive nervous spirit, so sensitive that it could meet the real world only when fortified by stimulants. Yet it is the expression of this very sensitivity in the poet for which the world values him.

The reminiscences of some of the neighbors who lived about the Spring Garden cottage in Philadelphia, where, for a time, the house of Usher was situated,—before it, too, like its dream prototype collapsed and crumbled,—recorded a variety of things.

The house, in the days when Poe lived there, was situated in a part of the city which still wore a semi-rural aspect. The dwelling was surrounded by a garden, and shaded by a giant pear tree. In the summer, there was a riot of bright flowers and tangled vines. "The little garden in summer and the house in winter were overflowing with choice flowers of the poet's selection." In the little parlor, Poe sat and wrote to Lowell

---

[610] Poe to G. W. Eveleth, New York, February 29, 1848. Harrison, *Life and Letters,* vol. II, page 285, gives one version, but for the complete text see *Letters of Edgar A. Poe to George W. Eveleth,* edited by James Southall Wilson, *Alumni Bulletin,* University of Virginia, January, 1924.

and Dickens, or to his friend Thomas. Mrs. Clemm, in her widow's cap and gingham apron, sought the shade under the pear tree and peeled potatoes, or moved about the garden with her expert shears. Here *The Gold-Bug* was written while Poe let his dreams wander back to the days of youth and the lonely, idle hours on Sullivan's Island near Fort Moultrie, recalling the very sound of the palmettos as they grated in the sea breeze. In the Summer, there was a blaze of hollyhocks and geraniums, and a noise of bees, while the teachers and children next door remembered hearing the sound of a subdued girlish singing, and of having seen the pale face of Virginia at the upper casement. Poe had carried her harp upstairs.

Here Eliza White came again to call, Poe's old Richmond friend; her father, the good editor of the *Messenger,* was in ill health and dying. Mary Devereaux also visited "over from Jersey City." Sometime in 1842 Mrs. James Warden (Miss Herring), Poe's cousin and Baltimore sweetheart (now widowed), came to call with her parents. She had unexpectedly met Mrs. Clemm and Virginia on Chestnut Street one day. The Grahams, Petersons, Hirst, English with his whiskers, "like antennæ," Alexander, the printer, Sartain, Dr. Mitchell, Captain Mayne Reid, F. W. Thomas, Mr. Thomas Clarke, Louis Godey, F. O. C. Darley, the artist, and many others came, too. The neighbors and their children, in love with Virginia, were much in and out. Even Rufus Griswold came to see, and was softened, almost to tenderness, in spite of himself. It was here, perhaps, that he heard that inspired conversation of which he was afterward moved to speak, even while damning the lips that could no longer reply.

His conversation was at times almost supra-mortal in its eloquence. His voice was modulated with astonishing skill, and his large and variably expressive eyes looked repose or shot fiery tumult into theirs who listened, while his own face glowed or was changeless in pallor, as his imagination quickened his blood, or drew it back frozen to his heart. His imagery was from the worlds no mortal can see but with the vision of genius—Suddenly starting from a proposition exactly and sharply defined in terms of utmost simplicity and clearness, he rejected the forms of customary logic, and in a crystalline process of accretion, built up his ocular demonstrations in forms of gloomiest and ghostliest grandeur, or in those of the most airy and delicious beauty, so minutely, and so distinctly, yet so rapidly, that the attention which was yielded to him was chained till it stood among his wonderful creations—, till he himself dissolved the spell, and brought his hearers back to common and base existence, by vulgar fancies or by exhibitions of the ignoble passions. . . .[611]

But it was no Watteau pastoral that the Spring Garden house was to frame. It was poverty complete and devastating, with both Poe and Virginia ill, and the salary from *Graham's* cut off, Mrs. Clemm was soon forced to her old expedients, and they were now, sometimes, all in vain.

---

[611] From *The Ludwig Article*—Griswold's obituary notice of Poe.

We hear from Hirst of shad and waffles; but we also hear from Mrs. Catherine Bergin, of a Philadelphia charitable society, that Mrs. Clemm applied to her for aid in the Summer of 1842, when there was nothing in the house but bread and molasses, and not very much of that. Adding up everything that Poe received during 1842 for all that he wrote, what the family lived on is still a mystery. The piano disappeared, and various other articles, until, in a year or two, the house was almost bare and Mrs. Clemm had a handful of pawn tickets. Only a few chairs, and a beautiful red carpet that she clung to till the last, and the beds were left. It was fortunate, indeed, that marketing was cheap.

About Midsummer, Virginia had another attack which drove Poe almost mad. It was his custom to slip out by the Wistar Lane door and go downtown, entering public houses as he passed, till Mrs. Clemm followed and brought him back. Philip Wagner, who kept a conveyancing office at the corner of Seventh and Spring Garden Streets, saw the sad tipsy return with the pleading, anxious woman; and the Baileys, good neighbors on Seventh Street, close by, also remembered.

Virginia, it appears, despite her invalidism, was often merry and loved to receive visitors. Among them was the little daughter of Thomas C. Clarke, who used to call frequently, and sit by her bedside. She afterward remembered singing a comic little tune, to which she had supplied some childish jargon, with a chorus about "The Wife of Mr. Poe." This delighted Virginia, who received it with "peal after peal of merry laughter."

It was a life of enormous, absurd, and grotesquely tragic contrasts. There would be an afternoon spent idly with Henry Hirst talking poetry; snatches of great conversation, while Poe warmed to some ethereal theme, and conjured cloud palaces and domes. Then followed a popping of Hirst's pistol at a mark set up in some country lane, or a mad shot at a badly scared farmer's chicken ("he once shot a chicken on the wing at fifty yards"),[601] then a walk back to town, and a pouring of drinks at Henry's "law office." Poe would return in an agony of remorse at the thought of the day wasted, of "Muddie" waiting stark with anxiety. The night would be spent with Virginia, trying to stop her terrible choking. He would walk the floor with her, the tell-tale red spots on his shirt bosom next morning driving him half insane. And yet—the *Penn* was to come out January first!

From June to September there was scarcely a line from his pen. At times he was delirious that Summer. Dr. Mitchell, a good Scotchman from Ayrshire, who had lived in Richmond, doubtless had many a talk with him about the High Street at Irvine, where Poe had played and gone to school as a little boy, and of the Allans and Galts and Fowlds— and what might have been. The doctor took a remarkable interest in his patient, and may have interested the lady at Saratoga Springs to invite him there about Midsummer. There was not enough money to take Virginia along, but Dr. Mitchell somehow secured cash, and letters of introduction for Poe. In August, he left.[612]

In the Summer of 1842, Poe was seen at Saratoga Springs, then the most fashionable watering place in America, driving in a handsome carriage with a married woman from Philadelphia, well enough known to have her name worth talking about.[613] Every day, for a week or so, he came with her in the morning and took the water.

Near the lady's house was a garden with big trees and trout ponds where a little boy played. And there is something more than a legend that the child gradually became fond of the gentleman in black with the flashing eyes and strange gestures, who walked in that garden and talked to himself, telling a story over and over again to no one visible, about a raven that talked and whose name was "Nevermore"—a word which the gentleman boomed out and waved his hands over. One day the boy remarked that he never heard of a bird with a name like that, at which the gentleman appeared much delighted and wrote something down. Later on other people read about it:

> For we cannot help agreeing that no living human being
> Ever yet was blest with seeing bird above his chamber door—
> Bird or beast upon the sculptured bust above his chamber door,
> With such name as 'Nevermore.'—

And it was perfectly true; no one ever had. At any rate, in the Summer of 1842 or 1843, while at the Barhyte Trout Ponds, at Saratoga Springs, Poe showed a draft of *The Raven* to a correspondent of the *New York Mirror*.

Unfortunately, some Philadelphians, summering at the Springs, noticed that Mr. Poe, the distinguished-looking editor of *Graham's Lady's and Gentleman's Magazine,* was there without his wife and driving out with a married woman! A great deal of foul talk, that later on played its part in driving that editor out of the Quaker City, got under way.

Poe returned to Philadelphia, where Virginia had been having hemorrhages about that time, and almost succumbed to an attack of heart failure himself, the third since 1834-35. This, as usual, seems to have brought him up with a round turn, and he seems again to have given up alcohol for a time. The trip to Saratoga, on Dr. Mitchell's advice and advances, was probably a step in the right direction. Poe was in a condition now where he could not do without stimulants.

Mrs. Warden, his cousin, was now much at the house. She was con-

---

[612] Poe, in his reply to Thomas Dunn English.
[613] See Mrs. Susan Archer Weiss, *Home Life of Poe,* pages 103-104; for an account of the Saratoga incident, pages 105-107. See Woodberry, 1909, vol. II, pages 112-113, for further remarks on the Saratoga incident. The source for the Saratoga story is mainly Dr. W. E. Griffis in the *Home Journal* for November 5, 1884.

siderably concerned over the state of affairs, and sat often by Virginia's bedside. To the invalid she brought small gifts from time to time— wine glasses and a little perfume bottle—greatly cherished by the girl-wife who looked "only fourteen years of age." Mrs. Warden (Miss Herring) contributed an important piece of evidence. She says that about this time *"she had often seen him [Poe] decline to take even one glass of wine but . . . that for the most part, his periods of excess were occasioned by a free use of opium. . . . During these attacks he was kept entirely quiet, and they did all possible to conceal his faults and failures."* [614]

During the entire year 1842, a more or less faithful correspondence went on between Poe and his friend, F. W. Thomas, in Washington, with a notable hiatus during the months of July and August. From these letters, a rather intimate insight into Poe's doings may be gleaned. The chief affairs discussed were literary, personal, and the plan to secure for Poe the benefits of government employ.

The lever chosen to move the stone of political indifference was Robert Tyler, a son of the President, to whom Poe was known by reputation. The entering wedge was made by Poe's first expressing a favorable opinion of one of Robert Tyler's poems. Thomas brought this to young Tyler's notice on a visit to the White House, and then wrote to Poe:

. . . Robert Tyler expressed himself highly gratified with your favorable opinion of his poems which I mentioned to him. He observed that he valued your opinion more than any other critic's in the country,—to which I subscribed. I am satisfied that any aid he could extend to you would be extended with pleasure. Write me frankly upon the subject. . . . [615]

The plan at first was to interest Robert Tyler in the scheme for the new magazine, the *Stylus,* about which Thomas was enthusiastic. It was hoped that Tyler would invest, or use his influence to throw some government printing in the way of the new magazine, but this plan was soon abandoned as impracticable, and Poe, after calling on Judge Blythe in Philadelphia, who evidently had the local federal patronage in hand, wrote to Robert Tyler [616] saying he thought with his continued influence that an appointment at the Philadelphia Custom House might be secured.

Tyler replied (March 31, 1842) giving the required recommendation. The matter, as usual in such cases, dragged on. On May 21,

---

[614] Woodberry, 1909, vol. II, *Poe and Opium,* page 428, prints a letter from Miss Poe to him (August 28, 1884) in which Miss Herring is quoted.
[615] Thomas to Poe, Washington, February 6, 1842.
[616] Poe to Robert Tyler—letter in the University of Wisconsin collection. Young Robert Tyler and his actress wife, the mistress of the White House, gathered about them such wits, *literati,* and material for a salon as the muddy Capital City then afforded. Virginians and Southerners were especially welcome, which accounts for Thomas being so often at the White House, and for Robert Tyler's interest in Poe being so cordial.

1842, we find Thomas again writing to Poe, after another visit to see young Tyler at the White House.

. . . Last night I was speaking of you, and took occasion to suggest that a situation in the Custom House, Philadelphia, might be acceptable to you, as Lamb [Charles] had held a somewhat similar appointment, etc., etc., and as it would leave you leisure to pursue your literary pursuits. Robert replied that he felt confident that such a situation could be obtained for you in the course of two or three months at farthest, as certain vacancies would then occur. What say you to such a plan? Official life is not laborious—and a situation that would suit you and place you beyond the necessity of employing your pen, he says he can obtain for you there. . . .

The essential reason for Poe's desire to secure government patronage comes out in his reply to Thomas four days later ·

. . . Nothing would more precisely meet my views. Could I obtain such an appointment, I would be enabled thoroughly to carry out all my ambitious projects. It would relieve me of all care as regards a mere subsistence, and thus allow me time for thought, which, in fact, is action.

What Mr. Poe thought of the relative value of being apprenticed to such men as Burton and Graham, and of the necessity of leisure for literature stands out plainly here.

Poe was now again pressing the *Stylus* project earnestly. In July, he writes to Thomas about it:

I feel that now is the time to strike. The delay after all, will do me no injury. My conduct of *Graham's* has rendered me better and I hope more favorably known than before. I am anxious, above all things, to render the journal one in which the *true*, in contradistinction from the merely factitious, genius of the country shall be represented. I shall yield nothing to great names—nor to the circumstances of position. I shall make war to the knife against the New England assumption of 'all the decency and all the talent.'

In letters written to Thomas Holley Chivers on June 6th, Poe had proposed that the latter finance the new magazine, a proposal which Chivers did not accept, although he promised to help with lists. Nothing daunted by this, however, Poe again announced in August, to one of his Georgia Poe relatives, that the first issue would certainly come out the first of the new year. Prudently regarding the Custom House appointment as merely a basis of living upon which to carry out the magazine scheme, Poe had been exerting himself in Philadelphia, probably immediately after his return from Saratoga, definitely to secure the place. In angling for a position he was, of course, confronted by the local condition of affairs in the contemporary political carp pond. It was very muddy.

The Whigs had elected their candidate, Harrison, largely on an anti-Jackson policy of treasury reform. Harrison's death, a month after his inauguration, brought in Tyler, the first Vice-President to succeed to the Presidency. Tyler refused to carry out the fiscal policies of his party, with the result that he split the Whigs and attempted to build up a party of his own, composed of both Whigs and Democrats, but based almost wholly on a ruthless use of the veto and a merciless chopping off of heads in federal patronage. Tyler was especially unpopular in Philadelphia, and the "T party" there was composed of the most blatant type of politicians in a city famous for bad politics. It was with such an Ali Baba company that Poe was now trying to ingratiate himself. One Smith was Collector of the Port, by virtue of his vices.

Towards the end of August, just after his breakdown, and while still nervous and depressed, Poe began to pay his political calls after a reassuring message, through a friend, from "Rob" Tyler. "I have, also, paid my respects to General J. W. Tyson, the leader of the T. party in the city, who seems especially well disposed,—but, notwithstanding *all this,* I have my doubts. A few days will end them. . . ." he writes Thomas. "My poor wife still continues ill, I have scarcely a faint hope of her recovery. . . ." [617] It was a most trying time, and Poe seems again to have resorted to his usual palliatives for sorrow.

Towards the end of September, 1842, F. W. Thomas paid a visit to the Poes at Spring Garden Street, while on a political and literary business trip to Philadelphia. His account of the house and its inmates at that time is straightforward and significant:

Poe was living in a little home on the rural outskirts of the city in a house that is described by Thomas as small but quite comfortable within. Although the whole aspect of the cottage testified to the poverty of its tenants, the rooms impressed the visitor as being neat and orderly. Thomas arrived quite late in the morning but found Mrs. Clemm busy cooking Poe's breakfast. The caller produced quite an evident confusion by his sudden advent, and there was some difficulty in arranging to include him at the board. In the meanwhile, Virginia entertained the guest. Thomas found the poet's wife to be both graceful and agreeable, and he remarked not only her regular and well-formed features but the most expressive pair of eyes that had ever gazed upon him. Nevertheless, her excessive pallor, a consumptive cough, and the deep facial lines caused him to look upon her as a victim to be claimed by an early grave. Both Virginia and Mrs. Clemm were much concerned about their "Eddie," and made it quite plain to Thomas that they hoped most ardently that the head of the house might soon be able to secure some steady work.

Poe, who had evidently just arisen, now appeared to greet his friend. A mop of dark hair tangled carelessly over his high forehead, and contrary to his general habit, his clothes were rather slovenly. Poe's greeting to Thomas was cordial, although a little restrained, and Thomas noted that his friend complained of feeling unwell. Poe told him that he had gone to New York to find employment, and also remarked that an effort to publish a new edition of his tales had been unsuccessful. Like so many others who visited the Poes, Thomas was forever impressed by Poe's pathetic tenderness and loving manner toward Virginia, but the visitor from Washington could not help but observe at the same

---

[617] Poe to Thomas, August 27, 1842.

time, and with the deepest regret, that his friend had again been yielding to intemperate habits. Thomas was so worried as to venture to remonstrate with Poe who admitted that he had lately been drinking "while in New York"—and then changed the subject by relating a humorous dialogue of Lucian.

Later on during the same day, the two friends visited town together. Thomas says that Poe was sober when they parted and they were to meet by appointment next day.[618]

Poe had promised to be present to hear Thomas make a political speech on Saturday night at Independence Hall, and to say good-bye to him before his departure. A few days later, September 21, 1842, Poe writes:

> . . . The will to be with you was not wanting—but, upon reaching home on Saturday night, I was taken with a severe chill and fever—the latter keeping me company all next day. I found myself too ill to venture out, but nevertheless, would have done so had I been able to obtain the consent of all parties. As it was I was quite in a quandary, for we keep no servant and no messenger could be procured in the neighborhood. I contented myself with the reflection that you would not think it necessary to wait for me very long after nine o'clock, and *that you were not quite so implacable in your resentments as myself.* I was much in hope that you would make your way out of the afternoon. Virginia and Mrs. were much grieved at not being able to bid you farewell. . . .

For a rare glimpse, Poe opens the door of his own home in this. Thomas was by no means "implacable" and again interested himself in his friend's behalf in Washington. Why Mr. Poe had chills and fever Saturday night, and why his wife and mother-in-law would not let him go out, Thomas knew only too well.

A few days later, Mr. Smith thrust a rude thumb into the bubble of political preferment. On November 19th—the time for announcing the Custom House appointments had come and passed—Poe writes to Thomas:

> . . . Some of the papers announced four removals and appointments. Among the latter I observed the name of ———— Pogue. Upon inquiry among those behind the curtain, I soon found that no such person as ———— Pogue had any expectation of an appointment, and that the name was a misprint or rather a misunderstanding of the reporters, who had heard my *own* name spoken of at the Customs House.[619]

Poe waited for two days before calling on the genial Mr. Smith, who had promised "that he would send for me when he wished to swear me in." He had already called thrice before. Mr. Smith had promised to swear him in in four days. When Mr. Poe called to hold up his hand Mr. Smith was out. Mr. Smith and Mr. Poe seem to have engaged in a game of hide-and-go-seek in which Mr. Poe was "it." Mr. Poe again

---

[618] J. H. Whitty, *Memoir,* large edition of *Complete Poems,* pages xliii and xliv, prints Thomas' text. The above gives the essential facts as related by Thomas.

[619] Poe to Thomas, November 19, 1842.

called and was informed that a messenger would be sent for him when Mr. Smith was ready, but the latter neglected to take the former's address. Mr. Poe then waited a month and called again, but he was not asked to take a seat—"I will *send* for you, Mr. Poe"—and that was all. Yet once more the unsent-for Mr. Poe reappeared, when the following colloquy took place:

'Have you no good news for me?'
'No. I am instructed to make no more removals.'
'But I have heard from a friend, from Mr. Robert Tyler, that you were requested to appoint me.'
'From *whom* [*sic*] did you say?'
'From Mr. *Robert* Tyler.'
(I wish you could have seen the scoundrel,—for scoundrel, my dear Thomas, in your private ear, *he is*—)
'From Mr. Robert Tyler!' says he—'Hem! I have received orders from *President* Tyler to make no more appointments, and shall make none.' [619]

Before Mr. Poe left, Smith, however, vouchsafed one other remark. He *had,* it seems, made just *one* more appointment. It was that of another man to the place that had been promised to Poe, who now returned to Spring Garden Street to write a furious letter to Thomas.

You can have no idea of the low ruffians and boobies—men, too, without a shadow of political influence or *caste*—who have received office over my head. If Mr. Smith had the feelings of a gentleman, he would have perceived that from the very character of my claim,—by which I mean *want* of claim—he should have made my appointment an early one. . . . I would write more, my dear Thomas, but my heart is too heavy. You have felt the misery of hope deferred, and will feel for me. . . .

Thus ended the first of the very few instances in which the United States customs service has been sought out to provide oats for Pegasus. Another occurred in the "reign" of Theodore Roosevelt, who had such a taking way, even with customs officers, that the United States Government for a brief while was surprised into cherishing literature. Mr. Tyler and his "T party" proved less sustaining to Mr. Poe.

The Fall of the year 1842 is also notable, in the annals of Poe, for the commencement of an intimate correspondence with James Russell Lowell. Poe admired Lowell's work, and had said so in print on several occasions. Towards the end of 1842, Lowell was busily engaged in arranging for the début of his new magazine, the *Pioneer,* that was to begin to appear monthly with January, 1843. Poe now wrote to him from Philadelphia,—"I should be glad to furnish a short article each month of such a character and upon such terms as you could afford in the beginning." Lowell replied immediately that he had already intended to ask Poe to contribute to the *Pioneer* because ". . . it assures me of the friendship of almost the only *fearless* American critic. . . .

Had you not written you would soon have heard from me. I give you *carte blanche* for prose or verse as may best please you—with one exception. . . ." [620]

This "exception" was to the spiteful article, entitled *Rufus Dawes: A Retrospective Criticism,* which had appeared in *Graham's* the month before. The "retrospect" was Poe's own remembrance of Dawes' paper's treatment of *Al Aaraaf* when it appeared in Baltimore in 1829.[354] The bitter taste had remained in Poe's mouth for almost fourteen years, and, in the columns of *Graham's,* in October, 1842, he spit it back venomously. Lowell did not like this rancorous vein in Poe, one from which he himself suffered at Poe's hands later, and, at the beginning, he took good care to give Poe notice that the pages of the *Pioneer* would not be open for the prosecution of any literary vendettas —"I do not wish an article like that of yours on Dawes, who, although I think with you that he is a bad *poet,* has yet I doubt not tender feelings as a *man* which I should be chary of wounding." [620] This was a point of view which nature had made it impossible for Poe to understand. He was the first to complain of the lack of it in others, and the last to recognize its absence in himself.

The inadvertent revelation of self in the letters of these two men is highly intriguing. Although no matters of very great moment were discussed between them, little tell-tale phrases and typical attitudes towards life leap out, from time to time, revealing the soul that directed the pen. Although these letters bear the postmarks of Philadelphia and Boston respectively, in reality they passed each other bound for the antipodes. Poe lived at the north pole of egotism, and Lowell in the more genial lands of an altruistic hemisphere. To Poe the inhabitants of that place "did walk upon their hands." He could not, for the life of him, get a correct view of their actual mode of locomotion. The icebergs that surrounded the north pole of egotism compelled Poe to rule, as the lonely and mysterious wizard, over the frozen deserts of his own nature. It was a strange land of almost perpetual night, lit fearfully by the sardonic face of a tottering moon, and wheeling zodiacal signs that marked the lairs of lions and the houses of dragons. On the borders of this country, which marched afar off with the faintly rumored kingdoms of humanity, the griffins of imagination trafficked with the sons of men for gold. The full summer sun never rose there, and it was haunted only by the wailing ghosts of dead women. Nothing disturbed it, and the wizard who ruled there, except the recurrence of terrific earthquakes. Then the ice would be melted by the hot volcanic springs that burst up from beneath,

[620] Poe to Lowell, November 16, 1842, and Lowell to Poe, November 19, 1842.

As the scoriac rivers that roll . . .
That groan as they roll down Mount Yaanek
In the realms of the boreal pole.

Diplomatic relations with the king of this realm were always difficult, and there were few postmen who continued to deliver letters there for any considerable time. For some time Mr. Lowell's persisted. It was the news from this strange realm of Poe's which Lowell most desired from him—"for good stories (imaginative ones) and if you are inspired to mystery of that kind I shall be glad to get it." [620] Poe was to receive $13 for every article. Sometime in December, 1842, he arranged to place the manuscript of his story *The Tell-Tale Heart* in Lowell's hands for the first number of the *Pioneer*. The flourish of trumpets in the correspondence about this is typical:

LOWELL

MY DEAR FRIEND,—I ought to have written to you before, but I have had so much to distract me, and so much to make me sick of pen and ink *I could not.* Your story of *The Tell-Tale Heart* will appear in my first number. Mr. Tuckerman (perhaps your chapter on Autographs is to blame) would not print it in the 'Miscellany,' and I was glad to get it for myself. It may argue presumptuousness in me to dissent from his verdict. . . .[621]

On Christmas Day, 1842, Poe mailed his answer to Lowell:

MY DEAR FRIEND,—I send you a brief poem for No. 2, with my best wishes. I . . . thank you for reversing the judgment of Mr. Tuckerman,—the author of the *Spirit of Poesy* which, by the way, is somewhat of a misnomer—since no spirit appears. . . . Should he, at any time, accept an effusion of mine I should ask myself what twattle I had been perpetrating, so flat as to come within the scope of his approbation. He writes . . . 'If Mr. Poe would condescend to furnish more quiet articles. . . .' All I have to say is that if Mr. T. persists in his *quietude,* he will put a *quietus* on the Magazine. . . .

After which, no doubt, Mr. Poe enjoyed his Christmas dinner, if there was one, all the more. Lowell's *Pioneer* came out with *The Tell-Tale Heart* the first of the new year, but there was no sign of the *Stylus*. Nevertheless, it was the main issue now being considered by Poe. So sure of its success was he that he had refused an offer of Mr. Graham to return to his old position at a better salary and with more influence.[622] Mr. Griswold was proving satisfactory only to himself. The bells of Philadelphia rang merrily for New Year's, 1843.

1843

The late Winter and Spring of 1843 were largely given up to the schemes for publishing the *Stylus,* which was the new name chosen for

---

[621] Lowell to Poe, December 17, 1842.
[622] Poe to Thomas, September 12, 1842. Graham had made Poe an offer to return at advantageous terms on account of dissatisfaction with Griswold.

the old *Penn,* due to the fact that under a new title the promotion of
the same project had a fresh disguise. This plan to start a magazine
of his own was a central fact in Poe's literary history. He never gave
it up, and even at the time of his death, six years later, the *Stylus* was
still being actively projected.[623]

In 1843, he came nearer than at any other time to seeing himself
actually ensconced in his own sanctum. The cause of his failure must
soon be recounted. It constituted, perhaps, the literary, if not the
moral crisis of his life, as all his hopes, ambitions, and prospects were
bound up with it. Poe felt that the delay with the *Penn,* and the experience he had gained on *Graham's,* were in reality to his advantage.
He so wrote Thomas, who encouraged him, and there is no doubt his
greatly enhanced reputation as editor of *Graham's* was all in his favor.

In the meantime he strove to support himself by doing hack work of
any kind, and selling stories here and there. Some of these were taken
by Lowell. *Graham's* still continued to carry his work. During the
year, two reviews of some importance appeared there from his hand.
Another periodical, however, at this period was more used by him. This
was the *Philadelphia Saturday Museum.*

The exact nature of Poe's connection with the *Saturday Museum,*
an obscure sheet of which no complete file is known, is very indefinite.
He was in some way closely associated with it, and the paper announced,
early in 1843, that he was to become its assistant editor. It is likely
that Poe allowed the owners to think that he might do this, and so kept
them in good fettle while he used the sheet for his own purposes. It
had for a time a considerable circulation and was a good medium for
advertising himself and pushing the *Stylus.* That he never intended to
connect himself with it permanently is shown by his own statement in
a letter to Lowell in March, 1843, in which he says the announcement
had been made "prematurely." Hirst also wrote for the *Museum,*
and Poe took advantage of that for his own advancement.

During January and February, Poe spent much of his time at Hirst's
office and at the house of Thomas C. Clarke at 206 South Twelfth
Street, Philadelphia, where the prospects for the new magazine were
earnestly discussed. Mr. Clarke was a publisher, an editor, and a gentleman of some means, and was finally persuaded by Poe and Hirst, now
bosom friends, and by the favorable letters and encomiums from Thomas
in Washington, to back Poe financially. Thomas, as a writer and a
politician, had much influence with Clarke, who depended upon Poe's
Washington friend to obtain the subscriptions and endorsements, of

---

[623] See Poe to E. H. N. Patterson as late as August 7, 1849, only two months before
Poe's death. On October 1, 1849, Poe told Mrs. Weiss (Susan Archer Talley) that he
was preparing a critique of her poems for the *Stylus*—for January, 1850. See *Last
Days of Edgar Poe, Scribner's Monthly,* March, 1878, Mrs. Weiss.

prominent men in the Capital City. In some way or other, the scheme to get Poe a government position, which had not been entirely abandoned, was bound up with the magazine. By the end of January the matter had been arranged, and Poe, Hirst, F. O. C. Darley, an artist, and W. D. Riebsam, a friend of Hirst's, all met with Thomas Clarke, when an agreement with Darley was signed by Clarke and Poe, for the artist to furnish illustrations to the new magazine. Hirst and Riebsam signed as witnesses.[624]

The agreement carried out Poe's ideas as to the nature of magazine illustration which he had earlier enunciated in the *Penn* prospectus. Darley was one of the best illustrators in Philadelphia, and has left sketches which have successfully captured the peculiar aspect of the times. The signing of an agreement with a well-known artist who bound himself not to work for other magazines for the ensuing year, shows that the financial arrangements for the *Stylus* were completed, and that the final success of the scheme now rested with Poe. It was his great opportunity; one which he lost.

The next move was to advertise Poe himself as a literary figure, and to announce the new magazine widely. To do this, the columns of the *Saturday Museum* were employed.

Poe wrote in February to Thomas asking him to do a sketch of his life for the *Museum*. Congress was in session and Thomas, on account of a press of work, had to refuse.[625] The material, notes, and clipped items of praise for Poe's work were then turned over to Hirst, who wrote the sketch, which was accompanied by a portrait, a poor one, and was published in the *Museum* about the end of February, 1843. Through influence or good will, other papers noticed it.

The *Spirit of the Times* (Philadelphia) remarked:

The *Saturday Museum* of this week contains a very fine likeness of our friend Edgar Allan Poe, Esq., with a full account of his truly eventful life. We look upon Mr. Poe as one of the most powerful, chaste, and erudite writers of the day, and it gives us pleasure to see him placed through the public press in his proper position before the world.

The *Saturday Museum* then took up the cry and replied:

We are glad to hear so good a paper as the *Times* speak thus highly of Mr. Poe, not only from the justice which it renders that powerful writer, but because

---

[624] Agreement between Felix O. C. Darley and Thomas C. Clarke with Edgar A. Poe signed January 31, 1843. Witnesses, present, Henry B. Hirst, W. D. Riebsam. For text see Harrison, *Life and Letters of Edgar Allan Poe,* vol. II, pages 126-127.

[625] F. W. Thomas said: That Poe sent him the notes for the *Museum* biography, but he had evaded writing them. Thomas told Poe afterwards that he knew more of Poe's history than had been sent him. Poe was amused and laughed the matter off by admitting that the story was intended to help the magazine project. . . . All of which throws a sidelight on Poe's statements about his own life. See also Thomas' letter to Poe, Washington, February 1, 1843.

we have been so fortunate as to secure his services as associate editor of the *Saturday Museum,* where we intend it (*i. e.,* his fame) shall be placed beyond the reach of conjecture. So great was the interest excited by the biography and poems of Mr. Poe published in the *Museum* of last week, that to supply those who were disappointed in obtaining copies we shall be at the expense of an extra edition, which will be printed with corrections and additions. Of this extra we shall publish an edition on fine white paper. It will be ready for delivery at the office Saturday morning.

In Hirst's "biography," Poe included some of his cryptograms and elaborated on his skill in solving them. Other papers copied this, as far off as Baltimore. It was a good lay, and throws an amusing light on the current methods of puffing. A little later the prospectus of the *Stylus,* practically a repetition of Poe's doctrines of magazine publishing given in the prospectus of the *Penn* a year before, was published in the *Museum.* Thomas showed a copy of the biography to Robert Tyler and other Washington friends, who were impressed.[626] Poe's articles on cipher, and his stories had created a considerable stir in Washington, and, through the efforts of Thomas and others, arrangements were now made for him to go on and deliver a lecture there, be received at the White House, and secure the endorsements and subscriptions of prominent men and government clerks. It was his great chance to make the darling project of his literary ambition a fact. Mr. Clarke advanced the necessary cash, and, on March 8, 1843, with a little money in his pocket and hopes never higher, Poe took the train for Washington at the old Eleventh and Market Street Station, and set out. He was, of course, as always on important occasions, laboring under great nervous excitement and a sublime egotistic confidence.

Thomas, who was a bachelor, had his rooms at *Fuller's Hotel.* Luck, as usual, was against Poe, and upon his arrival at the hostelry to which he had been bidden by his friend, he found Thomas ill. It was an unimportant fact apparently, but it was another crux in Poe's literary career. Had his good friend been well he might have protected Poe against himself. The fact was, he was not able to go about with him, and turned him over to a mutual friend, J. E. Dow, who was known to his friends, not without good cause, as "Rowdy Dow."

Mr. Fuller, the proprietor of the hostelry, was a famous host, and on the evening of Poe's arrival, there was a party in which the *Fuller House* port wine played an important part. Dow says Poe was "overpersuaded" to take some port wine. Mr. Fuller was a host who would not be denied. The next day Poe was ill and had evidently spent all his money, for he had a shave and hair cut in preparation for the presi-

---

[626] "Yes, I saw the *Saturday Museum* in Mr. Robert Tyler's room, and happened to light upon the article in which we are mentioned. I read that portion of it to him and shall take care that he is not misinformed on the subject. I remember Mr. Hirst." Thomas to Poe, Washington, February 1, 1843.

dential interview at the barber shop just above *Fuller's*. He could not pay the "levy" fee and had to let it go on credit. The next day (March 11th) he was better, and went through all of the government departments getting subscriptions. On account of his condition, however, Dow, who accompanied him, would not take him to the White House. On returning to the *Hotel Fuller,* Poe, being out of cash, wrote the following letter to his financial backer, Mr. Clarke:

Washington, *March* 11, 1843

My Dear Sir,—I write merely to infoʀm you of my well doing, for, so far, I have done nothing.

My friend, Thomas, upon whom I depended, is sick. I suppose he will be well in a few days. In the meantime I shall have to do the best I can.

I have not seen the President yet.

My expenses were more than I thought they would be, although I have economized in every respect, and this delay [Thomas being sick] puts me out sadly. *However,* all is going right. I have got the subscriptions of *all* the departments, President, etc. I believe that I am making a *sensation* which will tend to the benefit of the magazine.

Day after to-morrow I am to lecture. Rob Tyler is to give me an article, also Upsher. Send me $10 by mail as soon as you get this. I am grieved to ask you for money in this way, but you will find your account in it twice over.

Very truly yours,

Edgar A. Poe

Thos. C. Clarke, *Esq.*

Mr. Poe was certainly making a *sensation,* but not one calculated to benefit the magazine. Upon calling at the White House later with Dow, he had been in such a state as to make his condition evident to Robert Tyler, and it was thought best that he should not see the President. Mr. Poe, as usual, wore a Spanish-looking cloak and it was his peccadillo while in Washington to insist upon wearing it wrongside out, an eccentricity that certainly did cause somewhat of a sensation, evidently not a comfortable one to Dow, who upon the evening of the fourth day also felt called upon to address Mr. Carke.

Washington, *March* 12, 1843

Dear Sir,—I deem it to be my bounden duty to write you this hurried letter in relation to our mutual friend E. A. P.

He arrived here a few days since. On the first evening he seemed somewhat excited, having been over-persuaded to take some port wine.

On the second day he kept pretty steady, but since then he has been, at intervals, quite unreliable.

He exposes himself here to those who may injure him very much with the President, and thus prevent us from doing for him what we wish to do if he is himself again in Philadelphia. He does not understand the ways of politicians nor the manner of dealing with them to advantage. How should he?

Mr. Thomas is not well and cannot go home with Mr. P. My business and the health of my family will prevent me from so doing.

Under all circumstances of the case, I think it advisable for you to come on and see him safely back to his home. Mrs. Poe is in a bad state of health, and I charge you, as you have a soul to be saved, to say not one word to her about him until he arrives with you. I shall expect you or an answer to this letter by return mail.

Should you not come, we will see him on board the cars bound for Philadelphia, but we fear he might be detained in Baltimore and not be out of harm's way.

I do this under a solemn responsibility. Mr. Poe has the highest order of intellect, and I cannot bear that he should be the sport of senseless creatures, who, like oysters, keep sober, and gape and swallow everything.[627]

I think your good judgment will tell you what course you ought to pursue in the matter, and I cannot think it will be necessary to let him know that I have written you this letter; but I cannot suffer him to injure himself here without giving you this warning.

Yours respectfully,
J. E. Dow

To Thos. C. Clarke, *Esq.*
Philadelphia, Pa.

This is evidently the letter of a kindly and thoughtful, but very worried gentleman. It is one of the most forbearing and yet wisest letters that was ever written about Poe. That Dow should have thought it necessary to inform Clarke, from whom it was important to keep such facts under ordinary circumstances, tells the story. His remark about Baltimore is almost prophetic. Poe was to have delivered a lecture in Washington on the thirteenth, but that had to be given up. He borrowed money from both Thomas and Dow and succeeded in making a spectacle of himself.

On New York Avenue near Thirteenth and H Streets, Poe, Dow, one Dr. Lacey, Brady, who afterwards distinguished himself taking photographs of Civil War scenes, and a man who was apparently a Spaniard (*sic*), held a roaring party in which mint juleps played the star rôle. Poe, whose risibilities were always stirred by mustachios, made considerable fun of those adorning the countenance of the "Don," and trouble ensued. Mr. Poe was taken back to *Fuller's.*[628] No sign of Mr. Clarke's appearing, and apparently no word from him, induced Thomas and Dow to persuade Poe to return immediately. His appearance in Washington in clothes turned wrongside out, and in an excited state, talking, gesticulating and rowing with bearded gentlemen, after being puffed as the "most powerful, chaste, and erudite writer of the day,"

---

[627] The italics have been supplied here. This is one of the most significant remarks ever made about Edgar Allan Poe.

[628] According to Thomas' account and Poe's own letter to Thomas and Dow after arriving home, "the party" was continued at *Fuller's.* Dr. Fraily, for whom Poe had solved a cryptogram some time before, was present at the hotel, and came in for some abuse from Poe. Poe must have been hurried off home without further delay that night, as he breakfasted at Baltimore next morning.

was a fatal outcome.   Dow took Poe home, where, it appears, he caused considerable chagrin to his friend, whose wife was ill.

It had been the hope of Thomas to present Poe at the White House to the President, and secure the official promise of the first reversion of the Custom House job at Philadelphia.   Smith, the Collector there, had been appointed *ad interim* by Tyler and was having difficulty in being approved by Tyler's recalcitrant Congress.   Hence Dow's worry over Mr. Poe's appearance on being presented to political friends.   Washington, indeed, was the last place Poe should have appeared in.   The convivial way of politicians, and hotel life at the Capital, was an impossible gantlet for him to run.   It had been a fatal adventure.   The oysters who "keep sober, and gape and swallow everything" could not believe that in the funny, maudlin gentleman to whom they were introduced, they beheld the greatest literary figure of their age.   The lecture had been canceled.   Mr. Robert Tyler, it appears, was shocked, and Poe's worst weaknesses exhibited in the White House parlor itself.   It was all a huge fiasco.   Worst of all, Mr. Clarke knew why.   Dow, it seems, had to tell Poe that he had written Clarke, probably in order to prevail upon him to return.

Poe departed on the night of the thirteenth, the date of his lecture, evidently in such a condition that it was necessary to notify Mrs. Clemm to meet him.   On the way home he began to realize the necessity of smoothing matters over with Mr. Clarke, for he got a shave and a good breakfast in Baltimore and returned by the Susquehanna Railroad, lunching on the way.   Mrs. Clemm was waiting for him "at the car office," in what state of mind can be imagined.   Poe's appearance, he himself describes "as quite decent."   Nevertheless, he went home for supper, did his best to soothe Virginia, and took a warm bath.   He then called to make his peace with Mr. Clarke.   The rest can best be told in his letter written from Spring Garden Street (March 16, 1843) to—

MY DEAR THOMAS AND DOW,—

I never saw a man in my life more surprised to see another.   He [Clarke] thought by Dow's epistle that I must not only be dead but buried, and would as soon have thought of seeing his great-great-great-grandmother.   He received me, therefore, very cordially, and made light of the matter.   I told him what had been agreed upon—that I was a little sick, and that Dow, knowing I had been, in times past, given to spreeing upon an extensive scale, had become unduly alarmed, etc., etc., that when I found he had written, I thought it best to come home.   He said my trip had improved me, and that he had never *seen me looking so well!*—and I don't believe I ever did.   This morning I took medicine, and, as it is a snowy day will avail myself of the excuse to stay at home—so that by to-morrow I shall be *really* as well as ever.   Virginia's health is about the same; but her distress of mind has been even more than I anticipated.   She desires her *kindest* remembrances to both of you—as also does Mrs. C.

Clarke, it appears, wrote to Dow, who must have received the letter this morning. Please reënclose the letter to me, here, so that I may know how to guide myself. And, Thomas, do write immediately as proposed. If *possible*, enclose a line from Rob Tyler—but I fear under the circumstances, it is not so. I blame no one but myself.

The letter which I looked for, and which I wished returned, is not on its way —reason no money forthcoming—Lowell has not yet sent it. He is ill in New York, of ophthalmia. Immediately upon receipt of it, or before, I will forward the money you were both so kind as to lend, which is eight to Dow, and three and a half to Thomas. What a confounded business I have got myself into, attempting to write a letter to two people at once!

However, this is for Dow. My dear fellow, thank you a thousand times for your kindness and great forbearance, and don't say a word about the cloak turned inside out, or other peccadilloes of that nature. Also, express to your wife my deep regret for the vexation I must have occasioned her. Send me, also if you can, the letter to Blythe. Call, also, at the barber's shop just above *Fuller's* and pay for me a levy which I believe I owe. And now, God bless you, for a nobler fellow never lived.

And this for Thomas. My dear friend, forgive me my petulance and don't believe I meant, all I said. Believe me, I am very grateful to you for your many attentions and forbearances, and the time will never come when I shall forget either them or you. Remember me to the Don, whose mustachios I do admire after all, and who was about the finest figure I ever beheld—also to Dr. Fraily. Please express my regret to Mr. Fuller for making such a fool of myself in his house, and say to him (if you think necessary) that I should not have got half so drunk on his port wine but for the rummy coffee with which I was forced to wash it down. I should be glad, too, if you would take an opportunity of saying to Mr. Rob Tyler that if he *can* look over matters and get me the inspectorship I will join the Washingtonian's forthwith. I am serious as a judge—and much [more] so than many. I think it would be a feather in Mr. Tyler's cap to save from the perils of mint julep—and 'Port Wines'—a young man of whom all the world thinks so well and who thinks so remarkably well of himself.

And now, my dear friends, good-bye, and believe me most truly yours,

EDGAR A. POE

F. W. Thomas put a note on this letter which coming from the hand of Poe's best friend has an important bearing on his character:

This letter explains itself. While his friends were trying to get Poe a place he came on to Washington in the way he mentions. He was soon quite sick, and while he was so Dow wrote to one of his friends in Philadelphia about him! Poor fellow. A place had been promised his friends for him, and in that state of suspense which is so trying to all men, and particularly to men of imagination, he presented himself in Washington certainly not in a way to advance his interests. I have seen a great deal of Poe, and it was his excessive and at times marked sociality which forced him into his 'frolics,' rather than any morbid appetite for drink, but if he took but one glass of weak wine or beer or cider, the rubicon of the cup had been passed with him, and it almost always ended in excess and sickness. But he fought against the propensity as hard as ever Coleridge fought against it, and I am inclined to believe, after his sad experience and suffering, if he could have gotten office with a fixed salary, beyond the need of literary labour, that he would have redeemed himself at least this time. The accounts of his derelictions in this respect after I knew him were much exaggerated. I have seen men who drank bottles of wine to Poe's wine-glasses who yet escaped all imputations of intemperance. His was one of those temperaments whose only safety is total abstinence. He suffered terribly after any indiscretion. And after all what Byron said of Sheridan was truer of Poe:—

> '. . . Ah, little do they know
> That what to them seemed vice
> might be but woe'

and, moreover, there is a great deal of heartache in the jestings of this letter.

This is kindly and well meant, but like much interested evidence offered to the jury must be largely struck out as irrelevant. Whether Poe drank by the bottle or the cup, steadily or at infrequent intervals, is all beside the mark. The point is, after all, that from some cause, drink he did; and, when he did so, the results were disastrous. With an already shattered nervous system the effect of alcohol was to make him impossible. All the evidence points to the fact that, when alcoholically inspired, he was insufferable. To this, and his own implacable literary vendettas, he owed the worst and most inveterate enemies he made. His intellectual greatness, judgment, and his pompous dignity, his morbid sensitiveness, were alike set at naught and outraged by the caricature of himself which he exhibited when under the influence. Leonardo da Vinci once remarked, "The worst thing in the world is a bad reputation—the cause of a bad reputation is vice." Poe's spiritual excuse lies in the fact that he was not vicious. He did not drink because he was abandoned, but because a nervous weakness demanded the artificial courage of a stimulant of some kind to enable him to confront the world.[610] It was, at once, an escape and an apparent means to temporary strength. Conviviality no doubt played a part. What is there "mysterious" about all this? A million such persons walk the streets to-day. The inevitable results of such excesses, and the hopelessness of appeal to those whose will power is subservient to a chemical reaction, is an universal phenomenon familiar to all mankind. In the case of Poe, it was a concomitant rather than a cause. His prime trouble lay infinitely deeper.

To those who are familiar with some of the outstanding types of American character, there is a niche into which Edgar Allan Poe fits to a certain extent in his *minor* aspects. It is that of the proud, quixotic, cavalierly-mannered, and superficial Southerner with a little military training; more specifically, a Virginian of a certain brand. For some reason, probably partially connected with slavery, the old South of the plantation system conserved and bred this type to perfection. It is picturesque, professionally ardent, and regards itself so unmistakably as a social ornament and boon, that its superficial ear marks are often accepted at more than par value. Its motive force is a provincial pride.

Add a little, or a great deal of alcohol, as the case may be, or any other "spiritual" irritant to this human compound, and the result is more than usually insufferable: Pride becomes arrogance; manners become mannerisms; courage becomes foolhardiness; and self-assurance turns to insult.   The predicament, never understood by themselves, in which such types are then placed, is one of hostility with the world at large—a much larger world than provincialism permits them to surmise.   To the immigrant generations following the American Civil War this "cavalier type" has become harmless and romantic.   At an earlier date, its social and political implication to the times was more clearly understood.   In some quarters, therefore, there was, to such a gentleman from the plantations, a smoldering hostility rooted in fear.

Poe had been brought up in Richmond, Virginia, in a family which aspired to, and partially succeeded in, establishing itself in the aristocracy of the plantation.   That he had not been included, that to a certain extent he had been thrust out of its bosom, only confirmed in him the determination to persist in the characteristic manners and attitudes of the Cavalier School.   "I am a Virginian—at least I was born and raised in Richmond," is his own statement of the case.   He had chosen to reside in the North.   When "the great Southern Poet" went on a spree, the world in general was not privy to any more subtle cause for the trouble which followed, than the liquor from the same bottle out of which it also replenished its own glass.   The results with Mr. Poe were abnormal, but they were nevertheless characteristic.   In these abandoned years, a discourse on the technique of carrying liquor is not in order.   The year 1843, however, was more exacting, and, without digressing, it may be safely inferred that whatever small skill Mr. Poe may have had in that gentlemanly art hailed from south of the Potomac.   To his own unpsychological generation, he appeared upon numerous occasions in the then well-known character of "A Bad Man from Virginia on a spree"; nor is this by any means so superficial a characterization as might, at first blush, appear.   Differences of manners and custom, indicating, as they often do, the springs of moral action, are among the most profound which provoke the antipathies of men.

Poe's behavior on the trip to Washington in March, 1843, seems to have been a case in point.   He lost and alienated many friends.   Thomas was forced to apologize to himself and others about him, as we have seen; and Dow, who was certainly not one to be squeamish, was hardly very glad.   He never resumed intercourse with Poe on the same cordial basis.   The fact that he never received back the eight dollars which he lent to Poe may have had some bearing in so personal a matter.[721]   Poe, it must be said, was indeed hard pressed from now on—close-followed by misfortune after misfortune.   The last scene of the comedy to obtain for him the government position now took place in Washington, as his next stroke of ill luck.

On March 26th, Thomas visited the White House. He there had an interview with President Tyler who inquired in a kindly way about Mr. Poe. Robert Tyler was out, but the President's other son John, who was in the room, bluntly told his father that he wished he would appoint Poe to an office in Philadelphia. Before the President could reply, a servant entered and called him out. The interruption was fatal, for the necessary executive "remark," whatever it might have been, was never made.[629]

If matters up to a certain point had fared well for the *Stylus,* Lowell's venture with the *Pioneer* proved to have been planted in stony ground. The magazine failed with the fourth number in March, 1843, leaving Lowell bankrupt, while, for a time, it appeared that he was going blind. The omissions in the letters he wrote to Poe at this time show that he could hardly see, yet a kindly spirit and a great courage breathe through them. Both Poe and Lowell were under great tribulations in the Spring of 1843 and yet, in their touch, both seem to have brought out the best in each other's nature. When Lowell wrote to Poe (March 24, 1843) telling him of the wreck of his hopes, but promising to pay for *The Tell-Tale Heart* and other items, Poe replied:

MY DEAR FRIEND,—I have just received yours of the 24th, first that you should have been so unfortunate, and secondly that you should have thought it necessary to offer me any apology for your misfortunes. As for the few dollars you owe me—give yourself not one moment's concern about *them.* I am poor, but must be very much poorer, indeed, when I think of demanding them. . . .[630]

How he could have been much poorer than he was when he wrote this, it is hard to surmise. The wolf was once more at the door. Poe and Lowell continued to write each other through the Spring and early Summer. In the same letter in which he reassures Lowell about his debts to him, Poe announces that the *Stylus* is to appear the first of July following, and asks Lowell to obtain an article from Hawthorne for the first number. Later on Lowell himself is requested to contribute a sketch of his life and a portrait, which he promises to do. He also contributed a poem. Their communication in this time of adversity was affectionate.[631] "With all truth and love I remain your friend, J. R. L." —and with Poe it was "My dear Friend," a most unusual form of address for him. Lowell had retired to his father's house in Cambridge to write *Prometheus.* His eyes had recovered.

---

[629] Thomas to Poe, Washington, March 27, 1843.

[630] Poe to Lowell, March 27, 1843.

[631] Lowell to Poe, May 8, 1843, "Your early poems display a maturity which astonishes me and I recollect no individual (and I believe I have read all the poetry that was ever written) whose early poems were anything like as good. Shelley is nearest, perhaps."

My address will be 'Cambridge, Mass.,' in future. I do hope and trust *your* magazine will succeed. Be very watchful of your publisher and agents. They must be driven as men drive swine, take your eyes off them for an instant and they bolt between your legs and leave you in the mire.[632]

J. R. L.

It was more of a prophecy than a warning. Less than a month later Poe writes Lowell, "Alas! my magazine scheme has exploded." Mr. Clarke had withdrawn. Poe lays it to his "idiocy" and "imbecility," but that was probably only a disappointed man's expression for the common sense of his more cautious partner.

The Washington irregularities seem to be indicative of what went on, quite frequently, through the rest of the year. Mr. Clarke's faith was no doubt thoroughly shaken by the events of the trip, after Dow's letter, and ensuing lapses seem to have confirmed him in the opinion that, however brilliant Poe may have been as an editor or from a literary standpoint, he was by no means the type of man, from a business perspective, upon which one could risk a considerable and hard accumulated capital. The *Stylus* was dead! Poe never gave it up; he had come so near! The engravings and the articles were all ready—Lowell's poem went to Griswold—but the magazine remained a dream that never materialized. It failed to take form, as it failed again, for the same cause.[623]

Poe's financial predicament was now of the worst. There was literally not a *sou* in the house, and Virginia was again very ill, as this letter shows:

DEAR GRISWOLD,—Can you not send me $5? I am sick and Virginia is almost gone. Come and see me. Peterson says you suspect me of a curious anonymous letter. I did not write it, but bring it along with you when you make the visit you promised to Mrs. Clemm. I will try to fix the matter soon. Could you do anything with my *note?* [633]

Yours truly,
E. A. P.

That Poe should have had to appeal to Griswold shows that his need was indeed extreme. The money, it appears, was sent. Poe had been playing fast and loose with Griswold in his reviews of the latter's anthology and had used the columns of the *Museum* to poke a good deal of annoying sarcasm at "Dr. Driswold."

Griswold was living in a boarding house at Eighth and Chestnut Streets where he had met a lady who was supposed to be wealthy. The pair were married, and the wealth proved to be a dream. As the lady is said to have been possessed of even less beauty than gold, Mr. Griswold's state of mind was for some time quite savage.[600] It seems to

---

[632] Lowell to Poe, April 17, 1843.
[633] Written on June 11, 1843, to Griswold at the office of *Graham's Magazine*.

have been about this time that he began to persecute his colleague, Peterson, by anonymous letters and articles. Mr. Graham afterward discharged him for this. It is probably such a letter to which Poe refers and denies writing. Griswold had evidently attempted to pin the blame on Poe. He knew that Poe had again been offered the chair at *Graham's,* that Mr. Graham was dissatisfied with him (Griswold), and that Peterson was an able man. The inference, taking the character of the Reverend Doctor into consideration, seems plain.

It was about this time that Poe himself began to be greatly troubled by anonymous rumors circulated in Philadelphia about him. For those in regard to his drinking he had himself to blame. In addition to this, however, his name was coupled in a highly scandalous manner with the good lady who had opened her house to him at Saratoga Springs while he was ill.[634] The sources of these rumors can never be proved, but one of them may be strongly suspected. The beginnings of a nervous state of mind which later permitted Poe to harbor genuine delusions of persecutions were already present, and these rumors were undoubtedly a prime cause in driving him out of Philadelphia. It was a *dénouement* which, in certain quarters, was highly welcome.

During these periods when Poe was ill, Mrs. Clemm's strength and efforts alone supported the household. What little strength Poe had, was used up in writing, and he had no energy left with which to vend his wares.

She was the ever-vigilant guardian of the home watching it against the silent but continuous sap of necessity, that appeared every day to be approaching closer and closer. She was the sole servant, keeping everything clean; the sole messenger, doing the errands, making pilgrimages between the poet and his publishers, frequently bringing back such chilling responses as 'The article not accepted,' or, 'The check not to be given until such and such a day,' often too late for his necessities. And she was also the messenger to the market; from it bringing back not 'the delicacies of the season,' but only such commodities as were called for by the dire exigencies of hunger.

Thus runs the evidence of Captain Mayne Reid who was much about the Spring Garden Street house at that time. The Sunday morning breakfasts with Hirst must have now been few and far between, although Poe was still a great deal at his office.

As a consequence on July 19, 1843, he registered in the District Court of Philadelphia as a student of law with Henry B. Hirst for legal pre-

---

[634] Thomas Dunn English, *Reminiscences of Poe,* in *The Independent,* October 22, 1896, speaking of Poe's reasons for leaving Philadelphia: "I happen to know why, and there were several others who knew all about it. They are all, I believe, dead, I am the sole possessor of the scandalous secret, and as its recital would do no good to any one, the whole affair shall be buried with me." See also Woodberry, 1909, vol. II, notes, page 424.

ceptor. This, of course, came to nothing, and was probably merely a result of his interest in copyright law and Hirst's influence.[600]

After the *Stylus* bubble had burst, Poe addressed a letter to his cousin William Poe of Baltimore asking for a loan of $50, and describing his misfortunes. The latter had replied (May 15, 1843) refusing the loan, and evidently reproaching Poe for his weakness. By this time, the news seems to have been pretty well abroad. Poe did not reply, and, in a second letter a month later, his cousin in a somewhat softened tone again writes him congratulating him on winning a prize offered by the *Dollar Newspaper*. One passage in the letter is significant and much quoted:

There is one thing I am anxious to caution you against and which has been a great enemy to our family,[635]—I hope, however, in your own case, it may prove unnecessary,—'a too free use of the Bottle.' Too many, and especially literary characters, have sought to drown their sorrows and disappointments by this means, but in vain, and only, when it has been too late, discovered it to be a deeper source of misery. But enough of this say you, and so say I. . . .

The only outstanding success of the year 1843 was the prize secured by Poe's most widely read story, *The Gold-Bug.* He had originally written it, probably in 1842, for publication in the *Stylus.* That not being possible, he had offered it to Mr. Graham who had accepted it. The *Dollar Newspaper,* published just below *Graham's* in the same building, had later offered a prize of $100 for the best short story submitted under the terms of a contest. Poe now begged the story from Mr. Graham who returned the manuscript, accepting a critical article instead. The *Dollar Newspaper* was edited by Joseph Sailor who knew Poe well. Although this had no bearing on the award of the prize, which was made by a committee of judges, Sailor's notices of the award were exceedingly laudatory of Poe. *The Gold-Bug* appeared in the *Dollar Newspaper* for June 21 and 28, 1843, and was again reprinted as a whole with two other prize stories, as a supplement for July 12th. It was by far the most popular of any tale Poe had done and had a large success, attracting wide notice and printed comment. The story was cleverly illustrated by F. O. C. Darley who was to have been the artist for the defunct *Stylus.*

The great popularity of this story was undoubtedly partly due to the fact that, in it, the morbid strain so predominant in Poe was largely absent. A few skulls and corpses crept in, but they might be expected in a story of pirate gold. The retrospective tendency, which Poe had already shown in several of his other stories, was, in this, especially strong, and the author seems to have remembered with almost photographic accuracy the details of his environment on Sullivan's Island

---

[635] Too much has been made of this quotation. The same remark might be made about almost any "family." There are few who cannot remember hearing of several bibulous relatives.

fifteen years before.[636]   The only characteristic of the Philadelphia
period which crept into it was the cryptogram, a subject which Poe could
not then get out of his mind.   The example of cipher writing Poe gives
here is comparatively simple.   That he had taken great pains with the
story, there can be no doubt.   As first printed, the cryptogram was not
entirely correct, and several years later Poe was at some pains to correct
it and make further minor alterations and additions to the text.[299]

Not long after *The Gold-Bug* appeared, the *United States Saturday
Post,* which was a temporary disguise assumed by the *Saturday Evening
Post,* published a charge that the story had been plagiarized from one
called *Imogene, or the Pirate's Treasure* by a Miss Sherburne, in the
Spirit of the Times.   That publication made considerable noise in favor
of Miss Sherburne, but a refutation in the *Dollar Newspaper* for July
12th put the ghost to rest.   The real merit of *The Gold-Bug* lay in the
originality of the plot and the sheer fascination of narrative.   The characters are only sketched, and the realism lies in the accurate reproduction
of the scenes.   This tale, in reality, belongs, in spirit, to the "grotesques."

The only other stories of importance, published in the year 1843, were
The Tell-Tale Heart, probably an imaginative rendering of Poe's attack
of heart disease in 1842, and *The Black Cat* in the *United States Saturday Post* for July.   The latter shows a strongly marked tendency to
return to the horrors of *Arthur Gordon Pym,* and accentuates the fact,
that no matter what the plot, Poe's consciousness insisted upon forcing
upon him the same kind of imagery, regardless of the medium or the
material he used.   The treatment the cat received from its master, the
terrible effect of its eye, and the punishment which fell upon its perse-
cutor represent the fact that Poe could not help but revel in such cruelty,
yet he must condemn it too, and bring punishment upon the perpetrator.
He thus attempted to absolve himself from the feeling of conscious
condemnation which his involuntary dreams aroused.   In *The Murders
in the Rue Morgue,* the moral issue is entirely dodged by making the
criminal an ape; thus a double horror was invoked without the necessity
of blame.[637]

---

[636] For a full discussion of *The Gold-Bug* and the environment from which it sprang,
see Chapter XI, "Israfel in Carolina."

[637] The attempt to use these stories and other works of Poe as models which young
"authors," desirous of obtaining a mechanical proficiency in writing the short story, can
follow is one of the most absurd exercises yet devised by the academic mind attempting
to be a wet nurse to the creative.   No consciousness except the peculiar and abnormal
one of Poe could conceive such imagery, the events, or the order in which they occur.
The suggestion that, by their logical analyses, a similar deranged and morbid product
will be fostered in the pupil is the inference that must be drawn.   Nor is Poe's style to
be "taught."   Style above all things is the man himself.   The fascination of these stories
lies in the fact that their logic is the mad rationalization of a dream.   Both the dream
and the order of words in which it congealed are the product of a peculiar personality
which, to try to reproduce in the alembic of the classroom, is a laughable waste of time.

The high tide of Poe's creative ability had been reached in 1841-42. *The Gold-Bug, The Tell-Tale Heart,* and *The Black Cat,* although published later, belong to the earlier period of his working crest, as well as the, for him, singularly charming and innocent sketch about the elk. From 1842 on, Poe began physically and mentally to disintegrate. In 1843 the process was rapid, most of his work was of the hack variety, or critical articles of doubtful value. In August, he writes his friend Tomlin, "I was obliged to make a vow I would engage in the solution of no more cryptographs." The reason he gives is, that by the number offered for solution, he was "absolutely overwhelmed." In reality he had neither the vigor nor the inclination to continue. There was never any period when he had more time. He now grew more irritable and suspicious, scented plagiarism in the air, and became more biting in his criticism. Even his friend Henry B. Hirst was partially cast off some time before Poe left Philadelphia. Hirst, it seems, had committed the unpardonable sin of parodying Poe—

> Never seraph spread a pinion
> Over fabric half so fair !

had been rendered by the madcap young lawyer—

> Never nigger shook a shin-bone
> In a dance-house half so fair !

The breakfasts at Spring Garden Street and the Sunday excursions were immediately a thing of the past.[638]

There is some evidence that, in the Summer of 1843, Poe again visited at the house of the lady at Saratoga Springs, but the matter is somewhat confused.[613] He was greatly worried by the talk which now went around about it, however, and there was other gossip which found its way into print and private letters.

During the Summer, an anonymous article containing a peculiarly vicious attack on Poe appeared in one of the Philadelphia newspapers. Poe very rightly suspected Griswold, who had by that time been dismissed by Mr. Graham for the similar attempt on Charles Peterson, the source of which had been traced down. Whatever unfortunate basis of truth there was behind the assertions of Poe's bibulous and, at times, irresponsible conduct, it still remains as a cold fact that Rufus Griswold undoubtedly played the part to Poe during his life, and after his death, of a false friend. After sending the $5 which Poe had begged from him in the letter in June, [633] Griswold had visited next day at Spring Garden Street and afterward described the cottage:

---

[638] Statement by T. H. Lane. This cannot be entirely substantiated. Poe seems later, according to Mr. J. H. Whitty, to have helped both Hirst and his relatives in placing poems with the *Southern Literary Messenger.*

When he once sent for me to visit him, during a period of illness caused by protracted and anxious watching at the side of his sick wife, I was impressed by the singular neatness and the air of refinement in his home. It was a small house, in one of the pleasant and silent neighborhoods far from the center of the town, and though slightly and cheaply furnished everything in it was so tasteful and so fitly disposed that it seemed altogether suitable for a man of genius. For this and for most of the comforts he enjoyed, in his brightest as in his darkest years, he was chiefly indebted to his mother-in-law, who loved him with more than maternal devotion and constancy.

There can be no doubt that it was in Philadelphia, during the Spring and Summer of 1843, that Griswold became unhappily familiar with the presence of Mrs. Clemm, who was frequently at that time forced to carry Edgar's manuscripts to *Graham's,* or the offices of other publications, and to call upon the editors to dun them for payment or advances while playing upon their sympathy. Through Mrs. Clemm, Griswold and others became privy to the inmost troubles of the Poe household and the shadow of its tragedy. That Griswold used this information to strike with a concealed hand against Poe, and that he afterward exploited Mrs. Clemm in her dire poverty, while at the same time realizing upon the writings of his dead friend and damning his reputation, is a proven fact which must be remembered when taking his evidence.

Poe also suspected his friend, L. A. Wilmer of intimate Baltimore memories, of attacking him, and on August 28, 1843, writes to his friend Tomlin, the literary postmaster at Jackson, Tennessee, as follows:

And now my dear friend, have you forgotten that I asked you, some time since, to render me an important favor. You can surely have no scruples in a case of this kind. I have reason to believe that I have been maligned by some envious scoundrel in this city, who has written you a letter respecting myself. I believe I know the villain's name. It is Wilmer. In Philadelphia no one speaks of him. He is avoided by all as a reprobate of the lowest class. . . .

This was going it a bit strong. Wilmer had indeed, for a while, been treading the primrose path, knocking about from one newspaper to another, and burning the candle at both ends. He was not without many friends, however, and later on—having sowed the fields of youth with considerable zest—settled down to a decided minor success. After Poe's death, he became one of his most zealous defenders against the attacks of Griswold, whom he detested. Tomlin enclosed Wilmer's letter to Poe which proved harmless enough, in reality, although disturbing:

Edgar A. Poe (you know him by character, no doubt, if not personally) has become one of the strangest of our literati. He and I are old friends, and have known each other from boyhood, and it gives me inexpressable pain to notice the vagaries to which he has lately become subject. Poor fellow; he is not a teetotaller by any means, and I fear he is going to destruction, moral, physical and intellectual. . . .

It was the pity in this, as much as anything else, that would offend Poe. But there can be little doubt that Wilmer's statement was literally true.

August, 1843, to the Spring of 1844, when Poe left Philadelphia, may be regarded as a swift slope in the life of Poe, down which he slid rapidly to emerge on the plain of New York a man much altered for the worse. The main causes for this must be seen in the sick-bed of Virginia in the Spring Garden cottage, and the stimulants which, at this time, Poe resorted to for surcease from troubles which were more than he could bear.

As we have seen, Virginia represented for him a compromise with the driving passion of life, which was necessary to his peace of mind. The explanation which is reluctantly forced upon one, as the whole of the facts of his strange marriage and Poe's relations with other women are passed in review, and calmly considered, is that Poe was psychically inhibited. That he was actually physically impotent does not appear, either in the appearance of the man, the facts of his history, or the record of his creative work. There is a virility, even if a thwarted and sometimes morbid kind, in his creative and critical writing which is decidedly masculine. His continued interest in women is also indicative. To state that Poe was literally impotent is to assume a theory that is beyond the realm of proof.

The difficulty in presenting and understanding Poe and the relation of his personality to his creative work is that his physical and psychic make-up were enormously and peculiarly complex. Any simple and easy explanation, however desirable and superficially attractive to a biographer and his audience, is bound to be misleading and contrary to fact.

At best, since the man himself is removed beyond the realms of a direct, medical inquiry, only an approach to the problem can be made, though the evidence strongly points to the conclusion that the root of Poe's misfortunes, agony, and shipwreck, as well as his power as a literary artist, lay in some inhibition of his sexual life.

That Virginia could never have provided for him the normal relations of the adult married state is scarcely to be rationally disputed. She was a child of thirteen when he married her, and her rapid progress down the steep glacis of tuberculosis precludes the possibility of any considerable time when normal relations could have been established. In Philadelphia, in January, 1842, as we have seen, her invalidism became acute with periods of sinking and hemorrhages of the lungs. From then on she was dying. At times both Poe and Mrs. Clemm gave her up for lost. There is also the evidence of Mrs. Clemm about the nature of his marriage with her daughter, the character of which she afterward did not attempt to disguise. A Mrs. Phelps who knew her says: [639]

---

[639] *Newark Courier,* July 19, 1900.

. . . Mrs. Clemm, his aunt, was my mother's dear friend. I know something about . . . [the marriage] having *heard my mother and Mrs. Clemm discuss it.* He did not love his cousin, except as a dear cousin, when he married her, but she was fondly attached to him and was frail and consumptive. While she lived he devoted himself to her with all the ardor of a lover. . . .

Why was it, then, that he devoted himself to her "with all the ardor of a lover," as there can be no doubt that he did, and that the very thought of losing her at times drove him temporarily mad? It was not because he was physically incapable, but because, consciously or unconsciously, he feared the devastating effects upon himself of being released to other women, where the full implications of love were inevitably involved. That Poe pitied and "loved" Virginia with the yearning of a truly noble sympathy it is useless and cruelly narrow to deny, but that his madness at the contemplation of her loss involved himself primarily and her secondarily is also and more pertinently true.

The man was so nervously and complexly organized that the strong emotions of sex, the most profound and disturbing in the world, threatened not only to make all creative work impossible but literally to drive him insane. The anticipation of it was more than he could bear; the realization of it, after Virginia's death at Fordham, confirmed his fears. In a few months, after a desperate effort to attain again some basis of physical and mental equilibrium, he was thrown off the edge of the world by the momentum of his own hopeless troubles with a cry for mercy to the Spirit of the gulf beyond. Strange as it may seem, while she existed, this frail, barren, and tubercular little girl constituted for Edgar Allan Poe, the dreamer, an essential compromise with reality. His decline was largely coincident with hers. As the pale blue flame of her life flickered and jumped at the wick and threatened to go out, he solaced himself and found refuge in drugs and alcohol. These, in turn, produced and added their own fatal elements to the facts of disintegration so that the result was vastly accelerated. It was in the Summer of 1843 that Wilmer writes to his friend Tomlin, "I fear he is going to destruction, moral, physical and intellectual." Mr. Poe was angry, but his friend was right.

A few weeks later, September 13, 1843, Poe himself writes to Lowell. "Since I last wrote you [June 20th], I have suffered much from domestic and pecuniary misfortune, and at one period, had nearly succumbed." He is then forced to ask him for the $10 due, which Lowell remitted although in great financial distress. For the most part Poe was now sitting by Virginia's bedside nursing her, but ill himself, and in an agony of apprehension. When he did sally forth it was to wander about the streets in that condition described afterward by Griswold who knew him most intimately at this time:

. . . He walked the streets, in madness or melancholy, with lips moving in indistinct curses, or with eyes upturned in passionate prayers, (never for himself.

for he felt, or professed to feel, that he was already damned), but for their happiness who were at the moment the objects of his idolatry; or with his glance introverted to a heart gnawed with anguish, and with a face shrouded in gloom, he would brave the wildest storms; and at night, with drenched garments and arms wildly beating the wind and rain he would speak as if to spirits that at such times only could be evoked by him from that Aidenn close by [behind] whose portals his distributed soul sought to forget the ills to which his constitution subjected him. . . .

It was such wanderings as this that gave rise to the rumors that so troubled him. When he was thus loose in the streets, there was no telling where he might go, and it was generally Mrs. Clemm who rescued him and nursed him back to some resemblance to normal manhood. The rambles of Poe, however, were not always so spiritually romantic as the style of Dr. Griswold might lead us to believe.

Howard Paul, a young Philadelphian, the nephew of Mr. Clarke who had backed the *Stylus,* remembered Poe vividly and tells of him in a convivial and social hour, "warmed with wine and in a genial, glowing mood"—of his brilliant, and, as the dinner progressed, erratic conversation. Paul has left an excellent word picture of Poe as he appeared in 1843:

Poe was a slight, small boned, delicate looking man, with a well-developed head, which at a glance, seemed out of proportion to his slender body. His features were regular, his complexion pale; and his nose was Grecian and well-moulded, his eyes large and luminous, and when excited, peculiarly vivid and penetrating. He dressed with neatness, and there was a suggestion of hauteur in his manner towards strangers. He was impatient of restraint or contradiction, and when his Southern blood was up, as the saying goes, he could be cuttingly rude and bitterly sarcastic.[640]

Thomas Dunn English also noticed the small bones—"the hands like bird claws"—and the rest of Paul's description tallies with several others. From Paul also comes the information that Poe about this time had again turned his attention to drama. There is here a unique mention of the scenario of a tragedy that he projected about this time with a Philadelphia friend, Dr. Bird. About this "play" nothing more is known.

When the generosity of his friends or his connection with the press would permit, he visited the theater, and, it is said, he became friends with the father of Edwin Booth (J. B. Booth). Returning from the play one night, when both were in a high-flown condition, they laid hands upon an unfortunate Jew who offended them and suspended him "by his breeches on the spikes of a convenient area railing, where they left him kicking and howling while they pursued their tortuous way in gladsome mood." It was precisely the kind of joke which would have appealed to the practical side of the curious humor of Mr. Poe.

---

[640] Howard Paul in *Munsey's Magazine* for September, 1892.

After Dr. Griswold's dismissal from *Graham's,* Poe began once again to contribute, to some extent, to the critical columns. It was apparently in the Winter of 1843-44, when his fortunes were at so low an ebb, that he attempted to sell an early draft of *The Raven* to his old friend and editor there. According to Rosenbach, who had known Poe on both *Burton's* and *Graham's,* the poet came into the office one day with the manuscript of the poem in his pocket saying that his wife and Mrs. Clemm were starving and that he was destitute of funds. The poem was then read by those in the office, Graham, and probably Charles Peterson, who did not care to accept it. Godey seems also to have been present. Poe, however, was insistent both as to the poem's merits and his own needs. So Mr. Graham, in order to arrive at some solution, called in the rest of the magazine force and agreed to abide by their decision. Poe then read *The Raven* himself to the audience of clerks and ink-faced printers' devils, who agreed with Mr. Graham. The poem was not accepted, but out of commiseration for its author, and pity for their former editor, the hat was passed among those present and $15 was collected for Virginia and Mrs. Clemm. The money was given to Mrs. Clemm. Godey contributed. It would appear from this that the nadir had about been reached. It was greatly to the benefit of the poem, however, for Poe continued to work upon it for several years.

Almost all of the work and projects of this time bear the marks of having been undertaken by a man in a nervous state who could not carry any long task to a conclusion. With the waning of his power to do long sustained work in prose, Poe now began, after an interval of some years, to turn his attention to poetry. He was, as we have seen, working sporadically at *The Raven.* January, 1843, had seen his first notable new poem for some time, *The Conqueror Worm,* published in *Graham's.* Lowell had received *Lenore,* a vastly improved version of the verses written first at West Point, and dealing with the lost loves of the Richmond period. Naturally enough, with Virginia's state, the theme was again brought to mind, and Death stalked notably in *The Conqueror Worm.*

Poe now, also, again attempted another issue of his collected prose tales published in Philadelphia sometime during the Fall of 1843. This was to have been a cheap edition for popular consumption to be completed by further numbers. Evidently the project failed, probably through lack of sales, and only one issue is known in paper covers, originally priced at 12½ cents, entitled: *The Prose Romances of Edgar A. Poe. . . . No. I. The Murders in the Rue Morgue and The Man that was Used Up.* 1843, 8vo, pp. 40, paper. Philadelphia: published by William H. Graham, No. 98 Chestnut Street, 1843.

In the list of Poe's books, this may be considered his seventh "vol-

THE

PROSE ROMANCES OF EDGAR A. POE,

AUTHOR OF THE GOLD-BUG," "ARTHUR GORDON PYM," "TALES
OF THE GROTESQUE AND ARABESQUE,"
ETC. ETC. ETC.

UNIFORM SERIAL EDITION.

EACH NUMBER COMPLETE IN ITSELF.

No. I.

CONTAINING THE

MURDERS IN THE RUE MORGUE,

AND THE

MAN THAT WAS USED UP.

PHILADELPHIA:
PUBLISHED BY WILLIAM H. GRAHAM
NO. 98 CHESTNUT STREET

Price 12½ cents.

Title Page of *The Prose Romances of Edgar A. Poe*

Combined wrapper and title page of the rare paper-bound edition of "The Murders
in the Rue Morgue" and "The Man that was Used Up." — No. I.

The seventh in the series of Poe's publications

Courtesy of a New York Collector

Note. *The Murders in the Rue Morgue* is known to exist under this title alone
in an octavo pamphlet. As this is thought to have been a salesman's dummy,
and so not published, it is not reproduced here as a "published work." It is the
rarest of all Poe items

The Fashions of the Literati

A fashion plate from *Godey's Lady's Book*

Portrait of Edgar A. Poe

Which appeared with LOWELL's sketch of his life in *Graham's* for February, 1845.
A very poor portrait. Painted(?) in Philadelphia by A. C. SMITH, a local artist

From the original portrait in Graham's
Courtesy of John T. Snyder, Esq., of Pelham, New York

The House in which *The Raven* was finished in 1844, near Eighty-
fourth Street and Broadway, New York City

From a photograph taken in the 1870's, after grading
Courtesy of the Pennsylvania Historical Society

ume." It was handled by at least two bookstores in Philadelphia with small success, and was soon allowed to go out of print with no further numbers added to the unique "No. I." Copies of it are excessively rare.

As neither his work nor his publishing ventures brought him enough to live on, like many another poet in a similar financial quandary, Poe now began to lay plans to deliver lectures. In March, 1843, he had published in *Graham's* his *Rationale of Verse*. Lowell tried to obtain for him an appearance before the Boston Lyceum, but the proposal received a cold shoulder, a fact which may have influenced Poe in his hostility to the same audience some years later, as he never forgot a repulse. On November 25th he delivered a lecture before the William Wirt Literary Institute in Philadelphia on "American Poetry," in which he took the occasion to pay his respects to Griswold in revenge for the anonymous article. The affair created a considerable stir at the time. Both the Doctor and his anthology came in for some well-placed and very caustic criticism. He and Poe were not "on terms" again for about two years. This was the only occasion upon which Poe appeared personally before a fashionable "Quaker" audience. On January 11, 1844, he repeated the same lecture at Odd Fellows' Hall in Baltimore. The returns, of course, were small.

Poe was now about at the end of his string in Philadelphia. He had "withdrawn" from the editorship of two magazines; failed to start one of his own; and was known to be unreliable in his habits and a doubtful quantity to deal with personally in a dozen other magazine sanctums and newspaper offices in the town. Mrs. Clemm had made her rounds; publishers had found his tales a useless venture and—worst of all—scandal was busy with his name. With the outstanding literary reputation of the locality, Poe's personality, misfortunes, and irregularities, in a place where they were common gossip, made further advantageous contacts and associations impossible. The situation was much the same in both Baltimore and Richmond. His attacks on Longfellow and the New England school had also marked Boston off the list of possible removes. New York was therefore the only great literary center left where he might still hope to make a new place for himself.

For the first four months of 1844, the whereabouts and doings of Poe cannot be satisfactorily traced. Some little time before leaving Philadelphia the family must have given up the Spring Garden Street house, whence most of the pawnable articles had disappeared already. During Poe's occupancy of the place it had changed hands, having been bought from the landlord, William M. Alburger, who owned it when Poe first rented it, by Jessie White on January 7, 1843. Before the end came, Mrs. Clemm had evidently resorted to every known means to keep the kettle boiling. A schoolteacher who lived nearby describes the

appearance of the little house with its giant pear tree, the scraggly rose-
bush, carefully pruned by Mrs. Clemm, that grew over the little porch,
and the dooryard with the grass plot and garden.

Twice a day, on my way to and from school, I had to pass their house; and in
summer time often saw them. In the mornings Mrs. Clemm and her daughter
would be generally watering the flowers, which they had in a bed under the
windows. They seemed always cheerful and happy, and I could hear Mrs. Poe's
laugh before I turned the corner [Seventh and Spring Garden]. Mrs. Clemm
was always busy. I have seen her of mornings clearing the front yard, washing
the windows and the stoop, and even white-washing the palings. You would
notice how clean and orderly everything looked. She rented out her front rooms
to lodgers, and used the middle room, next to the kitchen for their own living
room or parlor. They must have slept under the roof. We never heard they
were poor, and they kept pretty much to themselves in the two years we lived
near them. I don't think that in that time I saw Mr. Poe half a dozen times.
We heard he was dissipated, but he always appeared like a gentleman, though
thin and sickly looking. . . . .[641]

From the same evidence it also appears that Mrs. Clemm was a dress
and coat maker, and that Virginia helped her and was at times to be
seen sewing on the front stoop. "She was pretty, but not noticeably so.
She was too fleshy."

Towards the end of the Philadelphia stay, in the Spring of 1844, Poe,
it appears, was much away from the house.

His dissipation was too notorious to be denied; and for days, and even weeks at a
time, he woud be sharing the bachelor life and quarters of his associates, who
were not aware that he was a married man. He would, on some evenings when
sober, come to the rooms occupied by himself and some other writers for the
press and, producing the manuscript of The Raven, read to them the last additions to it, asking their opinions and suggestions. He seemed to be having difficulty with it, and to be very doubtful as to its merits as a poem. The general
opinion of these critics was against it. . . .[642]

Even the published work of this Spring, which was, of course, written some time before it appeared, reflects the exigencies of the period.
The attempt to gain an English publishing contact through the influence of Dickens having failed,[602] Poe now took up the work of an
obscure English playwright by the name of R. H. Horne, and in the
March issue of Graham's gave his cabinet play Orion a tremendous
puff, saying that, in some respects, it surpassed Milton. Some correspondence then passed between the astonished but delighted Englishman and his American reviewer, in which Poe sought to have his favors

[641] From a description given by the schoolteacher to Mrs. Weiss. The school was
probably the one next door to the Poes' on the corner of Spring Garden and North
Seventh Streets.
[642] Col. John J. Du Solle, editor of Noah's New York Sunday Times, to Mrs. Weiss.
See her Home Life of Poe, page 99. Du Solle was, for a long time, a Philadelphia newspaper man and editor there of the Spirit of the Times. See illustration, page 301.

returned by endeavoring to use Horne to arrange for a London edition of the *Tales*. This also came to nothing, although Horne evidently tried.[643]

The rest of the literary output that came to print now was for the most part retrospective or contemplative. *Morning on the Wissahiccon,* and a strong return to the past in *A Tale of the Ragged Mountains,* published in *Godey's Lady's Book* for April, 1844. This story harked back to schooldays at the University of Virginia. In the beautiful mountains where he had walked in 1826, dreaming of Elmira Royster, he now took refuge again in vivid imagination from a sea of troubles.

Diddling Considered as one of the Exact Sciences, which later appeared in the *Broadway Journal,* is a grotesque essay on the various dodges of cheats; how to get something for nothing, dishonestly but cleverly. This is one of the most elaborate of Poe's attempts to be humorous. Evidently Poe derived considerable amusement from the distress and surprise of those despoiled. The petty crooks and scoundrels of the story are the heroes, and the laugh is supposed to come when the victim discovers his loss. There is a curious parallel between this effusion and Poe's own childish and almost unbalanced delight in a hoax of any kind. For those who wish a sidelight on a curious ramification of the man's character, *Diddling Considered as one of the Exact Sciences* supplies the text. Poe used tobacco, like most of the male population, juvenile and adult, in the '40's, and was hard put to it in his dire poverty at times to secure a plug of even so humble a sedative. In *Diddling* we are told how one may secure a plug for nothing by confusing a stupid shopkeeper about the change. A year later a shopkeeper in New York tells us how Poe came into his shop after looking into the window wistfully for some time.[644] "In a moment he entered and asked the price of tobacco. When I had told him he made no move to buy, and after a few general remarks started to leave. . . . So I offered the man a piece of tobacco. He accepted, thanked me and departed." In the story the clever hero confuses the shopkeeper by his superior ways and secures the tobacco as a prize. Mr. Poe was too honest actually to do that. It was beneath the dignity of a gentleman, but in his imagination he reveled in gulling the poor tradesmen whose wares he needed, but whose calling he despised. In the story Poe takes revenge, imaginatively, not only upon tobacco merchants, but upon furniture dealers, boarding-house keepers, and clerks. There is no doubt

---

[643] See this chapter, page 424. Also note 602.

[644] In 1844, Gabriel Harrison, an actor-politician, kept a store at Broadway and Prince Street, New York City. Poe used to loaf at this corner-shop and the description is taken from Mr. Harrison's *Reminiscences*. These appeared in the *New York Times* in March, 1899.

That *Diddling* was written in Philadelphia appears from the fact that Poe mentions it in a letter, Poe to Lowell, New York, May 28, 1844.

that, at the time the story was written, their importunities and even kindnesses must have been more than usually annoying to the poverty-stricken but always clever and proud Mr. Poe.

At the beginning of April, 1844, Poe seems rather suddenly to have decided to leave Philadelphia to try to break ground anew in New York. His life in Philadelphia had become, for him, a nightmare of physical suffering and mental and spiritual confusion. Whispers and scandals about his drinking, the destitution of his family, and the Saratoga Lady already began to lay the basis of a sense of persecution, to which his abnormally sensitive nature made him prone. All his former openings were closed, and it was also probably psychically important to change the scene to a place where every aspect, and chance acquaintances met on the street, did not evoke some ramification of the memories of failure. He had no particular plan in mind, and knew neither what he would do nor where he would live. A vague hope, again to persuade his friend, Professor Anthon, to induce Harpers to publish his collected tales was the only shred of plan in his mind. Mrs. Clemm was left to dispose of the miserable remnant of his effects and affairs. A few friends remembered, and cherished the cuttings from the garden which she and Virginia now gave them. The landlady afterward told of some carpets and plain painted chairs that she reluctantly claimed for the long arrears of rent. After Poe's departure Mrs. Clemm sold off his little library to William A. Leary, a neighboring bookseller on North Seventh Street.[645] There was not enough money to take her to New York, and she was left alone with her memories, her forebodings, and the cat. Catarina, having no marketable value, alone remained. She was a large tortoiseshell, beloved by Virginia, and the pet of a childless house.

Taking Virginia with him,—"Sissy coughed none at all,"—with only $11 in his pocket, Poe left Philadelphia in the early Spring morning. The train via the Perth Amboy route left at six o'clock A.M., but, on the morning of April 6, 1844, it was almost an hour late.[646] After some dispute with the driver over the baggage fee, Poe took Virginia over to the *Depot Hotel* while he read the morning newspapers con-

---

[645] See the *Poe-Duane Letters.* Endorsement by William Duane, once Secretary of the Treasury, on Poe's letter to him from New York, January 28, 1845, relative to borrowed copies of the *Southern Literary Messenger* which "was sold by the said Poe among a lot of books belonging to himself to William A. Leary, a bookseller on North Seventh Street. . . ." This bookseller would have been not far from the Poe cottage on the same street. See also Chapter XXII, page 468, for a full discussion of the "Poe-Duane Controversy" over the matter. Poe's postscript to Mrs. Clemm, April 7, 1844, shows that Mrs. Clemm knew about the books.

[646] The statements in this description are literally exact. From Poe's letter to Mrs. Clemm next day (April 7, 1844), from contemporary descriptions of the locality of the railroad station, prints, and from Table No. 16, of *The Traveler's Guide, A Map of the Railroads, Roads, Canals, and Steamboat Routes of the United States,* by H. S. Tanner, Philadelphia, Oberholtzer's *Literary History of Philadelphia,* etc., etc.

temptuously and waited. It was near the Walnut Street wharf, and the streets were alive with the early morning venders and their cries.

> De hominy man am on his way
> From de navy yahd
> Wid his hominy.

Or the more alluring chant over a little brazier trundled on wheels—

> Pepper-pot!
> All hot, all hot!
> Makee back strong
> Makee live long
> Come buy pepper-pot . . .

About seven o'clock a small locomotive with a huge diamond-shaped smoke-stack and a large brass bell puffed and clanged its way out of town, the pale face of Virginia looking out of one of the car windows, framed, like the proscenium of a toy stage, with little red-plush curtains. Doubtless the gallant Mr. Poe had secured for "Sissy" a seat, nearby, but not too close to the stove. The roar of the drays on the cobbles of the Philadelphia waterfront died away. As the train gathered speed, Poe may well have clutched his "Spanish looking cloak" closer about him and shivered. For him, Philadelphia had become the City of Dreadful Night. They changed at Perth Amboy to the steamer, and arrived late that afternoon in New York in the midst of a downpour. The next morning, Poe wrote to Mrs. Clemm after breakfast.

CHAPTER TWENTY-TWO

THE RAVEN AND HIS SHADOW

New York, Sunday Morning,
April 7, (1844) just after breakfast

MY DEAR MUDDY,—We have just this minute done breakfast, and I now sit down to write you about everything. I can't pay for the letter, because the P. O. won't be open to-day. In the first place we arrived safe at Walnut St. wharf. The driver wanted to make me pay a dollar, but I wouldn't. Then I had to pay a boy a levy to put the trunks in the baggage car. In the meantime I took Sis in the *Depot Hotel.* It was only a quarter past six, and we had to wait till seven. We saw the *Ledger* and *Times*—nothing in either—a few words of no account in the *Chronicle.* We started in good spirits, but did not get here until nearly three o'clock. We went in the cars to Amboy, about forty miles from N. York, and then took the steamboat the rest of the way. Sissy coughed none at all. When we got to the wharf [*New York*] it was raining hard. I left her on board the boat, after putting the trunks in the Ladies' cabin, and set off to buy an umbrella and look for a boarding-house. I met a man selling umbrellas, and bought one for twenty-five cents.[647] Then I went up Greenwich St. and soon found a boarding-house. It is just before you get to Cedar St., on the west side going up—the left-hand side. It has brown stone steps, with a porch with brown pillars. 'Morrison' is the name on the door.[648] I made a bargain in a few minutes and then got a hack and went for Sis. I was not gone more than half an hour, and she was quite astonished to see me back so soon. She didn't expect me for an hour. There were two other ladies waiting on board—so she wasn't very lonely. When we got to the house we had to wait about half an hour before the room was ready. The house is old and looks buggy [*letter cut here by a signature vandal*] . . . the cheapest board I ever knew, taking into consideration the central situation and the living. I wish Kate[649] could see it—she would faint. Last night, for supper, we had the nicest tea you ever drank, strong and hot,—wheat bread and rye bread—cheese—tea-cakes (elegant), a great dish (two dishes) of elegant ham, and two of cold veal, piled up like a mountain and large slices—three dishes of the cakes and everything in the greatest profusion. No fear of starving here. The landlady seemed as if she couldn't press us enough, and we were at home directly. Her husband is living with her—a fat, good-natured old soul. There are eight or ten boarders—two or three of them ladies—two servants. For breakfast we had excellent-flavoured coffee, hot and strong—not very clear and no great deal of cream—veal cutlets, elegant ham and eggs and nice bread and butter. I never sat down to a more plentiful or a nicer breakfast. I wish you could have seen the eggs—and the great dishes of meat. I ate

---

[647] It should be remembered that the purchasing power of money at this date was several times what it is now. In any sum mentioned, in connection with the times portrayed here, this basis of comparison must be borne in mind.

[648] Poe evidently gives explicit directions here to enable Mrs. Clemm to find the house when she herself arrived later on.

[649] A reference to "Catarina," the Poes' pet cat.

the first hearty breakfast I have eaten since I left our little home. Sis is delighted, and we are both in excellent spirits. She has coughed hardly any and had no night sweat. She is now busy mending my pants which I tore against a nail. I went out last night and bought a skein of silk, a skein of thread, two buttons, a pair of slippers, and a pan for the stove.[650] The fire kept in all night. We have now got four dollars and a half left. To-morrow I am going to try and borrow three dollars, so that I may have a fortnight to go upon. I feel in excellent spirits, and haven't drank a drop—so that I hope soon to get out of trouble. The very instant I scrape together enough money I will send it on. You can't imagine how much we both do miss you. Sissy had a hearty cry last night because you and Catterina weren't here.[649] We are resolved to get two rooms the first moment we can. In the meantime it is impossible we could be more comfortable or more at home than we are. It looks as if it were going to clear up now. Be sure and go to the P. O. and have my letters forwarded. As soon as I write Lowell's article, I will send it to you, and get you to get the money from Graham. Give our best love to C.[649]

(Signature cut away)

(P. S.) Be sure and take home the *Messenger* to Hirst. We hope to send for you very soon.

This is notable, in Poe's correspondence, as being the only one of his letters on record in which the mask is entirely dropped. All the rest seem to have been written under some strong emotion, for a set purpose, or wrapped in the ample folds of his literary and critical cloak. Here for about one brief hour—about nine o'clock on a rainy Sunday morning in April, 1844,—we see "Israfel," the hollow-eyed, cloak-wrapped figure with the ravens circling about his head, the man of gloomy destiny, the cabalistic seer, the mighty reasoner, the haunter of graves— stripped of all this legendary make-up—stripped even of his trousers, sitting up in bed, full of "elegant ham," writing "Muddie" a real honest letter about this workaday world. Virginia is sitting near the stove while the rain patters on the roof,—"She is now busy mending my pants which I tore against a nail," snuffling a little bit now and then because she misses her "Muddie," and her pussy cat away off there in Philadelphia. For sheer personal insight into the personal habits of the human animal known as Edgar Allan Poe, this letter is worth a whole barrel of confectionery to Helen Whitman, and the philosophy meant for Lowell or Chivers.

There seem to have been only two persons, in this life, in whom Poe ever fully confided. One of those was his foster-mother Frances Allan —("if only *she* hadn't died!")[380]—and the other was his aunt, Maria Clemm. She knew him as a human being, body and soul. That the intellect, the world of his imagination was utterly beyond her makes Poe's letters to her, and this one in particular, all the more important as a sheer literal record of physical fact. The facts which emerge from

---

[650] Spools did not come into general use until the late '60's.

it are not at all mysterious. They are, indeed, immemorially familiar to humanity; poverty, drink, tuberculosis, domestic love, and brave, useless hope.

Whole flocks of dove-like persons have cooed rapturously over this lone epistle for well-nigh two generations. The cat, of course, *is* very fetching; quite smoothable in fact. Taken out of its frame of surrounding facts, and read as a lonely item, this letter, as Mrs. Hale says, "is a subject upon which we could lucubrate indefinitely." Once returned to that frame, however, it is merely a very intimate and unique confirmation, from Poe's own hand, of what went before, and what came after. As such it is deserving of more than sentimental attention.

The nervous poverty of one whose only stock in trade is dreams runs in every line. There is the familiar argument with the cab driver over the customary fare, the little penny pan purchased to make the landlady's coal last all night, the mended clothes, the "elegant" board in the house that looks buggy—at nothing a week—three dollars to be borrowed plus four dollars and a half left, "so that I may have a fortnight to go upon"! Let those who can rhapsodize do so. Rhapsody should be made of softer stuff.

The man who wrote this letter had recently been starving. His descriptions of food read like the enthusiasm of a diet patient for his favorite café. Then there is the shadow of invalidism, the unusual absence of Sis' cough and night sweats, she who is called only by the name of sister. All this is carefully detailed to Mrs. Clemm, waiting in some boarding house in Philadelphia until Eddie could raise the $3 fare by way of Perth Amboy ($1 less than by the Trenton line). Things had come to a desperate pass, indeed, when the mainstay of the family had been left behind with the cat. Scarcely one item is wanting to complete the picture. Mr. Poe, snorting over the worthless Philadelphia papers, "a few words of no account," even as he left the town where he was no longer an editor, and then—"I feel in excellent spirits, and haven't drank a drop—*so that I hope soon to get out of trouble.*" Evidently Mrs. Clemm knew what the cause of trouble was. Even over the postscript to this pathetic letter, so determinedly cheerful, to encourage poor, lonely "Muddie," an angry controversy arose.

Poe,[651] it will be remembered, had written to Snodgrass some years

---

[651] The petty incidents of the Poe-Duane controversy are detailed here, not for their inherent importance, but because this incident furnishes a type of the many small misunderstandings which served to estrange Poe from his contemporaries. The difficulties of a detached mind in conflict with a practical world are, here, implicit. Other similar incidents have been deliberately left out as being brakes on the wheel of narrative, and this may be regarded as a symbol of the rest. The incident has been pieced together from the correspondence between Poe and Duane, and Duane and Hirst. Mrs. Clemm's position is easily inferred, quite human and natural. This incident may have *caused* the estrangement with Hirst.

before to obtain bound volumes of the numbers of the *Messenger* he had edited. Snodgrass could not get them, it seems, and, through Hirst, Poe had borrowed a copy belonging to William Duane, at one time Secretary of the Treasury. This is why Poe writes to Mrs. Clemm, "Be sure and take home the *Messenger* to Hirst." Mrs. Clemm had already inadvertently pawned the book with others, but was, it seems, afraid to tell this to Poe. She informed him that she had left it at Hirst's office with his brother. Duane then wrote Poe asking for the volume and Poe told him what Mrs. Clemm had said. In the meantime Hirst had fallen out with Poe and, Duane wrote him, "the statement was pronounced by Mr. Hirst to be a damned lie." Subsequent events showed that Mr. Hirst was right in denying having received the volume—"Mr. Poe having sold the books—I hope unintentionally." Further angry correspondence between the three now thoroughly angry parties to the controversy followed. Hirst went about Philadelphia saying that Poe had stolen the book and pawned it. Duane made a considerable pother over it and (after receiving a characteristic letter from Poe in which he was told to "Settle your difficulties with Hirst, and insult me with no more of your communications"), finally found the book in a second-hand store in Richmond, Virginia, thus confirming him in his suspicions of Poe. During all this fire-spitting, Mrs. Clemm was the only one who knew. The incident is important only as being typical of many similar minor difficulties and accusations that followed Poe. Here were two gentlemen, one a close friend and the other an acquaintance, suddenly calling Poe liar and thief, when he had gone to considerable pains to be punctilious. It was all very bewildering, only to be set down to the pure devilishness of human nature. That must be it! "Insult me no more," Poe writes Mr. Duane, who doubtless paid three cents to get the letter. *"Bombastes Furioso Poe,"* endorses Duane upon it. "Liar," shrieks Hirst. Mr. Griswold and Mr. English chuckle. The tale makes its sorry rounds, while Mrs. Clemm sticks to her story.[652]

The boarding house at which Poe and Virginia found themselves in New York was located at 130 Greenwich Street.[653] The funds for remaining there, and for bringing Mrs. Clemm on from Philadelphia, seem to have been provided by the perpetration of one of those elaborate literary jokes in which Poe so delighted. During the first weeks in which he was in New York, Poe must have called on the editor of the *Sun* and sold him the manuscript of *The Balloon Hoax,* for, on the

---

[652] Mr. J. H. Whitty says that Poe used the Duane volume of the *Messenger* to prepare his *Tales* in 1840, and that he (Whitty) found the identical volume in a Boston second-hand bookshop. See *Complete Poems,* J. H. Whitty, *Memoir,* page xlviii, large edition.

[653] The street number is taken from addresses on letters forwarded to Poe at this time.

Saturday following his arrival, the regular morning issue of the paper
for April 13th contained an apparently hastily inserted announcement
in double leads that the news of a balloon's having crossed the Atlantic
had just been received, and that an extra giving full particulars would
be issued at ten o'clock the same morning. The promised extra, which
appeared at the promised hour, contained Poe's story printed as if it
were a "scoop" by the *Sun*.[654] The clever, and "imaginative realism"
of Poe's style was successful in temporarily cozening the multitude who
read, gaped, and believed. Many a beaver hat or poke bonnet waggled
with astonishment over the—

ASTOUNDING

N E W S !

BY EXPRESS VIA NORFOLK!

THE

ATLANTIC CROSSED

in

THREE DAYS!

———

Signal Triumph

of

Mr. Monck Mason's

FLYING

MACHINE!!!!

Arrival at Sullivan's Island
near Charleston, S. C.
of Mr. Mason, Mr. Robert
Holland, Mr. Henson, Mr.
Harrison Ainsworth, and
four others, in the Steer-
ing Balloon "Victoria"—
After a passage of
Seventy-Five Hours
From Land to Land[655]

---

[654] The *New York Sun*, which was the first penny newspaper in New York, would
naturally have been chosen by Poe for this hoax. The paper was even then going in
for a peculiarly American and, in some respects, sensational method of treating news
which it may be said to have inaugurated, as a feature of the new, native journalism.

[655] Of these headlines, Poe, in a later edition of the collected *Tales*, says:
"The subjoined *jeu d'esprit* with the preceding heading in magnificent capitals, well
interspersed with notes of admiration, was originally published, as matter of fact, in
the *New York Sun*, a daily newspaper, and therein fully subserved the purpose of creat-
ing indigestible ailment for the *quidnuncs* during the few hours intervening between a
couple of the Charleston mails. The rush for the 'sole paper which had the news,' was
something beyond even the prodigious; and, in fact, if (as some assert) the 'Victoria'
did not absolutely accomplish the voyage recorded, it will be difficult to assign a reason
why she *should* not have accomplished it."

The beach at Sullivan's Island near Fort Moultrie, which seems to have left an undying impression upon Poe's mind, had again been returned to in *The Balloon Hoax,* as in *The Gold-Bug,* to lend authentic local color.[290] The journalism of the time, when news still depended upon the uncertain arrival of sailing ships, travelers' tales, and the timely letters of special correspondents, lent itself occasionally to hoaxing the public on a large scale, without the fear of contradiction by telegraph, which would now follow instantly. Wonders were in the air, and Mr. Poe's story was unusually clever, interesting, and circumstantial. As a matter of fact he had only anticipated the news by about a century. Strangely enough, the report in the New York papers of the first transatlantic balloon journey recorded almost the same number of hours and many of the same incidents found in Mr. Monck Mason's hypothetical log. From the author's standpoint, it was an excellent way to circulate a short story. It created a thundering lot of talk.

But there was something more than that. Mr. Poe's peculiar joy at having sold his fellow mortals was much deeper than his satisfaction at having sold a manuscript, even though the reward was never so welcome. To have taken in many justified him in that contempt for the mob which several of his other essays and stories exhibit to a marked degree, while it pandered to his own self-esteem. It was incense to that legend of the mob's inferiority, which the very weaknesses of his nature demanded. To keep the air clouded with this fragrant smoke was necessary, so that he, and the world he gazed upon, might appear through the haze other than they actually were. Lastly, it tickled his own curious sense of humor, so closely involved with his essential vanity. Remembering the headless goose at West Point that was made to pass for a gory human head, and the advertisement of himself as the master of mysterious cryptograms, one cannot help but recognize some of the features of "Count" Cagliostro.[377]

The perpetrator of the hoax was, of course, sooner or later tracked to his lair at 130 Greenwich Street, where the immediate result of the sale of the manuscript had been an enlarged apartment. Poe and Virginia now occupied two rooms. Mrs. Clemm was sent for, and seems to have arrived a week or so after her family, doubtless with tears of joy in her eyes, and a basket containing "Catarina." The literary town was soon aware that Mr. Poe was in its midst, but his position was an anomalous one.

He had now been editor of three important publications, but both his literary and personal excesses and peculiarities were known. If he was admired, he was also feared. There were few niches into which he would fit. Editors' chairs are neither easily vacated, nor readily filled, and there can be no doubt that Poe was very averse to filling any sub-

ordinate position. Neither his personality nor his inclinations fitted
him for that. As always, since the days on the *Messenger,* the ambitious ghost of the great national magazine was at his elbow as one of
the directing forces of his literary career. The wraith of this ambition,
always about to become embodied, walked with him to the very last.

During the first few months of his second sojourn in New York,
Poe existed mainly on the meager returns from hack work of one kind
or another. It is probable that his tale of *The Oblong Box,* which appeared in *Godey's Lady's Book* for September, 1844, was finished at
130 Greenwich Street, as its preoccupation with the scenes about
Charleston Harbor connects it with the same locality mentioned in *The
Balloon Hoax* of a few weeks before. *Dreamland* appeared in *Graham's*
for June, 1844. In *The Balloon Hoax,* Poe had rested on the more
popular, and more cheerfully realistic method of *The Gold-Bug* which,
he found, was by far the most popular of his stories. From now on,
however, he returned for the most part to the ideal world created by
his imagination. *The Oblong Box* was, of course, a coffin. Corpses,
premature burials, and those unique and haunted landscapes of his
poems show the strange paths that he took in his dreams, and the melancholy comfort which he found in the realms of the imagination alone.
Physically Poe had come from Philadelphia to New York, actually he
had arrived—

> By a route obscure and lonely
> Haunted by ill angels only,
> Where an *Eidolon,* named NIGHT,
> On a black throne reigns upright,
> I have reached these lands but newly
> From an ultimate dim Thule—
> From a wild weird clime that lieth, sublime,
> Out of SPACE—out of TIME.[656]

This poem may be said to mark the beginning of another resurgence
of creative poetical activity that lasted with some blank interludes from
the Spring of 1844 to the early part of 1849. This, the last flowering
of his creative harvest, was notable for the production of his greatest
poetry. *Dreamland, The Raven, Ulalume, The Bells,* the greatly improved *Valley of Unrest, Eldorado,* and *Annabel Lee,* besides some
minor things, seem to have followed each other in fairly rapid succession. On the other hand, the prose shows a distinct falling off in the
shaping power of imagination, and the criticism, a tendency to degen-
erate into hack work, or vicious personal attacks alternating with per-
fervid puffing.[657] From now on, for the most part, in his criticism,

---

[656] The first stanza of Poe's *Dreamland.*

[657] An exception to this statement about the prose of this period must be made in
favor of the charming landscape sketches of the latter years: *Landor's Cottage, The
Domain of Arnheim,* etc.

Poe seems to have been unable to dissociate himself from the purely personal, in his attitude towards his contemporaries, and anger, jealousy, irritation, or affection colored most of his reviews.

A survey of Poe's literary works from the end of the Philadelphia period to his final disappearance in 1849 shows that it bears indubitably the marks of his own psychic and physical fluctuations. The excesses of the last two years in Philadelphia, combined with what was probably the ordained and inherited tendency of his life curve to take a downward direction early in life, had left him more than ever nervously disorganized, and confirmed his tendency to turn inward even more than before. Hence, he was unequal to the more sustained effort necessary for creative prose, which now, for the most part, with the exception of a few landscape sketches, took on the guise of journalistic comment or correspondence, and we find him, after a period of more than a decade, turning again to poetry, which was at once the expression of the troubles of his inner life and a confession of his almost total withdrawal from any vital contact with the objective world. His consciousness, indeed, during the last five years of his life, seems to have busied itself almost entirely with the problems of self. That the painful events which went on about him in the outside world, during the last years of his life, helped to confirm him in this tendency to psychic withdrawal, there can be no doubt. Over some of these events he had no control. But it is also true that the progressive disorganization, which went on within, produced for him a corresponding chaos in the world without, so that a vicious circle was formed that tightened about him like a noose. One of the accompanying phenomena of this latter period, which must ever be borne in mind as its events are detailed, a psychic phenomenon which largely explains many of the events themselves, was a growing and accelerated tendency to an exaltation of the ego. By 1848, with the appearance of *Eureka,* this tendency had already passed the last admitted borders of sanity.

The tendency to this lamentable condition can be traced far back into his youth. Once given Poe's peculiar nervous constitution and the events which overtook him, and it seems hard to admit of any other outcome. Richmond, and the home life there, had driven him in upon himself. By the time he went to the University of Virginia, he was already a pompous youth possessed of a tremendous, certainly an eccentric, desire for fame. Literature had been his method of approach to the ideal, and had necessitated a constant introspection and years of brooding, that had inevitably set him apart. His open and avowed profession of the name of poet had, at once, sequestered him and exalted him to a strange degree. The profession of literature had involved poverty. This, in turn, had thrust upon him an incidental feeling of inferiority that he had offset by a correspondingly exalted pride. The very time and places in which he found himself, an age and country which could not understand the motives of an esthetic life, thrust upon him almost inevitably the necessity of exalting himself in his own eyes, to defend himself from the opinions of a world that regarded objective attainments and possessions as the only criteria of human success. All these were pertinent and tremendously significant factors in the progress and catastrophe of Edgar Allan Poe. Whether these, however, in themselves would have been sufficient to produce a completely abnormal result may well be doubted.

To all of these factors had been added another, which undoubtedly served to enlarge the already exalted ego of Mr. Poe clear out of the realm of the eccentric into the uncertain shadows of the insane. This was his use of opium. To what degree he indulged in this, and at just what intervals, it is impossible accurately to detail. "The poison, which, taken alternately with opium, kept him half his days in madness," is certainly an exaggeration.[658] That such a statement could be made at all by one who knew him intimately is nevertheless peculiarly significant. It is in the obvious effects upon him, however, that the main evidence exists. The end of that man who indulges in opium is frequently an intense exaltation of the ego. In describing this effect, with which he was peculiarly familiar, Baudelaire, who admired, and rapturously recognized in Poe the records of the effects of opium, goes on to say:

Finally, the drugged man admires himself inordinately; he condemns himself, he glorifies himself; he realizes his condemnation; he becomes the centre of the universe, certain of his virtue as of his genius. Then, in a stupendous irony, he cries: *Je suis devenu Dieu!* One instant after he projects himself out of himself, as if the will of an intoxicated man had an efficacious virtue, and cries, with a cry that might strike down the scattered angels from the ways of the sky: *Je suis un Dieu!"* [659] .

Now this is so precise and perfect a description of Poe's state of mind, particularly during the last years of his life, that, if it cannot be at least partly traced to the same cause, it is one of the most remarkable coincidences of effects on record. For Poe not only struck down the scattered angels when he seized the harp of Israfel, but he also, as many people testify, frequently thought of himself as damned. At the same time, he regarded himself as an epitome of genius. In the pages of

---

[658] William Wallace, in a reply to John Neal's sketch, after Poe's death. See a discussion of this in Woodberry, 1909, vol. II, notes, page 429. English, who saw much of Poe in New York in 1845-46, says he saw "no sign of it," *i.e.*, the opium habit. Rosalie Poe, on a visit to Fordham in 1846, tells of Poe's demanding morphine, however, and Sartain tells of Poe's begging for drugs in Philadelphia in 1849.

[659] *Charles Baudelaire, A Study,* by Arthur Symons, pages 72-73.

Eureka he follows precisely the course of the drug addict as described in the last sentence just quoted from Baudelaire. He finds that he is becoming God, for his exalted intelligence (ego) has, he thinks, permitted him to penetrate the secret of the universe. "One instant after he projects himself out of himself . . . and cries, 'Eureka,'—what does the word mean but that 'I have found.'" What he "found" was the secret of the universe. To find the secret of all things implies one's equality with God.

The final result of this growing tendency of Poe, to the final condition of an ego expounded to the *n*th power, has been delineated here somewhat out of the order of the time of its complete inflation, because it is imperative to bear it in mind, in order to understand the chronicle of the last years, which must now follow. Why the "godlike" soul of this man was so much irritated by the petty doings of many mortal men and women, the nature of the well-spring from which his poetry took its source, his alternating fits of despair and exaltation, and the nature of the tragedies which now rapidly overwhelmed him,—will, in the light of his psychic condition, undoubtedly become less mysterious.

In the Spring of 1844, Poe was writing a biographical sketch of James Russell Lowell which was highly laudatory, especially of his poetry which Poe genuinely admired. Lowell was also writing Poe's biography, a much more solid piece of criticism, which contained some excellent remarks on the contemporary conditions of American letters. The sketch appeared with a rather poor portrait of Poe painted (*sic*) by A. C. Smith and engraved by Welch and Walter among "Our Contributors" in *Graham's* for February, 1845.

There was considerable friendly correspondence between the two friends upon their labors in behalf of each other, about this time. Lowell's final opinion of Poe may be summed up roughly in the statement that he admired Poe's work as an imaginative artist, but shied at its abnormal implications; the better part of Poe's criticism Lowell held in high esteem while deprecating its animosity. The man himself he admired circumspectly, and pitied charitably. The comment of this generous and understanding man, probably the greatest contemporary with whom Poe had vital contact, constitutes an important judgment.

In a letter written to Lowell in May, 1844, enclosing data for his biography, Poe includes a list of six unpublished stories which were, he says, then in the hands of editors.[660] These tales, no doubt, represented the latter fruits of his labors during the Philadelphia period. The long delays to which he was subjected, not only before publishing,

---

[660] Poe to Lowell, New York, May 20, 1844. The unpublished stories were: *The Oblong Box, The Premature Burial, The Purloined Letter, The System of Doctor Tarr and Professor Fether, Mesmeric Revelation, Thou Art the Man.*

but before payment, are here made painfully clear and exhibit vividly an exasperating cause of his poverty.[661]

Since the early 1830's, Poe had been writing steadily and professionally. During that time he had produced both prose and poetry which even his detractors admitted to be of extraordinary quality. It was certainly as good as, if not better than any other imaginative literature then being produced in the United States. Yet he was not only poorly rewarded; he was still in abject poverty. His reputation had been literally his only gain rolled up by the years. Even this, in some quarters, was doubtful. His collected works had been given away to be sold without royalty, and, even then, they had not been successful in achieving circulation. Despite his not infrequent lapses, due to constitutional ill health and other causes, it must be remembered that Poe had worked desperately hard at his profession. The mere bulk of his work is conclusive evidence of this.[662] Hundreds of columns of reviews, editorials, and notes; a sufficient number of stories to make up five "ordinary novel volumes"; three books of poems, the editorship of three periodicals, and the conduct of an exacting and always active correspondence in the laborious medium of longhand—had barely sufficed to keep the wolf from the door, and had dumped Poe a derelict in New York in April, 1844, with $4.50 in his pockets.

It is preposterous to suppose that this was "all his own fault." To do so leaves out of account the very practical consideration that the main cause of Mr. Poe's poverty was that he was underpaid. Only the lower order of his literary labors, his journalism, had any marketable value. For his great art, the condition of taste, the copyright law, and the flood of English books that annually glutted the American market, left scarcely a purchaser. He could not, in fact, even successfully give away his stories or poems, when they were bound in book form. In this, he was groping against the wall which confronted everyone who wrote imaginatively in English on the western side of the Atlantic.

It was due to this condition that Poe continued, from 1835 to 1845, to make persistent and vain efforts to reap even a harvest of reputation from a successful circulation of his collected tales. Upon his removal to New York, he now once more addressed himself to the matter, and again turned to a former acquaintance. Professor Charles Anthon was to solicit, in Poe's interest, with Harpers, for whom Anthon was a literary adviser, in order to get them to bring out an edition comprising

---

[661] Woodberry, 1909, vol. II, pages 71-72, gives an excellent discussion of this matter, together with the full text of the correspondence with Lowell and Anthon about this time.

[662] See Poe to Prof. Charles Anthon, June, 1844.

the collected stories to date. In a passage in a letter to Anthon the vicissitudes of Poe's literary career, which may be taken as typical of those of many another American author of the day, are made sufficiently clear:

Holding steadily in view my ultimate purpose,—to found a Magazine of my own, or [one] in which at least I might have a proprietary right,—it has been my constant endeavor in the mean time, not so much to establish a reputation great in itself as one of that particular character which should best further my special objects, and draw attention to my exertions as Editor of a Magazine. Thus I have written no books, and have been so far essentially a Magazinist [defective MS.] bearing, not only willingly but cheerfully, sad poverty and the consequent contumelies and other ills which the condition of the mere Magazinist entails upon him in America, where, more than in any other region upon the face of the globe, to be poor is to be despised.

The one great difficulty resulting from this course is unless the journalist collects his various articles he is liable to be grossly misconceived and misjudged by men of whose good opinion he would be proud, but who see, perhaps, only a paper here and there, by accident—often only one of his mere extravaganzas, written to supply a particular demand. He loses, too, whatever merit may be his due on the score of versatility—a point which can only be estimated by collection of his various articles in volume form and all together. This is indeed a serious difficulty—to seek a remedy for which is my object in writing you this letter.[662]

The remedy, of course, was the proposed edition of collected tales which Poe says, "are in number sixty-six. They would make, perhaps, five of the ordinary novel-volumes." As a result of Professor Anthon's having been on his summer vacation, he did not answer Poe's letter until five months later. The tenor of his reply was entirely cordial. He had proposed the matter to Harpers, who, while they admitted Poe's reputation and the quality of his work, apparently refused to undertake publication for him on account of his connection with the textbook on conchology in Philadelphia, in 1839, a publication of a rival firm to which Poe had lent his name, and that had been designed to drive a similar book, under the Harper copyright, off the market. As Harpers had previously published *Arthur Gordon Pym* for Poe, their "complaints" were not without some basis. "The Harpers also entertain, as I heard from their own lips, the highest opinion of your talents, but—"[663] Poe had the option of calling upon the Harpers to make explanations, but it is doubtful if he did so. The project in that direction was permitted to languish.

With the arrival of Mrs. Clemm in New York, sometime during the Spring of 1844, the two rooms at 130 Greenwich Street were given up completely to Virginia and her mother, while Poe himself took up quarters with a Mrs. William (*sic*) Foster at Number 4 Ann Street.

---

[663] Anthon to Poe, New York, November 2, 1844.

Here he seems to have shared bachelor quarters with C. C. Curtis, and to have led a more or less poverty-stricken and haphazard existence, not without certain Bohemian interludes. In the cellar of one Sandy Welsh, who kept a tavern on Ann Street, during the Spring of 1844 Poe met a number of congenial spirits, journalists and others, and read *The Raven* to them, stanza by stanza, in the form in which it then existed. The poem was criticized by those present, sometimes in a humorous mood, and suggestions, some of which Poe is said to have adopted, were offered. Specific instances have been given of the emendations thus said to have been made by others, but the matter is extremely nebulous at best.[664]

The rest of Poe's time seems to have been largely occupied with making the rounds of the newspapers, and supplying out-of-town correspondents with light comments, items of news, and other literary comment. It is probable that, in slack periods, he resorted to this type of writing more than is generally suspected, and that all of these minor effusions have not been traced. On June 18th, he wrote for the editors of the *Columbia Spy* at Columbia, Pennsylvania:

New York Harbor in June, 1844

By *Edgar A. Poe*

In point of *natural* beauty, as well as of convenience, the harbor of New York has scarcely its equal in the northern hemisphere; but, as in the case of Brooklyn, the Gothamites have most generously disfigured it by displays of landscapes and architectural taste. More atrocious *pagodas,* or what not, for it is indeed difficult to find a name for them,—were certainly never imagined than the greater portion of those which affront the eye, in every nook and corner of the bay, and more particularly, in the vicinity of New Brighton. If these monstrosities appertain to taste, then it is taste in its dying agonies. . . .

How completely the world had changed since Poe had seen the same harbor on his way home from West Point in 1831, and how little he relished the change, can be seen in this sketch.[665] Poe's taste was, as was inevitable, affected by the standards of before the Mexican War days, but that, in the main, it rose above the monstrosities of the time, and looked back to the Georgian architecture and costumes of his early Richmond and English schooldays with regret, is vastly to his credit. For the little boy who played about Frances Allan's charming drawing room on Russell Square, London, in 1818, the "pagodas" of New Brighton were not to be swallowed without gasping.[666]

---

[664] See Woodberry, 1909, vol. II, page 114, note 1. *The Raven* was claimed to have been "submitted by Poe piecemeal to the criticism . . . of his intimates [at Welsh's] until it was voted complete." This is, of course, fancy run wild (Woodberry merely notes the claim). See *Scribner's* for October, 1875, F. G. Fairchild.

[665] For the contrast implied see Chapter XIV, pages 244-257.

[666] For the reasons for Poe's choice of the word "pagodas" to describe architectural houses see the illustration, page 333.

An amusing subject for a social essay on early nineteenth century America would be a comparison of the prevailing types of architecture with the current types of foreign novels, in which was imported not only thought, but taste.   Classic, Gothic, Moresque, and Victorian seems to have been the order of obsession, roughly speaking, in both books and buildings.   On the seaboard, the trade with the Orient had strange esoteric manifestations.

As the classical culture and the imported Renaissance patterns of the eighteenth century Colonial, and the later Georgian went out of style, there was a brief but determined attempt to follow the political conception of the "fathers" and make America, in outward appearance, the reflection of the classical republic of which such statesmen as Jefferson dreamed—hence "Thy groves and templed hills," embalmed in the national hymn.   This tendency continued to haunt the South.   A little later, there was a restless desire to become Gothic which "almost succeeded."   In the '40's a great many people had settled upon being Moresque or even Oriental, hence, as Poe says, the "pagodas."

Into a country that had a weak cultural digestive tract was poured a plethora of ideas that gorged it intellectually and artistically, with the result of astounding regurgitations in literature and architecture.   The terrible speed of the first machine era had, in the United States and elsewhere, already broken away from all the former bounds of taste, and progress swooped drunkenly forward.   American architecture had started upon the orgy of ugliness which culminated in the delirium tremens epoch of the Centennial.

. . . a collection of tags, thrown at random against a building.   Architectural forms . . . brought together by a mere juxtaposition of materials held in place by neither imagination nor logic. . . .[667]

As a symbol of the complete esthetic anarchy, and the barbarous romanticism of the era, one may take Colonel Colt's mansion near Hartford, Connecticut.   It was called Armsmear, and it was described as late as 1876 in the *Art Journal,* as a "characteristic type of the unique."[667]

Armsmear was a long, grand, impressive, contradictory, beautiful strange thing. . . . An Italian villa in stone, massive, noble, refined, yet not carrying out any decided principles of architecture, it is like the mind of its originator, bold and unusual in its combinations. . . . There is no doubt it is a little Turkish among other things, on one side it has domes, pinnacles, and light, lavish ornamentation, such as Oriental taste delights in. . . . Yet, although the villa is Italian and cosmopolitan, the feeling is English.   It is an English home in its substantiality, its home-like and comfortable aspects.

---

[667] Lewis Mumford.   The description of Armsmear, and its application, is taken from *Sticks and Stones.*   Lewis Mumford, Boni and Liveright, 1924.   The original of the description comes from the *Art Journal* for 1876.   Armsmear was built between 1855 and 1862, but it was the result of the type of culture prevalent a little earlier.

This masterpiece of paradox, in which confusion supplied the only unity, was typical of the leveling and imitative democratic mind, which cannot see that distinction implies difference. It is one of the most powerful arguments for the genius of Poe that, although he moved in a scene of monstrous and self-satisfied confusion, he conferred upon his own material a memorable unity.

In the 1840's the ferment of disintegration of all ancient orders whatsoever was rapidly going on. The process was visibly impressed upon the objective world. Wood was enormously plentiful and correspondingly cheap. So cheap, frame structures imitating the Alhambra, and aping the Oriental, began to blotch and to make inroads upon the erstwhile semi-classical landscape. Cast-iron balconies and jigsaw fretwork, "relieved" by Arabian inlays of garish tile and imitation stone, staggered horribly across the fronts of banks. Meticulous and useless finials, threatening architraves, and weak newel posts mutinied under the apparently colossal weight of false fronts. The world was losing all sense of proportion. America no longer imagined itself to be an ancient Roman or Greek state, it already knew better. The last of the fathers in knee breeks had now departed. Classical names for cities were out of style. Villes, Burgs, and Smith Cities began to infest the land. For a time there was even an attempt to be vaguely Egyptian in reservoirs and jails.[668]

The fashions were equally eclectic. Uncomfortable little boys dressed like Scottish chiefs, were led about by negro nurses. Hoopskirts and gentility swept the streets, and everything else. Delicate chinless ladies with lacquered heart-shaped fans and heelless cloth slippers rested their Chinese feet upon "balzerine" pillows and "listed" to Swiss music boxes. Plumbers fitted the chandeliers with umbilical gas pipes. Old ladies who had known Aaron Burr and the *macaronis* of *Fraunces' Tavern,* were now discreetly confined with other family skeletons to upstairs apartments, where their granddaughters could not hear them swearing in the grand old style, and complaining of the prudish younger generation, of their insipid conversation, of the lack of capable partners at whist, and the lamentable dearth of drink.

Little girls were laced tightly at home, but so much tighter at boarding schools, that a lady who lost a portion of her respectability by delivering lectures to mixed audiences, ventured to remark, in the privacy of her diary, that "the results were doubtful." Transatlantic Victorianism was in full swing. The forties were now four years old, and the famous unknown poetasters and poetesses gathered themselves

---

[668] Types of the "Egyptian" were the municipal reservoir at Forty-second Street and Fifth Avenue, New York, on the site of the present Public Library, and Moyamensing Prison, Philadelphia. See illustration, page 588. The Old "Tombs" in New York City, and the Richmond Medical College, still standing, were also "Nilesque."

in the salons of the Manhattan of 325,000 souls—exactly as they do now. In 1844, they were known to each other as the *literati*. Mr. Poe, the distinguished-looking Southern gentleman with the soulful eyes, was sardonically preparing to make their obscurity visible to the future.

The most amazing thing about this curious era is that not a doubt of its superiority to all the other ages that had preceded it seems ever to have disturbed its collective mind. The apparently soon to be completed control of nature by machinery had suggested a doctrine of "progress," hitherto unheard of, but now extended to everything from politics to petticoats. The magazines, the newspapers, public speeches, essays, and novels all reeked with gratulatory self-complacence. The philosophy of the time was so completely saturated with the notion that nine *yeas* must necessarily be a more profound judgment than eight *nays,* and that humanity was bound to be a little better on Tuesday than it had been on Monday—that not an objection could be publicly registered. Above all, taste was "more genteel."

"And here," contemptuously says a notice in the "Editor's Table" of *Godey's Lady's Book*—"here are the full dress and the walking costume of 1800."

The beginning of a new century, thus far in its progress, has developed most astonishingly the resources of mechanical arts, and better applied them to human convenience, comfort and improvement, than has ever before, in the history of the world, been effected. And we think, among other improvements, that the ladies have decidedly improved their fashions of dress. Look on these pictures, [*i.e.,* fashions of 1800] and then turn to our 'Fashion Plate,' and thank the Publisher of the *Lady's Book* for thus showing by contrast, the beauty and becomingness of our present costume.[669]

This was the same magazine to which Poe was glad to contribute *A Tale of the Ragged Mountains,* and to be thankful it was accepted. *Godey's Lady's Book,* in fact, was yet to play a rather important little part in his career, and those of certain ladies. Louis Godey, its editor, and Mrs. Hale were still his good friends. He needed them to live.

No wonder that, at times, Poe became impatient, or sardonic; he was practically alone in his protests and jest makings at the expense of his age. To expect that he should rise above it completely, is to ask the impossible. As a matter of fact, he did the best he could—he withdrew further and further into himself. When he did come out, it was generally to deliver a sting. That Poe felt a considerable amount of justifiable artistic and philosophic antipathy toward the America of the '40's, and that it was not all due to his own peculiarities, there can be no doubt. There was an immense cleavage between his artistry and his time. "Progress" had left him enormously alone.

In the Summer of 1844, with the arrival of hot weather, it became

---

[669] *Godey's Lady's Book* for April, 1844, page 199.

necessary to move Virginia to a cooler place in the country. The rural retreat chosen for the summer residence was an old farmhouse with Revolutionary traditions, on a farm along Bloomingdale Road, some five of six miles out of town. The house, which was for long known as "the house where *The Raven* was written," was situated in 1844 on what was then a rather conspicuous and rocky knoll, a few hundred feet from the northeast corner of the present Eighty-fourth Street and Broadway.[670 and 671]

The dwelling itself was of a familiar type of Colonial farm architecture. A large main building with a smaller and lower annex extended from one side. There were two low brick chimneys, one in the middle gable, and the other at the end of the annex. The dooryard of the house opened into Broadway just above Eighty-fourth Street. The path from the farm gate led past a little pond made by the spring, where wagoners stopped frequently to refresh themselves. The house and low outbuildings were well shaded by old trees, and the roof overtopped by a weeping willow, said to have been taken from a shoot by Napoleon's tomb at St. Helena. It was really the rear of the house that one approached from Bloomingdale Road (Broadway). The front with its square windows and square-framed door, exhibited that curious aspect of half-horrified surprise which lends an almost human expression to some dwellings. Its windows stared down over Bloomingdale into the valley of the Hudson, and from the rock-ledged knoll upon which it stood, there was a magnificent sweep of unbroken rural landscape up and down the river. The fields before the dwelling sloped down to the river where the steamboats passed. There was a glimpse of the roofs of old Claremont about two miles above, and the cliffs of the New Jersey shore opposite. For miles, the meadows, woods, and little roads seemed pouring themselves into the valley as if in haste to tumble into the stream. Some distance above, at what is now Ninety-sixth Street, was a dock where the side-wheel steamers landed, and a cluster of roofs in a deep vale where a stream entered the Hudson. Here, passengers

---

[670] The sources for the descriptions of the house and its environment, and of the events that took place there, are taken from Gill's *Life of Poe,* 1877, pages 147-150, and from illustrations made of the house while it was still standing. Also from photographs taken in 1876, reproductions, in the possession of the author. Also from the account in Woodberry, 1909, vol. II, page 113. The following original sources were also consulted. *Poe and the Raven,* by Gen. James R. O'Beirne (husband of Martha Brennan), in the *New York Mail and Express.* Also *Frank Leslie's Illustrated Weekly,* an article by Tyrrell, September, 1883. Also material having to do with the removal of the Brennan mantel to the Hall of Philosophy, Columbia University; maps, city plans, prints of the neighborhood, and two private letters of neighbors of the Brennans in 1845, in which Poe is not mentioned.

[671] Gen. J. R. O'Beirne—"In those days . . . Patrick Brennan owned a farm of 216 acres, extending from a point about 200 feet west of Central Park to the Hudson River. . . . The homestead stood on 84th St. between Amsterdam Ave. and Broadway, . . ." See Harrison, vol. I, page 224.

left from the neighboring farms for New York on the seven o'clock boat in the morning, fortifying themselves for the trip down at *Stryker's Bay Tavern,* kept by a fat host, Joseph Francis, who dispensed the neighborhood news, and cups of kindness. An occasional wagon or stage raised the dust along the farm fence, on its way down Bloomingdale Road to New York. The fare on the regular trips in the morning was one shilling, or "two bits," according to the year in which one was born. Most of the silver coins in general circulation were those adorned by the Mexican eagle holding the snake in his claws between two pillars.[672]

Sometime during the Spring, perhaps on a stroll out Bloomingdale Road, Poe had become acquainted with Mr. and Mrs. Patrick Brennan "of similar Melanesian descent, a hospitable agriculturist and his consort," who with their daughter Martha, a young girl of about fourteen years, and five or six younger children, lived on the farm of 216 acres where they raised truck for the city markets, fruit, and flowers. The Brennans occupied the place for nearly fifty years, and seem to have taken boarders from time to time, especially in the Summer. Poe evidently struck a bargain with them for himself, Mrs. Clemm, and Virginia. He was quite enchanted with the spot, the magnificent view, the excellent food, and the good nature of his hosts.

About the beginning of July, 1844, he gave up his room on Ann Street, forsook Sandy Welsh's cellar and other haunts about town, and gathering up Mrs. Clemm and Virginia at 130 Greenwich Street, drove out to the Brennans'. Despite the numerous children and dogs, he described the place later as "a perfect heaven." The last perfectly peaceful and happy hours that he was to know were passed under its roof. It still seemed possible, for those who could hope against hope, that in a place such as this Virginia *might* get well.

To Mrs. Clemm and Virginia, after the period of disintegration of the home in Philadelphia, and the anxious days on Greenwich Street, with Edgar roaming about the journalistic purlieus, and no assurance of where the next week's board was to come from, "Bloomingdale on the Hudson" must have seemed a little paradise. Poe was removed from influences which kept Mrs. Clemm in continual anxiety, Virginia was in healthful surroundings, and "Muddie" herself was in a place where she could luxuriate in the space, plenty, and respectability of being a matronly boarder. Doubtless she and Mrs. Brennan were soon

---

[672] Up until at least 1850, most of the older generation continued to reckon orally in shillings and pence. It was long doubtful whether dollar marks should go before or after figures (see, for instance, Poe's letters to John Allan). Owing to defective coinage laws, and the gold and silver parity, United States coins were exported and "change" was largely confined to Mexican money. This went at face value as long as the eagle and pillars on the coin were visible. See also Sumner, *History of American Currency.*

on excellent gossiping terms. The simple friendship between the good Irish couple and the Poes was long kept up, and seems to have had something to do with the latter's subsequent removes and places of residence. Poe was now sufficiently well known to be an object of considerable curiosity to simple folk; his mode of life was noted and afterward remembered.

Mrs. Clemm is said to have had a room downstairs. Poe and Virginia occupied a garret under the eaves, beneath which, running clear across the house with a door that looked out upon Bloomingdale Road, and a large open fireplace with a rather handsomely carved mantel, was the poet's study. It was in this room that *The Raven* was completed, and as some of its furnishings have entered the realm of eternity in imaginative literature, its contents have been the subject of curious inquiry.

The room, it seems, had been occupied by a former boarder of the Brennans', a Frenchman who had been an officer under Napoleon, and had gone into exile after the collapse of the first imperial régime. The walls were decorated with French military prints; there was a clock; heavy hangings, of some sort, after the Empire manner; several pieces of heavy, cloth-lined furniture; a bookcase; and an upright flat-topped desk. Two rather small windows with the usual square panes of old-fashioned, thick glass gave a view across the Hudson to New Jersey on the front, while a door in the rear opened out on the dooryard towards Broadway. In addition to this, there was an interior door that led into the center hallway.

Above the door opening into the hallway, stood the 'pallid bust of Pallas.' It was a little plaster cast and occupied a shelf nailed to the door casing, immediately behind the bust, and occupying the space between the top casing and the ceiling; a number of little panes of smoked glass took the place of the partition.[673]

On stormy nights, the wind swept up and down the Hudson Valley, just as it now scours along Riverside Drive, and shook the exposed house perched on the knoll. That some of these seemingly trivial objects and circumstances served to furnish forth part of the scenery and machinery of *The Raven* during the long hours of the Summer and Fall of 1844, when it was taking its final shape in this apartment, there can be little doubt.

The Brennans afterward recalled many of the incidents of Poe's sojourn with them: the long hours he spent in the room downstairs writ-

[673] Description from Gen. James O'Beirne (husband of Martha Brennan) long familiar with the Brennan house. O'Beirne continues—"This bust of Minerva was either removed or broken by one of the Brennan tenants after the family had moved to the city." *New York Mail and Express,* see notes 670, 671. It must be remembered that Gen. O'Beirne's description of the position of the bust with the light *behind* it, was written *after* the controversy had arisen about the shadow on the floor. Poe is said to have suggested such a solution himself in Richmond in 1849.

ing, of Poe and Virginia seated at the western windows watching the sunsets across the Hudson, of the leaves of manuscript and correspondence scattered over the broad planked floor of the room with the bust, and of the hours which Poe spent dreaming on a bench by the pond, under a shade tree whence the children would call him in to meals. Young Tom Brennan remembered how the fascinating gentleman with the cane drew designs in the dust, and how Poe used to wander off to Mount Tom and sit for hours gazing at the Hudson and dreaming. Martha Brennan, who was described by the neighbors as a dark-haired Irish beauty with blue eyes, drove her family to early mass, dressed in a black silk bodice with a narrow lace collar, and a lace-trimmed poke bonnet, tied under her chin with a black satin bow. She was about fifteen during the Summer of the Poes' stay, and made an ideal companion for Virginia whom she saw pasting Poe's manuscript together into the long rolls of which the child-wife was very proud, although having little conception of their meaning. Their size and shape, the beautiful characters engrossed upon them by her husband's copper-plate pen, and their marvelous length when unrolled, constituted her literary appreciation. Mrs. Clemm was more understanding. She listened patiently, in the rôle of a professional enthusiast, to much of Poe's work, and brewed him coffee when he grew tired. It seems to have been Poe's custom to rely greatly upon the effects of his stories and poems when spoken, and there can be no doubt that his strong sense of euphony and of the sonorous would lead him to read aloud or recite to whosoever would listen. There is testimony that he did so, and, lacking an audience, he was overheard to be composing aloud.

Poe was free of visitors on the farm, but made occasional trips to New York, walking when he did not have the fare, as was frequently the case. Mrs. Brennan said that the board was always paid. During the Summer, Poe must have relied for his "income" on three stories sent to Godey, a good friend who would pay him in advance, the article on Lowell placed with *Graham's,* and his contributions to the *Columbian Magazine* of *The Angel of the Odd* and *Mesmeric Revelation,* a subject which, together with spiritualistic manifestations, was then much in the public mind. In *The Literary Life of Thingum Bob, Esq.,* one of Poe's most highly autobiographical and ironical sketches, he again returned to the scenes of his youth in Richmond, in a satiric vein, and probably took a secret pleasure in placing it in his home town with the *Southern Literary Messenger,* where it appeared in December, 1844, and was copied into the *Broadway Journal* a little later. *The Premature Burial* also returned for its literal setting to some boat trip on the James, years before, perhaps with Burling. This story, first published at Philadelphia in the *Dollar Newspaper* for July 31, 1844, is one of the most genuinely morbid of any that Poe tossed off. It seems to have arisen from the sense of oppression and inevitable catastrophe which had long been a concomitant of his melancholia, or some dream of smothering, perhaps due to his heart trouble.[674]

What the rather tired-looking gentleman was thinking about as he sat on the bench under the trees at the Brennans', while the bees hummed, would no doubt have astonished the little folks who called him to dinner from time to time could they have been familiar with the recesses of his mind. Poe was not calmly reveling in the pastoral scene about him. Somehow or other, in the alembic of his nature, it was thus that he beheld the world:

I looked; and the unseen figure, which still grasped me by the wrist, had caused to be thrown open the graves of all mankind; and from each issued the faint phosphoric radiance of decay; so that I could see into the innermost recesses, and there view the shrouded bodies in their sad and solemn slumbers with the worm. But, alas! the real sleepers were fewer, by many millions, than those who slumbered not at all; and there was a feeble struggling; and there was a sad unrest; and from out of the depths of the countless pits there came a melancholy rustling from the garments of the buried. And, of those who seemed tranquilly to repose, I saw that a vast number had changed, in a greater or less degree, the rigid and uneasy position in which they had originally been entombed.[675]

Perhaps all of the coffee which Mrs. Clemm brewed after such a recital was not consumed by Edgar. It was from the sale of such dreams as these, some of which were composed amid the charming surroundings of the lower Hudson Valley, that Poe attempted to support himself during the Summer of 1844. He seems to have just managed to pay his board. In May, he had been so poor as not to be able to lift from the post office letters written to him from Georgia by Dr. Chivers. The postage was about twelve cents.[676]

That *The Raven* assumed its final form at Eighty-fourth Street and Broadway there can be no doubt. That Poe had brought an earlier draft of it with him when he arrived there is equally certain. As has already been shown, the germ of the idea had originated in Philadelphia

---

[674] Poe's story of *Loss of Breath,* and *The Tell-Tale Heart* both belong to this same type of thing. Dreams caused by a bad heart, a sense of oppression, the waking struggle with a consequent feeling of apprehension, and the fear of dying while asleep, or being buried while in a torpor, may account for much of the machinery of the plot and the imagery in such stories. For instance:

"In all that I endured there was no physical suffering, but of moral distress an infinitude. My fancy grew charnal. I talked 'of worms, of tombs, and epitaphs.' I was lost in reveries of death, and the idea of premature burial held continual possession of my brain. The ghastly Danger to which I was subjected, haunted me day and night. In the former, the torture of meditation was excessive, in the latter supreme."—Poe's *Premature Burial.*

[675] From Poe's *Premature Burial.*

[676] Chivers to Poe, Oakey Grove, Georgia, May 15, 1844. Postage between Poe and Chivers was evidently a considerable difficulty. See Chivers' reference to the matter in his letter to Poe of September 26, 1842.

about four years before with Poe's review of *Barnaby Rudge* in which the bird is found.   Lowell recognized this in his *Fable for Critics:*

> Here comes Poe with his Raven, like Barnaby Rudge,
> Three fifths of him genius, and two fifths sheer fudge. . . .

It now seems highly probable that the early poem was discussed with Hirst in the rambles about Philadelphia, and that Hirst may have contributed some ideas to it that led to his later claims to have "written" it.[601]   The story told by Mrs. Weiss, which she says Poe related to her in Richmond shortly before his death, that the bird was originally an owl, will bear inspection.[677]   That the poem was in existence in some form as early as the Summer of 1842 seems fairly certain, as it was then shown by Poe to Mrs. Barhyte, a contributor to the *New York Mirror*.   It was then, or in the next Summer, of 1843, that the lines suggested by a child were introduced.[612]   The next definite news about it is from Rosenbach, the Philadelphia acquaintance, who said that as early as the winter of 1843-44 he had read *The Raven,* and relates that about the same time it was offered to Graham when the collection for Mrs. Clemm was taken up.   Colonel Du Solle also tells that, early in 1844, Poe was trying it on journalistic friends about Philadelphia.[642] After the removal to New York, we again hear of its being read and receiving emendations at the hands of friends meeting in Sandy Welsh's cellar on Ann Street in the late Spring.[664]   Thus the period of its incubation which followed Poe's typically slow method of verse composition can be fairly certainly traced.   It was this manuscript which he brought with him to the Brennans' in the Summer of 1844.

"Events not to be controlled have prevented me from making, at any time, any serious effort in what, under happier circumstances, would have been the field of my choice," said Poe; and adds, "With me, poetry has not been a purpose, but a passion; and the passions should be held in reverence; they must not—they cannot at will be excited, with an eye to the paltry compensations, or the more paltry commendations, of mankind." [678]   At the farm overlooking the Hudson, for a very brief time, the "happier circumstances" seem to have been approached, and so, with an eye to no paltry compensations, Poe now turned himself

---

[677] *Home Life of Poe,* page 185.
"His first intention, he said, had been to write a short poem only, based upon the incident of an *Owl*—a night-bird, the bird of wisdom—with its ghostly presence and inscrutable gaze entering the window of a vault or chamber where he sat beside the bier of the lost *Lenore*.   Then he had exchanged the owl for the Raven, for the sake of the latter's 'Nevermore'; and the poem, despite himself, had grown beyond the length originally intended . . . the Owl, a night-bird—should be . . . attracted by the lighted window, and . . . would be more appropriate to the . . . Owl, Minerva's Bird," etc.
[678] Poe to Lowell, July 2, 1844.

diligently to finishing what he held to be his popular masterpiece, in the room where, despite Mrs. Brennan's protestations, he once absent-mindedly carved his name on the mantelpiece.

Much of the composition must have gone on during the quiet hours of the night. It was now that he probably saw the whole poem in its complete form; and added, to the already conceived antiphonal responses of the bird, the grotesque, eery, and romantic scenery and incidents that he knew so well how to blend. During the autumn nights when the drafty farmhouse was shaken by the blasts, when the fire was dying, the tree branches tapping at the windows, and the light behind the transom threw the shadow of the bust of Pallas on the floor, the mind of the poet fused the actual scene in which he found himself with the furniture of that ideal apartment of his dreams. Into this room, he introduced the raven from *Barnaby Rudge* with the improvement he had already suggested, that "Its croakings might have been prophetically heard in the course of the drama."

The sense of utter despair and inevitable frustration came from within the man himself, as an expression of his own melancholy, the reasons for which may be traced in his nature, and the tragic events of his life. The introduction of Poe's favorite theme of the "Lost Belovéd," taken together with the fatal implication of the Raven's remark, seems to indicate plainly that the author had, by this time, fully realized that his attempt, or the necessity that had been forced upon him by the nature of his marriage, to substitute a dream for the reality of love, led inevitably to despair. Nor was there now any hope for him successfully to capture, in ideality, what had been denied him in fact. On reading the poem, R. H. Horne wrote Poe about a year later : [679]

I am of the same opinion as Miss Barrett [Mrs. Browning] about *The Raven,* and it also seems to me that the poet intends to represent a very painful condition [of] mind, as of an imagination that was liable to topple over into some delirium or an abyss of melancholy, from the continuity of one unvaried emotion.

Now this is such an excellent description of Poe's exact state of mind, and of what actually occurred, that a professional psychologist could do no better. That the "continuity of one unvaried emotion" was of a sexual nature is plain from the use of a lost woman to shadow it forth. "As a lover I am done," says Poe in effect; "Nevermore!" Nor was there any hope in the hereafter. The thought burned into his heart with the eyes of a demon, and he could not drive it away. It was always there, "one unvaried emotion"—"that was liable to topple over into some delirium." That, at times, it did so topple, is perfectly clear. It is the kind of despair that drives men to suicide, and three years later

---

[679] Horne to Poe, Fitzroy Park, Highgate, London, May 17, 1845.

we find the still young man—who found this unhappy bird perched triumphant over the symbol of all his learning and art—trying to commit suicide by drinking laudanum. Those who think *The Raven* is a mere literary *tour de force* often disregard its genuine emotion because it is dramatically and logically presented.

Nor does a mere exposition of literary sources explain the psychic machinery in the use of the material, which, as in every poem, came from somewhere. Poe was almost certainly influenced in the refrain of *The Raven* by such poems as Thomas Holley Chivers' *Lament on the Death of My Mother*. A few lines will serve to illustrate:

> . . . Not where the pleasures of the world are sought—
> Not where the sorrows of the earth are found!
> Nor on the borders of the great deep sea,
> Wilt thou return again from Heaven to me—[680]
> No, never more!

And this, from Chivers' *To Allegra Florence in Heaven*,[681] is even more suggestive in both meter and refrain:

> Thy dear father will to-morrow
> Lay thy body, with deep sorrow,
> In the grave which is so narrow—
> There to rest for evermore!

Whole stanzas and poems might be quoted, especially *Isadore;* and General Pike's poems, with which Poe was familiar by review, are also aspirants to the honors of originals, as their author proclaimed. Hirst, Chivers, Pike, and a host of other little fellows, all claimed to have a finger in the big pie. It is possible, by using the magnifying glass of erudite research, to find the trace of their thumb marks on the crust even now. Mr. Poe, however, was the cook; he mixed it, baked it, and served it up piping hot.

Poe's own explanation of how the poem was concocted in *How I Wrote the Raven,* or *The Philosophy of Composition,* is, in the final analysis, not an explanation at all. It was simply his own effort to rationalize upon, and to make apparently logical *to himself,* his own creative processes. This critical essay was part of his attempt to project himself as the almighty reasoner, as it was also part of his propaganda for making *The Raven* popular. People asked him the question, "Mr. Poe, how did you write *The Raven?*" The essay was a *perfectly reasonable* reply. Instead of falling back on the old theory of mysterious

---

[680] In the Middletown, Connecticut, *Sentinel and Witness,* 1837.

[681] This appeared in Chivers' volume, *The Lost Pleiad.* There is mention of previous publication of this poem in 1842. The manuscript passed through Poe's hands. Chivers' poem of *Isadore* supplies a complete equivalent for the dramatic machinery of *The Raven.* Poe praised it as "original."

and divine inspiration, which has ever been the poet's method of dodging self-analysis, Poe, by his reply, not only silenced the Philistines but also added to his reputation as a logical genius. Among those whom he was trying to convince, he included himself. The real question would have been not, "Mr. Poe, *how* did you write *The Raven?*" but "*Why* did you, Mr. Poe?" For in *How I Wrote the Raven,* Poe, as he must do to keep from facing the realities of his own condition, utterly dodges the issue as to why it was that his psyche was drawn towards the type of material it selects to mold as it did. The explanation of the critical essay does not explain what it was meant as a rationalization to conceal.

There is this, however, to be said. The long period over which the composition of *The Raven* stretched, a period of four years at least, shows that, into the arrangement and composition of it went a deal of critical thinking, artistic analysis, a logical arrangement of effects, and a painstaking construction of the spinal narrative which no mere emotion could have provided. In it is the deliberate device of a musical counter-theme, and effects of assonance, rhyme, and meter which show a profoundly reasoned knowledge of the poet's art. That the images in many instances produced, seemingly simultaneously, the words and the rhythms with which to express themselves there can be small doubt.[682] But that Poe was artist enough to manufacture successfully during the long fabrication of the poem those sections where such "inspiration" did not occur, is only to say that he was a fine poet. No lyric warbler would have been equal to the task. In *How I Wrote the Raven* a part of this process of ratiocination is certainly shadowed forth on a critical basis. There is value in that.

The whole matter can be generally summed up by saying that the choice of the material was involuntary, but its method of treatment a highly reasoned and critical process. Above and beyond all this remains the fact that, in the case of *The Raven,* the perfect blending of these two processes became a unity which resulted in a work of art. The ghost of nothing had been endowed with memorable form.

By the end of the Summer of 1844, certainly in the Autumn, the poem was complete. It was about this time that we hear of Poe reciting it to William R. Wallace, a young New York lawyer who dabbled in verse himself, although not as extensively as Hirst.[683] It was Poe's custom, it seems, to spend part of his time on the porch of the old *Stryker's Bay Tavern* that overhung the stream which, then, ran into the

---

[682] See Coleridge: *Of the Fragment of Kubla Khan,* page 52. *Christabel, Kubla Khan,* etc., 1816 edition.

[683] In the Summer or Fall of 1848, Wallace took Poe to Mathew B. Brady to have a daguerreotype taken, at 205 Broadway. See full-page advertisement in the New York Directory for 1848-9 for location of Brady's galleries.

Hudson at Ninety-sixth Street, near the old ferry dock about a mile from the Brennan farm.   The region about Stryker's Bay: Blooming-dale Village, just in front of the Brennan House, Sylvan Grove between One Hundred Twenty-first and One Hundred Twenty-second Streets, where the steamboats from the foot of Wall Street landed, indeed the entire Harlem region was then the summer playground of New York. The river was the scene of constant steamboat races between such old favorites of the '40's as the "Globe," the "Champion," and the "Cleo-patra."   These, in their hurry, frequently failed to stop to pick up passengers at side landings, and rushed by, steam-pipes roaring, smoke and sparks belching from the stacks, while the gentlemen passengers gathered at the bar forward to bet on the result.

At the *Stryker's Bay Tavern,* Poe again met Thomas Dunn English who had given up editing in Philadelphia and had come, like Poe, to live in New York.   There Poe read *The Raven* to Wallace, whose ex-pressions of appreciation, it appears, were not thought by the poet to be adequate to the occasion.   Poe, on his part, assured his auditor that he had just listened to the greatest poem in the language.   Some allow-ance must be made for the poet's still being in the full flush of his first enthusiasm after composition.   That Poe did not think *The Raven* the best poem he wrote, seems evident from his own theories of poetry, and other remarks afterward.   That it was his show piece, and that he never lost a chance to further it, is also evident.   He felt it to be pitched in a popular key, and a certain forensic and dramatic value in it made it his favorite for recitations on every occasion.

Still another account of Poe's reading of *The Raven,* and of his life on the farm, comes from Martha Brennan, the farmer's daughter.   In it the pitiable condition of Virginia is plainly evident:

During two years she knew him intimately and never saw him affected by liquor or do aught that evinced the wild impetuous nature with which he has been accredited.   He was the gentlest of husbands and devoted to his invalid wife. *Frequently when she was weaker than usual, he carried her tenderly from her room to the dinner-table and satisfied every whim.*

Mrs. Brennan was noted for her kindheartedness and sympathetic nature, and once I heard her say that Poe read *The Raven* to her one evening before he sent it to the *Mirror.* . . .

On other days he would wander through the surrounding woods, and, return-ing in the afternoon, sit in the big room, as it used to be called, by a window and work unceasingly with pen and paper, until the evening shadows. . . .[670]

During the Summer, Poe continued his correspondence with James Russell Lowell.   The principal item of their "epistolary conversations" was the biography of Poe which Lowell was preparing for the forth-coming September issue of *Graham's.*   Lowell writes Poe that he is in one of his fits of constitutional indolence, and has delayed starting to

write. The indolence, he says, "was not counteracted by proper training
in my childhood. You may be sure I am not one of those who follow
a fashion which is hardly yet extinct, and call upon the good, easy world
to accept my faults in proof of my genius." [684] This kind of disguised
preaching was probably not very acceptable to Poe. In the same letter,
Lowell asks him for "some sort of a spiritual biography . . . *your own
estimate of your life."*

In an earlier letter to Lowell, Poe had complained of an article on
"American Poetry" in the *London Foreign Quarterly* in which he had
been referred to as an imitator of Tennyson. [685] This article Poe felt
had been written or inspired by Dickens—"I have private personal reasons for knowing this." The reasons were that this article contained
items of information which Poe had given to Dickens in letters, and
in his interviews in Philadelphia. Lowell writes Poe later that the
article had been written by one Foster, but Poe, on good grounds, remained unconvinced that Dickens had not had a hand in it.

At the beginning of July, Poe wrote Lowell, in answer to a request
for his "spiritual biography," a letter which throws an important light
on his character. [686] Of this letter Professor George E. Woodberry
aptly remarks :

> A poet's analysis of his original temperament, if it be sincere, is of the highest
> value ; for a man's conception of his own character, particularly if he be of an
> introspective turn, counts often as one of the most powerful influences that shape
> his acts. [687]

In the letter mentioned, Poe says that he can sympathize with Lowell
in his fits of constitutional indolence, which is one of his own besetting
failings. He is, he says, slothful and extremely industrious by fits.
At times, any intellectual activity becomes a kind of torture, and the
only pleasure he has in life was in solitary communion with nature
while rambling amid the mountains and the woods, "the altars" of
Byron. This theory is further made plain in his poem of *In Youth
Have I Known,* often entitled *Stanzas,* which took its flight from the
poem of Byron called *The Island.* It was a powerful influence on his
thought and artistic expression. Poe also tells Lowell that he is only
negatively ambitious, and is only spurred on now and then to excel fools
because he cannot bear to let foolish persons imagine they can excel
him. He says he really understands the vanity of temporal life, and
lives in a continual reverie concerning the future. How far removed
Poe was from the driving doctrine of his age, "Progress," may be seen

---

[684] Lowell to Poe, Elmwood, June 27, 1844.
[685] Poe to Lowell, New York, May 28, 1844.
[686] Poe to Lowell, New York, July 2, 1844.
[687] Woodberry, 1909, vol. II, page 90.

Edgar A. Poe about 1845

From a photograph of a daguerreotype taken by Brady, engraved and reproduced
in Harper's New Monthly Magazine *for December*, 1889
Courtesy of Harper and Brothers

N. P. Willis

Editor of the New York *Evening Mirror* and later of *The Home
Journal*

*From the portrait affixed to a volume of his poems mentioned by Poe in his
sketch of Willis*

Property of the author

*Dr.*Thomas Holley Chivers

of Oakey Grove, Georgia

A close friend of Poe, and an interesting but largely forgotten figure, whose
story deserves to be told

From a photograph

Frances Sargent Osgood

From an old engraving

in the lines of this letter, where he says that he feels that he has no faith in human perfectibility, and that the exertions of man do not appreciably affect his nature, that we are no happier, nor wiser than we were 6000 years ago—

> The result will never vary—and to suppose that it will, is to suppose that the foregone man has lived in vain—that the foregone time is but the rudiment of the future—that the myriads who have perished have not been upon equal footing with ourselves—nor are we with our own posterity. I cannot agree to lose sight of man the individual in man the mass.—I have no belief in spirituality.[686]

In this paragraph, Poe definitely rejects the three darling concepts of his time and place, progress, democracy, and supernaturalism. The rest of this letter is concerned with the poet's theories about spirit, matter, time, and space, and his conception of the nature of the universe and of man. About the same time, Poe was conducting a correspondence with Dr. Chivers dealing with the same themes, and a discussion of the transcendental philosophy of the time. In *Mesmeric Revelation,* a tale published in the *Columbian Magazine* in August, he elaborated upon such matters, and sent a copy of the periodical to both Lowell and Chivers.[688] After an interval of over a year, Poe now once more resumed his correspondence with Thomas:

New York, *Sept.* 8, 1844

MY DEAR THOMAS,—I received yours with sincere pleasure, and nearly as sincere surprise; for while you were wondering that I did not write to *you,* I was making up my mind that you had forgotten *me* altogether.

I have left Philadelphia, and am living, at present about five miles out of New York. For the last seven or eight months I have been playing hermit in earnest, nor have I seen a living soul out side of my family—who are well and desire to be kindly remembered. When I say 'well,' I only mean (as regards Virginia) as well as usual. Her health remains excessively precarious.

Touching *The Beechen Tree* [a poem by Thomas] I remember it well and pleasantly. I have not yet seen a published copy, but will get one forthwith and notice it as it deserves—and it deserves high praise—at the first opportunity I get. At present I am so much out of the world that I may not be able to do anything immediately.

Thank God! Richard (whom you know) is himself again. Tell Dow so; but he won't believe it. I am working at a variety of things (all of which you shall behold in the end)—and with an ardor of which I did not believe myself capable.

Let me hear from you soon, my dear Thomas, and believe me *ever*

Your friend,   POE

---

[688] Poe attended the lectures of Andrew Jackson Davis, given in New York about this time, in which mesmerism, transcendental theories, and psychic phenomena were discussed. Poe's reaction to this kind of "thought" was one of contempt. See his remark on Andrew Jackson Davis in his *Marginalia.* Some of the ideas gathered from Davis and similar "philosophers" were used by Poe in his stories. *Mesmeric Revelation* was republished in England. Also see note 700. *Valdemar* attracted the attention of the Brownings, see note 707.

Poe had indeed retired from the world. He was, during the Summer of 1844, as he desired to be, completely withdrawn from it. The effect upon his imagination, while he had been playing hermit, had been most satisfactory. Unfortunately, the means for continuing this secluded creative existence appear, now, to have been completely exhausted. Winter was approaching, and with it would come the end of the stay on the farm. To Mrs. Clemm, the great question must have been not, "Where will *The Raven* be published?" but "Wherewithal shall we continue to exist?" Like a schoolboy after a long vacation, "Eddie" shrank from, and deferred to the last minute, a renewed contact with the working world. Towards the end of September, 1844, Mrs. Clemm, in desperation, took the matter in her own hands. She went to the city to look up work for Poe, and no doubt at his own suggestion, called upon the editor of the *Weekly Mirror,* Nathaniel Parker Willis. Poe had been in correspondence with Willis some time before, and both were known to each other by reputation. Mr. Willis has left an account of his first, but by no means last, interview with Mrs. Clemm:

> Our first knowledge of Mr. Poe's removal to this city [New York] was by a call which we received from a lady who introduced herself to us as the mother of his wife. She was in search of employment for him, and she excused her errand by mentioning that he was ill, and that her daughter was a confirmed invalid, and that her circumstances were such as compelled her taking it upon herself. The countenance of this lady, made beautiful and saintly with an evidently complete giving up of her life to privation and sorrowful tenderness, her gentle and mournful voice, urging its plea, her long forgotten but habitual and unconsciously refined manners, and her appealing, and yet appreciative mention of the claims and abilities of her son, disclosed at once the presence of one of those angels upon earth that women in adversity can be. . . .[689]

Many sad rehearsals of this pathetic act had made Mrs. Clemm perfect in word and gesture. Mr. Willis, who was a fine Christian man, could not deny the widow in distress, and took the occasion to hire a very great editor at a very small salary.

About the time that Mrs. Clemm paid her visit, Mr. Willis was preparing to enlarge the scope of his business by slightly changing the title of his paper, and bringing it out both daily and weekly as the *Evening Mirror,* the weekly issue to be a kind of review of current events, news, politics, and literary affairs. In this scheme, a man with Poe's abilities, reputation, and experience would be a valuable aid. Edgar Allan Poe was therefore engaged as a "mechanical paragraphist," the nearest approach to the modern columnist, which the journalistic hierarchy then afforded. In addition to doing journalistic repartee, clipping sundry items, writing reviews, arranging for reciprocal puffs, and scribbling short articles, it is probable that Poe was also asked to look over the

---

[689] N. P. Willis in the *Home Journal,* October 13, 1849, just after Poe's death.

contributions sent in by mail, to retouch copy, and help with the layout. It was the kind of a job which he satirized in the little sketch of *X-ing a Paragrab*, a story, by the way, taken from a French source.

Poe was given a desk in the corner, where he came every morning at nine o'clock and worked steadily till the paper went to press. During Poe's connection with the *Evening Mirror*, Willis bears testimony that he saw but one side of Poe's character—"one presentiment of the man —a quiet, patient, industrious, and most gentlemanly person, commanding the utmost respect and good feelings by his unvarying deportment and ability." [689] Poe was not only industrious, but complied with his chief's suggestions when asked to make the tone of his criticisms less acrid, or to modify his irony to a more cheerful strain. On October 7, 1844, the new *Evening Mirror* first appeared, and in it were items which could have come from no pen but Poe's.

The new position provided the means of existence, but it was undoubtedly galling to Poe to occupy a subordinate position after filling so important a chair as the editorship of *Graham's*. Nevertheless he made the best of it. In the second number there was a highly favorable mention of Miss Barrett (afterwards Mrs. Browning) that was followed later by another. Through Horne and Miss Barrett, Poe hoped to draw the attention of Tennyson and others to himself and thus to further his English fame. *The Raven* he was then playing as his lucky card, and before he left Willis, he had persuaded the editor to publish it. In various other ways, legitimately enough, Poe used the columns of the *Mirror* to further his views. The *Stylus* was moribund but by no means buried, and Poe was only looking for another chance to climb into a better saddle. During the Autumn of 1844 he was doubtless introspective enough after the long Summer of dreaming and isolation, and the constant good nature and talkative, sunny temper of Willis was no doubt, at times, a severe trial to Poe.

The family still remained at the Brennans', on account of the comfortable living, its reasonable cost, and Virginia's health. The residence on the farm, however, necessitated a five-mile journey each way for Poe, who did not always have the bus or boat fare, and these walks required more energy than he possessed. In November, 1844, he therefore moved Mrs. Clemm and Virginia back to town, where he could be near the office. Poe's own estimate of his job, and of the importance of the paper he was now engaged with, may be found in a few lines about it sent to the *Columbia Spy* the June before. [690]

—The literary world of Gotham is not particularly busy. Mr. Willis, I see, has issued a very handsome edition of his poems—the only complete edition— with a portrait. Few men have received more abuse, deserving it less than the

[690] See page 478.

author of *Melanie*. I never read a paper from his pen, in the *New Mirror* without regretting his abandonment of Glen Mary, and the tranquillity and leisure he might there have found.   In its retirement he might have accomplished much, both for himself and for posterity, but, chained [to the] oar of a mere weekly paper, professedly addressing the frivolous and the fashionable, what can he now hope for but for a gradual sinking into the slough of the Public disregard? For *his* sake, I do sincerely wish the *New Mirror* would go the way of all flesh.

It was this same oar to which Poe now found himself chained, while no doubt regretting his seclusion at the Bloomingdale Farm.   Mr. Willis, however, was a good friend, kindly, a man of wide reputation, and one who exercised a considerable influence upon Poe's life and fame. He was one of the outstanding figures of the *literati* in the Manhattan of the '40's, one of those secondary literary-journalistic figures which the time produced, who exercised a forgotten but important influence upon the contemporary American scene.   "He will be remembered," says his biographer in 1869, "not as a philosopher or a celestial genius, but as a man eminently human, with almost unique endowments, who contributed his share to the good-will, cheerful enjoyment, and intellectual life of the present."

Nathaniel Parker Willis [691] was a native of Portland, Maine, where he was born in January, 1806.   His father was also a journalist who published an early religious journal, the *Boston Recorder,* founded in 1816.   Young Willis attended the Boston Latin School, and graduated from Yale in 1827.   He early became a poet, and published a youthful volume of a religious cast but combining a few pieces of pleasant fancy.

After college, Willis devoted himself to literature and edited the *Legendary,* a series of volumes of tales published by S. G. Goodrich. He then established the *American Monthly Magazine* in Boston.   His "Editor's Table" in the *American* "in which he treated of current literary topics, of art, books, and personal experience, was eminently sparkling and reasonable," and he gathered about him a rather felicitious but unimportant group.

By this time Willis had become a force in contemporary journalism and criticism.   He became friends with George P. Morris, and merged his magazine with the *New York Mirror,* conducted heretofore by Morris.   The policy of the paper combined that of the cheaper magazines of the day and the policies of "penny paper" journalism, first inaugurated by the *New York Sun.*[654] In short, Willis was one of the early exploiters of modern publicity and advertising methods.   The

---

[691] The material for this brief sketch of Willis has been drawn from various sources, chiefly a biography appended to *The Poems, Sacred, Passionate, and Humorous,* Nathaniel Parker Willis, Clark and Maynard, publishers, 5 Barclay Street, New York, 1869; *The Diary* of Elizabeth Oakes Smith; Poe's notice of Willis in *The Literati;* letters; notices; and other minor mention.

policy was a success, and he was, consequently, able to visit Europe in 1834.

Willis' impressions of the Old World were communicated to the columns of the *Mirror* with considerable grace and gusto. This type of feature and travel reporting was then a novelty, and his letters created a sensation that led to a widespread fame and considerable financial success.[692] He bore letters which gave him *entrée* to English literary circles of some repute, where his natural charm rendered him popular and enabled him to write sketches of such literary personages as Moore, Disraeli, D'Orsay, Bulwer-Lytton, and Lady Blessington. Mr. Willis had a considerable social, and a minor literary success abroad, due to the influence of his friends. In 1835, he married Mary Leighton Stace, the daughter of the Commissary-General at Woolwich Arsenal, and returned to the United States with his bride, where they purchased a farm, known as Glenmary on the Susquehanna. From here he wrote his *Letters from Under a Bridge,* a series of apt landscape sketches and pictures of rural life.

Deaths and financial misfortunes soon followed, forcing him to abandon Glenmary, and to return to New York where, with a Dr. Porter, he established the *Corsair* in the late '30's. Returning to England again, he secured Thackeray as a contributor, and published a volume of prose and poetry under the title of *Loiterings of Travel*. Two plays followed, *Bianca Visconti* and *Tortesa*. The latter was reviewed by Poe in the *Pittsburgh Literary Examiner* for July, 1839, and shortly afterward, in 1841, Poe and Willis began correspondence.[693]

Upon Willis' second return to the United States, he abandoned publication of the *Corsair* with Porter, and again resumed relations with Morris of the *New Mirror*. In October, 1844, this paper became the *Evening Mirror,* and it was at this time that Willis secured the assistance of Poe. In January, 1845, the *Evening Mirror* printed Poe's *Raven,* for which it is chiefly remembered. Willis and Morris afterward sold the *Evening Mirror* and founded the *Home Journal,* one of the outstanding and most successful ventures of the time, which left a lasting mark on American magazines. Willis was known to, and familiar with most of the literary and journalistic figures of his generation. He was especially popular with women, and enjoyed their society, moving in a rather higher realm than most of the *literati*. The best portrait of Willis has been left by Poe in his sketch of the man:

Whatever may be thought of Mr. Willis's talents, there can be no doubt about the fact that, both as an author and as a man, he has made a good deal of noise

---

[692] The fashion, thus created by Willis, was followed later by Bayard Taylor, and by Henry Ward Beecher in some of his *Star Papers*. To modern eyes these offerings appear superficial, pretty, and insipid.

[693] See page 395, also Woodberry, 1909, vol. I, page 287.

in the world—at least for an American. His literary life, in especial, has been one continual *émeute;* but then his literary character is modified or impelled in a very remarkable degree by his personal one. His success (for in point of fame, if in nothing else, he has certainly been successful) is to be attributed, one third to his mental ability and two thirds to his physical temperament—the latter goading him into the accomplishment of what the former merely gave him the means of accomplishing.

At a very early age, Mr. Willis seems to have arrived at an understanding that, in a republic such as ours, the *mere* man of letters must ever be a cipher, and endeavored, accordingly, to unite the *éclat* of the *littérateur* with that of the man of fashion or of society. He 'pushed himself,' went much into the world, made friends with the gentler sex, 'delivered' poetical addresses, wrote 'scriptural' poems, traveled, sought the intimacy of noted women, and got into quarrels with notorious men. All these things served his purpose—if, indeed, I am right in supposing that he had any purpose at all. . . . Mr. Willis's career has naturally made him enemies among the envious host of dunces whom he has outstripped in the race for fame; and these his personal manner (a little tinctured with reserve, *brusquerie,* or even haughtiness) is by no means adapted to conciliate. He has innumerable warm friends, however, and is himself a warm friend. He is impulsive, generous, bold, impetuous, vacillating, irregularly energetic—apt to be lured into error, but incapable of deliberate wrong.

Mr. Willis' career was in many ways close to the ideal of that which Poe would have planned for himself. He had received so many of the rewards for which the of-course-more-talented Mr. Poe longed that there seems to be some indication that the author of *The Raven* followed some of the receipts for fame that he had outlined as being in Mr. Willis' cook book. During the years that followed their acquaintance, Mr. Poe also "sought the intimacy of noted women, and got into quarrels with notorious men." If they were not noted or notorious at the time Poe met them, they soon became so.

Poe had lately been disappointed in one thing: Lowell had not finished the sketch of Poe's life in time to insert it in the September number of *Graham's* as had been arranged with Dr. Griswold. The publication of the "Life" would undoubtedly do much to enhance Poe's fame, and help him to the more important posts which he coveted. Lowell did not finish the sketch till the end of September. On a brief visit to New York, at the end of the month, he left the manuscript in a package.

You will find the package at No. 1 Nassau Street, *upstairs.* It was addressed to the care of *C. F. Briggs.* If his name is not upon the door, you will probably see the name of 'Dougherty' or 'Jones.' [694]

Poe secured the package; he probably sent "Muddie" for it. At any rate he did not then meet Briggs, which evidently was part of Lowell's scheme to bring the two together. A few months later Poe and Briggs

[694] Lowell to Poe, Elmwood, September 27, 1844.

became partners in the poet's last journalistic venture. It was almost a month later that Poe replied:

> MY DEAR FRIEND,—A host of small troubles growing from the *one* trouble of poverty . . . have hitherto prevented me from thanking you for the Biography and all the well intended flatteries it contains. . . .[605]

It was shortly after this that the Poes moved from the farm on the Bloomingdale Road (Eighty-fourth Street and Broadway) to a rooming house at 15 Amity Street. The final revisions of *The Raven* before going to press must have taken place there. The house was of a four-story Georgian type still familiar about Greenwich Village, and the family apartment consisted of two rooms on the second floor. After the comparative freedom of the farm, it must have seemed cramped quarters. Virginia was soon ill in bed again, and during a considerable portion of the time, her husband, doubtless rendered depressed and restless by the constant confusion of a sickroom, led a more or less bachelor existence about town. Since leaving Philadelphia he had been doing little or no drinking; in the Fall of 1844 he was so poor as not to be able to buy himself tobacco.

In the middle '40's, in what is now lower Manhattan, there was a charming man resembling "a delicate miniature of Napoleon III," who kept a store at the corner of Broadway and Prince Street. Here, with a minor success, he dispensed comestibles, tobacco, mild wines, and conversation about a large old-fashioned stove which in the wintertime assumed a comfortable cherry glow. The name of the gentleman with the imperial was Gabriel Harrison. He had been born in 1818, and had studied elocution and oratory. He drew and painted acceptably; acted in minor professional parts; and took an active interest in local and national politics. He also enjoyed, and took an acceptable part in the conversation of authors and newspaper men who gathered about his stove in the corner-shop to feast on canned delicacies, jams, and port wine. In short, Mr. Harrison combined passably well the twin virtues of appearing romantic and being a kindly man.

In the Autumn and early Winter of 1844, when Henry Clay and James K. Polk were running for President, when the annexation of Texas, the Oregon boundary, and the slavery dispute were in the air,

---

[605] Poe to Lowell, October 28, 1844. In this letter Poe also refers to a scheme, which he had suggested to Lowell before leaving Philadelphia, "a scheme for protecting ourselves from the imposition of publishers by a coalition." This plan called for a stock company of a dozen leading American writers to publish a magazine "of high character." Shares to be taken by the authors at $100 each, each to furnish one article a month. Only contributions from members, or other unpaid contributors, to be published. Members to be taken as far as possible from persons connected otherwise with the press. A system of black balling to be used in coöpting. Work to be anonymous.

This was another effort to launch the *Stylus*. Lowell did not reply to what he considered an impracticable plan.

Mr. Harrison was President of the *White Eagle Political Club,* and dispensing political gossip, literary chit-chat, and more substantial cheer in his corner-shop. In the midst of this campaign, he happened, one chilly evening, to look through the square panes of his small store window, and beheld a rather seedy-looking gentleman with a large head, and the air of an actor, looking wistfully through the panes at the display of twist and plug tobacco. The stranger was, apparently, possessed of a countenance that it was difficult to forget. After some hesitation, he entered the store and asked the price of tobacco. Mr. Harrison himself must now be placed on the stand.

I had told him the price, he made no move to buy, and after a few general remarks started to leave. I was struck by a certain indefinite something in his manner, by his voice, and by his fine articulation. . . . So I offered the man a piece of tobacco. He accepted, thanked me and departed. Two or three weeks later he came in again. . . .[696]

Poe was, evidently, on the second visit still out of funds. After some conversation with Mr. Harrison upon politics, into which Poe's experience in Philadelphia had given him some insight, he wrote a campaign song for the "White Eagle Club" that began

> See the White Eagle soaring aloft to the sky,
> Wakening the brood Welkin with his loud battle cry;
> Then here's the White Eagle, full daring is he,
> As he sails on his pinions o'er valley and sea.

I was delighted and wanted to pay him something for his trouble, but the only thing he would accept was a bag of my best coffee. As he was going I said that I should like to know his name.

'Certainly,' he answered, with a faint smile, 'Thaddeus Perley, at your service.'[696]

Mr. Poe evidently liked the coffee and the warmth of the stove, and shortly afterward returned. When he returned Fitz-Greene Halleck entered with Harrison and found Poe standing by the counter.

'Why, good evening, Mr. Perley,' I began. Halleck interrupted me. 'Great heavens, Poe, is this you!' he exclaimed. 'Poe?—this is Mr. Perley,' I broke in.

Poe looked at me and then at Halleck and after an instant's hesitation said, 'The fact of the matter is, Halleck, I have made this gentleman's acquaintance under the name of Perley; no harm was intended and none done. I knew that the facts would develop themselves. I have walked several miles through the sleet and rain, and, seeing a light here, thought that perhaps Mr. Harrison would let me warm up somewhat.'

'Why, of course,' I answered; 'here is the stove behind the tea boxes almost red hot. Take off your coat and dry it. What will you have, some of this old port?' I spread out some crackers, an old English pineapple cheese, and we all

---

[696] Reminiscences of Gabriel Harrison, *New York Times,* March, 1899. Harrison is one of the minor characters who was intimate with Poe in the New York period, from 1844 to 1847.

nibbled and bent our elbows in homage to his majesty, the old port, and talked of pleasant things till my big clock struck the hour of midnight. Poe left with Halleck and stopped at his house that night.[696]

Harrison became firm friends with Poe, and saw much of him about the store, and around town. Doubtless Mrs. Clemm learned from Eddie where the bag of coffee had come from. After Poe's death, the attacks on his memory troubled Harrison considerably. He was much interested in defending and keeping alive the memory of his friend, and undertook to paint a portrait of him based on a daguerreotype "as I remember him I think in 1849 or '50." Mrs. Clemm also kept Harrison's kindness in mind, and correspondence went on between them as late as October 6, 1865.[697] The portrait is now in the rooms of the Long Island Historical Society in Brooklyn.

It was at this time, evidently November, 1844, that Poe went for a short while to Philadelphia, to supervise a third edition of the *Conchologist's First Book*.[698] He now removed his name from the title page and substituted the initials E. A. P. Nevertheless, the publication of the edition was followed, soon after, by a charge of plagiarism in the Philadelphia newspapers. The truth is that much more ado has been made over this charge than the facts warrant. When the whole American publishing world was engaged in one vast filibustering expedition among foreign books, to single out Poe as a "plagiarist" was ludicrous. His reply that *"All* school-books are necessarily made in the same way," must be understood in the contemporary state of the American trade, and be accepted as literal and sufficient. Poe's name or initials on the title page, as an editor, did not necessarily imply that he claimed to have written the context. He was not "posing as a scientist" but trying to turn an "honest" penny or two, as hundreds of other editors of American school texts did at the time. Philadelphia was the center from which poured a flood of such materials. *Murray's Reader* from which Poe had been taught to read was a case in point. It may have been upon this trip that Poe also made arrangements for his *Marginalia* and for the review of Amelia Welby which appeared the following month in the *Philadelphia Democratic Review*.

These *Marginalia* were largely republished items from the *Pinakidia* that had appeared in the *Messenger* while he was its editor, and gleanings from his commonplace book.[699] The idea for these, the spirit, the form, and the nature of the contents was partly suggested by the similar aphorisms, epigrams, and puns in the *Letters* of Coleridge which Poe

---

[697] For the text of a letter to Harrison by Mrs. Clemm, showing his interest in Poe, years later, see Appendix VIII.

[698] See Chapter XIX, page 356, also notes 532, and 792.

[699] See Chapter XVII, page 324, for a fuller discussion of these items. Also see Woodberry, 1909, vol. I, pages 178, 179.

had reviewed in the *Messenger* years before.[700]   Poe gave to his collection his own peculiar twist, and they deserve to be read in the body of his work, as an interesting example of his wide range of curiosity, and a witty, and sometimes profound comment on the America of his day. Poe has been assaulted for these by scholars, because he sometimes invented sources. The admiration of the pedants at their own cleverness in unearthing the "deception," and in hallooing over the fact that Poe read translations, in some cases, instead of the original texts, has thrown a shade over these sparkling little comments and penetrating asides that has dimmed the ironical sunshine of their wit.

In December, 1844, Lowell visited his friend, Charles F. Briggs, at 1 Nassau Street, New York.   Briggs wrote under the *nom de plume* of "Harry Franco," and was then about to undertake the issue of a new weekly to be called the *Broadway Journal*. He was looking for an able editorial assistant or partner, and to him Lowell suggested Poe. Lowell, had, indeed, been a faithful friend. As early as October, 1844, he had attempted to bring Poe and Briggs together, and had also written to H. G. Colton of the *American Whig Review* recommending Poe. Poe, however, had annoyed Colton by his criticism, and he would not employ Poe.[701]   Lowell's praises, however, of the author of *The Raven* may have had something to do with Colton's acceptance of the poem for the *Review,* when it was offered to him through J. A. Shea, or what is even still more likely, Colton's hostility to Poe may account for the fact that *The Raven* was offered to him anonymously, and only accepted through the good offices of a third party.   At any rate, it was Lowell who was responsible for bringing Poe in touch with Briggs, and this finally resulted in the contact with the *Broadway Journal*.

By the close of 1844, Poe was prepared to sever connections with the *Evening Mirror* and to take up his duties on the *Broadway Journal.* Mr. Willis saw him about to leave the *Evening Mirror,* with regret, and with nothing but cordiality, perhaps blent with a little natural chagrin at his leaving.   Most of Poe's contributions in the *Mirror* had been purely perfunctory.   His notices of Elizabeth Barrett Barrett, and his review of Longfellow's *Waif* were, perhaps, the only exceptions. In the main, the purely subordinate position which he was forced to occupy, accounts for this.   He had, however, made good use of the paper to further his own interests, by personal favorable mention of himself and his friends, and before he left he arranged with Willis for

---

[700] A specific instance of the similarity of Coleridge's and Poe's jottings may be found in *Letters, Conversations, and Recollections* of S. T. Coleridge, Harper and Brothers, 1836, letter XIII, pages 82-87.   This is only one given instance. Compare these with Poe's in the *Democratic Review* for December, 1844. See note 490.

[701] Lowell to Poe, December 12, 1844. Colton was the author of a "poem" called *Tecumseh.*

New-York Mirror:

A JOURNAL OF LITERATURE, NEWS AND THE FINE ARTS.

PUBLISHED EVERY SATURDAY MORNING.

THREE DOLLARS A YEAR.]	OFFICE OF PUBLICATION, CORNER OF NASSAU AND ANN STREETS.	[PAYABLE IN ADVANCE.
VOLUME 1.	NEW-YORK, SATURDAY, FEBRUARY 8, 1845.	NUMBER XVIII.

We are permitted to copy (in advance of publication) from the 2d No. of the American Review, the following remarkable poem by EDGAR POE. In our opinion, it is the most effective single example of "fugitive poetry" ever published in this country; and unsurpassed in English poetry for subtle conception, masterly ingenuity of versification, and consistent, sustaining of imaginative lift and "pokerishness." It is one of these "dainties bred in a book" which we *feed* on. It will stick to the memory of everybody who reads it.

The Raven.

Once upon a midnight dreary, while I pondered, weak and
    weary,
Over many a quaint and curious volume of forgotten lore,
While I nodded, nearly napping, suddenly there came a
    tapping,
As of some one gently rapping, rapping at my chamber
    door.
"'Tis some visiter," I muttered, "tapping at my cham-
    ber door—
                Only this, and nothing more."

Ah, distinctly I remember it was in the bleak December,
And each separate dying ember wrought its ghost upon
    the floor.
Eagerly I wished the morrow;—vainly I had tried to bor-
    row
From my books surcease of sorrow—sorrow for the lost
    Lenore—
For the rare and radiant maiden whom the angels name
    Lenore—
                Nameless here for evermore.

And the silken sad uncertain rustling of each purple cur
    tain
Thrilled me—filled me with fantastic terrors never felt
    before;
So that now, to still the beating of my heart, I stood re-
    peating
"'Tis some visiter entreating entrance at my chamber
    door—
Some late visiter entreating entrance at my chamber
    door;—
                This it is, and nothing more."

Presently my soul grew stronger; hesitating then no
    longer,
"Sir," said I, "or Madam, truly your forgiveness I im-
    plore;
But the fact is I was napping, and so gently you came
    rapping,
And so faintly you came tapping, tapping at my chamber
    door,
That I scarce was sure I heard you"—here I opened wide
    the door;—
                Darkness there, and nothing more.

Part of the First Text of *The Raven*
Published under Poe's own name in the *New York Mirror*
From the original. Courtesy of John T. Snyder, Esq., of Pelham, New York

the publication, in advance, and anonymously, from the pages of the *American Whig Review,* of *The Raven.* This, more than any other item of his work, enhanced his contemporary fame. It may be said without exaggeration to have insured his reputation. By his thirty-sixth birthday, January 19, 1845, Edgar Allan Poe was within a few days of becoming a famous man

1 8 4 5

Poe's connection with the *Broadway Journal* began in a rather casual way. Briggs was probably inclined to try him out a bit before making any very definite offers, so, during the early months of the New Year, Poe contributed to the new journal at the rate of $1 a column, while still maintaining his connection with Willis. The first issue of the *Broadway Journal* appeared on January 4, 1845, when Poe's main efforts were bent on getting *The Raven* published.

Poe had resumed an old friendship, dating from West Point days, with J. A. Shea, a former commissary clerk at West Point, upon whom he relied considerably for literary advice and influence in placing his work.[702] There is no doubt that a carefully conceived campaign was worked out by Poe, for the publication of the poem, in order to obtain as wide a distribution as possible, and to create the utmost talk and controversy.

> . . . I wrote it for the express purpose of running just as I did *The Gold Bug* you know. The bird beat the bug all hollow.[703]

The scheme of publication called for as many nearly simultaneous appearances of the poem as possible, introductory notices to insure that its excellencies, and the effects it sought to produce, should not be misunderstood, and anonymous publication in order to pique the curiosity of the public. Even during the beginning of January, 1845, at 15 Amity Street, a few days before it appeared, the process of altering it went on. The last alterations, indeed, were made so late as not to have been included.

By arrangement with N. P. Willis, probably from an advance proof of the poem as it was to appear in the *American Whig Review,* the *Evening Mirror* printed *The Raven* in advance of any other publication on

---

[702] John Augustus Shea was not a "classmate" of Poe at West Point, but had been a clerk in the commissary. According to the son, Judge George Shea of the Marine Court of New York, Poe had been intimate with J. A. Shea while at the Point, and remembered George Shea as a child there in 1830-1. The Sheas seem to have known Poe intimately in New York about 1845. See Harrison, vol. I, pages 218, 220. Also see Woodberry, 1909, vol. II, page 114, with note of Judge Shea's personal reminiscence to Prof. Woodberry about *The Raven.* Also see this work, Chapter XXIII, page 228.
[703] Poe to Thomas, May 4, 1845. The statement must not of course be taken too literally.

January 29, 1845, "by Quarles," with an introductory paragraph that shows the inspiration of Poe and the style of Willis. This was the poem's first appearance in print. It was an enormous and complete success.

Even after the publication by the *Mirror,* Poe was still at work improving his lines. In hopes to change the text before the poem appeared in the *New York Tribune,* evidently sometime about the end of January, Poe dispatched the following undated note to his friend John Augustus Shea containing some further alterations.

DEAR SHEA,—Lest I should have made some mistake in the hurry I transcribe the whole alteration. Instead of the whole stanza commencing 'Wondering at the stillness broken,' etc., substituting this:

> Startled at the stillness broken by reply so aptly spoken,
> 'Doubtless,' said I, 'what it utters is its only stock and store
> Caught from some unhappy master whom unmerciful Disaster
> Followed fast and followed faster till his song one burden bore,
>   'Nevermore—oh Nevermore!'

At the close of the stanza preceding this, instead of 'Quoth the raven Nevermore,' substitute 'Then the bird said "Nevermore!"'

Truly yours, POE [704]

The back of the letter shows the address *J. August Shea, Esq., To be delivered as soon as he comes in.*

This shows that Poe had probably been making alterations on a text in Shea's hands, and he now sent a *résumé* of them to insure that they would be correctly included in the version about to appear in the *New York Tribune* with which Shea was connected.[704] Nevertheless, the poem was again reprinted without these alterations in the *American Whig Review* for February, 1845, with the stanza uncorrected, and in an obviously inferior form, as follows:

> Wondering at the stillness broken by reply so aptly spoken,
> 'Doubtless,' said I, 'what it utters is its only stock and store
> Caught from some unhappy master whom unmerciful Disaster
> Followed fast and followed faster—so, when Hope he would adjure,
> Stern Despair returned, instead of the sweet Hope he dared adjure—
>   That sad answer, "Nevermore!"'

This is an interesting example of the method Poe followed in perfecting his poems and also tends to throw light on the nature of "the *sweet* Hope he dared adjure." Shea, who was by way of being a bit of a *littérateur* and a poetaster himself, was at first credited, by some,

---

[704] There are several newspaper clippings that give this letter. The letter was found among Judge Shea's papers after his death. See Harrison, vol. I, page 220. The revisions sent to Shea were included in the poem as it appeared in the *New York Tribune* of February 4, 1845. Prof. Killis Campbell supplies the Shea *New York Tribune* connection.

with being the author as was Willis, but a second appearance of the poem in the *Evening Mirror* attributing it to Poe, and one in the *Broadway Journal* (I.6.), and the *Southern Literary Messenger* (March, 1845), soon discovered the name of the real author.[705] Even earlier than this the *Howard District Press* of Ellicotts, Maryland, for February 15, 1845, had reported the poem with the following notice.

POETRY

We are permitted to copy (in advance of publication from the 2d No. of the American Review) the following remarkable poem by Edgar Poe. In our opinion, it is the most effective single example of 'fugitive poetry' ever published in this country, and unsurpassed in English poetry for subtle conception, masterly ingenuity of versification, and consistent sustaining of imaginative lift and 'pokerishness.' It is one of these 'dainties bred in a book' which we *feed* on. It will stick to the memory of everybody who reads it.— *Mirror.*[706]

This typical bit of inspired *Americana* heralded *The Raven* all over the country. No American poem had ever achieved so instant, and so wide a success. The raven, indeed, "threatened to displace the eagle as the national bird," the busy editorial scissors of the day reduplicated it in endless publications, for a week or so everybody was demanding who the author was, and mouthing over the stanzas. Not until Mark Twain contributed his jingle of

> Punch, brothers, punch, and punch with care;
> Punch in the presence of the *passengaire* . . .

was there anything that became so rapidly and so universally familiar. With the revelation of the author's name, Poe found himself instantly famous, the object of curiosity, and the strange, romantic, diabolic, and tragic figure that he has ever since remained. It was not long before the stanzas carrying his fame spread to England.[707] Poe's manuscripts became property, and his letters now began to be sought. Autograph hunters were then ubiquitous, and the disastrous snipping instantly began.

Probably the editors, who had almost emptied their pigeon-holes of his accumulated contributions, were sorry that they had not delayed longer. . . . It

---

[705] See the reproduction of the *The Raven* from the *Evening Mirror,* page 503.

[706] From an original copy of the *Howard District Press* loaned to the author by the courtesy of John T. Snyder, Esq., of Pelham, N. Y.

[707] Elizabeth Barrett Barrett (Mrs. Browning) to Poe, from 5 Wimpole Street, London, April, 1846.
". . . Your *Raven* has produced a sensation, a 'fit horror,' here in England. Some of my friends are taken by the fear of it and some by the music. I hear of persons haunted by the 'Nevermore,' and one acquaintance of mine who has the misfortune of possessing a 'bust of Pallas' never can bear to look at it in the twilight. I think you will like to be told that our great poet, Mr. Browning . . . was struck much by the rhythm of that poem. . . ."

happened—and for this Godey and Graham must have blessed their stars, that in their respective magazines of this same month [February, 1845] the former published "The 1002 Tale," the voyage of Sinbad among the wonders made known by modern science, and the latter Lowell's sketch of Poe.[708]

Lowell's "Sketch" was soon republished by Willis from *Graham's,* which answered in a dignified way the new universal curiosity and questions about Poe. An authoritative glamour was thus lent to the strongly focused limelight, and Poe found himself actually occupying the breathless heights that he had dreamed himself upon, certainly since 1824. No time was lost in striking again while the iron glowed.

On February 28, 1845, Poe, now in the first full blossom of fame, delivered a lecture to the New York Historical Society before an audience of almost three hundred people, composed of minor society personages, his journalistic friends, authors, and a number of the *literati.* This occasion may be looked upon as his début among them, under the auspices of Willis. The lecture was much the same as that delivered at Philadelphia. It was couched in Poe's characteristic vein of hostility towards the favoritism of editors, the sins of log-rolling reviewers, and the bathos and ignorance of poetasters. His "monologue" seems to have been largely composed of the gleanings from his reviews. Bryant, Dana, the two Davidsons, Halleck, Longfellow, Mrs. Sigourney, Seba Smith, and others came in for a touching-up relieved by an occasional passage of praise. The praise, as a counterbalance to the rather caustic tone of his remarks, was somewhat exaggerated. Among those who were praised fulsomely was Mrs. Osgood. This lecture was notable for the fact that the bitter attack on Griswold which had so enlivened Poe's remarks in Philadelphia two years before was now notable by absence.

Of the impression Poe made upon this audience there remain two accounts by persons who were present, N. P. Willis and Judge Shea. Willis said in his characteristic style:

He becomes a desk,—his beautiful head showing like a statuary embodiment of Discrimination; his accent drops like a knife through water, and his style is so much purer and clearer than the pulpit commonly gets or requires that the effect of what he says, besides other things, pampers the ear.

Shea's account is more intimate and somewhat less in the lady's book vein:

It was my good fortune to be present when Poe and my father read and recited to each other. I remember distinctly Poe's rendering of *Florence Vane* [a poem by P. P. Cooke] and *Annabel Lee,* and more than once his own *Raven.* His reading of *The Raven* left upon the mind a very different impression from that which it inspires in print. It was a weird, rapturous invocation as to an actual

[708] Woodberry, 1909, vol. II, pages 110-111.

presence. Poe was among the first of the authors that took to reading and lecturing as a professional occupation. I heard him in the society library in New York in March 1845. He told me that he recalled me in my early childhood . . . at West Point. . . . The portraits of Poe represent him with a mustache. I do not recall that he wore one when I saw him. He had a graceful walk, a beautiful olive complexion, was strikingly handsome, but had a weak chin.[702]

Outwardly at least, Poe and Griswold had now resumed diplomatic relations, although the old rancor still burned underneath. Since coming to New York, Poe had met Griswold at the office of the *Tribune*, where the occasion had been somewhat strained. "I could make no advances when we met," writes Poe, "although I longed to do so." [709] This longing was occasioned by the fact that Griswold was getting out through Carey & Hart, in Philadelphia, his *Prose Writers of America*, and revising his poetical anthology for another edition. Poe was anxious to be included in the first, and to revise some of his poems in the second. On January 10, 1845, he resumed correspondence with Griswold with those ends in view. Fearful of what Griswold's comment might be, he says:

> . . . but with your present feelings you can hardly do me justice in any criticism, and I shall be glad if you will simply say after my name: 'Born 1811; published *Tales of the Grotesque and the Arabesque* in 1834; has resided latterly in New York.' [710]

The replies, however, were ostensibly cordial, and a *rapprochement* ensued. Griswold sent Poe a package of books, and Poe sent Griswold his prose manuscripts and verse corrections. Both of these men were too necessary to each other to be able to remain literary enemies. Poe was now too important to be ignored or mentioned slightingly, and he, on his part, realized the necessity of the friendship of the anthologist. Griswold seems to have pretty well won Poe's trust by his advances, and to have made the most of it. The Reverend Doctor, however, had by no means forgiven Poe. At the same time that he was writing to Poe assuring him of his liberal attitude and esteem, he took the opportunity to pour scandal into the ears of Briggs with all the rest of Poe's Philadelphia history. In January, Briggs wrote to Lowell:

> I like Poe exceedingly well; Mr. Griswold has told me shocking bad stories about him which his whole demeanor contradicts.[711]

The causes of Griswold's hatred of Poe, for such it was, probably lay deep within certain idiosyncrasies of the Doctor's nature. He was one who took violent likes or prejudices, even with men, as his friend, C. G. Leland, testifies:

---

[709] Poe to Griswold, New York, January 16, 1845.
[710] Poe to Griswold, New York, January 10, 1845.
[711] Briggs to Lowell, New York, January 6, 1845.

To the end of his life I was always with him a privileged character, and could take, if I chose, the most extraordinary liberties, though he was one of the most irritable and vindictive men I ever met if he fancied he was in any way too familiarly treated.[712]

Griswold also thoroughly disliked Poe, for very ordinary human reasons, and undertook to ruin him in so far as in him lay. For professional reasons he dissembled this, and succeeded in gaining Poe's confidence, who thus delivered himself into the hands of the enemy.[713] That Griswold and Poe were rivals for Mrs. Osgood's favor is by no means a remote possibility. The suggestion has been ably defended, if not conclusively proved.

Despite the kind offices of the good Doctor, Briggs' estimate of Poe was at first favorable, and by the middle of January, 1845, the author of *The Raven* had secured a one-third interest in the *Broadway Journal*. That paper announced him very early in March as having become one of the three editors, *i.e.*, Briggs, Poe, and Bisco. Henry S. Watson filled the post of music critic, in which department he wielded considerable authority and prestige—at that time. Poe, it seems, had rather forced the issue by insisting that his own name would bring additional subscribers. At the time of Poe's joining on, Briggs wrote to Lowell:

Poe is only an assistant to me, and will in no manner interfere with my own way of doing things.

In this estimate, Mr. Charles F. Briggs was profoundly mistaken. From the time of Poe's arrival at the office of the *Broadway Journal*, Mr. Briggs was forced to play a very second fiddle in what was by no means an orchestral harmony.

The Little Longfellow War was now transferred from the columns of the *Mirror* to those of the *Broadway Journal*. For the first time, Poe found himself at liberty to write without any softening influence from above, and charges of plagiarism flew about without let. Even Lowell came in for a passing "charge" which was unfounded; this, under the circumstances of his kindness, can only be regarded as an "honest stab in the back." Plagiarism had become a monomania with Poe.[714]

The publication of *The Raven,* with the consequent success and adu-

---

[712] The quotation is from C. G. Leland's *Memoirs*, 1893. See also Woodberry, 1909, vol. II, appendix VI, *Griswold's World*. From Leland's *Memoirs*.

[713] "One day I found in [Griswold's] desk, which he had committed to me, a great amount of further material collected to Poe's discredit. I burnt it all up at once, and told the Doctor what I had done, and scolded him well into the bargain. He took it all very amiably." (See note 712.) The "material" was evidently letters from various ladies of the *literati*. This was after Poe's death.

[714] The subject has been treated here as a whole for convenience, although out of the order of the narrative. The lessening importance of the Longfellow controversy has led to its being treated in a very limited way in the text.

lation which it brought, together with the unfounded hopes for the new journal, produced in Poe an air of feverish excitement which, about the Spring of 1845, began to become evident in his actions and writings. He was experiencing, too, a social contact with many people, and especially with women, more generally than for years past. During the months spent in New York in 1844, he had been abstemious, as the united testimony of the Brennans, Willis, and Mrs. Barhyte, who saw him constantly about the office of the *Mirror*, shows. He now once more began to drink, and more heavily than ever before. March, 1845, may be regarded as the beginning of the final steep slope that pitched ever more steeply, with only a few interludes, to the end.

Briggs almost immediately became dissatisfied, and, from now on, began a series of irritated and rather weak complaints to Lowell.[715] Lack of sufficient capital to assure his position, and a quarrel with John Bisco, another partner in the enterprise, began rapidly to press Briggs out of his "control." Mr. Poe's pressure was evidently very real, and from the time he took up his duties at the desk, he was evidently regarded by all those connected with the publication as "the boss."

Poe had been going about town in the Winter of 1845 with a number of theatrical people. His double rôle of dramatic critic on the *Journal* and author of *The Raven* gave him considerable theatrical prestige. Among those whom he had persuaded to recite *The Raven* in public was James E. Murdock, a genuinely notable actor of the time with a majestic voice. What Alec, the office boy, thought when Mr. Murdock read Mr. Poe's *Raven* is on record:

It was one cold day in winter, when everybody in the . . . *Journal* office from myself on up was busily at work, that Poe came into the office, accompanied by the great actor named Murdock. They went to Poe's desk, and Mr. Poe summoned the entire force, including myself, about him. There was less than a dozen of us and I was the only boy.[716]

Doubtless Poe had in his mind a similar reading some years before at *Graham's*, when, out of charity, the hat was passed and the poem voted a failure He was now having a magnificent revenge, having *The Raven* read to the employees of his own magazine as the most famous poem in America. There was balm in that. The little crowd of employees, wondering at the sudden halt of the clanking hand presses, gathered, perhaps anxiously, about the desk and the two men standing there, who were both professional tragedians.

When we were all together, Poe drew the manuscript of *The Raven* from his pocket and handed it to Murdock. He had called us to hear the great elocutionist

---

[715] The Briggs-Lowell correspondence during 1845. See Woodberry, 1909, vol. II; Prof. Woodberry was given access to the entire Lowell-Poe-Briggs, etc., correspondence by James Russell Lowell.

[716] Alexander T. Crane (once office boy on the *Broadway Journal*) in the *Sunday World-Herald*, Omaha, Nebraska, July 13, 1902.

read his newly written poem . . . with the combined art of two masters I was entranced. It is the most cherished memory of my life that I heard the immortal poem read by one whose voice was like a chime of silver bells."[716]

It is this trivial incident, obscurely preserved by an ex-office boy, which more than any other has accidentally captured and preserved the symbol of Poe's literary life. There is the background of the magazine office and the presses; the editor's desk; the drama, personified by Mr. Murdock, but introduced as usual by Mr. Poe; the production of the manuscript; its effect upon an ignorant audience; and the one intelligent heart that remembered long, long after the boss of the whole pathetic little show was dead.

One could *almost* laugh at the "great" elocutionist—at the vacancy of printers' faces, signed with ink, grinning, startled, gaping, white under the black—as a great dark bird, that somehow lived in Mr. James E. Murdock's voice, suddenly swooped into the gray office, filling it with diabolical repetition of croakings, and musical mutterings. Then, for a moment, they were all sad lovers; grieving; walking in the forever of a minute, in the black moonlight that had been poured out upon them from the soul of the pale, tired-looking man standing by the proof-sodden desk, his mouth twisted with the pain of an impossible triumph.

Yet, if one is still intelligent enough to admire the Mystery Play of the Imagination more than the Punch and Judy Show of the educated mind, then it is a question if, after all, one *can* laugh even at Mr. James E. Murdock, who was merely a means to an end. Just as poor little White of the *Messenger,* and Billy-buffoon Burton, and Graham—and all the rest had been. But then there is Mr. Poe.

Why does Poe continue to remain? There has been a deal of effort to explain him away on moralistic, psychological, medical, and critical grounds. The shelf grows larger every year, yet publishers continue to find a lucrative sale in his collected works, and the price of his rare first editions mounts astonishingly. All this is indicative of the fact that there continues to be found in Poe a permanency of values. These values lie in the realm of the imagination. Poe was able to create there something new and something unique. It is a world never heard of before, peopled with characters who breathe only in its atmosphere, beings moved by motives and passions wholly sufficient for the sphere to which they have been called, hitherto unheard of and unsuspected, but dying like spiritual fish when they are removed, even for a brief examination, from the water of dreams into the air of reality. This is the great glory and the triumph of their creator. A new Nowhere was added by him to the empire of literature. Once created, such a kingdom lies beyond the strictures and the cavilings of the pedantic, the literal, and the moral. There is no use discussing its right to be. It already exists. Not to visit it because of critical quarantines or moral taboos is to remain unaware of one of the most fascinating and terrifying Nowheres on the map of literature. It is a comparatively small tract, to be sure, this Island of Poe, but it is quite permanently a part of the imaginative world. "This island," say the professors, "does not rest on a sound scholarly basis." "There is a terrible bone-rending ogre who lives there with dead ladies," say the psychologists. "No realism here," exclaim the critics, "no resemblance to anything in the real world!" That, indeed, is a serious charge from sovereign Reality who makes the cripple Imagination, whom he keeps as a jester, hop as directed.

. . . the king loved his *practical* jokes, and took pleasure in forcing Hop-Frog to drink and (as the king called it) 'to be merry.'

'Come here, Hop-Frog,' said he as the jester . . . entered the room; 'swallow this bumper to the health of your absent friends . . . and then let us have the benefit of your invention. We want characters—*characters,* man,—something novel—out of the way. We are wearied with this everlasting sameness.' . . .

'I will equip you as ourang-outangs,' proceeded the dwarf, 'leave all that to me. The resemblance shall be so striking, that the company of masqueraders will take you for real beasts. . . .'[717]

The terrible revenge which the enslaved and debauched Imagination took upon his tormentors may be read in *Hop-Frog.* He escapes with "Fancy" who

. . . had been the accomplice of her friend in his fiery revenge . . . together, they effected their escape to their own country; for neither was seen again.[717]

The crowd is left gaping at the hideous remains.

Lecturing was just then beginning to be especially popular, and Poe intended to take advantage of the opportunity to deliver his lecture of February 27th before another audience, about the end of March. Evidently the employees about the *Journal* were much impressed by their new editor, for the office boy attended and left an account:

The night set for the second lecture was a very bad one. It stormed incessantly, with mingled rain and hail and sleet. In consequence there was scarcely a dozen persons present when Poe came upon the platform and announced that, under the circumstances, the lecture could not be given.[716]

The entrance money was returned at the door, but Poe was bitterly disappointed.

I was one of those present, as Poe had given me a complimentary ticket to the lecture, and badly as I was disappointed, I could see upon his face that my master was much more so. It was a little thing, it is true, but he was a man easily upset by little things.[716]

---

[717] From Poe's *Hop-Frog.* The allegory of this story seems to have been generally overlooked.

Poe came to the office next morning so much under the influence that he arrived leaning on the arm of a friend.[716]

He was, at that time, still living at 15 Amity Street. Virginia was now obviously beyond hope. It was only a matter of time. As we have seen, this thought was peculiarly terrifying to Poe. He must now, of necessity, have begun sincerely to consider the future. Sometime during the Spring, Willis introduced him to the poetess, Mrs. Frances Osgood, whom he had praised in his lecture. The occurrence may be said to have marked the beginning of a series of hectic, "platonic" friendships that succeeded and overlapped each other while Virginia continued alive, and led, later on, to the strange wooings and retreats which followed her death. The renewal of associations with women, with the consequent excitement which ensued, was from now on a large factor in the course of Poe's rapid disintegration. Mrs. Osgood's was the first affair, and she may be said to have kindled a fatal flame that rapidly consumed Poe.

Willis lived in rather sumptuous style at the *Astor House* where he entertained the *literati* and gathered about him, in the parlors there, the group of which he was the central figure and the literary nabob. Mrs. Osgood had been much flattered by Poe's praise, as he meant her to be. She describes their meeting in the Spring of '45 after the publication of *The Raven,* after Poe had sent the poem to her by Willis with a request for her "judgment" and the favor of an interview.

I shall never forget the morning when I was summoned to the drawing-room by Mr. Willis to receive him. With his proud beautiful head erect, his dark eyes flashing with the electric light of feeling and of thought, a peculiar, an inimitable blending of sweetness and hauteur in his expression and manner, he greeted me, calmly, gravely, almost coldly, yet with so marked an earnestness that I could not help being deeply impressed by it. From that moment until his death we were friends, although we met only during the first year of our acquaintance.

Mrs. Osgood lost no time in cultivating a romantic editor. On April 5th, in the *Broadway Journal,* "Israfel" was invoked. He replied with some verses *To F . . .* She, of course, did not know that they were being made to serve a second time, having years before been meant for Eliza White, in the *Messenger.* Mrs. Osgood, however, could have had little to complain of, for she also sent to Griswold a valentine in which the names of Osgood and Griswold were interwoven. Poe saw a good deal of her. The intimacy grew, and eventually aroused the wrath of a suspicious family. Mrs. Clemm, and Virginia who was apparently resigned, or incapable of being jealous, encouraged it, at first.

Frances Sargent Osgood (born Locke) was the wife of an American painter, Samuel S. Osgood, of some minor ability, who painted the portrait of Poe now in the possession of the New York Historical

Society. She had early been much given to the scribbling of sentimental verses that, then and later, achieved wide magazine publication, and in the late '30's while on a visit to England with her husband who was studying there, she had published a volume of poems that had a second American edition in 1842. Her verse was compounded of a bombastic rhetoric, sentimentality, and a certain "grace" for which Poe chiefly praised her.

"She has occasional passages of true imagination," says Poe, "but scarcely the gloomy vigorous, and sustained ideality of Mrs. Maria Brooks—or even in general, the less ethereal ideality of Mrs. Welby"— by which illustrious company Mrs. Osgood may be placed.

In character she is ardent, sensitive, impulsive—the very soul of truth and honor; a worshipper of the beautiful, with a heart so radically artless as to seem abundant in art; unusually admired, respected and beloved. In person she is about the medium height, slender even to fragility, graceful whether in action or repose; complexion usually pale, hair black and glossy; eyes a clear, luminous grey, large, and with singular capacity for expression.[718]

Such was the little woman who now began to exercise upon Poe a charm of sufficiently definite nature to cause a scandal, a copious flood of praise from the "great critic," and compromising correspondence.

Poe was now at the apex of his contemporary fame. *The Raven* was on everybody's lips, and the Longfellow War making a considerable noise. As dramatic critic of the *Broadway Journal* he was now much at the theater. One night at the Park, an actor who knew him saw him sitting in the audience. Into the lines of his part as the scene progressed, he interpolated, "Nevermore, Nevermore." "A thrill ran through the audience and a profound sensation was produced." Nothing shows the effect of the poem on the public more distinctly than this. Poe afterward referred to this event, which may be said to have marked the *ne plus ultra* of his reputation, "not with vanity, but with large, supernal eyes, as if the dirge were an ever present echo." The actor may possibly have been Murdock.

In 1845, in Flatbush there lived a rather remarkable woman, Mrs. Anna Cora Mowatt,[719] who has the distinction of being the first American lady to risk, and retain her social standing by an intimate connection with the stage. She was, in her own field, a portent of the movement for the emancipation of women of which Mrs. Oakes Smith was another example, a movement that in the middle forties was just

---

[718] This brief sketch of Mrs. Osgood is taken from the *Diary* of Elizabeth Oakes Smith and from Poe's notice of her in the *Literati Papers*.

[719] Material for the remarks on Mrs. Mowatt, Edwin Forrest, and the contemporary American stage has been gathered from a wide variety of sources—chiefly Poe; Oberholtzer's *Literary History of Philadelphia; The Romance of the American Stage,* M. C. Crawford, Little, Brown and Co., 1925; Letters of Forrest loaned to the author; contemporary dramatic notices, etc., etc.

beginning to get well under way. The "lady-like" field of literature was naturally the first area in which the bounds of convention began to give way. One could write poetry and publish it, and still retain one's reputation. The advocates of political rights were still considered to be dangerous, and *Godey's Lady's Book* had published in 1844 a solemn warning, from the pure pen of the author of *Ten Nights in a Barroom,* meant to admonish the sex. It was noticeable, however, that no less a person than Park Benjamin had rejoined on the other side! In a certain sense, the hectic salons of the *literati* were merely one of the phenomena of feminine discontent of the period, of the inevitable repercussion of democracy, and the social flux of society in a new republic, where the martial and feudal tradition of womanly inferiority no longer held sway. In this movement New York, Concord, and Boston were at the forefront.

In 1845, Mrs. Mowatt defied all tradition by writing, staging, and successfully presenting a play. It was a social satire on the manners and the sentimentality of the period, called *Fashion,* and it marked a distinctly new trend in the traditions of the American theater.

For the most part nothing but English plays had been produced in America, rhetorical melodramas, at the present, impossible to imagine. These had been somewhat relieved by "spectacles" and mellifluous tableaus which, about this time, began to go out of fashion by legal pressure.

Edwin Forrest had appeared in an American play by Stone, a young Philadelphian. *Metamora, or the Last of the Wampanoags* was the characteristic title. This was an Indian play in which Forrest appeared as King Philip to such effect that, in Boston, some Indians who attended it became so excited that they stood up and chanted a dirge at the death of the chief. *The Broker of Bogota* was another favorite. These plays of Forrest "represented the *alter ego* of the namby-pamby magazines." The star strode and strutted through them, "screeching and howling and tearing passions to tatters" watched by a breathless audience of "faint ladies, spruce clerks, spindling fops, and perfumed dandies . . . well nigh thrown into convulsions over their favorite's collossal poses, gestures, and thunderbolts of speech." Into this dramatic *mélange* Mrs. Mowatt injected a decidedly more civilized note with her comedy of manners and social satire *Fashion.* The patronizing audiences who saw this play in a recent modern revival did not seem to realize that it was meant, even at the time of its conception, as a satire.

The opening night was March 24, 1845. The play was largely and importantly attended. Many of Poe's friends among the *literati* knew Mrs. Mowatt. Epes Sargent had prevailed on Simpson, the manager of the Park Theater, to accept the comedy, and Poe attended for several nights running in order to do it justice in his review, first writing to Mrs. Mowatt to obtain a manuscript of the play. This was sent to him.[720] The review of *Fashion* appeared March 20th, in the *Broadway Journal*.

> The play is not without merit. It may be commended especially for its simplicity of plot. What the Spanish playwrights mean by dramas of intrigue, are the worst acting dramas in the world; the intellect of an audience can never safely be fatigued by complexity. The necessity for verbose explanation, however, on the part of Trueman, at the close of the play, is in this regard a serious defect. A *dénouement* should in all cases be taken up with action—with nothing else. Whatever cannot be explained by such action should be communicated at the opening of the story.
> In the plot, however estimable for simplicity, there is of course not a particle of originality of invention. Had it, indeed, been designed as a burlesque upon the arrant conventionality of stage incidents in general, it might have been received as a palpable hit. There is not an event, a character, a jest, which is not a well-understood thing, a matter of course, a stage-property time out of mind. The general tone is adopted from *The School for Scandal*, to which, indeed, the whole composition bears just such an affinity as the shell of a locust to the locust that tenants it—as the spectrum of a Congreve rocket to the Congreve rocket itself. In the management of her imitation, nevertheless, Mrs. Mowatt has, I think, evinced a sense of theatrical effect or point which may lead her, at no very distant day, to compose an exceedingly taking, although it can never much aid her in composing a very meritorious drama. *Fashion,* in a word, owes what it had of success to its being the work of a lovely woman who had already excited interest, and to the very commonplaceness or spirit of conventionality which rendered it readily comprehensible and appreciable by the public proper. It was much indebted, too, to the carpets, the ottomans, the chandeliers and the conservatories, which gained so decided a popularity for that despicable mass of inanity, the *London Assurance* of Boucicault.

Resemblances of characters in the play to well-known figures about town were traced by the audience, and the lady playwright was under the necessity of explaining that "Mrs. Tiffany," her heroine, the wife of a newly rich business man, was not meant as a caricature of any individual, as some of the critics alarmingly claimed. *Fashion* was a great success, and went on a wide tour "down east" and to Philadelphia.

Matters at the office of the *Journal* were not going any too easily for Poe. Briggs was in financial straits, and was evidently much shocked by Poe's flirtation with Mrs. Osgood, which now began to be talked of among the *literati* confirming Griswold's tittle-tattle of the Saratoga episode, but he was even more shocked by the conversation of the "Raven" himself. Mr. Poe had no faith in reformers. He regarded the Bible as a rigmarole. He was a monomaniac on the subject of plagiarism. Worst of all, he sided with Bisco, the other partner, and

---

[720] Anna Cora Mowatt to Poe: "Thursday evening"—[1845] "Edgar A. Poe, Esq.,—(I regret that I have not a more legible manuscript of the Comedy [*Fashion*] to submit to your perusal, or even one made containing all the corrections made at the suggestion of critical advisers. . . .) Your criticisms will be prized . . ." etc. Griswold collection.

was undoubtedly preparing to continue the *Journal* himself with that gentleman when Mr. Briggs, as it now seemed likely, should withdraw.[715] There is all the evidence here of a very conventional and unimaginative gentleman being greatly shocked by hearing, for the first time, the conversation of a genius who didn't give a damn. Poe's lordly airs about the office were also hard to bear, and the worshipful attitude towards him of office boys and the staff. Above all, Mr. Poe was irreligious which, at that time, was so unusual as to be thought a species of madness.

On the other hand, there is no doubt that the now great poet's growing egotism was harder and harder to stand, and that Mr. Briggs' *Journal* having insulted many of Mr. Briggs' friends, by the pen of Poe, at the cost of Mr. Briggs' slender capital, made a sore issue. Briggs would like to have hauled Poe's name down, but was told that Mr. Poe was even then considering retiring to the country to write, so Briggs might do as he liked.

Besides, Poe *was* doing most of the work. Columns of articles on Street Paving, Secrets of the Magazine Prison House, Anastatic Printing, replies to "Outis," Hirst's *Coming of the Mammoth*, the *Antigone*, and what not, continued to pour from the pen of the man with the big head, besides review after review, from *The Dictionary of Greek and Roman Antiquities* to Mr. Lord's *Poems*. On May 4th, Poe wrote to Thomas:

In the hope that you have not yet *quite* given me up as gone to Texas, or elsewhere, I sit down to write you a few words. . . . The fact is, that being seized of late with a fit of industry, I put so many irons in the fire all at once that I have been quite unable to get them out. For the last three or four months I have been working fourteen or fifteen hours a day,—hard at it all the time. I never knew what it was to be a slave before.

And yet, Thomas, I have made no money. I am as poor now as ever I was in my life—except in hope, which is by no means bankable. I have taken a third pecuniary interest in the *Broadway Journal,* and for everything I have written for it have been, of course, so much out of my pocket. In the end, however, it will pay me well—at least the prospects are good. Say to Dow for me that there never has been a chance for my repaying him, without putting myself to greater inconvenience than he himself would have wished to subject me to, had he known the state of the case.[721] Nor am I able to pay him now. The Devil himself was never so poor. Say to Dow, also that I am sorry he has taken to dunning in his old age—it is a diabolical practice, altogether unworthy 'a gentleman and a scholar'—to say nothing of the Editor of the *Madisonian*. . . .

There is no one in the world I would rather see this moment than yourself; and many are the long talks we have about you and yours. Virginia and Mrs. Clemm beg to be remembered to you in the kindest terms.

---

[721] This refers to the $8, still unpaid, which Poe had borrowed from Dow in Washington, see Chapter XXI, page 449. Dow was in sore straits, having lost his government position, and in debt for the *Madisonian* which he edited.

Besides all this, there were visitors from out of town, parties with the *literati,* and with Harrison, Shea, and bachelor friends Poe took Virginia to call on Mrs. Oakes Smith, and he was also in constant pursuit of Mrs. Osgood. He was having his portrait painted by Osgood, arranging a volume of the projected *Literary America,* and his collected poems for Wiley & Putnam, corresponding with Chivers and Horne, answering letters about *The Raven,* and much, too much about town.[750]

Sometime in May, Poe and his family moved to 195 Broadway where they occupied a back room on the third story in a house that had seen better days in the time of a rich merchant, and was now by way of being a tenement. Poe was now drinking a good deal, and his health was consequently precarious. The new lodgings were a symptom of his almost complete poverty. It was there that Lowell came to see him. Lowell was on his way home from Philadelphia, where, during his honeymoon, he had stopped, and spent a few months writing for the *Pennsylvania Freeman,* while living at 127 Arch Street where the Poes had stayed in 1839. Lowell and his wife left Philadelphia in a carriage with Mr. and Mrs. E. M. Davis, Lucretia Mott's daughter, about the end of May, journeyed through Chester County and came to call on Poe in New York. He had chosen an unfortunate time.

Poe was soggy with drink; "not tipsy—but as if he had been holding his head under a pump to cool it." Poe was evidently rancorous and sarcastic. Mrs. Clemm never left the room, but evidently felt great chagrin, for five years later she wrote an apologetic letter about the interview to Lowell. "The day you saw him in New York *he was not himself."* Lowell described Poe as being small, with a chalky, clammy complexion, fine dark eyes under broad temples, and with a brow that receded sharply back from the eyes. In manner, he was very formal and pompous. Poe, on his part, was disappointed in Lowell and wrote Chivers that he did not fulfill his idea of an intellectual man—"He was not half the noble-looking person that I expected to see." [722]

It was probably about this period that Mr. Saunders, the librarian of the Astor Library, one day met Poe on Broadway. It was sometime after the publication of *The Raven.* Poe, he said, was effusive and maudlin, and declared that he was going to read *The Raven* before Queen Victoria and the royal family. Mr. Saunders says he knew Poe quite well at that time, and that, after he had been drinking, which happened frequently, he would talk of nothing but himself, his work, and the jealousy of other writers. It is now that the first evidence of a persecution delusion is found.

---

[722] Woodberry, 1909, vol. II, pages 137-138; also prints the letter to Lowell from Mrs. Clemm about this visit, dated Lowell, March 9, 1850.

The next time I saw him he was very much depressed, and was suffering from a fit of melancholia to which he was subject. *He spoke of a conspiracy among the other authors of America to belittle his genius and to smother* his work. 'But posterity shall judge,' he said, with a gleam of pride in his eye. 'Future generations will be able to sift the gold from the dross, and then *The Raven* will be beheld, shining above them all, as a diamond of the purest water.'

The progress of enlarged ego and the beginning of delusion of persecution are here plain. Three years later they were at times complete.

About the beginning of July, Dr. Thomas Holley Chivers of Oakey Grove, Georgia, came to New York to arrange for the publication of a volume of poetry called *The Lost Pleiad and Other Poems.* Poe was very anxious to secure the aid of Chivers in supplying capital for the *Stylus,* which was still on his mind. The correspondence between the two had been affectionate, and dealt with transcendental and metaphysical subjects. Chivers had a great admiration for Poe. One day he found Poe in a sadly intoxicated state on Nassau Street, and was helping him home when they met the editor of the *Knickerbocker,* Lewis Gaylord Clark. Poe thought some wrong had been done him by Clark and threatened to attack him despite all that his friend could do. Understanding the situation, Mr. Clark bowed himself out of the scrape. Poe was to have given a reading before the literary societies at New York University apparently that evening, but continued on a spree and could not be found when Chivers called next day. The following morning Mrs. Clemm told Chivers that Poe was ill, probably to explain his absence. After some delay, the Georgia poet gained access to his room and found him in bed reading Macaulay. Chivers continued for some time in New York, and was much with Poe who noticed his book in the *Broadway Journal* in August. The capital for the *Stylus,* however, was, naturally enough under the circumstances, not forthcoming. It was the old story over again.

In June, Briggs had withdrawn from the *Broadway Journal* and left its fate, which was never in doubt, in the hands of Poe. The *Journal* had become notorious for the inveterate character of the Longfellow War, and its criticisms. Of these Longfellow himself remarked:

The harshness of his criticisms [Poe's] I have never attributed to anything but the irritation of a sensitive nature, shaped by some indefinite sense of wrong.[723]

Longfellow was essentially correct and generous in this. The indefinite sense of wrong was fast becoming a persecution complex. Briggs had hoped to get rid of Poe by the end of the first volume of the *Journal* in July. He had a friend upon whom he counted to buy out Bisco, the other partner, but the latter demanded an exorbitant sum, and scared

---

[723] *Southern Literary Messenger,* November, 1849.

off the prospective purchaser. Briggs then withdrew, persuading Bisco to carry on the *Journal* himself, Briggs retaining his claims. At this juncture the paper suspended for a week. Poe then went on a drunken spree and, of course, claimed that Briggs was insulting him and not using him fairly, although he owed him money. The upshot of it was that, in order not to lose everything, the sadly burdened Mr. Briggs allowed Poe and Bisco to continue the sheet from which Briggs now withdrew from any active participation.

The first number of the second volume in July described Poe as the sole editor, and one-third proprietor. Poe now made every effort to buy out the interests of the other partners and, in order to do this, involved himself in debt by floating notes with his friends about town, Horace Greeley being one of the unfortunate endorsers. He also implored William Poe, J. P. Kennedy, Chivers, Fitz-Greene Halleck, and probably N. P. Willis, towards the end of the year, to save him. The bulk of the notes came due the first of the new year; many had already been renewed, and Poe was unable to continue. The *Journal* increased its advertisements, but fell off in subscriptions. Kennedy wrote a kindly and cordial note, but could or would not assist his protégé with funds. It was the last letter that passed between them. From Midsummer on, the *Broadway Journal* was simply approaching its end, its life blood depending upon timely transfusions of borrowed funds. Poe was frantic at seeing his longed-for opportunity slowly slipping from his grasp, and continued to labor, to correspond, and to hope to the last. His drinking had now again undermined what little physical reserve he had. He was ill, poor, in debt, and despondent. Another period of collapse was approaching.

Some further indications of Poe's many activities at this time, and of the course of his difficulties, have recently come to light. About the time he had left the *Mirror,* in April, 1844, Poe had made a special arrangement with B. B. Minor, the editor of the *Southern Literary Messenger,* to publish *The Raven* with an especial type display. At the same time it seems he had undertaken to supply the *Messenger* with monthly installments of a *critique raisonnée* on forthcoming foreign and American books. Bisco, probably through Poe, had, at the same time, made arrangements with Minor to take subscriptions in the South for the *Broadway Journal.* A dispute arose about these over the amount. Bisco had paid Poe his share, apparently without authority, and no returns were made to the *Messenger.* The matter was never accommodated, and Poe ceased to contribute to his old paper until J. R. Thompson, a new editor, took the chair some years later.[724]

In June, 1845, while Poe was still living at 195 Broadway, he was

---

[724] J. H. Whitty notes this in his *Memoir* to the *Complete Poems.*

visited by R. H. Stoddard, who gives us an intimate glimpse of the author of *The Raven* that is rather illuminating. Stoddard was, at that time, a young, unknown poet who had been inspired by an Englishman, one Major Richardson.

It struck my fancy, ineffective as it was, for I was then under the spell of Keats. Yes, I was a poet also, and since my master had written an *Ode on a Grecian Urn*, I must needs write a companion piece. Like all early writing it was crude, but there was promise in it. I worked over it, made a copy of it, and sent it to the editor of the *Broadway Journal*, in which I hoped it might appear. A week or two passed, and as it did not appear, I went to ascertain its fate. It was a hot afternoon in June, and with the direction furnished me by the publisher [Briggs], I sought the residence of Mr. Poe. He received me with the courtesy habitual with him when he was himself, and gave me to understand that my ode would appear in the next number of his journal. The next number appeared, but not my ode. It was mentioned however, in 'Notices to Correspondents,' and dismissed with the curt remark that the editor declined to publish it unless he could be assured of its authenticity. . . .
'To the author of the lines on the "Grecian Flute." We fear that we have mislaid the poem.'
And a month later, this: *'We doubt the originality of the "Grecian Flute," for the reason that it is too good at some points to be so bad at others. Unless the author can reassure us, we decline it. . . .'*
. . . Of course I called within a few days to authenticate my trifle. It was a forenoon, and a very hot one, in July. I plodded down from the east side of the town, southwardly, westwardly, through Lewis Street, Division Street, and Chatham Street, until I reached Clinton Hall, on the southwest corner of Beekman and Nassau Streets. It was then past noon, and of course the potent editor of the *Broadway Journal* had gone out to his luncheon, with Briggs, or English, or some other Bohemian with whom he had not yet fallen out. 'Not in, sir,' ejaculated the fatuous publisher. I walked away, and cooled myself by wandering in and out of the Park, in the intolerable July afternoon. Returning with my blood at fever-heat, I was informed that Poe was in his *sanctum*. He was awakened either by myself or his publisher, and was in a very stormy mood. When summoned back to earth he was slumbering uneasily in a very easy chair. He was irascible, surly, and in his cups.
'Mr. Poe,' I ventured to remark meekly, 'I saw you two or three weeks ago, and I read in your paper that you doubted my ability to write—'
'I know,' he answered, staring up wildly. 'You never wrote the Ode to which I lately referred. You never—'
But the reader may imagine the rest of this unfortunate sentence. I was comminated, and threatened with condign personal chastisement. I left quickly, but was not, as I remember, downcast. On the contrary, I was complimented. The great American Critic had declared that I could not write what I *had* written. . . .[725]

There is something very vivid and immediate about this. It gives us a glimpse into the hot little old New York on a July day, 1845,—shows us a pathetically anxious young poet strolling about the Park, and Clinton Hall, "on the southwest corner of Beekman and Nassau Streets,"—the

---

[725] R. H. Stoddard, *Edgar Allan Poe*. From the text of the original article, courtesy of John T. Snyder, Esq., of Pelham, New York.

fast beating heart of the young man over his first poem in the hands of the "great editor"—asleep in his office chair, after lunch with English and the customary glass of whiskey at the bar—and the unfortunate awakening.   In the glamour and dancing heat of that lost afternoon of nearly a century ago, we see young Stoddard darting down the stairs with the curses of Poe ringing in his ears, and wiping his forehead as he stands amazed on the fiery brick sidewalks under the sign of the *Broadway Journal*.   But, above all, stands out clearly the disastrous effect of a drink, even a drink after lunch, on Mr. E. A. Poe.   The courteous reception of the young poet at 195 Broadway, when Poe was sober, makes the contrast plain.   He must have had a sympathy for young poets, he had himself been one.   Yet the effect of egotism and a casual glass was sufficient to hurl a sensitive, and, as we know from other records, a rather diffident young man, headlong into the street, with curses and threats ringing in his ears.   The incident was never forgiven, and years later, the pen that had written the *Grecian Flute* was employed with damning effect against Edgar Allan Poe.

How natural, and yet how unfortunate, it all was.   One of the last glimpses we have into that office at Nassau and Beekman Streets, where the phantom figures of genius were rapidly ceasing to move to "a lute's well-tunèd law," is another day in that hot Summer of 1845.   This time, let us believe, it is a record of the real self, Israfel, and not his demon.   It was a hot afternoon in August, so hot that Alec, the office boy, "was overcome with heat and fainted dead away."

. . . Poe was writing at his desk.   When I recovered consciousness I was stretched out on the long table at which I had been at work and Poe was bending over me bathing my wrists and temples in cold water.   He ministered to me until I was able to stand up, and then sent me home in a carriage.

This act of kindness, coupled with his uniform gentle greetings when he entered the office of a morning, together with personal inquiries and words of encouragement, made me love and trust my editor.[716]

All of the evidence about Poe is like this, paradoxical, contradictory, and *true*.   The witnesses for and against him must all be listened to with respect.   The whole of their evidence is required to picture the man.   "I am unable," says the just and careful Professor Woodberry, years later (1909), "to fall into that judgment which divides them into the goats and the sheep—the 'malignant' and the 'amiable'; they all, divergent as they are, seem to me to have written, according to their knowledge and their conscience, sincerely."   There can be no doubt that the scholar is correct.   The same man who drove young Stoddard into the street with every outrageous insult he could summon to his lips, a month later bent tenderly over the limp form of the child who had fainted, bathing his wrists and temples.   The motives of both actions are sufficiently plain.

Alcohol, however, was not the only irritant that was contributing to the disorganization of Poe's nervous system. With the progressive failure of Virginia's health, now approaching the inevitable end, Poe had been taking a renewed interest in women. Chief of these was Mrs. Fanny Osgood, upon whom he called frequently and who came to see him. In the Spring and Summer of 1845 there was a good deal of talk about this devotion, as Mrs. Oakes Smith shows when she describes a call that Poe made upon her, in company with Virginia.

The first time I ever saw Mr. Poe, he called upon me with his pretty child-wife, who must have been to him as near as anything earthy could be, 'Lenore,' with her long lustrous eyes, and serious lovely face. I had been inclined to a prejudice against him, from some gossip [evidently about Mrs. Osgood] that had come to my ears, but seeing him disarmed it all. I noted his delicate organization—the white, fine skin of a face that had upon it an expression of questioning like that of a child, a shade of anxiety, a touch of awe, of sadness; a look out of the large, clear eyes of intense solitude.

I felt a painful sympathy for him, just as one would feel for a bright, over-thoughtful child. I said at once, 'Ah, Mr. Poe, this country affords no arena for those who live to dream.'

'Do you dream? I mean sleeping dream?' he asked quickly.

'Oh, yes. I am a perfect Joseph in dreaming, except, that my dreams are of the unknown, the spiritual.'

'I knew it,' he said softly, 'I knew it by your eyes; and I—the great shadowy realm of dreams, whose music hidden from mortal ears, swells through all space, and gleams of more than mortal beauty ravish the eyes, comes to me—that is to dream!' and his eyes were far off in expression as if he saw them upon the instant. Suddenly he asked:

'Do those sweet, shadowy faces wear to you an expression of pain?'

'Not so much of pain as grave thoughtfulness—a tender sympathy.'

'Ah, that is *your* mind—to me they wear a look of suffering—patient suffering—almost an appeal—and I spread out my hands to reach them. I call to them in my dreams. I am more to them than they to me. I call to them to speak, but they are silent, and float away, pointing onward.' [726]

This is certainly one of the most important pieces of reporting on Poe's conversation and psychology that we have. Virginia's remarks are not recorded. It was her custom to sit silently by and say nothing.

In the Midsummer of 1845 the Poes again moved, this time from 195 Broadway to slightly better quarters at 85 Amity Street, not far from their old lodgings there. The necessity for the change was doubtless due to Virginia's health, who found the heat lower downtown to be weakening. This house was not far from Washington Square, and there, in one or two rooms, they remained during the ensuing Fall and Winter, Poe going to work at Nassau Street. Like Spring Garden Street, it was a residence of forlorn hope. Here, Mrs. Osgood came to visit them. This time we get a more definite impression of Virginia.

[726] *Diary* of Elizabeth Oakes Smith, Lewiston Journal Co., Lewiston, Maine, page 116.

Mrs. Anna Cora Mowatt
Authoress of "Fashion"

"Her figure is slight, even fragile. Her face is a remarkably fine one, and of that precise character best adapted to the stage. The forehead is, perhaps, the least prepossessing feature, although it is by no means an unintellectual one. Hair light auburn, in rich profusion, and always arranged with exquisite taste. The eyes are gray, brilliant and expressive, without being full. The nose is well formed, with the Roman curve, and indicative of energy. This quality is also shown in the somewhat excessive prominence of the chin. The mouth is large, with brilliant and even teeth and flexible lips, capable of the most instantaneous and effective variations of expression. A more radiantly beautiful smile it is quite impossible to conceive."

E. A. P.

From a portrait owned by "The Players," New York City

T A L E S

BY

EDGAR A. POE.

NEW YORK:
WILEY AND PUTNAM, 161 BROADWAY.

1845.

Title Page of *Tales*, by Edgar A. Poe
New York, 1845
EDGAR ALLAN POE'S eighth work to be published in volume form. Bound
in single, and double volumes

THE RAVEN

AND

OTHER POEMS.

BY

EDGAR A. POE.

NEW YORK:
WILEY AND PUTNAM, 161 BROADWAY.

1845.

Title Page of *The Raven and Other Poems*
New York, 1845
The ninth of POE's works issued during his lifetime
Courtesy of the New York Public Library

Virginia Poe
Wife of Edgar Allan Poe

*From a photograph (?) of a water color drawing made after Virginia's death
at Fordham in 1847, in the possession of Ingram*

Courtesy of the Bookman, *London, and of W. Van R. Whitall, Esq.*

It was in his own simple yet poetical home that to me the character of Edgar Poe appeared in its most beautiful light. Playful, affectionate, witty, alternately docile and wayward as a petted child, for his young, gentle, and idolized wife, and for all who came, he had, even in the midst of his harassing duties, a kind word, a pleasant smile, a graceful and courteous attention. At his desk beneath the romantic picture of his loved and lost Lenore, he would sit, hour after hour, patient, assiduous, and uncomplaining, tracing, in an exquisitely clear chirography, and with almost superhuman swiftness, the lightning thoughts—as they flashed through his wonderful and ever-wakeful brain. I recollect, one morning, toward the close of his residence in this city [New York], when he seemed unusually gay and light-hearted, Virginia, his sweet wife, had written me a pressing invitation to come to them; and I, who never could resist her affectionate summons, and who enjoyed his society far more in his own home than elsewhere, hastened to Amity Street. I found him just completing his series of papers entitled *The Literati of New York*. 'See,' said he, displaying in laughing triumph several little rolls of narrow paper (he always wrote thus for the press), 'I am going to show you by the difference of length in these, the different degrees of estimation in which I hold all you literary people. In each of these one of you is rolled up and fully discussed. Come, Virginia, help me!' And one by one they unfolded them. At last they came to one that seemed interminable. Virginia laughingly ran to one corner of the room with one end, and her husband to the opposite with the other. 'And whose lengthened sweetness long drawn out is that?' said I. 'Hear, hear!' he cried, 'just as if her little vain heart didn't tell her it's herself.' [727]

Mrs. Osgood greatly excited Poe. Doubtless, she had about her that *expression of the eyes* which mainly attracted him to women. Virginia seems to have been a complacent cipher, even a willing go-between. Later on, at least, Mrs. Clemm became alarmed. Poe followed Mrs. Osgood—"I went to Albany, and afterwards to Boston and Providence to avoid him." [728] Talk flew about, and Mrs. Osgood's family became alarmed. All of this, of course, was vastly disturbing to Poe. An active and dangerous correspondence continued between them, and exchanges of poetry in the columns of the *Journal*.

During the same month (July), Poe appeared at the commencement exercises of the Rutgers Institute, held in the Rutgers Street Church before a large audience. On this occasion he sat on the stage with Dr. J. W. Francis, Professors Lewis, Elias Loomis, and Tellkamp, and served on a committee consisting of himself, W. D. Snodgrass, and Henry T. Tuckerman. They awarded a prize to the best poetical composition from the graduating class of "young, cultured, and refined females." The prize poem which began "Deep in a glade by trees o'erhung," and went on for over a hundred equally chaste lines, was read

---

[727] Griswold, lii, liii, also see further account of Poe by Mrs. Osgood in the *Home Journal*, October 13, 1849, written on her death-bed. This reminiscence evidently applies to the time when Poe was engaged upon the *Literati* articles, perhaps early in 1846.

[728] This "visit" at Albany, and the trip to Boston and Providence seem to have taken place in the Summer of 1845. See page 527. The exact duration of Poe's association with Mrs. Osgood is somewhat obscure.

by the author of *The Raven*. The school had considerable social prestige, and Poe's presence was an indication of his notoriety at the time. This occasion served to patch up a quarrel with Tuckerman. There were seven pages of notice in the *Evening Mirror* for July 19th given over to the event.

During his sway on the *Broadway Journal,* Poe had not neglected the opportunity of using the columns of his own paper further to broadcast his works. Many of his stories and essays which had appeared in obscure places, and apparently failed to elicit any considerable notice or attention, were now, in many cases, revised and republished in the columns of the *Broadway Journal.* The prestige of the poet of *The Raven,* and a certain notoriety which surrounded their author, now served to bring them afresh to the notice of a larger and more important audience. The *Journal* was watched by other publications, especially during the period of the Longfellow War, and the skirmish with the transcendentalists. Many of its offerings were clipped and republished, a custom which Poe was very apt at stimulating Both his poetry and prose were now much discussed by the *literati* and others, and attracted more important attention than they had before. In addition to this, the editor-author maintained his connection with both *Godey's* and *Graham's,* the *Democratic Review* in Philadelphia, and the *Whig Review* in New York. This premeditated and carefully cultivated insurance against oblivion had been further increased in June, 1845, by the republication of some of Poe's tales by a New York publisher. For the first time he did not have to give his work away. He received a royalty of 8 cents on the sale of every volume!

Tales by Edgar A. Poe, New York: Wiley & Putnam, 161 Broadway; 1845, was the eighth bound volume of Poe's work which had appeared since 1827, if the abortive attempt to reissue the *Tales* in paper covers, in Philadelphia, can be counted as a "volume." The book was without a preface and contained 228 pages of prose, twelve tales in all. They were *The Gold-Bug, The Black Cat, Mesmeric Revelation, Lionizing, The Fall of the House of Usher, A Descent into the Maelström, The Colloquy of Monos and Una, The Conversation of Eiros and Charmion, The Murders in the Rue Morgue, The Mystery of Marie Rogêt, The Purloined Letter,* and *The Man of the Crowd.* The volume was Number 2 in Wiley & Putnam's *Library of American Books.*[729]

The volume of tales which Poe had sent to Anthon in the Spring of 1844, to present to Harpers, had contained seventy stories, according to Poe's own reckoning. The volume which now appeared in 1845 contained twelve. The selection for Wiley & Putnam had been made by

---

[729] For the use of first editions of the 1845 *Tales* and *The Raven and Other Poems,* from which the descriptions are taken, and for the reproductions of the title pages, I am indebted to the New York Public Library.

Evert A. Duyckinck, an able editor connected with the firm, who had chosen with an eye for sales, rather than artistic merit. Poe, however, was very dissatisfied, as the selection, he felt, did not give any idea of a point he was constantly harping on, *i.e.,* the versatility of his genius. The stories chosen were largely from the tales of ratiocination. It has been said that Duyckinck showed able judgment by choosing the tales upon which the fame of Poe mainly rests. This literary judgment may be questioned, as it is quite likely that the popularity of these stories *resulted* from the fact of their achieving wide circulation before the others were again made available in volume form. A number of these volumes contain Poe's autograph and inscription, as he is known to have kept copies by him, and to have used them for presentation purposes. During the printing and publication of this volume of collected prose tales, Poe was also preparing a volume of his collected verse which appears to have gone to the same publisher sometime in September. At the same time, he was also engaged upon a book which he refers to under the various titles of *The American Parnassus* and *Literary America*. This he also hoped to have Wiley & Putnam publish. *The American Parnassus* was probably an anthology planned to contain critical data and biographical sketches of contemporaries. For various reasons, like the *Stylus,* it was never to see the light.

Sometime during the Summer of 1845, although the exact time is not now very plain, Poe was much disturbed by the withdrawal of Mrs. Osgood to Albany, where she went to live. Whether this was to avoid Poe or not, is by no means clear. Other circumstances seem to have been the deciding factors. Poe was much exercised, however, at her departure and went to pay her a visit at Albany, the events of which are obscure. Mrs. Osgood later went to Boston, it is said, to avoid him. He saw her there, nevertheless, soon afterward, perhaps about the time of his lecture (*sic*). From Boston they went to Providence, Rhode Island, or met there one evening.

Poe had once seen some poems that had been contributed to the *Democratic Review* by Mrs. Helen Whitman, a poetess who lived in Providence, Rhode Island. Through them, he thought he recognized in her a spiritual sister. She was a widow in fair circumstances and a transcendentalist. In addition, her name was *Helen,* and she was said to be beautiful. The combination of circumstances aroused Poe's interest. There were moods in her poetry which he thought were peculiar to himself. Mrs. Osgood, who was alarmed at Poe's attentions, and yet probably feared to dismiss him in the state of mind in which she found him, was, it appears, anxious to have him meet Mrs. Whitman, and had waited for him after a lecture and poetry recital, when they had wandered about the town till a rather late hour.

It was upon this visit to Providence that Poe first saw Mrs. Whitman. Griswold says in a garden of roses by moonlight, relying on Poe's lines *To Helen,* in which he so places the scene. Writing later to Mrs. Whitman, Poe alludes to the meeting.

You may remember that once when I passed through Providence with Mrs. Osgood I positively refused to accompany her to your house, and even provoked her into a quarrel by obstinacy and the seeming unreasonableness of my refusal.

At a late hour, however, on this summer night, Poe became restless and left the hotel. He strolled past Mrs. Whitman's house at the corner of Benefit and Church Streets. There was moonlight, and Mrs. Whitman happened to be standing in the street door taking the air. She afterward wrote in a letter:

I was not 'wandering in a garden of roses' as Dr. Griswold has seen fit to describe me but standing on the side-walk or in the open doorway of the house on that sultry 'July evening' when the poet saw me and 'dreamed a dream' about me which afterwards crystallized into immortal verse.

The impression upon Poe, nevertheless, seems to have been profound. He never forgot her, and the incident was one of several which led later on to a now famous courtship.

The intimacy with Mrs. Osgood was now at an end so far as personal interviews were concerned. She continued to be his benefactor when occasion served, but from Albany. Mrs. Osgood was dying of tuberculosis.

The Fall of 1845 marked the end of the last period in Poe's life when any long and sustained publishing or creative activity in prose was possible. The work of the years following, with the exception of one or two poems, was decidedly less important in range or quality to what had gone before. In the only considerable piece of creative prose which he attempted, *Eureka,* the signs of hallucination and disorganization are plain. In October, 1845, the period of collapse that always followed a time of feverish activity was about to overtake him again. After the Summer of rest at the Brennans', he had driven himself relentlessly. The attainment of his great dream to own his own magazine seemed almost in his grasp. To keep up the pace, stimulants, this time alcohol, without doubt, had been rather constantly resorted to for a period of at least six months. In the fall of the year, Virginia again began to have hemorrhages. This was always maddening to Poe. In addition, he was undoubtedly in a condition of considerable psychic excitement over Mrs. Osgood, and other women with whom he had now begun to consort intimately. Poverty can, of course, be taken for granted. The result was an attack of what amounted to incipient insanity. He was very close to the edge—sometimes he was clear over it.[730] The result was fatal to all his hopes and effort. In October, 1845, he became sole proprietor and editor of the *Broadway Journal*—and utterly collapsed.

A sad evidence of his inability any longer to cope adequately with the affairs of this world was the fiasco of his appearance on October 16th at the Odeon, in Boston, to deliver a lecture and reading before the Lyceum of that city. Poe was the second on the program to appear in the Lyceum that evening, the first talk being delivered by Caleb Cushing.

A great deal of comment had been caused in Boston by Poe's attacks on Longfellow and transcendentalism; Lowell had secured the invitation to Poe, and a large and expectant audience greeted his appearance. He was to have written an original poem for the occasion, but he was in such a disturbed state that he could not do this, and confessed as much to English shortly before the event. English advised him to give up his appearance under the circumstances, but Poe persisted, to his own discomfiture. This was just after a spree, it seems.

The lecture was initiated by some general and rather admonitory remarks about the heresies of didacticism, after which Poe read the worst poem he could have picked for the occasion, *Al Aaraaf*. It was long and utterly unsuited for oral delivery, and one of his earliest efforts. *The Raven* was greeted with applause. The occasion was a distinct disappointment to Poe and his friends.

Poe had gone to Boston with an assumed attitude of superiority, and the memory of the long controversy with "Outis"—from which he had by no means come off with flying colors—rankling in his mind. Out of sheer bravado, it seems, he had announced that he would write a new poem for the occasion and show the "Frog-Pondians" what a real original poet could do. Then he found that he was in such a nervous condition that he could not write at all. The result was *Al Aaraaf,* and the sight of backs as well as faces, followed by some severe press comments on the affair, and rejoicing in the camp of his enemies.

Some of the New York papers, after the custom of the time, republished the unfavorable notices from Boston, and ignored the more favorable ones which also appeared. The truth is, a great deal more was made of the incident than it deserved. Poe's condition had not enabled him to live up to his reputation, and several persons had been bored. With the appearance of the notices in New York, Poe was goaded into a series of rather pettish replies in the *Broadway Journal*. In order to cover up his condition, he tried to pass the matter off as a hoax. His enemies, whom he had made himself, would not permit the

---

[730] Poe's own statements in a letter to E. A. Duyckinck written from 85 Amity Street, New York, November 13, 1845, are the basis for this assertion.

matter to drop, and his own rejoinders became less and less dignified. The reader can best judge for himself by a specimen of the extremes of both sides. The following are some of Poe's replies, and Thomas Dunn English's accusations made about a year later, after a physical encounter with Poe.

POE IN THE *Broadway Journal,* 1845

The facts of the case seem to be these:—We were invited to 'deliver' (stand and deliver) a poem before the Boston Lyceum. As a matter of course, we accepted the invitation. The audience was 'large and distinguished.' Mr. Cushing preceded us with a very capital discourse. He was much applauded. On arising we were most cordially received. We occupied some fifteen minutes with an apology for not 'delivering' as is usual in such cases, a didactic poem: a didactic poem being in our opinion no poem at all. After some further words —still of apology—for the 'indefiniteness' and 'general imbecility' of what we had to offer—all so unworthy of a Bostonian audience—we commenced and with many interruptions of applause, concluded. Upon the whole the approbation was considerably more [the pity too] than that bestowed upon Mr. Cushing.

When we had made an end, the audience, of course, rose to depart—and about one tenth of them, probably, had really departed, when Mr. Coffin, one of the managing committee, arrested those who remained by the announcement that we had been requested to deliver *The Raven.* We delivered *The Raven* forthwith—(without taking a respite)—were very cordially applauded again—and this was the end of it—with the exception of the sad tale invented to suit her own purpose by that amiable little enemy of ours, Miss Walters. It would scarcely be supposed that we would put ourselves to the trouble of composing for the Bostonians anything in the shape of an *original* poem. We did not. We had a poem (of about five hundred lines) lying by us—one quite as good as new. . . . *That* we gave them—it was the best we had—for the price. . . . The poem is what is occasionally called a 'juvenile poem'—but the fact is, it is anything but juvenile now, for we wrote it, printed it and published it, in book form, before we had fairly completed our tenth year. . . . Over a bottle of champagne that night, we confessed to Messrs. Cushing, Whipple, Hudson, Fields, and a few other natives who swear not altogether by the frog-pond—we confessed, we say, the soft impeachment of the hoax. . . .

THOMAS DUNN ENGLISH IN THE *Evening Mirror,* 1846

. . . He accepted an invitation to deliver a poem before a Boston institution— the Lyceum, I think. When I remonstrated with him on undertaking a task he could not perform, he alleged that he was in want of the money they would pay him, and would continue to 'cook up something.' Want of ability prevented him from performing his intention, and he insulted his audience, and rendered himself a laughing-stock, by reciting a mass of ridiculous stuff, written by some one, and printed under his name when he was about 18 years of age. It had a peculiar effect on his audience, who dispersed under its infliction; and when he was rebuked for his fraud; he asserted that he had intended a hoax. Whether he did or not is little matter, when we reflect that he took the money offered for his performance—thus committing an act unworthy of a gentleman, though in strict keeping with Mr. Poe's previous acts. . . .

Thus the war of the crane and the frogs continued with considerable rippling of the shallows in the frog-pond. Despite the mixture of metaphors, it was a typhoon in a teapot from which all hands emerged with black eyes and bleeding noses.

Poe had become sole owner of the *Broadway Journal* by paying $50 to Mr. Bisco in the shape of a personal note endorsed by Horace Greeley. Fitz-Greene Halleck also signed notes, the only eventual value of which, to the endorsers, was the autograph of Poe. Even this seems to have been of small avail, as Horace Greeley testifies in *Recollections of a Busy Life*. Chivers was also again appealed to, but staved the decision off until the *Journal* succumbed. In Poe's condition there was, indeed, no hope for it. On November 13, 1845, Poe wrote to his publishers a letter which makes sufficiently plain his physical, mental, and financial situation.

> Thursday Morning-13th 1845
> 85 Amity Street.

> My Dear Dr. Duyckinck,—For the first time during two months, I find myself entirely myself—dreadfully sick and depressed, but still myself. I seem to have just awakened from some horrible dream, in which all was confusion and suffering—relieved only by a constant sense of your kindness, and that of one or two other considerate friends. I really believe that I have been mad—but indeed I have had abundant reason to be so. I have made up my mind to a step which will preserve me, for the future, from at least the greater portion of the troubles which have beset me. In the mean time, I have need of the most active exertion to extricate myself from the embarrassments into which I have already fallen—and my object in writing you this note is (once again), to beg your aid. Of course I need not say to you that my most urgent trouble is the want of ready money. I find that what I said to you about the prospects of the B. J. is strictly correct. The most trifling immediate relief would put it on an excellent footing. All that I want is time to look about me; and I think that it is [in] your power to afford me this.

> I have already drawn from Mr. Wiley, first $30—then 10 (from yourself)—then 50 (on account of the *Parnassus*)—then 20 (when I went to Boston)—and finally 25—in all 135. Mr. Wiley owes me, for the *Poems* 75, and admitting that 1500 of the *Tales* have been sold, and that I am to receive 8 cts. a copy—the amount which you named, if I remember—admitting this, he will owe me $120, on them: in all 195. Deducting what I have received there is a balance of 60 in my favor. If I understood you, a few days ago, Mr. W. [Wiley] was to settle with me in February. Now, you will already have anticipated my request. It is that you would ask Mr. W. to give me, to-day, in lieu of all farther claims, a certain sum whatever he may think advisable, so dreadfully am I pressed, that I would willingly take even the $60 actually due (in lieu of all farther demand) than wait until February:—but I am sure that you will do the best for me that you can.

> Please send your answer to 85 Amity Street and believe me—with most sincere friendship and ardent gratitude.

> Yours,   Edgar A. Poe

Chivers was again appealed to two days later, and at the end of November, Mr. George Poe of Baltimore. Poe had also resumed correspondence with his cousin Neilson.

The *Journal* needed only $140 to preserve it, it seems, but, despite desperate efforts to meet this amount, which would be due the first of the new year, Poe was unable to raise the sum.[731] Some of his notes must already have gone to protest, and his failings were too well known to enlist any further capital.

An affected gleam of optimism still continued to color the *Journal's* columns, but even to Poe the finale must now have been plain. "The brandy nosed Mr. Briggs," an epithet which Poe had used to insult his former partner, no doubt did nothing to help, although Briggs' share of the venture was still unsettled. The crows began to gather, some with considerable satisfaction. Greeley's note went to protest; Halleck, who had already sent $100, would do nothing more, and there was no further response. During the last of the year Poe used the columns of the *Journal*, even while its death rattle was going on, to annoy his enemies and puff his friends in his old style, meanwhile contributing to two other magazines.[732] The last items in the *Journal,* of any note, from his pen were *The Brook Farm* (review), on December 13th, and a notice of Leigh Hunt, on December 20th. Poe's movements, and the incidents of the demise of the *Broadway Journal* during the last few days of 1845, can be traced.[733]

On December 6th, the offices of the *Journal,* probably on account of inability to pay the rent, were removed from Clinton Hall, at Beekman and Nassau Streets, to 103 Broadway, where Thomas H. Lane, who was a great admirer of Poe, had a lodging that he and Thomas Dunn English shared between them, keeping one servant. Lane evidently paid for the printing of the last two or three issues of the *Journal.*

On December 20th, Poe called, and left material for the next issue lacking two columns. He was ill and despondent, and Virginia was thought to be dying. Poe then announced to Lane and English his intention of forthwith drowning his troubles by going on a spree. Lane tried to dissuade him, but failing to do so, decided to put an end to the agony, and it seems probable at this time that he secured a farewell card from Poe.

Christmas was doubtless spent at 85 Amity Street by Virginia's bed, and in deepest gloom. The day after, an issue of the *Broadway Journal* appeared. There still being some unused copy on hand, English and

---

[731] Poe to Chivers, November 15, 1845.

[732] Stories republished in the *Broadway Journal* about this time were: *Some Words with a Mummy, The Devil in the Belfry, A Tale of the Ragged Mountains, Four Beasts in One, The Oblong Box, Mystification,* and *Loss of Breath.* Poe also published for the second time *The Spectacles,* the manuscript of which he had sent to Horne in England, in 1843. It first appeared in the *Dollar Newspaper* for March 27, 1844 (Prof. Killis Campbell).

[733] The account of the last days of the *Broadway Journal* is taken from the reminiscences of Thomas H. Lane and Thomas Dunn English.

Lane then made up a final number which appeared January 3, 1846, with the following brief farewell.

VALEDICTORY

Unexpected engagements demanding my whole attention, and the objects being fulfilled so far as regards myself personally, for which the *Broadway Journal* was established, I now, as its editor, bid farewell—as cordially to foes as to friends.

EDGAR A. POE

The *Broadway Journal* was seen no more. The only record of protest now appears on sundry notes cherished as autographs. One gleam remained to light the otherwise complete gloom. In the month of October had been published a volume of poems.

The Raven and Other Poems by Edgar A. Poe, New York: Wiley & Putnam, 1845. This book presented the collected poems of the author covering a period of almost two decades and was Poe's ninth volume. The youthful poems were here included with the important, and in many cases, saving revisions, which they had undergone, during that time in many and varied publications. It was the most important volume of poetry that had been issued up until that time in America, and contained in order: *The Raven, The Valley of Unrest, Bridal Ballad, The Sleeper, The Coliseum, Lenore, Catholic Hymn, Israfel, Dreamland, Sonnet—To Zante, The City in the Sea, To One in Paradise, Eulalie—A Song, To F——s S. O——d, To F——, Sonnet—Silence, The Conqueror Worm, The Haunted Palace, Scenes from Politian.*

Poems Written in Youth, containing an old footnote here reprinted, followed next with: *Sonnet—To Science, Al Aaraaf, Tamerlane, A Dream, Romance, Fairy-land, To ——, To the River ——, The Lake — To ——, Song,* and *To Helen.*[729]

Whatever may have been the shipwreck of hope in the world of reality, in this little volume, the weary, wayworn wanderer had successfully reached his own native shore in the realm of the imagination. If he found "the Condor years" intolerable, he had also discovered a memorable escape.

ROMANCE

Romance, who loves to nod and sing,
With drowsy head and folded wing,
Among the green leaves as they shake
Far down within some shadowy lake,
To me a painted paroquet
Hath been—a most familiar bird—
Taught me my alphabet to say—
To lisp my very earliest word
While in the wild wood I did lie,
A child—with a most knowing eye.
Of late, eternal Condor years

So shake the very Heaven on high
With tumult as they thunder by,
I have no time for idle cares
Through gazing on the unquiet sky.
And when an hour with calmer wings
Its down upon my spirit flings—
That little time with lyre and rhyme
To while away—forbidden things!
My heart would feel to be a crime
Unless it trembled with the strings.

CHAPTER TWENTY-THREE

THE LITERATI AND THE FORDHAM PASTORAL

EDGAR POE was living in a time between times. There were a great many ideas in the air—a great many things were happening—but in America, at least, nothing had yet solidified politically, socially, or intellectually. Literature, as a consequence, was equally chaotic. There was a restless drift to the free lands of the West. Individuals found the answer to individual problems by abandoning the environment and atmosphere which had produced them. The East was thus relieved of the pressure of solving what could happily be left to future and more crowded generations.

"The period from 1846 to 1860 was our period of comparative free trade. . . . It was a period of very great and very solid prosperity . . . the manufacturers did not perish, (nor did they) gain sudden and exorbitant profits. They made steady and genuine progress." [734] The bows of Yankee clipper-ships clove the most distant seas, from which the seaboard cities from Boston to New Orleans reaped a noble harvest. They were the homes of a stable merchant class, influenced to a considerable degree by European culture and Oriental importations. Already the Parthenon was beginning to mate with the pagoda. Hospitality was lavish. There was a supporting stream of immigration, and plenty of room for all. Consequently life still moved fairly leisurely, and with a self-assurance, and a certainty of abundance, that it has seldom attained elsewhere.

In New York, which was then verging on the half-million mark in population, the literary and social problems of the day were eagerly and constantly discussed in the various "parlors" of those who were benefiting by a prosperous order of things; but discussed with a perfunctory ardor, and a sentimental perfervidness possible only to people who, as yet, failed to understand the esthetic and social implications of questions which they restlessly agitated without feeling a compelling necessity to solve. Three great movements were already well initiated: abolition, prohibition, and woman suffrage. Thus matters went on in the colorless administration of James K. Polk, and the days of the Wilmot Proviso.

Could we now be suddenly introduced into one of the numerous salons of the time in Manhattan, after the shock of the costumes of the time had passed, we should then notice, as the chief difference thrust upon

---

[734] Sumner, page 54.

our attention, the accent and mannerisms of the vigorous speech of the time.[735]   The spoken language was still largely that of the provincial English of the Eighteenth or even of the Seventeenth Century, inherited from colonial ancestors, and, as yet, undenatured by the debilitating and "refining" toil of three generations of sure but mistaken school "marms." "Calm" and "clam" were still pronounced alike, as they were meant to be.   The Lord and lard were still confounded in sound, after the manner of Pope, and the grand vigorous "r" still rolled in "thunder," undenounced as yet by such expatriates as Henry James, and Rhodes scholars accustomed to the English curate's "Swahd of the Lahd and Gideon" affectations.   "Umbrellers" were invariably carried in New England where the drive against the "r" began.[736]   In the South where babies were nursed, and often suckled by "mammies" and "dahs" not long from the Congo or its tributaries, the Ethiopian accent was already fixed, and a matter of pride.   The hard dry nasal twang pressed westward with the frontier.   It was a difficult country in which to write classical English poetry.   There were few who made capital of the condition as Poe did.

As the days of 1846 began to flap back on the calendar, the nation began to drift with a complacent, imperial, and largely slave owner's optimism into war with Mexico.   In July, 1845, Texas had accepted a Congressional proposal of annexation.   In May, the President had sent a message to Congress "announcing a state of war."   The Mexicans, he said, had invaded *our* territory and shed the blood of fellow citizens *on our own soil!*   A vast new territory was ruthlessly annexed, and the problem of slavery or free soil became more explicit.   Henceforth politics, literature, and journalism began more and more to be given over to slavery *vs.* abolition, federal *vs.* states rights.   In such an atmosphere, the purely artistic products of poetical imaginations were less and less thought about or valued.   Whittier's innumerable stanzas on "bondsman and proud Sothrons," and the atmosphere for *Uncle Tom's Cabin* were soon to be created.[737]   In 1846, such literature was getting under way.

----

[735] It must be remembered that the written speech of the time was the reverse face of the situation, the attempt to be refined and genteel.   Americans were greatly troubled by the criticisms of English travelers and authors of the time, who laughed at the accent and use of words which were inherited from English grandfathers.   North American English early began to go its own way, in vocabulary, spelling, and syntax. See the remarks of Noah Webster in his early dictionaries.   Also *The American Language,* Mencken, and Professors Krapp and Lounsbury's comments in their various articles and books.   The effect of the hardy Scotch and Scotch-Irish immigrants, and of the Irish and German immigrants upon the language spoken in the United States has seldom been given full credit for its virile and enriching contributions.

[736] In rhyming Poe occasionally was inconsistent with the terminal "r."   In John Allan's household it would have been rolled; in Virginia neglected.

[737] The anti-slavery propaganda content of New England's literature was largely the cause of its contemporary popularity in the North, and its present eclipse.

Underneath all of this, there was a blind political and social optimism difficult to understand.[738] To the spread of American political institutions, there was practically no effective resistance in North America. It was a vast field, and the inference was easily arrived at that the wings of the eagle were rapidly to overshadow the world. The statements of statesmen, politicians, and journalists of the time make the outbreak of imperialism in the 1890's seems like the maiden dreams of a child. "At no remote date the American continent will rejoice under the beneficent shadow of our free institutions destined to spread their blessings upon all from pole to pole." [739] It is impossible to exaggerate the ridiculous bombast that rolled in rhetorical periods from rostrums, stumps, and editorial sanctums. "Our destiny is bounded only by the world!"

The enormous impetus given to "progress" [740] by the suddenly acquired power conferred by mechanical inventions, and the application of machinery, led naturally to the expectation that the fields of psychology and art would be as rapidly exploited. The world was credulously prepared for the announcement of any new wonders. To an age which seemed to be, and actually was, swiftly acquiring a mastery over natural forces at an unprecedented speed, it seemed only natural that the realm of the supernatural might soon be annexed, explored, and exploited as a kind of spiritual Texas. In a few years, spiritualism, "psychic phenomena," and new religions were in full swing. Mormonism was already prospering alarmingly. The America of the 1840's and 1850's added new comments and offshoots to the Christianity of the era, the most powerful and, in numbers, the most far-reaching which had agitated men since the Reformation. A transatlantic Protestantism long cut off from its source, under new conditions, was following out its "natural destiny" of splitting up again and again into an infinite variety of mutually antagonistic sects. The same Philadelphia *Dollar Newspaper* which had conferred the $100 prize on Poe's *Gold-Bug* was filled with the pictures and doings of Prophet Joseph Smith and his adherents. The vast unsettled lands of the great American desert revived and excused the institution of polygamy. In a few years, thousands of Americans were to dress themselves in white and calmly await upon

---

[738] Americans in the 1840's had a blind faith in the *form* of their own government as the "best" for all peoples.

[739] By turning to the *Congressional Record* of 1845-49 any number of similar bombastic manifestos may be enjoyed *ad lib.* Many of the speeches if made by contemporary Congressmen would now lead to an interchange of notes, and the withdrawal of ambassadors, especially by South American countries.

[740] "This disconcerted us so greatly that we thought it advisable to vary the attack to Metaphysics. *We sent for a copy of a book called the 'Dial' and read out of it a chapter or two about something which is not very clear, but which the Bostonians call the 'great Movement of Progress.'* The Count merely said that *Great Movements* were awfully common things in his day, as for *Progress*, it was at one time quite a nuisance." Poe in *Some Words with a Mummy.* Italics supplied.

housetops the second coming of Christ. Almost anything might happen, for almost everything had. In 1849, Eldorado was actually found.[741]

Such were some of the movements and cross-currents which agitated the more simple members of the new republican community. Even the more cultured and refined were leavened by the general ferment. The control of the conservatism of the New England and the plantation communities was fast passing away. In the fourth generation, the sense of their being homogeneous communities with distinct European ideals was being absorbed, and weakened by the general continental mass. Puritanism, Quakerism, and Calvinism, all alike were in process of distintegration, and felt keenly the infringement upon them of the ideas and ideals of the new industrial democracy, against which, in self-protection, the "cavaliers" two decades later appeared in arms. Literature, as a reflection of all this, was no exception. It was stirred by strange, and, to us, vague and naïve currents.

About Boston and Concord, the Puritan elements, still holding to some of their old tenets, were embarked upon the adventure of transcendentalism in religion and philosophy, or the social experiments of *Brook Farm* and *Fruitlands*. The whole northeastern seaboard from Maine to Virginia was stirred by the beginnings of spiritualism. New York was a hotbed. All classes, from the hard-headed Horace Greeley to the grandsons of patroons, attended lectures on mesmerism, the possibilities of galvanic resuscitation, and phrenology. Trance poets, phrenological professors, and psychically sensitive ladies were going about lecturing and writing for magazines. The society which had conquered nature by the machine, now felt itself to be on the verge of solving the mysteries of the intellect and of the spiritual world.

In western Pennsylvania the colonies of "Economists" and their like,[742] the last of the eighteenth century social experiments akin to the "Pantisocracy" of the Lake School, were going out of business from natural causes. In eastern Pennsylvania, Quakerism, Dunkerism, and the Mennonites still held firm. The Philadelphia Wistar Parties were continued among the aristocratically elect, and intellectually impotent Brahmins.[743] The brief light which the *Tusculum* group had shed in Baltimore in the '20's had proved a will-o'-the-wisp. That locality was absorbed in commercial enterprise, and the profitable planting of the Eastern Shore; Washington was conducting a war, and preparing for the duel between Calhoun and Webster; Richmond was given over to tobacco, politics, genealogy, and entertaining. The *Southern Literary*

---

[741] See Poe's poem on his own idea of "Eldorado" written at the time of the Gold Rush, Chapter XXVI, page 638.

[742] At "Economy" on the Ohio River below Pittsburgh. These people being celibates, strange doings ensued. This and similar colonies are an interesting paragraph in American history.

[743] See Chapter XIX, page 345.

Messenger already pointed with pride to the days of Poe, and grew querulous over abolition. In South Carolina, Simms and Paul Hamilton Hayne suffered between literary admiration and social contempt, while the Charlestonians planted rice and engaged in their horse racing and gardening. In Georgia, one solitary and pathetic man strove in vain against his environment, inventing new poetic meters, and silk-spinning machines. Chivers was troubled with the visions of transcendentalism, and wrote to Poe about the nature of God and "how do you pronounce 'Melpomene'?" He published volumes of poems composed of stanzas of pure inspiration followed by other stanzas of unutterable bathos. It was a new, a strange, a pregnant, and a baffling world to understand.

It is all very well now to patronize and belittle it through the easily-assumed lenses of hindsight, but it was all very real and we may be sure very confusing to those who were swimming in the contemporary whirlpool, unable to get their heads above the level of its troubled waters to see the grand rapids ahead. Not to have some understanding of it is to continue in an ignorantly patronizing attitude, and to throw an unnecessary cloak of mystery about such a man as Poe.[744] In one sense he was inevitably a part and parcel of it all. His stories of scientific mystery, *Von Kempelen and His Discovery, Mesmeric Revelation, or The Facts in the Case of M. Valdemar,* must be read as the products of their time, an exploitation of its great expectations for physical and psychic science.

Of course I shall not pretend to consider it any matter for wonder, that the extraordinary case of M. Valdemar has excited discussion. . . .

says Poe—under the circumstances of time and place, of course, not! It did so. The world was ready for it. Such facts were taken seriously by many on both sides of the water—

SIR,—As a believer in Mesmerism I respectfully take the liberty of addressing you to know, if a pamphlet lately published in London (by Short & Co., Blooms-bury) under the authority of your name and entitled Mesmerism, in *Articulo-Mortis* is genuine.[745]

That was from a druggist in Stonehaven, Scotland.

Boston, *December* 16, 1845

DEAR SIR,—Your account of M. Valdemar's case has been universally copied in this city, and has created a very great sensation. It requires from me no apology in stating, that I have not the least doubt of the *possibility* of such a phenomenon,

---

[744] Myriad attempts in the literature of the day to be mysterious, horrible, and mystical can be found. They lacked the essential element of imagination.

[745] Arch Ramsay, Stonehaven, Scotland, to Poe, November 30, 1846. Poe replied "explaining," and asking news of his Allan "relatives" in Ayrshire. Ramsay could not locate them.

for I did actually restore to active animation a person who died from excessive drinking of ardent spirits. He was placed in his coffin ready for interment.[746]

And in old England Mrs. Browning was greatly interested. No doubt her own interest extended to her group.

That these stories are so well constructed that their manner is still convincing and interesting is simply to say that Poe exploited, successfully, certain of the thought currents of his time in the realm of imaginative art. That he was greatly impressed, but by no means wholly taken in by the pseudo-science and secondary philosophies of the time was due to his reliance upon reason, his scorn of mob emotion, and his egotistic certainty in his own powers of analysis. It must be remembered that his seeming and, sometimes, actual technical familiarity with many of the sciences and pseudo-sciences was due to the special material which he elaborated with special pleading to develop his themes. It was the power of his imagination which gave to this material a peculiar life. Hundreds of similar attempts to use it now lie forgotten in the unread pages of Middle American magazines and dusty volumes.[744]

In the Winter of 1845, and through the Spring of 1846, Poe was, for the first time since early Richmond days, certainly for the first time during his mature manhood, made welcome to the drawing rooms and to the circles of a contemporary American society that had some claim to consider itself of importance, and actually did at that time make an audible noise in the world.[747]

In Baltimore, his poverty and youth had made such association impossible. The return to Richmond, as we have seen, had found many doors closed to him for family reasons; in Philadelphia, the tradition of exclusiveness had made it impossible. New York was already more cosmopolitan, and with the fame that had accrued to him since the publication of *The Raven,* in certain circles, Mr. Poe found himself not only able to appear, but actually much sought after. If the "parlors," and in some cases the salons, which he now found thrown open to him were not the most exclusive, they were certainly the most active in a literary way, and the most interesting in New York. That Poe was anxious for social recognition, that the old sting of his repulse in Richmond now found some balm in another Gilead, and that his appearance in drawing rooms of both fashion and pretension, was part of the reward of fame, and sweet to one who had had to stomach much that was

---

[746] Collyer to Poe, Boston, date given.

[747] Poe never entered the magic realm of the then 400 in New York. This centered about Coventry Waddell's Gothic Villa!—at Fifth Avenue and Thirty-eighth Street. The contribution of this group to "American civilization" was the invention of policemen's uniforms by James G. Gerard at a fancy dress ball at the Villa where he appeared in "full uniform." The tattered "rattle watch" was forthwith a thing of the past. Mr. Poe was denied the privilege of association with such intellectual giants, a fact which has recently been lamented in the public prints.

bitter, there can be no doubt at all. "This is a world of sweets and sours—" he had written years before. Most of his experience had been with the sours. The effect upon him of the sweets was somewhat peculiar. The records of it are to be found in the history of his flirtations and the papers of the *Literati*.

After the demise of the *Broadway Journal,* Poe was now to be found more frequently than before at the houses of such *literati,* and dispensers of hospitality and conversation, as Miss Anna C. Lynch, Mrs. Fanny Osgood, the Reverend Orville Dewey, Mrs. Seba (Elizabeth Oakes) Smith, Margaret Fuller, Marcus Spring, James Lawson, and Dr. Manly. In Brooklyn, then and later, Poe was seen frequently at the home of Sarah Anna Lewis, a poetess of immense sentimental capacities. About these people, and in their parlors, gathered the literary, journalistic, and the outer fringe of the social life of the city. There, were to be found the many women then actively interested in writing but more so, in their own literary reputations, so aptly called "The starry sisterhood." The journalists and anthologists upon whom they battened and were battened upon were also present, and certain poets, minor authors, and artists. Occasionally, but not frequently, their busy system was disturbed by the transit through its midst of some larger, and less nebulous star. The galaxy of New York had satellites, and was in communication with solar systems to the north, chiefly with Boston, Concord, and Providence.

The queen regnant of the *literati,* whose parlor was the most eagerly thronged, and which approached more nearly to the dignity of a genuine salon than any other, was Miss Anna C. Lynch (afterward, in 1855, the wife of Professor Vincenzo Botta). Miss Lynch entertained frequently in the evening at her house on Waverley Place. She was an occasional contributor to the contemporary magazines, newspapers, and parlor annuals, and was even ambitious enough to have attempted, with some success, *A Handbook of Universal Literature.* Miss Lynch is described as having been very pretty with a flair for repartee, with the tact of a Frenchwoman, and as generally quite charming. She had also a reputation for social exclusiveness which enhanced the value of her invitations. In the Spring of 1846 her hospitality was frequently extended to Edgar Allan Poe. According to Poe, her talent as a poetess, which he sardonically characterized as "unusual," "rested" upon her *Bones in the Desert* and her *Farewell to "Ole Bull."* [748]

Visitors to Miss Lynch's salon were admitted by a trim twelve-year-

---

[748] The sources for the descriptions of the salons and personalities of the *literati* are all taken from contemporary sources,—letters, diaries, magazines, prefaces to "works," and old prints. Some of the most important are, Poe, Stoddard, N. P. Willis, Elizabeth Oakes Smith, *Godey's Lady's Book,* the *Home Journal,* and files of contemporary newspapers. In order to avoid a senseless profusion of notes, the curious reader is referred generally to the grotesque literature of the time available at a public library—especially Poe's own papers on the *literati* in *Godey's Lady's Book.*

old maid, and ushered upstairs to *two* parlors, warmed at either end of a vista of "corded and machicolated draperies by opposite coal fires." Before one of these, neatly framed by a black mantel, it was the custom of Miss Lynch to receive her guests—"In person she is rather above the usual height, somewhat slender with dark hair and eyes." Beside her stood her elderly mother, and her sister, Mrs. Charles Congden, who had the rather fearsome reputation of being a lady humorist. Thither came the ladies of the *literati* in hoopskirts, and ostrich plumes, head-dresses, hair parted in the middle with thick water curls, or with heavy looped and taffy-like coiffures.

Evening ball dresses are very pretty when each skirt is bordered with triple embroidery, such as those of gauze, and colored silk and gold upon a white background, and others in tulle, upon which are placed flowers formed of dots of lace, each being encircled with a light silver thread, producing an effect somewhat resembling that of silver lace, and which is really beautiful when worn over a skirt of pale pink and blue. Those of the tarlatan muslin retain favor; they are generally embroidered in a stripe or wreath, embroidered in silk to imitate gold. The corsage green, and open single skirt, also *à la grecque*.[749]

The gentlemen arrived in stove-pipe hats, black cloaks, and shawls. All except Horace Greeley.

The guests to be met at Miss Lynch's were certainly interesting. There was Miss Bogart, the spinster, who wrote solemn lyrics, the authoress of *He Came Too Late;* Mrs. Fanny Osgood—"she sparkled, exhaled and went to Heaven"; Mr. W. W. Gillespie, a mathematical genius who stuttered; and Dr. J. W. Francis, a florid, and delightfully good-humored, and wise old man with long white flowing locks. It was he who sometimes treated Poe. Thither also came the silent and somewhat Olympian William Cullen Bryant and his chatty wife, Fitz-Greene Halleck, now a little cynical, and G. P. Morris of *Woodman, Spare that Tree.* Mrs. Oakes Smith, somewhat feared for her radical woman's rights proclivities, was frequently present, accompanied by her two young sons in roundabouts—Mr. Poe had just used up *Powhatan* and Mr. Seba Smith, its author, preferred to remain at home.[750] But there were also Dr. Griswold, and Ann Stephens, the dangerous, gossipy Mrs. Ellet, Mrs. Embury, Mrs. Hewitt, and many others.

In the plainly furnished room at one corner stands Miss Lynch with her round cherry face, and Mrs. Ellet, decorous and lady-like, who had ceased her conversation when Poe broke into his lecture. On the sofa in the side of the room I [T. D. English] sit with Miss Fuller, afterward the Countess Ossoli, on my

---

[749] 𝄇 "It is useless for others to *pretend* to give fashions, for *Godey's Lady's Book* is the standard that governs the female dress of this republic."

[750] *Powhatan;* a metrical romance in seven cantos, by Seba Smith (husband of Mrs. Smith), New York: Harper and Brothers, 1846. Poe remarked of this author, "We doubt whether he could distinctly state the difference between an epic and an epigram."—*Literati.*

right side, and Mrs. Elizabeth Oakes Smith on my left. At my feet little Mrs. Osgood, doing the infantile act, is seated on a footstool, her face upturned to Poe, as it had been previously to Miss Fuller and myself. In the centre stands Poe, giving his opinions in a judicial tone and occasionally reciting passages with telling effect. . . .

I had been talking with Catherine Sedgwick, (says Mrs. Oakes Smith) who was admired through a long life for her literary achievements, and Mr. Poe joined us. Mr. Poe, I thought, had not much praised me in a critique upon 'autographs,' but this did not disturb me so much as the injustice which he had done my husband. The conversation became animated, and I soon saw that . . . *The Raven* was really Mr. Poe: that he did not from another mental phase produce *Lenore*, or any other poem, but the idiosyncrasy of the author's mind continued in each like his dream within a dream. Then I laid aside my bit of personal pique and recognized the weird poet for such as he was.

'I am afraid my critique upon you did not please you,' he said, with his large eyes anxiously fixed upon me; I was half inclined to take him seriously to task, and now I wish I had done so, but I only replied:

'I have no right to complain. I suppose you wrote as you thought.'

'I meant great praise,' he replied . . .

Poe was an adroit and elegant flatterer for the time being, his imagination being struck by some fine woman. His language was refined, and abounded in the finer shades of poetry, praising a woman's eyes, he likened them to 'the brown leaf which had fallen by still waters.' Asked to define grace, he gave the name of a woman who had passing touched his fancy. He was always deferential; he paid a compliment to a woman's understanding no less than to her personal charms. He had an exquisite perception of all the graces of manner and shades of expression, was an admiring listener, and an unobtrusive observer. . . . His manners were refined, and the scope of his conversation that of the gentleman and the scholar. His wife, being an invalid, dared not encounter the night air, but he spoke of her tenderly and often.[748]

Richard Henry Stoddard, the youth whom Poe had so offended some months before, also came to Miss Lynch's—"I was introduced into her salon either by Dr. Rufus Wilmot Griswold or by Mr. Bayard Taylor."

I know that the night was a cold one, in November, I fancy, and that, chilled through and through, in spite of a thick cloak, which I wore, I stooped and chafed my hands before her glowing coal fire. Many a day passed before I heard the last story about my blundering *gaucherie* on that woeful night.[751] The Willises were there, the poet who wrote *Scripture Sketches* in his youth and . . . letters from all quarters of the world—his second wife and his daughter, Imogen. But before those I see Miss Lynch, tall, gracious, kindly. . . . Present also, were two of the swarming sisterhood of American singers, one elderly Spinster Miss Bogart . . . etc. On a later occasion, early the following spring I met another singer of tender memories . . . thirty eight summers had touched her lightly, she was in a decline, reminding her friends, after her soul had taken its flight of Young's *Narcissa* . . . Mrs. Osgood was a paragon. For, loved of all men who knew her, she was hated by no woman who ever felt the charm of her presence. Poe was enamored of her, *felt or fancied that he was which with him was the same thing.*[752]

---

[751] Stoddard had warmed his hands before shaking hands with his hostess!
[752] Italics supplied—one of many such remarks by persons who knew Poe.

Here we must leave the romantic young Stoddard sheepishly warming his hands before Miss Lynch's coal fire to visit Mrs. Seba Smith, at home in Greenwich Street.

We were somewhere near the old mansion of Bishop Moore, which at that time was a fine, picturesque dwelling, the grounds walled up and several feet higher than the street. Near Thirty-Third Street was the Asylum for the Blind, and all in this vicinity was pasture land, rocks, and wild flowers, and now and then a cow or a few sheep grazing. I was very homesick for a long time after my arrival in New York and used to take long walks with my children in the outskirts of the city in the hope of dissipating my discontent, for it must be remembered that above the present Thirtieth Street was a wilderness of rocks, bushes, and thistles with here and there a farm house.[753]

I had my well-attended salon like Dr. Dewey and many others. Conversation was certainly more of a fine art in those days than it now is,[754] and art, humor, and enthusiasm won a more respectful and appreciative response. Society was smoldering over the existence of slavery at the South and there was now and then a scintillating gleam of the national passionateness that culminated in the great Civil War. People everywhere, even in social circles, were intensely in earnest. I was talking in my rooms upon Woman Suffrage, and I think did not quite relish much of the light badinage that came to the surface by the wits of the period. . . .

Perhaps no one received any more marked attention than Edgar A. Poe. His slender form, intellectual face and weird expression of eye never failed to arrest the attention of even the least observant. He did not affect the society of men, rather that of highly intellectual women with whom he liked to fall into a sort of eloquent monologue, half dream, half poetry. Men were intolerant of all this, but women fell under his fascination and listened in silence. . . .[748]

Mrs. Smith's gatherings were held fortnightly, on Sunday nights, and it is at her house, probably in the Winter of 1846, that we hear of Virginia's appearing in public for the last time. She was dressed in a home-made gown of some red stuff, trimmed with rather quaint homemade yellow lace, and sat silently, pale but smiling by the fire, while her husband recited *The Raven* to an applauding little company. One never hears of Mrs. Clemm's being at any of these parties, but it is known that she capitalized "Eddie's friendship," and borrowed money from Poe's lady friends, which put him in great embarrassment, and sometimes obligated him for favorable reviews or revisions of their poetry. There was no other way to pay back such favors. On the other hand, Mrs. Clemm, no doubt, found that there was no other way to live. A good many of the "starry sisterhood," it seems, called from time to time at Amity Street, and later on at Fordham. There was now a great deal of curiosity about Poe. His domestic tragedy was interesting, and his association with Mrs. Osgood the theme of much gossip.

---

[753] This description is a little earlier than 1846, but holds substantially true for Poe's time in New York.

[754] In the late 1860's, that is.

I meet Mr. Poe very often at the receptions [says a correspondent of Mrs. Whitman in a letter dated January 7, 1846]. He is the observed of all observers. His stories are thought wonderful and to hear him repeat *The Raven,* which he does very quietly, is an event in one's life. People seem to think there is something uncanny about him, and the strangest stories are told, and, what is more, *believed,* about his mesmeric experiences, at the mention of which he always smiles. His smile is captivating. . . . Everybody wants to know him; but only a few people seem to get well acquainted with him.[748]

The legend of "Israfel," "The Raven," and all the rest was already well under way. The story about Mrs. Osgood and Poe, and how Virginia was ill, and Mrs. Clemm was forced to borrow money, and that Dr. Griswold was in love with Mrs. Osgood, etc., etc., went around and about the town, as such stories do. "But Poe had a rival in her affections in Dr. Griswold, whom she transformed for the moment into an impassioned poet," says Stoddard. The remark is not without significance in view of the Doctor's obituary style after Poe's death. Mrs. Osgood, after a while, gave up seeing the "Raven." The exact time of her decision is somewhat obscure. In the meantime there were doubtless a good many who remembered the lines addressed *To F——,* and cherished a clipping from the *Broadway Journal—*

> Beloved! amid the earnest woes
>   That crowd around my earthly path—
> (Drear path, alas! where grows
> Not even one lonely rose)—   ·
>   My soul at least a solace hath
> In dreams of thee, and therein knows
> An Eden of bland repose.
>
> And thus thy memory is to me
>   Like some enchanted far-off isle
> In some tumultuous sea—
> Some ocean throbbing far and free
>   With storms—but where meanwhile
> Serenest skies continually
> Just o'er that one bright island smile.[755]

Rufus Wilmot Griswold came frequently to Mrs. Oakes Smith's soirées, and at other times. She describes him:

, In person, Mr. Griswold was tall and slender with slight stoop of the shoulders and unbecoming to him; his head was picturesque, and his eyes large, soft, and beautiful. A general sensuousness rather than intellectuality was observable in his makeup. He was capable of a caustic satire in conversation, mingled with a playful wit, which made him always attractive to a circle, for the absence of any marked positivity in his character made his humors not only to be tolerated but admired, and even those who might have suffered from his strictures, were

---

[755] *Broadway Journal,* I, 17. One of Poe's poems frequently republished since July, 1835, with some eight or nine revisions, "going the rounds of the press." There were a number of other items published for Mrs. Osgood by Poe in the *Broadway Journal.*

more likely to laugh than reprehend. . . . Under an appearance of almost indo-
lent ease, he covered untiring, indefatigable industry, and the matter-of-fact
industry conflicting with the intimations of his own genius, gave him that half-
humorous, half-pathetic cast of mind and character, which rendered him attractive to the friends who best knew him. . . . That he was capricious and allowed
his personal predilections and prejudices to sway him is most true, for he had
the whims of a woman coupled with a certain spleen which he took no pains to
conceal yet he was weakly placable. . . . Mr. Griswold was in the habit of going
about with bits of criticism in his pocket and scraps of poetry which he had
picked up, these he would read and comment upon. He had the laugh of a child
and was strangely unable to see the world as an arena for forms, ceremonies
and proprieties.[748]

Despite the accusation of a certain canine strain by another acquaintance, the strong feline characteristics of the Reverend Doctor Griswold
are here plainly manifest. The same lady noticed that, like Poe, Dr.
Griswold had "a lonely soul." It was not one that could forgive criticism, or forget jealousy. Griswold also knew that Poe was preparing
an anthology. This afterward seems to have fallen into his hands,
and it doubtless contained reversals of his own judgments, and criticisms which were perhaps hard to stomach. Griswold could neither
like nor forgive Poe his superior gifts and airs. There is something
cat-like in his playing and flattering while Poe lived and was to be feared,
and something equally feline in the swift pounce upon him as soon as
he died. For a time the claws remained hidden in the soft, swift paws.

Through all this busy self-important life of the *literati,* one catches
intriguing little glimpses of a defunct, but withal, fascinating enough
time. Willis, bearded like a pard, and extremely youthful, is seen entertaining lavishly, far too lavishly, at the *Astor House,* with the fairy-like
little Imogen by his side. Poe and Mrs. Osgood meet there. Horace
Greeley comes tramping in, trousers half tucked into his boots, a dingy
white coat, and affectedly uncouth manners. For some years he had been
a vegetarian, but the hasty pudding and milk that his wife, who "abhorred dress and fashion," set before him at breakfast had caused him
to return to flesh to supply the tremendous energy which he poured out
into the columns of the *Tribune.* His conversation always dealt with
timely *isms* that might further his political hopes. "His stock in trade
was truth, honesty, and human equality." Greeley was kindly enough to
sign notes for Poe, and too hard-headed ever to forget their having gone
to protest. Margaret Fuller, who was the literary critic of the *Tribune*
from 1842 to 1845, lived with the Greeleys, and was one of the best
critics of her day.

Parties are also to be glimpsed at Marcus Spring's, a New York merchant of literary proclivities. There Poe saw Lydia Maria Child, a New
England novelist, one of Spring's protégées. There were other affairs
at the residence of James Lawson, a Scotch merchant with whom Poe

was anxious to be on good terms, for the prosperous Scotchman was fond of the society of authors, and knew many booksellers. Thomas Dunn English, Hart, the sculptor, Mary Gove Nichols, Mrs. Embury, and Mary Hewitt were all much about in the evenings and afternoons from house to house.

It was not such a large town then, and intimacies were bound to be intimate. Mr. Poe, in some quarters, began to find it very intimate indeed. Across the town is to be traced the invisible web of correspondence, which the letters, that Griswold afterward allowed to be destroyed, began to weave about Poe,—letters to Mrs. Osgood, Mrs. Ellet, Margaret Fuller, and a half dozen others—and their replies. These accumulated in the rooms at Amity Street, and they were read by Mrs. Clemm, as it will appear later.

Virginia's health was bad, much worse! Eddie was consequently despondent, much shaken and agitated by society, provided with no regular employment, and yet writing and corresponding frantically. It is a rather vivacious picture of Poe that one gets in the drawing rooms of the *literati,* but once out in the darkness, tramping the streets, his face seems to have fallen back into the old lines as his brain and feet traveled again and again the familiar, ever-present grooves of despair.

The last time that I remember to have seen him [says Stoddard] was in the afternoon of a dreary autumn day. A heavy shower had come up suddenly, and he was standing under an awning. I had an umbrella, and my impulse was to share it with him on his way home; but something—certainly, not unkindness—withheld me. I went on and left him there in the rain, pale, shivering, miserable, the embodiment of his own

Unhappy master,
Whom unmerciful disaster
Followed fast, and followed faster.

The recollection seems to apply about this time, *i.e.,* shortly after the *Broadway Journal* had failed, perhaps in the Fall of 1846.[756]

Poe's social experiences among the writers of New York in 1845-46, his knowledge of the opinions in which they were held by their own contemporaries, through his personal contacts, and in conversations among them, were now turned to professional use in a series of papers that began to appear in *Godey's Lady's Book* in Philadelphia with the Spring of 1846.

Since November, 1845, *Godey's Lady's Book* must have been the main source of his livelihood. He had contributed criticism to every number since the month mentioned, in which Bryant, W. G. Simms, Mrs. Osgood, Mrs. Hewitt, Mrs. Seba Smith, and Mathews had been

[756] R. H. Stoddard *Memoir,* 1874, page 81. A most untrustworthy compilation, except in regard to the author's own personal recollections of Poe.

commented upon. In addition to this, *Graham's* had carried some of the *Marginalia* in March, 1846, and *The Philosophy of Composition* in April. This last contained the so-called analysis of how he wrote *The Raven.*[757] The series in *Godey's*, which had already appeared, was now followed by another series of papers dealing with thirty-eight writers, men and women, then resident in New York, and known to Poe.

These papers, known as *The Literati*, began to come out in *Godey's Lady's Book* in May, 1846, and continued through the November issue. As we have already seen, Poe was preparing a book "on American Letters generally," *Literary America*, that was to have rivaled and superseded Griswold. He is known to have been busily engaged upon it as late as December, 1846, and later.[758] The papers, which now began to appear in *Godey's*, probably represented what would now be called the advance magazine publication of that section of the projected critique dealing with New York authors. Combined with this was some material included and incorporated from former book reviews.

In considering these sketches, it must be remembered that they were not the critical judgments of Poe himself, but for the most part merely his *obiter dicta*, and his record of the current impression of an author's importance at the time. The critical judgments, which creep in, will be found for the most part to have been taken from his previous book reviews, where a more formal evaluation of the writer's work had been attempted. These papers on the *literati*, because of the contemporary stir which they provoked, have been only too often confounded with the more serious part of Poe's criticism, and quoted against him. The truth is, they were hastily done, frankly journalistic sketches meant for contemporary consumption, and to make a noise. They were to fill the author's purse, and the pages of an anthology. This book was to sell by force of the personal interest of the writers included, and their friends, like other anthologies.

The series, from the standpoint of contemporary discussion and excitement, was an immense success. Poe treated the subjects of his sketches with an alarming degree of candor, and a personal knowledge that, in some cases, was felt to amount to a betrayal of conversational confidences. Naturally enough, the interest was at fever heat. There was no telling who might be the next to be elevated or gridironed, or what remarks made to Mr. Poe by somebody about anybody might not appear cunningly incorporated in the next number of *Godey's*, with consequent necessity for explanations or denials. Hence the series was

---

[757] See Chapter XXII, page 490.
[758] For Poe's own description of this projected critique on his contemporaries, see Poe to George W. Eveleth, New York, December 15, 1846, *Poe-Eveleth Letters*, Prof. J. S. Wilson, *Alumni Bulletin*, University of Virginia, January, 1924, page 10. See Poe to Ticknor, December 24, 1846,—from Fordham, text reproduced, page 578.

an immense hit from the standpoint of the circulation manager, while the author was automatically elevated to the throne of judgment—with no appeal. For there was no other critic whose pen marched with so great authority and reputation for savage candor. There was a great flutter in all the hen roosts of the coteries.

For the most part, Poe's judgments, such as they were, have been sustained. Such songsters as Willis, Halleck, Margaret Fuller, and Mrs. Embury were justly evaluated, and their now forgotten reputations discussed as they deserved. The too-current idea that these papers constituted a general and jealously caustic attack on his fellow writers is entirely unjust to Poe. A great deal of praise is generally wisely distributed, as any critic must do when considering living authors from a contemporary standpoint. On the other hand, the clipping of wings amid the Plymouth Rocks and bantams, who essayed the eagle's flight, was salutary. Unfortunately, particularly for Poe, there were several exceptions in which the spleen of his personal grudges was allowed full sway. Briggs, against whom Poe certainly had no just complaint, but whose attitude during the episode of the *Broadway Journal* was anathema to Poe, came in for a tremendous doing-up, as did Lewis Gaylord Clark, the editor of the *Knickerbocker*. This magazine, not being hospitable to Poe, was therefore included by him with the *North American Review* as in a category beyond the pale. Clark was now repaid in full with compound interest.

Mr. Clark once did me the honor to review my poems—I forgive him. . . . As the editor has no precise character, the magazine, as a matter of course can have none. When I say 'no precise character,' I mean that Mr. C., as a literary man, has about him no determinateness, no distinctiveness, no point—;—an apple, in fact, or a pumpkin has more angles. He is as smooth as oil or a sermon from Dr. Hawkes; he is noticeable for nothing in the world except for the markedness by which he is noticeable for nothing.

This was not so pleasant as it might have been, but one can recover from being compared with an apple or a pumpkin. With the article on "Thomas Done Brown," there were no vegetable comparisons. The animal kingdom, in the person of a long-eared equine, was drawn upon, and Mr. English's personal appearance held up to ridicule:

Mr. Brown had, for the motto on his magazine cover, the words of Richelieu—

> . . . Men call me cruel,
> I am not:—I am *just*.

Here the two monosyllables "an ass" should have been appended. . . . I do not personally know him. About his personal appearance there is nothing remarkable—except that he exists in a perpetual state of vacillation between mustachio and goatee. In character a *windbeutel*.[759]

---

[759] "Thomas Done Brown"; Poe's article on English in *The Literati*. English was a doctor, lawyer, editor, poet, controversialist, and finally—a Congressman.

In addition to this, English was held up to the world as an ignoramus who could neither spell, nor write grammatically. Poe as a matter of fact, as we have seen, knew him well, too well in fact to feel comfortable. English knew a great deal about Poe's life in Philadelphia. Lane, who lived with English, and had assisted in getting out the last number of the *Broadway Journal,* says that when the poet was inebriated, English drove Poe frantic, probably by making fun at him. In Philadelphia, English had quarreled with a number of people and, on several occasions, been worsted in encounters, notably by Henry Beck Hirst (*sic*). It seems, he had taken some of the castigations rather tamely. Hence Poe dubbed him "Thomas Done Brown," and wrote him up in a manner vindictive, remembering his own humiliations when he was helpless. No man, who was not dead-alive, could have refrained from replying.

The truth is, English was a bit of a cad. In descending to meet him on his own ground, Poe had done himself a great wrong, and forgot that Thomas was not done so brown but that he might give Mr. Poe's goose a hot turn on the spit. He soon did so—and with telling effect—of which more hereafter.

The upshot of *The Literati* was that, in one way or another, Poe was one of the most talked of men among literary circles in the United States. Unfortunately, all this kind of thing had nothing to do with what real fame rests upon, *i.e.,* contributions to imaginative literature. *The Raven* had made Poe famous; *The Literati* had rendered him notorious. Mr. Godey felt called upon to issue a card in which he refused to bow to blandishments or threats. But the editor of the *Lady's Book* did not, we may be sure, care very much for the rôle of the fearless editor which had, thus gratuitously, been thrust upon him. In the meantime Poe existed, and did little more than that, on the proceeds of his articles.

Behind all of this apparently facile social and literary activity went on the private and momentous physical and imaginative life of the man. There was a growing melancholy, and a good cause for it. The curious cast of his temperament, which thrust upon him a growing and ever more overshadowing conviction of impending disaster, was now forced to behold its darkest forebodings being rapidly fulfilled in the ever-hastening dissolution of Virginia. Her health during the last months of 1845, and the early part of 1846, gave somber symptoms of the rapid approach of her death. Moving feebly through the rooms, or sitting weakly coughing in a chair by the man who so glibly characterized-the *literati* in *Lady's Book* paragraphs, was the dying girl-wife, suffering, gasping, sweating, and bleeding.

The little rooms at 85 Amity Street, where Mrs. Clemm and Virginia lived, and the curious *literati* came to call, and then went away to gossip, were rapidly becoming intolerable. To Poe, there was something almost morbidly sequestered about his home. To admit strangers into the precincts was to reveal to them, and to prying feline eyes, the rapt secrets of his inmost life. Poe could not bear it. Mrs. Clemm loved nothing better than her own house—and Virginia needed the bracing help of country breezes, and the soothing quiet of country air. Remembering the blessed solitude of the Summer at Bloomingdale, where he had written *The Raven,* Poe once more made arrangements with the Brennans to take Mrs. Clemm and Virginia to the farm for a few weeks.

Sometime in April, 1846, Poe made a trip to Baltimore, the events of which are obscure. There was probably another lecture there, after which, upon his return, the family went to the country. There they remained until sometime later in the Spring, before removing to the vicinity of Turtle Bay. It was a good five-mile walk to the Brennans', or a long ride. Bus or steamboat fare was not always forthcoming, and it sometimes happened that Poe was unable to return at night to his fast sinking little wife. This seems to have been the great drawback to the sojourn on the farm, and at Fordham later on. Of Poe's consequently somewhat lonely life about New York during the Spring of 1846, only a few glimpses can be recaptured.

There seem to have been a good many calls upon Mrs. Osgood. Mrs. Marie Louise Shew was also resorted to, then, or later on, for hospitality and sympathy. Mrs. Shew, who had great sympathy for Poe, had been a nurse for many years with hospital experience. She, more than anyone else, seems to have realized his true physical condition. She became the Poes' good angel at Fordham, and, in town, made her house a haven of refuge and rest. She was well known to able physicians, Dr. Mott, and John Wakefield Francis, M.D., whom Poe had commemorated in an article, on account of the doctor's contributions to medical magazines. Dr. Francis was later called in to attend Poe, and frequently met him at the different salons in the *literati.* He was genial and liberal in his tendencies, and included, in his life of wide interests, an enthusiasm for literature, and the conversation of authors. Poe was helped by him at times of need, and has left a rather intimate and exceedingly cordial sketch of him in the papers of *The Literati:*

. . . His person and manner was richly peculiar. He is short and stout, probably five feet eight in height, limbs of great muscularity and strength, the whole frame indicating prodigious vitality and energy—the latter is, in fact, the leading trait in his character. His head is large, massive—the features in keeping; complexion dark florid; eyes piercingly bright; mouth exceedingly mobile and expressive; hair gray, and worn in matted locks about the neck and shoulders— eyebrows to correspond, jagged and ponderous. His age is about fifty-eight. His general appearance is such as to arrest attention.

His address is the most genial that can be conceived, its bonhommie irresistible. He stands habitually, with his head thrown back and his chest out; never waits for an introduction to anybody; slaps a perfect stranger on the back and calls him 'Doctor' or 'Learned Theban'; pats every lady on the head, and (if she is pretty and petite) designates her by some such title as 'My Pocket Edition of the Lives of the Saints.' His conversation proper is a sort of Roman punch made up of tragedy, comedy, and the broadest of all possible farce. He has a natural, felicitous flow of talk, always overswelling its boundaries and sweeping everything before it right and left. He is very earnest, intense, emphatic; thumps the table with his fists; shocks the nerves of the ladies. His forte, after all, is humor, the richest conceivable—a compound of Swift, Rabelais, and the clown in the pantomime. . . .

It is quite possible that this genial and wise old doctor, "whose professional duties and purse are always at the command of the needy," was called upon to give advice and help in the hopeless case of Virginia Poe. It is certain he did so in the case of her husband.[760]

Poe, now much talked about, because of the papers on the *literati*, and unfortunately, too, on account of his sick wife and Mrs. Osgood, was also to be found occasionally at *Frank's Place* "on Barclay Street where a convivial company gathered." In the early Winter of 1846, we hear of a dinner at the old *United States Hotel* on Fulton Street attended by Henry Ward Beecher, Dr. Francis Lister Hawkes—whose sermons Poe was now at some pains to proclaim boresome—and others.

February brought the last Valentine Day which Virginia was to know. At Amity Street she received an envelope addressed in a well-known hand.[761]

Poe was now getting farther into the clutches of Mrs. "Estelle" Lewis of Brooklyn, who decorated her studio with a bust of Pallas presided over by a stuffed raven. She was known as "Stella." Her husband was a fairly prosperous lawyer, who indulged his wife in the funds necessary to purchase fame, and to run a salon in Brooklyn.[762]

Sometime in the early Spring of 1846—the second stay at Bloomingdale was a short one—Poe again moved his wife and Mrs. Clemm to another secluded boarding place, then situated in a country district at the foot of Forty-seventh Street on the East River, in a section known as Turtle Bay.[763]

This change again brought Virginia and Mrs. Clemm nearer to town, and, at the same time, enabled Poe to walk conveniently to the city for what calls he had to pay, or the slack business he had to transact. Poverty, a dire pennilessness, was now once more oppressively bearing down

---

[760] Poe, in his reply to English, speaks of Dr. Francis as having intimate knowledge of the reasons for his (Poe's) drinking, and by inference, of Virginia's illness.

[761] *Century Magazine*—October, 1909.

[762] "Estelle's" real name was Sarah Anna. She scorned this baptismal handicap in the literary race for fame, and even persuaded her husband to pay Griswold to make the alteration in a complimentary article. An acrostic written by Poe to "Sarah Anna" did not produce the desired effect upon "Stella."

[763] The Brennans at Bloomingdale seem to have had something to do with recommending the Poes to former friends, at both Turtle Bay and Fordham. Mrs. Brennan and her daughter Martha drove Mrs. Clemm about the country a good deal.

upon him. The papers in *Godey's* could have done little more than pay the board. What the Poes contrived to live upon, how Mrs. Clemm provided medicines and the necessary dainties for Virginia, is a mystery of which only she knew the ramifications.

With Turtle Bay began that period of sickness, calamity, delirium, and desire for sequestration from the world which lasted from the Summer of 1846 through the Fordham episode, up into the Winter of 1848. It would seem as if Poe had withdrawn as much as possible from gratuitous human contact in order to spend the last days with Virginia, to see her through the inevitable last agony, to nurse his own jangled nerves, and to ponder upon the primordial nature of the universe! Such was the strange *mélange* of the experiences and events about to follow. Yet he was by no means able to suffer, recuperate, and ponder undisturbed. The period of hermitage at Turtle Bay and Fordham was intruded upon by some of the most lamentable and belittling episodes of the poet's life.

He was, indeed, helplessly in the clutch of psychic and worldly circumstances, half crazed at the thought of losing Virginia. Nevertheless, the inevitable immediate presence of the shadow on his threshold warned him of the release to come, and of the implications which must follow. In a short while, she, who had been at once his despair and consolation, would be no more. The writing in all its glowing and shadowed characters was even now being traced on the wall. He was greatly attracted by Mrs. Osgood, of that there can be no doubt; yet Mrs. Osgood was married. With the passing of Virginia, he would be released only to confront a new problem, one to which, no matter who the person was that embodied it, there seemed to be no solution. Then, too, he craved comfort, rest, and sympathy, the peculiar spiritual comradeship and understanding which he found only in women.

It is not hard to understand why this man, under all of these strange pressures and long-continued stresses,—the slowly stretching wires of inmost being that were tightened and tightened as the years went on, that every turn of the screw made more vibrant and brought a little nearer the breaking point,—it is not hard to understand why he sometimes felt himself to be going mad. Indeed, it is more difficult to understand why he did not go entirely insane. That, from time to time, he attempted to relieve the stress on the now nearly snapping cords and harp strings, by reverting to drugs and alcohol, seems now, if it ever could be, to have been excusable. Never was there a more delicate or more tormented being that had cried out so long and so unsuccessfully for surcease, that had longed for companionship and found none.

The Summer of 1846 was one of the hottest that had ever been known. As the sweltering May and June days settled down upon Turtle Bay, and over the steepled town about the lower end of Manhattan,—the

dusty roads, baking brick sidewalks, awnings, and the sleepy rumble
of clumsy busses that was then New York,—the *literati* began to withdraw to their several summer pagodas.   Mr. Poe was left more and
more alone with his agonies and cogitations, while the heat lightning
flashed and the distant thunder rolled.

The Poes, at Turtle Bay, boarded near to the farm of a Mr. John L.
Miller, a large, shaded farmhouse, and its environs of several acres
planted with orchards that stretched along the shores of the East River.
Here in the spring days, Mrs. Clemm, impeccable as ever, neat, but sad,
desirous of sharing her troubles with sympathetic gossips, came to sit
in the parlor, or upon the veranda, to watch the Sound steamers go by,
and to tell her troubles, very real ones, to Mrs. Miller.   Poe sometimes
came with her.   Virginia was generally too feeble to go out.   Sarah,
Mrs. Miller's little girl, remembered.[764]

When I was a little girl we lived in a house facing Turtle Bay, on the East
River, near the present 47th Street.   Among our nearest neighbors was a charming family . . . consisting of Mr. Poe, his wife Virginia, and his mother-in-law,
Mrs. Clemm.   Poor Virginia, was very ill, at the time and I never saw her leave
home.   Poe and Mrs. Clemm would frequently call on us.   He would also run
over every little while to ask my father to lend him our row-boat, and then he
would enjoy himself pulling at the oars over to the little islands just south of
Blackwell's Island, for his afternoon swim.

Mrs. Clemm and my mother soon became the best of friends, and she found
mother a most sympathetic listener to all her sad tales of poverty and want.   I
would often see her shedding tears as they talked.   As I recall her she always
seemed so wonderfully neat and orderly, and invariably wore a full white collar
around her neck. . . .

This personification of placidity and domestic order, this epitome of
dameliness and respectability, from which the burdens of Promethean
sorrows wrung reluctant tears, is one of the enormous contrasts, one
of those almost ghostly enigmas which fate seems to have thrust, in a
spirit of sardonic mischief or ironical sympathy, into the life cycle of
Edgar Allan Poe.   During his youth, he had been impossibly linked with
the strongest guardian that ever a poet had; in later life Maria Clemm
had, as if in compensation, been mercifully provided.   She remained
the only constant factor of all the years of Poe's manhood.   Despised,
deprecated, and sometimes ridiculed, a poor, boresome, but saintly old
woman, she continued her devotion of a lifetime by her domestic epilogue
and eulogy when he died.

All who saw Mrs. Clemm during Poe's lifetime, men, women, and
children, were impressed by an orderliness, an intense cleanliness, a preternatural neatness in her appearance, which, as the record is assembled
and grows, becomes spiritual rather than physical in its implications.

---

[764] *Bulletin* of the North Side (Bronx) Board of Trade for January, 1909,—Poe
Memorial Issue.

It was she who introduced into the career of this man, whose life had been a chaos of passion since his birth, that essential quality of orderly continuity and cleanly comfort without which he must soon have perished miserably, or existed more pathetically than Lazarus himself. When the imagination and toil of genius were insufficient to wring from obstinate hands and pockets even the paltry coppers that fall willingly to the blind man's whine, Maria Clemm went forth with her basket and returned sadly but triumphantly to place the proceeds of her noble beggary before her fainting son and dying daughter.

It is impossible to exaggerate the majestic, because invisible, abnegations and ministrations of Mrs. Clemm. At evening the fields have seen her, armed with a spade, digging in the twilight among the turnips which farmers had planted to feed to cows in the wintertime, filling her basket with humble, earthy loot to make soup for her wonderful Eddie and her poor Virginia. At Fordham, even this resource failed, and she was seen in the very early mornings by the neighbors, walking down secret country lanes, culling the yellow dandelions to make a salad or a mess of "greens" for Edgar Allan Poe.

In the immense and catholic scheme of things, which requires and insists upon the widest possible variations in the scale of human character, Edgar Poe and Maria Clemm, although spiritual hemispheres apart, were brought together, yoked as it were, by Virginia, into an effectual, though astonishing team. Under the occasional lyric ecstasies and majestic dirges that her son-in-law caught up, from time to time, in poetry or prose, behind the harmony that he wrung magnificently out of conflict and chaos, is the inaudible but fundamental monotone of this woman's cherishing affection.

Yet she must not be regarded as some simple saint, blindly devoted to the devastating ideal of unintelligent self-sacrifice. She was always, it seems, doing the most common-sense thing under the circumstances, or finding the only way that there was out of a difficulty. In the Spring of 1846, both the condition of Virginia's health and Poe's difficulties and misfortunes made some removal to a more remote scene desirable. Mrs. Clemm must have longed for a place where her daughter could die in peace, and her son might live with some dignity—where their poverty would not be spied upon, and their tragedies be made the theme of idle gossip. In all this Poe would have heartily concurred. Sometime about the end of May, 1846, they moved to the Fordham cottage. Little Sarah Miller remembered the Poes leaving Turtle Bay, and her visit to Fordham soon afterward. The cherry trees were in bloom—

In the midst of their friendship they came and told us they were going to move to a distant place called Fordham, where they had rented a little cottage, feeling sure the pure country air would do Mrs. Poe a world of good. Very soon a cordial invitation arrived for us all to come and take luncheon, which was very daintily served on the first floor. As I remember, the front door led directly into the apartment. I recall most clearly their bringing me a small wooden box to sit on at the table, instead of a chair. Always kind and smiling and very fond of children, Poe's handsome and attractive appearance always impressed me. He would come up to me and patting me on the shoulder, tell me I was a nice little girl. One of the most prized treasures is a small Chinese puzzle of carved ivory given to me by Poe himself.[764]

This dinner with the Turtle Bay Millers—little Sarah, wide-eyed and smiling on a box—is one of the first glimpses to be had of the Poes at Fordham. One cannot help wondering what Poe thought, looking at the child sitting at the table where there had never been any necessity to provide high-chairs for children. The cat was there; we hear of her shortly afterward, lying upon Virginia's hollow bosom. Some puzzles cannot be given away. Poverty, for instance! A bed had been left behind at Turtle Bay in lieu of board. And one wonders, too, just how they *did* furnish the cottage.[765]

It was a very pleasant, a humble, but a beautiful little place. It would have been an ideal setting for a pastoral. There was the rose-embowered, the blossom-showered cottage of a poet; chimes from a neighboring monastery sounding across the fields; cloudy woods and distant, sun-flashing waterways; the lulling sound of cowbells nearing home at twilight.

The stage setting for the great American tragedy was enormously, almost cosmically ironical. The corpse-like Virginia, and the pale brow of madness were about to be wreathed in honeysuckle and roses. Through the months of her gasping, and above the busy noise of her husband's occasional delirium, sounded the soothing boom of greedy bees. The contrast of the psychic drama and the physical scenery could have been conceived only by that exquisite lord of tragedy, Reality.

Shortly after the removal to Fordham, Poe departed on a business trip which ended in bitter disappointment. Then the fitness of the bucolic scenery was completely complemented by the arrival from Richmond, on a family visit, of the eccentric and slightly childish sister, Rosalie. Rosalie was a great trial to Mrs. Clemm. She was childish, and willful, and yet possessed of a certain shrewdness, so often conferred upon such children of the moon, as if by way of compensation. She observed, she talked; and Mrs. Clemm feared her tongue. Rosalie, on her part, did not care very much for "Aunty Clemm." She preferred

---

[765] Kindly attempts by biographers to furnish the Fordham cottage in May, 1846, with funds received from the libel suit settled in February, 1847, are hardly ingenious, to say the least. The *opinion* of the author is, that the cottage was not in any sense "furnished," until Mrs. Shew gave the Poes the articles contributed by charity, in December, 1846, and after. See Mrs. Weiss for the description of articles pawned by Mrs. Clemm.

Mrs. Maria Clemm

From a daguerreotype taken in 1849

"My mother — my own mother, who died early,
　Was but the mother of myself; but you
Are mother to the one I loved so dearly,
　And thus are dearer than the mother I knew
By that infinity with which my wife
　Was dearer to my soul than its soul-life."

Poe's Sonnet, "*To My Mother.*"

EUREKA:

A PROSE POEM.

BY

EDGAR A. POE.

NEW-YORK:
GEO. P. PUTNAM,
OF LATE FIRM OF "WILEY & PUTNAM,"
155 BROADWAY.
MDCCCXLVIII.

Title Page of *Eureka*

New York, 1848

The tenth and last of Poe's works issued in his lifetime

Courtesy of a New York Collector

Robert Stanard
Son of Jane Stith Stanard, Poe's "Helen"
Reproduced by permission of W. G. Stanard, Esq.

Sarah Helen Whitman
After a painting by C. J. Thompson
Courtesy of Charles Scribner's Sons

Poe's Mystical Association of the name of "Helen"

Edgar A Poe

From a daguerreotype taken in the Autumn of 1848 at Providence, R. I.

About this time Poe was paying attention to *Mrs.* Helen Whitman, complicated by tender relations with *Mrs.* Richmond, "Annie." On November 15, 1848, in a fit of despair, he attempted to commit suicide while in Providence, Rhode Island, by swallowing an ounce of laudanum. The overdose proved an emetic, and he survived

Poe's Cottage at Fordham

Still preserved in Poe Park, Fordham, New York City

From a sketch made before its removal to the present site

to sit chattering idly by the bedside or near the chair of Virginia [766] while Poe was in town.

Of some unsuccessful business interview and of the high hopes aroused in vain, this, the only letter known to have been sent by Poe to Virginia, is a memorial:

June 12, 1846.

MY DEAR HEART—MY DEAR VIRGINIA,—Our mother will explain to you why I stay away from you this night. I trust the interview I am promised will result in some substantial good for me—for your dear sake and hers—keep up your heart in all hopefulness and trust yet a little longer. On my last great disappointment I should have lost my courage but for you—my little darling wife. You are my greatest and only stimulus now, to battle with this uncongenial, unsatisfactory, and ungrateful life.

I shall be with you to-morrow . . . P.M., and be assured until I see you I will keep in loving remembrance your last words, and your fervent prayer!

Sleep well, and may God grant you a peaceful summer with your devoted Edgar.[767]

The attempt to show that this letter was written just prior to an interview with Mrs. Osgood is not borne out by the order of events that followed. The reference, in the letter itself, to "substantial good" is palpably one of financial import.[768] The real interpretation is the obvious one. It is one of grief, anxiety, and affectionate solicitude in ink.

Mrs. Clemm had to send money to Poe for his return. He was scolded, says Rosalie, and then put to bed for a night of delirium. He was in a terrible way; he cried out, *and demanded morphine*. One catches other glimpses of him about New York, trying to place articles, or writing again about the *Stylus*—always unsuccessfully.

Yet, that Poe forecast and ever dramatized the departure of Virginia, there can be little doubt, for it was at the time of this early summer visit, in 1846, that we hear from Rosalie of *Annabel Lee*. She definitely remembered having heard it read. After Poe's death there was a host of lady candidates, each claiming in a long, tedious, angry, and jealous correspondence with Poe's English biographer, Ingram, to be the only genuine and original "Annabel." In so far as any of Poe's vague heroines can be traced to any definite personality of the

---

[766] The character of Rosalie Poe has been greatly misunderstood by several biographers, who have fastened upon her the names of "idiot," "imbecile," and so forth. Rosalie was a little eccentric—undeveloped. This was later made worse by misfortunes sufficient to turn the head of many a normal old woman. She wrote a fair letter, taught writing in a school in Richmond, and understood, far too well, what was going on at Fordham, to please Mrs. Clemm. In 1846, Rose was still living with the Mackenzies in Richmond. Mrs. Clemm put her to sewing while she stayed at the cottage. See Mrs. Clemm's letters to Rosalie, also Mrs. Weiss, *Home Life of Poe*.

[767] Ingram,—from the *Griswold Collection,* also published by Woodberry and Harrison.

[768] See Mrs. Weiss, *Home Life of Poe,* for a doubtful interpretation of this letter.

world of reality, it may be said, in passing, that his wife Virginia is more closely shadowed forth in the poem than anyone else. "I was a child, and she was a child," and "our love—it was stronger by far than the love of those who were older than we—of many far wiser than we"— seems to refer beyond cavil to the strange incidents of his marriage to a *child,* and the opposition of relatives. In this poem is the long dirge of the waves on Sullivan's Island during the years he walked its beaches alone, and the death of Virginia at Fordham. In the Summer of 1846, all of this was in his past, or in the near future by inevitable implication. It was a magnificent and lyrical rendering, a dirgelike expression of his own and Virginia's tragedy.

Sixteen miles from the city was no barrier at all to the visitations of curiosity. There were trains on the Harlem Railroad, stages, and various of the starry sisterhood possessed well-to-do husbands and carriages. Callers were not infrequent. Many were desirous of favorable reviews or criticism from Mr. Poe. From some of these women, Mrs. Clemm had borrowed money, so little favors from "Eddie" were now in order.[769] One could also appear gracefully by bringing a basket for that poor darling, Mrs. Poe—and Mrs. Clemm, who was lonely, *did* like to gossip. Great trouble for Poe ensued.

Mrs. Gove was an occasional visitor. Mrs. "Estelle" Lewis of the Brooklyn salon was frequently to be found seated in Mrs. Clemm's Fordham kitchen.[770] Her husband had given Poe "$100" to revise his wife's verses—the critical remarks which followed were, also expected, to be tempered by so salubrious a wind. All of this was exasperating. Mrs. Oakes Smith, it seems, had also used the lever of her hospitality, and probable favors to Mrs. Clemm, to extract an article from the "Raven" in which the two hundred verses of her poem on *The Sinless Child* were vaguely eulogized through a veil of gauzy irony.

The execution of the Sinless Child is as we have already said inferior to its conception.

The quotations, when removed from the context, were excellent.

Mrs. Smith was, we learn, a child of nature. Birds lit upon her fingers. Her poem contained a sinless type of passion which intrigued Poe, who, between the millstones of his gratitude and specialized admiration, contrived to grind out of chaff the meal of praise, mixed with the broken glass of irony.

One day in June, Mrs. Clemm—Poe, it appears, was absent—was

---

[769] It must be remembered that Mrs. Clemm was haunted by the horror of going to the poor-house, a fate which she escaped by going to a church home. She mentions the poor-house in letters to Rosalie, in 1846.

[770] From later correspondence between Mrs. Houghton and Mrs. Whitman, it is quite evident that "Stella" got hold of Poe through Mrs. Clemm, and that he, at first, detested her. Poe also spoke bitterly to Mrs. Gove of the reviews wrung from him by lucre, and his terrible misery.

visited by an authoress, and poetess, a certain Mrs. Elizabeth Frieze Lummis Ellet. Mrs. Ellet had learned her gossip's trade in the most talented school for scandal on the continent. Her talk with Mrs. Clemm was evidently most pumping, alarming, and consoling, and Mrs. Clemm soon made the mistake of reading to her some of the sugar-and-spice letters of Mrs. Osgood. In New York, sixteen miles away, there was an explosion in the literary teapot.

Mrs. Osgood became greatly alarmed, more alarmed than ever. She had, it seems, already ceased to see Poe, through fear of gossip, and the new outbreak was doubly unwelcome. A committee of the *literati,* headed by Mrs. Elizabeth Frieze Lummis Ellet, was commissioned by Mrs. Osgood, "about the time the cherry trees bloomed," to call upon Poe and to demand her letters. Many of the starry ones, who had also written letters, must have been somewhat disturbed to learn that they were being read aloud to the sisterhood by Mrs. Clemm.

Mr. Poe was considerably nettled. He was *not* glad to see the commission of Mrs. Ellet, Margaret Fuller, and Miss Lynch, and evidently said so, hinting that Mrs. Ellet might be equally solicitous about her own correspondence. She was. The bundle of Mrs. Osgood's letters was returned instantly, and the committee withdrew bearing them back to New York. The talk went on, however.

After the irate committee left, Poe, who was sorry that his anger had led him to make an unchivalric remark to Mrs. Ellet, took her letters and left them at her door. There is no doubt that in all this affair there was little else than gossip, and a genuine malignity on the part of Mrs. Ellet, who soon afterward denied that she had received her letters.

Mr. Lummis, Mrs. Ellet's brother, next appeared, demanding his sister's letters from Poe. He doubted, or did not know that they had been returned. Mrs. Ellet naturally remained reticent. Poe's sacred word was doubted, and many hard things said about Mrs. Osgood. Mr. Lummis was soon said to be going about New York, with his coat-tail full of pistols, looking for Poe. A duel, then not at all unusual in literary and political circles, was in order. Mr. Poe called upon Mr. Thomas Dunn English at his and T. H. Lane's apartment at 304 Broadway, in a very excited state, to ask Mr. English to be his second in the quarrel.

Poe was probably in debt to English for sums due upon the demise of the *Broadway Journal,* and English had also been held up to ridicule by Poe in *Godey's* in the sketches of the *literati.*[771]

In January, 1846, Poe, while intoxicated, had had a row with English, probably over the death of the *Journal,* in which violence had been re-

---

[771] Poe denied his being in debt to English in the reply in the Philadelphia *Spirit of the Times,* July 10, 1846.

sorted to. Lane says that English was entirely exasperating to Poe when the latter was in his cups. It was upon Mr. English that Poe now called to do him the good offices of a friend! Strangely enough, John H. Tyler, who must have heard of similar singular scenes in Washington upon Poe's visit there, was present when Poe arrived. Mr. English's account follows.[772]

Mr. Poe having been guilty of some most ungentlemanly conduct, while in a state of intoxication, I was obliged to treat him with discourtesy. Sometime after this, he came to my chambers, in my absence in search of me. He found there, a nephew of one of our ex-presidents. To that gentleman he stated, that he desired to see me in order to apologize to me for his conduct. I entered shortly after, when he tendered me an apology and his hand. The former I accepted, the latter I refused. He told me that he came to beg my pardon, because he wished me to do him a favor. Amused at this novel reason for an apology, I replied that I would do the favor, with pleasure, if possible, but not on the score of friendship. He said that though his friendship was of little service his enmity might be dangerous. To this I rejoined that I shunned his friendship and despised his enmity. He beseeched a private conversation so abjectly, that, finally, moved by his humble entreaty, I accorded it. Then he told me that he had villified a certain well known and esteemed authoress, of the South [Mrs. Ellet], then on a visit to New York, that he had accused her of having written letters to him which compromised her reputation; and that her brother (her husband being absent) had threatened his life unless he produced the letters named. He begged me for God's sake to stand his friend, as he expected to be challenged. I refused, because I was not willing to mix myself in his affairs, and because having once before done so, I had found him at the critical moment, to be an abject poltroon. These reasons I told him. He then begged the loan of a pistol to defend himself against an attack. This request I refused, saying that his surest defence was a retraction of unfounded charges. He at last grew exasperated and using offensive language, was expelled from the room. . . .

So much for Mr. English's statement of the case in the *New York Mirror*. Unfortunately for that gentleman, although justly exasperated, his statement was mixed with an alloy which lightens considerably the pure gold of truth. From other passages in his career, it is known that he was an insufferable cock on his own dung hill; that he enjoyed the vituperation of controversy, and shunned the incidents of a fair fight. He had long been friends with Poe, who had helped to get out English's paper in Philadelphia when the latter was himself on a spree, and his statement of Poe's having been a poltroon was the exact reverse of the fact.

He might, therefore, have overlooked the episode in January. An old acquaintance shattered in nerves, hounded and pursued over a quarrel initiated by gossips, came to his house humbling his pride in his extremity, and holding out his hand. Mr. English accepted the apology

---

[772] The text of the original articles in the *New York Mirror* is here used by the courtesy of John T. Snyder, Esq., who supplied the author with the originals in his possession.

but would not take the hand, and boasted of it in print. Poe was no doubt greatly shaken, and overrated Mr. Lummis; English would not involve himself where a real encounter threatened. He even refused, as a careful lawyer, to loan Poe a pistol.[773] In the quarrel which followed, he did not merely put Poe out of the door, but beat him up first, after having his own face pummeled in the encounter. Poe was led out by Professor Ackerman, and was in bed for some days afterward, in the usual state of collapse to which any kind of excitement, love, stimulants, or anger reduced him. He was, in fact, a complete nervous wreck. Dr. Francis, realizing his condition, carried a letter to Lummis, who by this time must have found out that his sister after all had her letters.

Mrs. Osgood went to Albany, and the affair was hushed up. "Poe," says English, "fled the city." This meant that Poe returned to Fordham, where he lived. Mr. English remained, only to make a necessary temporary exit later. He had received a very sharp and unmannerly peck from the beak of the "Raven" in *Godey's,* and now discovered, in his own replies, some of the qualities of the bill of the vulture. On May 30, 1846, the *New York Mirror* had carried T. D. English's reply to *The Literati* paper in which he used the knowledge acquired during his intimate contact with Poe to sneer, not without considerable force, at Poe's own affectations of learning.

Mr. Poe's articles were to have still greater currency given them by uniting the *Godey's Book* with *Arthur's Magazine* and publishing them with the latest Paris fashions, Americanized and expressed from Paris. A still greater impetus was to be given to Mr. Poe's opinions; they were even to be accompanied with autographs of the New York *Literati.* It is said that all Division Street was put in an uproar by this tremendous announcement, and two milliner's apprentices never slept a wink one whole night, for thinking about it. Some of the students in Dr. Arthur's grammar school made a pilgrimage to Bloomingdale to gaze upon the asylum where Mr. Poe was reported to be confined, in consequence of his immense mental efforts having turned his brain . . . [and so on through several columns]—

To conclude, after the fashion of our Thersitical Magazinist, Mr. Poe is about 39. He may be more or less. If neither more nor less, we should say he was decidedly 39. But of this we are not certain. In height he is about 5 feet 1 or two inches, perhaps 2 inches and a half. His face is pale and rather thin; eyes gray, watery, and always dull; nose rather prominent, pointed and sharp; nostrils wide; hair thin and cropped short; mouth not very well chiselled, nor very sweet, his tongue shows itself unpleasantly when he speaks earnestly, and seems too large for his mouth; teeth indifferent; forehead rather broad, and in the region of ideality decidedly large, but low, and in that part where phrenology places conscientiousness and the group of moral sentiments it is quite flat; chin narrow and pointed, which gives his head, upon the whole, a balloonish appearance, which may account for his supposed light-headedness; he generally

---

[773] See also English writing October 29, 1896, in the *Independent.* "One word led to another and he [Poe] rushed toward me in a menacing manner."

carries his head upright like a fugleman on drill, but sometimes it droops considerably. His address is gentlemanly and agreeable at first, but it soon wears off and leaves a different impression after becoming acquainted with him; his walk is quick and jerking, sometimes waving, describing that peculiar figure in geometry denominated by Euclid, we think, but it may be Professor Farrar of Cambridge, Virginia fence. In dress he affects the tailor at times, and at times the cobbler, being in fact excessively nice or excessively something else. *His hands are singularly small, resembling birds claws;* his person slender; weight about 110 or 115 pounds, perhaps the latter; his study has not many of the Magliabechian characteristics, the shelves being filled mainly with ladies magazines; he is supposed to be a contributor to the *Knickerbocker,* but of this nothing certain is known; he is the author of *Politian,* a drama, to which Prof. Longfellow is largely indebted, it is said by Mr. Poe, for many of his ideas. Mr. Poe goes much into society, but what society we cannot positively say; he formerly lived at West Point; his present place of residence is unknown. He is married.[772]

Through the stifling days of June and July, while the heat lightning continued to flicker, the stage thunder of the controversy rolled on. On June 23rd, in reply to some further proddings, the following appeared as a paid card in the *New York Mirror:*

THE WAR

OF

THE LITERATI

———————

MR. ENGLISH'S REPLY

TO

MR. POE

———————

A TERRIFIC REJOINDER!

The War of the Literati—We publish the following terrific rejoinder of one of Mr. Poe's abused literati, with a twinge of pity for the object of its severity. But as Mr. Godey, 'for a consideration,' lends the use of his battery for an attack on the one side, it is but fair that we allow our friends an opportunity to exercise a little 'self-defence' on the other

(A CARD)

MR. ENGLISH'S REPLY TO MR. POE

As I have not, of late replied to attacks made upon me through the public press, I can easily afford to make an exception, and still keep my rule a general one. A Mr. Edgar A. Poe, has been engaged for some time past in giving to the public, through the medium of the *Lady's Book,* sketches of what he facetiously calls *The Literati of New York City.* These he names by way of distinction, I presume, from his ordinary writings, 'honest opinions.' He honors me by including me in the very numerous and remarkably august body he affects to describe. Others have converted the paper on which his sketches are printed to its legitimate use—like to like—but as he seems to covet a notice from me, he shall be gratified.

Mr. Poe states in his article, 'I do not personally know Mr. English.' That he does not know me is not a matter of wonder. The severe treatment he received at my hands for brutal and dastardly conduct, rendered it necessary for him if possible, to forget my existence. Unfortunately, I know him; and by the blessing of God, and the assistance of a grey-goose quill, my design is to make the public know him also.

I know Mr. Poe by a succession of his acts—one of which is rather costly. I hold Mr. Poe's acknowledgement for a sum of money which he obtained of me under false pretences. As I stand in need of it at this time, I am content he should forget to know me, provided he acquits himself of the money he owes me. I ask no interest, in lieu of which I am willing to credit him with the sound cuffing I gave him when I last saw him.

Another act of his gave me some knowledge of him. A merchant of this city had accused him of committing forgery. He consulted me on the mode of punishing his accuser, and as he was afraid to challenge him to the field, or chastise him personally, I suggested a legal prosecution as his sole remedy. At his request, I obtained a counsellor who was willing, as a compliment to me, to conduct his suit without the customary retaining fee. But, though so eager at first to commence proceedings, he dropped the matter altogether, when the time came for him to act—thus virtually admitting the truth of the charge.

As the matter contained in the last paragraph quoted above was libelous, the publisher, Fuller, tried to guard himself, by the introductory notice, a precaution which was futile. Poe replied in the Philadelphia *Spirit of the Times* on July 10, 1846:

To THE PUBLIC.—A long and serious illness of such character as to render quiet and perfect seclusion in the country of vital importance, has hitherto prevented me from seeing an article headed *The War of the Literati. . . .*

Full justice was done to the occasion in Poe's characteristic style. He was unable to defend himself fully against English's story of his conduct when intoxicated, but contributed enough biographical material about English sufficiently to demonstrate his character. Of his own weakness he remarks:

The errors and frailties which I deplore, it cannot at least be asserted that I have been the coward to deny. Never, even, have I made attempt at extenuating a weakness which is (or by the blessing of God, *was*) a calamity, although those who did not know me intimately had little reason to regard it as other than a crime. For, indeed, had my pride, or that of my family permitted, there was much—very much—there was everything to be offered in extenuation.

The charge of forgery was completely denied. Park Benjamin had quoted the alleged remark of a New York merchant, Edward J. Thomas of Broad Street, to English who had rashly rushed into print. Poe dispatched a letter to Thomas, who replied:

New York, *July* 5, 1845.

E. A. POE, *Esq.,* New York

DEAR SIR,—I had hoped ere this to have seen you, but as you have not called, and as I may soon be out of the city, I desire to say to you that, after repeated effort, I saw the person on Friday evening last, from whom the report originated to which you referred in your call at my office. [The contemptuous silence in respect to the communication sent through Mr. E. will be observed.] He denies it *in toto*—says he does not know it and never said so—and it undoubtedly arose from the misunderstanding of some word used. It gives me pleasure thus to trace it, and still more to find it destitute of foundation in truth, as I thought would be the case. I have told Mr. Benjamin the result of my inquiries, and shall do so to—— [the lady referred to as the common friend] by a very early opportunity—the only two persons who know anything of the matter, as far as I know.

> I am, Sir, very truly
> Your friend and obed't St.
> (*Signed*) EDWARD J. THOMAS [774]

"These are the facts which, in a court of justice, I propose to demonstrate," says Poe—and he did so. The *New York Mirror* was sued, for libel. The case came to trial February 22, 1847, before Justice Samuel Jones of the Superior (City) Court. English did not appear for the *Mirror,* and the verdict went to Poe who received $225 damages and costs. The total sum amounted to $492. Out of this, E. L. Fancher, Poe's attorney, received, it is said, a good fat fee. This was after the death of Virginia at Fordham.

The most unfortunate part of the whole miserable affair was, that largely due to unnecessary attacks on English in *Godey's,* the weaknesses of Edgar Poe had been advertised to the world. It was the English controversy, more than any other, which tarnished Poe's good name. Had it not been for that, we should now hear very much less about "Poe's drinking." The weaknesses of many another literary man, kept private, have been forgotten. The failings of Poe were trumpeted, and reprinted in a chain of little newspapers and magazines whose editors dealt out the vindictive journalistic personalities of an era when neighborhood gossip was news. It is hard now to get a perspective on the havoc which this kind of thing wrought upon so sensitive and so easily irritated a nature as Poe's.

There was not a single day in [the] year that he did not receive, through the post, anonymous letters from cowardly villains which so harrowed up his feelings that he at length, was driven to the firm belief that the whole world of Humanity was nothing less than the veritable devil himself tormenting him here on earth for nothing. [775]

One can easily trace, in this, the germs of a conviction of persecution as this went on from year to year.

Were I now called upon from the bottom of my heart, to give a faithful exhibition of this man's real nature, I would say that he was the Incarnation of the Greek

---

[774] Printed in Poe's reply to English in the *Spirit of the Times.*
[775] Thomas Holley Chivers, quoted by Prof. Woodberry in the *Century Magazine,* February, 1903.

Prometheus chained to the Mount Caucasus of demi-civilized Humanity, with the black Vulture of Envy, feeding on his self-replenished heart; while upon his trembling lips sat enthroned the most eloquent persuasion alternating with the bitterest, triumphant and God-like scorn. . . .[775]

This estimate was made by Thomas Holley Chivers who knew Poe well, and who had visited him on July 8, 1845, at 195 Broadway. From Fordham, on July 22, 1846, Poe wrote Chivers a significant letter, only a small part of which is here given.

I am living out of town about 13 miles, at a village called Fordham, on the railroad leading north. We are in a snug little cottage, keeping house, and would be very comfortable but that I have been for a long time dreadfully ill. I am getting better, however, altho slowly, and shall get well. In the meantime the flocks of little birds of prey that always take the opportunity to peck at a sick fowl of larger dimensions, have been endeavoring with all their power given them to effect my ruin. My dreadful poverty, also has given them every advantage. In fact, my dear friend, I have been driven to the very gates of despair more dreadful than death, and I had not even one friend, out [side] of my family, with whom to advise. What would I have not given for the kind pressure of your hand. . . .

Let not anything in this letter impress you with the belief that I *despair* even of worldly prosperity. On the contrary although I feel ill, and ground into the very dust with poverty, there is a sweet hope in the bottom of my soul. . . .[776]

We also learn, in this letter, that Poe had not been contributing to the magazines since February, 1846, and that the money received from Godey had long ago been exhausted.[765]

Of the life led by Poe and his family about Fordham, of the contemporary conditions of the neighborhood, and of its appearance and the location of the cottage itself, many carefully authenticated documents and much testimony remain.[777]

Fordham was a sleepy little village, in the 1840's, strung out along the Kingsbridge Road, the old stage line northward. The place dated from a New York manor, created in 1676. When the Poes moved there, it was just beginning to feel the influx of families from New

---

[776] Prof. Woodberry publishes the whole letter in the *Century Magazine* for February, 1903.

[777] Descriptions of the cottage and the life led at Fordham by Poe and his family come from *Transactions of the Bronx Society of Arts, Sciences and History,* vol. I, part V; *The Poe Cottage at Fordham,* R. G. Bolton; reminiscences attributed (correctly) to Mrs. Gove Nichols, the *Sixpenny Magazine,* February, 1863; Items: *New York Sun,* October 3, 1915; Church Records of Fordham and West Farms. *Poe's Mary,* see note 422; pamphlets and material available at the Poe cottage at Fordham; *Boston Herald,* January 20, 1909; *Appleton's Journal,* July 18, 1874; the *Book Buyer* for January, 1903; maps, street plans, and several clippings and letters loaned the author by collectors, not available for reference; bill for the widening of the Kingsbridge Road, *New York State Archives;* Petition of the Poe Memorial Association to the Legislature and Governor of New York, April 8, 1896, etc., etc. Also obviously autobiographical descriptions in *Landor's Cottage,* and other stories by Poe. Also letters of Mrs. Shew in the *Ingram Correspondence* at the University of Virginia. Personal visits to the Poe cottage.

York.   The Lorillards and others already had summer homes in the neighborhood, and the Roman Catholic College of St. John had been built nearby on Rose Hill.   A station had recently been constructed to take care of the two trains daily on the Harlem Railroad at Williamsbridge, a mile and a half to the north.   There was not even a post office. Poe had to walk for his mail about a mile, to West Farms.

The cottage occupied a triangular plot of ground of about an acre where the Kingsbridge Road began to turn east up to Fordham, at present marked by the line of East One Hundred Ninety-second Street. It was not a "Dutch Cottage," as it has so often been described, but a simple, frame, workman's dwelling built when the Colonial influence still prevailed, some time after the Revolution, as the hand-cut laths, and nails, and the mud plaster employed in its construction show.   It seems to have been erected a little previous to 1816.   The property in 1846 was owned by a neighboring farmer, a member of the Fordham Dutch Reformed Church, who, in the Spring of 1846, leased it to Poe.

The little house had broad paneled doors and small-paned windows. There were four rooms, two on each floor, a kitchen with an open fireplace, added soon after the building was erected, and a cow-shed lean-to.

In front, there was a small porch.   Poe himself describes "the pillars of the piazza enwreathed in jasmine, and sweet honeysuckle—the numerous pots of gorgeous flowers, the vivid green of the tulip tree leaves that partially overshadowed the cottage . . . the large, flat, irregular slabs of granite . . . imbedded in delicious turf not nicely adapted, but with velvety sod filling frequent intervals between the stones [leading] hither and thither from the house."   In the poet's day the entire dwelling seems to have been covered with the broad, dark-pine shingles then common.

The main room on the ground floor was the parlor where Poe wrote. "The more substantial furniture consisted of a round table, a few chairs (including a large rocking chair) and a sofa or rather settee . . . its material was plain maple painted a creamy white slightly understriped with green."   Poe also speaks in *Landor's Cottage,* evidently from life, of a vase of blooming flowers on the parlor table and "the fireplace nearly filled with a vase of brilliant geraniums."   There were more flowers, vases on the shelves and mantel, and clustered violets about the windows.   Such was the room in which he wrote in the summer days. The family evidently ate, after the manner of rural dwellers, in the kitchen.

Next to the parlor was a cubbyhole of a bedroom which Mrs. Clemm at first occupied, but into which Virginia was brought to be nursed later. Here she died.   The two garret rooms were evidently Poe's and Virginia's.   The east attic room was, at first, occupied by Virginia before the cold weather came, as her bedstead now shows the knobs cut off on one side, in order to allow it to fit under the low eaves. Poe's own room was next to Virginia's in the garret, "a low, cramped chamber, lighted by little square windows like port-holes." [778] The furnishings were poverty-stricken, but, as always, Mrs. Clemm was able to make the place gleaming and spotless. The walls were not papered, but covered with a lime wash. A little winding staircase led to the rooms above, and there were broad, plain, scoured, plank floors.

The surroundings were in keeping. The house itself stood facing west, close to the road, with a little dooryard filled with lilac bushes, and a large cherry tree. A few blue flagstones led from the gate to the porch. There was a wood, and an apple orchard just north—across what is now Poe Park. The hill sloped away to the south, almost from the verge of the porch, dipping down into Mill Creek Valley. To the south, down a slope of lawn, there were wide, sweeping views over the farms of the Bronx. The most living, contemporary description has been given by Mrs. Gove Nichols:

On this occasion [probably a visit in the Summer of 1846] I was introduced to the young wife of the poet, and to the mother, then more than sixty years of age. She was a tall, dignified old lady, with a most lady-like manner, and her black dress, though old and much worn, looked really elegant on her. She wore a widow's cap, of the genuine pattern, and it suited her exquisitely with her snow-white hair. Her features were large, and corresponded with her stature, and it seemed strange how such a stalwart and queenly woman could be the mother of her *petite* daughter. Mrs. Poe looked very young; she had large black eyes, and a pearly whiteness of complexion which was a perfect pallor. Her pale face, her brilliant eyes, and her raven hair gave her an unearthly look. One felt that she was almost a disrobed spirit, and when she coughed, it was made certain that she was rapidly passing away.

The mother seemed hale and strong, and appeared to be a sort of universal Providence to her strange children.

The cottage had an air of gentility that must have been lent to it by the presence of its inmates. So neat, so poor, so unfurnished, and yet so charming a dwelling I never saw. The floor of the kitchen was white as wheaten flour. A table, a chair, and a little stove it contained seemed to furnish it completely. The sitting room was laid with check matting; four chairs, a light stand, and a hanging bookshelf completed its furniture. There were pretty presentation copies of books on the little shelves, and the Brownings had posts of honor on the stand. With quiet exultation Poe drew from his inside pocket a letter he had recently received from Elizabeth Barrett Browning. He read it to us. It was very flattering. . . . On the bookshelf there lay a volume of Poe's poems. He took it down, wrote my name in it and gave it to me. I think he did this from a feeling of sympathy, for I could not be of advantage to him, as my two companions could. . . . He was at this time greatly depressed. Their extreme poverty, the sickness of his wife, and his own inability to write sufficiently accounted for this. We spent half an hour in the house, when some more company came, which included ladies, and then we all went to walk.

We strolled away into the woods, and had a very cheerful time, till someone

---

[778] Prof. Woodberry, 1909, vol. II, page 213.

proposed a game at leaping. I think it must have been Poe, as he was expert in the exercise. Two or three gentlemen agreed to leap with him, and though one of them was tall and had been a hunter in times past, Poe still distanced them all. But alas! his gaiters, long worn and carefully kept, were both burst in the grand leap that made him victor. . . . I was certain he had no other shoes, boots, or gaiters. Who amongst us could offer him money to buy a new pair? . . . When we reached the cottage, I think all felt that we must not go in, to see the shoeless unfortunate sitting or standing in our midst. I had an errand, however—and I entered the house to get it. The poor old mother looked at his feet with a dismay that I shall never forget. 'Oh, Eddie!' said she, 'how did you burst your gaiters?' Poe seemed to have come into a semi-torpid state as soon as he saw his mother. 'Do answer Muddie,' now said she coaxingly—I related the cause of the mishap, and she drew me into the kitchen.

'Will you speak to Mr. ——,' she said, 'about Eddie's last poem?' Mr. —— was the reviewer. 'If he will only take the poem, Eddie can have a pair of shoes. He has it—I carried it last week, and Eddie says it is his best. You will speak to him about it, won't you?'

We had already read the poem in conclave, and Heaven forgive us, we could not make head or tail of it.[783] It might as well have been in any of the lost languages, for any meaning we could extract from its melodious numbers. I remember saying that I believed it was only a hoax that Poe was passing off for poetry, to see how far his name would go in imposing upon people. But here was a situation. The reviewer had been actively instrumental in the demolition of the gaiters.

'Of course, they will publish the poem,' said I, 'and I will ask C—— to be quick about it.'

The poem was paid for at once, and published soon after. I presume it is regarded as genuine poetry in the collected poems of its author, but then it bought the poet a pair of gaiters, and twelve shillings over.

At my next visit Poe grew very confidential with me.

'I write,' said he, 'from a mental necessity—to satisfy my taste and my love of art. Fame forms no motive power with me. What can I care for the judgment of a multitude, every individual of which I despise?'

'But, Mr. Poe,' said I, 'there are individuals whose judgment you respect.'

'Certainly, and I would choose to have their esteem unmixed with the mean adulation of the mob.'

'But the multitude may be honestly and legitimately pleased,' said I.

'That may be *possible*,' said Poe, musingly, 'because they may have an honest leader, and not a poor man who has been paid a hundred dollars to manufacture opinions of them and fame for an author.'

'Do reviewers sell their literary conscience thus unconscionably?' said I.

'A literary critic must be loath to violate his taste, his sense of the fit and the beautiful. To sin against these, and praise an unworthy author, is to him an unpardonable sin. But if he were placed on the rock, or if one he loved better than his own life were writhing there, I can conceive of his forging a note against the Bank of Fame, in favour of some would-be poetess, who is able and willing to buy his poems and opinions.'

He turned almost fiercely upon me, his fine eyes piercing me, 'Would you blame a man for not allowing his sick wife to starve?' said he.

I changed the subject. . . .

At my next visit, Poe said, as we walked along the brow of the hill, 'I can't look out on this loveliness till I have made a confession to you. I said to you when you were here last, that I despised fame.'

'I remember,' said I.

'It is false,' said he. 'I love fame—I dote on it—I idolize it—I would drink to the very dregs the glorious intoxication. I would have incense ascend in my honour from every hill and hamlet, from every town and city on this earth. Fame! Glory!—they are life-giving breath, and living blood. No man lives, unless he is famous! How bitterly I belied my nature, and my aspirations, when I said I did not desire fame, and that I despised it.'

One must remember that fame was the only reward that he could expect, in compensation for a life that had been spent in toil and devoid of any apparent reward. Yet this outburst shows to what an exalted point the ego had attained. It was only a year before *Eureka* was written, when the climax of self-exaltation was achieved.

This outburst from the hidden depths of the man's nature reveals a more than rational ambition. Fame had become the craving, the morbid thirst of a soul condemned to solitary confinement. To be universally upon all lips, even after death, would somehow, he felt, identify him with men and bring them closer. Life had been a dream. His children were only dreams. To make them live, was to survive, in part, himself. "No man lives unless he is famous!"—glory would be his only immortality. One wonders—Mrs. Gove's recollections were published in the *Sixpenny Magazine!*[777]

The presence of so marked a character as Mr. Poe did not pass unnoticed in the annals of so quiet a neighborhood. The visitors from town, the sufferings of his wife, and the various shifts to which he was put by his obvious poverty were, no doubt, the commonplace of much rural gossip. Mrs. Clemm was forced occasionally to borrow a shilling from some of the neighbors to get Eddie's mail when he was unable to walk to the West Farms Post Office, and the priests and students at St. John's College remembered meeting Poe, from time to time, walking along the lanes, often at nightfall, muttering, lost in his dreams, a lonely and mysterious figure.

He occasionally walked out the Kingsbridge road to visit the Macombs, or down to the village of Tremont, where he had struck up an acquaintance with the resident physician at a home for incurables. The Valentines were also good and kind neighbors; their name recalled boyhood memories to Poe, a fact which would have been of considerable import to him, for he was almost superstitious about such associations. It was probably the deciding reason for his having rented the cottage from them! Virginia and Mrs. Clemm were especially good friends with the neighbors on the Van Cott farm nearby, and, from a Miss Susan Cromwell, another neighbor, comes a particularly tragic anecdote.[778]

Miss Cromwell lived a little beyond the Poes. In the Spring of 1846, as she was passing by the cottage up the Kingsbridge Road, she noticed Poe up in the cherry tree gathering the red, ripe fruit, and tossing it to Virginia, who caught it in her lap, laughing and calling back, as she sat dressed in white on a green sod bank beneath. Poe was standing on a branch above her, about to toss another bunch of cherries into the bright red pile already gathered in Virginia's apron, when white and crimson suddenly became one in the tide which leaped from her lips. Poe sprang from the branches, clasped Virginia in his arms, and vanished with her fainting in his arms, through the door of the little cottage. "They were," said the literal Miss Cromwell, "*awful* poor."

Through all the years, Poe had retained his West Point cloak or over-coat, for during the Fordham episode, we hear of it several times. It was stolen from him once, after he had left it in a tavern near the Harlem Railroad Station, but seems to have been recovered through a warrant issued by his friend Justice Lorillard. So marked a garment, in so small a neighborhood, was not hard to trace down. It was this same cape or coat which played such a tragic rôle in the Winter that followed.

From a family by the name of Bushby nearby comes the information that, while at Fordham, Poe was sponsor at the baptism of a child named for him. Significantly enough, he did not desire the boy to bear his middle name, and the namesake was baptized "Edgar Albert." [779] It was also noted that the Rector of the Episcopal Church at West Farms paid some visits to the cottage, and that Poe became friends with one of the priests in the seminary nearby.

Far from being a restful, and a quiet retirement, Fordham, in 1846, was to Poe a place of confusion. There was, of course, Virginia. He was torn between his pride and the trammelings of poverty. His health and unstrung nervous condition precluded any work, except intermit-tently, perhaps upon a few poems. The ideas of *Eureka* must, in spite of everything, have already been taking shape. These dreams had been dis-turbed by his domestic tragedy, the henpecks of the *literati,* and the an-noying affair with English. Rosalie had returned to Richmond in July.

During all this time, the usual active correspondence of a prominent literary man had been under way. [780] It was, under the circumstances of his health, a considerable tax at that time upon him. The most inti-

---

[779] Poe is known to have signed his name Edgar *Allan* Poe, only twice. (News of a letter said to belong to the early Baltimore period (*sic*) so signed, has recently been rumored to be in a collector's hands in Berlin.) Griswold was responsible for using the full name habitually. Poe evidently desired to suppress it. Poe, in his works, frequently refers in a disguised way to his middle name, and the reason for it. See *Three Sundays in a Week, The Literary Life of Thingum Bob Esq.*, etc., notes 191 to 197 in this volume.

[780] Griswold, Miss Barrett, Eveleth, Duyckinck, Godey, Miss Lynch, Cooke, Ramsay, Willis, and a half dozen or so others engaged Poe's time in letters and replies in 1846.

mate, and sympathetic letter of 1846 belongs to the correspondence with Thomas Holley Chivers. In July, Poe received a whole bundle of his letters, which the landlady at his former lodging, 195 Broadway, had neglected to forward. He hastened to reply. The intercourse of the two was most illuminating and intimate. Chivers afterward prepared a life of Poe.[781] At the beginning of the year, and continued throughout, there was an interchange of letters between Duyckinck and Poe. The former was now acting as Poe's literary agent, having published his poems and tales. Poe was anxious to get out another collection of his tales giving a fuller selection, and in January, 1846, he had sent the proposed collection to Duyckinck, proposing that Mr. Wiley advance him $50 for the copyright. About the same time he wrote to Griswold asking him to further the plan. He was dissatisfied with the narrow range of his stories in the published edition.

> Wiley and Putnam's reader has what he thinks a taste for ratiocination . . . and has accordingly made up the book mostly of analytic stories. . . .

Neither Dr. Griswold nor Mr. Duyckinck agreed, and nothing further came of the matter. In April, Poe received the letter from Elizabeth Barrett which so pleased him. With Duyckinck there was also, in April, further correspondence about the anthology upon which Poe seems to have worked spasmodically at Fordham, and in June a short note concerning the reply to English, and a review of Poe's *Tales* to be written up at the suggestion of Martin Farquhar in the *Literary Gazette*.

In April, Poe had been chosen by a concurrent vote of the literary societies of the University of Vermont, as the poet for an anniversary celebration in August. He was unable, on account of ill health and poverty, to go, but he wrote to Duyckinck asking to have the invitation given publicity. He also offered to sell that part of his correspondence containing the autographs of "statesmen," to Wiley & Putnam. Much of the correspondence of the Summer deals with the miserable English controversy. There were letters to Willis, Godey, Duyckinck and William Gilmore Simms. Simms' reply—he was then in New York—on July 30, 1846, is one of the best advised that Poe received. Poe had asked Simms to aid him in the English controversy.

> I note with regret the very desponding character of your last letter. I surely need not tell you how deeply and sincerely I deplore the misfortunes which attend you,—the more so as I see no prospect for your relief and extrication but such as must result from your own decision and resolve. No friend can help you in the struggle which is before you. Money, no doubt, can be procured; but this is not altogether what you require. Sympathy may soothe the hurts of Self Esteem, and make a man temporarily forgetful of his assailants;—but in what

---

[781] For an account of this *Life of Poe* by Chivers see Prof. Woodberry's article in the *Century Magazine* for February, 1903, reference note 775 above.

degree will this avail, and for how long, in the protracted warfare of twenty or thirty years?

You are still a very young man, and one too largely and too variously endowed, not to entertain the conviction—as your friends entertain it—of a long and manful struggle with, and a final victory over, fortune. But this warfare, the world requires you to carry on with your own unassisted powers. It is only in your manly resolution to use these powers, after a legitimate fashion, that it will countenance your claims to its regards and sympathy; and I need not tell you how rigid and exacting it has been in the case of the poetical genius, or, indeed, the genius of any order.

Suffer me to tell you frankly, taking the privilege of a true friend, that you are now perhaps in the most perilous period of your career—just in that position—just at that time of life—when a false step becomes a capital error—when a single leading mistake is fatal in its consequences. You are no longer a boy. 'At thirty wise or never!' You must subdue your impulses; etc., in particular let me exhort you to discard all associations with men, whatever their talents, whom you cannot esteem as men.

Pardon me for presuming thus to counsel one whose great natural and acquired resources should make him rather the teacher of others. But I obey a law of my own nature, and it is because of my sympathies that I speak. Do not suppose yourself abandoned by the worthy and honorable among your friends. They will be glad to give you welcome if you will suffer them. They will rejoice—I know their feelings and hear their language—to countenance your return to that community—that moral province in society—of which, let me say to you, respectfully and regretfully,—you have been, according to all reports but too heedlessly, and, perhaps, too scornfully indifferent.

Remain in obscurity for awhile. You have a young wife—I am told a suffering & an interesting one,—let me entreat you to cherish her, and to cast away those pleasures which are not worthy of your mind, and to trample those temptations under foot, which degrade your person, and make it familiar to the mouth of vulgar jest.

You may do all this, by a little circumspection. It is still within your power. Your resources from literature are probably much greater than mine. I am sure they are just as great. You can increase them, so that they shall be ample for all your legitimate desires; but you must learn the worldling's lesson of prudence;—a lesson, let me add, which the literary world has but too frequently & unwisely disparaged. It may seem to you very impertinent,—in most cases it is impertinent—that he who gives nothing else should presume to give counsel. But one gives that which he can most spare, and you must not esteem me indifferent to a condition which I can in no other way assist.

I have never been regardless of your genius, even when I knew nothing of your person. It is some years since I counselled Mr. Godey to obtain the contributions of your pen. He will tell you this. I hear that you reproach him. But how can you expect a magazine proprietor to encourage contributions which embroil him with all his neighbors? These broils do you no good—vex your temper, destroy your peace of mind, and hurt your reputation. You have abundant resources upon which to draw even were there no Grub Street in Gotham. Change your tactics and begin a new series of papers with your publisher.

The printed matter which I send you, might be quoted by Godey, and might be ascribed to me. But, surely, I need not say to you that, to a Southern man, the annoyance of being mixed up in a squabble with persons whom he does not know, and does not care to know—and from whom no Alexandrine process of cutting loose, would be permitted by society, would be an intolerable grievance. I submit to frequent injuries and misrepresentations, content though annoyed by the slaves [*sic*], that the viper should amuse himself upon the file, at the expense of his own teeth.

As a man, as a writer, I shall always be solicitous of your reputation & success. You have but to resolve on taking and asserting your position, equally in the social and the literary world, and your way is clear, your path is easy, and you will find true friends enough to sympathize in your triumphs.

Very sincerely though sorrowfully, Yr. obdt, Servt.

W. GILMORE SIMMS [782]

—all of which was most excellent advice. Amid the *pot pourri* of Poe's correspondence, against the emotional confusion of his nature, and his growing egotism, such letters availed little. What he more desired was admiration and sympathy. This was liberally supplied to him in the letters from Philip Pendleton Cooke, another poet, whose nature, judging from the passages in the works of Poe which he most admired, was in peculiar sympathy with Poe's. Miss Lynch continued her kindly interest in the family at Fordham, and, despite Poe's despairing letters to her, wrote, cheering him, and was of great charitable assistance. Poe was hardly in town at all at this period. One of the few references to his appearances in New York is contained in an undated letter from Miss Lynch (Mrs. Botta) in which his reciting a poem, perhaps *Ulalume,* at a Tuesday evening party is mentioned. [783]

Poe did little literary work at Fordham in 1846. In a letter to Chivers, in July, he notices the fact, and, on December 15th, he writes:

For more than six months I have been ill—for the greater part of that time, dangerously so, and quite unable to write even an ordinary letter. My magazine papers appearing in this interval were all in the publishers hands before I was taken sick. Since getting better, I have been, as a matter of course, overwhelmed with the business accumulating during my illness. [776]

Part of this business was loose ends, left over from the *Broadway Journal.* Some of the correspondence of the period was with G. W. Eveleth, a Maine man, who read Poe's work with admiration, took a keen interest in him personally, and has left some excellent contemporary criticisms of Poe. [784] June had brought a letter from Nathaniel Hawthorne, then at Salem, about *Mosses from an Old Manse* written on the seventeenth. He says:

[782] Postscript omitted—Simms was in New York, and too busy with a book on the press to visit Poe at Fordham, for which he apologizes. Letter frequently reprinted. The paragraphing has been supplied here. Letter in *Griswold Collection,* reprinted by Prof. Harrison and Prof. Woodberry.

[783] This seems to be the same recitation referred to by Mrs. Gove Nichols. See page 570.

[784] For the Poe-Eveleth correspondence see a *Bulletin of the New York Public Library,* edited by Dr. Thomas Ollive Mabbott. Also Prof. James Southall Wilson's *The Letters of Edgar A. Poe to George W. Eveleth, Alumni Bulletin,* University of Virginia, January, 1924.

. . . I have read your occasional notices of my productions with great interest—not so much because your judgment was, upon the whole favourable, as because it seemed to be given in earnest. I care for nothing but the truth. I confess, however, that I admire you [more] as a writer of tales than as a critic upon them, I might often—and often do—dissent from your opinions in the latter capacity, but would never fail to recognize your force and originality in the former.[785]

During the Summer and Autumn, by hook or crook, the inmates of the cottage at Fordham had managed to exist. As the Winter closed down upon them exceptionally cold (as the Summer had been unusually hot), poverty dire and inescapable, hunger and lack of clothing were now made doubly intolerable by extreme cold. There was a little stove in the kitchen, and an open fireplace in the parlor. The only cheerful recollections of the entire Winter came from the Catholic priest, who dropped in sometimes of evenings to spend a few hours before the fire with Poe, and engaged him in metaphysical conversation. As the Winter advanced, fuel was scarce. It became impossible to heat the little garret upstairs, and Virginia was moved down into the tiny bedroom next to the parlor. She was now unable to leave bed often, the end was so near. The Bathhursts, some kindly neighbors, sent food and fuel. In the snow-drifts the visits of the *literati* had ceased, and Poe and Mrs. Clemm were left alone to listen to the wolf howling at the door, and the whines of the winter wind that swirled the snow down the Kingsbridge Road. Mrs. Clemm alone ventured out, to "borrow" a few eggs or potatoes.

Virginia lay on a straw mattress, wrapped in Poe's cloak, for there were no blankets, hugging the cat to keep warm. In the little bedroom Poe could see her faint breath, as he bent over her holding her hands or feet to keep them from aching with cold. There must have been days when even the spring was frozen solid, and fuel was low; dark, winter afternoons and long, terrifying nights as Virginia fluttered down into the abyss, when it seemed as if all three must inevitably perish. Through it all persisted Mrs. Clemm's unceasing nursing of her two children, and the pride of "Israfel" and "Lucifer." Only the neighbors knew, pitied, and mercifully helped.

By what seems to have been a special dispensation, Mrs. Gove Nichols was impelled to make a visit to Fordham, apparently early in December, 1846. Poe and Mrs. Clemm were battling to keep Virginia alive.

I saw her in her bed-chamber. Everything here was so neat, so purely clean, so scant and poverty stricken, that I saw the poor sufferer with such a heartache as the poor feel for the poor.

There was no clothing on the bed, which was only straw, but a snow-white counterpane and sheets. The weather was cold, and the sick lady had the dreadful chills that accompany the hectic fever of consumption. She lay in the straw bed, wrapped in her husband's great coat, with a large tortoiseshell cat in her

---

[785] See, for a full discussion, Poe's review of Hawthorne in *Godey's Lady's Book* for November, 1847, Harrison reprints, vol. XIII, pages 141-155.

bosom. The wonderful cat seemed conscious of her great usefulness. The coat and the cat were the sufferer's only means of warmth, except as her husband held her hands, and her mother her feet. Mrs. Clemm was passionately fond of her daughter, and her distress on account of her illness and poverty was dreadful to see.

As soon as I was made aware of these painful facts, I came to New York and enlisted the sympathies and services of a lady, whose heart and hand were ever open to the poor and miserable. . . .[777]

Mrs. Shew, for it was to her that Mrs. Gove Nichols had appealed, sent "a feather bed and an abundance of bed-clothing and other comforts." She also headed a subscription among friends, and brought Mrs. Clemm $60 the next week, after which her visits and ministrations were untiring. The whole affair started a great deal of talk among the *literati* and in journalistic circles, now to a more humane and admirable tune. Indeed, in this matter, all the natural kindliness of the good but foolish women who had surrounded Poe, and of the editors and his social friends, comes out with a clear and merciful light. All the bigotries of literary cliques were temporarily forgotten, and natural human kindness came to the fore.

Mrs. Osgood received a letter from Mrs. Hewitt, written December 20th, which informed her of Poe's bitter plight.

The Poes are in the same state of physical and pecuniary suffering—indeed worse than they were last summer for now the cold weather is added to their accumulation of ills. I went to inquire of Mr. Post about them. He confirmed all that I had previously heard of their condition. Although he says Mrs. Clemm has never told him they were in want, yet she borrows a shilling often, *to get a letter from the office* . . . etc.

Mrs. Osgood was touched, and undoubtedly helped materially. She also spread the news, and wrote to her sister-in-law, Mrs. Locke, at Lowell, Massachusetts. Mrs. Locke sent Poe some verses and more substantial help. Mrs. Hewitt had undertaken to get up a subscription for the Poes among editors, so the matter got into print. "I fear it will hurt Poe's pride to have his affairs made so public." Soon afterward, greatly to Poe's own chagrin, this paragraph appeared in the *New York Express:*

We regret to learn that Edgar A. Poe and his wife are both dangerously ill with the consumption, and that the hand of misfortune lies heavy upon their temporal affairs. We are sorry to mention the fact that they are so far reduced as to be barely able to obtain the necessaries of life. This is indeed a hard lot, and we hope the friends and admirers of Mr. Poe will come promptly to his assistance in his bitterest hour of need.

N. P. Willis was much moved by this notice, and with his characteristic kindness, gentleness, and tact, published in the *Home Journal,* which he was then editing, an appeal and a touching eulogy of Poe. In this, under the guise of an appeal for his former editor, he advocated a house of refuge for authors. This was enclosed to Poe with a kindly note.

Poe was shocked that his affairs had thus been noised abroad, and replied, thankfully, but guardedly, saying that he had many private friends to whom he could have appealed, but that he deprecated public charity. The upshot of the whole matter was, that largely through the efforts of Marie Louise Shew, the Poe household was saved, and Virginia enabled to die at home surrounded by a few primary comforts.

Behind it all is the ghost of this poor little sufferer, seeming to revive at times, for her natural temperament was childishly merry, when little gifts were brought her, and she was surrounded for a while by the voices and kindly faces of friends. She had been married as a child to the loneliest and most ambitious man in the world. She seems to have clung to him pathetically, knowing him as no one else could. All attempts to present her real character must be forever baffled. What she was to others, she remains to us, an immature, sweet, and trusting, but scarcely visible girl-wife and invalided woman, caught by fate in the net of a tragedy, the strength of whose meshes she could no more glimpse than a fish seized upon by the trawler in dayless submarine valleys. About her there was, it must ever be remembered, the strange dignity of suffering and unfulfillment that requires, and yet mocks at tears.

Even at this desperate pass, we catch a glimpse of Poe *at work* in the little "parlor" at Fordham, the day before Christmas:

New York, *Dec.* 24, '46.

Wm. D. Ticknor, *Esq.* (Ticknor of Ticknor & Fields, Pub.).
Dear Sir,
I am engaged on a book which I will probably call *Literary America,* and in which I propose to make a general survey of our Letters. I wish, of course, to speak of Oliver Wendell Holmes, and as I can say nothing of him to which, you as his publisher, could object, I venture to ask you for a copy of his *Poems,* and any memoranda, literary or personal, which may serve my purpose, and which you may have it in your power to supply. If you could procure me his autograph, also, I would be greatly obliged to you.

You will of course understand that I should not feel justified in asking these favors, unless I thought, as all men do, *very* highly of Holmes.

Please send anything for me, to the care of Freeman Hunt, Esq., Merchants' Magazine Office, N. York.

Very truly and respectfully yours—
Edgar A. Poe [786]

Christmas Day, 1846, was passed with Virginia hovering upon the verge. During the last days of the year, Poe seems to have been working on the pages of his anthology while Mrs. Clemm, between intervals of nursing Virginia and receiving Mrs. Shew and others, went to get the mail, and scanned the papers eagerly for any mention of Eddie. The many reports about the family, and the echoes of the English contro-

---

[786] Letter in the *Justice Holmes Collection* in the Library of Congress, Washington, D. C. Courtesy of the Librarian of Congress, and the Honorable Justice Holmes.

versy had no doubt sharpened her eyes. The last hours of Virginia had been made more miserable by anonymous letters which were sent her, enclosing various reports circulated about the family's misery, and English's attack. Among the worst of these persecutors was the inveterate and ingenious Mrs. Ellet. Poe said that Virginia's end was hastened by Mrs. Ellet's pen.

Poe was now somewhat cheered to learn from Mrs. Clemm's gleanings from the public prints that his work was being republished, and attracting attention in England, Scotland, and France. The sight of Poe writing and corresponding, while Mrs. Clemm used her shears on the newspapers before the fire in the living room, with Virginia dying in the little room scarcely twenty feet away, is a curious but yet natural one. The wife's illness had become the familiar condition of the household for many years. Catarina walked about the cottage, her tail in the air, sometimes perching upon Poe's shoulder, or lying upon Virginia's bed. Mrs. Shew or Mrs. Gove Nichols dropped in, bringing dainties and comforts from the town.

On December 30th, Poe wrote his guarded and carefully calculated reply to Willis, and another letter to Duyckinck enclosing the news of his French republication, and the letter from Stonehaven, Scotland. The clock ticked on, and 1846 glided into 1847.

New Year's brought the shadow to the door. By the close of January it had reached to Virginia's bedside, and the end was at hand. On the twenty-ninth of January, 1847, the relatives and friends had begun to gather at Fordham. Among those who arrived on that day was Poe's "Mary," his old Baltimore sweetheart, to whom Virginia had carried notes as a little girl. To her surprise she found Virginia sitting up.

> The day before Virginia died I found her in the parlor. I said to her, 'Do you feel any better to day?' and sat down by the big armchair in which she was placed. Mr. Poe sat on the other side of her. I had my hand in hers, and she took it and placed it in Mr. Poe's, saying, 'Mary, be a friend to Eddie, and don't forsake him; he always loved you—didn't you, Eddie?' We three were alone, Mrs. Clemm being in the kitchen.[422]

One can see the poor, little, wasted body with the still plump face sitting propped up in the chair, gazing into the fire, with Poe and Mary on either side, thinking not of herself, but of what the future was to bring to her husband. She felt he needed friends. Mary went back that afternoon to New York, and Mrs. Smith (Miss Herring), the Poes' and Clemms' Baltimore cousin, arrived.[593 and 614] Towards evening, Virginia evidently began to sink rapidly, for Poe wrote to Mrs. Shew a letter that must have been delivered by a friend.

KINDEST—DEAREST FRIEND,—My poor Virginia still lives, although failing fast and now suffering much pain. May God grant her life until she sees you and thanks you once again! Her bosom is full to overflowing—like my own—with a boundless—inexpressible gratitude to you. Lest she may never see you more—she bids me say that she sends you her sweetest kiss of love and will die blessing you. But come—oh, come to-morrow! Yes, I *will* be calm—everything you so nobly wish to see me. My mother sends you, also, her 'warmest love and thanks.' She begs me to ask you, if possible, to make arrangements at home so that you may stay with us To-morrow night. I enclose the order to the Postmaster. Heaven bless you and farewell!

EDGAR A. POE

Fordham, *January 29, '47.*

Mrs. Shew came out the next morning. On the way to Fordham on the stage, she met "Poe's Mary" also bound for the cottage, and as they drove along through the bitter cold, they talked about Virginia.

Virginia was now lying again in her little cubbyhole of a bedroom on the ground floor. During the afternoon, she was still rational, and there was a final gleam. Mrs. Shew and Mrs. Smith were sitting by her bedside when Virginia took from beneath her pillow a picture of Poe, and the jewel case which had belonged to Mrs. Poe, the poet's mother, and gave them to Mrs. Shew. She also asked for two letters from Mrs. Allan which she had read to Mrs. Shew.[40] These, it appears, had been written to Poe after his running away from Richmond in 1827, were couched in affectionate terms, and begged him to return. They exonerated Poe from blame for the troubles in the Allan household. The letters, then or later, fell into the hands of Poe's cousin, Mrs. Smith. Eliza White also remembered having seen these letters. Could they be found, they might constitute an important piece of evidence in the story of Poe.[787]

Mrs. Shew said that Poe had denied himself many necessaries, and had suffered both cold and hunger to provide food and medicines for Virginia. At the time of her death, he was very ill. Virginia's passing must have had, for him, all the imaginative attributes of the mystic horror with which he regarded death, and her tiny bedroom have become the chamber where "Ligeia" strove fearfully to enter the corpse of "Rowena." Nothing was spared him. After nightfall apparently, Virginia smothered to death.

About all the tragedies that dogged the career of the man there was a complete, an ironically artistic, and certainly a Poesqueness that made them inimitable. After the death of Virginia, it was remembered that

---

[787] This incident constitutes an important link in the Poe-Allan mystery. Through Mrs. Shew is also traced the miniature of Mrs. David Poe (see note 40), also Mrs. Poe's jewel box, given to Rosalie in 1811. Rosalie may have brought this with her to Fordham on the visit in 1846. It shows, at least, that Mrs. Poe's mementoes and, by inference, her *letters* (see note 41) were also *still* preserved. Mrs. Shew says in her diary that the letters she heard read were from the *second* Mrs. Allan. This is an obvious mistake. It is impossible that the *second* Mrs. Allan should have written to Poe. It is *known* that she did not. All authorities agree on this. The letters were from the *first* Mrs. Allan, Poe's foster-mother.

there was no picture of her which the family possessed. Accordingly, while she still lay dead, propped up in her bed, a water color sketch of her was hastily made by one of the ladies present, showing her after she had succumbed, with her eyes closed. The sketch was apparently afterward retouched in its reproductions, and the eyes of the dead woman opened. It is this picture of Virginia with which the public has become familiar, through infinite reduplication. About it is all the air of tragedy and mortality, a certain creepiness which is associated with the popular legend of Poe.

Mrs. Shew provided a beautiful linen dress in which to bury Virginia, and she and Mrs. Clemm were assisted in their last ministrations by Mary, the adopted daughter of John Valentine, the owner of the little cottage.

On the day of the funeral, Virginia's coffin lay on the writing table before the windows in the little parlor. Some of the neighbors, the Valentines, and others came in. N. P. Willis, solicitous, and kindly to the last, came out from the city with G. P. Morris, his partner. It was very cold. Mary remained at the house. Poe, wrapping himself in the cloak which had but lately been used to keep Virginia warm, followed her to the grave. Mrs. Shew had hidden it but he had nothing adequate to wear, and the day was cold and gray. Virginia was borne down an alley of funereal trees, and left in the burial vault of the Valentine family in the graveyard of the Fordham Dutch Reformed Church, in the presence of her husband, Mrs. Clemm, Mrs. Shew, Mrs. Ann S. Stephens, and a few others.[788] Poe returned to the house where he was in a state of numbed collapse for some weeks afterward. Mrs. Clemm, in the desperation of poverty, tried to sell Virginia's gold thimble to Mary Devereaux before she left. Mary was too poor to buy it. Thus ended a long and haggard chapter of suffering. The tragedy of Israfel was about to enter upon its final phase.

---

[788] In 1875, owing to the destruction of the cemetery in which Virginia had been buried, the contents of the graves and vaults at Fordham were removed, or scattered. Virginia's remains were rescued by Gill, Poe's biographer, put in a box under his bed, etc.,—and, after exciting considerable gruesome and nauseous curiosity as the "bones of Annabel Lee," were finally taken to Baltimore and buried beside Poe, where they now rest. Thus fate was gruesomely consistent to the last.

CHAPTER TWENTY-FOUR

THE UNIVERSE AND MRS. SHEW

THE period from the death of Virginia, at the beginning of 1847, to the disappearance of Poe himself in October, 1849, may be regarded, conveniently, as exhibiting three stages, *i.e.,* a brief attempt at recuperation, and the staging of a literary come-back in 1847, under the care of Mrs. Clemm and Mrs. Shew,—which ended in failure and despair; the effort to find a refuge from self in two notable affairs with "Annie" and Helen Whitman in 1848,—also ending in despair and an attempt at suicide; the last Richmond period, lit by a brief gleam of the sunshine of old memories and the engagement to Mrs. Shelton,—followed swiftly by the end, at Baltimore in 1849.[789]

For some time after the death of Virginia, Poe was too ill to leave Fordham at all. Had it not been for both Mrs. Clemm and Mrs. Shew, it is morally certain he could not have survived. Nothing had appeared from his pen since the last of the *Literati Papers* in the October *Godey's Lady's Book* of 1846, except *The Cask of Amontillado,* probably written months before.[790]

Mrs. Shew now once more exerted herself, and was able to raise a purse of $100, to which General Scott—whose mind must have traveled back to a harum-scarum lad in Richmond at a ghost party years before, and to John Allan's handsome protégé at West Point—contributed, with some evidences of emotion, it is said.[356] Through Mrs. Shew, Dr. Valentine Mott had also been interested in Poe, and he and Dr. Francis saw him from time to time. There is considerable reason to suspect that it was the advice and warnings of this trained medical woman, and the two doctors that restrained Poe and enabled him to recover in so far as he did.

Even the first intense period of grief was broken in upon by the coming to trial of the libel suit in February.[791] The money received, and doubtless too, the sense of final vindication and triumph over his enemies, recalled Poe somewhat from his nightmare of sorrows.[791] At the same

---

[789] These divisions, of course, are purely convenient ones.

[790] Poe may have contributed about this time to the *Literary World,* contributions as yet untraced—see (Eveleth) correspondence, also Poe's reference to his file of this periodical to Mrs. Clemm from Richmond, September, 1849.

[791] See Poe to G. W. Eveleth, New York, March 11, 1847. Prof. James Southall Wilson's *The Letters of Edgar A. Poe to George W. Eveleth, Alumni Bulletin,* University of Virginia, January, 1924, page 14. Also see Chapter XXIII, page 566.

time, he was further annoyed by the charges of plagiarism made in Philadelphia over the book on conchology.[792]

Mrs. Clemm, poor old "Muddie," released from her long years of constant nursing of Virginia, now found herself with a new patient in Eddie. Nevertheless, she went out and bought some comfortable things. A new tea set, some carpets, and a lamp were the proceeds of the libel money. She and Eddie now had a few guests in to tea, and it was commented upon unfavorably that Mrs. Clemm took much pride in her new teapot, and that Eddie seemed fond of Mrs. Shew. To be sure Mrs. Shew *had* saved their lives—but then, "How could they forget poor, dead Virginia, so soon?"

In 1847 it was a great romantic advantage to be dead. Even the wailing harp of Israfel was not quite sufficient unto the woes with which it was so liberally furnished. Besides, in the notes from those strings, there had been detected a passionate, an almost lunar grief, that was not quite pretty. It was a little out of place in the drawing rooms where the weeping willow, and the lilies, and violets were appreciated,—but not the tomb itself. Mr. C. C. Burr, however, was adequate to the occasion and insisted that this was what his friend Poe was doing.[793]

Many times, after the death of his beloved wife, was he found at the dead hour of a winter-night, sitting beside her tomb almost frozen in the snow, where he had wandered from his bed weeping and wailing.

The age insisted upon it. Perhaps it *was* true. Mrs. Clemm tells us that Poe could not sleep; that the darkness and the lonely nights drove him frantic; and that she sat with him for hours with her hand on his forehead until, thinking him asleep, she would try to leave—only to hear him whisper, "Not yet, 'Muddie,' not yet."

There was a rocky ledge overhung by maples near the house that he particularly haunted. And there was a walk along the aqueduct path that, to the northward, at High Bridge, suddenly seemed to leave the earth behind, leading out on to a succession of granite arches, where, in the daytime, one could then look out over a great sweep of landscape, filled with blowing woods, white villages, and meadows that rolled away northward into the highlands and islands about Pelham Bay; or sank away eastward into the far, shimmering mirror of the Sound, streaked by the trailing plumes of steamboats, and flecked with sails. Down in the little graveyard below him, Virginia slept in the borrowed tomb

---

[792] Published in the *Saturday Evening Post*. See Poe to Eveleth, New York, February 16, 1847, Prof. James Southall Wilson's *The Letters of Edgar A. Poe to George W. Eveleth, Alumni Bulletin,* University of Virginia, January, 1924, page 12. In this letter appears Poe's defense, quoted in this book from another source. See Chapter XIX, page 356. Also see note 532, also Chapter XXII, page 501, and note 698.

[793] Charles C. Burr was a friend of Poe in Philadelphia. See Chapter XXVI, pages 649, 650, 651.

under the cypresses and pine trees.   Out of the sea behind Long Island
rose the moon.

> And now, as the night was senescent,
>   And the star-dials pointed to morn—
>   As the star-dials hinted of morn—
> At the end of our path a liquescent
>   And nebulous lustre was born,
> Out of which a miraculous crescent
>   Arose with a duplicate horn—
> Astarte's bediamonded crescent
>   Distinct with its duplicate horn. . . .

Since childhood Poe had loved the·stars, since the days of the telescope
at John Allan's house.[794]   In the pages of innumerable magazines he had
carefully read the astronomical notes, and followed the news of the
progress of that science as it was reported, decade by decade, in their
columns.[795]   And all this had led him to Laplace, and Newton, Dr.
Nichol, obscure works on physics and mathematics, Kepler, and
Boscovitch.

As Poe paced the arches of the High Bridge through the spring and
summer nights of the year A.D. 1847, the mysterious sleeping world
seemed to be cut away from beneath his feet, while over his head marched
flashing rank on rank "the armies of unalterable law."   He pondered
upon it all, upon himself, and upon the place of man in the scheme of
things, and he essayed to solve the mystery, which his own exalted ego
whispered that he could solve.   He could not bear to think that even God
should elude him.   There were two comments upon all this at Fordham
—*Ulalume* and *Eureka*.[796]   The poet's comment was strangled, but
withal splendidly strangled by the "Magnificent Logician."

In *Ulalume,* Poe, the poet, personified the constellations, reading into
them an allegory of his soul's predicament.   Once more, as in *William
Wilson,* he saw his own double.   It was Psyche, his soul, this time.
Bound on the great adventure of life, he and Psyche wandered together
in search of the beloved one, and came to the doors of a tomb.

There was a white, frosty starlight caught in these lines; a terror of
the great caverns of space haunted by the beasts of the zodiac; an element
of irresponsible cosmic will in the fatal hour marked by the star-dials;
a titanic alley of cypress for a mystic adventure with his own soul in a
demon landscape lit by the star-glimmering, miraculous crescent of the
goddess of passion.

---

[794] See Chapter VII, page 107, also note 183.

[795] The *Baltimore North American:* See *Poe's Brother,* George H. Doran Co., 1926.
Even as early as 1827 the *Baltimore North American* carried astronomical news typical of the "scientific" notes that interested Poe.

[796] The pronunciation of U-lalume as "Oolalume" is contrary to Poe's obvious fondness for the sound, "U" long ($\bar{u}$), repeated often in such words as "Eulalie." The "U"
in *Ulalume* is like the "U" in Uranus, Urania, etc.

> Astarte's bediamonded crescent
> Distinct with its duplicate horn.

A fancy from Hirst's or Chivers' trite verses had been transmitted, by genius, into an imaginative figure, an allegory of enormous significance.[601] Virginia, the little invalid maid who had represented for Israfel the maiden-like and chaste love of Diana, had passed away. For her, his tears were hardly dry when he beheld rising into the skies of his life, triumphant over all the lion dens of misery, the crescent of Astarte, who represented physical passion:

> And I said—'She is warmer than Dian:
> She rolls through an ether of sighs—
> She revels in a region of sighs:
> She has seen that the tears are not dry on
> These cheeks, where the worm never dies,
> And has come past the stars of the Lion,
> To point us the path to the skies—
> To the Lethean peace of the skies—'

And then a colloquy takes place between the poet and his own soul. A strange foreboding of love, of Astarte, has been discovered by his Psyche.

> But Psyche, uplifting her finger,
> Said—'Sadly this star I mistrust—
> Her pallor I strangely mistrust:—
> Oh, hasten!—oh, let us not linger!
> Oh, fly!—let us fly!—for we must!'
> In terror she spoke, letting sink her
> Wings until they trailed in the dust—

And then the alter ego "I," pacifies the soul, and kisses her out of her gloom, and conquers her scruples,

> And we passed to the end of the vista,
> But were stopped by the door of a tomb—

All the world knows the rest. " 'Tis the vault of thy *lost* Ulalume." It was only last year, Poe cries, "On *this* very night of last year . . . that I brought a dread burden down here." Just below him, in the misty lowlands among the trees, was the vault of Virginia.

> Well I know, now, this dank tarn of Auber,
> This ghoul-haunted woodland of Weir.[707]

In the few months that followed, the poet was to tempt his Psyche down the same vista at least three separate times. At the end, he inevitably found the same locked door of the tomb, until it opened for

---

[707] In *The Domain of Arnheim* and *Landor's Cottage* will be found descriptions of the same landscape under mist, and mystery that these two lines symbolize.

him alone. It was a species of despair that can be expressed only by the dirge-like name which he found written on the door. What it was in his nature that thus ended every love quest, whether it was the long frustration of his marriage, or a fear, even more deep-seated and abysmal, is a question that, if solvable, would go far to explain within him the conviction of tragedy and emotional disaster that rested upon him heavily for almost twenty years.

Thus the poet in him adventured with his soul and the stars. The mind of the man, now convinced of its great logical powers,[798] and under the necessity of so believing in itself, reached out even further into the abysses, and setting no bounds to its activities, beheld God breathing and inbreathing—through an endless succession of eternal cycles—atoms, and universes of stars. *Eureka* was written at Fordham. Let us descend from the aqueduct a moment into the cottage with Mrs. Clemm.

> He never liked to be alone, and I used to sit up with him, often until four o'clock in the morning, he at his desk, writing, and I dozing in my chair. When he was composing 'Eureka,' we used to walk up and down the garden, his arm around me, mine around him, until I was so tired I could not walk. He would stop every few minutes and explain his ideas to me, and ask if I understood him. I always sat up with him when he was writing, and gave him a cup of hot coffee every hour or two. At home he was simple and affectionate as a child, and during all the years he lived with me I do not remember a single night that he failed to come and kiss his 'mother,' as he called me, before going to bed.[799]

There is an enormous, an almost sardonic irony between the domestic scene, as described by Mrs. Clemm, and what was going on in the poet's mind. *Eureka* must have consumed a deal of coffee, and Mrs. Clemm would have been nearly walked to death. It was nothing less than the Eternal Spirit, brooding on the abyss and making it pregnant, streams of atoms "ruining along the illimitable inane" which now obsessed the poet's mind. Indeed, there is a close resemblance between Poe when he was pondering *Eureka* and "Lucretius," maddened by the love philter, and the enormous visions he was no longer able to save from the confusion of insane dreams.[800] The parallel in many ways is a true one, even to the events which followed.

It was a strange thing, this prose poem, a compound of many tides of thought at the time. It is the sophistry which Poe was forced to introduce into its pages in order to try to fuse its imponderable but antagonistic elements, by which the work finally falls. What was meant

---

[798] See Poe's comparison, in a note in *Eureka*, of his logical process in the prose poem with the same in his detective stories.

[799] R. E. Shapley in a Philadelphia newspaper, quoted by Woodberry, 1909, vol. II, page 236.

[800] See Tennyson's *Lucretius*,—and *De Rerum Natura*, by Lucretius, for the references. Harrison also mentions this parallel.

to be a chemical solution of ideas is found in reality upon analysis to be only an emulsion, but let us grant the fact, cleverly even subtly mixed. The unity is purely mechanical and literary, but *Eureka,* despite the bitter criticisms which it has received, remains a creditable piece of dialectic. Philosophically it is an Alexandrine concoction, but with this exception—it is animated by the imagination of an abnormally detached and exalted mind.

One hears very little of or from Poe during the Spring and Summer of 1847. The *Home Journal,* of March 13th, carried his lines addressed *To M. L. S.*—— (Marie Louise Shew) which are an expression of passionate gratitude to her for his preservation. Into those lines had already crept an attitude that was something more than gratitude, and a little less than love. Mrs. Shew had now been added to the pantheon of Poesque Angels in lines—

> By him who, as he pens them, thrills to think
> His spirit is communing with an angel's.

The next week Willis in the *Home Journal* inserted a notice announcing *The Authors of America, In Prose and Verse,* by Edgar A. Poe, as about to appear. This was evidently an advance puff for the projected anthology which never came out. Willis, from now on, printed and reprinted Poe's poems whenever he could in the *Home Journal,* and kept the legend of his genius alive by commendation and notices. He was, in short, a kindly disposed friend, inclined and able to be a good press agent. Willis undoubtedly desired to encourage Poe out of the despondency that had fallen upon him. He liked Poe, understood the cause of his weaknesses, and admired his genius. The effect of this championing by Willis in the *Home Journal* had an important bearing upon the rapid growth of Poe's fame. It was a powerful help. Poe kept writing to Willis, from time to time, telling him of his plans, and Mrs. Clemm called upon him frequently. The large spirit of Nathaniel P. Willis understood, condoned, helped, and still admired.

March, 1847, also saw the publication of *The Domain of Arnheim* in the *Columbian Magazine.* This was a revamped version of *The Landscape Garden,* evidently worked over to be resalable. The retouches, as usual, were great improvements, and shadowed forth vaguely some of the Hudson's vistas, or what is perhaps Harlem river scenery near Fordham. "Arnheim" is certainly the poet's name for his domain of retreat, but applies more strictly to "A mass of semi-Gothic semi-Saracenic architecture" that appears at the end of the story. This story, together with its earlier version of *The Landscape Garden,* alluded to before, is therefore a compound of early Richmond days and the Fordham period.[185] In it is the glorification of hermitage.

And a hermit Poe remained during the entire year of 1847. What few excursions he made into the world seem to have ended in disaster. He was then in such a delicate and precarious state of health that the least indulgence produced a state of collapse. Only while he remained at Fordham was he safe in Mrs. Clemm's care. We catch only a few glimpses of him in this sequestered existence.

Eureka and *Ulalume,* we know, were under way during this period. In the Summer, most of Poe's time seems to have been taken with gardening, enjoying country walks, and, probably, some boating (we hear in *Arnheim* about canoes). Poe was passing the time with "Muddie," the caged birds, and with the still flourishing and fondly cherished Catarina. Mrs. Shew occasionally came out to call, and once there were some English writers and travelers, who were charmed by this pastoral presentation of the poet in his garden with his cat, his flowers, and his caged birds.[801]

As spring advanced, he and Mrs. Clemm laid out some flower beds in the front garden and planted them with flowers and vines given by the neighbors, until when in May the cherry tree again blossomed the little abode assumed quite an attractive appearance. Upon an old "settle" left by a former tenant, and which Mrs. Clemm's skillful hands had mended and scrubbed and stained into respectability and placed beneath the cherry tree as a garden-seat, Poe might now often be seen reclining; gazing up into the branches, where birds and bees flitted in and out, or talking and whistling to his own pets, a parrot and bobolink, whose cages hung in the branches. A passer-by was impressed by the picture presented quite early one summer morning of the poet and his mother standing together on the green turf, smilingly looking up and talking to these pets. Here, on the convenient *settle,* on returning from one of his long sunrise rambles, he would rest until summoned by his mother to his frugal breakfast . . . "a pretzel and two cups of strong coffee"; or, when there was no pretzel, the crusty part of a loaf with a bit of salt herring as a relish. . . . He was fond of fruit, and his sister said of buttermilk and curds, which they obtained from their rural neighbors. . . . Most of his time, said Mrs. Clemm, was passed out of doors. He did not like the loneliness of the house, and would not remain alone in the room in which Virginia had died.[802]

About the beginning of August, 1847, Poe made a visit to Philadelphia, taking with him some articles to sell to *Graham's.* By August 10, 1847, he was back again at Fordham writing to someone connected with *Graham's Magazine* (probably Charles J. Peterson) from which it appears that—

Without your aid, at the precise moment and in the precise manner in which you rendered it, it is more than probable that I should not now be alive to write you this letter. . . .[803]

---

[801] The Englishmen speak of "rare tropical birds." There were a bobolink, a parrot, and canaries.

[802] *Home Life of Poe,* S. A. Weiss, pages 149, 150, 151. Mrs. Weiss constructed her accounts from various authentic recollections in this case. See note 777.

[803] This letter at the University of Virginia is minus an address, but was probably written to Peterson, the assistant editor of *Graham's Magazine.* Poe to ————, August 10, 1847, quoted by Harrison, vol. I, pages 270, 271, *Life and Letters.*

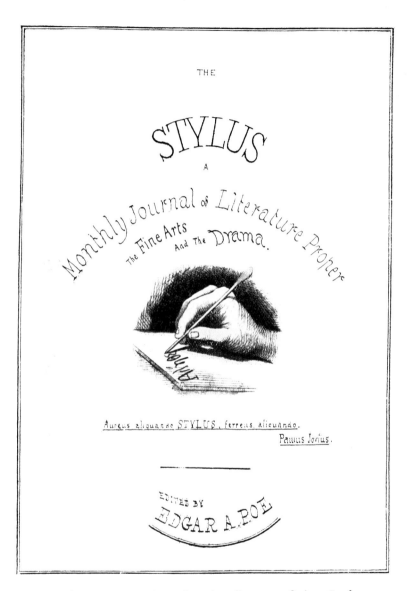

THE

STYLUS

A

Monthly Journal of Literature Proper

The Fine Arts And The Drama.

Aureus aliquande STYLUS, ferreus aliquando.

Paulus Jovius.

EDITED BY

EDGAR A. POE

Poe's Own Design for the Cover of the *Stylus*

Courtesy W. Van R. Whitall, Esq., of Pelham, New York

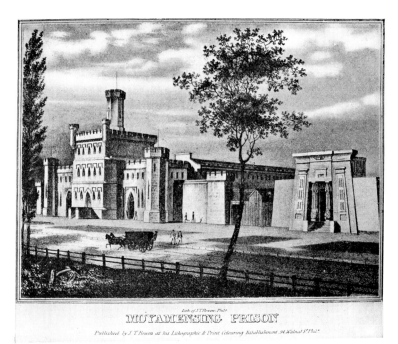

Where Poe was imprisoned for a night in September, 1849

Courtesy of the Pennsylvania Historical Society

Robert Sully
Portrait of the Artist by a friend

ROBERT SULLY was a close friend of POE from boyhood days. He was a nephew of THOMAS SULLY, and a son of MATTHEW SULLY, who had played on the stage with *Mrs.* POE. An artist of considerable ability, who is thought to have painted a portrait of POE

From a photograph of the original sketch
Courtesy of Miss Julia Sully and of the Edgar Allan Poe Shrine

The Fatal Letter

The "Lost Lenore" picture, thought to deal with POE's early love affair with
ELMIRA ROYSTER, and to represent the "Lenore" of *The Raven*. Given to
ROBERT SULLY, the artist, by POE with his own signature and a reference to *The
Raven* on the back, now obliterated

From a photograph of the original with signature
Courtesy of the Edgar Allan Poe Shrine, Richmond, Virginia

As to the meaning of which, there can be little doubt. Poe, in his already dreadfully disorganized condition, had taken a drink. He was, he said, "exceeding ill—so much so that I had *no hope* except in getting home immediately." [803]   He received an advance of $10 from Mr. Graham, who was kindly in his reception. Poe already owed Mr. Graham about $50.   Leaving two articles with the magazine, he now returned to Fordham. The first excursion, from the hermitage into the world of reality, had ended in swift, almost fatal disaster.

Poe's condition at this time, towards the end of 1847, is very difficult to apprehend justly. He seems to have been reduced to a quivering bundle of sensitive nerves by the privations preceding the great shock, for shock it was, of Virginia's death. From a medical diagnosis, upon which considerable faith may be put, only a few months later, it also appears that his heart was giving out, and that he was suffering from something akin to lesion of the brain. The trip to Philadelphia seems to show that the slightest indulgence in alcohol was to court death.

He was also troubled by a growing platonic affection for Mrs. Shew, upon whom, next to Mrs. Clemm, he now relied for help and sympathy. There can be very little doubt that, from time to time at Fordham, he resorted to drugs; Rosalie Poe specifically mentions morphine. He had now arrrived at that state of ego, with the writing and completion of *Eureka,* in which, as he phrases it, "My whole nature revolts at the idea that there is any Being in the Universe superior to *myself."* He states that he felt this feeling to be only natural in all men.[804]   In *Eureka* he had, by his metaphysical-cosmic theories, succeeded, he thought, in identifying all life as being a part of God, and, from that, he doubtless derived considerable comfort. By the end of 1847 he was now, once more, preparing to appear in the world, and to startle men by the announcement of his "discoveries."   Through Willis, he arranged to deliver *Eureka* as a lecture.

In December, *Ulalume* appeared anonymously in the *American Whig* as *The Raven* had done. Following out precisely the same scheme of calling notice to it, Poe now wrote to Willis who reprinted it the following month in the *Home Journal* with an inspired query as to its author.[805] Some minor interest was evoked. With the beginning of the new year, another instalment of the *Marginalia* appeared in *Graham's,* and a biography of Poe, by P. P. Cooke, came out in Richmond in the *Messenger.* Cooke's article was entitled,

Edgar A. Poe, an estimate of his literary merits. By P. P. Cooke,—the following paper is a sequel to Mr. Lowell's memorial (so-called) of Mr. Poe, published two or three years since in *Graham's Magazine.*[806]

---

[804] *Eureka.*
[805] Poe to Willis, Fordham, December 8 (1847).
[806] Poe to Cooke, New York, August 9, 1846. The notice had been arranged for the year before it appeared. Cooke's admiration for Poe continued.

The article concluded with what was, probably, an inspired paragraph by Poe, complaining about the small number, and the confined choice of Wiley & Putnam's edition of his *Tales*. "A reader gathering his knowledge of Mr. Poe from this Wiley & Putnam issue would perceive nothing of the diversity and variety for which his works are remarkable." A complete edition is thus hinted as being desirable.[806]

The lecture *On the Cosmogony of the Universe,* advertised to take place February 3, 1848, at the Society Library in New York, was to raise funds for the *Stylus,* now about to be resuscitated again, fortune permitting. In January, Poe had sent out the old prospectus again, with the added promise of articles on *Literary America*—a "faithful account of the literary productions, literary people, and literary affairs of the United States"—by the editor, of course. The Classical Department was announced as being in the hands of "the most distinguished of American scholars." This was Professor Charles Anthon, Poe's acquaintance of years past.[791]

Poe's friend, Freeman Hunt of the *Merchant's Magazine,* to whom Poe's mail was sent, had raised money for his own publication by making a personal canvass through the country for subscribers. Poe now decided to follow his friend's scheme. In January he had written to G. W. Eveleth that his plan was to go through the South and West, and there try to get enough subscribers to be able to commence with a list of at least five hundred.[807] The lecture on the universe was to provide the necessary traveling funds. N. P. Willis did his best through the columns of the *Home Journal* to advertise the lecture, and to smooth the way for the *Stylus.*

But even the weather was opposed to the *Stylus.* The night of the lecture was cold and stormy, and the hall none too well heated. Some sixty odd persons assembled, and listened to a rapturous address of lyrical logic for about two hours and a half. Poe must have read to them nearly the whole text of *Eureka,* or most copious extracts. Despite the disadvantages of the occasion, and the difficulties of the theme, the personality and eloquence of the lecturer made a memorable impression upon many of the auditors.

Poe's natural abilities as an orator and actor came out strongly upon such occasions as this. He is said, by people who had seen him, to have resembled Edwin Booth in some of the gestures and attitudes he used, and in certain aspects of his countenance.[808] His voice was thrilling, and wonderfully modulated. It must be remembered that he came

---

[807] Poe to Eveleth, January 4, 1848. Prof. James Southall Wilson's *The Letters of Edgar A. Poe to George W. Eveleth, Alumni Bulletin,* University of Virginia, January, 1924, page 19.

[808] Edward V. Valentine of Richmond to the author, July, 1925. Mr. Valentine made a bust of Edwin Booth, and also saw Poe.

of actor parents, and seems to have markedly inherited their gifts. There was always about him the air of the stage, something startling, arresting and dramatic. He seemed, to many, like a great tragedian off-stage, yet forever in the pose of his part. In the lecture on *Eureka,* Poe became the high priest unveiling the mysteries of God and Nature. So convinced was he himself, that, while the play lasted, the audience remained spell-bound, going away impressed, only to wonder later what it was all about.

The reports in the papers were of course ludicrous. Poe was grieved, and enclosed abstracts of the lecture to his friends, "to eke out a chance of your understanding what I really did say: I add a loose summary of my propositions and results":

The General Proposition is this—Because Nothing was, therefore All Things are.

1. An inspection of the universality of Gravitation—*i.e.,* of the fact that each particle tends, not to any one common point, but to every other particle—suggests perfect totality or absolute unity, as the source of the phenomenon.

2. Gravity is but the mode in which is manifested the tendency of all things to return into their original unity—is but the reaction of the first Divine Act.

3. The law regulating the return—*i.e.,* the law of Gravitation—is but a necessary result of the necessary and sole possible mode of equable irradiation of matter through space: this equable irradiation is necessary as a basis for the Nebular Theory of Laplace.

4. The Universe of Stars (contradistinguished from the Universe of Space) is limited.

5. Mind is cognizant of Matter only through its two properties, attraction and repulsion: therefore Matter is only attraction and repulsion: a finally consolidated globe-of-globes, being but one particle, would be without attraction—*i.e.,* gravitation: the existence of such a globe presupposed the expulsion of the separative ether which we know to exist between the particles as at present diffused: thus the final globe would be matter without attraction and repulsion: but these are matter: then the final globe would be matter without matter—*i.e.,* no matter at all: it must disappear. Thus Unity is Nothingness.

6. Matter, springing from Unity, sprang from Nothingness—*i.e.,* was created.

7. All will return to Nothingness, in returning to Unity. . . . What I have propounded will (in good time) revolutionize the world of Physical and Metaphysical Science. I say this calmly—but I say it.[809]

For obvious reasons, in a biographical narrative, it is not possible to discuss *Eureka* here. It contains what is, at *best,* a highly and cleverly elaborated sophistry. There are irreconcilable inconsistencies of thought in its thesis, with misapplications and misapprehensions of the data of science, even at the time that it was written (1847). Its chief virtue resides, even now, in a certain grandeur of imagination, and a vast breadth of detached vision, almost lyrically expressed at times in magnificent cosmic analogies. A successful apology for it cannot be made, and there is no necessity for doing so, when the central figure of a

---

[809] Poe to Eveleth, New York, February 29, 1848.

biography is not projected with the bias of a prejudice which calls for heroic propaganda. In justice, however, it must be said that *Eureka* cannot be easily brushed aside. It is by no means a fit subject for the sallies of "rash bavin wits." It must be remembered, in considering it in connection with Poe's life and the nature of his intellect, that the man was very ill, mentally and physically, when he wrote it. Despite that fact, it shows a certain logical ingenuity of no mean stamp, and a surprising scope and vigor as a synthesis of certain tendencies in early nineteenth century thought. Considerably more is to be learned from *Eureka,* even now, by pointing out and comprehending exactly where and why Poe was *wrong,* than by understanding why many of his contemporaries, who did not dare, nor fail so greatly, are so unimportantly right.[810]

One thing can be chronicled with certainty. The lecture on the universe did not provide sufficient cash to enable Poe to start on his mundane tour to solicit subscribers for the *Stylus.* Poe had hoped for three or four hundred in his audience. He had been forced to ask the Society Library to waive the payment in advance for the lecture hall, $15, and must, in the end, have come out of the affair with something less than $50 at best.[811] His enthusiasm for his theories was not a bit abashed by this, however. One catches a glimpse, about this time, of a man exalted. He now offered *Eureka* to George P. Putnam, lately of the firm which had published *The Collected Tales* and *The Poems,* and, in an interview with the publisher, discovered his unbounded hopes and faith in the importance of the "discoveries" in *Eureka* by suggesting an edition of 50,000 at once. Mr. Putnam was patient and kindly. He divided the estimate of the enthusiastic and exalted author by 100, and published an edition of 500, which sold very slowly.

Eureka: A Prose Poem. By Edgar A. Poe. New York: Geo. P. Putnam, of late firm of "Wiley & Putnam," 155 Broadway. MDCCCXLVIII,—a small book in board bindings published in March, 1848, was Poe's tenth published volume, the last of his lifetime. It was a 12mo of 143 pages. "With profound Respect," this work is dedicated to Alexander von Humboldt.

---

[810] A critique of *Eureka* has been left out of the text here as the bulk of an adequate discussion precludes its being included in a work of limited and biographical scope. There is no adequate discussion of *Eureka* extant. An attempt to relate it with modern discoveries in physics and astrophysics would be valuable and interesting. Einstein, and recent experiments in the nature of electricity, the behavior of atoms, and cathode rays might be included in the discussion.

[811] Poe to H. D. Chapin, Fordham, January 17, 1848. Mrs. Shew aided Poe to get permission to use the Library hall. At this time, Poe also thought of seeing John Neal about delivering a lecture at Portland, Maine.

PREFACE

To the few who love me and whom I love—to those who feel rather than to those who think—to the dreamers and those who put faith in dreams as in the only realities—I offer this Book of Truths, not in its character of Truth-Teller, but for the Beauty that abounds in its Truth; constituting it true. To these I present the composition as an Art-Product alone:—let us say as a Romance; or, if I be not urging too lofty a claim, as a Poem.

What I here propound is true:—therefore it cannot die:—or if by any means it be now trodden down so that it die, it will "rise again to the Life Everlasting."

Nevertheless it is as a Poem only that I wish this work to be judged after I am dead.

E. A. P.

After which follow 136 pages of text.

The returns from the book were small, and very slow to come in, so Poe now went ahead with plans to lecture elsewhere, *i.e.,* at Lowell and Providence. The Lyceum idea was just getting under way. It had developed from the Sunday lecture. These were often delivered in the afternoon, and even in the evenings from pulpits. The inevitable opposition of the clergy to anything secular or interesting invading their sacrosanct field, soon developed, and various societies were organized over the country that imported lecturers and people of note to the local circle of *literati* or *cognoscenti*. New England, the East, the middle West, and a few places in the South took up the idea eagerly, and lecturers and propagandists of all kinds began to make the rounds of city, town, and village. Mrs. Oakes Smith was the first woman to appear publicly before circles of some prestige. Later on, these Lyceums were turned over to the slavery question and trouble ensued. In 1848, Poe was preparing a new lecture to raise money for the *Stylus*. *Eureka* proving not to be a popular subject, he now turned to his *Philosophy of Composition* and *The Poetic Principle* which Graham had bought in manuscript, and began to turn them to account on the platform. These lectures included the recitation of poetry, his own, and selected bits from others with which he was able to make an impression.

In February, 1848, there was a Valentine Party at Miss Lynch's which Poe did not attend, as he was now *persona non grata* to most of the *literati*. At this gathering some verses from Mrs. Helen Whitman addressed to *The Raven* were read. These later on paved the way to an important affair with the "Seeress of Providence."

The rest of the Spring and Summer was taken up with the publication of *Eureka,* correspondence with Eveleth, and the disturbing vicissitudes of the friendship with Mrs. Shew. Of all the women with whom Poe was intimate during the latter years, Marie Louise Shew seems to have shown the most sterling essentials of a well-rounded vigorous personality. She was the daughter of a doctor, and, as has been previously noticed, herself a nurse with considerable medical education and experience, as well as the friend of physicians. This practical acquaintance, and familiarity with the essential physical verities of life endowed her with a genuine pity and humanity, and saved her from the quagmire of spiritualism and esthetic sentimentality in which so many of the starry sisterhood wallowed. She understood Poe, although she did not read his poetry and stories, unless addressed to herself, and she sympathized with the difficulties of his temperament, and his physical infirmities. More than this, she brought him food and clothing in time of bitter need, and made her house a haven for him after the death of Virginia.

Poe, on his part, began by regarding her with respect and gratitude, and ended by allowing her sympathy to lead him into an utter dependency, worship, and affection which became so pronounced that Mrs. Shew was forced to end her ministrations and association. In the Spring of 1848, Poe was much at her house. After Virginia's death it was like a second home to him.

Mrs. Shew had permitted him to help, and gladly accepted his aid in furnishing her drawing rooms. This he had done after the canons of taste announced in his *Philosophy of Furniture*.[534]

Louise! my brightest, most unselfish of all who ever loved me! . . . I shall have so much pleasure in thinking of you and yours in that music room and library. Louise, I give you great credit for taste in these things, and I know I can please you in the purchases. During my first call at your house after my Virginia's death, I noticed with so much pleasure the large painting over the piano, which is a masterpiece, indeed; and I noticed the size of all your paintings, the scrolls instead of set figures of the drawing room carpet, the soft effect of the window shades, also the crimson and gold. . . .[534] I was charmed to see the harp and piano uncovered. The pictures of Raphael and the 'The Cavalier' I shall never forget—their softness and beauty! The guitar with the blue ribbon, music-stand and antique jars! I wondered that a little country maiden like you had developed so classic a taste and atmosphere. . . .[812]

"The little country maiden" had also developed a classic common sense that read Mr. Poe, if she did not read his works, like a book. Poe was more than willing to be her "patient," and under her tactful care and diagnosis. He regarded her, like all women who showed marked sympathy, with

> The desire of the moth for the star,
> Of the night for the morrow—

lines, from Shelley, which he once pointed out as the truest characteristic of hopeless love that he knew. Poe, it seems, could not think of

[812] Poe to Mrs. Shew, undated, "Sunday night,"—Spring of 1848. Harrison, *Letters,* vol. II, page 297, quotes.

any love but the "highest love," *i.e.,* a hopeless love, and was fond of harping on the theme in both ink and conversation.

The Shew house was close to a large New York church and there, after the death of Virginia, we hear of Poe's attending service with Mrs. Shew. He sang well, she remarked, in a fine "tenor" voice, and knew all the responses. His mind must have traveled back to the old Monumental Church at Richmond, with Frances Allan standing hand in hand with a child in long past, golden days. It is one of the few records known of Poe in church in manhood.[813] The sermon touched on a theme that reminded him of Virginia, and reduced him to despair.

Sometime later in the Spring of 1848, Poe paid a visit to Mrs. Shew's house which resulted in the writing of *The Bells,* next to *The Raven* his most popular poem.[814]

Poe and Mrs. Shew retired to a little conservatory overlooking a garden, where they had tea. He complained to his hostess that he had to write a poem, but had no inspiration. Mrs. Shew, to help him, brought pen, ink, and paper, and, while they sat there, the sound of church bells filled the air, and fell almost like a blow of pain on Poe's hypersensitive ears and jangled nerves. He pushed the paper away saying, "I dislike the noise of bells to-night, I cannot write. I have no subject, I am exhausted." Mrs. Shew then wrote on the paper, "The bells, the little, silver bells"—and Poe finished a stanza, again almost relapsing into a state of coma. Mrs. Shew then urged him again, beginning a second stanza with "The heavy iron bells." Poe finished two more stanzas, heading them "by Mrs. M. L. Shew," after which he was completely unable to proceed. After supper he was taken upstairs and put to bed, where he appears to have lapsed into a coma. Mrs. Shew called Dr. Francis in. The doctor and Mrs. Shew sat by the bedside and noted his symptoms. The pulse was very weak and irregular, and caused the doctor to say, *"He has heart disease, and will die early in life."* Mrs. Shew had previously noted the symptoms also. Both of them felt that Poe was nearly dying, and that he was close to the verge of insanity. He remained for the night, but did not seem to realize his danger. The end was indeed near.

During the remainder of 1848, and part of 1849, *The Bells* went through many revisions. Three versions of it are known before it made its final public appearance in *Sartain's Union Magazine* for November, 1849, with the following notice:

There is a curious piece of literary history connected with this poem. . . . It illustrates the gradual development of an idea in the mind of a man of original

---

[813] Poe attended church with Mrs. Shelton in Richmond in 1849.

[814] Ingram: from a portion of Mrs. Shew's diary. Parts of this diary were read to the author by Prof. James Southall Wilson of the University of Virginia in July, 1925. Ingram gives only portions of the full account.

genius. This poem came into our possession about a year since—[December, 1848]. It then consisted of eighteen lines! They were as follows:

THE BELLS,—A SONG

The Bells!—hear the bells!
The merry wedding-bells!
The little silver bells!
How fairy-like a melody there swells
From the silver tinkling cells
Of the bells, bells, bells!
Of the bells!

The bells!—ah, the bells!
The heavy iron bells!
Hear the tolling of the bells!
Hear the knells!
How horrible a monody there floats
From their throats—
From their deep-toned throats!
How I shudder at the notes
From the melancholy throats
Of the bells, bells, bells!
Of the bells!

About six months after this we received the poem enlarged and altered nearly to its present size and form, and about three months since, the author sent an alteration and enlargement, in which condition the poem was left at the time of his death.

This kind of revision was typical of Poe's method.

The poem, however, was not of such a sudden birth as Mrs. Shew imagined. It would be possible to show that the poet had long contemplated writing a poem on the subject. Chateaubriand's *Génie du christianisme,* a source from which Poe adapted a number of items, suggests a poem on the subject of bells. A clipping said to have been found in Poe's notebook from *Poulson's Philadelphia American Daily Advertiser,* an obscure sheet, supplied the source of the word "tintinnabulation." This extract concerned St. Paulinus, Bishop of Nola, a source also drawn upon by Coleridge. This Bishop is said to have first introduced bells for the use of Christian churches in the Roman Campagna in A.D. 409. Pliny has recorded that ages before the Christian era the pagans used bells and called them *tintinnabula.*[815]

The inference is plain. It seems more truly the mark of a great creative mind that, out of such dross as this, Poe was able to seize the

---

[815] J. H. Whitty, *Poems,* notes on *The Bells.* The final draft of the poem was finished February 8, 1849; see Poe to Annie, same date. F. W. Thomas had a manuscript copy of *The Bells.* Poe also told Thomas that Dickens' *Chimes* was the final inspiration; from it comes the "high, high, higher up." See Poe's remark on lines in *The Valley of Unrest* in the *American Whig Review* of April, 1845, etc., etc., etc. This poem has one of the longest and most intricate histories of any of Poe's poems.

nugget of the word which most people suppose him to have coined. It was from such dry sources that the inspiration came, and not from the bottle.[816]

Mrs. Shew speaks of Poe's sleeping twelve hours after this collapse, and of his being taken home to Fordham by Dr. Francis—"the old man was odd but very skilful." Poe was evidently close to exhaustion. One must regard him, now, as being so delicately overstrung that the slightest emotional stress produced results out of all proportion to the cause. He was now, beyond doubt, in a thoroughly abnormal condition, and subject to delirious spells, and hours of wandering out of which he emerged to remember nothing of what had happened. At times his sleep resembled a coma. It seems to have been during the approach of one of these periods, when in a half-exhausted, sub-conscious state, that he produced the first draft of *The Bells*. It was finished and given an intellectual unity, from time to time, later on.[814]

On one occasion, Mrs. Shew says that Poe, in a half-dreamlike state, told her of a trip he had made to Spain where he had fought a duel, and had been nursed by a Scotch lady whose name he could not divulge. He showed Mrs. Shew a scar on his arm or shoulder which he said he had then received. From Spain, Poe went to Paris, where he said he wrote a novel that had later been brought out under Eugène Sue's name, etc., etc. This, of course, was a half-delirious recital of mythical events that has tended to confuse some biographers who desired to lay stress on Poe's foreign experiences and background.[814]

Friendship with a man in this state was exceedingly difficult. Poe's dependence, and affection for Mrs. Shew alarmed a woman of her experience and common-sense type. She realized that it could not go on. At the same time, she plainly saw that he needed the care and affection that only an acknowledged member of his family circle could provide. She undoubtedly advised Poe to look about him, and to marry someone who could, at once, provide him the means of existence and the care of a wife. Dr. Francis is said to have warned the poet that, unless he gave up all stimulants and excesses, the end was near. For a short time Poe seems to have heeded this, and to have restrained himself. Mrs. Shew now withdrew in a kindly, but firm way from further intercourse, realizing that she had done all that she could, and that any further intimacy would find her involved in the same kind of gossip which had driven Mrs. Osgood to Albany. In June, Poe received a letter from Mrs. Shew saying that her visits to Fordham and his visits to her must cease.[817] It was kindly but explicit. A glimpse into Poe's state of mind,

---

[816] Also see Woodberry, 1909, vol. II, pages 258, 259, for a similar version of the sources of *The Bells*.
[817] This is distinctly implied in Poe's reply.

and the result of his platonic friendship with this fine woman who had saved his life, and who now refused to be compromised, may best be obtained by reading the poet's reply written from his retreat at Fordham:

> Can it be true, Louise, that you have the idea fixed in your mind to desert your unhappy and unfortunate friend and patient? You did not say so, I know, but for months I have known you were deserting me, not willingly, but none the less surely—my destiny—

> 'Disaster, following fast and following faster, till his song one burden bore—
> Till the dirges of his Hope that melancholy burden bore—
>   Of "Never-nevermore." '

> So I have had premonitions of this for months. I repeat, my good spirit, my loyal heart! Must this follow as a sequel to all the benefits and blessings you have so generously bestowed? Are you to vanish like all I love, or desire, from my darkened and 'lost soul'? I have read over your letter again and again, and cannot make it possible, with any degree of certainty, that you wrote it in your right mind. (*I know you did not without tears of anguish and regret.*) Is it possible your influence is lost to me? Such tender and true natures are ever loyal until death; but you are not dead, you are full of life and beauty! Louise you came in [refers to some time when Mrs. Shew had been nursing him] in your floating white robe—'Good morning, Edgar.' There was a touch of conventional coldness in your hurried manner, and your attitude as you opened the door to find Muddie, is *my last remembrance of you.* There was love, hope, and *sorrow* in your smile, instead of love, hope, and *courage,* as ever before. O Louise, how many sorrows are before you! Your ingenious and sympathetic nature will be constantly wounded in its contact with the hollow, heartless world; and for me, alas! *Unless some true and tender, and pure womanly love saves me, I shall hardly last a year longer alive!* [818] A few short months will tell how far my strength (physical and moral) will carry me in life here. How can I believe in Providence when *you* look coldly upon me? Was it not you who renewed my hopes and faith in God? . . . and in humanity? Louise, I heard your voice as you passed out of my sight leaving me . . . ; but I still listen to your voice. I heard you say with a sob, 'Dear Muddie,' I heard you greet *my Catarina* [the cat] but it was only as a memory . . . nothing escaped *my ear,* and I was convinced it was not your generous self . . . repeating words so foreign to your nature—to your tender heart! I heard you sob out your sense of duty to my mother, and I heard her reply, 'Yes, Loui . . . yes,' . . . Why turn your soul from its true work for the desolate to the thankless and miserly world? . . . I felt my heart stop, and was sure I was then to die before your eyes. Louise, it is well—it is fortunate—you looked up with a tear in your dear eyes, and raised the window, and talked of the guava you had brought for my sore throat. Your instincts are better than a *strong man's reason for me*—I trust they may be for *yourself.* Louise, I feel I shall not prevail—a shadow has already fallen upon your soul, and is reflected in your eyes. It is *too late*—you are floating with the cruel tide . . . it is not a common trial—it is a fearful one to me. Such rare souls as yours so beautify this earth! So relieve its toils and cares, it is hard to lose sight of them even for a short time . . . but you must know

---

[818] These italics are here supplied as being prophetic, and as Poe's own comment on his need for feminine affection, and as an indication of his precarious health. He lived only a little over a year after this letter.

and *be assured* of my regret and sorrow if aught I have written has hurt you. *My heart never wronged you.* I placed you in *my esteem—in all solemnity—* beside the friend of my boyhood—the mother of my schoolfellow, of whom I told you, and as I have repeated in the poem [*To Helen*] . . . as the truest, tenderest of this world's most womanly souls, and an angel to my forlorn and darkened nature. I will not say 'lost soul' again, for your sake. I will try to overcome my grief for the sake of your unselfish care of me in the past, and in life or death. I am ever yours gratefully and devotedly.[819]

EDGAR A. POE

Thus Mrs. Shew had departed, leaving her words of farewell ringing in his ears—and her advice. *Feminine sympathy* was now essential to Poe. He seems to have desired an angel rather than a woman, and he now deliberately set about to bring one home to his cottage whence both his good angels, Virginia and Marie Louise, had departed.

In the poetry of Helen Whitman, Poe thought that he detected that quality and temperament which was his necessity, and he now set about to find this kindred soul. Strangely enough, disastrously, in fact, across this spiritual chase passed the vision of another woman whom he accidentally met. It was Mrs. Annie Richmond. To these, to make emotional confusion thrice confounded, was shortly added the name of his boyhood love, Sarah Elmira Royster (Mrs. Shelton),—and, through it all, danced the ghost of a magazine striving to be born.

Never was so fast disintegrating a nature torn amid so many woes and loves. Behind it all was "Muddie," patient, but ever hoping and urging, conniving, when necessary, in little harmless, but important subterfuges, to provide her dear Eddie with a wife who might bring him a competence, and the protection of a preserving love. "Muddie" was no longer his mother-in-law and aunt, but his mother in every act and thought. Mrs. David Poe had now been sleeping in her unmarked grave at St. John's in Richmond for thirty-seven years. Her husband's sister had long taken her place:

> Because I feel that, in the Heavens above,
>   The angels, whispering to one another,
> Can find, among their burning terms of love,
>   None so devotional as that of 'Mother',
> Therefore by that dear name I long have called you—
>   You who are more than mother unto me,
> And fill my heart of hearts, where Death installed you
>   In setting my Virginia's spirit free.
> My mother—my own mother, who died early,
>   Was but the mother of myself; but you
> Are mother to the one I loved so dearly,
>   And thus are dearer than the mother I knew
> By that infinity with which my wife
>   Was dearer to my soul than its soul-life.[820]

---

[819] *Ingram,* II, pages 157-159. Woodberry also quotes, 1909, **vol. II**, pages 261-264.
[820] Probably written later than the time order implied in the text indicates. Published in *The Flags of Our Union,* Boston, July 7, 1849, under title of *To My Mother.*

Despite Poe's attempt to lead a secluded life at Fordham, perhaps no period of his life was more carefully described by visitors and friends. Both his growing fame and the necessities of his poverty, coupled with the illness of Virginia, served inevitably to bring interruptions.   A portrait of him which was previously stated to have been painted about this time by Charles Hine, a Connecticut artist, has since been shown to be a posthumous picture.[821]

---

[821] *Facts About Poe,* Prof. James Southall Wilson. This is the most authentic text for the discussion of portraits of Poe. Hine also painted a portrait of Walt Whitman.

CHAPTER TWENTY-FIVE

A HANDKERCHIEF SOAKED IN ETHER

SARAH HELEN WHITMAN, the "Seeress of Providence," whom Poe had seen once, "once only," three years before, standing in her doorway, one night on Benefit Street, was the recipient of "some of the most perfect literary love letters" ever written.[822] To her they were the greatest, and withal, the most mysterious event of a life largely given over to listening to noises on the alleged other side of the veil,—to the rappings, the twitterings, and flutterings which intrigued, mystified, amused, and bemused an entire generation of Americans who traveled the road to Endor.

In the Summer of 1848, the ghosts held a caucus, principally in the northeastern part of the United States. Tables began to jig and dance, curtains became pregnant with the spirit of nothing, ladies went into trances—and hysterics. Spiritualism and kindred movements became the rage. There were few who were not at least impressed. It was a movement that had its roots much deeper, in the peculiar suppressions and conventions, the great underlying sadness of North America that has been mistaken for a literary convention, but that gripped the country, especially the young men and the middle-aged women, from 1820 to 1860, if pens ever wrote truth and pages can be read aright.

We can laugh, now, because we have forgotten, or do not know any longer what it was that drove thousands of rational people into intolerable little parlors, to holding hands, to listening expectantly—hoping for great messages from old tables about which their grandparents had gathered to discuss tea and politics, or cards and wine—we have forgotten what it was that made it necessary to "get beyond." There were, in 1848, two principal ways to escape the intolerant and, *par conséquence,* intolerable boredoms of what may be termed the official family existence of the Republic. One way was to go West; the other was to go "Beyond." Both, in the final analysis, were spiritual adventures upon different planes.

This restlessness for escape, inspiration, hysteria, or adventure, by whatever term one may choose to denominate it, was widespread, and had deep ramifications all over the country.[823] New England, of course,

---

[822] See Chapter XXII, page 528.
[823] Family letters and diaries in the author's collection show that, by 1852, spiritualism had emigrated, and was in full swing in Oregon and Washington Territory among the families of the pioneers. Séances were held in covered wagons.

claimed for its own manifestations the usual endemic virtues.   Yet the ghosts there might merely be said to be a little more rampant, if ghosts can be, their spirituality, especially about Boston and Concord, seven times refined.   Providence, Rhode Island, was, to a certain extent, included in the holy territory.   There, in the '40's and '50's, "the local citizens of the world of souls of Transcendentalism" discussed, as other groups were doing elsewhere, the life of the spirit transcendent above all material or physical demands, and discussed it so well and long that mysticism and idealism slipped imperceptibly into occultism, mesmerism, and spiritualism.

Mrs. Helen Whitman was the inspiration of the Providence group, and of quite an important little vortex of correspondence, and scattered friends who came under her influence.   She was delicately beautiful, veiled, mysterious, and elusive.   She dressed in light silken draperies, and, as she passed, shielding her eyes from the too garish light of day by a fan, one glimpsed a spiritual dream of womanhood gliding by upon dainty slippers, followed by undulating scarfs—and a faint, deathly-sweet odor of a handkerchief soaked in ether.

Life was just a little too vivid for this "Helen of a Thousand Dreams"—that is, real life—"her pleasant rooms were never pervaded by anything but a subdued light," and the ether seems, upon occasions, to have helped to blunt the too-keen edge of things.   She had never been very well.   She had heart trouble, and was much given to premature announcements by letter of her imminent departure, and to sorrowful but thrilling farewells to her friends.

Mrs. Whitman had her own troubles, however, and her means of escape must be charitably left to her own often notable and admirable devices.   Mrs. Nicholas Power, her mother, was of a very powerful turn of mind, so far as opinions went.   With many of these, her husband seems to have disagreed.   During the War of 1812, upon a voyage to the West Indies, he was captured by the British.   His return to freedom in 1815, however, did not coincide by some nineteen years with his return to his family in Providence.   They had been expecting him in the meanwhile until faith took on the foolish look of credulity.   Then Nicholas returned, suddenly.   The occasion was thus commemorated by his equally eccentric daughter Anna:

> Mr. Nicholas Power left home in a sailing vessel bound for St. Kitts,
> When he returned, he frightened his family out of their wits.—[824]

Helen's early life had thus been overshadowed.   The eccentric younger sister was a great trial.   The girls' father passed away leaving

---

[824] *Poe's Helen*, by Caroline Ticknor, Charles Scribner's Sons, 1916.   This book, one of the best in the Poe bibliography of comment, treats the Whitman-Poe incident in full, and gives an excellent idea of a remarkable American woman of the Nineteenth Century and her contemporaries.   The author is in great debt to the volume.

their common-sense mother in charge of three daughters, and a little property of her own. Helen had a passion for flowers, and spent much time in the rose garden behind the red house at Providence, and at the home of her aunt, Mrs. C. J. Bogart at Jamaica, Long Island, where, for a time, she went to a Quaker School. The Bogarts gave Helen her first taste of the world. She developed a fondness for reading novels and for parties, for scribbling verse and dabbling in poetry. In 1828, after a long engagement, she married, at the house of her aunt on Long Island, John Winslow Whitman of Pembroke, Massachusetts, a young lawyer with a sensitive archangelic face. After a few years he died, and, in 1835, Mrs. Whitman went back to live with her mother on Benefit and Church Streets in Providence. In 1838 her portrait, by which she is best known, was painted by Giovanni Thompson. This shows her at thirty-five years of age, as a young widow, ten years before she met Poe.[825]

Mrs. Whitman, who published poetry from time to time, about the end of the 1840's became greatly interested in spiritualism, in which she and Mrs. Oakes Smith found a congenial field. Trances, mediums, and the entire "experimental field" were explored by them. Mrs. Whitman was of too high a quality of mind to be hoaxed. She was "subliminally interested." Mrs. Oakes Smith, although apparently a more virile person, at last completely succumbed. The last reminiscences and utterances of Mrs. Smith, who did much toward the emancipation of women in America, were a babble of "spiritual" twaddle.

It will perhaps serve to throw some light upon Mrs. Whitman to follow her upon a trip to Niagara Falls with Mrs. Oakes Smith, "Mrs. Gould, the trance-poet, and others—made possible by the munificence of a wealthy merchant of New York—seven of us, so companionable that our journey was a dream of enjoyment."[826]

Travelers learn much of each other to be learned in no other way. Mrs. Whitman conformed but slightly to prevailing fashions or conventionalities. Her dress expressed herself: a slight lace tucker, a veil—now on the head, now in the hand—an invariable fan. Altogether she was a unique and attractive little person. Angels have a right to their own way, and it was natural that we should see only sweetness in the ways of Helena.

As we went through the long corridors of the *Cataract House,* it was needful for someone to follow and pick up the scatterings of our friend. In the flow of conversation, away went a shawl that had been tied carelessly about the waist; this was carefully picked up and retained not to interrupt the flow of the sweet voice in its gentle cadence of words. Next, down went the fan, followed by the veil; but the loss of this was final. In the cars, Mr. Day had provided India rubber aircushions, which made a nice rest for the head. Mrs.

---

[825] Mrs. Whitman was forty-five years old, and had been a widow for ten years when Poe came a-courting.
[826] *Diary* of Mrs. Oakes Smith, wife of Seba Smith. Extracts are here rearranged out of their order in the *Diary.*

Whitman had adjusted hers by the open window, but the intervention of some pleasant thought induced a turn of the head, *and out went the cushion!* . . . Sarah Helen Whitman once said of John Neal, 'He is remarkable amongst remarkable men—unique, wonderful.' She said this when we together met Mr. Neal at Niagara, and listened to his conversation which was great, even with the stupendous Niagara for accompaniment.

Mr. Neal's pen name it may be recalled was "Jehu O'Cataract."[827] It must be remembered that all this was Mrs. Whitman seen through the eyes of Mrs. Smith, who doted on her. There was another, and a genuine side. Men such as John Hay, George W. Curtis, Ellery Channing, Horace Greeley, and several others of considerable note, corresponded with her and visited at Providence. Her conversation, at its best, was witty and even biting. She was familiar with French and German literature, and interested in music and painting. Her poetry was the best of any writen by the *literati,* and on one or two occasions, attained a genuine note. Mrs. Whitman was aware of what was going on in her world, and played quite an important minor rôle in it. She was undoubtedly the most "civilized" woman whom Poe had ever approached.

Poe, on his part, as we have seen, was not unscathed by the occultism of his time, yet he managed to keep his head above it. His dabbling in it was for purely literary reasons. From it he obtained dramatic material for his art in story and verse, and the pleasure of indulging in enigmatic smiles, and scoffing asides. Andrew Jackson Davis, whose lectures on mesmerism Poe had attended, supplied, for his first book, perhaps the initial idea for *Eureka.*[828] Shortly before Poe and Mrs. Whitman met, we hear from Davis of a visit which Poe paid to his rooms, apparently in search of technical data for *The Case of M. Valdemar.* Davis, who claimed to be able "to look through people," beheld a strange, dark shadow that always lay before Poe, and a background of very dark hills, a sort of mystic and dolorous landscape about his head.

Poe's own mysticism was purely personal, and the subliminal landscapes which he created in his poetry, prose, and landscape sketches were the refuges and spiritual lands of his own darkened soul. It was for this reason that his poetry was more original than that of any other American poet of the age. It employed a symbolism which was

---

[827] See Chapter XII, page 207. John Neal was by no means the fool that this passage makes him out, nor is it characteristic of Mrs. Smith. This part of her diary is gushing over Mrs. Whitman.

[828] The author is indebted to S. Foster Damon, Esq., of Brown University, author of *William Blake, His Philosophy and Symbols,* for calling his attention to the influence of Davis upon Poe. Several interesting references to Poe occur in Davis' books that deserve the further attention of students. Davis' first book presents a cosmogony. See Davis' *The Magic Staff,* page 217, *Events in the Life of a Seer,* pages 18 and 19, *Answers to Questions,* page 63, all referring to Poe.

personally unique, but which yet finds an echo, and provides a refuge for those who can glimpse within themselves, or through experience, the islands of spiritual exile, and the scenery along the highways and byways of despair. Such experiences are deep and primary ones, vastly more important than the rational or decorative, and must remain forever an important field for the preoccupation of the poet's art.

Poe's refuge from life was not at the spiritual séance, or in becoming a pioneer. His adventure lay inward down into the ever darker and more mysterious gulfs within. In 1849, there was a great rush to the gold fields of California. It was an Eldorado that attracted many. The comment of Poe was this:

ELDORADO

Gayly bedight,
A gallant knight,
In sunshine and in shadow,
Had journeyed long,
Singing a song,
In search of Eldorado.

But he grew old—
This knight so bold—
And o'er his heart a shadow
Fell as he found
No spot of ground
That looked like Eldorado.

And, as his strength
Failed him at length;
He met a pilgrim shadow—
'Shadow,' said he,
'Where can it be—
This land of Eldorado?'

'Over the Mountains
Of the Moon,
Down the Valley of the Shadow,
Ride, boldly, ride,'
The shade replied—
'If you seek for Eldorado!' [829]

Poe was now definitely bound "down the Valley of the Shadow." The physical man, who was about to set out in search of a wife, and to encounter Annie and Helen Whitman, was a sadly jangled bundle of nerves. Any excess of emotion, he was unable to sustain without the use of stimulants, and stimulants were a fatal method of relief. Occa-

---

[829] First published in *The Flag of Our Union*, Boston, 1849; Griswold, 1850. See *Dreamland* for an earlier reference to "Eldorado." This is evidently one of Poe's last poems, about the time of the Gold Rush.

sionally, only two or three times now, before he disappeared over the edge of the world, the troubles of his impossible situation were embodied in a notable expression. For the rest, his pen was all but useless. A contrast of the bibliography of the last three years of Poe's life with those that had preceded it will, in bulk alone, disclose the evidence, and depict the story of his disintegration.

The appearance of the completely unstrung man from the refuge at Fordham, in the midst of the lives of the three women with whom he was now about to come in contact, was fraught, as might be expected, with tragedy, agony, and frustration. Knowing this, there were, nevertheless, motives which urged him on. He must once more bring someone home to the cottage who could supply that cherishing sympathy and physical nursing which he could not do without.[818] Means for the support of the home, and for establishing the *Stylus,* the "darling dream of his life," were included. In this course he was supported by the advice of Mrs. Shew, and the necessities of Mrs. Clemm, to whom he owed everything. But, by his pen alone, without the assistance of a dowry, he could no longer support Mrs. Clemm. In the Summer of 1848, sometime in June, the process of wooing began.

As early as February, Mrs. Whitman herself had opened the door. Miss Lynch, at her Valentine Party, to which she had invited N. P. Willis, Horace Greeley, Miss Sedgwick, Morris, Grace Greenwood, Bayard Taylor, Harte, C. M. Clay, Furness, Margaret Fuller, and Charles Dana, asked Mrs. Whitman to contribute a valentine.[830] Mrs. Whitman had been greatly moved by *The Raven.* Her birthday was the same as Poe's, and she felt drawn to him by his poetry, as he had been attracted by hers. Whispers of Poe's deep impression of the night in Providence, when he had first seen her, had reached her ears. N. P. Willis was addressed at the party as a "City Pigeon," and Mrs. Whitman's valentine poem was to the "Raven." Poe was not going about with the *literati* at the time, as he was under a cloud, but the reading of the valentine made a great sensation.

> Oh! thou grim and ancient Raven,
> From the Night's plutonic shore,
> Oft in dreams, thy ghastly pinions
> Wave and flutter round my door—
> Oft thy shadow dims the moonlight
> Sleeping on my chamber door.
>
> Romeo talks of 'White doves trooping,
> Amid crows athwart the night,'
> But to see thy dark wing swooping
> Down the silvery path of light,

[830] See Chapter XXIV, page 593.

Amid swans and dovelets stooping,
Were, to me, a nobler sight. . . .

Then, Oh! Grim and Ghastly Raven!
Wilt thou to my heart and ear
Be a Raven true as ever
Flapped his wings and croaked 'Despair'?
Not a bird that roams the forest
Shall our lofty eyrie share.[831]

Providence, R. I.—*Feb.* 14, 1848.

These verses were sent to Poe by Miss Lynch through Mrs. Osgood. Poe recognized the writing, having seen some of Mrs. Whitman's poetry before. Shortly after, "the Valentine" appeared in the *Home Journal* through the good offices of the "City Pigeon." Poe was thrown into a state of ecstasy upon beholding the lines. He took down his own volume of poems and read *To Helen.* The mystic circle was almost complete.[832]

Shortly afterward, Mrs. Osgood, who understood the reference to the "swans and dovelets," wrote to Mrs. Whitman.

I see by the *Home Journal* that your beautiful *invocation* has reached the 'Raven' in his eyrie (at Fordham) and I suppose, ere this, he has swooped upon your little dovecote in Providence. May Providence protect you if he has! for his croak is the most eloquent imaginable. He is in truth 'A glorious devil, with large heart and brain. . . .'

Poor little Fanny Osgood was dying of a cough, "which is killing me by inches, and there are not many inches left." She was anxious for news. The "Raven" had not yet "swooped" but he was about to do so.

In June, Mrs. Shew had broken with Poe. At a moonlight party at a neighbor's house at Fordham soon afterward, Maria McIntosh, one of the *literati,* was present and heard Poe raving about Mrs. Whitman, whom he had never met. Apparently, he was as much in love with her *then* as he ever was. Shortly afterward, Miss McIntosh went to Providence. She was a friend of Mrs. Whitman. There the matter rested for a while. A bewildering succession of events now intervened, which greatly help to explain the real nature of Poe's affair with Mrs. Whitman.

Since the publication of *Eureka* in March, aside from his correspond-

---

[831] Five stanzas omitted. See *The Poems of Sarah Helen Whitman.* Mrs. Whitman's sense in the last stanza quoted is "Wilt thou be (as) true a Raven as . . ."

[832] Statements in the text about Poe and Mrs. Whitman are made from the letters that passed between them, and from letters of Mrs. Whitman to Mrs. Hewitt, and others of the *literati,* after Poe's death.

ence, Poe had written nothing at all.[833]   In July, 1848, through Mrs.
Locke, Mrs. Osgood's sister-in-law, Poe arranged for a lecture to be
given at Lowell, Massachusetts, Mrs. Locke's home town.   The lecture was on *The Poetic Principle,* and was delivered on July 10th.   A
lady, who was present, described Poe upon the occasion:

> I saw him first in Lowell, and there heard him give a lecture on poetry, illus-
> trated by readings.   His manner of rendering some of the selections constitutes
> my only remembrance of the evening which so fascinated me.   Everything
> was rendered with pure intonation, and perfect enunciation, marked attention
> being paid to the rhythm.   He almost sang the more musical versifications.
> I recall more perfectly than anything else the undulations of his smooth baritone
> voice as he recited the opening lines of Byron's *Bride of Abydos,—*
>
> > Know ye the land where the cypress and myrtle
> > Are emblems of deeds that are done in their clime,—
>
> measuring the dactylic movement perfectly as if he were scanning it.   The effect
> was very pleasing.
>
> He insisted strongly upon an even, metrical flow in versification, and said that
> hard, unequally stepping poetry had better be done into prose.   I think he made
> no selections of a humorous character, either in his public or parlor readings.
> He smiled but seldom, and never laughed, or said anything to excite mirth in
> others.   His manner was quiet and grave. . . .   In thinking of Mr. Poe in later
> years I have often applied to him the line of Wordsworth's sonnet,—
>
> > 'Thy soul was like a star, and dwelt apart.'

It was on this visit to Lowell that Poe met Mrs. Annie Richmond,
about whom *Landor's Cottage* is woven.   In the story is a description
of his first meeting with Annie.[834]   Again it was the expression about
the eyes which attracted him, the abstraction of womanliness, rather
than the woman herself.   His great need of, and his desire for sympathy,
for some escape from his loneliness, is here evident.

> As no bell was discernible, I rapped with my stick against the door, which
> stood half open.   Instantly a figure advanced to the threshold—that of a young
> woman about twenty-eight years of age—slender, or rather slight, and some-
> what above the medium height.   As she approached, with a certain modest
> decision of step altogether indescribable, I said to myself, 'Surely here I have
> found the perfection of natural, in contradistinction from artificial grace.'   The
> second impression which she made on me, but by far the more vivid of the two,
> was that of enthusiasm.   So intense an expression of romance, perhaps I should
> call it, or of unworldliness, as that which gleamed from her deep-set eyes, had
> never so sunk into my heart of hearts before.   *I know not how it is, but this
> peculiar expression of the eye, wreathing itself occasionally into the lips, is the*

---

[833] An exception to this is the sonnet, *An Enigma,* in the *Union Magazine* for March,
1849, addressed to Sarah Anna Lewis, "Stella," the manuscript was sent to Mrs. Lewis
in 1847.   Mrs. Lewis was not pleased with the "Sarah Anna"; see Chapter XXIII,
page 552.   Griswold, 1850, follows the Lewis manuscript text.

[834] Poe himself makes this plain by various statements in letters to Annie and elsewhere.   He set great store by *The Domain of Arnheim,* and its pendant *Landor's Cottage* as having a hidden "spiritual" meaning.

most powerful, if not absolutely the sole spell, which rivets my interest in woman.
'Romance,' provided my readers fully comprehend what I would here imply by
the word—'romance' and 'womanliness' seem to me [835] convertible terms: and,
after all what man truly loves in woman, is, simply, her womanhood. The eyes
of Annie (I heard some one from the interior call her 'Annie, darling!') were
'spiritual grey'; her hair, a light chestnut; this is all I had time to observe of her.

It is to be noted in this story that, while the description of the woman
is that of Annie Richmond, the description of the cottage is of Poe's
own at Fordham, and that Poe thus imagined Annie at home in *his
own house* where he so often longed to see her.

There can be no doubt that it was she, of all women, who now most
attracted him. He was as near in love with her as he could be, and the
hours spent in the bosom of her family with her husband, her sister
Sarah, and little Caddy, seemed to him a dream of delight. Both Annie
and Sarah, Poe soon called by the name of "sister," the dearest epithet
he employed. His experience with Mrs. Richmond ran much the same
course as that with Mrs. Shew. The impossible and intricate relationship which followed was crossed by the malignant and the well-meant
letters of others with whom he had gone through the same formula of
platonic friendship.

Poe brought himself to the verge of the grave over Annie. His affair
with her, and the simultaneous one with Mrs. Whitman, were too much.
The resulting catastrophe revealed to him the inevitable *cul de sac* of his
wooings. In the terrible tangle he, at last, attempted to commit suicide.
Yet, at the very last, it was to Annie that his thoughts turned, even when
he became engaged to Mrs. Shelton in the Fall of 1849.[836]

Bearing with him the remembrance of Annie, with whom shortly
afterward he began to correspond, Poe returned to New York after
the lecture at Lowell. He arrived home July 13th. The proceeds of
the lecture, and two advances from George P. Putnam made on *Eureka,*
now supplied him with sufficient funds to start South in order to get
subscriptions for the *Stylus.*[837] On July 16th, Poe left New York,
while Mrs. Clemm remained at Fordham. Three days later he arrived
at Richmond. Here, once more among the acquaintances and haunts
of his boyhood, he gave way to drink, and disappeared for two weeks in
the lower haunts of the town. John R. Thompson, the editor of the
Southern Literary Messenger, was accidentally informed that the former and now famous editor of his paper was in a serious plight somewhere along the waterfront. He charitably set out to rescue him:

---

[835] This expression, or its equivalents, occurs again and again in Poe's stories and
poems. It is undoubtedly peculiarly significant as a symbol. Italics supplied here.

[836] Nearly all of Poe's commentators pick this or that woman "as the great love of
the poet's life." A list of Poe authors, and their favorite candidates for Poe's affection,
could be compiled. The reader is here left to nominate his own.

[837] Woodberry is followed here.

If you have ever visited Richmond, you may perhaps know that the business portion of the town and the sites occupied by residences exclusively are distant from the shipping by a mile and a half, so that very few persons not actually engaged in commercial affairs ever visit the landing at all. As soon as I heard the name Poe in this connection my worst suspicions were excited, and I at once took a carriage and went to seek him. It was a very warm day . . . When I reached the purlieus of this abandoned quarter, I learned that such a person had indeed been there, drunk, for two weeks, and that he had gone a few hours previous, without hat or coat, to the residence of Mr. John MacKenzie, some three miles distant in the country, alone and on foot. It was Poe. The next day he called on me with Mr. [Jack] MacKenzie. . . . I did all I could to restrain his excesses and to relieve the pressure of his immediate wants (for he was extremely indigent), but no influence was adequate to keep him from the damnable propensity to drink.[838]

Once at Duncan Lodge, the old home of the Mackenzies, Poe was in good hands. He had been welcome there since childhood, and Jack Mackenzie was still a firm friend. Rosalie was also still living there, and Poe paid frequent visits.[839] Most of his time, however, was spent in newspaper haunts. He made the office of the *Messenger* his head-quarters. Thompson's descriptions of Poe's doings in Richmond at this time are thought on good authority to be exaggerated.[840]

Poe, it seems, was able to call on Thompson at the *Messenger* office shortly after the spree along the waterfront, and he seemed little the worse for wear. He was also at this time seen about town by Charles M. Wallace, a local historian of some ability and accurate memory, who noted that, although Poe was drinking, he was never in a condition when he could not take care of himself. On one occasion Mr. Wallace was called from his bed by a prominent Richmond newspaper man, probably Thompson or Daniel, to meet Poe who was in a gay but select company of convivial spirits gathered at a neighboring tavern. The company was listening to Poe declaiming *The Raven* and *Eureka*.

When Wallace arrived, he found his famous fellow townsman discussing current events. Poe bowed in a very dignified way when introduced to Wallace, and although the poet's face was flushed and his manner nervous, he was by no means intoxicated. At the request of the by-standers, Poe then began his discourse, which, although it went on for fully an hour, proved to be eloquent and entertaining. It was probably on the atomic nature of the Universe.

J. R. Thompson apparently did not see as much of Poe on this visit

---

[838] Thompson to Patterson, November 9, 1849, *The American,* April 11, 1889. Harrison reprints, vol. XVII, page 403. Woodberry abridges (as followed here), 1909, vol. II, pages 270-271.

[839] Miss Rosalie Poe continued to make her home with the Mackenzies till the Civil War, and its attendant misfortunes overtook the family. An interesting account of a visit by Rosalie Poe to the ruined Duncan Lodge in 1865 occurs in Mrs. S. A. Weiss' *Home Life of Poe.*

[840] See J. H. Whitty, *Poems,* large edition, Memoir, pages lxvi, lxvii, also for the account of the "Daniel Duel," Whitty, pages 444, 445, notes.

as some of his later remarks would seem to indicate. In a letter to P. P. Cooke, written October 17, 1848, only part of which has been published,[841] Thompson said that Poe had left Richmond sometime before, after remaining three weeks in a terribly drunken condition, and after having declaimed *Eureka* in the barrooms. This is perhaps an exaggerated statement of the incident related by Wallace. According to Thompson, friends tried in vain to get Poe to sober up so that he could write. Thompson himself could get nothing from him but *The Rationale of Verse*, already prepared as a lecture. This he took, he says, out of charity. Poe's periods of lucidity were few and far between. One overhears in these accounts the shuffling of feet in barrooms, the exalted voice of Poe discoursing in a supra-inspired tone of the atom streams pulsing from the beating heart of Nothing, as *Eureka* is intoned above the clinking of glasses. Mr. Thompson was moved to close his letter to Mr. Cooke with words to the effect that Poe *was* a peculiar fellow.[841]

Despite some ponderable evidence to the contrary, it seems most likely that Poe did not see Mrs. Shelton (Elmira) while in Richmond in 1848. Thompson's statement of his constant intoxication is weakened greatly by many columns of matter which he wrote in his beautiful script at this time, part of which Thompson afterward gave away. There was a review of Mrs. Lewis's poems that appeared in the *Messenger* and a *Literati Paper* about her sent to the *Democratic Review*.

Of Poe's further doings in Richmond at this time, a number of recollections still exist. He remained about six weeks, passing his time about Duncan Lodge, the offices of newspapers, and his bachelor quarters with Pleasants, editor of the *Richmond Whig*. Very little work was done on the *Stylus* scheme, but there were readings in the parlors of friends. Poe saw Dr. Ambler, his old friend Robert Stanard, "Helen's" son, and Robert Sully, the artist, who, it is thought, may have done a portrait of him at this time, or in 1849.[842] He also attempted to call on his first sweetheart, Catherine Poitiaux, but was apparently in a condition which denied him admittance. The second Mrs. Allan and her family were no doubt informed of his presence in town and that he was indulging in drink. John Allan had been buried, and had been sleeping beside his wife Frances, for fourteen years. The second Mrs. Allan and her children, although still known as "the Scotch Allans," were much about in society, and had made the big house at Main and Fifth Streets famous for a rather lavish hospitality.[843] There is no

---

[841] John R. Thompson to P. P. Cooke, Manuscript, as noted by Mr. Whitty.

[842] Edward V. Valentine, Esq., informed the author in Richmond, in May, 1926, that he knew this portrait had been painted. It is thought to have been lost in a fire.

[843] The following reference fifteen years later is significant:
"Mrs. Scotch Allan (Edgar Allan Poe's patron's wife) sent me ice-cream and lady-cheek apples from her farm. John R. Thompson the sole literary fellow I know in Richmond, sent me *Leisure Hours in Town*, by a country parson." *Diary* of Mrs. James Chestnut, Jr., Richmond, November 30, 1863, page 258.

record of Poe having seen his "Aunt Nancy" Valentine, now a jolly but aging woman of a "charitable and social turn of mind." There were many affairs at the Mackenzies', however. Mrs. Weiss says that Mrs. Mackenzie had written to Poe, suggesting that he come to Richmond to try his fortunes with his old sweetheart, Elmira (Mrs. Shelton). This, however, is doubtful.

In Richmond, Poe again came into contact with a Mrs. Clarke, now a widow, with whom he had boarded at the Worthingtons' in 1835, while on the *Messenger*. To her he paid a good deal of attention. Mrs. Clarke deposes about such calls and gives a rather pompous picture:

> If there happened to be friends present he was often obliging enough to read, and would sometimes read some of his own poems; but he would never read *The Raven* unless he felt in the mood for it. . . . One day he came in with his sister and two of the Mackenzies and stopped with me. There were some other people present, and he read *The Raven* for us. He shut out the daylight and read by an astral lamp on the table. When he was through all of us that had any tact whatever spared our comments and let our thanks be brief; for he was most impatient of both. . . . I enjoyed a good deal of his society during the visit in 1847 [*sic*]. On his last visit I saw less of him. He was then said to be engaged to a Mrs. Shelton. Some said he was marrying her for her money. There was a good deal of gossip at that time concerning Poe. His intemperate habits especially were exaggerated and made the most of by those who did not like him . . . When he was in company at a party, for instance—you might see a little of him in the earlier part of the evening, but he would presently be off somewhere. . . . when a very young man he imitated Byron.[844]

The most intimate reminiscences of Poe, at this time, came from the Mackenzies at Duncan Lodge. It must be remembered that, to Poe, Richmond was home. It was the only place where he did not feel an outcast, but met old boyhood chums on the street. Here his fame was a boon instead of an annoyance and, for the first time since the death of Virginia, he seems to have cast off gloom, and to have returned to a semblance of the more merry and normal self of boyhood days.

> I am convinced that a great deal of Poe's unhappiness and apparent reserve and solitariness was owing to his obscure home life, which kept him apart from all genial social influences. At the North wherever seen out of his business hours, he appears to have been 'alone and solitary, proud and melancholy looking,' . . . With a few he was on friendly terms, but of intimate friends or associates he had not one so far as is known.[844]

In Richmond, all this was reversed, and the better and more human part of the man emerged. There can be do doubt that the visit in 1848 prolonged his life for a year. Martha Mackenzie, Jack's sister, was a charming girl, a compound of gaiety and happiness. . . . The stories of

---

[844] Mrs. Clarke afterward moved to Louisville, where she reminisced. Mrs. Weiss quotes, pages 159-161, 165, 166, 167. Mrs. Weiss, who can be followed safely in matters relating to the Mackenzies, is also further drawn on for the incidents at Duncan Lodge.

her wedding in October, 1848, and of the two weeks' celebration, are still remembered in Richmond as a golden streak in silver days.[844]

One evening, quite late, an alarm of fire was raised, and all the young men of Duncan Lodge, accompanied by Poe, hastened to the scene of disaster, about a mile further in the country. Finding a great crowd collected, and that their services were not required, they sat on a fence looking on, and it was past midnight when they thought of returning home. Gay young Dr. 'Tom' Mackenzie remarked that it would never do to return in their immaculate white linen suits, as they would be sure to get a 'wigging' from the old ladies for not having helped to put out the fire, and, besides, they were all hungry, and he knew how they could get a good supper. With that he seized a piece of charred wood and commenced besmirching their white garments and their hands and faces, including Poe's. Arriving at home in an apparently exhausted condition, they were treated by Mrs. Mackenzie herself, who would not disturb her servants, to the best that the pantry afforded, nor was the trick discovered until the following day. Mrs. Mackenzie laughed, but from Mrs. Carter, the mother of two of the culprits, and who was gifted with eloquence, they got the 'wigging' which they had been anxious to avoid. . . . Poe enjoyed it all immensely.[844]

In the garden at Duncan Lodge a number of the young men played leap-frog. Poe, as happy and boyish as they, indulged himself in a sport at which he excelled, and he was seen in the long green alleys of the garden, leaping and skinning over the backs of the others like a bird, easily excelling where his old friend Jack Mackenzie fell down. It is one of the few merry scenes, and almost the last, in which Poe is to be discovered.[844]

Besides private readings at the houses of friends, Poe appeared once in public. Mrs. Mackenzie, it appears, suggested that he should do so, and a reading was announced to be held in the music hall of the old *Exchange Hotel,* for which one hundred tickets were advertised at fifty cents apiece. It was Midsummer, and most of the better class of people were out of town. On the night of the reading only thirteen people, including the janitor, appeared. Among them *was said to have been* Mrs. Shelton (Elmira), who sat directly in front of Poe, before the platform. "Poe was cool and self-possessed, but his delivery mechanical and rather hurried, and on concluding he bowed abruptly and retired." Under the circumstances one could not expect much enthusiasm.[845]

By this time Poe's funds were no doubt exhausted. Thompson had helped him by allowing him to write for the *Messenger,* but about the beginning of September, Poe became involved in a quarrel with John M. Daniel, editor of the *Examiner,* that developed into a typically Poesque affair. Bad blood, it seems, existed between Poe and Daniel from the start.[846]

---

[845] This is very doubtful. Mrs. Weiss gives the account but, in this case, seems to have confused Elmira's attendance at the lecture in 1849 with the earlier one. Poe, we may feel fairly certain, did *not* see Mrs. Shelton in 1848.

The two could not agree about literature, and there was also a dispute over a debt of some kind. More serious than this, however, Daniel knew one of the Whitman family relations, and was overheard airing his doubts as to the motives of Poe's attentions to Helen Whitman. This came to Poe's ears while he was sitting in a newspaper office. He was infuriated, and wrote forthwith a challenge to Daniel scrawled on a newspaper headsheet. This he had carried to Daniel who refused to take the matter seriously. Poe's newspaper friends also regarded the matter lightly. The great poet, it seems, was not then in a condition to fight a duel. Nevertheless, under the code, satisfaction must be allowed him. After some little time, the matter was arranged.

Daniel, under the plea of not wishing to give publicity to the affair, consented to an interview at the office of the *Examiner*. There he waited alone and met Poe by appointment.

When Poe entered the sanctum, Mr. Daniel was seated quietly at his desk upon which were prominently displayed two very large, old-fashioned but murderous-looking pistols. Poe drew himself up very haughtily and demanded the reason for the interview. Daniel then explained that in order to avoid trouble with the authorities, the usual formalities might be dispensed with, and the two gentlemen present could satisfactorily settle their difficulties by simply walking to opposite ends of the room and taking a shot at each other.

Poe looked about him. The room was large; Mr. Daniel was very collected; and the two pistols seemed to offer a dilemma rather than the choice which had been officially tendered. The grotesque nature of the situation appealed to Poe's sense of humor, and, as he grew more sober and contemplated the pistols, caution gained the day. A few questions and explanations were exchanged and the trouble was patched up.

With evident relief, Poe then, in his inimitable manner, began to relate the story of the challenge sent by Edward Coote Pinkney, the Maryland poet, to Poe's old friend John Neal. There was a decided point to the anecdote as Poe asked Daniel not to turn his affair into ridicule in the columns of the *Examiner* next day, in the same way that Neal had ridiculed Pinkney. This was very neat, as it was Neal who had refused to meet Pinkney. Daniel appears to have appreciated how cleverly Poe had saved his own face by thus putting him, Daniel, in a parallel case with Neal. The matter then ended in laughter, much aided by the arrival of several mutual friends who had remained hidden close by in no very great apprehension of hearing pistol shots, it is said.

Poe then capped the climax by reciting as only he could, Pinkney's well-known toast:

> I fill this cup to one made up of loveliness alone,
> A woman, of her gentle sex the seeming paragon;

after which "all hands" retired to a neighboring barroom where other toasts confirmed the reign of peace.

Helen Whitman now once more enters upon the somewhat jangled scene. During the Summer, in July, Miss McIntosh and Miss Blackwell, who had both visited Poe at Fordham, were walking in the moonlight with Mrs. Whitman in her garden. Miss McIntosh then detailed to Mrs. Whitman Poe's remarks about her made about a month before. Miss Blackwell warned her friend about Poe, but in spite of that, Mrs. Whitman sent him a poem which was unsigned but in her own handwriting. This was sent to Fordham, and, after some delay, reached Poe in Richmond on September 10th shortly after or about the same time as the abortive "duel" with Daniel.[846] The lines were an obvious bid on Mrs. Whitman's part for the interview which she knew Poe was seeking:

> A low bewildering melody
> Is murmuring in my ear—
> Tones such as in the twilight wood
> The aspen thrills to hear
> When Faunus slumbers on the hill
> And all entrancéd boughs are still.
>
> The jasmine twines her snowy stars
> Into a fairer wreath—
> The lily through my lattice bars
> Exhales a sweeter breath—
> And, gazing on night's starry cope,
> I dwell with 'Beauty which is Hope.'

Of these lines Poe afterward wrote to Mrs. Whitman:

. . . but I have not yet told you that your Ms. lines reached me in Richmond on the very day in which I was about to depart on a tour and an enterprise which would have changed my very nature—steeped me in a stern, cold, and debasing, although brilliantly gigantic ambition—and borne me 'far, far away' and forever from *you,* sweet, sweet Helen, and from this divine dream of your love.[846]

It is quite plain from the context of this, and from the ostensible reason of Poe's trip to Richmond and the South, that he is not referring either to a possible wooing of Mrs. Shelton, or to the "duel" with Daniel, but to his plans to "tour" the South on the "enterprise" of promoting the *Stylus.*[847] The necessity for the controversy which has centered about this paragraph is difficult to understand. Poe's "gigantic ambition," of course, was to become the arbiter of American letters as editor of the *Stylus.* This was now given up to pursue Mrs. Whitman. He left Richmond immediately, probably on September 10th or 11th, and returned to "Muddie" at Fordham, prepared for his Provi-

---

[846] Poe to Mrs. Whitman, October 18, 1848.
[847] Considerable controversial material exists about this matter.

dence campaign. Mrs. Clemm, it is said, did not favor this particular
match. Her opposition, if she did oppose, made no difference with Poe,
as his subsequent moves clearly demonstrate.

He now secured a letter of introduction from his friend, Miss Mc-
Intosh, but, before leaving for Providence, took the precaution of
writing a note in a disguised hand, and signed "Edward S. T. Grey,"
purporting to be from an autograph collector. From the reply to this
ruse, he ascertained that Mrs. Whitman was at home. About the end
of September, apparently, Poe appeared in Providence, and presented
the letter of introduction.[824]

No time was lost: Poe declared that he was in love. "During a walk
in the cemetery I said to you while the bitter, bitter, tears sprang to my
eyes—'Helen I love now—now for the first and only time.'" This was
in a letter to Mrs. Whitman of October 1, 1848, with which a notable
series of love letters began.

The love letters of Edgar Poe and Helen Whitman have come to
occupy such an important place in the story of the man, and, of course,
the place in the history of the woman, that it has been difficult, in the
past, justly to evaluate them as records of human passion, or to see them
in their proper perspective in the biographies of the authors.

A considerable body of literature, mostly controversial, has grown
up about these letters, and the events which they detail, the very bulk
of which has caused them to loom with an undue importance in the eyes
of those who have turned them over, and commented upon them. Several collections of these letters exist in separate places, not only of the
love letters themselves, but of Mrs. Whitman's epistles written to Mrs.
Hewitt, Ingram, Gill, and others after Poe's death. Mrs. Whitman
was a prolific letter writer. She rushed into the breach to defend Poe,
and incidentally herself, after the Griswold attack. She became involved
in the miserable squabble that went on among the aging and jealous
survivors of the *literati* after Poe departed hence, which perplexed, annoyed, and exhausted Ingram, his English biographer.

Ingram attempted, through the conflicting and often deliberately
deceptive correspondence of these women, to get at the facts. Most
of the petty problems, such as, who was the original of "Annabel Lee"?
—and who did the most for Poe at Fordham?—and to just what extent
had Griswold lied, forged, and tampered with Poe documents and letters?—have now been satisfactorily settled, or allowed to rest as unimportant.

In reality, all of the aftermath inherent in the Ingram-*literati* correspondence can now be brushed aside, and must be evaluated as a purely
cluttering-up process in the difficult work of reconstructing the so extraordinary elements of Poe's character and doings. Those who carefully
sifted out the facts in the past deserve credit, but the time has now come

when the aura of academic controversy, and the fictitious value of collections of letters, and material dealings with what so and so long *after* Poe's death, must be cast into the limbo to which the scaffolding which has aided in the erection of the edifice of biography belongs.

The time has also arrived when the love affairs of the poet, and the correspondence in connection with them, must take their true place in his history, in conformity with the value which the events that brought them forth, and the known peculiarities of Poe's nature inevitably demand that they should take. This applies peculiarly to the Whitman episode.

In the first place, it must be remembered that both Poe and Helen Whitman were literary persons, and specialists in simulating, or recording passion and sentimental love in literary form. In other words, they could, upon demand, write an excellent love letter. The expressions in such letters, when taken at face value, imply a genuine passion behind them. Taken in connection with the known causes, events, and the final outcome of the affair,—and also considered along with the remarks made by both parties at the time and afterward,—the whole correspondence is removed from the electric rays of genuine human passion at white heat, into the phosphorescent glow of self-interest, romantic adventure, and secondary sentimental lovers' phraseology.

The Poe-Whitman letters will be considered here as documents emanating from persons whose idiosyncrasies are known, and as records in connection with the events which they delineate. The Helen Whitman incident, when considered in the perspective of the whole of Poe's biography, boils down to a hectic affair with one of three women who interested Poe from 1848 through 1849. Helen Whitman was one of *two* widows, each of whom, there can be little doubt, Poe hoped to marry for reasons necessary to his domestic comfort, and the realization of his ambitions. She was one of *three* women who engaged his attentions at the last. Of these three, Mrs. Annie Richmond seems to have received the type of affection from Poe which most nearly resembles love.

It is very doubtful if Poe at this time, in his depleted and disorganized condition of body and mind, could, in reality, support, or provide a genuine and complete manly passion for any woman at all. His whole appeal to Helen Whitman was on a sentimental "spiritual comradeship" basis. He appealed to her imagination, her literary self-importance, and her ambition. A year later, Poe became engaged to another widow, this time with the prospect of considerable property. He then disappeared over the edge of the world. To Poe, Helen was an incident disturbing to his pride; to Mrs. Whitman, Poe was the great adventure. To the day of her death she went on attitudinizing, sentimentalizing, worshiping, not her lover but "The Raven"; dressing up as Pallas, and writing second-rate poetry.

Let us be carefully just, and admit that there was inevitably some affection and respect involved. Mrs. Whitman was beautiful, professionally mysterious, and a personage. Poe was handsome, intriguing, romantic, and "divine." The friction of two such stars inevitably generated, perhaps at the time, considerable surface heat. It was only skin deep, however. The difficulties they encountered in their courtship are overcome a thousand times every day by normal lovers. Had they really possessed for each other the divine passion they professed, the opposition of relatives, and the tittle-tattle of gossip would have been brushed aside, and Mrs. Whitman would have become famous or pitied as the gifted and romantic partner of Edgar Allan Poe.

In the hectic championing of Poe by Mrs. Whitman, after his death, one senses a feeling of lost opportunity, and the necessity for the worship of an ideal to offset the reality. Poe seems, for awhile, to think that he had found his ideal of disembodied, angelic love. It must also be remembered that both correspondents had their literary reputations to live up to in writing love letters, and that the letters were phrased in the peculiar lovers' conventions of the mid-Nineteenth Century.

Abstractly, the Poe-Whitman correspondence is the essence of romantic passion; historically, it is a record of the flame of sentimental affection under forced draft. It blazed, wavered, and went out. The fuel of sustaining physical love was absent.

Those who desire a purely literary love feast can turn to the available publications of these love letters. For the reasons given above, they will be used here only as throwing light upon the events they serve to narrate. To these events we must now pass on.

Mr. Poe's letter of introduction to Mrs. Whitman was dated September 15, 1848, which leads one to date the first interview in the graveyard at Providence, as about that time. On October 1st we find Poe writing the first of his literary rhapsodies to Mrs. Whitman. On September 20th he wrote an open letter to C. F. Hoffman connected with the *Literary World* in reply to a critique on *Eureka*, in which he said, speaking of Laplace: "The *ground* covered by the great French astronomer compares with that covered by my theory, as a bubble compares with the ocean on which it floats," *i.e.*, Laplace was talking about the solar system and nebulæ; Poe was talking about the universe. In the meanwhile, the affair with Mrs. Whitman had already taken its first unfavorable twist.

In the first interview in the cemetery, Poe had compared his love for Mrs. Whitman to that ideal love of his *boyhood* for "Helen" Stanard. It seems to have been from this interview that the story about Poe's haunting "Helen" Stanard's grave, for the most part, took its origin, although he had also told about this early affair in Richmond to Mrs. Shew. Mrs. Whitman afterward gave the details of Poe's own story in *Poe and His Critics* (since published as *Was Poe Immoral?*), in which she explains the genesis of the early verses *To Helen*. Poe evidently laid great stress on the similarity of the name; Mrs. Whitman "discovered" that she and Poe were descended from the same ancestry (*sic*),[848] and that their birthdays were the same! Thus the stars had fated their coming together. At the very first Mrs. Whitman had shown Poe her poetry, which expressed a foreboding that he protested against:

> Oh then, beloved, I think on thee
> And on that life so strangely fair,
> Ere yet one chord of Memory
> Hath gathered in Hope's golden hair . . .

Oh, Helen, *why* did you show them to me? There seemed, too, so very especial a purpose in what you did. Their very beauty was cruelty *to me*. . . .

And now, in the most simple words I can command, let me paint to you the impression made upon me by your personal presence. As you entered the room, pale, hesitating, and evidently oppressed at heart; as your eyes rested for one brief moment upon mine, I felt, for the first time in my life, and tremblingly acknowledged, the existence of spiritual influences altogether out of the reach of the reason. I saw that you were Helen—my Helen—the Helen of a thousand dreams. . . . She whom the great Giver of all good had preordained to be mine—mine only—if not now, alas! then hereafter and for ever in the Heavens.— You spoke falteringly and seemed scarcely conscious of what you said. I heard no words—only the soft voice more familiar to me than my own. . . .

Your hand rested within mine and my whole soul shook with a tremulous ecstasy: and then, but for the fear of grieving or wounding you, I would have fallen at your feet in as pure—in as real a worship as was ever offered to Idol or to God.

And when, afterwards, on those two successive evenings of all-heavenly delight, you passed to and fro about the room—now sitting by my side, now far away, now standing with your hand resting on the back of my chair, while the preternatural thrill of your touch vibrated even through the senseless wood into my heart—while you moved thus restlessly about the room—as if a deep sorrow or a most pronounced joy haunted your bosom—my brain reeled beneath the intoxicating spell of your presence, and it was with no merely human senses that I either saw or heard you. It was my soul only that distinguished you there. . . .

On the very first visit to Providence, Poe, it appears, had proposed marriage. After the interview, before leaving Providence, Poe again visited the cemetery where, characteristically, he had chosen to propose to Mrs. Whitman.

In the morning [after the interview] I revisited the cemetery. At 6 P.M. I left the city on the Stonington train for New York. I cannot explain to you— since I cannot myself comprehend—the feeling which urged me not to see you again before going—not to bid you a second time *farewell*. I had a sad fore-

---

[848] Mrs. Whitman seizing on the similarity of sound between her family name "Power," and that of "Poe," invented a magnificent common ancestry for herself and Poe. "He was of the old Norman family of Le Poer, a name conspicuous in Irish annals," etc., etc.

boding at heart. In the seclusion of the cemetery you sat by my side—on the
very spot where my arm first tremblingly encircled your waist.

Mrs. Whitman had not given her consent, and shortly after Poe's
second visit wrote him raising objections, and giving vent to her forebodings. She was, she felt, not suited or able to support the burdens
and incidents which marriage would entail. She was older than Poe,
a widow, and an invalid. Four lines carefully scratched out in her letter
suggest that there were very definite reasons for not marrying—"I find
that I cannot tell you all that I promised. I can only say to you" . . .
(here follow the obliterated lines). In addition to this, Mrs. Whitman
had already been warned, probably by the Osgoods and others, of the
difficulties which might follow an entanglement with "The Raven."
The stories of the English controversy and of the Ellet-Lummis affair
had been detailed to her, and her whole letter palpitated with doubt.
That Poe's tempestuous wooing had shaken her, there can be no doubt.

It was to this letter that Poe had replied on October 18th from Fordham, pleading, defending himself, and exalting the love of the soul
which should transcend all entirely worldly considerations. This was
a powerful argument with the transcendental and spiritual Helen. How
much Poe believed in this himself it is difficult to say. He was now
laboring under great emotional excitement. The ugly head of gossip,
raised by Mrs. Whitman's letter, drove him frantic. Her personality
had undoubtedly moved him, and all his pride of nature was involved.
Failure threatened to strip him spiritually naked.

Very soon after Poe's letter of Oct. 18, 1848 and before I had replied to it,
he came again to Providence. During this visit he told me much of his earlier
life—much of his intimate history—and I became more and more deeply interested in him. He seemed to connect me strangely with his memories of Helen
Stanard and often declared to me that he had known and loved me ages ago.
    The name of Helen had a strange charm for him from an incident that hap-
pened in his boyhood. The mother of one of his schoolmates, who had spoken
a few kind words to the imaginative child, died suddenly and left a sweet and
sorrowful memory in his heart that seems never to have faded.
    I believe that the spirit of her who bore this beloved name, has always hovered
around him and that it was in some way, through *her* influence that he was dearer
to me. You may think this fanciful, but many strange incidents suggestive of
such psychical influences occurred to me at that period of my life. One evening
just after dusk, I went into a room dimly lighted by a coal fire. Poe was sitting
dreamily musing by the fireside. In a corner of the room hung an unframed
picture painted on a very dark background. . . . As I entered the room Poe
started up and said, 'Helen, I have had such strange dreams since I have been
sitting here that I can hardly believe myself awake! Your picture in the dim
light looked so like the face of Robert Stanard that it startled me. You remember that he was the schoolmate of whom I have spoken to you, the son of Mrs.
Stanard whom I loved so well. I never noticed the resemblance before, but
when you *see him*, as one day you will, you will see how strikingly this picture
resembles him.'

Duncan Lodge

The Home of the Mackenzies, foster-parents of Rosalie Poe and friends of the Poet

Duncan Lodge, named for MARY DUNCAN, was on Broad Street, just above old Richmond College and "Belleville"

From a photograph.   Courtesy of the Edgar Allan Poe Shrine, Richmond, Virginia

Poe's Trunk and Boot Hooks

Courtesy of the Poe Shrine

For the history of this trunk, now at the Edgar Allan Poe Shrine, Richmond, Va., see the *Valentine Museum Poe Letters*

The visit to Richmond had evidently renewed in Poe most vividly his memories of his boyhood upon which he now, in a half ecstatic and highly nervous state, pondered and dreamed. Richmond, it may be taken for granted, was the home to which his wandering and exiled heart returned all through his life. From his remarks to Mrs. Whitman it would seem that, after marrying her, he planned to live in Richmond.

From Providence, Poe went on to Lowell, Massachusetts, where he delivered another lecture. Here he once more visited "Annie". (Mrs. Richmond) at the village of Westford. That Annie greatly moved Poe it is perfectly evident. She and her sister Sarah, both of whom he called "sister," he took into his confidence. In his harassed and nervous state, the quiet and peace of the normal home of the Richmonds seemed like heaven to him. There were walks "to look at the hills," in the landscape evidently under the haze of the love that he endowed it with in *Landor's Cottage*. Mrs. Richmond's sister, Sarah, a young girl at the time, describes him:

> My memory photographs him, sitting before an open wood fire, in the early autumn evening, gazing intently into the glowing coal, holding the hand of a dear friend—'Annie'—while for a long time no one spoke, and the only sound was the ticking of the tall old clock in the corner of the room.

Poe remained some days with the Richmonds, soothed by Annie's comforting presence. He was awaiting Mrs. Whitman's decision.

About the second of November, he received from her an indecisive letter. This, and the complication of his now undoubtedly affectionate feeling for Mrs. Richmond, threw him into a state of nervous excitement closely akin to insanity. Poe wrote to Mrs. Whitman that he would see her in Providence on November 4th, and left the Richmond house for the interview with Helen, first extracting a promise from Mrs. Richmond that she (Annie) would visit him upon his death-bed. While Poe was at Westford, waiting to hear from Mrs. Whitman, *he had discovered that he could not live without Mrs. Richmond!* In his disorganized and weakened condition, the emotional conflict was more than he could bear.

Nevertheless, in a half-comatose condition, he set out for Providence, but once arrived there, the agony of his emotional dilemma reduced him to a state that made him forget, or unable to bring himself to see Mrs. Whitman. He says, in a letter written three weeks later to Annie:

> I remember nothing distinctly from that moment [the parting with 'Annie'] until I found myself in Providence. I went to bed and wept through a long, long, hideous night of Despair—When the day broke, I arose and endeavored to quiet my mind by a rapid walk in the cold, keen air—but all *would* not do—the Demon tormented me still. Finally, I procured two ounces of laudanum, and without returning to my hotel, took the cars back to Boston. . . .

Arrived in Boston, a town filled with many unhappy memories for Poe, it now occurred to him, in the emotional impasse at which he had arrived, to put an end to his existence in the same town where it had begun thirty-nine years before. Whether or not the conflict which went on in his nature was a primary one can best be judged by what occurred. He had now arrived at the confines of endurance. Whatever happened, however, he desired Annie to come to his death-bed, for—

... When I arrived [in Boston] I wrote you [Annie] a letter in which I opened my whole heart to you—to *you*. ... I told you how my struggles were more than I could bear. I then reminded you of that holy promise which was the last I exacted from you in parting—that promise that under all circumstances, you would come to me on my bed of death. I implored you to come *then*, mentioning the place where I should be found in Boston. Having written this letter, I swallowed about half the laudanum, and hurried to the Post Office, *intending not to take the rest until I saw you*—for I did not doubt for one moment, that Annie would keep her sacred promise. But I had not calculated on the strength of the laudanum, for before I reached the Post Office my reason was entirely gone, and the letter was never put in. Let me pass over—my darling sister—the awful hours that succeeded. A friend was at hand, ·who aided me. ... It appears that, after the laudanum was rejected from my stomach, I became calm, and to a casual observer, sane—so that I was suffered to go back to Providence.

Having thus failed to obtain another interview with Mrs. Richmond, even at the cost of trying to make it his death-bed scene—evidently Poe desired to die in her arms,—he now descended upon Providence to continue his suit with Mrs. Whitman. His face was distorted by his terrible sufferings, his eyes out of focus, and his mouth drawn all awry. It is that countenance which, unfortunately, has become best known to the world; the distorted face, the two sides of the man at conflict, which suggests his own terrible predicament, and perhaps a lesion of the brain.

Wandering about Providence half distracted, and without any sense of social conventions, he called upon Mrs. Whitman at so early an hour that she could not see him. She wrote to him at the hotel suggesting a meeting at the Athenæum later on, a favorite classical haunt of Mrs. Whitman. Poe replied (November 7, 1848) saying he was *very* ill and should, if possible, go home, but begs her for some word of love, and to say that "under all circumstances" she would be his.

During the night Poe had been taken care of at the hotel by a Mr. Mac-Farlane, a friend of the Whitmans. With considerable sense of the importance of the great poet whom he had in his care, MacFarlane took the opportunity, and led Poe around next morning, still half mad, to the establishment of Masury & Hartshorn where a daguerreotype was taken of him, probably at the very hour when he looked the worst that he ever looked in his life.[849] Mrs. Whitman, justly enough, labeled this

---

[849] Reproduced, page 557.

the *Ultima Thule* portrait, as it showed Poe immediately after being snatched back from the ultimate world's end of horror.

After thus helplessly having had the lineaments of his despair preserved for future generations by a solicitous fool, Poe now called at the Whitman house on Benefit Street—

> . . . in a state of wild and delirious excitement calling upon me to save him from some terrible impending doom. The tones of his voice were appalling and rang through the house. Never have I heard anything so awful, awful even to sublimity.

Mrs. Whitman was afraid to see him. Evidently the reports of his appearance were alarming; on the other hand, she was afraid of the consequences of a refusal. Her mother, who was opposed to the marriage, advised her to grant the distracted man an interview,—"moved by his suffering she urged me to soothe him by promising all that he might require of me." Mrs. Whitman's mother then endeavored to calm him for two hours while Helen, upstairs, was summoning courage to go down. Finally, in her usual dramatic manner, she entered. Of the dream which now burst upon the half-crazed vision of Poe we have an account:

> As she came flitting into the room and gave you her small, nervous hand, you saw a slight figure, a pale, eager face of fine spiritual expression and irregular features, the dreamy look of deep-set eyes that gazed over and beyond, but never at you. Her movements were very rapid, and she seemed to flutter like a bird, so that her friends asserted that she was always in the process of transformation either to or from the condition of a lapwing.[850]

It is perfectly plain that Poe regarded the comfort of the love of some woman as necessary to his salvation. He hailed Helen as if she had been an angel sent to save him from damnation, and clung to her dress so frantically that a piece of the floating muslin drapery was torn away. Mrs. Whitman's mother, as a calm common-sense soul, had some hot coffee brought to him. After a little while the older woman sent for a friend, Dr. A. H. Okie, who advised Poe's removal for rest to the house of another friend, W. J. Pabodie, "where he was most kindly cared for."[851]

[850] Description by Miss Sarah S. Jacobs, Helen's friend. Quoted *Poe's Helen,* Ticknor, page 5.

[851] The following facts of the events of the last few days in Providence are not "reconstructions," but come largely from a letter written by "Sarah H. Whitman" to her friend, Mrs. Mary E. Hewitt, on October 4, 1850, eight pages of fine script, detailing with great care the exact order of events, her own emotions, what occurred, who was present, etc., etc., at the time the engagement to Poe was broken. The author does not have the right to quote from the letter. New light has been cast on the Poe-Whitman affair by the following:

"The Yale University Press has published in pamphlet form a group of *New Letters about Poe,* reprinted from the *Yale Review* for July, 1925. The letters deal with the romance of Edgar Allan Poe and Mrs. Sarah Helen Whitman, and their broken engagement. The pamphlet is edited by Stanley T. Williams."

There were several interviews with Helen at the Athenæum, where Mrs. Whitman asked Poe if he had seen a poem called *Ulalume* that had appeared in *Colton's American Review* for December, 1847, a copy of which was then in the building. Poe then acknowledged to her that he was the author, and, as they bent over the verses, he read them to her and signed them. The magazine is still preserved at the Athenæum in Providence. In the same building, Mrs. Whitman gave her conditional consent to marry Poe, and at the same time extorted from him a sacred promise to let stimulants absolutely alone. It was the proviso upon which her own promise rested—and a loophole—a barn door of escape:

Poe left Providence on the 14th of November, and wrote back to Helen:

. . . It is five o'clock and the boat is just being made fast at the wharf. I shall start on the train that leaves New York at 7 for Fordham. I write this to show you that I have not *dared* to break my promise to you. And now, dearest Helen, be true to me

Of the parting that morning at Providence, and of the events of the day which followed, Mrs. Whitman has left an account which explains much of what afterward occurred. Poe had left with Helen's promise to marry him, given as we have seen on the advice of her mother, who evidently regarded it as merely a soothing formula to dismiss the half-mad suitor. A great deal of gossip was of course started by Poe's peculiar actions, and the sight of the pair wandering about together. Neighbors no doubt "called." Two or three hours after Poe left, the Whitmans were informed by "kind friends" of the whole Ellet-Lummis-Osgood affair, and of Poe's habits. Mrs. Whitman's mother was driven wild. Helen, it seems, had become more interested in the romantic Virginia poet than the New England relatives had thought possible. She spent, consequently, a very miserable day—her relatives beseeched and argued—property was involved.

Walking in her garden that night, Mrs. Whitman looked up and beheld Arcturus, a star beloved by Poe who had pointed it out to her. "During the painful scenes which followed, which I would if possible banish forever from my remembrance, I chanced to look toward the western horizon and saw there Arcturus shining resplendently through an opening in the clouds, while of all the neighboring constellations, I could see only Orpheus, in the head of the serpent, still glimmering near with a pale and sickly luster." Having in mind the serpent of gossip which was threatening her lover's star, Mrs. Whitman retired to her chamber and in "prophetic exaltation" wrote

ARCTURUS

(Written in October)

'Our star looks through the storm.'

Star of resplendent front! thy glorious eye
Shines on me still from out yon clouded sky,—
Shines on me through the horrors of a night
More drear than ever fell o'er day so bright,—
Shines till the envious Serpent slinks away,
And pales and trembles at thy steadfast ray.
Hast thou not stooped from heaven, fair star! to be
So near me in this hour of agony?—
So near,—so bright,—so glorious, that I seem
To lie entranced as in some wondrous dream,—
All earthly joys forgot,—all earthly fear,
Purged in the light of thy resplendent sphere:
Kindling within my soul a pure desire
To blend with thine its incandescent fire,—
To lose my very life in thine, and be
Soul of thy soul through all eternity.[852]

About the same time that Mrs. Whitman was looking allegorically upon Arcturus, Poe was drawing into Fordham on the little train to be met by "Muddie," no doubt in tears, and trembling over the terrible change for the worse visible in the face of her darling. *Arcturus* was sent to Poe soon afterward.

In the week that followed, Poe, in a half-delirious condition—Mrs. Clemm says he was "hardly recognizable,"—continued in the fitful fever of his conflict between Annie and Helen. He wrote to both Annie and Helen: to Annie, the account of his attempt to commit suicide; and to Helen a defense against the accusations of various kinds. In the last letter, the persecutions of Mrs. Ellet, which had hastened the death of Virginia, disclose the agony of a sensitive and quixotically constituted man under the torture of relentless gossips. Mrs. Ellet's part in the whole affair over her own letters, the threatened duel, and poor little Fanny Osgood's "honor"—she was now gasping out life in Albany—stands out clearly as a fine piece of feminine deviltry. All this was leading up to a conviction of persecution on the part of the

---

[852] Poe on receipt of these lines makes a reply that throws considerable light on his *own* methods of composition: "Your lines *To Arcturus* are truly beautiful. I would retain the Virgilian words—omitting the translation. The first note leave out.—61 Cygni has been proved nearer than Arcturus and Alpha Lyrae is presumably so—Bessel, also, has shown 6 other stars to be nearer than the brighter one(s)+ of this hemisphere—There is obvious tautology in 'pale candescent.' To be candescent is to become *white* with heat. Why not read—'To blend with thine its incandescent fire?' . . ." Mrs. Whitman made some of the changes, as the poem as printed here shows. Note— "Written in October" is romance to make the poem fall into Poe's "most immemorial year."

nervously shipwrecked man at Fordham, nursed by "Muddie," between periods of writing frantic appeals to Annie and her sister, love letters and epistles of defense to Helen, and a desperate appeal to Edward Valentine, his foster-mother's cousin, who had loved him as a little boy. This last was a request dated November 20, 1848, for $200 to start the *Stylus*.[853]

> If for the sake of 'auld lang syne' you will advance me the sum needed, there are no words which can express my gratitude.

It was to the same cheerful gentleman, now a minister, who had once felt the child's arms tighten about him in terror, thirty-four years before, as they passed a graveyard, riding upon the same horse.

Annie did not reply. Mrs. Richmond had also been illuminated by the same "kind friends," and was naturally alarmed. In a letter to Annie's sister, Sarah, Poe says, "Her silence fills my whole soul with terror."

To Annie

Indeed, indeed, Annie, there is *nothing* in this world worth living for except love—love *not* such as I once thought I felt for Mrs. Osgood but such as burns in my very soul for *you*—so pure—so unworldly—a love which would make all sacrifices for your sake. . . . Could I have accomplished what I wish, no sacrifice would have seemed to me too great, I felt so burning, so intensely passionate a longing to show you that I loved you. Write to me—. I am resolved to *get rich*—to triumph—for your sweet sake. Kiss dear Sarah for me . . . we talk so much of her. . . . Remember me to *all*—to your father and mother and dear little Caddy, and Mr. R[ichmond] and Mrs. C. . . .— And now good-bye, my own dear sister Annie. . . .

To Mrs. Whitman

22nd of November, 1848

I wrote you yesterday, sweet Helen, but through fear of being too late for the mail omitted some things I wished to say. I fear, too, that my letter must have seemed cold—perhaps even harsh or selfish—for I spoke nearly altogether of my own griefs. Pardon me, my Helen, if not for the love I bear you, at least for the sorrows I have endured—more I believe than have often fallen to the lot of man. How much have they been aggravated by my consciousness that, in too many instances, they have risen from my own culpable weakness or childish folly! My sole hope now is in you, Helen. As you are true to me or fail me, so do I live or die. . . .

Was I right, dearest Helen, in my first impression of you?—you know I have implicit faith in first impressions—was I right in the impression that you are ambitious? If so, and if you will have faith in me, I can and will satisfy your wildest desires. It would be a glorious triumph, Helen, for us—for you and me.

I dare not trust my schemes to a letter—nor indeed have I time to hint at them here. When I see you I will explain all—as far, as I dare explain all my hopes even to you.

---

[853] At the same time Poe wrote a letter to Miss Susan Archer Talley (Mrs. Weiss), to Richmond, asking her as a friend to use her influence with Valentine. Miss Talley replied in a formal note promising to do what she could.

Would it not be 'glorious,' darling, to establish, in America, the sole unquestionable aristocracy—that of intellect—to secure its supremacy—to lead and to control it? All this I can do, Helen, and will—if you bid me—and aid me.

To ANNIE (*November* 16, 1848)

Two days after returning from Providence with Mrs. Whitman's
promise of marriage

. . . I am so *ill*—so terribly hopelessly *ill* in body and mind, that I *cannot* live, unless I can feel your sweet, gentle loving hand pressed upon my forehead— oh, my *pure, virtuous, generous, beautiful sister Annie!* Is it not *possible* for you to come—if only for one little week? Until I subdue this fearful agitation, which if continued, will either destroy my life or drive me hopelessly mad. . . .

During all this time, Poe existed on the proceeds of his recent lectures. The *Stylus,* of course, was to make him rich (for Annie), and to enable him to reign as the arbiter of American letters with Helen by his side. To what confusion the death of Virginia had released him is apparent.

In the meantime, relatives were using their persuasive powers in Providence to break off the match there. Mrs. Whitman reserved her decision. On December 12th, or thereabouts, Poe again visited Helen, when matters went so far as to cause Poe to write a note to a minister, Dr. Crocker, asking him to have the banns of the marriage published on "Sunday and Monday" (following). Dr. Crocker was to perform the ceremony when the day had been decided upon. The relatives had failed to break off the engagement, but knowing Poe's failings, they insisted that an arrangement should be made to protect the family estate.

On December 15th, a marriage contract was drawn up between Poe and Mrs. Whitman at Providence, in which Mrs. Whitman's estate, consisting of about $8300 worth of bank notes and mortgages, was transferred to Mrs. Power, "our said mother for her own use." Poe, Anna Power, Sarah Helen Whitman, and her sister, Susan Anna Power, signed this in the presence of Henry Martin and William J. Pabodie, as witnesses. As Poe had stayed at the house of Pabodie, who was said to be in love, and long a suitor of Mrs. Whitman's (*sic*), much can be read between the lines.

Poe returned for a short stay at Fordham, informing Mrs. Clemm of what had taken place, and doubtless discussing with her the preparation of the cottage for the new bride. Mrs. Clemm was patient but saddened. The opposition of Mrs. Power to her daughter's marriage, and the transfer of the property that she insisted upon, had angered Poe and alarmed Mrs. Clemm, who was now about to be presented with a penniless daughter-in-law by no means used to the poverty in which Virginia had lived and died. Poe wrote to Helen saying *his* mother would return good for evil—and to expect him in Providence, Wednesday the twentieth. On that date, he left New York to go to Providence to deliver a lecture before the Franklin Lyceum. At the New York station he met Mrs. Hewitt, all agog over the marriage reports, who said to him,—"Mr. Poe, are you going to Providence to be married?" "I am going," replied he, "to deliver a lecture on Poetry"—and then added after a little hesitation—"that marriage may never take place."

The lecture was delivered successfully before an audience of about 1800 enthusiastic auditors. The next morning, Poe wrote to Annie!— "I hope that I distinguished myself at the lecture—I *tried* to do so, for your sake. . . . Give my dearest love to all—"

The lecture had been on Wednesday, December 20, 1848; the note to Annie is dated Thursday. It was probably upon this same day that he obtained Mrs. Whitman's final consent to marry him on the following Monday. On Friday the twenty-second, a further consent to the release of the property of Mrs. Whitman was signed by Poe in the presence of Pabodie, to whom Poe, next day, Saturday, gave the note to the minister to publish the banns. Pabodie did not deliver it. At the same time, Poe wrote a letter to Mrs. Clemm:

MY OWN DEAR MOTHER—We shall be married on Monday, and will be at Fordham on Tuesday, in the first train.

This was on Saturday, December 23rd, and Poe expected Dr. Crocker to publish the banns on the morrow at church.

On the morning of the same day (Saturday), he and Mrs. Whitman took a drive together. Helen then returned to the house to pack, and met Poe later in the afternoon at a circulating library. Here a letter was handed to Mrs. Whitman cautioning her against the marriage, and informing her of Poe's interest in Mrs. Richmond, which had created a scandal at Lowell. Mrs. Whitman also learned, possibly through Pabodie, that the same morning, at the bar of the *Earl House,* Poe had been seen drinking wine with some gay young friends there at the bar. This convinced her that her influence would be futile in reforming him.[851]

On the way home, Helen informed Poe of what she had heard, and while he was still present, countermanded the publication of the banns. Poe vehemently denied that he had been drinking, and there was no evidence whatever in his manner that he had been doing so, so Mrs. Whitman says. She listened to his remonstrances and denials with despair, she adds, yet not unsolaced by the sense of relief that his infringement of his promise had released her from her own. It was plain to her now that Poe's plea to save him had imposed upon her a responsibility, and a mission which, in spite of all, would be in vain. The incident at the *Earl House* bar showed her that her marriage with him could bring no benefits to either, and nothing but misery on them both.[851] There can be no doubt that, so far as human wisdom can see, Mrs. Whitman was eminently correct in her forebodings.

Poe withdrew, and Mrs. Whitman informed her mother of what had occurred. That lady, anxious to have Poe out of town, sent for him in the late afternoon to put a final quietus upon the affair, and to return some papers to him. Pabodie accompanied Poe to the house where Mrs. Whitman and her mother, Mrs. Power, received the gentlemen in the same parlor where the courtship had gone on. Helen was worn out by argument and appeal, nearly hysterical, and about to faint.

With trembling hands she returned to Poe certain letters and papers, and overcome by her emotions fell back on a couch pressing the anesthetic kerchief to her face. Poe came over beside her and begged her to say that it was not to be a final interview. Mrs. Power here interposed to save her daughter by mentioning the hour of the departure of the next train for New York, and hoping fervently that Mr. Poe would not miss it. At this, Poe fell upon his knees, begging Helen to reconsider. Finally she murmured, "What can I say?"

"Say that you love me, Helen!" he begged. Pressing closer he heard the last words that she ever spoke to him, "I love you"—whispered in accents of despair through a handkerchief soaked in ether.

Mr. Pabodie accompanied Mr. Poe to the station.

CHAPTER TWENTY-SIX

LENORE AND THE EDGE OF THE WORLD

MRS. CLEMM, poor soul, who had no doubt been wondering what her status would be in the household with the new wife, was greatly relieved when the train pulled into Fordham with Eddie—and no bride. Poe's reactions to the whole affair were curious. He was one of those personalities in whom pride and conscience are synonymous. His pride had been wounded, and he never forgave that. He hoped to pass the whole matter off quietly, by giving out that the engagement had been postponed. In this report he desired Mrs. Whitman to join.

The emotional tempest which he had just passed through had worn itself out, and, as it were, cleared the atmosphere. From the total of the correspondence which immediately followed, one gathers a distinct feeling of relief, and a sense of settling down to the real business of his life, writing. The last Christmas was spent with "Muddie" at Fordham, and, along with a feeling of relief and a deceptive vigor, there was a temporary rise in the tide of well-being, even a sense of returning health as the New Year's bells rang for 1849.

What the world thought of the engagement with Helen Whitman is caught in the lines of a letter that Horace Greeley wrote to Griswold in January—evidently he had not yet learned that the engagement was broken.

Do you know Sarah Helen Whitman? Of course, you have heard it rumored that she is to marry Poe. Well, she has seemed to me a good girl, and—you know what Poe is. Now I know a widow of doubtful age will marry almost any sort of a white man, but this seems to me a terrible conjunction. Has Mrs. Whitman no friend within your knowledge that could faithfully explain Poe to her? I never attempted this sort of thing but once, and the net product was two enemies and the hastening of the marriage; but I do think she must be deceived. Mrs. Osgood must know her. . . .[854]

About the same time, Poe was writing to Annie, saying that "a great burden is taken off my heart by my rupture with Mrs. W., for I have fully made up my mind to break the engagement." He was not able to maintain this pose, however, as the reports of the doings in Providence were soon flying about, with the usual tendency of the gossips' snowball to grow into an avalanche, when once set rolling. Towards the end of

---

[854] *Griswold's Correspondence,* page 249. Printed by Harrison, *Life,* page 290.

January, Poe again wrote to Annie enclosing, to her, a letter to Mrs. Whitman to be read first by Annie, then to be sealed, and mailed to Mrs. Whitman. This was to clear himself with Annie, who had heard the gossip about the last scenes at Providence, and, at the same time, to assure Mrs. Whitman that he was not responsible for the reports going about, "No amount of provocation shall enduce me to speak ill of you [Helen] even in my own defense."[855]

The truth is, Poe was heartily sick of it all. He was still determined to do something to alleviate his poverty, which left him no chance to rest, but, in the same letter to Annie, in which he enclosed Mrs. Whitman's, he boils over and remarks:

. . . Of one thing rest assured, from this day forth, I shun the pestilential society of literary women. They are a heartless, unnatural venomous, dishonorable set, with no guiding principle but inordinate self-esteem. Mrs. Osgood is the only exception I know. . . .[856]

It was a natural, although certainly, under the circumstances of the letter and its enclosure, not a delicate thing to say.

About the room in the cottage of Fordham, where he now began once more to throw himself into writing almost as a feverish refuge, an immense web of gossip began to gather. It had, as a matter of fact, very little to do with what has made him famous. The curious student may still follow its scandalous, and ludicrous, mystic mazes through reams of correspondence, and learn nothing but the nature of the petty characters of those who surrounded Poe. It is now fairly plain what happened.[857]

All the realities of life lay, for Poe, in the realm of the imagination. It was only there that he could, in any way, integrate the world. He longed for a logical, and a complete, consistency never found in the realm of the physical, and the world which he constructed for himself was a refuge that suited the peculiarities of his nature. There can be no doubt that, whatever the cause, he was not capable of enduring, during his later years, the excitement of passion, and at the same time remain sane.[858] Love, like everything else, could be perfect for him

---

[855] The statements made in this text about the aftermath of the Whitman affair will be found verified in the various letters to Mrs. Richmond (Annie) about this time, and the letter to Mrs. Whitman mentioned. Many of these letters are reprinted in full by Prof. Woodberry and Harrison. See also *The "Annie" Letters,* published by Ingram, the source of most of this correspondence.

[856] This statement, together with the publication of *The "Annie" Letters* by Ingram, is said to have caused Mrs. Whitman great chagrin later on.

[857] Ingram's well-meant activities, as T. D. English said in a letter to Griswold, served to rake many things from the dust which had better have remained there. Prof. Woodberry also regrets the publication of much of the petty scandals of the letters.

[858] Joseph Wood Krutch in his *Edgar Allan Poe, A Study in Genius,* has gone so far as to claim that Poe was impotent. The reader who is interested should read Mr.

only imaginatively. Only in the imagination could he find an ideal satisfaction. Every woman whom he loved was exalted into the dream angel whom he could worship imaginatively, rather than physically enjoy. Virginia, for a while, had provided for him an ideal personality so to exalt. The physical implications, there, must have been reduced to the minimum, if present at all. As her dissolution approached, and after her death occurred, it became necessary to find other women upon whom to center the sensations which he exalted into the ideal love of his soul. Several ladies followed in quick succession. Mrs. Osgood, Mrs. Shew (and Mrs. Richmond and Mrs. Whitman simultaneously). The very fact that they were, in some cases, married helped to remove them from the physical realm. Poe's attitude toward each was the same, and in each case the ideal woman, the angel, emerged from his imagination. It was a mere accident who produced the effect. Someone who was near, kind, sympathetic, and comforting was all that was needed. About them all, he managed to throw the glamour of his psychic romance.

All this was hard, impossible, at the time, to understand. Mrs. Shew and Mrs. Richmond seem to have grasped the situation. Mrs. Whitman did so afterward. It was "spiritual love"; she enthroned him as her ideal. Unfortunately for Poe, such a futile and hopeless equipment for the realities of physical life involved him with the world, which could not grasp his motives, in a conflict, and a maze of difficulties that helped to hound him to death.

Husbands, who found "Israfel" rhapsodizing in their wives' parlors, could not understand that the gentleman, the dangerously romantic poet, who seemed to be talking to Fanny, or Louise, or Annie, as the case might be, was in reality merely addressing the accidental embodiment which "Lenore," or "Helen," or "Ligeia," or "Annabel Lee" had, at that particular date, assumed. Other interests of a more mundane nature were naturally inferred. Trouble, swift, sure, and devastating, ensued. And "Israfel" was once more left alone.

To women, it was all enormously intriguing. All the passion of the man, all of the life instinct lived and burned in his conversation and letters. They had never dreamed of such talk from a man. The banal "pass the coffee," of James or Henry, was suddenly, by Poe's lips, transformed, exalted into the accents of archangels upon the tongue of man. It is easy to discount or laugh at this now, but it was quite different, quite another thing, to sit listening to the news from Aidenn leaning against the same sofa back with Edgar Allan Poe.

Krutch's book. There is no attempt here to prove any particular theory about Poe's condition. Poe's letters to various women, from 1847 to 1849, prove that his attitude towards them was a peculiar one. This author does not know whether Poe was impotent or not, but is quite sure that, in 1848 and 1849, Poe was nervously disorganized and abnormal.

If this aspect of the man at first overwhelmed, and attracted women, his boundless need, and pathetic pleas for sympathy, and utter spiritual possession of the object of his admiration knew no bounds. As it was impossible to be an angel in paradise, "to dwell alone in a world of moan," the "Helen" or "Annie," who had been enticed there, always withdrew, sometimes regretfully and tactfully, sometimes indignantly—but always, as was perfectly natural and feminine, disappointed. In the meantime, during the celestial episode, a great deal of mundane talk had been going on.

Such a man as Poe was bound to arouse a stir in feminine circles. There is an almost psychic sense with women that leads them, instinctively, to feel when the normal attitude of the male to the female is altered, or lacking. With Poe it was present; it aroused them, and yet,—it was elusive, strange, something new. They pursued him and persevered. They wanted to find him out. To the spectator males, there was only one, the universal, obvious explanation.

For Poe, the man, it was a fatal and a disastrous predicament. It involved a nature, endowed with the mad pride of Lucifer, in squabbles and predicaments so ludicrous, and petty, as to produce in him a spiritual nausea. All the flashing glades of heaven, the bowers of paradise, wreathed with fairy fruits and flowers, were invaded by gesticulating old women shouting about real estate, or Mr. Lummises with derringers in their coat-tails. Imaginatively, the bowers of love were removed farther and farther away, out of space, out of time. They became Valleys of Many-Colored Grass, or the heavily curtained chamber of Rowena, yet all would not do. Mrs. Elizabeth Frieze Ellet penetrated—discovered even the lone isles in the sea—and the dreams, the lovely, supernal visions, vanished in the sulphur smoke of gossip, accusations of seduction, or the horrible whiskered face of an English, glimmering through an alcoholic mist over pistols on the table. No, Poe would have to apologize, cringe, make a cur of himself—or next morning the *New York Mirror* would tell why—and it did.

But, then again, there was something else—had he not written, twenty years before in *Tamerlane,* dreaming of Elmira?—"Tamerlane," the great "Tamerlane," was dying, thinking of why love had been lost and snatched from him—just as "Israfel," the great "Israfel," was dying now—and still murmuring:

> Young Love's first lesson is—the heart:
>   For 'mid that sunshine, and those smiles,
> When, from our little cares apart,
>   And laughing at her girlish wiles,
> I'd throw me on her throbbing breast,
>   And pour my spirit out in tears—
> There was no need to speak the rest—

> No need to quiet any fears
> Of her—who ask'd no reason why,
> But turn'd on me her quiet eye!

And yet—and yet

> How was it that Ambition crept
> Unseen, amid the revels there,
> Till growing bold, he laugh'd and leapt
> In the tangles of Love's very hair? [859]

No, he could stand them no longer; the terrible gossips in hoop-skirts, the suspicious husbands, the little gad-fly magazines, hounding him, printing coarse parodies of the immortal dreams, beloved faces vanishing, always vanishing. And was he not sick with long months of headache,[860] haunted by terrific visions, poor as Lazarus, a laughing-stock, and yet great? He knew it,—capable of putting into words, at lucky intervals, dreams that would haunt eternity, music that, with a melancholy magic, covers the tragedy of humanity with a pall of stars. He only, of all the millions of beings who have spoken English, caught up in the meshes of language the cosmic sorrow of the ocean while, from the sounding beaches, the angels abducted his "Annabel Lee." This was no small thing. No one had done it before, and no one will ever do it again in just his way.

But it was all getting quite unbearable now, in 1849,—something must be done. Even before Helen Whitman withdrew, he wrote:

. . . for the terrible agony which I have so lately endured—an agony known only to my God and to myself—seems to have passed my soul through fire and purified it from all that is weak. Henceforward I am strong:—this, those who love me shall see—as well as those who have so untiringly endeavored to ruin me. It needed only some such trials as I have undergone to make me what I was born to be, by making me conscious of my strength.[861]

What was his strength? In the Winter of 1849, the balked and nervously ruined man who had again retreated to the cottage at Fordham, pursued by the hissing and laughter of the world, seems compounded of weakness. His strength was his imagination.

The very elements that were fast making his physical existence impossible had been so mixed in him that all the passion, and love, the tenderness that yearned over the happy fireside of Annie, and wished to be identified with it, overflowed through his pen, and became embodied in the only world he could control, and order as he desired, the sphere of imaginative literature. All else about him dissolved, withdrew, vanished away into time, until the objective world itself, its con-

---

[859] Lines from *Tamerlane* published in John Neal's *Yankee* in 1829. The last four lines refer specifically to the dying "Tamerlane."

[860] Poe specifically complains to Annie of months of headache.

[861] Poe to Mrs. Whitman.

crete things, and its three-dimensioned denizens seemed more dream-like, less palpably real than his dream within a dream.

And they have remained so to the generations that followed. The era, the peculiar mid-Nineteenth Century in which he lived and moved, has become a lost country to those who have followed. It is more remote and peculiar than Siam. As one looks at its queer costumes, its strange rococo architecture, its faiths, prejudices, hopes, and ambitions, its now meaningless conventions that bounded its motives,—but above all, as one attempts to approach it through its popular literature,—it seems like a strange ocean of mist in which, through vaguely glimpsed streets in dreamfully grotesque towns, there move, for forgotten reasons, the ghosts of costumes. Out of this vaguely-agitated, and grayly-twinkling land, like a steeple above a city fog, beneath which the noise of unseen traffic rolls on, a few objects stand forth, outlined and clearly defined. One of these is the imaginative prose and poetry of Edgar Allan Poe.

The time will perhaps come when it will be found necessary to penetrate down into the mist of "middle America," and to examine more fully the edifice upon which the pinnacles rest. The spirits who once lived there moved in the boundaries and the conventions of their time. The Athens of Plato, the Florence of Dante, the Paris of Villon, and the London of Dr. Johnson are comparatively plain. We are at great pains to understand them, whilst the cities of our grandfathers glimmer mysteriously as Atlantis, despised and discounted, within the yellow borders of old prints.

Yet there was a great stir there. Something important and significant was going on. All the potentialities of the past were being released. Out of the thirteen republics—the words have almost been forgotten—that lined the Atlantic Seaboard, arose a giant that has laid his hand heavily upon the home of man. The time will come when it will not be thought beneath the dignity of scholars both to profess and really to know.

The paragraph about the literary women with whom he would have no more to do, penned irritably in the letter to Annie, was no mere caprice. It was the result of an experience so painful, so real a reality, that it penetrated even the dream world of Poe. To traffic any longer with such witches was to barter away his soul. From now on, he would devote himself to writing! This time, the *Stylus* would become a fact! From January to June of 1849, the preparations for the great campaign went on. Helen would not come to sit beside him on the throne which he would occupy. Be it so then, he would reign there alone. The last, the briefest, but one of the most important of his creative periods began. Out of it came the finished *Bells,* and the great ballad of *Annabel Lee.*

Nor is the half-mad, the apparently insane ambition to be despised. Humbleness in the great, in the "sports" of intellect, is, at best, but a lubricant upon the contemporary wheels that manufacture fame, a wise, though not a necessary stock in trade.   Genius knows itself the rose that justifies its tree; a blossom upon the fruitless bushes of ambition. Only madmen, according to grocers' standards, retire to caverns to be fed by ravens; it is insane to pit fishermen and tent-makers against pro-consuls and Cæsars; masons can see no monumental material in paper, yet the dreams of poets outlast the golden countenances of kings.   Were it not for the magnificent eccentrics, society, like a community of insects, would crystallize forever in the ignoble efficiency of caste.

And all of these mad dreamers, the glorious company of egoists who fear not the god of their neighbors, always fail.   Columbus sails for Cathay, and only finds another world; Napoleon fails to found a dy-nasty.   Shelley leaves God alone with Oxford; Coleridge was unable to finish *Christabel* or *Kubla Khan*.   Yet the same line which marks the extremity of such failures becomes the boundary of political empires, and of literary kingdoms.

Poe had also greatly failed.   His mad dream of becoming the arbiter of American letters was never, could not, in the nature of things, have been attained.   He succeeded only in achieving a niche in the literature of the English language.   Whether an humble heart is consonant with such an eventuality may well be doubted.   Poe was very proud.   And, on the whole, there was distinctly something to be proud of.   It was doing fairly well for the poor orphan boy, the lonely clerk who had pored over the columns of English reviews, in the dim book loft of *Ellis & Allan* in the provincial town of Richmond, only twenty years before.   He had triumphed over enormous handicaps.

Poe has been accused of being unreliable, flighty, and inconsistent. From the standpoint of a Burton or a Graham, this was true.   But in one thing he had been supremely faithful, driving steadily through pov-erty, disease, death, frustration, and the despair of his weaknesses—he had been faithful to his literary work:

How I labored—how I toiled—How I wrote! Ye Gods, did I *not* write? I knew not the word 'ease.' By day I adhered to my desk, and at night, a pale student, I consumed the midnight oil. You should have seen me— you *should*. I leaned to the right. I leaned to the left. I sat forward. I sat backward. I sat upon end. I sat *tête baissée*, . . . bowing my head close to the alabaster page. And . . . through good report and through ill report, I—*wrote*. Through sun-shine and through moonshine, I—*wrote*. *What* I wrote it is unnecessary to say. The *style!*—that was the thing. . . .[862]

The letters which Poe sent to Annie from Fordham in the early months of 1849 plainly show that he had now made up his mind

---

[862] Last paragraphs of Poe's *Literary Life of Thingum Bob, Esq.*

to devote himself to literature with the objects of enhancing his fame and gaining enough money to raise him out of poverty, and put him in the way of starting the *Stylus*. Women, love, and the troubles these brought upon him, he fondly believed he had, after his recent terrible experience, dropped out of his life. In the stanzas *For Annie,* which he addressed to Mrs. Richmond about this time, occur some significant lines:

> Thank Heaven! the crisis—
> The danger is past,
> And the lingering illness
> . Is over at last—
> And the fever called 'Living'
> Is conquered at last. ·. . . .
>
> And oh! of all tortures
> That torture the worst
> Has abated—the terrible
> Torture of thirst
> For the naphthaline river
> Of Passion accurst :—
> I have drunk of a water
> That quenches all thirst :—

And about the end of January he writes:

. . . I am so busy, now, and feel so full of energy. Engagements to write are pouring in upon me every day. I had two proposals within the last week from Boston. I sent yesterday an article to the *Am. Review,* about *Critics and Criticism.* Not long ago I sent one to the *Metropolitan* called *Landor's Cottage* it has something about 'Annie' in it, and will appear, I suppose in the March number. To the *S. L. Messenger* I have sent fifty pages of *Marginalia,* five pages to appear each month of the current year. I have also made permanent engagements with another magazine, called *The gentlemen's.* So you see that I have only to keep up my spirits to get out of all my pecuniary troubles. The least price I get is $5 per *'Graham* page,' and I can easily average 1½ per day— that is $7½. As soon as 'returns' come in I shall be out of difficulty.[863]

By the middle of February, he evidently felt he was on his feet again. Several allusions to a sense of returning health belong to this period, and, on February 14th we find him resuming, after a long interval, his correspondence with F. W. Thomas, who had left government employ in Washington and was, at that time, engaged in editing the *Louisville* (Kentucky) *Chronicle.*

. . . Right glad am I to find you once more in a true position—'in the field of letters.' Depend upon it after all, Thomas, literature is the most noble of professions. In fact, it is about the only one fit for a man. For my own part there is no seducing me from the path. I shall be a littérateur at least, all my life; nor would I abandon the hopes which still lead me on for all the gold in California. Talking of gold and temptations at present held out to 'poor-devil authors' did

---

[863] Poe to Annie.

it ever strike you that all that is really valuable to a man of letters—to a poet in especial—is absolutely unpurchasable? Love, fame, the dominion of intellect, the consciousness of power, the thrilling sense of beauty, the free air of Heaven, exercise of body and mind, with the physical and moral health which result—these and such as these are really all that a poet cares for :—then answer me this—*why* should he go to California? . . .[864]

The excitement of the gold rush was evidently a good deal on Poe's mind. As we have seen, he felt that his own richest vein of ore lay within. It is almost certain that the poem, *Eldorado,* dates from about this time. The theme was also treated by him in prose. On March 8th, Poe wrote to Duyckinck enclosing "the Von Kempelen Article," which he hoped his literary agent could place for him. He had, he said, prepared the story to be published as a hoax in Boston in the *Flag of Our Union,* but he thought it would be "thrown away" in that publication.

The story purported to relate the arrest, in Bremen, of a certain American chemist, Von Kempelen, suspected of counterfeiting. A chest of gold was found in his room, which turned out to be the result of alchemy—"All that yet can fairly be said to be known is" that "Pure gold can be made at will, and very readily from lead in connection with certain other substances, in kind and proportions, unknown." [865] It was of this story that Poe wrote to Duyckinck.

My sincere opinion is that nine persons out of ten (even among the best-informed) will believe the quiz (provided the design does not leak out before publication) and that this, acting as a sudden although, of course, a very temporary, check to the gold fever, it will create a *stir* to some purpose.[866]

In a letter to Eveleth, at the end of February, occurs the first reference to Poe's contemplated move to Richmond,[867] "I mean to start for Richmond on the 10th [of] March." Poe and Mrs. Clemm had intended to go to Lowell to be near the Richmonds, but a serious cloud had overshadowed the poet's intentions to be near Annie and her family. Mrs. Locke, Mrs. Osgood's sister-in-law, had assumed the rôle of Mrs. Ellet. A great many of the doings at Providence were detailed to Mr. and Mrs. Richmond, together with the history of Poe's relations with the Osgoods.[868] Mr. Richmond and his wife seem to have acted with a great deal of judgment and cool-headedness in the matter. Although they were alarmed, they still continued to cherish a warm, and even an affectionate regard for Poe.

[864] Poe to Thomas, February 14, 1849. This is Poe's ideal of literary life. He, of course, took no such physical care of himself. It was what he had been advised to do. See notes by Kennedy, White, Thomas.

[865] From the text, the central "fact" of the story.

[866] Poe to Duyckinck, March 8, 1849.

[867] Poe to Eveleth, February 29, 1849.

[868] Partly an inference, but a certain one. Mrs. Locke was Mrs. Osgood's sister-in-law. The rest is inherent in the text of letters from Poe to Annie.

The whole affair is now remote and obscure. As nearly as can be made out, Poe, on his lecture at Lowell, had gone there largely through the influence of Mrs. Locke, who was delighted to play the rôle of patroness which she had really played to some purpose just after Virginia's death. Poe, it seems, after meeting Mrs. Richmond, paid very little attention to Mrs. Locke, even staying at the Richmonds' in preference to the other lady's house. Mrs. Locke was in communication with Helen Whitman, who said that "She [Mrs. Locke] conceived herself to have been deeply wronged. . . . I saw that she was too much under the influence of pride to exercise a calm judgment in the matter." Mrs. Locke was doubly indignant at having to watch Poe go through all the same motions with Annie which had marked his affair with Mrs. Osgood, who was then dying of consumption. Mrs. Locke, therefore, determined to produce, if possible, an end to the affair with Annie similar to that of Mrs. Osgood's. She was partially successful in a rôle which the long aftermath of her acrimonious and tittle-tattling correspondence discloses her to have been well fitted for. Mrs. Richmond was alarmed, although she, who undoubtedly understood Poe, refused to misconstrue his attentions to her.

A large part of the correspondence between Poe and Mrs. Richmond, during the early months of 1849, is concerned with the charges, countercharges, and rebuttals that Mrs. Locke's activities involved.[869] The letters of both Annie and Sarah to Poe, and especially to Mrs. Clemm, now took a tone which made it plain to Mrs. Clemm, at least, that a residence in the neighborhood of the Richmonds, or any further visits there on Poe's part, would be decidedly unwelcome.[870]

Mrs. Clemm called Poe's attention to this, and it would seem that it was her attitude which induced him to give up the scheme. It is probable, although it cannot be proved by letters, that it was at this time that Mrs. Clemm suggested to Poe his going to Richmond, with the possibility of looking up Elmira Royster (Mrs. Shelton) again. A great deal of conversation must have taken place between the two about their plans for a new place of residence, if the lease on the Fordham cottage were allowed to expire, as it was about to do.[871] For a

[869] The correspondence which is the source of the statements made in the text is plainly indicated. Specific references to the dates of letters is avoided here, as anyone particularly interested in this peculiar phase of Poe's love affairs will have to read the Whitman, "Annie," Griswold, Poe, Osgood, letters of this time, and after Poe's death, to glean the ramifications of this miserable affair. Margaret Fuller, and Mrs. Hewitt, and Mrs. Ellet are also concerned in the spider web. See also the Woodberry and Harrison biographies of Poe.

[870] Sarah was Annie's sister.

[871] In May, 1849, Mrs. Clemm writes Annie that the lease will be allowed to expire. A change of plan then occurred. Mrs. Susan Archer Weiss says that Mrs. Mackenzie had written, in the Summer of 1848, urging the Elmira affair upon Poe. This is doubtful. The cottage was leased in 1849 for another year by Poe, and Mrs. Clemm was living there when he died.

time, Poe seemed to have felt it best that even the correspondence with Annie should cease. On February 19th, he wrote to her:

I cannot and *will* not have it on my conscience that I have interfered with the domestic happiness of the only being in the whole world, whom I have loved at the same time with truth and with purity . . . you have not *said* it to me, but I have been enabled to glean from what you *have* said, that Mr. Richmond has permitted himself (perhaps without knowing it) to be influenced against me by the malignant misrepresentations of Mr. and Mrs. [Locke]. . . .

Poe's initial quarrel with the Lockes had arisen over Mrs. Locke's assertions about Mrs. Richmond, so Poe states to Annie. His decision not to come to Lowell evidently greatly relieved matters, for correspondence was resumed with the Richmonds, and also went on with the Lockes. Ten days after the letter quoted above, Poe writes Eveleth he is going to Richmond.

All seemed going well, when the usual tide of misfortune, that always overtook Poe at crucial times, now delivered a double blow. Most of the periodicals for which he had been so briskly writing, and upon which he depended for his livelihood, either suspended or defaulted payment, and he was simultaneously attacked by a relapse into ill health attended by sinking spells, and an unaccountable depression. He was, indeed, in a process of physical dissolution. Even poor, patient "Muddie" now writes to Annie, "I thought he would die several times. God knows I wish we were both in our graves. It would I am sure, be far better." A little later, Poe writes to Annie that he is better,—but—

. . . You know how cheerfully I wrote to you not long ago—about my prospects —hopes—how I anticipated being soon out of difficulty. Well! all seems to be frustrated—at least for the present. As usual, misfortunes never come single, and I have met one disappointment after another. The *Columbian Magazine,* in the first place, failed—then Post's *Union* (taking with it my principal dependence); then the *Whig Review* was forced to stop paying for contributions —then the *Democratic*—then (on account of his oppression and insolence) I was obliged to quarrel, finally, with ——; and then, to crown all, the '—— ——' (from which I anticipated so much and with which I had made a regular engagement for $10 a week throughout the year) has written a circular to correspondents, pleading poverty and declining to receive any more articles. More than this, the *S. L. Messenger* which owed me a good deal, cannot pay just yet, and altogether, I am reduced to Sartain and Graham both very precarious. No doubt, Annie, you attribute my 'gloom' to these events—but you would be wrong. It is not in the power of any mere *worldly* considerations, such as these, to depress me. . . . No, my sadness is *unaccountable,* and this makes me the more sad. I am full of dark forebodings. *Nothing* cheers or comforts me. My life seems wasted—the future looks a dreary blank: but I will struggle on and 'hope against hope.' . . . What do you think? I have received a letter from Mrs. Locke. She says she is about to publish a detailed account of *all* that occurred between us, under guise of romance, with fictitious names, etc.,—that she will make me appear noble, generous, etc., etc.,—nothing bad—that she will 'do justice to my motives,' etc., etc. . . .[872]

Poe's illness was undoubtedly a relapse after the serious illness following the Whitman affair. His periods of relapse were now accentuated, and came upon him suddenly after any excitement or exertion. He had worn himself out in the period between December, 1848, and March, 1849, composing, sending off articles and poems to the magazines, to the newspapers, and to Griswold, and by conducting a feverish correspondence.

Every line in manuscript and correspondence was, of course, in those days carried on in longhand. Poe was too poor to afford, at any time, an amanuensis, and he was pedantically meticulous about his manuscripts. The labor of composing, redrafting, and editing, and then making perfect fair-copies, with the added labor of writing long, and often beautifully composed letters, is almost impossible to exaggerate. Much of this, at a time of weakness and depression, was now found of no avail, by the failure of magazines, and some of the manuscripts were thrown back on his hands. *Landor's Cottage,* which, for Annie's sake, he had spent much labor upon, and that he was therefore doubly anxious to publish, had met the latter fate.

The records of his illnesses from 1847 on show that his heart was giving out. Mrs. Shew, as we have seen, together with Dr. Francis, felt that he could not live long, even two years before. This condition, we can be morally certain, was the cause of that depression that he could not explain. In addition, the symptoms of a lesion of the brain, which were several times medically noted, now became more acute. He is described, about now, as having had periods of "brain fever" that point to some sort of cerebral inflammation and congestion, and he complains to Annie of a headache that lasted for months.

Poe's periods of collapse and depression had, hitherto, occurred at long intervals. From 1847 to 1849 the process is obviously accelerated, the recovery less complete, and the intervals of prostration greatly prolonged.

It is highly probable that, during the end of the stay at the cottage in Fordham, he again resorted to drugs for stimulation and surcease. There is no mention of alcohol, but a few months later, in June, 1849, immediately after leaving New York, Poe appeared to a friend in Philadelphia completely unmanned, shaking, and begging for laudanum.[873] The same drug had been procured by him in Providence in December, 1848, when he intended to commit suicide, so he was evidently familiar with it. The dose then taken, he said, acted as an

---

[872] Poe to Annie, March, 1849.
[873] The friend was Sartain, see page 650.

emetic, but it was sufficient to have killed any normal person not inured to its effects. He had swallowed about an ounce. It was in such a debilitated condition that he continued to pour forth great poetry and distinguished prose.

The Winter and early Spring of 1849 were marked by the publication of *Mellonta Tauta* in *Godey's Lady's Book* for February. This had been written before *Eureka,* for Poe quoted from it in the introduction to the latter.

Mellonta Tauta, under the guise of being written on April Fool's Day, 2848, contains some of the most important of Poe's inferences about the future that are, in many instances, prophetic. The philosophy in it elaborates many of the points made in *Eureka,* and it is probable that it was meant for an introduction to the prose poem or, at least, as a companion piece. The author's satire on his own times, its social theories, fashions, and architecture is decidedly interesting.

Poe had also been contributing to the *Flag of Our Union,* an obscure Boston sheet, that had the sole merit of paying him promptly and fairly well. In it appeared the little-understood allegory of *Hop-Frog,* the sonnet *To My Mother,* and *A Valentine,* written in 1846, and addressed to Mrs. Osgood—these during February and March. The *Southern Literary Messenger* published a review of Lowell's *Fable for Critics,* also in March. It is during the same period that we hear of the composition of *The Bells, Annabel Lee, For Annie, Lenore,* and, by inference, *Eldorado.* All of these belonged to the finest order of his works.

With the correspondence in hand, it is not difficult to glance into the cottage at Fordham, and see what was going on. On February 8th, Poe writes:

. . . I have been so busy, 'Annie' ever since I returned from Providence—six weeks ago. I have not suffered a day to pass without writing from a page to three pages. Yesterday, I wrote five, and the day before a poem considerably longer than *The Raven.* I call it *The Bells.* How I wish 'Annie' could see it! . . . The five prose pages I finished yesterday are called—what do you think? —I am sure you will never guess—*Hop-Frog!*

About a month later we find him writing to Griswold (undated).

I enclose perfect copies of the lines *For Annie* and *Annabel Lee,* in hopes that you may make room for them in your new edition. As regards *Lenore* (which you were kind enough to say you would insert) I would prefer the concluding stanza to run as here written. . . .[874]

Poverty now once more had him in its grip, but both he and Mrs. Clemm appear to have been relieved somewhat by the generosity of "Stella" (Mrs. S. A. Lewis), whose literary reputation Poe was fur-

---

[874] This was evidently the last stanza as it appeared in *Griswold* in 1850. Poe later made still further changes in the last stanza of *Lenore.* See note 299.

thering. His review of "Stella's" poem *The Child of the Sea,* in the September, 1848, *Southern Literary Messenger,* was undoubtedly colored by the relief which she had, even then, brought to his desperate necessities. Mrs. Clemm had become quite intimate with Mrs. Lewis, and Poe, who at first detested her, had become reconciled, and had even grown to like her. The friendship and correspondence with Mrs. Shew were also resumed about now, and she from time to time once more appeared at Fordham. On March 30th, he writes:

You see that I am not yet off to Richmond as I proposed. I have been detained by some very important and unexpected matters which I will explain when I see you. What is the reason you have not been out?[875]

All through the correspondence of the spring months of 1849 is to be found a running reference to the constantly deferred trip to Richmond. Along with this, as another biographer has noted, there is, in the "Annie" letters, what amounts to a chorus of, "I must get rich, get rich." [876] The postponement of the Richmond trip was, of course, due to poverty, and this Poe knew he could no longer cope with in his debilitated condition. To continue to exist, to provide a home for Mrs. Clemm, and to start the *Stylus,* a life of decent comfort freed from the fear of the wolf was necessary. This was undoubtedly the controlling motive in the last year of Poe's life, and the key to his contemplated trip to Richmond, and engagement with Mrs. Shelton. He desired to be with Annie, but that could not be. Mrs. Lewis, to a minor degree, was now playing the part of Mrs. Shew, both as lady bountiful and as the "dear friend." The perverse fate which the nature of the man invoked, but which circumstances united strangely, all through his life, to make dramatically perfect, now, in the guise of a friend interested in the *Stylus,* stepped in to provide the means to speed him towards the gulf. The passive instrument of fate was an innocent young man in Illinois, one Edward Howard Norton Patterson.[877]

Oquawka, or Yellow Banks, was a small town in Illinois, first settled in the early 1830's on the Mississippi River, halfway between the Des Moines and the Rock Island Rapids. In 1837, an old Philadelphia map describes it as being laid out in two sections on an extensive scale. "The soil was sandy." By 1849, although the anticipation of the "extensive scale" had not yet been realized, the "two large warehouses, one grocery, two taverns and *several* dwelling houses" had increased to

---

[875] Poe to Mrs. Shew, March 30, 1849.

[876] Prof. Woodberry so comments.

[877] Some of the Poe-Patterson correspondence has been published by Gill, Prof. Woodberry, and Prof. Harrison. The account and the letters here drawn upon are taken from *Some Letters of Edgar Allan Poe to E. H. N. Patterson of Oquawka, Illinois,* with comments by Eugene Field, Caxton Club Publication, 189 copies, Chicago, 1898.

several dwelling houses more.   There was "a neat and substantial bridge" over the Henderson River, and a weekly newspaper, the *Oquawka Spectator.*[878]

This sheet had been founded by J. B. Patterson from Winchester, Virginia, who arrived in Oquawka in September, 1835.   In the years that followed, he had become a local literary light, written a *Life of Black Hawk,* edited the *Spectator,* and passed to his reward, leaving a tidy little sum to his son Edward, who came of age in 1849.   The son continued to edit the *Spectator.*

For some years, young Patterson had been reading the columns of exchanges which came to the little office of the *Spectator.*   Poe's work in *Graham's, Godey's,* and other sheets had attracted his attention, and he admired.   Some announcements and plans for the great American magazine had also become known to him, and, in 1849, being in possession of his father's money, ambitious, and inexperienced, out of a clear sky he wrote to Poe, making a proposition tantamount to backing the *Stylus.*   Patterson wrote his first letter on December 18, 1848, but the poverty-stricken Mr. Poe did not receive it until April, 1849.   It must have dropped into his lap like manna.   He immediately replied:

No doubt you will be surprised to hear that your letter, dated Dec. 18, has only this moment [about the middle of April] reached me.   I live at the village of Fordham, about 14 miles from New York, on the Harlem Rail-Road—but as there is no Post Office at the place, I date always from New York, and get all my letters from the city Post Office.   When by accident or misapprehension letters are directed to me at Fordham, the clerks—some of them who do not know of my arrangements—forward them to West Farms, the nearest Post Office town, and one which I rarely visit.   Thus it happened with your letter. . . . Should you not have changed your mind on the subject, I should be pleased to hear from you again. . . .

Experience, not less than the most mature reflection on this topic, assured me that no *cheap* magazine can ever again prosper in America.   We must aim high—address the intellect—the higher classes—of the country (with reference, also, to a certain amount of foreign circulation) and put the work at $5:—going about 112 pp. (or perhaps 128) with occasional wood-engravings in the first style of the art, but only in obvious illustrations of the text.   Such a Mag. would begin to pay after 1000 subscribers; and with 5000 would be a fortune worth talking about:—but there is no earthly reason why, under proper management, and with energy and talent, the work might not be made to circulate, at the end of a few years—(say 5) 20,000 copies in which case it would give a clear income of 70 or 80,000 dollars—even if conducted in the most expensive manner. . . . I need not add that such a Mag. would exercise a literary and other influence never yet exercised in America.   I presume you know that during the second year of its existence, the *S. L. Messenger* rose from less than 1000 to 5000 subs., and that *Graham,* in 8 months after my joining it, went up from 5000 to 52,000.

[878] It was from this "center" that the great American magazine was to appear.   Poe afterward balked at this, and proposed or accepted Patterson's proposal of dating the Eastern edition of the *Stylus* from New York, and the Western from St. Louis, Missouri.

I do not imagine that a $5 Mag. could even be forced into so great a circulation as this latter; but under certain circumstances, I would answer for 20,000. The whole income from *Graham's* 52,000 never went beyond 15,000$:—the proportioned expenses of the $3 Mags. being so much greater than those of $5 ones.

My plan, in getting up such work as I propose, would be to take a tour through the principal States—especially West and South—visiting the small towns more particularly than the large ones—lecturing as I went, to pay expenses—and staying sufficiently long in each place to interest my personal friends (old college and West Point acquaintances scattered all over the land) in the success of the enterprise. By these means, I could guarantee in 3 months (or 4) to get 1,000 subs. in advance, with their signatures—nearly all pledged to pay at the issue of the first number. Under such circumstances, success would be certain. I have now about 200 names pledged to support me whenever I venture on the undertaking—which perhaps you are aware I have long had in contemplation—only awaiting a secure opportunity. . . .

I will endeavor to pay you a visit at Oquawka, or meet you at any place you suggest. . . .[879]

Patterson replied on May 7th next, rather enthusiastically, and at great length. He was youthfully in earnest. ". . . My plan then (with certain modifications which we can agree upon) is this":

I will furnish an office and take upon myself the sole charge and expense of Publishing a Magazine (name to be suggested by you) to be issued in monthly numbers at Oquawka, Illinois, containing in every number, 96 pages . . . at the rate of $5 per annum. Of this magazine you are to have the entire editorial control, furnishing at your expense, matter for its pages, which can be transmitted to me by mail or as we may hereafter agree upon. . . . You can make your own bargains with authors and I am to publish upon the best terms I can . . . and we are to share the receipts equally. . . . If my plan accords with your views, you will immediately select a title, write me to that effect, and we will both commence operations. We ought to put out the first number January next. Let me hear from you immediately.

Poe did reply encouragingly, under date of May 23rd, enclosing a design for the cover of the *Stylus* and remarking:

. . . Today I am going to Boston & Lowell, to remain a week; and immediately afterwards I will start for Richmond, where I will await your answer to this letter. Please write to me *there*, under cover, or to the care of John R. Thompson, Ed^r. of the "South. Lit. Messenger." On receipt of your letter (should you still be in the mind you now are) I will proceed to St. Louis and there meet you. . . .

I fancy that I shall be able to meet the current expenses of the tour by lecturing as I proceed; but there is something required in the way of outfit; and as I am not overstocked with money (what poor devil author *is?*) I must ask you to advance half of the sum I need to begin with—about $100. Please, therefore, enclose $50 in your reply, which I will get at Richmond. . . .

Leaving the matter of the *Stylus* thus, in a highly promising condition, Poe now departed on his trip northward, and paid a visit of

---

[879] Poe to Patterson, New York (Fordham), April 8, 1849.

about a week to Annie.   Matters in Lowell had then been accommodated, and, for a few days, he was happy by the fireside of those he
loved, and who returned his almost childlike affection.   Here he wrote
the third draft of *The Bells,* and returned to Fordham a few days later.

The cottage there, as we have seen, had been taken for another year.
Poe was in arrears for rent, and desperately pressed, so poor in fact
that he could not raise the carfare to Richmond.   He was, therefore,
under the necessity of writing to Richmond to ask that Patterson's letter containing the $50 be forwarded to him in New York.   Just as Mr.
Clarke had paid for a trip to Washington to start the magazine in 1843,
Mr. Patterson was now paying for a trip to Richmond in 1849—with
the same result.   Yet such were the inexplicable contradictions of Poe
that, on June 26th, he wrote to Eveleth :

. . . I am awaiting the *best opportunity* for its issue; and if by waiting until the
day of judgment I perceive still increasing chances of ultimate success, why
until the day of judgment I will patiently wait.   I am now going to Richmond
to 'see about it'—and *possibly* I may get out the first number next January. . . .

All of which means, if it means anything, that Poe did not intend to
get out the *Stylus* at all.   It too, like all his great dreams, he preferred
to have remain where they could be perfect, *i.e.,* in the realms of the
imagination.[880]   There were sordid aspects to conducting a real magazine in a workaday world, which Poe could no longer bring himself to
face.   In the meantime he would go to Richmond.   New York had become, like Philadelphia in 1844, a town haunted with strangely hostile
ghosts.   How had it all come about?   He was not quite certain—not
his fault, of course!   He would show them all yet—wait till the *Stylus*
was started!   In the meantime he would—go home!

But from the first, there was a certain fatality about it, a sense of
finality.   He was again inexplicably depressed.   Another attack was
coming on.   The heart that had been pounding away for forty years,
sometimes fluttering and throbbing, was giving out.   His nerves were
tautened to the last notch, and the birdlike hands were trembling.   There
were never to be any more great poems or weird stories from that brain.
It was still filled with visions, but they were too strange, too overpowering now for utterance.   They were almost insane, like a mad rattle in
the shell of a man.   The cottage at Fordham was "temporarily closed."
The "50$" had come.   Eddie was leaving for Richmond, and, for the
time being, "Muddie" was to stay with the kind Mrs. Lewis, in the
house in Brooklyn where the stuffed raven perched over Pallas.   It
was the end of June, 1849.

Poe wrote to Dr. Griswold, asking him to superintend the collection of his works.   Willis was to write the accompanying biography.

---

[880] Poe *may* already have had in mind "the better opportunity" of conducting the
Stylus from Richmond on Mrs. Shelton's money (*sic*).

The fame of E. A. Poe seemed to him to have been left in good hands. One catches a final glimpse of him upon a sunny morning in Manhattan, nigh a century ago. It is in the parlor of Elizabeth Oakes Smith. As they sat in the long-vanished room chatting, Mrs. Smith's canary, that had been let out of its cage for morning exercise, fluttered about the apartment, and alighted upon the head of Apollo on the mantelpiece.[881]

'See, Mr. Poe,' I said, 'I do not keep a raven but there is song to song. Why did you not put an owl on the head of Pallas? However, there would have been no poem then.'

'No, there is mystery about the raven.'

Then he referred to Mrs. Whitman. . . .

'Such women as you and Helena, and a few others ought to be installed as queens, and artists of all kinds should be privileged to pay you court. They would grow wise and holy under such companionship. . . .'

The last time I saw him he called when my carriage was at the door on my way to Philadelphia, where I was to lecture. He seemed greatly disappointed, even grieved, saying over and over:

'I am sorry I cannot talk with you, I had so much to say. So very much I wished to say.'

And so she left him, as the carriage went down the street, haunted always afterwards by ". . . his look of pain, his unearthly eyes, his weird look of desolation" as he stood there in the sunshine, looking greatly disappointed and murmuring, "I had . . . so much, so very much, I wished to say."

The plans which finally interrupted all further conversation were completed by June 29th.[882] On that day, in company with Mrs. Clemm, in great distress at the prospect of parting, Poe crossed the ferry to Brooklyn where he and "Muddie" spent the night at the house of Mr. and Mrs. Sylvanus D. Lewis, the latter the poetess frequently mentioned, a Baltimore girl of some attainments, and the author of *The Child of the Sea,* which Poe had lately and favorably reviewed.

The Lewises were most kindly, and the parting the next morning, darkened by the poet's prophetic gloom, and conviction of impending disaster, was affectionately dramatic. One catches a fleeting glimpse of the little group on the steps of the old Brooklyn house at 125 Dean Street. There is the legal-looking Sylvanus, "Stella," with her coiffure of luxuriant ringlets, Mrs. Clemm crying, and Edgar, also weeping, standing on the sidewalk, with his carpetbag in his hand. He turned to say good-bye to Mrs. Lewis:

---

[881] From the *Diary* of Elizabeth Oakes Smith. Mrs. Smith was about to depart for a lecture in Philadelphia in the Summer of 1849, one of her first, it appears, which places the time of the last interview with Poe.

[882] There is some indication that the cottage at Fordham was closed about the middle of June and that, during the interval between that time and his departure, Poe lived with a friend in New York. The matter is not clear.

He took my hand in his, and looking in my face, said, 'Dear Stella, my much beloved friend. You truly understand and appreciate me—I have a presentiment that I shall never see you again . . . If I never return write my life. You can and will do me justice.' [883]

Then he and Mrs. Clemm left together for the boat.

'God bless you, my own darling mother. Do not fear for Eddy! See how good I will be while I am away from you, and will come back to love and comfort you.' [884]

These were the last words the trembling woman heard as the boat pulled out, leaving her to return to spend weeks of helpless anxiety. Eddie did not return. The mission which fate had conferred upon Maria Clemm was over. Her reward was a pair of painfully rheumatic, and absolutely empty hands.

The traveler to Richmond via Philadelphia continued on his way. He was passing over the same route which he had followed eighteen years before, but he was now speeding on the last lap of his voyage much more rapidly. The city he gazed back upon for the last time had grown, as if by magic. In two decades the face of nature had been altered. The smoke was darker, and there was an enormous convention of stacks and sails. One wonders what the author of *Mellonta Tauta* thought as he gazed behind him at the Island, and, none too hopefully, before thinking, prophetically, perhaps, of "the entire area . . . densely packed with houses, some of them twenty stories high, land (for some unaccountable reason) being considered as especially precious in just this vicinity. . . . They were by no means civilized, however, but cultivated various arts and sciences after the fashion of their time. . . ." [885]

Mr. James K. Polk was in the White House. The War with Mexico was over, and, in Philadelphia, the lithographers were thriving at reprinting American maps. A red tinge had leaped southwestward to the Pacific. Mr. Poe remarked that, "The women . . . were oddly deformed by a protuberance of the region just below the small of the back—although most unaccountably, this deformity was looked upon altogether in the light of beauty." [885] The steamboat went on, faster than it had in 1831, locomotives also were swifter. Mr. Poe must have hurtled into Philadelphia amid a shower of sparks, sometime about the late afternoon of July 1, 1849.

In his scantily packed, but flowered carpetbag, there were two lectures, one of them certainly on *The Poetic Principle*,—and in his pockets

---

[883] Mrs. Lewis has left a careful description of the scene, *Ingram*. She never felt capable of undertaking Poe's biography, she says later. This was fortunate for Poe.
[884] Mrs. Clemm.
[885] From *Mellonta Tauta*.

there may have been as much as $40.[886]   The station was not far from
the waterfront, and the waterfront was then roaring with all the mad
excitement of the Gold Rush of 1849.   There were many saloons, all
of them liberally patronized, and in one of them it is certain, that after
the dusty ride in the cars from Perth Amboy, somewhere along the hot
cobbled streets of Philadelphia, Mr. Poe entered and took a drink. As
one of the minor consequences, he remained in Philadelphia for a fortnight.

The precise order of the events and calamities which now overtook
the man can never be precisely reconstructed.[887]   His affairs no longer
moved by any means to a lute's well tunéd law.   Confusion, utter and
horrible, surrounded him, because confusion was complete within.   He
was overtaken by delirium tremens. From the mercifully reticent recollections of his friends, and some correspondence, a few facts remain.

The office of John Sartain, then the proprietor of *Sartain's Magazine,*
was invaded suddenly, one July day, by a disheveled and trembling
caricature of a great poet crying out for protection, and fleeing from
the imaginary pursuers who were in conspiracy against him.   This was
an habitual hallucination with Poe when in a condition approaching collapse.   The long years of embittered controversy, the frequent receipt
of angry, and sometimes threatening and scandalous letters, had left
an indelible impress on his sensitive mind.   As he walked the streets of
Philadelphia, it seemed to him that the corner loungers looked at him
malevolently, and that conspirators were on his tracks.   His old friend,
Sartain, took him home, where Poe demanded a razor to shave off his
mustache, in order to disguise himself from his imaginary tormentors.
This, for obvious reasons, was refused.   With difficulty, Sartain persuaded him to lie down, and watched through the night, as he was afraid
to leave him alone, and Poe felt that he needed protection.   The attentions of the friend continued all next day while

. . . without cessation Poe poured forth, in the rich, musical tones for which
he was distinguished the fevered imageries of his brilliant but over-excited imagination.   The all absorbing theme which still retained possession of his mind,
was a fearful conspiracy that threatened his destruction.   Vainly his friend
endeavored to reassure and persuade him.   He rushed on with unwearied steps,
threading different streets, his companion striving to lead him homeward but
still in vain.[888]

---

[886] With the remainder of the money sent by Patterson, $50, Poe probably bought
some clothes, "outfit,"—see Poe to Patterson May 7, 1849.   The fare to Philadelphia
was about $4.

[887] The story of Poe's experience in Philadelphia comes from John Sartain's reminiscences, also letters of Poe to Mrs. Clemm between July 7 and July 18, 1849, and
the article and correspondence published by C. C. Burr in the *Nineteenth Century*
(February, 1852), pages 19-33.   The most available reference is Woodberry, 1909,
vol. II, pages 309-312.   See also Poe to Patterson, Richmond, July 19, 1849.   Also
Gill's *Life of Poe* for an account of the Sartain incident, from whom Gill had it direct.

[888] Gill's *Life of Poe,* page 235.

During this terrific ramble, Poe led Sartain to the Fairmount Reservoir, where they climbed together the steep flights of stairs leading to the top, while the infernal-heavenly tongue went on and on, hinting at suicide, "insisting upon the imminence of peril, and pleading touchingly for protection." After some persuasion, Poe returned with his companion to the house. The experience of the kindly and patient Sartain seems to have given him an incandescent glimpse into landscapes beyond Pennsylvania. Nor were his trials yet over. Poe escaped from the house and wandered off to spend the night in a field. Here he "fell into a slumber" in which a white-robed vision appeared to him, and warned him against suicide. It was probably a dream of Virginia. This seems to have quieted him somewhat.

Just how the days passed, neither Poe nor his friends ever knew. He was completely beyond himself, incapable of explanation. He was arrested for being intoxicated, and taken to Moyamensing Prison where he spent a night.[889]

Here on the battlements appeared a white female form that addressed him in whispers. "If I had not heard what she said," he declared, "it would have been the end of me." Next morning he was haled in with the other unfortunates before Mayor Gilpin, and was recognized. "Why, this is Poe, the poet," was remarked, and he was dismissed without a fine. When asked by Sartain why he had been incarcerated, he replied, probably troubled by remembrance of the English accusations, that he had forged a check. A symptom, frequent in cases suffering from Poe's complaint, now developed, one which Poe mentions as "cholera."

His wandering evidently continued for some time. He was under hallucinations about the death of Mrs. Clemm, and, while with Sartain, *begged him persistently for laudanum.* Two old friends, Charles Chauncey Burr and George Lippard, the latter the poet-novelist who had known him in the days of friendship with Henry Beck Hirst, now rescued him from the streets, and cared for him. On July 7th, he was able to write to Mrs. Clemm: [890]

MY DEAR, DEAR MOTHER,—I have been so ill—have had the cholera, or spasms quite as bad, and can now hardly hold the pen.

The very instant you get this come to me. The joy of seeing you will almost compensate for my sorrows. We can but die together. It is of no use to reason

---

[880] Prof. Woodberry considers Poe's imprisonment to have been an hallucination, but both Poe and Sartain refer to it as a fact, with details, while the hallucinations are specifically described in contradistinction. That Poe would have been arrested in his condition is the most probable thing that could have happened.

[890] This letter was dated from "New York," an obvious slip of the pen made by a sick man. Poe afterwards refers to the dreadful handwriting in the letters to Mrs. Clemm from May 7th to July 14th. His handwriting was an accurate index of his condition at any time.

with me now; I must die. I have no desire to live since I have done *Eureka*. I could accomplish nothing more. For your sake it would be sweet to live, but we must die together. You have been all—all to me, darling ever beloved mother, and dearest truest friend.

I was never really insane except upon occasions when my heart was touched.

I have been taken to prison once since I came here for getting drunk; but then I was not. It was about Virginia.

Poe evidently had little remembrance of what Sartain had done for him.[891] He remained in the care of his friends, Burr and Lippard. The latter called upon Poe's old employers for help, and Graham with his usual charity spoke of Poe with great pity, and contributed $5. Charles Peterson, who was still in the office at Poe's old desk, did likewise. It was probably he who had helped Poe in August, 1847, under similar circumstances.[892] The old friends in Philadelphia understood it all only too well—and helped when they could. Burr now purchased a steamboat ticket for Poe as far as Baltimore, and provided with the $10 contributed by Graham and Peterson, he set out for Richmond with his carpetbag that had been lost for ten days. The lectures had been stolen, and the discovery of this loss was a staggering blow. He was accompanied to the dock by the faithful Burr. It was Friday, the thirteenth.

The trip from Philadelphia to Richmond is, for so obscure an event, remarkably clear. A boat leaving Baltimore for Richmond on Friday evening was taken by the traveler, and, as it neared Richmond, he wrote a short note in the cabin to Mrs. Clemm:

Near Richmond

The weather is awfully hot, and besides all this, I am so homesick I don't know what to do. I never wanted to see any one half so bad as I want to see my own darling mother. It seems to me that I would make any sacrifice to hold you by the hand once more, and get you to cheer me up for I am terribly depressed. I do not think that any circumstances will ever tempt me to leave you again. When I am with you I can bear anything, but when I am away from you I am too miserable to live.[893]

The parting from Mrs. Clemm, with its almost immediately fatal results, brings out clearly the fact that Poe's existence had been prolonged by her. Poe was genuinely worried about having to leave her alone, but there runs through all of his thoughts and delusions in Philadelphia about Mrs. Clemm, an undercurrent of fear that with Virginia buried, and he himself away, she might make a home for herself some place else. Nothing was further from her thoughts.

Her movements and doings, during the time of Poe's trip to Richmond, have been preserved in her letter written July 9, 1849, to Annie. She had evidently not received the letter written to her by Poe from

---

[891] Poe gives Burr and Lippard most of the credit for saving him.
[892] See Chapter XXIV, page 588.
[893] Poe to Mrs. Clemm, July 14, 1849 (first letter of that date).

Philadelphia on the seventh. She said she had not heard from Eddie
for ten days. "Eddy was obliged to go through Philadelphia and I
much fear for him. . . . Oh, if any evil has befallen him what can
comfort me?" The day after Poe had left New York, Mrs. Clemm had
left Mrs. Lewis' house for Fordham. On the way out she called on a
"rich friend," who had made her promises of help, but who had never
been told the whole desperate situation. Mrs. Clemm unburdened herself, at which the friend advised her to leave Poe. "Anyone to propose
to *me* to leave my Eddy," she says, "what a cruel insult! No one to
nurse him and take care of him when he is sick and helpless!" A few
days later she must have received every confirmation of her worst fears,
by the delivery of his shocking letters. He was, of course, in the deepest
gulf of remorse, gloom, and self-disgust after the Philadelphia interval,
and appears, upon his arrival in Richmond, to have almost succumbed.

Poe arrived in Richmond on the night of the fourteenth, and went
by instinct directly to Duncan Lodge.[894] There he was assured of tender
care from Rosalie and the Mackenzies, and that his infirmities, and terrible condition of body, clothes, and mind would be decently concealed.
He seems to have remained there, at most, for only a very few days. On
the evening of his arrival, a few hours after the note written on the
steamer, he again addressed a letter to Mrs. Clemm:

. . . I got here with two dollars over—of which I enclose you one. Oh, God,
my Mother, shall we ever meet again? If possible, oh COME! My clothes
are so horrible and I am so ill. Oh, if you could come to me, my mother. Write
instantly—Oh do not fail. God forever bless you.

EDDY [895]

A few days later Poe moved to the *Old Swan Tavern,* between Eighth
and Ninth on Broad Street, which had once been a place of considerable
repute, but was now of a distinctly past reputation, the boarding place
of bachelor business men, and their associates. In a small frame house
on Broad Street next to the *Swan,* there lived, at that time, Dr. George
Rawlings, who, during the early days of Poe's stay, was called in to
visit him. This was apparently during the aftermath of the Philadelphia experience. Dr. Rawlings said Poe was still violent at intervals,
and at one time drew a pistol and threatened to shoot him.[896] He soon
afterwards recovered and writes Mrs. Clemm, "I have not drank anything since Friday morning, and then only a little Port Wine." This

---

[894] Mrs. Weiss so states.
[895] Poe to Mrs. Clemm, July 14, 1840 (second letter of that date). The fare from
Baltimore was $7. Poe started from Philadelphia, ticket paid by Burr to Baltimore,
with $10. Meals probably cost $1. This left him $2 in Richmond, one of which he
here sends to Mrs. Clemm. A typical piece of Poesque finance.
[896] J. H. Whitty, *Memoir,* large edition, page lxxiii.

Baltimore in 1849

A street scene in the city where Poe died under circumstances of extreme
tragedy, and where he now lies buried

From an old print
Courtesy of the Maryland Historical Society

was on the nineteenth, and "Friday" refers to the day he left Philadelphia the week before.

Once in the hands of kind friends and medical attention, his recovery was rapid. He received a letter from Mrs. Clemm which greatly cheered him, and five days after his arrival he wrote to "Muddie" again in a more hopeful mood:

Richmond, Thursday, *July* 19

My Own Beloved Mother—You will see at once by the handwriting of this letter, that I am better—much better in health and spirits. Oh! if you only knew how your dear letter comforted me! It acted like magic. Most of my sufferings arose from the terrible idea that I could not get rid of—the idea that you were dead. For more than ten days I was totally deranged, although I was not drinking one drop; and during this interval I imagined the most horrible calamities.

All was hallucination, arising from an attack which I had never before experienced—an attack of *mania-á-potu.* May heaven grant that it prove a warning to me for the rest of my days. . . .

All is not lost yet, and 'the darkest hour is just before daylight.' Keep up courage, my own beloved mother—all may yet go well. I will put forth all my energies. . . .

On the same date, he also dispatched a letter to Patterson, giving an attack of cholera in Philadelphia as the cause of his delay in acknowledging the $50, and for interrupting his correspondence. For a short time now the ghost of the *Stylus* and other troublesome things were laid aside. Israfel had come home to the only part of the real world that he loved.

As the gloom of the pit which he had just escaped was deep, so was the old familiar light upon the hills and streets, that he knew and loved from boyhood, bright, and tinged with the amber glow of melancholy memory so dear to his heart. It is pleasant to record that the scene in which he now, for the first time, took an accepted and applauded part, just before the curtain fell, was enacted in the atmosphere of an Indian Summer of youth, and a renaissance of old loves and friendships. Richmond had changed, and had grown, but not to a disturbing degree. A new generation had grown up, but many of the old places, the old faces, the customs and manners, the tricks of speech, and the Southern attitude of living for being rather than for possessing,—which so well suited his own temperament,—were still there. An infinite host of memories must have rushed in and transported him, as he breathed once more the syrupy odor of tobacco, peculiar to the Richmond air. Before he remembered anything at all, it was through this Virginia atmosphere that Frances Allan had carried him home from the milliner's house to Tobacco Alley.

During the last day, in what must be regarded as his native city, the returned exile divided his time very largely among the houses of his friends: the Mackenzies' at Duncan Lodge, Mrs. Shelton's house on Church Hill, and Talavera, the home of the Talleys.

Broad Street . . . extended several miles in a straight line from Chimborazo Heights and Church Hill on the east, where Mrs. Shelton [Elmira] had her residence, to the western suburbs, where Duncan Lodge and our own home of "Talavera" were situated. This was the route which Poe traversed in his visits to Mrs. Shelton. There were no street cars in those days, hacks were expensive, and the walk from "the Swan" to Church Hill was long and fatiguing. Poe would break his journey by stopping to rest at the office of Dr. John [*sic*] Carter, a young physician . . . about half-way between these two points.[897]

This young doctor had considerable influence with Poe, and later on attended him at Duncan Lodge. The poet's fame, the report that he was in the city to pay attention to Mrs. Shelton, and the influence of Mrs. Julia Mayo Cabell, who entertained for him, thus in a sense lifting the family ban, made Poe's reception in Richmond entirely different from any that he had received before.[898] The bitter feeling in regard to "his conduct to his guardian" had largely subsided, except in a few implacable directions, and open doors were more frequent, and wider than ever before.

Poe, on his part, was most careful in his social attitude. His manner was now not only dramatic, but assured and distinguished, and he was careful, knowing the old prejudice against him, to make no advances, especially to women. Although the younger generation, particularly, were anxious to meet him, he seems to have confined himself very largely to the society of old friends.

Of Poe in his latter years, while in Richmond, there are several excellent descriptions by competent observers. Basil C. Gildersleeve, the great classical scholar, then a youth, remembered meeting him frequently upon Broad Street.

A poetical figure, if there ever was one, clad in black as was the fashion then— slender—erect—the subtle lines of his face fixed in meditation. I thought him wonderfully handsome, the mouth being the only weak point.[899]

Poe's fame was even then quite startling. Professor Gildersleeve told of being too shy to seek an introduction, but of obtaining, through J. R. Thompson, Poe's autograph, of which the lad was extremely proud. Edward V. Valentine, then a young boy of about twelve, remembered seeing Poe pass the house, and hearing his uncle say, "There goes Edgar Poe," whereupon he jumped up, ran out into the street,

---

[897] Susan Archer Weiss, *Home Life of Poe*. Many of the Richmond incidents must be drawn from this source (with care). Mrs. Weiss, then Miss Talley, lived in Richmond, and saw much of Poe in 1849.

[898] See a previous reference to a Mrs. Mayo, a protagonist of Poe of former times, Chapter XVII, page 315.

[899] Given by Harrison, *The Life and Letters of Edgar Allan Poe,* vol. I, pages 315-316.

and peered up into the famous gentleman's face, who smiled and passed on. All these were small straws that showed how the wind blew.

He was now greatly pestered to read *The Raven,* which he did on several occasions at various houses. Rosalie also, it appears, annoyed him a good deal by following him about like the lamb which Mrs. Hale forever conferred upon Mary. Rosalie was tremendously fond of her brother; delighted at the applause when he read; and was always seeking to do him little kindnesses. Rosalie Poe was, *by no means, the feeble-minded woman* that she has been represented to be. She was, says a personal acquaintance,[900] "rather pretty, and resembled 'himself' somewhat in appearance, but was as different as possible in mental capacity (*i.e.*), she was amiable, and sweet-tempered, but as a companion wholly tiresome and monotonous. She seemed to have little or no individuality or force of character." Miss Poe had taught writing at Miss Jane Mackenzie's school for nine years, and was an "elegant needlewoman." Rosalie was, at worst, a rather high grade moron. Various other lower mental classifications used to describe her have been technically misapplied. Poe was, nevertheless, much annoyed by her upon occasions, particularly when calling upon Mrs. Shelton. The same curiosity which had annoyed Mrs. Clemm at Fordham in 1846, now bothered him. He would send her home, or elsewhere, upon suddenly remembered and mythical errands.

The wooing of Elmira now went on apace. Mrs. A. Barrett Shelton had now been a widow for some years. She had borne two daughters, both named for her, and both of whom died in infancy, and a son who was then a youth.[901] Mr. Shelton had been a successful merchant, and had left the income of a considerable property to his wife. The estate, on her death, was to go to other heirs. Not long after his arrival in Richmond, Poe called upon her. She was then a rather personable middle-aged woman, with a good deal of self-possession, and pious.

Upon being informed by the servant that a gentleman had called, Mrs. Shelton came downstairs. It was Sunday, and she was dressed for church. Upon her entering the room, Poe rose, saying, with considerable emotion, "Oh! *Elmira,* is it you!" Mrs. Shelton knew him at once, and received him cordially but continued on her way to church, with which she said she never allowed anything to interfere. She asked Poe to call again. He did so. Old times were talked over, and Poe now proposed that Elmira keep the promise which she had made to him twenty-four years before.[902] She at first thought he was jesting ro-

---

[900] Mrs. Clarke, previously mentioned in the Summer of 1848.
[901] Inscription on Mrs. Shelton's tombstone in Shockoe Cemetery in Richmond. Her own name is lacking, but burial records confirm. Also Edward V. Valentine to the author in Richmond, in May, 1926.
[902] See Chapter VIII, page 119.

mantically, but he soon convinced her he was in earnest. At this time, probably towards the end of July, she arrived at what she later described as an "understanding" with her old flame.

The relations between the two are now fairly clear. Poe's early love for the little Elmira was undoubtedly one of the most normal and complete that he ever experienced. It was even more than "Helen" Stanard's the great romance of his youth; *Tamerlane,* Henry Poe's contributions in Baltimore,[903] *Merlin,* by L. A. Wilmer, and a mass of biographical references all prove this. It was partly the loss of Elmira which had driven Poe from Richmond. Elmira, on her part, had found herself deceived by her parents into marrying Mr. Shelton, and, as we have seen, had cherished an affection for her boy-lover, whose letters from the University had never reached her. Her resentment over the affair had afterward alarmed her husband. As the years went on, all this had, of course, been laid aside, but the memory of it with all its connotations, must have made Poe's renewal of his old suit seem like a revival of her girlhood. It was a refreshing draught from the fountain of romance and of youth. Poe, we may be sure, approached her on the basis of the fulfillment of her old promise. He was now famous, an embodiment of his own words in *Tamerlane.*

> Her own Alexis, who should plight
> The love he plighted *then*—again,
> And raise his infancy's delight,
> The bride and queen of Tamerlane—[238]

She remembered him leaning over her at the piano, while they sang. It is certain that all this, flimsy as it may seem, played a great part in the renewal of their friendship. She asked Poe to give her one of the little sketches that he had made for her in 1825. He wrote to Mrs. Clemm about it, and later on must have found it after all, for it was discovered among her effects.[904]

Of the other and worldly considerations there is little need to speak. They were undoubtedly present. Poe saw in Elmira a woman for whom he had once cherished an ardent flame, and who may still have been attractive to him. She could make him comfortable, provide him with a home, and the basis of a social reputation in Richmond, where he intended now to remain on one of the newspapers, and it is also probable that he hoped to be able, under these circumstances, to use his intended wife's fortune as a better basis upon which to conduct the *Stylus* than that offered by Patterson. Above all, he would be living

---

[903] Particularly *The Pirate* in the *Baltimore North American* for 1827. See *Poe's Brother,* Doran, 1926.

[904] Poe's reference to this picture in a letter to Mrs. Clemm from Richmond, September, 1848, is most amusing, and illuminating as to the little domestic artifices practiced by Poe and his mother-in-law. See Harrison, vol. II, pages 369 and 370.

in Richmond, and Mrs. Clemm would be provided with a home. He was very explicit, and anxious about that, as Mrs. Shelton's letter to Mrs. Clemm discloses. Such were some of the factors which, in all probability, entered into this Indian Summer romance. Poe told Mrs. Shelton that she was his "Lost Lenore."

To Robert Sully, his old boyhood friend, of whom he now once more saw a great deal, spending hours with him in his studio, he gave the picture, called the "Fatal Letter," which Mrs. Osgood had noticed hanging over his desk at 85 Amity Street. It seems to have been an illustration for one of Byron's poems, and to Poe represented the despair of Elmira when she had discovered one of his own love letters after her engagement to Mr. Shelton. There was an inscription on the back, now obliterated, with some reference to the Lost Lenore in *The Raven,* and his signature.[905]

The course of true love was not all smooth even now, however. Poe's reputation was, of course, known to Elmira, who, it is said, was somewhat worried about her fortune, and not especially enthusiastic about the *Stylus* scheme. She now made some arrangements to protect her property that are said to have nettled Poe. They had been seen at church together, and talk of the engagement was rife, but, about the beginning of August, a coolness arose between them that threatened for a while to break off the affair. Mrs. Shelton wrote demanding her letters, and she was for a while publicly avoided by Poe.[906]

On August 7th, he lectured before a small but enthusiastic audience of his friends and admirers in the *Exchange* Concert Rooms on *The Poetic Principle.* Several accounts of the occasion remain. Mrs. Shelton was present, but, after the talk was concluded, Poe ignored her and joined the Talley party from Talavera. All the press notices were entirely laudatory except that written by Daniel, whom Poe had "challenged" the Summer before. This appeared in the *Richmond Examiner* two weeks later, and was, in part, as follows:[907]

Poe's subject was *The Poetic Principle* and he treated it with all the acuteness and imagination that we had expected from him. We were glad to hear the lecturer explode what he properly pronounced to be the poetic 'heresy of modern times,' to wit: that poetry should have a purpose, an end to accomplish beyond that of ministering to our sense of the beautiful. . . .

Mr. Poe made good his distinction with a great deal of acuteness and in a very clever manner. His various pieces of criticism upon the popular poets of the country were for the most part just, and were very entertaining. But we were disappointed in Mr. Poe's recitations. We had heard a good deal of his manner, but it does not answer our wants. His voice is soft and distinct,

---

[905] Edward V. Valentine to the author in Richmond, May, 1926. Robert Sully started a painting of the scene of *The Raven* never finished. See Mrs. Weiss.

[906] Mrs. Weiss. She tells of a call of Mrs. Shelton upon Mrs. Mackenzie, to get the latter to prevail upon Poe to return her letters.

[907] *Richmond Examiner,* August 21, 1849.

but neither clear nor sonorous. He does not make rhyme effective; he reads all verse like blank verse; and yet he gives it a sing-song of his own more monotonous than any versification. On the two last syllables of every sentence he invariably falls a fifth. He did not make his own *Raven* an effective piece of reading. At this we would not be surprised were any other than the author its reader. The chief charm perhaps of that extraordinary composition is the strange and subtle music of the versification. As in Mr. Longfellow's rhythm we can hear it with our mind's ear while we read it ourselves, but no human organs are sufficiently delicate to weave it into articulate sounds. For this reason we are not surprised at ordinary failures in reading these pieces. But we anticipated some peculiar charm in their utterances by the lips of him who created the verse, and in this we were disappointed. A large audience was in attendance. Indeed the concert room was completely filled. Mr. Poe commenced his career in this city, and those who had not seen him since the days of his obscurity of course felt no little curiosity to behold so famous a townsman. Mr. Poe is a small thin man, slightly formed, keen visaged, with dark complexion, dark hair, and we believe dark eyes. His face is not an ordinary one. The forehead is well developed and the nose somewhat more prominent than usual. Mr. Poe is a man of very decided genius. Indeed we know of no other writer in the United States who has half the chance to be remembered in the history of literature. But his reputation will rest on a very small minority of his compositions. Among all his poems there are only two pieces which are not execrably bad,—*The Raven* and *Dream-Land*. . . . Had Mr. Poe possessed talent in the place of genius, he might have been a popular and money-making author. He would have written a great many more good things than he has; but his title to immortality would not and could not be surer than it is. For the few things that the author has written which are at all valuable are coins stamped with the unmistakable die. They are of themselves; *sui generis,* unlike any diagram in Time's kaleidoscope, either past, present, or to come—and gleam with the hues of Eternity.

On the other hand, the *Richmond Whig* hoped that Mr. Poe's lecture would be repeated. Basil Gildersleeve was present, and remembered Poe's reading of *The Raven*. Professor Gildersleeve said that upon that occasion Poe was *not* dramatic in his delivery, but was so sensitive to the music of his own verse that he emphasized it markedly in his delivery. Poe was greatly elated over his success, and reception, and made enough money to exist. However, he writes Mrs. Clemm that he can, as yet, send her nothing, commenting enthusiastically upon his press notices, nevertheless.

There were also frequent readings of *The Raven* at the houses of friends, once at the Talleys' where he was especially *en rapport,* and we hear of one occasion when a June-bug ruined the solemnity of the occasion while an old lady tried to protect the poet from the attentions of the insect with her fan. Poe was vastly annoyed.

On the same date as the lecture (August 7th), Poe again wrote to Patterson, once more alluding to the effects of cholera, calomel, and a state akin to congestion of the brain, as the cause for his not having written more. In this letter, which closed the correspondence,[908] Poe balked at the idea of a $3 magazine which Patterson was inclined to favor, and argued for his favorite figure of $5. He was now evidently inclined to put the matter off, probably on account of other prospects, and suggests meeting Patterson at St. Louis, and deferring the appearance of the *Stylus* to July 1, 1850. It was the last glimmer of a ghost that had haunted him since the 1830's.[453] He had, as he hinted to Eveleth that he might do, put its appearance off until the Day of Judgment. The darling dream of his ambition thus slipped unnoticed into the glimmering oblivion of eternity.

A round of parties and entertainments continued. Poe did not have a dress coat, and was embarrassed—and there were other complications. It was hard *not* to take what was pressed upon him, and in August he was again overtaken by another attack of his old trouble, and was attended at Duncan Lodge by his friend on Broad Street, Dr. Carter. There had been another occasion earlier, when he had been nursed in his rooms at the *Old Swan* by the Mackenzies. On the second occasion he was taken home by them. It was very serious. In his condition, one drink would have been sufficient to bring it on. Only the skill of a medical man saved him, and Dr. Carter warned him that one more indulgence would certainly be fatal. The conversation was long and earnest.

Poe told the medical friend of his own desperate efforts to free himself from the clutch of alcohol, and how earnestly he desired to do so. *There is no use denying that his condition, his history, and his admissions mark him at this time as a dipsomaniac.* At this interview with Dr. Carter, he burst into tears, asserting with all the solemnity and pathetic earnestness that any soul could be capable of, that he *would* restrain himself, that he *would* hereafter withstand the temptation. There can be no doubt that he meant it, and trembled at the thought of failure.

To give all possible force to his own resolutions, of whose weakness he knew only too well, it seems to have been shortly after this last seizure that he joined the Shockoe Hill Division of the Sons of Temperance, where he was administered the oath to abstain totally by W. J. Glenn, the presiding officer of the Society. Glenn avers that, until Poe's death in Baltimore, nothing irregular was noticed in his conduct, although a brother teetotaler of the same lodge, who kept a cobbler's shop on Broad Street, was awakened one night shortly afterward, about two

---

[908] Continued after Poe's death by J. R. Thompson, the editor of the *Southern Literary Messenger*.

hours before daylight, by the loud knocks of E. A. Poe demanding a pair of boots that had been left with the shoemaker some days before for repairs.[909] A notice of Mr. Poe's having joined the ranks of the Sons of Temperance appeared in the *Philadelphia Bulletin,* copied from the *Richmond Whig* early in September. His doings, in fact, were noticed widely. Notices of the successful lecture appeared even in the *Cincinnati Atlas.*[909]

As Summer neared its end, Poe was much seen about Broad Street. He still spent some of his time at the office of the *Messenger* with his friend Thompson. In August, a long review of Mrs. Osgood's poems appeared in that paper, where a series of the *Marginalia,* Numbers 11 to 15 inclusive, had been coming out from May to September, 1849. Thompson, who knew Poe's strength and weakness, was uniformly kind, and practically helpful.

Poe had now made for himself a new journalistic connection in his home town. He was a newspaper man, and felt at home in journalistic offices, drawn to the noise of presses, and the desk piled with proof. Like many professional writers, he connected the pen and the press, and must often have composed in the same building where his manuscript went to print. Dressed in a white linen coat and trousers, a black velvet vest, and a broad, planter's Panama hat, Mr. Poe might have been seen in the late Summer of 1849 about the office of the *Richmond Examiner.*

. . . He was the most notable figure among the group of specialists that gathered around John M. Daniel, editor of the *Richmond Examiner.* Daniel was an electric battery, fully charged, whose touches shocked the staid and lofty-minded leaders in Virginia politics. There was about him that indefinable charm that draws men of genius towards one another, though differing in the quality and measure of their endowment. There was Robert W. Hughes, with his strong judicial brain, just starting on his path of distinction. There was Patrick Henry Aylett, a descendant of the great orator, and a rising young lawyer. There was Arthur Petticolas, who had an æsthetic touch that gave his dissertations on Art a special charm and value. The *Examiner* under Daniel was a free lance: it made things lively for all sorts of readers.

Mr. Poe naturally found his way thereto as literary editor. He had already attained celebrity as a writer whose prose and poetry was unlike those of all other persons. The reading public was watching him expectantly, looking for greater things. There was about him something that drew especial notice. His face was one of the saddest ever seen. His step was gentle, his voice soft, yet clear; his presence altogether winning. Though unlike in most particulars, Poe and Daniel affiliated in dealing with a world in which sin and folly on the one hand provoked their wrath and scorn, and on the other appealed to their pity and helpfulness.

---

[909] W. J. Glenn to Prof. J. A. Harrison, Richmond, Virginia, December 4, 1900. Published by Harrison, *The Life and Letters of Edgar Allan Poe,* vol. I, pages 320-322. Also see J. H. Whitty, *Memoir, Collected Poems,* large edition, page lxxiii.

That Mr. Poe was battling with tragic threatenings at this time, now seems pretty clear. The literary public of Richmond knew enough of him to elicit a profound interest in his behalf. . . .[910]

Mr. John M. Daniel was the same "electric battery" with whom, only the Summer before, Mr. Poe had been on the verge of fighting a duel.

Most of the August days of 1849 must have been spent at the office of the *Examiner.* Judge Robert W. Hughes tells of Poe sitting hour after hour revising his poems, and having them set up in the composing room for reference. On the proofs which were then taken, Poe made corrections and alterations. Only two poems were published at the time, *The Raven* in its final form, and *Dreamland,* but the proofs were afterward put into the hands of Poe's good friend, F. W. Thomas, when he came East as literary editor of the *Enquirer.* Thus the time was spent to advantage, even as the last sands were running out.[911]

He was much seen upon Broad Street, going to and from the hotel,—forward looking, erect, close buttoned, the haunting poetical face leaving a memorable impression, with the eyes burning, and mystical under the broad brows and the brim of the Panama hat. Many of the old haunts were revisited. The Allan house, of course, was closed to him, but there must have been a heart-thrilling walk past the real house of his youth, still unaltered, at Fourteenth Street and Tobacco Alley. The ghosts of Frances Allan and "Pa" were there, and the proud wraith of an orphan boy. These old days haunted the inmost recesses of his brain Memory with Poe was a passion.

The Hermitage, the old Mayo house, full of lost ghosts and old cherished dreams, where he had once gone with Rob Stanard, and old "Uncle Billy" to gather chinquapins, was now deserted and falling into ruin, a visible symbol of the loss of his youth. One afternoon he went there with Susan Archer Talley:

On reaching the place our party separated, and Poe and myself strolled slowly about the grounds. I observed that he was unusually silent and preoccupied, and, attributing it to the influence of memories associated with the place, forebore to interrupt him. He passed slowly by the mossy bench called the 'lover's seat,' beneath two aged trees, and remarked, as we turned toward the garden, 'There used to be white violets here.' Searching amid the tangled wilderness of shrubs, we found a few late blossoms, some of which he placed carefully between the leaves of a notebook. Entering the deserted house, he passed from room to room with a grave, abstracted look, and removed his hat, as if involuntarily, on entering the salon, where in old times many a brilliant company had assembled. Seated in one of the deep windows, over which now grew masses

---

[910] Bishop O. P. Fitzgerald; Harrison, *Life and Letters of Edgar Allan Poe,* vol. I, pages 316-320, an address made at the University of Virginia; some parts of this are unreliable.

[911] J. H. Whitty, *Memoir,* gives the best account of Poe's work at the *Examiner* at this time.

of ivy, his memory must have borne him back to former scenes, for he repeated
the familiar lines of Moore:

> 'I feel like one
> Who treads alone
> Some banquet hall deserted,'

and paused with the first expression of real sadness I had ever seen on his face.
The light of the setting sun shone through the drooping ivy-boughs into the
ghostly rooms, and the tattered and mildewed paper-hangings, with their faded
tracery of rose garlands, waved fitfully in the autumn breeze. *An inexpressibly
eerie feeling came over me. . . .*[912]

The overpowering effect of such reveries, and the melancholy mood
that suddenly overwhelmed him, was noticeable to all during this final
interlude, even when mixing in the gay society of those days, and in the
circles he best knew.

For a while he would stand exchanging repartee with all his old pleasure; his face would light up as some old friend approached, and as time
went on he began to lose the haunted and haggard look, and the reserve
of hauteur and cold civility. The men whom he knew he greeted cordially, and his old Byronic air with women now returned, mixed with a
quixotic reverence that was found delightful. He was often seen laughing and talking with young people—then suddenly—as if he felt it all
to be a dream—a melancholy would fall upon him and he would retire
to sit alone or to wander with a solitary friend through the garden, talking musically of vanished days. His personality left an indelible impression upon all. He was a figure that seemed to personify poetic fame,
speaking with a modulated voice of things fit to be rapt in poetic numbers. "Here is something to be remembered," thought those who walked
with him. The world, which forgets so easily, went on record as being
impressed. It was this living human quality that friends afterward
insisted upon talking about, that they tried to preserve for those to follow. And it is just *that* which we must miss in all that has been written
about the man, that no one now can ever really know.

By the beginning of September, he was once more in the good graces
of Mrs. Shelton, and sometime shortly before September 5th they became engaged to be married, for on that date he writes to Mrs. Clemm,
still at Fordham, plainly indicating that the engagement had definitely
taken place.

. . . And now, my own precious Muddy, the very moment I get a definite answer
about everything I will write again and tell you what to do. Elmira talks about
visiting Fordham, but I do not know whether that would do. I think, perhaps,
it would be best for you to give up everything there and come on here in the
Packet. Write immediately and give me your advice about it, for you know

[912] S. A. Weiss, *Scribner's Magazine*, vol. XV, 5, page 712, March, 1878.

best. Could we be happier in Richmond or Lowell? for I suppose we could never be happy at Fordham, and Muddy, I *must* be somewhere where I can see Annie. . . .[913]

He could not forget Mrs. Richmond. A little later in the same letter he returns to the same theme and says, "we could easily pay off what we owe at Fordham, but I want to live *near Annie.* . . . I got a sneaking letter to-day from Chivers. Do not tell me anything about Annie—I cannot bear to hear it now—unless you can tell me that Mr. [Richmond] is dead. I have got the wedding ring, and shall have no difficulty, I think, in getting a dress-coat." So, at the last, it *was* Annie after all. But Mr. Richmond, after the obstinate manner of husbands, survived Poe, who was also worried as to how he was going to appear at his wedding to Elmira without a dress-coat. It was certainly a difficult world!

In the meantime, poor "Muddie" at Fordham had nearly starved to death. She did not have enough money to get into town to make the rounds of her friends. Since the last of June she had received $1 from Poe. He had no more to send. There were promises and hopes. Mr. St. Leon Loud had called at the *Examiner,* and offered Poe $100 to edit his wife's poems. She was a Philadelphia poetess,—"Of course I accepted . . . the whole labor will not occupy me three days . . ." but this brought no bread into the cottage at Fordham, where "Muddie" now waited, alone with her memories. On August 27th, she had been forced to appeal to Griswold in a piteous letter for a "small sum,"— "Indeed I *have* suffered." A week went by and she wrote again. By this time she was back again living with Mrs. Lewis in Brooklyn. Griswold was elusive. He had already written a letter to Poe, promising to accept the commission to edit his works in case of Poe's sudden death.[914]

Meanwhile, in Richmond, time was getting on, while Israfel was spending his last few hours with Lenore upon the edge of the world. It was as if, for a while, the traveler had emerged upon a happy plateau at sunset, and walked with renewed confidence to the edge of the gulf. Early in September, Mrs. Shelton left for the country on a brief visit, while Poe remained in town. All the little last appearances of the man were now remembered, and afterward set down with the peculiar care and atmosphere of importance that last happenings inevitably assume. One catches final glimpses of him going about of evenings, calling on his old friends, as the darkness began to fall.

On September 3rd, he called at the Strobias', and on September 4th, on his old sweetheart Catherine Poitiaux. She had refused to see him

[913] *Griswold,* Prof. Woodberry, 1909, publishes, vol. II, pages 326-329, complete available text.

[914] Mrs. Clemm's condition is known from two of her letters to Griswold, one from Fordham, August 27, 1849, and the other New York, September 4, 1849, both in *Griswold,* published by Woodberry, 1909, vol. II, pages 323-325.

the year before.   Now he came into the room where she was sitting and
greeted her as an old friend who would not be denied.   Catherine was
Frances Allan's god-child.   Poe and she had climbed apple trees together
in long vanished gardens, and she had written him his first "love letter." [915]   He stayed only a few minutes, and then rose to go.   A shade
seemed to fall upon his face, which she felt even then as the shadows
she had seen on the countenances of the dying.   She asked when she
might expect to see him again.   Looking at her, he repeated the words
of *The Raven,* and was gone.

At Sanxey's old bookstore (where he had met Thomas Bolling in
1829, and talked over adventures with the newly printed *Al Aaraaf* in
his hand), J. W. Randolph, who now kept the place, remembered Poe
as he dropped in one day to browse, and how he inquired if old Sanxey,
who, in other days, had loaned him many a volume, was still alive.
Hearing that Sanxey was too feeble to go out, he delighted the old heart
by paying a call.   There were also calls at the Lamberts', and the Bern-
ards', relatives of Thomas White and Frances Allan.[916]

Before Elmira returned, he went to deliver a lecture at Norfolk, probably leaving Richmond on Saturday, September 8th.   At Norfolk, he
called upon some friends, the Ingrams, and made himself especially
agreeable to Miss Susan, the younger daughter of the house.   As the
custom then was, a party was organized, and Poe with several others
went over to take Sunday dinner at the hotel on the beach at Old Point
Comfort.   Over half a century later, Miss Ingram still vividly recalled
the scene.

It was a warm September night and the little company, consisting
mostly of young folks, sat on the beach talking quietly.   There were
Poe, a young collegian, the girls, and Susan's aunt by way of chaperon.
Behind them loomed the large frame bulk of the old *Hygeia House.*
The distant dance music from the hotel orchestra, and bugle calls from
Fortress Monroe, came over the moonlit water full of many sad, secret
memories for an ex-sergeant major, late of the First United States
Artillery:

Mr. Poe sat there in that quiet way of his which made you feel his presence.
After a while my aunt, who was nearer his age, said: 'This seems to be just
the time and place for poetry, Mr. Poe.   And it was.   We all felt it.   The old
Hygeia stood some distance from the water, but with nothing between it and
the ocean.   It was moonlight, and the light shone over everything with that undimmed light that it has in the South.   There were many persons on the long
verandas that surrounded the Hotel, but they seemed remote and far away.   Our
little party was absolutely cut off from everything except that lovely view of

---

[915] Published Chapter V, page 61.
[916] J. H. Whitty, *Memoir, Collected Poems,* large edition, page lxxxii.   Mr. Whitty
also adds some information of Miss Poitiaux, page lxxxi.

the water shining in the moonlight, and its gentle music borne to us on the soft breeze. Poe felt the influence. How could a poet help it? And when we seconded the request that he recite for us he agreed readily. He recited, *The Raven*, *Annabel Lee* and last of all *Ulalume* with the last stanza of which he remarked that he feared it might not be intelligible to us, as it was scarcely clear to himself. . . .

We went from Old Point Comfort to our home near Norfolk, and he called on us there, and again I had the pleasure of talking with him. Although I was only a slip of a girl and he what then seemed to me quite an old man, and a great literary one at that, we got on together beautifully. He was one of the most courteous gentlemen I have ever seen, and that gave a great charm to his manner. . . .

I remember one little instance that illustrated how loyal he was to the memory of those that had been kind to him. I was fond of orris root and always had the odor of it about my clothes. One day when we were walking together he spoke of it. 'I like it, too,' he said. 'Do you know what it makes me think of? My adopted mother. Whenever the bureau drawers in her rooms were opened there came from them a whiff of orris root, and ever since when I smell it I go back to the time when I was a little boy and it brings back thoughts of my mother.' [917]

Perhaps Miss Susan's orris root drew its memory-evoking strength from deeper ground than she knew. On Monday evening after the party, Poe sent his young friend a wistfully charming note enclosing *Ulalume*.

I have transcribed *Ulalume* with much pleasure, Dear Miss Ingram—as I am sure I would do anything at your bidding. . . . I would endeavor to explain to you what I really meant—or what I fancied I meant, by the poem, if it were not that I remembered Dr. Johnson's bitter and rather just remarks about the folly of explaining what, if worth explanations, would explain itself. . . . Leaving *Ulalume* to its fate, therefore, and in good hands. . . . [917]

One ponders at the perfumed ghost of Frances Allan, little Susan, and *Ulalume,* all recalled by one of the last letters that bore the signature "Edgar A. Poe." It was the last touch of moonlight, that evening by the sea.

Through the week, while at Norfolk, Poe called upon his friends several times. On Friday, September 14th, he delivered his lecture in the Norfolk Academy on *The Poetic Principle.* A round of entertainments followed, some of the most brilliant that he had received. For three days, the Norfolk *American Beacon* announced, reported, and praised him to his heart's content. Norfolk was quite a little triumph. "I cleared enough to settle my bill at the *Madison House* with $2 over," he writes Mrs. Clemm from Richmond, September 18th, the night after returning—"Elmira has just got home from the country. I spent last evening with her. I think she loves me more devotedly than I ever knew and I cannot help loving her in return."

[917] *New York Herald,* February 19, 1905, article by Miss Susan Ingram.

Everything was coming out all right after all. On Tuesday, he tells Mrs. Clemm, he will leave for Philadelphia. A day there will do for Mrs. Loud's poems, then (with the $100 in his pocket) *"possibly on Thursday I may start for New York."* He would go straight over to Mrs. Lewis', and send out to Fordham for "Muddie." There were too many sorrowful memories for him to go to Fordham now. "It will be better for me not to go—don't you think so?" As yet he could not send Mrs. Clemm even one dollar, although—"the papers here are praising me to death . . . keep up my file of the *Literary World."* Mrs. Clemm, no doubt, faithful to the last, kept up the file, wondering what she would wear at Eddie's wedding.

At the end of September it seemed as if the pleasant, level plateau over which his feet had for a brief time carried him, sloped suddenly. Down it he walked unusually confident. There was a brief acceleration of human events, a whirl of delirious horror at the edge of the gulf, and then—

On the twenty-second of September he spent the evening at Mrs. Shelton's. All was happily arranged. The marriage was set for October 17th. He was especially happy, for Elmira had consented to write to Mrs. Clemm, which she now did. For a moment it seemed as if all the story might end with the old fairytale formula. Poe had given Elmira a large cameo brooch, from which she would never afterward be parted. After Edgar left, she sat down and wrote to Mrs. Clemm.

Richmond, *Sept. 22nd,* 1849

My dear Mrs. Clemm,—You will no doubt be much surprised to receive a letter from one whom you have never seen, although I feel as if I were writing to one whom I love very devotedly, and whom to *know* is to *love.* . . . Mr. Poe has been very solicitous that I should write to you, and I do assure you, it is with emotions of pleasure that I now do so. I am fully prepared to *love* you, and I do sincerely hope that our spirits may be congenial. There shall be nothing wanting on my part to make them so.

I have just spent a very happy evening with your dear Edgar, and I know it will be gratifying to you to know that he is all that you could desire him to be, sober, temperate, moral, & much beloved. He showed me a letter of yours, in which you spoke affectionately of me, and for which I feel very much gratified & complimented. . . . Edgar speaks frequently & very affectionately of your daughter & his Virginia, for which I love him but the more. I have a very dear friend (to whom I am much attached) by the name of *Virginia Poe.* She is a lovely girl in character, tho' not as beautiful in person as your beloved one.

I remember seeing Edgar, & his lovely wife, very soon after they were married. . . . It is needless (I know) for me to ask you to take good care of him when he is (as I trust he soon will be) again restored to your arms.

'I trust a kind Providence' will protect him and guide him in the way of truth, so that his feet slip not. I hope, my dear friend, that you will write to me, and as Edgar will perhaps reach you as soon as this does, he will direct your letter.

It has struck 12 o'clock, and I am encroaching on the Sabbath, and will therefore conclude. 'Good night, Dear friend,' may Heaven bless you and shield you, and may your remaining days on earth be peaceful and happy. . . .

Thus prays your attached tho' unknown friend.

ELMIRA[918]

Poe's trip back North was to close the cottage at Fordham, certainly to see Griswold, who had undertaken to edit the *Collected Works,* and to bring "Muddie" back to Richmond for the marriage. His last movements in Richmond can be confidently traced.

On Monday, September 24th, he delivered his final lecture, again on *The Poetic Principle,* before an audience of friends who had now, hearing rumors of his engagement, and guessing his necessity, gathered in considerable numbers at the *Exchange Hotel* "with a view to giving him pecuniary assistance in a delicate way . . . there was a touch of old Virginia in the way this was done." At this lecture, from various accounts, it would seem that a decent sum must have been raised. It was sufficient at least for him to start North to get Mrs. Clemm.[919]

The next afternoon (Tuesday the twenty-fifth) he spent at Talavera with his old friends the Talleys, where he told his future biographer, Susan Talley (Mrs. Weiss), that his trip to Richmond had been the happiest experience of many years, and that when he finally left New York to come South, he would feel that he was shaking off the dust of the trouble and vexation of his past life. "On no occasion had I seen him so cheerful and hopeful as upon this evening." He sat chatting to the Talleys in the sitting room, avoiding a party of guests in the parlors to have a few last words with his intimate friends. He was sorry to have to leave Richmond at all, he said, but he would certainly be back again in two weeks. He begged them to write to him while he was away. The other guests left slowly. Poe remained, hating to cut the thread. His hostess and her daughters went to the door with him to say a final good-bye. To the very last, all accidents with him were weirdly consistent—none of them ever forgot the one that followed:

We were standing in the portico, and after going a few steps he paused, turned, and again lifted his hat in a last adieu. At that moment a brilliant meteor appeared in the sky directly over his head, and vanished. . . .[920]

---

[918] Mrs. Shelton to Mrs. Clemm, September 22, 1849. Harrison, vol. II (from manuscript belonging to Miss A. F. Poe).

[919] Bishop O. P. Fitzgerald says $1500, but this is evidently wrong. Mrs. Weiss corrects this statement. The amount was probably helpful but small. There are also *rumors* that Mrs. Shelton gave Poe money to go North, and to return. He "borrowed" $5 from Thompson the day before he left Richmond.

[920] Mrs. Weiss, also quoted by Gill, Chatto & Windus, 1878, page 231. Mrs. Weiss was not superstitious, and says that after the incident they "laughed." The story is undoubtedly true, and one of the dramatic circumstances that seemed to haunt Poe.

Poe went to Duncan Lodge where he spent the night, depressed and thoughtful, smoking in the open window of his room. The next morning he had his trunk packed, and carried down to the *Swan Tavern.* As it was being carried out of the house, a lamp was broken, and Rosalie remarked to Mrs. Mackenzie that no complaint should be made as it was broken by a poet.[921] It was the last time that Poe slept beneath the mercifully sheltering roof of Duncan Lodge. Mrs. Mackenzie continued to shelter Rose. The trunk, "most of his estate," was a small black leather one, bound with iron hoops, and containing manuscripts, and a few other belongings. Its subsequent history was curious.[922] Dr. William Gibbon Carter and Dr. Mackenzie accompanied him to town.

Wednesday, September 26th, Poe spent about Richmond with his friends. He called upon Thompson of the *Messenger,* who advanced him $5, and, as he left, Poe turned to him and said, "By the way, you have been very kind to me,—here is a little trifle that may be worth something to you." He then handed Thompson a small roll of paper with *Annabel Lee* written on it in his beautiful script. Poe passed the rest of the day with some of his friends about town. During the afternoon, Miss Susan Talley was visited by Rosalie, bearing a note from Poe in which he enclosed the lines *For Annie.* Towards evening he went to Church Hill for a final call upon Elmira. At this interview he appeared very sad, and Mrs. Shelton said *he complained of being quite sick.* She felt his pulse, and found him to be distinctly feverish, and she did not think him able to travel next morning.[923]

Walking along Broad Street on his way back from Mrs. Shelton's, he stopped in at Dr. Carter's office where he read the newspaper and left, taking, by mistake, the doctor's Malacca cane and leaving his own. He went across the street to *Sadler's Restaurant,* a well-known place of entertainment in Richmond, which informed its customers by way of a slogan that "Thirteen old gentlemen were made sick by eating Turtle Soup at Sadler's." Here Poe met J. M. Blakey, and some other acquaintances. The party was a cheerful one, conversation went on to a late hour, and was joined in by the host, Mr. Sadler. Poe, it was said, appeared cheerful himself and was sober.

---

[921] Edward V. Valentine to the author in Richmond in May, 1926. From an item contributed by a lady who was present at the Mackenzies' when Poe left (in Mr. Valentine's diary).

[922] For the history of this trunk, now at the Edgar Allan Poe Shrine, Richmond, Virginia, see the *Valentine Museum Poe Letters,* edited by Mary Newton Stanard, page 179.

[923] Mrs. Shelton to Mrs. Clemm. Letter in the Poe-Chivers papers, quoted from Prof. Woodberry, 1909, vol. II, page 341.

Judge Hughes of Richmond afterward said that both Sadler and Blakey told him they distinctly remembered meeting Poe at the restaurant that night, and that they did not think he was drinking. He was talking of going North, and when they saw him last, shortly before his departure, they were certain he was quite sober.[924]

Some of the party accompanied Poe to the wharf, and saw him off. The boat left for Baltimore at four o'clock on the morning of September 27, 1849. Next morning Elmira, who was uneasy about him, came downtown to look him up. She was surprised to find that he had gone so suddenly, and recorded her anxiety. Thus Elmira was left in Richmond, while Edgar proceeded rapidly toward the edge of the world.

---

[924] J. H. Whitty prints this information in his *Memoir* to the *Complete Poems*.

CHAPTER TWENTY-SEVEN

AN APPEAL TO HIGHER AUTHORITY

THE steamer for Baltimore continued on its way. It was then a voyage of about forty-eight hours from Richmond with many stops. Several things might have happened on the route, and on most steamboats at that time there was a bar forward, for the refreshment of gentlemen travelers. The contingencies will bear being kept in mind.[925]

There is little doubt that, when he left Richmond, Poe was once more approaching one of his periods of collapse. The usual symptoms of great depression, amounting almost to melancholia, had been noted by many as he took his leave, and Elmira noticed that he had a feverish pulse.[923] It was probably the heart again. He had been quite active for some time, and was laboring under considerable excitement over the move South, and his approaching marriage. Under the circumstances, an attack was due. His sudden departure at four A.M., surprising Elmira, seems to show that, even at the time of leaving Richmond, he was a bit irrational.[926] What happened at *Sadler's,* or what took place on the boat, it is impossible to be sure about. Poe was in that peculiar condition, a physical dilemma in fact, that few who have discussed his failings seem to realize, *i.e., his failing heart required a stimulant which would be disastrous to his brain.* So far, largely through the good fortune of falling into the hands of friends, and of a latent power of recovery, he had survived. His strength was now exhausted, and Dr. Carter had warned him that one more lapse would bring on a fatal attack. He ventured to overstep the mark, and this time he did not fall into the hands of friends. The result was, as had been medically predicted, fatal.

---

[925] Steamers stopped by signal from plantation wharfs. Poe may have changed to the Norfolk-Baltimore steamer at Old Point Comfort. From a contemporary map (1850) in the writer's possession, the steamboat route from Richmond to Baltimore was by way of Eppe's Island, Windmill Point, Powhatan, Sandy Point, Hog Island, Day's Point, Old Point Comfort, Rappahanoc River, Smith's Point, Point Lookout, Patuxent River, Cove Point, Sharp's Island, Herring Bay, Annapolis, Sandy Point, North Point, Baltimore (Map, tables 3 and 5). In 1815, the round trip, steamboat, from Baltimore to Norfolk, required a week. In 1820, the time was cut to twenty hours; by 1840 it required thirteen or fourteen, where it remained for some time. The trip to Richmond from Baltimore in 1849 must have taken at least forty-eight hours with stops. See *Steamboat Days* by F. E. Dayton.

[926] Woodberry shows conclusively that Poe's departure from Richmond at 4 A.M. was somewhat of a whim.

When, or how, he took the drink is a futile discussion. There is no doubt that he did. An attack, such as that which he had experienced at Philadelphia with similar delirium, ensued. The chronicle of the next few days is consequently involved in the lurid mists of confusion.

The steamer landed at Baltimore, probably during the forenoon of Saturday, September 29th. What now happened must be pieced out, if possible, by the most plausible conjectures available, made by those familiar with the locality and its customs. We know that Poe was ostensibly upon his way to Philadelphia where he expected to revise Mrs. St. Leon Loud's poems for a fee of $100. It also seems that, on passing through Baltimore, he expected to call upon some of his friends, for he actually attempted to do so. The trains for Philadelphia left at nine A.M., and eight P.M., and there would therefore have been several hours to wait. If Poe went to a hotel, he would most naturally have chosen the *United States Hotel,* then just opposite the Baltimore and Ohio Railroad Station, or possibly old *Bradshaw's,* nearby.[927] Whether he did so is not known. Sometime during the day he called at the residence of his friend, Dr. Nathan C. Brooks, at which time he was said to have been intoxicated. A void of five days then took place in his history, about which nothing certain can ever be ascertained.[928]

There was an election going on in Baltimore, at the time, for members of Congress and representatives to the State Legislature. The town was notoriously corrupt politically, and terrorized by gangs of hoodlums. Voters were not registered, and anyone who would, or could hold up his hand before a judge of elections, and face the ordeal of a "challenge," was permitted to take the oath. Thus the party which could round up the greatest number of helpless "voters" could win any election. For several days before balloting such helpless unfortunates as political gangs could sandbag or intimidate were "mobilized," and kept docile with drugs and whiskey at various places called "coops." They were then repeatedly voted.

There was an election due in Baltimore on October 3, 1849, and, five days before it began, Poe arrived. He was, therefore, in Baltimore while the "campaign" for voters was going on. That he was, when in

---

[927] *New York Herald,* March 27, 1881 (Spencer), a discussion of Dr. Snodgrass' *The Facts of Poe's Death and Burial, Beadle's Monthly,* 1867.

[928] Several other stories about Poe's doings during these five days exist. He is said to have taken a train to Philadelphia, and to have been put off at Havre de Grace, Maryland, and sent back (Conductor George Rollins)—evidence second-hand and very flimsy. Bishop O. P. Fitzgerald mentions Poe's attending a birthday party, and drinking a toast to the "fair hostess"—certainly apocryphal. The election incident story is given here not as certain, but as the *most probable.* The best discussions are in Woodberry and Harrison.

an already helpless condition, seized upon and "cooped" is not only quite a possible but by far the most probable explanation of what happened. The reasons for supposing so follow : [929]

On High Street, in the rear of an old engine-house, there was a Whig "coop," notorious as the "Fourth Ward Club." It is said that in 1849 there were imprisoned there between 130 and 140 "voters." Poe was found, upon election day, within two squares of this place at *Cooth & Sergeant's Tavern* in Lombard Street, near High Street. From now on we are once more dealing with witnesses and facts.

On October 3, 1849, James E. Snodgrass, M. D.,[547] an old friend of Poe, who lived at 103 High Street within about two blocks of *Cooth & Sergeant's Tavern,* received a note scrawled in pencil that read:

> Baltimore City, 3d, 1849
>
> DEAR SIR,—There is a gentleman, rather the worse for wear, at Ryan's 4th ward polls, who goes under the cognomen of Edgar A. Poe, and who appears in great distress, and he says he is acquainted with you, and I assure you he is in need of immediate assistance.
>
> Yours in haste,
>
> To Dr. J. E. Snodgrass   Jos. W. WALKER [930]

Dr. Snodgrass recognized the signature as that of a compositor on the *Baltimore Sun* whom he knew slightly.[931] It is evident that Walker recognized Poe as a *gentleman* in the wrong surroundings, and sent the note to Snodgrass, because Poe knew him, and because he (the doctor) lived near, and was a medical man.

Dr. Snodgrass hastened through the rainy, chill October weather to the tavern, where he found Poe in the barroom, sitting helpless in an armchair, surrounded by ruffians.

His face was haggard, not to say bloated, and unwashed, his hair unkempt and his whole physique repulsive. His expansive forehead . . . and those full-orbed and mellow, yet soulful eyes for which he was so noticeable when himself, now lusterless as shortly I could see, were shaded from view by a rusty, almost brimless, tattered and ribbonless palm leaf hat. His clothing consisted of a sack-coat of thin and sleezy black alpaca, ripped more or less at intervals of its seams, and faded and soiled, and pants of a steel-mixed pattern of cassinett, half worn and

---

[929] The author examined various files of the Baltimore newspapers for October, 1849, at the Maryland Historical Society in Baltimore in May, 1926, also various pamphlets dealing with hospitals and church homes in Baltimore, for some of the facts given in this chapter. Directories of the day were also consulted.

[930] The version of the note given here is a copy from the original. See Harrison, *The Life and Letters of Edgar Allan Poe,* vol. I, pages 327-328. This note has been frequently misquoted, due to Dr. Snodgrass' garbled version. Note copied by W. Hand Browne for Prof. Harrison.

[931] J. W. Walker, printer, was afterwards drowned, so no further evidence from him appears.

badly fitting, if they could be said to fit at all. He wore neither vest nor neck cloth, while the bosom of his shirt was both crumpled and badly soiled. . . ."[932]

Dr. Snodgrass, at first, tried to get a private room for Poe at the "tavern," but while this was being prepared, with confusion and delay, Mr. Herring, Poe's cousin, arrived.[933] After some consultation, it was decided that Poe had better be taken to the Washington Hospital. A carriage was sent for, and the dying man was carried to the conveyance, still grasping Dr. Carter's Malacca cane that he had brought by mistake from Richmond. The unconscious, but still muttering wreck of a great poet was now drawn by horses through the streets of Baltimore, and delivered at the Washington Hospital into the hands of the physician on duty, Dr. J. J. Moran, at the hour of 5 P.M. This was on Wednesday, October 3rd.

Poe remained unconscious until three o'clock next morning. The mercy of oblivion was then withdrawn. Drenched in perspiration, with shaking limbs, pale, and talking constantly in a "busy but not violent or active delirium, the whole chamber seethed for him, and with vacant converse he talked to the spectres that withered and loomed on the walls."

Dr. Moran was now called in, and endeavored to obtain some information about where he lived, and his relatives. "But his answers were incoherent and unsatisfactory." He told the physician that he had a wife in Richmond, doubtless thinking of Elmira. Sometime during the day Neilson Poe called, but could not be allowed to see his cousin. Changes of linen, and all comforts were sent him. The Poe and Herring relatives left nothing lacking.

Seeing that he was a gentleman, the doctor had Poe placed in a room not far from the living quarters of his family, and the bedside of the sufferer was visited by the physician's wife, Mrs. Mary O. Moran.

The key to his trunk was found in his clothes, but he could not remember what had become of the trunk. He seems to have left it at the *Old Swan Tavern* in Richmond. Dr. Moran, seeing his case was hopeless, strove to cheer him by telling him that in a few days "he would be able to rejoin the society of his friends." The thought seems to have

---

[932] The account here is taken from *The Facts of Poe's Death and Burial,* by J. E. Snodgrass, M.D., in *Beadle's Monthly,* pages 283 to 288 (1867), original text furnished by John T. Snyder, Esq. The author is aware of the doubtful elements in part of this story, written eighteen years later, but, as Dr. Snodgrass *was present,* his testimony is that of a direct witness, the only one available. The fact that the doctor's memory of dates failed him does not vitiate his memory of Poe's appearance, and the events. Note that Poe wore a "planter's" hat in Richmond, and still had the wreck of it as described by Dr. Snodgrass.

[933] How he was informed does not appear. That he was informed is evident.

maddened the patient instead of soothing him, for he "broke out with much energy and said the best thing his best friend could do would be to blow out his miserable brains with a pistol—that when he beheld his miserable degradation he was ready to sink into the earth." All that he had lost must now have flashed upon him in "concentrated despair." Worn out, he dozed,—when the doctor returned a little later two nurses were struggling to keep him in bed. A demon, worse than all that he had imagined, tormented him in a long and violent delirium.

It went on for days. Neither Mrs. Clemm nor "Annie" knew. They did not come. In the desperate struggles and agonies of remorse, what was left of him was worn away. Dr. Moran's wife, hearing he was quiet at last, came down the passage from the wing where she kept house, to take down his last directions, thinking he had something tangible to leave.

He asked her if there was any hope. She replied, thinking he meant, hope for recovery, that her husband thought him a very ill man. He then said, "I meant hope for a wretch like me beyond this life." She tried to comfort him, "with the words of the Great Physician," and read him the fourteenth chapter of *St. John.* Wiping the beads of perspiration from his brow, she smoothed his pillow, gave him a soothing draught, and departed to make his shroud. What Poe thought no one will ever know. Nothing less heartrending can truthfully be said, than that the death of Edgar Allan Poe was more painful than his life.

He lived from Wednesday, the third, to the Sunday following. On Saturday night he began to dream of the past. It would be grateful to record, or to suppose that he sank back into the sunny valley of his childhood, and saw Mrs. Stanard again, that he wandered in gardens with little Rob and Elmira, or that Frances Allan might have come to his bedside, as she used, to soothe his troubled sleep. But we know this was not what happened. Nothing was spared him.

On the last night, as the shadow fell across him, it must have been the horrors of shipwreck, of thirst, and of drifting away into unknown seas of darkness[934] that troubled his last dreams, for, by some trick of his ruined brain, it was the scenes of *Arthur Gordon Pym* that rose in his imagination, and the man who was connected most intimately with them. "Reynolds!" he called, "Reynolds! Oh, Reynolds!" The room rang with it. It echoed down the corridors hour after hour all that

---

[934] J. N. Reynolds connected with a project for the exploration of the South Polar Seas. Poe was interested in this in Richmond during the time he was on the *Messenger* there, and writing *Arthur Gordon Pym.* He may have had interviews with Reynolds in New York, where *Pym* was published in 1838. See also Poe's review of J. N. Reynolds' pamphlet, *South Sea Expedition,* in the *Southern Literary Messenger* for January, 1837. See note 503 and context, this text.

Saturday night. The last grains of sand uncovered themselves as they slipped away, during the Sunday morning of October 7, 1849. He was now too feeble to call out any more. It was three o'clock in the morning and the earth's shadow was still undisturbed by dawn.

He became quiet, and seemed to rest for a short time. Then, gently moving his head, he said, "Lord help my poor soul."

for the terrible agony which I have so lately endured — an agony known only to my God and to myself — seems to have passed my soul through fire and purged it from all that is weak Henceforward I am strong :— this those who love me shall see — as well as those who have so relentlessly endeavored to ruin me

Facsimile of part of a letter of Poe to Mrs. Helen Whitman

APPENDICES

NOTES ON POE'S ANCESTRY

PATERNAL

EDGAR (ALLAN) POE'S ancestry, on his father's side, was Scotch-Irish, and can be traced back into the Parish of Fenwick in Ayrshire, Scotland, where there were intermarriages with some of the remote ancestors of the Allans and Galts. The Poes belonged to the Protestant Scotch who went to Ireland. There is some indication that their name is one of the variants of Powell, Powr, Power, etc. All attempts to be dogmatic about the immediate ancestry of the poet, prior to the early Eighteenth Century, must be regarded as whimsically doubtful.

By about 1745, there are some genuine documents and records to be traced, with authentic mention of the Poes about Dring, in the Parish of Kildallen, County Cavon, Ireland. Here one *David Poe* (great-great-grandfather of the poet) departed this vale of tears shortly before August, 1742, leaving a will containing considerable theological sophistry, and some tangible biological records. Upon his wife, Sarah, he had begotten, in the order named, Alexander, John, and Anna.

Alexander Poe came to America about 1739, and settled at Marsh Creek, near the present Gettysburg Battlefield in Lancaster County, Pennsylvania. He prospered, and must have written home to brother *John Poe,* still in Ireland, and now married to Jane McBride. *John Poe* and Jane McBride Poe, bringing with them two young sons, *David Poe* and George Poe, therefore left Ireland about 1748, or a little earlier (date not certain), and landing at Newcastle, Delaware, at first went to settle in Pennsylvania. John Poe and Jane, his wife, had ten children in their family. It was their son, *David Poe,* who was the poet's grandfather. This *David Poe* lived in Pennsylvania where he married a Miss Elizabeth Cairnes, whose family also hailed from Ireland, but had been living in Lancaster County, Pennsylvania.

Sometime prior to the outbreak of the American Revolution, *David Poe* and his wife Elizabeth moved to Baltimore where his pursuits were various, ranging from making furniture and spinning-wheels to driving the British and Tories out of Baltimore. In 1778 he was appointed as "Assistant Deputy Quartermaster" of the Continental forces, which meant that he was a purchasing agent for the Revolutionary Army. He is said to have been of great assistance to La Fayette (I have not been able to trace the sources except for some minor mention that tends to confirm the tradition). His services caused him to be spoken of as "General." From 1790 on, there is no difficulty in tracing him. The Federal Census of 1790 shows David Poe to have owned four slaves, to have had nine "free white males" in his household (four under 16 years of age), and two free white females. By the aid of old Baltimore directories, he can now be traced as follows:

About 1800—173 West Baltimore Street,—Store and Residence
"   1807   17 Camden Street, Fish Inspector
"   1810   19 Camden Street, [number probably changed (?)]
"   1812   Park Lane
October 19, 1816—Death notices.

This brief sketch of the poet's grandfather, David Poe, in many respects a remarkable man, must end here, except to note that he had by his wife Elizabeth Cairnes seven children. Three only, of these seven, concern us:

1. *David Poe* (eldest son, father of Edgar)
2. Maria Poe (afterward Mrs. Maria Clemm) *aunt and mother-in-law* of Edgar Poe, the poet.
3. Eliza Poe (afterward Mrs. Henry Herring)

David Poe, the poet's father married a widow, Mrs. Elizabeth Hopkins (born Arnold), and had three children:

> William Henry Leonard Poe (no issue)
> *Edgar Poe*—(the poet)   (no issue)
> Rosalie Poe   (no issue)

Note: To avoid confusion, all accounts of collateral relatives springing from *brothers of the poet's grandfather, David Poe,* are here omitted.

MATERNAL

Trace of Poe's ancestry, on the maternal side, is to be found in play bills and pamphlets, not readily obtainable in America, of the Drury Lane Theatre, London, and in the records of St. George's Parish, London. The maternal great-grandfather of the poet was *William Smith,* an actor of some repute, and occasional flattering mention. His daughter, *Elizabeth Smith,* married *Henry Arnold,* the son of one William Henry Arnold, author of some comedies produced at the Drury Lane about the end of the Eighteenth Century. The brother of William Henry Arnold, James Arnold, became manager of the Drury Lane Theatre in 1812. (*It has not been possible to collect much data on these Arnolds in America. What material has been available, all points to the fact that they were persons of considerable executive, literary, and histrionic talents. Names and dates were checked by a friend of the author from old play bills and pamphlets in England.*)

Henry Arnold and *Elizabeth Arnold* (born Smith) were the maternal grandparents of Edgar Allan Poe. From Church Records at St. George's, London, where many "theatrical marriages" were performed, it appears that the couple were married about June, 1784. Sometime in the Spring of 1787 (*Ingram*), a daughter was born to them, baptized "Elizabeth." *Elizabeth Arnold* was the mother of Edgar Allan Poe.

Henry Arnold's name, the author is informed by an English correspondent, disappears from the play bills about 1783 (*sic*). He appears to have died, leaving his widow with the young *Elizabeth* Poe to support. Her mother (Poe's maternal grandmother) acted at the Covent Garden Theatre Royal, London, and appears on the play bills there of the 1790's, as a singer. Early in 1796, taking the young Elizabeth (Poe's mother) with her, she came to America, and landed at Boston. Either before, or immediately after her arrival in the United States, she married a Mr. Charles Tubbs who acted (danced?) and played the pianoforte. The appearances of Mr. and Mrs. Tubbs, and of the young Elizabeth Arnold from 1796 on, can be plainly traced in old American play bills at Boston, Portland, Newport, Rhode Island, New York, Charleston, South Carolina, etc., etc., and in the dramatic notices in the newspapers of the time. (Professor Woodberry gives a nearly complete list of Miss Arnold's, Mrs. Poe's, appearances from 1796 to 1811.)

In the Summer of 1802, *Elizabeth Arnold* married an actor by the name of C. D. Hopkins; apparently an American. C. D. Hopkins died October 26, 1805, leaving his widow, *Elizabeth Arnold Hopkins,* childless. In January, 1806, the widow, *Elizabeth Arnold Hopkins,* married *David Poe,* an actor in the same company with her. There were born of this union three children:

> William Henry Leonard Poe—Boston, 1807
> *Edgar (Allan) Poe*—Boston, January 19, 1809
> Rosalie Poe—Norfolk, December 10, 1810 [?]

The last date entered in the Mackenzie Bible is not certain, nor is Rosalie's parentage.

Mrs. David Poe (Elizabeth Arnold) died in Richmond, Sunday, December 8, 1811, and was buried at ten o'clock Tuesday, December 10th, at St. John's Episcopal Church, in Richmond, Virginia, where she now lies, in a grave until recently unmarked. Of her three children, all were childless.

GALT CORRESPONDENCE, ETC.

THE following miscellaneous items deal with the early Richmond days of Poe's childhood, or the trip of the Allans to England from 1815 to 1820.

ONE

Letter from John Allan's niece Mary Fowlds at Kilmarnock, Scotland, to John Allan, Esq., at 47 Southampton Row, London:

MY DEAR UNCLE—   Kilmarnock, 11*th Nov.* 1815

I observed by your letter to Father that you were extremely fond I should have a sweetheart. I think they would only be lumber at present but I don't intend to be an old maid the more of that but when my education is over then will I make a bold push and see what I can do. I hope Miss Valentine has got a beau to make a husband of by this time as she is in the Capitol. I suppose they will be as the midges in a summers' evening and when she is served herself I hope she will send down a gross or two as they are a scarce commodity here and she may rely upon the thanks of all the ladies in Kilmarnock. I must finish this love story. Hope Mrs. Allan has got quite well again and able to go about and see all the curiosities as I understand they are great in number. We are often wondering how you are all coming on indeed when we are all met together at night (as you know I am always engaged at school through the day) you generally engross part of our conversation. We dined and spent the evening at Mrs. Fowlds (grandmother) on Halloween and according to the custom of Scotland we burnt our nuts and pulled our stocks. I was just making the observation had you been here you would have enjoyed [it] highly. We are all pretty well at present. My mother was engaged in making puddings yesterday and while she was filling the skins she was just saying how happy she would be if you would all come in on her and assist in eating them. I have no news to give you— the people here are just as you left them. All the family join me in love to you, Mrs. Allan, Miss Valentine and little Edgar [*Poe*]. I am my Dear Uncle your affectionate niece. I shall be hoping to hear from you soon.

                                                          MARY FOWLDS

The above letter fixes the address of the Allans at 47 Southampton Row, London, as early as November, 1815, and the fact that young Poe was then in London. *From Galt-Allan correspondence, courtesy of E. V. Valentine, Esq.*

TWO

(a) Allan Fowlds addresses a letter to John Allan "at 47 Southampton Row, Near Russell Square, London," from Kilmarnock, Scotland, May 27, 1817.

(b) Mary Allan writes to her brother, John Allan, from Troon, Scotland, August 22, 1817, addressing him at "18 Basing Hall, London."

(c) *Unpublished portion of a letter quoted in the text, Jane Galt to Mary Allan:*

MY DEAR MARY   Damlish, *Oct.* 24, 1818

Mrs. Allan intended to have wrote herself to day but is very Weak.—? and is afraid she will feel too much fatigued to write. We leave this on Monday for

Sidmouth where Mrs. Elwell proposes staying two days we will let you know from there what day we shall have the pleasure of seeing you in Southhampton Row. Mrs. Allan seems to dread very much the returning to London as she will enter it about the first of November. (See text, Chapter V, note 127.)

(d) In a letter to John Allan at Richmond, Virginia, Mary Allan writes from Kilmarnock, March 24, 1815.

. . . by your letter to Mrs. Fowlds I am sorry to read that Mrs. Allan had been so indisposed. I hope by this time she is quite well and that her face will not be injured by the fracture. . . .

This accident to Mrs. Allan seems to have delayed the trip of the family to England for some months.

Three

Notices in Old Richmond Newspapers of Mrs. David Poe (Supplied by E. V. Valentine, Esq.).

(a) First mention of David and Mrs. Poe as a married couple, in Richmond papers—July, 1806.

(b) Last notice of Mrs. Poe's Richmond benefit. *Patriot,* November 29, 1811. (Last appearance was Tuesday, October 8th.) (Mrs. Poe died Sunday, December 8, 1811.) Death notice in *Richmond Enquirer* for December 10, 1811, "By the death of this . . ." etc. The *Richmond Patriot* for December 10, 1811, contained a notice of her funeral at ten o'clock.

(c) In 1804, Mr. and Mrs. C. D. Hopkins appeared with David Poe in plays given in Richmond, in an old carriage shop used as a temporary theater, situated just behind what was later the Allan residence at Fifth and Main. (*Hopkins*—Mrs. Poe's first husband.)

Sully

(d) Mrs. Poe (as Mrs. Hopkins) acted with Matthew Sully, brother of the artist, Thomas Sully, in 1803 in Norfolk. The Sullys had just then come over from England. Robert Sully, Poe's friend, was a son of the actor Matthew Sully.

Usher

(e) The name of Usher, as early friends of the Poes, occurs frequently in old play bills. These Ushers appear later to have settled in Baltimore, and to have known the Poes there. In the *Baltimore North American* for Saturday, October 27, 1827, occurs this notice:

Died . . . On Friday evening, the 12th inst. Elizabeth Usher, daughter of the late Thomas Usher, sen. of the county of Antrim, Ireland, and formerly a merchant of this city.

Four

Data concerning Poe's Foster-Mother, Frances Allan

Mrs. Allan (Frances Keeling Valentine) and her sister, Anne Moore Valentine, were early left orphans. At eleven and twelve years of age, respec-

tively, they appeared in Hustings Court, on January 12, 1795, and volun-
tarily took John Dixon (a Richmond printer, who seems earlier to have
had affiliations in Williamsburg on the *Government Gazette*) as guardian.
The two girls were brought up by this printer. Frances Valentine married
John Allan in 1803. Young Poe was much about the house of John Dixon
during boyhood days. Poe's early experience brought him much into contact with printing and book-selling. Ebenezer Burling's father, Thomas
Burling, was also a printer. A Richmond correspondent says that John
Dixon sheltered Poe from some of the "coarse influences" he was early
subjected to.

FIVE

Miscellaneous Legal Notices, etc.

(a) *Richmond Compiler,* April 24, 1832—sale of John Allan's property
on deed of trust, corner of Main and Fifth Streets, Clay Street house, advertised. See Book Number 7, page 580. *Ellis & Allan.*

(b) John Allan elected Secretary of Amiable Society Club.—*Richmond
Whig,* November 27, 1830.

(c) Sale of property of *Ellis & Allan,* advertised in *Richmond Compiler*
for May 13, 1822. This was bought in by an advance of $10,000 on a note
endorsed by William Galt now in the *Ellis & Allan Papers.*

WILLS OF WILLIAM GALT AND JOHN ALLAN

THE following correspondence and legal documents are here appended, in full, as tending to clear up many erroneous and vague statements of years past, concerning the matters with which the letters and wills, here printed, deal. As all of the persons mentioned in the wills, here appended, have long been dead, and the matters to which they relate are almost a century (in some cases more than a century) of past date,—the only genuine interest which now attaches to them is purely literary, in so far as they tend to throw light upon the early condition of affairs in Richmond in Poe's boyhood, the persons surrounding him, and the causes of the troubles in the Allan household. The will of John Allan, in particular, is, in itself, a striking comment on the character of Edgar Allan Poe's guardian. It is felt that much of the text, and the construction put upon events in Poe's boyhood, in the earlier part of this biography, will be materially strengthened by thus publishing the chief documents upon which many of the assertions made in the body of the text must, in the final analysis, rely for proof.

For three quarters of a century the character of Edgar Allan Poe has been persistently under a cloud, in regard to his relations with his guardian. The second Mrs. Allan charged Poe with forgery, and he was supposed to have been callously ungrateful for the "tender cherishing" he received at John Allan's hands. Poe, on his part, it must be remembered, must inevitably have known of all the facts here shown, and *more*. The present biographer is in possession of still further facts, casting additional light on still other domestic relations of Poe's guardian which, for reasons at the present, still cogent and delicate, it is not felt advisable to print. The documents printed below are:

One: A letter from Thomas Bolling of "Cobbs" in Chesterfield County, Virginia, to Colonel William Bolling of Bolling Hall in Goochland County, Virginia, dated Richmond, November 29, 1800. This letter is from a Virginia planter of good family who was a customer of William Galt, John Allan's uncle, the founder of the Allan fortune. It is here printed to show the opinion in which William Galt, and Scotch merchants of his type, were held by gentleman planters. It tends to throw a humorous light on the opening sentences of William Galt's Will. The letter is printed by courtesy of the Edgar Allan Poe Shrine, Richmond, Virginia.

Two: Letters from the County Clerk's Office, Goochland, Virginia, to the author.

Three: The Will of William Galt (*Sr.*).

Four: The Will of John Allan (foster-father of Edgar Allan Poe).

Five: Comments on some legal aspects of John Allan's Will.

ONE

Richmond, *29th Nov.*, 1800

My DEAR SON

Your favor of the 26th Inst. I recd. yesterday inclosing me a draught upon P. P. & Johnston, which I'm sorry to inform you, was rejected, owing to a mistake of Mr. S. Saunder's drawing it upon a 25. stamp when it should have been upon one of 50. the Genl. informs me, that if he will renew it upon a stamp of 50. Cents that they will still pay it on the 10th of next Month. I thank you, for the attention paid me, with respect to Saunder's Flour, if his Flour is very fine, I wish you to engage 6 Barrels of it for me, I shall this Day pay off your account with Biscoes & Galt. Biscoes account is £35.15.5½ and to old Galt £61.15.11. you will perhaps be surprised when I have to inform you, that I have engaged with the Old skinflint again, when I came up yesterday Morning he asked me, if it was not time for P. M. Boyce to come down for my Negroes Cloathing. I told him that I expected that he, or Mr. Ragland would be down this Day, but that I was done with him, that I had called upon him for your account and mine, that I intended to sell my Tobacco, pay him off our account and have nothing more to do with him; he appeared to be much surprised, and a more anxious Man, you never saw, than he was, to have me continue my dealings with him, however, I told him, I was much vexed at my last Year's account and that I could not deal with him any longer, and went up to Polloc's, when I got there he refused to furnish me with any article, but at the runing rates, of course I could not engage with him, as that was his mode of dealing, and fortunately as I thought, when returning, I met D. Ragland who told me, that Mr. Galt called him in, and told him to endeavor with me to take my Goods of him, if he should meet with me, I accordingly went. The Old Man told me that I must not leave him, that he would be bound I should have no fault to find with my account after taking them up, he assured me that I should [get] my New Goods at 100% ["100%," *the meqning is not clear here, perhaps a slip of the pen for 10%*] from the prime cost and gave me 33/6 for my Tobacco, which was 16 more than any other person would give and I could not tell where to apply, after leaving Polloc. Ragland is pleased with the Goods. Give my kind Love to my dear little William Bolling and tell him in addition to his Order or rather request, I have sent him a Cap which I hope will please, and will be delivered to him by Mr. Dudley Ragland, if the Shoes does not fit, they can be changed. The Puttie glass and only one Bunch of Nail Rod, as it is quite too large, and smaller is not now to be had in Town, for Mr. R and one of Mr. Galts young men, has been all over the Town of Richmond, and can not get any smaller. I thought it best to send one bunch, tho it was too large. I am in great haste with most affectionate Love to You all

Your Ever Affectionate Father

THOMAS BOLLING

N. B. I have paid your account to B. J. Shephard, £7.

Two

County Clerk's Office

GOOCHLAND COUNTY

Goochland, Virginia

P. G. MILLER, *Clerk*

HERVEY ALLEN, *Esq.*,   *November 28, 1925*
DEAR SIR:—

Replying to your letter of the 24th instant. The will of John Allan (1834) is not recorded here. You will find a copy of the will recorded in the Chancery Court of the City of Richmond, in Will Book No. 2, page 457. The will of

William Galt (copy) is recorded in the same office in Deed Book 117-B, page 99. Mr. Chas. O. Saville is the clerk of the Chancery Court of the City of Richmond.

Yours very truly,

P. G. MILLER

(*Clerk*)

(P. S.) The "Byrd" lands, comprising upwards of 6000 acres, were devised to John Allan by will of Wm. Galt. This estate, so named possibly, from Byrd Creek, a stream running through it, was situated on the James River, in Goochland County (and partly in Fluvanna Co.) about 50 miles West of Richmond. It has been subdivided into smaller farms, among the most fertile and productive in the County.

Following receipt of the above, request was made to the Clerk's Office, Chancery Court of the City of Richmond, Richmond, Virginia, for certified copies of the wills of William Galt, and of John Allan deceased, which are here printed verbatim from the copies supplied.

THREE

Last Will and Testament of William Galt

I, WILLIAM GALT, of the City of Richmond, State of Virginia, bearing always in mind, and admonished by the circumstances of my present state, as well as by the word of truth, recorded in Sacred Scripture, which I cherish as the foundation of my firm faith and the anchor of my hope for happiness in an eternal state, how uncertain is the tenure of human life, as it now exists, and being desirous, while it is permitted me, to dispose of my temporal means and estate, the result, under Divine Providence, of my own, I trust, honest exertions, as it becometh my duty and my relations to God and man, do make this my last will and testament, which it is my desire should bear witness to my firm faith in the Gospel of our Lord and Savior Jesus Christ, the source of all my existing hope and consolation.

1st. I desire that all my just debts be paid, they are few and small, compared with my means. Intending an equitable distribution of my visible estate in Virginia, with the exception after mentioned, among my near kinsmen near me, namely, John Allan, William Galt, Jun. and his brother James Galt, all of the City of Richmond, the first my nephew, the other two, nearest kinsmen of my name, children of my adoption and nurture.

2nd. I give, devise and bequeath to the said John Allan, my three landed estates, named the "Byrd," lying and being situate in the Counties of Goochland and Fluvanna, on the Byrd Creek, with the slaves, stocks and property of all kinds belonging thereto; also, the following real estate in the City of Richmond, to-wit: my land and tenements on E Street, now occupied by Hall & Moore, and Mrs. Higginboth, with the stores of the latter tenement; my vacant lot corner of F and 2nd Streets, opposite the residence of Charles Ellis; my land and tenement on 14th Street, now in his occupation, and my land and store on 15th Street, occupied by Ellis and Allan, wooden tenement on the same street, occupied by Pascal, and my square parcel of land in the rear thereof, having some old buildings thereon, which, and the other property on 15th Street, I purchased at a sale of the property of Ellis & Allan, to him, the said John Allan, his heirs, and lawful distributees, in absolute property forever. I give and bequeath to Mrs. Allan, the wife of said John, my Carriage and horses.

3rdly. I give, devise and bequeath to the said William Galt, Junior, one equal moiety in value of my landed estate in Fluvanna, named "The Fork" containing at this time three several plantations on the Fluvanna or James River, with a like moiety of the slaves, stocks and property of all kinds belonging thereto. Also the following real estate in the City of Richmond, to-wit: my land and tenement fronting on E Street occupied by myself as a dwelling house, by Norman Stewart, and by William and William Galt, Jun. for their business, that is to say, for a store and lumber house; the land and tenement on 14th Street the ground floor whereof is occupied by the Clerk of the United States Court, for his office, to the said William Galt, Junr. his heirs and lawful distributees in absolute property forever, with all the appurtenances thereunto belonging.

4thly. I give and bequeath to the said James Galt, one equal moiety in value, of all my slaves, stocks and property of all kinds belonging to the Fork estate, whereof the other moiety has been, in the last article given and bequeathed to William Galt, Jun. his brother; but as the said James Galt is a native of Scotland, and although he has sometime since, in due form of law, declared his intention to become a citizen of the United States of America, and in pursuance thereof has abjured allegiance to his native Soverign, yet has not been actually naturalized, and so may not, according to law, be capable of taking and holding real estate. I give and devise to the said John Allan and William Galt Junior, and the survivor of them, and his heirs, upon the trust and condition after mentioned, the other equal moiety in value of my said landed estate named "the Fork" whereof one such moiety I have already herein given to the said William Galt, junior, in absolute property, together with the following real estate in the City of Richmond, to-wit: my parcel of land on 13th Street, whereon is a tenement occupied by Shepherd & Pollard, and a lumber house occupied by Otis, Dunlop & Company, my land and tenements corner of E and 13th Street, partly occupied by Charles Z. Abraham, as an Apothecary's Shop, with the land and tenements in the rear thereof on 13th Street, and the strip of land adjoining Poore's property, which I purchased of Gallego's estate, and whereon Dr. Tazewell, when my tenant, had a stable, with the appurtenances, but charged with the payment to the said James Galt of the sum of ninety thousand dollars, within twelve months after the time limited by law, pursuant to his declaration aforesaid, for being admitted a citizen of the United States, or to his lawful representatives; but upon this express trust and condition, that the said charge shall be satisfied and acquitted if the said John Allan and William Galt, Jun. the survivor of them, or his heirs, do, within the time aforesaid, by deed sufficient in the law, convey to the said James Galt, or his heirs, able to take and hold real estate in fee by the laws of Virginia, all the said lands tenements and appurtenances hereby to them as aforesaid devised, in absolute property and inheritance, together with the nett mesne rents, issues and profits thereof, or so dispose thereof, with the assent and consent of the said James Galt, or his aforesaid, that he or they may receive the actual and true nett proceeds thereof.

5thly. It is my will and desire that the men of my married slaves, if both husband and wife belong to me, shall be considered as belonging to and accompanying the plantation on which their wives respectively reside; and that the division of the Fork estate hereinbefore mentioned, be so made, that the slaves, stocks &c upon and attached to the upper plantation, may remain thereon, and those belonging to the two lower plantations may remain upon the same, but so as not to infringe the foregoing arrangement designed by me for the comfort of married persons.

6thly. I give and devise to the said John Allan and William Galt, jun. in equal and undivided moieties, my lumber house, stables and lots of land inclosed on Tobacco Alley, between 13th and 14th Streets, to them and their heirs forever.

7thly. I give and bequeath my household furniture to William Galt, Jun. and my watch and wearing apparel to the said James Galt.

8thly. It is my will and desire that the business carried on in the City of Richmond under the firm of William & William Galt, jun. be continued for the benefit, from its commencement, of the said John Allan, William Galt, jun. and James Galt, each being equally, that is to say, one third interested; and that the said James Galt be in relation to such interests be admitted by the said John Allan and William Galt, jun. and actually exist as a partner in the said business, as soon as he attains his full age of twenty one years; to which effect, and that this my desire may be fulfilled. I give and bequeath my funds appropriated to the said business or which ought to accrue to me therefrom, and substitute the said John Allan and James Galt in my place, and give to each of them one third share of the interest therein, that is to say, a moiety to each, of my two thirds of the concern and my slave Dandridge to the concern.

9thly. I give, devise and bequeath to Elizabeth Galt, the land and brick tenement now occupied by her, with the adjoining two vacant lots of land in the said City, all of which I purchased at the sale of John Lesslie's estate, and also the negro woman Annie, with her increase, to her and her heirs forever.

10thly. I give and bequeath to John Allan and William Galt, jun, and the survivor of them, in trust, that they and he shall hold and apply the same to and for the sole use and benefit of the said Elizabeth Galt and her children, fifty shares of the new stock of the Bank of Virginia, and fifty shares of the stock of the Farmers' Bank of Virginia.

11thly. I desire that the acting executor or executors hereinafter named set free my negro woman Patty and my negro boy Belmour, and thereupon give the former twenty, the latter forty dollars.

12thly. I release to the Rev. John H. Rice and to Phill Pleasants, the debt which each respectively owes me.

13thly. I direct, authorize and empower my Executors hereinafter named or such of them as are qualified to act, to sell my plantation in the Counties of Campbell and Amherst, on the part whereof in Amherst a Merchant Mill has been built, with the slaves, stock and property of all kinds thereon; also all the real estate which I own in the town of Lynchburg, and the vacant lot opposite the Monumental Church, which I purchased of Mayo.

14th. I give and bequeath to the trustees of Hampden Sidney College in addition to the permanent fund of the Theological Seminary, thirty shares of the Stock of the Farmers' Bank of Virginia.

15th. I desire that ten shares of my old stock of the Bank of Virginia, be secured to the use of the First Presbyterian Church, in the City of Richmond, so that the profits accruing therefrom, be applied in aid of the Minister's salary; and I enjoin it upon my Executors to have this well and lawfully done.

16th. I give and bequeath to the Rev. Mr. Armstrong, Pastor of the First Presbyterian Church, one thousand dollars.

17th. I give and bequeath to Miss Ann M. Valentine, two thousand dollars.

18th. Should any balance upon the settlement of the business of Galt & Galt appear against John Garth, such balance is to be remitted and given up to him, upon condition that he surrender to my executors any real property he may have purchased with the funds of the concern.

19th. I give and bequeath to James Galt five hundred dollars, in addition to what is before given him, to equalize my disposition of the furniture &c &c.

20th. I give and bequeath to Miss Rosanna Dixon, one thousand dollars.

21. I give and bequeath to my friend and man of business, John Forbes, One thousand dollars, which is to be in full of all accounts between us, and a testimony of my good will.

21. I give and bequeath to the said John Allan, William Galt, Jr. and James Galt, the survivors and survivor of them in trust to the sole use and benefit of Elizabeth Forbes, wife of the said John Forbes, and her family, that is to say her children, twenty shares of old stock of the Bank of Virginia.

22. I can rely on my executors for paying the foregoing legacies without needless delay; but none are to be demanded until after they shall have collected of my debts sufficient to satisfy the same without leaving any unsatisfied.

23. I give my pew in the First Presbyterian Church to the said John Allan, William Galt, Jr. and James Galt.

I give and bequeath to Doctor James Black in trust for and to the exclusive use of Mrs. William Dennison, one thousand pounds sterling.

I give and bequeath to Miss Mary Allan, one thousand pounds sterling.

I give and bequeath to Jane Walch one thousand pounds sterling on condition that she marry with the consent of Mr. Miller, Mrs. Fowlds and her father, or of the survivors or survivor of them; to be paid within twelve months after her marriage with such consent shall have been certified to my acting executors or either of them.

All the residue of my estate not herein previously disposed of exclusive of six hundred pounds sterling to be remitted to Mr. Fowlds during the summer of this year, I give and bequeath to Mrs. Fowlds, Mrs. Johnston, Mrs. Miller, Mrs. Black, Doctor James Black in trust for Mrs. Dennison, Miss Mary Allan and Miss Jane Walch.

Lastly, revoking all wills and testaments by me heretofore made I hereby name and appoint the said John Allan, William Galt, Jr. and James Galt, executors of this my last will and testament; but the said James Galt is not to act as such, until he be of full age, and I hereby direct that my said executors be not required to give security as such, nor to ask or require security or indemnity from my legatees in Scotland.

In witness whereof, I the said William Galt, the testator have to this my last will and testament, set my hand and seal this twenty fifth day of March, in the year of our Lord, one thousand eight hundred and twenty five.

WILLIAM GALT   W. G.

(*Seal*)

Signed, sealed, published and declared by William Galt, Sen'r, as and for his last will and testament, in the presence and hearing of us, who at his request, in his presence, and in the presence of each other, have subscribed our names as witnesses attesting the same.

ROBERT GORDON
JAMES H. BROWN
NORMAN STEWART

At a Superior Court of Law for Henrico County, held at the Capitol in the City of Richmond, on Tuesday the twenty-ninth day of March, in the year 1825.

This last will and testament of William Galt, late of the City of Richmond, deceased, was proved according to law by the oaths of Robert Gordon, James H. Brown and Norman Stewart, witnesses thereto, and ordered to be recorded. And on the motion of John Allan and William Galt, two of the executors named in the said last will and testament (the said William Galt being therein appointed by the name of William Galt, Junior) who made oath thereto and entered into and acknowledged a bond in the penalty of Two hundred and fifty thousand dollars, conditioned as the law directs, but without security (the said William Galt, deceased, having by his said will directed that none should be required of them) certificate is granted them for obtaining a probate of the said will in due form; liberty being reserved to the other executor in the said will named to join in the probate when he shall attain the full age of twenty one years.

Teste:

J. ROBINSON, *Clerk,*

A copy,

J. ROBINSON, *Clerk,*

A copy,

Teste:

CHARLES O. SAVILLE, *Clerk.*

FOUR

Last Will and Testament of John Allan (foster-father of Edgar Allan Poe)

IN THE name of God, Amen: I, John Allan, of the City of Richmond, being of sound mind and disposing memory, do make and ordain this my last will and testament, revoking all other wills by me heretofore made.

Item 1. I desire that my executors shall as soon as possible, pay all my just debts.

Item 2nd. I devise unto Miss Ann Moore Valentine, three hundred dollars annually, and her board, washing and lodging to be paid and found her by my executors out of my estate during her natural life, but this provision is to be in lieu and in discharge of the sum of two thousand dollars which I have in my possession belonging to her, and of which she is to discharge and acquit my estate in case she accepts of this bequest.

Item 3rd. I give and bequeath to my sisters Nancy Fowlds, Jane Johnston and Elizabeth Miller of Scotland three hundred pounds sterling each and to my sister Mary Allan one hundred pounds sterling.

Item 4th. I will and desire that my whole estate, real and personal shall be kept together and under the management of my executors hereinafter named, until my eldest child arrives to the age of twenty one years, except my present residence, with all the ground thereto attached, & the lot of ground at the intersection of F and 2nd Streets, opposite the present residence of Charles Ellis, which property I hereby authorize and empower my executors, or such of them as may act, to sell at the expiration of five years from this date if they shall think it advisable, and invest the proceeds arising from such sales in Bank Stocks or other public or private securities, which is to be held as the residue of my estate.

Item 5th. I give and bequeath to my beloved wife, Louisa Gabriella Allan, one third of the nett annual income of my whole estate during her natural life, or until our eldest child becomes of age, to be paid her annually by my executors. If she should be living when our eldest child becomes of age and the division of my estate takes place, then I desire that my beloved wife shall have during her natural life one third of my whole estate, to be so laid off as to include in her share my whole property in the City of Richmond, which may then remain unsold, but if the net annual rent or value of my property in Richmond shall not be equal to one third of the nett annual rent or value of all my estate then I desire and request that the difference may be made up to her out of some other part of my estate, and in case it shall exceed the one third of the net annual rent or value of my estate, then I desire that so much of the property in Richmond as may produce the excess may be withdrawn from her share.

Item 6th. I desire that the remaining two thirds of the income of my estate shall be applied by my executors to the support, maintenance & education of my children or so much thereof as may be necessary, and the balance invested for their benefit in stocks or other securities.

Item 7th. I give and bequeath all the residue of my estate to my children who may be living at the time of my death and to such as may be born after my death of which my wife at the time may be enscient, to be divided among them when the eldest becomes of age in the following manner, viz: if they shall all be boys then I desire that the division may be equal among them, or if they shall all be girls, then that the division shall also be equal among them, but if I should have children living at the time of both sexes, then I will and desire that the shares or parts of the boys shall be double that of the girls.

Item 8th. I will and desire that the part of my estate above devised to my wife for life, shall at her death be divided among my children in the same manner, and in the same proportions as the residue of my estate is above directed to be divided.

Item 9th. In the event all my children should die before they marry or arrive at the age of twenty one years, I then give and devise to my relations William Galt and James Galt and to Mr. Corbin Warwick and to the survivors and survivor of them and the heirs, executors and administrators of such survivor, all my estate, real and personal hereinabove devised to my children. Upon this special trust and confidence that they or the survivors of them or the survivor of them, and the heirs, executors and administrators of such survivor shall and will sell publickly or privately, as to them may seem best, the said estate real and personal, and pay over and apply four fifths of the proceeds of such sales to the sole and separate use and benefit of John Allan Fowlds son of my sister Nancy Fowlds, William Galt Johnston, son of my sister Jane Johnston and to the eldest son of my sister Elizabeth Miller, but in the event that they or either of them may be dead at that time, then I desire that the parts or shares of such of them as may be dead, may be divided among the brothers and sisters which he may have living, the remaining one fifth part of the proceeds I wish held and disposed of as I may hereafter by codicil direct and appoint. I desire that my relations shall out of my estate give to —— and —— a good English education.

Lastly, I constitute and appoint my beloved wife, Louisa Gabriella Allan and James Galt and Corbin Warwick executrix and executors of this my last will and testament. In testimony whereof I have hereunto set my hand and affixed my seal this Seventeenth day of April, in the year of our Lord one thousand eight hundred and thirty two.

JOHN ALLAN (*Seal*)

Signed, sealed, published & declared by John Allan, as & for his last will & testament in our presence & attested by us in his presence.

TH. NELSON
M. CLARK
ROBERT H. CABELL

Mrs. Louisa Gabriella Allan, wife of Jno. Allan
John Allan, child & 1 *enseignt*
1/3^1 3/3 n for life of 1/3 of *perisha* estate

1st pay all my debts.

2nd. My whole estate to be kept under the management of my exors. hereinafter mentioned until my eldest child becomes of age, the house and all the ground contiguous and attached to the same, I hereby authorize and empower my executors, or such of them as may act, to sell if they shall think it advisable after the expiration of 5 years from this date, also lot at intersection of F and 2nd Street, opposite Mr. Ellis, money arising from such sales to be invested in Bank Stocks or other public securities in discretion of exors. 1/3 of the net annual income of my whole estate to be paid to my beloved L. G. A. during her natural life or until my eldest child becomes of age. At the division of my estate I desire that my wife shall have one third of my estate for her life to be so laid off as to include the Town property, which if it should not amount to one third of the nett annual income then the same is to be made up to her out of some other part of my estate, if it should exceed it, then a part of it is to be deducted.

To Miss Ann Moore Valentine $300. per annum and her board lodging and washing to be paid and found her out of my estate during her natural life, and this provision is to be in lieu of $2000. which I hold of her money, and of which my estate is to be discharged if she accepts this bequest. To each of my sisters Nancy Fowlds, Jane Johnston, Elizabeth Miller £300 Sterling, and to my sister Mary Allan £100 Sterling, all residing in Scotland. I devise the whole of my estate among my children which may be alive at the time of my death and of such as my wife may at that time prove to be ensignt, in case they should be all boys I then desire that the estate may be equally divided among them in case of the birth of a daughter or daughters then I desire that my son or sons as the case may be shall be entitled to double what my daughters may have, my children to take the part of such of them as may die under age. In case of the death of all my children without being married or arriving at the age of 21 years I then give and devise to my relations Wm. Galt & Jas. Galt & to Corbin Warwick & to their heirs, exors. & admrs, all the estate given above to my children, upon this special trust and confidence that they or such of them as may act, shall sell all the estate, real and personal, and out of the proceeds apply 4/5ths for the sole, separate use and benefit of John Allan Fowlds son of sister Nancy Fowlds, William Galt Johnston, son of my sister, Jane Johnston and to the eldest son of my sister Elizabeth Miller, and in case of the death of either or all of them before my own death, before the death or marriage of my children, then and in that event I wish the brothers and sisters of such of them as may be dead to take his or their part or share, the remaining 1/5th part I wish disposed of in such manner as I may hereafter appoint by codicil. I desire that my executors shall out of my estate provide give to ———— a good english education for two boys sons of Mrs. Elizabeth Wills, which she says are mine, I do not know their names, but the remaining fifth, four parts of which I have disposed of must go in equal shares to them or the survivor of them but should they be dead before they attain the age of 21 years then their share to go to my sister's Fowlds children in equal proportions with the exception of three thousand dollars, which must go to Mrs. Wills and her daughter in perpetuity.

JOHN ALLAN, Dec. 31st, 1832

[Originally in John Allan's own Handwriting]

This memo, in my own handwriting is to be taken as a codicil and can be easily proven by any of my friends.

The notes preceding are in the handwriting of my friend, Jno. G. Williams.

The twins were born sometime about the 1st of July, 1830. I was married the 5th October 1830 in New York, my fault therefore happened before

I ever saw my present wife and I did not hide it from her. In case therefore these twins should reach the age of 21 years & from reasons they cannot get their share of the fifth reserved for them, they are to have $4000. each out of my whole estate to enable them to prosecute some honest pursuit, profession or calling.

March 15th, 1833, I understand one of Mrs. Wills' twin sons died some weeks ago, there is therefore one only to provide for.

My wife is to have all my furniture, books, bedding, linen, plate, wines, spirits &c &c, Glass & China ware.

JOHN ALLAN

At a Circuit Superior Court of Law and Chancery held for Henrico County at the Capitol in the City of Richmond, the 8th day of May, 1834. This last will and testament of John Allan, deceased, and codicil thereto annexed, were produced in Court by James Galt, an Executor in the said will named, and the said will was thereupon proved according to law by the oaths of Thomas Nelson, Micajah Clarke and Robert H. Cabell, the witnesses thereto; and there being no subscribing witnesses to the said codicil, William Galt and the said Thomas Nelson were sworn and severally deposed that they are well acquainted with the testators handwriting, and verily believe that the parts of the said codicil stated therein to have been written by the testator and his name thereto in two instances subscribed are of the said testators proper handwriting. Whereupon the said will and codicil and the notes written on the same sheet of paper with the codicil and mentioned in the latter, are ordered to be recorded, and at the same Circuit Superior Court, continued and held at the Capitol aforesaid on the 26th day of the same month of May, 1834. Louisa G. Allan, widow and relict of the said John Allan, deceased, and executrix named in his said last will and testament, appeared in Court and renounced the Executorship, and also declared that she will not take or accept the provision or any part thereof made for her by the said will, and renounced all benefit which she might claim thereby.

And on the motion of the aforesaid James Galt, one of the executors in the said will named, who made oath thereto according to law and with William Galt and the said Louisa G. Allan, his securities, entered into and acknowledged a bond in the penalty of one hundred thousand dollars, conditioned as the law directs, certificate is granted the said James Galt for obtaining a probate of the said will in due form. Liberty being reserved to the other executor named in the said will to join in the probate when he shall think fit.

Teste:

J. ROBINSON, C. C.

A Copy,

Teste:

J. ROBINSON, C. C.

A Copy,

Teste:

CHARLES O. SAVILLE, Clerk.

FIVE

Comments on Some Legal Aspects of John Allan's Will

The document probated May 8, 1834, consists of a will of nine Items executed April 17, 1832, some notes said by the testator to be in the handwriting of "my friend, Jno. G. Williams," and an undated holographic codicil signed without witnesses, on the same sheet as the notes, which from reference in its fourth clause can be ascribed to March 15, 1833, or some date subsequent thereto. This description has the authority of the Circuit Superior Court of Law and Chancery for Henrico County, Virginia. The certificate states "and his name thereto in two instances subscribed" refers to the two signatures of John Allan appearing respectively at the bottom and the top of the holographic codicil. The first is obviously not *subscribed* to the codicil. Since notes and codicil are on the same sheet, in the order named, the first of the two signatures, if subscribed to anything, was subscribed to the notes with the intention of constituting them as a first codicil. There would seem to be no other explanation for the signature beneath the notes and above the holographic codicil, and it is made more probable by the fact that the notes are written in the first person throughout as though intended for execution by the testator, and in form as good as, or better than, the holographic provisions. Inasmuch as the notes are adopted as part of the holographic codicil by the testator by reference, they were probated along with the will and holographic codicil, so that the error, if the above surmise be correct, would be of importance only in regard to the sequence of separate codicils. While this might be of the greatest importance in a given case it appears to be of little moment here except as a matter of interest.

The will proper, the notes and the holographic codicil constitute an odd legal document. The will and the notes bear internal evidence of having been composed by the same person, either a layman with some conceit of legal learning or a singularly ignorant lawyer. "Enceinte" has two forms, both misspellings, in the will, and a third variant misspelling in the notes, which would point rather to their joint authorship than to the contrary. Aside from this and some minor errors which a professional scrivener might be expected to avoid, the will and notes are inexpertly drawn. Both are couched in pseudo-legal phraseology apt to be affected by lay friends who "have had a great deal of experience drawing wills"; expressions of outright ambiguity are used; incongruous or even conflicting provisions occur; ordinary contingencies, the test of intelligent forethought, are ignored; clauses are inserted as afterthoughts, out of legal or logical order; certain provisions achieve absurdity which it is hard to believe the testator intended, as for instance in the bequest of a share of his estate to twins, where he leaves them equal shares of one-fifth, as though they were one child! As a whole the document is the very type and example of the litigation-breeding will, such as frequently proves the reliance and mainstay of a local bar for a generation.

A very few examples in point appear in the following:

1. Makes bequests of money, presumably to be paid forthwith out of capital as such bequests usually are, then in Item 4th directs that "my whole estate" be held in trust until eldest child is 21, thereby raising the conflicting presumption that the money bequests are to be paid only out of income. Which?

2. Does not by appropriate words constitute his executors testamentary trustees. Provides for the distribution of his estate on his eldest child becoming twenty-one, which would give their shares to minors, the remaining children; but appoints no testamentary guardians of minor children's estates until they become of age.

3. "My eldest child" does not specify whether eldest at testator's death or merely first surviving child to reach 21; if eldest child at his death dies before 21, how is time of distribution of estate determined? If guessing were permitted in interpreting a will it would be a fair venture that the testator really had in mind his youngest child instead of eldest, and became confused in terms; substitution of youngest for eldest, however, leaves distribution equally indeterminate, as to date.

4. "At the expiration of five years from this date" (Item 4th) apparently meant in the testator's mind "from my death," since he might not die for more than five years from "this date," namely, the date of execution of the will. This is almost certain from the fact that during the interval from the execution of the will to his death, whenever that might be, he would have control and discretion over the sale of any of his property *himself*, and discretion in his executors could not inhere until he died. He obviously wanted *them* to have five years in which to await a good market and exercise their discretion. This sheer oversight lends probability to the hazard as to "eldest child" above.

5. "My children" includes legitimate as well as illegitimate offspring. Inasmuch as this testator is believed to have had several of the latter in various places, this unequivocal language creates a flat inconsistency with the later division of the estate into *fifths*. Which is the oversight? Appellate courts take successive guesses at such problems until the estate goes in fees.

6. Share of boys to be double that of girls. *Quaere:* if one boy and several girls, would share of boy be double that of *all* the girls? According to wording in notes, the answer would be Yes. But did testator mean this?

7. "And to the survivors and survivor of them and the heirs, executors and administrators of such survivor, all my estate, real and personal, hereinabove devised to my children," etc., (Item 9th). This is almost Gilbertian. John Allan actually devises *in præsentia* to the heirs, administrators and executors of a *survivor*. These do not have heirs, etc., who can inherit until they *cease* to survive. Technically one does not devise personal property. This is less than an untechnical will; it is grossly stupid and ineffectual. The holographic codicil by Allan himself in private makes no pretense at legal verbiage. John Allan doesn't say whether the specific bequest of furniture, etc., is to be taken as *part of* or in *addition to* his wife's share provided in the will—a very important financial question to the other heirs.

8. The codicil which John Allan wrote himself in private was really not

actuated by a desire to make any additional devise (real estate) or bequest (personal property). It was a mere subterfuge to save his face, square himself with his conscience, or bolster up his post-mortem reputation. It was not a *devise* but a *device*.

He was either shamed into it by the mother of the twins, or by the discovery of his "fault" by his wife. Note: he had already provided the "fifth" for these twins; the codicil giving them $4000. each, if they could not get their shares of the fifth, was a subterfuge; unnecessary, since, if they could not get the "fifth," they could not get $8000. either;—both depended on the same will and the same "reasons" would inhere.

All of the holographic codicil was written at *one sitting*. The date inserted in the body of it, meant to give the impression that the death of one of the twins had occurred—or become known to him—just after he had written the first few sentences—is palpable stage-business. The proof of this is that had he written the first part of the codicil separately, *he would at the same time* have signed his *name* beneath it, to give it effect. He did not do so, showing it was all written at one time and signed as a whole.

He therefore knew that one twin was dead before he started to write the codicil at all. The real excuse for writing it is the exculpation passage where he says his "fault" occurred before he met his present wife. This in law is known as "self-serving testimony." Such narrative statements, like dissertations on history, religion, etc., have no proper place in a will. Like all extraneous passages in any legal document they are called "surplusage." Allan's remarks had no *testamentary* value and should have been left out. They were, however, the real purpose and object of the codicil. The futility of the $4000. bequest is at once apparent when it is reduced to its simplest terms: "If you can't get what I left you on page 2 of this same will, then get what I leave you on page 3." It was a subterfuge in order to get in his self-serving testimony about himself.

The final paragraph—furniture, books, etc.—was a palpable sop to the wife after the disclosure of the illegitimate children. Its effect would be likely to get her into litigation over the total amount of her share—whether the furniture, books, etc., were to be counted into her third, like the residence property, or to be in addition to it. The value of the furniture, books, etc., might make this an important question to all concerned.

There is no doubt that the wife wisely dodged a lot of trouble by renouncing all her rights under the will and electing to take her share under the intestate law. This would be determined once for all by the court.

No attempt at the pseudo-legal verbiage adorns the codicil. It is colloquial in every word, straight from the heart. But it is the heart of a man not aching to provide for the fatherless and to comfort a bereaved wife, but suddenly stung with shame and torn with anxiety over his own post-mortem reputation.

[A legal opinion contributed by an attorney-at-law
of Washington, D. C.]

IV

WILLIAM HENRY LEONARD POE, the elder brother, by two years, of Edgar Allan Poe, was born in Boston in 1807 while his parents, David Poe and Elizabeth Arnold Poe, were filling an engagement at the Federal Street Theater in that city. The child seems to have first seen the light sometime between January 12 and February 22, 1807, as the unusual interruptions in the appearances of his mother, who was then playing in Shakespearean parts, "Ophelia," "Cordelia," and "Blanche," indicate. The parents of the Poe boys were both poor, and seem to have been unable to care for their first child, for, on a visit to Baltimore during the theatrical vacation, sometime between May 25 and September 14, 1807, the boy was left with his paternal grandfather, "General" David Poe, who then resided at Number 19 Camden Street, Baltimore. It was thus in the family of his grandparents that he was "adopted" and brought up.

David and Elizabeth Poe returned to play in Boston where, on January 19, 1809, Mrs. Poe gave birth to her afterward famous son, Edgar. Her husband, David, deserted her, or died, in New York in July, 1810, after which Mrs. Poe went South, playing in Richmond, Norfolk, Charleston, South Carolina, and other places in the Southern circuit. In December, 1810, the date is not certain, she gave birth to her third child, Rosalie, in Norfolk, Virginia. These three children, William, Edgar, and Rosalie, constituted therefore the family of David and Elizabeth Poe. In December, 1811, Mrs. Poe died in Richmond, Virginia, in the house of a milliner, in circumstances of great poverty and extreme tragedy. Edgar was "adopted" or taken into the house of John and Frances Allan, and Rosalie, or Rose, was taken home and cared for by a Mrs. William Mackenzie, both Mr. Allan and Mr. Mackenzie being Scotch merchants in comfortable circumstances. In the meantime, William Henry Leonard Poe, the eldest, had remained with his grandparents in Baltimore.

The first mention of "Henry," as he was called, occurs in a letter written on February 8, 1813, from Baltimore by Eliza Poe (afterward Mrs. Herring), the paternal aunt of Henry and Edgar, to Mrs. John Allan in Richmond. The letter deals, for the most part, with Edgar, whom the Poes were anxious to care for, but goes on to say:

. . . Henry frequently speaks of his little brother and expresses a great desire to see him, tell him he sends his best love to him and is greatly pleased to hear that he is so good as also so pretty a boy as Mr. Douglas represented him to be. . . .

Mr. Douglas was a Baltimore gentleman who had seen young Edgar, then only four years old, in company with his foster-parents, the Allans, at the Virginia Hot Springs.

Edgar's foster-mother seems to have been afraid that the Baltimore relatives might claim her little "son," and there was consequently little contact

---

[935] Reprinted here slightly altered and abridged from *Poe's Brother, The Poems of William Henry Leonard Poe,* by Hervey Allen and Thomas Ollive Mabbott, George H. Doran Company, Publishers, New York, 1926.

between the two orphan brothers. After the return of the Allans from England in 1820, some correspondence between the two boys seems to have taken place, for, in November, 1824, John Allan writes to Henry Poe, then seventeen years of age, a letter in which he complains bitterly of Edgar, attacks the legitimacy of Rosalie, and apparently attempts to estrange the two young men. In this letter there is reference to a correspondence between the two brothers as follows:

DEAR HENRY:

I have just seen your letter of the 25th ult. to Edgar and am much afflicted he has not written you . . . etc.

Mr. Allan appears to have had his own private reasons for wishing to estrange the two brothers, but in this he was not successful, for, sometime during the Summer of 1825, William Henry Leonard paid a visit to his brother, Edgar Allan, then living at the corner of Main and Fifth Streets in Richmond with his foster-parents, the Allans.[936] Edgar was at that time paying attention to, and was undoubtedly very much in love with a little girl who lived nearby, Sarah Elmira Royster, and Miss Royster has left a recollection of a visit paid to her by the two Poe brothers, in company with a friend of Edgar's by the name of Ebenezer Burling.

Henry was, at this time, either in the Navy or the Merchant Marine, probably the former as a letter of his from Montevideo shows, and Miss Royster remembered his appearing in a nautical uniform, seemingly that of a midshipman. The difficulties in the Allan household about 1825 were serious; Edgar was already "on the outs" with his foster-father, and the visit of his blood brother at such a time must have cemented their already natural affection.

From the early poetry left by both Edgar and Henry Poe, it plainly appears that both brothers were of a similar, poetically inclined, and somewhat melancholy temperament. Both inherited the same traits and predilections, and, it would seem, also the same weaknesses for Henry, even earlier than Edgar, went into ill health. He was said to have been a delicate, sensitive, and willowy youth, and it is known that he died early of tuberculosis and drink.

Of Henry Poe's life about Baltimore, of the twenties and early thirties of the last century, very little is known. From a great variety of sources, hints in correspondence, and obscure recollections, it has been possible to piece together the following:

Henry Poe remained with his grandparents Mr. and Mrs. David Poe, Sr., up until the time of the death of the grandfather, October 19, 1816. when the family seems to have been living at Park Lane in the Western precincts (now Raborg Street), according to the old directories. Henry Poe seems also to have been helped and cared for by a Mr. Henry Didier, who had been a law student with David Poe, Jr. before the latter went on the stage. The widowed grandmother was left in poor circumstances, de-

---

[936] J. H. Whitty prints in his *Memoirs to the Collected Poems of Edgar Allan Poe* a notice of F. W. Thomas alluding to an earlier visit of Henry Poe to Richmond.

pendent on a small pension. Soon after the death of her husband, she became paralyzed and went to live with her daughter, Mrs. Maria Clemm, afterward Poe's mother-in-law, whither Henry also accompanied her.

In the meantime, however, probably about the time of the break-up of his grandparents' household, he went to sea. From various incidents which Edgar Poe afterward "incorporated" into his own biography, it seems likely that Henry visited the Mediterranean, the West Indies and South America, the near East, and possibly Russia. His adventures at least furnished forth a chapter of life which was afterward appropriated, and perhaps enlarged upon by his younger brother for "trade" purposes. It now appears, indeed, that many of the "standard" biographies of E. A. Poe are in reality a synthesis of Henry and Edgar, especially in regard to the years 1827-1829.

About the time that Edgar went to Boston in 1827, Henry Poe seems to have completed his experience at sea, for, from that time on, there is a fairly consecutive running reference to him as being in Baltimore. F. W. Thomas, afterward Edgar's close friend, says of Henry about 1826:

Your brother and I were then intimate—and rather rivals in a love affair.

Thomas was then living in Baltimore, and much about town with a rather gay, young, literary, social, and political set to which Henry Poe must also have belonged. He is known to have been rather wild, to have early developed a fondness for drink, to have been fond of female society—and to have died young. That he must also have possessed a considerable charm, not a little latent talent, a somewhat precocious development, and a vivid imagination, what little we have from his immature pen seems clearly to indicate. In appearance, he was said to have resembled strangely his brother, Edgar, but to have been somewhat taller. From 1826 on, Henry's whereabouts and what scanty information we have about his doings must be traced mainly through those of his brother, Edgar.

Edgar Poe matriculated at the University of Virginia, February 14, 1826. Before leaving Richmond, he had obtained the promise of Elmira Royster to marry him, and, upon departure, had presented her with a locket engraved with initials in which the engraver had made an error. It is also known that he sent back a letter to his sweetheart by James Hill, the Allans' darkey coachman and slave, who drove Poe and his foster-mother to the University. This was probably the last letter which Elmira or "Myra," as he called her, received from Poe until a year or so before his death (1849), when he again became engaged to her. Owing to Mr. Allan's undoubtedly calculated parsimony—Poe was in debt upon his arrival at the University from lack of funds—the young Edgar engaged in the game of Loo at which he was unfortunate. Having no cash, he exploited his credit with Charlottesville merchants, and ran up a considerable debt in order to pay his classmates. Poe had "plunged" deeper than he realized, and when Mr. Allan was presented with the bills, *he took the opportunity* of removing Poe from the University at the end of the year. In the meantime, Mr. and Mrs. Royster had intercepted all of Poe's letters to Elmira, and had persuaded their daughter to become engaged to a Mr. A. Barrett

Shelton, a young gentleman of considerable means and social status. The Roysters had, at one time, loaned Mr. Allan considerable sums, and were well enough known to him to be assured that Poe's prospects for an inheritance, although he had been brought up as a foster-son, were nil. Otherwise it is not likely that they would have opposed his suit. Upon returning to Richmond, Poe found that his sweetheart, who doubtless supposed him indifferent, had been removed and was engaged to his rival. The blow was a telling one. He was heart-broken, pursued by warrants for debt, and in disgrace with his "father" who desired him to be a lawyer. He quarreled with Mr. Allan, and left home going to Boston under the assumed name of *Henri Le Rennét*. Here, probably on a little money furnished him by Mrs. Allan and his "aunt," Miss Anne Valentine, he "published" his first volume of poems, called *Tamerlane and Other Poems,* printed by a tyro printer named Calvin F. S. Thomas. The title poem dealt with his love affairs with Elmira Royster.

It now seems, from poetry published by Henry Poe in Baltimore in 1827, in the *North American,* that Poe sent a copy of this book to his elder brother who inserted certain selections from it, in the magazine mentioned, under his own initials. Edgar seems also to have written the full particulars of his tragic little love affair to William Henry Poe in Baltimore, after arriving at Fort Moultrie, Sullivan's Island, Charleston Harbor, South Carolina.

It was during this time, or shortly before, that he evidently communicated with his brother Henry. The result of these communications may be read in *The Pirate,* in the *Baltimore North American* for 1827. Whether the story is by E. A. Poe, or a romantic rendering of Edgar's letter to him by William Henry Poe, is hard to tell, probably the latter. . . .

In 1829, Henry Poe was known to have been employed in the office of one Henry Didier, a former law student with his father David, and to have been living with Mrs. Maria Clemm, his aunt, in Mechanics Row, Milk Street, Baltimore. His constant writing for the magazine, in 1827, implies that he had been in Baltimore some time. It is the opinion of this writer that Henry Poe's last voyage was made not later than 1827. That he (Henry) was in sailor togs in 1825, we know by his visit to Miss Royster. In 1827 we find him settled and writing for the *North American* in Baltimore. He must also have been entering now upon his period of decline for, in 1829, there is record of his illness and despairing drinking. A short time later he died of tuberculosis at Mrs. Clemm's.

The probabilities are, therefore, that the material that appeared in the *North American* in 1827 was his own, and Edgar's poems, copied from *Tamerlane.* Henry's romancing upon his brother's love affair with Elmira Royster, was exactly the tragic-romantic type of star-crossed lover plot which most tickled the sentimental-lugubrious palate of the period, and appealed especially to romantic youth. That Edgar had lost his sweetheart, and run away on an adventurous career, was an opportunity which Henry could not neglect. Hence *The Pirate.* That this story refers to the Elmira incident there cannot be the shadow of doubt. Henry had been taken to call upon her, Edgar had written him the particulars of the later affair.

Henry having treated the incident in prose, L. A. Wilmer, another contributor to the *North American,* now did it in poetry, and produced *Merlin* in which Elmira's name is used, and the machinery of the same plot more imaginatively exploited. In *Merlin* Elmira's "habitation" is given as near the "Hudson" instead of the James.

It is now in order to detail what is known of the rest of Henry Poe's short life. In 1829, Edgar Poe returned to Richmond, left the Army, visited Washington, and then went to live for a while in Baltimore during the Summer and Winter of 1829. At that time he lived certainly for a while with Henry and his aunt, Mrs. Clemm, and the little girl, Virginia, whom he afterward married in Baltimore. On May 20, 1829, Edgar Poe writes to John Allan from Baltimore, *"I have succeeded in finding Grandmother and my relatives."* On August 10, 1829, Edgar Poe, still in Baltimore, again writes to John Allan, *"My Grandmother is extremely poor and ill* [paralytic]. *My Aunt Maria* [Mrs. Clemm] *if possible still worse and Henry entirely given over to drink and unable to help himself, much less me"*—a statement that sufficiently indicates Henry's condition at the time. In July, 1830, Edgar entered West Point, and we again hear of Henry through him in another letter to John Allan, June 28 (1830). *"I take the first opportunity since arriving here of acknowledging the receipt of your letter of 21st May inclosing a U. S. note for $20 I received it three days ago —it has been lying sometime in the W. P. post office where it was forwarded from Baltimore, by Henry."* On his way to West Point from Richmond, Edgar had again visited his brother Henry in Baltimore in May and June, 1830.

Edgar Poe left West Point about February 18, 1831, after being dismissed by court-martial. He stayed a short time in New York, and evidently arrived in Baltimore about the end of March, 1831, when he went to live with his Aunt Maria Clemm at Mechanics Row, Milk Street, in the Fells Point district. There were then in the household, Mrs. Clemm, Virginia Clemm, old Mrs. David Poe, the grandmother, Henry Poe, Henry Clemm, and to them was now added Edgar. Henry Poe was very ill, was dying in fact. Edgar must have spent much of his time nursing his elder brother for whom he had gone into debt. On August 2, 1831, the following notice appeared in the *Baltimore American:*

Died last evening, W. H. Poe aged 24 years. His friends and acquaintances are invited to attend his funeral this morning at 9 from the dwelling of Mrs. Clemm in Milk Street.

William Henry Leonard Poe was buried in the graveyard of the old First Presbyterian Church in Baltimore where his younger brother now lies. Edgar Allan Poe survived Henry by eighteen years.

V

FIRST MARRIAGE OF POE AND VIRGINIA CLEMM

OWING to conflicting statements as to the date of Poe's alleged *first* marriage to Virginia Clemm (in Baltimore), now current in biographies, the following letter and certificate are here printed showing that the license was issued September 22, 1835, and *not* 1834 as sometimes wrongly stated.

License Number 409

THE STATE OF MARYLAND

[SEAL]   *Baltimore City, SCT.*   [SEAL]

I hereby Certify to all whom it doth or may Concern, That on the twenty-second day of September in the year of our Lord one thousand eight hundred and thirty-five a LICENSE issued from the OFFICE OF THE CLERK OF BALTIMORE COUNTY COURT, directed to the Reverend Mr. ——— or any other person qualified by Law to CELEBRATE THE RITES OF MARRIAGE between a certain Edgar A. Poe and Virginia E. Clemm of Baltimore County, according to Law, there appearing to him no lawful cause, or just impediment by reason of any consanguinity or affinity to hinder the same, as by the records of said Court appears, which records are now in my keeping.

THE
SUPERIOR COURT
OF BALTIMORE
IN THE
8th. JUDICIAL
CIRCUIT OF
MARYLAND

IN TESTIMONY WHEREOF, I hereto subscribe my name and affix the Seal of the Superior Court of Baltimore City, this twentieth .... day of February, A.D., 1926.

STEPHEN C. LITTLE,

Clerk of the Superior Court of Baltimore, City

No direct proof of the marriage of Edgar A. Poe and Virginia Clemm in Baltimore in 1835, prior to their later public marriage in Richmond, can be found. The inference that it took place is not only aroused by the fact of a license having been issued, but made more certain by a reluctant admission, later on, by Mrs. Clemm, that such a private marriage had taken place in Baltimore. The so-called "family tradition," assigning the place of marriage in Baltimore Old Christ Church, is difficult to trace to its source. The tradition was that the marriage had been performed by the Reverend John Johns, later Bishop of Virginia. In 1900, Professor James A. Harrison was informed by Mr. A. S. Johns, a son of the Bishop, that no tradition of such a marriage *was known to the Johns family,* and Professor Harrison was then referred to the records at Christ Church, Baltimore, where no record of the first Poe-Clemm marriage can be found. Similar searches at St. Paul's Parish, made for Professor Woodberry in September, 1884, and for Professor Harrison in November, 1900, by Charles Handfield Wyatt, showed that Mr. Wyatt *may* have been mistaken as to the date of the marriage—"I think it was prior to 1828." Further search was therefore made again at St. Paul's.

704

SAINT PAUL'S PARISH

Baltimore, Maryland

February 24, 1926

MY DEAR MRS. KINSOLVING [937]

I have examined the Parish books, in my possession as Registrar, and find therein no record of the marriage of the late Edgar Allan Poe.

Cordially yours

C. T. GOULD

Registrar

The search has not been carried on exhaustively so far. The author has examined the columns of the available files of the Baltimore newspapers for September and October, 1835, without result. Further search in other church records of the date in and *about* Baltimore might bring results. It must be remembered that Poe was, at the time, anxious to conceal this marriage with a child from the relatives in Baltimore, hence no clergyman's record. It may have been before a justice of the peace. Such a marriage would have been kept doubly secret, at the time, as it was a social disgrace. Thus—a newspaper clipping of about a century ago—

A marriage before a Justice of Peace is shocking to morals and good manners. It goes further than the design of degrading and insulting the Church; it humbles and degrades the parties, particularly that party, which the ceremony is chiefly intended to benefit and exalt,—the woman. A marriage of this kind would have more the appearance of indentures of apprenticeship in the city, or of hiring servants at a statute fair, than of any serious or solemn class of contract and obligation. We scarcely need add, how little suitable it would be to a country which has always been remarked for the delicacy and modesty of its women. *Baltimore North American.*

---

[937] Search was made for the author by the kindness of Mrs. Sally Bruce Kinsolving, wife of the Rector of St. Paul's Parish, Baltimore, Maryland.

HISTORY OF POE'S FRIEND, F. W. THOMAS

F. W. THOMAS' association with Poe, the Poe-Thomas correspondence, and the many reminiscences which Thomas has left of his friend, seem to make it worth while to collect here a more complete account of the man. The biography itself is of interest as it throws light on some of the remarks in the Poe-Thomas letters, and adds some authentic facts to the background of contemporary American life from 1775 to 1841; covering two generations in the persons of E. S. Thomas and F. W. Thomas, father and son, the latter, Poe's friend.

The data for Ebenezer S. Thomas has been kindly supplied by John Bennett, Esq., of Charleston, South Carolina, from a great mass of early American notes and data collected by him. The Life of F. W. Thomas is contained in a letter written by him to Poe in Philadelphia, August 3, 1841, probably to supply Poe with biographical material to use in notices of Thomas' books in some of the periodicals for which Poe wrote. The allusion to Henry Poe and early Baltimore days is of peculiar interest. The reason for the political and journalistic influence of F. W. Thomas will, in the light of the facts given below, now be more apparent:

EBENEZER S. THOMAS: Book-seller, Stationer; Editor,
CITY GAZETTE, Charleston, S. C.

Father of F. W. Thomas, author of *Clinton Bradshaw* and *East and West.* Another son edited the Louisville, Kentucky, *Daily Herald.* Born in Lancaster, Massachusetts, 1775. A nephew of Isaiah Thomas, publisher of the Worcester *Massachusetts Spy,* the famous Revolutionary journal, on which his father was employed as circulation agent and distributor.

ISAIAH THOMAS: his uncle: LL.D.: book-publisher, printer, binder, and book-seller; printed the American first editions of *Bell's Surgery, Cullen's Practice, Blackstone's Commentaries, Millott's Elements of Ancient and Modern History, Harvey's Works,* besides the first folio and royal quarto editions of the Bible printed in America. Known in England as 'The American Baskerville.'

Founder of the American Antiquarian Society; author of a *History of Masonry,* and the widely known *History of Printing,* in 2 vols.

Isaiah Thomas, as a journeyman printer, followed and perfected himself in his trade on the *Halifax Gazette,* Nova Scotia, where he got into political trouble for his freely-expressed opinions.

ISAIAH THOMAS was in business in Charleston, South Carolina, for two years, 1767-1768: I find no impression he made on the community, if he made any.

EBENEZER S. was apprenticed to ISAIAH, his uncle, to learn the printing, book-binding, and stationery business, in 1788, at the age of 13 years.

He left his uncle's shop in 1792, at termination of his apprenticeship, and was employed as a book-binder in Boston until 1795, in which year he came to Charleston, South Carolina, and here became a partner of CALEB CUSHING, printer, book-binder, book-seller, and stationer.

CUSHING was a Boston man; whether any relative of the later politician of the same name I cannot say. He died in Charleston of yellow fever, leaving the book-business to THOMAS, located, in 1802, at 117 Tradd Street, dwelling above the shop, as was customary, in Scotch fashion, at that time. In 1803 he removed his business to the now more fashionable street,—to 121 Broad Street, as book-seller and stationer.

An ambitious man of more than ordinary abilities and outlook, THOMAS, desiring to establish personal relations with the book-publishing firms of Great Britain, in 1800 . . . and annually thereafter . . . went to England and Scotland, . . . that is, London and Edinburgh . . . to select and to purchase his own stock, and form personal acquaintances abroad who should act correspondents on whom he might depend for future advices and supplies generally. He had friendly relations with Constable, Scott's publisher; became intimately acquainted with Hone, the book and print-seller of Ludgate Hill; made the familiar acquaintance of Washington Irving, then Consul in London; and established business relations with the old firm of Vernor & Hood, afterward Vernor, Hood & Sharp, with which house he attained unlimited credit, and through them, throughout England and Scotland, acquaintance of great benefit.

In 1803 he took into partnership, James Male, under the firm-name of Thomas & Male, and made his fourth purchasing voyage to England and Scotland, visiting many friends of position, and touring the Continent as a means of cultivation and information.

He returned from England from this trip with a printed catalogue of 50,000 volumes, in every branch of literature, arts, and sciences, travels, fiction, and religion, belles lettres and textbooks, then by far the largest importation ever made into the United States by a book-dealer.

In that year, 1803, the African slave-trade was reopened for a term of five years; the reaction upon literature and book-buying was immediate and disastrous. There were then in Charleston four considerable book-selling houses, Young's, Bailey & Waller, Crow & Query, and E. S. Thomas. Bailey & Waller failed, and were sold out at public auction by Henry Smerdon, vendue master, a remnant stock, of 'novels, history, poetry, voyages, etc., etc., at No. 16 Broad Street, opposite the State Bank.'

THOMAS, embarking elsewhere in business, (while continuing to work off his stock here,) with Messrs. Christopher and Nathaniel Olney, in 1804-5, as partners, built, at Providence, R. I., the fifth cotton factory in the U. S.

In the fall of 1804 or 1805, returning to Charleston, he evidently made a 'whirlwind courtship'; for he married, during that brief stay, here, a Miss Fonerdon, daughter of Adam Fonerdon, Esq., of Baltimore, who was in Charleston on her way to Italy with a sister and brother-in-law. These last continued their journey, . . . she remained; and the following Spring returned to Providence and the cotton-mill. THOMAS closed out his book-shop here in 1807. He also sold out from the cotton-mill business at Providence.

BUT, in 1810, returned to Charleston, having purchased the plant and good-will of the *City Gazette,* of Charleston, from Peter Freneau; its editor and publisher: (Freneau & Paine, and afterward Freneau & Williams).

PETER FRENEAU: Brother of Philip Freneau, the 'Poet of the Revolution.' There were then but two papers in Charleston, and but three in the State. The ancient *State Gazette,* Timothy & Mason, was on its last legs. Freneau was a correspondent of Thos. JEFFERSON, and an ardent supporter of the Jeffersonian republican party, which the *City Gazette* espoused, as against the Federalists.

On January 1st, 1810 the paper became Thomas's; proprietor, publisher, and editor; though FRENEAU remained associated with its editorial staff until his death, contributed to its political animus and power.

Thomas published the *City Gazette* as a daily, and the old *South Carolina Gazette* as a weekly, and was successful with both, his net profit on both during the established years of his management reaching $12,000 per annum. The

Gazette was the one and only republican (Jeffersonian), paper in the city, and was strongly supported, and backed by prominent men.

Among intimate friends of Thomas during his years as book-seller and editor in Charleston were Robert Y. Hayne, ex-governor Charles Pinckney, Hon. William Lowndes, John Ceddes, governor of S. C., and Col. Thomas Lehre, one of the prominent leaders of the Jeffersonian party, Peter Freneau, and Hon. Wm. Loughton Smith, U. S. Ambassador to Portugal, a brilliant man, and like Hayne and Lowndes, a statesman of no mean rank. Pinckney, Freneau, and Lehre formed the committee of consultation of the Jeffersonian party, and Thomas was known as 'the lever of the Triumvirate,' they being dubbed the Triumvirs, and he their official spokesman through the *City Gazette:* they were nicknamed Caesar, Pompey, and Lepidus, by the Federal party.

Among journalistic friends made at this period Thomas counted Maj. M. M. Noah, afterward editor of the *N. Y. Evening Star,* one time Consul at Tunis, and known among pamphleteers as 'Muly Mulack' from his signed contributions to the *N. Y. Times,* Townsend, of the *N. Y. Express* also was an old friend of Thomas's.

Thomas supported Langdon Cheves for Congress, and that campaign sent Calhoun, Lowndes and Cheves from South Carolina, such a 'constellation of talent and statesmanship' says one, pretty truly, 'as seldom has been sent to that body from one State.'

It was through Thomas's publication of a political letter from M. M. Noah, attacking Jos. Alston, for alleged participation in Burr's so-called conspiracy, and for alleged misconduct of an election which made Alston governor of S. C., that Thomas was prosecuted by Jos. Alston for libel, found technically guilty by the jury, was escorted from his prison by a brass band and parade of admirers; and shot at through a window by some un-identified supporter of Alston's.

It was at Thomas's suggestion to David Ramsay, the historian, that the latter undertook his *Life of Washington;* . . . and it was at the very moment of the conclusion of Thomas's trial in the Charleston court that a loud report of a pistol was heard from the street near by . . . when Ramsay was shot by one Lining whom Ramsay, as a consulting physician, had pronounced insane. This is just incidental.

His health having suffered from the climate of Carolina, especially through the several summers he had lived in the city, Thomas sold out the *City Gazette,* in January, 1816; after what he afterward called the happiest six years of his life, though during five of the six the country had suffered economically from embargo, non-intercourse, and war.

With the competent fortune amassed here by the *Gazette* he retired to Baltimore, his wife's former home, and with his family settled on a considerable landed property he had bought near Baltimore. There he was a notable demonstrator of science as applied to agriculture, and did much to promote expert farming; is so referred to occasionally by authorities at that time. But the great decline in the value of crops and real estate broke him, in 1827; he sold his property to pay his debts, and removed West, to Cincinnati, where he established the *Daily Commercial-Advertiser,* 1828; which he styled the second daily paper in the western country. In 1835 he established the Cincinnati *Daily Evening Post;*—and, retiring from active editorial work, in 1839, toured the States campaigning for Wm. Henry Harrison.

He was an ardent supporter of the Federal Union, and an antagonist of John C. Calhoun from the discovery of the end and aim of Nullification onward. Revisiting Charleston in 1840, he found himself, much to his regret, *persona non grata* to many of his old acquaintances, owing to the increasing bitterness of national questions . . . and his vigorously maintained position on Nullification, States Rights, and Secession (as a threat).

He seems to have been really a discriminating and genuine amateur appreciator of the fine arts, and cultivated his appreciation during his travels abroad. It is the tradition that it was he who discovered and encouraged Hiram Powers, the Cincinnati sculptor, whose Greek Slave was considered in its day the acme of American sculptural art . . . Thorwaldsen being then the arbiter and mode. The date of his death I do not know.—J. B.

Frederick W. Thomas, Poe's friend.[938]
From a letter written to Poe in Philadelphia by F. W. Thomas, Washington, District of Columbia, August 3, 1841,—original in *Griswold Collection,* also in Harrison, vol. II, pages 95-99.

Washington, 3 *August,* 1841

My family, by the father's side, were among the early settlers of New England. Isaiah Thomas, the founder of the American Antiquarian Society at Worcester (Mass.), and the author of *The History of Printing,* was my father's uncle. . . . My Father, E. S. Thomas, . . . emigrated to Charleston, S. C., where he, after establishing himself in the book-business, met my mother, who was then on a visit from Baltimore, of which city she was [a native] . . . Shortly after the marriage of my father he removed from Charleston to Providence, Rhode Island, where I was born in, I think, the fall of 1808. I left Rhode Island a child in the nurse's arms and have never been back—so I hold myself to be a Southerner— as my parents returned to Charleston with me. (My family consists of myself, then Lewis, Frances, Susan, Mary, Martha, Belle and Calvin.) I was a delicate child, and, at the age of four, I fell from a furniture box on which I was playing, and injured my left leg. I went into the house crying, as a child would, and soon returned to play again. My limb, a few weeks afterwards, became very painful, my health gradually declined, and the physicians advised my parents to send me to a healthier climate. In charge of my aunt I was sent to Baltimore, and placed under the care of my aunt Foulke. There I grew robust and recovered from my lameness except an occasional weakness in my limb, when I over-exercised myself at play. When about eight or nine, in running to the window, over a wet floor, to look at the soldiers passing, I got a fall, which, after long confinement (a year or more), threw me, a skeleton, on crutches. I used them until five years since, when the contrivance I now use was suggested to me. I went to school very little in consequence of my lameness and frequent indisposition, and when I was seventeen I commenced the study of law. I have never been to college. The first attempt I made at scribbling was at this time. I wrote a poetical satire on some fops about town, and they became exasperated with the printer of the paper, I forget its name—a scurrilous penny-sheet—and tore his office to pieces, making Pi of his type. I attended at this time a debating society, which had a great many visitors, and there I used to hold forth with the rest. I was invited one Fourth of July to make a speech before the society on a steamboat excursion, and, getting some little credit for it I was invited by my political friends to address their meetings which I did, being then rated with Jacksonism. . . . Your brother and I were then intimate—and rather rivals in a love affair. Scott, my fellow student, studied hard,—I often stole out to the Baltimore

---

[938] Prof. Lewis Chase first prints an interesting letter from Poe to F. W. Thomas written from Philadelphia, October 27, 1841, in *American Literature,* Duke University Press, March, 1934, pages 66-67, followed by some interesting comment.

Library and devoured the works upon Poetry, Oratory and Biography. Just after I was admitted to practice, my father, who had lost a handsome fortune, emigrated with his family, leaving myself, to Cincinnati and established the *Commercial Advertiser*. I practiced a few months, and then from ill health, retired to the country, where, after a year's sojourn, I emigrated to Cincinnati in 1832 and assisted my father in editing his paper. We soon differed upon political matters, and I commenced the practice of the law, but in bad health. I defended a great many criminals, I believe with some success, and lectured before the Lyceum. In descending the river I wrote several stanzas expressive of my feelings, which I published in my father's paper. They were noticed and complimented by the contemporary press, and I wrote out some farther impressions which the new scenes had made on me, and upon invitation delivered them before the Lyceum, in the shape of a rambling poem called *The Emigrant, or Reflections in Descending the Ohio*. This took, if I may so say, before the Lyceum and I was requested to publish it, which I did in 1833. . . .

After this, when Judge McLean was brought out for the Presidency, I was selected to publish his organ in Cincinnati, which I called the *Intelligencer*. I had it for about six months, and was compelled to quit the editorial chair, in consequence of bad health. While confined to my house and bed, I remarked one day to my *sister Frances* that I felt like trying to write a novel. She insisted upon my doing it, and daily brought paper and pen to my bedside, where most of *Clinton Bradshaw* was written. I should have mentioned that my best friend in Cincinnati was Charles Hammond of the Cincinnati *Gazette*, who is now dead, but who was esteemed the best editor and lawyer in Ohio. To him I dedicated my *Emigrant*, and he defended me with true chivalry against all critical attacks. In his paper, too, I wrote many satires upon folks about town, which made me some enemies.

When I had finished *Clinton Bradshaw*, with letters of introduction in my pocket to Mathew Carey, from Mr. Hammond and General Harrison, I started for Philadelphia which I reached in the dusk of the evening. Unknown and unknowing, in bad health and worse spirits, I wandered on not knowing what to do with myself, and shall never forget stopping before a house in Chestnut Street struck with a tune that some fair one was playing, as if with a familiar voice. The discovery that the song was mine, *'Tis said that absence conquers love*, changed the whole current of my feelings.

Mr. Carey (this was in 1835) introduced me to Carey, Lea & Co. and they undertook the publication of my work. Let me say that Mr. Carey treated me with the greatest kindness. He was lame too, but a philosopher, and he felt and expressed a real sympathy for me. I was frequently his guest, and he often came to see me. In proof of his benevolent character let me say that he often annoyed me, or rather provoked my sensitiveness, by sending some lame man or woman or other he had picked up in the street, to consult with me upon my superior powers of locomotion. Most of the characters in *Clinton Bradshaw* were drawn from persons living in Baltimore. 'Glassman' was meant for Charles Mitchell, a very distinguished lawyer, who was dissipated. 'Old Nancy' for old Nelly, who is still an apple woman in Baltimore. 'Cavendish' was drawn from a young, eccentric friend of mine, named Kelley, who is since dead. 'Shaffer' was a portraiture of Jennings, etc.

East and West was published in 1836. It was an attempt to portray the every day scenes of life occurring to a fallen family emigrating from the east to the west, most of the characters there were from life. *Howard Pinckney* was published in 1840. I have by me in MS. the poem which you have seen called— (I believe I will so call it)—*The Adventures of a Poet*, which consists of 1800 lines; and two volumes of sketches of such persons as Wirt, John Randolph, Simon Kenton (the Last of the Pioneers), with tales, etc. . . .

In the May number of the *Southern Literary Messenger,* for 1838, you will find a sketch of your humble servant by Ingraham.

While writing my books I travelled through the west to Louisville, St. Louis, &c., and in the last canvass held forth in those places on the Harrison side. Sometimes upon invitation, in these cities and in Cincinnati, I delivered lectures upon literary subjects such as Oratory, Poetry, etc., Odd-Fellow addresses, and Fourth of July addresses. I was a delegate to the Baltimore May convention in '40, where I held forth, and after which I made your acquaintance in Philadelphia and got pelted by the people as you remember—or rather by the Locos.

I came on East last March to get my books out, but the death of General Harrison, and the uncertainties about the currency and the bank have prevented my publishing. Here I was invited to lecture before different societies, and in Alexandria, and did so to full houses, gratis—which were followed by empty puffs; but you know what Goldsmith says about the Muse—

> Thou source of all my bliss and all my woe
> That found me poor at first and keeps me so.

(Don't say of me that I am in office, as it is only a temporary appointment.)

I am now engaged in writing a novel upon the events of the present day, many of the scenes of which are laid in Washington. My object is to describe life in the varieties in which I have seen it in Missouri, New Orleans and here among the holders and seekers. I have written occasionally for these three or four years past for the *Knickerbocker, Graham's,* the *Ladies Companion* and the *Southern Literary Messenger.* . . .

One of the first persons who noticed me in the West was General Harrison, who shortly after my arrival in Cincinnati invited me to the Bend, where I went and was his guest for some weeks,—I was engaged there in one of my first law cases against his eldest son (now dead), William Harrison.

Note. The subsequent history of Thomas' association with Poe is narrated in the body of the text.

VII

THE following four items are here included by courtesy of the Edgar Allan Poe Shrine of Richmond, Virginia: They are:

One: A letter from Thomas Bolling, a classmate of Poe, to his mother from the University of Virginia dated April 1, 1825.

Two: A letter from Thomas Bolling from the University of Virginia to his father, Colonel William Bolling of Bolling Hall, dated May 10, 1826.

Three: A letter from Alen Garrett of Charlottesville, Virginia, a friend of the Bolling family and also known to Poe.

Four: A document signed by G. Thomas from the University of Virginia, to Colonel William Bolling for installments due.

Note—the first two letters are printed to show the relations between father and son in the Bolling family who lived close to the estate of John Allan, in Goochland County. This family were personal friends of Poe and John Allan.

Letter *three* shows the manner in which the financial affairs, and the word of honor of a young scion of a Virginia planter's family were treated by his parents and friends.

Letter *four* shows Colonel Bolling not only sending his son to the University and paying his way, but also contributing to the "Educational Fund" for the University by subscription.

All of these items, it is thought, may tend to throw an interesting contemporary light on the indignation of Poe at his guardian's highly contrasted methods of procedure with his "son." Thomas Bolling is referred to in the text (*Originals in author's possession*).

ONE

April 1, 1825

MY DEAR MOTHER

Thinking it a duty incumbent on me to thank you for your very affectionate postscript, and the Dr. having concluded to tarry longer, I determined at least to write you, that the number of letters which I have written to my Father, will not reproach me, when I see you again which will not be untill December, unless you should repeat your trip this summer, which I am inclined to think will be very pleasing as I expect this will be a very long summer and you so seldome go from home, that when ever you do, the clouds seem to be drawn from every quarter of the Globe.

There are sixty students at present and are gradually increasing, the people around us seem to be trying to get in with us by exhibiting every imaginable attention. My father my getting a mattress which I should prefer but for one reason. That is if me and my room mate were to fall out, I should take another room, and then the bed would be far preferable, so I have only to request you to send it as soon as convenient, and indeed I had as leave, sleep in it in summer as not. As yet I have every necessary article and a plenty of paper but will thank you to send a *Horrice Delphini* which is in my press, my candles I hope you will not fail to send though I am not in immediate need of them, I think by sending my trunk and bed together, you might make a better bargain as to the price of convayance, You need not put yourself to any trouble about my violin as I am very little concerned and can get one here when ever I choose, and indeed

I rather you should not, because they might bowrow it to serenade and might get it ruined, there are several of my Breme Students here among whom are Anderson whom I am very fond of, I forgot to credit my father for not having taken snuff and abuse him for not having practised on the Violin, and I hope you will not lay it by in the prime of your life one of you must write when my trunk comes and excuse these unconnected sentences. My love and sincere well wishes for you all and Believe me ever your affectionate Son

THOMAS BOLLING

P. S. I have begun this letter to my mother but have addressed myself principally to my father.

Farewell
your Son
THOS. BOLLING

Thinking that it will be agreeable to my Father I enclose a copy of the Laws—

TWO

University of Virginia, *May 10th,* 1826

MY EVER DEAR FATHER.

I have both to acknowledge the receipt of your letter and the enclosure, both of which contributed greatly to my satisfaction, not only the pleasure of hearing that you were well, but many other things quite agreeable to my eye, one in particular that of your safe arrival home, and my dear Father I was glad to hear of your intended trip to Lynchburge for several reasons, especially at this time since I know that you will meet with our relation *Meade* whom I have been in company with for several nights at Mr. Garretts, and have to acknowledge much kind treatment from them to me, and what rendered my time still more agreeable, was to meet with Mistress Chattoria and the Miss Carry's and must inform you of a most agreeable trip I took with them to Retten's Mountain on Thursday last. On Wednesday evening I was invited to spend the evening at Mrs. Carr's, about 7 miles on the way which being performed left 15, which was a very agreeable distance to go and return the next and the view I can only say surpassed all conception. I possessed a pleasing melancholy, arising from my being able to see far below my dear home, without being able to forward my body with my sight, and to spare you my anxiety to perform the trip, I will attempt to describe my *noble Beast,* a *sorrel horse* 6 feet, string Halted in both hind legs, could neither *pace,* gallup or *trot,* and still he performed all, that is a confused higgledy, piggledy of the whole, and I never backed a more sure footed animal, which is the *sum* of his merits, and afforded more laughter, than anything we met with the whole day, and finally he has the exact character of the Horse that *Shakespeare* describes so admirably in one of his plays. I have some idea of buying him and trading for that colt you mentioned, as you mentioned it would be a difficult matter to *barter* you out of. I had a very pleasing dream last nit. that you and myself were hunting, I with my gun and pointer, and the conversation we carried on together was happiness *below,* and only regret it had not been in reality, I think at this time there is some probability of Mrs. Garretts going down next month if so it is more than probable I will accompany her as far as (B. H.) and was truly rejoiced that I de—— myself of that pleasure, which some of my comrades did, since I know that you would have been dissatisfied, for I have lived to the age to know that there is nothing in the bounds of reason that you will spare to gratify my wants and inclinations, and it would give me pleasure by way of a variety for you to refuse, for if I could call to mind any circumstance of my *past* life I could not recollect a single demand or request which has not been granted to me by you, and if you were to refuse now I could hardly think anything of it. I must now give you some information res our College affairs. We have lately lost a student by the name of Thomas Barclay, expelled for a very trivial offence, and suspended for the Session, and I Clarke whom Mr. Wessiger is acquainted for months, the latter particularly was the most inconsidered act I have known the Faculty to be guilty of, for he was considered a very studious fellow, inoffensive in every respect, and Nature was as liberal towards him in the way of sense, as most of people, and I am in hopes that his sentence will be reconsidered, and his punishment abolished. I would request of you to send my old hat by the first opportunity as my present one is declining fast, it was a very indifferent one. Cousin Meade gave me three books, and   [*torn*]   and 2 for Jane Rolf, which I am in hopes she will be able to read with fluency, and if so I will certainly procure her promised present. I have arrived at the part of Nat. Philosophy which is considered the most difficult part of the course, namely, Astronomy, and although I consider it quite difficult, I must acknowledge it more or less pleasant, and I sincerely trust that the next, may at least, be my last College year, and then I shall be able to enjoy the company of whose value, is the sole importance and consideration of this world to me, and in your next I must beg a *history* of your visit to Lynchburge and when my thirst for seeing you will be quenched, by a movement on one part or the other, though at present there is little probability of my visiting you, as I would be afraid during the warm month, and were I to put it off for the fall, then our vacation would be so near that it would scarcely be worth undertaking, and now I have arrived at the limits of my paper and having penned all the news I contain at present, I will bid you adieu, with love to all by assuring you of the unremitted attachment of one who professes and calls himself by the name of your affectionate Son

Thomas Bolling

Three

Charlottesville 21*st*, *April* 1826

My Dear Sir

I avail myself of the first leasure moment I have had since my last letter to you to answer the remaining part of your favour of the 27th ult. I regret exceedingly, that Thomas should have thought it necessary, to mention to you the occurrence between him and myself in relation to the fifty dollars deposited with me the last summer, because it shows that he still doubts whether or not I was satisfied as to the correctness of his statement. I had hoped that all his fears on that score had been removed by me upon our second interview upon the subject, and that he was perfectly satisfied with the reasons I then gave him accounting for my seeming forgetfulness and hesitation at the moment of his application for the money. The truth is that the length of time which elapsed between the deposit and his application and that time having been occupied by such a variety and multiplicity of business always pressing upon me, the deposit had escaped my recollection, and my hesitation at the moment, while I was endeavoring to refresh my recollection, I presume struck Thomas as doubts with me as to the deposit, yet without further hesitation I furnished him the money. Afterwards in reflecting upon the subject, I was enabled to recollect something of the circumstances, and upon seeing Thomas I hoped I had removed all uneasiness with him on that score. Since the receipt of your letter, I have refrained from renewing the matter to him least I might not be able by assurances to remove entirely his doubts in regard to it, and must ask your aid in accomplishing their removal. I assure you that I am perfectly satisfied with the statement he made to me of the deposit, although at the moment of his application for the money, I confess it had escaped my recollection, and while with Thomas (young as he is) such forgetfulness would seem unaccountable, yet to you, who knows the effect which a constant pressure of public and private business has upon our frail memories, such forgetfulness is excusable, and therefore it is that I ask your friendly aid, for I assure you it would be a source of no little uneasiness to me, to believe that Thomas still doubts my sincerity in the assurances already given him upon this subject.

While it is admitted that the delay already taken place in our intended visit to you and family, would seem to authorize you to insist on 'no further continuances.' Yet circumstances not under our command, may in spite of our most anchious wishes, controls our movements, and as they have heretofore been found so unyielding, I cannot but still hope that should they continue their obstinacy, we shall still find with you further indulgence, should unavoidable circumstances render the asking of it on our part indispensably necessary, we however at present hope we shall find it in our power to redeem our promise some time in June next in the mean time we need not add any further assurances of the pleasure we should receive from a visit so long and so anchiously wished for on our part. My family are in their usual good health, all of whom join in offering to yourself and Mrs. Bolling renewed assurances of affectionate regard, & I beg leave to repeat to you the most friendly and respectful regards with which

I remain

Yours most sincerely

ALEN GARRETT

P. S. Thomas was with us two days ago. he is quite well.

FOUR

MR. WILLIAM BOLLING

In Account with UNIVERSITY OF VIRGINIA

1818	April 1st	To Installment due this day	$ 25.00
1819	April 1st	" " " " "	25.00
1820	April 1st	" " " " "	25.00
1821	April 1st	" " " " "	25.00

$100.00

CR.

1818	March	23	By deposit in Bank of Va.........	$25.00	
1819	Sept.	30	" ditto	25.00	
1820	Oct.	24	" ditto	25.00	75.00

Balance due $ 25.00

Charlottesville, *Oct.* 21, 1822

DEAR SIR

The Tuitors of the University having lately appointed me to Collect the balances due on Subscriptions: I take the liberty of making a statement of Your Acct. which you will Perceive above amounting to the sum of Twenty-Five Dollars, and ask the favor of you, either to transmit to me by mail to this Place or deposit in the Bank of Va. Richmond to the Credit of the Bursar of the University the amt. As the Legislature will shortly meet it will afford a safe opportunity to forward the money by one of your representatives to be deposited in Bank as above. This course is desirable as it will save me the trouble and the University the expense of my waiting on you in Person.

Yrs. Respy.

G. THOMAS

Dec. 21, 1822 Then received of Col. Wm. Bolling Twenty-five Dollars on acct. of the above.

G. THOMAS

Colr.

VIII

LETTERS FROM MARIA CLEMM AND DR. J. J. MORAN

TWO letters by Mrs. Maria Clemm ("Muddie"), Poe's aunt and mother-in-law, are here printed from the originals by the courtesy of James F. Drake, Esq., of New York City.

One—Written by Mrs. Clemm from the house of Mrs. Annie Richmond at Lowell, Massachusetts, on April 11, 1850, a few months after Poe's death concerning the copyright on Poe's *Collected Works* that Griswold had in possession to her undoing. The letter is to John Neal at Portland, Maine.

Two—This letter from Mrs. Clemm, written from the Church Home in Baltimore, on October 6, 1865, shows the pitiable state of her crippled hands, by the deranged script. It is written to Gabriel Harrison of New York, then at work on his portrait of Poe, and evidently in reply to a letter of his, written to her, asking for information as to the personal appearance of Poe as data for his portrait, based upon memory and a daguerreotype (last supplementary letter of Harrison to Mrs. Clemm to that of January 31, 1865,—see J. A. Harrison, vol. II, pages 433-434).

ONE

Lowell, *April* 11*th* 1850

DEAR SIR

Will you pardon me for again intruding on your time, but the kindness you have evinced for me in your kind letters encourages me to do so. I have had a letter from New York, in which I have been asked if I would say what I would take for the copyright of my dear Eddie's works, but at the same time requested not to mention to any of my friends that they have passed out of my hands. Do you think this would be right? Will you have the kindness to advise me how to act? I have written Mr. Willis on the subject, and will be entirely guided by his and your advice. I am told the work is selling very well, but have heard nothing from the publisher concerning it. I received the paper with your kind notice, and thank you most sincerely. Will Graham think you publish the other that you mentioned having written?

God bless you dear Mr. Neal, and believe me to be your grateful and sincere friend.

MARIA CLEMM

TWO

(To Gabriel Harrison)

Baltimore *Oct.* 6, '65

MY DEAR FRIEND

I have just received your most welcome letter for it has been so very long since I have heard from you. I am better again, and as soon as I am able I will comply with request, now I can scarcely write these few lines. No, I have not heard from Mr. Lewis or the press either. God help any poor soul that is obliged to ask a favor, altho I am just going to ask one of you, but I feel so sure if it is in your power you will grant it I want $5 or even *three* more than I ever did in my whole life, cannot you procure it for me somehow, oh if you could only know how much I am in need of it, you would try to send it to me, if possible write by *return* of mail. I am very sad to day for tomorrow is the anniversary of my darling Eddie's death. please excuse this peice of paper I have no other and have not the means of getting it I am ever your true friend

"Muddie"
(Maria Clemm)

Dr. J. J. Moran Items

The following letter from Dr. J. J. Moran who attended Poe on his death-bed in Baltimore, on October 7, 1849, is of interest as recording an interview with Mrs. A. B. Shelton (Elmira Royster), thirty-three years after Poe's death. *If* the doctor can be believed, Mrs. Shelton was still able to weep for Poe. This is quite possible, of course.

The point is here, however, that Dr. Moran was on one of his lecture trips in which he went about the country telling about the death of Poe. At every recital the "demise of our great poet" became more edifying. At this particular stage, a really beautiful and touching climax had been achieved. A comparison of this letter with the one which Dr. Moran wrote to Mrs. Clemm on November 15, 1849, provides an insight into the growth of a certain kind of Poe legend.

Falls Church *Va Febry 27*, 1882

Mr. Edward Abbott

Dear Sir

Yours recd. did not reach me until I had returned from a lecture tour to Richmond, the home of his *Annabel Lee,* who yet lives, is near her three score and ten. Yet she was at the lecture, 32 years have intervened since his death, and she and I, met for the first time after that period, it was a meeting I shall never forget—so deeply were we impressed, that our tears could not be re-strained—but to the question asked in reference to the slip of paper sent, I answer, it is correct in the main or chief part. The word rode, should be arched—his decrees legibly &c. he was in my hands 16 hours, and 15 out the 16, was rational and perfectly conscious—I have some hope of getting Boston soon to deliver my lecture have been written to for that purpose—have also a letter from G. W. Childs of Pha In haste as I have a great number of letters to answer

I remain yours
Respectfully—
J. J. Moran—

(*Courtesy of James F. Drake, Esq.*)

(Report of one of Dr. Moran's Garbled Lectures about Poe's death)

Dr. J. J. Moran, of Falls Church, Va., who was with Edgar Allan Poe in his dying hours, in a recent lecture said that the slander had been reiterated that Poe died while under the influence of liquor, and nothing could be further from the fact. Upon his arrival at the hospital the doctor questioned the hackman who brought him there, and he declared that Poe was not drunk, nor was there the smell of liquor about him when he lifted him into his vehicle. As Poe's last hour approached, Dr. Moran said that he bent over him and asked if he had any word he wished communicated to his friends. Poe raised his fading eyes and answered 'Nevermore.' In a few moments he turned uneasily and moaned, 'Oh God, is there no ransom for the deathless spirit?' Continuing he said: 'He who rode the heavens and upholds the universe has His decrees written on the frontlet of every human being.' Then followed murmuring, growing fainter and fainter, then a tremor of the limbs, a faint sigh, 'and the spirit of Edgar Allan Poe had passed the boundary line that divides time from eternity.'

(*Courtesy of James F. Drake, Esq.*)

POE-NEAL CORRESPONDENCE, AND ''POLITIAN''

THE brief glimpse of Poe and John Neal, in the letters printed below, gives a rather amusing sidelight on both "Quarles" and "Jehu O'Cataract," *i.e.,* Poe and John Neal. Neal gave Poe his first public notice in the *Yankee* in 1829 in the squib about *Al Aaraaf,* which, although helpful, was pedantically patronizing in its corrections of Poe's verbiage and metrics. Neal had lately been residing in Baltimore, knew the Poes, and looked upon Edgar as a little poetaster to be helped for old friends' sake, but also to be patted on the shoulder with the admonitory air of a great editor. Young Poe, on his part, already regarded himself as a poet and a critic, and had his own opinion about Mr. John Neal. On July 28, 1829, he writes to Carey, Lea & Carey from Baltimore:

. . . notwithstanding the assertions of M^r. J^n Neal to the contrary, who now & then hitting thro' sheer impudence, upon a correct judgment in matters of authorship, is most unenviably rediculous whenever he touches the fine arts—

Thus Poe had the *first* word, meant only for the private eye of Mr. Lea. Poe cannot be accused of ingratitude to Neal who, not until two months later, was patting him on the back and then giving him a little kick. See page 168 of the September, 1829, *Yankee,* followed in December by four pages more (295–298) in which the patting was more pronounced, and the kicks reduced to three minor ones from footnotes.

Eleven years later the following letters were exchanged, disclosing both still at the same game, *i.e.,* Poe striving to further his own reputation; John Neal correcting Poe's grammar with all the patronizing attitude of the New Englander, "alarmed *at a style that is beginning to prevail at the South.*"

Poe was attempting to get the *Penn* (magazine) launched in Philadelphia, and wrote to Neal asking his influence.

Philadelphia, *June 4th,* 1840

MY DEAR SIR : As you gave me the first jog in my literary career, you are in a measure bound to protect me and keep me rolling. I therefore now ask you to aid me with your influence in whatever manner your experience shall suggest.

It strikes me that I never write you except to ask a favor. But my friend Thomas will assure you that I bear you always in mind, holding you in the highest respect and esteem.

Most truly yours,
EDGAR A. POE

To which he received this characteristic reply, collect postage:

Portland, *June 8, '40*

MY DEAR SIR : Yours of June 4, directed to New York, reached me but yesterday. I am glad to hear of your new enterprise and hope it may be all that you desire; but I cannot help you. I have done with the newspapers—have abandoned the journals—and have involved so many of my friends of late by becoming editor, or associate editor of so many different things for a few months at a time—and always against my will—that I haven't the face to ask any person to subscribe for anything on earth.

But, as I have said before, I wish you success, and to prove it, allow me to caution you against a style, which I observe, to my great alarm, is beginning to prevail at the South. You say 'I will be pardoned' for 'I shall be pardoned.' For assurance that 'I will fulfill,' &c., for 'shall,' &c. Are you Irish—the well-educated Irish I mean? They always make this mistake, and the Scotch, too, sometimes; and you, I am persuaded, are either connected by blood or habits with the Irish of the South. Forgive me this liberty, I pray you, and take it for granted that I should not complain of these two little errors if I could find anything else to complain of.

Yours truly,
JOHN NEAL

These letters were published in the *New York Times Book Review* for June 17, 1917, under the title of *Poe and John Neal* by Edwin B. Hill. The Poe letter is to be found on page 256 of Neal's *Wandering Recollections of a Somewhat Busy Life*. The letter is incomplete.

Neal's letter to Poe (folded sheet) is addressed to "Mr. Edgar A. Poe, Philadelphia, Pa.," and in Poe's hand is the filing endorsement, "John Neal, June 8, 1840." In 1917 it was in the possession of Mr. E. B. Hill.

(*Courtesy of the* New York Times, Inc.)

The following reprint abridged from a review of Poe's tragedy of *Politian,* edited by Thomas Ollive Mabbott, and first published in 1923, *Richmond, The Edgar Allan Poe Shrine,* is here given as showing how Poe used contemporary material in his work. The review by H. I. Brock appeared in the *New York Times Book Review* for November 11, 1923.

. . . Notes in Mr. Mabbott's edition serve to recall enough of the details of a story which in 1825—ten years before Poe made literary use of it—set the tongues of the country wagging as eagerly as more recently they wagged over the murder case of Mrs. Hall. Newspapers were not what they are now, but this story enjoyed a considerable publicity in print. And Poe whose first published poem, *Tamerlane,* saw the light in 1827, had ready to his pen a rich scenario.

Briefly, a certain Colonel Solomon P. Sharp had done grievous injury to a lady of good family, Miss Ann Cook. In her shamed seclusion she was wooed by another Kentuckian, Jereboam O. Beauchamp, a young lawyer. The lady consented to marry this new and ardent admirer only upon condition that before the wedding day he should kill the man who had wronged her.

The enamored Beauchamp agreed and promptly, after the approved manner of the time and country, challenged Sharp to fight a duel. Both were buried in one grave at Bloomfield, Ky.

Such is the story, grim and bloodstained enough to satisfy even Poe's insatiate fancy for the sombre. Tricked out with Italian names, titles, scenery, accessories of princely state, the story of *Politian* is the same. A Duke's son betrays the lady Lalage, his father's lovely ward, and by his ducal father is betrothed to a highborn lady, his kinswoman. The forsaken one despairs and vows vengeance on a dagger. Then comes to Rome from far-away Britain, Politian, Earl of Leicester, and falls a victim to those so lately despised charms. He woos lorn Lalage in a moonlit garden—which is familiar Poe enough. 'A deed is to be

INDEX

Titles of books by Poe are in capitals and small capitals. Titles of stories, poems, and articles by Poe are all in italic. Titles of books, stories, poems, etc., by others are all in italic, the name of the author being given where it does not already occur in the title. The names of newspapers and magazines are also in italic. American newspapers and periodicals are listed under title, not under city of publication.

ABBOT, MR., astronomer: 413
Abbott, Edward: 717
Abraham, Charles Z.: 688
Adams, Dr., Mayor of Richmond: 100
Adams, John: 121
Adams, John Quincy: 251, 322
Addison, Joseph: 82, 355
Adelphi House, New York: 340
Adventures of a Poet, The, by F. W. Thomas: 710
Afloat in the Forest by Captain Mayne Reid: 391
Al Aaraaf: 180, 207, 250, 533, 664; quoted: 141, 209, 210, 335; published: 146, 209-212; attempts to publish: 197-199, 203, 204, 205; reviewed: 207, 209, 211, 259, 284, 439, 719; read to Boston Lyceum: 529
Alburger, Mr., Poe's landlord: 429, 461
Alciphron by Thomas Moore, reviewed by Poe: 382, 407
Alderman, Dr. Edwin A.: 121
Alexander, Charles, printer: 365, 378, 391, 431
Alexander's Weekly Messenger: 347, 361, 383, 409; Poe in: 174
Allan & Ellis: 63, 73
Allan, Frances Keeling (Mrs. John), foster-mother of Poe: 32, 47, 53-56, 61, 64, 83, 86, 107, 118, 152, 153, 187, 273, 303, 362, 478, 595, 611, 664; urges Poe's adoption: 16, 28, 35, 36, 37, 42; takes Poe at death of mother: 18-20, 653, 699; described: 28; receives letter from Eliza Poe: 38, 207, 699; and Poe: 40, 41, 48, 58-60, 70, 115, 136, 147, 161, 219; early influence of, on Poe: 43, 44, 84; illness of: 62, 71, 72, 76, 77, 92, 104, 117, 150, 162, 185, 682; learns of husband's faithlessness: 95; accompanies Poe to University: 120, 122, 148; helps Poe: 112, 160; in will of William Galt: 120, 688; Poe's memory of: 183, 206, 211, 212, 233, 236, 249, 305, 358, 661, 665, 674; death of: 187-189, 214, 238; writes Poe: 580; an orphan: 683

Allan, John, Poe's guardian: x, 24, 44, 70, 81, 120, 181, 222, 223, 274, 291, 292, 308, 362, 582, 611; will of: x, 226, 237, 272, 274, 279, 287-290, 685, 686—quoted: 691-695—legality of: 696-698; letter to W. H. L. Poe: 12, 101, 103, 116, 117, 261, 700; house of: 16, 22, 584, 661; meets Poe: 16; regarding adoption of Poe: 16, 20, 31, 39, 42, 699; described: 23, 134, 162, 338; estate of: 27; financial embarrassment of: 28, 82, 96; early attitude towards Poe: 31, 32, 35, 37, 40, 41, 44, 62; sails to Portugal: 31; illegitimate children of: 35, 36, 49, 95, 195, 238, 274, 279, 694, 697; discipline of: 48, 85; to Europe with family: 53-56; in Scotland: 56-58; in England: 58, 64, 70-74, 682, 683; returns to Richmond: 73, 75-77; relations with the Ellises: 76, 77, 86; attitude towards poetry: 84, 207, 208; differences with Poe: 91, 114-117, 119; Poe's attitude towards: 95, 96, 102, 103, 112; inherits William Galt's fortune: 96; new house of: 105, 107, 165; inkstand of: 107, 218; borrowed money from Roysters: 110, 702; social aspirations of: 112, 118, 181; and the University: 130, 131, 140, 220, 701, 712; and Poe's expenses: 132-137, 148, 163, 206, 702; visits Poe at University: 144, 145; hounds Poe: 147, 153-157; and Poe's gambling debts: 148-150; final break with Poe: 156-161, 262; and Poe's discharge from the Army: 181, 182, 183, 184-188, 192; moved by death of wife: 188, 189; sends Poe to West Point: 190, 191, 197, 201, 214, 218, 229; letter to Secretary of War: 196; refuses to finance *Al Aaraaf:* 199; corresponds with Poe: 205, 297, 309, 326, 483, 703; Poe's last visit to: 210-215, 286-287; proposes to Miss Valentine: 214; becomes engaged to Miss Patterson: 217; second marriage of: 226, 230, 259; and Sergeant Graves: 235, 236; Poe's accusations from West Point: 236-238; affection for Poe: 238;

723

Poe, Rosalie (Rose)—*Continued*
Mackenzies: 19, 20, 37, 39, 80: described: 85, 274; lack of development of: 85, 117, 311, 559, 655; legitimacy of, questioned: 103, 116, 117, 238, 261, 700; quoted: 299, 474; visits at Fordham: 556, 559, 580
Poe, Sarah, great-great-grandmother of E. A. P.: 679
Poe, Virginia Maria (Clemm) (Mrs. Edgar Allan): 203-206, 215, 257, 258, 260, 263, 277, 296, 301, 305, 311, 316, 321, 322, 328, 330, 332, 336, 340, 341, 353, 361, 370, 371, 381, 384, 385, 404, 408, 428, 431, 436, 446, 460, 462, 464-469, 471, 477, 482, 514, 519, 582, 583, 585, 588, 589, 594, 599, 600, 612, 625, 627, 639, 650, 651, 666, 703; death of: 162, 579-581; marries Poe: vii, 262, 291, 309, 704; carries notes: 267, 270, 294; described: 271, 311-313, 358; Poe's feeling for: 286, 291, 358, 391, 457, 458, 632, 793; marriage to Poe opposed: 306, 308; second marriage to Poe: 318-320; sickness of: 383, 425, 427, 429, 432-434, 451, 491, 514, 524, 528, 532, 545, 547, 552; and Mrs. Graham: 391; collapse of: 417, 419; at Bloomingdale: 483-499, 551; Mrs. Osgood's comments on: 525; last public appearance of: 544; at Turtle Bay: 552-556; at Fordham: 556-561, 567, 568-581; Poe's letter to: 559
Poe, Virginia, friend of Mrs. Shelton: 666
Poe, William, of Augusta: 306, 318
Poe, William, of Baltimore: 383, 453, 521
Poe, William Henry Leonard: xi, xiii, 238, 262, 310, 381, 680, 681; adopted by "General" Poe: 4, 9, 11, 38, 699, 701; John Allan's letter to: 12, 23, 101, 103, 104, 116, 261, 700; as an author: 20, 117, 168, 323, 656; and Poe: 117, 258, 259; a midshipman: 117, 170; lives with Mrs. Clemm: 203, 206, 215, 257, 702; sickness of: 246, 259, 312; death of: 260, 703; Poe endorses note of: 264; sketch of: 699-703
Poe in Philadelphia by Alexander Harvey: 392, 421
Poe Memorial Association: 567
"Poe Canon" by Killis Campbell: viii
POEMS: 245; published: 247; dedication of: 247
Poems by Edgar Allan Poe with an Original Memoir by R. H. Stoddard: 84, 134, 153, 547
Poems by Thomas Campbell: 106, 229
Poems by Mr. Lord: 518
Poems by O. W. Holmes: 578
Poems of Sarah Helen Whitman, The: 608
Poems by Two Brothers, Tennyson: 165

Poems, Sacred, Passionate, and Humorous, The, by N. P. Willis: 496
Poems of Poe by Killis Campbell: 164
Poems Written in Youth: 533
Poe's Brother, The Poetry of William Henry Leonard Poe by Allen and Mabbott: xiii, 20, 168, 584, 656, 699
Poe's Collected Works: 421, 667; Griswold withholds copyright of, from Mrs. Clemm: 717
Poe's Gold-Bug from the Standpoint of an Entomologist by Prof. A. Smyth, Jr.: 176
Poe's Helen by Miss Ticknor: 602, 623
Poe's Mary by A. Van Cleef: 268, 427
Poe's Philadelphia Homes by E. P. Oberholtzer: 343
Poe's Reading by Killis Campbell: 107
Poetic Principle, The: 249, 593, 608, 648, 657, 665, 667
Poets and Poetry of America, Anthology, by Griswold: 397
Pogue, misprint for Poe: 437
Poland, rebellion of: 246
Polk, James K., President: 499, 535, 648
Politian: 276, 278, 313, 323, 564; reviewed: 720; sources of: 720
Polloc's: 686
Poore, Mr.: 688
Poore, Mrs., Poe's landlady: 304, 305, 308, 311
Pope, Alexander: 82, 536
Porter, Dr., editor: 497
Porter, Miss: 400
Poitiaux, Catherine Elizabeth, Poe's first sweetheart: 43, 54, 59, 61, 611, 663
Portland, Me.: Elizabeth Arnold's stage début in: 4
Post, Mr., editor: 640
Poulson's Philadelphia American Daily Advertiser: 596
Power, Susan Anna: 602, 627
Power, Nicholas: 602
Power, Mrs. Nicholas: 602, 627, 629
Powers, Hiram, sculptor: 709
Powhatan by Seba Smith, reviewed by Poe: 407, 542
P. P. & Johnston: 685
Premature Burial, The: 415, 475; quoted: 485, 486
Press, Philadelphia: 392, 421
Preston, Col. (Hon.) James P.: 196, 197
Prince, Mr.: 340
Prince's Linnæan Garden: 340
Prometheus by Lowell: 450
PROSE ROMANCES OF EDGAR A. POE, published: 460
Prose Writers of America by Griswold: 509
Prothero, Rowland E.: 71
Pundit: 412